McDougal Littell

THE LANGUAGE OF
LITERATURE

WORLD LITERATURE

McDougal Littell

THE LANGUAGE OF
LITERATURE

WORLD LITERATURE

Arthur N. Applebee

Andrea B. Bermúdez

Sheridan Blau

Rebekah Caplan

Peter Elbow

Susan Hynds

Judith A. Langer

James Marshall

McDougal Littell
A HOUGHTON MIFFLIN COMPANY
Evanston, Illinois • Boston • Dallas

Acknowledgments

Reading Model

Parabola and Paul Jordan-Smith: "Green Willow," retold by Paul Jordan-Smith, from *Parabola: The Magazine of Myth and Tradition* 8.1 (January 1983). Copyright © 1983 by Paul Jordan-Smith. Reprinted by permission of *Parabola* and the author.

Unit One

Penguin Books: Excerpts from *The Epic of Gilgamesh*, translated by N. K. Sandars (Penguin Classics, 1960; third edition, 1972). Copyright © 1960, 1964, 1972 by N. K. Sandars. Reproduced by permission of Penguin Books Ltd. "Creation Hymn" and "Burial Hymn," from *The Rig Veda*, translated by Wendy Doniger O'Flaherty (Penguin Classics, 1981). Copyright © 1981 by Wendy Doniger O'Flaherty. Reproduced by permission of Penguin Books Ltd.

Henry Holt and Company: Excerpt from the Book of the Dead, from *Wings of the Falcon*, translated by Joseph Kaster. Copyright © 1968 by Joseph Kaster. Reprinted by permission of Henry Holt and Company, LLC.

University of Texas Press: "I'm going downstream on Kingswater Canal" and "Whenever I leave you, I go out of breath," from *Love Songs of the New Kingdom*, translated from the ancient Egyptian by John L. Foster. Copyright © 1969, 1970, 1971, 1972, 1973, 1974 by John L. Foster. Reprinted by permission of the University of Texas Press.

Simon & Schuster: Excerpts from the Book of Genesis and the Book of Psalms, from *The Bible, Designed to Be Read as Living Literature*, edited by Ernest Sutherland Bates. Copyright © 1936 by Simon and Schuster, Inc. Copyright renewed © 1964 by Simon and Schuster, Inc. Reprinted with the permission of Simon & Schuster.

Continued on page R180

Senior Consultants

The senior consultants guided the conceptual development for *The Language of Literature* series. They participated actively in shaping prototype materials for major components, and they reviewed completed prototypes and/or completed units to ensure consistency with current research and the philosophy of the series.

Arthur N. Applebee Professor of Education, State University of New York at Albany; Director, Center for the Learning and Teaching of Literature; Senior Fellow, Center for Writing and Literacy

Andrea B. Bermúdez Professor of Studies in Language and Culture; Director, Research Center for Language and Culture; Chair, Foundations and Professional Studies, University of Houston–Clear Lake

Sheridan Blau Senior Lecturer in English and Education and former Director of Composition, University of California at Santa Barbara; Director, South Coast Writing Project; Director, Literature Institute for Teachers; Former President, National Council of Teachers of English

Rebekah Caplan Senior Associate for Language Arts for middle school and high school literacy, National Center on Education and the Economy, Washington, D.C.; served on the California State English Assessment Development Team for Language Arts; former co-director of the Bay Area Writing Project, University of California at Berkeley

Peter Elbow Emeritus Professor of English, University of Massachusetts at Amherst; Fellow, Bard Center for Writing and Thinking

Susan Hynds Professor and Director of English Education, Syracuse University, Syracuse, New York

Judith A. Langer Professor of Education, State University of New York at Albany; Co-director, Center for the Learning and Teaching of Literature; Senior Fellow, Center for Writing and Literacy

James Marshall Professor of English and English Education; Chair, Division of Curriculum and Instruction, University of Iowa, Iowa City

Contributing Consultants

Linda Diamond Executive Vice President, Consortium on Reading Excellence (CORE); co-author of *Building a Powerful Reading Program*

Lucila A. Garza ESL Consultant, Austin, Texas

Jeffrey N. Golub Assistant Professor of English Education, University of South Florida, Tampa

William L. McBride, Ph.D. Reading and Curriculum Specialist; former middle and high school English instructor

Sharon Sicinski-Skeans, Ph.D. Assistant Professor of Reading, University of Houston–Clear Lake; primary consultant on *The InterActive Reader*

Multicultural Advisory Board

The multicultural advisors reviewed literature selections for appropriate content and made suggestions for teaching lessons in a multicultural classroom.

Julie A. Anderson English Department Chairperson, Dayton High School, Dayton, Oregon

Vikki Pepper Ascuena Meridian High School, Meridian, Idaho

Dr. Joyce M. Bell Chairperson, English Department, Townview Magnet Center, Dallas, Texas

Linda F. Bellmore Livermore High School, Livermore, California

Dr. Eugenia W. Collier Author; lecturer; Chairperson, Department of English and Language Arts; Teacher of Creative Writing and American Literature, Morgan State University, Maryland

Dr. Bill Compagnone English Department Chairperson, Lawrence High School, Lawrence, Massachusetts

Kathleen S. Fowler President, Palm Beach County Council of Teachers of English, Boca Raton Middle School, Boca Raton, Florida

Jan Graham Cobb Middle School, Tallahassee, Florida

Barbara J. Kuhns Camino Real Middle School, Las Cruces, New Mexico

Patricia J. Richards Prior Lake, Minnesota

Continued on page R168

Teacher Review Panels

The following educators provided ongoing review during the development of the tables of contents, lesson design, and key components of the program.

CALIFORNIA

Steve Bass 8th Grade Team Leader, Meadowbrook Middle School, Ponway Unified School District

Cynthia Brickey 8th Grade Academic Block Teacher, Kastner Intermediate School, Clovis Unified School District

Karen Buxton English Department Chairperson, Winston Churchill Middle School, San Juan School District

Bonnie Garrett Davis Middle School, Compton School District

Sally Jackson Madrona Middle School, Torrance Unified School District

Sharon Kerson Los Angeles Center for Enriched Studies, Los Angeles Unified School District

Continued on page R168

Manuscript Reviewers

The following educators reviewed prototype lessons and tables of contents during the development of *The Language of Literature* program.

David Adcox Trinity High School, Euless, Texas

Carol Alves English Department Chairperson, Apopka High School, Apopka, Florida

Jacqueline Anderson James A. Foshay Learning Center, Los Angeles, California

Kathleen M. Anderson-Knight United Township High School, East Moline, Illinois

Anita Arnold Thomas Jefferson High School, San Antonio, Texas

Cassandra L. Asberry Dean of Instruction, Carter High School, Dallas, Texas

Jolene Auderer Pine Tree High School, Longview, Texas

Don Baker English Department Chairperson, Peoria High School, Peoria, Illinois

Continued on page R169

World Literature Teacher Panel

The following educators provided guidance during the initial development of this book.

Renee Bartholomew Crystal Lake Central High School, Crystal Lake, Illinois

Johanna Brocker Wells Community Academy, Chicago, Illinois

Ken Filas Round Lake High School, Round Lake, Illinois

Elizabeth Kenny Adlai E. Stevenson High School, Lincolnshire, Illinois

Allan Ruter Glenbrook South High School, Glenview, Illinois

Margaret Sinclair Glenbard High School, Carol Stream, Illinois

Judith Soltis, Ph.D. Homewood-Flossmoor High School, Flossmoor, Illinois

Patty Van Lehn St. Charles High School, St. Charles, Illinois

Charles Venegoni, Ph.D. John Hersey High School, Arlington Heights, Illinois

Suzanne Zweig Sullivan High School, Chicago, Illinois

The following people provided assistance with Lakota and West African pronunciations.

Jim Green Lakota Instructor, Language Department, South Dakota State University

Robert Launay Professor or Anthropology, Northwestern University

Elikem Tomety Consultant from Ghana

UNIT ONE Literature of the Ancient World

3000 B.C.–A.D. 500

Part 1 Mesopotamian, Egyptian & Hebrew Literature
Part 2 Literature of India

LITERARY FOCUS
The Epic

SKILL FOCUS
Writing Workshop: Autobiographical Incident
Grammar: Using Elements in a Series
Vocabulary: Words with Multiple Meanings

UNIT TWO The Classical Age of Greece and Rome 800 B.C.–A.D. 200

Part 1 Literature of Ancient Greece
Part 2 Literature of Ancient Rome

LITERARY FOCUS
The Epics of Greece and Rome

SKILL FOCUS
Communication Workshop: Writing and Staging a Scene
Grammar: Using Participles
Vocabulary: Analyzing Word Parts— Greek and Latin Roots

UNIT THREE Traditions in Chinese and Japanese Literature 1500 B.C.–A.D. 1800

Part 1 Literature of Ancient China
Part 2 Literature of Japan

LITERARY FOCUS
Moral Teaching Through Literature

SKILL FOCUS
Writing Workshop: Lyric Poetry, Problem-Solution Essay
Grammar: Using Parallelism for Effect, Creating Compound and Complex Sentences
Vocabulary: Homophones, Homonyms, and Homographs; Using Reference Tools

UNIT FOUR Literature of the Middle East and Africa A.D. 300–1900

Part 1 Persian and Arabic Literature
Part 2 West African Oral Literature

SKILL FOCUS
Writing Workshop: Personality Profile
Grammar: Using Adverbs and Adverb Phrases
Vocabulary: Using Context Clues

UNIT FIVE Europe in Transition 400–1789

Part 1 Literature of the Middle Ages
Part 2 Literature of the Renaissance & Enlightenment

LITERARY FOCUS
The Sonnet

SKILL FOCUS
Writing Workshop: Subject Analysis
Communication Workshop: Persuasive Speech
Grammar: Changing Word Order for Sentence Variety, Using Noun Clauses
Vocabulary: Understanding Analogies, Analyzing Word Parts—Affixes

UNIT SIX 19th-Century European Literature 1789–1899

Part 1 The Age of Romanticism
Part 2 The Emergence of Realism

LITERARY FOCUS
Romanticism
Realism

SKILL FOCUS
Writing Workshop: Cause-and-Effect Essay
Grammar: Using Adverb Clauses
Vocabulary: Recognizing Denotations and Connotations

UNIT SEVEN Modern and Contemporary Literature 1900–Present

Part 1 Expressions of Modernism
Part 2 Responses to War and Conflict
Part 3 Contemporary Nobel Prize Winners

LITERARY FOCUS
Modernism
Magical Realism

SKILL FOCUS
Writing Workshops: Literary Interpretation, Research Report
Grammar: Using Adjective Phrases and Clauses, Varying Sentence Length
Vocabulary: Recognizing Word Families, Choosing Word Attack Strategies

Student Resource Bank

Reading Handbook
Writing Handbook
Communication Handbook
Grammar Handbook
Academic Reading Handbook
Glossary of Literary Terms
Glossary of Words to Know in English and Spanish

Literature Connections

Each of the books in the *Literature Connections* series combines a novel or play with related readings—poems, stories, plays, personal essays, articles—that add new perspectives on the theme or subject matter of the longer work.

Listed below are some of the titles that can be used along with this World Literature anthology:

The Tempest by William Shakespeare

Hamlet by William Shakespeare

Macbeth by William Shakespeare

Julius Caesar by William Shakespeare

Canterbury Tales by Geoffrey Chaucer

Tess of the d'Urbervilles by Thomas Hardy

1984 by George Orwell

Kaffir Boy by Mark Mathabane

Nervous Conditions by Tsitsi Dangarembga

A Place Where the Sea Remembers
by Sandra Benítez

Things Fall Apart by Chinua Achebe

The Underdogs by Mariano Azuela

When Rain Clouds Gather by Bessie Head

THE LANGUAGE OF
LITERATURE

Reading Strategies

Tools for Active Reading   6
   STRATEGIES FOR READING

Reading Literature   8
   READING MODEL
     Green Willow
     Japanese folk tale retold by Paul Jordan-Smith

Reading Handbook
   READING FOR DIFFERENT PURPOSES   R2
   READING FOR INFORMATION   R4
     Text Organizers   R4
     Reading a Magazine Article   R6
     Reading a Web Page   R7
   PATTERNS OF ORGANIZATION   R8
     Main Idea and Supporting Details   R9
     Chronological Order   R10
     Comparison and Contrast   R11
     Cause and Effect   R12
     Problem and Solution   R13
   FUNCTIONAL READING   R14
     Transit Map   R14
     Workplace Document   R15
   ENRICHING YOUR VOCABULARY   R16

Academic Reading Handbook   R91
   Analyzing Text Features   R91
   Understanding Visuals   R95
   Recognizing Text Structures   R99
   Reading in the Content Areas   R109
   Reading Beyond the Classroom   R115

UNIT ONE

Literature of the *Ancient World*

2500 B.C.—A.D. 300 14

Spiritual Beginnings 16

Part 1 Mesopotamian, Egyptian, & Hebrew Literature

INTERNET
CONNECTION

Mesopotamia: History, Arts, and Culture 18
Egypt: History, Arts, and Culture 20
The Ancient Hebrews: History, Arts, and Culture 22
Searching for the Past 24
Time Line 26
Connect to Today: The Legacy of the Ancient Middle East 28

**Learning the Language of Literature:
Foundations of Early Literature** 30

Mesopotamian Literature

from **The Epic of Gilgamesh** EPIC POETRY 32
 • GUIDE FOR READING
 • CONNECT TO TODAY: THE QUEST TO FIND GILGAMESH 49

Egyptian Literature

from the **Book of the Dead** SCRIPTURE 50
 Adoration of the Disk

New Kingdom Poetry POETRY 56
 I'm going downstream on Kingswater Canal
 Whenever I leave you, I go out of breath
 • THE TRANSLATOR AT WORK: DECODING HIEROGLYPHICS 61

Comparing Literature Across Cultures 62
Creation Literature

Hebrew Literature

from **The Hebrew Bible** SCRIPTURE 63
 from **Genesis**
  Creation and the Fall
  Noah and the Flood

Mayan Literature

Popol Vuh MYTH 76
 • GUIDE FOR READING

Standardized Test Practice Writing About Literature 87

Hebrew Literature	*from* **The Hebrew Bible**	SCRIPTURE	88
	Psalms 23, 104		
	The Book of Ruth		
	from **The New Testament**	SCRIPTURE	98
	The Parable of the Prodigal Son		
	PART WRAP-UP		100
	Reflect and Assess		
	Extend Your Reading		

Sacred and Practical Teachings

Part 2   **Literature of Ancient India**   102

INTERNET
CONNECTION

Historical Highlights	104
People and Society	106
Arts and Culture	108
Time Line	110
Connect to Today: The Legacy of Ancient India	112

	from the **Rig Veda**	SCRIPTURE	114
	Creation Hymn		
	Burial Hymn		
	Learning the Language of Literature: The Epic		120
	from the **Mahabharata**	EPIC	122
	Arjuna, the Mighty Archer		
	Milestones in World Literature:		
	The Bhagavad-Gita		128
Valmiki	*from the* **Ramayana**	EPIC	130
	Rama and Ravana in Battle		
	Related Reading		
Jonah Blank	*from* **Arrow of the Blue-Skinned God**	NONFICTION	141
	• CONNECT TO TODAY: MODERN VIEWS OF		
	RAMA AND SITA		145
	from the **Panchatantra**	TALES	146
	Slow, the Weaver		
	The Brahman's Dream		

WRITING WORKSHOP	
Personal and Reflective Writing Autobiographical Incident	150
Standardized Test Practice Revising and Editing	155
Building Vocabulary Words with Multiple Meanings	156
Sentence Crafting Using Elements in a Series	157
PART WRAP-UP	158
Reflect and Assess	
Extend Your Reading	

UNIT TWO

The Classical Age of *Greece* and *Rome*

800 B.C.—A.D. 200

160

The Heroic Tradition
Part 1   Literature of Ancient Greece   162

INTERNET
CONNECTION

Historical Highlights   164
People and Society   166
Culture   168
Arts and Humanities   170
Time Line   172
Connect to Today: The Legacy of Ancient Greece   174

**Learning the Language of Literature:
The Epics of Greece and Rome**   176

Homer   *from the* **Iliad**   EPIC POETRY   178
 • GUIDE FOR READING
from **Book 1: The Rage of Achilles**
from **Book 6: Hector Returns to Troy**
from **Book 22: The Death of Hector**
from **Book 24: Achilles and Priam**
 • THE TRANSLATOR AT WORK: HOMER AND THE ORAL TRADITION   225

Sappho   **Some say thronging cavalry . . .**   POETRY   226
He Is More Than a Hero
To Aphrodite of the Flowers, at Knossos

Thucydides   *from* **History of the Peloponnesian War**   NONFICTION   232
Pericles' Funeral Oration
 • CONNECT TO TODAY: NELSON MANDELA
    CELEBRATES A NATIONAL HERO   245

Plato   *from the* **Apology**   NONFICTION   246

Milestones in World Literature: Greek Drama   256

Sophocles   **Oedipus the King**   DRAMA   258
 • GUIDE FOR READING

	Related Reading		
Muriel Rukeyser	**Myth**	POETRY	329

COMMUNICATION WORKSHOP
Speaking and Listening Writing and Staging a Scene		332
Standardized Test Practice Revising and Editing		339
Building Vocabulary Analyzing Word Parts—Greek and Latin Roots		340
Sentence Crafting Using Participles		341

PART WRAP-UP	342
Reflect and Assess	
Extend Your Reading	

The Tradition Continues

Part 2 Literature of Ancient Rome 344

INTERNET CONNECTION

Historical Highlights	346
People and Society	348
Arts and Culture	350
Time Line	352
Connect to Today: The Legacy of Ancient Rome	354

Virgil	*from the* **Aeneid**	EPIC POETRY	356
	from **Book 2: The Fall of Troy**		
	• GUIDE FOR READING		

Comparing Literature Across Cultures			382
Perspectives on Helen of Troy			
Sara Teasdale	**Helen of Troy** UNITED STATES	POETRY	383
Edgar Allan Poe	**To Helen** UNITED STATES	POETRY	388
	Standardized Test Practice Writing About Literature		391

Horace	**Seize the Day**	POETRY	392
	Better to live, Licinius		
Ovid	*from* **Metamorphoses**	POETRY	398
	The Story of Daedalus and Icarus		
	Related Reading		
William Carlos Williams	**Landscape with the Fall of Icarus**	POETRY	403
	• CONNECT TO TODAY: THE URGE TO FLY		405
Tacitus	*from* **The Annals**	NONFICTION	406
	The Burning of Rome		

PART WRAP-UP	410
Reflect and Assess	
Extend Your Reading	
Standardized Test Practice Reading and Writing for Assessment	412

UNIT THREE

Traditions in *Chinese* and *Japanese Literature*

1500 B.C.–A.D. 1800

418

From Observation to Insight

Part 1 **Literature of Ancient China** 420

INTERNET CONNECTION

Historical Highlights 422
People and Society 424
Arts and Culture 426
Time Line 428
Connect to Today: The Legacy of Ancient China 430

Learning the Language of Literature:
Moral Teaching Through Literature 432

| Confucius | *from the* **Analects** | NONFICTION | 434 |
| Lao-tzu | *from the* **Tao Te Ching** | NONFICTION | 440 |

Related Reading
Chuang Tzu	**Taoist Tale: The Fish Rejoice**	FICTION	444
Anonymous	*from the* **Book of Odes**	POETRY	446
	Mulberry on the Lowland		
	We Pick Ferns, We Pick Ferns		
Li Po	**The River-Merchant's Wife: A Letter**	POETRY	452
	Still Night Thoughts		
	Gazing at the Lu Mountain Waterfall		
	• THE TRANSLATOR AT WORK: TRANSLATING CHINESE POETRY		461
Tu Fu	**Dreaming of Li Po**	POETRY	462
	Jade Flower Palace		

Related Reading
Percy Bysshe Shelley	**Ozymandias**	POETRY	467
Tu Fu	**Song of P'eng-ya**	POETRY	468
	• CONNECT TO TODAY: REFUGEES—PEOPLE WITHOUT A COUNTRY		471
Li Ch'ing-chao	**Two Springs**	POETRY	472
	On Plum Blossoms		

WRITING WORKSHOP
Narrative and Literary Writing Lyric Poetry 476
Standardized Test Practice Revising and Editing 481
Building Vocabulary Homophones, Homonyms, and Homographs 482
Sentence Crafting Using Parallelism for Effect 483

PART WRAP-UP 484
Reflect and Assess
Extend Your Reading

Capturing the Moment

Part 2 **Literature of Japan** 486

INTERNET
CONNECTION

Historical Highlights 488
People and Society 490
Arts and Culture 492
Time Line 494
Connect to Today: The Legacy of Japan 496

Sei Shōnagon *from* **The Pillow Book** NONFICTION 498
Milestones in World Literature: *The Tale of Genji* 508

Musō Soseki **Zen Teachings** NONFICTION 510
Anonymous **Zen Parables**
• CONNECT TO TODAY: ZEN—ALIVE AND WELL 517

Noh Drama
Zeami Motokiyo **The Deserted Crone** DRAMA 518
• GUIDE FOR READING

Tanka Poetry
Ono Komachi **I've gone to him** POETRY 534
Lady Ise **Spring rains weaving**
Ki Tsurayuki **In this world**
Saigyō **As I look at the moon**

Comparing Literature Across Cultures 540
Haiku Across the Centuries

Japanese Haiku
Matsuo Bashō **Haiku** POETRY 541
Yosa Buson
Kobayashi Issa

Related Reading: Primary Source
Kobayashi Issa *from* **The Spring of My Life** NONFICTION 544

Haiku in the 20th Century
José Juan Tablada **Haiku** MEXICO POETRY 547
Richard Wright **Haiku** UNITED STATES

Standardized Test Practice Writing About Literature 551

WRITING WORKSHOP
Informative Exposition Problem-Solution Essay 552
Standardized Test Practice Revising and Editing 557
Building Vocabulary Using Reference Tools 558
Sentence Crafting Creating Compound and Complex Sentences 559

PART WRAP-UP 560
Reflect and Assess
Extend Your Reading

UNIT FOUR

Literature of the *Middle East* and *Africa*

A.D. 300–1900

562

Mysticism, Morals, Magic
Part 1 **Persian and Arabic Literature** 564

INTERNET CONNECTION

Historical Highlights 566
People and Society 568
Arts and Culture 570
Time Line 572
Connect to Today: The Legacy of Persia and Arabia 574

from **The Koran** SCRIPTURE 576
The Exordium
Faith in God
Night
Daylight

from **The Thousand and One Nights** TALE 582
The Second Voyage of Sindbad the Sailor
• CONNECT TO TODAY: SINDBAD YESTERDAY,
TODAY, AND TOMORROW 591

Milestones in World Literature:
The Shahnameh—Epic of Persia 592

Omar Khayyám   *from the* **Rubáiyát** POETRY 594
• THE TRANSLATOR AT WORK: FITZGERALD'S *RUBÁIYÁT* 599

Rumi   **Birdsong from Inside the Egg** POETRY 600
The Grasses

Sadi   *from the* **Gulistan** ANECDOTES 606

PART WRAP-UP 610
Reflect and Assess
Extend Your Reading

Giving Guidance, Praising Greatness

Part 2   West African Oral Literature   612

INTERNET CONNECTION

Historical Highlights	614
People and Society	616
Arts and Culture	618
Time Line	620
Connect to Today: The Legacy of West Africa	622

Fulani	**How the World Was Created from a Drop of Milk**	MYTH	624
Soninke	**The First Bard Among the Soninke**	LEGEND	628
Mandinka	*from* **Sundiata** **Childhood** **The Lion's Awakening**	EPIC	632
Yoruba	**Praise Songs for Orishas** **Obatala** **Shango** **Oshun**	SONGS	642
	• CONNECT TO TODAY: ORISHAS IN THE AMERICAS		649

Comparing Literature Across Cultures   650
Trickster Tales

Ashanti	**Tales of Anansi the Spider** **All Stories are Anansi's** **Anansi Plays Dead**	TALES	651
Lakota	**Tales of Iktomi the Spider** NORTH AMERICA **Iktomi and the Wild Ducks** **Iktomi Takes Back a Gift**	TALES	658
	Standardized Test Practice Writing About Literature		663

Various	**West African Proverbs**	NONFICTION	664

WRITING WORKSHOP

Observation and Description Personality Profile	668
Standardized Test Practice Revising and Editing	673
Building Vocabulary Using Context Clues	674
Sentence Crafting Using Adverbs and Adverb Phrases	675

PART WRAP-UP   676
Reflect and Assess
Extend Your Reading

Standardized Test Practice Reading and Writing for Assessment	678

UNIT FIVE

Europe in *Transition*
400–1789

684

Heroic Quests

Part 1 Literature of the Middle Ages   686

INTERNET
CONNECTION

Historical Highlights	688
People and Society	690
Arts and Culture	691
Time Line	692
Connect to Today: The Legacy of the Middle Ages	694

Anonymous	*from* **The Song of Roland** FRANCE	EPIC	696
Chrétien de Troyes	*from* **Perceval: The Story of the Grail** FRANCE	ROMANCE	708
	• GUIDE FOR READING		
	• CONNECT TO TODAY: THE GRAIL LEGEND IN FILM AND STORY		723
Marie de France	**The Lay of the Were-Wolf** FRANCE	TALE	724

DANTE ALIGHIERI   **AUTHOR STUDY**   ITALY

Life and Times		732
INTERNET CONNECTION		
from **The Inferno**	POETRY	736
Cantos 1, 3, 5, 34		
• GUIDE FOR READING		
from **La Vita Nuova**	MEMOIR	757
The Author's Style		760

NETACTIVITIES:
Author Exploration

WRITING WORKSHOP

Informative Exposition Subject Analysis	762
Standardized Test Practice Revising and Editing	767
Building Vocabulary Understanding Analogies	768
Sentence Crafting Changing Word Order for Sentence Variety	769

PART WRAP-UP   770
Reflect and Assess
Extend Your Reading

Human Possibility

Part 2 Literature of the Renaissance & Enlightenment

INTERNET CONNECTION

Historical Highlights		774
People and Society		776
Arts and Culture		778
Time Line		780
Connect to Today: The Legacy of the Renaissance and Enlightenment		782

Giovanni Boccaccio	*from* **The Decameron** ITALY **Federigo's Falcon**	FICTION	784
Andreas Capellanus	*Related Reading: Primary Source* *from* **The Art of Courtly Love** FRANCE	NONFICTION	791
Sir Thomas More	*from* **Utopia** ENGLAND • CONNECT TO TODAY: SEARCHING FOR UTOPIA	FICTION	794 803
	Learning the Language of Literature: The Sonnet		804

The Sonnet Poets

Francesco Petrarch	**Sonnet 3** ITALY	POETRY	806
Pierre de Ronsard	**To Hélène** FRANCE • THE TRANSLATOR AT WORK: DEALING WITH THE SONNET	POETRY	808 811
William Shakespeare	**Sonnet 29** ENGLAND **Sonnet 30** **Sonnet 64**	POETRY	812
	Milestones in World Literature: The Plays of Shakespeare		818

	Comparing Literature Across Cultures *Sonnets by Women*		820
Louise Labé	**Sonnet 23** FRANCE	POETRY	821
Sor Juana Inés de la Cruz	**Stay, shadow of contentment** MEXICO	POETRY	824
	Standardized Test Practice Writing About Literature		827

Miguel de Cervantes	*from* **Don Quixote** SPAIN	FICTION	828
Jorge Luis Borges	*Related Reading* **A Soldier of Urbina** ARGENTINA	POETRY	843
	Milestones in World Literature: The Plays of Molière		846
Voltaire	*from* **Candide** FRANCE	FICTION	848

COMMUNICATION WORKSHOP		
Speaking and Listening Persuasive Speech		858
Building Vocabulary Analyzing Word Parts: Affixes		864
Sentence Crafting Using Noun Clauses		865

PART WRAP-UP		866
Reflect and Assess		
Extend Your Reading		

UNIT SIX

19th-Century *European Literature*
1798–1899

868

Expressions of the Heart
Part 1 **The Age of Romanticism** 870

 INTERNET CONNECTION

Historical Highlights 872
Arts and Culture 874
Time Line 876

Learning the Language of Literature: Romanticism 878

Johann Wolfgang von Goethe
from **Faust** GERMANY VERSE DRAMA 880
• GUIDE FOR READING
Related Reading: Primary Source
from **Letter to His Friends** NONFICTION 895

Comparing Literature Across Cultures 898
Romantic Poetry

William Wordsworth
The World Is Too Much With Us ENGLAND POETRY 899
My Heart Leaps Up

Related Reading: Primary Source
Dorothy Wordsworth
from the **Grasmere Journals** ENGLAND NONFICTION 902

Romantic Poetry from Other Cultures

José Martí from **Simple Verses** CUBA POETRY 905
Uvavnuk **Shaman Song** INUK/ESKIMO POETRY 907

Standardized Test Practice Writing About Literature 909

Heinrich Heine **The Lorelei** GERMANY POETRY 910

Victor Hugo from **The Expiation** FRANCE POETRY 914
Russia 1812
• CONNECT TO TODAY: VICTOR HUGO ON STAGE AND SCREEN 921

Charles Baudelaire **Invitation to the Voyage** FRANCE POETRY 922
The Albatross

Arthur Rimbaud	**The Sleeper in the Valley** FRANCE	POETRY	928
Paul Verlaine	**Autumn Song** FRANCE	POETRY	930
	PART WRAP-UP **Reflect and Assess** **Extend Your Reading**		932

Life's Lessons

Part 2 **The Emergence of Realism** 934

INTERNET CONNECTION

Historical Highlights		936
Arts and Culture		938
Time Line		940

Learning the Language of Literature: Realism		942

Guy de Maupassant	**A Piece of String** FRANCE	FICTION	944

LEO TOLSTOY **AUTHOR STUDY** RUSSIA

Life and Times INTERNET CONNECTION		954
How Much Land Does a Man Need?	FICTION	958
Letter to His Editor	NONFICTION	974
What Men Live By	FICTION	976
from **Sonya Tolstoy's Diary**	NONFICTION	993
The Author's Style		995

NETACTIVITIES: Author Exploration

Comparing Literature Across Cultures *Aspects of Realism*		998

Anton Chekhov	**A Problem** RUSSIA	FICTION	999
Rabindranath Tagore	**The Artist** INDIA	FICTION	1008

Standardized Test Practice Writing About Literature		1015

Milestones in World Literature: The Novels of Fyodor Dostoyevsky		1016

Henrik Ibsen	**A Doll's House** NORWAY	DRAMA	1018
	• GUIDE FOR READING		
	• THE TRANSLATOR AT WORK: TRANSLATING DRAMA		1063
	• CONNECT TO TODAY: WOMEN IN SOCIETY		1083

WRITING WORKSHOP	
Informative Exposition Cause-and-Effect Essay	1084
Standardized Test Practice Revising and Editing	1089
Building Vocabulary Recognizing Denotations and Connotations	1090
Sentence Crafting Using Adverb Clauses	1091

PART WRAP-UP **Reflect and Assess** **Extend Your Reading**	1092

UNIT SEVEN

Modern and Contemporary Literature

1900–PRESENT

1094

The Changing World	1096
Time Line	1098
Literary Map of the World	1100

Worlds of Change

Part 1 **Expressions of Modernism** 1102

INTERNET
CONNECTION

Cultural Highlights of Modernism 1104

Learning the Language of Literature: Modernism 1106

Franz Kafka	**Metamorphosis** CZECH REPUBLIC	FICTION	1108
	• GUIDE FOR READING		
Rainer Maria Rilke	**The Panther** CZECH REPUBLIC	POETRY	1150
Federico García Lorca	**The Guitar** SPAIN	POETRY	1152
	• THE TRANSLATOR AT WORK: TRANSLATING MODERN POETRY		1155
Virginia Woolf	**Professions for Women** ENGLAND	NONFICTION	1156
James Joyce	**Eveline** IRELAND	FICTION	1166
Yasunari Kawabata	**The Jay** JAPAN	FICTION	1174
Léopold Sédar Senghor	**And We Shall Be Steeped** SENEGAL **Prayer to Masks**	POETRY	1182
	• CONNECT TO TODAY: APPRECIATING CULTURAL ROOTS		1187
Gabriela Mistral	**Time** CHILE	POETRY	1188

WRITING WORKSHOP

Responding to Literature Literary Interpretation	1190
Standardized Test Practice Revising and Editing	1195
Building Vocabulary Recognizing Word Families	1196
Sentence Crafting Using Adjective Phrases and Clauses	1197

PART WRAP-UP   1198
Reflect and Assess
Extend Your Reading

When Worlds Collide
Part 2 Responses to War and Conflict   1200

INTERNET
CONNECTION
Historical Highlights: Through World War II   1202
Historical Highlights: Post World War II   1204

Luigi Pirandello   **War** ITALY   FICTION   1206
                        **Milestones in World Literature: *All Quiet on
                        the Western Front***   1214

Anna Akhmatova   **I Am Not One of Those Who Left the Land** RUSSIA POETRY 1216
                        • CONNECT TO TODAY: LIVING DANGEROUSLY—WRITERS
                          IN THE 20TH CENTURY   1219

Bertolt Brecht   **The Spy** GERMANY   DRAMA   1220

Elie Wiesel   *from* **The World Was Silent** ROMANIA   NONFICTION   1232

                        Related Reading
Nelly Sachs   **When in Early Summer** GERMANY   POETRY   1241
                        • CONNECT TO TODAY: THE HOLOCAUST
                          AND HUMAN RIGHTS   1243

Albert Camus   **The Guest** ALGERIA   FICTION   1244
                        • GUIDE FOR READING

                        Comparing Literature Across Cultures   1260
                        The Prison Experience
Aleksandr Solzhenitsyn **Freedom to Breathe** RUSSIA   PROSE POETRY   1261

Mahmud Darwish   **The Prison Cell** PALESTINE   POETRY   1265

                        Standardized Test Practice Writing About Literature 1269

CHINUA ACHEBE   **AUTHOR STUDY** NIGERIA

                        Life and Times   1270
                        INTERNET CONNECTION

                        Dead Men's Path   FICTION   1274

                        from **An Interview with Chinua Achebe** NONFICTION   1280
                        by Bill Moyers

                        Keeper of the Vigil, a poem for Chinua Achebe POETRY 1284
                        by Yusef Komunyakaa

                        Civil Peace   FICTION   1286

NETACTIVITIES: **The Author's Style**   1292
Author Exploration

| Isabel Allende | *from* **Paula** CHILE | NONFICTION | 1294 |
| Yehuda Amichai | **The Diameter of the Bomb** ISRAEL | POETRY | 1304 |

WRITING WORKSHOP
Report Research Report 1306
Standardized Test Practice Revising and Editing 1315
Building Vocabulary Choosing Word Attack Strategies 1316
Sentence Crafting Varying Sentence Length 1317

PART WRAP-UP 1318
Reflect and Assess
Extend Your Reading

Critics and Dreamers
Part 3 **Contemporary Nobel Prize Winners** 1320

INTERNET CONNECTION
The Nobel Prize and World Literature 1322

Nadine Gordimer	**Amnesty** SOUTH AFRICA	FICTION	1324
	• CONNECT TO TODAY: FARM WORKERS IN THE NEW SOUTH AFRICA		1335
Wole Soyinka	**After the Deluge** NIGERIA	POETRY	1336
Wislawa Szymborska	**The End and the Beginning** POLAND	POETRY	1336

Learning the Language of Literature:
Magical Realism 1344

| Gabriel García Márquez | **The Handsomest Drowned Man** COLOMBIA **in the World** | FICTION | 1346 |

Milestones in World Literature: *One Hundred Years of Solitude* 1356

Pablo Neruda	**Ode to the Lizard** CHILE	POETRY	1358
	Ode to the Watermelon		
	• THE TRANSLATOR AT WORK: ON TRANSLATING NERUDA		1365
Naguib Mahfouz	**Half a Day** EGYPT	FICTION	1366

Related Reading
| Judith Wright | **Counting in Sevens** AUSTRALIA | POETRY | 1371 |
| Octavio Paz | **January First** MEXICO | POETRY | 1374 |

PART WRAP-UP 1378
Reflect and Assess
Extend Your Reading

Student *Resource Bank*

Reading Handbook R2
  Reading for Different Purposes R2
  Reading for Information .R4
  Functional Reading R14
  Enriching Your Vocabulary .R16

Writing Handbook R18
  The Writing Process .R18
  Building Blocks of Good Writing R22
  Descriptive Writing R27
  Narrative Writing .R29
  Explanatory Writing .R31
  Persuasive Writing .R35
  Research Report Writing .R37
  Business Writing .R43

Communication Handbook R45
  Inquiry and Research R45
  Study Skills and Strategies R47
  Critical Thinking R49
  Speaking and Listening R50
  Viewing and Representing R52

Grammar Handbook R55
  Quick Reference: Parts of Speech R55
  Nouns R56
  Pronouns R57
  Verbs R59
  Modifiers R62
  Prepositions, Conjunctions, and Interjections R64
  Quick Reference: The Sentence and Its Parts R66
  The Sentence and Its Parts R67

  Phrases R69
  Verbals and Verbal Phrases R69
  Clauses R71
  The Structure of Sentences R72
  Writing Complete Sentences R73
  Subject-Verb Agreement .R74
  Quick Reference: Punctuation R77
  Quick Reference: Capitalization R79
  Little Rules That Make a Big Difference R80
  Grammar Glossary R85

Academic Reading Handbook R91
  Analyzing Text Features .R91
  Understanding Visuals R95
  Recognizing Text Structures R99
  Reading in the Content Areas R109
  Reading Beyond the Classroom R115

Glossary of Literary Terms R125

Glossary of Words to Know in English and Spanish R144

Index of Fine Art R156

Index of Skills R163

Index of Titles and Authors R176

Acknowledgments R180

Art Credits R187

Selections by Genre

Epic

from the **Aeneid** 356
    Virgil
from **The Epic of Gilgamesh** 32
from the **Iliad** 178
    Homer
from the **Mahabharata** 122
from the **Ramayana** 130
    Valmiki
from **The Song of Roland** 696
from **Sundiata** 632

Myths, Tales, and Legends

The First Bard Among the Soninke 628
How the World Was Created from a Drop of Milk 624
The Lay of the Were-Wolf 724
    Marie de France
from the **Panchatantra** 146
Popol Vuh 76
Tales of Anansi the Spider 651
Tales of Iktomi the Spider 658
from **The Thousand and One Nights** 582

Romance

from **Perceval: The Story of the Grail** 708
    Chrétien de Troyes

Scripture

Adoration of the Disk 50
from the **Book of the Dead** 50
The Book of Ruth 88
    Hebrew Bible
from **Genesis** 63
    Hebrew Bible
from **The Koran** 576
The Parable of the Prodigal Son 98
    The New Testament
Psalms 23, 104 88
    Hebrew Bible
from the **Rig Veda** 114

Fiction

Amnesty 1324
    Nadine Gordimer
The Artist 1008
    Rabindranath Tagore
from **Candide** 848
    Voltaire
Civil Peace 1286
    Chinua Achebe
Dead Men's Path 1274
    Chinua Achebe
from **Don Quixote** 828
    Miguel de Cervantes
Eveline 1166
    James Joyce
Federigo's Falcon *from* **The Decameron** 784
    Giovanni Boccaccio
The Fish Rejoice 444
    Chuang Tzu
The Guest 1244
    Albert Camus
from the **Gulistan** 606
    Sadi
Half a Day 1366
    Naguib Mahfouz
The Handsomest Drowned Man in the World 1346
    Gabriel García Márquez
How Much Land Does a Man Need? 958
    Leo Tolstoy
The Jay 1174
    Yasunari Kawabata
Metamorphosis 1108
    Franz Kafka
A Piece of String 944
    Guy de Maupassant
A Problem 999
    Anton Chekhov
from **Utopia** 794
    Sir Thomas More
War 1206
    Luigi Pirandello
What Men Live By 976
    Leo Tolstoy

Nonfiction

from the **Analects** 434
Confucius

from the **Apology** 246
Plato

from **Arrow of the Blue-Skinned God** 141
Jonah Blank

from **The Art of Courtly Love** 791
Andreas Capellanus

The Burning of Rome *from* **The Annals** 406
Tacitus

from the **Grasmere Journals** 902
Dorothy Wordsworth

from **An Interview with Chinua Achebe** 1280
Bill Moyers

Letter to His Editor 974
Leo Tolstoy

from **Letter to His Friends** 895
Johann Wolfgang von Goethe

from **Paula** 1294
Isabel Allende

Pericles' Funeral Oration *from* **History of
   the Peloponnesian War** 232
Thucydides

from **The Pillow Book** 498
Sei Shōnagon

Professions for Women 1156
Virginia Woolf

from **Sonya Tolstoy's Diary** 993
Sonya Tolstoy

from **The Spring of My Life** 545
Kobayashi Issa

from the **Tao Te Ching** 440
Lao-tzu

from **La Vita Nuova** 757
Dante Alighieri

West African Proverbs 664

from **The World Was Silent** 1232
Elie Wiesel

Zen Parables 510

Zen Teachings 510
Musō Soseki

Poetry

After the Deluge 1336
Wole Soyinka

The Albatross 922
Charles Baudelaire

And We Shall Be Steeped 1182
Léopold Sédar Senghor

As I look at the moon 534
Saigyō

Autumn Song 928
Paul Verlaine

Better to live, Licinius 392
Horace

Birdsong from Inside the Egg 600
Rumi

from the **Book of Odes** 446

Counting in Sevens 1371
Judith Wright

The Diameter of the Bomb 1304
Yehuda Amichai

Dreaming of Li Po 462
Tu Fu

The End and the Beginning 1336
Wislawa Szymborska

Freedom to Breathe 1261
Aleksandr Solzhenitsyn

Gazing at the Lu Mountain Waterfall 452
Li Po

The Grasses 600
Rumi

The Guitar 1150
Federico García Lorca

Haiku 541, 547
Matsuo Bashō, Yosa Buson, Kobayashi Issa,
José Juan Tablada, and Richard Wright

He Is More Than a Hero 226
Sappho

Helen of Troy 383
Sara Teasdale

I Am Not One of Those Who Left the Land 1216
Anna Akhmatova

I'm going downstream on Kingswater Canal 50

from **The Inferno** 736
Dante Alighieri

In this world 534
Ki Tsurayuki

Invitation to the Voyage 922
Charles Baudelaire

I've gone to him 534
Ono Komachi

Jade Flower Palace 462
Tu Fu

January First 1374
Octavio Paz

Keeper of the Vigil 1284
Yusef Komunyakaa

Landscape with the Fall of Icarus 403
William Carlos Williams

The Lorelei 910
Heinrich Heine

My Heart Leaps Up 899
William Wordsworth

Myth 329
Muriel Rukeyser

Ode to the Lizard 1358
Pablo Neruda

Ode to the Watermelon 1358
Pablo Neruda

On Plum Blossoms 472
Li Ch'ing-chao

Ozymandias 467
Percy Bysshe Shelley

The Panther 1150
Rainer Maria Rilke

Praise Songs for Orishas 642

Prayer to Masks 1182
Léopold Sédar Senghor

The Prison Cell 1265
Mahmud Darwish

The River-Merchant's Wife: A Letter 452
Li Po

from the **Rubáiyát** 594
Omar Khayyám

Russia 1812 from **The Expiation** 914
Victor Hugo

Seize the Day 392
Horace

Shaman Song 905
Uvavnuk

from **Simple Verses** 905
José Martí

The Sleeper in the Valley 928
Arthur Rimbaud

A Soldier of Urbina 843
Jorge Luis Borges

Some say thronging cavalry 226
Sappho

Song of P'eng-ya 468
Tu Fu

Sonnet 3 806
Francesco Petrarch

Sonnet 23 821
Louise Labé

Sonnets 29, 30, 64 812
William Shakespeare

Spring rains weaving 534
Lady Ise

Stay, shadow of contentment 824
Sor Juana Inés de la Cruz

Still Night Thoughts 452
Li Po

The Story of Daedalus and Icarus from
  Metamorphoses 398
Ovid

Time 1188
Gabriela Mistral

To Aphrodite of the Flowers, at Knossos 226
Sappho

To Helen 388
Edgar Allan Poe

To Hélène 806
Pierre de Ronsard

Two Springs 472
Li Ch'ing-chao

Whenever I leave you, I go out of breath 50

When in Early Summer 1241
Nelly Sachs

The World Is Too Much With Us 899
William Wordsworth

Drama

The Deserted Crone 518
Zeami Motokiyo

A Doll's House 1018
Henrik Ibsen

from **Faust** 880
Johann Wolfgang von Goethe

Oedipus the King 258
Sophocles

The Spy 1220
Bertolt Brecht

Special Features of This Book

Author Study

Dante Alighieri 732
Leo Tolstoy 954
Chinua Achebe 1272

Comparing Literature Across Cultures

Creation Literature 62
Perspectives on Helen of Troy .382
Haiku Across the Centuries 540
Trickster Tales 650
Sonnets by Women 820
Romantic Poetry 898
Aspects of Realism 998
The Prison Experience 1260

Learning the Language of Literature

Foundations of Early Literature 30
The Epic 120
The Epics of Greece and Rome 176
Moral Teaching through Literature 432
The Sonnet 804
Romanticism 878
Realism 998
Modernism 1106
Magical Realism 1344

Milestones in World Literature

The Bhagavad-Gita 128
Greek Drama 256
The Tale of Genji 508
The Shahnameh—Epic of Persia 592
The Plays of Shakespeare 818
The Plays of Molière 846
The Novels of Fyodor Dostoyevsky 1016
All Quiet on the Western Front 1214
One Hundred Years of Solitude 1356

Connect to Today

The Quest to Find Gilgamesh 49
Modern Views of Rama and Sita 141
Nelson Mandela Celebrates a National Hero 245
The Urge to Fly 405
Refugees—People Without a Country 471
Zen—Alive and Well 517
Sindbad Yesterday, Today, and Tomorrow 591
Orishas in the Americas 649
The Grail Legend in Film and Story 723
Searching for Utopia 803
Victor Hugo on Stage and Screen 921
Women in Society 1083
Appreciating Cultural Roots .1187
Living Dangerously—Writers in the 20th Century 1219
The Holocaust and Human Rights 1243
Farm Workers in the New South Africa 1335

The Translator at Work

Decoding Hieroglyphics 61
Homer and the Oral Tradition 225
Translating Chinese Poetry 461
FitzGerald's *Rubáiyát* 599
Dealing with the Sonnet 811
Translating Drama 1063
Translating Modern Poetry 1155
On Translating Neruda 1365

Writing Workshop

Autobiographical Incident 150
Lyric Poetry 476
Problem-Solution Essay 552
Personality Profile 668
Subject Analysis 762
Cause-and-Effect Essay 1084
Literary Interpretation 1190
Research Report 1306

Communication Workshop

Writing and Staging a Scene 332
Persuasive Speech 858

Building Vocabulary

Words with Multiple Meanings 156
Analyzing Word Parts—Greek and
    Latin Roots 340
Homophones, Homonyms, and
    Homographs 482

Using Reference Tools 558
Using Context Clues 674
Understanding Analogies 768
Analyzing Word Parts—Affixes 864
Recognizing Denotations and Connotations 1090
Recognizing Word Families 1196
Choosing Word Attack Strategies 1316

Sentence Crafting

Using Elements in a Series 157
Using Participles 341
Using Parallelism for Effect 483
Creating Compound and Complex Sentences 559
Using Adverbs and Adverb Phrases 675
Changing Word Order for Sentence Variety 769
Using Noun Clauses 865
Using Adverb Clauses 1091
Using Adjective Phrases and Clauses 1197
Varying Sentence Length 1317

Assessment Pages

Reading and Writing for Assessment
412, 678

Standardized Test Practice: Revising and Editing
155, 481, 557, 673, 767, 1089, 1195, 1315

Standardized Test Practice: Writing About Literature
87, 391, 551, 663, 827, 909, 1015, 1269

Reflect and Assess
100, 158, 342, 410, 484, 560, 610, 676, 770, 866, 932, 1092, 1198, 1318, 1378

Why Study World Literature?

To Become Culturally Literate

What is the story behind the Trojan horse? What's the name of Chinua Achebe's most famous novel? Someday you may need to know this, for an exam or even a quiz show. If you read world literature, you'll be ready.

To Experience the World— Past and Present

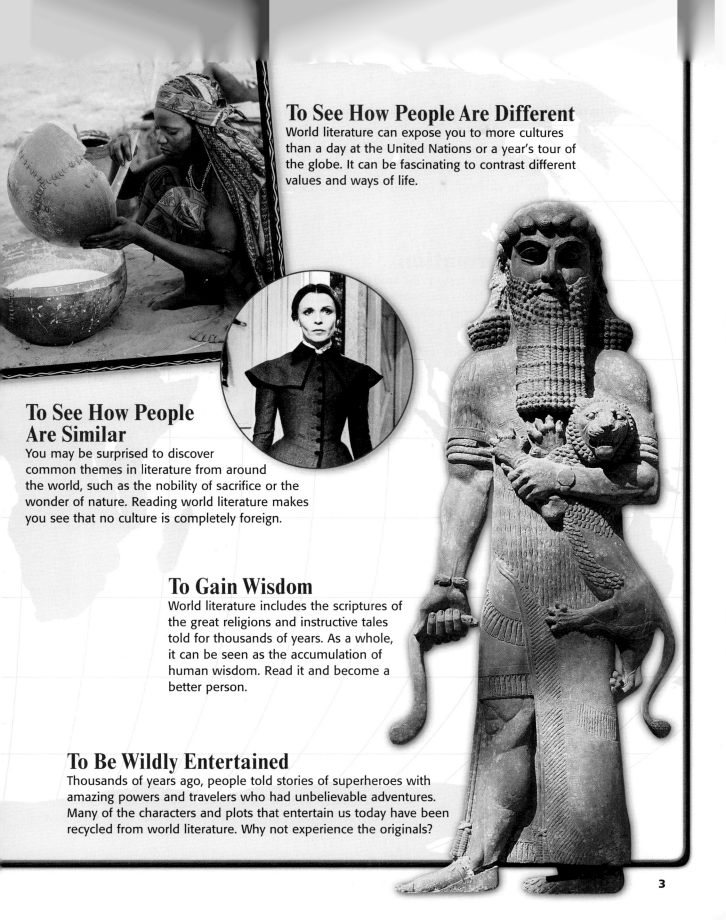

To See How People Are Different

World literature can expose you to more cultures than a day at the United Nations or a year's tour of the globe. It can be fascinating to contrast different values and ways of life.

To See How People Are Similar

You may be surprised to discover common themes in literature from around the world, such as the nobility of sacrifice or the wonder of nature. Reading world literature makes you see that no culture is completely foreign.

To Gain Wisdom

World literature includes the scriptures of the great religions and instructive tales told for thousands of years. As a whole, it can be seen as the accumulation of human wisdom. Read it and become a better person.

To Be Wildly Entertained

Thousands of years ago, people told stories of superheroes with amazing powers and travelers who had unbelievable adventures. Many of the characters and plots that entertain us today have been recycled from world literature. Why not experience the originals?

As rewarding as world literature can be, it can some-times present special challenges. Reading literature from a foreign or ancient culture can be a strange experience. Who are these people? Why are they doing what they're doing? What do these words I never heard of mean?

Seek Out Information

Learning something about the history, the land, the people, and the author before you read helps you overcome these challenges. World literature comes alive when you understand the context in which it was written.

The following features in this book will help you open new doors to literature from around the world:

Introductions

Why did stories from Ancient Greece often tell of long voyages across the sea? Why is storytelling such an important part of West African literature? Introductions provide answers to these and other questions. They are quick guides to the cultures and time periods that produced the literature you will read. Each introduction includes maps, information about history and society, a time line of important events, and a feature showing the contributions of that culture or period to today's world.

PART 1 In the Name of Honor

Literature of Ancient G...

Why It Matters
Greece is a small mountainous country, yet it gave birth to some of the most cherished ideas of Western civilization. The Greeks championed individual freedom, developed an early form of democracy, and demonstrated the power of rational thought. Greek ideals of beauty and justice have spread throughout the world. Greek literature, especially poetry and drama, continues to inspire writers today.

or Links to Ancient Greece, click on:

HUMANITIES
CLASSZONE.COM

LEARNING the Language of Literature

The Epics of Greece and Rome

Learning the Language of Literature

These two-page features introduce you to types of literature associated with certain cultures and time periods. Read about the development of the epic. Learn how literary movements, such as Romanticism and Realism, left their mark on the world.

4

② A Mountainous Terrain Mountain ranges divide mainland Greece into various regions. The Greeks believed that their gods and goddesses lived at the top of the highest mountain in Greece—Mount Olympus (shown above). Greek **mythology** greatly influenced the literature of the Western world.

③ Cradle of Democracy The largest and most influential of the Greek city-states, **Athens** was the birthplace of democracy, drama, and philosophy. Athenian sculpture and architecture are still imitated today. Athens was named for Athena, the gray-eyed goddess of war and wisdom. A statue of Athena is shown here.

④ Land of City-States The chains of mountains kept people isolated from one another and led to the creation of city-states—small independent areas centered around a single city. **Sparta** was a strong city-state known for its military way of life. Sparta and Athens were the main rivals in a war that lasted 27 years.

Author Biography and Build Background

Prereading pages give background that will help you understand each selection more fully. Learn about an author's life, study important terms, and find out more about the history and culture of the selection you're about to read.

Online Background

Background information doesn't stop there. Visit our Web site to learn even more about the cultural contributions of each time and place.

HUMANITIES
CLASSZONE.COM

Reader's Notebook

Putting your thoughts on paper can help you understand and connect with literature. Many readers record their ideas in a 📖 **READER'S NOTEBOOK**. You can use almost any kind of notebook for this purpose. Below are two ways you can use your notebook.

① IMPROVE YOUR READING SKILLS

Complete the 📖 **READER'S NOTEBOOK** activity on the **Preparing to Read** page of each selection. This activity will help you apply an important skill as you read.

PREPARING to Read

What **Men** Live By

Leo Tolstoy
Translated by Louise and Aylmer Maude

Question	Prediction
1. Who's the stranger that appears in section one?	1. He'll turn out to be someone who's the opposite of what he seems to be.

② RECORD YOUR THOUGHTS

Write down ideas, responses, connections, and questions before you read, while you read, and after you read a selection. Summarize important passages, and collect any ideas that may later be a springboard to your own writing.

Connect to Your Life

Would you give your last dollar to your friend? to a stranger? Discuss the idea of giving with your classmates. Then create a few moral guidelines that people could use when making decisions about giving.

Focus Your Reading

LITERARY ANALYSIS: FORESHADOWING
Foreshadowing is a writer's use of hints or clues to suggest what will happen later. For example, in "How Much Land Does a Man Need?" Pakhom's dream in section VII foreshadows his fate at the end. As you read, look for clues that foreshadow what's to come.

ACTIVE READING: PREDICTING
Predicting what will happen next in a story can alert you to foreshadowing. Keep in mind what you know about Tolstoy, and always use your own ability to figure things out in making your predictions.

📖 **READER'S NOTEBOOK** "What Men Live By" has many strange events that are not explained until the end of the story. As you come across each event in your reading, write a question about it and then a brief **prediction** that might answer the question. Use a chart like this one to keep track of your predictions.

Question	Prediction
1. Who's the stranger that appears in section 1?	1.

Working Portfolio

Artists and writers keep portfolios to store their works in progress or the works they are most proud of. Create your own **Working Portfolio**, using a folder, a box, or a notebook. As the year progresses, fill it with examples of your papers, your creative writing, your summaries of projects, and your own goals and accomplishments as a reader and writer.

Tasha Edwards
PORTFOLIO

Date	Project	Comments
10/6	Essay on Tolstoy's stories	Finished
11/19	Report on realism	Best paper I've written
12/8	Essay on "A Doll's House"	Need more supporting details

Strategies for Reading

Reading world literature presents special challenges and often requires more background than what you need to read literature from your own culture. However, once you begin reading, you apply the same reading strategies that you would for any piece of literature. Don't forget to **monitor** how well you're using these strategies during reading.

Predict Try to figure out what will happen next and how the selection might end. Then read on to see how accurate your guesses were.

Visualize Visualize characters, events, and setting to help you understand what's happening. Use the art to help you imagine faraway places. Pay attention to the images that form in your mind as you read.

Connect Connect personally with what you read. Think of similarities between the descriptions in the selection and what you have personally experienced, heard about, and read about. In spite of the obvious differences, you may find you have things in common with people from other times and cultures.

Question While you read, question what happens. Searching for reasons behind events and characters' feelings can help you feel closer to literature from another time and place.

Clarify Stop occasionally to review your understanding of what you read. You can do this by **summarizing** what you have read, identifying the **main idea**, and **making inferences**—drawing conclusions from the information you are given. As necessary, reread passages and background information. Also watch for answers to questions you had earlier.

Evaluate Form opinions about what you read, both while you're reading and after you've finished. Develop your own ideas about characters, events, time periods, and cultures.

On the following pages, you will see how one reader tackles a World Literature selection—how she uses background information and the Strategies for Reading above to understand literature from a different time and culture.

Green Willow

Japanese Folk Tale
Retold by Paul Jordan-Smith

In the era of Bummei there lived a young samurai, Tomotada, in the service of the daimyo of Noto. He was a native of Echizen, but had been accepted at a young age into the palace of the Lord of Noto, where he proved himself a good soldier and a good scholar as well, and enjoyed the favor of his prince. Handsome and amiable, he was admired also by his fellow samurai.

One day, the Lord of Noto called for Tomotada and sent him on a special quest to the Lord of Kyoto. Being ordered to pass through Echizen, Tomotada asked and was granted permission to visit his widowed mother. And so he set out on his mission.

Winter had already come; the countryside was covered with snow, and though his horse was among the most powerful in the Lord of Noto's stable, the young man was forced to proceed slowly. On the second day of his journey, he found himself in mountain districts where settlements were few and far between. His anxiety was increased by the onslaught of a heavy snowstorm, and his horse was showing signs of extreme fatigue. In the very moment of his despair, however, Tomotada caught sight of a cottage among the willows on a nearby hill. Reaching the dwelling, he knocked loudly on the storm doors which had been closed against the wind. Presently the doors opened, and an old woman appeared, who cried out with compassion at the sight of the noble Tomotada, "Ah, how pitiful! Traveling in such weather, and alone! Come in, young sir, come in!"

"What a relief to find a welcome in these lonely passes," thought Tomotada, as he led his horse to a shed behind the cottage. After seeing that his horse was well sheltered and fed, Tomotada entered the cottage, where he beheld the old woman and her husband, and a young girl as well, warming themselves by a fire of bamboo splints. The old couple respectfully requested that he be seated, and proceeded to warm some rice wine and prepare food for the warrior. The young girl, in the meantime, disappeared behind a screen, but not before Tomotada had observed with astonishment that she was extremely beautiful, though dressed in the meanest attire. He wondered how such a beautiful creature could be living in such a lonely and humble place. His thoughts, however, were interrupted by the old man, who had begun to speak.

"Honored Sir," he began. "The next village is far from here and the road is unfit for travel. Unless your quest is of such importance that it cannot be delayed, I would advise you not to force yourself and your horse beyond your powers of endurance. Our hovel is perhaps unworthy of your presence, and we have no comforts to offer; nevertheless, please honor us by staying under this miserable roof."

Alongside this story are comments that high school student **Nicola Shorobura** made as she read the story for the first time. Her comments will give you a glimpse into the mind of a reader actively engaged in the process of reading. To get the most from this reading model, first read the story on you own and record your responses to it in your 📖 READER'S NOTEBOOK. Then read Nicola's comments below and respond to each of the prompts labeled "YOUR TURN."

Nicola: This sets the mood really well and helps you picture what's happening.
VISUALIZING/EVALUATING

Nicola: I'm wondering who the old woman is. Maybe it'll say further on in the story.
QUESTIONING

Nicola: I bet that the girl will be a main character in this story.
PREDICTING

Nicola: He doesn't even know these people. They're being really nice to him and taking him in. They're apologizing for their place.
EVALUATING

➤ YOUR TURN
What details help you form a mental picture of the girl?
VISUALIZING

Tomotada was touched by the old man's words—and secretly, he was glad of the chance afforded him to see more of the young girl. Before long, a simple meal was set before him, and the girl herself came from behind the screen to serve the wine. She had changed her dress, and though her clothes were still of homespun, her long loose hair was neatly combed and smoothed. As she bent to fill his cup, Tomotada was amazed to see that she was even more beautiful than he had at first thought: she was the most beautiful creature he had ever seen. She moved with a grace that captivated him, and he could not take his eyes from her. The old man spoke apologetically, saying, "Please forgive the clumsy service of our daughter, Green Willow. She has been raised alone in these mountains and is only a poor, ignorant girl." But Tomotada protested that he considered himself lucky indeed to be served by so lovely a maiden. He saw that his admiring gaze made her blush, and he left his wine and food untasted before him. Suddenly struck by inspiration, he addressed her in a poem.

> As I rode through the winter
> I found a flower and thought,
> "Here I shall spend the day."
> But why does the blush of dawn appear
> When the dark of night is still around us?

Without a moment's hesitation, the girl replied:

> If my sleeve hides the faint color of dawn,
> Perhaps when morning has truly come
> My lord will remain.

Nicola: Her reply kind of seems like she's asking him to stay on.
CLARIFYING

➤ YOUR TURN
Do you agree with Nicola?
CLARIFYING

Then Tomotada knew that the girl had accepted his admiration, and he was all the more taken by the art of her verse and the feelings it expressed. "Seize the luck that has brought you here!" he thought to himself, and he resolved to ask the old couple to give him the hand of their daughter in marriage.

Alas for the Lord of Noto's quest!

The old couple were astonished by the request of Tomotada, and they bowed themselves low in gratitude. After some moments of hesitation, the father spoke: "Honored master, you are a person of too high a degree for us to consider refusing the honor your request brings. Indeed our gratitude is immeasurable. But this daughter of ours is merely a country girl, of no breeding and manners, certainly not fit to become the wife of a noble samurai such as yourself. But since you find the girl to your liking, and have condescended to overlook her peasant origins, please accept her as a gift, a humble handmaid. Deign, O Lord, to regard her henceforth as yours, and act towards her as you will."

Nicola: In this culture, I guess the parents have control over the girl's future.
EVALUATING/QUESTIONING

Seven Spring Herbs (c. 1918), Kaburaki Kiyokata. Color on silk, 139 cm × 48 cm. Yokohama Museum of Art, Japan.

Now a samurai was not allowed to marry without the consent of his lord, and Tomotada could not expect permission until his quest was finished. When morning came, Tomotada resumed his journey, but his heart grew more apprehensive with every footfall of his horse. Green Willow rode behind her lord, saying not a word, and gradually the progress of the young man slowed to a halt. He could not tear his thoughts from the girl, and did not know whether he should bring her to Kyoto. He was afraid, moreover, that the Lord of Noto would not give him permission to marry a peasant girl, and afraid also that his daimyo might be likewise captivated by her beauty and take her for himself. And so he resolved to hide with her in the mountains, to settle there and become himself a simple farmer. Alas for the Lord of Noto's quest!

For five happy years, Tomotada and Green Willow dwelt together in the mountains, and not a day passed that did not bring them both joy and delight in each other and their life together. Forgotten was the time before Green Willow had come into his life. But one day, while talking with her husband about some household matter, Green Willow uttered a loud cry of pain, and became very white and still. "What is it, my wife?" cried Tomotada as he took her in his arms. "Forgive me, my lord, for crying out so rudely, but the pain was so sudden . . . My dear husband, hold me to you and listen—do not let me go! Our union has been filled with great joy, and I have known with you a happiness that cannot bear description. But now it is at an end: I must beg of you to accept it."

Nicola: Why is the quest so important to him? He says he wants to marry the girl. Why not just do it? Maybe this has something to do with the samurai code of honor mentioned in **Build Background** at the beginning. QUESTIONING/CLARIFYING

Nicola: It seems Tomotada doesn't have a lot of confidence in what he does. He's scared of what's going to happen because in this society, his lord has total control of his life. EVALUATING/CLARIFYING

Nicola: The kind of love he has for her reminds me of Romeo and Juliet. Their love is more important than anything else. CONNECTING

Nicola: They brought each other joy and happiness. Why does it have to come to an end? Why is she ending it? QUESTIONING

Toba (Su Dongpo)
(1820–1832), Katsushika
Hokusai. Woodblock
print, 516 mm × 227 mm.
Honolulu (Hawaii)
Academy of Arts, gift of
James A. Michener, 1970
(15, 943).

"Ah!" cried Tomotada, "It cannot be so. What wild fancies are these? You are only a little unwell, my darling. Lie down and rest, and the pain shall pass."

"No, my dearest, it cannot be. I am dying—I do not imagine it. It is needless to hide from you the truth any longer, my husband. I am not a human being. The soul of a tree is my soul, the heart of a tree my heart, the sap of a willow is my life. And some one, at this most cruel of moments, has cut down my tree—even now its branches have fallen to the ground. And this is why I must die! I have not even the strength left to weep, nor the time . . ."

With another cry of pain, Green Willow turned her head and tried to hide her face behind her sleeve. In the same moment, her form seemed to fold in upon itself, and before Tomotada's astonished and grief-stricken eyes, her robes crumpled in the air and fell empty to the ground.

Many years after this, an itinerant monk came through the mountain passes on his way to Echizen. He stopped for water beside a stream, on the banks of which stood the stumps of three willow trees—two old and one young. Nearby, a rude stone memorial had been set up, which showed evidence of regular care unusual in such a remote place. He inquired about it from an old priest who lived in the neighborhood and was told the story of Green Willow.

"And what of Tomotada?" asked the mendicant, when the priest had finished his tale. But the old man had fallen into a reverie and gazed at the shrine, oblivious of his guest.

"Alas for the Lord of Noto's quest!" the old man sighed to himself and fell silent. The air grew chill as the evening drew on. At length, the old priest shook himself from his dreams.

"Forgive me!" he told his guest. "As age creeps upon me, I sometimes find myself lost in the memories of a young samurai."

Nicola: *Is this really happening, or is she just comparing herself to a tree that's been cut down? Her name is Green Willow, so maybe this is for real. Folk tales sometimes have unusual things happen.*
QUESTIONING/CLARIFYING

➤ YOUR TURN
What's your take on what has just happened?
CLARIFYING

Nicola: *Who is this monk? Why is he inquiring of the priest? What's the significance?*
QUESTIONING

➤ YOUR TURN
Who do you think the old priest might be?
PREDICTING

Nicola: *By the process of elimination, I figure that the priest was the samurai. He must have set up the memorial. This ending is really good. It's kind of magical.*
CLARIFYING/EVALUATING

Literature of the Ancient World
3000 B.C. – A.D. 500

Nakht hunting with his family (18th dynasty). From the tomb of Nakht, scribe and priest under Pharaoh Thutmose IV, in the cemetery of Sheikh Abd al-Qurnan, Luxor-Thebes, Egypt.
Photograph copyright © Erich Lessing/Art Resource, New York.

*"Man dies, his body is dust,
 his family all brought low to the earth;
But writing shall make him remembered,
 alive in the mouths of any who read."*

—PAPYRUS INSCRIPTION
(c. 1300–1100 B.C.)

PART 1
Spiritual Beginnings:
Mesopotamian, Egyptian, and
Hebrew Literature 16–101

PART 2
Sacred and Practical Teachings:
Literature of Ancient India 102–159

Mesopotamian, Egyptian, and Hebrew Literature

Why It Matters

The ancient Middle East is often called the cradle of civilization. In prehistoric times, people gathered in the fertile river valleys of Mesopotamia, Canaan, and Egypt— the Fertile Crescent—to farm. From their interactions arose the basic elements of civilization: law, commerce, arts, religion, education, and literature. On this foundation were built many later cultures, including our own.

For Links to the Ancient Middle East, click on:

HUMANITIES
CLASSZONE.COM

❶ River Cultures

The earliest civilizations in the arid Middle East grew up around rivers. Rivers provided water necessary for people, livestock, and agriculture. The **Nile, Tigris,** and **Euphrates Rivers** flooded each year, depositing silt that produced a rich topsoil good for planting. Rivers also provided an easy means of travel, promoting commerce and social interaction.

Mediterranean Sea

C A N A A N

❸

Samaria

Jordan River

Jerusalem

❶

Giza ❹
Memphis

E G Y P T

Nile River

❹ Egypt

The record for a single civilization's occupying a single area of land in the ancient Middle East belongs to the Egyptians, whose history spanned 3,000 years. The cities of Egypt were scattered up and down the upper third of the **Nile,** the longest river in the world. Protected on either side by vast deserts, Egypt was spared the constant warfare and shifts of power that troubled other regions. Egypt's famous **pyramids** are not only the tombs of Egyptian rulers but also the source of some of the world's oldest literature.

Red Sea

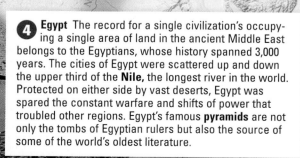

• *Thebes*

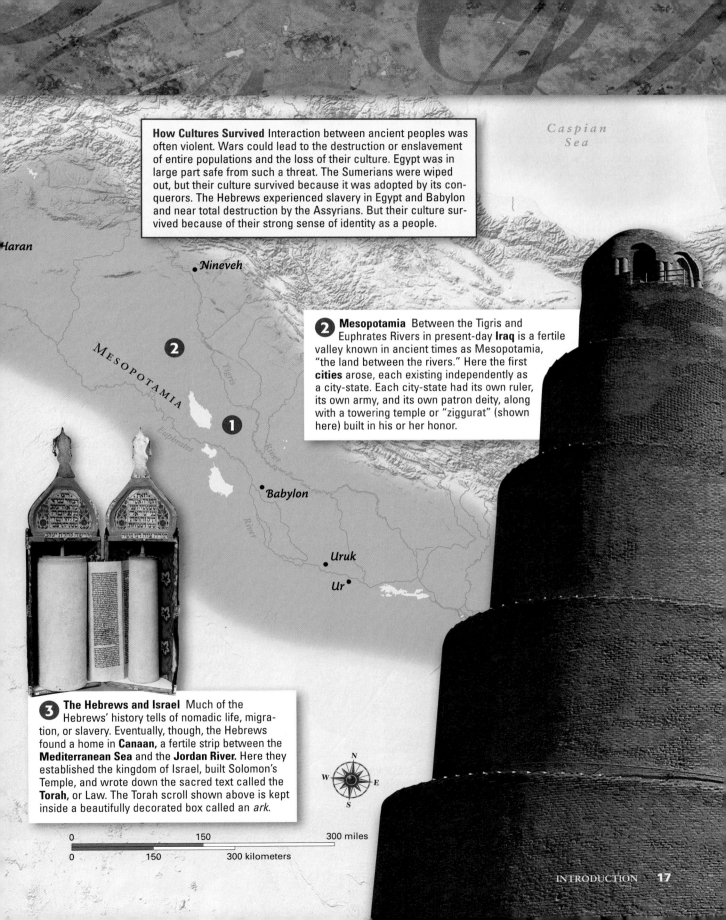

How Cultures Survived Interaction between ancient peoples was often violent. Wars could lead to the destruction or enslavement of entire populations and the loss of their culture. Egypt was in large part safe from such a threat. The Sumerians were wiped out, but their culture survived because it was adopted by its conquerors. The Hebrews experienced slavery in Egypt and Babylon and near total destruction by the Assyrians. But their culture survived because of their strong sense of identity as a people.

Caspian Sea

Haran

Nineveh

2 Mesopotamia Between the Tigris and Euphrates Rivers in present-day **Iraq** is a fertile valley known in ancient times as Mesopotamia, "the land between the rivers." Here the first **cities** arose, each existing independently as a city-state. Each city-state had its own ruler, its own army, and its own patron deity, along with a towering temple or "ziggurat" (shown here) built in his or her honor.

M E S O P O T A M I A

Tigris

Euphrates

1

2

River

Babylon

River

Uruk

Ur

3 The Hebrews and Israel Much of the Hebrews' history tells of nomadic life, migration, or slavery. Eventually, though, the Hebrews found a home in **Canaan,** a fertile strip between the **Mediterranean Sea** and the **Jordan River.** Here they established the kingdom of Israel, built Solomon's Temple, and wrote down the sacred text called the **Torah,** or Law. The Torah scroll shown above is kept inside a beautifully decorated box called an *ark*.

| 0 | | 150 | | 300 miles |
| 0 | 150 | | 300 kilometers | |

Mesopotamia: History, Arts, and Culture

After being settled by the Sumerians, Mesopotamia was dominated by a series of empires created by successive invaders. As a rule, however, the conquerors preserved the culture of the peoples they defeated.

Sumerians
c. 3500–2350 B.C.

Recorded history began with the Sumerians, who invented writing around 3000 B.C. A mysterious people possibly of Central Asian origin, they had settled southern Mesopotamia about 500 years earlier and taken up farming in the area, which became known as **Sumer.** By 3000 B.C. their villages had grown into large city-states, such as **Ur** and **Uruk.** Each had a different ruler and worshiped a different god or goddess.

Akkadians
c. 2350–2000 B.C.

Around 2350 B.C. a group of **Semites**—people who spoke a language related to Hebrew and Arabic—invaded Sumer from the north. Led by Sargon of Akkad, the **Akkadians** conquered the city-states of Sumer and unified them and the adjoining regions into the world's first empire. The Akkadians adopted much of Sumerian culture, including its religion and literature.

Babylonians
c. 2000–1570 B.C.

The Babylonians, a Semitic people who spoke Akkadian, conquered Mesopotamia about 2000 B.C., establishing an empire with Babylon, on the Euphrates River, as its capital. Like the Akkadians, the Babylonians adopted the culture of the Sumerians, including their literature. The Babylonian empire reached its peak from 1792 to 1750 B.C. under **King Hammurabi,** who established one of the first sets of laws—the **Code of Hammurabi.** Around 1570 B.C. the Babylonian empire fell to Kassite invaders, who ruled for more than 400 years.

Mask of King Sargon of Akkad

Assyrians
c. 850–612 B.C.

Various peoples vied for control of the region in the 300 years following Kassite rule. Around 850 B.C. one of these groups—the Assyrians, a warlike people from northern Mesopotamia—began to consolidate a great empire. They extended their rule from Mesopotamia to Egypt and Asia Minor. Known for ruthlessness in battle, the Assyrians destroyed the kingdom of Israel and dispersed its inhabitants (see page 22). However, the Assyrian capital of **Nineveh** became an important learning center. There **King Ashurbanipal** established an early library, preserving many Sumerian and Babylonian writings.

Neo-Babylonians
c. 612–539 B.C.

In 612 B.C. Chaldean invaders conquered the Assyrians, destroying Nineveh and founding the second Babylonian empire. This empire, which conquered and enslaved the remaining Jews of Palestine, endured until it was conquered by the Persians in 539 B.C.

SUMERIANS

c. 3500 B.C.

Cities, Civilization, and Culture

The Development of Cities Mesopotamian agriculture had begun well before the Sumerians arrived in about 3500 B.C. However, it was their effort to control the flooding of the Tigris and Euphrates for regular irrigation that forced people to become more organized, encouraging the growth of cities. This led to the following developments:

Architecture Some ancient Mesopotamian cities had magnificent buildings and gardens. A towering ziggurat could be seen from miles away. Walls, city gates, and thoroughfares were often decorated with impressive relief carvings or mosaics.

Technology The *shaduf*—a long pole on a fulcrum with a bucket on one end and a weight on the other—made it possible to lift water above river level and create terraced or "hanging" gardens and even fountains. Other Mesopotamian inventions include the wheel, the sail, and the plow.

Law Established sets of laws like the Code of Hammurabi made justice more consistent and made it easier for large groups of people to live together in harmony.

Writing The Sumerians invented the world's first writing. Known as **cuneiform,** or "wedge-shaped" script, it was made by pressing the ends of reeds into clay, which was then hardened by baking. Writing was essential to the development of commerce, law, government, religion, and literature.

Math and Science Using arithmetic, geometry, and astronomy, the Mesopotamians developed a calendar to help with irrigation needs and even a "map of the world," shown at left.

People and Society

The Upper Class
In most Mesopotamian cities, the aristocracy, or upper class, included members of the ruling family, high-ranking government officials, military leaders, priests, large landowners, and some very wealthy merchants.

The Common Folk
Lower on the social scale were merchants and farmers; artisans skilled in crafts, such as toolmakers, stonemasons, and potters; and scribes, who kept records of religious events and trade or government transactions.

The Slaves
On the bottom rung of the social ladder, slaves performed society's lowliest tasks. Some slaves were foreigners conquered in war; others were locals sold into slavery by impoverished parents.

The Women
Sumerian women had far more opportunities than women in most other ancient civilizations. They could farm, take up crafts, become merchants, even join the priesthood. Some of the world's oldest surviving written poetry is a series of sacred hymns composed by a moon priestess named Enheduanna, daughter of King Sargon of Akkad.

		NEO-BABYLONIANS ▼
AKKADIANS	BABYLONIANS	ASSYRIANS
c. 2350 B.C.	c. 2000 B.C.	c. 1570 B.C. c. 850 B.C. 539 B.C.

Egypt: History, Arts, and Culture

Egyptian history is divided into three "kingdoms." Each consisted of several dynasties, or successions of rulers from the same family or line.

Old Kingdom
c. 2660–2180 B.C.

By 3200 B.C., farming villages along the upper and lower Nile had organized into two separate kingdoms, Upper Egypt and Lower Egypt. These were united about 3100 B.C. by **King Menes,** who established the first dynasty. Little is known of the first two dynasties, but extensive records were kept in the third, which begins the Old Kingdom. During this time, powerful pharaohs built gigantic **pyramids** to serve as royal tombs. The Old Kingdom ended about 2180 B.C. Five weak dynasties followed in the First Intermediate Period.

Pharaoh Khafre (fourth dynasty), builder of the second of the great pyramids at Giza

Middle Kingdom
c. 2080–1640 B.C.

The Middle Kingdom began when a family of ruling nobles in Thebes emerged victorious in its struggles with the rulers of other cities, seized control of the entire kingdom, and established a powerful central government in Thebes. Amenemhet I, founder of the 12th dynasty, and his heirs strengthened the realm both politically and commercially, conquering the African kingdom of Nubia in the south and trading with Asian neighbors in the east. After the prosperity of the Middle Kingdom, weak rulers and internal strife allowed Semitic invaders called the **Hyksos** to conquer Egypt.

New Kingdom
c. 1570–1075 B.C.

The New Kingdom began when native Egyptian rulers banded together to drive out the dreaded Hyksos. Fighting with bronze weapons and two-wheeled chariots, New Kingdom pharaohs went on to make Egypt the world's strongest power. Thutmose III expanded his kingdom farther into Africa; Ramses II fought and later formed an alliance with the Hittites, an Indo-European people living in what today is Turkey. The weak rule of the 20th dynasty marks the end of the New Kingdom and the beginning of a long period of decline that culminated when Egypt was invaded and sacked by the Assyrians in 671 B.C.

History to Literature

EVENT IN HISTORY	EVENT IN LITERATURE
Ancient Egyptians believe in an afterlife.	Egyptian hymns, poems, and spells are collected in the Book of the Dead.
New Kingdom pharaoh Akhenaten institutes exclusive worship of the sun god Aten.	Akhenaten and his wife, Nefertiti, compose the "Hymn to Aten," or "Adoration of the Disk."

OLD KINGDOM

c. 2660 B.C.

MIDDLE KINGDOM

c. 2180 B.C.   c. 2080 B.C.

Life and the Afterlife

The culture of the ancient Egyptians was dominated by a religious outlook focused on preparation for the afterlife. Much of their technology and craftsmanship went into this effort. The construction of the great pyramids utilized the Egyptians' skill in mathematics and engineering, and the art of mummification benefited from their advances in medicine. The Egyptians' vision of paradise was an idealized version of life on earth. For this reason, preparations for the afterlife became a focal point for Egyptian artistic creativity as well.

This work of art was found in the tomb of King Tutankhamen. The image decorates the back of a throne intended for the king's use in the afterlife. The scene depicts the queen anointing the king with perfume. Overlooking the couple is the sun god, one of the most important Egyptian deities, who blesses them with hands extended on rays of light. The Egyptians believed that pictures and words describing their hopes for the afterlife could help make those hopes come true.

This famous painted bust of Queen Nefertiti was found in the workshop of a royal sculptor. The bust is not only a magnificent work of art in itself; it also gives us a visual representation of Egyptian fashion in cosmetics, clothing design, and jewelry.

People and Society

The Upper Class
In addition to the ruling family, who were considered divine, the upper class included wealthy landowners, government officials, high-ranking priests, and military leaders. Medicine was quite advanced, and most doctors were also in the upper class.

The Middle Class
This group included merchants, craftspeople, artisans, and other skilled workers. These people could sometimes move into the upper class through marriage.

The Lower Class
Farm laborers, who formed the bulk of the Egyptian lower class, also worked on building projects such as the pyramids. Even lower on the social scale were slaves. Though assigned heavy labor and lowly chores, slaves could marry, own property, and sometimes even buy their freedom.

The Women
Upper- and middle-class women had almost the same rights as men. They could own land, run businesses, and even propose marriage. Women in ruling families sometimes took the reins of power. Queen Ahhotep helped drive out the Hyksos, and a woman named Hatshepsut even reigned successfully as pharaoh.

NEW KINGDOM

c. 1640 B.C.   c. 1570 B.C.   c. 1075 B.C.

The Ancient Hebrews: History, Arts, and Culture

Hebrew civilization is associated more with a particular people than a geographical region. At different times, the Hebrews occupied nearly every part of the ancient Middle East and interacted with many of its other civilizations.

The Early Hebrews
c. 2000–1200 B.C.

The Semitic people known as the Hebrews or Jews trace their history to **Abraham,** a shepherd who lived in the Mesopotamian city of Ur about 2000 B.C. According to the Bible, he and his family crossed over the Euphrates River (the root of the word *Hebrew* means "cross over"), wandered along the Fertile Crescent to Egypt, and eventually settled in the land of Canaan. Abraham's son Isaac had a son named **Jacob,** also called **Israel,** whose twelve sons were the ancestors of the Twelve Tribes of Israel.

The Exodus
c. 1200–1020 B.C.

To escape famine, the Hebrews migrated once again to Egypt. There they multiplied over the centuries but were enslaved and forced into hard labor. Finally **Moses** brought them across the Sinai Desert back to Canaan. The Hebrews fought for two centuries to establish themselves and grew as a military power.

The Kingdom of Israel
c. 1020–922 B.C.

About 1020 B.C. the Hebrews united under a king named **Saul** to form the nation called Israel. Saul was succeeded by his son-in-law **David,** a popular king who established **Jerusalem** as Israel's capital; David was succeeded by his son **Solomon,** a powerful king who built the great Temple of Solomon in Jerusalem.

After Solomon's death, internal fighting divided the nation into two kingdoms—Israel in the north and Judah in the south.

The Divided Kingdom
c. 922–539 B.C.

Over the next 200 years, Israel and Judah sometimes fought each other and sometimes allied against outside enemies. The most powerful of these enemies were the Assyrians, to whom Israel fell in 722 B.C. About 150 years later, Judah fell to the Babylonian king Nebuchadnezzar II, who vanquished Jerusalem and destroyed the Temple in 586 B.C. Most of the surviving Jews were exiled to Babylon, where they stayed until King Cyrus the Great of Persia conquered Babylonia in 539 B.C. and let the Jews return to Jerusalem and rebuild the Temple.

King Solomon, Anagni Cathedral, Italy/The Art Archive/Dagli Orti.

History to Literature

EVENT IN HISTORY	EVENT IN LITERATURE
A flood devastates the Middle East.	The story of Noah in the Bible's Book of Genesis
Moses leads the Hebrews out of captivity in Egypt.	The Bible's Book of Exodus

THE EARLY HEBREWS

c. 2000 B.C.

The Center of Cultural Life

The Hebrews' change from nomads to city dwellers and citizens of a kingdom had a tremendous impact on their culture. Nomadic life does not encourage the creation of beautiful buildings or works of art or promote the development of technology. With their own land, the Hebrews had more opportunities for cultural expression.

The Temple A dramatic example of this expression is the construction of Solomon's Temple in Jerusalem. For many years the Hebrews carried their holiest relic, the tablets on which were inscribed the Ten Commandments, in a special chest with handles that was called the Ark of the Covenant. When the Temple was built, the tablets were permanently housed in its most sacred area, the "Holy of Holies."

In addition to being a monumental work of architecture, the Temple provided one of the most important settings for Hebrew cultural life. Psalms were sung there, and histories and stories that would become part of the Bible were read. Traditions of worship developed that continue in the practice of the Jewish faith to this day.

Esther Scroll (1848). Iraq, handwritten with ink, illustrated with tempera on parchment. Read annually for the festival of Purim. Collection of the Israel Museum, Jerusalem (H 95 L 1740 mm). Photograph copyright © Israel Museum.

People and Society

The Most Powerful
The early Hebrews followed tribal patriarchs, or "fathers," similar to tribal chiefs; later, judges presided as important military leaders; still later, the Hebrews united under a king. In a society dominated by faith, however, prophets and priests wielded great influence, even over judges and kings.

In the Middle
Landowners and warriors formed something of a middle class, which merchants and artisans gradually joined with the growth of Hebrew cities.

The Least Powerful
Most Hebrews were simple herders and farmers or worked as servants or hired help. During periods of military conquest, the Hebrews also made slaves of conquered peoples, as was the custom of the day.

The Women
Like most cultures of the ancient Middle East, Jewish society was dominated by males, and women had few rights and privileges outside the home. Nevertheless, they occasionally rose to positions of influence. For example, one of the most powerful military leaders was a female judge named Deborah.

THE EXODUS	THE KINGDOM OF ISRAEL	THE DIVIDED KINGDOM	
c. 1200 B.C.	c. 1020 B.C.	c. 922 B.C.	539 B.C.

Searching for the Past

Here are some of the major breakthroughs in the quest to reconstruct the history of ancient Middle Eastern cultures.

Tokens representing different items of trade

How Writing Was Invented

For years mysterious clay tokens had been found in the Middle East, some of them from as early as 8000 B.C. Researchers also noticed another mystery: many cuneiform tablets were curved rather than flat. Then in the 1990s archaeologist Denise Schmandt-Besserat hypothesized that the small images were a very early form of writing. Sumerian merchants used the tokens to record shipments of goods. For every sheep or jar of oil loaded on a boat, a token would be sealed into a clay envelope. The recipient could break the envelope to make sure a shipment was complete. In time, people also made impressions with the tokens on the outside of the envelopes so that they could be "read" without being broken. Eventually, pictures drawn on the clay with a reed replaced tokens altogether. These pictures in turn evolved into cuneiform, and scribes continued to make tablets rounded like the outside of an envelope.

Clay envelope showing both impressions made with tokens and drawn images

Breaking the Code

Egyptian hieroglyphics remained undeciphered for many years. But in 1799, near Rosetta, Egypt, soldiers in Napoleon's army found a large stone with three bands of writing on it: two in forms of hieroglyphics and one in Greek. Because the three texts on the **Rosetta Stone** contained the same message, scholars were able to use the known language— Greek—to decipher hieroglyphics.

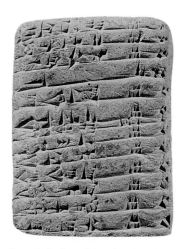

Rounded clay tablet showing the more advanced cuneiform script

The Rosetta Stone

A Library in the Sand

While serving as a British diplomat in the Middle East, Austen Henry Layard grew fascinated with the possibility of locating lost cities mentioned in the Bible. In 1849 he located the ruins of Nineveh, capital of ancient Assyria, and unearthed the once-magnificent library of Ashurbanipal, the seventh-century-B.C. Assyrian king. Housing some 25,000 broken clay tablets, the library was a virtual gold mine of early Mesopotamian literature, including the Gilgamesh epic, which had been lost for 24 centuries.

King Tut's Tomb

Although most Egyptian royal tombs were looted over the centuries, the tomb of the young king Tutankhamen survived with many of its riches intact. Its discovery by a British expedition in 1922 captured the world's imagination. In the burial chamber was a coffin of solid gold where the mummy of the young pharaoh rested, wearing a magnificent golden mask. Decorative hieroglyphic inscriptions identifying and honoring the dead king were meant to ease his way into the afterlife. In the treasury area was an array of valuables also aimed at making the king's afterlife comfortable—boats, thrones, golden goddess figurines, and even a chariot.

The Dead Sea Scrolls

In 1947 a young shepherd hunting for a lost goat in the desert near the Dead Sea came upon some caves that no one had entered for centuries. The caves contained earthenware jars that stored ancient scrolls carefully wrapped in linen to preserve them from the elements. Some of the scrolls turned out to be the oldest surviving texts of many sections of the Bible. Scholars date the scrolls to the time of Jesus. Most think the scrolls were likely the work of the Essenes, a Jewish sect living in the area at that time, possibly in contact with early Christians. To prevent damage, the Israeli government has allowed only a few experts to handle the scrolls, but their contents are now available for reading on the Internet.

The Search Continues

The library of King Ashurbanipal had been destroyed, and in its remains were found only broken tablets. However, in 1986 near Sippar, Iraq, an ancient library was discovered that contained unbroken tablets still on their shelves. The Gulf War and subsequent UN sanctions have prevented this find from being fully explored. But the library at Sippar may one day yield up literary treasures from the ancient world that we now can only imagine.

Time Line

c. approximately
B.C. before Christ
A.D. after Christ

ANCIENT MIDDLE EAST (3000 B.C.–A.D. 70)

| 3000 B.C. | A.D. 1 | PRESENT |

EVENTS IN LITERATURE

3000 B.C.	2500 B.C.	2000 B.C.
c. 2700 B.C. Earliest pyramid texts in Egypt	**c. 2500 B.C.** Earliest legends of Gilgamesh orally composed	**c. 2000 B.C.** First coffin texts in Egyptian tombs
	c. 2275 B.C. Enheduanna, priestess daughter of King Sargon, records some of the world's earliest surviving written poems	**c. 1700 B.C.** Old Babylonian version of Gilgamesh epic
	c. 2100 B.C. Sumerian Gilgamesh epics begin to be composed	
	c. 2040 B.C. Earliest versions of the Egyptian "Tale of the Shipwrecked Sailor"	

EVENTS IN THE ANCIENT MIDDLE EAST

3000 B.C.	2500 B.C.	2000 B.C.
c. 3000 B.C. Sumerians develop cuneiform writing	**c. 2350 B.C.** Sargon of Akkad conquers and unites city-states of Sumer	**c. 2000 B.C.** Babylonians conquer Akkadians in Mesopotamia; Hebrews migrate to Canaan
c. 3000 B.C. Egyptians begin using hieroglyphic writing	**c. 2180 B.C.** Egypt's Old Kingdom ends; period of weak rulers follows	**c. 1790 B.C.** Babylonian king Hammurabi issues ➤ his code of laws
c. 2750 B.C. Gilgamesh is king in Sumerian city-state of Uruk	**c. 2080 B.C.** Beginning of Egypt's Middle Kingdom (to c. 1600 B.C.)	**c. 1570 B.C.** Beginning of Egypt's New Kingdom (to c. 1075 B.C.)
c. 2556 B.C. Great Pyramid of Giza is built during Egypt's Old Kingdom		**c. 1570 B.C.** Kassites take control in Mesopotamia

Inscription of code

EVENTS IN WORLD HISTORY

3000 B.C.	2500 B.C.	2000 B.C.
c. 3000 B.C. New Stone Age in northern Europe	**c. 2500 B.C.** First cities in India's Indus Valley	**c. 2000 B.C.** Late Bronze Age in Greece; Minoan civilization flourishes on Crete
c. 2750 B.C. Beaker People of Britain build Stonehenge ➤		**c. 2000 B.C.** First cities emerge along China's Yellow River
		c. 1600 B.C. Mycenean culture flourishes on the Greek mainland
		c. 1600 B.C. Beginning of China's Shang Dynasty

1500 B.C.   1000 B.C.   500 B.C.

c. 1500 B.C. Egyptian Book of the Dead assembled from earlier texts

c. 1375 B.C. "Adoration of the Disk" ("Hymn to Aten") composed

c. 1300 B.C. Standard version of *Epic of Gilgamesh* written down

c. 1300 B.C. Oldest New Kingdom love lyrics composed

c. 1000 B.C. Hebrew Torah assembled; many biblical psalms composed

c. 650 B.C. Gilgamesh epic collected or copied for Ashurbanipal's library

c. 612 B.C. Ashurbanipal's library buried; Gilgamesh epic lost for next 24 centuries

c. 600 B.C. Bible's Book of Ruth

c. 300 B.C. Entire Hebrew Bible assembled

c. A.D. 100 New Testament Gospels completed

1500 B.C.   1000 B.C.   500 B.C.

c. 1472 B.C. Hatshepsut is female pharaoh of Egypt

c. 1365 B.C. Amenhotep IV (Akhenaten) briefly establishes a monotheistic religion in Egypt

c. 1350 B.C. Tutankhamen (King Tut) succeeds Akhenaten as pharaoh

c. 1205 B.C. Moses leads Hebrew people from captivity in Egypt

c. 1020 B.C. Hebrews establish kingdom of Israel, with Saul as first king

922 B.C. Death of King Solomon; Hebrew kingdom divided into Israel and Judah

650 B.C. Assyrian empire at its peak

586 B.C. Nebuchadnezzar II captures Jerusalem; Hebrews' Babylonian captivity begins

539 B.C. Persia's Cyrus the Great conquers the Babylonians and ends Babylonian captivity

c. 332–331 B.C. Alexander the Great conquers Egypt and Persia and brings the Hebrews under Hellenistic (Greek) control

63 B.C. Romans gain control of Judah, which they call Judea

c. A.D. 29 Crucifixion of Jesus

c. A.D. 70 Fall of Jerusalem; Jews dispersed in the Diaspora

1500 B.C.   1000 B.C.   500 B.C.

c. 1500 B.C. Aryans, Indo-European speakers of central Asia, invade India

c. 1200 B.C. Olmec civilization flourishes on Mexico's Gulf Coast

c. 1200 B.C. City of Troy defeated by ancient Greeks

c. 1050 B.C. Chou overthrow China's Shang Dynasty and establish their own

776 B.C. First recorded Greek Olympic Games

c. 563 B.C. Birth of Siddhartha Gautama, founder of Buddhism

551 B.C. Birth of Chinese philosopher Confucius

c. 500 B.C. Nok culture develops iron-making technology in West Africa

c. 500 B.C. Zapotec civilization at its height in Mexico

c. 204 B.C. Emperor Shih Huang Ti completes first Great Wall of China

27 B.C. Augustus (Octavian) becomes emperor of Rome

Modern Hebrew
Over the centuries, Jews continued to study the Hebrew language and use it in worship. When the modern state of Israel was proclaimed in 1948, a modernized form of Hebrew became one of its official everyday languages.

Law
The Code of Hammurabi and the Mosaic Code of the Torah are the ancestors of all Western laws. The Ten Commandments— the most important laws of the Torah—remain basic to both Jewish and Christian moral teachings.

Christianity

Judaism

Islam

Birthplace of Three Religions
Jewish monotheism gave birth to Christianity, and both faiths influenced Islam as well. Christians accept the Hebrew Bible as part of their own, and Muslims recognize Moses and other biblical figures as important prophets.

Libraries
Modern libraries carry on the mission established by the ancient libraries of Mesopotamia: to preserve the written works of our culture.

Architecture
The magnificent pyramids and obelisks of ancient Egypt have left their mark on Western architecture. The Washington Monument in Washington, D.C., and the glass pyramid at the Louvre in Paris are just two illustrations of Egyptian influence.

Writing
The invention of the written word enabled people to record, store, and retrieve information. Today, computers can perform these operations in record time, but they still depend heavily on the written word.

Foundations of Early Literature

Why It Matters

To explain the world's mysteries, to sing praise and express one's faith, to impart wisdom, to record great deeds and landmark events—these are some of the universal human needs and desires that gave rise to early literature. It is hard for us today to understand the importance of literature in early societies. We tend to think of literature as something far removed from real life. Yet in early societies, literature was at the center of life. It connected people to their cultures' strongest beliefs, traditions, and values.

Detail of *Moses Receiving the Ten Commandments* (16th century), Raphael

From Oral to Written Literature

The world's earliest literature was oral, passed along by word of mouth from one person to another and from one generation to the next. This literature was always connected with some important activity—singing, storytelling, religious or social ritual, prayer, teaching, or even magic. As civilizations progressed, however, they began to use writing to preserve their literature. This had the advantage of giving works a stable and lasting form. But it often separated the works from the activities they were related to, so that it is harder for us today to fully appreciate their importance.

Early Literary Forms

Early literature took different forms to serve different purposes:

▶ **Myths** are traditional stories— often about gods and goddesses— that serve to explain natural phenomena, the human situation, and the origins of beliefs and rituals. *The Epic of Gilgamesh* incorporates several Sumerian myths into its plot.

▶ **Heroic literature** records and celebrates the great deeds of heroes and heroines. Probably as early as 2500 B.C., Gilgamesh, king of Uruk, was celebrated in Sumerian oral **legends.** In time, these evolved into an **epic,** a long poem celebrating the exploits of this important hero in Sumerian culture.

▶ **Sacred verse,** such as **hymns, prayers,** and **psalms,** expresses religious faith and is usually written to be chanted or sung. Some of the world's oldest surviving written poems are hymns praising Sumerian gods and goddesses. The Egyptian Book of the Dead contains hymns to the god Osiris.

▶ **Wisdom literature** instructs or advises human beings about wise and moral behavior. Sometimes it takes the form of memorable sayings, like the **proverbs** of the Bible. At other times, brief stories are used to illustrate moral messages, as in the New Testament **parables.**

▶ **Folk tales** focus on ordinary people having extraordinary experiences. Often they feature magic, exaggeration, and humor. Ancient Egypt produced one of the world's oldest folk tales about a shipwrecked sailor. The tale probably inspired the famous tales of Sindbad that appear in *The Thousand and One Nights.*

Literature Across Time and Cultures

The literature of every culture reflects the culture's distinctive qualities. Yet when we look at many works from different cultures over the ages, we find some startling similarities. Certain types of situations, characters, and images seem to occur again and again, even in works from cultures having no knowledge of one another.

For example, *The Epic of Gilgamesh* and the Book of Genesis both tell of a great flood that nearly destroyed humanity. The *Popol Vuh,* which could not have been influenced by either of the other two works, tells of a similar event. Another recurring story element is a **quest,** a journey to find a treasure, achieve a goal, or undergo a personal transformation. Many ancient works of literature are quest stories, including *The Epic of Gilgamesh,* the *Odyssey,* the *Aeneid,* and the biblical stories of Abraham and Moses.

Archetypes

Common elements such as situations, characters, or images that appear again and again in literature and art are called **archetypes.** Scholars sometimes explain archetypes in terms of psychology. Stories about quests, for example, may be common because a quest is a good analogy for life. A journey to the underworld or to the bottom of the sea can stand for a person's exploration of hidden parts of his or her psyche. Archetypes reflect universal characteristics of human experience. They apply to all people, regardless of time or culture.

YOUR TURN Can you think of recent books or movies that tell stories about quests?

Armand Assante in TV production of the *Odyssey*

Strategies for Reading: Early Literature

1. Before reading, learn as much as you can about the culture and time from which the work comes.

2. Notice what the literary form of the work is—for example, myth, heroic literature, or sacred verse. Think about the purposes of the form, and look for ways in which the work fulfills them.

3. If the work is lengthy, use a list or diagram to help keep track of characters and major events.

4. If a passage confuses you, go back and summarize its main idea.

5. If the work is a short one, such as a song or a prayer, read it through once without stopping, then read it again carefully line by line.

6. When reading *The Epic of Gilgamesh* (page 32) and the *Popol Vuh* (page 76), use the accompanying Guides for Reading to help clarify meaning.

7. Monitor your reading strategies, and modify them when your understanding breaks down. Remember to use the strategies for active reading: **predict, visualize, connect, question, clarify,** and **evaluate.**

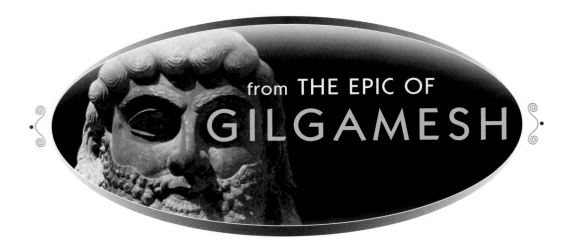

from THE EPIC OF
GILGAMESH

Build Background

What Is *The Epic of Gilgamesh?*

The Epic of Gilgamesh is one of the oldest works of literature in existence. The earliest versions of the story date back over 4,000 years to a time more than 1,000 years before the *Iliad* and the *Odyssey* or the first books of the Bible. Yet the story is one that modern readers can understand and enjoy because it deals with concerns that still matter to people today: friendship, heroism, mortality, and the desire to control one's destiny.

Gilgamesh is two parts god and one part human. In the first half of the story, Gilgamesh explores his godlike side. Using superhuman powers, he performs amazing feats and even defies the gods. But along with his extraordinary abilities come extraordinary flaws. Gilgamesh is arrogant, boastful, selfish, and destructive; he represents both the best and the worst that a person can be.

In the second half of the story, Gilgamesh explores the human side of his character as he faces unexpected limitations of his power. These limitations not only show his human weaknesses; they also give him the opportunity to develop human strengths. This part of the epic also contains a flood story remarkably like the one in the Bible.

How the Epic Evolved *The Epic of Gilgamesh,* like most epics, is based to some degree on fact. Scholars believe that Gilgamesh was a Sumerian king who ruled over the city-state of Uruk around 2700 B.C. In the centuries following his death, stories about him circulated orally and tales of his adventures grew. Through this oral tradition of storytelling, Gilgamesh developed over time into a figure of legendary proportions.

The evolution of this oral tradition into the written epic that we have today was the work of nearly 1,000 years. Written stories about Gilgamesh existed in the Sumerian language by 2000 B.C. By then, however, the Sumerians had been invaded and defeated twice, first by the Akkadians and then by the Babylonians. The Babylonians put an end to Sumerian civilization. However, they valued the culture of the Sumerians and integrated it into their own. Using the older culture's cuneiform script, the Babylonians preserved and translated the Gilgamesh texts and continued to develop them. The "standard" version of the epic that we have today was put together and written down by a Babylonian scribe around 1300 B.C.

For a humanities activity, click on:

HUMANITIES
CLASSZONE.COM

How the Epic Survived The Assyrian king Ashurbanipal (668–627 B.C.) set out to compile the world's first great library in his capital city of Nineveh. He sent representatives all over the ancient Middle East to collect, copy, and translate famous texts. Among these were at least 35 copies of *The Epic of Gilgamesh.* However, when the Assyrian empire fell to its enemies in 612 B.C., Nineveh was leveled. The library was destroyed, and *The Epic of Gilgamesh* lost.

Nearly 2,500 years later, in 1849, a young archaeologist named Austen Henry Layard unearthed the remains of the buried library. What he found was more than 25,000 broken tablets. It was not until the mid-1850s that the scholars Henry Rawlinson and George Smith deciphered the cuneiform script found on the broken tablets. Years later, Smith announced a remarkable discovery: among the newly excavated writings was a story of a great flood like the one described in the Bible, but much older. What Smith had discovered was part of *The Epic of Gilgamesh.*

To date, none of the 11 Gilgamesh tablets have been completely restored, but by comparing fragments of different copies, scholars have been able to fill in many gaps in the text. Much of the epic is still missing, however. Translators must use their imaginations, their literary skills, and their knowledge of cuneiform to bring this masterpiece to the modern reader.

Archaeological excavation in progress at the site of the ancient city of Ebla in Syria. Cuneiform tablets found at this site reveal a civilization that flourished in the third millennium B.C. To date, more than half a million tablets have been found in the Middle East.

Connect to Your Life

In this story the main character experiences a loss that he finds hard to accept. Think of some disappointments or defeats that you or people you know have experienced—for example, moving away from friends to a new town or breaking up with a boyfriend or girlfriend. In each case, how easy was it to accept the situation?

Focus Your Reading

LITERARY ANALYSIS: THE QUEST STORY
The Epic of Gilgamesh may be the oldest quest story in existence. On page 31, you learned that a **quest story** is a kind of story that is common to many cultures. In a quest story, a hero goes on a journey and tries to achieve a goal, such as bringing back a valuable object or acquiring knowledge. Usually, a **quest hero** has special powers or special friends that help (or hinder) him or her on the journey. As you read this story, notice what powers and friends Gilgamesh has and what roles they play in his quest.

ACTIVE READING: CAUSE AND EFFECT
Events in a plot are often related by **cause and effect.** One event in the story causes another event, which is the effect. The effect may in turn cause another event, and so on. For example, on page 35, Gilgamesh's behavior causes people to complain about him. As a result of these complaints, the gods take action against him.

📖 **READER'S NOTEBOOK** As you read this story, keep track of cause-and-effect relationships by using a chart. Remember that some events may appear first as effects and then again as causes.

Causes	Effects
→	
→	

WORDS TO KNOW **Vocabulary Preview**

allot	musing	prevail	teem
incantation	ominous	stupor	transit
lament	ordain		

from The Epic of Gilgamesh

Translated by N. K. Sandars

• CHARACTERS AND PLACES IN THE EPIC •

Anu (ā′nōō): father of the gods, who had an important temple in Uruk

Anunnaki (ä-nōō-nä′kē): gods who judge the dead and control destinies

Belit-Sheri (bĕl′ēt-shĕr′ē): scribe and recorder of the underworld gods

Dilmun (dĭl′mən): a paradise in the world of the gods

Ea (ā′ä): god of waters and of wisdom and one of the creators of mankind, toward whom he is usually well-disposed

Enkidu (ĕn′kē-dōō): Gilgamesh's friend. Molded by Aruru, goddess of creation, out of clay, he is wild or natural man.

Enlil (ĕn′lĭl): god of earth, wind, and spirit; carries out tasks for Anu

Ereshkigal (ĕ-rĕsh′kē′gäl): queen of the underworld

Gilgamesh (gĭl′gə-mĕsh′): king of Uruk and the hero of the epic

Irkalla (ĭr-kä′lə): another name for Ereshkigal, the queen of the underworld

Ishtar (ĭsh′tär): goddess of love, fertility, and war, called the Queen of Heaven

Nergal (nĕr′gäl): husband of Ereshkigal and coruler of the underworld

Ninurta (nə-nĕr′tə): warrior and god of war, wells, and irrigation

Shamash (shä′mäsh): sun god, judge and giver of laws

Siduri (sə-dōō′rē): divine winemaker and brewer, who lives on the shore of the sea in the garden of the sun

Urshanabi (ûr′shə-nä′bē): ferryman of Utnapishtim, who sails daily across the waters of death that divide the garden of the sun from the paradise where Utnapishtim lives

Uruk (ōō′rŏŏk′): biblical Erech, modern Warka, in southern Babylonia between Fara and Ur; shown by excavation to have been an important city from very early times, with great temples to the gods Anu and Ishtar

Utnapishtim (ōōt′nə-pēsh′təm): friend of the god Ea, with whose help he survives the flood, together with his family and with "the seed of all living creatures." He and his wife are the only mortals to be granted the gift of eternal life.

Gilgamesh and Enkidu slaying Humbaba. Photograph courtesy of the Royal Ontario Museum, ©ROM.

GUIDE FOR READING

FOCUS In this section, Enkidu tells Gilgamesh about a dream of a visit to the underworld, the place where people go after they die. As you read, look for passages that help you understand what the ancient Mesopotamians expected the afterlife to be like.

THE DEATH OF ENKIDU

The hero Gilgamesh, king of Uruk, is "two-thirds a god, one-third a man." In this epic, we see him exploring both sides of his character.

Gilgamesh is first presented as a superhuman ruler who has let his power go to his head. He has begun taking advantage of his subjects rather than taking care of them. The gods hear the people's complaints and create Enkidu, a "hairy-bodied wild man" equal in strength to Gilgamesh, to fight him. Instead of fighting, however, Enkidu and Gilgamesh become best friends. Together they fight and defeat Humbaba, a monster created by the gods to guard a sacred grove.

After the victory, the goddess Ishtar falls in love with Gilgamesh. When he rejects her, she has her father, Anu, send the Bull of Heaven to punish him. Together, Gilgamesh and Enkidu kill the bull. For this and other offenses, the gods decree, one of the two heroes must die. Enkidu, who is not part god, is chosen. Before he dies, Enkidu has a dream of what waits for him in the afterlife.

As Enkidu slept alone in his sickness, in bitterness of spirit he poured out his heart to his friend. "It was I who cut down the cedar, I who leveled the forest, I who slew Humbaba and now see what has become of me. Listen, my friend, this is the dream I dreamed last night. The heavens roared, and earth rumbled back an answer; between them stood I before an awful being, the somber-faced man-bird; he had directed on me his purpose. His was a vampire face, his foot was a lion's foot, his hand was an eagle's talon. He fell on me and his claws were in my hair, he held me fast and I smothered; then he transformed me so that my arms became wings covered with feathers. He turned his stare towards me, and led me away to the palace of Irkalla, the Queen of Darkness, to the house from which none who enters ever returns, down the road from which there is no coming back.

"There is the house whose people sit in darkness; dust is their food and clay their meat. They

"THE DREAM WAS MARVELOUS BUT THE TERROR WAS GREAT."

are clothed like birds with wings for covering, they see no light, they sit in darkness. I entered the house of dust and I saw the kings of the earth, their crowns put away for ever; rulers and princes, all those who once wore kingly crowns and ruled the world in the days of old. They who had stood in the place of the gods like Anu and Enlil, stood now like servants to fetch baked meats in the house of dust, to carry cooked meat and cold water from the water-skin. In the house of dust which I entered were high priests and acolytes,[1] priests of the <u>incantation</u> and of ecstasy; there were servers of the temple, and there was Etana, that king of Kish whom the eagle carried to heaven in the days of old. I saw also Samuqan, god of cattle, and there was Ereshkigal the Queen of the Underworld; and Belit-Sheri squatted in front of her, she who is recorder of the gods and keeps the book of death. She held a tablet from which she read. She raised her head, she saw me and spoke: "Who has brought this one here?" Then I awoke like a man drained of blood who wanders alone in a waste of rushes; like one whom the bailiff has seized and his heart pounds with terror."

Gilgamesh had peeled off his clothes, he listened to his words and wept quick tears, Gilgamesh listened and his tears flowed. He opened his mouth and spoke to Enkidu: "Who is there in strong-walled Uruk who has wisdom like this? Strange things have been spoken, why does your heart speak strangely? The dream was marvelous but the terror was great; we must treasure the dream whatever the terror; for the dream has shown that misery comes at last to the healthy man, the end of life is sorrow." And Gilgamesh <u>lamented</u>, "Now I will pray to the great gods, for my friend had an <u>ominous</u> dream."

This day on which Enkidu dreamed came to an end and he lay stricken with sickness. One whole day he lay on his bed and his suffering increased. He said to Gilgamesh, the friend on whose account he had left the wilderness, "Once I ran for you, for the water of life, and I now have nothing." A second day he lay on his bed and Gilgamesh watched over him but the sickness increased. A third day he lay on his bed, he called out to Gilgamesh, rousing him up. Now he was weak and his eyes were blind with weeping. Ten days he lay and his suffering increased, eleven and twelve days he lay on his bed of pain. Then he called to Gilgamesh, "My friend, the great goddess cursed me and I must die in shame. I shall not die like a man fallen in battle; I feared to fall, but happy is the man who falls in the battle, for I must die in shame." And Gilgamesh wept over Enkidu. . . .

PAUSE & REFLECT How would you describe the afterlife depicted in Enkidu's dream?

---

1. **acolytes** (ăk′ə-līts′): assistants at religious services.

WORDS TO KNOW

incantation (ĭn′kăn-tā′shən) *n.* a set of words chanted or sung as part of a religious ritual
lament (lə-mĕnt′) *v.* to express grief or sorrow
ominous (ŏm′ə-nəs) *adj.* threatening; signaling evil to come

· THE SEARCH FOR EVERLASTING LIFE ·

Enkidu dies. For the first time, Gilgamesh is faced with a situation he cannot control. He also experiences for the first time the human emotions of grief and fear.

Bitterly Gilgamesh wept for his friend Enkidu; he wandered over the wilderness as a hunter, he roamed over the plains; in his bitterness he cried, "How can I rest, how can I be at peace? Despair is in my heart. What my brother is now, that shall I be when I am dead. Because I am afraid of death I will go as best I can to find Utnapishtim whom they call the Faraway, for he has entered the assembly of the gods." So Gilgamesh traveled over the wilderness, he wandered over the grasslands, a long journey, in search of Utnapishtim, whom the gods took after the deluge;[2] and they set him to live in the land of Dilmun, in the garden of the sun; and to him alone of men they gave everlasting life.

At night when he came to the mountain passes Gilgamesh prayed: "In these mountain passes long ago I saw lions, I was afraid and I lifted my eyes to the moon; I prayed and my prayers went up to the gods, so now, O moon god Sin, protect me." When he had prayed he lay down to sleep, until he was woken from out of a dream. He saw the lions round him glorying in life; then he took his axe in his hand, he drew his sword from his belt, and he fell upon them like an arrow from the string, and struck and destroyed and scattered them.

So at length Gilgamesh came to Mashu, the great mountains about which he had heard many things, which guard the rising and the setting sun. Its twin peaks are as high as the wall of heaven and its paps reach down to the underworld. At its gate the Scorpions stand guard, half man and half dragon; their glory is terrifying, their stare strikes death into men, their shimmering halo sweeps the mountains that guard the rising sun. When Gilgamesh saw them he shielded his eyes for the length of a moment only; then he took courage and approached. When they saw him so undismayed the Man-Scorpion called to his mate, "This one who comes to us now is flesh of the gods." The mate of the Man-Scorpion answered, "Two thirds is god but one third is man."

Then he called to the man Gilgamesh, he called to the child of the gods: "Why have you come so great a journey; for what have you traveled so far, crossing the dangerous waters; tell me the reason for your coming?" Gilgamesh answered, "For Enkidu; I loved him dearly, together we endured all kinds of hardships; on his account I have come, for the common lot of man has taken him. I have wept for him day and night, I would not give up his body for burial, I thought my friend would come back because of my weeping. Since he went, my life is nothing; that is why I have traveled here in search of Utnapishtim my father; for men say he has entered the assembly of the gods, and has found everlasting life. I have a desire to question him concerning the living and the dead." The Man-Scorpion opened his mouth and said, speaking to Gilgamesh, "No man born of woman has done what you have asked, no mortal man has gone into the mountain; the length of it is twelve leagues[3] of darkness; in it there is no light, but

2. **deluge** (dĕl′yo͞oj): an unusually heavy, destructive flood.

3. **twelve leagues:** roughly thirty-six miles.

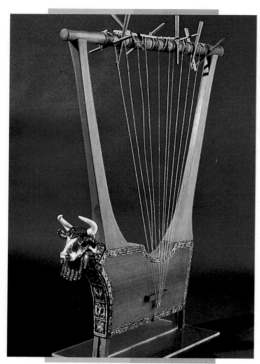

Sumerian bull-headed lyre. The British Museum, London.

haematite and rare stones, agate,[4] and pearls from out of the sea. While Gilgamesh walked in the garden by the edge of the sea Shamash saw him, and he saw that he was dressed in the skins of animals and ate their flesh. He was distressed, and he spoke and said, "No mortal man has gone this way before, nor will, as long as the winds drive over the sea." And to Gilgamesh he said, "You will never find the life for which you are searching." Gilgamesh said to glorious Shamash, "Now that I have toiled and strayed so far over the wilderness, am I to sleep, and let the earth cover my head for ever? Let my eyes see the sun until they are dazzled with looking. Although I am no better than a dead man, still let me see the light of the sun."

PAUSE & REFLECT What quality or behavior do you think is most helpful to Gilgamesh in overcoming obstacles on his journey?

the heart is oppressed with darkness. From the rising of the sun to the setting of the sun there is no light." Gilgamesh said, "Although I should go in sorrow and in pain, with sighing and with weeping, still I must go. Open the gate of the mountain." And the Man-Scorpion said, "Go, Gilgamesh, I permit you to pass through the mountain of Mashu and through the high ranges; may your feet carry you safely home. The gate of the mountain is open." . . .

Gilgamesh must walk 12 leagues in total darkness to pass through the mountain. But at last he reaches a wonderful world no mortal has seen.

There was the garden of the gods; all round him stood bushes bearing gems. Seeing it he went down at once, for there was fruit of carnelian with the vine hanging from it, beautiful to look at; lapis lazuli leaves hung thick with fruit, sweet to see. For thorns and thistles there were

FOCUS As you read the next section, look for the paragraph in which Siduri offers advice to Gilgamesh. Then look for the paragraph in which Gilgamesh responds to this recommendation.

Beside the sea she lives, the woman of the vine, the maker of wine; Siduri sits in the garden at the edge of the sea, with the golden bowl and the golden vats that the gods gave her. She is covered with a veil; and where she sits she sees Gilgamesh coming towards her, wearing skins, the flesh of the gods in his body, but despair in his heart, and his face like the face of one who has made a long journey. She looked, and as she scanned the distance she said in her own heart, "Surely this is some felon; where is he going now?" And she

---

4. **carnelian** (kär-nēl′yən) . . . **lapis lazuli** (lăp′ĭs lăz′ə-lē) . . . **haematite** (hē′mə-tīt′) . . . **agate** (ăg′ĭt): gemstones of various colors. Carnelian is red or reddish-brown, lapis lazuli is deep blue, haematite is a dull metal shade, and agate often has multicolored stripes.

barred her gate against him with the cross-bar and shot home the bolt. But Gilgamesh, hearing the sound of the bolt, threw up his head and lodged his foot in the gate; he called to her, "Young woman, maker of wine, why do you bolt your door; what did you see that made you bar your gate? I will break in your door and burst in your gate, for I am Gilgamesh who seized and killed the Bull of Heaven, I killed the watchman of the cedar forest, I overthrew Humbaba who lived in the forest, and I killed the lions in the passes of the mountain."

Then Siduri said to him, "If you are that Gilgamesh who seized and killed the Bull of Heaven, who killed the watchman of the cedar forest, who overthrew Humbaba that lived in the forest, and killed the lions in the passes of the mountain, why are your cheeks so starved and why is your face so drawn? Why is despair in your heart and your face like the face of one who has made a long journey? Yes, why is your face burned from heat and cold, and why do you come here wandering over the pastures in search of the wind?"

Gilgamesh answered her, "And why should not my cheeks be starved and my face drawn? Despair is in my heart and my face is the face of one who has made a long journey, it was burned with heat and with cold. Why should I not wander over the pastures in search of the wind? My friend, my younger brother, he who hunted the wild ass of the wilderness and the panther of the plains, my friend, my younger brother who seized and killed the Bull of Heaven and overthrew Humbaba in the cedar forest, my friend who was very dear to me and who endured dangers beside me, Enkidu my brother, whom I loved, the end of mortality has overtaken him. I wept for him seven days and nights till the worm fastened on him. Because of my brother I am afraid of death, because of my brother I stray through the wilderness and cannot rest. But now, young woman, maker of wine, since I have seen your face do not let me see the face of death which I dread so much."

She answered, "Gilgamesh, where are you hurrying to? You will never find that life for which you are looking. When the gods created man they <u>allotted</u> to him death, but life they retained in their own keeping. As for you, Gilgamesh, fill your belly with good things; day and night, night and day, dance and be merry, feast and rejoice. Let your clothes be fresh, bathe yourself in water, cherish the little child that holds your hand, and make your wife happy in your embrace; for this too is the lot of man."

But Gilgamesh said to Siduri, the young woman, "How can I be silent, how can I rest, when Enkidu whom I love is dust, and I too shall die and be laid in the earth. You live by the seashore and look into the heart of it; young woman, tell me now, which is the way to Utnapishtim, the son of Ubara-Tutu? What directions are there for the passage; give me, oh, give me directions. I will

"NO MORTAL MAN HAS GONE THIS WAY BEFORE, NOR WILL, AS LONG AS THE WINDS DRIVE OVER THE SEA."

WORDS TO KNOW
allot (ə-lŏt') *v.* to give as a share or portion

cross the Ocean if it is possible; if it is not I will wander still farther in the wilderness." . . .

Siduri tells Gilgamesh that he must cross the ocean with the boatman Urshanabi. When she hints that Urshanabi might refuse to take him, Gilgamesh loses his temper. He smashes Urshanabi's sacred stones and the tackle and mast of his boat. Urshanabi explains that Gilgamesh has destroyed the very things that would protect them both from the waters of death. To make up for his actions, Gilgamesh must cut poles and push the boat himself. Eventually, he has to use his own body and clothing for a sail.

So Urshanabi the ferryman brought Gilgamesh to Utnapishtim, whom they call the Faraway, who lives in Dilmun at the place of the sun's transit, eastward of the mountain. To him alone of men the gods had given everlasting life.

Now Utnapishtim, where he lay at ease, looked into the distance and he said in his heart, musing to himself, "Why does the boat sail here without tackle and mast; why are the sacred stones destroyed, and why does the master not sail the boat? That man who comes is none of mine; where I look I see a man whose body is covered with skins of beasts. Who is this who walks up the shore behind Urshanabi, for surely he is no man of mine?" So Utnapishtim looked at him and said, "What is your name, you who come here wearing the skins of beasts, with your cheeks starved and your face drawn? Where are you hurrying to now? For what reason have you made this great journey, crossing the seas whose passage is difficult? Tell me the reason for your coming."

He replied, "Gilgamesh is my name. I am from Uruk, from the house of Anu." Then Utnapishtim said to him, "If you are Gilgamesh,

why are your cheeks so starved and your face drawn? Why is despair in your heart and your face like the face of one who has made a long journey? Yes, why is your face burned with heat and cold; and why do you come here, wandering over the wilderness in search of the wind?" . . .

Gilgamesh explains that he is grieving over the death of his friend and afraid of dying himself. He has come to Utnapishtim to learn the secret of everlasting life.

Utnapishtim said, "There is no permanence. Do we build a house to stand for ever, do we seal a contract to hold for all time? Do brothers divide an inheritance to keep for ever, does the flood-time of rivers endure? It is only the nymph of the dragon-fly who sheds her larva and sees the sun in his glory. From the days of old there is no permanence. The sleeping and the dead, how alike they are, they are like a painted death. What is there between the master and the servant when both have fulfilled their doom? When the Anunnaki, the judges, come together, and Mammetun the mother of destinies, together they decree the fates of men. Life and death they allot but the day of death they do not disclose."

Then Gilgamesh said to Utnapishtim the Faraway, "I look at you now, Utnapishtim, and your appearance is no different from mine; there is nothing strange in your features. I thought I should find you like a hero prepared for battle, but you lie here taking your ease on your back. Tell me truly, how was it that you came to enter the company of the gods and to possess everlasting life?" Utnapishtim said to Gilgamesh, "I will reveal to you a mystery, I will tell you a secret of the gods."

PAUSE & REFLECT Why doesn't Gilgamesh take Siduri's advice?

WORDS TO KNOW

transit (trăn′sĭt) *n.* passage
musing (myōō′zĭng) *adj.* thoughtfully questioning or meditating **muse** *v.*

THE STORY OF THE FLOOD

Y ou know the city Shurrupak, it stands on the banks of Euphrates? That city grew old and the gods that were in it were old. There was Anu, lord of the firmament,[5] their father, and warrior Enlil their counselor, Ninurta the helper, and Ennugi watcher over canals; and with them also was Ea. In those days the world teemed, the people multiplied, the world bellowed like a wild bull, and the great god was aroused by the clamor. Enlil heard the clamor and he said to the gods in council, 'The uproar of mankind is intolerable and sleep is no longer possible by reason of the babel.'[6] So the gods agreed to exterminate mankind. Enlil did this, but Ea because of his oath warned me in a dream. He whispered their words to my house of reeds, 'Reed-house, reed-house! Wall, O wall, hearken reed-house, wall reflect; O man of Shurrupak, son of Ubara-Tutu; tear down your house and build a boat, abandon possessions and look for life, despise worldly goods and save your soul alive. Tear down your house, I say, and build a boat. These are the measurements of the barque as you shall build her: let her beam[7] equal her length, let her deck be roofed like the vault that covers the abyss;[8] then take up into the boat the seed of all living creatures.'

"When I had understood I said to my lord, 'Behold, what you have commanded I will honor and perform, but how shall I answer the people, the city, the elders?' Then Ea opened his mouth and said to me, his servant, 'Tell them this: I have learned that Enlil is wrathful against me, I dare no longer walk in his land nor live in his city; I will go down to the Gulf to dwell with Ea my lord. But on you he will rain down abundance, rare fish and shy wild-fowl, a rich harvest-tide. In the evening the rider of the storm will bring you wheat in torrents.'

"In the first light of dawn all my household gathered round me, the children brought pitch and the men whatever was necessary. On the fifth day I laid the keel and the ribs, then I made fast the planking. The ground-space was one acre, each side of the deck measured one hundred and twenty cubits,[9] making a square. I built six decks below, seven in all, I divided them into nine sections with bulkheads between. I drove in wedges where needed, I saw to the punt-poles,[10] and laid in supplies. The carriers brought oil in baskets, I poured pitch into the furnace and asphalt and oil; more oil was consumed in caulking, and more again the master of the boat took into his stores. I slaughtered bullocks for the people and every day I killed sheep. I gave the shipwrights wine to drink as though it were river water, raw wine and red wine and oil and white wine. There was feasting then as there is at the time of the New Year's festival; I myself anointed my head. On the seventh day the boat was complete.

"Then was the launching full of difficulty; there was shifting of ballast[11] above and below till two thirds was submerged. I loaded into her all that I had of gold and of living things, my family, my kin, the beast of the field both wild

---

5. **firmament:** the vault of the heavens; the sky.

6. **babel:** loud, unpleasant noise.

7. **beam:** the width of a ship.

8. **vault that covers the abyss:** the sky as it stretches across the depths below.

9. **cubits:** ancient units of measure, originally equal to the length of the forearm from the elbow to the tip of the middle finger. Length ranges from 17 to 22 inches.

10. **punt-poles:** poles that are pushed against the bottom of a body of water in order to propel a boat.

11. **ballast** (băl'əst): heavy material placed into the bottom of a boat to enhance stability.

WORDS TO KNOW

teem (tēm) v. to be filled to overflowing

"I DARE NO LONGER WALK IN HIS LAND NOR LIVE IN HIS CITY."

and tame, and all the craftsmen. I sent them on board, for the time that Shamash had <u>ordained</u> was already fulfilled when he said, 'In the evening, when the rider of the storm sends down the destroying rain, enter the boat and batten her down.' The time was fulfilled, the evening came, the rider of the storm sent down the rain. I looked out at the weather and it was terrible, so I too boarded the boat and battened her down. All was now complete, the battening and the caulking; so I handed the tiller to Puzur-Amurri the steersman, with the navigation and the care of the whole boat.

"With the first light of dawn a black cloud came from the horizon; it thundered within where Adad, lord of the storm was riding. In front over hill and plain Shullat and Hanish, heralds of the storm, led on. Then the gods of the abyss rose up; Nergal pulled out the dams of the nether[12] waters, Ninurta the war-lord threw down the dikes, and the seven judges of hell, the Annunaki, raised their torches, lighting the land with their livid flame. A <u>stupor</u> of despair went up to heaven when the god of the storm turned daylight to darkness, when he smashed the land like a cup. One whole day the tempest raged, gathering fury as it went, it poured over the people like the tides of battle; a man could not see his brother nor the people be seen from heaven. Even the gods were terrified at the flood, they fled to the highest heaven, the firmament of Anu; they crouched against the walls, cowering like curs. Then Ishtar the sweet-voiced Queen of Heaven cried out like a woman in travail:[13] 'Alas the days of old are turned to dust because I commanded evil; why did I command this evil in the council of all the gods? I commanded wars to destroy the people, but are they not my people, for I brought them forth? Now like the spawn of fish they float in the ocean.' The great gods of heaven and of hell wept, they covered their mouths.

"For six days and six nights the winds blew, torrent and tempest and flood overwhelmed the world, tempest and flood raged together like warring hosts. When the seventh day dawned the storm from the south subsided, the sea grew calm, the flood was stilled; I looked at the face of the world and there was silence, all mankind was turned to clay. The surface of the sea stretched as flat as a roof-top; I opened a hatch and the light fell on my face. Then I bowed low, I sat down and I wept, the tears streamed down my face, for on every side was the waste of water. I looked for land in vain, but fourteen leagues distant there appeared a mountain, and there the boat grounded; on the mountain of Nisir the boat held fast, she held fast and did not budge. One day she held, and a second day on the mountain of Nisir she held fast and did not budge. A third day, and a fourth day she held fast on the mountain and did not budge; a fifth day and a sixth day she held fast on the mountain. When the seventh day dawned I loosed a dove and let her go. She flew away, but finding no resting-place she returned. Then I loosed a swallow, and she flew away but finding no resting-place she returned. I loosed a raven, she saw that the waters had retreated, she ate, she flew

---

12. **nether:** lower.

13. **travail** (trə-vāl′): the pain of childbirth.

around, she cawed, and she did not come back. Then I threw everything open to the four winds, I made a sacrifice and poured out a libation[14] on the mountain top. Seven and again seven cauldrons I set up on their stands, I heaped up wood and cane and cedar and myrtle. When the gods smelled the sweet savor, they gathered like flies over the sacrifice. Then, at last, Ishtar also came, she lifted her necklace with the jewels of heaven that once Anu had made to please her. 'O you gods here present, by the lapis lazuli round my neck I shall remember these days as I remember the jewels of my throat; these last days I shall not forget. Let all the gods gather round the sacrifice, except Enlil. He shall not approach this offering, for without reflection he brought the flood; he consigned my people to destruction.'

"When Enlil had come, when he saw the boat, he was wroth and swelled with anger at the gods, the host of heaven, 'Has any of these mortals escaped? Not one was to have survived the destruction.' Then the god of the wells and canals Ninurta opened his mouth and said to the warrior Enlil, 'Who is there of the gods that can devise[15] without Ea? It is Ea alone who knows all things.' Then Ea opened his mouth and spoke to warrior Enlil, 'Wisest of gods, hero Enlil, how could you so senselessly bring down the flood?

Lay upon the sinner his sin,
Lay upon the transgressor[16] his transgression,
Punish him a little when he breaks loose,
Do not drive him too hard or he perishes;
Would that a lion had ravaged mankind
Rather than the flood,
Would that a wolf had ravaged mankind
Rather than the flood,
Would that famine had wasted the world
Rather than the flood,
Would that pestilence had wasted mankind
Rather than the flood.

It was not I that revealed the secret of the gods; the wise man learned it in a dream. Now

take your counsel what shall be done with him.'

"Then Enlil went up into the boat, he took me by the hand and my wife and made us enter the boat and kneel down on either side, he standing between us. He touched our foreheads to bless us saying, 'In time past Utnapishtim was a mortal man; henceforth he and his wife shall live in the distance at the mouth of the rivers.' Thus it was that the gods took me and placed me here to live in the distance, at the mouth of the rivers."

PAUSE & REFLECT What would you say is the main reason Utnapishtim is favored by the gods?

FOCUS As you read on, notice places in the text that show how Utnapishtim responds to the visit from Gilgamesh.

THE RETURN

U tnapishtim said, "As for you, Gilgamesh, who will assemble the gods for your sake, so that you may find that life for which you are searching? But if you wish, come and put it to the test: only prevail against sleep for six days and seven nights." But while Gilgamesh sat there resting on his haunches, a mist of sleep like soft wool teased from the fleece drifted over him, and Utnapishtim said to his wife, "Look at him now, the strong man who would have everlasting life, even now the mists of sleep are drifting over him." His wife replied, "Touch the man to wake him, so that he may return to his own land in peace, going back through the gate by which he came." Utnapishtim said to his wife, "All men are deceivers, even you he will attempt to deceive;

---

14. **libation:** liquid given as an offering to a god.
15. **devise** (dǐ-vīz´): plan or think out.
16. **transgressor:** a person who breaks a command or law.

WORDS TO KNOW
prevail (prǐ-vāl´) *v.* to hold out; triumph

HUMANITIES CONNECTION This relief carving of Gilgamesh, approximately 15 feet high, once adorned a wall in the palace of the Assyrian king Sargon II.

therefore bake loaves of bread, each day one loaf, and put it beside his head; and make a mark on the wall to number the days he has slept."

So she baked loaves of bread, each day one loaf, and put it beside his head, and she marked on the wall the days that he slept; and there came a day when the first loaf was hard, the second loaf was like leather, the third was soggy, the crust of the fourth had mold, the fifth was mildewed, the sixth was fresh, and the seventh was still on the embers. Then Utnapishtim touched him and he woke. Gilgamesh said to Utnapishtim the Faraway, "I hardly slept when you touched and roused me." But Utnapishtim said, "Count these loaves and learn how many days you slept, for your first is hard, your second like leather, your third is soggy, the crust of your fourth has mold, your fifth is mildewed, your sixth is fresh and your seventh was still over the glowing embers when I touched and woke you." Gilgamesh said, "What shall I do, O Utnapishtim, where shall I go? Already the thief in the night has hold of my limbs, death inhabits my room; wherever my foot rests, there I find death."

Then Utnapishtim spoke to Urshanabi the ferryman: "Woe to you Urshanabi, now and for ever more you have become hateful to this harborage; it is not for you, nor for you are the crossings of this sea. Go now, banished from the shore. But this man before whom you walked, bringing him here, whose body is covered with foulness and the grace of whose limbs has been spoiled by wild skins, take him to the washing-place. There he shall wash his long hair clean as snow in the water, he shall throw off his skins and let the sea carry them away, and the beauty of his body shall be shown, the fillet[17] on his forehead shall be renewed, and he shall be given clothes to cover his nakedness. Till he reaches his own city and his journey is accomplished, these clothes will show no sign of age, they will wear like a new garment." So Urshanabi took Gilgamesh and led him to the washing-place, he washed his long hair as clean as snow in the water, he threw off his skins, which the sea carried away, and showed the beauty of his body. He renewed the fillet on his forehead, and to cover his nakedness gave him clothes which would show no sign of age, but would wear like a new garment till he reached his own city, and his journey was accomplished.

Then Gilgamesh and Urshanabi launched the boat on to the water and boarded it, and they made ready to sail away; but the wife of Utnapishtim the Faraway said to him, "Gilgamesh came here wearied out, he is worn out; what will you give him to carry him back to his own country?" So Utnapishtim spoke, and Gilgamesh took a pole and brought the boat in to the bank. "Gilgamesh, you came here a man wearied out, you have worn yourself out; what shall I give you to carry you back to your own country? Gilgamesh, I shall reveal a secret thing, it is a mystery of the gods that I am telling you. There is a plant that grows under the water, it has a prickle like a thorn, like a rose; it will wound your hands, but if you succeed in taking it, then your hands will hold that which restores his lost youth to a man."

PAUSE & REFLECT Do you think Utnapishtim treats Gilgamesh fairly?

---

17. **fillet** (fĭl′ĭt): narrow cloth or ribbon worn as a headband.

When Gilgamesh heard this he opened the sluices so that a sweet-water current might carry him out to the deepest channel; he tied heavy stones to his feet and they dragged him down to the water-bed. There he saw the plant growing; although it pricked him he took it in his hands; then he cut the heavy stones from his feet, and the sea carried him and threw him on to the shore. Gilgamesh said to Urshanabi the ferryman, "Come here, and see this marvelous plant. By its virtue a man may win back all his former strength. I will take it to Uruk of the strong walls; there I will give it to the old men to eat. Its name shall be 'The Old Men Are Young Again'; and at last I shall eat it myself and have back all my lost youth." So Gilgamesh returned by the gate through which he had come, Gilgamesh and Urshanabi went together. They traveled their twenty leagues and then they broke their fast; after thirty leagues they stopped for the night.

Gilgamesh saw a well of cool water and he went down and bathed; but deep in the pool there was lying a serpent, and the serpent sensed the sweetness of the flower. It rose out of the water and snatched it away, and immediately it sloughed[18] its skin and returned to the well. Then Gilgamesh sat down and wept, the tears ran down his face, and he took the hand of Urshanabi; "O Urshanabi, was it for this that I toiled with my hands, is it for this I have wrung out my heart's blood? For myself I have gained nothing; not I, but the beast of the earth has joy of it now. Already the stream has carried it twenty leagues back to the channels where I found it. I found a sign and now I have lost it. Let us leave the boat on the bank and go."

After twenty leagues they broke their fast, after thirty leagues they stopped for the night; in three days they had walked as much as a journey of a month and fifteen days. When the journey was accomplished they arrived at Uruk, the strong-walled city. Gilgamesh spoke to him, to Urshanabi the ferryman, "Urshanabi, climb up on to the wall of Uruk, inspect its foundation terrace, and examine well the brickwork; see if it is not of burnt bricks; and did not the seven wise men lay these foundations? One third of the whole is city, one third is garden, and one third is field, with the precinct of the goddess Ishtar. These parts and the precinct are all Uruk."

This too was the work of Gilgamesh, the king, who knew the countries of the world. He was wise, he saw mysteries and knew secret things, he brought us a tale of the days before the flood. He went a long journey, was weary, worn out with labor, and returning engraved on a stone the whole story. ❖

---

18. **sloughed** (slŭft): cast off; shed.

Connect to the Literature

1. What Do You Think? How did you react when you learned the result of Gilgamesh's quest for immortality?

Comprehension Check
- Why does Gilgamesh want to find Utnapishtim?
- What story does Utnapishtim tell Gilgamesh?
- How does Utnapishtim become immortal?

Think Critically

2. What three adjectives would you use to describe Gilgamesh? Explain your choices.

3. Why can't Gilgamesh accept the fact that human beings die?

THINK ABOUT
- what Gilgamesh says when he decides to go in search of Utnapishtim
- what Gilgamesh says to Shamash after passing through the mountain
- what Gilgamesh tells Siduri when she asks him why his cheeks look starved and his face drawn

4. Why do you think the story ends with Gilgamesh proudly showing Urshanabi the city of Uruk?

5. ACTIVE READING: ANALYZING CAUSE AND EFFECT Look back in your 📖 READER'S NOTEBOOK at the examples of **cause-and-effect** relationships you recorded. What event in the story do you think had the strongest effect on Gilgamesh?

Extend Interpretations

6. What If? How do you think the story of Gilgamesh might continue? What kind of person—and king—will he be in the future?

7. Connect to Life In our world today, what are some different attitudes that people take toward death?

LITERARY ANALYSIS: THE QUEST STORY

A **quest story** is a story in which an individual known as the quest hero goes on a journey in order to achieve a goal. A quest hero may be part god or have friends (or enemies) who are gods. Because of this, he or she often has access to supernatural powers. However, quest heroes usually have ordinary human traits as well, both good and bad, that allow us to identify with them. Often, quest stories reflect the history, values, and beliefs of a particular culture.

Activity Analyze Gilgamesh as a quest hero by creating a diagram like the one started here.

> **Superhuman Qualities**
> **1.** Is not afraid of lions or scorpion people
> **2.** Can journey beyond the human world
> **3.**
> **4.**

> **Gilgamesh the Quest Hero**

> **Human Qualities**
> **1.** Is sad about the death of his friend
> **2.** Is afraid of his own death
> **3.**
> **4.**

> **Cultural Qualities**
> **1.** Believes in an afterlife
> **2.** Prays to the moon god for protection
> **3.**
> **4.**

Writing Options

1. Definition of Heroism How would you define heroism? Before writing, think about the kind of heroism Gilgamesh shows at different points in the story. Consider how your ideal hero would compare with Gilgamesh. Then write a paragraph giving your definition. Be sure to include some specific examples of heroic behavior.

2. Gilgamesh Adventure Write another episode of *The Epic of Gilgamesh,* in which Gilgamesh has an encounter with a strange person or creature who either helps him or stands in his way.

Writing Handbook
See page R29: Narrative Writing.

Activities & Explorations

1. Gilgamesh Illustration Choose a memorable scene from *The Epic of Gilgamesh,* such as Enkidu's dream, Gilgamesh's encounter with the scorpion people, the garden of the gods, the flood, or the serpent stealing the flower that restores youth. Illustrate the scene as you envision it. ~**ART**

2. City Plan Using books or the Internet, find out what the ancient city of Uruk might have looked like. Then create a model or blueprint of the city, with labels indicating the most important structures and places. ~**VIEWING AND REPRESENTING**

Inquiry & Research

Report on a Lost Civilization The Sumerians are a mystery in the history of the ancient world. No one knows for sure where they came from, and their language was not related to that of any other people in the region. Yet their influence on future civilizations—even our own—was vast. Find out more about this lost civilization, and present your findings in an oral report.

Communication Handbook
See page R45: Finding Sources.

Vocabulary in Action

EXERCISE: SYNONYMS On a piece of paper, write the letter of the word in each set that is not related in meaning to the other words in the set.

1. (a) lament, (b) moan, (c) wail, (d) sing
2. (a) teeming, (b) cavernous, (c) filled, (d) crowded
3. (a) considering, (b) forgetting, (c) reflecting, (d) musing
4. (a) allot, (b) give, (c) distribute, (d) deny
5. (a) daze, (b) stupor, (c) spell, (d) sadness
6. (a) fortunate, (b) lucky, (c) ominous, (d) favored
7. (a) prayer, (b) incantation, (c) shrine, (d) chant
8. (a) forbid, (b) ordain, (c) decree, (d) establish
9. (a) refuse, (b) succeed, (c) prevail, (d) win
10. (a) transit, (b) roadblock, (c) obstruction, (d) barrier

Building Vocabulary

For a lesson on using a thesaurus to find synonyms, see page 558.

The Quest to Find *Gilgamesh*

If Gilgamesh is "two-thirds a god, one-third a man," then the fictional archaeologist Indiana Jones could be described as two-thirds an adventurer and one-third a scholar. Most archaeology is not as hair-raising as the predicaments Indy gets into, but it too is often full of mystery and excitement.

One of the unsolved mysteries of contemporary archaeology is the text of the Gilgamesh epic itself. In the more than 150 years since the first fragments were discovered in the ruins of Nineveh, only about 80 percent of the story has been pieced together. The quest to find the rest continues today.

Piecing Together the Puzzle

Recently the American scholar Theodore Kwasman found the long-lost opening lines of the epic—not seen by human eyes for 24 centuries. Kwasman made his discovery among the tablet fragments found at Nineveh in 1849, but he did his detective work at the British Museum in London, where the majority of the fragments are now housed.

To make his discovery, Kwasman not only had to read cuneiform; he also had to know the text of *Gilgamesh* well enough to connect a known passage to an unknown one.

Fragments connected by Theodore Kwasman. Tablet with opening lines of *Gilgamesh*. The British Museum, London.

What Happens Next? More work needs to be carried out by archaeologists. Their efforts to uncover ruins may someday give us a complete *Gilgamesh.* However, many obstacles remain, some of which would challenge Indiana Jones himself.

The region near Nineveh, now part of Iraq, has been torn by war in recent years, just as it was when Nineveh was destroyed in 612 B.C. Since the Gulf War in 1991, historical sites have been neglected—and even looted. Researchers from outside Iraq have been prevented from visiting the sites, and we have no way of knowing how much of this ancient treasure has been lost.

Small-Group or Whole-Class Discussion Many people feel that archaeological treasures removed from ancient Mesopotamian cities by Layard and others should be returned to Iraq. Other people, because of wars and political tension in the region, are glad that many artifacts are in places like the British Museum. What is your opinion? Who owns the treasures of the ancient world?

from the
BOOK OF THE DEAD
THE CHAPTER OF NOT LETTING THE BODY PERISH

ADORATION OF THE DISK
KING AKHENATEN and PRINCESS NEFERTITI

NEW KINGDOM POETRY
I'M GOING DOWNSTREAM ON KINGSWATER CANAL
WHENEVER I LEAVE YOU, I GO OUT OF BREATH

Build Background

Egyptian Culture The selections you are about to read reflect three important features of ancient Egyptian culture:

- concern about the afterlife
- worship of a sun god
- delight in everyday life

[handwritten annotation: Need to know for test]

[handwritten annotation: Raw]

As different as these features might seem to be, they are interrelated. The Egyptians believed that in the afterlife people would have the same interests and experience the same pleasures as in earthly life. They saw the sun god as the giver of life to all of nature.

Book of the Dead The Book of the Dead is based upon the most important myth in Egyptian culture— the myth of Osiris. Osiris was a benevolent god who taught human beings agriculture and other arts of civilization. His younger brother Set became jealous and killed him for the throne. Isis, the sister of Osiris, found her brother's body and brought it back to life. Osiris then became lord of the otherworld.

Throughout their history, the Egyptians based many of their burial practices on this myth. In the Old Kingdom, they believed that when a pharaoh died, he rose, like Osiris, from the dead. In fact, they believed

that the king became Osiris himself. To celebrate this event, the king's followers recited hymns and prayers based on the Osiris story and carved them permanently into the walls of the pyramids where the kings were buried. Such "pyramid texts" are the earliest works of Egyptian literature that have survived.

By the time of the Middle Kingdom, the privilege of becoming Osiris had been extended to all the nobility. This trend was taken a step further in the New Kingdom. They believed that a glorious afterlife as Osiris was available to anyone who had lived a good life and for whom the proper prayers were said. These prayers, based once again on the myth of Osiris, were written on papyrus scrolls and buried along with the dead. The Egyptians called these burial scrolls the Chapters of Coming Forth by Day, a name that shows their positive expectations for the afterlife.

The selection on pages 52–53 is taken from the burial papyrus of a man named Nu, who worked as a steward or property manager.

For a humanities activity, click on:

HUMANITIES
CLASSZONE.COM

[handwritten annotation: Set = Osiris brother who killed Osiris]
[handwritten annotation: Nu wrote this poem to Osiris]

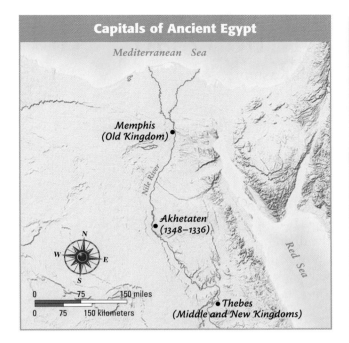

Capitals of Ancient Egypt

Mediterranean Sea

Memphis
(Old Kingdom)

Nile River

Akhetaten
(1348–1336)

Red Sea

N
W E
S

0   75   150 miles
0   75   150 kilometers

Thebes
(Middle and New Kingdoms)

Adoration of the Disk The second example of ancient Egyptian literature was written by the pharaoh Akhenaten, who ruled Egypt about 1353–1336 B.C. Akhenaten rejected the traditional worship of many gods and goddesses. Instead, he declared that the sun god Aten was the only true god and built a new capital city in his honor. Akhenaten also wrote in Aten's honor the poem you will read on page 54.

New Kingdom Poetry The ancient Egyptians were obviously fascinated with death and the afterlife. This fact has led to a popular image of their culture as being as dried up and lifeless as one of their mummies. The truth is that the ancient Egyptians were a people who knew how to enjoy life immensely. This was especially true during the period of the New Kingdom, a time of unparalleled prosperity and cultural enrichment—the result of political expansion and international commerce.

The New Kingdom produced a body of excellent lyric poetry that reflects the Egyptians' joy in life. Like much poetry throughout the ages, many of these poems celebrate one of the great vital forces of human life—romantic love. On pages 57–58, you will find two examples of New Kingdom love poems.

Connect to Your Life

Each of these selections reveals something about what the ancient Egyptians valued. What do you think is most greatly valued in your own culture? Share your ideas with your classmates.

Focus Your Reading

LITERARY ANALYSIS: SPEAKER

In a work of literature, the **speaker** is the voice that speaks the ideas presented. The speaker is not necessarily the writer; he or she may be a creation of the writer, much like a character in a play. As you read these four works, try to form an impression of the person speaking based on what he or she says.

ACTIVE READING: IDENTIFYING CULTURAL CHARACTERISTICS

In order to understand a culture different from your own, you need to consider the culture's values, its philosophical and religious beliefs, the stories its people tell, and the images they use.

READER'S NOTEBOOK As you read these Egyptian selections, look for clues that help you identify **cultural characteristics** of the ancient Egyptians. Keep track of the clues you find by recording them in a chart like the one started here.

Selection	Clue	What It Reveals About the Egyptians
Book of the Dead	"Grant that I may descend into the Land of Eternity"	They wanted to live forever.

from the Book of the Dead

Translated by Joseph Kaster

[handwritten: Dont let my body rot.]

THE CHAPTER OF NOT LETTING THE BODY PERISH

Words spoken by the Osiris Nu:

Hail to thee, O my Divine Father Osiris! I came to heal thee! Do thou heal me, that I may be complete, and that I may be, indeed, like unto my divine father Khepri,[1] the divine type of him who never corrupted. Come, then, make powerful my breath, O Lord of Breath, who exalts those divine beings who are like him! Come, make me endure, and fashion me, O thou Lord of the Sarcophagus![2]

[handwritten: Another name for Raw]

[handwritten: Peutrafi = rot]

Grant that I may descend into the Land of Eternity, according as that which was done to thee together with thy father Atum,[3] whose body did not see corruption, nor did he himself see decay.

I have never done that which thou hatest, but have acclaimed[4] thee among those who love thy Divine Essence. Let me not putrefy, as you do unto every god and every goddess, every animal and every reptile, when they perish, when their animating spirits go forth after their death.

Hail to thee, O my father Osiris! Thou livest with thy members. Thou didst not decay, thou didst not become worms, thou didst not wither, thou didst not putrefy. I am Khepri, and my limbs shall have eternity! I shall not decay, I shall not rot, I shall not putrefy, I shall not become worms, I shall not see corruption before the eye of Shu![5] I shall exist! I shall exist! I shall live! I shall live! I shall flourish! I shall flourish!

I shall wake up in contentment; I shall not putrefy; my intestines shall not perish; I shall not suffer injury. My eye

---

1. **Khepri** (kĕp′rē): the god Ra in the form of the rising sun.
2. **sarcophagus** (sär-kŏf′ə-gəs): a stone coffin.
3. **Atum** (ä′təm): Ra in the form of the setting sun and creator of the world.
4. **acclaimed:** praised highly.
5. **Shu** (shōō): the god of the air.

[handwritten: He wants to become with body]

shall not decay; the form of my face shall not disappear; my ear shall not become deaf. My head shall not be separated from my neck. My tongue shall not be removed, my hair shall not be cut off. My eyebrows shall not be shaved away, and no evil defect shall befall me.

My body shall be enduring, it shall not perish. It shall not be destroyed, nor shall it be turned back whence it entered into this Land of Eternity!

Papyrus from the *Book of the Dead* of Nakht (18th Dynasty, 1350–1300 B.C.). Photograph copyright © The British Museum.

HUMANITIES CONNECTION The Book of the Dead consists of papyrus scrolls that were found in the tombs of important individuals of the New Kingdom period. This scroll shows a nobleman and his wife making an offering to Osiris in order to win his blessing in the next world.

Adoration of the Disk
King Akhenaten and Princess Nefertiti

Translated by Robert Hillyer

[handwritten: Akhenaten was creator of life]

Thy dawn, O Ra, opens the new horizon,
And every realm that thou hast made to live
Is conquered by thy love, as joyous Day
Follows thy footsteps in delightful peace.

5 And when thou settest, all the world is bleak;
Houses are tombs where blind men lie in death;
Only the lion and the serpent move
Through the black oven of the sightless night.

[handwritten: Metaphores]

Dawn in the East again! the lands awake,
10 And men leap from their slumber with a song;
They bathe their bodies, clothe them with fresh garments,
And lift their hands in happy adoration.

The cattle roam again across the fields;
Birds flutter in the marsh, and lift their wings
15 Also in adoration, and the flocks
Run with delight through all the pleasant meadows.

Both north and south along the dazzling river
Ships raise their sails and take their course before thee;
And in the ocean, all the deep-sea fish
20 Swim to the surface to drink in thy light.

For thou art all that lives, the seed of men,
The son within his mother's womb who knows
The comfort of thy presence near, the babe
To whom thou givest words and growing wisdom;

25 The chick within the egg, whose breath is thine,
Who runneth from its shell, chirping its joy,
And dancing on its small, unsteady legs
To greet the splendor of the rising sun.

[handwritten right margin: What is the disk? The Sun]

[handwritten right margin: Animals + people praise sungod]

Handwritten annotations:
Day is Metaphor Life
Night = Death

He said the only god is the sun god

They think raw created bird, animal and men,

Akhenaten offers a sacrifice to Aten, the sun god
(c. 1350 B.C.). Relief from Amarna, Egypt. Archaeological Museum,
Cairo. Photograph copyright
© Erich Lessing/Art Resource, New York.

HUMANITIES CONNECTION Here, Akhenaten, Nefertiti, and
their eldest daughter worship the sun god Aten. The royal
couple hold up libations, or ritual offerings of drink. The rays
coming from the sun's disk end in hands for extending
blessings and receiving the libations. This relief carving is
from Akhenaten's palace.

Thy heart created all, this teeming earth,
30 Its people, herds, creatures that go afoot,
Creatures that fly in air, both land and sea,
Thou didst create them all within thy heart.

Men and their fates are thine, in all their stations,
Their many languages, their many colors,
35 All thine, and we who from the midst of peoples,
Thou madest different, Master of the Choice.

And lo, I find thee also in my heart,
I, Akhenaten, find thee and adore.
O thou, whose dawn is life, whose setting, death,
40 In the great dawn, then lift up me, thy son.

Kat-Tep and his wife, Hetepheres (fourth dynasty). Painted limestone statue. The British Museum, London.
Photograph copyright © Michael Holford.

HUMANITIES CONNECTION This is a tomb sculpture of the high official Kat-Tep and his wife, Hetepheres. The depiction of them side by side and of equal height is unusual in Egyptian art. The difference in color between the two figures shows that Hetepheres' sphere of activity was indoors and Kat-Tep's outdoors.

I'm going downstream on Kingswater Canal

Translated by John L. Foster

I'm going downstream on Kingswater Canal,
        with leave to attend Sun Festival;
I want to wander there where the tents
        are pitched at the far end of Mertiu Lagoon.
5 I'll hurry along—I can hardly keep silent—
        thinking of God's holy Day,
For maybe I'll see my truelove go by
        bound for the Houses of Offering.

I'll stand there with you at the mouth of the Mertiu
10   (heart, are you with me or back in Ra's city?),
Then we'll turn back to Offeringhouse Orchard,
        where I'll steal from the grove by the chapels
A branch for a festival fan.
        There I can watch the whole celebration.

15 With my eyes upturned toward the holy garden,
        and my arms full of flowering branches,
And my hair heavy with sweetsmelling unguents,
        what a splendid Lady I'll be!—
Dressed fine like a princess, for Ra,
20   Lord of Two Lands, on His feast day.

Fine like a bride, love,
        I'll stand there (waiting) beside you.

17 unguents (ŭng′gwənts): ointments.

Whenever I leave you, I go out of breath

Translated by John L. Foster

Whenever I leave you, I go out of breath
        (death must be lonely like I am);
I dream lying dreams of your love lost,
        and my heart stands still inside me.
5 I stare at my favorite datecakes—
        they would be salt to me now—
And pomegranate wine (once sweet to our lips)
        bitter, bitter as birdgall.

Touching noses with you, love, your kiss alone,
10   and my stuttering heart speaks clear:
Breathe me more of your breath, let me live!
        Man meant for me,
God himself gave you as his holy gift,
        my love to outlast forever.

8 birdgall: a bitter substance derived from the liver of a bird.

[handwritten note: Sonnet = 14 line Love poems]

Relief from the tomb of Vizier Ramose (18th dynasty), Thebes.
Photograph copyright © Michael Holford.

Connect to the Literature

1. **What Do You Think?** Which of the four selections you just read seems most memorable to you? Why?

Think Critically

2. In the excerpt from the Book of the Dead, how would you describe the **tone,** or attitude, of Nu's speech? How does the tone relate to the situation described in the text?

3. In "Adoration of the Disk," why does the **speaker** think that Ra should be praised?

4. In "I'm going downstream . . .," why does the speaker delight in dreaming of herself standing like a bride beside her love?

5. **ACTIVE READING: IDENTIFYING CULTURAL CHARACTERISTICS** Look back at the list of **cultural characteristics** that you recorded in your 📖 READER'S NOTEBOOK. Get together with a few classmates and compare clues and interpretations for one selection. Then report your group's findings to the class as a whole.

Extend Interpretations

6. **Comparing Texts** Which of the selections gave you the strongest sense of the speaker as a person? Explain your answer.

7. **Comparing Texts** In both "I'm going downstream on Kingswater Canal" and "Whenever I leave you, I go out of breath," a female speaker addresses her absent beloved. What are some ways in which the poems differ?

8. **Connect to Life** Their literature and art show that the ancient Egyptians both appreciated everyday life and prepared extensively for death. How do their attitudes compare with those of your society?

LITERARY ANALYSIS: SPEAKER

The **speaker** in a work of literature is the voice that speaks the ideas presented. The speaker is not necessarily the writer, although in some cases he or she may be. The speaker relates ideas from his or her point of view. Sometimes, a writer will create a speaker with a distinct identity in order to achieve a certain effect.

Activity Choose one of the four selections, and jot down some notes describing your impression of the person speaking. Then, using your notes, read the selection aloud to the class in a way you think expresses the speaker's personality.

Writing Options

1. Autobiographical Papyrus Scroll What would you like people to find written about you when they open your tomb thousands of years from now? Would it be instructions for what to say in the next world, your deepest thoughts about life and death, or a description of your unique qualities as an individual? Use your answers to these questions to write your own Book of the Dead papyrus scroll. Place the scroll in your **Working Portfolio.** 📁

2. Praise Poem In "Adoration of the Disk" the speaker praises all of creation. Make a list of some praiseworthy things in your own environment. Use the list to write a poem praising your surroundings.

Writing Handbook
See page R27: Descriptive Writing.

Activities & Explorations

Pyramid Cutaway Find out what the internal structure of one of the Egyptian pyramids was like and why it was designed that way. Then create a cutaway model, drawing, or blueprint to illustrate the structure to your classmates.
~ **VIEWING AND REPRESENTING**

Inquiry & Research

Papyrus Demonstration The Book of the Dead was written on scrolls of papyrus, a kind of paper made by the Egyptians from the stems of rushes. Find out how papyrus was made, and explain the method to your classmates, using drawings, photographs, or (if possible) real materials.

RESEARCH STARTER
CLASSZONE.COM

Excavations of the Metropolitan Museum of Art, 1929; Rogers Fund, 1930 (30.3.31). Photograph © 1978 The Metropolitan Museum of Art.

Decoding Hieroglyphics

The form of writing used by the ancient Egyptians is known as hieroglyphics. For more than 3,000 years these picture-signs were used not only to record words but also to decorate buildings, sacred monuments, and works of art. Hieroglyphic writing was often included in burials to give the deceased people speech in the afterlife.

The Rosetta Stone Thousands of examples of hieroglyphic texts survived the age of the pharaohs, but for almost 2,000 years no one could read them. Then, in 1799, after Napoleon's conquest of Egypt, French soldiers digging in the sand found a polished black stone covered in writing. The stone contained the same message in three different forms of writing: hieroglyphics, demotic (a simpler form of hieroglyphics), and Greek. Because ancient Greek was well known, it was possible to compare the texts and piece together the meaning of the hieroglyphics. By 1822 the French scholar Jean-François Champollion had broken the code.

How Hieroglyphics Work There's much more to reading hieroglyphics than knowing what each picture represents. Ancient Egyptian grammar was complex, and the hieroglyphics were used in several different ways. A hieroglyphic could represent an object, an idea related to the object, a letter, a syllable, or a grammatical relationship. For example, the hieroglyphic 〰〰〰 , which represents a ripple of water, can stand for the word *ripple*, the idea of motion, the preposition *to*, or the sound *n*.

Pady-mahes (745–656 B.C.). Gray granite statue. Brooklyn (New York) Museum of Art, Charles Edwin Wilbour Fund.

Below is the name of Akhenaten, author of "Adoration of the Disk."

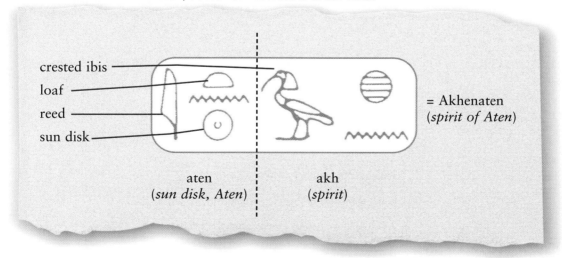

crested ibis
loaf
reed
sun disk

aten
(*sun disk, Aten*)

akh
(*spirit*)

= Akhenaten
(*spirit of Aten*)

Activity Design picture-signs of your own for the following words: *family, education, happy.* Share your designs with your classmates, and discuss why you chose to represent the words in the way you did.

Creation Literature

OVERVIEW

Genesis   63

Popol Vuh   76

Standardized Test Practice:
Writing About Literature   87

Many cultures have stories about the creation of the world and of the human race. Such stories, even from unrelated cultures, can be remarkably similar, suggesting that the stories may reflect beliefs and values held by all people. However, the differences between creation stories are also revealing. Differences in particular details can reflect differences in the cultures from which the stories come.

In the pages that follow, you will be asked to compare and contrast the creation stories in the Hebrew Bible and the *Popol Vuh,* a work from the Mayan culture of Central America. You will explore what these two creation stories have in common and also reflect on their differences. On the basis of your comparison, you will decide what the stories reveal about the cultures from which they come.

Points *of* Comparison

The following list shows the basic plot of many creation stories. As you will later see, there are variations, but knowing this plot structure is a good place to start.

Creation Literature Plot Structure

- A creator creates people to inhabit the world.
- The creator has certain expectations of the people.
- The people do or do not meet these expectations.
- The creator punishes or rewards the people.

Analyzing Creation Literature Use a chart like the one shown to help you take notes about the stories. Add any other questions that you think will help you compare the two accounts.

Questions for Analysis	Genesis	*Popol Vuh*
What do the creators want the people they have created to do?		
How do the people meet or fail to meet the creators' expectations?		
What do the creators do in response?		
In the end, how do things get resolved?		
What do these details reveal about the culture?		

Standardized Test Practice: Comparison-and-Contrast Essay After you read both selections, you will have the opportunity to write a comparison-and-contrast essay. Your notes will help you plan and write the essay.

FROM Genesis

Build Background

The Hebrew Bible The Hebrew Bible is not just a literary work of the ancient Hebrews; it is the sum total of their literature. It contains histories, biographies, laws, genealogical records, census figures, songs, love poetry, stories, proverbs, and other kinds of writing. The Hebrews had a rich and diverse literary tradition, but they thought of it as all belonging together in a single sacred book, or Bible.

One reason for their way of thinking may be that, as a people, the ancient Hebrews were not as rooted in a particular geographical region as the peoples of Mesopotamia and Egypt. Not having a permanent homeland to define them, the Hebrews may have felt more keenly than others the value of literature as an expression of their culture's identity.

Another reason for the ancient Hebrews to view their entire literary tradition as sacred was that their religion was monotheistic. Unlike most other ancient peoples, the Hebrews believed in a single all-powerful deity, all-knowing and present everywhere. They also believed that they had a covenant with God—a special relationship in which God watched over them and guided their destiny. As a result, they wrote little that did not touch in some way on their religion.

The Bible as Literature Despite its close attachments to Hebrew history and culture, the Hebrew Bible contains many stories, images, and themes dealing with matters that are important to all people. It also contains many fine examples of various literary forms.

The Hebrew Bible has strong connections to our own culture for yet another reason. For hundreds of years, English-speaking writers have loved the Bible and have incorporated its stories, images, themes, and turns of phrase into literary works of their own. To know the English language and the English literary tradition is to be profoundly influenced by the Hebrew Bible.

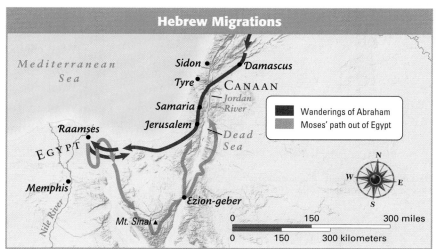

Hebrew Migrations

Mediterranean Sea

Sidon • • *Damascus*

Tyre • CANAAN

Samaria • — Jordan River

Jerusalem • — Dead Sea

Raamses •

EGYPT

Memphis •

Nile River

Mt. Sinai ▲

• Ezion-geber

Wanderings of Abraham
Moses' path out of Egypt

N / W — E / S

0   150   300 miles
0   150   300 kilometers

The Book of Genesis The Book of Genesis is the first book in the Hebrew Bible. It tells the history of the Hebrew people from the creation of the world to their migration to Egypt because of a famine. In Egypt they became slaves, but they eventually fled that land under the leadership of Moses—events that are recounted in the Book of Exodus.

Genesis focuses on the interactions between God and particular human beings with whom he has a special relationship. The first of these are Adam and Eve, the first man and woman, whom God created after creating the heavens, the earth, plants, and animals. The story of Noah takes place at a later time, when the descendants of Adam and Eve have populated the world.

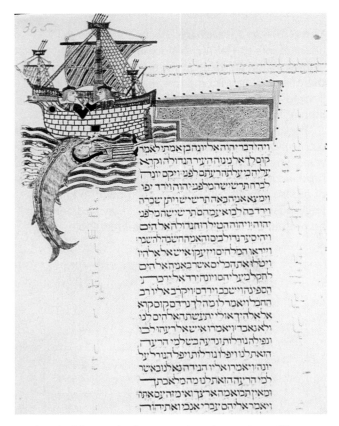

Jonah in the fish's mouth. Illumination from the Kennicott Bible. Courtesy of the Bodleian Library, Oxford University, Oxford, England.

Connect to Your Life

What comes to mind when you hear the names Adam and Eve? What do you know about the Garden of Eden or Noah and the Flood? With a group of classmates, share recollections of these biblical stories and discuss your impressions of them.

Focus Your Reading

LITERARY ANALYSIS: SACRED LITERATURE

Texts that convey the traditions, beliefs, and rituals of particular religions are often referred to as **sacred literature,** or **scriptures.** Although there is something to be learned from every good work of literature, sacred literature usually has as one of its main purposes the teaching of cultural values. As you read the two stories from Genesis, be alert for the teachings that they may contain.

ACTIVE READING: READING SACRED LITERATURE

Sacred literature usually has a higher status in a culture than ordinary literature, and it is often used in special ways. However, a work of sacred literature always has a literary form as well; it may be a story, a poem, a history, a biography, a song, a proverb. A good way to approach a work of sacred literature is to focus on the text itself. Read the words carefully, and ask the same questions you would of any other work of literature:

- What characters do I learn about?
- What conflicts are presented, and how are they resolved?
- What kind of language is used?
- What images or symbols are used?
- What themes does the work deal with?

READER'S NOTEBOOK As you read, look for answers to your questions and jot them down.

from Genesis
King James Bible

Creation AND THE Fall

In the beginning God created the heaven and the earth. And the earth was without form, and void; and darkness was upon the face of the deep. And the Spirit of God moved upon the face of the waters. And God said, "Let there be light": and there was light. And God saw the light, that it was good: and God divided the light from the darkness. And God called the light Day, and the darkness he called Night.

And the evening and the morning were the first day.

And God said, "Let there be a firmament in the midst of the waters, and let it divide the waters from the waters." And God made the firmament, and divided the waters which were under the firmament from the waters which were above the firmament: and it was so. And God called the firmament Heaven.

And the evening and the morning were the second day.

And God said, "Let the waters under the heaven be gathered together unto one place, and

The Creation of Adam, Michelangelo Buonarroti. Sistine Chapel, Vatican Palace, Vatican State. Scala/Art Resource, New York.

HUMANITIES CONNECTION In this detail from Michelangelo's paintings on the ceiling of the Sistine Chapel, God and Adam touch each other with extended hands. Through his act of creation, God is bridging the gap between heaven and earth. Adam also plays a role in creation: he must actively receive God's blessing.

let the dry land appear": and it was so. And God called the dry land Earth; and the gathering together of the waters called he Seas: and God saw that it was good. And God said, "Let the earth bring forth grass, the herb yielding seed, and the fruit tree yielding fruit after his kind, whose seed is in itself, upon the earth": and it was so. And the earth brought forth grass, and herb yielding seed after his kind, and the tree yielding fruit, whose seed was in itself, after his kind: and God saw that it was good.

And the evening and the morning were the third day.

And God said, "Let there be lights in the firmament of the heaven to divide the day from the night; and let them be for signs, and for seasons, and for days, and years; and let them be for lights in the firmament of the heaven to give light upon the earth."

And it was so. And God made two great lights; the greater light to rule the day, and the lesser light to rule the night: he made the stars also. And God set them in the firmament of the heaven to give light upon the earth. And to rule over the day and over the night, and to divide the light from the darkness: and God saw that it was good.

And the evening and the morning were the fourth day.

And God said, "Let the waters bring forth abundantly the moving creature that hath life, and fowl that may fly above the earth in the open firmament of heaven." And God created great whales, and every living creature that moveth, which the waters brought forth abundantly, after their kind, and every winged fowl after his kind: and God saw that it was good. And God blessed them, saying, "Be fruitful, and multiply, and fill the waters in the seas, and let fowl multiply in the earth."

And the evening and the morning were the fifth day.

And God said, "Let the earth bring forth the living creature after his kind, cattle, and creeping thing, and beast of the earth after his kind": and it was so. And God made the beast of the earth after his kind, and cattle after their kind, and every thing that creepeth upon the earth after his kind: and God saw that it was good.

God said, "Let us make man in our image, after our likeness: and let them have dominion[1] over the fish of the sea, and over the fowl of the air, and over the cattle, and over all the earth, and over every creeping thing that creepeth upon the earth." So God created man in his own image, in the image of God created he him; male and female created he them. And God blessed them, and God said unto them, "Be fruitful, and multiply, and replenish[2] the earth, and subdue it: and have dominion over the fish of the sea, and over the fowl of the air, and over every living thing that moveth upon the earth." And God said, "Behold, I have given you every herb bearing seed, which is upon the face of all the earth, and every tree, in the which is the fruit of a tree yielding seed; to you it shall be for meat. And to every beast of the earth, and to every fowl of the air, and to everything that creepeth upon the earth, wherein there is life, I have given every green herb for meat." And it was so. And God saw every thing that he had made, and, behold, it was very good.

And the evening and the morning were the sixth day.

Thus the heavens and the earth were finished, and all the host of them.

And on the seventh day God ended his work which he had made; and he rested on the seventh day from all his work which he had made. And God blessed the seventh day, and sanctified it: because that in it he had rested from all his work which God created and made.

---

1. **dominion:** authority; control.
2. **replenish:** fill with people.

In the day that the Lord God made the earth and the heavens, and every plant of the field before it was in the earth, and every herb of the field before it grew (for the Lord God had not caused it to rain upon the earth, and there was not a man to till the ground) there went up a mist from the earth, and watered the whole face of the ground. And the Lord God formed man of the dust of the ground, and breathed into his nostrils the breath of life; and man became a living soul.

And the Lord God planted a garden eastward in Eden; and there he put the man whom he had formed. And out of the ground made the Lord God to grow every tree that is pleasant to the sight, and good for food; the tree of life also in the midst of the garden, and the tree of knowledge of good and evil. And a river went out of Eden to water the garden; and from thence it was parted, and became into four heads. The name of the first is Pison:[3] that is it which compasseth the whole land of Havilah,[4] where there is gold; and the gold of that land is good: there is bdellium[5] and the onyx stone. And the name of the second river is Gihon:[6] the same is it that compasseth the whole land of Ethiopia. And the name of the third river is Hiddekel:[7] that is it which goeth toward the east of Assyria. And the fourth river is Euphrates.

And the Lord God took the man, and put him into the garden of Eden to dress it and to keep it. And the Lord God commanded the man, saying, "Of every tree of the garden thou mayest freely eat: but of the tree of the knowledge of good and evil, thou shalt not eat of it: for in the day that thou eatest thereof thou shalt surely die."

And the Lord God said,

"It is not good that the man should be alone; I will make him a help meet for him." And out of the ground the Lord God formed every beast of

> "Of every tree in the garden thou mayest freely eat: but of the tree of the **knowledge of good and evil,** thou shalt not eat of it: for in the day that thou eatest thereof thou shalt surely die."

the field, and every fowl of the air; and brought them unto Adam to see what he would call them: and whatsoever Adam called every living creature, that was the name thereof. And Adam gave names to all cattle, and to the fowl of the air, and to every beast of the field; but for Adam there was not found a help meet for him.

And the Lord God caused a deep sleep to fall upon Adam, and he slept: and he took one of his ribs, and closed up the flesh instead thereof; and the rib, which the Lord God had taken from man, made he a woman, and brought her unto the man.

And Adam said,

"This is now bone of my bones,
  and flesh of my flesh:
She shall be called Woman,
  because she was taken out of Man."

Therefore shall a man leave his father and his mother, and shall cleave unto his wife: and they shall be one flesh. And they were both naked, the man and his wife, and were not ashamed.

Now the serpent was more subtle than any beast of the field which the Lord God had made.

And he said unto the woman,

---

3. **Pison** (pē-sōn′).

4. **Havilah** (hăv-ē-lä′).

5. **bdellium** (děl′ē-əm): a gum resin obtained from various shrubs and trees, used as a medicine.

6. **Gihon** (gē-hōn′).

7. **Hiddekel** (hĭ-děk′ĕl).

"Yea, hath God said, 'Ye shall not eat of every tree of the garden'?"

And the woman said unto the serpent,

"We may eat of the fruit of the trees of the garden; but of the fruit of the tree which is in the midst of the garden, God hath said, 'Ye shall not eat of it, neither shall ye touch it, lest ye die.'"

And the serpent said unto the woman,

"Ye shall not surely die: for God doth know that in the day ye eat thereof, then your eyes shall be opened, and ye shall be as gods, knowing good and evil."

And when the woman saw that the tree was good for food, and that it was pleasant to the eyes, and a tree to be desired to make one wise, she took of the fruit thereof, and did eat, and gave also unto her husband with her; and he did eat. And the eyes of them both were opened, and they knew that they were naked; and they sewed fig leaves together, and made themselves aprons.

And they heard the voice of the Lord God walking in the garden in the cool of the day: and Adam and his wife hid themselves from the presence of the Lord God amongst the trees of the garden.

And the Lord God called unto Adam, and said unto him,

"Where art thou?"

And he said,

"I heard thy voice in the garden, and I was afraid, because I was naked; and I hid myself."

And he said,

"Who told thee that thou wast naked? Hast thou eaten of the tree, whereof I commanded thee that thou shouldest not eat?"

And the man said,

"The woman whom thou gavest to be with me, she gave me of the tree, and I did eat."

And the Lord God said unto the woman,

"What is this that thou hast done?"

And the woman said, "The serpent beguiled[8] me, and I did eat."

And the Lord God said unto the serpent,

"Because thou hast done this,
thou art cursed above all cattle,
and above every beast of the field;
upon thy belly shalt thou go,
and dust shalt thou eat
all the days of thy life:
And I will put enmity[9] between thee and the
woman,
and between thy seed and her seed;
it shall bruise thy head,
and thou shalt bruise his heel."

Unto the woman he said,

"I will greatly multiply thy sorrow and thy
conception;
in sorrow thou shalt bring forth children;
and thy desire shall be to thy husband,
and he shall rule over thee."

And unto Adam he said,
"Because thou hast hearkened unto the voice of thy wife, and hast eaten of the tree, of which I commanded thee, saying, 'Thou shalt not eat of it':

Cursed is the ground for thy sake;
in sorrow shalt thou eat of it all the days of
thy life.
Thorns also and thistles shall it bring forth to
thee;
and thou shalt eat the herb of the field;
in the sweat of thy face shalt thou eat bread,
till thou return unto the ground;
for out of it wast thou taken:
For dust thou art,
and unto dust shalt thou return."

---

8. **beguiled** (bĭ-gīld'): deceived; tricked; misled.

9. **enmity:** hatred; hostility.

The Judgement of Adam and Eve: "So Judged He Man" (1807), William Blake. The Huntington Library, Art Collections, and Botanical Gardens, San Marino, California/SuperStock.

And Adam called his wife's name Eve; because she was the mother of all living. Unto Adam also and to his wife did the Lord God make coats of skins, and clothed them.

And the Lord God said, "Behold, the man is become as one of us, to know good and evil: and now, lest he put forth his hand, and take also of the tree of life, and eat, and live for ever—" therefore the Lord God sent him forth from the garden of Eden, to till the ground from whence he was taken. So he drove out the man; and he placed at the east of the garden of Eden Cherubims,[10] and a flaming sword which turned every way, to keep the way of the tree of life.

---

10. **Cherubims** (chĕr'ə-bĭmz): angels.

Noah AND THE Flood

And it came to pass, when men began to multiply on the face of the earth, and daughters were born unto them, that the sons of God saw the daughters of men that they were fair; and they took them wives of all which they chose.

And the Lord said, "My spirit shall not always strive with man, for that he also is flesh; yet his days shall be a hundred and twenty years."

There were giants in the earth in those days; and also after that, when the sons of God came in unto the daughters of men, and they bore children to them, the same became mighty men which were of old, men of renown.[11] And God saw that the wickedness of man was great in the earth, and that every imagination of the thoughts of his heart was only evil continually. And it repented the Lord that he had made man on the earth, and it grieved him at his heart.

And the Lord said, "I will destroy man whom I have created from the face of the earth; both man, and beast, and the creeping thing, and the fowls of the air; for it repenteth me that I have made them."

But Noah found grace in the eyes of the Lord.

Noah was a just man and perfect in his generations, and Noah walked with God. And Noah begot three sons, Shem, Ham, and Japheth.[12]

And God said unto Noah, "The end of all flesh is come before me; for the earth is filled with violence through them; and, behold, I will destroy them with the earth. Make thee an ark of gopher wood; rooms shalt thou make in the ark, and shalt pitch it within and without with pitch. And this is the fashion which thou shalt make it of: the length of the ark shall be three hundred cubits, the breadth of it fifty cubits, and the height of it thirty cubits. A window shalt thou make to the ark, and in a cubit shalt thou finish it above; and the door of the ark shalt thou set in the side thereof; with lower, second, and third stories shalt thou make it. And, behold, I, even I, do bring a flood of waters upon the earth, to destroy all flesh, wherein is the breath of life, from under heaven; and everything that is in the earth shall die. But with thee will I establish my covenant;[13] and thou shalt come into the ark, thou, and thy sons, and thy wife, and thy sons' wives with thee. And of every living thing of all flesh, two of every sort shalt thou bring into the ark, to keep them alive with thee; they shall be male and female. Of fowls after their kind, and of cattle after their kind, of every creeping thing of the earth after his kind, two of every sort shall come unto thee, to keep them alive. And take thou unto thee of all food that is eaten, and thou shalt gather it to thee; and it shall be for food for thee, and for them."

Thus did Noah; according to all that God commanded him, so did he. And the Lord said unto Noah, "Come thou and all thy house into the ark; for thee have I seen righteous before me in this generation. Of every clean beast thou shalt take to thee by sevens, the male and his female: and of beasts that are not clean by two, the male and his female. Of fowls also of the air by sevens, the male and the female; to keep seed alive upon the face of all the earth. For yet seven days, and I will cause it to rain upon the earth forty days and forty nights; and every living substance that I have made will I destroy from off the face of the earth."

And Noah did according unto all that the Lord commanded him. And Noah went in, and his sons, and his wife, and his sons' wives with him,

---

11. **renown:** fame based on good deeds.

12. **Japheth** (jā′fəth).

13. **covenant:** a formal agreement.

into the ark, because of the waters of the flood. Of clean beasts, and of beasts that are not clean, and of fowls, and of every thing that creepeth upon the earth, there went in two and two unto Noah into the ark, the male and the female, as God had commanded Noah. And it came to pass after seven days that the waters of the flood were upon the earth. In the six hundredth year of Noah's life, in the second month, the seventeenth day of the month, the same day were all the fountains of the great deep broken up, and the windows of heaven were opened. And the waters prevailed, and were increased greatly upon the earth; and the ark went upon the face of the waters. And the waters prevailed exceedingly upon the earth; and all the high hills, that were under the whole heaven, were covered. Fifteen cubits upward did the waters prevail; and the mountains were covered. And all flesh died that moved upon the earth, both of fowl, and of cattle, and of beast, and of every creeping thing that creepeth upon the earth, and every man. All in whose nostrils was the breath of life, of all that was in the dry land, died. And every living substance was destroyed which was upon the face of the ground, both man, and cattle, and the creeping things, and the fowl of the heaven; and they were destroyed from the earth: and Noah only remained alive, and they that were with him in the ark. And the waters prevailed upon the earth a hundred and fifty days.

And God remembered Noah, and every living thing, and all the cattle that was with him in the ark: and God made a wind to pass over the earth, and the waters assuaged.[14] The fountains also of the deep and the windows of heaven were stopped, and the rain from heaven was restrained; and the waters returned from off the earth continually: and after the end of the hundred and fifty days the waters were abated.[15] And the ark rested in the seventh month, on the

seventeenth day of the month, upon the mountains of Ararat. And the waters decreased continually until the tenth month: in the tenth month, on the first day of the month, were the tops of the mountains seen.

And it came to pass at the end of forty days that Noah opened the window of the ark which he had made: and he sent forth a raven, which went forth to and fro, until the waters were dried up from off the earth. Also he sent forth a dove from him, to see if the waters were abated from off the face of the ground; but the dove found no rest for the sole of her foot, and she returned unto him into the ark, for the waters were on the face of the whole earth: then he put forth his hand, and took her, and pulled her in unto him into the ark. And he stayed yet other seven days; and again he sent forth the dove out of the ark; and the dove came in to him in the evening; and lo, in her mouth was an olive leaf plucked off: so Noah knew that the waters were abated from off the earth. And he stayed yet other seven days; and

> And the waters prevailed upon the earth a hundred and fifty days.

sent forth the dove; which returned not again unto him any more. And it came to pass in the six hundredth and first year, in the first month, the first day of the month, the waters were dried up from off the earth: and Noah removed the covering of the ark, and looked, and, behold, the face of the ground was dry. And in the second month, on the seven and twentieth day of the month, was the earth dried.

And God spoke unto Noah, saying, "Go forth of the ark, thou, and thy wife, and thy sons, and

---

14. **assuaged** (ə-swājd′): became calm or smooth.

15. **abated:** reduced or removed altogether.

The building of the Ark (Gen. 6:13–17), the Flood (Gen. 8:6–11, leaving the Ark (Gen. 8:18–19), the sacrifice of Noah (Gen. 8:20–9:15) (c. 1250 A.D.). The Pierpont Morgan Library, New York.

HUMANITIES CONNECTION This manuscript illumination shows four scenes from the story of Noah and the Flood. Before the invention of the printing press, the Bible and other books had to be copied by hand. Individual copies often included illuminations—hand-painted illustrations and decorations—that made each volume unique.

thy sons' wives with thee. Bring forth with thee every living thing that is with thee, of all flesh, both of fowl, and of cattle, and of every creeping thing that creepeth upon the earth; that they may breed abundantly in the earth, and be fruitful, and multiply upon the earth."

And Noah went forth, and his sons, and his wife, and his sons' wives with him. Every beast, every creeping thing, and every fowl, and whatsoever creepeth upon the earth, after their kinds, went forth out of the ark.

And Noah builded an altar unto the Lord; and took of every clean beast, and of every clean fowl, and offered burnt offerings on the altar. And the Lord smelled a sweet savor; and the Lord said in his heart,

"I will not again curse the ground any more for man's sake; for the imagination of man's heart is evil from his youth; neither will I again smite[16] any more every thing living, as I have done.

> *While the earth remaineth,*
> *seedtime and harvest, and cold and heat,*
> *and summer and winter, and day and night*
> *shall not cease."*

And God blessed Noah and his sons, and said unto them, "Be fruitful, and multiply, and replenish the earth. And the fear of you and the dread of you shall be upon every beast of the earth, and upon every fowl of the air, upon all that moveth upon the earth, and upon all the fishes of the sea; into your hand are they delivered. Every moving thing that liveth shall be meat for you; even as the green herb have I given you all things. But flesh with the life thereof, which is the blood thereof, shall ye not eat. And surely your blood of your lives will I require; at the hand of every beast will I require it, and at the hand of man; at the hand of every man's brother will I require the life of man.

> *Whoso sheddeth man's blood,*
> *by man shall his blood be shed;*
> *for in the image of God*
> *made he man."*

And God spoke unto Noah, and to his sons with him, saying,

"And I, behold, I establish my covenant with you, and with your seed after you; and with every living creature that is with you, of the fowl, of the cattle, and of every beast of the earth with you; from all that go out of the ark, to every beast of the earth. And I will establish my covenant with you; neither shall all flesh be cut off any more by the waters of a flood; neither shall there any more be a flood to destroy the earth."

And God said,

"This is the token of the covenant which I make between me and you and every living creature that is with you, for perpetual generations:

> *I do set my bow in the cloud,*
> *and it shall be for a token of a covenant*
> *between me and the earth.*
> *And it shall come to pass,*
> *when I bring a cloud over the earth,*
> *that the bow shall be seen in the cloud*

and I will remember my covenant, which is between me and you and every living creature of all flesh; and the waters shall no more become a flood to destroy all flesh. And the bow shall be in the cloud; and I will look upon it, that I may remember the everlasting covenant between God and every living creature of all flesh that is upon the earth."

And God said unto Noah, "This is the token of the covenant, which I have established between me and all flesh that is upon the earth." ❖

---

16. **smite:** punish with a severe blow.

Connect to the Literature

1. What Do You Think?
How did you react to the punishment given to Adam and Eve? Did you react in the same way to the punishment of the Flood?

Comprehension Check
- Why does Eve eat the forbidden fruit?
- How are Adam and Eve punished for disobeying God?
- Why does God decide to destroy all living things with a flood?
- How does Noah know when dry land has reappeared?

Think Critically

2. In these stories, what qualities is God portrayed as having?

THINK ABOUT

- God's feelings about his creation, especially human beings
- his reaction after learning that Adam and Eve have disobeyed him
- his decision to destroy all living creatures with a flood
- the covenant he establishes with Noah and his descendants

3. What qualities of human beings are portrayed in these stories?

4. ACTIVE READING: READING SACRED LITERATURE
Review the questions on page 62 and the answers that you wrote in your 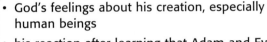 **READER'S NOTEBOOK**. How did your observations about the literature help you to understand it?

Extend Interpretations

5. What If? What might have happened in the story of Adam and Eve if Eve had not listened to the serpent?

6. Comparing Texts *The Epic of Gilgamesh* and Genesis both contain stories of a flood that wipes out almost all living things. Compare these stories and their heroes, Utnapishtim and Noah. How might you account for the similarities between the two stories?

7. Connect to Life In the world today is goodness usually rewarded and evil usually punished? Give some examples to support your opinion.

LITERARY ANALYSIS: SACRED LITERATURE

A sacred text, or **scripture,** is a work of literature that has a special status in the culture from which it springs. It may be seen as divinely inspired and may be used in worship and viewed with reverence. It may also be a work of great beauty and artistry.

More than many other kinds of literature, sacred literature is likely to have teaching as one of its main purposes. What it teaches generally has to do with a culture's most important concerns: the basic principles of morality, the meaning of human existence, and the relationship between the human and the divine.

Cooperative Learning Activity
With your classmates, create a list of the teachings to be found in the two stories from Genesis. Write the list on the board; then, next to each teaching, record the events or details that convey the teaching.

Genesis	
Teaching	What Conveys the Teaching
Don't blame others for your mistakes.	dialogue between God and Adam after Adam ate the forbidden fruit

Writing Options

Guide-for-Living Comparison

According to the scholar Joseph Campbell, one purpose of religious and mythological stories is to guide people through the trials of living. How does the kind of guidance found in *The Epic of Gilgamesh* compare with that found in Genesis? Explore this question in an essay. Before writing, list some of the trials faced by Gilgamesh, Adam, Eve, and Noah. Next to each trial, jot down what the person did—or perhaps should have done—to deal with the situation. Use the list as a source of supporting examples as you write.

Writing Handbook
See page R31: Compare and Contrast.

Activities & Explorations

1. Bible Storyboard Choose a story from Genesis and make a storyboard showing how you would turn it into a movie. Include drawings, dialogue, director's tips, music ideas, and any other necessary information. Present your storyboard to the class. Be ready to explain why you think your movie would be effective. ~ **ART/VIEWING AND REPRESENTING**

2. Good vs. Evil Debate In the story of Noah and the Flood, God says that "the imagination of man's heart is evil from his youth." Do you think that people are more naturally inclined to do wrong or to do good? Debate the question with a classmate who has a different opinion. ~ **SPEAKING AND LISTENING**

Inquiry & Research

1. Bible Report Investigate the Hebrew Bible further by exploring a book other than Genesis. Find out what the book is about, what kind of writing it is, what significance it has in Jewish history and culture, and what influence it has had on other literature. Present your findings in the form of an oral report.

2. Genesis in the Arts Over the years, scenes from Genesis have been the subjects of many famous paintings. Use museum Web sites or art-history books to search for at least two such paintings. In a presentation to the class, display these works. Explain what scene each work depicts and which one you prefer.

RESEARCH STARTER
CLASSZONE.COM

Points *of* Comparison

Review the excerpt from Genesis and fill in the "Genesis" column of your comparison-and-contrast chart.

Paired Activity Compare your chart with that of a classmate and discuss the similarities and differences between them. On the basis of your discussion, decide whether you want to change any of your answers before going on to the next part of this lesson.

Questions for Analysis	Genesis	*Popol Vuh*
What do the creators want the people they have created to do?	Live happily in the Garden of Eden, obey God's commands	
How do the people meet or fail to meet the creators' expectations?		
What do the creators do in response?		
In the end, how do things get resolved?		
What do these details reveal about the culture?		

PREPARING to *Read*

Now that you have read one of the best-known creation stories, it's time to turn your attention to a less-familiar one, from a culture very different from the ancient Hebrews'. As you will see, the Mayan account of creation differs in many ways from that in Genesis. But there are also many surprising similarities between the accounts.

Build Background

Mayan Civilization The selection you are about to read is an excerpt from an important Mayan work—the *Popol Vuh.* The Maya were a Native American people who lived in what is now southern Mexico and Guatemala. They developed an advanced civilization that flourished from A.D. 250 to 900. Their cities were magnificent, with grand temples. Around 900, for reasons not completely understood, they abandoned the cities and migrated into the surrounding countryside. Spanish invaders entered their territory in the early 1500s, and by the middle of the century, most of the Maya had been conquered by the Spaniards.

The Maya excelled in painting and sculpture and developed advanced forms of mathematics and astronomy. Using paper prepared from fig-tree bark, they even made books. Other Mayan inventions include an accurate yearly calendar based on precise astronomical measurements and a complex system of hieroglyphic writing. Like the ancient Egyptians, the Maya used their written language to decorate as well as communicate.

In addition to their yearly calendar, the Maya created a sacred calendar of 260 days. Each day was associated with a particular god or goddess. Mayan priests used the calendar as a way of harmonizing their activities with divine forces. In the *Popol Vuh,* when the gods speak of "keeping days," they are referring to the use of the sacred calendar.

The *Popol Vuh,* or "book of the community," contains the Mayan story of the creation of the world. It was written not long after the Spanish conquest by an anonymous Mayan noble, who may have been trying to keep the work from becoming lost as a result of his people's defeat.

from

POPOL
VUH

Translated by Dennis Tedlock

We get a calender from them
Soveregn Plumed Serpent = god of sea Sea
Heart of Sky

Heart of Sky = Hurrican
thunder
Hurricane
Newborn +
sudden
thunder

GUIDE FOR READING

FOCUS In the opening section, you will learn about the very beginning of the world. As you read, notice how the gods think and talk about their creation.

This is the beginning of the Ancient Word, here in this place called Quiché.[1] Here we shall inscribe, we shall implant the Ancient Word, the potential and source for everything done in the citadel of Quiché, in the nation of Quiché people. . . .

This is the account, here it is:

Now it still ripples, now it still murmurs, ripples, it still sighs, still hums, and it is empty under the sky.

Here follow the first words, the first eloquence:

There is not yet one person, one animal, bird, fish, crab, tree, rock, hollow, canyon, meadow, forest. Only the sky alone is there; the face of the earth is not clear. Only the sea alone is pooled under all the sky; there is nothing whatever gathered together. It is at rest; not a single thing stirs. It is held back, kept at rest under the sky.

Whatever there is that might be is simply not there: only the pooled water, only the calm sea, only it alone is pooled.

Whatever might be is simply not there: only murmurs, ripples, in the dark, in the night. Only the Maker, Modeler alone, Sovereign Plumed Serpent, the Bearers, Begetters are in the water, a glittering light. They are there, they are enclosed in quetzal[2] feathers, in blue-green.

Thus the name, "Plumed Serpent." They are great knowers, great thinkers in their very being. And of course there is the sky, and there is

Mayan cylindrical vessel decorated with mythological scene (seventh to eighth century). The Metropolitan Museum of Art (New York), The Michael C. Rockefeller Memorial Collection, Purchase, Nelson A. Rockefeller Gift, 1968.

also the Heart of Sky. This is the name of the god, as it is spoken.

And then came his word, he came here to the Sovereign Plumed Serpent, here in the blackness, in the early dawn. He spoke with the Sovereign Plumed Serpent, and they talked, then they thought, then they worried. They agreed with each other, they joined their words, their thoughts. Then it was clear, then they reached accord[3] in the light, and then humanity was clear, when they conceived the growth, the generation of trees, of bushes, and the growth of life,

---

1. **Quiché** (kē-chä′).
2. **quetzal** (kĕt-säl′): Central American bird, with brilliantly covered plumage, often identified with the Sovereign Plumed Serpent.
3. **accord:** agreement.

First thing they created was land

AND THEN THE EARTH AROSE BECAUSE OF THEM, IT WAS SIMPLY THEIR WORD THAT BROUGHT IT FORTH. FOR THE FORMING OF THE EARTH THEY SAID "EARTH."

of humankind, in the blackness, in the early dawn, all because of the Heart of Sky, named Hurricane. Thunderbolt Hurricane comes first, the second is Newborn Thunderbolt, and the third is Sudden Thunderbolt.

So there were three of them, as Heart of Sky, who came to the Sovereign Plumed Serpent, when the dawn of life was conceived:

"How should the sowing be, and the dawning? Who is to be the provider, nurturer?"

"Let it be this way, think about it: this water should be removed, emptied out for the formation of the earth's own plate and platform, then should come the sowing, the dawning of the sky-earth. But there will be no high days and no bright praise for our work, our design, until the rise of the human work, the human design," they said.

And then the earth arose because of them, it was simply their word that brought it forth. For the forming of the earth they said "Earth." It arose suddenly, just like a cloud, like a mist, now forming, unfolding. Then the mountains were separated from the water, all at once the great mountains came forth. By their genius alone, by their cutting edge alone they carried out the conception of the mountain-plain, whose face grew instant groves of cypress and pine.

And the Plumed Serpent was pleased with this:

"It was good that you came, Heart of Sky, Hurricane, and Newborn Thunderbolt, Sudden Thunderbolt. Our work, our design will turn out well," they said.

And the earth was formed first, the mountain-plain. The channels of water were separated; their branches wound their ways among the mountains. The waters were divided when the great mountains appeared.

Such was the formation of the earth when it was brought forth by the Heart of Sky, Heart of Earth, as they are called, since they were the first to think of it. The sky was set apart, and the earth was set apart in the midst of the waters.

Such was their plan when they thought, when they worried about the completion of their work.

PAUSE & REFLECT How do the gods seem to feel about their creation at this point?

FOCUS Now the gods will create the animals. As you read, notice what the gods expect of the animals and how they react to the animals' behavior.

Now they planned the animals of the mountains, all the guardians of the forests, creatures of the mountains: the deer, birds, pumas, jaguars, serpents, rattlesnakes, fer-de-lances,[4] guardians of the bushes.

A Bearer, Begetter speaks:

"Why this pointless humming? Why should there merely be rustling beneath the trees and bushes?"

"Indeed—they had better have guardians," the others replied. As soon as they thought it and said it, deer and birds came forth.

---

4. **fer-de-lances** (fĕr′dl-ăn′səz): poisonous tropical snakes.

And then they gave out homes to the deer and birds:

"You, the deer: sleep along the rivers, in the canyons. Be here in the meadows, in the thickets, in the forests, multiply yourselves. You will stand and walk on all fours," they were told.

So then they established the nests of the birds, small and great:

"You, precious birds: your nests, your houses are in the trees, in the bushes. Multiply there, scatter there, in the branches of trees, the branches of bushes," the deer and birds were told.

When this deed had been done, all of them had received a place to sleep and a place to stay. So it is that the nests of the animals are on the earth, given by the Bearer, Begetter. Now the arrangement of the deer and birds was complete.

And then the deer and birds were told by the Maker, Modeler, Bearer, Begetter:

"Talk, speak out. Don't moan, don't cry out. Please talk, each to each, within each kind, within each group," they were told—the deer, birds, puma, jaguar, serpent.

"Name now our names, praise us. We are your mother, we are your father. Speak now:

'Hurricane,
Newborn Thunderbolt, Sudden Thunderbolt,
Heart of Sky, Heart of Earth,
Maker, Modeler,
Bearer, Begetter,'

Speak, pray to us, keep our days,"[5] they were told. But it didn't turn out that they spoke like people: they just squawked, they just chattered, they just howled. It wasn't apparent what language they spoke; each one gave a different cry. When the Maker, Modeler heard this:

"It hasn't turned out well, they haven't spoken," they said among themselves. "It hasn't turned out that our names have been named. Since we are their mason and sculptor, this will

not do," the Bearers and Begetters said among themselves. So they told them:

"You will simply have to be transformed. Since it hasn't turned out well and you haven't spoken, we have changed our word:

"What you feed on, what you eat, the places where you sleep, the places where you stay, whatever is yours will remain in the canyons, the forests. Although it turned out that our days were not kept, nor did you pray to us, there may yet be strength in the keeper of days, the giver of praise whom we have yet to make. Just accept your service, just let your flesh be eaten.

"So be it, this must be your service," they were told when they were instructed—the animals, small and great, on the face of the earth.

And then they wanted to test their timing again, they wanted to experiment again, and they wanted to prepare for the keeping of days again. They had not heard their speech among the animals; it did not come to fruition and it was not complete.

And so their flesh was brought low: they served, they were eaten, they were killed—the animals on the face of the earth.

PAUSE & REFLECT How do the gods change their expectations of the animals?

FOCUS As you read the next section, notice what the gods say about their expectations and how they react to the mud person and the people of wood.

Again there comes an experiment with the human work, the human design, by the Maker, Modeler, Bearer, Begetter:
"It must simply be tried again. The time for the planting and dawning is nearing. For this we must make a provider and nurturer. How else

---

5. **keep our days:** pray to us according to the regular movements and rhythms of a calendar.

can we be invoked[6] and remembered on the face of the earth? We have already made our first try at our work and design, but it turned out that they didn't keep our days, nor did they glorify us.

"So now let's try to make a giver of praise, giver of respect, provider, nurturer," they said.

So then comes the building and working with earth and mud. They made a body, but it didn't look good to them. It was just separating, just crumbling, just loosening, just softening, just disintegrating, and just dissolving. Its head wouldn't turn, either. Its face was just lopsided, its face was just twisted. It couldn't look around. It talked at first, but senselessly. It was quickly dissolving in the water.

"It won't last," the mason and sculptor said then. "It seems to be dwindling away, so let it just dwindle. It can't walk and it can't multiply, so let it be merely a thought," they said.

So then they dismantled, again they brought down their work and design. Again they talked:

"What is there for us to make that would turn out well, that would succeed in keeping our days and praying to us?" they said. Then they planned again:

"We'll just tell Xpiyacoc,[7] Xmucane,[8] Hunahpu Possum, Hunahpu Coyote, to try a counting of days, a counting of lots," the mason and sculptor said to themselves. Then they invoked Xpiyacoc, Xmucane.

Then comes the naming of those who are the midmost seers: the "Grandmother of Day, Grandmother of Light," as the Maker, Modeler called them. These are names

HUMANITIES CONNECTION This picture of Mayan warriors and their prisoners of war comes from Bonampak, a Mayan city that flourished 1,200 years ago. One building at Bonampak contains three rooms of murals, the most complete set of ancient paintings yet discovered in the New World.

of Xpiyacoc and Xmucane.

When Hurricane had spoken with the Sovereign Plumed Serpent, they invoked the daykeepers, diviners, the midmost seers:

"There is yet to find, yet to discover how we are to model a person, construct a person again, a provider, nurturer, so that we are called upon and we are recognized: our recompense[9] is in words.

Midwife, matchmaker,
our grandmother, our grandfather,

---

6. **invoked:** prayed to.

7. **Xpiyacoc** (shpē′yä-kōk′).

8. **Xmucane** (shmōō′kä-ně′).

9. **recompense** (rěk′əm-pěns′): payment; reward.

Xpiyacoc, Xmucane,
let there be planting, let there be the dawning
of our invocation, our sustenance, our
    recognition
by the human work, the human design,
the human figure, the human form.
So be it, fulfill your names:
Hunahpu Possum, Hunahpu Coyote,
Bearer twice over, Begetter twice over,
Great Peccary, Great Coati,
lapidary, jeweler,
sawyer,[10] carpenter,
plate shaper, bowl shaper,
incense maker, master craftsman,
Grandmother of Day, Grandmother of Light.

You have been called upon because of our work,
our design. Run your hands over the kernels of
corn, over the seeds of the coral tree, just get it
done, just let it come out whether we should
carve and gouge a mouth, a face in wood," they
told the daykeepers.

And then comes the borrowing, the counting
of days; the hand is moved over the corn kernels,
over the coral seeds, the days, the lots.

Then they spoke to them, one of them a
grandmother, the other a grandfather.

This is the grandfather, this is the master of
the coral seeds: Xpiyacoc is his name.

And this is the grandmother, the daykeeper,
diviner who stands behind others: Xmucane is
her name.

And they said, as they set out the days:

"Just let it be found, just let it be discovered,
say it, our ear is listening,
may you talk, may you speak,
just find the wood for the carving and
    sculpting
by the builder, sculptor.
Is this to be the provider, the nurturer
when it comes to the planting, the dawning?
You corn kernels, you coral seeds,
you days, you lots:

may you succeed, may you be accurate,"

they said to the corn kernels, coral seeds, days,
lots. "Have shame, you up there, Heart of Sky:
attempt no deception before the mouth and face
of Sovereign Plumed Serpent," they said. Then
they spoke straight to the point:

"It is well that there be your manikins, woodcarvings, talking, speaking, there on the face of
the earth."

"So be it," they replied. The moment they
spoke it was done: the manikins, woodcarvings,
human in looks and human in speech.

This was the peopling of the face of the earth:

They came into being, they multiplied, they
had daughters, they had sons, these manikins,
woodcarvings. But there was nothing in their
hearts and nothing in their minds, no memory
of their mason and
builder. They just
went and walked
wherever they
wanted. Now they
did not remember
the Heart of Sky.

And so they fell,
just an experiment
and just a cutout
for humankind.
They were talking
at first but their
faces were dry.
They were not yet
developed in the
legs and arms. They
had no blood, no
lymph. They had no
sweat, no fat. Their
complexions were
dry, their faces were

**AND SO THEY
FELL, JUST AN
EXPERIMENT
AND JUST A
CUTOUT FOR
HUMANKIND.**

---

10. **lapidary . . . sawyer:** gemstone cutter . . . cutter of timber.

crusty. They flailed[11] their legs and arms, their bodies were deformed.

And so they accomplished nothing before the Maker, Modeler who gave them birth, gave them heart. They became the first numerous people here on the face of the earth.

Again there comes a humiliation, destruction, and demolition. The manikins, woodcarvings were killed when the Heart of Sky devised a flood for them. A great flood was made; it came down on the heads of the manikins, woodcarvings.

The man's body was carved from the wood of the coral tree by the Maker, Modeler. And as for the woman, the Maker, Modeler needed the hearts of bulrushes for the woman's body. They were not competent, nor did they speak before the builder and sculptor who made them and brought them forth, and so they were killed, done in by a flood:

There came a rain of resin from the sky.

There came the one named Gouger of Faces: he gouged out their eyeballs.

There came Sudden Bloodletter: he snapped off their heads.

There came Crunching Jaguar: he ate their flesh.

There came Tearing Jaguar: he tore them open.

They were pounded down to the bones and tendons, smashed and pulverized even to the bones. Their faces were smashed because they were incompetent before their mother and their father, the Heart of Sky, named Hurricane. The earth was blackened because of this; the black rainstorm began, rain all day and rain all night. Into their houses came the animals, small and great. Their faces were crushed by things of wood and stone. Everything spoke: their water jars, their tortilla griddles, their plates, their cooking pots, their dogs, their grinding stones, each and every thing crushed their faces. Their dogs and turkeys told them:

"You caused us pain, you ate us, but now it is *you* whom *we* shall eat." And this is the grinding stone:

"We were undone because of you.

Every day, every day,
in the dark, in the dawn, forever,
r-r-rip, r-r-rip,
r-r-rub, r-r-rub,
right in our faces, because of you.

This was the service we gave you at first, when you were still people, but today you will learn of our power. We shall pound and we shall grind your flesh," their grinding stones told them.

And this is what their dogs said, when they spoke in their turn:

"Why is it you can't seem to give us our food? We just watch and you just keep us down, and you throw us around. You keep a stick ready when you eat, just so you can hit us. We don't talk, so we've received nothing from you. How could you not have known? You *did* know that we were wasting away there, behind you.

"So, this very day you will taste the teeth in our mouths. We shall eat you," their dogs told them, and their faces were crushed.

And then their tortilla griddles and cooking pots spoke to them in turn:

"Pain! That's all you've done for us. Our mouths are sooty, our faces are sooty. By setting us on the fire all the time, you burn us. Since *we* felt no pain, *you* try it. We shall burn you," all their cooking pots said, crushing their faces.

The stones, their hearthstones were shooting out, coming right out of the fire, going for their heads, causing them pain. Now they run for it, helter-skelter.

They want to climb up on the houses, but they fall as the houses collapse.

They want to climb the trees; they're thrown off by the trees.

---

11. flailed: thrashed; beat.

FOCUS As you continue to read, notice what the first human beings are made of and how they behave.

Quetzalcoatl, the Plumed Serpent (center), fashioning a human being. *The Creation of Man*, Diego Rivera. Page from *Popol Vuh*, water color on paper. Copyright © 2001 Banco de México Diego Rivera & Frida Kahlo Museums Trust. Av. Cinco de Mayo No. 2, Col. Centro, Del. Cuauhtémoc 06059, México, D.F./Bridgeman Art Library.

And here is the beginning of the conception of humans, and of the search for the ingredients of the human body. So they spoke, the Bearer, Begetter, the Makers, Modelers named Sovereign Plumed Serpent:

"The dawn has approached, preparations have been made, and morning has come for the provider, nurturer, born in the light, begotten in the light. Morning has come for humankind, for the people of the face of the earth," they said. It all came together as they went on thinking in the darkness, in the night, as they searched and they sifted, they thought and they wondered.

And here their thoughts came out in clear light. They sought and discovered what was needed for human flesh. It was only a short while before the sun, moon, and stars were to appear above the Makers and Modelers. Split Place, Bitter Water Place[12] is the name: the yellow corn, white corn came from there.

And these are the names of the animals who brought the food: fox, coyote, parrot, crow. There were four animals who brought the news of the ears of yellow corn and white corn. They were coming from over there at Split Place, they showed the way to the split.

And this was when they found the staple[13] foods.

And these were the ingredients for the flesh of the human work, the human design, and the water was for the blood. It became human blood, and corn was also used by the Bearer, Begetter.

And so they were happy over the provisions of the good mountain, filled with sweet things, thick with yellow corn, white corn, and thick with pataxte and cacao, countless zapotes,

They want to get inside caves, but the caves slam shut in their faces.

Such was the scattering of the human work, the human design. The people were ground down, overthrown. The mouths and faces of all of them were destroyed and crushed. And it used to be said that the monkeys in the forests today are a sign of this. They were left as a sign because wood alone was used for their flesh by the builder and sculptor.

So this is why monkeys look like people: they are a sign of a previous human work, human design—mere manikins, mere woodcarvings. . . .

PAUSE & REFLECT Why do you think the gods treat the people of wood so harshly?

---

12. **Split Place, Bitter Water Place:** the site of a stronghold of the Quiché lords.

13. **staple:** principal; most basic.

anonas, jocotes, nances, matasanos,[14] sweets—the rich foods filling up the citadel named Split Place, Bitter Water Place. All the edible fruits were there: small staples, great staples, small plants, great plants. The way was shown by the animals.

And then the yellow corn and white corn were ground, and Xmucane did the grinding nine times. Food was used, along with the water she rinsed her hands with, for the creation of grease; it became human fat when it was worked by the Bearer, Begetter, Sovereign Plumed Serpent, as they are called.

After that, they put it into words:

the making, the modeling of our first mother-
  father,
with yellow corn, white corn alone for the
  flesh,
food alone for the human legs and arms,
for our first fathers, the four human works.

It was staples alone that made up their flesh.

These are the names of the first people who were made and modeled.
This is the first person: Jaguar Quitze.
And now the second: Jaguar Night.
And now the third: Not Right Now.
And the fourth: Dark Jaguar.
And these are the names of our first mother-fathers. They were simply made and modeled, it is said; they had no mother and no father. We have named the men by themselves. No woman gave birth to them, nor were they begotten by the builder, sculptor, Bearer, Begetter. By sacrifice alone, by genius alone they were made, they were modeled by the Maker, Modeler, Bearer, Begetter, Sovereign Plumed Serpent. And when they came to fruition, they came out human:
They talked and they made words.
They looked and they listened.
They walked, they worked.
They were good people, handsome, with looks

of the male kind. Thoughts came into existence and they gazed; their vision came all at once. Perfectly they saw, perfectly they knew everything under the sky, whenever they looked. The moment they turned around and looked around in the sky, on the earth, everything was seen without any obstruction. They didn't have to walk around before they could see what was under the sky; they just stayed where they were.

As they looked, their knowledge became intense. Their sight passed through trees, through rocks, through lakes, through seas, through mountains, through plains. Jaguar Quitze, Jaguar Night, Not Right Now, and Dark Jaguar were truly gifted people.

PAUSE & REFLECT How do the first human beings behave?

FOCUS As you read to the end, notice what the gods do not like about the new kind of person and what they do about it.

And then they were asked by the builder and mason:

"What do you know about your being? Don't you look, don't you listen? Isn't your speech good, and your walk? So you must look, to see out under the sky. Don't you see the mountain-plain clearly? So try it," they were told.

And then they saw everything under the sky perfectly. After that, they thanked the Maker, Modeler:

"Truly now,
double thanks, triple thanks

---

14. **pataxte and cacao . . . matasanos:** Pataxte (pä′täsh-tä′) and cacao (kə-kou′) are two varieties of seeds from which chocolate is made. Zapotes (zə-pō′dēz), anonas (ə-nō′nəz), jocotes (hō-kō′täz), nances (nän′säz), and matasanos (măd′ə-sä′nōz) are kinds of tropical fruits.

They know to much and see to much

that we've been formed, we've been given
our mouths, our faces,
we speak, we listen,
we wonder, we move,
our knowledge is good, we've understood
what is far and near,
and we've seen what is great and small
under the sky, on the earth.
Thanks to you we've been formed,
we've come to be made and modeled,
our grandmother, our grandfather,"

they said when they gave thanks for having been
made and modeled. They understood everything
perfectly, they sighted the four sides, the four
corners in the sky, on the earth, and this didn't
sound good to the builder and sculptor:

"What our works and designs have said is no
good:

'We have understood everything, great and
small,' they say." And so the Bearer, Begetter
took back their knowledge:

"What should we do with them now? Their
vision should at least reach nearby, they should
see at least a small part of the face of the earth,
but what they're saying isn't good. Aren't they
merely 'works' and 'designs' in their very names?
Yet they'll become as great as gods, unless they
procreate, proliferate at the sowing, the dawning, unless they increase."

"Let it be this way: now we'll take them apart
just a little, that's what we need. What we've
found out isn't good. Their deeds would become
equal to ours, just because their knowledge
reaches so far. They see everything," so said

the Heart of Sky, Hurricane,
Newborn Thunderbolt, Sudden Thunderbolt,
Sovereign Plumed Serpent,
Bearer, Begetter,
Xpiyacoc, Xmucane,
Maker, Modeler,

as they are called. And when they changed the
nature of their works, their designs, it was
enough that the eyes be marred by the Heart of
Sky. They were blinded as the face of a mirror is
breathed upon. Their vision flickered. Now it
was only from close up that they could see what
was there with any clarity.

And such was the loss of the means of understanding, along with the means of knowing
everything, by the four humans. The root was
implanted.

And such was the making, modeling of our
first grandfather, our father, by the Heart of Sky,
Heart of Earth. ❖

[Handwritten notes:]

Creations to praise
① Animals - could not talk or worship

② Mud - nothing

③ Wood - could multiply but had nothing in mind or hearts

✻ Faces got crushed and the people who got away were Monkeys

Describe the mood the heart of sky brings on the Wood?

④ Corn → Xmucane grinds corn 9 times of faces, shaper of heads, tearing Jaguar + I move

corn = flesh
water = blood

Rain of sticky came down, gouger

Connect to the Literature

1. What Do You Think? What surprised you the most as you read this excerpt from the *Popol Vuh?*

Comprehension Check
- What do the gods not like about the last kind of person they create?
- How do the gods correct this characteristic of their creatures?

Think Critically

2. How would you describe the gods in the *Popol Vuh?*

3. How would you describe the relationship between people and the gods?

4. What wisdom or values do you think this creation story conveys?

Points of Comparison

Paired Activity Now that you have read and studied both creation stories, work with a partner to compare and contrast them. First, review the answers about the Book of Genesis in your and your partner's comparison-and-contrast charts. Then, together, fill in answers under *"Popol Vuh."*

Questions for Analysis	Genesis	*Popol Vuh*
What do the creators want the people they have created to do?	Live happily in the Garden of Eden, obey God's commands	Praise the gods and "keep their days"
How do the people meet or fail to meet the creators' expectations?		
What do the creators do in response?		
In the end, how do things get resolved?		
What do these details reveal about the culture?		

Standardized Test Practice

Writing About Literature

PART 1   Reading the Prompt

In writing assessments, you may be asked to compare and contrast works of literature that have similar topics or belong to the same type, such as the two creation stories that you have read. You are now going to practice writing an essay that involves this type of comparison.

> **Writing Prompt**
>
> Many cultures have creation stories that have been told for generations. Creation stories from different cultures often show remarkable similarities, reflecting beliefs and values common to all people. Such stories may, however, differ in significant ways that can reveal differences between cultures.
>
> In a short essay, compare and contrast the creation accounts in the **①** Book of Genesis and the *Popol Vuh*. Show what the two stories have in **②** common; then look at differences between the two stories. Cite evidence **③** from the texts to support your analysis. In your conclusion, summarize **④** what the similarities and differences reveal about the two cultures.

> **STRATEGIES**
> IN ACTION
>
> **①** I have to **compare and contrast** two creation stories.
>
> **②** I need to show **what the stories have in common** and **how they are different.**
>
> **③** I need to include **details, examples,** or **quotations** from the stories to support my ideas.
>
> **④** I need to develop a **conclusion** about what the similarities and differences reveal about the two cultures.

PART 2   Planning a Comparison-and-Contrast Essay

- Review the comparison-and-contrast chart that you filled out for Genesis and the *Popol Vuh.*
- In your chart, find examples of similarities and differences to point out in your essay.
- Create an outline to organize your ideas.

PART 3   Drafting Your Essay

Introduction Begin by introducing your topic. Identify the shared elements that make the stories comparable. Then explain briefly how you think they differ.

Body Discuss the similarities and differences in more detail. Use your comparison-and-contrast chart as a source of specific ideas and examples.

Conclusion Briefly summarize the major similarities and differences between the stories. Explain what you think they reveal about the cultures the stories came from.

Revision Check your use of signal words—such as *similarly, also, like, but, unlike,* and *while*—to make sure that your comparisons and contrasts are clear.

PSALM 23
PSALM 104
THE BOOK OF RUTH

Build Background

The Book of Psalms The Book of Psalms is the hymnal of ancient Israel. The word *psalm* (säm) comes from a Greek word meaning "to play the harp." Like many other lyric poems, psalms were originally intended to be sung. Most of the psalms were written to be used during worship in the Temple. Many are attributed to King David, who ruled over Israel around 1000 B.C. Before becoming king, David was a shepherd. Shepherds spent long hours watching their flocks and often sang and played the harp to pass the time.

The Book of Psalms contains 150 songs on a wide variety of topics. Each describes a particular way God influences people or events in the world. Psalm 23 focuses on the relationship between God and a single individual. Psalm 104 describes God's connection to all of nature. Many of the psalms, like these, are songs of praise.

The Book of Ruth If the Book of Psalms presents us with some of the first lyric poems, the Book of Ruth gives us one of the first and most memorable short stories. Ruth is very different from earlier biblical heroes. When the story begins, she is not an important person at the center of Hebrew history. In fact, as a woman who is widowed, childless, and foreign, she is at the bottom of the social scale. Our interest in Ruth is in her story—in what motivates her as a character, in the conflict that she faces, and in how it gets resolved.

Connect to Your Life

The Book of Ruth is a story about a person who is completely dependent on the kindness of others. Think of a time when you had to depend on another person for something important. Did the person come through? What were your feelings throughout the experience? Discuss your experience with a classmate.

Focus Your Reading

LITERARY ANALYSIS: DESCRIPTION
Psalm 23, Psalm 104, and the Book of Ruth come alive through **description**—writing that helps readers picture scenes, events, and **characters.** Good description often involves the use of vivid language:

> *The trees of the Lord are full of sap,*
>   *the cedars of Lebanon, which he hath planted,*
>   *where the birds make their nests;*
>   *as for the stork,*
>   *the fir trees are her house.*

As you read, think about the effects created by the descriptive details you encounter.

ACTIVE READING: VISUALIZING
When you **visualize,** you use your imagination to form pictures in your mind. The more precise the **details** a writer supplies, the better a reader is able to visualize a work's **setting, characters,** and events.

📖 **READER'S NOTEBOOK** As you read these selections, write down the details that help you easily visualize what is being described.

Psalm 23

King James Bible

The Lord is *my shepherd;*
    I shall not want.[1]
    He maketh me to lie down in green pastures;
    he leadeth me beside the still waters;
5 he restoreth my soul.
    He leadeth me in the paths of righteousness
    for his name's sake.
    Yea, though I walk through the valley
    of the shadow of death,
10 I will fear no evil: for thou art with me;
    thy rod and thy staff they comfort me.
    Thou preparest a table before me
    in the presence of mine enemies:
    Thou anointest my head with oil; my cup runneth over.[2]
15 Surely goodness and mercy shall follow me
    all the days of my life,
    and I will dwell in the house of the Lord forever.

---

1. **want:** be in need.
2. **Thou preparest . . . runneth over:** In this verse, the Lord is presented as a generous host who offers his guest food, oil for grooming, and an overflowing cup of wine. In ancient times, olive oil was used as a cleansing agent and was quite expensive.

David, the young shepherd, plays his pipe and a bell (I Samuel 16: 5–11). French manuscript illustration. The Granger Collection, New York.

Psalm 104

King James Bible

Bless *the* Lord, *O my soul.*
O Lord my God, thou art very great;
   thou art clothed with honor and majesty.
Who coverest thyself with light as with a garment?
5   Who stretchest out the heavens like a curtain?
Who layeth the beams of his chambers in the waters?
Who maketh the clouds his chariot?
Who walketh upon the wings of the wind?
Who maketh his angels spirits,
10   his ministers a flaming fire?
Who laid the foundations of the earth,
   that it should not be removed for ever?
Thou coveredst it with the deep as with a garment;
   the waters stood above the mountains.
15   At thy rebuke they fled;
   at the voice of thy thunder they hastened away.
They go up by the mountains,
they go down by the valleys
   unto the place which thou hast founded for them.
20 Thou hast set a bound that they may not pass over,
that they turn not again to cover the earth.
   He sendeth the springs into the valleys,
   which run among the hills.
   They give drink to every beast of the field;
25   the wild asses quench their thirst.
By them shall the fowls of the heaven have their habitation,
   which sing among the branches.
He watereth the hills from his chambers:
   The earth is satisfied with the fruit of thy works.
30 He causeth the grass to grow for the cattle,
   and herb for the service of man:

Detail of *St. John the Baptist in the Wilderness*, Geertgen tot Sint Jans. 42 cm × 28 cm.
Gemäldegalerie, Berlin. G. Westermann/Artothek.

That he may bring forth food out of the earth;
    and wine that maketh glad the heart of man,
    and oil to make his face to shine,
35   and bread which strengtheneth man's heart.
The trees of the Lord are full of sap,
    the cedars of Lebanon, which he hath planted,
    where the birds make their nests;
    as for the stork,
40   the fir trees are her house.
The high hills are a refuge for the wild goats,
    and the rocks for the conies.[1]
He appointed the moon for seasons;
    the sun knoweth his going down.[2]

---

1. **conies:** animals similar to hares or rabbits.

2. **the sun knoweth his going down:** The sun knows when
  to set.

45 Thou makest darkness, and it is night,
   wherein all the beasts of the forest do creep forth.
The young lions roar after their prey,
   and seek their meat from God.
The sun ariseth, they gather themselves together,
50   and lay them down in their dens.
Man goeth forth unto his work
   and to his labor until the evening.
O Lord, how manifold are thy works!
In wisdom hast thou made them all;
55   the earth is full of thy riches.
      So is this great and wide sea,
      wherein are things creeping innumerable,
      both small and great beasts.
There go the ships;
60   there is that leviathan,[3]
   whom thou hast made to play therein.
These wait all upon thee,
that thou mayest give them their meat in due season.
That thou givest them they gather;
65 thou openest thine hand, they are filled with good.
      Thou hidest thy face, they are troubled;
thou takest away their breath, they die,
      and return to their dust.
Thou sendest forth thy spirit, they are created,
70   and thou renewest the face of the earth.
The glory of the Lord shall endure for ever;
   the Lord shall rejoice in his works.
He looketh on the earth, and it trembleth;
   he toucheth the hills, and they smoke.
75 I will sing unto the Lord as long as I live;
I will sing praise to my God while I have my being.
      My meditation of him shall be sweet;
      I will be glad in the Lord.
Let the sinners be consumed out of the earth,
80   and let the wicked be no more.
Bless thou the Lord, O my soul.
      Praise ye the Lord.

---

3. leviathan: a monstrous sea creature sometimes identified
with the whale.

The Book of Ruth

Jewish Publication Society of America

In the days when the chieftains ruled, there was a famine in the land; and a man of Bethlehem in Judah, with his wife and two sons, went to reside in the country of Moab.[1] The man's name was Elimelech,[2] his wife's name was Naomi,[3] and his two sons were named Mahlon and Chilion—Ephrathites[4] of Bethlehem in Judah. They came to the country of Moab and remained there.

Elimelech, Naomi's husband, died; and she was left with her two sons. They married Moabite women, one named Orpah and the other Ruth, and they lived there about ten years. Then those two—Mahlon and Chilion—also died; so the woman was left without her two sons and without her husband.

She started out with her daughters-in-law to return from the country of Moab, for in the country of Moab she had heard that the Lord had taken note of His people and given them food. Accompanied by her two daughters-in-law, she left the place where she had been living; and they set out on the road back to the land of Judah.

But Naomi said to her two daughters-in-law, "Turn back, each of you to her mother's house. May the Lord deal kindly with you, as you have dealt with the dead and with me! May the Lord grant that each of you find security in the house of a husband!" And she kissed them farewell. They broke into weeping and said to her, "No, we will return with you to your people."

But Naomi replied, "Turn back, my daughters! Why should you go with me? Have I any more sons in my body who might be husbands for you? Turn back, my daughters, for I am too old to be married. Even if I thought there was hope for me, even if I were married tonight and I also bore sons, should you wait for them to grow up? Should you on their account debar yourselves from marriage? Oh no, my daughters! My lot is far more bitter than yours, for the hand of the Lord has struck out against me."

They broke into weeping again, and Orpah kissed her mother-in-law farewell. But Ruth clung to her. So she said, "See, your sister-in-law has returned to her people and her gods. Go follow your sister-in-law." But Ruth replied, "Do not urge me to leave you, to turn back and not follow you. For wherever you go, I will go; wherever you lodge, I will lodge; your people shall be my people, and your God my God. Where you die, I will die, and there I will be buried. Thus and more may the Lord do to me if anything but death parts me from you." When [Naomi] saw how determined she was to go with her, she ceased to argue with her; and the two went on until they reached Bethlehem.

When they arrived in Bethlehem, the whole city buzzed with excitement over them. The women said, "Can this be Naomi?" "Do not call me Naomi," she replied. "Call me Mara,` for Shaddai[5] has made my lot very bitter. I went away full, and the Lord has brought me back empty. How can you call me Naomi, when the Lord has dealt harshly with me, when Shaddai has brought misfortune upon me!"

Thus Naomi returned from the country of Moab; she returned with her daughter-in-law Ruth the Moabite. They arrived in Bethlehem at

---

1. **Moab** (mō´ăb): an ancient kingdom east of the Dead Sea.
2. **Elimelech** (ĕl-ē-mĕl´ĕk).
3. **Naomi** (nā-ō´mē): a name meaning "pleasantness" in Hebrew.
4. **Ephrathites** (ē´frə-thīts´).
5. **Mara . . . Shaddai** (shə-dä´ē): *Mara* means "bitterness" in Hebrew; *Shaddai* is God.

Summer, or Ruth and Boaz (1660), Nicolas Poussin.
Musée du Louvre, Paris/SuperStock.

the beginning of the barley harvest.

Now Naomi had a kinsman on her husband's side, a man of substance, of the family of Elimelech, whose name was Boaz.[6]

Ruth the Moabite said to Naomi, "I would like to go to the fields and glean[7] among the ears of grain, behind someone who may show me kindness." "Yes, daughter, go," she replied; and off she went. She came and gleaned in a field, behind the reapers; and, as luck would have it, it was the piece of land belonging to Boaz, who was of Elimelech's family.

Presently Boaz arrived from Bethlehem. He greeted the reapers, "The Lord be with you!" And they responded, "The Lord bless you!" Boaz said to the servant who was in charge of the reapers, "Whose girl is that?" The servant in charge of the reapers replied, "She is a Moabite girl who came back with Naomi from the country of Moab. She said, 'Please let me glean and gather among the sheaves behind the reapers.' She has been on her feet ever since she came this morning. She has rested but little in the hut."

Boaz said to Ruth, "Listen to me, daughter. Don't go to glean in another field. Don't go else-where, but stay here close to my girls. Keep your eyes on the field they are reaping, and follow them. I have ordered the men not to molest you. And when you are thirsty, go to the jars and drink some of [the water] that the men have drawn."

She prostrated herself with her face to the ground, and said to him, "Why are you so kind as to single me out, when I am a foreigner?"

Boaz said in reply, "I have been told of all that you did for your mother-in-law after the death of your husband, how you left your father and mother and the land of your birth and came to a people you had not known before. May the Lord reward your deeds. May you have a full recom-pense from the Lord, the God of Israel, under whose wings you have sought refuge!"

She answered, "You are most kind, my lord, to comfort me and to speak gently to your maid-servant—though I am not so much as one of your maidservants."

At mealtime, Boaz said to her, "Come over here and partake of the meal, and dip your morsel in the vinegar." So she sat down beside the reapers. He handed her roasted grain, and she ate her fill and had some left over.

When she got up again to glean, Boaz gave orders to his workers, "You are not only to let her glean among the sheaves, without interfer-ence, but you must also pull some [stalks] out of the heaps and leave them for her to glean, and not scold her."

She gleaned in the field until evening. Then she beat out what she had gleaned—it was about an *ephah*[8] of barley—and carried it back with

---

6. **Boaz** (bō′ăz).

7. **glean:** gather the remains after a crop has been harvested.

8. *ephah* (ē′fə): slightly more than a bushel.

her to the town. When her mother-in-law saw what she had gleaned, and when she also took out and gave her what she had left over after eating her fill, her mother-in-law asked her, "Where did you glean today? Where did you work? Blessed be he who took such generous notice of you!" So she told her mother-in-law whom she had worked with, saying, "The name of the man with whom I worked today is Boaz."

Naomi said to her daughter-in-law, "Blessed be he of the Lord, who has not failed in His kindness to the living or to the dead! For," Naomi explained to her daughter-in-law, "the man is related to us; he is one of our redeeming kinsmen."[9] Ruth the Moabite said, "He even told me, 'Stay close by my workers until all my harvest is finished.'" And Naomi answered her daughter-in-law Ruth, "It is best, daughter, that you go out with his girls, and not be annoyed in some other field." So she stayed close to the maidservants of Boaz, and gleaned until the barley harvest and the wheat harvest were finished. Then she stayed at home with her mother-in-law.

Naomi, her mother-in-law, said to her, "Daughter, I must seek a home for you, where you may be happy. Now there is our kinsman Boaz, whose girls you were close to. He will be winnowing[10] barley on the threshing floor tonight. So bathe, anoint yourself, dress up, and go down to the threshing floor. But do not disclose yourself to the man until he has finished eating and drinking. When he lies down, note the place where he lies down, and go over and uncover his feet and lie down. He will tell you what you are to do." She replied, "I will do everything you tell me."

She went down to the threshing floor and did just as her mother-in-law had instructed her. Boaz ate and drank, and in a cheerful mood went to lie down beside the grainpile. Then she went over stealthily and uncovered his feet and lay down. In the middle of the night, the man gave a start and pulled back—there was a woman lying at his feet!

"Who are you?" he asked. And she replied, "I am your handmaid Ruth. Spread your robe over your handmaid, for you are a redeeming kinsman."

He exclaimed, "Be blessed of the Lord, daughter! Your latest deed of loyalty is greater than the first, in that you have not turned to younger men, whether poor or rich. And now, daughter, have no fear. I will do in your behalf whatever you ask, for all the elders of my town know what a fine woman you are. But while it is true I am a redeeming kinsman, there is another

> Naomi said to her daughter-in-law, "Blessed be he of the Lord, who has not failed in His kindness to the living or to the dead!

redeemer closer than I. Stay for the night. Then in the morning, if he will act as a redeemer, good! let him redeem. But if he does not want to act as redeemer for you, I will do so myself, as the Lord lives! Lie down until morning."

So she lay at his feet until dawn. She rose before one person could distinguish another, for he thought, "Let it not be known that the woman came to the threshing floor." And he said, "Hold out the shawl you are wearing." She held it while he measured out six measures of barley, and he put it on her back.

When she got back to the town, she came to her mother-in-law, who asked, "How is it with you, daughter?" She told her all that the man had done for her; and she added, "He gave me

---

9. **redeeming kinsmen:** According to Hebrew law, if a man died without a son, that man's brother or another male relative could take possession of the man's property and marry his widow.

10. **winnowing:** separating grain kernels from their tough outer covering.

these six measures of barley, saying to me, 'Do not go back to your mother-in-law empty-handed.'" And Naomi said, "Stay here, daughter, till you learn how the matter turns out. For the man will not rest, but will settle the matter today."

Meanwhile, Boaz had gone to the gate and sat down there. And now the redeemer whom Boaz had mentioned passed by. He called, "Come over and sit down here, So-and-so!" And he came over and sat down. Then [Boaz] took ten elders of the town and said, "Be seated here"; and they sat down.

He said to the redeemer, "Naomi, now returned from the country of Moab, must sell the piece of land which belonged to our kinsman Elimelech. I thought I should disclose the matter to you and say: Acquire it in the presence of those seated here and in the presence of the elders of my people. If you are willing to redeem it, redeem! But if you will not redeem, tell me, that I may know. For there is no one to redeem but you, and I come after you." "I am willing to redeem it," he replied. Boaz continued, "When you acquire the property from Naomi and from Ruth the Moabite, you must also acquire the wife of the deceased, so as to perpetuate[11] the name of the deceased upon his estate." The redeemer replied, "Then I cannot redeem it for myself, lest I impair[12] my own estate. You take over my right of redemption, for I am unable to exercise it."

Now this was formerly done in Israel in cases of redemption or exchange: to validate any transaction, one man would take off his sandal and hand it to the other. Such was the practice in Israel. So when the redeemer said to Boaz, "Acquire for yourself," he drew off his sandal. And Boaz said to the elders and to the rest of the people, "You are witnesses today that I am acquiring from Naomi all that belonged to Elimelech and all that belonged to Chilion and Mahlon. I am also acquiring Ruth the Moabite, the wife of Mahlon, as my wife, so as to perpetu-ate the name of the deceased upon his estate, that the name of the deceased may not disappear from among his kinsmen and from the gate of his home town. You are witnesses today."

All the people at the gate and the elders answered, "We are. May the Lord make the woman who is coming into your house like Rachel and Leah, both of whom built up the House of Israel! Prosper in Ephrathah and per-petuate your name in Bethlehem! And may your house be like the house of Perez whom Tamar bore to Judah[13]—through the offspring which the Lord will give you by this young woman."

So Boaz married Ruth; she became his wife, and he cohabited with her. The Lord let her con-ceive, and she bore a son. And the women said to Naomi, "Blessed be the Lord, who has not withheld a redeemer from you today! May his name be perpetuated in Israel! He will renew your life and sustain your old age; for he is born of your daughter-in-law, who loves you and is better to you than seven sons."

Naomi took the child and held it to her bosom. She became its foster mother, and the women neighbors gave him a name, saying, "A son is born to Naomi!" They named him Obed; he was the father of Jesse, father of David.

This is the line of Perez: Perez begot Hezron, Hezron begot Ram, Ram begot Amminadab, Amminadab begot Nahshon, Nahshon begot Salmon, Salmon begot Boaz, Boaz begot Obed, Obed begot Jesse, and Jesse begot David.[14] ❖

---

11. **perpetuate:** cause to last or be remembered forever. If a redeeming kinsman marries Ruth, their son will be recog-nized as the heir of her first husband.

12. **impair:** weaken; damage.

13. **may your house be like . . . Judah:** Perez, the son of Judah, was an ancestor of Boaz. His mother, Tamar, had been a widow like Ruth.

14. **the line of Perez . . . David:** Through this lineage, Ruth is established as an ancestor of David, the famous king of Israel.

Connect to the Literature

1. What Do You Think?
Which scene in these three selections stands out most clearly in your mind? Describe the scene and discuss what interests you about it.

Comprehension Check
- In Psalm 23, what kind of relationship does the person speaking have with the Lord?
- How does Ruth react when Naomi decides to return to her homeland?
- What must Boaz do before he can marry Ruth?

Think Critically

2. In Psalm 23, why does the speaker expect goodness and mercy to follow him all the days of his life?

3. In Psalm 104, why does the speaker describe God's hiding his face and taking away his creatures' breath as well as all the good things he does?

4. In the Book of Ruth, why does Boaz marry Ruth?

THINK ABOUT
- why Boaz praises Ruth for leaving her parents and homeland and coming to a people she had not known before
- why Naomi suggests that Ruth visit Boaz on the threshing floor
- why Boaz thinks that Ruth's coming to him shows more loyalty than staying with Naomi
- what it means to be a "redeeming kinsman"

5. ACTIVE READING: VISUALIZING Think about the visual details that you wrote down in your 📖 **READER'S NOTEBOOK**. How did visualizing help you understand and appreciate these selections?

Extend Interpretations

6. What If? How do you think the story of Ruth would have turned out if the other kinsman had agreed to marry her?

7. Comparing Texts How is Psalm 104 (pages 90–92) similar to and different from "Adoration of the Disk" (pages 54–55)? Support your response.

8. Connect to Life Can Ruth be a role model in our time, even though today's women are not completely dependent on or subservient to men?

LITERARY ANALYSIS: DESCRIPTION

Description is the process by which a writer creates a word picture of a scene, event, or **character.** Good descriptive writing appeals to the senses, helping the reader to see, hear, smell, taste, or feel the subject being described. It usually features vivid, precise language. Notice how descriptive details in the following passage bring to life Boaz's kindness to Ruth:

> *At mealtime, Boaz said to her, "Come over here and partake of the meal, and dip your morsel in the vinegar." So she sat down beside the reapers. He handed her roasted grain, and she ate her fill and had some left over.*

Paired Activity With a partner, go through one of the selections and look for details that appeal to one or more of the senses. Create a chart like the one started below.

Detail	Senses				
	sight	sound	smell	taste	touch
"dip your morsel in the vinegar"	✓		✓	✓	

FROM THE NEW TESTAMENT   KING JAMES BIBLE

The Parable of the PRODIGAL SON

THE NEW TESTAMENT

In this part of Unit One, you have read several examples of sacred literature. In reflecting on some of them, you have thought about ways in which stories can be used to convey moral and spiritual truths. Now you will read a story from another sacred text—the New Testament.

The 27 books of the New Testament, together with the Hebrew Bible (Old Testament), make up the Christian Bible. The New Testament focuses on the teachings of Jesus of Nazareth and his apostles. Jesus often conveyed his teachings by telling a kind of story known as a **parable.** Parable *comes from a Greek word that means "to compare." Parables illustrate abstract truths using comparisons to familiar activities, such as farming, housekeeping, or family life.*

In the Gospel of Luke the parable of the Prodigal (wastefully extravagant) Son follows two other parables about finding lost things. Jesus tells these stories in response to a question about why he associates with sinners. As you read, ask yourself:

1. Why does the father act as he does?

2. What does this story teach?

The Return of the Prodigal Son (1773), Pompeo Baton. Oil on canvas, 173 cm × 122 cm. Kunsthistorisches Museum Gemäldegalerie, Vienna. Photograph copyright © Erich Lessing/Art Resource, New York.

"And the son said unto him, 'Father, I have sinned against heaven, and in thy sight, and am no more worthy to be called thy son.'"

And he[1] said, "A certain man had two sons: and the younger of them said to his father, 'Father, give me the portion of goods that falleth to me.' And he divided unto them his living. And not many days after the younger son gathered all together, and took his journey into a far country, and there wasted his substance with riotous living. And when he had spent all, there arose a mighty famine in that land; and he began to be in want. And he went and joined himself to a citizen of that country; and he sent him into his fields to feed swine. And he would fain[2] have filled his belly with the husks that the swine did eat: and no man gave unto him.

"And when he came to himself, he said, 'How many hired servants of my father's have bread enough and to spare, and I perish with hunger! I will arise and go to my father, and will say unto him, "Father, I have sinned against heaven, and before thee, and am no more worthy to be called thy son: make me as one of thy hired servants."'

"And he arose, and came to his father. But when he was yet a great way off, his father saw him, and had compassion, and ran, and fell on his neck, and kissed him. And the son said unto him, 'Father, I have sinned against heaven, and in thy sight, and am no more worthy to be called thy son.' But the father said to his servants, 'Bring forth the best robe, and put it on him; and put a ring on his hand, and shoes on his feet: and bring hither the fatted calf, and kill it; and let us eat, and be merry: for this my son was dead, and is alive again; he was lost, and is found.' And they began to be merry.

"Now his elder son was in the field: and as he came and drew nigh to the house, he heard music and dancing. And he called one of the servants, and asked what these things meant. And he said unto him, 'Thy brother is come; and thy father hath killed the fatted calf, because he hath received him safe and sound.' And he was angry, and would not go in: therefore came his father out, and intreated[3] him. And he answering said to his father, 'Lo, these many years do I serve thee, neither transgressed I at any time thy commandment: and yet thou never gavest me a kid,[4] that I might make merry with my friends: but as soon as this thy son was come, which hath devoured thy living with harlots, thou has killed for him the fatted calf.' And he said unto him, 'Son, thou art ever with me, and all that I have is thine. It was meet[5] that we should make merry, and be glad: for this thy brother was dead, and is alive again; and was lost, and is found.'"

---

1. **he:** Jesus.

2. **fain:** gladly.

3. **intreated:** entreated; urged.

4. **kid:** young goat.

5. **meet:** fitting; proper.

Mesopotamian, Egyptian, and Hebrew Literature

Reflect and Assess

What did you learn about ancient Mesopotamian, Egyptian, and Hebrew cultures from reading the selections in Unit One, Part 1? Did you discover anything unusual or unexpected? Use the following options to help you explore what you have learned.

The Flood (Gen. 8:6–11) (c.1250). The Pierpont Morgan Library, New York.

Reflecting on the Literature

Being Human In different ways, each of the selections in this part of the book explores what it means to be human and how best to live one's life. Think about the works you have read, and identify three pieces of wisdom that you think still apply today. In your own words, explain what the wisdom is and how it still applies.

Reviewing Literary Concepts

Kinds of Heroes A traditional hero has good qualities that help him or her triumph over a difficult opponent or situation. In this section you have encountered a wide range of heroes—from Gilgamesh, who is powerful enough to defy the gods, to Ruth, who has almost no power at all. Pick three heroes from the works you have read, and identify one or two good qualities each hero possesses. Then explain how these qualities help the heroes to triumph. Which hero impressed you the most? Why?

⌐ Building Your Portfolio

Writing Options Look back at the various Writing Options you completed for the lessons in this part of the book. Choose one that you think represents your best work. Write a cover note explaining the reasons for your choice and add the assignment to your **Presentation Portfolio.** ⌐

Self ASSESSMENT

📖 **READER'S NOTEBOOK**

Below are some important names and terms that you learned in this part of the book. Explain what each one means and what significance it has in the study of early literature. If you have trouble with a term, look back at the place where it is introduced, or look it up in the **Glossary of Literary Terms** (page R91).

oral tradition
myth
quest story
Hebrew Bible
cuneiform
archetype
parable
The Book of the Dead
King Ashurbanipal's library
sacred literature
The Epic of Gilgamesh

Setting GOALS

What did you find to be the biggest challenge as you worked with the selections in Unit One, Part 1? Write down two strategies that you think will help you deal with this kind of challenge as you read other literature in this book.

Extend Your *Reading*

Conversations with Mummies

NEW LIGHT ON THE LIVES OF ANCIENT EGYPTIANS

Rosalie David and Rick Archbold

This fascinating book describes how scientists use state-of-the-art technology, such as CAT scanners and electron micro-scopes, to study Egyptian mummies. Researchers have discovered what these ancient people ate, how they may have looked, what they died from, and more.

The Illustrated Hebrew Bible

75 SELECTED STORIES

Ellen Frankel

Frankel, editor in chief of the Jewish Publication Society, has chosen 75 of the most important stories from the Hebrew Bible, beginning with the Creation. They are retold in accessible language and beautifully illustrated with pictures of ancient artifacts, illuminated manuscripts, synagogue mosaics, and masterpieces by such artists as Rembrandt, Michelangelo, Titian, and Chagall.

And Even *More* . . .

Books

Echoes of Egyptian Voices John L. Foster
These fresh translations of ancient Egyptian texts include "The Tale of the Shipwrecked Sailor," which may have inspired later stories of Sindbad the sailor.

Gilgamesh the King Robert Silverberg
This novel is an imaginative retelling of the epic by a noted science fiction writer.

A Dictionary of Creation Myths David Adams Leeming with Margaret Adams Leeming
This reference work retells creation myths from all over the world. Cross-references in entries guide readers to similar myths, and information on sources is included.

Other Media

History Through Literature: Civilization and Writing
Part 1 of an acclaimed series traces the move from oral to written literature in ancient river-valley civilizations. SVE & Churchill Media. (VIDEOCASSETTE AND CD-ROM)

Mysteries of Egypt
Using spectacular location shots and historical reenactments, Omar Sharif tells the story of ancient Egypt's rise and fall. National Geographic. (VIDEOCASSETTE AND DVD)

The Bible: A Literary Heritage
Shot in Israel, this film re-creates scenes from the Bible, showing the different genres of literature it contains. Learning Corporation of America. (VIDEOCASSETTE)

Genesis: World of Myths and Patriarchs

Ada Feyerick

Drawing on archaeological discoveries, this book examines Mesopotamia, Canaan, and Egypt and their influence on the book of Genesis. Included are helpful maps, photographs of artifacts and places, excerpts from ancient literature, and quotations from archaeologists who excavated important sites.

Literature of Ancient India

Why It Matters

The vast subcontinent of India has one of the world's oldest and most influential cultures. Two great world religions, Hinduism and Buddhism, arose there; the ancient hymns, stories, and epics associated with them are known to millions today. India also has a rich folk-tale tradition, from which many well-known European folk tales were borrowed. India produced exquisite and inspirational visual arts and contributed much to math and science.

For Links to Ancient India, click on:

HUMANITIES
CLASSZONE.COM

AFRICA

1 **Aryan Invasions** Aryans were warriors and seminomadic herdsmen. About 1500 B.C., they came riding on horseback through the treacherous mountain passes of the Hindu Kush. They brought their families, livestock, and traditions into the lush valley of the Indus River and conquered the native inhabitants.

Diverse People and Cultures
India remains one of the world's most diverse countries. Its rich diversity began with the interaction of Aryan and non-Aryan people about 1500 B.C. Centuries later, waves of invaders from Persia, Greece, and Central Asia added new languages and customs to the cultural mix.

4 **Home of Hinduism** This depiction of the Hindu god Shiva is from a temple in Madurai. There are more than 750 million practicing Hindus in the world today. That's over twice the number of people living in the entire United States. Hinduism is the world's oldest religion, tracing many of its beliefs back to the Aryan tribes that invaded India.

3 Birthplace of Buddhism
The founder of Buddhism was a wealthy prince born in Kapilavastu in about 563 B.C. He abandoned his life of luxury in search of life's basic truths. After attaining enlightenment, he taught others the way. His followers spread Buddhist teachings across India and the rest of Asia.

2 Land of Kingdoms
Over the centuries, Aryan tribal settlements expanded into warring kingdoms, the largest being Magadha in the lower Ganges region. By 250 B.C., most of India had been united in one vast empire ruled by the benevolent Asoka. Throughout his realm, Asoka erected stone pillars inscribed with his humane policies.

HINDU KUSH MTS.

ASIA

Indus River

1 • Harappa

HIMALAYAS

Mohenjo-Daro •

Hastinapura

Indraprastha
(Delhi)

3

KOSALA • Kapilavastu

Ayodhya

Ganges River

2 MAGADHA

INDIA

Arabian
Sea

Bay of
Bengal

4

(SRI LANKA)

N
W E
S

INDIAN OCEAN

| 0 | 250 | 500 miles |
| 0 | 250 | 500 kilometers |

Historical Highlights

In ancient India, the link between literature and history was religion. From earliest times, literature expressed religious belief, which in turn drove the political and social forces that molded India's unique history.

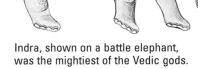

Indra, shown on a battle elephant, was the mightiest of the Vedic gods.

Indus Valley Civilization

2500–1500 B.C.

About the time the Egyptians were building pyramids, people in the Indus Valley were creating complex cities. In the largest cities, Mohenjo-Daro and Harappa, brick public buildings and private homes stood on a grid of broad avenues and smaller cross streets. Most houses had indoor bathrooms and sewer connections. After flourishing for centuries, however, this advanced civilization mysteriously declined.

Carved stone seals like this one were probably used by Indus Valley merchants to stamp their goods. The writing on them has never been translated.

Early Vedic Age

1500–1000 B.C.

After the decline of the Indus Valley civilization, Indo-European tribes invaded India from what is now Iran. They called themselves Aryans, "the ones of noble birth," and referred to the darker-skinned Indus Valley people as *dasas*, "the dark ones." The conquering Aryans introduced their religion, their class system, and their language, Sanskrit, which is related to English and other languages in the Indo-European language family. This period of Indian history is called the Vedic age after the Aryan sacred literature known as the Vedas, four collections of hymns, prayers, magic spells, and rituals. Some basic concepts of Hinduism—such as the caste system and the belief in an afterlife—originally came from the *Rig Veda*, the oldest of the Vedas.

Late Vedic Age

1000–500 B.C.

The Aryans spread southeast along the Ganges River, settling in farms and villages. As powerful clans organized larger areas, violent conflicts arose over who should rule. Priests also grew more ambitious, causing concerns about their power.

India's great national epics, the *Mahabharata* and the *Ramayana*, describe political struggles of this period and also explain important social and religious concepts. The *Upanishads* interpreted Vedic hymns and introduced new spiritual principles of Hinduism—such as belief in one universal spirit, reincarnation, and *karma*.

INDUS VALLEY CIVILIZATION	EARLY VEDIC AGE
2500 B.C.	1500 B.C.

Rise of Buddhism and Jainism

560–321 B.C.

Buddhism and Jainism were new belief systems that attracted followers from all social classes.

Buddhism was founded by a young prince named Siddhartha Gautama. His religion was based on ethical behavior and nonviolence rather than worship of gods. Known as the Buddha, or "enlightened one," he preached throughout India for about 40 years.

Jainism also emphasized individual morality and nonviolence but was more strict. Its founder, Mahavira, believing that all living creatures had a soul, refused to harm even an insect.

The Buddha is shown with earlobes stretched long by the costly earrings he wore before giving up his wealth.

Age of Empires

321 B.C.–A.D. 500

India's first empire builder, Chandragupta Maurya, succeeded in politically uniting the northern part of India for the first time. His adviser Kautilya wrote a "how-to" handbook for emperors, called the *Arthasastra*.

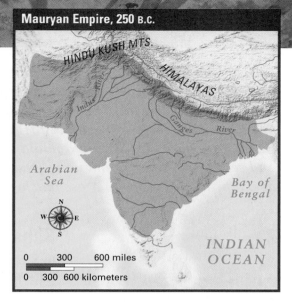

Mauryan Empire, 250 B.C.

HINDU KUSH MTS.
HIMALAYAS
Indus River
Ganges River
Arabian Sea
Bay of Bengal
INDIAN OCEAN

0   300   600 miles
0   300   600 kilometers

Chandragupta's grandson Asoka further expanded the empire through war but promoted peace after he converted to Buddhism.

The Mauryan Empire began to break up soon after Asoka's death in 232 B.C., as waves of invaders poured into northern India. Stability returned about 500 years later during the Gupta Empire. The Gupta rulers presided over a golden age in which literature and the arts flourished.

History to Literature

EVENT IN HISTORY	EVENT IN LITERATURE
Aryans invade the Indus Valley about 1500 B.C.	The *Rig Veda* contains sacred hymns celebrating the Aryan way of life.
A civil war erupts in the large Bharata kingdom about the tenth century B.C.	The *Mahabharata* describes a war between factions of the Bharata tribe: the Kauravas, ruling from their capital at Hastinapura, and the Pandavas, ruling from Indraprastha.
Aryan religious beliefs are questioned during the late Vedic age and after the fall of the Mauryan Empire.	Holy men outline many principles of Hinduism in the *Upanishads;* later, the *Bhagavad-Gita* clarifies important Hindu concepts.
India enjoys a golden age during the Gupta Empire.	The great poet Kalidasa writes plays for Emperor Chandra Gupta II's court.

LATE VEDIC AGE	RISE OF BUDDHISM AND JAINISM	AGE OF EMPIRES	
1000 B.C.	560 B.C.	321 B.C.	A.D. 500

People and Society

Perhaps the most durable Aryan tradition in India is the caste system, which still persists. According to the Rig Veda, *four basic social classes emerged, in descending order, from the body of Purusha, the first man. These castes were based on occupation and skin color* (varna), *and separated Aryans from non-Aryans. In the late Vedic age, a fifth class division arose outside the caste system.*

Brahmans

The **brahmans**, or priests, sprang from the mouth of Purusha. The Aryans devised their ranking system according to the purity and dignity they thought attached to an occupation. Since priests performed sacred rituals, they were considered the purest class and wore white clothes to distinguish themselves. Brahmans rose from being second in status in early Vedic times to being more powerful than kings in the late Vedic age.

Kshatriyas

Kshatriyas were warriors and rulers, who came from Purusha's arms. They wore red and commanded the most respect in early Vedic society.

A characteristic feature of the caste system is the concept of **dharma,** or roughly translated, "duty." Each class had sacred duties to perform to maintain the order of the universe. If you were born a warrior, you went to battle; you couldn't, for instance, sell vegetables in the market. As the god Krishna says in the *Bhagavad-Gita,* "It is better to do one's own duty badly than to do another's duty well."

Vaishyas

The vaishya caste consisted of farmers, merchants, and tradespeople such as carpenters and physicians. Most artisans, including poets and dancers, belonged to this caste. They emerged from Purusha's thighs and were assigned the color yellow.

The vaishyas, kshatriyas, and brahmans made up the three highest classes. During the late Vedic age, this social order hardened into a rigid hierarchy. Membership in a caste was strictly hereditary and usually not subject to change. One exception was that men in the top two castes could choose wives from a lower caste, although a lower-caste man could not marry up. That is, a priest could marry a farmer's daughter, but a farmer could not marry a priest's daughter.

Warriors were members of the kshatriya caste.

The British Library/The Art Archive.

Street sweepers belonged to the category of outcastes.

Shudras

Shudras—servants and menial laborers—were the lowest of the four main castes. They came from Purusha's feet and wore the color black. This caste also included **dasas**, indigenous people conquered by Aryan tribes. Aryans gradually came to use the word *dasa* to mean "slave." Although a shudra's quality of life probably depended on his or her employer, it couldn't have been very satisfying. By the late Vedic age, it was legal to beat or even kill a shudra.

An interesting crack in the caste structure occurred during the shift from hereditary rule by tribal chiefs to the government of kingdoms by powerful monarchs. Although members of the kshatriya caste continued to rule local communities, most kings came from shudra families.

Outcastes

In later Vedic times, a new class division arose outside the caste system. **Outcastes,** also called **untouchables,** were thought to be so unclean, so polluted, that merely touching them endangered a person's purity. Generally, the nature of their work condemned outcastes: digging graves, for instance, or disposing of animal and human waste. Even butchers and leatherworkers fell into the category because they handled dead animals. Upper-caste Hindus went to extreme measures to avoid untouchables, requiring them to ring a bell as a warning of their presence.

Hindus believed that they could be born into a higher or lower caste in the next life, depending on their actions in their present life.

Women in Ancient India

Like most ancient peoples, the Aryans were patriarchal. In general, males ruled. Sons were favored over daughters, and women faced stricter moral standards than men. Warriors customarily had several wives. On the positive side, a woman usually chose the man she married, and widows could remarry. Girls attended school and could engage in religious activities when they grew up. Some of the hymns of the Vedas were composed by women.

Life got worse for women under Hinduism. Hindus considered women inferior, sinful, and a source of contamination.

Around the first century B.C., the Laws of Manu set down a detailed code of conduct for Hindus. Here are a few of the laws relating to women:

- Brides could be as young as eight.
- Warriors could abduct a bride and murder her family.
- Women were forbidden to own property or otherwise be independent.
- A wife couldn't displease her husband, even after he died.

Victoria & Albert Museum, London.

Arts and Culture

Perhaps the most important contribution of ancient India is its religious traditions. Hinduism and Buddhism share a reverence for the inner life and remind us of the riches to be found within ourselves. The literature, art, music, and dance that grew from these traditions are beautiful and moving, inspirational to people across the world.

Literature

The literature of ancient India remains a living tradition, tied to religion and moral instruction. Although Hinduism has changed significantly from the Aryan beliefs recorded in the Vedas, Hindus still chant hymns from the *Rig Veda* at weddings and funerals. The great epics, the *Mahabharata* and the *Ramayana,* contain exciting tales for children to enjoy as well as philosophical ideas for adults to ponder. The fables of the *Panchatantra* and the Jataka tales of the Buddha's past lives appeal to readers of all ages. The classic drama of the poet Kalidasa—known as the Shakespeare of India—is still performed on Indian stages.

A separate literary tradition developed in southern India among speakers of the Tamil language. Unlike Sanskrit, Tamil is not an Indo-European language. It is Dravidian. The earliest Tamil poetry dates from the first century A.D.

How Was Literature Presented?

The sacred Vedas were composed orally hundreds of years before they were written down. Priests kept the Vedas alive by memorizing them and teaching them to the next generation of priests. The hymns and rituals had to be recited perfectly to have the desired religious effect. This practice required extraordinary feats of memory. The *Rig Veda* alone contains more than 1,000 hymns.

The British Library/The Art Archive.

Religion

Hinduism began as a blending of Aryan and non-Aryan traditions and developed over a period of more than 2,500 years. Hindus basically believe in one god, Brahman. More an abstract spirit than a being, however, Brahman exists everywhere, both within all living things and in the surrounding cosmos. Below Brahman—and yet part of him—are three other gods: Brahma, the creator; Vishnu, the preserver; and Shiva, the destroyer. Vishnu is said to have come to earth in ten bodily forms, or avatars. The most important of these avatars are the mythical Krishna of the *Bhagavad-Gita,* the legendary king Rama of the *Ramayana,* and the historical Buddha.

Central to Hindu belief as well as to India's caste system is the concept of reincarnation. An individual soul *(atman)* evolves in a cycle of earthly existence by which it passes from one body at death to be reborn in another body. A person's quality of life depends on his or her actions, or *karma,* in a previous life. For example, an evil ruler might come back

Text of the *Sri Bhagavata* Purana. Puranas explained Vedic concepts to ordinary people.

as an untouchable; a greedy merchant could return as a crow. The goal of existence is *moksha*—perfect understanding of the universe and, ultimately, a release from the cycle of rebirth and union with Brahman.

Buddhism arose as a reaction to Hinduism's complex rituals and the power of the Vedic priests. Buddhists accept the Hindu belief in reincarnation with the ultimate goal being enlightenment and union with the universal spirit *(nirvana)*. But Buddhists reject the caste system and don't worship Hindu gods. The way to salvation lies in moderation, specifically by following the Buddha's Middle Way, between desire and self-denial. Buddhists practice meditation, nonviolence, and religious toleration. After some of its ideas were absorbed by Hinduism, Buddhism eventually died out in India. It gained a stronger foothold in Sri Lanka, East Asia, and Southeast Asia.

Jainism, like Buddhism, arose in response to the power of the Vedic priests. Jains practice extreme forms of self-denial and nonviolence. The sect still exists in India today, but it never spread widely outside of India.

Arts and Architecture

Ancient Indian arts had a religious purpose. The classic Indian architectural form is the Hindu temple, made of stone blocks and carved with images of deities. Buddhist monuments, or *stupas*, were built in the shape of mounds, to symbolize the universe. Beautiful paintings line caves where Buddhist monks once worshiped, and some of the most famous Indian sculptures depict Hindu gods, such as Shiva.

Shiva the Destroyer

Shiva is worshiped as both the destroyer and the creator of life.

In his upper right hand, he holds a drum that represents the pulse of creation.

His lower right hand blesses his followers.

He tramples the dwarf of ignorance with his right foot.

Shiva's dance maintains the movement of the universe, symbolized by the ring of fire.

Shiva dancing. Courtesy of the Trustees of the Victoria & Albert Museum, London.

Time Line

ANCIENT INDIA (2500 B.C.–A.D. 500)

3000 B.C.	A.D. 1	PRESENT

EVENTS IN INDIAN LITERATURE

2000 B.C.	1600 B.C.	1200 B.C.

1500–900 B.C. Hymns of the *Rig Veda* are composed

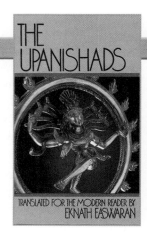

THE UPANISHADS

TRANSLATED FOR THE MODERN READER BY
EKNATH EASWARAN

EVENTS IN INDIAN HISTORY

2000 B.C.	1600 B.C.	1200 B.C.

c. 2500–1700 B.C. Advanced civilization flourishes in the Indus River valley ➤

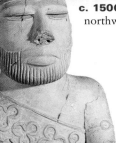

Sculpture of a priest-king from the Indus culture

c. 1500 B.C. Aryan tribes invade northwest India

c. 1100s B.C. Bharata tribe's victory in the Battle of the Ten Kings increases its power

1000–500 B.C. Aryan communities begin to appear in the Ganges River basin

900s B.C. Descendants of the Bharata kings fight for control of the kingdom

EVENTS IN WORLD HISTORY

2000 B.C.	1600 B.C.	1200 B.C.

2080–1640 B.C. Middle Kingdom in Egypt

c. 2000 B.C. Indo-European nomadic tribes begin migrating from what is now southern Russia, eventually spreading across Europe, Turkey, Iran, and India

1792–1750 B.C. Hammurabi reigns at the height of the Babylonian empire

c. 1400 B.C. Phoenicians develop an alphabet

1200–400 B.C. Olmec civilization thrives in southern Mexico

1050–221 B.C. Chou Dynasty rules in China

c. 1020 B.C. King Saul unites the Hebrews

800 B.C.	400 B.C.	A.D. 1

750–550 B.C. Teachings of the *Upanishads* are written

400–100 B.C. *Mahabharata* and *Ramayana* are composed

c. 304 B.C. Chandragupta Maurya's chief adviser writes the *Arthasastra*

c. 200 B.C. Traditional fables are collected in the *Panchatantra*

c. 100 B.C. *Bhagavad-Gita* is added to the *Mahabharata*

A.D. 100s Tamil poetry and drama flourish in southern India

A.D. 320–500 Under Gupta rulers, India experiences a golden age, with achievements in art, literature, religion, science, and mathematics

A.D. 400s Kalidasa writes poetry and drama, including the famous play *Shakuntala*

800 B.C.	400 B.C.	A.D. 1

c. 599 B.C. Birth of Mahavira, founder of Jainism

c. 563 B.C. Birth of Siddhartha Gautama, founder of Buddhism

500s B.C. Aryan kingdom of Magadha expands by taking over smaller kingdoms

326 B.C. Alexander the Great invades the Indus Valley and temporarily brings it under Greek control

c. 321–301 B.C. Chandragupta Maurya unites northern India in the Mauryan Empire

269–232 B.C. Asoka brings Mauryan Empire to its height

A.D. 320 Chandra Gupta I, from Magadha, begins building the Gupta Empire

A.D. 415 Death of Chandra Gupta II weakens Gupta Empire

A.D. 499 Aryabhata, an Indian mathematician, calculates the value of pi (π) and the number of days in a solar year

A.D. 500s Huns and other Central Asian nomads overrun India

800 B.C.	400 B.C.	A.D. 1

551 B.C. Birth of Confucius in China

550–539 B.C. Cyrus the Great builds the Persian Empire

338 B.C. Phillip II of Macedon conquers Greece

332–323 B.C. Alexander the Great conquers Persia and spreads Greek culture throughout his empire

c. 200 B.C. Emergence of Nazca culture in Peru

146 B.C. Romans destroy Carthage in North Africa and expand their empire

c. A.D. 29 Jesus is crucified

c. A.D. 65 First Buddhist monastery is built in China

c. A.D. 105 Chinese invent paper

c. A.D. 391 Christianity is declared the official religion of the Roman Empire

A.D. 449 Anglo-Saxons invade England

Connect to Today: The Legacy of Ancient India

Yoga and Meditation
Pre-Aryan artifacts show people sitting in the cross-legged positions associated with yoga. Yoga (Sanskrit for "union") is an ancient spiritual discipline involving special postures, controlled breathing, and meditation, or mental concentration. First introduced to the United States in 1893, yoga is practiced by more than 15 million Americans today.

Ancient "New Age" Ideas

Many other popular trends and practices of today originated in ancient India.

Vegetarianism was linked to the belief in nonviolence held by Jains, Buddhists and Hindus. Today, growing numbers of people have stopped eating meat, many for ethical and health reasons.

Animal rights also followed from nonviolence. Today, groups protest experimentation and product testing on animals.

Gurus, or personal spiritual teachers, taught Vedic wisdom to pupils who lived with them. Now the term is applied broadly to people who are experts in a particular area.

Ayurvedic medicine is gaining more practitioners in the West. This Indian system of healing, described in the ancient *Atharva Veda,* is based on body type.

Chess and Dice
The game of chess evolved from *chaturanga,* a four-player war game played in northwest India in ancient times. The pieces had different powers, and victory was based on exposing or capturing the king. Dice, too, came from India. Dice carved of nuts were found at the pre-Aryan site of Mohenjo-Daro.

Nonviolence

Nonviolence, or *ahimsa,* was one of the central beliefs of Jainism. It became part of Buddhism and Hinduism as well. The technique of passive resistance that 20th-century leader Mohandas Gandhi used in gaining Indian independence was based on *ahimsa.* Gandhi's strategy, in turn, influenced Martin Luther King, Jr.'s efforts in the U.S. civil rights movement.

Mathematics and Science

Some of the greatest achievements of ancient India were in math and science. Indians invented modern numerals, the concept of zero, and the decimal system—all of which we use today. Ancient Indian scientists figured out that the earth was round and that a solar year had 365 days.

58.675555

365 days

0

7.66

1 2 3 4 5 6 7 8 9

0

365 days

1 2 3 4 5 6 7 8 9

0

from the

Rig Veda

Build Background

Book of Hymns The *Rig Veda* (rĭg-vā′də) is one of the sacred scriptures of the Aryans, who invaded India around 1500 B.C. The oldest of four Vedas, or books of wisdom, it contains 1,028 hymns to Aryan gods. Ancient priests called *hotars* chanted these hymns at ritual sacrifices. The hymns were passed down orally for generations before finally being written down sometime around 600 B.C. Today in India they are still recited at weddings and other ceremonies, in exactly the same form.

Thirty-three gods are mentioned in the *Rig Veda.* Indra, a thunderbolt-hurling war god, is the most important. He is praised for conquering the *dasas,* the people who lived in northern India before the Aryans came. Other gods named are Agni, the fire god, who consumes the sacrifices, and Yama, the god of death.

Aryan Life The hymns in the *Rig Veda* are not merely songs in praise of the gods; they also reveal much about the daily concerns of the ancient Aryans. Some of these concerns seem surprisingly contemporary. One hymn, for example, describes how gambling destroys family life. "Let someone else fall into the trap of the brown dice," it urges. Another hymn encourages people to give charity to the poor, for "the riches of the man who gives fully do not run out."

The two hymns you will read are different in style and subject. The first, "Creation Hymn," speculates about how the world was created. "Burial Hymn" is essentially a funeral sermon.

Connect to Your Life

Have you ever heard or read a statement that seemed to contradict itself or express the impossible? "I know that I know nothing" is one such statement. Jot down some others and share them with a classmate.

Focus Your Reading

LITERARY ANALYSIS: PARADOX
Even the translator, Wendy Doniger O'Flaherty, admits that "Creation Hymn" is hard to understand. She writes, "It is meant to puzzle and challenge, to raise unanswerable questions, to pile up paradoxes." A **paradox** is a statement that seems contradictory or impossible yet suggests a truth. The line "There was neither death nor immortality" is a paradox. Look for others in the hymn, and try to take the translator's advice: "Be as open to the words as possible, letting them move [you] when they can."

ACTIVE READING: MAKING INFERENCES
To understand "Burial Hymn" you will have to **make inferences** about, or guess from clues, what is taking place during the funeral ritual. For example, reading the words "this wall" and "this hill," you might infer that the mourners are outdoors.

📖 **READER'S NOTEBOOK** As you read, try to picture whom the priest is speaking to at different points in the ritual. Also imagine what actions he and the mourners are performing. Use a chart like the one below to organize your inferences.

Who is addressed?	What is happening?

from the Rig Veda

Translated by Wendy Doniger O'Flaherty

CREATION HYMN

1 There was neither non-existence nor existence then; there was neither the realm of space nor the sky which is beyond. What stirred? Where? In whose protection? Was there water, bottomlessly deep?

2 There was neither death nor immortality then. There was no distinguishing sign of night nor of day. That one breathed, windless, by its own impulse. Other than that there was nothing beyond.

3 Darkness was hidden by darkness in the beginning; with no distinguishing sign, all this was water. The life force that was covered with emptiness, that one arose through the power of heat.

4 Desire came upon that one in the beginning; that was the first seed of mind. Poets seeking in their heart with wisdom found the bond of existence in non-existence.

5 Their cord was extended across. Was there below? Was there above? There were seed-placers; there were powers. There was impulse beneath; there was giving-forth above.

6 Who really knows? Who will here proclaim it? Whence was it produced? Whence is this creation? The gods came afterwards, with the creation of this universe. Who then knows whence it has arisen?

7 Whence this creation has arisen—perhaps it formed itself, or perhaps it did not—the one who looks down on it, in the highest heaven, only he knows— or perhaps he does not know.

2 That one: the unknown force that caused the creation of the world.

4 Desire . . . was the first seed of mind: Thought grew out of desire.

5 cord: something used as a boundary to separate the elements from one another.

6 The gods came afterwards: In other words, the gods are not the source of creation.

Indra, King of Three Worlds, from the Temple Car. Courtesy of the Trustees of the Victoria & Albert Museum, London.

HUMANITIES CONNECTION
Indra, the greatest of the Vedic gods, is shown in this woodcarving from southern India. He holds his thunderbolt weapon, Vajra, as a scepter and sits on an elephant.

BURIAL HYMN

1 Go away, death, by another path that is your own, different from the road of the gods. I say to you who have eyes, who have ears: do not injure our children or our men.

2 When you have gone, wiping away the footprint of death, stretching farther your own lengthening span of life, become pure and clean and worthy of sacrifice, swollen with offspring and wealth.

3 These who are alive have now parted from those who are dead. Our invitation to the gods has become auspicious today. We have gone forward to dance and laugh, stretching farther our own lengthening span of life.

4 I set up this wall for the living, so that no one else among them will reach this point. Let them live a hundred full autumns and bury death in this hill.

5 As days follow days in regular succession, as seasons come after seasons in proper order, in the same way order their life-spans, O Arranger, so that the young do not abandon the old.

6 Climb on to old age, choosing a long life-span, and follow in regular succession, as many as you are. May Tvastr who presides over good births be persuaded to give you a long life-span to live.

7 These women who are not widows, who have good husbands—let them take their places, using butter to anoint their eyes. Without tears, without sickness, well dressed let them first climb into the marriage bed.

2 you: the mourners at the burial.

3 auspicious (ô-spĭsh'əs): favorable; successful.

6 Tvastr (tə-väsh'tər): creator of the gods and protector of all living things.

7 butter: Purified by ritual, the butter is to protect the women mourners' eyes; **let them first . . . the marriage bed:** that is, before they are old or die.

Government Museum and National Art Gallery, Madras.

HUMANITIES CONNECTION This 11th-century stone sculpture depicts Agni, the Vedic fire god. One of his roles was the purification of sacrifices.

8   Rise up, woman, into the world of the living. Come here; you are lying beside a man whose life's breath has gone. You were the wife of this man who took your hand and desired to have you.

9   I take the bow from the hand of the dead man, to be our supremacy and glory and power, and I say, "You are there; we are here. Let us as great heroes conquer all envious attacks."

10   Creep away to this broad, vast earth, the mother that is kind and gentle. She is a young girl, soft as wool to anyone who makes offerings; let her guard you from the lap of Destruction.

11   Open up, earth; do not crush him. Be easy for him to enter and to burrow in. Earth, wrap him up as a mother wraps a son in the edge of her skirt.

12   Let the earth as she opens up stay firm, for a thousand pillars must be set up. Let them be houses dripping with butter for him, and let them be a refuge for him here for all his days.

13   I shore up the earth all around you; let me not injure you as I lay down this clod of earth. Let the fathers hold up this pillar for you; let Yama build a house for you here.

14   On a day that will come, they will lay me in the earth, like the feather of an arrow. I hold back speech that goes against the grain, as one would restrain a horse with a bridle. ❖

8 Rise up, woman: The dead man's widow would have lain down beside his body.

13 let Yama build a house for you here: Yama, the lord of the dead, should build a structure to protect the dead man's remains.

Thinking through the LITERATURE

Connect to the Literature

1. What Do You Think?
What is the most interesting or puzzling idea you found in these hymns from the *Rig Veda?*

Comprehension Check
- Who knows how the universe was created, according to "Creation Hymn"?
- What does the priest ask of the earth in "Burial Hymn"?

Think Critically

2. What questions does "Creation Hymn" raise about how the universe was created? What answers does it give?

3. What are you told about "that one" who is mentioned in "Creation Hymn"?

4. ACTIVE READING: MAKING INFERENCES From the words of "Burial Hymn," what did you infer was happening during the funeral ritual? Refer to the chart you made in your **READER'S NOTEBOOK**.

5. Judging from "Burial Hymn," how would you say the ancient Aryans viewed death?

> **THINK ABOUT**
> - what they believed would happen to the dead man
> - how desirable or frightening death seemed

Extend Interpretations

6. Comparing Texts How would you compare the account of creation in "Creation Hymn" with the accounts from Genesis and the *Popol Vuh?*

> **THINK ABOUT**
> - what existed before creation
> - the role played by the gods

7. Connect to Life How do the sentiments in "Burial Hymn" compare with those you've heard at modern funerals?

LITERARY ANALYSIS: PARADOX

A **paradox** is a statement that appears to be contradictory yet expresses a certain truth. "There was neither non-existence nor existence then" is a paradox and certainly hard to visualize, yet it helps the reader imagine a state before the most basic dimensions of our world were present. Religious and spiritual writings often contain paradoxes. Such paradoxes shake readers out of their normal ways of thinking and point them toward a higher level of understanding.

Cooperative Learning Activity
With a small group of classmates, find other paradoxical statements in "Creation Hymn" and write them in a chart like the one below. Discuss each statement, exchanging ideas about what you think it means or what it makes you visualize. Choose one of the statements and summarize your discussion of it for the rest of the class.

Paradox	Interpretations
"There was neither non-existence nor existence then."	This was a time before all things or even the idea of things.

The Development of the Epic

In the Beginning Were Stories

Before written language and literature, there were stories. People told stories for entertainment, certainly. But they also created stories to define themselves as human beings and to explain their place in the universe. These stories, passed on orally from one generation to the next, became an early form of history.

The Nature of an Epic

These stories from the oral tradition provided the raw material for one of the oldest forms of literature, the epic. An **epic** is a long narrative poem that tells the deeds of a great person, an **epic hero.** In epics, myth and legend are woven into rich tapestries that express the core values and beliefs of particular cultures. Epics can also serve religious and nationalistic purposes. The *Mahabharata* and the *Ramayana,* two great epics of India, are as sacred to Hindus as the Bible is to Christians. The *Shah-nameh,* the national epic of Persia, glorifies Persia's past and justifies the rule of its kings.

Some of the translations of ancient epics you will encounter are in prose. Most likely, you've read an epic silently, alone. But all epics were originally composed as poetry for public performance. They were sung or recited by professional poets, known in different cultures as scops (Anglo-Saxon), bards (Celtic), *sutas* (Indian), or *dielis* (West African). Some epics existed for hundreds of years before being written down.

Rama. V&A Picture Library. Courtesy of the Trustees of the Victoria & Albert Museum, London.

Features of Epic Poetry

A feature of many epic poems is the **repetition** of particular words, phrases, and grammatical structures. In some cases, perhaps, such repetition served to help the poet with the difficult task of memorization. For example, when Gilgamesh stands at Siduri's gate, he identifies himself in this way:

> . . . I am Gilgamesh who seized and killed the Bull of Heaven, I killed the watchman of the cedar forest, I overthrew Humbaba who lived in the forest, and I killed the lions in the passes of the mountain.
> —*The Epic of Gilgamesh*

Siduri replies by repeating what Gilgamesh just said: "If you are that Gilgamesh who seized and killed the Bull of Heaven, . . ." When epics were recited, repetitions also served as summaries of already presented actions, to help listeners remember what had happened before.

Another feature of many epics is the use of **epithets**—words or short phrases that highlight key qualities of characters or objects. For example, in the excerpt from the *Mahabharata,* the hero Arjuna is called "king of men" and "Terrifier."

A Larger-Than-Life Hero

An epic hero has to be larger than life—the strongest, the smartest, the bravest, the best—because such a hero represents a culture's ideal. Most epic heroes are part divine. Gilgamesh is "two-thirds a god." The Pandava brothers in the *Mahabharata* were fathered by gods. In the *Ramayana,* Prince Rama is actually an embodiment of the god Vishnu.

Even an epic hero who is semidivine, however, usually has very recognizable human traits. Gilgamesh may have superhuman strength and courage, but he suffers and dies like the rest of us mortals. He also makes mistakes, such as losing the magic plant that could have restored his youth. Arjuna, the "king of men" in the *Mahabharata*, seems perfect until Book 6 of the epic, when he loses his will to fight. In this episode, called separately the *Bhagavad-Gita*, the god Krishna has to convince Arjuna to do his duty (see page 128).

Characteristics of an Epic

Epics from different cultures can be very different. The Hindu epics are much more spiritual than the earthy *Epic of Gilgamesh*, for instance. However, most epics share these basic characteristics:

- The epic hero is usually male and holds a high position in society. He may be a king or a prince and is almost always an important historical or legendary figure.

- The hero's actions reflect the values of a culture; the hero's character embodies the culture's ideals.

- The epic setting is vast in scope, often involving the heavens and the underworld.

- The plot may be complicated by supernatural beings or events, and it may involve a dangerous journey.

- The tone of the epic is serious; characters often make long, formal speeches.

- The epic treats universal themes, such as good and evil, and expresses universal values, such as honor and courage.

The Epic Today

The epic is alive and well in the world today. Traditional and newly imagined epics offer writers and filmmakers a ready source of themes, action heroes, and special effects. A television version of the *Ramayana* captivated Indian viewers for 78 weeks in the late 1980s. Western audiences have never tired of the Greek *Odyssey*. Epic conflicts and heroes enliven much science fiction and fantasy, such as *Star Wars* and the *Dune* novels.

In the United States today, perhaps the closest equivalents of epic heroes can be found in the pages of comic books. Superman, Wonder Woman, and the X-Men all have supernatural powers and fight evil to save the world. Perhaps when you were young, you dreamed of being such a hero.

YOUR TURN What have you read or seen lately that contained elements of an epic? Who was the hero?

Strategies for Reading: The Epic

1. Notice which specific character traits help the epic hero to succeed.

2. Decide what values the epic hero reflects.

3. Determine whether these values are still valid today.

4. Keep a list or chart of supernatural events to see how important they are in the epic.

5. Reread passages that appear confusing.

6. Monitor your reading strategies, and modify them when your understanding breaks down. Remember to use the strategies for active reading: **predict, visualize, connect, question, clarify,** and **evaluate.**

from the
Mahabharata

Build Background

The World's Longest Epic The *Mahabharata* (mə-hä-bä′rə-tə) is the longest epic in the world. Composed of 100,000 Sanskrit couplets in 18 books, it is eight times the length of the *Iliad* and the *Odyssey* combined. It was recited by bards for generations before being written down sometime between 400 B.C. and A.D. 400. The author is said to be Vyasa (vyä′sə), a legendary sage who also appears in the story as the grandfather of the main characters.

The translator of the epic, J. A. B. van Buitenen, describes it as an encyclopedia of Brahman-Indian civilization, containing "history, legend, edification; religion and art; drama and morality." Children in India today are taught stories from the *Mahabharata*, and both ancient and modern writers have drawn on it for inspiration. The English director Peter Brook has produced Broadway and film versions of the epic for Western audiences.

The *Mahabharata* Story

Clashing Cousins *Mahabharata* means "great epic of the Bharata dynasty." The Bharatas were an ancient ruling family of India; in fact, the official name of the Republic of India is Bharat. The conflict in the story centers on two branches of the Bharata family: the Kauravas ("descendants of Kuru") and the Pandavas ("descendants of Pandu"). These cousins are rivals for a kingdom in north-central India.

The Kauravas are the 100 sons of the blind king Dhrtarastra (drĭ-tə-räsh′trə). They are demons in human form, born from pieces of flesh that were incubated in separate pots. The oldest is Duryodhana, a jealous plotter. The Pandavas are the five sons of Dhrtarastra's brother, Pandu. These sons—Yudhisthira, Bhima, Arjuna, and the twins Nakula and Sahadeva—were actually fathered by gods. Yudhisthira, being the oldest of the cousins, is the rightful heir to the kingdom, but Duryodhana arranges to have the Pandavas exiled. He then burns down their house, but they escape.

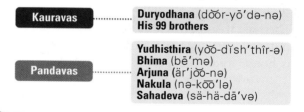

Kauravas	**Duryodhana** (dŏŏr-yō′də-nə) **His 99 brothers**
Pandavas	**Yudhisthira** (yŏŏ-dĭsh′thîr-ə) **Bhima** (bē′mə) **Arjuna** (är′jŏŏ-nə) **Nakula** (nə-kŏŏ′lə) **Sahadeva** (sä-hä-dā′və)

Connect to Your Life

You will read an excerpt from early in the epic, when the Pandavas and Kauravas (also called Kurus) are boys being raised together. Guided by the great teacher Drona, they are training to be warriors. Recall a time when you were part of a group learning a discipline, such as martial arts, music, or running. Perhaps there was a student who did better than others in the group. What set him or her apart?

Focus Your Reading

LITERARY ANALYSIS: CHARACTERIZATION IN AN EPIC

The word **characterization** refers to the techniques a writer uses to develop characters. In an epic, the hero is usually developed through his superhuman actions, his noble speeches, and the admiring or fearful reactions of other characters. **Epithets,** brief descriptive phrases such as "king of men," also point out a hero's greatness.

ACTIVE READING: SEEING CONTRASTS

Epics celebrate qualities that are admired in a culture. Arjuna's admirable qualities stand out when he is **contrasted** with, or shown as different from, others around him. For example, Arjuna is equally skillful with all weapons, whereas each of the other students excels with only one kind of weapon.

📖 **READER'S NOTEBOOK** As you read this excerpt, make a list of the personal qualities Arjuna reveals. Also list qualities shown by the other students.

Arjuna	Other Students

WORDS TO KNOW **Vocabulary Preview**

esoteric   honed   invincible   peer   unvanquished

While the Pandavas are in exile, the great warrior Arjuna wins the hand of the princess Draupadi (drou′pə-dē) by stringing a bow that no one else can bend and hitting a target. When he gets home and tells his mother that he has won a prize, she tells him to share it with his brothers. Because he cannot disobey, all five brothers share Draupadi as a wife.

A Necessary War The Pandavas eventually return home. For a while, they and the Kauravas split the kingdom and rule different parts, but Duryodhana goads Yudhisthira into wagering his right to the kingdom in a dice game. When Yudhisthira loses, the Pandavas must go into exile again for 13 years. At the end of the 13 years, the Pandavas come back to claim the kingdom, but Duryodhana refuses to give it up. The cousins go to war.

One ally of the Pandavas is their cousin Krishna. Krishna serves as Arjuna's charioteer, but he is also a deity, an incarnation of the supreme god, Vishnu. He has descended to earth to restore *dharma* (law and righteousness). When Arjuna hesitates to fight against his kinsmen, Krishna lectures him on his duty. This moral lecture, the *Bhagavad-Gita*, is the most famous part of the *Mahabharata* (see page 128). After an 18-day battle, almost everyone is killed except the five Pandava brothers, and Yudhisthira is crowned king.

from the Mahabharata

Translated by J. A. B. van Buitenen

●

ΑRJUNA,
THE MIGHTY ARCHER

Of the Kurus who studied with Drona, Duryodhana and Bhima excelled in combat with clubs. Asvatthaman[1] surpassed all in all the <u>esoteric</u> arts. The twins were masters on the sword hilt, beyond all other men. Yudhisthira was the best on chariots. But Arjuna was the best on every weapon. The Pandava, chief of the chiefs of warriors, was renowned on earth as far as the ocean for his insight, application, strength, and enterprise in all weapons. Both in weaponry and devotion to his guru, the mighty Arjuna was distinguished by his excellence, even though the arms drills were the same for all; among all the princes he was the outstanding warrior. The evil-minded sons of Dhrtarastra could not stand the superior vigor of Bhimasena[2] and the expertness of Arjuna, O king of men.

When all their studies were completed, Drona assembled them all to test their knowledge of weaponry, bull among men. He had craftsmen fashion an artificial bird and attach it to a tree-top where it was hardly visible, and proceeded to point out the target to the princes.

Drona said:

Hurry, all of you! Quickly take your bows, put your arrow to the string, and take your position aiming at this bird. As soon as I give the word, shoot off its head. I shall order you one after the other, and you do it, boys!

Vaisampayana[3] said:

The great Angirasa[4] first turned to Yudhisthira. "Lay on the arrow, <u>invincible</u> prince," he said, "and as soon as I have ceased talking let go of it!" Yudhisthira then first took his loud-sounding bow and at his guru's command stood aiming at the bird. And while the Kuru prince stood there with his bow tensed, Drona said to him after a while, "Do you see the bird in the treetop, prince?" "I see it," Yudhisthira replied to his teacher. After a while Drona again said to him, "Now can you see the tree or me, or your brothers?" "Yes," he said to each question, "I see the tree, and yourself, and my brothers, as well as the bird." Then Drona said, dissatisfied, "Run off then!" and scolded him: "You won't be able to hit that target." Then the famous teacher questioned Duryodhana and the other sons of Dhrtarastra one after the other in the same way, to put them to the test; and also Bhima and the other pupils and the foreign kings. They all said that they could see everything, and were scolded.

Thereupon Drona spoke smilingly to Arjuna, "Now you must shoot at the target. Listen. As soon as I give the word you must shoot the arrow. Now first stand there for a little while, son, and keep the bow taut." The left-handed archer

---

1. **Asvatthaman** (əsh-və-tä′mən): Drona's son.
2. **Bhimasena** (bē′mə-sā′nə): Bhima.
3. *Vaisampayana* (vī′shəm-pä′yə-nə): one of the reciters of the epic. He learned it from his teacher Vyasa, the reputed author.
4. **Angirasa** (än-jîr′ə-sə): title given to Drona, identifying him as a follower of the great teacher Angiras.

WORDS TO KNOW
esoteric (ĕs′ə-tĕr′ĭk) *adj.* understood by only a certain group
invincible (ĭn-vĭn′sə-bəl) *adj.* unable to be conquered

Drona at the Well, Bhaktisiddhanta.

stretched the bow until it stood in a circle and kept aiming at the target as his guru had ordered. After a while Drona said to him in the same way, "Do you see this bird sitting there? And the tree? And me?" "I see the bird," Arjuna replied, "but I don't see the tree or you." Satisfied, the <u>unvanquished</u> Drona again waited a spell, then said to the bull-like warrior of the Pandavas, "If you see the bird, describe it to me." "I see its head, not its body." At Arjuna's words Drona shuddered with pleasure. "Shoot!" he said, and the Partha[5] shot without hesitation, cut off the tree-perching bird's head with the <u>honed</u> blade of his arrow, and made the target tumble to the ground.

When Phalguna[6] had succeeded in the task, Drona embraced him and deemed Drupada and his party laid low in battle.[7]

A few days later the great Angirasa went with his pupils to the Ganges[8] to bathe, O bull among Bharatas. When Drona had plunged into the water, a powerful crocodile that lived in the river grabbed him by the shin, prompted by Time. Although he was quite able to save himself, he ordered his pupils, "Kill this crocodile and save me!" hurrying

them on. He had not finished speaking before the Terrifier[9] with a burst of five arrows killed the crocodile under the water, while the others were still coming from everywhere in great confusion. And upon seeing the Pandava make such quick work of his task, Drona deemed him the best of all his students and was mightily pleased. The crocodile, cut to many pieces by the Partha's arrows, let go of the shin of the great-spirited Drona and returned to the five elements. Drona Bharadvaja then said to the great-spirited warrior, "Receive from me, strong-armed Arjuna, this outstanding invincible weapon that is named Brahma-Head, along with the instructions of how to release and return it. It should never be used against human beings, for if it is unleashed on one of little luster, it might burn up the world. This weapon, son, is said to be without its match in all three worlds.[10] Therefore you must hold it carefully; and listen to my word: should ever a superhuman foe oppress you, hero, use this weapon to kill him in battle."

The Terrifier gave his promise with folded hands and took that ultimate weapon. And the guru again said to him, "No man in the world shall be your <u>peer</u> as an archer!" ❖

---

5. **the Partha** (pär′tə): Arjuna. This title designates him as a son of Prtha-Kunti.

6. **Phalguna** (pəl-goo′nə): Arjuna.

7. **deemed Drupada** (droo′pə-də) **. . . laid low in battle:** Drona had agreed to teach the princes only if they would later attack King Drupada, Drona's former friend, who had snubbed him.

8. **Ganges** (găn′jēz′): a river in India, sacred to Hindus.

9. **the Terrifier:** title given to Arjuna.

10. **all three worlds:** the earth, the atmosphere, and the sky.

WORDS TO KNOW

unvanquished (ŭn′văng′kwĭsht) *adj.* undefeated
honed (hōnd) *adj.* finely sharpened **hone** *v.*
peer (pîr) *n.* equal

Connect to the Literature

1. What Do You Think?
What was your reaction to Arjuna?

Comprehension Check
- How does Drona test his students' skills in archery?
- How does Arjuna show that he is the best student?
- How does Drona reward Arjuna?

Think Critically

2. ACTIVE READING: SEEING CONTRASTS Review the two lists you made in your **READER'S NOTEBOOK**. In what ways is Arjuna different from the rest of the students?

3. Judging from your list of Arjuna's qualities, which traits do you think were admired in ancient India?

4. What is your opinion of Drona as a teacher?

THINK ABOUT

- how he responds to Arjuna
- why he scolds the other students
- why he does not save himself from the crocodile

5. Why do you think Indian parents still tell this story to their children? What lessons does it contain?

Extend Interpretations

6. Comparing Texts Does Drona remind you of any other figure from literature, films, or comics? Explain.

7. Connect to Life Think about any lesson you found in the story. Based on your own experiences, do you think this lesson is true?

LITERARY ANALYSIS: CHARACTERIZATION IN AN EPIC

The word **characterization** refers to the techniques that a writer uses to develop a character. A writer may
- describe a character's physical appearance
- present the character's actions, words, thoughts, or feelings
- present other characters' reactions to the character
- make direct comments about the character

Epithets are a form of direct commentary often used in epics. They are brief descriptive phrases, such as "bull among men," that suggest a character's qualities.

Activity What alerts you that Arjuna is a hero? Go back through the selection and identify techniques used to characterize Arjuna.

Physical Description	Character's Actions/Words/Thoughts
Other Characters' Reactions	Narrator's Direct Comments/Epithets

Choices & CHALLENGES

Writing Options

1. Dramatic Monologue
Imagine that you are Duryodhana, the jealous cousin of Arjuna. How might you feel about Drona's archery tests? Write a monologue in which you express your feelings to your Kaurava brothers after the tests.

2. Remembering a Teacher
Recall the best teacher you ever had, in any subject. Think about his or her methods of getting you to excel. Was this teacher like or unlike Drona? Present your ideas in a brief reflective essay. Then place the essay in your **Working Portfolio.**

Writing Handbook
See page R31: Explanatory Writing.

3. Paragraph on Excellence
For the Connect to Your Life activity on page 123, you recalled a student who excelled in a particular discipline. What would you say is the most important quality needed to succeed in this discipline? Share your thoughts in a paragraph.

Activities & Explorations

1. Dramatic Reading
Give a dramatic reading of this selection for younger students. You will need readers to take the parts of the narrator and the characters. Decide how much action you will show and whether you will use props or costumes. Simplify the text so that it can be easily spoken. Also present enough background for children to understand the story.
~ PERFORMING

2. Cover Illustration
Imagine that this selection is being published as a children's book. Create an illustration that could be used on the cover. You might look at examples of Indian art for an appropriate style. **~ ART**

Inquiry & Research

More *Mahabharata* Look in the library or on the Internet for other famous episodes from the *Mahabharata,* such as the stories of Shakuntala, Nala, and Savitri. Read these stories to the class.

RESEARCH STARTER
CLASSZONE.COM

Vocabulary in Action

EXERCISE: SYNONYMS AND ANTONYMS For each pair of words, write *S* if the words are synonyms or *A* if they are antonyms.

1. unvanquished—subdued
2. esoteric—secret
3. honed—dull
4. invincible—unbeatable
5. peer—superior

Building Vocabulary

Some of the Words to Know contain affixes. For an in-depth lesson on affixes, see page 864.

Bhagavad-Gita

The *Bhagavad-Gita* (bŭg′ə-vəd-gē′tä)—literally, "song of the Lord"—is the most beloved and most widely translated religious work in India. Consisting of an 18-chapter episode in the *Mahabharata,* it begins on the eve of battle as the warrior-prince Arjuna sees his uncles, cousins, friends, and teachers lined up on the field against him. Overcome with grief, Arjuna suddenly refuses to fight. Mentioning his great-uncle and his teacher by name, he cries out in despair:

Krishna, how can I fight
against Bhishma and Drona
with arrows
when they deserve my worship?

It is better in this world
to beg for scraps of food
than to eat meals
smeared with the blood
of elders I killed.

Below:
Arjuna is led into battle by his charioteer, the god Krishna.

Over the next 700 verses, the god Krishna explains to Arjuna the universal truth about existence and teaches him how to understand and act on that truth. Through a series of questions and answers, the *Gita* defines the basic ideas of Hindu philosophy.

One of these ideas is that of *dharma,* or sacred duty. Each of the four social classes—priests, warriors, tradespeople, and servants—has specific duties, which must be upheld to maintain the social and cosmic order. As a warrior, Arjuna has a sacred duty to fight—and to kill if necessary.

Another concept central to Hindu belief is that of reincarnation, or rebirth in another form. The cycle of death and rebirth depends on a person's actions, or *karma,* in each life. For example, by committing a crime, a person would generate negative karma that he or she would have to work through in the next life—say, by becoming the victim of another's crime. But as Arjuna's dilemma shows, following *dharma* (his duty as a soldier) can create negative *karma* (killing members of his own family). "Conflicting sacred duties confound my reason," Arjuna laments in the *Gita.* It also seems that one can never escape the cycle of death and rebirth or the suffering it involves.

But Krishna gives answers to Arjuna's dilemma. First, he reminds Arjuna that although the body dies, the spirit lives on eternally:

> Our bodies are known to end,
> but the embodied self is enduring,
> indestructible, and immeasurable;
> therefore, Arjuna, fight the battle!

Krishna then offers two ways to achieve *moksha,* or union with God and release from the cycle of reincarnation. The first way is to do one's duty without feeling attached to the results—to act without desire, in other words. For Arjuna, this means fighting the battle but taking no personal responsibility for its success or failure. Whatever happens will be God's will.

The other path to enlightenment is through meditation. Krishna tells Arjuna that by disciplining the mind to withdraw completely from the senses and fix itself on a single point, one can realize union with God. But even for the truly devout, this supreme goal may require many births to attain. Fortunately, there is the *Bhagavad-Gita* to show the way.

Above:
The Bhagavad-Gita *influenced the 19th-century American writer Henry David Thoreau.*

Below:
New translations of the Bhagavad-Gita *continue to be written.*

MILESTONE LINKS
CLASSZONE.COM

PREPARING to *Read*

FROM THE

RAMAYANA

Wise Man of the Forest

Valmiki
c. 400 B.C.?

The *Ramayana* (rä-mä′yə-nə), or "journey of Rama," is India's second great epic and may be even more popular than the *Mahabharata.* Most of what is known about its author, Valmiki (väl-mē′kē), comes from the epic itself, for Valmiki is a character in the story.

According to the prologue, Valmiki was a wise man who lived deep in the forest. One day Narada, messenger of the gods, visited him and told him the story of Rama, the ideal man. Although very moved, Valmiki didn't feel capable of writing an epic worthy of so great a hero.

Inspired by Nature

Later, as he was walking by the river, Valmiki spotted a pair of herons nesting in a tree. Suddenly, a hunter shot the male heron with an arrow. Valmiki was so affected by the female's grief for her mate that he cursed the hunter for causing such misery. He uttered this curse in a rhymed verse form that had never been heard before. He called it a *sloka* (shlō′kə), after *soka,* the Sanskrit word for grief. Valmiki realized that the *sloka* was the perfect medium to convey the story of Rama and his sorrowful separation from his wife, Sita.

Above: Detail of illustration, Valmiki teaches the *Ramayana* in Dandak Forest. Copyright © The British Museum, London.

India's First Poet

The classical poets who came after Valmiki hailed him as the first true poet of India and praised his artistry. Later poets such as Kamban and Tulsidas used Valmiki's *Ramayana* as the basis of their own versions in the popular languages of India. The epic lives on in folk songs and dramatic performances, even in non-Hindu countries such as Thailand and Indonesia. As R. K. Narayan says in the introduction to his English translation, "Everyone knows the story but loves to listen to it again."

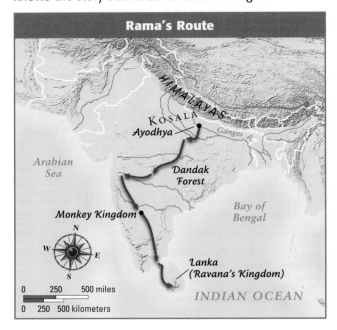

Build Background

The Story of Rama

Hero in Exile Rama is the son of King Dasaratha, the ruler of Kosala. Exceptionally strong and brave, he wins the hand of the princess Sita by bending and stringing a bow that no other man could lift. King Dasaratha intends that Rama shall be his heir. However, the king's second wife—whom he had earlier promised to grant any two wishes—demands that her own son, Bharata, be given the throne and that Rama be exiled to the forest for 14 years. The king cannot break his promise, so Rama must leave. Sita and Lakshmana, Rama's loyal brother, go with him.

In the forest, Rama and Lakshmana kill demons who have been harassing holy men. Lakshmana cuts off the ears and nose of a female demon whose brother, Ravana, rules the island of Lanka. Ravana is immensely powerful, with 10 heads and 20 arms. He kidnaps Sita in revenge.

Monkeys Versus Demons Searching all of India for Sita, Rama makes an alliance with Sugreeva, the king of the monkeys. Hanuman, the monkey general, proves to be a particularly loyal and valuable ally. He leaps to the island of Lanka and finds the captive Sita. He watches as Ravana begs her to become his wife, whereupon Sita protests that she will have no other man but Rama. When they are alone, Hanuman offers to carry Sita back to Rama, but she refuses to be touched by any male but her husband. Hanuman returns to Rama, and they prepare to wage war on Ravana. The monkeys build a bridge across the sea to Lanka, and the battle begins.

Guide for Living In India, the *Ramayana* is not just an entertaining story, but a guide for living. Rama is viewed as the ideal man and ruler. He is worshiped as an incarnation of the god Vishnu. The devoted Sita is seen as the ideal wife; millions of Indian women are urged to be like her.

For a humanities activity, click on:

HUMANITIES
CLASSZONE.COM

Connect to Your Life

Recall a grand battle between good and evil, perhaps presented in a movie, TV show, comic book or novel. Who was the hero and who was the villain? What was at stake? What powers or weapons were used? Who won? Make some notes for later comparison.

Focus Your Reading

LITERARY ANALYSIS: CONFLICT IN AN EPIC

A **conflict** is a struggle between opposing forces that moves a plot forward. In an epic, conflict is often on a grand scale—supreme good versus monstrous evil, life versus death for thousands. In epic battles, the hero and his opponent often use supernatural powers and are aided by the gods. Look for such elements in the battle between Rama and Ravana.

ACTIVE READING: CLASSIFYING CHARACTERS

There are many characters in this battle, and their names are probably unfamiliar. It may help you to **classify,** or sort, these characters as allies of either Rama or Ravana. Vibishana, for example, is Ravana's brother, but he is on Rama's side.

READER'S NOTEBOOK As you read, put the characters in two groups according to their loyalty, either to Rama or to Ravana. Beside each name, write down something that will help you remember the character—such as a description of a physical or personality trait—and note the character's role in the battle.

WORDS TO KNOW **Vocabulary Preview**

benediction	impervious	intermittently	primordial
dejectedly	incarnation	parrying	pristine
formidable	ineffectually		

from the Ramayana

Retold by R. K. Narayan

RAMA AND RAVANA IN BATTLE

Every moment, news came to Ravana of fresh disasters in his camp. One by one, most of his commanders were lost. No one who went forth with battle cries was heard of again. Cries and shouts and the wailings of the widows of warriors came over the chants and songs of triumph that his courtiers arranged to keep up at a loud pitch in his assembly hall. Ravana became restless and abruptly left the hall and went up on a tower, from which he could obtain a full view of the city. He surveyed the scene below but could not stand it. One who had spent a lifetime in destruction, now found the gory spectacle intolerable. Groans and wailings reached his ears with deadly clarity; and he noticed how the monkey hordes revelled in their bloody handiwork. This was too much for him. He felt a terrific rage rising within him, mixed with some admiration for Rama's valour. He told himself, "The time has come for me to act by myself again."

He hurried down the steps of the tower, returned to his chamber, and prepared himself for the battle. He had a ritual bath and performed special prayers to gain the <u>benediction</u> of Shiva;[1] donned his battle dress, matchless armour, armlets, and crowns. He had on a protective armour for every inch of his body. He girt his sword-belt and attached to his body his accoutrements[2] for protection and decoration.

---

1. **Shiva** (shē′və): an important Hindu god.
2. **accoutrements** (ə-ko͞o′tər-mənts): military equipment other than uniforms and weapons.

Rama fights Ravana. Courtesy of the Trustees of the Victoria & Albert Museum, London.

HUMANITIES CONNECTION Rama has dark blue skin because he is a form of the god Vishnu. Vishnu's blue skin represents endlessness or infinity.

When he emerged from his chamber, his heroic appearance was breathtaking. He summoned his chariot, which could be drawn by horses or move on its own if the horses were hurt or killed. People stood aside when he came out of the palace and entered his chariot. "This is my resolve," he said to himself: "Either that woman Sita,[3] or my wife Mandodari,[4] will soon have cause to cry and roll in the dust in grief. Surely, before this day is done, one of them will be a widow."

The gods in heaven noticed Ravana's determined move and felt that Rama would need all the support they could muster. They requested Indra[5] to send down his special chariot for Rama's use. When the chariot appeared at his camp, Rama was deeply impressed with the magnitude and brilliance of the vehicle. "How has this come to be here?" he asked.

"Sir," the charioteer answered, "my name is Matali.[6] I have the honor of being the charioteer of Indra. Brahma, the four-faced god and the creator of the Universe, and Shiva, whose power has emboldened Ravana now to challenge you, have commanded me to bring it here for your use. It can fly swifter than air over all obstacles, over any mountain, sea, or sky, and will help you to emerge victorious in this battle."

Rama reflected aloud, "It may be that the rakshasas[7] have created this illusion for me. It may be a trap. I don't know how to view it." Whereupon Matali spoke convincingly to dispel the doubt in Rama's mind. Rama, still hesitant, though partially convinced, looked at Hanuman[8] and Lakshmana[9] and asked, "What do you think of it?" Both answered, "We feel no doubt that this chariot is Indra's; it is not an illusory creation."

Rama fastened his sword, slung two quivers full of rare arrows over his shoulders, and climbed into the chariot.

The beat of war drums, the challenging cries of soldiers, the trumpets, and the rolling chariots speeding along to confront each other, created a deafening mixture of noise. While Ravana had instructed his charioteer to speed ahead, Rama very gently ordered his chariot-driver, "Ravana is in a rage; let him perform all the antics he desires and exhaust himself. Until then be calm; we don't have to hurry forward. Move slowly and calmly, and you must strictly follow my instructions; I will tell you when to drive faster."

Ravana's assistant and one of his staunchest supporters, Mahodara[10]—the giant among giants in his physical appearance—begged Ravana, "Let me not be a mere spectator when you confront Rama. Let me have the honour of grappling with him. Permit me to attack Rama."

"Rama is my sole concern," Ravana replied. "If you wish to engage yourself in a fight, you may fight his brother Lakshmana."

Noticing Mahodara's purpose, Rama steered his chariot across his path in order to prevent Mahodara from reaching Lakshmana. Whereupon Mahodara ordered his chariot-driver, "Now dash straight ahead, directly into Rama's chariot."

The charioteer, more practical-minded, advised him, "I would not go near Rama. Let us keep away." But Mahodara, obstinate and intoxicated with war fever, made straight for Rama. He wanted to have the honour of a direct encounter with Rama himself in spite of Ravana's advice; and for this honour he paid a heavy price, as it was a moment's work for Rama to destroy him, and leave him lifeless and shapeless on the field. Noticing this, Ravana's anger mounted further. He commanded his driver, "You will not slacken now. Go." Many ominous signs were seen

---

3. **Sita** (sē′tä): Rama's wife.
4. **Mandodari** (mən-dō′də-rē).
5. **Indra** (ĭn′drə): a warrior god, the lord of rain and thunder.
6. **Matali** (mä′tə-lē).
7. **rakshasas** (räk′shə-səz): demons.
8. **Hanuman** (hŭn′ŏŏ-mən): a monkey ally of Rama's.
9. **Lakshmana** (lŭk′shmə-nə): Rama's brother.
10. **Mahodara** (mə-hō′də-rə).

now—his bow-strings suddenly snapped; the mountains shook; thunders rumbled in the skies; tears flowed from the horses' eyes; elephants with decorated foreheads moved along dejectedly. Ravana, noticing them, hesitated only for a second, saying, "I don't care. This mere mortal Rama is of no account, and these omens do not concern me at all." Meanwhile, Rama paused for a moment to consider his next step; and suddenly turned towards the armies supporting Ravana, which stretched away to the horizon, and destroyed them. He felt that this might be one way of saving Ravana. With his armies gone, it was possible that Ravana might have a change of heart. But it had only the effect of spurring Ravana on; he plunged forward and kept coming nearer Rama and his own doom.

When he emerged from his chamber, his heroic appearance was breathtaking. He summoned his chariot, which could be drawn by horses or move on its own if the horses were hurt or killed.

Rama's army cleared and made way for Ravana's chariot, unable to stand the force of his approach. Ravana blew his conch[11] and its shrill challenge reverberated through space. Following it another conch, called "Panchajanya,"[12] which belonged to Mahavishnu[13] (Rama's original form before his present incarnation), sounded of its own accord in answer to the challenge, agitating the universe with its vibrations. And then Matali picked up another conch, which was Indra's, and blew it. This was the signal indicating the commencement of the actual battle. Presently Ravana sent a shower of arrows on Rama; and Rama's followers, unable to bear the sight of his body being studded with arrows, averted their heads. Then the chariot horses of Ravana and Rama glared at each other in hostility, and the flags topping the chariots—Ravana's ensign of the Veena[14] and Rama's with the whole universe on it—clashed, and one heard the stringing and twanging of bow-strings on both sides, overpowering in volume all other sound. Then followed a shower of arrows from Rama's own bow. Ravana stood gazing at the chariot sent by Indra and swore, "These gods, instead of supporting me, have gone to the support of this petty human being. I will teach them a lesson. He is not fit to be killed with my arrows but I shall seize him and his chariot together and fling them into high heaven and dash them to destruction." Despite his oath, he still strung his bow and sent a shower of arrows at Rama, raining in thousands, but they were all invariably shattered and neutralized by the arrows from Rama's bow, which met arrow for arrow. Ultimately Ravana, instead of using one bow, used ten with his twenty arms, multiplying his attack tenfold; but Rama stood unhurt.

Ravana suddenly realized that he should change his tactics and ordered his charioteer to fly the chariot up in the skies. From there he attacked and destroyed a great many of the

---

11. **conch** (kŏngk): a large spiral seashell, sometimes used as a trumpet.

12. **Panchajanya** (pän′chə-jŭn′yə).

13. **Mahavishnu** (mə-hä′vĭsh′nōō): Hinduism's supreme god, who divides himself into the trinity of Brahma, Vishnu, and Shiva.

14. **ensign of the Veena** (vē′nə): a flag depicting a stringed musical instrument.

WORDS TO KNOW

dejectedly (dĭ-jĕk′tĭd-lē) *adv.* sadly; in a depressed way
incarnation (ĭn′kär-nā′shən) *n.* a bodily form taken on by a spirit

monkey army supporting Rama. Rama ordered Matali, "Go up in the air. Our young soldiers are being attacked from the sky. Follow Ravana, and don't slacken."

There followed an aerial pursuit at dizzying speed across the dome of the sky and rim of the earth. Ravana's arrows came down like rain; he was bent upon destroying everything in the world. But Rama's arrows diverted, broke, or neutralized Ravana's. Terror-stricken, the gods watched this pursuit. Presently Ravana's arrows struck Rama's horses and pierced the heart of Matali himself. The charioteer fell. Rama paused for a while in grief, undecided as to his next step. Then he recovered and resumed his offensive. At that moment the divine eagle Garuda was seen perched on Rama's flagpost, and the gods who were watching felt that this could be an auspicious sign.

After circling the globe several times, the duelling chariots returned, and the fight continued over Lanka. It was impossible to be very clear about the location of the battleground as the fight occurred here, there, and everywhere. Rama's arrows pierced Ravana's armour and made him wince. Ravana was so insensible to pain and impervious to attack that for him to wince was a good sign, and the gods hoped that this was a turn for the better. But at this moment, Ravana suddenly changed his tactics. Instead of merely shooting his arrows, which were powerful in themselves, he also invoked several supernatural forces to create strange effects: He was an adept in the use

There followed an aerial pursuit at dizzying speed across the dome of sky and rim of the earth.

of various asthras[15] which could be made dynamic with special incantations. At this point, the fight became one of attack with supernatural powers, and parrying of such an attack with other supernatural powers.

Ravana realized that the mere aiming of shafts with ten or twenty of his arms would be of no avail because the mortal whom he had so contemptuously thought of destroying with a slight effort was proving formidable, and his arrows were beginning to pierce and cause pain. Among the asthras sent by Ravana was one called "Danda," a special gift from Shiva, capable of pursuing and pulverizing its target. When it came flaming along, the gods were struck with fear. But Rama's arrow neutralized it.

Now Ravana said to himself, "These are all petty weapons. I should really get down to proper business." And he invoked the one called "Maya" —a weapon which created illusions and confused the enemy.

With proper incantations and worship, he sent off this weapon and it created an illusion of reviving all the armies and its leaders— Kumbakarna[16] and Indrajit[17] and the others— and bringing them back to the battlefield. Presently Rama found all those who, he thought, were no more, coming on with battle

---

15. **asthras** (ŭs′thrəz): arrows or other weapons powered by supernatural forces.

16. **Kumbakarna** (kŏŏm′bə-kûr′nə): Ravana's brother.

17. **Indrajit** (ĭn′drə-jēt): Ravana's son.

WORDS TO KNOW

impervious (ĭm-pûr′vē-əs) *adj.* unable to be affected
parrying (păr′ē-ĭng) *n.* a warding off or turning aside **parry** *v.*
formidable (fôr′mĭ-də-bəl) *adj.* hard to overcome

Rama cuts off Ravana's heads. Copyright © The British Library, London.

HUMANITIES CONNECTION This painting is one of about 400 from a 17th-century *Ramayana* manuscript created for Jagat Singh I, ruler of Udaipur. It presents a sequence of events in Rama and Ravana's battle, so the same figures appear more than once.

cries and surrounding him. Every man in the enemy's army was again up in arms. They seemed to fall on Rama with victorious cries. This was very confusing and Rama asked Matali, whom he had by now revived, "What is happening now? How are all these coming back? They were dead." Matali explained, "In your original identity you are the creator of illusions in this universe. Please know that Ravana has created phantoms to confuse you. If you make up your mind, you can dispel them immediately." Matali's explanation was a great help. Rama at once invoked a weapon called "Gnana"[18]—which means "wisdom" or "perception." This was a very rare weapon, and he sent it forth. And all the terrifying armies who seemed to have come on in such a great mass suddenly evaporated into thin air.

Ravana then shot an asthra called "Thama," whose nature was to create total darkness in all the worlds. The arrows came with heads expos-

ing frightening eyes and fangs, and fiery tongues. End to end the earth was enveloped in total darkness and the whole of creation was paralyzed. This asthra also created a deluge of rain on one side, a rain of stones on the other, a hail-storm showering down intermittently, and a tornado sweeping the earth. Ravana was sure that this would arrest Rama's enterprise. But Rama was able to meet it with what was named "Shivasthra."[19] He understood the nature of the phenomenon and the cause of it and chose the appropriate asthra for counteracting it.

Ravana now shot off what he considered his deadliest weapon—a trident[20] endowed with extraordinary destructive power, once gifted to Ravana by the gods. When it started on its journey there was real panic all round. It came

---

18. **Gnana** (gnä′nə).

19. **Shivasthra** (shĭ-vŭs′thrə).

20. **trident** (trīd′nt): a spear with three prongs.

on flaming toward Rama, its speed or course unaffected by the arrows he flung at it.

When Rama noticed his arrows falling down ineffectively while the trident sailed towards him, for a moment he lost heart. When it came quite near, he uttered a certain mantra[21] from the depth of his being and while he was breathing out that incantation, an esoteric syllable in perfect timing, the trident collapsed. Ravana, who had been so certain of vanquishing Rama with his trident, was astonished to see it fall down within an inch of him, and for a minute wondered if his adversary might not after all be a divine being although he looked like a mortal. Ravana thought to himself, "This is, perhaps, the highest God. Who could he be? Not Shiva, for Shiva is my supporter; he could not be Brahma, who is four faced; could not be Vishnu, because of my immunity from the weapons of the whole trinity. Perhaps this man is the primordial being, the cause behind the whole universe. But whoever he may be, I will not stop my fight until I defeat and crush him or at least take him prisoner."

With this resolve, Ravana next sent a weapon which issued forth monstrous serpents vomiting fire and venom, with enormous fangs and red eyes. They came darting in from all directions.

Rama now selected an asthra called "Garuda" (which meant "eagle"). Very soon thousands of eagles were aloft, and they picked off the serpents with their claws and beaks and destroyed them. Seeing this also fail, Ravana's anger was roused to a mad pitch and he blindly emptied a quiver full of arrows in Rama's direction. Rama's arrows met them half way and turned them round so that they went back and their sharp points embedded themselves in Ravana's own chest.

Ravana was weakening in spirit. He realized that he was at the end of his resources. All his learning and equipment in weaponry were of no avail and he had practically come to the end of his special gifts of destruction. While he was going down thus, Rama's own spirit was soaring up. The combatants were now near enough to grapple with each other and Rama realized that this was the best moment to cut off Ravana's heads. He sent a crescent-shaped arrow which sliced off one of Ravana's heads and flung it far into the sea, and this process continued; but every time a head was cut off, Ravana had the benediction of having another one grown in its place. Rama's crescent-shaped weapon was continuously busy as Ravana's heads kept cropping up. Rama lopped off his arms but they grew again and every lopped-off arm hit Matali and the chariot and tried to cause destruction by itself, and the tongue in a new head wagged, uttered challenges, and cursed Rama. On the cast-off heads of Ravana, devils and minor demons, who had all along been in terror of Ravana and had obeyed and pleased him, executed a dance of death and feasted on the flesh.

Ravana was now desperate. Rama's arrows embedded themselves in a hundred places on his body and weakened him. Presently he collapsed in a faint on the floor of his chariot. Noticing his state, his charioteer pulled back and drew the chariot aside. Matali whispered to Rama, "This is the time to finish off that demon. He is in a faint. Go on. Go on."

But Rama put away his bow and said, "It is not fair warfare to attack a man who is in a faint. I will wait. Let him recover," and waited.

When Ravana revived, he was angry with his charioteer for withdrawing, and took out his sword, crying, "You have disgraced me. Those who look on will think I have retreated." But his

---

21. **mantra** (măn′trə): a word, sound, or phrase used as a prayer or spell.

primordial (prī-môr′dē-əl) *adj.* first-existing; original

charioteer explained how Rama suspended the fight and forbore to attack when he was in a faint. Somehow, Ravana appreciated his explanation and patted his back and resumed his attacks. Having exhausted his special weapons, in desperation Ravana began to throw on Rama all sorts of things such as staves, cast-iron balls, heavy rocks, and oddments he could lay hands on. None of them touched Rama, but glanced off and fell <u>ineffectually</u>. Rama went on shooting his arrows. There seemed to be no end of this struggle in sight.

Now Rama had to pause to consider what final measure he should take to bring this campaign to an end. After much thought, he decided to use "Brahmasthra,"[22] a weapon specially designed by the Creator Brahma on a former occasion, when he had to provide one for Shiva to destroy Tripura,[23] the old monster who assumed the forms of flying mountains and settled down on habitations and cities, seeking to destroy the world. The Brahmasthra was a special gift to be used only when all other means had failed. Now Rama, with prayers and worship, invoked its fullest power and sent it in Ravana's direction, aiming at his heart rather than his head; Ravana being vulnerable at heart. While he had prayed for indestructibility of his several heads and arms, he had forgotten to strengthen his heart, where the Brahmasthra entered and ended his career.

Rama watched him fall headlong from his chariot face down onto the earth, and that was the end of the great campaign. Now one noticed Ravana's face aglow with a new quality. Rama's arrows had burnt off the layers of dross,[24] the

> While he had prayed for indestructibility of his several heads and arms, he had forgotten to strengthen his heart.

anger, conceit, cruelty, lust, and egotism which had encrusted his real self, and now his personality came through in its <u>pristine</u> form—of one who was devout and capable of tremendous attainments. His constant meditation on Rama, although as an adversary, now seemed to bear fruit, as his face shone with serenity and peace. Rama noticed it from his chariot above and commanded Matali, "Set me down on the ground." When the chariot descended and came to rest on its wheels, Rama got down and commanded Matali, "I am grateful for your services to me. You may now take the chariot back to Indra."

Surrounded by his brother Lakshmana and Hanuman and all his other war chiefs, Rama approached Ravana's body, and stood gazing on it. He noted his crowns and jewelry scattered piecemeal on the ground. The decorations and the extraordinary workmanship of the armour on his chest were blood-covered. Rama sighed as if to say, "What might he not have achieved but for the evil stirring within him!"

At this moment, as they readjusted Ravana's blood-stained body, Rama noticed to his great shock a scar on Ravana's back and said with a smile, "Perhaps this is not an episode of glory for me as I seem to have killed an enemy who was turning his back and retreating. Perhaps I was wrong in shooting the Brahmasthra into

---

22. **Brahmasthra** (brə-mŭs′thrə).

23. **Tripura** (trĭ-pōō′rə).

24. **dross** (drŏs): waste matter; impurities.

WORDS TO KNOW
ineffectually (ĭn′ĭ-fĕk′chōō-ə-lē) *adv.* in a useless manner
pristine (prĭs′tēn′) *adj.* pure; uncorrupted

Rama and Sita enthroned. Courtesy of the Trustees of the Victoria & Albert Museum, London.

him." He looked so concerned at this supposed lapse on his part that Vibishana,[25] Ravana's brother, came forward to explain. "What you have achieved is unique. I say so although it meant the death of my brother."

"But I have attacked a man who had turned his back," Rama said. "See that scar."

Vibishana explained, "It is an old scar. In ancient days, when he paraded his strength around the globe, once he tried to attack the divine elephants that guard the four directions. When he tried to catch them, he was gored in the back by one of the tuskers and that is the scar you see now; it is not a fresh one though fresh blood is flowing on it."

Rama accepted the explanation. "Honour him and cherish his memory so that his spirit may go to heaven, where he has his place. And now I will leave you to attend to his funeral arrangements, befitting his grandeur." ❖

_____

25. **Vibishana** (vĭ-bē′ shə-nə).

from ARROW OF THE BLUE-SKINNED GOD:
RETRACING THE RAMAYANA THROUGH INDIA

JONAH BLANK

In 1990, the anthropologist and journalist Jonah Blank traveled through India, following the path Rama took in the Ramayana. *In his book* Arrow of the Blue-Skinned God, *Blank relates this famous epic to life in India today and tells what the epic means to him.*

Rama and the archer in a carriage attack Ravana.
Copyright © The British Library, London.

When I was a boy, like most boys, I longed to become a knight in shining armor. My heroes were Sir Lancelot, King Richard the Lionheart, and . . . Saint George. I believed that there really had been a time when brave men devoted their lives to the cause of right. I would read Thomas Malory[1] entire afternoons and evenings, and desperately wish to slip back to those times. It always made me sad to put the book down and look out the window at the mundane[2] world, the world in which "Sir" was what a waiter called my father if he wanted a tip.

I did not bother to think that the Saracens[3] slain by valiant Crusaders were fighting a holy war of their own, knights just as righteous or unrighteous as the thundering chivalry of Europe. Nor did I think much about the women and children slaughtered by the Lionheart for the crime of being Muslim. My heroes had not yet been demythologized.[4] . . . But even then the knight with whom I most identified was Saint

---

1. **Thomas Malory:** author of *Le Morte d'Arthur,* a collection of tales about King Arthur and such knights as Sir Lancelot.
2. **mundane** (mŭn-dān′): ordinary; everyday.
3. **Saracens** (săr′ə-sənz): Muslims from the time of the Crusades, against whom Richard the Lionheart and others did battle.
4. **been demythologized** (dē′mĭ-thŏl′ə-jīzd′): had the mythical or mysterious elements removed.

George. Because he, more than any other, personified the triumph of good over evil. . . .

What Saint George represented, without my realizing it, was an entire world view in which good *always* beats evil, without even working up a sweat. When he kills the dragon, it is not a titanic clash between equally powerful enemies. For the knight, slaughtering a monster is no more difficult than swatting a mosquito. There is little drama, no chance that the dragon might actually win. Virtue *must* prevail—that is the natural order of the universe. It is an immensely comforting notion of life.

It is also the notion of life that underlies the Ramayana. I don't want to spoil the suspense (and I won't reveal the kicker), but in the end Rama wins. It was fated from the beginning. All the characters know it. Even the Demon King's counselors tell their master that he will lose, and only suicidal arrogance lets him ignore their warning. All Indians know how the epic turns out, yet they cluster around their televisions, radios, and school stages just the same.

Everyone, I think, longs for a world where good always trounces evil. When we go to the movies we know the hero will win out and the villain will be crushed, but we still grip the armrests in anticipation. What are action-thriller films if not morality plays? Does the sadistic[5] drug lord *ever* walk away unpunished? It is the same in most popular forms of fiction: right must defeat wrong, or else we'd feel cheated.

In real life, it is quite often evil that triumphs. In real life, rapists and murderers go free on judicial technicalities, slumlords and stock manipulators flourish as respected members of society. In real life, good, honest, hard-working people lose their livelihoods at the flick of a corporate raider's pen. Perhaps that is why we so desperately seek escape. We ache for a world where good always wins, because that is not the real world we inhabit. We long for Saint George. We long for Rama.

If you look at the icons of these two holy warriors, you notice that both faces wear the same untroubled expression. Both mouths are tinged with the same faint shadow of a placid smile. It is a smile of inner serenity, of divine self-confidence, of quiet contentment, a smile that comes from utter certainty that good is destined to prevail. ❖

---

5. **sadistic** (sə-dĭs′tĭk): loving or delighting in cruelty.

Saint George and the Dragon (17th century). Ivory. Cavalry Museum Pinerolo/The Art Archive/Dagli Orti.

Thinking through the LITERATURE

Connect to the Literature

1. What Do You Think?
What is your reaction to the battle between Rama and Ravana?

Comprehension Check
- What kinds of weapons do Rama and Ravana use against each other?
- How does Rama finally win the battle?
- How does Rama treat Ravana after killing him?

Think Critically

2. Ravana, with his 10 heads and 20 arms, would seem to have an advantage over Rama. Why do you think Rama is able to defeat him?

3. ACTIVE READING: CLASSIFYING CHARACTERS
Review the chart of characters you classified in your **READER'S NOTEBOOK**. How much do Rama's and Ravana's allies affect the course of the battle?

4. How would you describe Rama's heroic code—that is, the set of rules that he, as a hero, must follow?

> **THINK ABOUT**
> - the chance he gives Ravana to recover
> - his strategy and behavior in battle
> - what he tells Ravana's brother after Ravana has been killed

5. Do you think that Ravana is heroic? Support your answer.

Extend Interpretations

6. Critic's Corner Barbara Powell writes of the *Ramayana,* "While it is alive with exciting action, intrigue, and profound emotions, it is sublimely spiritual as well." What spiritual or religious dimensions do you see in this excerpt?

7. Comparing Texts How would you compare Rama with Arjuna from the *Mahabharata?*

8. Comparing Texts In *Arrow of the Blue-Skinned God* (page 141), Jonah Blank compares Rama to Saint George. Name other heroes whom you would compare to Rama. Do you agree with Blank about why people need such heroes?

9. Connect to Life What similarities can you see between Rama and Ravana's struggle and the battle between good and evil that you recalled for the Connect to Your Life activity?

Writing Options

1. Comparison Essay Compare the battle between Rama and Ravana with a struggle between good and evil in modern culture. You might see echoes of the *Ramayana* in *Star Wars,* or superhero comic books, for example.

2. Battle Lines Try to put the *Ramayana* back into its original form—poetry. Take a scene from this selection and rewrite it in rhymed or unrhymed verse suitable for reciting with music. Perform the poem.

3. Definition Essay What did it take to be a hero in ancient India? Write a definition based on the *Ramayana* and the *Mahabharata.* Use Rama, Arjuna, or any other characters from the epics as examples to support your ideas.

Activities & Explorations

1. Battle Scene In India, people frequently perform the *Ramayana* in folk plays. Write dialogue, then stage the battle between Rama and Ravana. Use masks or makeup to express the characters' larger-than-life qualities. Invent creative ways to suggest supernatural events that would be difficult to show on-stage. ~ **PERFORMING**

2. Comic Book The *Ramayana* was once published as a comic book of more than 100 pages. Draw a few comic-book panels of your own to depict the battle scene. How do you envision the terrifying Ravana? ~ **ART**

Inquiry & Research

The Epic Performed Research a performance tradition based on the *Ramayana.* You might investigate *Ramlilas,* or annual drama festivals; *wayang kulit,* or Indonesian shadow-puppet plays; or *kathakali* or *bharatnatyam,* forms of Indian classical dance. Present your findings in an oral report that includes photographs or a videotape.

Communication Handbook
See page R45: Finding Sources.

RESEARCH STARTER
CLASSZONE.COM

Vocabulary in Action

EXERCISE: WORDS IN CONTEXT For each underlined word, write the Word to Know that could substitute for it in the context.

The two armies fought on aimlessly and (1) <u>unproductively</u>. Neither had realized how (2) <u>overpowering</u> the other's forces were; both had considered themselves (3) <u>invulnerable</u> to attack. But in truth they were evenly matched: the (4) <u>avoidance</u> of an attack by one brought on an equally clever move by the other. And so the battle went on (5) <u>periodically</u> for days.

The countries of the two armies were long-standing enemies, almost since the (6) <u>earliest</u> days of the world. Worshippers of different gods, both had gone into battle with a special (7) <u>blessing</u> from their priests to bring on victory. At a certain point one army thought they saw the (8) <u>personification</u> of their chief god floating high and (9) <u>uncorrupted</u> over the battlefield. But the image disappeared, and they went (10) <u>sadly</u> back into battle.

WORDS TO KNOW

benediction	impervious	intermittently	primordial
dejectedly	incarnation	parrying	pristine
formidable	ineffectually		

Building Vocabulary
For an in-depth lesson on using context clues, see page 674.

Modern Views of Rama and Sita

In Indian culture, Rama and his wife, Sita, embody such virtues as strength, leadership, devotion, and purity. However, some Indians question whether Rama and Sita are good role models in today's world. Their actions in the seventh book of the *Ramayana,* the *Uttara Kanda,* are particularly troubling to many people.

Unhappy Ending After Rama slays Ravana, he rejects Sita, saying he doubts she has remained pure during her captivity. She demands a trial by fire, and the god Agni, knowing she is innocent, saves her from the flames. Rama then states he had put Sita through the ordeal to prove her innocence before all his subjects. Months later, however, the people remain suspicious of Sita. For the good of the kingdom, Rama orders his brother Lakshmana to abandon Sita in the forest. There the pregnant Sita takes refuge with the poet Valmiki and gives birth to twin sons. These sons learn to recite the *Ramayana,* and eventually they perform it before Rama's court. When Rama realizes who they are, he invites Sita to return to him. He asks her to prove her purity once more, but she refuses and asks Mother Earth to swallow her up. Her wish is granted, and she disappears.

Are Rama and Sita Heroic? Given these events, modern Indians disagree about how to view Rama and Sita. Contemporary rural women sing folk songs calling Rama heartless and expressing sympathy for Sita. A 1998 exhibit, "Sita in the City," showed that South Asian immigrants in New York held wildly varying views of Sita. One mother saw Sita's chastity as something for teenage girls to emulate, but an activist against domestic violence called Sita "a lousy role model for women." Some people admiringly compared Sita to a modern single mother raising children alone. Some saw her fire test as a sign of virtue and strength, while others saw it as proof of women's oppression.

Group Discussion Who are some of the men and women—real or fictitious—held up as ideals in your own culture? Would you want to imitate them? Have they ever been challenged as proper role models? Explain.

Rama and Sita are seen as role models for modern Indian couples.

FROM THE

PANCHATANTRA

Translated by **ARTHUR W. RYDER**

In this part of the book, you have read classic stories from ancient India and seen how they offer spiritual and practical lessons. Now you will read from another famous book of instructive stories from India. The Panchatantra *(pŭn´chə-tän´trə) is a collection of Sanskrit fables probably gathered around 200* B.C. *Over the centuries it has been translated into more than 50 languages, including Arabic, Greek, and Hebrew, and its stories have spread all over the world. So many familiar tales can be traced back to the* Panchatantra *that it has been called the Mother of Folklore.*

Panchatantra means "five books." The introduction explains that a king wanted to educate his three foolish sons. For this purpose he hired a Brahman, who proceeded to teach the principles of life by means of stories. These stories are arranged under five themes, or lessons. Often, stories are told within other stories, a technique repeated in such works as The Thousand and One Nights.

The two stories you will read are taken from the fifth book. They deal with the theme of hasty action. A wheel bearer is telling the stories to his friend, a gold finder. As you read, consider the following questions:

1. *What lessons do the tales teach?*
2. *Do the tales seem familiar to you?*
3. *What similarities and differences can you find between the tales and other pieces of Indian literature you've read?*

❧ SLOW, THE WEAVER ❧

He who, lacking wit, does not
      Harken to a friend,
Just like weaver Slow, inclines
      To a fatal end. . . .

In a certain town lived a weaver named Slow. One day all the pegs in his loom broke. So he took an axe, and in his search for wood, came to the seashore. There he found a great sissoo[1] tree, and he thought: "This seems a good-sized tree. If I cut it down, I can make plenty of weaving-tools." He therefore lifted his axe upon it.

Now there was a fairy in the tree who said: "My friend, this tree is my home. Please spare it. For I live here in utter happiness, since my body is caressed by breezes cool from contact with ocean billows."

"But, sir," said the weaver, "what am I to do? While I lack apparatus made of wood, my family is pinched by hunger. Therefore, please move elsewhere, and quickly. I intend to cut it down."

"Sir," said the fairy, "I have taken a liking to you. Ask anything you like, but spare this tree."

"In that case," said the weaver, "I will go home and return after asking my friend and my wife." And when the fairy consented, the weaver started home. On entering the town, he encountered his particular friend, the barber, and said: "My friend, I have won the favor of a fairy. Tell me what to ask for."

And the barber said: "My dear fellow, if it is really so, ask for a kingdom. You can be king, and I will be prime minister. So we shall both taste the delights of this world before those of the world to come."

"Quite so, my friend," replied the weaver. "However, I shall ask my wife, too." "Don't," said the barber. "It is a mistake to consult women. As the saying goes:

Give a woman food and dresses
(Chiefly when her trouble presses);
Give her gems and all things nice;
Do not ask for her advice.

And again:

Where a woman, gambler, child,
As a guide is domiciled,[2]
Death advances, stage by stage—
So declares the ancient sage.

And once again:

Only while he does not hear
Woman's whisper in his ear,
May a man a leader be,
Keeping due humility.

Women seek for selfish treasures,
Think of nothing but their pleasures,
Even children by them reckoned
To their selfish comfort second."

And the weaver rejoined: "You may be right. Still, I shall ask her. She is a good wife."

So he made haste and said to her: "My dear wife, today we won the favor of a fairy. He offers anything we want. So I have come to ask you to tell me what to say to him. Here is my friend, the barber, who tells me to ask for a kingdom."

---

1. **sissoo** (sĭs′o͞o) **tree:** a kind of East Indian tree known for its strong, useful timber.

2. **domiciled** (dŏm′ĭ-sīld′): residing; making a home.

"Dear husband," said she, "what sense have barbers? Do not take his advice. For the proverb says:

> All advice you may discard
> From a barber, child, or bard,
> Monk or hermit or musician,
> Or a man of base[3] condition.

"Besides, this king-business means a series of dreadful troubles and involves worry about peace, war, change of base, entrenchment, alliance, duplicity, and other matters. It never gives satisfaction. And even worse,

> His very sons and brothers wish
> The slaughter of a king;
> As this is kingship's nature, who
> Would not reject the thing?"

"Yes," said the weaver, "you are right. But tell me what to ask for." And she replied: "As it is, you turn out one piece of cloth a day, and this meets all our expenses. Now ask for a second pair of arms and an extra head, so that you may produce one piece of cloth in front and another behind. The price of one meets the household expenses, with the price of the other you may put on style and spend the time in honor among your peers."

On hearing this, he was delighted and said: "Splendid, my faithful wife! You have made a splendid suggestion. I am determined to follow it."

So the weaver went and laid his request before the fairy: "Well, sir, if you offer what I wish, pray give me a second pair of arms and an extra head." And in the act of speaking he became two-headed and four-armed.

But as he came home, delight in his heart, the people thought he was a fiend, and beat him with clubs and stones and things so that he died.

"And that is why I say:

> He who, lacking wit, does not, . . .

and the rest of it."

Kanduri cloth from Uttar Pradesh (c. 1900). The Metropolitan Museum, New York. Collection of Michael and Margaret Lecomber.

Then the wheel-bearer continued: "Yes, any man becomes ridiculous when bitten by the demon of extravagant hope. There is sense in this:

> Do not indulge in hopes
> Extravagantly high:
> Else, whitened like the sire
> Of Moon-Lord, you will lie."

"How was that?" asked the gold-finder. And the other told the story of the Brahman's dream. ❖

---

3. **base:** low; inferior.

❧ THE BRAHMAN'S DREAM ❧

In a certain town lived a Brahman named Seedy, who got some barley-meal by begging, ate a portion, and filled a jar with the remainder. This jar he hung on a peg one night, placed his cot beneath it, and fixing his gaze on the jar, fell into a hypnotic reverie.[4]

"Well, here is a jar full of barley-meal," he thought. "Now if famine comes, a hundred rupees[5] will come out of it. With that sum I will get two she-goats. Every six months they will bear two more she-goats. After goats, cows. When the cows calve, I will sell the calves. After cows, buffaloes; after buffaloes, mares. From the mares I shall get plenty of horses. The sale of these will mean plenty of gold. The gold will buy a great house with an inner court. Then someone will come to my house and offer his lovely daughter with a dowry.[6] She will bear a son, whom I shall name Moon-Lord. When he is old enough to ride on my knee, I will take a book, sit on the stable roof, and think. Just then Moon-Lord will see me, will jump from his mother's lap in his eagerness to ride on my knee, and will go too near the horses. Then I shall get angry and tell my wife to take the boy. But she will be busy with her chores and will not pay attention to what I say. Then I will get up and kick her."

Being sunk in his hypnotic dream, he let fly such a kick that he smashed the jar. And the barley-meal which it contained turned him white all over.

"And that is why I say:
> Do not indulge in hopes, . . .

and the rest of it." ❖

---

4. **reverie** (rĕv′ə-rē): daydream.

5. **rupees** (rōō-pēz′): units of Indian money.

6. **dowry** (dou′rē): money or property given with a bride at marriage.

Writing Workshop

For the memory books . . .

From Reading to Writing The excerpt from the *Ramayana* tells of Rama's fight to the death with Ravana. A full-scale battle always makes an exciting story. However, even a small-scale battle, such as a girl's internal struggle about changing her appearance, can make for good reading. An **autobiographical incident** is an event from a writer's own life. No matter how ordinary an event is, it can always be told with color and drama.

For Your Portfolio

WRITING PROMPT Write an essay about a memorable incident from your own life.

Purpose: To share and reflect upon a personal experience

Audience: Your classmates, friends, and family

Basics in a Box

Autobiographical Incident at a Glance

Beginning

• Introduces the incident, including the people involved and the setting

Middle

• Re-creates the incident using descriptive details
• Makes the significance clear

End

• Concludes by reflecting on the outcome and significance
• Presents the writer's feelings about the experience

RUBRIC Standards for Writing

A successful autobiographical incident should

• focus on a well-defined incident or series of related incidents

• provide background information for the incident

• use elements such as plot, character, and setting as appropriate

• make the order of events clear

• use description or dialogue as appropriate

• include precise language and specific details

• show why the experience was significant

• maintain a consistent tone and point of view

Analyzing a Student Model

Emily Craighead
Naperville Central
High School

I'm Gonna Wash That Dye Right Outta My Hair

"Don't you dare touch that," my mother reprimanded lightly. I pulled back my plastic-gloved hand and refrained from taking a book from the pine bookcase. Instead, I scratched my moist head, which was coated with a slimy orange substance. This slimy orange substance, I hoped, would turn my hair a radiant golden blonde. Sighing, I cautiously sat down on the edge of my bed and waited for the ring of the timer, which would allow me to rinse the dye from my hair.

Interrupting the stillness of the sticky August day, a welcome breeze swept through my open window and toyed with the pictures on my bulletin board. I thought about how I had succeeded in persuading my mother to allow me to dye my hair. The idea had first been planted in my head by my friends, many of them brunettes, who wanted to spend the next summer as ravishing blondes. A group of them were even having a hair-dyeing party on the last day of school. Of course, I felt compelled to join their ranks because I did not want to be a light-brown-haired misfit. Much to my surprise, my moderately conservative mother was happy to let me dye my hair, although not permanently. We must have spent at least an hour comparing and contrasting the plethora of hair-coloring kits crowded onto the shelves of the drugstore.

"Well, this one is much too light for you," my mother informed me.

"No it isn't. It is too dark," I contradicted her.

Finally, after much discussion, we purchased a golden-honey dye that would wash out in a week. This way, if the product did indeed turn my hair green as my mother threatened, my hair would return to its natural color by the time school started.

Dring! The timer sounded and I eagerly leapt off the bed and dashed into the bathroom. I thrust my head under the faucet, paying no heed to the water that splashed across the counter. When the water ran clear, I pulled a comb through the tangles and plugged in the blow dryer. The fierce, warm wind of the blow dryer roared deafeningly in my ears, but all that I could hear was a powerful voice in my head declaring how beautiful my golden locks would be, glinting beneath the blazing summer sun by the side of a turquoise pool.

"You will be completely transformed," the voice complimented me, "and everyone will notice you, and only you." I turned off the blow dryer and, my eyes shut tightly, I ran my brush through my hair once more. I shook my mane of hair and opened my eyes expectantly.

Staring back at me in the mirror was a slightly rounded face, with big blue eyes shining. This same face had returned my glance in the mirror before I applied the coloring, only now the waves of hair encircling the visage were a

❶ Introduces essay with dialogue, bringing event immediately to life

Another Option:
- Begin with background for the incident.

❷ Gives background on the writer's decision to color her hair

❸ Sensory language adds life to the description.

❹ Writer reveals her own character by relating her thoughts.

LANGUAGE SKILLS

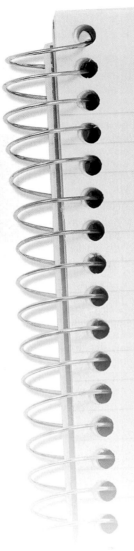

more intense blonde. Observing the face in the mirror, where the corners of the mouth now drooped, I wondered why I wasn't seeing the face of a supermodel. Of course, I hadn't expected a new beauty that would attract guys like a magnet, but now, it seemed as though my new orangish hair would do nothing at all for me.

I walked into my room to show my mother my new look. She smiled and, as any mother would, told me how beautiful I looked. As she left to drive my sister to a friend's house, I sat down at my desk. I ran my hands through my hair but quickly wrenched them free from the curls that entangled them, as though they had touched something filthy. The strands of hair that fell through my fingers were like straw, not like the silk I had expected. When I pulled my hand away, the locks fell limply over my shoulders and I shivered. Sighing, I lowered my head into the cradle of my arms but quickly sat up straight again. Without raising my eyes from the face of a bleach-blonde-haired movie star on the cover of the magazine that lay on a pile of mail, I extended my hand and lifted the first page. In one fluid motion, I ripped that picture-perfect face from my sight and folded the glossy sheet so that a crease ran directly down the center of that unblemished face. Satisfied, I tossed it into the trash can beside my desk. I realized that I did not want to dye my hair at all, even if it did make me look good. It felt so artificial and alien. Dyeing my hair also made me just like any other American teenage girl, using something fake and changing her appearance as though it meant that she would belong more fully to society. My dreams had nothing to do with ending up on the cover of a magazine as a soulless slave to fashion. I did not want to be a clone; I wanted to be an individual. Not necessarily to stand out but to be original in both personality and appearance. The desire to be another bikini-clad 15-year-old sunbathing by the side of the neighborhood pool deserted me.

⑤ Reflects on the significance of her decision

I walked back into the bathroom and lowered my head beneath a current of cool water. I let the stream slide over my scalp and flow down my neck. I leaned into the sink again, into the icy, refreshing water. I scrubbed some more and rinsed again. One down, six to go. I would wash that dye right out of my hair and I would be myself again. Down the drain swirled the soapy water, along with my naïve conceptions of the meaning of belonging to a group. I would become the person I really wanted to be all along; a girl brimming with hope for the future and full of original ideas, unencumbered by the weight of fads and conformity. I suppose, though, that if I had never dyed my hair, I always would have wondered whether a new hair color would have made me a new person. Despite the unnatural tint of her hair, the girl in the mirror smiled now, and her eyes sparkled.

⑥ Uses actions to resolve the event

Writing Your Autobiographical Incident

❶ Prewriting

Begin by choosing the incident you want to write about. You might choose to write about a major event that marked a turning point in your life, or perhaps you'll choose a smaller event that taught you a particular lesson.

Brainstorm a list of events from your life. To jog your memory, look through old photo albums and journals or diaries. Think about the first time you did certain things: your first day at a new school, or the first time you met your best friend. What stories do you like to tell your friends about yourself? After you choose an event, follow the steps below.

Planning Your Autobiographical Incident

▶ **1. Test your topic.** Do you remember the incident well enough to write about it accurately? Is it a memory you can comfortably share with your class? What point will you make about this event?

▶ **2. Think about your purpose and audience.** How will you show readers how and why the incident affected you?

▶ **3. Sketch out ideas.** When and where did the incident take place? Was there something special about the setting? What were the key events? Who were the people involved? How did they look, act, and talk?

❷ Drafting

Start by writing down your memory of the incident as it comes to you. Don't worry about how it sounds or whether you've gotten it completely right; you can fix it later. Concentrate on getting the information from the beginning to the end, and don't worry about the details. As you draft, keep the following things in mind:

- Use elements of short story writing—**plot, character,** and **setting.** Include any background information your reader might need.

- Use **dialogue** when you can.

- Describe **sensory** details—sights, sounds, smells, tastes, and textures. This will make your writing more immediate.

- **Organize** your ideas. **Chronological order** is usually the clearest way to tell a story, but sometimes using **flashbacks** makes a great impact. Flashback is the technique of starting a story in the middle and then relating events from an earlier time.

- Write a **conclusion** that sums up your impression of the event or what you've learned from it.

After you finish your first draft, let it sit for a while. Then reread it. You might also want to ask your peer readers for their reactions.

IDEABank

1. Your Working Portfolio 📁
Build on the **Writing Options** you completed earlier in this unit:

- **Autobiographical Papyrus Scroll**
  p. 60
- **Remembering a Teacher**
  p. 127

2. Lifeline To jog your memory, create a time line of your life showing significant events from your life at school, at home, with your friends, and in your community. Choose one event to write about.

3. Family Resources
Sometimes people in your family remember things that have escaped your memory. Ask a family member to recall significant events in your life. This may help you remember something you'd like to write about. Make a few notes on these events, and write about one of them.

Need help with your autobiographical incident?

See the **Writing Handbook**
Narrative Writing,
pp. R29–R30

LANGUAGE SKILLS

Ask Your Peer Reader

- Why do you think this experience was important for me?

- Which part of the incident is described most vividly?

- What parts are unnecessary or need more explanation?

Need help with run-on sentences?

See the **Grammar Handbook,** p. R73

Publishing IDEAS

- Gather a group of classmates and read your works aloud to one another.
- Read your work to your family. Ask whether your recollection of the events matches theirs.

PUBLISHING OPTIONS
CLASSZONE.COM

❸ Revising

The Law of Editing: For every vision, there is an equal and opposite revision.

TARGET SKILL ▶ MAINTAINING A CLEAR FOCUS Your writing will have a stronger impact if you include only the most important ideas and details. Extra details will distract your reader from the main point. When writing about your own life, it is sometimes tempting to include everything that comes to mind; however, leaving out irrelevant details can be as important as including the relevant ones.

> Much to my surprise, my moderately conservative mother was happy to let me dye my hair, although not permanently. ~~My mother is a very successful attorney.~~

❹ Editing and Proofreading

TARGET SKILL ▶ RUN-ON SENTENCES Even experienced writers can make the mistake of running two or more sentences together. Run-ons fail to show where one idea ends and another begins. This is incorrect and often confusing. To fix a run-on sentence, use the correct punctuation or a conjunction to separate the two ideas.

> The fierce, warm wind of the blow dryer roared deafeningly in my ears, *but* all that I could hear was a powerful voice in my head declaring how beautiful my golden locks would be, glinting beneath the blazing summer sun by the side of a turquoise pool.

❺ Reflecting

FOR YOUR WORKING PORTFOLIO What did you learn or remember about your life as you wrote? Did it cause you to change your mind about the incident? How important does it seem now? Attach your reflections to your finished essay. Save your autobiographical incident in your **Working Portfolio.**

Read this paragraph from the first draft of an autobiographical essay. The underlined sections may include the following kinds of errors:

- **run-on sentences**
- **capitalization errors**
- **fragments**
- **incorrect pronoun cases**

For each underlined section, choose the revision that most improves the writing.

I will never forget the first time I saw the ocean. <u>I was eight years old, my family</u> (1) got in the car and drove west. We lived in South Dakota, where the plains seemed to go on forever, but I could always see the other side of rivers and lakes. <u>My brother and me were</u> (2) very <u>excited. Because we'd never taken such a long trip.</u> (3) It took us two days to get to <u>Oregon; we kept</u> (4) pestering my parents, <u>asking, "are we there yet?"</u> (5) We drove across rushing rivers, through stunning deserts and mountain ranges. Finally we <u>reached the Oregon coast; It was magnificent!</u> (6) The waves crashed against the rocks, and the water seemed to extend forever. I wondered what was beyond the horizon. I knew that someday I would have to cross the ocean and find out for myself.

1. A. I was eight years old, because my family
   B. When I was eight years old, my family
   C. I was eight years old, but my family
   D. Correct as is

2. A. Me and my brother were
   B. My brother and myself were
   C. My brother and I were
   D. Correct as is

3. A. excited because we'd never taken such a long trip.
   B. excited, we'd never taken such a long trip.
   C. excited; Because we'd never taken such a long trip.
   D. Correct as is

4. A. Oregon, we kept
   B. Oregon: the whole time, we kept
   C. Oregon we kept
   D. Correct as is

5. A. asking: "are we there yet?"
   B. asking, "Are we there yet"
   C. asking, "Are we there yet?"
   D. Correct as is

6. A. reached the Oregon coast; it was magnificent!
   B. reached the Oregon coast, it was magnificent!
   C. reached the oregon coast. It was magnificent!
   D. Correct as is

Need extra help?

See the **Grammar Handbook**

Correcting Run-On Sentences, p. R73

Capitalization, p. R79

Correcting Fragments, p. R73

Pronoun Case, p. R57

TEST PRACTICE

Building Vocabulary

The English language changes constantly, gaining new words (such as *Internet*) and gaining new definitions for old words (such as *surf*). We are currently in a period of particularly rapid change. However, the language has been changing since it was first spoken. One result of this process is that many words have more than one meaning.

Words with multiple meanings can confuse a reader, who may not always know which meaning the writer intended. And if the writer is using the word in a way the reader has never seen, it can be especially puzzling.

Look at the model below. The word *mount* can mean "to get up on something, as a horse or bicycle" or "to increase in amount, extent, or intensity." Which of the two meanings do you think is correct here?

> Noticing this, Ravana's anger mounted further.
> —*Ramayana*

Strategies for Building Vocabulary

As you read, keep an eye out for words that do not seem to mean what you expect them to mean. Then use the following strategies to determine the author's intended meaning.

❶ **Use Context Clues to Determine Meaning** When you encounter a word that is used in an unexpected way, look at the surrounding sentences for clues. Consider the word *surveyed* in the following example.

> Ravana became restless and abruptly left the hall and went up on a tower, from which he could obtain a full view of the city. He surveyed the scene below but could not stand it.
> —*Ramayana*

One familiar meaning of *surveyed* is "conducted a statistical study on." However, it's clear from the context that Ravana did not pass around questionnaires. On the other hand, you know that he climbed a tower to get a full view of the city. From this clue you can infer that in this context, *surveyed* means "examined or looked at fully."

❷ **Refer to the Dictionary** When context clues don't help, consult a dictionary. Remember, words with multiple meanings have multiple definitions, so be sure to consider each of the numbered definitions given. Which one makes the most sense in the sentence?

You can quickly eliminate definitions with the wrong part of speech. For example, the word *survey* can be a noun as well as a verb. However, the sentence in the *Ramayana* makes it clear that the word is used as a verb.

In addition to definitions, many dictionary entries give sentences or phrases that show how a word is used. These examples can also help you determine which definition is the right one.

EXERCISE Use a dictionary or context clues to define each underlined word in these sentences from the *Ramayana*. Then choose a different definition for the same word and use it in your own sentence.

1. The gods in heaven noticed Ravana's <u>determined</u> move and felt that Rama would need all the support they could muster.
2. Rama fastened his sword, slung two <u>quivers</u> full of rare arrows over his shoulders, and climbed into the chariot.
3. Rama paused for a while in grief, undecided as to his next step. Then he recovered and resumed his <u>offensive.</u>
4. Ravana then shot an asthra called "Thama," whose <u>nature</u> was to create total darkness in all the worlds.
5. Rama's crescent-shaped weapon was continuously busy as Ravana's heads kept <u>cropping</u> up.

Sentence Crafting   Using Elements in a Series

Grammar from Literature Writers often link together a series of elements—nouns, verbs, modifiers, phrases, or clauses—in a single sentence. This technique makes ideas concise and often creates a pleasing rhythm, which can make a text easier to understand and remember.

A **series** consists of three or more elements that have the same function in a sentence. For example, they might be parts of a compound subject, a compound object, or a series of similar phrases. The elements are separated by semicolons or commas with, usually, at least one coordinating conjunction. Notice the series in the examples from the *Ramayana* below.

> series of direct objects
> **He had a ritual bath and performed special prayers to gain the benediction of Shiva; donned his** battle dress, matchless armour, armlets, **and** crowns.

> series of objects of a preposition
> **["]It can fly swifter than air over all obstacles, over any** mountain, sea, or sky, **and will help you to emerge victorious in this battle."**

> series of independent clauses
> **Many ominous signs were seen now—**his bow-strings suddenly snapped; the mountains shook; thunders rumbled in the skies; tears flowed from the horses' eyes; elephants with decorated foreheads moved along dejectedly.

Using Series in Your Writing Look for places where listing elements will help you reduce unnecessary repetition and create rhythm. Notice how creating a series eliminates wordiness in the following examples.

> WORDY
> **But Rama's arrows** diverted **Ravana's. They also** broke **some of Ravana's arrows, and they** neutralized **some others.**

> CONCISE
> **But Rama's arrows** diverted, broke, or neutralized **Ravana's.**

Usage Tip In a series, items that are parallel in meaning should also be parallel in structure. In the sentence below, the last item in the series is not grammatically parallel with the other two items.

> INCORRECT
>   adjective adjective   independent clause
> **In battle, Rama is** brave, strong, **and** the gods have blessed him with their gifts.

See page 483 for more instruction on parallel constructions.

> CORRECT
>   adjective adjective   adjective
> **In battle, Rama is** brave, strong, **and** blessed **with gifts from the gods.**

WRITING EXERCISE Combine each group of sentences below by creating a sentence containing a series.

1. Ravana heard cries of grief from his camp. He heard the wailing of widows. Groans of pain reached his ears.
2. In preparation for battle, Ravana bathed himself and prayed to the god Shiva. He also put on his suit of armor and emerged from his chamber.
3. Rama's chariot was large and brilliant. It was capable of flying over any obstacle.
4. Rama and Ravana both had great strength. They had powerful arms, too, and a desire to win.
5. Ravana shot thousands of arrows at Rama and attacked his army from the sky. Ravana also used supernatural forces called asthras.

GRAMMAR EXERCISE Rewrite the sentences below, correcting any errors in parallelism.

1. Because of an illusion, Rama thought he saw Ravana's defeated army come back to life, rise up on the battlefield, and moving forward with battle cries.
2. Ravana shot an asthra that plunged the world into darkness, paralyzed creation, and whose purpose was to send storms down to the earth.
3. Rama's cleverness, his physical strength, and being magical allowed him to fight back.
4. Ravana's gifts of destruction—his knowledge and to use special weaponry—were running out.
5. Rama's final weapon struck Ravana's heart, knocked him from his chariot, and is transforming him.

Reflect and Assess

What did you learn about ancient
Indian literature from reading the
selections in Unit One, Part 2? Did
the literature surprise you in any way?
Use the following options to help you
explore what you have learned.

Detail of illustration, Rama fights Ravana. Courtesy of the Trustees of the Victoria
& Albert Museum, London.

Reflecting on the Literature

Teaching Stories The ancient epics and folk tales of India are still
appreciated for the life lessons they present. Many people regard these
stories as guides for behavior, even in the modern world. Think back over
the selections you've read, and identify three lessons they teach. State each
lesson in your own words, and discuss how a person might apply it today.

Reviewing Literary Concepts

Developing Characters In this part of the book, you learned about techniques of characterization, particularly in epics. Pick three characters from
the Indian epics or folk tales you've read, and come up with one descriptive trait for each. Then note how you learned of this trait—whether
through the narrator's comments, through the character's actions, or
through some other technique. Which of the three characters was developed most effectively, in your opinion?

Building Your Portfolio

Writing Workshop and Writing Options Look back at the autobiographical
incident you wrote for the Writing Workshop and at the various Writing
Options you completed. Which represents your best work? Add that
assignment to your **Presentation Portfolio** , along with a cover note
explaining why you are especially proud of it.

Self ASSESSMENT

READER'S NOTEBOOK

Following are important terms that
relate to this part of the book.
Next to each term, write a sentence describing or defining it. If
you are unclear about any term, go
back through the unit or consult
the **Glossary of Literary Terms**
(page R91).

Aryans	characterization
Rig Veda	epithet
paradox	*Ramayana*
epic	conflict
Mahabharata	*Panchatantra*

Setting GOALS

Would you like to read more of a
particular work or of a certain
type of literature featured in Unit
One, Part 2? Ask your teacher or
a librarian to help you locate
works to read on your own.

Extend Your *Reading*

Folktales from India

EDITED BY A. K. RAMANUJAN

Ramanujan, an award-winning translator and poet, gathers 110 tales translated from 22 Indian languages. He selected only tales told in households, by amateur storytellers. Excluded are myths, legends, and tales taken directly from Sanskrit literary texts. The works in the book are arranged in six broad categories: male-centered stories, female-centered stories, stories about families, humorous tales, animal fables, and stories about stories. The result is a delightfully varied and fresh collection, enhanced by Ramanujan's informative introduction.

The Eternal Cycle: Indian Myth

Part of Time-Life's Myth and Mankind series, this beautiful volume contains stories from Hindu, Buddhist, and Jain mythology, including examples from the *Rig Veda,* the *Mahabharata,* and the *Ramayana.* Lavishly illustrated with full-color photos of art and sacred sites, the book also contains mini-essays on such topics as the caste system, the Ganges River, and Indian festivals. A concluding section, "The Legacy of Indian Myth," examines how such mythology has influenced politics, popular entertainment, and the practices of Indian immigrants abroad.

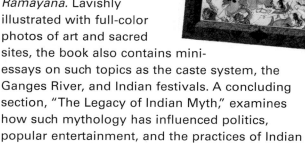

And Even *More . . .*

Books

Theater of Memory BARBARA STOLER MILLER
Contemporary translations of Kalidasa's three surviving Sanskrit plays, including *Shakuntala and the Ring of Recollection.*

Indian Art: A Concise History ROY C. CRAVEN
A fascinating overview of Indian art, from early Indus Valley examples, through Hindu and Buddhist masterpieces, to Rajput miniature paintings.

Women Writing in India: 600 B.C. to the Present EDITED BY K. LALITA AND SUSIE J. THARU
An anthology of works by Indian women writers, including Atukuri Molla, who wrote her own *Ramayana,* and Mirabai, who wrote famous love lyrics to the god Krishna.

Other Media
Mahabharata
A three-hour film version of the epic, directed by Peter Brook and starring actors of many different nationalities. Parabola Video Library. (VIDEOCASSETTE)

India and the Infinite: The Soul of a People
This visually stunning documentary, narrated by Professor Huston Smith, examines India's major religions. Hartley Film Foundation. (VIDEOCASSETTE)

Snakes and Ladders

GITA MEHTA

Mehta is an Indian-born writer and documentary filmmaker who sees her homeland as "an extraordinary world spinning through an extraordinary time." Her short, entertaining personal essays examine life in India today, focusing on the nation's many contradictions.

The Classical Age of Greece and Rome 800 B.C.–A.D. 200

Temple E at Selinus (Selinunte), Italy. Photograph by Anne and Henri Stierlin.

*"... To the glory that was Greece
And the grandeur that was Rome."*

—EDGAR ALLAN POE

PART 1
The Heroic Tradition:
Literature of Ancient Greece ... 162–343

ꙮ

PART 2
The Tradition Continues:
Literature of Ancient Rome 344–411

Literature of Ancient Greece

Why It Matters

Greece is a small mountainous country, yet it gave birth to some of the most cherished ideas of Western civilization. The Greeks championed individual freedom, developed an early form of democracy, and demonstrated the power of rational thought. Greek ideals of beauty and justice have spread throughout the world. Greek literature, especially poetry and drama, continues to inspire writers today.

① A Famous War
Perhaps the most famous war ever described in literature was the **Trojan War**, in which a coalition of Greek states fought the inhabitants of Troy. This war is the subject of the *Iliad*, a long narrative poem by Homer that is still popular today. According to legend, Greek soldiers hid in a massive hollow statue of a horse to gain entrance to Troy.

For Links to Ancient Greece, click on:

ⓘ HUMANITIES
CLASSZONE.COM

MACEDONIA

Mt. Olympus ②

Ionian Sea

GREECE

Ithaca

Delphi

Thebes
PELOPONNESUS *Athens*
Corinth ③
Mycenae
Olympia

Sparta
④

Aegean Sea

Lesbos

Chios

① *Troy*

A Seafaring People

Greece is surrounded by water and has little usable farmland. Thus, ancient Greeks set out in ships to trade with others. Shown here is a model of a 5th-century-B.C. Greek sailing ship.

Mediterranean Sea

Black Sea

ASIA MINOR

2 **A Mountainous Terrain** Mountain ranges divide mainland Greece into various regions. The Greeks believed that their gods and goddesses lived at the top of the highest mountain in Greece—Mount Olympus (shown above). Greek **mythology** greatly influenced the literature of the Western world.

3 **Cradle of Democracy** The largest and most influential of the Greek city-states, **Athens** was the birthplace of democracy, drama, and philosophy. Athenian sculpture and architecture are still imitated today. Athens was named for Athena, the gray-eyed goddess of war and wisdom. A statue of Athena is shown here.

4 **A Land of City-States** The chains of mountains kept people isolated from one another and led to the creation of city-states— small independent areas centered around a single city. **Sparta** was a strong city-state known for its military way of life. Sparta and Athens were the main rivals in a war that lasted 27 years.

N
W   E
S

0   100   200 miles
0   100   200 kilometers

Alexandria

EGYPT

Historical Highlights

Much of ancient Greek literature deals with the heroes, villains, triumphs, and setbacks of Greek history. To understand the stories and ideas in the part ahead, it is vital to know something about the historical events that inspired many of them.

The Heroic Age
2000–1200 B.C.

The early Greeks are known as **Mycenaeans** (mī′sə-nē′ənz), named after their leading city, Mycenae (mī-sē′ne). Mycenaeans were warriors and traders. They adapted an older writing system to the Greek language. Their kings gathered fortunes in gold and lived in palaces protected by stone walls. About 1250 B.C., Mycenaean warriors won a war against the wealthy city of **Troy** and may have burned the city to the ground.

The Decline
1200–800 B.C.

Not long after the defeat of Troy, Mycenaean civilization collapsed. A group of people from northern Greece—the Dorians—moved into the area the Mycenaeans had controlled. During the age that followed, knowledge of writing was lost. The Greeks kept their culture alive in songs and stories about the glories of their past, especially their heroes at Troy. **Homer** based his epic poems the *Iliad* and the *Odyssey* on these stories.

The Growth of City-States
800–500 B.C.

During this period, Greek tribal settlements grew into independent city-states. Because of the shortage of fertile land, numerous Greeks traveled great distances, from southern Italy to Asia Minor, to found new city-states.

Each city-state had its own army, its own system of government, and its own way of life. For example, **Sparta** developed into a military state, while **Athens** became a major cultural center and thus a magnet for artistic talent from all over Greece. Around 500 B.C., the ruling aristocrats of Athens took a bold step. They extended power to all Athenian citizens (men aged 18 or older who were neither slaves nor foreigners). Athens became the world's first **democracy.**

The Greek hero Achilles bearing the corpse of his friend Patroclus

THE HEROIC AGE		THE DECLINE
2000 B.C.		1200 B.C.

The Great Wars

500–400 B.C.

The Greek city-states often squabbled among themselves, but their biggest fear was an invasion by the Persians. When Persian forces landed on mainland Greece in 490 B.C., Athens defeated them. Later, the city-states joined together to fight their common enemy. The **Persian Wars** continued on and off for a number of years, with Greece ultimately the winner. At the end, Athens emerged more powerful than ever.

Athens' supremacy was eventually challenged by its rival, Sparta. The **Peloponnesian War** between the two city-states lasted 27 years. It ended in 404 B.C. with Athens' complete surrender.

Peloponnesian War Alliances

Aegean Sea

PERSIAN EMPIRE

•*Athens*

Sparta•

- Athens and allies
- Sparta and allies
- Other Greek areas

Macedonia and the Hellenistic Age

400–146 B.C.

With the fall of Athens, Greece had lost its center. Fighting between city-states continued, and the Greeks couldn't stop the army of **Philip II** of **Macedonia,** a kingdom north of Greece, from taking control of the region in 338 B.C. Philip's son, **Alexander the Great**, eventually united Greece, Persia, Egypt, and parts of India into one great empire.

Alexander died when he was only 33, and his empire fragmented shortly after his death.

A scene from a burial tomb, showing a battle between the Macedonians and Persians

However, his conquests helped bring about a new culture, the **Hellenistic culture**, which blended Greek (Hellenic), Egyptian, Persian, and Indian influences. The influence of Greek culture continued even after the Romans conquered Greece in 146 B.C.

History to Literature

EVENT IN HISTORY	EVENT IN LITERATURE
Greek warriors defeat Trojans, about 1250 B.C.	Homer's *Iliad* and *Odyssey* celebrate heroes of the Trojan War.
Greeks defeat Persians, 479 B.C.	The Greek playwright Aeschylus stages *Persians* in 472 B.C.
Athens becomes a major power, 5th century B.C.	Sophocles, who served as an Athenian general, explores issues of power and fate in his play *Oedipus the King,* performed in Athens c. 430 B.C.
War between Athens and Sparta, 431–404 B.C.	The Greek historian Thucydides explains the events that led to the war in his *History of the Peloponnesian War.*

THE GROWTH OF CITY-STATES		THE GREAT WARS	MACEDONIA AND THE HELLENISTIC AGE
800 B.C.		500 B.C. 400 B.C.	146 B.C.

People and Society

In ancient Greece, the way you lived depended on your position in society. If you were one of the lucky few, you were born into wealth and power; the unlucky might face a life of slavery. Of course, your fate also depended on where and when you were born. Two different societies are described here—Athens and Sparta. During the 400s B.C., these two city-states were the most powerful and influential in Greece.

Aesop telling a fable

Aristocrats

An aristocrat is a member of the nobility, the ruling or privileged class in society. In Athens, the aristocrats were wealthy landowners. They inherited their land and positions in society. Owning land and having others work it gave the aristocrats time to devote themselves to politics, to the life of the mind, and to hunting. After an era of kings, the aristocrats ruled Athens, but eventually they shared their power with other citizens.

Sparta did not have a true aristocracy. Instead, a small group of rulers had authority over the society. Two kings headed the army, while 5 magistrates and a council of 28 elders and the kings governed the city. Only native Spartans, those whose ancestry could be traced to the city's original inhabitants, enjoyed the full rights of citizenship.

Common Folk

A large number of farmers, merchants, and resident foreigners made up the middle and lower classes in Athens. Farmers and merchants who were born in Athens enjoyed the full rights of citizenship. The foreigners were not citizens but were protected by law and had both privileges and duties. Some foreigners became powerful merchants and bankers.

In Sparta, the commoners were neither citizens nor slaves. They were people who could not trace their ancestry to Sparta. Constituting a fairly small class, the commoners lived as free people in Sparta and typically worked as merchants and farmers.

Scene from a Greek vase showing family life

Slaves

The elegant life and leisure of the Athenian aristocracy could not have been possible without the existence of slaves, who did most of the manual labor. **Aesop,** whose fables you probably read as a child, is thought to have been a slave. In Athens at the height of its glory, more than one-third of the population were slaves.

In Sparta, people called helots were treated like slaves. They outnumbered the Spartans by seven to one. Helots farmed the land, working long hours and receiving in return only a little of the food they grew themselves. Because of their large numbers, the helots posed a threat to the Spartans. The Spartans routinely declared war on the helots so that they could kill any who seemed rebellious.

Warriors

Because warfare was a fact of Greek life, all young Athenian men received training as soldiers. Athens, however, only assembled an army in times of war. Soldiers served in the military and then returned to more peaceful ways of life. Although the Athenians were reluctant warriors, their navy dominated the Greek world.

By contrast, the entire life of a Spartan man revolved around military service. At the age of 7, male children were sent to military schools, which taught toughness and discipline. At the age of 20, Spartans became soldiers and lived together in barracks. These young soldiers could marry but were not allowed to live at home with their families until they turned 30. Even then, however, men continued to serve in the military until the age of 60.

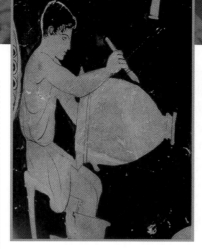

Detail from vase painting, showing a potter at work

Artists and Writers

Artists, including sculptors and potters, held an honorable position in Athenian society. Sculptors created the lifelike statues of gods that decorated the temples. Potters, who worked in a special quarter of the city, decorated their wares with scenes of gods and heroes as well as of everyday life. Many writers also enjoyed a special status in Athens. They were believed to have been inspired by the nine Muses, the goddesses of arts and sciences. Poets were often invited to read their latest works at banquets held in the homes of aristocrats.

While Athens was the cultural center of the Greek world, Sparta did not value the arts. As a result, the city produced few artists or writers. Spartans learned to read and write, but they mainly read works that praised the heroics of soldiers at war.

Greek armor

Women of Ancient Greece

In general, an Athenian woman's life was not that much better than a slave's. Denied education and any hope of equality, women and girls were confined to the home, and their contact with men was severely limited. A girl married shortly after puberty, probably at 15. Often her husband was twice her age. The young wife then raised her children, separated from their father, in the women's quarters of the home. She was not even allowed to eat with her husband and his male friends.

Spartan women were allowed much more freedom than their Athenian counterparts. Although women did not receive military training, their physical education was similar to that accorded the men. Girls took part in athletics, and women engaged in business and owned land. Wives ran their own households, since their husbands, after all, hardly ever lived at home.

Culture

The culture of ancient Greece—its unique way of life—encouraged creativity and excellence in all pursuits. From fierce athletic competitions to boldly ambitious educational programs, the Greeks aimed for the best in all things. In such an atmosphere, literature flourished.

Religion

Unlike the religions of Jews, Christians, and Muslims, the religion of the ancient Greeks had no sacred writings (such as the Bible) and no commandments. Worship centered on an elite group of gods—the 12 Olympians, headed by Zeus and his wife, Hera.

The Greeks developed a rich set of **myths**, or traditional stories, about their gods. The gods quarreled and competed with each other and showed human qualities such as love, hate, and jealousy. Unlike humans, however, the gods lived forever. The gods held the ultimate power and served as a reminder of human limitations.

The 12 Olympians

Zeus
king of all divinities, god of thunder

Hera
queen of all divinities, goddess of marriage

Poseidon
god of the sea and earthquakes

Athena
goddess of war and wisdom

Apollo
god of light, music, and poetry

Artemis
goddess of hunting

Ares
god of battle

Aphrodite
goddess of love and beauty

Hephaestus
god of fire and toolmaking

Demeter
goddess of agriculture

Hermes
messenger of the gods

Hestia
goddess of home and family

Political Life

Many Greek city-states expected all citizens to become involved in politics. The most extensive form of democracy in ancient Greece was found in Athens, where about one-fifth of the population could participate in government. A lawmaking body called the Assembly passed laws and elected generals. Any citizen could be a part of the Assembly and could submit a law for the Assembly to debate. Each year, 500 citizens were chosen at random to serve on the Council of Five Hundred, which proposed laws and advised the Assembly. Many positions were paid, so even poor citizens could hold office.

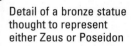

Detail of a bronze statue thought to represent either Zeus or Poseidon

School of Athens, a Renaissance painting by the artist Raphael. In the center stand Plato and Aristotle.

Education and Philosophy

The Greeks valued education because they believed that human beings could be perfected. Greek teachers—especially in Athens—taught their students to think for themselves, a privilege unique in the ancient world. Although such freedom caused conflict, it also produced some of the greatest minds of Western civilization.

Socrates dedicated himself to reason, truth, and virtue. He believed that true happiness depends on the goodness of one's soul.

Plato, Socrates' student and founder of the first school for higher education (the Academy), expanded Socrates' ideas into a wide-ranging philosophical system that examined the nature of reality.

Aristotle, Plato's student and tutor to Alexander the Great, emphasized scientific observation and studied plants, animals, the human body, language, literature, ethics, politics, and logic.

Athletics

Every four years, male athletes from all over the Greek world would stop what they were doing (even in times of war) and travel to the **Olympic Games.** Competitive events included ones still presented at the Olympics today—boxing, wrestling, the javelin and discus throws, and races of all kinds. The Greeks' love of games sometimes baffled their enemies. One Persian general reportedly exclaimed, "What kind of men have you brought us to fight against? It's not for money they compete, but for the mere achievement of excellence!"

Turning Points in Literature

The Alphabet

The alphabet we have today is the Roman version of the Greek alphabet, which the Greeks had developed from the Phoenician alphabet. Previous writing systems were extremely complicated and difficult to use, requiring years of training. The simplicity of using letters to represent all the sounds in the Greek language made widespread literacy a possibility for the first time in history.

Ancient and Modern Alphabets

Phoenician About 1000 B.C.	Greek About 500 B.C.	Modern
Ⱏ	Λ	A
ⴹ	Ᏼ	B
7	Γ	C

Greece forever influenced the art of the Western world. The ancient Greeks combined idealism—the quest for perfection—and realism to create works of great beauty. Even today, the influence of Greek architects, sculptors, and writers can be felt, from the design of many of our public buildings to the staging of the latest drama.

Sculpture

Greek sculptors were the first to portray the human body realistically. They created figures that were strong, graceful, and lifelike. Like Greek architects, Greek sculptors valued order, balance, and proportion in their work.

Many sculptors depicted the Greek gods and goddesses in idealized human form. One of the greatest sculptors, **Phidias,** created the statue of Athena that stood within the Parthenon. This statue no longer exists, but descriptions by Greek writers have enabled artists to create smaller copies of it. The original statue stood nearly 40 feet tall and was made of such precious materials as gold and ivory.

Music and Dance

The Greeks greatly valued music. The ancient poems that we read today are essentially song lyrics whose melodies have been lost. The word *lyric* comes from the name of the lyre, a small harp used to accompany the poet-singer. Even drama developed from the songs of religious ritual.

Dance also played a vital role in Greek life. No religious ritual, victory celebration, or festival was complete without a dancing chorus or dancing flute players. The Olympic Games held elaborate dance competitions.

Literature

Greek literature begins with the **epics** the *Iliad* and the *Odyssey,* believed to have been composed by the blind poet **Homer.** Although the written forms of these long narrative poems date from the 700s B.C., oral versions existed much earlier. The Trojan War, which probably took place around 1250 B.C., forms the backdrop for the two epics.

During the 600s B.C., a new kind of poetry arose—the **lyric.** Possibly reaching its fullest expression on the island of Lesbos with such poets as **Alcaeus** and **Sappho,** the lyric was shorter and more personal than the epic. The lyric allowed poets to express their thoughts and feelings. Sappho, in particular, told of her loves and hates.

During the 400s B.C., drama became the most important literary form. The Greeks created the dramatic forms of **tragedy—** a serious drama about the downfall of a **tragic hero—**and **comedy.** The three greatest tragic dramatists were **Aeschylus, Sophocles,** and **Euripides.** The comedies of **Aristophanes** often poked fun at customs, politics, and respected Athenians.

A statue of Demosthenes, who was famous for his public speaking

The Parthenon,
in Athens

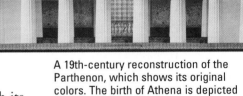

A 19th-century reconstruction of the
Parthenon, which shows its original
colors. The birth of Athena is depicted
at the top.

Architecture

Many of the buildings of ancient Greece now lie in ruins,
but among the structures remaining are astonishing examples of the Greek ideals of beauty, grace, and proportion.
One of the best remaining examples is the **Parthenon**, a
magnificent temple built to honor the goddess Athena. The
temple, located on the **Acropolis**, the hill overlooking Athens,
demonstrates the classical Greek ideals. It is so harmonious with its
site that it appears to grow out of the surrounding rock.

Greek architects also designed massive open-air theaters. The theater at Epidaurus, in the Peloponnesus, for example, could hold
14,000 spectators.

How Was Literature Presented?

Homer and poets like him probably sang their verses or recited
them to music in the palaces of ruling warrior princes. Later, after
the epics had been written down, they were memorized and
recited by professional **rhapsodes** to large audiences at religious
festivals. Lyric poetry was often sung—usually accompanied by
the music of the lyre and sometimes by dancing—at small social
gatherings, such as weddings and local festivals.

Dramatic festivals were such important public occasions that
prisoners were released on bail to attend them. As many as
20,000 spectators could crowd into the Theater of Dionysus in
Athens. Throughout the long Peloponnesian War, Athenian dramatic festivals continued uninterrupted behind the city walls.

Time Line

ANCIENT GREECE
(800 B.C.–150 B.C.)

3000 B.C.   A.D. 1   PRESENT

EVENTS IN GREEK LITERATURE

800 B.C.   **600 B.C.**

c. 800–700 B.C. Homer composes the *Iliad* and the *Odyssey*; Greeks develop a letter alphabet

c. 625 B.C. Alcman, one of the few Spartan poets, composes choral songs for festivals

c. 600–580 B.C. Alcaeus and Sappho compose lyric poetry

534 B.C. First dramatic festival held in Athens honors the god Dionysus

486 B.C. Comedy presented at the dramatic festival in Athens

472 B.C. Aeschylus' tragedy *Persians* first staged in Athens

c. 430 B.C. Sophocles' tragedy *Oedipus the King* performed in Athens

415 B.C. Euripides, called by Aristotle "the most tragic of poets," stages his tragedy *The Trojan Women*

Greek vase (about 540 B.C.)

EVENTS IN GREEK HISTORY

800 B.C.   **600 B.C.**

800–750 B.C. Rise of Greek city-states

776 B.C. First recorded athletic games held in Olympia to honor the god Zeus

c. 750–700 B.C. Greeks begin establishing trade and settlements in Sicily and Italy

c. 735–715 B.C. Sparta conquers neighboring Messenia and enslaves its people

594 B.C. Solon reforms Athenian laws, making it illegal to enslave people who owe money

508 B.C. Political reforms make Athens a democracy

490–479 B.C. During the Persian Wars, the Greeks battle the Persians, eventually defeating them

461–429 B.C. Under the rule of Pericles, Athenian democracy reaches its height

431–404 B.C. The Peloponnesian War between Athens and Sparta ends with the fall of Athens

430 B.C. Plague strikes Athens during a siege by the Spartans

EVENTS IN WORLD HISTORY

800 B.C.   **600 B.C.**

900-200 B.C. Assyrian Empire in Southwest Asia and North Africa

c. 800-400 B.C. Chavín civilization flourishes in Peru

753 B.C. Legendary date of the founding of Rome

750 B.C. Nubians unite the Nile Valley of Egypt

c. 700–500 B.C. Hindus write a series of philosophical works called the *Upanishads*

c. 563 B.C. Birth of Siddhartha Gautama, founder of Buddhism

550–539 B.C. Cyrus the Great of Persia builds an empire

538 B.C. Return of Hebrews to Jerusalem from Babylonian captivity

509 B.C. Founding of the Roman Republic

500 B.C. Speakers of the Bantu language begin migrating southward in Africa from what is now Nigeria

c. 500 B.C. Zapotec civilization flourishes in Mexico

479 B.C. Death of Confucius

400 B.C.

399 B.C. Socrates is tried and executed

387 B.C. Plato founds the Academy

367 B.C. Seventeen-year-old Aristotle becomes ➤ Plato's student

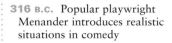

316 B.C. Popular playwright Menander introduces realistic situations in comedy

200 B.C.

200s B.C. Theocritus invents pastoral poetry—poems about nature and country life

200s B.C. Callimachus writes short poems about Greek mythology and history; later Roman poets imitate his style

200s B.C. Apollonius of Rhodes writes the *Argonautica*, a long romantic poem

400 B.C.

338 B.C. Philip II of Macedonia conquers Greece in the Battle of Chaeronea

332–323 B.C. Alexander the Great conquers Persia and spreads Greek culture throughout his empire

323 B.C. Alexander dies; his empire eventually splits into a number of independent states

c. 300 B.C. Museum and library built in Alexandria, Egypt, as a center for poets, scholars, and scientists

200 B.C.

146–30 B.C. Romans gradually conquer the territory that once belonged to Alexander the Great's empire

400 B.C.

400–100 B.C. Indian epic *Mahabharata* first written down

321–301 B.C. Mauryan Empire unites northern India

c. 250 B.C. Kingdom of Meroë at its height in East Africa

c. 214-204 B.C. Construction of first Great Wall in China completed

200 B.C.

c. 200 B.C. Nazca culture arises in Peru

146 B.C. Rome destroys Carthage

44 B.C. Assassination of Julius Caesar

27 B.C. Roman Empire established, with Augustus as emperor

Connect to Today: The Legacy of Ancient Greece

The Olympics

The first documented Olympic Games were held in Greece in 776 B.C. Like our modern Olympics, the Greek games were held every four years and included footraces, wrestling, and the javelin throw. The Greeks' contests in chariot racing and trumpeting are, however, no longer Olympic events!

Mythology

The gods and goddesses of ancient Greece still capture our imagination. The first humans to reach the moon did so in a spacecraft named for Apollo, the Greek god of light and truth.

Democracy

"Our constitution is called a democracy because power is in the hands not of a minority but of the whole people," the Athenian leader Pericles boasted in 431 B.C. Modern democracies, however, allow much larger segments of their populations to become citizens and voters than Athens did.

Comedy and Tragedy
Both of these forms of drama were invented in ancient Greece. Unlike today's plays, movies, and TV shows, Greek drama featured only male actors, who wore masks onstage. Many Greek plays, though, used special effects, including a crane that would let actors seem to descend from the sky.

Architecture
The marble columns and elegant lines of ancient Greek architecture are still admired and imitated today. The Lincoln Memorial, shown below, was designed on a plan similar to that of the Parthenon.

The Legacy of Language

Words and Phrases

You may not know how to speak Greek, but many of the words you use have Greek origins. For example, the word *democracy* comes from the Greek roots *dem,* meaning "people," and *crat,* meaning "rule." Here are just a few examples of English words that contain Greek roots.

Root	Meaning	English Words
ast(e)r	star	astronaut, asterisk, astronomy
bibl	book	bibliography, Bible
log	word	dialogue, monologue, eulogy
poli(t)	city, state	police, political, metropolis

The Epics of Greece and Rome

In Unit One, you read excerpts from three Eastern epics: *The Epic of Gilgamesh* from Mesopotamia and the *Mahabharata* and *Ramayana* from India. As you may recall, an **epic** is a long narrative poem that deals with a hero's adventures and deeds. An epic hero—Gilgamesh or Rama, for example—reflects a culture's ideals, values, and beliefs.

In this unit, you will read excerpts from two epics of Western cultures: the *Iliad* from ancient Greece and the *Aeneid*

Achilles Kills Hector (1630), Peter Paul Rubens

from ancient Rome. Many scholars believe that these epics and the epics of Eastern civilizations derive from the same tradition. You may therefore notice some similarities between the Eastern and the Western epics. As you will see, however, the Greeks and Romans put their own unique stamps on the epic genre.

Epic Conventions

In the Greek and Roman epics, you will notice certain conventions, or devices, found in other epics. For example, both the *Iliad* and the *Aeneid* tell about events set in a distant and glorious past. The events are majestic in scale—heroic battles and dangerous quests. Like Gilgamesh and Rama, the Greek and Roman epic heroes are larger-than-life figures who perform great deeds. Both Achilles, the hero of the *Iliad,* and Aeneas, the hero of the *Aeneid,* are half divine: each has a goddess for a mother. Supernatural elements are found in these epics too. Gods, goddesses, and magical creatures appear, at times taking part in human affairs.

Literary Style

One of the distinctive qualities of Greek and Roman epics is their attribution to particular authors. Though these epics still show clear traces of the oral tradition, they also reveal the hands of individual writers shaping materials to create unified wholes. The Greek and Roman epics are also distinguished for the richness and power of their language. Two devices that contribute to the epics' dignified style are the epithet and the epic simile.

- Homer's style is marked by an extensive use of **epithets**—descriptive words and phrases that characterize persons and things. For example, the adjectives "brilliant" and "godlike" frequently appear before Achilles' name. He is also identified as "the swift runner," "the headstrong runner," and "the proud runner."
- As you know, a simile is a comparison that contains the word *like* or *as.* An **epic simile** is a simile that extends over several lines. Often, epic similes serve to increase the dramatic power of the passages in which they occur, as in Aeneas' description of Troy in flames:

> "I knew the end then: Ilium was going down
> In fire, the Troy of Neptune going down,
> As in high mountains when the countrymen
> Have notched an ancient ash, then make their axes
> Ring with might and main, chopping away
> To fell the tree—ever on the point of falling,
> Shaken through all its foliage, and the treetop
> Nodding; bit by bit the strokes prevail
> Until it gives a final groan at last
> And crashes down in ruin from the height."
>
> —Virgil, *Aeneid*

The Importance of Honor

The Western epics reflect values that were important to Greek civilization and that later influenced ancient Rome. Honor was, certainly, one of these values. In the *Iliad,* heroes from all parts of Greece converge on Troy to fight for the honor of a betrayed king. Achilles, the greatest of these heroes, lives for honor. When his friend is slain in battle, Achilles fights with fury to avenge him and to reclaim his own honor. In the *Aeneid,* Aeneas is given a divine mission—to lead the Trojan refugees to Italy and to found the Roman people. Aeneas' sense of honor and duty ensures that he will remain true to his destiny.

The Power of Fate

The power of fate, or destiny, is a major theme in the epics of Greece and Rome. According to the Greeks, every person—hero or not—was given a distinct fate at birth. It was wise to accept one's fate; to attempt to avoid it was foolish. Such an attempt was a sign of pride, or hubris (hyo͞o′brĭs), and might lead to terrible consequences. For a long time, Achilles avoids his fate by refusing to take part in the fighting at Troy. As a result, many warriors are slain, and Achilles loses his best friend. Aeneas, on the other hand, accepts his fate and the sacrifices it demands. Again and again, he gives up his personal happiness—for example, the love of the queen of Carthage—to fulfill his destiny as the founder of Rome.

The Hero's Limitations

Like other epic heroes, Achilles and Aeneas are extraordinary but not perfect. They have human failings. Achilles, for example, sulks in his tent for a long time because he feels mistreated by his commander. Aeneas has lapses of judgment and moments of weakness. For example, as he carries his father from burning Troy he has a moment of panic:

> "I took fright,
> And some unfriendly power, I know not what,
> Stole all my addled wits. . . ."
> —Virgil, *Aeneid*

The *Iliad* and the *Aeneid* are masterpieces of Western civilization. Along with the great epics of Eastern civilizations, they show the tremendous vitality of the epic tradition in the ancient world.

Strategies for Reading: Greek and Roman Epics

1. Identify the epic hero's strengths and weaknesses.

2. Think about the values the epic hero represents.

3. Determine how the hero's actions affect his own life and the lives of other characters.

4. Consider the roles of fate and the gods in the events.

5. Look for epithets and epic similes, and consider what they add to the story.

6. Monitor your reading strategies, and modify them when your understanding breaks down. Remember to use the strategies for active reading: **predict, visualize, connect, question, clarify,** and **evaluate.**

FROM THE

ILIAD

HOMER

Homer
700s B.C.?

Author Mystery Homer has long been recognized as one of the world's greatest poets, but the man himself remains a mystery. Some scholars doubt that he ever actually existed, believing that the epics attributed to him are the work of many poets. Others agree with the ancient view that one great poet wrote both the *Iliad* and another famous epic, the *Odyssey.* If he existed, Homer was probably born somewhere in western Asia Minor (what is now Turkey). According to ancient tradition, Homer was blind. The story of his blindness, however, may have simply been a way of praising his wisdom, for Greek legends feature many stories of blind people with great insight.

Singers of the Trojan War It's likely that Homer heard singer-poets narrate tales about the Trojan War, a legendary ten-year war waged by Greeks against the wealthy city of Troy, or Ilium, in Asia Minor. Indeed, he may have himself been such a singer-poet, one who late in his life wrote down some of the stories he had told. Many scholars believe that the *Iliad* was created in the 700s B.C., though the circumstances of its composition remain unclear.

Homer as Teacher In later centuries, Homer's epics served as the centerpiece of Greek education. Children learned to read by studying his poems, and they memorized long passages. The epics kept alive the early Greeks' legends and myths and greatly influenced people's beliefs about the gods. Many read the poems not just for their exciting stories but because they believed that Homer had revealed important truths about human beings and their place in the universe.

Discovery of Troy In the late 19th century, archaeologists discovered the ruins of ancient Troy. The evidence they gathered has led many scholars to believe that Homer's tales about the Trojan War have some basis in fact. Greek armies probably did attack Troy sometime in the 1200s B.C., and they may have destroyed the city.

Ruins of ancient Troy

The messenger god Hermes (right) has brought together Hera (top left), Athena (with shield), and Aphrodite, who is accompanied by her child, Eros. *The Judgment of Paris* (16th century), Giulio Romano. Ducal Palace, Mantua, Italy.

Build Background

Origins of the Trojan War According to legend, the Trojan War resulted from an argument among the gods. Eris, the goddess of strife, was angry because she had not been invited to the wedding of Peleus, a mortal king, and Thetis, a sea goddess. To get revenge, Eris threw a golden apple, labeled "for the fairest," into the midst of the wedding guests. A dispute arose when three goddesses—Hera, Athena, and Aphrodite—claimed the prize. Paris, the son of the Trojan king Priam, was chosen to decide which of the three was in fact the most beautiful. Each goddess offered Paris a bribe, but he awarded the apple to Aphrodite, who had promised him Helen, the most beautiful woman in the world.

Abduction of Helen Helen was already married to Menelaus, the king of Sparta, when Paris went to Sparta, where he stayed as a guest of the king. According to the customs of the time, a host and a guest had sacred obligations to each other. Paris, ignoring his duty to his host, took Helen back to Troy with him. Menelaus and his brother Agamemnon then gathered warriors from all over Greece to attack Troy and retrieve Helen.

Siege of Troy and the *Iliad* The Greek forces sailed to Troy and surrounded the city, besieging it for ten years. The events recounted in the *Iliad* take place during the final year of the war. The poem focuses on Achilles, the greatest Greek warrior. When he was an infant, his goddess mother had held him by the heel and dipped him into the river Styx in the realm of the dead. After that, Achilles could not be hurt in any part of his body, except for his heel. He does, however, have a fierce temper, which proves costly to the Greeks.

Bitter Feud Homer's story begins with a quarrel between Achilles and Agamemnon, the commander of the Greek forces. Achilles, filled with anger, withdraws from the war. As a result, the Trojans, led by the brave Hector, are able to drive the Greeks back to their ships. Achilles returns to combat only after his best friend, Patroclus, has been killed by Hector. With unstoppable energy, Achilles kills every Trojan in his path until he finally meets Hector in a man-to-man battle outside the city walls.

For a humanities activity, click on:

HUMANITIES
CLASSZONE.COM

Cast of Major Characters

Gods

Aphrodite (ăf'rə-dī'tē): the goddess of love and beauty; favors the Trojans

Apollo (ə-pŏl'ō): the god of healing, music, poetry, and prophecy; favors and protects the Trojans

Athena (ə-thē'nə): the goddess of wisdom and warfare; protects the Greeks

Hera (hîr'ə): the queen of the gods, sister and wife of Zeus; favors the Greeks

Hermes (hûr'mēz): the messenger of the gods

Thetis (thē'tĭs): a sea goddess, mother of Achilles ⟨Greek⟩

Zeus (zōōs): the king of the gods, father of Aphrodite, Apollo, Athena, and Hermes; for the most part does not takes sides in the war

Greeks

Achilles (ə-kĭl'ēz): the mightiest Greek warrior, son of Thetis and the mortal king Peleus

Agamemnon (ăg'ə-mĕm'nŏn'): the king of Mycenae, brother of Menelaus and commander of all the Greek forces at Troy

Calchas (kăl'kəs): a priest and prophet

Helen (hĕl'ən): the wife of Menelaus, daughter of Zeus and the mortal woman Leda

Menelaus (mĕn'ə-lā'əs): the king of Sparta, whose wife, Helen, was carried off to Troy by Paris

Nestor (nĕs'tər): the king of Pylos, oldest and wisest of the Greek leaders

Odysseus (ō-dĭs'yōōs'): the king of Ithaca, known for his craftiness.

Patroclus (pə-trō'kləs): a young Greek warrior, best friend of Achilles

Trojans

Andromache (ăn-drŏm'ə-kē): the wife of Hector

Astyanax (ə-stī'ə-năks'): the infant son of Hector and Andromache

Chryses (krī'sēz'): a priest of Apollo, whose daughter has been captured by the Greeks

Hector (hĕk'tər): the leader and greatest warrior of the Trojan army

Hecuba (hĕk'yə-bə): the queen of Troy, wife of Priam and mother of Hector and Paris

Paris (păr'ĭs): the Trojan prince whose abduction of Helen from Greece was the cause of the Trojan War

Priam (prī'əm): the king of Troy, father of Hector and Paris

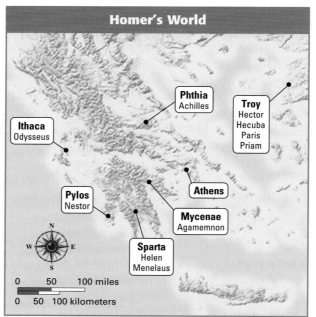

Homer's World

Phthia — Achilles
Troy — Hector, Hecuba, Paris, Priam
Ithaca — Odysseus
Athens
Pylos — Nestor
Mycenae — Agamemnon
Sparta — Helen, Menelaus

0   50   100 miles
0   50   100 kilometers

Connect to Your Life

When people talk about Greek epics, the word *hero* often comes up. Review the following definitions of the word from the *American Heritage Dictionary*.

1. In mythology and legend, a man, often of divine ancestry, who is endowed with great courage and strength, celebrated for his bold exploits, and favored by the gods.

2. A person noted for feats of courage or nobility of purpose, especially one who has risked or sacrificed his or her life: *soldiers and nurses who were heroes in an unpopular war.*

3. A person noted for special achievement in a particular field: *the heroes of medicine.*

Which of these definitions most closely matches your own idea of a hero? In your judgment, what does a person need to be or to accomplish in order to be considered a true hero?

Focus Your Reading

LITERARY ANALYSIS: EPIC HERO

An epic hero is a larger-than-life figure whose actions are central to an epic poem. Epic heroes take part in dangerous adventures and accomplish great deeds that require courage and superhuman strength. In the *Iliad*, Hector describes his role in the following words:

> . . . *To stand up bravely,*
> *always to fight in the front ranks of Trojan*
> *soldiers,*
> *winning my father great glory, glory for*
> *myself.*

Both Achilles and Hector may be considered epic heroes. As you will see, however, there are major differences between these two characters.

ACTIVE READING: EVALUATING

When you read, it is natural to form your own opinions about characters and events. In order to form reasonable opinions about those in the *Iliad*, keep the following points in mind:

- Try to examine why characters act the way they do, and look for the causes of major events.
- Remember that there's usually more than one perspective to consider. For example, in the quarrel between Achilles and Agamemnon, each man has a point.
- Look for evidence in the text to support your opinions.
- Be ready to change your mind if you gain new insights or find new evidence.

READER'S NOTEBOOK As you read, jot down your evaluations of key characters and events. The example shown here will help you get started.

Character or Event	Motive or Cause	My Evaluation
Agamemnon wants to take Briseis from Achilles.		As a commander, he should be concerned about his troops, not his own desires.

WORDS TO KNOW Vocabulary Preview

assent	gaunt	recoil	spurn
comply	lithe	recourse	waver
defile	pittance		

from the
Iliad
Homer

Translated by Robert Fagles

THE RAGE OF ACHILLES

GUIDE FOR READING

FOCUS In this excerpt from Book 1 of the *Iliad*, you will learn about the feud between Achilles and Agamemnon. As you read, evaluate the causes of the conflict between them and decide who is more to blame.

As the poem opens, the Greek army is suffering from a deadly plague. Apollo has sent the plague to punish the Greeks. The god is angry because Agamemnon, the Greek commander, has taken the daughter of Chryses, Apollo's priest, as a war prize. When a prophet reveals the cause of Apollo's anger, Agamemnon reluctantly agrees to give her up. He insists, however, on being given Achilles' war prize as compensation. Achilles feels insulted and in his fury threatens to kill Agamemnon. The wise Nestor tries to make peace, with only partial success.

Rage—Goddess, sing the rage of Peleus' son Achilles,
murderous, doomed, that cost the Achaeans countless losses,
hurling down to the House of Death so many sturdy souls,
great fighters' souls, but made their bodies carrion,
5 feasts for the dogs and birds,
and the will of Zeus was moving toward its end.
Begin, Muse, when the two first broke and clashed,
Agamemnon lord of men and brilliant Achilles.

1 Goddess: a Muse (goddess of poetry and music) whom the poet calls upon for inspiration.

2 Achaeans (ə-kē′ənz): Greeks.

4 carrion: decaying flesh.

Greek helmet and breast plate. Archaeological Museum, Sofia, Bulgaria.

What god drove them to fight with such a fury?
10 Apollo the son of Zeus and Leto. Incensed at the king
he swept a fatal plague through the army—men were dying
and all because Agamemnon spurned Apollo's priest.
Yes, Chryses approached the Achaeans' fast ships
to win his daughter back, bringing a priceless ransom
15 and bearing high in hand, wound on a golden staff,
the wreaths of the god, the distant deadly Archer.
He begged the whole Achaean army but most of all
the two supreme commanders, Atreus' two sons,
"Agamemnon, Menelaus—all Argives geared for war!
20 May the gods who hold the halls of Olympus give you
Priam's city to plunder, then safe passage home.
Just set my daughter free, my dear one . . . here,

10 Leto (lē′tō): a goddess;
incensed: enraged.

16 Archer: Apollo, who was
thought to be able to cause diseases by shooting people with his
arrows.

18 Atreus' (ā′trōōs′).

19 Argives (är′jīvz′): Greeks.

20 Olympus (ə-lĭm′pəs): the highest mountain in Greece, believed
to be the home of the gods.

<u>WORDS TO KNOW</u>

spurn (spûrn) *v.* to reject in a scornful way

ILIAD   **183**

accept these gifts, this ransom. Honor the god
who strikes from worlds away—the son of Zeus, Apollo!"

25   And all ranks of Achaeans cried out their <u>assent</u>:
"Respect the priest, accept the shining ransom!"
But it brought no joy to the heart of Agamemnon.
The king dismissed the priest with a brutal order
ringing in his ears: "Never again, old man,
30   let me catch sight of you by the hollow ships!
Not loitering now, not slinking back tomorrow.
The staff and the wreaths of god will never save you then.
The girl—I won't give up the girl. Long before that,
old age will overtake her in *my* house, in Argos,
35   far from her fatherland, slaving back and forth
at the loom, forced to share my bed!
                                        Now go,
don't tempt my wrath—and you may depart alive."

The old man was terrified. He obeyed the order,
turning, trailing away in silence down the shore
40   where the roaring battle lines of breakers crash and drag.
And moving off to a safe distance, over and over
the old priest prayed to the son of sleek-haired Leto,
lord Apollo, "Hear me, Apollo! God of the silver bow
who strides the walls of Chryse and Cilla sacrosanct—
45   lord in power of Tenedos—Smintheus, god of the plague!
If I ever roofed a shrine to please your heart,
ever burned the long rich bones of bulls and goats
on your holy altar, now, now bring my prayer to pass.
Pay the Danaans back—your arrows for my tears!"

50   His prayer went up and Phoebus Apollo heard him.
Down he strode from Olympus' peaks, storming at heart
with his bow and hooded quiver slung across his shoulders.
The arrows clanged at his back as the god quaked with rage,
the god himself on the march and down he came like night.
55   Over against the ships he dropped to a knee, let fly a shaft
and a terrifying clash rang out from the great silver bow.
First he went for the mules and circling dogs but then,
launching a piercing shaft at the men themselves,
he cut them down in droves—
60   and the corpse-fires burned on, night and day, no end in sight.

36 loom: a device used for weaving cloth, a principal job of women in ancient Greek households.

44 Chryse (krĭ'sē): Chryses' hometown, site of a temple of Apollo; **Cilla** (sĭl'ə): another Trojan town.

45 Tenedos (tĕn'ə-dŏs): a small island off the Trojan coast; **Smintheus** (smĭn'thōōs): a title of Apollo.

49 Danaans (də-nā'əns): Greeks.

50 Phoebus (fē'bəs): a title of Apollo in his role as god of the sun.

57 mules and circling dogs: the animals that are the first to be affected by the plague.

Nine days the arrows of god swept through the army.
On the tenth Achilles called all ranks to muster—
the impulse seized him, sent by white-armed Hera
grieving to see Achaean fighters drop and die.
65 Once they'd gathered, crowding the meeting grounds,
the swift runner Achilles rose and spoke among them:
"Son of Atreus, now we are beaten back, I fear,
the long campaign is lost. So home we sail . . .
if we can escape our death—if war and plague
70 are joining forces now to crush the Argives.
But wait: let us question a holy man,
a prophet, even a man skilled with dreams—
dreams as well can come our way from Zeus—
come, someone to tell us why Apollo rages so,
75 whether he blames us for a vow we failed, or sacrifice.
If only the god would share the smoky savor of lambs
and full-grown goats, Apollo might be willing, still,
somehow, to save us from this plague."

So he proposed
and down he sat again as Calchas rose among them,
80 Thestor's son, the clearest by far of all the seers
who scan the flight of birds. He knew all things that are,
all things that are past and all that are to come,
the seer who had led the Argive ships to Troy
with the second sight that god Apollo gave him.
85 For the armies' good the seer began to speak:
"Achilles, dear to Zeus . . .
you order me to explain Apollo's anger,
the distant deadly Archer? I will tell it all.
But strike a pact with me, swear you will defend me
90 with all your heart, with words and strength of hand.
For there is a man I will enrage—I see it now—
a powerful man who lords it over all the Argives,
one the Achaeans must obey . . . A mighty king,
raging against an inferior, is too strong.
95 Even if he can swallow down his wrath today,
still he will nurse the burning in his chest
until, sooner or later, he sends it bursting forth.
Consider it closely, Achilles. Will you save me?"

And the matchless runner reassured him: "Courage!
100 Out with it now, Calchas. Reveal the will of god,
whatever you may know. And I swear by Apollo

67 Son of Atreus: Agamemnon.

76–77 If only . . . full-grown goats:
If Apollo would accept an animal
sacrifice from the Greek forces.

80 seers: prophets.

81 scan the flight of birds: In
ancient Greece, the behavior of
birds was thought to provide signs
of future events.

dear to Zeus, the power you pray to, Calchas,
when you reveal god's will to the Argives—no one,
not while I am alive and see the light on earth, no one

105 will lay his heavy hands on you by the hollow ships.
None among all the armies. Not even if you mean
Agamemnon here who now claims to be, by far,
the best of the Achaeans."
                                    The seer took heart
and this time he spoke out, bravely: "Beware—

110 he casts no blame for a vow we failed, a sacrifice.
The god's enraged because Agamemnon spurned his priest,
he refused to free his daughter, he refused the ransom.
That's why the Archer sends us pains and he will
        send us more
and never drive this shameful destruction from the Argives,

115 not till we give back the girl with sparkling eyes
to her loving father—no price, no ransom paid—
and carry a sacred hundred bulls to Chryse town.
Then we can calm the god, and only then appease him."   **118 appease:** satisfy.

    So he declared and sat down. But among them rose

120 the fighting son of Atreus, lord of the far-flung kingdoms,
Agamemnon—furious, his dark heart filled to the brim,
blazing with anger now, his eyes like searing fire.
With a sudden, killing look he wheeled on Calchas first:
"Seer of misery! Never a word that works to my advantage!

125 Always misery warms your heart, your prophecies—
never a word of profit said or brought to pass.
Now, again, you divine god's will for the armies,
bruit it out, as fact, why the deadly Archer   **128 bruit it out:** report it.
multiplies our pains: because I, I refused

130 that glittering price for the young girl Chryseis.   **130 Chryseis** (krī-sē′ĭs): Chryses'
Indeed, I prefer *her* by far, the girl herself,   daughter.
I want her mine in my own house! I rank her higher
than Clytemnestra, my wedded wife—she's nothing less   **133 Clytemnestra** (klī′təm-nĕs′trə).
in build or breeding, in mind or works of hand.

135 But I am willing to give her back, even so,
if that is best for all. What I really want
is to keep my people safe, not see them dying.
But fetch me another prize, and straight off too,
else I alone of the Argives go without my honor.

140 That would be a disgrace. You are all witness,
look—*my* prize is snatched away!"

But the swift runner
Achilles answered him at once, "Just how, Agamemnon,
great field marshal . . . most grasping man alive,
how can the generous Argives give you prizes now?
145 I know of no troves of treasure, piled, lying idle,
anywhere. Whatever we dragged from towns we plundered,
all's been portioned out. But collect it, call it back
from the rank and file? *That* would be the disgrace.
So return the girl to the god, at least for now.
150 We Achaeans will pay you back, three, four times over,
if Zeus will grant us the gift, somehow, someday,
to raze Troy's massive ramparts to the ground."

But King Agamemnon countered, "Not so quickly,
brave as you are, godlike Achilles—trying to cheat *me*.
155 Oh no, you won't get past me, take me in that way!
What do you want? To cling to your own prize
while I sit calmly by—empty-handed here?
Is that why you order me to give her back?
No—if our generous Argives *will* give me a prize,
160 a match for my desires, equal to what I've lost,
well and good. But if they give me nothing
I will take a prize myself—your own, or Ajax'
or Odysseus' prize—I'll commandeer her myself
and let that man I go to visit choke with rage!
165 Enough. We'll deal with all this later, in due time.
Now come, we haul a black ship down to the bright sea,
gather a decent number of oarsmen along her locks
and put aboard a sacrifice, and Chryseis herself,
in all her beauty . . . we embark her too.
170 Let one of the leading captains take command.
Ajax, Idomeneus, trusty Odysseus or you, Achilles,
you—the most violent man alive—so you can perform
the rites for us and calm the god yourself."
A dark glance
and the headstrong runner answered him in kind:
"Shameless—
175 armored in shamelessness—always shrewd with greed!
How could any Argive soldier obey your orders,
freely and gladly do your sailing for you
or fight your enemies, full force? Not I, no.
It wasn't Trojan spearmen who brought me here to fight.
180 The Trojans never did *me* damage, not in the least,

145 **troves:** collections.

152 **raze:** demolish; **ramparts:** defensive walls.

162 **Ajax** (ā′jăks′): the strongest Greek warrior next to Achilles—known as the Greater Ajax to distinguish him from another warrior of the same name.

163 **commandeer** (kŏm′ən-dîr′): seize by force.

171 **Idomeneus** (ī-dŏm′ə-nōōs′): the ruler of the island of Crete.

they never stole my cattle or my horses, never
in Phthia where the rich soil breeds strong men
did they lay waste my crops. How could they?
Look at the endless miles that lie between us . . .

185 shadowy mountain ranges, seas that surge and thunder.
No, you colossal, shameless—we all followed you,
to please you, to fight for you, to win your honor
back from the Trojans—Menelaus and you, you dog-face!
What do *you* care? Nothing. You don't look right or left.

190 And now you threaten to strip me of my prize in person—
the one I fought for long and hard, and sons of Achaea
handed her to me.

My honors never equal yours,
whenever we sack some wealthy Trojan stronghold—
my arms bear the brunt of the raw, savage fighting,

195 true, but when it comes to dividing up the plunder
the lion's share is yours, and back I go to my ships,
clutching some scrap, some <u>pittance</u> that I love,
when I have fought to exhaustion.

No more now—
back I go to Phthia. Better that way by far,

200 to journey home in the beaked ships of war.
I have no mind to linger here disgraced,
brimming your cup and piling up your plunder."

But the lord of men Agamemnon shot back,
"*Desert,* by all means—if the spirit drives you home!

205 I will never beg you to stay, not on *my* account.
Never—others will take my side and do me honor,
Zeus above all, whose wisdom rules the world.
You—I hate you most of all the warlords
loved by the gods. Always dear to your heart,

210 strife, yes, and battles, the bloody grind of war.
What if you are a great soldier? That's just a gift of god.
Go home with your ships and comrades, lord it over your
Myrmidons!
You *are* nothing to me—you and your overweening anger!
But let this be my warning on your way:

215 since Apollo insists on taking my Chryseis,
I'll send her back in my own ships with *my* crew.
But I, I will be there in person at your tents
to take Briseis in all her beauty, your own prize—

182 Phthia (fthī′ə): Achilles' homeland.

193 sack: capture and loot.

212 Myrmidons (mûr′mə-dŏnz′):
Achilles' people.

213 overweening: arrogant.

218 Briseis (brī-sē′ĭs): a captive
Trojan woman who was given to
Achilles.

WORDS TO KNOW

188　　**pittance** (pĭt′ns) *n.* a small reward; tiny amount

Temple of Poseidon, Sounion, Greece.

so you can learn just how much greater I am than you
220   and the next man up may shrink from matching words
                with me,
         from hoping to rival Agamemnon strength for strength!"

PAUSE & REFLECT The angry Achilles has threatened
to take his men and return home. Why do Achilles and
Agamemnon become so enraged at each other, and, in
your judgment, who is more to blame?

FOCUS The anger of Achilles—"the most violent man
alive"—is always dangerous. Read to find out how various
characters, both human and divine, respond to his anger.

He broke off and anguish gripped Achilles.
         The heart in his rugged chest was pounding, torn . . .
         Should he draw the long sharp sword slung at his hip,
225   thrust through the ranks and kill Agamemnon now?—
         or check his rage and beat his fury down?
         As his racing spirit veered back and forth,
         just as he drew his huge blade from its sheath,
         down from the vaulting heavens swept Athena,
230   the white-armed goddess Hera sped her down:
         Hera loved both men and cared for both alike.
         Rearing behind him Pallas seized his fiery hair—
         only Achilles saw her, none of the other fighters—
         struck with wonder he spun around, he knew her at once,
235   Pallas Athena! the terrible blazing of those eyes,
         and his winged words went flying: "Why, why now?
         Child of Zeus with the shield of thunder, why come now?
         To witness the outrage Agamemnon just committed?
         I tell you this, and so help me it's the truth—
240   he'll soon pay for his arrogance with his life!"

         Her gray eyes clear, the goddess Athena answered,
         "Down from the skies I come to check your rage
         if only you will yield.
         The white-armed goddess Hera sped me down:
245   she loves you both, she cares for you both alike.
         Stop this fighting, now. Don't lay hand to sword.
         Lash him with threats of the price that he will face.
         And I tell you this—and I *know* it is the truth—

232 Pallas (păl'əs): a title of
Athena.

one day glittering gifts will lie before you,
250   three times over to pay for all his outrage.
Hold back now. Obey us both."
                                        So she urged
and the swift runner complied at once: "I must—
when the two of you hand down commands, Goddess,
a man submits though his heart breaks with fury.
255   Better for him by far. If a man obeys the gods
they're quick to hear his prayers."
                                        And with that
Achilles stayed his burly hand on the silver hilt
and slid the huge blade back in its sheath.
He would not fight the orders of Athena.
260   Soaring home to Olympus, she rejoined the gods
aloft in the halls of Zeus whose shield is thunder.

   But Achilles rounded on Agamemnon once again,   **262 rounded on:** attacked with
lashing out at him, not relaxing his anger for a moment: words.
"Staggering drunk, with your dog's eyes, your fawn's heart!
265   Never once did you arm with the troops and go to battle
or risk an ambush packed with Achaea's picked men—
you lack the courage, you can see death coming.
Safer by far, you find, to foray all through camp,   **268 foray:** raid.
commandeering the prize of any man who speaks against
        you.
270   King who devours his people! Worthless husks, the men
        you rule—
if not, Atrides, this outrage would have been your last.   **271 Atrides** (ā-trī′dēz′): "son of
I tell you this, and I swear a mighty oath upon it . . .   Atreus"—that is, Agamemnon.
by this, this scepter, look,
                                                            273 scepter: a rod symbolizing
that never again will put forth crown and branches,   authority, handed in turn to each
275   now it's left its stump on the mountain ridge forever,   speaker in the warriors' assembly.
nor will it sprout new green again, now the brazen ax
has stripped its bark and leaves, and now the sons of Achaea
pass it back and forth as they hand their judgments down,
upholding the honored customs whenever Zeus commands—
280   This scepter will be the mighty force behind my oath:
someday, I swear, a yearning for Achilles will strike
Achaea's sons and all your armies! But then, Atrides,
harrowed as you will be, *nothing* you do can save you—   **283 harrowed:** distressed.
not when your hordes of fighters drop and die,
285   cut down by the hands of man-killing Hector! Then—

WORDS TO KNOW

comply (kəm-plī′) *v.* to agree to a request or carry out an order; obey
ILIAD   **191**

then you will tear your heart out, desperate, raging
that you disgraced the best of the Achaeans!"
                                        Down on the ground
he dashed the scepter studded bright with golden nails,
then took his seat again. The son of Atreus smoldered,
290　glaring across at him, but Nestor rose between them,
the man of winning words, the clear speaker of Pylos . . .   **291 Pylos** (pī′lŏs′).
Sweeter than honey from his tongue the voice flowed on
　　and on.
Two generations of mortal men he had seen go down by now,
those who were born and bred with him in the old days,
295　in Pylos' holy realm, and now he ruled the third.
He pleaded with both kings, with clear good will,
"No more—or enormous sorrow comes to all Achaea!
How they would exult, Priam and Priam's sons   **298 exult:** rejoice.
and all the Trojans. Oh they'd leap for joy
300　to hear the two of you battling on this way,
you who excel us all, first in Achaean councils,
first in the ways of war.
                        Stop. Please.
Listen to Nestor. You are both younger than I,
and in my time I struck up with better men than you,
305　even you, but never once did they make light of me.
I've never seen such men, I never will again . . .
men like Pirithous, Dryas, that fine captain,   **307–309 Pirithous** (pī-rĭth′ō-əs),
Caeneus and Exadius, and Polyphemus, royal prince,   **Dryas** (drī′əs) . . . **Caeneus**
and Theseus, Aegeus' boy, a match for the immortals.   (sē′nyōōs′) **and Exadius** (ĭg-zăd′ē-əs)
310　They were the strongest mortals ever bred on earth,   . . . **Polyphemus** (pŏl′ə-fē′məs) . . .
the strongest, and they fought against the strongest too,   **Theseus** (thē′syōōs′), **Aegeus'**
shaggy Centaurs, wild brutes of the mountains—   (ē′jyōōs′) **boy:** heroes of the leg-
they hacked them down, terrible, deadly work.   endary war fought by the Lapiths
And I was in their ranks, fresh out of Pylos,   against the Centaurs (a monstrous
315　far away from home—they enlisted me themselves   race with bodies half human and
and I fought on my own, a free lance, single-handed.   half horse).
And none of the men who walk the earth these days
could battle with those fighters, none, but they,
they took to heart my counsels, marked my words.
320　So now you listen too. Yielding is far better . . .
Don't seize the girl, Agamemnon, powerful as you are—
leave her, just as the sons of Achaea gave her,
his prize from the very first.
And you, Achilles, never hope to fight it out
325　with your king, pitting force against his force:

Fresco of Athena restraining Achilles from killing Agamemnon (1757), Giambattista Tiepolo. Villa Valmarana, Vicenza, Italy. Scala/Art Resource, New York.

no one can match the honors dealt a king, you know,
a sceptered king to whom great Zeus gives glory.
Strong as you are—a goddess was your mother—
he has more power because he rules more men.
330   Atrides, end your anger—look, it's Nestor!
I beg you, cool your fury against Achilles.
Here the man stands over all Achaea's armies,
our rugged bulwark braced for shocks of war."

    But King Agamemnon answered him in haste,
335 "True, old man—all you say is fit and proper—
but this soldier wants to tower over the armies,
he wants to rule over all, to lord it over all,
give out orders to every man in sight. Well,
there's one, I trust, who will never yield to him!
340 What if the everlasting gods have made a spearman of him?

HUMANITIES CONNECTION Athena intervenes in the argument between Achilles and Agamemnon. Note that Achilles is drawing his sword while Agamemnon has reacted defensively.

333 bulwark: defensive barrier.

Have they entitled him to hurl abuse at *me*?"

"Yes!"—blazing Achilles broke in quickly—
"What a worthless, burnt-out coward I'd be called
if I would submit to you and all your orders,
345 whatever you blurt out. Fling them at others,
don't give me commands!
Never again, *I* trust, will Achilles yield to *you*.
And I tell you this—take it to heart, I warn you—
my hands will never do battle for that girl,
350 neither with you, King, nor any man alive.
You Achaeans gave her, now you've snatched her back.
But all the rest I possess beside my fast black ship—
not one bit of it can you seize against my will, Atrides.
Come, try it! So the men can see, that instant,
355 your black blood gush and spurt around my spear!"

Thinking Through the Literature

1. How do Athena, Agamemnon, and Nestor respond to the anger of Achilles?
2. Do you think Achilles or Agamemnon bears the greater share of the blame for their **conflict?** Explain your reasoning.
3. What do you learn about the **characters** of Agamemnon and Achilles in the excerpt from Book 1? Support your conclusions with details from the text.
4. Hera sends Athena to intervene in the conflict. Describe Athena's actions, and discuss what they suggest about the relationship between gods and mortals.
5. Review the oath that Achilles swears in lines 281–287. What future events might be **foreshadowed** by his words?

HECTOR RETURNS TO TROY

FROM BOOK 6

GUIDE FOR READING

FOCUS In the following scene, Hector's wife pleads with her husband to stay in the city with her. As you read, look for the reasons that she gives.

After Achilles withdraws from the war, the fighting between Trojans and Greeks begins again. Even without their best warrior, the Greeks do well on the battlefield. Hector, fearful that the Greeks are near victory, returns to Troy and tells the Trojans to ask the goddess Athena for help. He then visits his wife and child. Hector's wife, Andromache, pleads with him to stay in the city.

At that, Hector spun and rushed from his house,
back by the same way down the wide, well-paved streets
throughout the city until he reached the Scaean Gates,
the last point he would pass to gain the field of battle.

5   There his warm, generous wife came running up to meet him,
Andromache the daughter of gallant-hearted Eetion
who had lived below Mount Placos rich with timber,
in Thebe below the peaks, and ruled Cilicia's people.
His daughter had married Hector helmed in bronze.

10 She joined him now, and following in her steps
a servant holding the boy against her breast,
in the first flush of life, only a baby,
Hector's son, the darling of his eyes
and radiant as a star . . .

15 Hector would always call the boy Scamandrius,
townsmen called him Astyanax, Lord of the City,
since Hector was the lone defense of Troy.
The great man of war breaking into a broad smile,
his gaze fixed on his son, in silence. Andromache,

3 Scaean (skē'ən) **Gates:** a gateway in Troy's wall, facing the Greek camp.

6 Eetion (ē-ĕt'ē-ŏn').

8 Thebe (thē'bē): a town near Troy; **Cilicia's** (sĭ-lĭsh'əz) **people:** the inhabitants of the region surrounding Thebe.

15 Scamandrius (skə-măn'drē-əs).

HUMANITIES CONNECTION
This painting on a Greek vase shows a soldier preparing to leave home. The soldier is inspecting the entrails, or intestines, of an animal that has been sacrificed to the gods. The striped figure to the left is a slave in native dress.

Soldier leaving his family for battle. Bildarchiv Preuss, Kulturbesitz, Berlin, Germany.

20 pressing close beside him and weeping freely now,
    clung to his hand, urged him, called him: "Reckless one,
    my Hector—your own fiery courage will destroy you!
    Have you no pity for him, our helpless son? Or me,
    and the destiny that weighs me down, your widow,
25 now so soon. Yes, soon they will kill you off,
    all the Achaean forces massed for assault, and then,
    bereft of you, better for me to sink beneath the earth.
    What other warmth, what comfort's left for me,
    once you have met your doom? Nothing but torment!
30 I have lost my father. Mother's gone as well.
    Father . . . the brilliant Achilles laid him low
    when he stormed Cilicia's city filled with people,
    Thebe with her towering gates. He killed Eetion,
    not that he stripped his gear—he'd some respect at least—
35 for he burned his corpse in all his blazoned bronze,

27 bereft: deprived.

34 he'd some respect at least: Achilles showed respect for Eetion by not plundering his armor and by treating his corpse with appropriate ceremony.

35 blazoned bronze: decorated armor.

then heaped a grave-mound high above the ashes
and nymphs of the mountain planted elms around it,
daughters of Zeus whose shield is storm and thunder.
And the seven brothers I had within our halls . . .

40 all in the same day went down to the House of Death,
the great godlike runner Achilles butchered them all,
tending their shambling oxen, shining flocks.
                                        And mother,
who ruled under the timberline of woody Placos once—
he no sooner haled her here with his other plunder

45 than he took a priceless ransom, set her free
and home she went to her father's royal halls
where Artemis, showering arrows, shot her down.
You, Hector—you are my father now, my noble mother,
a brother too, and you are my husband, young and warm
        and strong!

50 Pity me, please! Take your stand on the rampart here,
before you orphan your son and make your wife a widow.
Draw your armies up where the wild fig tree stands,
there, where the city lies most open to assault,
the walls lower, easily overrun. Three times
55 they have tried that point, hoping to storm Troy,
their best fighters led by the Great and Little Ajax,
famous Idomeneus, Atreus' sons, valiant Diomedes.
Perhaps a skilled prophet revealed the spot—
or their own fury whips them on to attack."

PAUSE & REFLECT Why is it so important to Andromache that Hector not return to the battlefield?

FOCUS Hector is determined to fight, even though he believes that Troy is doomed. As you read, pay attention to his reasons for fighting, as well as his worries about his wife's future.

60 And tall Hector nodded, his helmet flashing:
"All this weighs on my mind too, dear woman.
But I would die of shame to face the men of Troy
and the Trojan women trailing their long robes
if I would shrink from battle now, a coward.
65 Nor does the spirit urge me on that way.
I've learned it all too well. To stand up bravely,

always to fight in the front ranks of Trojan soldiers,
winning my father great glory, glory for myself.
For in my heart and soul I also know this well:
70 the day will come when sacred Troy must die,
Priam must die and all his people with him,
Priam who hurls the strong ash spear . . .

                            Even so,
it is less the pain of the Trojans still to come
that weighs me down, not even of Hecuba herself
75 or King Priam, or the thought that my own brothers
in all their numbers, all their gallant courage,
may tumble in the dust, crushed by enemies—
That is nothing, nothing beside your agony
when some brazen Argive hales you off in tears,
80 wrenching away your day of light and freedom!
Then far off in the land of Argos you must live,
laboring at a loom, at another woman's beck and call,
fetching water at some spring, Messeis or Hyperia,
resisting it all the way—
85 the rough yoke of necessity at your neck.
And a man may say, who sees you streaming tears,
'There is the wife of Hector, the bravest fighter
they could field, those stallion-breaking Trojans,
long ago when the men fought for Troy.' So he will say
90 and the fresh grief will swell your heart once more,
widowed, robbed of the one man strong enough
to fight off your day of slavery.

                        No, no,
let the earth come piling over my dead body
before I hear your cries, I hear you dragged away!"

95   In the same breath, shining Hector reached down
for his son—but the boy recoiled,
cringing against his nurse's full breast,
screaming out at the sight of his own father,
terrified by the flashing bronze, the horsehair crest,
100 the great ridge of the helmet nodding, bristling terror—
so it struck his eyes. And his loving father laughed,
his mother laughed as well, and glorious Hector,
quickly lifting the helmet from his head,
set it down on the ground, fiery in the sunlight,
105 and raising his son he kissed him, tossed him in his arms,

83 Messeis (mə-sē′ĭs) . . . **Hyperia**
(hī′pə-rī′ə): springs in Greece.

WORDS TO KNOW

198   **recoil** (rĭ-koil′) v. to pull back in fear or surprise

Greek bust of Zeus. Museo Nazionale, Naples Italy. Photograph copyright © Alinari-Viollet.

lifting a prayer to Zeus and the other deathless gods:
"Zeus, all you immortals! Grant this boy, my son,
may be like me, first in glory among the Trojans,
strong and brave like me, and rule all Troy in power

110   and one day let them say, 'He is a better man than his
       father!'—
when he comes home from battle bearing the bloody gear
of the mortal enemy he has killed in war—
a joy to his mother's heart."

                         So Hector prayed
and placed his son in the arms of his loving wife.

115   Andromache pressed the child to her scented breast,
smiling through her tears. Her husband noticed,
and filled with pity now, Hector stroked her gently,
trying to reassure her, repeating her name: "Andromache,
dear one, why so desperate? Why so much grief for me?

120   No man will hurl me down to Death, against my fate.

And fate? No one alive has ever escaped it,
neither brave man nor coward, I tell you—
it's born with us the day that we are born.
So please go home and tend to your own tasks,
125 the distaff and the loom, and keep the women
working hard as well. As for the fighting,
men will see to that, all who were born in Troy
but I most of all."
                         Hector aflash in arms
took up his horsehair-crested helmet once again.
130 And his loving wife went home, turning, glancing
back again and again and weeping live warm tears.
She quickly reached the sturdy house of Hector,
man-killing Hector,
and found her women gathered there inside
135 and stirred them all to a high pitch of mourning.
So in his house they raised the dirges for the dead,
for Hector still alive, his people were so convinced
that never again would he come home from battle,
never escape the Argives' rage and bloody hands.

125 distaff (dĭs'tăf'): a device used in making wool or other fibers into thread.

136 dirges (dûr'jĭz): funeral songs.

Thinking Through the Literature

1. Why is Hector so determined to keep fighting?

2. What does Hector think the future holds for his wife?

3. Hector says that "no one alive has ever escaped" fate (line 121). How would you describe Hector's attitude toward fate? Use details from Hector's speech to his wife in lines 61–94 to support your judgment.

4. What do you learn about the **character** of Hector in the excerpt from Book 6? Consider his roles as husband, father, and warrior.

5. Review the description of an **epic hero** on page 181. In light of that description, who seems more heroic to you, Hector or Achilles? Use details from the poem to support your response.

THE DEATH OF HECTOR

GUIDE FOR READING

FOCUS This excerpt from Book 22 describes a battle to the death between Achilles and Hector. As you read, evaluate Hector's chance of winning the battle.

After Hector returns to battle, the Trojans gain the advantage. They drive the Greeks back to their ships and seem to have victory within reach. Greek leaders try to persuade Achilles to rejoin the fighting, offering many gifts. The proud Achilles still refuses to fight, though he does agree to keep his ships at Troy. After more fighting—and the fall of many Greek heroes— Achilles' best friend, Patroclus, appeals to him once more. Achilles refuses again, but he does agree to allow Patroclus to enter the battle. Wearing Achilles' armor and leading his troops, Patroclus succeeds in pushing the Trojans back. But Hector kills the brave Patroclus with the help of Apollo. He takes Achilles' armor from the corpse and wears it himself.

Enraged and grief-stricken, Achilles decides to avenge the death of his friend. When Achilles tells his mother of his decision, she tearfully informs him that he is doomed to an early death, for once he kills Hector, his own death will follow. Achilles accepts his fate and enters the battle, wearing magnificent new armor made by the smith of the gods. In relentless pursuit of Hector, Achilles slaughters every Trojan in his path.

As Book 22 opens, the Trojan warriors have fled to the safety of the city—all except Hector. Achilles chases Hector around the walls of Troy until the gods decide to intervene.

So he <u>wavered</u>,
waiting there, but Achilles was closing on him now
like the god of war, the fighter's helmet flashing,
over his right shoulder shaking the Pelian ash spear,

4 Pelian (pē'lē-ən): made of wood from Mount Pelion in Greece.

WORDS TO KNOW

waver (wā'vər) v. to have difficulty in making a decision

that terror, and the bronze around his body flared
like a raging fire or the rising, blazing sun.
Hector looked up, saw him, started to tremble,
nerve gone, he could hold his ground no longer,
he left the gates behind and away he fled in fear—
and Achilles went for him, fast, sure of his speed
as the wild mountain hawk, the quickest thing on wings,
launching smoothly, swooping down on a cringing dove
and the dove flits out from under, the hawk screaming
over the quarry, plunging over and over, his fury
driving him down to beak and tear his kill—
so Achilles flew at him, breakneck on in fury
with Hector fleeing along the walls of Troy,
fast as his legs would go. On and on they raced,
passing the lookout point, passing the wild fig tree
tossed by the wind, always out from under the ramparts
down the wagon trail they careered until they reached
the clear running springs where whirling Scamander
rises up from its double wellsprings bubbling strong—
and one runs hot and the steam goes up around it,
drifting thick as if fire burned at its core
but the other even in summer gushes cold
as hail or freezing snow or water chilled to ice . . .
And here, close to the springs, lie washing-pools
scooped out in the hollow rocks and broad and smooth,
where the wives of Troy and all their lovely daughters
would wash their glistening robes in the old days,
the days of peace before the sons of Achaea came . . .
Past these they raced, one escaping, one in pursuit
and the one who fled was great but the one pursuing
greater, even greater—their pace mounting in speed
since both men strove, not for a sacrificial beast
or oxhide trophy, prizes runners fight for, no,
they raced for the life of Hector breaker of horses.
Like powerful stallions sweeping round the post for trophies,
galloping full stretch with some fine prize at stake,
a tripod, say, or woman offered up at funeral games
for some brave hero fallen—so the two of them
whirled three times around the city of Priam,
sprinting at top speed while all the gods gazed down,
and the father of men and gods broke forth among them
    now:
"Unbearable—a man I love, hunted round his own city walls

21 **careered:** rushed.

22 **Scamander** (skə-măn′dər): the chief river of the plain below Troy.

41 **tripod** (trī′pŏd′): a three-legged cooking kettle. (Since all metal was very valuable in ancient Greece, tripods were often given as prizes in athletic contests.)

and right before my eyes. My heart grieves for Hector.
Hector who burned so many oxen in my honor, rich cuts,
now on the rugged crests of Ida, now on Ilium's heights.
50   But now, look, brilliant Achilles courses him round
the city of Priam in all his savage, lethal speed.
Come, you immortals, think this through. Decide.
Either we pluck the man from death and save his life
or strike him down at last, here at Achilles' hands—
55   for all his fighting heart."
                            But immortal Athena,
her gray eyes wide, protested strongly: "Father!
Lord of the lightning, king of the black cloud,
what are you saying? A man, a mere mortal,
his doom sealed long ago? You'd set him free
60   from all the pains of death?
                            Do as you please—
but none of the deathless gods will ever praise you."

And Zeus who marshals the thunderheads replied,
"Courage, Athena, third-born of the gods, dear child.
Nothing I said was meant in earnest, trust me,
65   I mean you all the good will in the world. Go.
Do as your own impulse bids you. Hold back no more."

So he launched Athena already poised for action—
down the goddess swept from Olympus' craggy peaks.

PAUSE & REFLECT Zeus feels sorry for Hector and
even wonders whether the gods should save him. Do you
think Hector has a fair chance to win the battle?

FOCUS Athena is coming down to earth to help Achilles.
As you read, notice how she assists Achilles.

And swift Achilles kept on coursing Hector, nonstop
70   as a hound in the mountains starts a fawn from its lair,
hunting him down the gorges, down the narrow glens
and the fawn goes to ground, hiding deep in brush
but the hound comes racing fast, nosing him out
until he lands his kill. So Hector could never throw
75   Achilles off his trail, the swift racer Achilles—
time and again he'd make a dash for the Dardan Gates,
trying to rush beneath the rock-built ramparts, hoping

49 Ida (ī′də): a mountain range
near Troy; **Ilium's** (ĭl′ē-əmz): Troy's.
50 courses: chases; hunts.

70 starts: frightens; **lair:** hiding
place.

76 Dardan Gates: a gateway in
Troy's wall.

men on the heights might save him, somehow, raining
        spears
but time and again Achilles would intercept him quickly,
80 heading him off, forcing him out across the plain
and always sprinting along the city side himself—
endless as in a dream . . .
when a man can't catch another fleeing on ahead
and he can never escape nor his rival overtake him—
85 so the one could never run the other down in his speed
nor the other spring away. And how could Hector have fled
the fates of death so long? How unless one last time,
one final time Apollo had swept in close beside him,
driving strength in his legs and knees to race the wind?
90 And brilliant Achilles shook his head at the armies,
never letting them hurl their sharp spears at Hector—
someone might snatch the glory, Achilles come in second.
But once they reached the springs for the fourth time,
then Father Zeus held out his sacred golden scales:

94 sacred golden scales: the balance used by Zeus to decide people's fates.

95 in them he placed two fates of death that lays men low—
one for Achilles, one for Hector breaker of horses—
and gripping the beam mid-haft the Father raised it high
and down went Hector's day of doom, dragging him down
to the strong House of Death—and god Apollo left him.

97 mid-haft: by the handle in the middle.

100 Athena rushed to Achilles, her bright eyes gleaming,
standing shoulder-to-shoulder, winging orders now:
"At last our hopes run high, my brilliant Achilles—
Father Zeus must love you—
we'll sweep great glory back to Achaea's fleet,
105 we'll kill this Hector, mad as he is for battle!
No way for him to escape us now, no longer—
not even if Phoebus the distant deadly Archer
goes through torments, pleading for Hector's life,
groveling over and over before our storming Father Zeus.

109 groveling (grŏv′ə-lĭng): throwing himself to the ground.

110 But you, you hold your ground and catch your breath
while I run Hector down and persuade the man
to fight you face-to-face."
                        So Athena commanded
and he obeyed, rejoicing at heart—Achilles stopped,
leaning against his ashen spearshaft barbed in bronze.
115 And Athena left him there, caught up with Hector at once,
and taking the build and vibrant voice of Deiphobus
stood shoulder-to-shoulder with him, winging orders:
"Dear brother, how brutally swift Achilles hunts you—

116 Deiphobus (dē-ĭf′ə-bəs): a son of Priam.

Pallas de Velletri, attributed to Kresilas. Marble, 305 cm. Musée du Louvre, Paris. Photograph copyright © Herve Lewandowski. Réunion des Musées Nationaux/Art Resource, New York.

coursing you round the city of Priam in all his lethal speed!
120 Come, let us stand our ground together—beat him back."

"Deiphobus!"—Hector, his helmet flashing, called out to her—
"dearest of all my brothers, all these warring years,
of all the sons that Priam and Hecuba produced!
Now I'm determined to praise you all the more,
125 you who dared—seeing me in these straits—
to venture out from the walls, all for *my* sake,
while the others stay inside and cling to safety."

The goddess answered quickly, her eyes blazing,
"True, dear brother—how your father and mother both
130 implored me, time and again, clutching my knees,
and the comrades round me begging me to stay!
Such was the fear that broke them, man for man,
but the heart within me broke with grief for you.
Now headlong on and fight! No letup, no lance spared!

125 these straits: this distress.

135   So now, now we'll *see* if Achilles kills us both
      and hauls our bloody armor back to the beaked ships
      or he goes down in pain beneath your spear."

       Athena luring him on with all her immortal cunning—
      and now, at last, as the two came closing for the kill
140   it was tall Hector, helmet flashing, who led off:
      "No more running from you in fear, Achilles!
      Not as before. Three times I fled around
      the great city of Priam—I lacked courage then
      to stand your onslaught. Now my spirit stirs me
145   to meet you face-to-face. Now kill or be killed!
      Come, we'll swear to the gods, the highest witnesses—
      the gods will oversee our binding pacts. I swear
      I will never mutilate you—merciless as you are—
      if Zeus allows me to last it out and tear your life away.
150   But once I've stripped your glorious armor, Achilles,
      I will give your body back to your loyal comrades.
      Swear you'll do the same."
                      A swift dark glance
      and the headstrong runner answered, "Hector, stop!
      You unforgivable, you . . . don't talk to me of pacts.
155   There are no binding oaths between men and lions—
      wolves and lambs can enjoy no meeting of the minds—
      they are all bent on hating each other to the death.
      So with you and me. No love between us. No truce
      till one or the other falls and gluts with blood
160   Ares who hacks at men behind his rawhide shield.
      Come, call up whatever courage you can muster.
      Life or death—now prove yourself a spearman,
      a daring man of war! No more escape for you—
      Athena will kill you with my spear in just a moment.
165   Now you'll pay at a stroke for all my comrades' grief,
      all you killed in the fury of your spear!"

148 mutilate you: hack up your body.

159 gluts: satisfies.

160 Ares (âr′ēz): the god of war.

PAUSE & REFLECT How does Athena help Achilles?

Although Hector knows that he is doomed to die, he will stand and fight. As you read, look for the ways in which Achilles insults Hector, both with words and with actions.

With that,
shaft poised, he hurled and his spear's long shadow flew
but seeing it coming glorious Hector ducked away,
crouching down, watching the bronze tip fly past
170 and stab the earth—but Athena snatched it up
and passed it back to Achilles
and Hector the gallant captain never saw her.
He sounded out a challenge to Peleus' princely son:
"You missed, look—the great godlike Achilles!
175 So you knew nothing at all from Zeus about my death—
and yet how sure you were! All bluff, cunning with words,
that's all you are—trying to make me fear you,
lose my nerve, forget my fighting strength.
Well, you'll never plant your lance in my back
180 as I flee *you* in fear—plunge it through my chest
as I come charging in, if a god gives you the chance!
But now it's for you to dodge *my* brazen spear—
I wish you'd bury it in your body to the hilt.
How much lighter the war would be for Trojans then
185 if you, their greatest scourge, were dead and gone!"

Shaft poised, he hurled and his spear's long shadow flew
and it struck Achilles' shield—a dead-center hit—
but off and away it glanced and Hector seethed,
his hurtling spear, his whole arm's power poured
190 in a wasted shot. He stood there, cast down . . .
he had no spear in reserve. So Hector shouted out
to Deiphobus bearing his white shield—with a ringing shout
he called for a heavy lance—
                    but the man was nowhere near him,
vanished—
                    yes and Hector knew the truth in his heart
195 and the fighter cried aloud, "My time has come!
At last the gods have called me down to death.
I thought he was at my side, the hero Deiphobus—
he's safe inside the walls, Athena's tricked me blind.
And now death, grim death is looming up beside me,
200 no longer far away. No way to escape it now. This,

185 scourge (skûrj): source of misery.

188 glanced: bounced.

this was their pleasure after all, sealed long ago—
Zeus and the son of Zeus, the distant deadly Archer—
though often before now they rushed to my defense.
So now I meet my doom. Well let me die—
205 but not without struggle, not without glory, no,
in some great clash of arms that even men to come
will hear of down the years!"
                                    And on that resolve
he drew the whetted sword that hung at his side,
tempered, massive, and gathering all his force
210 he swooped like a soaring eagle
launching down from the dark clouds to earth
to snatch some helpless lamb or trembling hare.
So Hector swooped now, swinging his whetted sword
and Achilles charged too, bursting with rage, barbaric,
215 guarding his chest with the well-wrought blazoned shield,
head tossing his gleaming helmet, four horns strong

208 whetted: sharpened.

209 tempered: hardened
by heating.

215 well-wrought: skillfully made.

Greek soldiers arming themselves. Copyright © Peter Connolly.

and the golden plumes shook that the god of fire
drive in bristling thick along its ridge.
Bright as that star amid the stars in the night sky,
220 star of the evening, brightest star that rides the heavens,
so fire flared from the sharp point of the spear Achilles
brandished high in his right hand, bent on Hector's death,
scanning his splendid body—where to pierce it best?
The rest of his flesh seemed all encased in armor,
225 burnished, brazen—*Achilles'* armor that Hector stripped
from strong Patroclus when he killed him—true,
but one spot lay exposed,
where collarbones lift the neckbone off the shoulders,
the open throat, where the end of life comes quickest—
         there
230 as Hector charged in fury brilliant Achilles drove his spear
and the point went stabbing clean through the tender neck
but the heavy bronze weapon failed to slash the windpipe—
Hector could still gasp out some words, some last reply . . .
he crashed in the dust—
                         godlike Achilles gloried over him:
235 "Hector—surely you thought when you stripped Patroclus'
      armor
that you, you would be safe! Never a fear of me—
far from the fighting as I was—you fool!
Left behind there, down by the beaked ships
his great avenger waited, a greater man by far—
240 that man was I, and I smashed your strength! And you—
the dogs and birds will maul you, shame your corpse
while Achaeans bury my dear friend in glory!"

   Struggling for breath, Hector, his helmet flashing,
said, "I beg you, beg you by your life, your parents—
245 don't let the dogs devour me by the Argive ships!
Wait, take the princely ransom of bronze and gold,
the gifts my father and noble mother will give you—
but give my body to friends to carry home again,
so Trojan men and Trojan women can do me honor
250 with fitting rites of fire once I am dead."

   Staring grimly, the proud runner Achilles answered,
"Beg no more, you fawning dog—begging me by my parents!
Would to god my rage, my fury would drive me now
to hack your flesh away and eat you raw—

217 the god of fire: Hephaestus, who made Achilles' armor and shield.

222 brandished: waved.

241 maul: mangle.

252 fawning: cringing.

255   such agonies you have caused me! Ransom?
No man alive could keep the dog-packs off you,
not if they haul in ten, twenty times that ransom
and pile it here before me and promise fortunes more—
no, not even if Dardan Priam should offer to weigh out
260   your bulk in gold! Not even then will your noble mother
lay you on your deathbed, mourn the son she bore . . .
The dogs and birds will rend you—blood and bone!"

259 Dardan: descended from Dardanus, ancestor of the Trojan kings.

262 rend: tear apart.

     At the point of death, Hector, his helmet flashing,
said, "I know you well—I see my fate before me.
265   Never a chance that I could win you over . . .
Iron inside your chest, that heart of yours.
But now beware, or my curse will draw god's wrath
upon your head, that day when Paris and lord Apollo—
for all your fighting heart—destroy you at the Scaean Gates!"

270   Death cut him short. The end closed in around him.
Flying free of his limbs
his soul went winging down to the House of Death,
wailing his fate, leaving his manhood far behind,
his young and supple strength. But brilliant Achilles
275   taunted Hector's body, dead as he was, "Die, die!
For my own death, I'll meet it freely—whenever Zeus
and the other deathless gods would like to bring it on!"

     With that he wrenched his bronze spear from the corpse,
laid it aside and ripped the bloody armor off the back.
280   And the other sons of Achaea, running up around him,
crowded closer, all of them gazing wonder-struck
at the build and marvelous, <u>lithe</u> beauty of Hector.
And not a man came forward who did not stab his body,
glancing toward a comrade, laughing: "Ah, look here—
285   how much softer he is to handle now, this Hector,
than when he gutted our ships with roaring fire!"

     Standing over him, so they'd gloat and stab his body.
But once he had stripped the corpse the proud runner Achilles
took his stand in the midst of all the Argive troops
290   and urged them on with a flight of winging orders:
"Friends—lords of the Argives, O my captains!
Now that the gods have let me kill this man

WORDS TO KNOW

     lithe (līŧħ) *adj.* limber and graceful

who caused us agonies, loss on crushing loss—
more than the rest of all their men combined—
295   come, let us ring their walls in armor, test them,
see what <u>recourse</u> the Trojans still may have in mind.
Will they abandon the city heights with this man fallen?
Or brace for a last, dying stand though Hector's gone?
But wait—what am I saying? Why this deep debate?
300   Down by the ships a body lies unwept, unburied—
Patroclus . . . I will never forget him,
not as long as I'm still among the living
and my springing knees will lift and drive me on.
Though the dead forget their dead in the House of Death,
305   I will remember, even there, my dear companion.
                                                                        Now,
come, you sons of Achaea, raise a song of triumph!
Down to the ships we march and bear this corpse on high—
we have won ourselves great glory. We have brought
magnificent Hector down, that man the Trojans
310   glorified in their city like a god!"
                                                        So he triumphed
and now he was bent on outrage, on shaming noble Hector.
Piercing the tendons, ankle to heel behind both feet,
he knotted straps of rawhide through them both,
lashed them to his chariot, left the head to drag
315   and mounting the car, hoisting the famous arms aboard,
he whipped his team to a run and breakneck on they flew,
holding nothing back. And a thick cloud of dust rose up
from the man they dragged, his dark hair swirling round
that head so handsome once, all tumbled low in the dust—
320   since Zeus had given him over to his enemies now
to be <u>defiled</u> in the land of his own fathers.

    So his whole head was dragged down in the dust.
And now his mother began to tear her hair . . .
she flung her shining veil to the ground and raised
325   a high, shattering scream, looking down at her son.
Pitifully his loving father groaned and round the king
his people cried with grief and wailing seized the city—
for all the world as if all Troy were torched and smoldering
down from the looming brows of the citadel to her roots.
330   Priam's people could hardly hold the old man back,
frantic, mad to go rushing out the Dardan Gates.

329 looming brows of the citadel
(sĭt′ə-dəl): jutting battlements of
the stronghold.

WORDS TO KNOW

recourse (rē′kôrs′) *n.* something turned to for help or protection
defile (dĭ-fīl′) *v.* to treat in a shameful way; destroy the beauty or honor of

ILIAD   **211**

He begged them all, groveling in the filth,
crying out to them, calling each man by name,
"Let go, my friends! Much as you care for me,
335 let me hurry out of the city, make my way,
all on my own, to Achaea's waiting ships!
I must implore that terrible, violent man . . .
Perhaps—who knows?—he may respect my age,
may pity an old man. He has a father too,
340 as old as I am—Peleus sired him once,
Peleus reared him to be the scourge of Troy
but most of all to me—he made my life a hell.
So many sons he slaughtered, just coming into bloom . . .
but grieving for all the rest, one breaks my heart the most
345 and stabbing grief for him will take me down to Death—
my Hector—would to god he had perished in my arms!
Then his mother who bore him—oh so doomed,
she and I could glut ourselves with grief."

Thinking Through the Literature

1. How does Achilles insult Hector with words and with actions?

2. What qualities of Hector's **character** stand out in the excerpt from Book 22?

- how Hector runs away from Achilles
- what persuades him to stand and fight
- how he faces his own certain death

3. Consider the roles played by Athena, Zeus, and Apollo in the excerpt from Book 22. To what extent do the gods seem to control human life? Support your conclusion with evidence from the text.

- the passage in which Zeus weighs the fates of Hector and Achilles (lines 93–99)
- Athena's words and actions
- Apollo's helping Hector to run away from Achilles (lines 86–89)

4. Do you think Achilles is justified in his treatment of Hector's corpse? Support your opinion with evidence from the text.

5. Review the reactions of Priam and Hecuba to Achilles' treatment of their son's corpse (lines 323–348). Why do you think Homer included a description of their grief?

ACHILLES AND PRIAM

GUIDE FOR READING

FOCUS As you read about the meeting of Achilles and Priam, pay attention to Achilles' reasons for taking pity on his enemy.

After Achilles kills Hector, the Greeks conduct funeral rites for Patroclus. In the following days, whenever Achilles is overcome by grief, he takes out his chariot and drags Hector's corpse around the grave of Patroclus. Apollo, still loyal to Hector, can do nothing to stop Achilles, but he does protect the corpse from all damage. Zeus, recognizing that Hector had always been faithful to the gods, sends a message to Achilles, telling him to give Hector's body to Priam in exchange for a ransom. Bowing to divine will, Achilles agrees. Zeus then sends a message to Priam, directing him to gather treasures and take them to Achilles. Aided by the god Hermes, Priam drives a wagonload of treasures to the enemy camp. Alone, he enters Achilles' hut to ask for the return of Hector's corpse.

The majestic king of Troy slipped past the rest
and kneeling down beside Achilles, clasped his knees
and kissed his hands, those terrible, man-killing hands
that had slaughtered Priam's many sons in battle.
5 Awesome—as when the grip of madness seizes one
who murders a man in his own fatherland and flees
abroad to foreign shores, to a wealthy, noble host,
and a sense of marvel runs through all who see him—
so Achilles marveled, beholding majestic Priam.
10 His men marveled too, trading startled glances.
But Priam prayed his heart out to Achilles:
"Remember your own father, great godlike Achilles—
as old as *I* am, past the threshold of deadly old age!

HUMANITIES CONNECTION This detail from a Roman sarcophagus (stone coffin) sculpture shows the body of Hector tied to a chariot. Imagine how King Priam felt when he had to witness the dragging of his son's corpse.

No doubt the countrymen round about him plague him now,
15 with no one there to defend him, beat away disaster.
No one—but at least he hears you're still alive
and his old heart rejoices, hopes rising, day by day,
to see his beloved son come sailing home from Troy.
But I—dear god, my life so cursed by fate . . .
20 I fathered hero sons in the wide realm of Troy
and now not a single one is left, I tell you.
Fifty sons I had when the sons of Achaea came,
nineteen born to me from a single mother's womb
and the rest by other women in the palace. Many,
25 most of them violent Ares cut the knees from under.
But one, one was left me, to guard my walls, my people—
the one you killed the other day, defending his fatherland,
my Hector! It's all for him I've come to the ships now,
to win him back from you—I bring a priceless ransom.
30 Revere the gods, Achilles! Pity me in my own right,
remember your own father! I deserve more pity . . .

I have endured what no one on earth has ever done
      before—
I put to my lips the hands of the man who killed my son."

Those words stirred within Achilles a deep desire
35 to grieve for his own father. Taking the old man's hand
he gently moved him back. And overpowered by memory
both men gave way to grief. Priam wept freely
for man-killing Hector, throbbing, crouching
before Achilles' feet as Achilles wept himself,
40 now for his father, now for Patroclus once again,
and their sobbing rose and fell throughout the house.
Then, when brilliant Achilles had his fill of tears
and the longing for it had left his mind and body,
he rose from his seat, raised the old man by the hand
45 and filled with pity now for his gray head and gray beard,
he spoke out winging words, flying straight to the heart:
"Poor man, how much you've borne—pain to break the
      spirit!
What daring brought you down to the ships, all alone,
to face the glance of the man who killed your sons,
50 so many fine brave boys? You have a heart of iron.
Come, please, sit down on this chair here . . .
Let us put our griefs to rest in our own hearts,
rake them up no more, raw as we are with mourning.
What good's to be won from tears that chill the spirit?
55 So the immortals spun our lives that we, we wretched men
live on to bear such torments—the gods live free of sorrows.
There are two great jars that stand on the floor of Zeus's
      halls
and hold his gifts, our miseries one, the other blessings.
When Zeus who loves the lightning mixes gifts for a man,
60 now he meets with misfortune, now good times in turn.
When Zeus dispenses gifts from the jar of sorrows only,
he makes a man an outcast—brutal, ravenous hunger
drives him down the face of the shining earth,
stalking far and wide, cursed by gods and men.
65 So with my father, Peleus. What glittering gifts
the gods rained down from the day that he was born!
He excelled all men in wealth and pride of place,
he lorded the Myrmidons, and mortal that he was,
they gave the man an immortal goddess for a wife.
70 Yes, but even on him the Father piled hardships,

55 the immortals spun our lives: the gods determined our fates.

62 ravenous (răv′ə-nəs): characterized by eager craving.

no powerful race of princes born in his royal halls,
only a single son he fathered, doomed at birth,
cut off in the spring of life—
and I, I give the man no care as he grows old
75   since here I sit in Troy, far from my fatherland,
a grief to you, a grief to all your children.
And you too, old man, we hear you prospered once:
as far as Lesbos, Macar's kingdom, bounds to seaward,
Phrygia east and upland, the Hellespont vast and north—
80   that entire realm, they say, you lorded over once,
you excelled all men, old king, in sons and wealth.
But then the gods of heaven brought this agony on you—
ceaseless battles round your walls, your armies slaughtered.
You must bear up now. Enough of endless tears,
85   the pain that breaks the spirit.
Grief for your son will do no good at all.
You will never bring him back to life—
sooner you must suffer something worse."

    But the old and noble Priam protested strongly:
90   "Don't make me sit on a chair, Achilles, Prince,
not while Hector lies uncared-for in your camp!
Give him back to me, now, no more delay—
I must see my son with my own eyes.
Accept the ransom I bring you, a king's ransom!
95   Enjoy it, all of it—return to your own native land,
safe and sound . . . since now you've spared my life."

    A dark glance—and the headstrong runner answered,
"No more, old man, don't tempt my wrath, not now!
My own mind's made up to give you back your son.
100   A messenger brought me word from Zeus—my mother,
Thetis who bore me, the Old Man of the Sea's daughter.
And what's more, I can see through you, Priam—
no hiding the fact from me: one of the gods
has led you down to Achaea's fast ships.
105   No man alive, not even a rugged young fighter,
would dare to venture into our camp. Never—
how could he slip past the sentries unchallenged?
Or shoot back the bolt of my gates with so much ease?

78 Lesbos (lĕz′bŏs), **Macar's** (măk′ärz′) **kingdom:** an island off the coast of Asia Minor, south of Troy, whose first king was Macar.

79 Phrygia (frĭj′ē-ə): a region of northwestern Asia Minor; **Hellespont** (hĕl′ĭ-spŏnt′): a strait just north of Troy.

101 Old Man of the Sea's daughter: daughter of the sea god Nereus.

So don't anger me now. Don't stir my raging heart still more.
110 Or under my own roof I may not spare your life, old man—
suppliant that you are—may break the laws of Zeus!"

111 suppliant: one who humbly begs.

PAUSE & REFLECT For what reasons does Achilles take pity on Priam?

FOCUS Though Achilles has agreed to release Hector's body, the Greek hero still struggles to control his anger. As you read, think about whether Achilles acts as a good host to his royal visitor.

The old man was terrified. He obeyed the order.
But Achilles bounded out of doors like a lion—
not alone but flanked by his two aides-in-arms,
115 veteran Automedon and Alcimus, steady comrades,
Achilles' favorites next to the dead Patroclus.
They loosed from harness the horses and the mules,
they led the herald in, the old king's crier,
and sat him down on a bench. From the polished wagon
120 they lifted the priceless ransom brought for Hector's corpse
but they left behind two capes and a finely-woven shirt
to shroud the body well when Priam bore him home.
Then Achilles called the serving-women out:
"Bathe and anoint the body—
125 bear it aside first. Priam must not see his son."
He feared that, overwhelmed by the sight of Hector,
wild with grief, Priam might let his anger flare
and Achilles might fly into fresh rage himself,
cut the old man down and break the laws of Zeus.
130 So when the maids had bathed and anointed the body
sleek with olive oil and wrapped it round and round
in a braided battle-shirt and handsome battle-cape,
then Achilles lifted Hector up in his own arms
and laid him down on a bier, and comrades helped him
135 raise the bier and body onto the sturdy wagon . . .
Then with a groan he called his dear friend by name:
"Feel no anger at me, Patroclus, if you learn—
even there in the House of Death—I let his father
have Prince Hector back. He gave me worthy ransom
140 and you shall have your share from me, as always,
your fitting, lordly share."

114 flanked: accompanied on either side.

115 Automedon (ô-tŏm′ə-dŏn′) . . . **Alcimus** (ăl′sĭ-məs).

122 shroud: wrap.

134 bier (bēr): a platform for laying out a corpse.

So he vowed
and brilliant Achilles strode back to his shelter,
sat down on the well-carved chair that he had left,
at the far wall of the room, leaned toward Priam
145 and firmly spoke the words the king had come to hear:
"Your son is now set free, old man, as you requested.
Hector lies in state. With the first light of day
you will see for yourself as you convey him home.
Now, at last, let us turn our thoughts to supper.
150 Even Niobe with her lustrous hair remembered food,
though she saw a dozen children killed in her own halls,
six daughters and six sons in the pride and prime of youth.
True, lord Apollo killed the sons with his silver bow
and Artemis showering arrows killed the daughters.
155 Both gods were enraged at Niobe. Time and again
she placed herself on a par with their own mother,
Leto in her immortal beauty—how she insulted Leto:
'All you have borne is two, but I have borne so many!'
So, two as they were, they slaughtered all her children.
160 Nine days they lay in their blood, no one to bury them—
Cronus' son had turned the people into stone . . .
then on the tenth the gods of heaven interred them.
And Niobe, <u>gaunt</u>, worn to the bone with weeping,
turned her thoughts to food. And now, somewhere,
165 lost on the crags, on the lonely mountain slopes,
on Sipylus where, they say, the nymphs who live forever,
dancing along the Achelous River run to beds of rest—
there, struck into stone, Niobe still broods
on the spate of griefs the gods poured out to her.

170   So come—we too, old king, must think of food.
Later you can mourn your beloved son once more,
when you bear him home to Troy, and you'll weep many
        tears."

    Never pausing, the swift runner sprang to his feet
and slaughtered a white sheep as comrades moved in
175 to skin the carcass quickly, dress the quarters well.
Expertly they cut the meat in pieces, pierced them with spits,
roasted them to a turn and pulled them off the fire.
Automedon brought the bread, set it out on the board
in ample wicker baskets. Achilles served the meat.

150 Niobe (nīʹə-bē).

161 Cronus' son: Zeus.
162 interred (ĭn-tûrdʹ): buried.

166 Sipylus (sĭpʹə-ləs): a mountain in western Asia Minor.
167 Achelous (ăkʹə-lōʹəs).
169 spate: flood.

WORDS TO KNOW
gaunt (gônt) adj. thin and drawn

HUMANITIES CONNECTION
Here is another detail from
a Roman sarcophagus
sculpture, this one showing
King Priam begging Achilles
to return the body of his
son, Hector.

180   They reached out for the good things that lay at hand
and when they had put aside desire for food and drink,
Priam the son of Dardanus gazed at Achilles, marveling
now at the man's beauty, his magnificent build—
face-to-face he seemed a deathless god . . .

185   and Achilles gazed and marveled at Dardan Priam,
beholding his noble looks, listening to his words.
But once they'd had their fill of gazing at each other,
the old majestic Priam broke the silence first:
"Put me to bed quickly, Achilles, Prince.

190   Time to rest, to enjoy the sweet relief of sleep.
Not once have my eyes closed shut beneath my lids
from the day my son went down beneath your hands . . .
day and night I groan, brooding over the countless griefs,
groveling in the dung that fills my walled-in court.

195   But now, at long last, I have tasted food again
and let some glistening wine go down my throat.
Before this hour I had tasted nothing."

                           He shook his head
as Achilles briskly told his men and serving-women

to make beds in the porch's shelter, to lay down
200 some heavy purple throws for the beds themselves
and over them spread blankets and thick woolly robes,
a warm covering laid on top. Torches held in hand,
they went from the hall and fell to work at once
and in no time two good beds were spread and made.
205 Then Achilles nodded to Priam, leading the king on
with brusque advice: "Sleep outside, old friend,
in case some Achaean captain comes to visit.
They keep on coming now, huddling beside me,
making plans for battle—it's their duty.
210 But if one saw you here in the rushing dark night
he'd tell Agamemnon straightaway, our good commander.
Then you'd have real delay in ransoming the body.
One more point. Tell me, be precise about it—
how many days do you need to bury Prince Hector?
215 I will hold back myself
and keep the Argive armies back that long."

    And the old and noble Priam answered slowly,
"If you truly want me to give Prince Hector burial,
full, royal honors, you'd show me a great kindness,
220 Achilles, if you would do exactly as I say.
You know how crammed we are inside our city,
how far it is to the hills to haul in timber,
and our Trojans are afraid to make the journey.
Well, nine days we should mourn him in our halls,
225 on the tenth we'd bury Hector, hold the public feast,
on the eleventh build the barrow high above his body—
on the twelfth we'd fight again . . . if fight we must."

    The swift runner Achilles reassured him quickly:
"All will be done, old Priam, as you command.
230 I will hold our attack as long as you require."

    With that he clasped the old king by the wrist,
by the right hand, to free his heart from fear.
Then Priam and herald, minds set on the journey home,
bedded down for the night within the porch's shelter.
235 And deep in his sturdy well-built lodge Achilles slept
with Briseis in all her beauty sleeping by his side.

PAUSE & REFLECT Is Achilles a good host to Priam?
Give evidence from the text to support your evaluation.

206 brusque: blunt; curt.

226 barrow: a mound of stones or earth placed over a burial site.

232 by the right hand, to free his heart from fear: using his weapon hand, to show that he is not going to attack Priam.

233 herald: the aide who accompanied Priam to the Greek camp.

FOCUS Read to find out what happens when Priam brings Hector's corpse to the gates of Troy.

Now the great array of gods and chariot-driving men
slept all night long, overcome by gentle sleep.
But sleep could never hold the running Escort—
240 Hermes kept on turning it over in his mind . . .
how could he convoy Priam clear of the ships,
unseen by devoted guards who held the gates?
Hovering at his head the Escort rose and spoke:
"Not a care in the world, old man? Look at you,
245 how you sleep in the midst of men who'd kill you—
and just because Achilles spared your life. Now, yes,
you've ransomed your dear son—for a king's ransom.
But wouldn't the sons you left behind be forced
to pay three times as much for *you* alive?
250 What if Atrides Agamemnon learns you're here—
what if the whole Achaean army learns you're here?"

The old king woke in terror, roused the herald.
Hermes harnessed the mules and team for both men,
drove them fast through the camp and no one saw them.

255 Once they reached the ford where the river runs clear,
the strong, whirling Xanthus sprung of immortal Zeus,
Hermes went his way to the steep heights of Olympus
as Dawn flung out her golden robe across the earth,
and the two men, weeping, groaning, drove the team
260 toward Troy and the mules brought on the body.
No one saw them at first, neither man nor woman,
none before Cassandra, golden as goddess Aphrodite.
She had climbed to Pergamus heights and from that point
she saw her beloved father swaying tall in the chariot,
265 flanked by the herald, whose cry could rouse the city.
And Cassandra saw *him* too . . .
drawn by the mules and stretched out on his bier.
She screamed and her scream rang out through all Troy:
"Come, look down, you men of Troy, you Trojan women!
270 Behold Hector now—if you ever once rejoiced
to see him striding home, home alive from battle!
He was the greatest joy of Troy and all our people!"

239 Escort: Hermes.

256 Xanthus (zăn′thəs): another name for the river Scamander.

262 Cassandra (kə-săn′drə): a daughter of Priam.

263 Pergamus (pûr′gə-məs): the stronghold of Troy.

Her cries plunged Troy into uncontrollable grief
and not a man or woman was left inside the walls.
275 They streamed out at the gates to meet Priam
bringing in the body of the dead. Hector—
his loving wife and noble mother were first
to fling themselves on the wagon rolling on,
the first to tear their hair, embrace his head
280 and a wailing throng of people milled around them.
And now, all day long till the setting sun went down
they would have wept for Hector there before the gates
if the old man, steering the car, had not commanded,
"Let me through with the mules! Soon, in a moment,
285 you can have your fill of tears—once I've brought him home."

Connect to the Literature

1. What Do You Think? Has your opinion of Achilles changed as a result of his reception of Priam? Explain.

Comprehension Check
- When Priam asks for pity, what person does he ask Achilles to remember?
- Why do Priam and Achilles cry?
- How does Achilles show hospitality to Priam?
- Besides returning the body of Hector, what does Achilles agree to?

Think Critically

2. Which character in this episode do you feel more sympathetic toward, Achilles or Priam? Explain your response, using details from the poem.

3. In most of the *Iliad,* Achilles is defined by his anger. What other qualities of his **character** are revealed in the episode with Priam?

 THINK ABOUT
- Achilles' feelings for his father
- his treatment of Priam and his concern that Priam not provoke his anger
- his words of advice to Priam

4. Review Achilles' statements about the two jars from which Zeus distributes his "gifts" to mortals (page 215, lines 57–64). What do his words suggest about the Greeks' view of fate?

5. ACTIVE READING: EVALUATING Review what you wrote in your ![] **READER'S NOTEBOOK.** Did you change your opinion about characters as you read further and learned more about them? What influenced your judgments about the major events? Compare your evaluations with those of your classmates, and discuss any differences you note.

Extend Interpretations

6. Critic's Corner The French philosopher Simone Weil wrote, "The true hero, the true subject, the center of the *Iliad* is force. Force employed by man, force that enslaves man, force before which man's flesh shrinks away." Are there any aspects of human life that the epic presents as *not* being ruled by force?

7. Connect to Life The *Iliad* depicts a warrior society far different from our own society. Do you think the poem contains a **theme,** or message, that applies to life today? Give reasons to support your opinion.

LITERARY ANALYSIS: EPIC HERO

An **epic hero** is a larger-than-life figure whose adventures are the focus of an epic poem. Epic heroes take part in dangerous adventures that are often of historical or cultural importance. Their deeds usually reflect the ideas and values of a people. They possess great courage and extraordinary strength; many are assisted by supernatural beings.

Paired Activity Working with a partner, compare Hector and Achilles as epic heroes. Fill out a Venn diagram like the one shown, identifying what the two heroes have in common and what sets them apart. In your judgment, which character is more heroic?

LITERARY ANALYSIS: EPIC SIMILES AND EPITHETS

Epic similes and epithets are descriptive devices frequently used by Homer. An **epithet** is an identifying word or phrase used with (or in place of) the name of a person or thing. For example, Achilles is often identified as "the swift runner."

An **epic simile** is a simile that stretches over a number of lines. One example can be found on page 202, lines 10–15, where Achilles is compared to a wild mountain hawk.

Activity Find at least two other examples of epithets and two other examples of epic similes in the poem. Discuss how they contribute to your understanding of characters and events.

Choices & CHALLENGES

Writing Options

1. Ancient Values Essay From what you have read, what seem to have been the most important values of Homer's culture? First, review the text and identify passages that suggest cultural values, such as Agamemnon's statement that it would be a "disgrace" to "alone of the Argives go without my honor" (page 186, lines 138–140). Then choose two or three values to write about. Explain the importance of each value, and give quotations from the poem to illustrate each.

2. Analysis of the Gods What did the ancient Greeks believe about the gods? In what ways were gods and human beings alike, and in what ways were they different? How were people supposed to relate to the gods? Analyze the Greeks' religious beliefs, using examples from the poem to illustrate each point.

3. Homeric Argument Some critics have argued that Homer condemns the tragic waste of warfare. Others have claimed that Homer celebrates warfare and the values of the warrior. Take a position on this widely debated issue, and present examples from the poem to support your position.

Writing Handbook
See page R35: Persuasive Writing.

Activities & Explorations

Classic Illustration Choose a scene from the *Iliad* to illustrate. Carefully review the relevant passage, writing down visual details. Then create one illustration or a series of illustrations representing the scene. ~ ART

Inquiry & Research

The Real Troy Find out more about the discovery of the ruins of Troy. What do archaeologists now know about the ancient city? What connections do scholars see between the archaeological remains and the accounts in the *Iliad*?

RESEARCH STARTER
CLASSZONE.COM

Vocabulary in Action

EXERCISE: CONTEXT CLUES Write the word that best fills the blank in each sentence.

1. We saw the Trojan slave _____ with the order being barked at her; she dared not disobey.
2. As a young woman in Troy, she had been agile and _____ in her movements.
3. Then, she had not been afraid to _____ anyone who questioned or challenged her.
4. Now she is a _____ old woman living in Greece, so thin and weak she can barely walk.
5. Her weakened condition often makes her _____ when she should make a quick decision.
6. When she pleases her Greek master, she is given a mere _____ as a reward.
7. If an enemy approaches her, she will usually _____ fearfully.
8. She quickly nods in _____ when commanded to turn over her money.
9. What _____ does she have but to do as she is told?
10. Eventually, captivity will _____ even the strongest spirit.

WORDS TO KNOW

assent	gaunt	recoil	spurn
comply	lithe	recourse	waver
defile	pittance		

Building Vocabulary
For an in-depth lesson on Greek and Latin roots, see page 340.

Homer and the Oral Tradition

When Robert Fagles began translating Homer, he could often be heard "mumbling and muttering" to himself. Fagles went on to translate not only the *Iliad* but also the *Odyssey*—nearly 28,000 lines of poetry—and his muttering continued to the end.

Robert Fagles

Fagles's mumbling had a purpose—he was trying to capture the oral quality of Homer's language. Homer's poetry, Fagles says, was intended to be recited before spellbound listeners: "These poems weren't meant as literature or words on a page to be read, but as a song in the air." According to Fagles, the oral tradition that gave birth to Homer's epics helps to explain what the poet Matthew Arnold called the "speed, directness, and simplicity" of their language.

Another translator, Robert Fitzgerald, focused more on the literary aspects of Homer's poetry. Read the following translations of the passage about Hector's death to see the differences between the two versions.

Fagles

Death cut him short. The end closed in
   around him.
Flying free of his limbs
his soul went winging down to the House
   of Death,
wailing his fate, leaving his manhood far behind,
his young and supple strength.

> Fagles begins with short sentences, which create emphasis when read aloud.

> The line that begins "Flying free" is the start of one long sentence. Note how this sentence is broken into short phrases.

Fitzgerald

Even as he spoke, the end came, and death
   hid him;
spirit from body fluttered to undergloom,
bewailing fate that made him leave his youth
and manhood in the world.

> Fitzgerald uses one long sentence.

> Notice the made-up word *undergloom.*

Questions to Consider

1. How would you describe the differences between the two translations?

2. Which translation do you think would be more effective when read aloud? Why?

POEMS BY
SAPPHO

Sappho
c. 630–580 B.C.

Greatest Female Poet

Sappho (săf'ō) is generally considered the greatest woman poet of the ancient world. Her image was stamped on coins and memorialized in statues and on vases. By the Middle Ages, however, all that survived of her work was quotations by other authors. Only two complete poems were preserved.

Celebrity of Her Era Most of what we know of Sappho's life comes through the writings of others. It is said that she was born into a wealthy family and was married to a prosperous businessman with whom she had had one daughter. While still in her youth, she became something of a celebrity, as much for her dynamic personality as for her poetry. It is likely that she was a central figure in a group of aristocratic women dedicated to the cultivation of poetry and the arts.

Freedom and Refinement Sappho lived more than a century after Homer, during a period of Greek culture marked by increased literacy, luxury, and leisure time. Prominent among the cultural centers of the time was the beautiful island of Lesbos, where Sappho spent most of her life. Located in the Aegean Sea off the coast of Asia Minor, Lesbos was unique in the ancient world for allowing women considerable freedom and social standing.

Personal Poetry Sappho often wrote about intensely personal subjects, such as her close friendships with other women and her relationship with her daughter. Because many of her poems appear to have been about love and several mention Aphrodite, the goddess of love, some people believe that she may have been the leader of a religious cult dedicated to Aphrodite. Others believe that she was simply following the poetic fashions of her time.

Connect to Your Life

The three poems you are about to read deal with forms of beauty, from the beauty of a beloved person to the beauty of nature. In the first poem, the speaker gives her opinion about "the most beautiful of sights the dark earth offers." In your judgment, what are some of the most beautiful sights in the world? What do your choices reveal about the kinds of things you value and appreciate?

Focus Your Reading

LITERARY ANALYSIS: LYRIC POETRY

A **lyric poem** is a short poem in which a speaker expresses personal thoughts and feelings. Sappho's lyrics are notable for their simple language and their expression of strong emotion, as in these lines:

> *. . . . If I meet*
> *you suddenly, I can't*
> *speak—my tongue is broken;*

As you read the following poems, try to form an impression of the speaker of each poem and to identify the feelings expressed.

ACTIVE READING: CLARIFYING

When you are studying poetry, it's important to reread to **clarify** your understanding. During the process of rereading, your appreciation of a poem may change and develop.

 **READER'S NOTEBOOK** As you read each poem, jot down what you learn about the speaker and the situation described. Also list any questions that come to mind. Then reread the poem to try to answer the questions and add to your understanding.

"Some say thronging cavalry . . ."

Speaker misses friend, Anactória

Build Background

Lyric Poetry By Sappho's time, the Homeric epic had given way to a shorter, more personal form of poetry called the lyric. Lyric poets customarily performed with musicians and dancers at festivals, weddings, and other gatherings. Although Sappho wasn't the first lyric poet, she raised the form to a high art.

The three poems you will read are typical of Sappho's poetry. "Some say thronging cavalry . . ." laments the absence of a woman named Anactória, who may have been a close friend of Sappho's. "He Is More Than a Hero" may be addressed to another close female friend, though no name is given. "To Aphrodite of the Flowers, at Knossos" is addressed to the goddess of love.

Recovery of Sapphic Fragments Since around 1900, archaeological digs in Egypt have unearthed fragments of ancient manuscripts of Sappho's poems. Most of the manuscripts had been ripped into strips and used to wrap mummies. In general, these discoveries have yielded only disconnected bits of Sappho's poetry—groups of words that seem to celebrate love, beauty, nature, and the goddess Aphrodite. Still, they give us a fascinating glimpse into the mind of this highly regarded poet.

Some say thronging cavalry . . .

Sappho

Translated by Jim Powell

Some say thronging cavalry, some say foot soldiers,
others call a fleet the most beautiful of
sights the dark earth offers, but I say it's what-
       ever you love best.

5 And it's easy to make this understood by
everyone, for she who surpassed all human
kind in beauty, Helen, abandoning her
       husband—that best of

men—went sailing off to the shores of Troy and
10 never spent a thought on her child or loving
parents: when the goddess seduced her wits and
       left her to wander,

she forgot them all, she could not remember
anything but longing, and lightly straying
15 aside, lost her way. But that reminds me
       now: Anactória,

she's not here, and I'd rather see her lovely
step, her sparkling glance and her face than gaze on
all the troops in Lydia in their chariots and
20   glittering armor.

Greek sculpture of a maenad (late fifth century B.C.). Marble, 56⅜″ (1.43 m). The Metropolitan Museum of Art, New York.

1 thronging cavalry: a large gathering of soldiers on horseback.

16 Anactória (ăn′ək-tôr′ē-ə): one of Sappho's friends, who had married and moved away.

19 Lydia (lĭd′ē-ə): a kingdom on the mainland of Asia Minor near Lesbos.

He Is More Than a Hero

Sappho

Translated by Mary Barnard

He is a god in my eyes—
the man who is allowed
to sit beside you—he

who listens intimately
5 to the sweet murmur of
your voice, the enticing

laughter that makes my own
heart beat fast. If I meet
you suddenly, I can't

10 speak—my tongue is broken;
a thin flame runs under
my skin; seeing nothing,

hearing only my own ears
drumming, I drip with sweat;
15 trembling shakes my body

and I turn paler than
dry grass. At such times
death isn't far from me

6 enticing: attractive; arousing desire.

To Aphrodite of the Flowers, at Knossos

Sappho

Translated by Willis Barnstone

Leave Krete and come to this holy temple
where the graceful grove of apple trees
circles an altar smoking with frank-
    incense.

5 Here roses leave shadow on the ground
and cold springs babble through apple branches
where shuddering leaves pour down pro-
    found sleep.

In our meadow where horses graze
10 and wild flowers of spring blossom,
anise shoots fill the air with a-
    roma.

And here, Queen Aphrodite, pour
heavenly nectar into gold cups
15 and fill them gracefully with sud-
    den joy.

1 Krete (krēt): Crete—a large island south of mainland Greece, site of the city of Knossos.

3–4 frankincense: a sweet-smelling tree resin burned as incense.

11 anise (ăn′ĭs): a fragrant herb.

Connect to the Literature

1. **What Do You Think?** Of the three poems, which do you think you understand best? Explain your reasons.

Think Critically

2. **ACTIVE READING: CLARIFYING** Look back at the comments and questions that you wrote in your **READER'S NOTEBOOK**. Which questions were you able to answer? How? Discuss any unanswered questions with your classmates.

3. In each poem the **speaker** describes a person, situation, or **setting.** In your own words, explain what the speaker is describing in each case.

> **THINK ABOUT**
> - why thinking about Helen of Troy makes the speaker think of Anactória's absence in "Some say thronging cavalry . . ."
> - how the speaker feels about the person spoken to in "He Is More Than a Hero"
> - the **setting** described in "To Aphrodite . . ."

4. On the basis of the three poems you have read, decide which two of the following statements best apply to Sappho. Use evidence from the poems to support your choices.

   She views life as a bitter struggle.

   She values intimate moments of friendship.

   She criticizes her culture's emphasis on beauty.

   She appreciates the beauty of nature.

Extend Interpretation

5. **Critic's Corner** The literary historian Peter Levi has described Sappho's poetry as "full of a pure, natural sweetness, and full of longing." Do you think his comment applies to any of these three poems? Explain why or why not.

6. **Connect to Life** If Sappho's poems were to be set to music today, what contemporary singer do you think would do them justice? Explain your choice.

LITERARY ANALYSIS: LYRIC POETRY

The ancient Greeks are credited with inventing lyric poetry. This form of poetry owes its name to the lyre (līr), a small harp that was used to accompany the recital or singing of poetry. Some lyrics, such as "He Is More Than a Hero," offer reflections on love and friendship. Others, such as "To Aphrodite of the Flowers, at Knossos," deal with reactions to nature. Today, any short poem in which a single speaker expresses his or her innermost thoughts and feelings is called a **lyric poem.**

Paired Activity Work with a partner to fill out a chart like the one shown. First, create a list of phrases or adjectives that describe the speaker of each poem. Then write phrases or sentences that tell what's important to the speaker.

Poem	Phrases That Describe Speaker	What Is Important to Speaker
"Some say thronging"		
"He Is More Than a Hero"		
"To Aphrodite"		

from HISTORY OF THE PELOPONNESIAN WAR

PERICLES' FUNERAL ORATION

THUCYDIDES

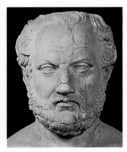

Thucydides
c. 460–404 B.C.

A Citizen Disgraced One of the great historians of the ancient world, Thucydides (thōō-sĭd′ĭ-dēz′) turned to writing only after he was disgraced in his native Athens. The great event of his lifetime was the bitter 27-year-long Peloponnesian War between Athens and Sparta. In 424 B.C., the citizens of Athens selected Thucydides as one of the ten *strategoi* (strə-tē′goi), or military leaders, of the city. Because of his rank and influence, he was given command of an Athenian fleet. However, when he failed to prevent the Spartans from capturing an important port city, he was recalled to Athens, put on trial, and exiled from his native city.

History for the Ages Thucydides turned his misfortune into an opportunity to work on the *History of the Peloponnesian War.* He wanted to provide a complete account of the war so that future generations could understand the events and their causes. To be as accurate and fair as possible, he traveled throughout the Peloponnesus (the peninsula forming the southern part of Greece), interviewing the Spartans and their allies.

In writing his history, Thucydides offered his own theories about how states interact with one another.

For example, he argued that interactions between states are fundamentally immoral, no matter how just each state may be toward its own citizens: "The strong do what they have the power to do and the weak accept what they have to accept." His keen insights into the nature of international relations continue to influence scholars and political leaders today.

Mysterious Death Thucydides was allowed to return to Athens after the final defeat of the city in 404 B.C. He probably died only a few years later—perhaps violently during the political turmoil of the time. He left the *History of the Peloponnesian War* unfinished; its account abruptly stops about seven years before the war's end.

Athens	v.	Sparta
Strong navy. Located near the Aegean, Athens developed a powerful navy.		**Strong army.** Landlocked and isolated by mountains, Sparta depended on its army.
Democracy. Citizens were encouraged to participate.		**Oligarchy.** Governed by a small group of rulers.
Education for citizens. Tutors and professional teachers educated male citizens.		**Military training.** Males taken from home at age 7 and educated in strict military school.
Artistic. Great achievements in poetry, drama, history, painting, philosophy, architecture.		**Athletic.** Spartan athletes won many first prizes at the Olympic Games.

Build Background

Who Was Pericles?

In writing his history, Thucydides recreated many important speeches. To do so, he relied on notes that he compiled from interviews as well as his own memory. Thucydides was probably in attendance early in 430 B.C. when Pericles (pĕr'ĭ-klēz') gave his funeral **oration,** or formal speech, to honor the Athenian warriors who had been killed during the first year of the Peloponnesian War.

Like Thucydides, Pericles served as one of Athens' *strategoi.* More importantly, he was the greatest Athenian politician of his time, greatly respected for his wisdom, leadership, and virtue. So influential was he that historians have named the middle decades of the 400s the Age of Pericles. This period saw many of Athens' greatest achievements in art and culture, including the building of the Parthenon.

The Achievements of Pericles

- Enabled common people to hold any state office by having salaries paid to public officials
- Built up navy and expanded Athenian empire throughout the Mediterranean world
- Beautified Athens by spending city's fortune to build huge temples—including the Parthenon—and other public buildings
- Supported drama and other arts, personally financing a production by the playwright Aeschylus

Connect to Your Life

What comes to mind when you hear the word *patriotism*? Do you think that citizens should always try to feel love and devotion for their country? For five minutes, do some focused freewriting on what patriotism means to you.

Focus Your Reading

LITERARY ANALYSIS: AUTHOR'S PURPOSE
Authors and speakers communicate for various purposes: to inform, to express opinions, to entertain, to persuade. Near the beginning of his speech, Pericles announces his purposes:

> *What I want to do is . . . to discuss the spirit in which we faced our trials and also our constitution and the way of life which has made us great. After that I shall speak in praise of the dead. . . .*

As you read, think about whether Pericles is convincing in his praise of Athens and of the soldiers who sacrificed their lives for their homeland.

ACTIVE READING: MAIN IDEA
To achieve his purposes, Pericles develops a number of ideas. Almost every paragraph sets forth a single main idea, which is then supported by details and examples. Sometimes, the main idea is clearly stated at the beginning of the paragraph, as in the second paragraph:

> *I shall begin by speaking about our ancestors, since it is only right . . . to pay them the honor of recalling what they did.*

In other paragraphs, the main idea may not come until later.

READER'S NOTEBOOK As you read, look for the main ideas expressed about Athens and the soldiers who died. Starting with the sixth paragraph of the speech, on page 236, record the main idea of each paragraph.

WORDS TO KNOW **Vocabulary Preview**

abiding	incredulous	revelation	undeterred
culmination	relinquish	tangible	versatility
incompatibility	reproach		

from History of the Peloponnesian War

Pericles' Funeral Oration

Thucydides

Translated by Rex Warner

In the same winter the Athenians, following their annual custom, gave a public funeral for those who had been the first to die in the war. These funerals are held in the following way: two days before the ceremony the bones of the fallen are brought and put in a tent which has been erected, and people make whatever offerings they wish to their own dead. Then there is a funeral procession in which coffins of cypress wood are carried on wagons. There is one coffin for each tribe, which contains the bones of members of that tribe. One empty bier[1] is decorated and carried in the procession: this is for the missing, whose bodies could not be recovered. Everyone who wishes to, both citizens and foreigners, can join in the procession, and the women who are related to the dead are there to make their laments at the tomb. The bones are laid in the public burial-place, which is in the most beautiful quarter outside the city walls. Here the Athenians always bury those who have fallen in war. The only exception is those who died at Marathon,[2] who, because their achievement was considered absolutely outstanding, were buried on the battlefield itself.

When the bones have been laid in the earth, a man chosen by the city for his intellectual gifts and for his general reputation makes an appropriate speech in praise of the dead, and after the speech all depart. This is the procedure at these burials, and all through the war, when the time came to do so, the Athenians followed this ancient custom. Now, at the burial of those who were the first to fall in the war Pericles, the son of Xanthippus,[3] was chosen to make the speech. When the moment arrived, he came forward from the tomb and, standing on a high platform, so that he might be heard by as many people as possible in the crowd, he spoke as follows:

"Many of those who have spoken here in the past have praised the institution of this speech at the close of our ceremony. It seemed to them a mark of honor to our soldiers who have fallen in

---

1. **bier** (bēr): a platform for laying out a corpse.
2. **Marathon:** the site of a famous Greek victory over the Persians in 490 B.C.
3. **Xanthippus** (zăn-thĭp′əs): a famous Athenian military commander.

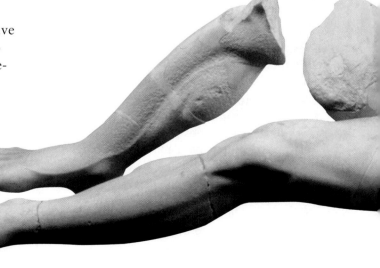

war that a speech should be made over them. I do not agree. These men have shown themselves valiant in action, and it would be enough, I think, for their glories to be proclaimed in action, as you have just seen it done at this funeral organized by the state. Our belief in the courage and manliness of so many should not be hazarded on the goodness or badness of one man's speech. Then it is not easy to speak with a proper sense of balance, when a man's listeners find it difficult to believe in the truth of what one is saying. The man who knows the facts and loves the dead may well think that an oration tells less than what he knows and what he would like to hear: others who do not know so much may feel envy for the dead, and think the orator over-praises them, when he speaks of exploits that are beyond their own capacities. Praise of other people is tolerable only up to a certain point, the point where one still believes that one could do oneself some of

the things one is hearing about. Once you get beyond this point, you will find people becoming jealous and <u>incredulous</u>. However, the fact is that this institution was set up and approved by our forefathers, and it is my duty to follow the tradition and do my best to meet the wishes and the expectations of every one of you.

"I shall begin by speaking about our ancestors, since it is only right and proper on such an occasion to pay them the honor of recalling what they did. In this land of ours there have always been the same people living from generation to generation up till now, and they, by their courage and their virtues, have handed it on

Fallen warrior. Glyptothek, Munich, Germany. Photography by Koppermann.

WORDS TO KNOW
incredulous (ĭn-krĕj′ə-ləs) *adj.* unwilling to believe; skeptical

PERICLES' FUNERAL ORATION   **235**

> **Our constitution is called a democracy because power is in the hands not of a minority but of the whole people.**

to us, a free country. They certainly deserve our praise. Even more so do our fathers deserve it. For to the inheritance they had received they added all the empire we have now, and it was not without blood and toil that they handed it down to us of the present generation. And then we ourselves, assembled here today, who are mostly in the prime of life, have, in most directions, added to the power of our empire and have organized our State in such a way that it is perfectly well able to look after itself both in peace and in war.

"I have no wish to make a long speech on subjects familiar to you all: so I shall say nothing about the warlike deeds by which we acquired our power or the battles in which we or our fathers gallantly resisted our enemies, Greek or foreign. What I want to do is, in the first place, to discuss the spirit in which we faced our trials and also our constitution and the way of life which has made us great. After that I shall speak in praise of the dead, believing that this kind of speech is not inappropriate to the present occasion, and that this whole assembly, of citizens and foreigners, may listen to it with advantage.

"Let me say that our system of government does not copy the institutions of our neighbors. It is more the case of our being a model to others, than of our imitating anyone else. Our constitution is called a democracy because power is in the hands not of a minority but of the whole people. When it is a question of settling private disputes, everyone is equal before the law; when it is a question of putting one person before another in positions of public responsibility, what counts is not membership of a particular class, but the actual ability which the man possesses. No one, so long as he has it in him to be of service to the state, is kept in political obscurity because of poverty. And, just as our political life is free and open, so is our day-to-day life in our relations with each other. We do not get into a state with our next-door neighbor if he enjoys himself in his own way, nor do we give him the kind of black looks which, though they do no real harm, still do hurt people's feelings. We are free and tolerant in our private lives; but in public affairs we keep to the law. This is because it commands our deep respect.

"We give our obedience to those whom we put in positions of authority, and we obey the laws themselves, especially those which are for the protection of the oppressed, and those unwritten laws[4] which it is an acknowledged shame to break.

"And here is another point. When our work is over, we are in a position to enjoy all kinds of recreation for our spirits. There are various kinds of contests and sacrifices regularly throughout the year; in our own homes we find a beauty and a good taste which delight us every day and which drive away our cares. Then the greatness of our city brings it about that all the good things from all over the world flow in to us, so that to us it seems just as natural to enjoy foreign goods as our own local products.

---

4. **unwritten laws:** customs.

"Then there is a great difference between us and our opponents, in our attitude towards military security. Here are some examples: Our city is open to the world, and we have no periodical deportations[5] in order to prevent people observing or finding out secrets which might be of military advantage to the enemy. This is because we rely, not on secret weapons, but on our own real courage and loyalty. There is a difference, too, in our educational systems. The Spartans, from their earliest boyhood, are submitted to the most laborious training in courage; we pass our lives without all these restrictions, and yet are just as ready to face the same dangers as they are. Here is a proof of this: When the Spartans invade our land, they do not come by themselves, but bring all their allies with them; whereas we, when we launch an attack abroad, do the job by ourselves, and, though fighting on foreign soil, do not often fail to defeat opponents who are fighting for their own hearths and homes. As a matter of fact none of our enemies has ever yet been confronted with our total strength, because we have to divide our attention between our navy and the many missions on which our troops are sent on land. Yet, if our enemies engage a detachment[6] of our forces and defeat it, they give themselves credit for having thrown back our entire army; or, if they lose, they claim that they were beaten by us in full strength. There are certain advantages, I think, in our way of meeting danger voluntarily, with an easy mind, instead of with a laborious training, with natural rather than with state-induced courage. We do not have to spend our time practicing to meet sufferings which are still in the future; and when they are actually upon us we show ourselves just as brave as these others who are always in strict training. This is one point in which, I think, our city deserves to be admired. There are also others:

"Our love of what is beautiful does not lead

Bust of Pericles (c. 425 B.C.) Marble, 18⅞″. Copyright © The British Museum.

to extravagance; our love of the things of the mind does not make us soft. We regard wealth as something to be properly used, rather than as something to boast about. As for poverty, no one need be ashamed to admit it: the real shame is in not taking practical measures to escape from it. Here each individual is interested not only in his own affairs but in the affairs of the state as well: even those who are mostly occupied with their own business are extremely well-informed on general politics—this is a peculiarity of ours: we

---

5. **deportations:** expulsions of noncitizens.
6. **engage a detachment:** fight a single unit.

Partial view of the Parthenon, Athens, Greece

do not say that a man who takes no interest in politics is a man who minds his own business; we say that he has no business here at all. We Athenians, in our own persons, take our decisions on policy or submit them to proper discussions: for we do not think that there is an incompatibility between words and deeds; the worst thing is to rush into action before the consequences have been properly debated. And this is another point where we differ from other people. We are capable at the same time of taking risks and of estimating them beforehand. Others are brave out of ignorance; and, when they stop to think, they begin to fear. But the man who can most truly be accounted brave is he who best knows the meaning of what is sweet in life and of what is terrible, and then goes out <u>undeterred</u> to meet what is to come.

"Again, in questions of general good feeling there is a great contrast between us and most other people. We make friends by doing good to others, not by receiving good from them. This makes our friendship all the more reliable, since we want to keep alive the gratitude of those who are in our debt by showing continued goodwill to them: whereas the feelings of one who owes us something lack the same enthusiasm, since he knows that, when he repays our kindness, it will be more like paying back a debt than giving something spontaneously. We are

WORDS TO KNOW

incompatibility (ĭn′kəm-păt′ə-bĭl′ĭ-tē) *n.* a lack of harmony; conflict
undeterred (ŭn′dĭ-tûrd′) *adj.* not discouraged

unique in this. When we do kindnesses to others, we do not do them out of any calculations of profit or loss: we do them without afterthought, relying on our free liberality.[7] Taking everything together then, I declare that our city is an education to Greece, and I declare that in my opinion each single one of our citizens, in all the manifold aspects of life, is able to show himself the rightful lord and owner of his own person, and do this, moreover, with exceptional grace and exceptional <u>versatility</u>. And to show that this is no empty boasting for the present occasion, but real <u>tangible</u> fact, you have only to consider the power which our city possesses and which has been won by those very qualities which I have mentioned. Athens, alone of the states we know, comes to her testing time in a greatness that surpasses what was imagined of her. In her case, and in her case alone, no invading enemy is ashamed at being defeated, and no subject can complain of being governed by people unfit for their responsibilities. Mighty indeed are the marks and monuments of our empire which we have left. Future ages will wonder at us, as the present age wonders at us now. We do not need the praises of a Homer, or of anyone else whose words may delight us for the moment, but whose estimation of facts will fall short of what is really true. For our adventurous spirit has forced an entry into every sea and into every land; and everywhere we have left behind us everlasting memorials of good done to our friends or suffering inflicted on our enemies.

"This, then, is the kind of city for which these men, who could not bear the thought of losing her, nobly fought and nobly died. It is only natural that every one of us who survive them should be willing to undergo hardships in her service. And it was for this reason that I have spoken at such length about our city, because I wanted to

> **Mighty indeed are the marks and monuments of our empire which we have left. Future ages will wonder at us, as the present age wonders at us now.**

make it clear that for us there is more at stake than there is for others who lack our advantages; also I wanted my words of praise for the dead to be set in the bright light of evidence. And now the most important of these words has been spoken. I have sung the praises of our city; but it was the courage and gallantry of these men, and of people like them, which made her splendid. Nor would you find it true in the case of many of the Greeks, as it is true of them, that no words can do more than justice to their deeds.

"To me it seems that the <u>consummation</u>[8] which has overtaken these men shows us the meaning of manliness in its first <u>revelation</u> and in its final proof. Some of them, no doubt, had their faults; but what we ought to remember first is their gallant conduct against the enemy in

---

7. **liberality:** generosity.
8. **consummation:** end.

WORDS TO KNOW

versatility (vûr′sə-tĭl′ĭ-tē) *n.* an ability to do many things well
tangible (tăn′jə-bəl) *adj.* capable of being felt or perceived; concrete
revelation (rĕv′ə-lā′shən) *n.* a making known; exposure

PERICLES' FUNERAL ORATION   **239**

defense of their native land. They have blotted out evil with good, and done more service to the commonwealth than they ever did harm in their private lives. No one of these men weakened because he wanted to go on enjoying his wealth: no one put off the awful day in the hope that he might live to escape his poverty and grow rich. More to be desired than such things, they chose to check the enemy's pride. This, to them, was a risk most glorious, and they accepted it, willing to strike down the enemy and relinquish everything else. As for success or failure, they left that in the doubtful hands of Hope, and when the reality of battle was before their faces, they put their trust in their own selves. In the fighting, they thought it more honorable to stand their ground and suffer death than to give in and save their lives. So they fled from the reproaches of men, abiding with life and limb the brunt of battle; and, in a small moment of time, the climax of their lives, a culmination of glory, not of fear, were swept away from us.

"So and such they were, these men—worthy of their city. We who remain behind may hope to be spared their fate, but must resolve to keep the same daring spirit against the foe. It is not simply a question of estimating the advantages in theory. I could tell you a long story (and you know it as well as I do) about what is to be gained by beating the enemy back. What I would prefer is that you should fix your eyes every day on the greatness of Athens as she really is, and should fall in love with her. When you realize her greatness, then reflect that what made her great was men with a spirit of adventure, men who knew their duty, men who were ashamed to fall below a certain standard. If they ever failed in an enterprise, they made up their minds that at any rate the city should not find their courage lacking to her, and they gave to her the best

> **They have blotted out evil with good, and done more service to the commonwealth than they ever did harm in their private lives.**

contribution that they could. They gave her their lives, to her and to all of us, and for their own selves they won praises that never grow old, the most splendid of sepulchers—not the sepulcher in which their bodies are laid, but where their glory remains eternal in men's minds, always there on the right occasion to stir others to speech or to action. For famous men have the whole earth as their memorial: it is not only the inscriptions on their graves in their own country that mark them out; no, in foreign lands also, not in any visible form but in people's hearts, their memory abides and grows. It is for you to try to be like them. Make up your minds that happiness depends on being free, and freedom depends on being courageous. Let there be no relaxation in face of the perils of the war. The people who have most excuse for despising death are not the wretched and unfortunate, who have no hope of doing well for themselves, but those who run the risk of a complete reversal in their lives, and who would feel the difference most

WORDS TO KNOW

relinquish (rĭ-lĭng′kwĭsh) *v.* to give up; hand over
reproach (rĭ-prōch′) *n.* blame; criticism
abiding (ə-bī′dĭng) *adj.* enduring **abide** *v.*
culmination (kŭl′mə-nā′shən) *n.* a high point or climax

Athenians voting. Kunsthistorisches Museum, Vienna, Austria.

intensely, if things went wrong for them. Any intelligent man would find a humiliation caused by his own slackness more painful to bear than death, when death comes to him unperceived, in battle, and in the confidence of his patriotism.

"For these reasons I shall not commiserate with those parents of the dead, who are present here. Instead I shall try to comfort them. They are well aware that they have grown up in a world where there are many changes and chances. But this is good fortune—for men to end their lives with honor, as these have done, and for you honorably to lament them: their life was set to a measure where death and happiness went hand in hand. I know that it is difficult to convince you of this. When you see other people happy you will often be reminded of what used to make you happy too. One does not feel sad at not having some good thing which is outside

one's experience: real grief is felt at the loss of something which one is used to. All the same, those of you who are of the right age must bear up and take comfort in the thought of having more children. In your own homes these new children will prevent you from brooding over those who are no more, and they will be a help to the city, too, both in filling the empty places, and in assuring her security. For it is impossible for a man to put forward fair and honest views about our affairs if he has not, like everyone else, children whose lives may be at stake. As for those of you who are now too old to have children, I would ask you to count as gain the greater part of your life, in which you have been happy, and remember that what remains is not long, and let your hearts be lifted up at the thought of the fair fame of the dead. One's sense of honor is the only thing that does not grow old, and the last pleasure, when one is worn out with age, is not, as the poet said, making money, but having the respect of one's fellow men.

"As for those of you here who are sons or brothers of the dead, I can see a hard struggle in front of you. Everyone always speaks well of the dead, and, even if you rise to the greatest heights of heroism, it will be a hard thing for you to get the reputation of having come near, let alone equaled, their standard. When one is alive, one is always liable to the jealousy of one's competitors, but when one is out of the way, the honor one receives is sincere and unchallenged.

"Perhaps I should say a word or two on the duties of women to those among you who are now widowed. I can say all I have to say in a short word of advice. Your great glory is not to be inferior to what God has made you, and the greatest glory of a woman is to be least talked about by men, whether they are praising you or criticizing you. I have now, as the law demanded, said what I had to say. For the time being our offerings to the dead have been made, and for the future their children will be supported at the public expense by the city, until they come of age. This is the crown and prize which she offers, both to the dead and to their children, for the ordeals which they have faced. Where the rewards of valor are the greatest, there you will find also the best and bravest spirits among the people. And now, when you have mourned for your dear ones, you must depart." ❖

Thinking through the LITERATURE

Connect to the Literature

1. What Do You Think?
From your reading of the speech, what is your impression of Pericles? What details in the speech influenced your impression?

Comprehension Check
- According to Pericles, who has political power in Athens: a single person, a small group, or all the people?
- Who trains more rigorously for war, Athenians or Spartans?
- Which of these words describe the Athenians: thrifty, adventurous, generous, careless?

Think Critically

2. ACTIVE READING: MAIN IDEA Compare your
 READER'S NOTEBOOK record of Pericles' main ideas with a partner's. What do you think are his most important ideas about Athens and the soldiers who died?

3. Pericles takes great pride in the democracy of Athens. Why is it important to him that all citizens participate in public life? Use details from the speech to support your conclusion.

4. Pericles says that Athens "deserves to be admired" for its approach to military security. Do you think he makes a convincing case? Explain why or why not.

> **THINK ABOUT**
> - his description of how the Spartans train for war
> - his comment about the Spartans' use of allies
> - the distinction he draws between "natural" and "state-induced" courage

5. Pericles asks his audience to "fix your eyes every day on the greatness of Athens" and to "fall in love with her." Why does Pericles think Athens is deserving of love? Use details from the text to support your response.

6. The soldiers who died, Pericles says, "won praises that never grow old." What do his comments reveal about the Athenians' view of honor?

Extend Interpretations

7. Comparing Texts Both Homer and Pericles celebrate military virtues, such as courage and honor. Discuss how Achilles' heroism compares with that of the Athenian soldiers memorialized by Pericles.

8. Connect to Life Do you think that Pericles' patriotism is still relevant today? Explain why or why not.

LITERARY ANALYSIS: AUTHOR'S PURPOSE

The most common purposes for writing or public speaking are to entertain, to inform or explain, to express an opinion, and to persuade. For example, a politician might give a speech to persuade people about an issue. A magazine writer might inform people about the same issue without taking a stand. Pericles announces his purposes on page 236, with the sentence that begins "What I want to do . . ."

Paired Activity Working with a partner, evaluate the success of Pericles' speech in fulfilling its purposes. Complete a chart like the one shown, giving a grade of 1 to 5 (with 1 being the lowest grade) for each purpose and explaining your reason.

Purpose	Success of Speech	
	Grade	Reason
To discuss the spirit of Athenians in facing trials		
To discuss Athens' constitution and the way of life that makes it great		
To speak in praise of the dead		

Writing Options

1. Extended Definition Write an extended definition of *patriotism* based on Pericles' speech. First, find passages of the speech that show how he feels about Athens. Then arrange the passages into categories, like "Respect for Homeland's Ideals." Structure your writing by devoting a paragraph to each category.

2. Analysis of Women's Role Write an analysis of the role of women in Athenian society. First review the speech to find all of the references to women. Then draw conclusions about how women lived and what was expected of them. In your writing, use quotations from the speech.

Writing Handbook
See page R33: Analysis.

Activities & Explorations

Athens vs. Sparta Debate With the class divided into two teams, debate the following question: Which city-state, Athens or Sparta, provides a better model for the way the United States should prepare for military conflict? Use examples from the speech to support your position. ~ **SPEAKING AND LISTENING**

Communication Handbook
See page R49: Critical Thinking.

Inquiry & Research

Legacy of Pericles Find out more about the life and achievements of Pericles. In your judgment, was Pericles a true hero? Give an oral report in which you share the results of your research, along with your evaluation of the man's character.

RESEARCH STARTER
CLASSZONE.COM

Vocabulary in Action

EXERCISE: MEANING CLUES Choose the discussion topic in which each word would most likely be used.

1. **incredulous:** (a) a report that a spacecraft has landed downtown, (b) an apple tree flowering in the spring, (c) a family visiting relatives in another state

2. **abiding:** (a) a village marketplace, (b) a house where a family has lived for 50 years, (c) a car with a new paint job

3. **relinquish:** (a) a lost wallet handed over to the police, (b) a party attended by 30 guests, (c) an old-fashioned pocket watch found in an attic

4. **versatility:** (a) a beach crowded with swimmers, (b) a comedian who also sings and dances, (c) a left-handed person

5. **culmination:** (a) a collection of stamps, (b) a steep descent into a mountain valley, (c) a high-school graduation

6. **incompatibility:** (a) a married couple struggling to get along with one another, (b) a large, hard-to-service appliance, (c) a child afraid to sleep without a night light

7. **reproach:** (a) a cornfield buried in heavy snow, (b) a mother lecturing a disobedient child, (c) the building of a new road between towns

8. **revelation:** (a) a friend too busy to stay in touch, (b) a victory parade, (c) the reading of a long-lost relative's will

9. **tangible:** (a) light, puffy clouds, (b) firm evidence connecting a suspect to a crime, (c) four strong riders on a bicycle team

10. **undeterred:** (a) a driver sitting impatiently in rush-hour traffic, (b) a light breeze rustling through the trees, (c) a climber who reaches the top of a mountain

Building Vocabulary

A number of Words to Know in this lesson contain prefixes and suffixes. For an in-depth lesson on affixes, see page 864.

Nelson Mandela Celebrates a National Hero

Like Pericles, modern political leaders are sometimes called upon to honor those who have died for their country or ideals. In 1977 a famous political prisoner, Stephen Biko, died in a South African prison. Biko was a leader in the fight against apartheid, a government policy of racial segregation that discriminated against nonwhites. Later investigations revealed that Biko had been beaten to death by police officers.

Stephen Biko

In September 1997, Nelson Mandela, then the president of South Africa, gave a speech to pay tribute to Biko. As you read the following excerpts from his speech, look for similarities to Pericles' funeral oration.

> *We are gathered here to pay homage to one of the greatest sons of our nation, Stephen Bantu Biko. His hope in life, and his life of hope, are captured by his resounding words: "In time, we shall be in a position to bestow on South Africa the greatest possible gift—a more human face." . . .*
>
> *Today's occasion speaks of our resolve to preserve the memories of our heroes and heroines; to keep alive the flame of patriotism which burnt in the hearts and minds of the like of Steve Biko; to redeem the pledge to give a more human face to a society for centuries trampled upon by the jackboot of inhumanity. . . .*
>
> *History called upon Steve Biko at a time when the political pulse of our people had been rendered faint by banning, imprisonment, exile, murder and banishment. . . .*
>
> *It is the dictate of history to bring to the fore the kind of leaders who seize the moment, who cohere the wishes and aspirations of the oppressed. Such was Steve Biko, a fitting product of his time; a proud representative of the re-awakening of a people. . . .*
>
> *In time, we must bestow on South Africa the greatest gift—a more humane society.*
>
> *We are confident that by forging a new and prosperous nation, we are continuing the fight in which Steve Biko paid the supreme sacrifice.*

Nelson Mandela (center) with Stephen Biko's sons

Discussion

1. What does Stephen Biko have in common with the Athenian soldiers praised by Pericles? Use quotations from both speeches to support your response.

2. Why was it important to Mandela to keep alive the memory of Biko? What did Mandela hope to accomplish for his country?

from the

APOLOGY

P L A T O

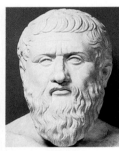

Plato
c. 427–347 B.C.

Influential Philosopher

Many regard Plato as the most influential philosopher in the history of the Western world. Most of what we know about Plato comes from his own writings. He was born, probably in Athens, to a high-ranking family. In his youth, he wrote poetry and reportedly was a champion wrestler. His life took an abrupt turn, however, when he became a devoted follower of Socrates.

Plato's Teacher, Socrates At this time, Socrates was an odd character—a poor old man who refused to wear shoes and who walked the streets of Athens in a shabby cloak. Socrates loved to engage people in philosophical conversations. Through a series of questions, he would lead people to examine their own thinking about concepts such as virtue, justice, and truth—a technique that became known as the Socratic method. Though Socrates was popular with the young, some Athenians viewed him as a threat to Athenian traditions and ideals. In 399 B.C., a group of citizens came together to prosecute him, charging him with neglecting the gods of Athens and corrupting its youth.

The Academy Socrates' conviction and execution for these "crimes" deeply affected Plato. He concluded that if humans were ever to rise above their narrow self-interest, they needed to be educated in philosophy. Around 387 B.C., Plato established a school, the Academy, where he invited only those individuals who were, in his words, "intoxicated to learn what was in their souls." The Academy—which some have called the first university of Europe—was actually a park, with groves of beautiful trees, running tracks, and shady walks, where students and teachers gathered to discuss ideas.

Plato's Legacy The Academy survived as a cultural institution for hundreds of years after Plato's death. In addition to influencing the development of mathematics, astronomy, philosophy, law, and political science, Plato's ideas have had a major impact on Jewish, Christian, and Islamic thought.

Other Works
Republic
Crito
Phaedo
Symposium

Connect to Your Life

In his speeches to the jury, Socrates refuses to compromise his principles, even though he knows his life is at stake. What is your attitude toward people who refuse to compromise their principles?

Focus Your Reading

LITERARY ANALYSIS: SPEECH

Most of Plato's works are **dialogues,** representations of conversations between two or more people. The *Apology,* however, consists of Socrates' speeches to the jury at his trial. You are about to read his concluding **speech,** or public talk, which takes place just after the jury has announced his death sentence. As you read, pay attention to how Socrates presents himself and to how he views the two sides of the jury—those who voted for his death and those who did not.

ACTIVE READING: PARAPHRASING

When you read a challenging work, such as this speech, it is often helpful to **paraphrase** passages, restating them in your own words. When you paraphrase, you try to express the author's meaning in a simpler way. The following passage is important for an understanding of Socrates' position:

> *But I suggest, gentlemen, that the difficulty is not so much to escape death; the real difficulty is to escape from doing wrong, which is far more fleet of foot.*

This passage may be paraphrased as follows: "Our greatest challenge in life is not avoiding death, but avoiding evil, which comes upon us more quickly than death."

📖 **READER'S NOTEBOOK** As you read, look for passages that you think are especially important or difficult. In your notebook, restate these passages in your own words.

WORDS TO KNOW **Vocabulary Preview**

annihilation	disparage	unscrupulous
culpable	reconcile	

Build Background

The Trial of Socrates

When Socrates was put on trial in 399 B.C., Athens was in a period of great turmoil. The city had been defeated by Sparta in 404 B.C. The Spartans forced Athens to install new rulers—a group known as the Thirty Tyrants—some of whom had been friends and followers of Socrates. These rulers, however, turned out to be corrupt and brutal. When democratic rule returned to Athens in 403 B.C., critics of Socrates blamed him for the abuses of the Thirty Tyrants, even though he had publicly disobeyed their orders.

Other citizens resented Socrates because he seemed to mock the traditions and values of Athens. Feelings of ill will intensified until Socrates, at age 70, was brought to trial. A jury of 500 male citizens heard the charges against him; then Socrates presented his own defense. Instead of trying to win the sympathy of the jury, Socrates refused to compromise. Even after he was found guilty, he might have escaped the death penalty by proposing a lesser penalty. But he proposed that the city reward him for his service to virtue and truth. Many jurors were insulted by his attitude, and, by a majority of votes, Socrates was sentenced to death. He was made to drink a potion containing hemlock, a deadly poison. Plato attended Socrates' trial and later based the *Apology* on his memory of what he had heard.

from the Apology
Plato
Translated by Hugh Tredennick

ell, gentlemen, for the sake of a very small gain in time you are going to earn the reputation—and the blame from those who wish to disparage our city—of having put Socrates to death, "that wise man"—because they will say I am wise even if I am not, these people who want to find fault with you. If you had waited just a little while, you would have had your way in the course of nature. You can see that I am well on in life and near to death. I am saying this not to all of you but to those who voted for my execution, and I have something else to say to them as well.

No doubt you think, gentlemen, that I have been condemned for lack of the arguments which I could have used if I had thought it right to leave nothing unsaid or undone to secure my acquittal. But that is very far from the truth. It is not a lack of arguments that has caused my condemnation, but a lack of effrontery[1] and impudence, and the fact that I have refused to address you in the way which would give you most pleasure. You would have liked to hear me weep and wail, doing and saying all sorts of things which I regard as unworthy of myself, but which you are used to hearing from other people. But I did not think then that I ought to stoop to servility[2] because I was in danger, and I do not regret now the way in which I pleaded my case. I would much rather die as the result of this defense than live as the result of the other sort. In a court of law, just as in warfare, neither I nor any other ought to use his wits to escape death by any means. In battle it is often obvious that you could escape being killed by giving up your arms and throwing yourself upon the mercy of your pursuers, and in every kind of danger there are plenty of devices for avoiding death if you are unscrupulous enough to stick at nothing. But I suggest, gentlemen, that the difficulty is not so much to escape death; the real difficulty is to escape from doing wrong, which is far more fleet of foot. In this present instance I, the slow old man, have been overtaken by the slower of the two, but my accusers, who are clever and quick, have been overtaken by the faster—by iniquity.[3] When I leave this court I shall go away condemned by you to death, but they will go away convicted by truth herself of depravity[4] and wickedness. And they accept their sentence even as I accept mine. No doubt it was bound to be so, and I think that the result is fair enough.

Having said so much, I feel moved to prophesy to you who have given your vote against me, for I am now at that point where the gift of prophecy comes most readily to men—at the point of death. I tell you, my executioners, that as soon as I am dead, vengeance shall fall upon you with a punishment far more painful than your killing of me. You have brought about my death in the belief that through it you will be delivered from submitting your conduct to

---

1. **effrontery** (ĭ-frŭn′tə-rē): rude boldness.
2. **servility** (sər-vĭl′ĭ-tē): disgracefully humble behavior.
3. **iniquity** (ĭ-nĭk′wĭ-tē): wickedness.
4. **depravity** (dĭ-prăv′ĭ-tē): evil; corruption.

WORDS TO KNOW

disparage (dĭ-spăr′ĭj) *v.* to speak in a slighting way of; belittle
unscrupulous (ŭn-skroō′pyə-ləs) *adj.* lacking a sense of right and wrong

248

Roman mosaic of the School of Plato. Museo Archeologico Nazionale, Naples, Italy. Alinari/Art Resource, New York.

HUMANITIES CONNECTION This Roman mosaic shows Plato at his Academy in Athens. Plato is holding a stick, which he may be using to draw a geometrical figure in the sand. The Acropolis is shown at top right.

THE BEST AND EASIEST WAY IS NOT TO STOP THE MOUTHS OF OTHERS, BUT TO MAKE YOURSELVES AS GOOD MEN AS YOU CAN.

criticism, but I say that the result will be just the opposite. You will have more critics, whom up till now I have restrained without your knowing it, and being younger they will be harsher to you and will cause you more annoyance. If you expect to stop denunciation[5] of your wrong way of life by putting people to death, there is something amiss[6] with your reasoning. This way of escape is neither possible nor creditable. The best and easiest way is not to stop the mouths of others, but to make yourselves as good men as you can. This is my last message to you who voted for my condemnation.

As for you who voted for my acquittal, I should very much like to say a few words to reconcile you to the result, while the officials are busy and I am not yet on my way to the place where I must die. I ask you, gentlemen, to spare me these few moments. There is no reason why we should not exchange fancies while the law permits. I look upon you as my friends, and I want you to understand the right way of regarding my present position.

Gentlemen of the jury—for *you* deserve to be so called—I have had a remarkable experience. In the past the prophetic voice[7] to which I have become accustomed has always been my constant companion, opposing me even in quite trivial things if I was going to take the wrong course. Now something has happened to me, as you can see, which might be thought and is commonly considered to be a supreme calamity; yet neither when I left home this morning, nor when I was taking my place here in the court, nor at any point in any part of my speech did the divine sign oppose me. In other discussions it has often checked me in the middle of a sentence, but this time it has never opposed me in any part of this business in anything that I have said or done. What do I suppose to be the explanation? I will tell you. I suspect that this thing that has happened to me is a blessing, and we are quite mistaken in supposing death to be an evil. I have good grounds for thinking this, because my accustomed sign could not have failed to oppose me if what I was doing had not been sure to bring some good result.

We should reflect that there is much reason to hope for a good result on other grounds as well. Death is one of two things. Either it is annihilation, and the dead have no consciousness of anything, or, as we are told, it is really a change—a migration[8] of the soul from this place to another. Now if there is no consciousness but only a dreamless sleep, death must be a

---

5. **denunciation** (dĭ-nŭn'sē-ā'shən): disapproval; condemnation.

6. **amiss:** wrong; faulty.

7. **prophetic voice:** Socrates believed that at times he heard a divine voice warning him to avoid particular actions.

8. **migration** (mī-grā'shən): movement.

marvelous gain. I suppose that if anyone were told to pick out the night on which he slept so soundly as not even to dream, and then to compare it with all the other nights and days of his life, and then were told to say, after due consideration, how many better and happier days and nights than this he had spent in the course of his life—well, I think that the Great King[9] himself, to say nothing of any private person, would find these days and nights easy to count in comparison with the rest. If death is like this, then, I call it gain, because the whole of time, if you look at it in this way, can be regarded as no more than one single night. If on the other hand death is a removal from here to some other place, and if what we are told is true, that all the dead are there, what greater blessing could there be than this, gentlemen? If on arrival in the other world, beyond the reach of our so-called justice, one will find there the true judges who are said to preside in those courts, Minos and Rhadamanthus and Aeacus and Triptolemus[10] and all those other half-divinities who were upright in their earthly life, would that be an unrewarding journey? Put it in this way. How much would one of you give to meet Orpheus and Musaeus, Hesiod[11] and Homer? I am willing to die ten times over if this account is true. It would be a specially interesting experience for me to join them there, to meet Palamedes and Ajax, the son of Telamon,[12] and any other heroes of the old days who met their death through an unfair trial, and to compare my fortunes with theirs—it would be rather amusing, I think. And above all I should like to spend my time there, as here, in examining and searching people's minds, to find out who is really wise among them, and who only thinks that he is. What would one not give, gentlemen, to be able to question the leader of that great host against Troy, or Odysseus, or Sisyphus,[13] or the thousands of other men and women whom one could mention, to talk and mix and argue with whom would be unimaginable happiness? At any rate I

AND ABOVE ALL I SHOULD LIKE TO SPEND MY TIME THERE, AS HERE, IN EXAMINING AND SEARCHING PEOPLE'S MINDS.

presume that they do not put one to death there for such conduct, because apart from the other happiness in which their world surpasses ours, they are now immortal for the rest of time, if what we are told is true.

You too, gentlemen of the jury, must look forward to death with confidence, and fix your minds on this one belief, which is certain—that

---

9. **the Great King:** the fabulously wealthy ruler of Persia.

10. **Minos** (mī'nəs) **and Rhadamanthus** (răd'ə-măn'thəs) **and Aeacus** (ē'ə-kəs) **and Triptolemus** (trĭp-tŏl'ə-məs): legendary rulers who were believed to serve as judges of the souls of the dead.

11. **Orpheus** (ôr'fyōōs) **and Musaeus** (myōō-sē'əs), **Hesiod** (hē'sē-əd): like Homer, famous early Greek poets. (The first two are almost certainly mythical figures.)

12. **Palamedes** (păl'ə-mē'dēz) **and Ajax** (ā'jăks'), **son of Telamon** (tĕl'ə-mŏn'): two legendary participants in the Trojan War. Palamedes was unjustly executed for treason; Ajax, after being judged less worthy than Odysseus to receive Achilles' armor, killed himself in a fit of insanity.

13. **Sisyphus** (sĭs'ə-fəs): the legendary founder of the city of Corinth, famous for his cleverness.

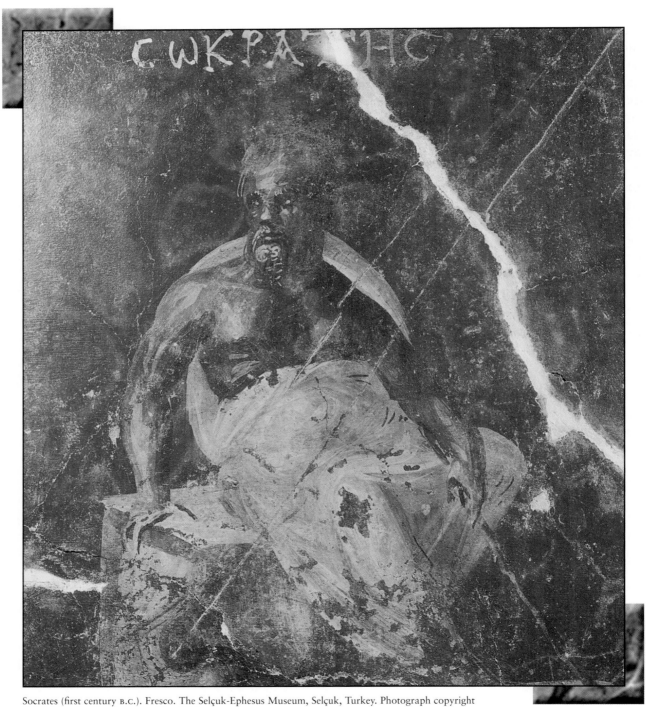

Socrates (first century B.C.). Fresco. The Selçuk-Ephesus Museum, Selçuk, Turkey. Photograph copyright © Erich Lessing/Art Resource, New York.

HUMANITIES CONNECTION This fresco—a painting done on fresh, moist wall plaster—depicting Socrates is from a Roman house at Ephesus (in what is now western Turkey).

nothing can harm a good man either in life or after death, and his fortunes are not a matter of indifference to the gods. This present experience of mine has not come about mechanically. I am quite clear that the time had come when it was better for me to die and be released from my distractions. That is why my sign never turned me back. For my own part I bear no grudge at all against those who condemned me and accused me, although it was not with this kind intention that they did so, but because they thought that they were hurting me; and that is culpable of them. However, I ask them to grant me one favor. When my sons grow up, gentlemen, if you think that they are putting money or anything else before goodness, take your revenge by plaguing them as I plagued you; and if they fancy themselves for no reason, you must scold them just as I scolded you, for neglecting the important things and thinking that they are good for something when they are good for nothing. If you do this, I shall have had justice at your hands, both I myself and my children.

Now it is time that we were going, I to die and you to live, but which of us has the happier prospect is unknown to anyone but God. ❖

Connect to the Literature

1. **What Do You Think?**
What are your impressions of Socrates as a person? Explain your judgment.

Comprehension Check
- Why didn't Socrates tell the jury what it wanted to hear?
- What does Socrates take as a sign that his death sentence is a "blessing"?
- What does Socrates say he would like about an afterlife?

Think Critically

2. **ACTIVE READING: PARAPHRASING** What do you think are the most important or difficult passages in this speech? Work with a partner to review and edit the paraphrases in your READER'S NOTEBOOK. Then read aloud to your classmates one text passage and your paraphrase of it.

3. Socrates says that death is either "annihilation" or "a migration of the soul from this place to another." Why do you think Socrates is so cheerful in the face of death?

4. What values are most important to Socrates? Support your judgment with evidence from the text.

> **THINK ABOUT**
> - the way he chooses to defend himself
> - the role that the "prophetic voice" plays in his life
> - his final request about his sons

Extend Interpretations

5. **Comparing Texts** Socrates and Pericles represent two very different kinds of **heroes**. Pericles embodied the Athenian ideal. He was a gifted leader and a wealthy aristocrat who was physically attractive and beloved by most citizens. Of these two men, which do you find more heroic? Use evidence from the *Apology* and Pericles' funeral oration to support your judgment.

6. **Critic's Corner** The scholar Gregory Vlastos has written that for Socrates "virtue matters more for your own happiness than does everything else put together." Do you think that Socrates was right? Give your reasons.

7. **Connect to Life** Earlier in the *Apology,* Socrates refers to himself as a "gadfly," an insect that annoys cattle. Socrates annoyed many Athenians because he made them think about their responsibility to be virtuous. Who are the gadflies of today? In what ways are they like Socrates?

LITERARY ANALYSIS: SPEECH

In ancient Greece, a **speech,** a formal talk in a public arena, was considered the most important form of communication. In fact, the Sophists (sŏf'ĭsts), Greek philosophers who were paid teachers, trained young men in the techniques of artful speaking. To be effective, a speech was supposed to express the character and authority of the speaker and appeal to the judgment and emotions of the audience.

Paired Activity With a partner, review Socrates' speech. Examine his description of his own character, as well as his attitudes toward the members of the jury who voted to convict him and toward those who voted to acquit him. Record your findings in a graphic organizer like the one shown.

How Socrates Describes His Character	*Says that he will not do things "unworthy" of himself*
Attitude Toward Those Who Voted to Convict	
Attitude Toward Those Who Voted to Acquit	

Choices & CHALLENGES

Writing Options

1. Dramatic Scene Imagine that Socrates meets with one of the prosecutors after his trial. Write a brief dramatic scene presenting the encounter. You may include other people in the scene, such as members of the jury and Socrates' friends. Drawing on what you have read about the trial, make up dialogue that you think would be believable. Place your writing in your **Working Portfolio.**

2. Newspaper Editorial The jury's decision in the trial of Socrates has been debated for centuries. Some people say that Socrates gave the jury no choice and brought about his own conviction. Others argue that the jury's decision was a great injustice. Read the rest of the *Apology* and decide whether the jury made the correct decision. Write a newspaper editorial that either praises or condemns the decision.

Writing Handbook
See page R35: Persuasive Writing.

Activities & Explorations

1. Philosophical Dialogue Socrates was famous for making people feel uncomfortable by asking them questions that challenged their whole way of thinking. With a partner, create an impromptu dialogue between Socrates and a prominent person in today's society. Socrates should ask a series of questions that challenge the values and beliefs of the other person.
~ PERFORMING

2. Socrates in Caricature Socrates often mocked his own physical appearance. Find physical descriptions of Socrates and draw a caricature of him— that is, a comic and exaggerated portrait. **~ ART**

Inquiry & Research

Philosopher in the Clouds
The comic playwright Aristophanes (ăr'ĭ-stŏf'ə-nēz) ridiculed Socrates in his play *The Clouds.* The play influenced public opinion and even played a role in Socrates' being brought to trial. Research how Aristophanes portrayed Socrates and decide whether it was a fair portrayal. Share your findings in an oral report.

 **RESEARCH STARTER**
CLASSZONE.COM

Vocabulary in Action

EXERCISE: WORD MEANINGS Answer the questions below to show your understanding of the boldfaced words.

1. If Socrates wanted to **disparage** someone, would he say something bad or something good about that person?
2. If a member of the jury felt **culpable** for how he voted, would he feel guilty or relieved? Why?
3. Socrates says it is possible that death may bring **annihilation.** What does he mean?
4. If a member of the jury accepted a bribe, would that make him **unscrupulous?** Why?
5. Socrates asks the jurors who sided with him to **reconcile** themselves to the decision. What does he want them to do?

Building Vocabulary
The word *culpable* comes from the Latin word *culpa,* meaning "fault." For an in-depth lesson on Greek and Latin roots, see page 340.

GREEK DRAMA

Classical drama began long ago in ancient Greece—in the sixth century B.C. At that time, a religious festival took place in Athens each spring in honor of Dionysus (dī′ə-nī′səs), the god of wine and fertility, or new growth. At this festival, a chorus of masked dancers performed on a circular stage, singing hymns to the god. In 535 B.C. Thespis of Icaria, a Greek poet, introduced the first actor onstage. The word *thespian,* meaning "actor," comes from his name. The actor impersonated various characters by wearing different masks and costumes and took part in a dialogue with the leader of the chorus. With this occurrence, the first plays were born. Religious in nature, these plays explored deep questions, such as the role of fate in human life or the relationship between mortals and the gods.

Throughout the sixth and fifth centuries B.C., Greek plays kept their religious purpose. The word *tragedy* reflects this purpose. It comes from the Greek word for a goat, an animal regarded as sacred to Dionysus.

Ruins of Greek theater at Epidaurus

As time passed, Greek plays became more entertaining. Writers competed for prizes by staging plays before thousands of spectators at the festival of Dionysus in Athens. Hundreds of Greek tragedies were performed at these festivals. Sadly, fewer than 35 have survived.

Modern production of Aeschylus' *Oresteia*

The greatest writers of tragedy in ancient Greece were Aeschylus, Sophocles, and Euripides. Aeschylus (ĕs′kyə-ləs) added a second actor onstage, creating a dialogue between two characters. Sophocles (sŏf′ə-klēz′) added a third actor, making plots more intriguing and complex. Euripides (yŏŏ-rĭp′ĭ-dēz′) created spectacular stage effects and portrayed characters in highly realistic ways. His play *Medea,* for example, explores the motives of a woman guilty of a horrid crime.

For the most part, these writers based their plays on familiar legends and myths. The audience knew the story behind the play, but the characters in the play, of course, did not. This contrast created an ironic perspective. Like the gods themselves, the audience looked on, knowing what would happen and yet caring deeply about the characters who suffered onstage.

Suffer they certainly did—bravely, passionately, and terribly. Consider Aeschylus' *Oresteia.* This set of three related plays tells the story of King Agamemnon's doomed family. This Greek commander sacrifices his daughter to the gods in return for a favorable wind so that his fleet can sail to Troy. When he returns home from the Trojan War, his wife murders him. Then Agamemnon's son, Orestes, kills his mother to avenge his father's murder and, to escape punishment, goes into exile. Another ill-fated family was that of Oedipus. Sophocles dramatized their sufferings in three masterful plays: *Oedipus the King* (page 258), *Antigone,* and *Oedipus at Colonus.*

Comedy was not as popular as tragedy among the ancient Greeks. The greatest writer of comedies was Aristophanes (ăr′ĭ-stŏf′ə-nēz). His satiric comedies poked fun at many well-known Athenians. *Lysistrata,* a domestic comedy, is still popular with audiences today. It shows clever and determined women banding together to stop their husbands from going to war.

Classical drama is a priceless legacy of ancient Greece. It includes several plays that rank as world masterpieces. These plays have inspired countless writers down through the centuries. In drama the Greeks developed a new literary form and showed its power. Even today Greek drama provides a way to ponder life's mysteries, to celebrate its glory, and to come to terms with its suffering.

Coins used by Greeks to gain admission to the theater

MILESTONE LINKS
CLASSZONE.COM

OEDIPUS *the* KING

— S O P H O C L E S —

Sophocles
496?–406 B.C.

Public Figure Sophocles lived a long life and, by all accounts, a happy one. It spanned almost the entire fifth century B.C.—a century of great achievements in Athens, both in politics and art.

When he was young, Sophocles was a skillful wrestler, dancer, and musician. Later, he had a successful career in public life. As a military leader, he worked alongside Pericles, the great statesman who dominated Athenian politics for more than 30 years. Sophocles also served as an ambassador, as a public treasurer, and, in his 80s, as a member of a special commission appointed to guide Athens through a time of crisis. In addition, he seems to have helped in establishing the first Athenian public hospital. Handsome, charming, friendly, and well educated, Sophocles was highly regarded.

Great Dramatist As a writer, Sophocles' achievements were truly amazing. One of the greatest dramatists of the golden age of Greek drama, he composed more than 120 plays. Unfortunately, only 7 of them have survived intact. For about 30 years, he competed in the annual Dionysian dramatic festival, taking first prize at least 18 times. By contrast, Aeschylus received only 13 first prizes, and Euripides won only 4.

Sophocles was an innovator in drama. He enlarged the chorus from 12 to 15 members, introduced painted scenery, and added a third speaking actor. His plays are noted for their powerful language, superb artistry, and unforgettable characters. Sophocles never stopped writing plays, keeping his intellectual powers until the end of his life. He completed one of his greatest plays, *Oedipus at Colonus,* when he was about 90.

Tragic Vision It is ironic that Sophocles—gifted, admired, and successful as he was—had so dark a view of human life. He was deeply aware of life's pain and sorrow. His plays feature towering heroes who remind the audience of the vast potential of human beings. However, the very qualities that make these heroes great also lead to their ruin.

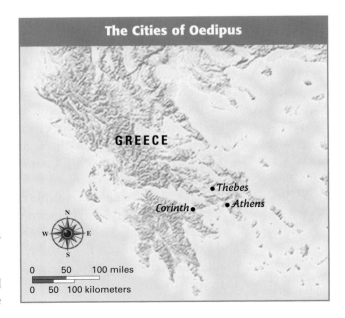

The Cities of Oedipus

GREECE

Corinth • Thebes • Athens

N W E S

0   50   100 miles
0   50   100 kilometers

Build Background

Sophocles' Theban Plays Of all Sophocles' tragic characters, the one who has touched the hearts of audiences most deeply is Oedipus. Sophocles himself was fascinated with this king and his family. Two of his surviving tragedies—*Oedipus the King* and *Oedipus at Colonus*—are about Oedipus, and *Antigone* centers on one of his daughters. These three plays are sometimes called the Theban plays. Thebes, an ancient city in central Greece, was once among the most powerful of Greek city-states. The city is important in the legend of Oedipus and in all three plays.

Aristotle and Tragedy In the 300s B.C., the Greek philosopher Aristotle wrote an essay about drama, the *Poetics*. In this essay, Aristotle examined several works of Greek literature, describing their structures and effects. He praised *Oedipus the King* as the model of a perfectly made tragedy.

On the basis of his study of Sophocles' play, Aristotle characterized a **tragedy** as "an imitation of an action that is serious, complete, and of a certain magnitude." He also stated that a tragedy triggers two emotions in its audience: pity and terror.

The Legend of Oedipus

His Origins *Oedipus the King,* like nearly every other Greek tragedy, is based on a legend that was familiar to the ancient Greeks. According to this legend, Oedipus was the son of King Laius and Queen Jocasta of Thebes. An oracle told Laius that a son born to him and Jocasta would kill him. When Jocasta gave birth to a son, Laius ordered a servant to pin the baby's feet together and leave him exposed on a mountain to die. The servant took pity on the baby, however, and entrusted him to a shepherd. The shepherd gave the baby to the childless king and queen of Corinth—Polybus and Merope. They named the baby Oedipus, from words meaning "swollen foot," and raised him as their son.

A Fateful Night Oedipus grew to manhood believing that he was the son of Polybus and Merope. One night at a banquet, a drunkard blurted out to Oedipus that he was not his father's son. Oedipus then visited the oracle at Delphi to try to discover the truth about his parents. The oracle did not reveal Oedipus' true identity but did deliver a terrible prophecy—that Oedipus would kill his father and marry his mother.

Murder at a Crossroad Horrified at this disclosure, Oedipus fled from Corinth in an effort to prevent the prophecy from coming true. Making his way toward Thebes, he came upon King Laius and his servants at a crossroad. Oedipus quarreled with them about who had the right of way. Not realizing that Laius was his real father, Oedipus killed him in a fit of rage.

Riddle of the Sphinx When Oedipus reached Thebes, a monster was terrorizing it. Known as the Sphinx, the monster had the face of a woman, the body of a lion, and the wings of a bird. It sang an intriguing riddle: "What is it that walks on four legs in the morning, on two at midday, and on three in the evening?" Anyone who could not solve the riddle was devoured by the Sphinx. Oedipus, however, figured out the answer. He promptly replied, "Man, for he crawls as a baby, walks erect in maturity, and uses a staff in old age." On receiving this answer, the Sphinx destroyed itself, and Thebes was freed from the terror.

Oedipus, Ruler of Thebes As a reward for saving the city, Oedipus was given the throne of Thebes and the hand of Jocasta, the late king's widow. Not knowing that he was actually her son, Oedipus married her. For 20 years he ruled Thebes in peace with his wife and her brother Creon.

As the play begins, Thebes is in trouble once more. The city is reeling from a terrible plague. Naturally, the citizens go to Oedipus for help, remembering that he had saved the city from the Sphinx long ago. In his effort to bring the plague to an end, Oedipus discovers the secret of his birth and hurtles headlong into unspeakable suffering.

For a humanities activity, click on:

HUMANITIES
CLASSZONE.COM

To get the most out of your reading, try to imagine yourself attending a performance of *Oedipus the King* in fifth-century Athens. At dawn, you make your way to the Theater of Dionysus, built on the slope of a hill. As you enter the outdoor theater, you look up and see the gleaming white columns of the Parthenon—a temple dedicated to the goddess Athena—catching the morning sun. Then, with perhaps 17,000 other spectators, you settle down to watch as the events of the tragedy unfold.

Cast of Characters

Oedipus (ĕd′ə-pəs), king of Thebes

A **Priest** of Zeus

Creon (krē′ŏn′), brother of Jocasta

A **Chorus** of Theban citizens and their **Leader**

Tiresias (tī-rē′sē-əs), a blind prophet

Jocasta (jō-kăs′tə) the queen, wife of Oedipus

A **Messenger** from Corinth

A **Shepherd**

A **Messenger** from inside the palace

Antigone (ăn-tĭg′ə-nē) and **Ismene** (ĭs-mē′nē), daughters of Oedipus and Jocasta

Guards and attendants

Priests of Thebes

Typical Greek Theater

The seats for the audience were built into the hillside. Actors wore large masks that could be seen from a distance. In addition to masks, the actors wore elevated shoes.

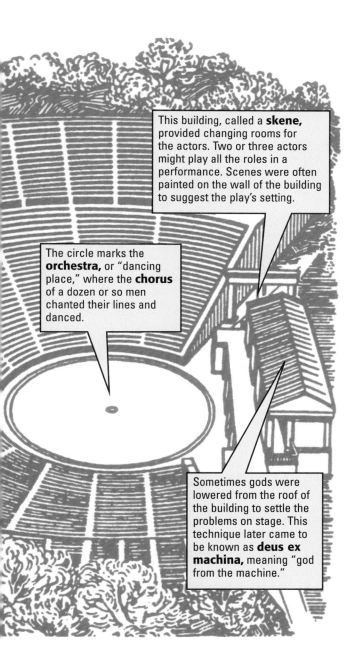

This building, called a **skene,** provided changing rooms for the actors. Two or three actors might play all the roles in a performance. Scenes were often painted on the wall of the building to suggest the play's setting.

The circle marks the **orchestra,** or "dancing place," where the **chorus** of a dozen or so men chanted their lines and danced.

Sometimes gods were lowered from the roof of the building to settle the problems on stage. This technique later came to be known as **deus ex machina,** meaning "god from the machine."

Connect to Your Life

In this play, Sophocles tells the story of a king who learns to look at his past in a new way. Think about some events in your own past that you look at differently now that you are older. Why do you think your understanding of the events has changed?

Focus Your Reading

LITERARY ANALYSIS: TRAGIC HERO

The central character in a tragedy is called a **tragic hero.** Such a character, though noble, has a defect, or flaw. The flaw—which may be poor judgment, great pride, or weakness—helps to bring about his or her downfall. As you read this play, think about Oedipus' qualities. Also ask yourself whether or not he has a flaw.

ACTIVE READING: STRATEGIES FOR READING GREEK DRAMA

Use these strategies when reading this play:

• **Visualize** the characters and the events as you read.
• Keep in mind the sequence of events that make up the **plot.**
• Think about the hero's **motivations,** noble qualities, and any flaw, or defect, he may have.
• Consider how the words and actions of **minor characters** help you to understand the main characters.
• **Question** what happens in the play, and stop reading occasionally to **clarify** your understanding.

READER'S NOTEBOOK As you read this play, record your answers to the Pause & Reflect questions found at various points in the play. Apply the strategies listed above, and note any other thoughts or questions you may have.

WORDS TO KNOW **Vocabulary Preview**

appall	foreboding	mortify	revile
denounce	futile	oblivion	surmise
despondent	loathed	retract	swarthy
explicit	menace	reverberate	

Oedipus the King
Sophocles
Translated by Robert Fagles

GUIDE FOR READING

FOCUS A terrible plague has struck the city of Thebes. Plants, animals, and people are dying in great numbers. The priests of the city seek help from Oedipus, their king. As you read, look for details that help you form impressions of Oedipus as a leader.

Time and Scene: *The royal house of Thebes. Double doors dominate the façade; a stone altar stands at the center of the stage.*

Many years have passed since Oedipus *solved the riddle of the Sphinx and ascended the throne of Thebes, and now a plague has struck the city. A procession of priests enters; suppliants, broken and* despondent, *they carry branches wound in wool and lay them on the altar.*

The doors open. Guards assemble. Oedipus *comes forward, majestic but for a telltale limp, and slowly views the condition of his people.*

> **Oedipus.** Oh my children, the new blood of ancient Thebes,
>   why are you here? Huddling at my altar,
>   praying before me, your branches wound in wool.
>   Our city reeks with the smoke of burning incense,
> 5 rings with cries for the Healer and wailing for the dead.
>   I thought it wrong, my children, to hear the truth
>   from others, messengers. Here I am myself—
>   you all know me, the world knows my fame:
>   I am Oedipus.

(*helping a* Priest *to his feet*)

3 branches wound in wool: tokens placed on altars by people seeking favors from the gods.

5 the Healer: the god Apollo, who could both cause and cure plagues.

WORDS TO KNOW

262   **despondent** (dǐ-spŏn′dənt) *adj.* sad; depressed

Christopher Plummer as Oedipus in a scene from the film *Oedipus the King* (1968).

HERE I AM MYSELF—
YOU ALL KNOW ME,
THE WORLD KNOWS MY FAME:
I AM OEDIPUS.

Speak up, old man. Your years,
10   your dignity—you should speak for the others.
           Why here and kneeling, what preys upon you so?
           Some sudden fear? some strong desire?
           You can trust me. I am ready to help,
           I'll do anything. I would be blind to misery
15   not to pity my people kneeling at my feet.

    Priest. Oh Oedipus, king of the land, our greatest power!
           You see us before you now, men of all ages
           clinging to your altars. Here are boys,
           still too weak to fly from the nest,
20   and here the old, bowed down with the years,
           the holy ones—a priest of Zeus myself—and here
           the picked, unmarried men, the young hope of Thebes.
           And all the rest, your great family gathers now,
           branches wreathed, massing in the squares,
25   kneeling before the two temples of queen Athena
           or the river-shrine where the embers glow and die
           and Apollo sees the future in the ashes.
                                   Our city—
           look around you, see with your own eyes—
           our ship pitches wildly, cannot lift her head
30   from the depths, the red waves of death . . .
           Thebes is dying. A blight on the fresh crops
           and the rich pastures, cattle sicken and die,
           and the women die in labor, children stillborn,
           and the plague, the fiery god of fever hurls down
35   on the city, his lightning slashing through us—
           raging plague in all its vengeance, devastating
           the house of Cadmus! And black Death luxuriates
           in the raw, wailing miseries of Thebes.

           Now we pray to you. You cannot equal the gods,
40   your children know that, bending at your altar.
           But we do rate you first of men,
           both in the common crises of our lives
           and face-to-face encounters with the gods.
           You freed us from the Sphinx, you came to Thebes
45   and cut us loose from the bloody tribute we had paid
           that harsh, brutal singer. We taught you nothing,
           no skill, no extra knowledge, still you triumphed.
           A god was with you, so they say, and we believe it—
           you lifted up our lives.

26 river-shrine: a shrine of Apollo in Thebes, where priests foretold the future by interpreting the way offerings to the god burned.

31 blight: a disease that withers plants.

37 Cadmus (kăd′məs): the founder of Thebes; **luxuriates** (lŭg-zhŏŏr′ē-āts′): takes pleasure.

45 bloody tribute: the human lives taken by the Sphinx.

<blockquote>So now again,</blockquote>

50 Oedipus, king, we bend to you, your power—
    we implore you, all of us on our knees:
    find us strength, rescue! Perhaps you've heard
    the voice of a god or something from other men,
    Oedipus . . . what do you know?
55 The man of experience—you see it every day—
    his plans will work in a crisis, his first of all.

    Act now—we beg you, best of men, raise up our city!
    Act, defend yourself, your former glory!
    Your country calls you savior now
60 for your zeal, your action years ago.
    Never let us remember of your reign:
    you helped us stand, only to fall once more.
    Oh raise up our city, set us on our feet.
    The omens were good that day you brought us joy—
65 be the same man today!
    Rule our land, you know you have the power,
    but rule a land of the living, not a wasteland.
    Ship and towered city are nothing, stripped of men
    alive within it, living all as one.

Oedipus.   My children,

70 I pity you. I see—how could I fail to see
    what longings bring you here? Well I know
    you are sick to death, all of you,
    but sick as you are, not one is sick as I.
    Your pain strikes each of you alone, each
75 in the confines of himself, no other. But my spirit
    grieves for the city, for myself and all of you.
    I wasn't asleep, dreaming. You haven't wakened me—
    I have wept through the nights, you must know that,
    groping, laboring over many paths of thought.
80 After a painful search I found one cure:
    I acted at once. I sent Creon,
    my wife's own brother, to Delphi—
    Apollo the Prophet's oracle—to learn
    what I might do or say to save our city.

85 Today's the day. When I count the days gone by
    it torments me . . . what is he doing?
    Strange, he's late, he's gone too long.

82 Delphi (dĕl′fī′): the site of a temple where prophecies were delivered by a priestess of Apollo.

MY CHILDREN,
I PITY YOU.

Oedipus speaks to the chorus in the Tyrone Guthrie film version, *Oedipus Rex* (1957).

But once he returns, then, then I'll be a traitor
if I do not do all the god makes clear.

90 **Priest.** Timely words. The men over there
are signaling—Creon's just arriving.

PAUSE & REFLECT What are your impressions of
Oedipus as a leader?

FOCUS Creon is returning from Delphi with news from
the god Apollo. Read to find out about the cause of the
plague in Thebes.

Oedipus (*sighting* Creon, *then turning to the altar*).
                              Lord Apollo,
let him come with a lucky word of rescue,
shining like his eyes!

Priest. Welcome news, I think—he's crowned, look,
95   and the laurel wreath is bright with berries.

95 laurel wreath: a crown of
leaves worn by those seeking the
help of the oracle at Delphi.

Oedipus. We'll soon see. He's close enough to hear—

(*Enter* Creon *from the side; his face is shaded with a* *wreath*.)

> Creon, prince, my kinsman, what do you bring us?
> What message from the god?

Creon. Good news.
> I tell you even the hardest things to bear,
100 > if they should turn out well, all would be well.

Oedipus. Of course, but what were the god's *words?* There's
>   no hope
> and nothing to fear in what you've said so far.

Creon. If you want my report in the presence of these
>   people . . .

(*pointing to the priests while drawing* Oedipus *toward the* *palace*)

> I'm ready now, or we might go inside.

Oedipus. Speak out,
105 > speak to us all. I grieve for these, my people,
> far more than I fear for my own life.

Creon. Very well,
> I will tell you what I heard from the god.
> Apollo commands us—he was quite clear—
> "Drive the corruption from the land,
110 > don't harbor it any longer, past all cure,
> don't nurse it in your soil—root it out!"

Oedipus. How can we cleanse ourselves—what rites?
> What's the source of the trouble?

Creon. Banish the man, or pay back blood with blood.
115 > Murder sets the plague-storm on the city.

Oedipus. Whose murder?
> Whose fate does Apollo bring to light?

Creon. Our leader,
> my lord, was once a man named Laius,
> before you came and put us straight on course.

117 Laius (lā′əs): the king of Thebes before Oedipus.

Oedipus. I know—
> or so I've heard. I never saw the man myself.

120 **Creon.** Well, he was killed, and Apollo commands us now—
> he could not be more clear,
> "Pay the killers back—whoever is responsible."

Oedipus. Where on earth are they? Where to find it now,
the trail of the ancient guilt so hard to trace?

125 **Creon.** "Here in Thebes," he said.
Whatever is sought for can be caught, you know,
whatever is neglected slips away.

Oedipus. But where,
in the palace, the fields or foreign soil,
where did Laius meet his bloody death?

130 **Creon.** He went to consult an oracle, Apollo said,
and he set out and never came home again.

Oedipus. No messenger, no fellow-traveler saw what
happened?
Someone to cross-examine?

Creon. No,
they were all killed but one. He escaped,
135 terrified, he could tell us nothing clearly,
nothing of what he saw—just one thing.

Oedipus. What's that?
One thing could hold the key to it all,
a small beginning give us grounds for hope.

Creon. He said thieves attacked them—a whole band,
140 not single-handed, cut King Laius down.

Oedipus. A thief,
so daring, so wild, he'd kill a king? Impossible,
unless conspirators paid him off in Thebes.

Creon. We suspected as much. But with Laius dead
no leader appeared to help us in our troubles.

145 **Oedipus.** Trouble? Your *king* was murdered—royal blood!
What stopped you from tracking down the killer
then and there?

Creon. The singing, riddling Sphinx.
She . . . persuaded us to let the mystery go
and concentrate on what lay at our feet.

Oedipus. No,
150 I'll start again—I'll bring it all to light myself!
Apollo is right, and so are you, Creon,
to turn our attention back to the murdered man.
Now you have *me* to fight for you, you'll see:
I am the land's avenger by all rights,
155 and Apollo's champion too.

154 avenger: one who punishes
wrongdoing.

But not to assist some distant kinsman, no,
for my own sake I'll rid us of this corruption.
Whoever killed the king may decide to kill me too,
with the same violent hand—by avenging Laius
160 I defend myself.

(*to the priests*)

                    Quickly, my children.
Up from the steps, take up your branches now.

(*to the guards*)

One of you summon the city here before us,
tell them I'll do everything. God help us,
we will see our triumph—or our fall.

(Oedipus *and* Creon *enter the palace, followed by the guards.*)

165 **Priest.** Rise, my sons. The kindness we came for
Oedipus volunteers himself.
Apollo has sent his word, his oracle—
Come down, Apollo, save us, stop the plague.

(*The priests rise, remove their branches and exit to the side.*)

PAUSE & REFLECT What is the cause of the plague in Thebes?

FOCUS The chorus enters and chants a plea to the gods, describing the people's sufferings. As you read, look for details that help you visualize the sufferings of the people of Thebes.

(Enter a Chorus, *the citizens of Thebes, who have not heard the news that* Creon *brings. They march around the altar, chanting.*)

Chorus.   Zeus!
Great welcome voice of Zeus, what do you bring?
170 What word from the gold vaults of Delphi
comes to brilliant Thebes? Racked with terror—
                            terror shakes my heart
and I cry your wild cries, Apollo, Healer of Delos
I worship you in dread . . . what now, what is your price?
175 some new sacrifice? some ancient rite from the past
come round again each spring?—

157 corruption: pollution; contamination.

173 Delos (dē′lŏs′): the island where Apollo was born.

. . . THE MISERIES NUMBERLESS,
GRIEF ON GRIEF, NO END—
TOO MUCH TO BEAR, WE ARE ALL
DYING

Masked members of the chorus, from a stage production of *Oedipus the King*, directed by Peter Hall (1996).

> what will you bring to birth?
> Tell me, child of golden Hope
>   warm voice that never dies!

180 You are the first I call, daughter of Zeus
deathless Athena—I call your sister Artemis,
heart of the market place enthroned in glory,
                    guardian of our earth—
I call Apollo, Archer astride the thunderheads of heaven—
185 O triple shield against death, shine before me now!
If ever, once in the past, you stopped some ruin
launched against our walls
          you hurled the flame of pain
far, far from Thebes—you gods
190   come now, come down once more!

                    No, no
the miseries numberless, grief on grief, no end—
too much to bear, we are all dying
O my people . . .
    Thebes like a great army dying

180–244 In this chant the chorus prays to various gods—Athena, Artemis, Apollo, Zeus, and Dionysus—for help and protection.

195 and there is no sword of thought to save us, no
and the fruits of our famous earth, they will not ripen
no and the women cannot scream their pangs to birth—
screams for the Healer, children dead in the womb
                and life on life goes down
200   you can watch them go
        like seabirds winging west, outracing the day's fire
down the horizon, irresistibly
                streaking on to the shores of Evening
                                                Death
so many deaths, numberless deaths on deaths, no end—
205 Thebes is dying, look, her children
stripped of pity . . .
        generations strewn on the ground
unburied, unwept, the dead spreading death
and the young wives and gray-haired mothers with them
210 cling to the altars, trailing in from all over the city—
Thebes, city of death, one long cortege
                and the suffering rises
                        wails for mercy rise
        and the wild hymn for the Healer blazes out
215 clashing with our sobs our cries of mourning—
        O golden daughter of god, send rescue
        radiant as the kindness in your eyes!
Drive him back!—the fever, the god of death
                        that raging god of war
220 not armored in bronze, not shielded now, he burns me,
battle cries in the onslaught burning on—
O rout him from our borders!
Sail him, blast him out to the Sea-queen's chamber
                        the black Atlantic gulfs
225   or the northern harbor, death to all
where the Thracian surf comes crashing.
Now what the night spares he comes by day and kills—
the god of death.

                O lord of the stormcloud,
you who twirl the lightning, Zeus, Father,
230 thunder Death to nothing!

Apollo, lord of the light, I beg you—
        whip your longbow's golden cord
showering arrows on our enemies—shafts of power

211 cortege (kôr-tĕzh'): funeral procession.

216 golden daughter of god: Athena.

223 Sea-queen's chamber: the ocean depths—home of Amphitrite, wife of the sea god Poseidon.

226 Thracian (thrā'shən) **surf:** the rough waters of the western Black Sea.

champions strong before us rushing on!

235   Artemis, Huntress,
torches flaring over the eastern ridges—
           ride Death down in pain!

God of the headdress gleaming gold, I cry to you—
your name and ours are one, Dionysus—
240   come with your face aflame with wine
           your raving women's cries
your army on the march! Come with the lightning
come with torches blazing, eyes ablaze with glory!
Burn that god of death that all gods hate!

239 your name and ours are one, Dionysus (dī′ə-nī′səs): Dionysus, god of wine, was born of a Theban woman.

PAUSE & REFLECT What details helped you visualize Thebes as a city of death?

FOCUS Oedipus will now speak to his people. Read to find out what he intends to do to the killer or killers of Laius.

(Oedipus *enters from the palace to address the* Chorus, *as if addressing the entire city of Thebes.*)

245   **Oedipus**. You pray to the gods? Let me grant your prayers.
Come, listen to me—do what the plague demands:
you'll find relief and lift your head from the depths.

I will speak out now as a stranger to the story,
a stranger to the crime. If I'd been present then,
250   there would have been no mystery, no long hunt
without a clue in hand. So now, counted
a native Theban years after the murder,
to all of Thebes I make this proclamation:
if any one of you knows who murdered Laius,
255   the son of Labdacus, I order him to reveal
the whole truth to me. Nothing to fear,
even if he must <u>denounce</u> himself,
let him speak up
and so escape the brunt of the charge—
260   he will suffer no unbearable punishment,
nothing worse than exile, totally unharmed.

255 Labdacus (lăb′də-kəs).

(Oedipus *pauses, waiting for a reply.*)

WORDS TO KNOW

    denounce (dĭ-nouns′) *v.* to condemn publicly

Next,
    if anyone knows the murderer is a stranger,
    a man from alien soil, come, speak up.
    I will give him a handsome reward, and lay up
265   gratitude in my heart for him besides.

(silence again, no reply)

    But if you keep silent, if anyone panicking,
    trying to shield himself or friend or kin,
    rejects my offer, then hear what I will do.
    I order you, every citizen of the state
270   where I hold throne and power: banish this man—
    whoever he may be—never shelter him, never
    speak a word to him, never make him partner
    to your prayers, your victims burned to the gods.
    Never let the holy water touch his hands.
275   Drive him out, each of you, from every home.
    He is the plague, the heart of our corruption,
    as Apollo's oracle has just revealed to me.
    So I honor my obligations:
    I fight for the god and for the murdered man.

280   Now my curse on the murderer. Whoever he is,
    a lone man unknown in his crime
    or one among many, let that man drag out
    his life in agony, step by painful step—
    I curse myself as well . . . if by any chance
285   he proves to be an intimate of our house,
    here at my hearth, with my full knowledge,
    may the curse I just called down on him strike me!

    These are your orders: perform them to the last.
    I command you, for my sake, for Apollo's, for this country
290   blasted root and branch by the angry heavens.
    Even if god had never urged you on to act,
    how could you leave the crime uncleansed so long?
    A man so noble—your king, brought down in blood—
    you should have searched. But I am the king now,
295   I hold the throne that he held then, possess his bed
    and a wife who shares our seed . . . why, our seed
    might be the same, children born of the same mother
    might have created blood-bonds between us
    if his hope of offspring had not met disaster—

274 holy water: water used for purification after a sacrifice to the gods.

285 intimate: friend.

300 but fate swooped at his head and cut him short.
So I will fight for him as if he were my father,
stop at nothing, search the world
to lay my hands on the man who shed his blood,
the son of Labdacus descended of Polydorus,

305 Cadmus of old and Agenor, founder of the line:
their power and mine are one.

                Oh dear gods,
my curse on those who disobey these orders!
Let no crops grow out of the earth for them—
shrivel their women, kill their sons,

310 burn them to nothing in this plague
that hits us now, or something even worse.
But you, loyal men of Thebes who approve my actions,
may our champion, Justice, may all the gods
be with us, fight beside us to the end!

315 **Leader.** In the grip of your curse, my king, I swear
I'm not the murderer, I cannot point him out.
As for the search, Apollo pressed it on us—
he should name the killer.

Oedipus.   Quite right,
but to force the gods to act against their will—

320 no man has the power.

Leader.   Then if I might mention
the next best thing . . .

Oedipus.   The third best too—
don't hold back, say it.

Leader.   I still believe . . .
Lord Tiresias sees with the eyes of Lord Apollo.
Anyone searching for the truth, my king,

325 might learn it from the prophet, clear as day.

Oedipus. I've not been slow with that. On Creon's cue
I sent the escorts, twice, within the hour.
I'm surprised he isn't here.

Leader.   We need him—
without him we have nothing but old, useless rumors.

330 **Oedipus.** Which rumors? I'll search out every word.

Leader. Laius was killed, they say, by certain travelers.

Oedipus. I know—but no one can find the murderer.

Leader. If the man has a trace of fear in him

304 **Polydorus** (pŏl′ə-dôr′əs).

305 **Agenor** (ə-jē′nôr′): Cadmus'
father.

335 he won't stay silent long,
not with your curses ringing in his ears.

Oedipus. He didn't flinch at murder,
he'll never flinch at words.

PAUSE & REFLECT What curse does Oedipus put on the
killer or killers of Laius?

FOCUS After the prophet Tiresias enters, he and Oedipus
quarrel bitterly. In the heat of anger, Tiresias blurts out the
identity of Laius' murderer. Read to find out whom Tiresias
names.

(*Enter* Tiresias, *the blind prophet, led by a boy with escorts
in attendance. He remains at a distance.*)

Leader. Here is the one who will convict him, look,
they bring him on at last, the seer, the man of god.
340 The truth lives inside him, him alone.

Oedipus.   O Tiresias,
master of all the mysteries of our life,
all you teach and all you dare not tell,
signs in the heavens, signs that walk the earth!
Blind as you are, you can feel all the more
345 what sickness haunts our city. You, my lord,
are the one shield, the one savior we can find.

We asked Apollo—perhaps the messengers
haven't told you—he sent his answer back:
"Relief from the plague can only come one way.
350 Uncover the murderers of Laius,
put them to death or drive them into exile."
So I beg you, grudge us nothing now, no voice,
no message plucked from the birds, the embers
or the other mantic ways within your grasp.   **354 mantic:** prophetic.
355 Rescue yourself, your city, rescue me—
rescue everything infected by the dead.
We are in your hands. For a man to help others
with all his gifts and native strength:
that is the noblest work.

Tiresias.   How terrible—to see the truth
360 when the truth is only pain to him who sees!
I knew it well, but I put it from my mind,

else I never would have come.

Oedipus. What's this? Why so grim, so dire?

Tiresias. Just send me home. You bear your burdens,
365   I'll bear mine. It's better that way,
please believe me.

Oedipus.   Strange response . . . unlawful,
unfriendly too to the state that bred and reared you—
you withhold the word of god.

Tiresias.   I fail to see
that your own words are so well-timed.
370   I'd rather not have the same thing said of me . . .

Oedipus. For the love of god, don't turn away,
not if you know something. We beg you,
all of us on our knees.

Tiresias.   None of you knows—
and I will never reveal my dreadful secrets,
375   not to say your own.

Oedipus. What? You know and you won't tell?
You're bent on betraying us, destroying Thebes?

Tiresias. I'd rather not cause pain for you or me.
So why this . . . useless interrogation?
380   You'll get nothing from me.

Oedipus.   Nothing! You,
you scum of the earth, you'd enrage a heart of stone!
You won't talk? Nothing moves you?
Out with it, once and for all!

Tiresias. You criticize my temper . . . unaware
385   of the one *you* live with, you <u>revile</u> me.

Oedipus. Who could restrain his anger hearing you?
What outrage—you spurn the city!

Tiresias. What will come will come.
Even if I shroud it all in silence.

390   **Oedipus.** What will come? You're bound to *tell* me that.

Tiresias. I will say no more. Do as you like, build your anger
to whatever pitch you please, rage your worst—

Oedipus. Oh I'll let loose, I have such fury in me—
now I see it all. You helped hatch the plot,
395   you did the work, yes, short of killing him

379 interrogation (ĭn-tĕr′ə-gā′shən): questioning.

WORDS TO KNOW
revile (rĭ-vīl′) *v.* to abuse verbally; criticize harshly

YOU WON'T TALK?
NOTHING MOVES YOU?
OUT WITH IT, ONCE AND FOR ALL!

Oedipus accuses Tiresias in a London stage production of *Oedipus the King*, with Laurence Olivier as Oedipus and Ralph Richardson as Tiresias (1945).

with your own hands—and given eyes I'd say
you did the killing single-handed!

Tiresias.   Is that so!
I charge you, then, submit to that decree
you just laid down: from this day onward
speak to no one, not these citizens, not myself.
You are the curse, the corruption of the land!

Oedipus. You, shameless—
aren't you <u>appalled</u> to start up such a story?
You think you can get away with this?

Tiresias.   I have already.
The truth with all its power lives inside me.

Oedipus. Who primed you for this? Not your prophet's
    trade.

Tiresias. You did, you forced me, twisted it out of me.

Oedipus. What? Say it again—I'll understand it better.

Tiresias. Didn't you understand, just now?
Or are you tempting me to talk?

Oedipus. No, I can't say I grasped your meaning.
Out with it, again!

Tiresias. I say you are the murderer you hunt.

Oedipus. That obscenity, twice—by god, you'll pay.

Tiresias. Shall I say more, so you can really rage?

Oedipus. Much as you want. Your words are nothing—
<u>futile</u>.

Tiresias. You cannot imagine . . . I tell you,
you and your loved ones live together in infamy,
you cannot see how far you've gone in guilt.

Oedipus. You think you can keep this up and never suffer?

Tiresias. Indeed, if the truth has any power.

Oedipus.   It does
but not for you, old man. You've lost your power,
stone-blind, stone-deaf—senses, eyes blind as stone!

Tiresias. I pity you, flinging at me the very insults
each man here will fling at you so soon.

Oedipus.   Blind,
lost in the night, endless night that nursed you!
You can't hurt me or anyone else who sees the light—

418 **infamy** (ĭn'fə-mē): disgrace.

400

405

410

415

420

425

you can never touch me.

Tiresias.   True, it is not your fate
to fall at my hands. Apollo is quite enough,
430   and he will take some pains to work this out.

Oedipus. Creon! Is this conspiracy his or yours?

Tiresias. Creon is not your downfall, no, you are your own.

Oedipus.   O power—
wealth and empire, skill outstripping skill
in the heady rivalries of life,   **434 heady:** violent; passionate.
435   what envy lurks inside you! Just for this,
the crown the city gave me—I never sought it,
they laid it in my hands—for this alone, Creon,
the soul of trust, my loyal friend from the start
steals against me . . . so hungry to overthrow me
440   he sets this wizard on me, this scheming quack,
this fortune-teller peddling lies, eyes peeled
for his own profit—seer blind in his craft!

Come here, you pious fraud. Tell me,
when did you ever prove yourself a prophet?
445   When the Sphinx, that chanting Fury kept her death-
       watch here,
why silent then, not a word to set our people free?
There was a riddle, not for some passer-by to solve—
it cried out for a prophet. Where were you?
Did you rise to the crisis? Not a word,
450   you and your birds, your gods—nothing.
No, but I came by, Oedipus the ignorant,
I stopped the Sphinx! With no help from the birds,
the flight of my own intelligence hit the mark.

And this is the man you'd try to overthrow?
455   You think you'll stand by Creon when he's king?
You and the great mastermind—
you'll pay in tears, I promise you, for this,
this witch-hunt. If you didn't look so senile
the lash would teach you what your scheming means!

460   **Leader.** I would suggest his words were spoken in anger,
Oedipus . . . yours too, and it isn't what we need.
The best solution to the oracle, the riddle
posed by god—we should look for that.

Tiresias. You are the king no doubt, but in one respect,
465   at least, I am your equal: the right to reply.
    I claim that privilege too.
    I am not your slave. I serve Apollo.
    I don't need Creon to speak for me in public.

                                   So,
    you mock my blindness? Let me tell you this.
470   You with your precious eyes,
    you're blind to the corruption of your life,
    to the house you live in, those you live with—
    who *are* your parents? Do you know? All unknowing
    you are the scourge of your own flesh and blood,
475   the dead below the earth and the living here above,
    and the double lash of your mother and your father's
        curse
    will whip you from this land one day, their footfall
    treading you down in terror, darkness shrouding
    your eyes that now can see the light!
                           Soon, soon
480   you'll scream aloud—what haven won't <u>reverberate</u>?
    What rock of Cithaeron won't scream back in echo?
    That day you learn the truth about your marriage,
    the wedding-march that sang you into your halls,
    the lusty voyage home to the fatal harbor!
485   And a crowd of other horrors you'd never dream
    will level you with yourself and all your children.

    There. Now smear us with insults—Creon, myself
    and every word I've said. No man will ever
    be rooted from the earth as brutally as you.

490 **Oedipus.** Enough! Such filth from him? Insufferable—
    what, still alive? Get out—
    faster, back where you came from—vanish!

Tiresias. I would never have come if you hadn't called me
    here.

Oedipus. If I thought you would blurt out such absurdities,
495   you'd have died waiting before I'd had you summoned.

Tiresias. Absurd, am I! To you, not to your parents:
    the ones who bore you found me sane enough.

Oedipus. Parents—who? Wait . . . who is my father?

Tiresias. This day will bring your birth and your destruction.

480 haven: place of safety.

481 Cithaeron (sĭ-thîr′ən): a mountain about 12 miles south of Thebes.

reverberate (rĭ-vûr′bə-rāt′) *v.* to reflect a noise; resound

500   **Oedipus.** Riddles—all you can say are riddles, murk and
           darkness.

       Tiresias. Ah, but aren't you the best man alive at solving
           riddles?

       Oedipus. Mock me for that, go on, and you'll reveal my
           greatness.

       Tiresias. Your great good fortune, true, it was your ruin.

       Oedipus. Not if I saved the city—what do I care?

505   **Tiresias.** Well then, I'll be going.

       (*to his attendant*)

                                        Take me home, boy.

       Oedipus. Yes, take him away. You're a nuisance here.
           Out of the way, the irritation's gone.

       (*turning his back on* Tiresias, *moving toward the palace*)

       Tiresias.   I will go,
           once I have said what I came here to say.
           I will never shrink from the anger in your eyes—
510   you can't destroy me. Listen to me closely:
           the man you've sought so long, proclaiming,
           cursing up and down, the murderer of Laius—
           he is here. A stranger,
           you may think, who lives among you,
515   he soon will be revealed a native Theban
           but he will take no joy in the revelation.
           Blind who now has eyes, beggar who now is rich,
           he will grope his way toward a foreign soil,
           a stick tapping before him step by step.

       (Oedipus *enters the palace.*)

520   Revealed at last, brother and father both
           to the children he embraces, to his mother
           son and husband both—he sowed the loins
           his father sowed, he spilled his father's blood!

           Go in and reflect on that, solve that.
525   And if you find I've lied
           from this day onward call the prophet blind.

       (Tiresias *and the boy exit to the side.*)

       PAUSE & REFLECT Whom does Tiresias name as the
       murderer of Laius?

The chorus describes the panic that the
murderer of Laius must now feel and then reflects on
Oedipus. As you read, look for details that suggest how
the chorus feels about Oedipus at this point in the play.

Chorus.   Who—
    who is the man the voice of god denounces
    resounding out of the rocky gorge of Delphi?
       The horror too dark to tell,
530   whose ruthless bloody hands have done the work?
    His time has come to fly
       to outrace the stallions of the storm
           his feet a streak of speed—
    Cased in armor, Apollo son of the Father
535   lunges on him, lightning-bolts afire!
    And the grim unerring Furies
          closing for the kill.
                  Look,
    the word of god has just come blazing
    flashing off Parnassus' snowy heights!
540   That man who left no trace—
    after him, hunt him down with all our strength!
    Now under bristling timber
       up through rocks and caves he stalks
          like the wild mountain bull—
545   cut off from men, each step an agony, frenzied, racing
       blind
    but he cannot outrace the dread voices of Delphi
    ringing out of the heart of Earth,
       the dark wings beating around him shrieking doom
          the doom that never dies, the terror—
550   The skilled prophet scans the birds and shatters me with
       terror!
    I can't accept him, can't deny him, don't know what to
       say,
    I'm lost, and the wings of dark <u>foreboding</u> beating—
    I cannot see what's come, what's still to come . . .
    and what could breed a blood feud between
555   Laius' house and the son of Polybus?
    I know of nothing, not in the past and not now,
    no charge to bring against our king, no cause

536 unerring: not turning aside;
relentless; **Furies:** terrifying goddesses who pursue and punish
criminals.

539 Parnassus' (pär-năs′əs) **snowy
heights:** the peaks of the mountain
that towers over Delphi.

555 the son of Polybus (pŏl′ə-bəs):
Oedipus, who believes himself to
be the son of Polybus, king of
Corinth.

WORDS TO KNOW
282   **foreboding** (fôr-bō′dĭng) *n.* a sense of evil or danger to come

to attack his fame that rings throughout Thebes—
　　not without proof—not for the ghost of Laius,
560　　　not to avenge a murder gone without a trace.

Zeus and Apollo know, they know, the great masters
　　　　of all the dark and depth of human life.
But whether a mere man can know the truth,
whether a seer can fathom more than I—　　　　　　　**564 fathom:** understand.
565　there is no test, no certain proof
　　　though matching skill for skill
a man can outstrip a rival. No, not till I see
these charges proved will I side with his accusers.
We saw him then, when the she-hawk swept against him,　**569 she-hawk:** the Sphinx.
570　saw with our own eyes his skill, his brilliant triumph—
　　　there was the test—he was the joy of Thebes!
　　　Never will I convict my king, never in my heart.

Thinking Through the Literature

1. Why does Oedipus send for Tiresias?

2. How does the chorus feel about Oedipus at this point in the play?

3. Why do you think Oedipus is so determined to discover the murderer of Laius?

 THINK ABOUT
　　• how he feels about the people of Thebes
　　• how he once saved the city from the Sphinx
　　• why he might feel especially close to the murdered king

What do each of these images suggest about the chorus? Study the gestures, postures, costuming, and physical positions.

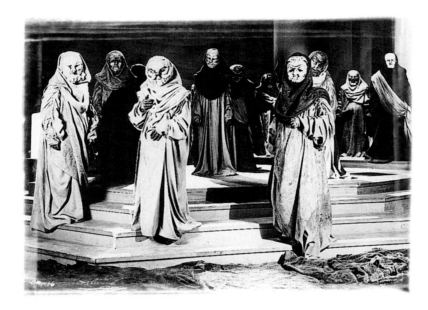

Tyrone Guthrie film
version, *Oedipus Rex*
(1957)

Peter Hall stage production
of *Oedipus the King* (1996)

FOCUS Creon defends himself against Oedipus' charge of treason. Read to find out how Oedipus treats Creon in this scene.

(*Enter* Creon *from the side.*)

Creon. My fellow-citizens, I hear King Oedipus
    levels terrible charges at me. I had to come.
575   I resent it deeply. If, in the present crisis,
    he thinks he suffers any abuse from me,
    anything I've done or said that offers him
    the slightest injury, why, I've no desire
    to linger out this life, my reputation in ruins.
580   The damage I'd face from such an accusation
    is nothing simple. No, there's nothing worse:
    branded a traitor in the city, a traitor
    to all of you and my good friends.

Leader.   True,
    but a slur might have been forced out of him,
585   by anger perhaps, not any firm conviction.

Creon. The charge was made in public, wasn't it?
    I put the prophet up to spreading lies?

Leader. Such things were said . . .
    I don't know with what intent, if any.

590 **Creon.** Was his glance steady, his mind right
    when the charge was brought against me?

Leader. I really couldn't say. I never look
    to judge the ones in power.

(*The doors open.* Oedipus *enters.*)

                    Wait,
    here's Oedipus now.

Oedipus.   You—here? You have the gall
595   to show your face before the palace gates?
    You, plotting to kill me, kill the king—
    I see it all, the marauding thief himself
    scheming to steal my crown and power!
                    Tell me,
    in god's name, what did you take me for,
600   coward or fool, when you spun out your plot?
    Your treachery—you think I'd never detect it
    creeping against me in the dark? Or sensing it,
    not defend myself? Aren't you the fool,
    you and your high adventure. Lacking numbers,

594 gall: rude boldness.

597 marauding: roaming in search of plunder.

605 powerful friends, out for the big game of empire—
you need riches, armies to bring that quarry down!

606 **quarry:** the object of a hunt.

Creon. Are you quite finished? It's your turn to listen
for just as long as you've . . . instructed me.
Hear me out, then judge me on the facts.

610 **Oedipus.** You've a wicked way with words, Creon,
but I'll be slow to learn—from you.
I find you a <u>menace</u>, a great burden to me.

Creon. Just one thing, hear me out in this.

Oedipus.   Just one thing,
don't tell *me* you're not the enemy, the traitor.

615 **Creon.** Look, if you think crude, mindless stubbornness
such a gift, you've lost your sense of balance.

Oedipus. If you think you can abuse a kinsman,
then escape the penalty, you're insane.

Creon. Fair enough, I grant you. But this injury
620 you say I've done you, what is it?

Oedipus. Did you induce me, yes or no,
to send for that sanctimonious prophet?

622 **sanctimonious** (săngk′tə-mō′nē-əs): making a show of being holy or pious.

Creon. I did. And I'd do the same again.

Oedipus. All right then, tell me, how long is it now
625 since Laius . . .

Creon.   Laius—what did *he* do?

Oedipus.   Vanished,
swept from sight, murdered in his tracks.

Creon. The count of the years would run you far back . . .

Oedipus. And that far back, was the prophet at his trade?

Creon. Skilled as he is today, and just as honored.

630 **Oedipus.** Did he ever refer to me then, at that time?

Creon.   No,
never, at least, when I was in his presence.

Oedipus. But you did investigate the murder, didn't you?

Creon. We did our best, of course, discovered nothing.

Oedipus. But the great seer never accused me then—why
not?

635 **Creon.** I don't know. And when I don't, *I* keep quiet.

Oedipus. You do know this, you'd tell it too—
if you had a shred of decency.

WORDS TO KNOW

286   **menace** (mĕn′ĭs) *n.* a threat

Creon.   What?
          If I know, I won't hold back.

Oedipus.   Simply this:
          if the two of you had never put heads together,
640   we would never have heard about *my* killing Laius.

Creon. If that's what he says . . . well, you know best.
          But now I have a right to learn from you
          as you just learned from me.

Oedipus.   Learn your fill,
          you never will convict me of the murder.

645 **Creon.** Tell me, you're married to my sister, aren't you?

Oedipus. A genuine discovery—there's no denying that.

Creon. And you rule the land with her, with equal power?

Oedipus. She receives from me whatever she desires.

Creon. And I am the third, all of us are equals?

650 **Oedipus.** Yes, and it's there you show your stripes—
          you betray a kinsman.

Creon.   Not at all.
          Not if you see things calmly, rationally,
          as I do. Look at it this way first:
          who in his right mind would rather rule
655   and live in anxiety than sleep in peace?
          Particularly if he enjoys the same authority.
          Not I, I'm not the man to yearn for kingship,
          not with a king's power in my hands. Who would?
          No one with any sense of self-control.
660   Now, as it is, you offer me all I need,
          not a fear in the world. But if I wore the crown . . .
          there'd be many painful duties to perform,
          hardly to my taste.
                              How could kingship
          please me more than influence, power
665   without a qualm? I'm not that deluded yet,
          to reach for anything but privilege outright,
          profit free and clear.
          Now all men sing my praises, all salute me,
          now all who request your favors curry mine.
670   I am their best hope: success rests in me.
          Why give up that, I ask you, and borrow trouble?
          A man of sense, someone who sees things clearly

665 qualm: feeling of uneasiness or doubt.

669 curry: seek by flattery.

would never resort to treason.
No, I have no lust for conspiracy in me,
675 nor could I ever suffer one who does.

Do you want proof? Go to Delphi yourself,
examine the oracle and see if I've reported
the message word-for-word. This too:
if you detect that I and the clairvoyant
680 have plotted anything in common, arrest me,
execute me. Not on the strength of one vote,
two in this case, mine as well as yours.
But don't convict me on sheer unverified <u>surmise</u>.
How wrong it is to take the good for bad,
685 purely at random, or take the bad for good.
But reject a friend, a kinsman? I would as soon
tear out the life within us, priceless life itself.
You'll learn this well, without fail, in time.
Time alone can bring the just man to light—
690 the criminal you can spot in one short day.

Leader.   Good advice,
my lord, for anyone who wants to avoid disaster.
Those who jump to conclusions may go wrong.

Oedipus. When my enemy moves against me quickly,
plots in secret, I move quickly too, I must,
695 I plot and pay him back. Relax my guard a moment,
waiting his next move—he wins his objective,
I lose mine.

Creon.   What do you want?
You want me banished?

Oedipus.   No, I want you dead.

Creon. Just to show how ugly a grudge can . . .

Oedipus.   So,
700 still stubborn? you don't think I'm serious?

Creon. I think you're insane.

Oedipus.   Quite sane—in my behalf.

Creon. Not just as much in mine?

Oedipus.   You—my mortal enemy?

Creon. What if you're wholly wrong?

Oedipus.   No matter—I must rule.

679 **clairvoyant:** person who can see the future—here, Tiresias.

683 **unverified:** not proved to be true.

Creon. Not if you rule unjustly.

Oedipus. Hear him, Thebes, my city!

705 **Creon.** My city too, not yours alone!

Leader. Please, my lords.

(*Enter* Jocasta *from the palace.*)

Look, Jocasta's coming,
and just in time too. With her help
you must put this fighting of yours to rest.

Jocasta. Have you no sense? Poor misguided men,
710 such shouting—why this public outburst?
Aren't you ashamed, with the land so sick,
to stir up private quarrels?

(*to* Oedipus)

Into the palace now. And Creon, you go home.
Why make such a furor over nothing?

715 **Creon.** My sister, it's dreadful . . . Oedipus, your husband,
he's bent on a choice of punishments for me,
banishment from the fatherland or death.

Oedipus. Precisely. I caught him in the act, Jocasta,
plotting, about to stab me in the back.

720 **Creon.** Never—curse me, let me die and be damned
if I've done you any wrong you charge me with.

Jocasta. Oh god, believe it, Oedipus,
honor the solemn oath he swears to heaven.
Do it for me, for the sake of all your people.

(*The* Chorus *begins to chant.*)

725 **Chorus.** Believe it, be sensible
give way, my king, I beg you!

Oedipus. What do you want from me, concessions?

727 concessions: favors.

Chorus. Respect him—he's been no fool in the past
and now he's strong with the oath he swears to god.

730 **Oedipus.** You know what you're asking?

Chorus. I do.

Oedipus. Then out with it!

Chorus. The man's your friend, your kin, he's under oath—
don't cast him out, disgraced
branded with guilt on the strength of hearsay only.

Oedipus. Know full well, if that is what you want

The Greek National Theater's performance of *Oedipus the King* in Rome's Colosseum (2000). Most of the figures shown here are statues, used to create a backdrop for the action.

735　　　you want me dead or banished from the land.

Chorus.　　　　　　　　　　　　　　　　Never—
　　　　no, by the blazing Sun, first god of the heavens!
　　　　　Stripped of the gods, stripped of loved ones,
　　　　let me die by inches if that ever crossed my mind.
　　　　But the heart inside me sickens, dies as the land dies
740　　　and now on top of the old griefs you pile this,
　　　　your fury—both of you!

Oedipus.　　　　　　　　　　　Then let him go,
　　　　even if it does lead to my ruin, my death
　　　　or my disgrace, driven from Thebes for life.
　　　　It's you, not him I pity—your words move me.
745　　　He, wherever he goes, my hate goes with him.

Creon. Look at you, sullen in yielding, brutal in your rage—
　　　　you will go too far. It's perfect justice:
　　　　natures like yours are hardest on themselves.

Oedipus. Then leave me alone—get out!

Creon.   I'm going.
750   You're wrong, so wrong. These men know I'm right.

(*Exit to the side.*)

> **PAUSE & REFLECT** Why does Oedipus turn against
> Creon?

> **FOCUS** As Creon leaves, Oedipus is still very angry.
> Jocasta tries to calm him down. Unintentionally, however,
> she awakens his deepest fears. Read to find out why he
> suddenly becomes afraid.

(*The* Chorus *turns to* Jocasta.)

Chorus. Why do you hesitate, my lady
                why not help him in?

Jocasta. Tell me what's happened first.

Chorus. Loose, ignorant talk started dark suspicions
755   and a sense of injustice cut deeply too.

Jocasta. On both sides?

Chorus.   Oh yes.

Jocasta.   What did they say?

Chorus. Enough, please, enough! The land's so racked already
                or so it seems to me . . .
                End the trouble here, just where they left it.

760 **Oedipus.** You see what comes of your good intentions now?
                And all because you tried to blunt my anger.

761 blunt: make less sharp.

Chorus.   My king,
                I've said it once, I'll say it time and again—
                    I'd be insane, you know it,
                senseless, ever to turn my back on you.
765   You who set our beloved land—storm-tossed,
                    shattered—
                straight on course. Now again, good helmsman,
                steer us through the storm!

(*The* Chorus *draws away, leaving* Oedipus *and* Jocasta *side
by side.*)

Jocasta.   For the love of god,
                Oedipus, tell me too, what is it?
                Why this rage? You're so unbending.

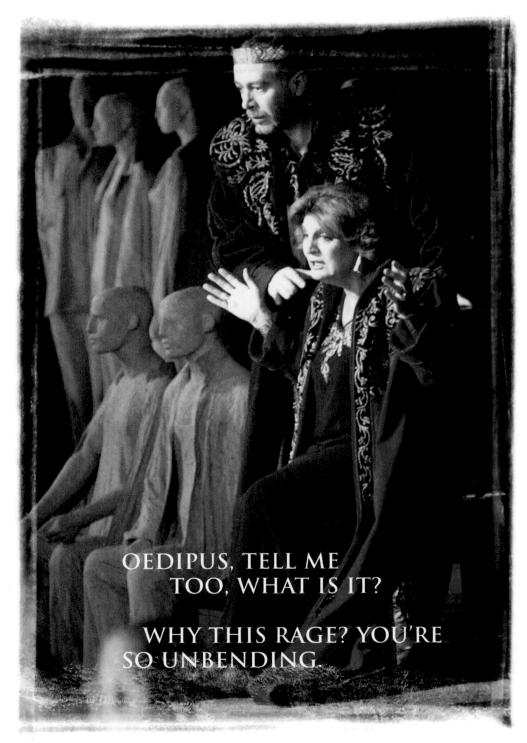

OEDIPUS, TELL ME
TOO, WHAT IS IT?

WHY THIS RAGE? YOU'RE
SO UNBENDING.

Oedipus and Jocasta in the Greek National Theater's *Oedipus Rex*, staged in Rome's Colosseum (2000).

770 **Oedipus.** I will tell you. I respect you, Jocasta,
　　　much more than these men here . . .

(*glancing at the* Chorus)

　　　Creon's to blame, Creon schemes against me.

Jocasta. Tell me clearly, how did the quarrel start?

Oedipus. He says *I* murdered Laius—I am guilty.

775 **Jocasta.** How does he know? Some secret knowledge
　　　or simple hearsay?

Oedipus. 　　　　　　　　Oh, he sent his prophet in
　　　to do his dirty work. You know Creon,
　　　Creon keeps his own lips clean.

Jocasta. 　　　　　　　　　　A prophet?
　　　Well then, free yourself of every charge!
780 　Listen to me and learn some peace of mind:
　　　no skill in the world,
　　　nothing human can penetrate the future.
　　　Here is proof, quick and to the point.

　　　An oracle came to Laius one fine day
785 　(I won't say from Apollo himself
　　　but his underlings, his priests) and it declared
　　　that doom would strike him down at the hands of a son,
　　　our son, to be born of our own flesh and blood. But Laius,
　　　so the report goes at least, was killed by strangers,
790 　thieves, at a place where three roads meet . . . my son—
　　　he wasn't three days old and the boy's father
　　　fastened his ankles, had a henchman fling him away

792 henchman: trusted follower.

　　　on a barren, trackless mountain.
　　　　　　　　　　　　　　　There, you see?
　　　Apollo brought neither thing to pass. My baby
795 　no more murdered his father than Laius suffered—
　　　his wildest fear—death at his own son's hands.
　　　That's how the seers and all their revelations
　　　mapped out the future. Brush them from your mind.
　　　Whatever the god needs and seeks
800 　he'll bring to light himself, with ease.

Oedipus. 　　　　　　　　　　　　Strange,
　　　hearing you just now . . . my mind wandered,
　　　my thoughts racing back and forth.

Jocasta. What do you mean? Why so anxious, startled?

Oedipus. I thought I heard you say that Laius
805   was cut down at a place where three roads meet.

Jocasta. That was the story. It hasn't died out yet.

Oedipus. Where did this thing happen? Be precise.

Jocasta. A place called Phocis, where two branching roads,
        one from Daulia, one from Delphi,
810   come together—a crossroads.

Oedipus. When? How long ago?

Jocasta. The heralds no sooner reported Laius dead
        than you appeared and they hailed you king of Thebes.

Oedipus. My god, my god—what have you planned to do
        to me?

815   **Jocasta.** What, Oedipus? What haunts you so?

Oedipus.   Not yet.
        Laius—how did he look? Describe him.
        Had he reached his prime?

Jocasta.   He was <u>swarthy</u>,
        and the gray had just begun to streak his temples,
        and his build . . . wasn't far from yours.

Oedipus.   Oh no no,
820   I think I've just called down a dreadful curse
        upon myself—I simply didn't know!

Jocasta. What are you saying? I shudder to look at you.

Oedipus. I have a terrible fear the blind seer can see.
        I'll know in a moment. One thing more—

Jocasta.   Anything,
825   afraid as I am—ask, I'll answer, all I can.

Oedipus. Did he go with a light or heavy escort,
        several men-at-arms, like a lord, a king?

Jocasta. There were five in the party, a herald among them,
        and a single wagon carrying Laius.

Oedipus.   Ai—
830   now I can see it all, clear as day.
        Who told you all this at the time, Jocasta?

Jocasta. A servant who reached home, the lone survivor.

Oedipus. So, could he still be in the palace—even now?

Jocasta. No indeed. Soon as he returned from the scene
835   and saw you on the throne with Laius dead and gone,

808 Phocis (fō′sĭs): a region of
central Greece, between Delphi
and Thebes.

809 Daulia (dô′lē-ə).

WORDS TO KNOW

swarthy (swôr′thē) *adj.* having a dark complexion

294

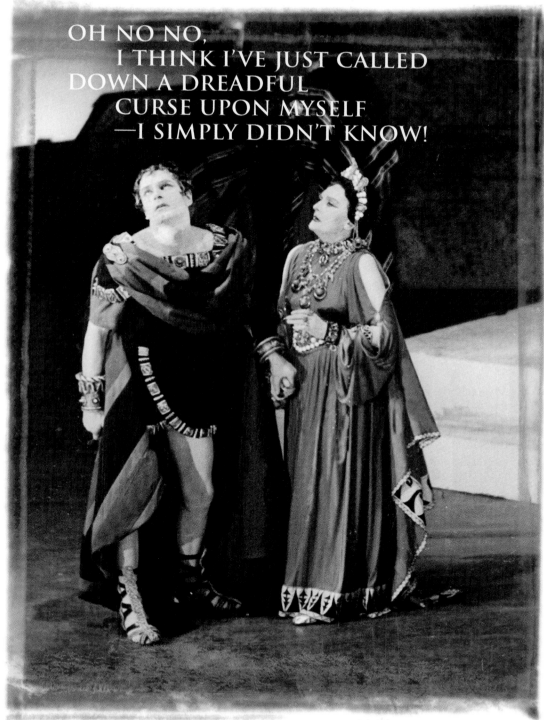

> OH NO NO,
>   I THINK I'VE JUST CALLED
> DOWN A DREADFUL
>   CURSE UPON MYSELF
>   —I SIMPLY DIDN'T KNOW!

Laurence Olivier and Sybil Thorndike playing Oedipus and Jocasta in a production at the New Theatre in London (1945).

he knelt and clutched my hand, pleading with me
to send him into the hinterlands, to pasture,
far as possible, out of sight of Thebes.
I sent him away. Slave though he was,
840   he'd earned that favor—and much more.

Oedipus. Can we bring him back, quickly?

Jocasta. Easily. Why do you want him so?

Oedipus.   I am afraid,
Jocasta, I have said too much already.
That man—I've got to see him.

Jocasta.   Then he'll come.
845   But even I have a right, I'd like to think,
to know what's torturing you, my lord.

Oedipus. And so you shall—I can hold nothing back from
      you,
now I've reached this pitch of dark foreboding.
Who means more to me than you? Tell me,
850   whom would I turn toward but you
as I go through all this?

My father was Polybus, king of Corinth.
My mother, a Dorian, Merope. And I was held
the prince of the realm among the people there,
855   till something struck me out of nowhere,
something strange . . . worth remarking perhaps,
hardly worth the anxiety I gave it.
Some man at a banquet who had drunk too much
shouted out—he was far gone, mind you—
860   that I am not my father's son. Fighting words!
I barely restrained myself that day
but early the next I went to mother and father,
questioned them closely, and they were enraged
at the accusation and the fool who let it fly.
865   So as for my parents I was satisfied,
but still this thing kept gnawing at me,
the slander spread—I had to make my move.
                                   And so,
unknown to mother and father I set out for Delphi,
and the god Apollo spurned me, sent me away
870   denied the facts I came for,
but first he flashed before my eyes a future
great with pain, terror, disaster—I can hear him cry,

853 Dorian (dôr′ē-ən): descended from Dorus, the ancestor of one of the main divisions of the Greek people; **Merope** (mĕr′ə-pē′).

866 gnawing at: biting at; tormenting.

867 slander: statements that unfairly harm a person's reputation.

869 spurned: rejected.

"You are fated to couple with your mother, you will
        bring
a breed of children into the light no man can bear to
        see—
875 you will kill your father, the one who gave you life!"
I heard all that and ran. I abandoned Corinth,
from that day on I gauged its landfall only
by the stars, running, always running
toward some place where I would never see
880 the shame of all those oracles come true.
And as I fled I reached that very spot
where the great king, you say, met his death.

Now, Jocasta, I will tell you all.
Making my way toward this triple crossroad
885 I began to see a herald, then a brace of colts
drawing a wagon, and mounted on the bench . . . a man,
just as you've described him, coming face-to-face,
and the one in the lead and the old man himself
were about to thrust me off the road—brute force—
890 and the one shouldering me aside, the driver,
I strike him in anger!—and the old man, watching me
coming up along his wheels—he brings down
his prod, two prongs straight at my head!
I paid him back with interest!
895 Short work, by god—with one blow of the staff
in this right hand I knock him out of his high seat,
roll him out of the wagon, sprawling headlong—
I killed them all—every mother's son!

Oh, but if there is any blood-tie
900 between Laius and this stranger . . .
what man alive more miserable than I?
More hated by the gods? *I* am the man
no alien, no citizen welcomes to his house,
law forbids it—not a word to me in public,
905 driven out of every hearth and home.
And all these curses I—no one but I
brought down these piling curses on myself!
And you, his wife, I've touched your body with these,
the hands that killed your husband cover you with
        blood.

910 Wasn't I born for torment? Look me in the eyes!
I am abomination—heart and soul!
I must be exiled, and even in exile
never see my parents, never set foot
on native ground again. Else I am doomed
915 to couple with my mother and cut my father down . . .
Polybus who reared me, gave me life.
                                    But why, why?
Wouldn't a man of judgment say—and wouldn't he be
    right—
some savage power has brought this down upon my
    head?

Oh no, not that, you pure and awesome gods,
920 never let me see that day! Let me slip
from the world of men, vanish without a trace
before I see myself stained with such corruption,
stained to the heart.

Leader. My lord, you fill our hearts with fear.
925 But at least until you question the witness,
do take hope.

Oedipus.   Exactly. He is my last hope—
I am waiting for the shepherd. He is crucial.

Jocasta. And once he appears, what then? Why so urgent?

Oedipus. I will tell you. If it turns out that his story
930 matches yours, I've escaped the worst.

Jocasta. What did I say? What struck you so?

Oedipus.   You said *thieves*—
he told you a whole band of them murdered Laius.
So, if he still holds to the same number,
I cannot be the killer. One can't equal many.
935 But if he refers to one man, one alone,
clearly the scales come down on me:
I am guilty.

Jocasta.   Impossible. Trust me,
I told you precisely what he said,
and he can't <u>retract</u> it now;
940 the whole city heard it, not just I.
And even if he should vary his first report
by one man more or less, still, my lord,
he could never make the murder of Laius

911 **abomination** (ə-bŏm′ə-nā′shən): a disgusting thing.

retract (rĭ-trăkt′) *v.* to take back; withdraw

truly fit the prophecy. Apollo was <u>explicit</u>:
945   my son was doomed to kill my husband . . . my son,
poor defenseless thing, he never had a chance
to kill his father. They destroyed him first.

So much for prophecy. It's neither here nor there.
From this day on, I wouldn't look right or left.

950 **Oedipus.** True, true. Still, that shepherd,
   someone fetch him—now!

Jocasta. I'll send at once. But do let's go inside.
   I'd never displease you, least of all in this.

(Oedipus *and* Jocasta *enter the palace.*)

PAUSE & REFLECT Jocasta has told Oedipus that Laius
was killed at "a place where three roads meet." Why
does Oedipus become fearful when he hears this piece of
information?

FOCUS The chorus now sings about the timeless laws
that rule human life. Read to find out how the chorus feels
about the old prophecies.

Chorus. Destiny guide me always
955   Destiny find me filled with reverence
           pure in word and deed.
        Great laws tower above us, reared on high
        born for the brilliant vault of heaven—
           Olympian Sky their only father,
960   nothing mortal, no man gave them birth,
        their memory deathless, never lost in sleep:
        within them lives a mighty god, the god does not
           grow old.

        Pride breeds the tyrant
        violent pride, gorging, crammed to bursting
965   with all that is overripe and rich with ruin—
        clawing up to the heights, headlong pride
        crashes down the abyss—sheer doom!
           No footing helps, all foothold lost and gone.
        But the healthy strife that makes the city strong—   **969 strife:** conflict.
970   I pray that god will never end that wrestling:
        god, my champion, I will never let you go.

WORDS TO KNOW
explicit (ĭk-splĭs′ĭt) *adj.* clear; definite

But if any man comes striding, high and mighty
　　in all he says and does,
no fear of justice, no reverence
975　for the temples of the gods—
　　let a rough doom tear him down,
repay his pride, breakneck, ruinous pride!
If he cannot reap his profits fairly
　　cannot restrain himself from outrage—
980　mad, laying hands on the holy things untouchable!

　　Can such a man, so desperate, still boast
　　he can save his life from the flashing bolts of god?
　　　　If all such violence goes with honor now
　　　　　　why join the sacred dance?

985　Never again will I go reverent to Delphi,
　　　　the inviolate heart of Earth
　　or Apollo's ancient oracle at Abae
　　or Olympia of the fires—
　　　　unless these prophecies all come true
990　for all mankind to point toward in wonder.
　　King of kings, if you deserve your titles
　　　　Zeus, remember, never forget!
　　You and your deathless, everlasting reign.

　　　　They are dying, the old oracles sent to Laius,
995　　　now our masters strike them off the rolls.
　　　　　　Nowhere Apollo's golden glory now—
　　　　　　　　the gods, the gods go down.

986 inviolate (ĭn-vī′ə-lĭt): pure.

987 Abae (ā′bē).

988 Olympia (ō-lĭm′pē-ə): the site of an oracle of Zeus.

Thinking Through the Literature

1. What did Oedipus do at "a place where three roads meet"?

2. Why did Oedipus run away from his home in Corinth?

3. How would you describe Jocasta's view of prophets and prophecies?

4. What is the chorus's attitude toward the old prophecies?

FOCUS Jocasta prays to the god Apollo, asking for help for her husband. Then a messenger arrives with startling news about Polybus, the king of Corinth. Read to find out what the news is.

(*Enter* Jocasta *from the palace, carrying a suppliant's branch wound in wool.*)

Jocasta. Lords of the realm, it occurred to me,
just now, to visit the temples of the gods,
1000   so I have my branch in hand and incense too.

Oedipus is beside himself. Racked with anguish,
no longer a man of sense, he won't admit
the latest prophecies are hollow as the old—
he's at the mercy of every passing voice
1005   if the voice tells of terror.
I urge him gently, nothing seems to help,
so I turn to you, Apollo, you are nearest.

(*placing her branch on the altar, while an old herdsman enters from the side, not the one just summoned by the king but an unexpected* Messenger *from Corinth*)

I come with prayers and offerings . . . I beg you,
cleanse us, set us free of defilement!
1010   Look at us, passengers in the grip of fear,
watching the pilot of the vessel go to pieces.

Messenger (*approaching* Jocasta *and the* Chorus).
Strangers, please, I wonder if you could lead us
to the palace of the king . . . I think it's Oedipus.
Better, the man himself—you know where he is?

1015 **Leader.** This is his palace, stranger. He's inside.
But here is his queen, his wife and mother
of his children.

Messenger.   Blessings on you, noble queen,
queen of Oedipus crowned with all your family—
blessings on you always!

1020 **Jocasta.** And the same to you, stranger, you deserve it . . .
such a greeting. But what have you come for?
Have you brought us news?

Messenger.   Wonderful news—
for the house, my lady, for your husband too.

Jocasta. Really, what? Who sent you?

1011 pilot of the vessel: Oedipus, who guides the "ship of state."

Messenger.   Corinth.
1025   I'll give you the message in a moment.
          You'll be glad of it—how could you help it?—
          though it costs a little sorrow in the bargain.

Jocasta. What can it be, with such a double edge?

Messenger. The people there, they want to make your
              Oedipus
1030   king of Corinth, so they're saying now.

Jocasta. Why? Isn't old Polybus still in power?

Messenger. No more. Death has got him in the tomb.

Jocasta. What are you saying? Polybus, dead?—dead?

Messenger.   If not,
          if I'm not telling the truth, strike me dead too.

Jocasta (*to a servant*).
1035   Quickly, go to your master, tell him this!

          You prophecies of the gods, where are you now?
          This is the man that Oedipus feared for years,
          he fled him, not to kill him—and now he's dead,
          quite by chance, a normal, natural death,
1040   not murdered by his son.

Oedipus (*emerging from the palace*).
                                    Dearest,
          what now? Why call me from the palace?

Jocasta (*bringing the* Messenger *closer*).
          Listen to *him,* see for yourself what all
          those awful prophecies of god have come to.

Oedipus. And who is he? What can he have for me?

1045 **Jocasta.** He's from Corinth, he's come to tell you
          your father is no more—Polybus—he's dead!

Oedipus (*wheeling on the* Messenger).
          What? Let me have it from your lips.

Messenger.   Well,
          if that's what you want first, then here it is:
          make no mistake, Polybus is dead and gone.

1050 **Oedipus.** How—murder? sickness?—what? what killed him?

Messenger. A light tip of the scales can put old bones to rest.

Oedipus. Sickness then—poor man, it wore him down.

1051 A light tip . . . to rest: A little disturbance can cause an old person to die.

Messenger.   That,
   and the long count of years he'd measured out.

Oedipus.   So!
   Jocasta, why, why look to the Prophet's hearth,
1055   the fires of the future? Why scan the birds
   that scream above our heads? They winged me on
   to the murder of my father, did they? That was my doom?
   Well look, he's dead and buried, hidden under the earth,
   and here I am in Thebes, I never put hand to sword—
1060   unless some longing for me wasted him away,
   then in a sense you'd say I caused his death.
   But now, all those prophecies I feared—Polybus
   packs them off to sleep with him in hell!
   They're nothing, worthless.

PAUSE & REFLECT What does Oedipus learn about
Polybus from the messenger?

FOCUS Read to find out how Oedipus happened to be
raised as the son of Polybus.

Jocasta.   There.
1065   Didn't I tell you from the start?

Oedipus. So you did. I was lost in fear.

Jocasta. No more, sweep it from your mind forever.

Oedipus. But my mother's bed, surely I must fear—

Jocasta.   Fear?
   What should a man fear? It's all chance,
1070   chance rules our lives. Not a man on earth
   can see a day ahead, groping through the dark.
   Better to live at random, best we can.
   And as for this marriage with your mother—
   have no fear. Many a man before you,
1075   in his dreams, has shared his mother's bed.
   Take such things for shadows, nothing at all—
   Live, Oedipus,
   as if there's no tomorrow!

Oedipus.   Brave words,
   and you'd persuade me if mother weren't alive.
1080   But mother lives, so for all your reassurances
   I live in fear, I must.

Jocasta.   But your father's death,
that, at least, is a great blessing, joy to the eyes!

Oedipus. Great, I know . . . but I fear *her*—she's still alive.

Messenger. Wait, who is this woman, makes you so afraid?

1085 **Oedipus.** Merope, old man. The wife of Polybus.

Messenger. The queen? What's there to fear in her?

Oedipus. A dreadful prophecy, stranger, sent by the gods.

Messenger. Tell me, could you? Unless it's forbidden
other ears to hear.

Oedipus.   Not at all.
1090 Apollo told me once—it is my fate—
I must make love with my own mother,
shed my father's blood with my own hands.
So for years I've given Corinth a wide berth,
and it's been my good fortune too. But still,
1095 to see one's parents and look into their eyes
is the greatest joy I know.

Messenger.   You're afraid of that?
That kept you out of Corinth?

Oedipus.   My *father*, old man—
so I wouldn't kill my father.

Messenger.   So that's it.
Well then, seeing I came with such good will, my king,
1100 why don't I rid you of that old worry now?

Oedipus. What a rich reward you'd have for that!

Messenger. What do you think I came for, majesty?
So you'd come home and I'd be better off.

Oedipus. Never, I will never go near my parents.

1105 **Messenger.** My boy, it's clear, you don't know what you're
doing.

Oedipus. What do you mean, old man? For god's sake,
explain.

Messenger. If you ran from *them,* always dodging home . . .

Oedipus. Always, terrified Apollo's oracle might come true—

Messenger. And you'd be covered with guilt, from both
your parents.

1110 **Oedipus.** That's right, old man, that fear is always with me.

Messenger. Don't you know? You've really nothing to fear.

> **1093 given Corinth a wide berth:**
> stayed far away from Corinth.

Oedipus. But why? If I'm their son—Merope, Polybus?

Messenger. Polybus was nothing to you, that's why, not in blood.

Oedipus. What are you saying—Polybus was not my father?

1115 **Messenger.** No more than I am. He and I are equals.

Oedipus.   My father—
how can my father equal nothing? You're nothing to me!

Messenger. Neither was he, no more your father than I am.

Oedipus. Then why did he call me his son?

Messenger.   You were a gift,
years ago—know for a fact he took you
1120   from my hands.

Oedipus.   No, from another's hands?
Then how could he love me so? He loved me, deeply . . .

Messenger. True, and his early years without a child
made him love you all the more.

Oedipus.   And you, did you . . .
buy me? find me by accident?

Messenger.   I stumbled on you,
1125   down the woody flanks of Mount Cithaeron.

Oedipus.   So close,
what were you doing here, just passing through?

Messenger. Watching over my flocks, grazing them on the slopes.

Oedipus. A herdsman, were you? A vagabond, scraping for wages?

Messenger. Your savior too, my son, in your worst hour.

Oedipus.   Oh—
1130   when you picked me up, was I in pain? What exactly?

Messenger. Your ankles . . . they tell the story. Look at them.

Oedipus. Why remind me of that, that old affliction?

Messenger. Your ankles were pinned together. I set you free.

Oedipus. That dreadful mark—I've had it from the cradle.

1135 **Messenger.** And you got your name from that misfortune too,
the name's still with you.

Oedipus.   Dear god, who did it?—
mother? father? Tell me.

1135 you got your name from that misfortune: Oedipus' name comes from Greek words meaning "swollen foot."

Messenger.   I don't know.
  The one who gave you to me, he'd know more.

Oedipus. What? You took me from someone else?
1140   You didn't find me yourself?

Messenger.   No sir,
  another shepherd passed you on to me.

Oedipus. Who? Do you know? Describe him.

Messenger. He called himself a servant of . . .
  if I remember rightly—Laius.

(Jocasta *turns sharply.*)

1145   **Oedipus.** The king of the land who ruled here long ago?

Messenger. That's the one. That herdsman was *his* man.

Oedipus. Is he still alive? Can I see him?

Messenger. They'd know best, the people of these parts.

(Oedipus *and the* Messenger *turn to the* Chorus.)

Oedipus. Does anyone know that herdsman,
1150   the one he mentioned? Anyone seen him
  in the fields, here in the city? Out with it!
  The time has come to reveal this once for all.

Leader. I think he's the very shepherd you wanted to see,
  a moment ago. But the queen, Jocasta,
1155   she's the one to say.

Oedipus. Jocasta,
  you remember the man we just sent for?
  Is *that* the one he means?

Jocasta.   That man . . .
  why ask? Old shepherd, talk, empty nonsense,
  don't give it another thought, don't even think—

1160   **Oedipus.** What—give up now, with a clue like this?
  Fail to solve the mystery of my birth?
  Not for all the world!

Jocasta.   Stop—in the name of god,
  if you love your own life, call off this search!
  My suffering is enough.

Oedipus.   Courage!
1165   Even if my mother turns out to be a slave,
  and I a slave, three generations back,
  you would not seem common.

Jocasta.   Oh no,
  listen to me, I beg you, don't do this.

Oedipus. Listen to you? No more. I must know it all,
1170   must see the truth at last.

Jocasta.   No, please—
  for your sake—I want the best for you!

Oedipus. Your best is more than I can bear.

Jocasta.   You're doomed—
  may you never fathom who you are!

Oedipus. (*to a servant*).
  Hurry, fetch me the herdsman, now!
1175   Leave her to glory in her royal birth.

Jocasta. Aieeeeee—
                      man of agony—
  that is the only name I have for you,
  that, no other—ever, ever, ever!

(*Flinging through the palace doors. A long, tense silence
follows.*)

PAUSE & REFLECT How did it come about that Oedipus
was raised as Polybus' son?

FOCUS Oedipus wants to solve the mystery of his birth.
What do you predict he will find out when he questions
the herdsman?

Leader. Where's she gone, Oedipus?
1180   Rushing off, such wild grief . . .
  I'm afraid that from this silence
  something monstrous may come bursting forth.

Oedipus. Let it burst! Whatever will, whatever must!
  I must know my birth, no matter how common
1185   it may be—I must see my origins face-to-face.
  She perhaps, she with her woman's pride
  may well be <u>mortified</u> by my birth,
  but I, I count myself the son of Chance,
  the great goddess, giver of all good things—
1190   I'll never see myself disgraced. She is my mother!
  And the moons have marked me out, my blood-brothers,
  one moon on the wane, the next moon great with power.

1192 on the wane: with its lighted
part getting smaller day by day.

WORDS TO KNOW

mortify (môr′tə-fī′) *v.* to embarrass or humiliate

That is my blood, my nature—I will never betray it,
never fail to search and learn my birth!

1195   **Chorus.** Yes—if I am a true prophet
                 if I can grasp the truth,
          by the boundless skies of Olympus,
         at the full moon of tomorrow, Mount Cithaeron
         you will know how Oedipus glories in you—
1200   you, his birthplace, nurse, his mountain-mother!
         And we will sing you, dancing out your praise—
         you lift our monarch's heart!
           Apollo, Apollo, god of the wild cry
              may our dancing please you!
                              Oedipus—
1205   son, dear child, who bore you?
       Who of the nymphs who seem to live forever
       mated with Pan, the mountain-striding Father?
       Who was your mother? who, some bride of Apollo
       the god who loves the pastures spreading toward
           the sun?
1210   Or was it Hermes, king of the lightning ridges?
       Or Dionysus, lord of frenzy, lord of the barren
           peaks—
       did he seize you in his hands, dearest of all his
           lucky finds?—
         found by the nymphs, their warm eyes dancing, gift
       to the lord who loves them dancing out his joy!

(Oedipus *strains to see a figure coming from the distance.*
Attended by palace guards, an old Shepherd *enters slowly,*
reluctant to approach the king.)

1215   **Oedipus.** I never met the man, my friends . . . still,
       if I had to guess, I'd say that's the shepherd,
       the very one we've looked for all along.
       Brothers in old age, two of a kind,
       he and our guest here. At any rate
1220   the ones who bring him in are my own men,
       I recognize them.

      (*turning to the* Leader)
                    But you know more than I,
       you should, you've seen the man before.

      Leader. I know him, definitely. One of Laius' men,
       a trusty shepherd, if there ever was one.

1206 nymphs (nĭmfs): minor nature goddesses.

1207 Pan: the god of forests, pastures, and shepherds.

1225   **Oedipus.** You, I ask you first, stranger,
      you from Corinth—is this the one you mean?

  Messenger. You're looking at him. He's your man.

  Oedipus. (*to the* Shepherd).
      You, old man, come over here—
      look at me. Answer all my questions.
1230   Did you ever serve King Laius?

  Shepherd.   So I did . . .
      a slave, not bought on the block though,
      born and reared in the palace.

  Oedipus. Your duties, your kind of work?

  Shepherd. Herding the flocks, the better part of my life.

1235   **Oedipus.** Where, mostly? Where did you do your grazing?

  Shepherd.   Well,
      Cithaeron sometimes, or the foothills round about.

  Oedipus. This man—you know him? ever see him there?

  Shepherd (*confused, glancing from the* Messenger *to the*
      King).
      Doing what?—what man do you mean?

  Oedipus (*pointing to the* Messenger).
      This one here—ever have dealings with him?

1240   **Shepherd.** Not so I could say, but give me a chance,
      my memory's bad . . .

  Messenger. No wonder he doesn't know me, master.
      But let me refresh his memory for him.
      I'm sure he recalls old times we had
1245   on the slopes of Mount Cithaeron;
      he and I, grazing our flocks, he with two
      and I with one—we both struck up together,
      three whole seasons, six months at a stretch
      from spring to the rising of Arcturus in the fall,
1250   then with winter coming on I'd drive my herds
      to my own pens, and back he'd go with his
      to Laius' folds.

  (*to the* Shepherd)
              Now that's how it was,
      wasn't it—yes or no?

  Shepherd.   Yes, I suppose . . .
      it's all so long ago.

  Messenger.   Come, tell me,

1249 Arcturus (ärk-tŏŏr′əs): a
bright star. (For the Greeks, its
rising just before the sun marked
the beginning of autumn.)

WHY, MASTER, MAJESTY—WHAT HAVE I DONE WRONG?

The shepherd in Peter Hall's stage production of *Oedipus the King* (1996).

1255   you gave me a child back then, a boy, remember?
        A little fellow to rear, my very own.

Shepherd. What? Why rake up that again?

Messenger. Look, here he is, my fine old friend—
        the same man who was just a baby then.

1260   **Shepherd.** Damn you, shut your mouth—quiet!

Oedipus. Don't lash out at him, old man—
        you need lashing more than he does.

Shepherd.   Why,
        master, majesty—what have I done wrong?

Oedipus. You won't answer his question about the boy.

1265   **Shepherd.** He's talking nonsense, wasting his breath.

Oedipus. So, you won't talk willingly—
        then you'll talk with pain.

(*The guards seize the* Shepherd.)

Shepherd. No, dear god, don't torture an old man!

Oedipus. Twist his arms back, quickly!

Shepherd. God help us, why?—
1270   what more do you need to know?

Oedipus. Did you give him that child? He's asking.

Shepherd. I did . . . I wish to god I'd died that day.

Oedipus. You've got your wish if you don't tell the truth.

Shepherd. The more I tell, the worse the death I'll die.

1275 **Oedipus.** Our friend here wants to stretch things out, does
     he?

(*motioning to his men for torture*)

Shepherd. No, no, I gave it to him—I just said so.

Oedipus. Where did you get it? Your house? Someone else's?

Shepherd. It wasn't mine, no, I got it from . . . someone.

Oedipus. Which one of them?

(*looking at the citizens*)

                        Whose house?

Shepherd. No—
1280   god's sake, master, no more questions!

Oedipus. You're a dead man if I have to ask again.

Shepherd. Then—the child came from the house . . .
     of Laius.

Oedipus.   A slave? or born of his own blood?

Shepherd.   Oh no,
     I'm right at the edge, the horrible truth—I've got to say
        it!

1285 **Oedipus.** And I'm at the edge of hearing horrors, yes, but I
     must hear!

Shepherd. All right! His son, they said it was—his son!
     But the one inside, your wife,
     she'd tell it best.

Oedipus. My wife—
1290   *she* gave it to you?

Shepherd. Yes, yes, my king.

Oedipus. Why, what for?

Shepherd. To kill it.

Oedipus. Her own child,
1295   how could she?

Laurence Olivier as Oedipus in the
London stage production (1945).

Shepherd. She was afraid—
frightening prophecies.

Oedipus. What?

Shepherd.   They said—
he'd kill his parents.

1300 **Oedipus.** But you gave him to this old man—why?

Shepherd. I pitied the little baby, master,
hoped he'd take him off to his own country,

far away, but he saved him for this, this fate.
If you are the man he says you are, believe me,
1305 you were born for pain.

Oedipus.   O god—
all come true, all burst to light!
O light—now let me look my last on you!
I stand revealed at last—
cursed in my birth, cursed in marriage,
1310 cursed in the lives I cut down with these hands!

(*Rushing through the doors with a great cry. The
Corinthian* Messenger, *the* Shepherd *and attendants exit
slowly to the side.*)

PAUSE & REFLECT What does Oedipus discover about
his birth?

FOCUS The chorus reacts to Oedipus' discovery of the
truth of his birth. Read to find out what the chorus thinks
of him now.

Chorus.   O the generations of men
the dying generations—adding the total
of all your lives I find they come to nothing . . .
            does there exist, is there a man on earth
1315 who seizes more joy than just a dream, a vision?
And the vision no sooner dawns than dies
blazing into oblivion.

You are my great example, you, your life
your destiny, Oedipus, man of misery—
1320 I count no man blest.

                    You outranged all men!
            Bending your bow to the breaking-point
you captured priceless glory, O dear god,
and the Sphinx came crashing down,
                    the virgin, claws hooked
1325 like a bird of omen singing, shrieking death—
like a fortress reared in the face of death
you rose and saved our land.

WORDS TO KNOW

oblivion (ə-blĭv′ē-ən) *n.* a state of being forgotten

From that day on we called you king
we crowned you with honors, Oedipus, towering over
        all—
1330   mighty king of the seven gates of Thebes.

But now to hear your story—is there a man more agonized?
More wed to pain and frenzy? Not a man on earth,
the joy of your life ground down to nothing
O Oedipus, name for the ages—
1335   one and the same wide harbor served you
                         son and father both
son and father came to rest in the same bridal chamber.
How, how could the furrows your father plowed
bear you, your agony, harrowing on
1340   in silence O so long?

                    But now for all your power
Time, all-seeing Time has dragged you to the light,
judged your marriage monstrous from the start—
the son and the father tangling, both one—
O child of Laius, would to god
1345   I'd never seen you, never never!
           Now I weep like a man who wails the dead
and the dirge comes pouring forth with all my heart!
I tell you the truth, you gave me life
my breath leapt up in you
1350   and now you bring down night upon my eyes.

1347 dirge (dûrj): funeral song.

Thinking Through the Literature

1. What did the shepherd do with the baby he was ordered to kill?

2. At this point in the play, how does the chorus regard Oedipus, the man who once saved Thebes?

3. How did Oedipus unknowingly bring about the thing he most tried to avoid?

4. What do you predict Oedipus will do now that he knows the truth about his birth?

FOCUS A messenger reveals the terrible events that have occurred offstage. Read to find out about these events.

(*Enter a* Messenger *from the palace.*)

Messenger. Men of Thebes, always first in honor,
what horrors you will hear, what you will see,
what a heavy weight of sorrow you will shoulder . . .
if you are true to your birth, if you still have

1355   some feeling for the royal house of Thebes.
I tell you neither the waters of the Danube
nor the Nile can wash this palace clean.
Such things it hides, it soon will bring to light—
terrible things, and none done blindly now,

1360   all done with a will. The pains
we inflict upon ourselves hurt most of all.

Leader. God knows we have pains enough already.
What can you add to them?

Messenger. The queen is dead.

Leader.   Poor lady—how?

1365 **Messenger.** By her own hand. But you are spared the worst,
you never had to watch . . . I saw it all,
and with all the memory that's in me
you will learn what that poor woman suffered.

Once she'd broken in through the gates,

1370   dashing past us, frantic, whipped to fury,
ripping her hair out with both hands—
straight to her rooms she rushed, flinging herself
across the bridal-bed, doors slamming behind her—
once inside, she wailed for Laius, dead so long,

1375   remembering how she bore his child long ago,
the life that rose up to destroy him, leaving
its mother to mother living creatures
with the very son she'd borne.
Oh how she wept, mourning the marriage-bed

1380   where she let loose that double brood—monsters—

husband by her husband, children by her child.
                                    And then—
but how she died is more than I can say. Suddenly
Oedipus burst in, screaming, he stunned us so
we couldn't watch her agony to the end,
1385   our eyes were fixed on him. Circling
like a maddened beast, stalking, here, there,
crying out to us—
                    Give him a sword! His wife,
no wife, his mother, where can he find the mother earth
that cropped two crops at once, himself and all his
      children?
1390   He was raging—one of the dark powers pointing the
          way,
none of us mortals crowding around him, no,
with a great shattering cry—someone, something leading
      him on—
he hurled at the twin doors and bending the bolts back
out of their sockets, crashed through the chamber.

1395   And there we saw the woman hanging by the neck,
cradled high in a woven noose, spinning,
swinging back and forth. And when he saw her,
giving a low, wrenching sob that broke our hearts,
slipping the halter from her throat, he eased her down,
1400   in a slow embrace he laid her down, poor thing . . .
then, what came next, what horror we beheld!

He rips off her brooches, the long gold pins
holding her robes—and lifting them high,
looking straight up into the points,
1405   he digs them down the sockets of his eyes, crying, "You,
you'll see no more the pain I suffered, all the pain I
      caused!
Too long you looked on the ones you never should have
      seen,
blind to the ones you longed to see, to know! Blind
from this hour on! Blind in the darkness—blind!"
1410   His voice like a dirge, rising, over and over
raising the pins, raking them down his eyes.
And at each stroke blood spurts from the roots,

splashing his beard, a swirl of it, nerves and clots—
black hail of blood pulsing, gushing down.

1415   These are the griefs that burst upon them both,
coupling man and woman. The joy they had so lately,
the fortune of their old ancestral house
was deep joy indeed. Now, in this one day,
wailing, madness and doom, death, disgrace,
1420   all the griefs in the world that you can name,
all are theirs forever.

Leader.   Oh poor man, the misery—
has he any rest from pain now?

(*A voice within, in torment.*)

Messenger.   He's shouting,
"Loose the bolts, someone, show me to all of Thebes!
My father's murderer, my mother's—"
1425   No, I can't repeat it, it's unholy.
Now he'll tear himself from his native earth,
not linger, curse the house with his own curse.
But he needs strength, and a guide to lead him on.
This is sickness more than he can bear.

(*The palace doors open.*)

                                 Look,
1430   he'll show you himself. The great doors are opening—
you are about to see a sight, a horror
even his mortal enemy would pity.

(*Enter* Oedipus, *blinded, led by a boy. He stands at the
palace steps, as if surveying his people once again.*)

Chorus.   O the terror—
the suffering, for all the world to see,
the worst terror that ever met my eyes.
1435   What madness swept over you? What god,
what dark power leapt beyond all bounds,
beyond belief, to crush your wretched life?—
godforsaken, cursed by the gods!
I pity you but I can't bear to look.
1440   I've much to ask, so much to learn,
so much fascinates my eyes,
but you . . . I shudder at the sight.

OH, OHH—
THE AGONY! I AM AGONY—

Laurence Olivier as Oedipus (1945).

Oedipus.   Oh, Ohh—
     the agony! I am agony—
     where am I going? where on earth?
1445   where does all this agony hurl me?
     where's my voice?—
          winging, swept away on a dark tide—
     My destiny, my dark power, what a leap you made!

Chorus. To the depths of terror, too dark to hear, to see.

1450 **Oedipus.** Dark, horror of darkness
     my darkness, drowning, swirling around me
     crashing wave on wave—unspeakable, irresistible
          headwind, fatal harbor! Oh again,
     the misery, all at once, over and over
1455   the stabbing daggers, stab of memory
     raking me insane.

     Chorus.   No wonder you suffer
     twice over, the pain of your wounds,
     the lasting grief of pain.

     Oedipus.   Dear friend, still here?
          Standing by me, still with a care for me,
1460   the blind man? Such compassion,
               loyal to the last. Oh it's you,
     I know you're here, dark as it is
     I'd know you anywhere, your voice—
     it's yours, clearly yours.

     Chorus.   Dreadful, what you've done . . .
1465   how could you bear it, gouging out your eyes?
     What superhuman power drove you on?

Oedipus. Apollo, friends, Apollo—
     he ordained my agonies—these, my pains on pains!
     But the hand that struck my eyes was mine,
1470   mine alone—no one else—
               I did it all myself!
     What good were eyes to me?
     Nothing I could see could bring me joy.

1468 ordained: decreed; commanded.

Chorus. No, no, exactly as you say.

Oedipus.   What can I ever see?
1475   What love, what call of the heart
     can touch my ears with joy? Nothing, friends.

Take me away, far, far from Thebes,
quickly, cast me away, my friends—
this great murderous ruin, this man cursed to heaven,
1480   the man the deathless gods hate most of all!

Chorus. Pitiful, you suffer so, you understand so much . . .
I wish you had never known.

Oedipus.   Die, die—
whoever he was that day in the wilds
who cut my ankles free of the ruthless pins,
1485   he pulled me clear of death, he saved my life
for this, this kindness—
                               Curse him, kill him!
If I'd died then, I'd never have dragged myself,
my loved ones through such hell.

1490 **Chorus.** Oh if only . . . would to god.

Oedipus.   I'd never have come to this,
my father's murderer—never been branded
mother's husband, all men see me now! Now,
<u>loathed</u> by the gods, son of the mother I defiled
coupling in my father's bed, spawning lives in the
        loins
1495   that spawned my wretched life. What grief can crown
        this grief?
                       It's mine alone, my destiny—I am Oedipus!

Chorus. How can I say you've chosen for the best?
Better to die than be alive and blind.

Oedipus. What I did was best—don't lecture me,
1500   no more advice. I, with *my* eyes,
how could I look my father in the eyes
when I go down to death? Or mother, so abused . . .
I have done such things to the two of them,
crimes too huge for hanging.
                               Worse yet,
1505   the sight of my children, born as they were born,
how could I long to look into their eyes?
No, not with these eyes of mine, never.
Not this city either, her high towers,
the sacred glittering images of her gods—
1510   I am misery! I, her best son, reared
as no other son of Thebes was ever reared,
I've stripped myself, I gave the command myself.

WORDS TO KNOW
320   **loathed** (lōthd) *adj.* intensely hated   **loathe** *v.*

All men must cast away the great blasphemer,
the curse now brought to light by the gods,
1515　the son of Laius—I, my father's son!

1513 **blasphemer** (blăs-fē′mər): a person who shows disrespect for sacred things.

Now I've exposed my guilt, horrendous guilt,
could I train a level glance on you, my countrymen?
Impossible! No, if I could just block off my ears,
the springs of hearing, I would stop at nothing—
1520　I'd wall up my loathsome body like a prison,
blind to the sound of life, not just the sight.
Oblivion—what a blessing . . .
for the mind to dwell a world away from pain.

1517 **train a level glance on you:** look you straight in the eye.

O Cithaeron, why did you give me shelter?
1525　Why didn't you take me, crush my life out on the spot?
I'd never have revealed my birth to all mankind.

O Polybus, Corinth, the old house of my fathers,
so I believed—what a handsome prince you raised—
under the skin, what sickness to the core.
1530　Look at me! Born of outrage, outrage to the core.

1530 **outrage:** a horribly offensive act.

O triple roads—it all comes back, the secret,
dark ravine, and the oaks closing in
where the three roads join . . .
You drank my father's blood, my own blood
1535　spilled by my own hands—you still remember me?
What things you saw me do? Then I came here
and did them all once more!
　　　　　　　　Marriages! O marriage,
you gave me birth, and once you brought me into the
　　　world
you brought my sperm rising back, springing to light
1540　fathers, brothers, sons—one murderous breed—
brides, wives, mothers. The blackest things
a man can do, I have done them all!
　　　　　　　　No more—
it's wrong to name what's wrong to do. Quickly,
for the love of god, hide me somewhere,
1545　kill me, hurl me into the sea
where you can never look on me again.

(*beckoning to the* Chorus *as they shrink away*)

Closer,
it's all right. Touch the man of grief.
Do. Don't be afraid. My troubles are mine
and I am the only man alive who can sustain them.

1549 **sustain:** endure.

PAUSE & REFLECT How and why does Oedipus blind himself?

FOCUS Read to find out what happens to Oedipus at the end of the play.

(*Enter* Creon *from the palace, attended by palace guards.*)

1550 **Leader.** Put your requests to Creon. Here he is,
just when we need him. He'll have a plan, he'll act.
Now that he's the sole defense of the country
in your place.

Oedipus.   Oh no, what can I say to him?
How can I ever hope to win his trust?
1555 I wronged him so, just now, in every way.
You must see that—I was so wrong, so wrong.

Creon. I haven't come to mock you, Oedipus,
or to criticize your former failings.

(*turning to the guards*)

                              You there,
have you lost all respect for human feelings?
1560 At least revere the Sun, the holy fire
that keeps us all alive. Never expose a thing
of guilt and holy dread so great it appalls
the earth, the rain from heaven, the light of day!
Get him into the halls—quickly as you can.
1565 Piety demands no less. Kindred alone
should see a kinsman's shame. This is obscene.

1566 **obscene:** disgusting.

Oedipus. Please, in god's name . . . you wipe my fears away,
coming so generously to me, the worst of men.
Do one thing more, for your sake, not mine.

1570 **Creon.** What do you want? Why so insistent?

Oedipus. Drive me out of the land at once, far from sight,
where I can never hear a human voice.

Creon. I'd have done that already, I promise you.
　　First I wanted the god to clarify my duties.

1575 **Oedipus.** The god? His command was clear, every word:
　　death for the father-killer, the curse—
　　he said destroy me!

Creon. So he did. Still, in such a crisis
　　it's better to ask precisely what to do.

Oedipus. 　　　　　　　　　　　　　　So miserable—
1580 　　you would consult the god about a man like me?

Creon. By all means. And this time, I assume,
　　even you will obey the god's decrees.

Oedipus. 　　　　　　　　　　　　　　　　I will,
　　I will. And you, I command you—I beg you . . .
　　the woman inside, bury her as you see fit.
1585 　　It's the only decent thing,
　　to give your own the last rites. As for me,
　　never condemn the city of my fathers
　　to house my body, not while I'm alive, no,
　　let me live on the mountains, on Cithaeron,
1590 　　my favorite haunt, I have made it famous.
　　Mother and father marked out that rock
　　to be my everlasting tomb—buried alive.
　　Let me die there, where they tried to kill me.

　　Oh but this I know: no sickness can destroy me,
1595 　　nothing can. I would never have been saved
　　from death—I have been saved
　　for something great and terrible, something strange.
　　Well let my destiny come and take me on its way!

　　About my children, Creon, the boys at least,
1600 　　don't burden yourself. They're men,
　　wherever they go, they'll find the means to live.
　　But my two daughters, my poor helpless girls,
　　clustering at our table, never without me
　　hovering near them . . . whatever I touched,

1604 hovering (hŭv′ər-ĭng): hanging about.

1605 　　they always had their share. Take care of them,
　　I beg you. Wait, better—permit me, would you?
　　Just to touch them with my hands and take
　　our fill of tears. Please . . . my king.
　　Grant it, with all your noble heart.
1610 　　If I could hold them, just once, I'd think

I had them with me, like the early days
when I could see their eyes.

(Antigone *and* Ismene, *two small children, are led in from
the palace by a nurse.*)

                        What's that?
O god! Do I really hear you sobbing?—
my two children. Creon, you've pitied me?

1615   Sent me my darling girls, my own flesh and blood!
Am I right?

Creon.   Yes, it's my doing.
I know the joy they gave you all these years,
the joy you must feel now.

Oedipus.   Bless you, Creon!
May god watch over you for this kindness,

1620   better than he ever guarded me.

                      Children, where are you?
Here, come quickly—

(*groping for* Antigone *and* Ismene, *who approach their
father cautiously, then embrace him*)

                    Come to these hands of mine,
your brother's hands, your own father's hands
that served his once bright eyes so well—
that made them blind. Seeing nothing, children,

1625   knowing nothing, I became your father,
I fathered you in the soil that gave me life.

How I weep for you—I cannot see you now . . .
just thinking of all your days to come, the bitterness,
the life that rough mankind will thrust upon you.

1630   Where are the public gatherings you can join,
the banquets of the clans? Home you'll come,
in tears, cut off from the sight of it all,
the brilliant rites unfinished.
And when you reach perfection, ripe for marriage,

1635   who will he be, my dear ones? Risking all
to shoulder the curse that weighs down my parents,
yes and you too—that wounds us all together.
What more misery could you want?
Your father killed his father, sowed his mother,

1640   one, one and the selfsame womb sprang you—
he cropped the very roots of his existence.

HOW I WEEP FOR YOU
—I CANNOT SEE YOU NOW . . .

Oedipus speaks words of pity to his daughters, from the film
Oedipus the King (1968), starring Christopher Plummer.

Such disgrace, and you must bear it all!
Who will marry you then? Not a man on earth.
Your doom is clear: you'll wither away to nothing,
1645   single, without a child.

(*turning to* Creon)

                              Oh Creon,
you are the only father they have now . . .
we who brought them into the world
are gone, both gone at a stroke—
Don't let them go begging, abandoned,
1650   women without men. Your own flesh and blood!
Never bring them down to the level of my pains.
Pity them. Look at them, so young, so vulnerable,
shorn of everything—you're their only hope.
Promise me, noble Creon, touch my hand!

(*reaching toward* Creon, *who draws back*)

1655   You, little ones, if you were old enough
to understand, there is much I'd tell you.
Now, as it is, I'd have you say a prayer.
Pray for life, my children,
live where you are free to grow and season.
1660   Pray god you find a better life than mine,
the father who begot you.

Creon.   Enough.
You've wept enough. Into the palace now.

Oedipus. I must, but I find it very hard.

Creon. Time is the great healer, you will see.

1665   **Oedipus.** I am going—you know on what condition?

Creon. Tell me. I'm listening.

Oedipus. Drive me out of Thebes, in exile.

Creon. Not I. Only the gods can give you that.

Oedipus. Surely the gods hate me so much—

1670   **Creon.** You'll get your wish at once.

Oedipus.   You consent?

Creon. I try to say what I mean; it's my habit.

Oedipus. Then take me away. It's time.

Creon. Come along, let go of the children.

Oedipus.   No—
    don't take them away from me, not now! No no no!

*(clutching his daughters as the guards wrench them loose
and take them through the palace doors)*

1675 **Creon.** Still the king, the master of all things?
    No more: here your power ends.
    None of your power follows you through life.

*(Exit Oedipus and Creon to the palace. The Chorus comes
forward to address the audience directly.)*

Chorus. People of Thebes, my countrymen, look on Oedipus.
    He solved the famous riddle with his brilliance,
1680   he rose to power, a man beyond all power.
    Who could behold his greatness without envy?
    Now what a black sea of terror has overwhelmed him.
    Now as we keep our watch and wait the final day,
    count no man happy till he dies, free of pain at last.

(Exit in procession.)

The images below come from two different productions of Oedipus the King. *One is a film version set amid the ruins of ancient Greece; the other is a theatrical production set in contemporary Africa. Study the images below. Which setting do you find more interesting? What are the advantages of a classical Greek setting? Why might a director choose a very different contemporary setting?*

Oedipus is helped by an elder of Thebes, after blinding himself. Hartford Stage's production of *Oedipus the King.*

Oedipus stands apart from Creon and Jocasta. Hartford Stage's production of *Oedipus the King,* directed by Jonathan Wilson, produced in 2001.

Two images of Oedipus, played by Christopher Plummer, in a 1968 film version of *Oedipus the King.*

MYTH
—MURIEL RUKEYSER—

Sphinx of Taharqa. Copyright © The British Museum, London.

Modern writers have often returned to the myths and legends of ancient Greece for their subjects. In this poem, a contemporary writer takes a humorous approach to Oedipus.

Long afterward, Oedipus, old and blinded, walked the
roads.   He smelled a familiar smell.   It was
the Sphinx.   Oedipus said, "I want to ask one question.
Why didn't I recognize my mother?"   "You gave the
wrong answer," said the Sphinx.   "But that was what
made everything possible," said Oedipus.   "No," she said.
"When I asked, What walks on four legs in the morning,
two at noon, and three in the evening, you answered,
Man.   You didn't say anything about woman."
"When you say Man," said Oedipus, "you include women
too. Everyone knows that."   She said, "That's what
you think."

Connect to the Literature

1. What Do You Think? How did you react to the ending of this play? Discuss your impressions.

Comprehension Check
- Why does Jocasta hang herself?
- Whom does Oedipus hold in his arms before going into exile?
- Who becomes the ruler of Thebes at the end of the play?

Think Critically

2. ACTIVE READING: STRATEGIES FOR READING GREEK DRAMA Review what you recorded in your **READER'S NOTEBOOK**. What strategies helped you the most in reading this play? What questions do you still have about the play?

3. Oedipus blinds himself and is filled with self-hatred when he discovers the truth about his past. Does Oedipus deserve what happens to him, or is he a victim of fate? Cite lines from the play to support your opinion.

4. Tiresias, the prophet, is the agent of the god Apollo. How would you compare and contrast Oedipus and Tiresias?

> THINK ABOUT
> - their physical condition
> - their attitude toward the gods
> - their insights into the truth

5. How would you describe the role of the chorus in this play? How does the chorus's attitude change as the play progresses?

Extend Interpretations

6. The Writer's Style The term **imagery** refers to words that appeal to the senses. One pattern of imagery in this play involves references to darkness and light, blindness and sight. Find some examples of such images in the play. Why do you think Sophocles used these images?

7. Comparing Texts Reread Muriel Rukeyser's poem "Myth" on page 329. What slant does the poet give to the story of Oedipus?

8. Connect to Life How much control do you think people actually have over their lives? Cite examples from your reading and your own experience as you explore this question.

LITERARY ANALYSIS: TRAGIC HERO

The term **tragic hero,** first used by Aristotle, refers to a dignified or noble character who is central to a drama. According to Aristotle, a tragic hero possesses a defect, or **tragic flaw,** that brings about or contributes to his or her downfall. This flaw may be poor judgment, pride, weakness, or an excess of an admirable quality. The tragic hero recognizes his or her own flaw but only after it is too late to change the course of events.

Paired Activity Determine to what extent Aristotle's definition of *tragic hero* applies to Oedipus. Consider whether the qualities that make him great also lead to his ruin.

LITERARY ANALYSIS: DRAMATIC IRONY

Irony is a contrast between what is expected and what actually exists or happens. **Dramatic irony** occurs when the reader or viewer of a play is aware of information that a character in the play is not aware of. For example, in line 119, Oedipus, speaking of King Laius, says that he "never saw the man." We readers realize—just as Sophocles' original audience did—that Oedipus has seen Laius. In fact, he killed him long ago. Reread a few scenes from the play, looking for examples of dramatic irony. Why do you think Sophocles used this technique?

Choices & CHALLENGES

Writing Options

1. Personal Response
Aristotle explained that a tragedy stirs two emotions in its audience—pity and terror. Write a personal-response essay, applying Aristotle's theory to your own reading of *Oedipus the King*. What events in the play evoked your deepest sympathy? What events in the play filled you with terror?

2. Diary Entry
Choose an important character other than Oedipus in this play—such as Jocasta, Creon, Tiresias, or the messenger from Corinth. Then write a diary entry expressing that character's thoughts and feelings.

3. Literary Analysis
The effect of the last scene would be different if the violent events—the death of Jocasta and the blinding of Oedipus—were dramatized onstage instead of being reported by a messenger. Write a brief essay explaining what a dramatist gains by making such events take place offstage rather than onstage.

Writing Handbook
See page R31: Explanatory Writing.

Activities & Explorations

1. Theater Model
On the basis of the stage directions in the play, create a model of the stage for *Oedipus the King*. Then prepare an oral report or a multimedia presentation on the theater in ancient Greece. **~ ART**

2. Role-Playing
With a few classmates, choose one important scene from the play and act it out for the rest of the class. Then share with the class the insights you gained by playing a particular character.
~ SPEAKING AND LISTENING

Inquiry & Research

Oedipus Complex Sigmund Freud (1856–1939) is known as the father of psychoanalysis. He was intrigued by Sophocles' play and the myth of Oedipus. Freud coined the term *Oedipus complex* as a name for certain unconscious urges in the human mind. Find out about Freud's use of this term. Then prepare an oral report to share your findings.

RESEARCH STARTER
CLASSZONE.COM

Vocabulary in Action

EXERCISE: SYNONYMS AND ANTONYMS Identify each pair of words as synonyms or antonyms.

1. **denounce**–criticize
2. **swarthy**–pale
3. **retract**–promote
4. **despondent**–happy
5. **oblivion**–prominence
6. **appall**–delight
7. **reverberate**–echo
8. **foreboding**–warning
9. **surmise**–fact
10. **explicit**– implied
11. **loathed**–despised
12. **mortify**–shame
13. **menace**–threat
14. **futile**–effective
15. **revile**–praise

Building Vocabulary

The word *foreboding* has interesting connotations, suggesting fear and anxiety. For an in-depth lesson on denotation and connotation, see page 1090.

Communication Workshop

Literature through performance

From the Page to the Stage Although you'll find *Oedipus the King* printed in many books, Sophocles wrote it for the stage. Writing **drama** is different from writing prose, which the reader experiences alone, in his or her own mind. With a staged drama, the viewer's understanding of the play is influenced by the interpretation of the director and the performers. Many playwrights like to direct their own plays for this reason.

For Your Portfolio

WRITING PROMPT Write and stage a dramatic scene.

Purpose: To entertain

Audience: Your classmates and other interested students and adults

---

Basics in a Box

RUBRIC Writing and Staging a Scene

A successful script should
- introduce the setting and characters in the opening stage directions
- use the setting and characters to create a convincing world
- develop a clear and interesting situation or conflict
- reveal the personalities of the characters through the dialogue
- advance the story through actions as well as dialogue
- include stage directions as necessary

A successful performance should
- demonstrate an awareness of the audience
- present a clear and consistent interpretation of the script
- maintain the audience's interest through strong acting, good pacing, and effective staging

Analyzing a Student Model

Matt Kirby
Nicolet High School

A Chip off the Old Block?

Characters: Michael *is a high school student working for his* **Father,** *a carpenter with his own furniture shop.*

Setting: *It is springtime, shortly before graduation. Michael is at work in his father's shop. The family lives in a small town.*

RUBRIC
IN ACTION

❶ Introduces the characters and the setting in the opening stage directions

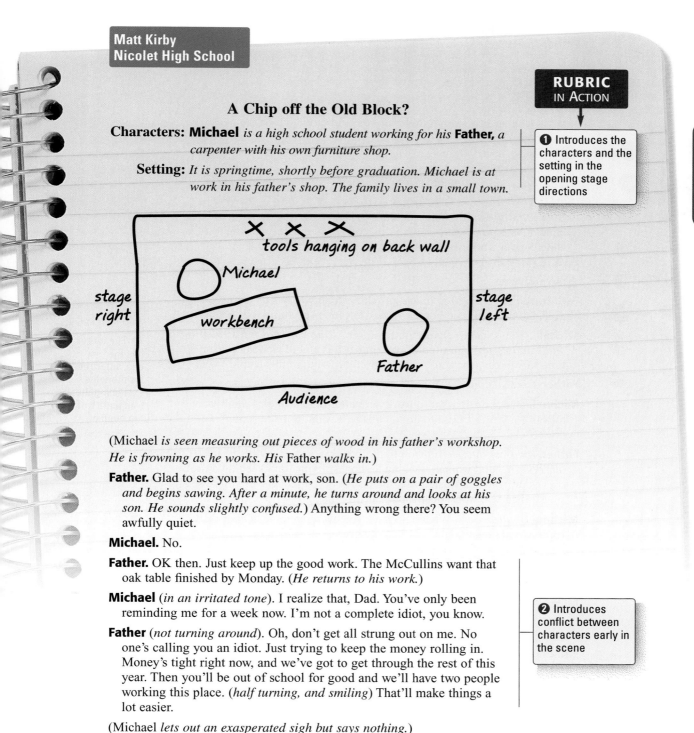

(Michael *is seen measuring out pieces of wood in his father's workshop. He is frowning as he works. His* Father *walks in.*)

Father. Glad to see you hard at work, son. (*He puts on a pair of goggles and begins sawing. After a minute, he turns around and looks at his son. He sounds slightly confused.*) Anything wrong there? You seem awfully quiet.

Michael. No.

Father. OK then. Just keep up the good work. The McCullins want that oak table finished by Monday. (*He returns to his work.*)

Michael (*in an irritated tone*). I realize that, Dad. You've only been reminding me for a week now. I'm not a complete idiot, you know.

Father (*not turning around*). Oh, don't get all strung out on me. No one's calling you an idiot. Just trying to keep the money rolling in. Money's tight right now, and we've got to get through the rest of this year. Then you'll be out of school for good and we'll have two people working this place. (*half turning, and smiling*) That'll make things a lot easier.

(Michael *lets out an exasperated sigh but says nothing.*)

❷ Introduces conflict between characters early in the scene

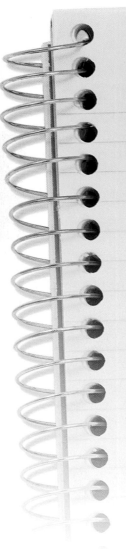

Father (*turning fully toward his son*). I'm not sure when this started exactly, but you've got an attitude problem. <u>You've been lippin' off to your mother and me, and frankly, we don't like it.</u> You better clean up your act, boy.

Michael (*in a much louder tone*). And what if I don't? I'm 18 years old, Dad. What are you going to do to me? Not let me out of the house? Forget it! I can do what I want. (*His Father stares at him, shocked. The Father turns back to his work, and silence overcomes the two. Michael's Father turns as if to say something, but Michael begins whistling to interrupt him. Thinking better of it, his Father turns to his work again.*)

Father (*turning back to Michael and trying again*). Look, son. I don't know what's gotten into you, but maybe we can just try to forget it and keep on working.

Michael. What's gotten into me? Oh, that's good. So I'm the one with the problem.

Father. You're reading too much into this. Don't worry. Once you graduate this year and come to work for me, everything will get better.

Michael. That's just it, Dad! Don't you see? (*throwing down his ruler and standing up*) <u>I'm tired of working at this stupid workshop. I'm tired of working for you.</u> And I'm tired of living in this stupid town!

Father. Control yourself. What exactly are you trying to say?

Michael. Dad, I don't want to work here after high school. I don't want to waste my life. I want to go to college. I want to make something of myself.

Father. (*pauses; then, icily*). You think that I've wasted my life? Fine. If marrying a good woman, making an honest living, and keeping a roof over your head is a wasted life, then I guess you're right. If you're so smart, then you won't need any help from me.

Michael (*in disbelief*). What help have you ever given me? Other than feeding and housing me, you've only ever given me orders or ignored me completely!

Father. Ignored you? You think I didn't pay attention to you? Or care about what you did?

Michael (*sarcastically*). Oh, sure, you cared. You cared when it involved sports or working in the shop. You cared what I did when you could gain something from it.

Father. How dare you talk to me that way!

---

❸ The writer has the father reveal information about himself and his son.
Another Option:
• Reveal information through the characters' actions.

❹ Indicates actions and tone of voice through stage directions

❺ The writer has the character reveal his thoughts, explaining the true nature of the conflict.

Michael. But you didn't care about the one thing I cared about—school. Have you ever noticed that? Did you ever notice how hard I work? That I always do my homework? You know, other kids get in trouble for failing a test. I bring the test home and you say, "Well, no matter. It's not important."

Father. So, I didn't yell at you! Are you going to be mad at me for that?

Michael (*almost in tears*). No, but it might have helped once in a while to notice and give me a little encouragement. Did you even know that in the last two years I've gone from a C-minus average to an A-minus? I have an *A-minus* in school, Dad. Does that mean anything to you?

Father (*distracted by* Michael's *emotion*). Son, don't cry. Men don't— (*stops, looks at* Michael *in astonishment*) You have an A-minus? (*visibly swelling with pride*) Well, I'll be. My boy, with an A-minus.

Michael (*looking up, wiping away a tear*). Dad?

Father. Imagine that. (*pauses*) I never knew you wanted to go to college. (Michael *nods.*) You know it costs a lot of money.

Michael (*with shy hopefulness*). Tuition at State isn't so bad. And they have scholarships . . .

Father (*thinking*). Can you work for me full-time this summer? And over breaks? (Michael *nods, and his* Father *grins.*) Think you could stand it?

Michael (*grinning too*). I think I could manage.

Father. Well, let's see what we can do.

Michael (*smiling more broadly and standing up*). Do you mean that? We could really look into it?

Father. Sure we can. You know I want the best for you, Michael.

(*The two move together in an awkward embrace, and* Michael *is heard whispering a faint "Thank you."*)

> **❻** Uses stage directions and dialogue to present the resolution of the conflict

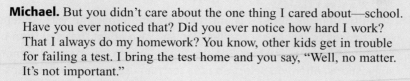

1. Your Working Portfolio
Build on the **Writing Option** you completed earlier in this unit:

• **Dramatic Scene,** p. 255

2. Fairy Tale Theater
Adapt a myth or fairy tale for the stage. You might want to consult a book of world folklore or mythology for ideas.

3. Conflict Chart
List conflicts that you have experienced, heard of, or read about. Build your scene around one of these conflicts.

Writing and Staging Your Scene

❶ Prewriting

Begin by thinking about a character or situation that interests you and that experiences or involves a conflict. You can also adapt material from books, movies, ballads, or folklore. See the **Idea Bank** in the margin for more suggestions. After you select an idea for your scene, follow the steps below.

Planning Your Script

1. Consider the basic elements of your scene. Fill out a chart like the one below to help you identify the elements you need to include.

Characters	Setting	Plot	Stage Directions
Who are the characters? How do they interact?	When and where does the scene take place?	What events will happen? In what sequence will they occur?	How will the characters speak? What is the pace of the scene?

2. Think about your audience. Who will watch your scene? What language is appropriate for them? What background information will they need in order to understand the setting, characters, and action?

3. Decide on a mood. What general feeling do you want to convey? How can you use dialogue, setting, and action to create that mood?

❷ Drafting

As you write your script, keep the following points in mind:

• Establish the **setting** and introduce the **characters** of your scene.
• Use **dialogue** to advance the plot and reveal details about the characters—personalities, interests, backgrounds, attitudes, and beliefs.
• Use **stage directions** to describe setting, costumes, lighting, sound effects, and props. Also use them to indicate gestures, tone of voice, and motion.

Need help with dialogue?

See the **Writing Handbook**,
p. R29.

❸ Revising

TARGET SKILL ▶ USING DIALOGUE EFFECTIVELY Your characters' words should sound natural when spoken, so read your dialogue aloud. Use contractions and sentence fragments to mimic actual speech. Indicate tone of voice or emotion with precise stage directions. For example, you might instruct your actors through such directions as "whispers," "shouts," and "shivers."

> **Father** (*thinking*). Can you work for me full-time this
> summer? ~~Can you work for me~~ <u>And</u> over breaks? ~~Do you~~
> think you could stand it? ^(Michael nods, and his
> Father grins.)

❹ Planning Your Performance

With a group of classmates, choose a script from among the ones group members have written. After selecting a script, follow the steps below.

Steps for Planning Your Scene

▶ **1. Assign acting roles.** You can hold auditions, draw straws, or assign roles by consensus.

▶ **2. List and assign responsibilities.** Consider the following jobs. Which are necessary? Who will perform them?

- director
- lighting manager
- prop manager
- set designer
- costumer
- sound engineer

▶ **3. Decide on an interpretation.** Discuss the scene and make collective decisions about the characters' motivations, actions, and emotions. What do you want the audience to think and feel after watching your scene?

▶ **4. Create a "director's script."** Mark a copy of the script with notes on the staging, sets, action, and delivery. This script will serve as a record of the group's interpretive decisions. In creating the director's script, consider movement, gesture, tone of voice, pacing, and technical effects.

▶ **5. Gather the props, costumes, and lighting materials you will need.** What materials will help to show the time and place of the scene and to establish the characters' personalities?

❺ Practicing and Presenting

The entire cast should practice the scene several times before presenting it.

- **Read through the parts.** The actors should learn their lines. Then they should mark their scripts with the appropriate emotions and actions.
- **Walk through the action.** Actors should physically act out their parts, rehearsing their entrances, exits, and other motions. Do the actions make sense?
- **Do a complete run-through.** Finally, set up the stage and rehearse the scene with the costumes, props, and lighting that you have decided upon.

After several rehearsals with just the cast, ask one or two other people to watch a rehearsal and offer feedback.

Ask Your Peer Reader

- What did you like best about the performance?
- Was there anything that didn't make sense to you? Explain.
- Which actions and emotions seemed most real to you? Which seemed awkward or unrealistic?
- Did you want to see more or less of anything? Explain.

PRACTICING TIP

Make audiotapes or videotapes of the rehearsals so that you can listen for dialogue that needs to be louder or clearer or can watch for awkward stage movements.

❻ Refining Your Performance

TARGET SKILL ▶ EVALUATING YOUR INTERPRETIVE CHOICES Use these standards to evaluate the decisions you made in interpreting your scene.

- **Naturalness and clarity** Do the actors speak and interact in a realistic way? Do they move naturally? Does the scene make sense to the audience?
- **Communication of mood and character** Do the actors' voices, movements, and timing work together to show the emotions and values of the characters?
- **Consistency** Does each actor's performance fit the overall interpretation of the scene? Do the technical aspects all work together to support this interpretation?

❼ Reflecting

FOR YOUR WORKING PORTFOLIO What did you you learn about writing and staging a scene? Attach your reflections to your marked-up script. Save your script in your **Working Portfolio.** 🗂

Publishing IDEAS

- Choose several scenes from your class to perform for other classes.
- Videotape your scene to show to family and friends. Make a copy for your school library.

PUBLISHING OPTIONS
CLASSZONE.COM

Read this paragraph from the first draft of a drama review. The underlined sections may include the following kinds of errors:

- **incorrect possessives**
- **inconsistent verb tenses**
- **missing or misplaced commas**
- **misspelled words**

For each underlined section, choose the revision that most improves the writing.

> The Surprising Puppet Theaters 11th annual Spring Pageant opened this
> (1)
> passed weekend. True to form, the company put on a show worthy of everyones'
> (2)   (3)
> time and attention. The company choses a theme for the pageant every year, and
> (4)
> this year's theme is farming. It may not sound exciting, but the company's use of
> puppets, which range from ten inches to ten feet in height brings new drama to
> (5)
> the popular notions about farm life. In one scene, a potato does battle with a
> giant slug. In another scene, the farmer plays a haunting tune on his fiddle,
> encouraging his little sweet peas to grow. The farmer and his vegetables
> (6)
> struggled with drought, flood, pests, and storms, ending the show with a glorious,
> victorious harvest. Excellent performances and beautifully crafted puppets make
> this show a must-see!

1. **A.** The Surprising Puppet Theater's
   B. The Surprising Puppet Theaters'
   C. The Surprising Puppet's Theater
   D. Correct as is

2. **A.** this passt weekend
   B. this past weekend
   C. this paste weekend
   D. Correct as is

3. **A.** everyones time
   B. everybodys time
   C. everyone's time
   D. Correct as is

4. **A.** company chose
   B. company choosed
   C. company chooses
   D. Correct as is

5. **A.** puppets which range from ten
      inches to ten feet in height
   B. puppets, which range from ten
      inches to ten feet in height,
   C. puppets, that range from ten
      inches to ten feet in height,
   D. Correct as is

6. **A.** The farmer and his vegetables
      have struggled
   B. The farmer and his vegetables
      struggle
   C. The farmer and his vegetables
      struggles
   D. Correct as is

Need extra help?

See the **Grammar Handbook**

Quick Reference: Punctuation, p. R77

Verb Tense, p. R60

TEST PRACTICE

Building Vocabulary

The History of English Many Modern English words come from Old English, a Germanic language related to German, Dutch, and Swedish. However, a good number of English words have origins in Latin, Greek, and French (which is descended from Latin). These words tend to be more difficult and specialized, as many of them were brought into English by scholars and priests to describe academic, religious, and political ideas. These words have changed over the years, but they still have recognizable word parts.

A **root** is the core part of a word, to which other roots or **affixes** (prefixes and suffixes) can be added to create new words. Consider the word *prophecies* in the example below. The Greek root *phet* means

"speaker," the prefix *pro-* means "before," and *-es* is a common suffix for plural nouns. *Prophet* refers to one who predicts an event or speaks of it before it happens; *prophecies* refers to the predictions themselves.

> "Seer of misery! Never a word that works to
>   my advantage!
> Always misery warms your heart, your
>   prophecies—
> never a word of profit said or brought to pass."
>
> —Homer, *Iliad*

Strategies for Building Vocabulary

Knowing how to break words into parts and recognizing common Greek and Latin roots can help you understand unfamiliar words.

❶ Break a Word into Parts When you first encounter an unfamiliar word, try to determine its root. For example, look at the word *appendage.* You might recognize the first and last syllables, *ap-* and *-age,* as a prefix and a suffix. That leaves the middle syllable, *pend,* as the most likely root.

❷ Make an Educated Guess Think about other words you know that contain the same root. *Pendant* refers to something that hangs from a necklace, and *suspend* can mean "to hang." Perhaps *appendage* refers to something that hangs from something else.

❸ Check Against the Dictionary Look up the word in a dictionary and compare its definition with your guess. One definition of *appendage* is "a limb or organ joined to the trunk of a body"; an arm is an example of an appendage. To be joined to a body is almost the same as to be hanging from it. The earlier guess was close, if not exactly right.

❹ Read the Etymology In a dictionary entry, you will often find a word's etymology, or history. This will give you insight into the word's root (or roots) and affixes. If the entry for *appendage* does not contain an etymology, look at nearby entries for related words, such as *append.* You will likely find an etymology that applies. As expected, the etymology for *append* traces it to the Latin word *pendere,* which means "to hang." The following tables contain more Greek and Latin roots.

Greek Root	Meaning	English Words
cycl	circle	bicycle, recycle
graph	write	autograph, photograph, graphic
soph	wise	philosopher, sophisticated

Latin Root	Meaning	English Words
corp	body	corporation, corpse, corpulent
junct	join	juncture, junction, adjunct
pend	hang	pendulum, suspend, appendix

EXERCISE Use a dictionary to identify the meaning and root of each of these words from the *Iliad.* Use the information you find to create a chart like the ones above for the words' Greek and Latin roots. Be sure to indicate whether each root is Greek or Latin.

1. incensed   **3.** colossal   **5.** commandeer

2. sacrosanct   **4.** intercept

Sentence Crafting Using Participles

Grammar from Literature A **participle** is a verb form used as an adjective. For example, in the passages below from Homer's *Iliad,* the word *terrifying* modifies *clash,* and *disgraced, brimming,* and *piling* modify *I.*

> Over against the ships he dropped to a knee, let fly a shaft and a terrifying clash rang out from the great silver bow.

> "I have no mind to linger here disgraced, brimming your cup and piling up your plunder."

A **participial phrase** consists of a participle and any other words that modify or complete it. In the passages below from the *Iliad,* notice the participial phrases in blue. Then see the modified words in red.

> The old man was terrified. He obeyed the order, turning, trailing away in silence down the shore

> . . . No way to escape it now. This, this was their pleasure after all, sealed long ago—

A participial phrase allows you to describe two different actions in one sentence while bringing one of them into focus. Look at the following sentence and revision.

> DRAFT
> The soldier cried out for revenge. He ran at his enemy.

> REVISION
> Crying out for revenge, the soldier ran at his enemy.

Usage Tip As with other adjectives, it is important to place a participial phrase near the word it modifies. A writer may make the mistake of placing a participial phrase so far from the word it modifies that the meaning of the sentence is unclear or incorrect. This mistake is known as a **misplaced participle.** In the example below, it is the seer, not the war, who is looking into the future.

> MISPLACED PARTICIPLE
> The seer predicted war looking into the future.

> REVISED
> Looking into the future, the seer predicted war.

A **dangling participle** is one that does not clearly modify any noun or pronoun in a sentence. To fix a dangling participle, you can add a noun or pronoun to be modified by the phrase, or you can revise the sentence completely.

> DANGLING PARTICIPLE
> Running from Achilles, it was a desperate race.

> REVISED
> Hector ran from Achilles in a desperate race.

WRITING EXERCISE Rewrite each sentence, changing the underlined words to a participle or participial phrase.

1. Andromache begged him to stay close to home. <u>She feared that Hector would die in battle.</u>
2. <u>Hector imagined what would happen to her if he died.</u> He felt torn about what to do.
3. <u>He smiled at his baby son</u> and reached down to touch him.
4. <u>Hector's armor frightened his son.</u> The boy shrank from Hector's touch.
5. Hector prayed to Zeus. <u>He asked that his son grow up to be a great warrior.</u>

GRAMMAR EXERCISE The following paragraph contains one dangling and one misplaced participial phrase. Find and rewrite the incorrect sentences.

After winning a battle, the Greek king Agamemnon kidnapped the daughter of Chryses, Apollo's priest. Chryses came to Agamemnon, begging for the return of his daughter, but the proud king refused. This made Apollo very angry. Sending a plague down on the Greek armies, both animals and men fell to the sickness. Burning day and night, Apollo watched the corpse-fires below. Achilles was the strongest of the Greek warriors. Wondering how they might appease Apollo, he called in Calchas, a prophet, to explain the god's anger.

Literature of Ancient Greece

Reflect and Assess

The selections in Unit Two, Part 1, introduced you to several masterpieces of ancient Greek literature. How has your understanding of ancient Greece been influenced by your readings? What are your strongest impressions of Greek thought and culture? Use the following options to review what you have learned.

Detail of fresco of Athena restraining Achilles from killing Agamemnon (1757), Giambattista Tiepolo. Villa Valmarana, Vicenza, Italy. Scala/Art Resource, New York.

Reflecting on the Literature

In Quest of Honor As you know, honor was very important to the ancient Greeks. Choose four characters or people from the selections, and discuss what honor means to each of them. Consider how each of your subjects can achieve honor and how honor can be lost. Do you think that the views of honor expressed in ancient Greece still have relevance today?

Reviewing Literary Concepts

Tragic Hero Review the meaning of **tragic hero,** as explained on pages 261 and 330. Then consider whether other historical figures or characters featured in the selections, besides Oedipus, might be considered tragic heroes. Choose two characters or historical figures and discuss how the term *tragic hero* can be applied to each of them.

⌐ Building Your Portfolio

Communication Workshop and Writing Options Review the dramatic scene that you wrote for the Communication Workshop on page 332 and the various Writing Options you completed in this part of the book. In your judgment, which piece of writing is the most successful? Write a cover note explaining what you like about the work you chose, and add the assignment to your **Presentation Portfolio.** ⌐

Self **ASSESSMENT**

📖 READER'S NOTEBOOK

The following list consists of important names and terms from this part of Unit Two. Work with a partner to create a true-false or multiple-choice test that can be used to measure other students' understanding of these terms. For additional help, make use of the Index or the **Glossary of Literary Terms** (beginning on page R91).

Greek epic	Socrates
epic simile	Plato
Greek drama	Oedipus
Pericles	tragedy
Peloponnesian War	lyric

Setting **GOALS**

The literature of the ancient world is often quite challenging to read, as you have probably experienced for yourself. Make a list of your strengths and weaknesses as a reader of such literature. Then circle those weaknesses that you would like to work on in the months ahead.

Extend Your *Reading*

The Greeks: Crucible of Civilization

PAUL CARTLEDGE

This book provides an introduction to the extraordinary achievements of ancient Greece by focusing on the lives of 15 men and women. The author, a professor of Greek history at Cambridge University, makes the past come alive through profiles of people such as the statesman Pericles, the poet Sappho, and the general Alexander.

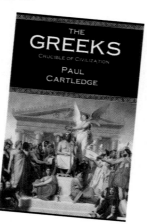

The Ancient City: Life in Classical Athens and Rome

PETER CONNOLLY AND HAZEL DODGE

This unique and compelling work gives the reader a tour of daily life in ancient Athens and Rome. Through a combination of detailed drawings, fine art, and brief explanations, the reader is given a close-up picture of the economy, popular culture, government, architecture, fashion, religious ceremonies, and public festivals.

And Even *More* . . .

Books

Four Plays by Aristophanes WILLIAM ARROWSMITH, ED.
The Athenian playwright blended satire with broad comedy. His four most celebrated masterpieces are included: *The Clouds, The Birds, Lysistrata,* and *The Frogs.*

Mythology: Timeless Tales of Gods and Heroes EDITH HAMILTON
Hamilton has collected the most popular myths of ancient Greece. Her readable and authoritative retellings of the myths have been enjoyed by readers for decades.

The Wars of the Ancient Greeks VICTOR DAVIS HANSON
This richly illustrated book shows how the Greeks fought their wars, from the man-to-man combat described by Homer to the complex military campaigns of Alexander the Great.

Other Media

Great Cities of the Ancient World: Athens and Ancient Greece
Through special effects and full-motion video, the ruins of ancient Greece are restored to their original beauty. Reconstructions are shown of 25 structures in Athens and five other cities, including the Acropolis, the theater of Dionysus, and the Temple of Apollo at Delphi. 78 minutes. Zenger Media. (VIDEOCASSETTE)

The Road to Ancient Greece
This interactive program provides an introduction to the history and culture of ancient Greece. Zenger Media. (CD-ROM)

Inside the Walls of Troy: A Novel of the Women Who Lived the Trojan War

CLEMENCE MCLAREN

Two woman provide their own perspectives on the events of the Trojan War. The first narrator is the beautiful Helen; the second is Cassandra, a daughter of King Priam. Cassandra has a gift of prophecy, but it is her fate that no one believes her visions of the future.

Literature of Ancient Rome

Why It Matters

The Roman Empire was one of the largest and greatest empires of Western civilization. The Romans united the diverse peoples of the Mediterranean world under one political system. Moreover, the Romans maintained the longest period of peace that Western civilization has ever known. Their language, Latin, developed into such modern languages as Italian, French, and Spanish. The literary heritage of Rome reflects the values cherished by this civilization.

For Links to Ancient Rome, click on:

HUMANITIES
CLASSZONE.COM

1 Creators of an Empire
Rome evolved from a small community of shepherds and farmers nestled in the hills along the **Tiber River,** in what is now central Italy. Over the centuries, the Romans built a vast empire. At its height, it extended into three continents—Europe, Asia, and Africa.

North Sea

BRITAIN

ATLANTIC OCEAN

3

E U R O P E

GAUL

Adriatic Sea

Tiber R.

1

Rome •

ITALY

Pompeii •

4

Mediterranean Sea

• Carthage

Roman Empire, A.D. 120

N
W   E
S

0   500   1,000 miles

0   500   1,000 kilometers

4 Pompeii Archaeologists have uncovered some of the splendors of ancient Roman life in the ruins of Pompeii, once a prosperous town in southern Italy. In A.D. 79, the volcano **Mount Vesuvius** erupted. It spewed gases that killed the people of Pompeii and volcanic ash that buried them, preserving forever the shape of their bodies as they died.

A F R I C A

Master Builders
The Romans turned Rome into a magnificent city, with massive public buildings, glorious temples, and huge amphitheaters. The Romans also constructed towns and cities throughout the empire. Still standing today are some of the **aqueducts,** such as the one pictured, that brought water into Roman cities and towns.

ASIA

2 **Christianity** An upstart religion from Judea, Christianity spread quickly throughout the empire. The apostle Paul, who claimed Roman citizenship, made Christianity more than just a local religion.

Black Sea

Caspian Sea

Aegean Sea

Tigris River

Antioch

SYRIA

Euphrates

Jerusalem

Alexandria

JUDEA

2

River

ARABIA

EGYPT

3 **A Nation Built by Soldiers** The Roman soldier, as this statue suggests, was a superb fighter. One of Rome's greatest generals, **Julius Caesar** wrote about his army's conquest of Gaul. The Roman army not only destroyed but also built—clearing forests and constructing roads, bridges, aqueducts, and the buildings of new Roman cities.

Historical Highlights

Rome's long history was a spectacle of grand passion, heroic sacrifice, and some really bad behavior. It provided plenty of subject matter for Roman writers. Even in our own time, writers, playwrights, and filmmakers dip into Rome's history for stirring events and characters.

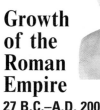

Growth of the Roman Empire
27 B.C.–A.D. 200

Augustus Caesar

Legendary Beginnings
753–509 B.C.

The Romans gave themselves mythic origins. According to Virgil's *Aeneid*, their ancestor was the Trojan hero **Aeneas,** who fled from Troy and sailed to Italy. According to legend, Aeneas' descendants were the twins **Romulus** and **Remus,** who were nursed by a wolf. In 753 B.C., Romulus founded a settlement, naming it Rome after himself.

From about 616 to 509 B.C., the early Romans were ruled by the **Etruscans,** who had a more advanced civilization. Rome gradually evolved from a village into a city.

The Roman Republic
509–27 B.C.

The Romans ultimately revolted against the Etruscan kings and established a **republic.** It changed over the years as members of the upper class struggled with other citizens for power. Meanwhile, the Romans greatly expanded their territory. In the **Punic Wars,** the Romans defeated the Carthaginians of North Africa for control of the western Mediterranean. By the 60s B.C., Rome ruled Greece, Macedonia, Asia Minor, Syria, and Judea. These conquests led to civil wars in Rome for the next 20 years. In 46 B.C., **Julius Caesar** seized control of the government; he ruled for about two years before he was assassinated.

The first emperor of Rome renamed himself **Augustus,** which means "exalted one." Born Gaius Octavius, he was Julius Caesar's grandnephew and handpicked heir. He became emperor after defeating the forces of **Mark Antony** and **Cleopatra** in the Battle of Actium. Augustus brought peace to war-weary Romans, restoring law and order. He solidified the empire by strengthening the local administration of its provinces. His reign marked the beginning of a 200-year period of stability called the Pax Romana (Roman Peace). The peace and prosperity ushered in a golden age of art, architecture, and literature. No other period in Roman history ever matched the **Augustan Age** for artistic achievement. At the end of his long reign,

Romulus marks the site for the foundation of Rome.

LEGENDARY BEGINNINGS	THE ROMAN REPUBLIC
753 B.C.	509 B.C.

boasted that he had found Rome a city of brick and left it a city of marble.

After Augustus' reign the empire grew only a little. In A.D. 43, the emperor **Claudius** invaded Britain, and later the emperor **Trajan** annexed parts of what is now Hungary and Romania.

However, the Augustan Age wasn't a golden age for everyone. Although the Pax Romana allowed **Christianity** to spread, Christians began to be persecuted in A.D. 64, when the emperor **Nero** blamed them for a fire that gutted Rome. Two **Jewish** rebellions against Roman rule met with swift and brutal retaliation. Those Jews who survived were exiled from their homeland for the next 1,800 years.

Decline and Fall of the Roman Empire

A.D. 200–476

One of the wisest of the Roman emperors was **Marcus Aurelius.** After he died in A.D. 180, Rome had a series of cruel and incompetent rulers. The empire also began to fray at the edges. Germanic tribes invaded from the north, disrupting trade and taxing the resources of the Roman army. Gradually, the structures of Roman society were overwhelmed. Economic problems weakened the empire as well.

From a combination of external and internal forces, the Roman Empire in the west gradually declined and eventually fell. Even Christianity, which became the official religion of the empire in A.D. 391, couldn't save it. In the end, hordes of invaders overran the empire. Like the legendary city of Troy, Rome was plundered of its riches at last.

History to Literature

EVENT IN HISTORY	EVENT IN LITERATURE
Rome is founded in 753 B.C.	Virgil's epic *Aeneid* celebrates Aeneas as the ancestor of the Roman people.
Julius Caesar conquers Gaul from 58 to 50 B.C.	Caesar describes his adventures in *Commentaries on the Gallic War.*
Julius Caesar is assassinated in 44 B.C.	William Shakespeare's play *Julius Caesar,* written about 1600, dramatizes Caesar's death and the fate of the conspirators.
During Nero's reign, a devastating fire engulfs Rome.	In the *Annals,* the Roman historian Tacitus writes a revealing account of the fire and Nero's response to it.

GROWTH OF THE ROMAN EMPIRE	DECLINE AND FALL OF THE ROMAN EMPIRE
27 B.C.	A.D. 200

A.D. 476

People and Society

Like the Greeks, the Romans were divided into classes. However, as the empire began to grow rapidly, money—more than class—became the great divider between people.

Patricians

Making up Rome's small but powerful upper class, the **patricians** were members of Rome's oldest and wealthiest families. Being a Roman patrician was more a matter of birth and bloodline than wealth.

Patricians exclusively ran the early republic, and their family organization became the model for Roman society. Basically, the father, or *paterfamilias,* was the head of the family. By law, he had absolute power over his property, his children, and his grand-children until the day he died. He alone determined whether a newborn child was to be killed, sold into slavery, or welcomed into the family. He arranged his children's marriages, resolved family disputes, and could banish another family member at will.

Plebeians

The **plebeians** were Roman citizens—both rich and poor—who weren't patricians. Not until the fourth century B.C. did the plebeians win political rights equal to those of the patricians. After Augustus became emperor, he looked for able plebeians to help administer the empire. Succeeding emperors kept up the practice, making government service a way for plebeians to improve their lives.

In addition to government jobs, the empire generated a booming business in trade. Enterprising Romans made money as importers, exporters, shipbuilders, merchants, and in other business-related activities. As a result, Roman society had the largest, most comfortable **middle class** of all ancient societies.

Roman bas-relief showing a middle-class family

The Urban Poor

For centuries, most Romans farmed small plots of land to make a living. When the empire expanded and farmers were required to serve in the army, they usually had to sell their farms to the big landowners. When the small farmers returned from military service, they found that slaves from the conquered territories now did most of the farm labor. The farmers had little choice but to follow the crowds flooding into Rome.

Of the 1 million people who lived in Rome in the Augustan Age, about three-fourths were unemployed and poor. The poor survived on free grain distributed by the government—one of the earliest known forms of welfare. They lived in some of the first **public housing** ever built: multistory, timber-frame tenement buildings. Overcrowded and hastily put up, these rickety structures were apt to collapse or catch fire, fatally trapping the inhabitants inside.

Coin with the image of Julius Caesar

The Army

One way to escape grinding poverty was to join the army. From the time of Augustus, the Romans had a standing army of about 300,000 men. There were two classes of soldiers: **legionaries,** who were Roman citizens, and **auxiliaries,** noncitizens from the provinces.

A typical Roman soldier enlisted as a teenager and served for 25 years. His pay, although not high, was more than a laborer's, and he received excellent medical care. Discipline was harsh and training rigorous—the keys to the army's consistent success on the battlefield. During peacetime, Roman soldiers constructed the roads, bridges, and buildings of the empire. To relax, they could socialize in the towns that grew up around their camps. Upon being discharged, a legionary could expect a plot of land or a cash payment as a pension. An auxiliary was given Roman citizenship.

Slaves

Like the Greeks, the Romans captured people during wartime and used them as servants and laborers. But as slaves—some of them educated and highly skilled—poured into Rome from the conquered territories, they began to be used for more specialized jobs as tutors, bookkeepers, and clerks.

Conditions for slaves in the countryside were exceptionally harsh. In 73–71 B.C., an escaped gladiator named **Spartacus** led an uprising of more than 70,000 slaves. The Spartacus rebellion was brutally crushed. Rebels who were captured were crucified. The roads leading into Rome were lined with the crosses of executed slaves.

To their credit, though, the Romans were actually quite generous in freeing their slaves. The Roman dramatist Terence, for example, was a freed slave originally from Carthage.

Women in Ancient Rome

Roman women enjoyed a much freer and more active life than did their counterparts in Greece. A Roman wife customarily ran the household, managing the money, organizing the work of the slaves, and taking care of the children. Although her marriage was arranged by her father, a woman could get divorced. Most Roman matrons took pride in their spinning and weaving. Girls received training in the textile arts from an early age.

Although they weren't citizens, many Roman women owned property, controlled their own money, appeared openly in public, wore makeup, and got their hair done. They could attend some public performances, even though they often had to sit separately from the men. Women played female roles in the pantomime skits so popular among Roman audiences, but they were barred from acting in serious dramas. Still, Roman men were quite used to seeing educated women at dinner parties and priestesses in the temples. Under the emperor Domitian, women even appeared as gladiators in the Colosseum.

Arts and Culture

Roman culture was a continuation of what the Greeks had started. To the Greek ideals of beauty, grace, and wisdom, the Romans added strength, integrity, and majesty. Greeks and Romans gave us the classical style, which we use today as a standard of comparison for all other Western art and literature.

Architecture and Engineering

It has been said that the true Roman artist was the engineer. The Romans basically adapted Greek architectural styles to suit their own purposes. What impressed the Romans was size rather than beauty. They invented **concrete** and perfected the **arch** as an architectural form so that they could build monumental structures worthy of a great empire—towering aqueducts and bridges, huge public baths, giant amphitheaters, and great domed rotundas. One of the Romans' greatest achievements was the network of **roads** that crisscrossed the empire—about 50,000 miles of paved highways and 200,000 miles of secondary roads. Some of them are still used today.

Public Entertainment

Roman emperors lavished free entertainments on their citizens, in part to pacify the poor. Chariot races were very popular. A huge U-shaped arena in Rome, the **Circus Maximus,** could accommodate 250,000 spectators. Just down the street, the 50,000-seat **Colosseum** showcased a variety of violent events. In the morning there might be organized hunts in which hundreds of tigers, leopards, bulls, lions, and elephants would be slaughtered. Next on the program, unarmed criminals (and in later years Christians) were led into the arena to be either killed by gladiators or eaten alive by wild beasts. In the afternoon came the star attraction—the gladiatorial contests. Usually, gladiators fought to win their freedom, but some returned to the arena for the sheer pleasure of life-or-death combat. In another spectacular event, the arena might be flooded to stage mock naval battles. One battle reportedly involved 24 ships and 19,000 men.

Law and Government

The Romans' most lasting contribution to the world was their system of law, which has influenced the legal systems of many nations—including the United States. These are the main principles of Roman law:

- All people have the right to equal treatment under the law.
- A person is considered innocent until proved guilty.
- The burden of proof rests with the accuser rather than the accused.

The governments of many nations, moreover, include a senate—in many ways similar to the legislative body of ancient Rome.

Colosseum

Art and Sculpture

Many Roman artists and sculptors imitated Greek models. But unlike the Greeks, who had idealized the human body, the Romans were sternly realistic. They excelled in painting. Large murals, called **frescoes,** decorated the walls of wealthy Romans' homes. Roman artists also contributed to two other art forms: the **bas-relief,** in which sculpted images stand out from a flat background, and the **mosaic,** in which small pieces of glass, stone, or tile are arranged to form designs or images on a flat surface.

Augustus Caesar

Religion

During the 300s B.C., the Romans adopted the major Greek gods, giving them Roman names. They singled out **Jupiter** (Zeus), **Juno** (Hera), and **Minerva** (Athena) as special favorites. Still, the earlier Roman household gods remained dear to Romans' hearts. Families regularly invoked **Vesta,** goddess of the hearth, to protect their homes. The temple of Vesta in Rome contained a sacred hearth, on which a fire was fed continually by "vestal virgins." Other popular deities included **Ceres,** goddess of the harvest, and **Janus,** the god who guarded doorways.

Literature

Roman writers borrowed freely from Greek literary models to create epic and lyric poems, comedies, and tragedies. But Roman literature, more than anything else, is about being Roman. From **Cicero's** philosophical essays to **Virgil's** poetry, **Horace's** odes, the histories of **Livy** and **Tacitus,** and the plays of **Plautus** and **Terence,** Roman literature illustrated the virtues of the Roman character— dignity, duty, integrity, and discipline—and inspired Romans to live up to their own ideals. Ovid narrated Roman as well as Greek myths in his *Metamorphoses* and accomplished for Roman literature what Augustus did for Rome: Ovid integrated the Greek and Roman cultures for the greater glory of Rome.

How Was Literature Presented?

When a Roman writer wanted an audience for his works, he had three options. He might hire a hall, invite some friends, and give a public recitation. This form of presentation was common because Romans had great respect for oratory and Roman literature was meant to be read aloud. Another way to publicize a literary work was to read it at a private party. Virgil, for example, recited his *Aeneid* at one of the emperor Augustus' dinner parties. Finally, a writer could buy writing materials and hire specially trained slave-copyists to produce a few books. The Roman version of a book was basically a rolled-up scroll of papyrus sheets.

Virgil reading from the *Aeneid*

Time Line

c. approximately
B.C. before Christ's birth
A.D. after Christ's birth

ANCIENT ROME
(753 B.C. –A.D. 200)

2500 B.C.   A.D. 1   PRESENT

EVENTS IN ROMAN LITERATURE

800 B.C.   600 B.C.   400 B.C.

240 B.C. Livius Andronicus' Latin version of a Greek play is performed before a Roman audience

c. 205 B.C. Comedy of Plautus first performed

EVENTS IN ROMAN HISTORY

800 B.C.   600 B.C.   400 B.C.

753 B.C. Legendary founding of Rome

Romulus and Remus

509 B.C. Romans overthrow the Etruscans and establish a republic

450 B.C. First Roman law code, the Laws of the Twelve Tables, is posted in the forum

338–264 B.C. Romans conquer Italy

264 B.C. First gladiatorial contests held in Rome

264–241 B.C. First Punic War between Rome and Carthage

218–201 B.C. In the Second Punic War, the Carthaginian general Hannibal crosses the Alps to fight the Romans; he is eventually defeated

EVENTS IN WORLD HISTORY

800 B.C.   600 B.C.   400 B.C.

c. 700s B.C. Homer composes the *Iliad* and the *Odyssey*

c. 563 B.C. Siddhartha Gautama, founder of Buddhism, born in India

c. 500 B.C. Nok culture in West Africa develops iron-making technology

c. 500 B.C. Zapotec civilization in Mexico builds Monte Albán, first city in the Americas

431–404 B.C. Peloponnesian War between Athens and Sparta

269–232 B.C. Asoka expands the Mauryan Empire in India

206 B.C. Beginning of Han Dynasty in China, which strengthens central government

MARCUS AURELIUS
MEDITATIONS

200 B.C.   **A.D. 1**

166 B.C. Comedy of Terence first performed

149 B.C. Publication of Cato's history of Rome

51 B.C. Publication of Julius Caesar's *Commentaries on the Gallic War*

19 B.C. Publication of Virgil's *Aeneid* after his death

8 B.C. Death of Maecenas, patron of Virgil, Horace, and others

A.D. 8 Ovid exiled to the shore of the Black Sea

A.D. 54 Publication of Seneca's philosophical works

A.D. 98 Tacitus publishes *Germania*, a study of the Germanic tribes

A.D. 100 Juvenal creates his *Satires*

A.D. 174–180 Marcus Aurelius writes his *Meditations*

200 B.C.   **A.D. 1**

149–146 B.C. In the Third Punic War, the Romans destroy Carthage

73–71 B.C. Spartacus leads a slave uprising in southern Italy

58–50 B.C. Julius Caesar's army conquers Gaul

44 B.C. Julius Caesar is assassinated

31 B.C. Octavian defeats Mark Antony in the Battle of Actium

27 B.C. Octavian becomes the emperor Augustus

A.D. 14 Death of the emperor Augustus

C. A.D. 29 Crucifixion of Jesus of Nazareth

A.D. 64 Fire damages Rome

A.D. 70 Romans destroy the Temple in Jerusalem

A.D. 79 Eruption of Mount Vesuvius buries the Roman towns of Herculaneum and Pompeii

A.D. 80 Completion of the Colosseum in Rome after ten years of work

A.D. 117 Roman Empire reaches its greatest extent under the emperor Trajan

A.D. 122–126 Hadrian's Wall is built across northern Britain

A.D. 180 Death of Marcus Aurelius and the end of the Pax Romana

200 B.C.   **A.D. 1**

c. 200 B.C. Nazca culture arises in Peru

185 B.C. End of the Mauryan Empire

C. A.D. 65 First Buddhist monastery built in ➤ China

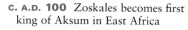

The Baiju monastery in Gyangze, China

C. A.D. 100 Zoskales becomes first king of Aksum in East Africa

A.D. 100–700 Moche culture flourishes in Peru

C. A.D. 105 Chinese invent paper

Connect to Today: The Legacy of Ancient Rome

Government at Work
The political system of the Romans strongly influenced modern governments. Like the senators of ancient Rome, the Congress of the United States carries on the business of government.

Action in the Arena
The citizens of Rome filled the Colosseum to watch gladiators fight to the death. The recent popularity of the film *Gladiator* points to our curiosity about this Roman spectacle. Today, spectators still fill modern arenas to watch athletes compete for victory.

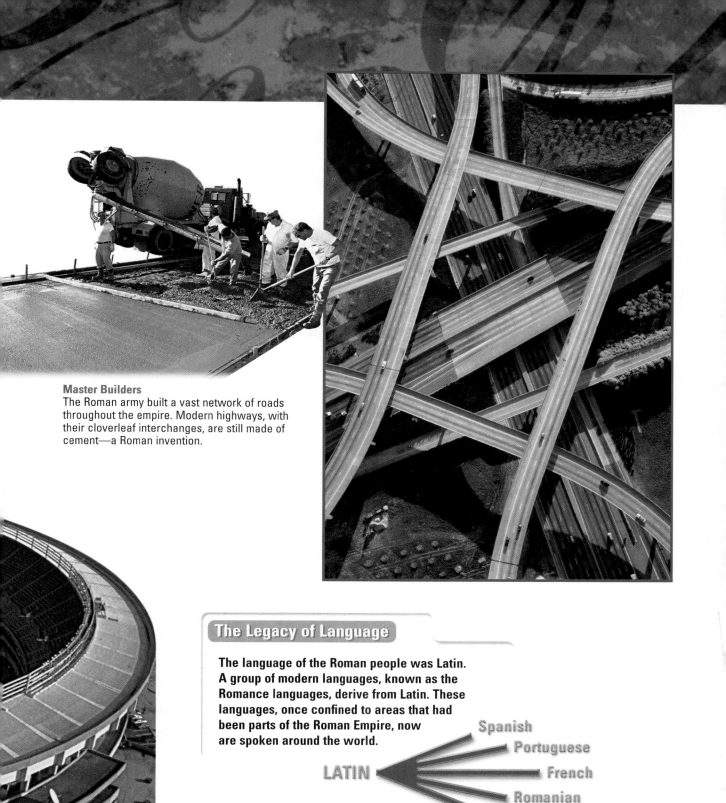

Master Builders
The Roman army built a vast network of roads throughout the empire. Modern highways, with their cloverleaf interchanges, are still made of cement—a Roman invention.

The Legacy of Language

The language of the Roman people was Latin. A group of modern languages, known as the Romance languages, derive from Latin. These languages, once confined to areas that had been parts of the Roman Empire, now are spoken around the world.

LATIN →
Spanish
Portuguese
French
Romanian
Italian

from the
AENEID
THE FALL OF TROY · VIRGIL

Virgil
70–19 B.C.

Rome's Favorite Poet The ancient Romans considered Virgil their greatest poet. He was loved by all who knew him—from his friend and fellow poet Horace to the emperor Augustus himself. Long after Virgil's death, the monks of the Middle Ages kept copying his works, unlike some of the writings of other Roman authors. For more than 1,500 years, Virgil was the most honored poet of Europe. He even appears as Dante's guide through hell and purgatory in that poet's *Divine Comedy,* one of the greatest poems of the Middle Ages. Many believe that only the Bible has had a greater influence on Western culture than Virgil.

Personal Life Little is known about Virgil's personal life. A farmer's son born in a small Italian village, Virgil spent his early years studying and writing poetry. He never married and was considered shy and gentle. He studied philosophy and rhetoric in Rome but preferred to live in the countryside that he loved.

For a humanities activity, click on:

Early Works Virgil's love of rural life inspired him to write pastoral poetry—poems that celebrate life in the country. His first known work, the *Eclogues,* is a collection of ten poems about the simple joys and sorrows of rural life. This popular work gained him the recognition of powerful men in the Roman government. Soon, Virgil found a patron, or sponsor, in Maecenas, one of the emperor Augustus' chief ministers. Virgil dedicated his second work, the *Georgics,* to Maecenas. This work celebrates rural values—such as discipline and hard work—as the basis of the Roman character.

Writing the National Epic Around 30 B.C., Virgil was asked to write a poem to honor Rome. The poem he wrote, the *Aeneid,* would become Rome's national epic. According to some historians, Augustus commissioned Virgil to write it in order to trace Rome's origin to a divine plan.

Imagine the pressure on Virgil, commanded to write his country's great epic while his emperor waited! Understandably, he at times felt overwhelmed by the responsibility. However, good Roman that he was, he stuck with it. For ten years, he worked steadily on the poem, creating almost 10,000 lines of verse. He planned to devote three more years to revising the poem. Unfortunately, he fell ill on a journey from Athens and died shortly after returning to Italy. Supposedly, Virgil had left word with his friends to burn the manuscript if anything were to happen to him. Luckily, Augustus stepped in, overruling this request. He had the poem published in its unpolished form—for Rome and for all time.

Build Background

Written Epic Virgil's *Aeneid* is an example of a written epic. This form evolved from oral stories about legendary heroes whose brave deeds helped their people.

Written Epics from Different Cultures	
Babylon	***Epic of Gilgamesh*** (the oldest existing epic)
France	***Chanson de Roland***
Spain	***Cantar de mío Cid***
England	***Beowulf***
Germany	***Nibelungenlied***
Finland	***Kalevala***
India	***Mahabharata*** and ***Ramayana***

The *Aeneid* and the Augustan Age Written in the Latin language, the *Aeneid* is Virgil's masterpiece and the national epic of ancient Rome. Virgil imitated the Greek poet Homer by using many of the elements found in Homer's epics. Virgil's hero is the Trojan prince Aeneas, who represents the ideal Roman. (The emperor Augustus considered himself a descendant of Aeneas.) The poem establishes the mythological roots of Rome, shows the nobility of its people, and foretells the coming of Augustus' glorious reign.

Virgil wrote the *Aeneid* between the years 30 and 19 B.C. In the year 31 B.C., the forces of Octavian (later to become the emperor Augustus) had defeated the fleets of Mark Antony and Cleopatra in the Battle of Actium. This battle marked the end of the Roman Republic and the beginning of the Roman Empire. Virgil felt that Augustus was ushering in a new era of peace, prosperity, and national pride after 20 years of bloody civil war.

Brimming with patriotism, Virgil set about to write an epic that would do for Roman civilization what Homer's *Iliad* and *Odyssey* had done for the people of Greece. Though based on these Greek epics, the *Aeneid* is Roman to its core, conveying Roman themes and emphasizing Roman values.

Aeneas as Epic Hero Throughout the epic, Virgil uses the Latin word *pius* to describe Aeneas. This term means "dutiful and loyal to family, to country, and to the gods." Aeneas is a good leader, a devoted father, and a loving son. No matter the cost, he always obeys the will of the gods. He endures terrible suffering but remains faithful to his mission. For example, he loses his wife before setting sail from Troy to Italy but still completes the journey. Through Aeneas' suffering, Virgil conveys a timeless truth about life: "At the heart of things there are tears."

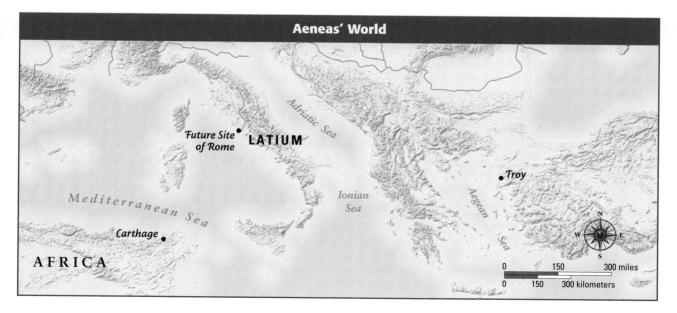
Aeneas' World

The Story of Aeneas

The *Aeneid* is divided into 12 books. The first 6 resemble Homer's *Odyssey* in that they deal with the hero's wanderings. Shortly after the end of the Trojan War, Aeneas, his father, and his son, together with a band of refugees, leave Troy. They sail westward for Italy, as the ghost of Aeneas' wife has told him to do. Near Sicily, a storm separates Aeneas from his companions, and he lands on the African coast. There he meets Dido, the beautiful queen of Carthage. Strongly attracted to Aeneas, she gives a banquet in his honor. At the banquet, Aeneas relates his adventures, including the fall of Troy. Aeneas and Dido fall deeply and passionately in love. Aeneas, however, must leave her to fulfill his divine mission of finding a new home for the Trojans—the settlement that will become the city of Rome. Sailing from Carthage, he notices the flames of a funeral pyre. Dido, heartbroken over his departure, has taken her life.

Later, Aeneas visits a prophetess, the Cumaean Sibyl. With her, he descends to the underworld, where he meets his now-dead father, who shows him a vision. Aeneas sees the future generations of Romans who will descend from him. The line of descent culminates in the emperor Augustus.

The last 6 books of the *Aeneid* deal with warfare, thus resembling Homer's *Iliad.* They describe Aeneas' arrival in Latium, near the future site of Rome. The local king, Latinus, offers him alliance and the hand of his daughter Lavinia. Turnus, one of Lavinia's suitors, attacks the Trojans, killing Pallas, a young soldier whom Aeneas has promised to protect. Before the two armies, Aeneas and Turnus fight in single combat. Enraged to find that Turnus is wearing the armor of Pallas, Aeneas kills him with a sword.

Cast of Characters

Gods

Juno (jōō′nō): the queen of the gods

Mars (märz): the god of war

Neptune (nĕp′tōōn′): the god of the sea

Pallas (păl′əs): the goddess of wisdom; also known as **Minerva** (mǐ-nûr′və)

Venus (vē′nəs): the goddess of love and beauty, mother of Aeneas

Greeks

Menelaus (mĕn′ə-lā′əs): a leader of the expedition against Troy; husband of Helen

Neoptolemus (nē′ŏp-tŏl′ə-məs): a mighty warrior, son of the hero Achilles; also known as **Pyrrhus** (pǐr′əs)

Sinon (sī′nən): a warrior purposely left behind in Troy when the Greeks sailed away, pretending to give up the fighting

Ulysses (yōō-lǐs′ēz′): a leader known for his wily schemes

Trojans

Aeneas (ǐ-nē′əs): the hero of the epic and the son of the goddess Venus and Anchises, a mortal

Anchises (ăn-kī′sēz′): the father of Aeneas

Cassandra (kə-săn′drə): a daughter of Priam, whose prophecies always come true but are never believed

Creusa (krē-ōō′zə): the wife of Aeneas

Hecuba (hĕk′yə-bə): the wife of Priam and queen of Troy

Helen (hĕl′ən): the wife of the Greek leader Menelaus, who betrayed him by running off with the Trojan prince Paris

Iulus (yōō′ləs): the young son of Aeneas and Creusa; also known as **Ascanius** (ăs-kā′nē-əs)

Laocoön (lā-ŏk′ō-ŏn′): a nobleman, brother of Anchises

Politēs (pə-lī′tēz′): a son of Priam

Priam (prī′əm): the king of Troy

Connect to Your Life

At the end of this excerpt, Aeneas sets out to lead a band of refugees from Troy to Italy. Think of people from different walks of life whom you regard as good leaders. They may be politicians, teachers, military officers, or even characters in books or movies. What qualities do good leaders have? How do they respond to adversity and misfortune? Share your ideas with a small group of classmates.

Focus Your Reading

LITERARY ANALYSIS: CULTURE HERO

A **culture hero** is a larger-than-life figure who reflects the values of a people. A culture hero provides a noble image to inspire and guide the actions of all who share that culture. As you read, think about the character of Aeneas. Consider the qualities that make him heroic.

ACTIVE READING: PREDICTING

As a reading skill, **predicting** involves using clues in a story, along with prior knowledge and experience, to make reasonable guesses about what will happen later in the story. Good readers make and revise predictions almost unconsciously as they read.

📖 **READER'S NOTEBOOK** As you read Aeneas' account of the fall of Troy, look for clues that seem to foreshadow future events. In a chart like the one below, jot down your predictions and the clues that led you to them. An example is shown.

Prediction	Clue
The wooden horse will bring about the destruction of Troy.	"...it cast a shadow / Over the city's heart." (lines 122–123)

from the Aeneid
The Fall of Troy

Virgil

Translated by Robert Fitzgerald

GUIDE FOR READING

FOCUS Aeneas is telling Queen Dido about the end of the Trojan War. After ten long years, the Greeks suddenly depart from Troy, leaving behind a huge wooden horse. Read to find out how the Trojans react to this parting gift.

"**K**nowing their strength broken in warfare, turned
Back by the fates, and years—so many years—
Already slipped away, the Danaan captains
By the divine handicraft of Pallas built
5   A horse of timber, tall as a hill,
And sheathed its ribs with planking of cut pine.
This they gave out to be an offering
For a safe return by sea, and the word went round.
But on the sly they shut inside a company
10   Chosen from their picked soldiery by lot,
Crowding the vaulted caverns in the dark—
The horse's belly—with men fully armed.

Offshore there's a long island, Tenedos,
Famous and rich while Priam's kingdom lasted,
15   A treacherous anchorage now, and nothing more.
They crossed to this and hid their ships behind it
On the bare shore beyond. We thought they'd gone,
Sailing home to Mycenae before the wind,
So Teucer's town is freed of her long anguish,
20   Gates thrown wide! And out we go in joy

3 Danaan (də-nāʹən): Greek.

6 sheathed: covered.

18 Mycenae (mī-sēʹnē): the city ruled by the Greek commander, Agamemnon.

19 Teucer's (tōōʹsərz) **town:** Troy. (Teucer was the first Trojan king.)

Wooden horse inside the city of Troy, surrounded by Trojans; scene from *Helen of Troy* (1955).

To see the Dorian campsites, all deserted,
The beach they left behind. Here the Dolopians
Pitched their tents, here cruel Achilles lodged,
There lay the ships, and there, formed up in ranks,
25 They came inland to fight us. Of our men
One group stood marveling, <u>gaping</u> up to see
The dire gift of the cold unbedded goddess,
The sheer mass of the horse.
                          Thymoetes shouts
It should be hauled inside the walls and moored
30 High on the citadel—whether by treason
Or just because Troy's fate went that way now.
Capys opposed him; so did the wiser heads:
'Into the sea with it,' they said, 'or burn it,
Build up a bonfire under it,
35 This trick of the Greeks, a gift no one can trust,
Or cut it open, search the hollow belly!'

21 Dorian (dôr′ē-ən): Greek.

22 Dolopians (də-lō′pē-ənz): a group of Greek allies.

27 the cold unbedded goddess: Pallas, protector of the Greeks.

28 Thymoetes (thī-mē′tēz′).

30 citadel (sĭt′ə-dəl): stronghold.

32 Capys (kăp′ĭs).

WORDS TO KNOW
gaping (gā′pĭng) *adj.* staring open-mouthed **gape** *v.*

Contrary notions pulled the crowd apart.
Next thing we knew, in front of everyone,
Laocoön with a great company

40 Came furiously running from the Height,
And still far off cried out: 'O my poor people,
Men of Troy, what madness has come over you?
Can you believe the enemy truly gone?
A gift from the Danaans, and no <u>ruse</u>?

45 Is that Ulysses' way, as you have known him?
Achaeans must be hiding in this timber,
Or it was built to butt against our walls,
Peer over them into our houses, pelt
The city from the sky. Some crookedness

50 Is in this thing. Have no faith in the horse!
Whatever it is, even when Greeks bring gifts
I fear them, gifts and all.'
                                    He broke off then
And rifled his big spear with all his might
Against the horse's flank, the curve of belly.

55 It stuck there trembling, and the rounded hull
Reverberated groaning at the blow.
If the gods' will had not been <u>sinister</u>,
If our own minds had not been crazed,
He would have made us foul that Argive den

60 With bloody steel, and Troy would stand today—
O citadel of Priam, towering still!

But now look: hillmen, shepherds of Dardania,
Raising a shout, dragged in before the king
An unknown fellow with hands tied behind—

65 This all as he himself had planned,
Volunteering, letting them come across him,
So he could open Troy to the Achaeans.
Sure of himself this man was, braced for it
Either way, to work his trick or die.

70 From every quarter Trojans run to see him,
Ring the prisoner round, and make a game
Of jeering at him. Be instructed now
In Greek deceptive arts: one barefaced deed
Can tell you of them all.

46 Achaeans (ə-kē'ənz): Greeks.

56 reverberated: echoed.

59 foul that Argive (är'jīv') **den:** slash the Greek hiding place.

62 Dardania (där-dā'nē-ə): the region surrounding Troy.

73 deceptive arts: trickery.

WORDS TO KNOW

ruse (rōōs) *n.* a trick
sinister (sĭn'ĭ-stər) *adj.* having an evil disposition or intent

*The Greek spy, Sinon, tells a convincing lie about the
Trojan horse. He explains that the Greeks built the wood-
en horse to win back the favor of the goddess Pallas. He
says that they were planning to sacrifice him to the goddess but he narrowly escaped. Sinon tells the Trojans to
treat the statue with respect and to bring it within their
city walls. If they do so, they will avoid doom and ensure
that the Greeks will meet a terrible fate.*

75 **A**nd now another sign, more fearful still,
    Broke on our blind miserable people,
    Filling us all with dread. Laocoön,
    Acting as Neptune's priest that day by lot,
    Was on the point of putting to the knife
80 A massive bull before the appointed altar,
    When ah—look there!
    From Tenedos, on the calm sea, twin snakes—
    I shiver to recall it—endlessly
    Coiling, uncoiling, swam abreast for shore,
85 Their underbellies showing as their crests
    Reared red as blood above the swell; behind
    They glided with great <u>undulating</u> backs.
    Now came the sound of thrashed seawater foaming;
    Now they were on dry land, and we could see
90 Their burning eyes, fiery and <u>suffused</u> with blood,
    Their tongues a-flicker out of hissing maws.   **91 maws:** mouths.
    We scattered, pale with fright. But straight ahead
    They slid until they reached Laocoön.
    Each snake enveloped one of his two boys,   **94 boys:** sons.

Sculpture of Laocoön (first century B.C.). Vatican Museums, Vatican State.

HUMANITIES CONNECTION This marble statue shows Laocoön and his two sons being crushed by sea serpents. Laocoön suffers for having warned his people about the Trojan horse. This statue was an original Hellenistic Greek work that may have been imported to Rome. Greek statues like this one met with great acclaim in the Roman world.

95   Twining about and feeding on the body.
    Next they ensnared the man as he ran up
    With weapons: coils like cables looped and bound him
    Twice round the middle; twice about his throat
    They whipped their back-scales, and their heads towered,
100 While with both hands he fought to break the knots,
    Drenched in slime, his head-bands black with venom,
    Sending to heaven his appalling cries   **102 appalling:** horrifying.
    Like a slashed bull escaping from an altar,
    The fumbled axe shrugged off. The pair of snakes
105 Now flowed away and made for the highest shrines,
    The citadel of pitiless Minerva,
    Where coiling they took cover at her feet
    Under the rondure of her shield. New terrors   **108 rondure:** circle.
    Ran in the shaken crowd: the word went round

110 Laocoön had paid, and rightfully,
For profanation of the sacred hulk
With his offending spear hurled at its flank.

'The offering must be hauled to its true home,'
They clamored. 'Votive prayers to the goddess
115 Must be said there!'
                    So we breached the walls
And laid the city open. Everyone
Pitched in to get the figure underpinned
With rollers, hempen lines around the neck.
Deadly, pregnant with enemies, the horse
120 Crawled upward to the breach. And boys and girls
Sang hymns around the towrope as for joy
They touched it. Rolling on, it cast a shadow
Over the city's heart. O Fatherland,
O Ilium, home of gods! Defensive wall
125 Renowned in war for Dardanus's people!
There on the very threshold of the breach
It jarred to a halt four times, four times the arms
In the belly thrown together made a sound—
Yet on we strove unmindful, deaf and blind,
130 To place the monster on our blessed height.
Then, even then, Cassandra's lips unsealed
The doom to come: lips by a god's command
Never believed or heeded by the Trojans.
So pitiably we, for whom that day
135 Would be the last, made all our temples green
With leafy festal boughs throughout the city.

As heaven turned, Night from the Ocean stream
Came on, profound in gloom on earth and sky
And Myrmidons in hiding. In their homes
140 The Teucrians lay silent, wearied out,
And sleep enfolded them. The Argive fleet,
Drawn up in line abreast, left Tenedos
Through the aloof moon's friendly stillnesses
And made for the familiar shore. Flame signals
145 Shone from the command ship. Sinon, favored
By what the gods unjustly had decreed,
Stole out to tap the pine walls and set free

110–112 Laocoön had paid . . . its flank: Pallas had punished Laocoön for treating the wooden horse with disrespect by throwing his spear at it.

115 breached: broke through.

119 pregnant: filled.

124 Ilium (ĭl′ē-əm): another name for Troy.

139 Myrmidons (mûr′mə-dŏnz′): Greeks.

140 Teucrians (tōō′krē-ənz): Trojans.

The Danaans in the belly. Opened wide,
The horse emitted men; gladly they dropped
150 Out of the cavern, captains first, Thessandrus,
Sthenelus and the man of iron, Ulysses;
Hand over hand upon the rope, Acamas, Thoas,
Neoptolemus and Prince Machaon,
Menelaus and then the master builder,
155 Epeos, who designed the horse decoy.
Into the darkened city, buried deep
In sleep and wine, they made their way,
Cut the few sentries down,
Let in their fellow soldiers at the gate,
160 And joined their combat companies as planned.

PAUSE & REFLECT Why do the Trojans bring the
wooden horse inside their city?

FOCUS Terrible fighting rages outside the palace of
Priam, the king of Troy. As you read, look for details that
help you visualize this fighting.

*The ghost of Hector visits Aeneas in his sleep, warning
him about the Greek invasion. Hector tells Aeneas to flee
the city so that one day he will be able to establish
another great city—Rome. Aeneas awakens, puts on his
armor, and goes out into the streets of the burning city.
He and his comrades defeat a small band of Greek
soldiers, take their armor, and put it on to disguise
themselves. They continue to fight the invaders.
Eventually, the Greeks see through the Trojans' disguise,
and many of Aeneas' companions are killed.*

150–155 **Thessandrus** (thə-săn′drəs)
. . . **Sthenelus** (sthĕn′ə-ləs) . . .
Acamas (ăk′ə-məs) . . . **Thoas**
(thō′əs) . . . **Machaon** (mə-kā′ŏn′)
. . . **Epeos** (ĕ-pē′əs).

The burning of Troy

Ashes of Ilium!
Flames that consumed my people! Here I swear
That in your downfall I did not avoid
One weapon, one exchange with the Danaans,
165 And if it had been fated, my own hand
Had earned my death. But we were torn away
From that place—Iphitus and Pelias too,
One slow with age, one wounded by Ulysses,
Called by a clamor at the hall of Priam.
170 Truly we found here a <u>prodigious</u> fight,
As though there were none elsewhere, not a death

167 Iphitus (ī'fĭ-təs) **and Pelias**
(pĕl'ē-əs): Trojan soldiers.

AENEID   **367**

In the whole city: Mars gone berserk, Danaans
In a rush to scale the roof; the gate besieged
By a tortoise shell of overlapping shields.
175　Ladders clung to the wall, and men strove upward
Before the very doorposts, on the rungs,
Left hand putting the shield up, and the right
Reaching for the cornice. The defenders
Wrenched out upperworks and rooftiles: these
180　For missiles, as they saw the end, preparing
To fight back even on the edge of death.
And gilded beams, ancestral ornaments,
They rolled down on the heads below. In hall
Others with swords drawn held the entrance way,
185　Packed there, waiting. Now we plucked up heart
To help the royal house, to give our men
A respite, and to add our strength to theirs,
Though all were beaten. And we had for entrance
A rear door, secret, giving on a passage
190　Between the palace halls; in other days
Andromachë, poor lady, often used it,
Going alone to see her husband's parents
Or taking Astyanax to his grandfather.
I climbed high on the roof, where hopeless men
195　Were picking up and throwing futile missiles.
Here was a tower like a promontory
Rising toward the stars above the roof:
All Troy, the Danaan ships, the Achaean camp,
Were visible from this. Now close beside it
200　With crowbars, where the flooring made loose joints,
We pried it from its bed and pushed it over.
Down with a rending crash in sudden ruin
Wide over the Danaan lines it fell;
But fresh troops moved up, and the rain of stones
205　With every kind of missile never ceased.

PAUSE & REFLECT What details helped you imagine
the fighting outside Priam's palace?

172 berserk: recklessly violent.

178 cornice (kôr'nĭs): a molding at
the top of a wall.

191 Andromachë (ăn-drŏm'ə-kē),
poor lady: Andromachë's husband,
the Trojan prince Hector, had been
killed by Achilles earlier in the war.

193 Astyanax (ə-stī'ə-năks'): the
son of Hector and Andromachë.

196 promontory (prŏm'ən-tôr'ē): a
ridge of land extending into a
body of water.

WORDS TO KNOW
respite (rĕs'pĭt) *n.* a rest

What do you predict will happen when the Greek
soldiers break into the palace?

Just at the outer doors of the vestibule
Sprang Pyrrhus, all in bronze and glittering,
As a serpent, hidden swollen underground
By a cold winter, <u>writhes</u> into the light,
210 On vile grass fed, his old skin cast away,
Renewed and glossy, rolling slippery coils,
With lifted underbelly rearing sunward
And triple tongue a-flicker. Close beside him
Giant Periphas and Automedon,
215 His armor-bearer, once Achilles' driver,
Besieged the place with all the young of Scyros,
Hurling their torches at the palace roof.
Pyrrhus shouldering forward with an axe
Broke down the stony threshold, forced apart
220 Hinges and brazen door-jambs, and chopped through
One panel of the door, splitting the oak,
To make a window, a great breach. And there
Before their eyes the inner halls lay open,
The courts of Priam and the ancient kings,
225 With men-at-arms ranked in the vestibule.
From the interior came sounds of weeping,
Pitiful commotion, wails of women
High-pitched, rising in the formal chambers
To ring against the silent golden stars;
230 And, through the palace, mothers wild with fright
Ran to and fro or clung to doors and kissed them.
Pyrrhus with his father's brawn stormed on,
No bolts or bars or men availed to stop him:
Under his battering the double doors
235 Were torn out of their sockets and fell inward.
Sheer force cleared the way: the Greeks broke through
Into the vestibule, cut down the guards,
And made the wide hall seethe with men-at-arms—
A tumult greater than when dikes are burst
240 And a foaming river, swirling out in flood,
Whelms every parapet and races on
Through fields and over all the lowland plains,
Bearing off pens and cattle. I myself
Saw Neoptolemus furious with blood

206 vestibule (vĕs′tə-byōōl′):
entrance hall.

214 Periphas (pə-rī′fəs) . . .
Automedon (ô-tŏm′ə-dŏn′).

216 the young of Scyros (skī′rəs):
the followers of Neoptolemus, who
lived on the island of Scyros.

238 seethe: boil; surge.

241 whelms every parapet:
overflows every protective wall.

WORDS TO KNOW

writhe (rīth) v. to twist about; squirm

245 In the entrance way, and saw the two Atridae;
Hecuba I saw, and her hundred daughters,
Priam before the altars, with his blood
Drenching the fires that he himself had blessed.
Those fifty bridal chambers, hope of a line
250 So flourishing; those doorways high and proud,
Adorned with takings of barbaric gold,
Were all brought low: fire had them, or the Greeks.

What was the fate of Priam, you may ask.
Seeing his city captive, seeing his own
255 Royal portals rent apart, his enemies
In the inner rooms, the old man uselessly
Put on his shoulders, shaking with old age,
Armor unused for years, belted a sword on,
And made for the massed enemy to die.
260 Under the open sky in a central court
Stood a big altar; near it, a laurel tree
Of great age, leaning over, in deep shade
Embowered the Penatës. At this altar
Hecuba and her daughters, like white doves
265 Blown down in a black storm, clung together,
Enfolding holy images in their arms.
Now, seeing Priam in a young man's gear,
She called out:
                            'My poor husband, what mad thought
Drove you to buckle on these weapons?
270 Where are you trying to go? The time is past
For help like this, for this kind of defending,
Even if my own Hector could be here.
Come to me now: the altar will protect us,
Or else you'll die with us.'
                                          She drew him close,
275 Heavy with years, and made a place for him
To rest on the consecrated stone.
                                          Now see
Politës, one of Priam's sons, escaped
From Pyrrhus' butchery and on the run
Through enemies and spears, down colonnades,
280 Through empty courtyards, wounded. Close behind
Comes Pyrrhus burning for the death-stroke: has him,
Catches him now, and lunges with the spear.

245 the two Atridae (ā-trī′dē): Menelaus and his brother Agamemnon.

263 embowered the Penatës (pə-nā′tēz): sheltered the images of the household gods.

279 colonnades (kŏl′ə-nādz′): rows of columns.

The boy has reached his parents, and before them
Goes down, pouring out his life with blood.
285 Now Priam, in the very midst of death,
Would neither hold his peace nor spare his anger.

'**F**or what you've done, for what you've dared,' he said,
'If there is care in heaven for atrocity,
May the gods render fitting thanks, reward you
290 As you deserve. You forced me to look on
At the destruction of my son: defiled
A father's eyes with death. That great Achilles
You claim to be the son of—and you lie—
Was not like you to Priam, his enemy;
295 To me who threw myself upon his mercy
He showed compunction, gave me back for burial
The bloodless corpse of Hector, and returned me
To my own realm.'
                    The old man threw his spear
With feeble impact; blocked by the ringing bronze,
300 It hung there harmless from the jutting boss.

288 atrocity (ə-trŏs′ĭ-tē): horrible cruelty.

291 defiled: stained; polluted.

296 compunction: pity.

299 feeble: weak.

300 jutting boss: the raised center of a shield.

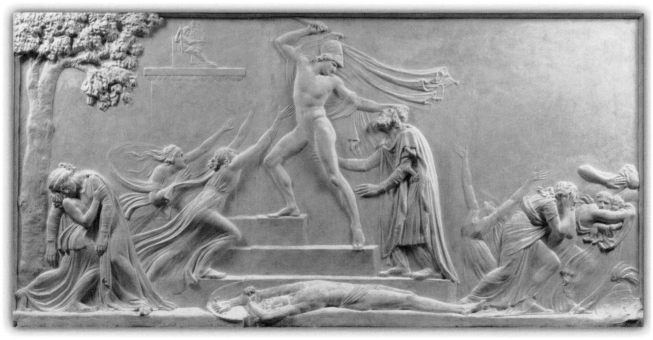

HUMANITIES CONNECTION In this bas-relief sculpture, Pyrrhus prepares to kill Priam as his wife and daughters look on in horror.

The Death of Priam (1787–1792), Antonio Canova. Museo Correr, Venice, Italy.

Then Pyrrhus answered:
                                  'You'll report the news
To Pelidës, my father; don't forget
My sad behavior, the degeneracy
Of Neoptolemus. Now die.'
                                  With this,

305   To the altar step itself he dragged him trembling,
Slipping in the pooled blood of his son,
And took him by the hair with his left hand.
The sword flashed in his right; up to the hilt
He thrust it in his body.
                                  That was the end
310   Of Priam's age, the doom that took him off,
With Troy in flames before his eyes, his towers
Headlong fallen—he that in other days
Had ruled in pride so many lands and peoples,
The power of Asia.
                                  On the distant shore
315   The vast trunk headless lies without a name.

302 Pelidës (pē-lī'dēz'): "son of Peleus"—that is, Achilles, who was killed earlier in the war.

303 degeneracy: decline into wickedness.

315 the vast trunk: Priam's huge body.

> **PAUSE & REFLECT** What does Pyrrhus do to Priam, the king of Troy?

> **FOCUS** Deeply moved by Priam's death, Aeneas notices Helen of Troy. He regards her as the cause of all the bloodshed. What do you predict he will do to Helen?

For the first time that night, inhuman shuddering
Took me, head to foot. I stood unmanned,
And my dear father's image came to mind
As our king, just his age, mortally wounded,
320   Gasped his life away before my eyes.
Creusa came to mind, too, left alone;
The house plundered; danger to little Iulus.
I looked around to take stock of my men,
But all had left me, utterly played out,
325   Giving their beaten bodies to the fire
Or plunging from the roof.
                                  It came to this,
That I stood there alone. And then I saw
Lurking behind the doorsill of the Vesta,

328 the Vesta: the temple of Vesta, goddess of the hearth.

In hiding, silent, in that place reserved,
330 The daughter of Tyndareus. Glare of fires
Lighted my steps this way and that, my eyes
Glancing over the whole scene, everywhere.
That woman, terrified of the Trojans' hate
For the city overthrown, terrified too
335 Of Danaan vengeance, her abandoned husband's
Anger after years—Helen, that Fury
Both to her own homeland and Troy, had gone
To earth, a hated thing, before the altars.
Now fires blazed up in my own spirit—
340 A passion to avenge my fallen town
And punish Helen's whorishness.

                     'Shall this one
Look untouched on Sparta and Mycenae
After her triumph, going like a queen,
And see her home and husband, kin and children,
345 With Trojan girls for escort, Phrygian slaves?
Must Priam perish by the sword for this?
Troy burn, for this? Dardania's littoral
Be soaked in blood, so many times, for this?
Not by my leave. I know
350 No glory comes of punishing a woman,
The feat can bring no honor. Still, I'll be
Approved for snuffing out a monstrous life,
For a just sentence carried out. My heart
Will teem with joy in this avenging fire,
355 And the ashes of my kin will be appeased.'

So ran my thoughts. I turned wildly upon her,
But at that moment, clear, before my eyes—
Never before so clear—in a pure light
Stepping before me, radiant through the night,
360 My loving mother came: immortal, tall,
And lovely as the lords of heaven know her.
Catching me by the hand, she held me back,
Then with her rose-red mouth <u>reproved</u> me:

                              'Son,
Why let such suffering goad you on to fury
365 Past control? Where is your thoughtfulness
For me, for us? Will you not first revisit
The place you left your father, worn and old,

330 the daughter of Tyndareus
(tĭn-dăr′ē-əs): Helen. (Tyndareus, although not actually Helen's father, was the husband of her mother, Leda.)

335–336 her abandoned husband's anger: the anger of Menelaus, the husband Helen deserted to run off with Paris.

342 Sparta (spär′tə): the city ruled by Menelaus.

345 Phrygian (frĭj′ē-ən): Trojan.

347 littoral (lĭt′ər-əl): seashore.

360 my loving mother: Venus.

364 goad: drive; urge.

Or find out if your wife, Creusa, lives,
And the young boy, Ascanius—all these
370   Cut off by Greek troops foraging everywhere?
Had I not cared for them, fire would by now
Have taken them, their blood glutted the sword.
You must not hold the woman of Laconia,
That hated face, the cause of this, nor Paris.
375   The harsh will of the gods it is, the gods,
That overthrows the splendor of this place
And brings Troy from her height into the dust.
Look over there: I'll tear away the cloud
That curtains you, and films your mortal sight,
380   The fog around you.—Have no fear of doing
Your mother's will, or balk at obeying her.—
Look: where you see high masonry thrown down,
Stone torn from stone, with billowing smoke and dust,
Neptune is shaking from their beds the walls
385   That his great trident pried up, undermining,
Toppling the whole city down. And look:
Juno in all her savagery holds
The Scaean Gates, and raging in steel armor
Calls her allied army from the ships.
390   Up on the citadel—turn, look—Pallas Tritonia
Couched in a stormcloud, lightening, with her Gorgon!
The Father himself empowers the Danaans,
Urges assaulting gods on the defenders.
Away, child; put an end to toiling so.
395   I shall be near, to see you safely home.'

She hid herself in the deep gloom of night,
And now the dire forms appeared to me
Of great immortals, enemies of Troy.
I knew the end then: Ilium was going down
400   In fire, the Troy of Neptune going down,
As in high mountains when the countrymen
Have notched an ancient ash, then make their axes
Ring with might and main, chopping away
To fell the tree—ever on the point of falling,
405   Shaken through all its foliage, and the treetop
Nodding; bit by bit the strokes prevail
Until it gives a final groan at last
And crashes down in ruin from the height.

370 foraging: plundering.

373 the woman of Laconia
(lə-kō′nē-ə): Helen.

385 undermining: digging under
the foundations.

390 Tritonia (trī-tō′nē-ə): a title of
Pallas.

391 Gorgon: the monstrous
Medusa, whose head Pallas bears
on her shield.

Now I descended where the goddess guided,
410 Clear of the flames, and clear of enemies,
For both retired; so gained my father's door,
My ancient home. I looked for him at once,
My first wish being to help him to the mountains;
But with Troy gone he set his face against it,
415 Not to prolong his life, or suffer exile.

PAUSE & REFLECT Why does Aeneas decide to spare Helen's life?

FOCUS Aeneas will try to lead his father, his wife, and his son through the burning city. Read to find out what happens to Aeneas' wife.

Unmoved by the protests of his family, Aeneas' father refuses to leave his home. However, he is finally persuaded by two divine signs. First, a small flame appears on the head of Iulus, Aeneas' son, touching the boy but not burning him. After Aeneas and his wife put out the flame, there comes the second sign—a crack of thunder outside, followed by a falling star.

Now indeed
My father, overcome, addressed the gods,
And rose in worship of the blessed star.

'Now, now, no more delay. I'll follow you.

420   Where you conduct me, there I'll be.

Gods of my fathers,

Preserve this house, preserve my grandson. Yours

This portent was. Troy's life is in your power.

I yield. I go as your companion, son.'

Then he was still. We heard the blazing town

425   Crackle more loudly, felt the scorching heat.

422 portent: a sign of future events; omen.

'Then come, dear father. Arms around my neck:

I'll take you on my shoulders, no great weight.

Whatever happens, both will face one danger,

Find one safety. Iulus will come with me,

430   My wife at a good interval behind.

Servants, give your attention to what I say.

At the gate inland there's a funeral mound

And an old shrine of Ceres the Bereft;

Near it an ancient cypress, kept alive

435   For many years by our fathers' piety.

By various routes we'll come to that one place.

Father, carry our hearthgods, our Penatës.

It would be wrong for me to handle them—

Just come from such hard fighting, bloody work—

440   Until I wash myself in running water.'

433 Ceres the Bereft: the goddess of grain, whose daughter Proserpina was stolen away by Pluto, god of the underworld.

When I had said this, over my breadth of shoulder

And bent neck, I spread out a lion skin

For tawny cloak and stooped to take his weight.

Then little Iulus put his hand in mine

445   And came with shorter steps beside his father.

My wife fell in behind. Through shadowed places

On we went, and I, lately unmoved

By any spears thrown, any squads of Greeks,

Felt terror now at every eddy of wind,

450   Alarm at every sound, alert and worried

Alike for my companion and my burden.

I had got near the gate, and now I thought

We had made it all the way, when suddenly

A noise of running feet came near at hand,

455   And peering through the gloom ahead, my father

Cried out:
               'Run, boy; here they come; I see
Flame light on shields, bronze shining.'
                              I took fright,
And some unfriendly power, I know not what,
Stole all my addled wits—for as I turned

460 Aside from the known way, entering a maze
Of pathless places on the run—
                         Alas,
Creusa, taken from us by grim fate, did she
Linger, or stray, or sink in weariness?
There is no telling. Never would she be

465 Restored to us. Never did I look back
Or think to look for her, lost as she was,
Until we reached the funeral mound and shrine
Of venerable Ceres. Here at last
All came together, but she was not there;

470 She alone failed her friends, her child, her husband.
Out of my mind, whom did I not accuse,
What man or god? What crueler loss had I
Beheld, that night the city fell? Ascanius,
My father, and the Teucrian Penatës,

475 I left in my friends' charge, and hid them well
In a hollow valley.
                 I turned back alone
Into the city, cinching my bright harness.
Nothing for it but to run the risks
Again, go back again, comb all of Troy,

480 And put my life in danger as before:
First by the town wall, then the gate, all gloom,
Through which I had come out—and so on backward,
Tracing my own footsteps through the night;
And everywhere my heart misgave me: even

485 Stillness had its terror. Then to our house,
Thinking she might, just might, have wandered there.
Danaans had got in and filled the place,
And at that instant fire they had set,
Consuming it, went roofward in a blast;

490 Flames leaped and seethed in heat to the night sky.
I pressed on, to see Priam's hall and tower.
In the bare colonnades of Juno's shrine
Two chosen guards, Phoenix and hard Ulysses,
Kept watch over the plunder. Piled up here

459 addled wits: confused powers of mind.

477 cinching: fastening tightly.

484 my heart misgave me: I had feelings of dread.

495 Were treasures of old Troy from every quarter,
Torn out of burning temples: altar tables,
Robes, and golden bowls. Drawn up around them,
Boys and frightened mothers stood in line.
I even dared to call out in the night;
500 I filled the streets with calling; in my grief
Time after time I groaned and called Creusa,
Frantic, in endless quest from door to door.
Then to my vision her sad wraith appeared—
Creusa's ghost, larger than life, before me.
505 Chilled to the marrow, I could feel the hair
On my head rise, the voice clot in my throat;
But she spoke out to ease me of my fear:

'What's to be gained by giving way to grief
So madly, my sweet husband? Nothing here
510 Has come to pass except as heaven willed.
You may not take Creusa with you now;
It was not so ordained, nor does the lord
Of high Olympus give you leave. For you
Long exile waits, and long sea miles to plow.
515 You shall make landfall on Hesperia
Where Lydian Tiber flows, with gentle pace,
Between rich farmlands, and the years will bear
Glad peace, a kingdom, and a queen for you.
Dismiss these tears for your beloved Creusa.
520 I shall not see the proud homelands of Myrmidons
Or of Dolopians, or go to serve
Greek ladies, Dardan lady that I am
And daughter-in-law of Venus the divine.
No: the great mother of the gods detains me
525 Here on these shores. Farewell now; cherish still
Your son and mine.'
                        With this she left me weeping,
Wishing that I could say so many things,
And faded on the <u>tenuous</u> air. Three times
I tried to put my arms around her neck,
530 Three times enfolded nothing, as the wraith
Slipped through my fingers, bodiless as wind,
Or like a flitting dream.
                        So in the end
As night waned I rejoined my company.
And there to my astonishment I found

503 wraith: ghost.

515 Hesperia (hĕ-spîr′ē-ə): "western land"—that is, Italy.

516 Lydian Tiber (lĭd′ə-ən tī′bər): the river beside which Rome would be built—called Lydian here because it flowed through the lands of the Etruscans, who originally came from Lydia in Asia Minor.

WORDS TO KNOW

378

tenuous (tĕn′yōō′əs) *adj.* thin or flimsy

Scene from *Helen of Troy* (1955).

535 New refugees in a great crowd: men and women
Gathered for exile, young—pitiful people
Coming from every quarter, minds made up,
With their belongings, for whatever lands
I'd lead them to by sea.
                              The morning star
540 Now rose on Ida's ridges, bringing day.
Greeks had secured the city gates. No help
Or hope of help existed.
So I resigned myself, picked up my father,
And turned my face toward the mountain range."

540 Ida's ridges: the crests of a
mountain range near Troy.

Thinking through the LITERATURE

Connect to the Literature

1. What Do You Think?
What was your reaction to Aeneas' loss of his wife?

Comprehension Check
- What trick do the Greeks use to conquer Troy?
- How do Laocoön and his two sons die?
- What does Aeneas do to help his old father reach safety?

Think Critically

2. ACTIVE READING: PREDICTING What predictions did you make in your READER'S NOTEBOOK as you read this epic poem? Discuss with a classmate the clues that prompted your predictions.

3. How would you describe the relationship between Aeneas and his wife?

4. Two supernatural characters appear to Aeneas: his mother (the goddess Venus) and the ghost of his wife. How would you compare these characters?

5. Do you think Aeneas always acts the way a hero should? Explain your opinion.

> **THINK ABOUT**
> - his flight with his family from the burning city
> - his intent to kill Helen
> - his reaction to the killing of Priam

6. What role does fate, or destiny, play in Aeneas' life?

Extend Interpretations

7. The Writer's Style As you know, a **simile** is a comparison that uses the word *like* or *as.* Virgil introduces **epic similes**—similes that extend over several lines—in lines 206–213 and 399–408. What makes each effective?

8. Critic's Corner Joe Paterno, longtime football coach at Penn State University, found the *Aeneid* deeply moving when he read it in high school: "Aeneas, as Virgil created him, was a totally new kind of epic hero. . . . He lives his life not for 'me' and 'I,' but for 'us' and 'we.' Aeneas is the ultimate team man." Do you agree with Paterno's view of Aeneas? Cite lines from the poem to support your opinion.

9. Connect to Life How would you compare Aeneas' qualities with those of the leaders you discussed for the Connect to Your Life activity on page 359?

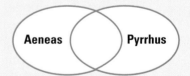

Writing Options

1. Interview with Aeneas
Write an interview for a newsmagazine, in which Aeneas discusses the role of fate, or destiny, in his life and his attitude toward the gods. Have Aeneas mention events that the gods controlled. Then have him explain how he felt about having little or no control over his future.

2. Creusa's Story
What do you think happened to Creusa after she was separated from Aeneas during their flight from Troy? Write a dialogue in which Creusa's ghost tells more of her story to Aeneas.

3. Compare-and-Contrast Essay
Whom do you admire more as a hero, Aeneas or Achilles, the hero of the *Iliad*? Why? Write a compare-and-contrast essay to explore your ideas.

Writing Handbook
See page R31: Compare and Contrast.

Activities & Explorations

1. Epic Storyboard
Imagine that this excerpt from the *Aeneid* is to be made into part of a TV miniseries. You are planning a 30-second preview of the episode. With two or three classmates, prepare a storyboard—a series of sketches with captions—outlining the action of the preview. ~ **ART**

2. Oral Reading
Imagine yourself as Aeneas, describing your adventures to Queen Dido at a banquet. Prepare an oral reading of a dramatic episode, such as the murder of Priam or your frantic search for Creusa. Practice reading with the appropriate tone of voice, pauses, and changes in pitch and volume. Then present your reading to the class. ~ **PERFORMING**

Inquiry & Research

Roman Influences The influence of Roman culture extends beyond literature. With a few classmates, find out more about Roman civilization and its effect upon later cultures of the world. Each group member may wish to do further research in one of the following categories, which are introduced on pages 350–351: Religion, Law and Government, Architecture and Engineering, Art and Sculpture.

RESEARCH STARTER
CLASSZONE.COM

Vocabulary in Action

EXERCISE: WORD MEANINGS For each sentence, write *T* if the statement is true or *F* if it is false.

1. Snakes are reptiles that **writhe,** or twist.
2. If you **reprove** your younger brother, you praise him.
3. A **tenuous** agreement is likely to be broken.
4. A **gaping** woman keeps her lips shut tight.
5. Some people seek a **respite** from their troubles by walking through the woods.
6. A **sinister** person is someone you can trust.
7. A **prodigious** weight is easy to lift.
8. Pretending to be ill can be a **ruse** to avoid work.
9. Fields of wheat blowing in the wind can be described as **undulating.**
10. Sometimes, the sky at sunset appears **suffused** with a rosy glow.

Building Vocabulary

For an in-depth lesson on using context clues, see page 674.

Perspectives on Helen of Troy

OVERVIEW

Helen of Troy	383
To Helen	388
Standardized Test Practice: Writing About Literature	391

The epics, myths, and legends of ancient Greece and Rome have stirred the imagination of writers for centuries. When modern writers return to the classic stories and characters, they often bring fresh perspectives.

This lesson includes two well-known poems about Helen of Troy—one by the 20th-century American writer Sara Teasdale, the other by the 19th-century American writer Edgar Allan Poe. As you may recall, Virgil's Aeneas hated Helen because he blamed her for the destruction of Troy. These two poems provide a more sympathetic view of Helen. In the pages that follow, you will be asked to compare and contrast the treatments of Helen in these poems. Your comparisons should help you appreciate how modern writers can breathe new life into the classics.

Points of Comparison

Use a chart like the one shown to take notes about each poem. The questions in the chart should help you identify similarities and differences in the poems. If other questions come to mind, feel free to add them to your chart. You may also replace questions in the chart with ones of your own.

	"Helen of Troy," Sara Teasdale	"To Helen," Edgar Allan Poe
Who is the speaker of the poem? How would you describe the speaker?		
What emotions are expressed by the speaker? Which lines help you identify those emotions?		
In your opinion, which poem presents a more favorable view of Helen?		
In your opinion, which poem is more memorable? Why?		

Standardized Test Practice: Comparison-and-Contrast Essay After you finish reading the two poems, you will have the opportunity to write a comparison-and-contrast essay. Your notes will help you plan and write the essay.

❧ HELEN of TROY ❧
~ Sara Teasdale ~

Sara Teasdale
1884–1933

A Popular and Honored Poet

Sara Teasdale was born and educated in St. Louis, Missouri. Her first volume of poetry, published in 1907, was praised for the delicate simplicity of the verse. In 1911 she published *Helen of Troy and Other Poems.* The first group of poems in this collection focuses on famous women of history, myth, and legend. In 1918 her book *Love Songs* won the Columbia University Poetry Society prize, the forerunner of the Pulitzer Prize in poetry. Although her works were widely read, her personal life was unhappy. Shy and withdrawn, she avoided public appearances and remained in semiseclusion after an unhappy marriage. She died at the age of 48, after a bout with pneumonia.

Build Background

"Helen of Troy" is set at daybreak, immediately after the Greek victory over the Trojans. As you may recall, the Greeks had built an enormous wooden horse, in which soldiers were hidden. The Trojans, tricked into believing that the horse was an offering to a goddess, had brought the horse into Troy. In the dark of night, the Greek soldiers emerged from the horse and attacked the city, killing many Trojans and setting fire to buildings. As the poem begins, Helen is looking at the flames of the burning city and reflecting on her life.

Connect to Your Life

According to legend, Helen of Troy was the most beautiful woman of the ancient world. Do you think that people gifted with physical beauty have an easier time in life than those who are ordinary in appearance? Are beautiful people and ordinary-looking ones treated differently? Use examples from your own experience to support your opinion.

Focus Your Reading

LITERARY ANALYSIS: SPEAKER

The **speaker** of a poem is the voice that "talks" in the poem, like the narrator in a story. In this poem, the poet has created a speaker far different from herself—the legendary Helen of Troy. By allowing Helen to speak for herself, the poet gives the reader a unique perspective on the events of the Trojan War.

ACTIVE READING: MAKING INFERENCES

As you read this poem, you will need to make **inferences,** or logical guesses, about its meaning. To make inferences about Helen, you will need to combine what you already know about her with what she states about herself. For example, she states that "I am she who loves all beauty—yet I wither it." You already know that Greeks battled the Trojans because of Helen. Her statement allows you to infer that she blames herself for the destruction of Troy.

📖 **READER'S NOTEBOOK** As you read, record your inferences about Helen in your notebook.

Helen of Troy

Sara Teasdale

Wild flight on flight against the fading dawn
The flames' red wings soar upward duskily.
This is the funeral pyre and Troy is dead
That sparkled so the day I saw it first,
5   And darkened slowly after. I am she
Who loves all beauty—yet I wither it.
Why have the high gods made me wreak their wrath—
Forever since my maidenhood to sow
Sorrow and blood about me? See, they keep
10 Their bitter care above me even now.
It was the gods who led me to this lair,
That though the burning winds should make me weak,
They should not snatch the life from out my lips.
Olympus let the other women die;
15 They shall be quiet when the day is done
And have no care to-morrow. Yet for me
There is no rest. The gods are not so kind
To her made half immortal like themselves.

It is to you I owe the cruel gift,
20 Leda, my mother, and the Swan, my sire,
To you the beauty and to you the bale;
For never woman born of man and maid
Had wrought such havoc on the earth as I,
Or troubled heaven with a sea of flame
25 That climbed to touch the silent whirling stars,
Blotting their brightness out before the dawn.
Have I not made the world to weep enough?
Give death to me.

3 pyre: a fire for burning a dead body.

6 wither it: cause it to fade.

7 wreak: inflict.

11 lair: hiding place.

18 half immortal: Helen was fathered by Jupiter, king of the gods, in the form of a swan; her mother, Leda, was human.

21 bale: evil.

Helen of Troy (1863), Dante Gabriel Rossetti. Oil on panel, 31 cm ×
27 cm. Photograph copyright © Elke Walford/Hamburger
Kunsthalle, Hamburg, Germany.

HUMANITIES CONNECTION Dante Gabriel Rossetti, one of
the most famous painters of the 1800s, was inspired by the
theme of romantic love. The bright colors and sharp details
in this painting of Helen of Troy are typical of his style.

> Yet life is more than death;
> How could I leave the sound of singing winds,
> 30 The strong clean scent that breathes from off the sea,
> Or shut my eyes forever to the spring?
> I will not give the grave my hands to hold,
> My shining hair to light oblivion.
> Have those who wander through the ways of death,
> 35 The still wan fields Elysian, any love
> To lift their breasts with longing, any lips
> To thirst against the quiver of a kiss?

33 oblivion (ə-blĭv′ē-ən):
forgetfulness.

35 wan fields Elysian (ĭ-lĭzh′ən):
pale land of the dead.

I shall live on to conquer Greece again,
To make the people love, who hate me now.
40 My dreams are over, I have ceased to cry
Against the fate that made men love my mouth
And left their spirits all too deaf to hear
The songs that echoed always in my soul.

I have no anger now. The dreams are done;
45 Yet since the Greeks and Trojans would not see
Aught but my body's fairness, till the end,
In all the islands set in all the seas,
And all the lands that lie beneath the sun,
Till light turn darkness, and till time shall sleep,
50 Men's lives shall waste with longing after me,
For I shall be the sum of their desire,
The whole of beauty, never seen again.
And they shall stretch their arms and starting, wake,
With "Helen!" on their lips, and in their eyes
55 The vision of me. Always I shall be
Limned on the darkness like a shaft of light
That glimmers and is gone. They shall behold
Each one his dream that fashions me anew;—
With hair like lakes that glint beneath the stars
60 Dark as sweet midnight, or with hair aglow
Like burnished gold that still retains the fire.
I shall be haunting till the dusk of time
The heavy eyelids that are filled with dreams.

I wait for one who comes with sword to slay—
65 The king I wronged who searches for me now;
And yet he shall not slay me. I shall stand
With lifted head and look into his eyes,
Baring my breast to him and to the sun.
He shall not have the power to stain with blood
70 That whiteness—for the thirsty sword shall fall
And he shall cry and catch me in his arms.
I shall go back to Sparta on his breast.
I shall live on to conquer Greece again!

46 aught: anything.

56 limned (lĭmd): painted.

61 burnished: polished.

65 The king I wronged: Menelaus, the husband Helen betrayed by running off with Paris to Troy.

Connect to the Literature

1. What Do You Think?
Do you admire the determination that Helen expresses in the last line of the poem? Explain.

Comprehension Check
- How does Helen feel about surviving Troy's destruction?
- Does Helen believe that her beauty will eventually fade?
- Does Helen think that her husband will forgive her?

Think Critically

2. ACTIVE READING: MAKING INFERENCES
Review the inferences you recorded in your
📖 **READER'S NOTEBOOK.** On the basis of your inferences, how would you describe Helen's difficulties?

3. Helen's feelings change significantly over the course of the poem. Review the sections of the poem and identify the feelings expressed in each.

4. In your opinion, is Helen's beauty more a blessing or a curse to her? Use quotations from the poem to support your judgment.

5. Do you think Helen takes personal responsibility for the destruction of Troy? Use evidence from the poem to support your conclusion.

LITERARY ANALYSIS: SPEAKER

In a poem, the **speaker** is the voice imagined as speaking the poem's words. Sometimes the speaker can be identified with the poet; but in the case of "Helen of Troy," the speaker is clearly not Sara Teasdale. Helen speaks for herself, so that the reader sees the events of the war from her point of view.

Paired Activity With a partner, create two descriptions of Helen's character. The first should present Helen's view of herself, as conveyed by the poem. The second should present Helen from the point of view of another person—her husband, perhaps, or a Trojan woman whose husband has been killed in battle. Share the descriptions with your classmates, and discuss which one is closer to your own view of Helen.

Points *of* Comparison

Paired Activity With a partner, review "Helen of Troy," using the questions in your comparison-and-contrast chart to help you analyze the poem. Fill in your answers to the questions pertaining to "Helen of Troy." Don't forget that you can change or add to the questions.

	"Helen of Troy," Sara Teasdale	"To Helen," Edgar Allan Poe
Who is the speaker of the poem? How would you describe the speaker?		
What emotions are expressed by the speaker? Which lines help you identify those emotions?	*bitterness (lines 7–10, lines 14–18)*	
In your opinion, which poem presents a more favorable view of Helen?		
In your opinion, which poem is more memorable? Why?		

PREPARING to *Read*

The poem by Sara Teasdale has given you one view of Helen—a portrait in her own words. Now you will see Helen from a very different perspective. Edgar Allan Poe's "To Helen" presents Helen from a male point of view.

Edgar Allan Poe
1809–1849

A Troubled Youth The son of traveling actors, Edgar Poe was orphaned at an early age and taken in by a wealthy Virginian couple. A moody adolescent, Poe began attending the University of Virginia. His heavy debts, however, led to a quarrel with his adoptive father, and he was forced to leave school. Later he was expelled from the U.S. Military Academy at West Point in 1831.

A Short Career Poe began his writing career by publishing a pamphlet of poems in 1827. He also worked as an editor and wrote stories and literary reviews, but money was scarce. For the most part, he was ignored until he won a literary prize in 1843. Illness, poverty, and the death of his beloved wife, Virginia, limited his literary production. Poe died at the age of 40 after being found sick and delirious on the streets of Baltimore.

An American Master Despite his troubled life, Poe was an originator of the modern short story and pioneered the detective mystery. His haunting poems are notable for their insistent sound effects, and his horror tales established him as a master of psychological terror.

Build Background

"To Helen" Poe seems to have been fascinated with the idea of Helen of Troy. Critics, however, are divided in their interpretations of "To Helen." Some believe that the poem is a tribute to the legendary Helen, a symbol of beauty. Others think that the poem was written about an actual woman, one whose beauty reminded Poe of the legendary Helen.

Detail of *Helen of Troy* (late 19th–early 20th century), Evelyn de Morgan. National Trust Photographic Library/From the De Morgan Foundation.

To Helen

Edgar Allan Poe

Helen, thy beauty is to me
  Like those Nicean barks of yore,
That gently, o'er a perfumed sea,
  The weary, way-worn wanderer bore
5 To his own native shore.

On desperate seas long wont to roam,
  Thy hyacinth hair, thy classic face,
Thy Naiad airs have brought me home
  To the glory that was Greece
10 And the grandeur that was Rome.

Lo! in yon brilliant window-niche
  How statue-like I see thee stand!
  The agate lamp within thy hand,
Ah! Psyche, from the regions which
15 Are Holy Land!

2 Nicean (nī-sē′ən) **barks:** ships of the ancient Mediterranean world.

6 wont: accustomed.

7 hyacinth (hī′ə-sĭnth): dark and curling.

8 Naiad (nā′əd) **airs:** manner like that of a Greek goddess of streams.

13–14 The agate lamp . . . Psyche (sī′kē): In an ancient tale, the young woman Psyche used an oil lamp to view her sleeping husband—Venus' son Cupid—who had forbidden her to behold him.

Connect to the Literature

1. What Do You Think?
Write down two questions that you have about the poem. Share them with your classmates, and see if anyone can answer them.

Comprehension Check
- List two details in the poem that describe Helen's beauty.
- What scene is described in the last stanza?

Think Critically

2. In the first stanza the speaker compares Helen to ancient ships that brought the "weary, way-worn wanderer" home. What does this comparison suggest about the speaker's attitude toward Helen?

3. In the second stanza the speaker refers to Greece and Rome in the past tense, which suggests that he is living in a different time. How might the beauty of Helen help to connect the speaker to "the glory that was Greece / And the grandeur that was Rome"?

4. Do you think the poem is about Helen of Troy, or is it about an actual woman who reminds the speaker of the legendary beauty? Can it be about both? Explain your reasoning.

Extend Interpretations

5. The Writer's Style Because of her beauty, Poe's Helen seems to possess a kind of godlike power. Do you think Poe exaggerates the power of beauty? Why or why not?

Points *of* Comparison

Paired Activity Now that you have read both poems about Helen, complete rows 1 and 2 of your comparison-and-contrast chart. Then work with a partner to discuss any remaining questions that you have and to complete the rest of the chart.

	"Helen of Troy," Sara Teasdale	"To Helen," Edgar Allan Poe
Who is the speaker of the poem? How would you describe the speaker?		*The speaker is an admirer of Helen.*
What emotions are expressed by the speaker? Which lines help you identify those emotions?	*bitterness (lines 7–10, lines 14–18)*	
In your opinion, which poem presents a more favorable view of Helen?		
In your opinion, which poem is more memorable? Why?		

Writing About Literature

PART 1 Reading the Prompt

In writing assessments, you may be asked to compare and contrast works of literature with a common subject, such as the two poems about Helen of Troy that you have just read. You are now going to practice writing an essay that involves this type of comparison.

> **Writing Prompt**
>
> Helen of Troy has fascinated writers for centuries. Compare and ❶ contrast the two perspectives on Helen provided by Sara Teasdale and Edgar Allan Poe. Consider what you learn about the two poems' speakers, and identify the emotions expressed in each poem. In your ❷ opinion, which poem provides a more favorable view of Helen? ❸ Which is the more memorable poem? Support your analysis with details and quotations from the poems. ❹

> **STRATEGIES** IN ACTION
>
> ❶ I have to **compare and contrast** two poems.
>
> ❷ For each poem, I need to discuss the **speaker** and the emotions expressed.
>
> ❸ I need to decide which poem is more favorable toward Helen and which is more memorable.
>
> ❹ I need to include **details** and **quotations** from the poems to support my analysis.

PART 2 Planning a Comparison-and-Contrast Essay

- Review the comparison-and-contrast chart that you completed for the Points of Comparison features in this lesson.
- Using your chart, find examples of similarities and differences to point out in your essay. If necessary, review the poems again to find more evidence.
- Create an outline to organize your ideas.

PART 3 Drafting Your Essay

Introduction After introducing Helen of Troy to the reader, share your thoughts about why so much has been written about her. Then explain that you will be comparing two poems and identify the basis of your comparison. Describe what you found to be the most interesting similarity or difference in the poems.

Body You might use the questions in your comparison-and-contrast chart as a guide to the key points of your comparison. In one paragraph, for example, you might compare and contrast the speakers of the poems.

Conclusion Wrap up your essay with a summary of the poems' major differences and similarities.

Revision Check your use of signal words, such as *by contrast, similarly, also, both,* and *in the same way.* Make sure that the connections between your ideas are clear.

PREPARING to *Read*

POEMS BY HORACE

Horace
65–8 B.C.

Simple Pleasures If you lived in ancient Rome, you might have enjoyed spending time with the poet Horace. He was a friendly host who served fine foods and good wines. He was a good listener and companion—easygoing and humorous. His views on life, love, and just about everything else under the Roman sun were wise, witty, and down-to-earth.

Early Struggles Horace rose from humble beginnings. His father was a former slave who owned land in Italy's central highlands. He made sure that his son received an excellent education, first in Rome and later in Athens. This was at a time when education was a privilege usually reserved for the wealthy. While in Athens, Horace was swept up in the civil war that erupted in Rome in 44 B.C., after the murder of Julius Caesar. At the battle of Philippi in 42 B.C., Horace fought on Brutus' side—the losing side—against the forces of Mark Antony and Octavian (later the emperor Augustus). After Brutus' defeat, Horace returned to Rome, heartsick and penniless.

Rise to Fame Back in Rome, Horace managed to find a government job and began writing poems. His verse soon caught the eye of the poet Virgil, who introduced him to Maecenas (mē-sē'nəs), a rich patron of the arts. From then on, Horace's career as a poet was assured. Maecenas gave Horace a farm in the Sabine Hills, northeast of Rome. For the rest of his life, Horace lived on this farm, writing poetry and enjoying his role in the literary life of Rome.

Ever Popular Horace's poetry has made him the most quoted of all the Latin poets. He valued moderation, good sense, and living for the present moment. Horace coined the expression *Carpe diem—* "Seize the day"—which is still widely used. This sentiment is summed up best in Horace's words: "He is master of himself and happy who as the day ends can say, I have lived—tomorrow come cloud, come sunshine."

Other Works
Ars Poetica
Satires

Build Background

To Teach and Delight Horace once said, "Everyone has his own way of enjoying himself. Mine is to put words into meter." He put words into meter during the Augustan Age of Latin literature. This was the period when the emperor Augustus ruled Rome and established the Roman Empire. Augustus took a personal interest in the literary works created during his reign. Together with Virgil and Ovid, Horace was recognized as one of the great poets of the time.

Horace earned this reputation mainly because of his **odes.** These are short poems—almost like songs—written with grace, charm, and precision of language. Often addressed to a particular person, an ode expresses careful thoughts rather than deep emotions. Down through the centuries, Horace's odes have continued to offer readers wise and witty comments about life.

Horace had two purposes for writing: namely, to teach and delight. The Romans believed that all the arts should influence their audience in positive ways. As a Roman poet, therefore, Horace felt a responsibility to use his poetry to serve a didactic, or teaching, purpose. He felt that literature should teach moral values, help strengthen character, and show people how to live. The poems "Seize the Day" and "Better to live, Licinius, . . ." do all of these things.

Connect to Your Life

The poems you are about to read offer practical advice on how to live. What pieces of good advice have helped you the most during your high school years? Share one or two "nuggets of wisdom" with a small group of classmates.

Focus Your Reading

LITERARY ANALYSIS: THEME

A **theme** is a message or central idea that a writer shares with readers. A theme may be a lesson about life or about people and their actions. As you read each of these poems, think about the theme that Horace wants to convey.

ACTIVE READING: UNDERSTANDING CONTRAST

In each of these poems, the speaker uses contrasts to convey ideas. When two or more things are contrasted, the differences are emphasized. For example, in the poem "Seize the Day," the speaker contrasts two things the future may bring: either a number of years—"many a winter"—or maybe only one—"the last [winter]." As you read these poems, look for additional examples of contrast.

READER'S NOTEBOOK In your notebook, use a chart like the one shown below to record the contrasts you find in "Seize the Day." Then create a similar chart to record the contrasts you find in "Better to live, Licinius, . . ."

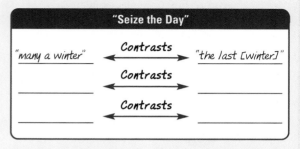

"Seize the Day"		
"many a winter"	←— Contrasts —→	"the last [winter]"
_____	←— Contrasts —→	_____
_____	←— Contrasts —→	_____

Seize the Day

Horace

Translated by David Mulroy

Ask not the forbidden question, the ends the gods
have assigned us, Leuconoe. Scorn Babylonian numbers.
Acceptance is better, whatever occurs—if Jove
has granted us many a winter or this is the last
5   that breaks the Etruscan sea against the rocks.
Be sensible, drink, and trim your hopes to fit
your limits. An envious age will have fled as we speak.
Seize the day with little faith in tomorrow.

2 Leuconoe (lōō-kŏn'ō-ē'): a
woman's name; **Babylonian numbers:** astrology—the belief that
the positions of the stars can be
used to predict earthly events.

3 Jove: Jupiter, king of the gods.

5 Etruscan sea: the Tyrrhenian
Sea—the part of the
Mediterranean west of Italy.

Pasquius Proculus and his wife. Wall painting from Pompeii. Museo Archeologico
Nazionale, Naples, Italy.

HUMANITIES CONNECTION This portrait depicts a working-class man
and woman. The woman holds writing implements, and the man holds
a scroll. These objects suggest the couple's intellectual pursuits.

Better to live, Licinius, . . .

Horace

Translated by Joseph P. Clancy

Pompeiian household shrine fresco. Ancient Art and Architecture Collection, Ltd.

Better to live, Licinius, not always
rushing into deep water, and not, when fear
of storms makes you shiver, pushing too close to
  the dangerous coast.

5 A man who prizes golden moderation
stays safely clear of the filth of a run-down
building, stays prudently out of a palace
  others will envy.

5 moderation: avoidance of extremes.

7 prudently: in a manner showing good sense.

Detail of Pompeiian household shrine fresco. Ancient Art and Architecture Collection, Ltd.

The giant pine is more often troubled by the
10 wind, and the tallest towers collapse with a
heavier fall, and bolts of lightning strike the
        tops of the mountains.

Hopeful in the bad times, fearful in the good times,
that is the man who has readied his heart for
15 the turn of the dice. Jupiter brings back foul
        winters; he also

takes them away. No, if things are bad now, they
will not remain that way: sometimes Apollo
wakes the silent Muse with his lyre and is not
20   always an archer.

When troubles come, show that you have a stout heart
and a stern face: but see that you have the good sense
to take in sail when it swells in a wind that's
        a little too kind.

18 Apollo (ə-pŏl′ō): the god of both music and archery.

19 lyre (līr): a stringed instrument like a small harp.

21 stout: brave; determined.

Connect to the Literature

1. **What Do You Think?** How did you react to the advice given in each of these poems?

Think Critically

2. In "Seize the Day," why does the speaker advise Leuconoe to live for today?

3. In your own words, explain what you think the speaker of "Better to live, Licinius, . . ." means by "golden moderation."

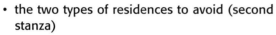

THINK ABOUT

- the two types of residences to avoid (second stanza)
- what happens to the "giant pine" and the "tallest towers" (third stanza)
- the ways to react in bad and in good times (fourth stanza)

4. **ACTIVE READING: UNDERSTANDING CONTRAST**
Review what you listed in your 📖 **READER'S NOTEBOOK**.
For each poem, decide which contrast is most effective in conveying an idea.

5. To what extent do these poems both teach and delight? Support your answer with details from each poem.

Extend Interpretations

6. **The Writer's Style** Writers often use descriptive words and phrases to re-create sensory experiences for the reader. Such words and phrases are known as imagery. Each image appeals to one or more of the five senses. Cite examples of images in each of these poems. Which image do you find particularly effective?

7. **Comparing Texts** Which poem do you think offers better advice, and why?

8. **Connect to Life** In "Seize the Day," the speaker says that it is important to "trim your hopes to fit your limits" (lines 6–7). Do you agree? Use examples from your own experience to support your opinion.

LITERARY ANALYSIS: THEME

In a literary work, a **theme** is a message or central idea that the writer wants to share with readers. A theme may be a lesson about life or about people and their actions. Sometimes, writers state themes directly. Often, however, the reader must **infer** a central message by reading between the lines. Different readers may even discover different themes in the same work.

Activity Write a letter to a friend, in which you give advice about how to live. Include a discussion of the theme of one of Horace's poems.

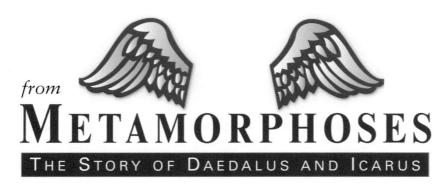

from

METAMORPHOSES

THE STORY OF DAEDALUS AND ICARUS

OVID

Ovid
43 B.C.–A.D. 18

A Poet's Poet Along with Horace and Virgil, Ovid was one of the great Roman poets during the reign of the emperor Augustus. His work had a lasting influence on later European literature, especially during the Middle Ages and the Renaissance. Both Geoffrey Chaucer (1340?–1400) and William Shakespeare (1564–1616) were greatly influenced by Ovid.

Early Years Ovid was born into a well-to-do family in 43 B.C.—one year after the murder of Julius Caesar. Educated in law and rhetoric, he held a few minor offices early in his working life and seemed destined for a career in public life. But against the wishes of his father, who urged him toward a career in law, Ovid began writing poems. His first work, the *Amores,* is a series of short and witty poems about a love affair. This work brought Ovid immediate success. Among his most popular works is the *Ars amatoria* [Art of love], published in 1 B.C. This handbook in verse offers lighthearted advice on ways to begin and maintain a romance.

Lasting Legacy Ovid's masterpiece is the *Metamorphoses.* This long narrative poem retells most of the important Greek and Roman legends and myths. Ovid, however, breathed new life into the old stories. He shaped them in imaginative ways, adding details and strengthening their structure. Ovid's retellings inspired European writers for centuries to come.

A Ruined Life Before Ovid was able to publish the *Metamorphoses,* he suffered a terrible misfortune. In A.D. 8, the emperor Augustus banished him from Rome. Ovid was exiled to Tomi, a remote fishing village on the Black Sea. The exact reason for this cruel punishment is not known. For Ovid, exile to the far reaches of the Roman Empire was a fate worse than death. He continued to write poems, however, and in some of them he pleaded to be allowed to return to Rome. These pleas fell on deaf ears, and Ovid died in exile in A.D 18.

Build Background

Stories About Magical Changes The *Metamorphoses* was Ovid's most ambitious work. It consists of nearly 12,000 lines of Latin verse. In it, some 250 stories, drawn mostly from Greek and Roman mythology, are retold. The poem begins with the creation of the world and ends with the transformation of the soul of Julius Caesar into a star in the sky. In most of the stories, a transformation, or metamorphosis, is important to the plot. For example, in one story, a maiden named Daphne, fleeing from the god Apollo, is transformed into a laurel tree.

In "The Story of Daedalus and Icarus," the main characters are living in exile—like Ovid himself in his later years. Daedalus and his son Icarus are prisoners on Crete, an island ruled by King Minos. Daedalus, whose name means "cunning craftsman," is a skillful architect, sculptor, and inventor. As the story begins, he is trying to find a way to escape from the island.

Sky and Water I (1938), M. C. Escher. In this woodcut an artist treats the idea of transformation, just as Ovid did in the *Metamorphoses*.

Connect to Your Life

In this story, Daedalus devises a clever plan to escape from Crete. Think about books, movies, or television shows in which characters attempt to escape from captivity. Which attempts succeed? With a few classmates, retell some adventure stories whose plots feature escapes.

Focus Your Reading

LITERARY ANALYSIS: MYTH
"The Story of Daedalus and Icarus" is a retelling of a **myth.** A myth is a traditional story that usually features superhuman beings and unlikely events. As you read this myth, consider the wondrous events in it and their possible meanings.

ACTIVE READING: READING NARRATIVE POETRY
Ovid presents this myth in a **narrative poem**— one that tells a story. A narrative poem has **characters, setting**, a **plot**, and a **point of view,** all of which serve to develop a **theme.**

While reading this excerpt, ask yourself the following questions:

- What sequence of events makes up the plot?

- In what setting do the events occur?

- What characters take part in the events?

- From whose point of view is the story told?

- What theme emerges from the story?

READER'S NOTEBOOK Create a sequence chain like the one shown below. In the boxes, summarize key events in the order they occur.

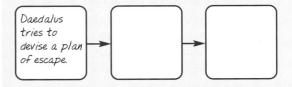

Daedalus tries to devise a plan of escape. → ☐ → ☐

from Metamorphoses
The Story of Daedalus and Icarus
Ovid
Translated by Rolfe Humphries

H omesick for homeland, Daedalus hated Crete
And his long exile there, but the sea held him.
"Though Minos blocks escape by land or water,"
Daedalus said, "surely the sky is open,
5   And that's the way we'll go. Minos' dominion
Does not include the air." He turned his thinking
Toward unknown arts, changing the laws of nature.
He laid out feathers in order, first the smallest,
A little larger next it, and so continued,
10 The way that pan-pipes rise in gradual sequence.
He fastened them with twine and wax, at middle,
At bottom, so, and bent them, gently curving,
So that they looked like wings of birds, most surely.
And Icarus, his son, stood by and watched him,
15 Not knowing he was dealing with his downfall,
Stood by and watched, and raised his shiny face
To let a feather, light as down, fall on it,
Or stuck his thumb into the yellow wax,
Fooling around, the way a boy will, always,
20 Whenever a father tries to get some work done.
Still, it was done at last, and the father hovered,
Poised, in the moving air, and taught his son:
"I warn you, Icarus, fly a middle course:
Don't go too low, or water will weigh the wings down;
25 Don't go too high, or the sun's fire will burn them.
Keep to the middle way. And one more thing,
No fancy steering by star or constellation,

10 pan-pipes: a musical instrument made up of a series of hollow tubes of varying lengths.

17 down: the soft feathers of a baby bird.

21 hovered (hŭv′ərd): remained suspended in the air.

The Fall of Icarus (17th century), Jacob Peter Gowy. Oil on canvas, 195 cm × 180 cm. Museo del Prado, Madrid, Spain. Copyright © Archivo Iconografico, S.A./Corbis.

Follow my lead!" That was the flying lesson,
And now to fit the wings to the boy's shoulders.
30 Between the work and warning the father found
His cheeks were wet with tears, and his hands trembled.
He kissed his son (*Good-bye,* if he had known it),
Rose on his wings, flew on ahead, as fearful
As any bird launching the little nestlings
35 Out of high nest into thin air. *Keep on,*
Keep on, he signals, *follow me!* He guides him
In flight—O fatal art!—and the wings move
And the father looks back to see the son's wings moving.
Far off, far down, some fisherman is watching
40 As the rod dips and trembles over the water,
Some shepherd rests his weight upon his crook,
Some ploughman on the handles of the ploughshare,
And all look up, in absolute amazement,
At those air-borne above. They must be gods!
45 They were over Samos, Juno's sacred island,
Delos and Paros toward the left, Lebinthus
Visible to the right, and another island,
Calymne, rich in honey. And the boy
Thought *This is wonderful!* and left his father,
50 Soared higher, higher, drawn to the vast heaven,
Nearer the sun, and the wax that held the wings
Melted in that fierce heat, and the bare arms
Beat up and down in air, and lacking oarage
Took hold of nothing. *Father!* he cried, and *Father!*
55 Until the blue sea hushed him, the dark water
Men call the Icarian now. And Daedalus,
Father no more, called "Icarus, where are you!
Where are you, Icarus? Tell me where to find you!"
And saw the wings on the waves, and cursed his talents,
60 Buried the body in a tomb, and the land
Was named for Icarus.

34 nestlings: young birds.

42 ploughshare: the cutting blade of a plow.

45–48 Samos (sā′mŏs′) . . . **Delos** (dē′lŏs′) . . . **Paros** (pâr′ŏs) . . . **Lebinthus** (lə-bĭn′thəs) . . . **Calymne** (kə-lĭm′nē): islands between mainland Greece and Asia Minor.

53 oarage: apparatus functioning as oars.

60–61 the land was named for Icarus: a reference to the island now named Ikaria.

Landscape with the Fall of Icarus (c. 1558), Pieter Brueghel the Elder. Museum of Fine Arts, Brussels, Belgium. Art Resource, New York.

LANDSCAPE WITH THE FALL OF ICARUS

WILLIAM CARLOS WILLIAMS

Ovid's story of Daedalus and Icarus has inspired many artists and writers. In the following poem, the speaker looks at a painting about the drowning of Icarus. As you read this poem, consider how the speaker views Icarus' death.

> According to Brueghel
> when Icarus fell
> it was spring
>
> a farmer was ploughing
> 5   his field
> the whole pageantry
>
> of the year was
> awake tingling
> near
>
> 10   the edge of the sea
> concerned
> with itself
>
> sweating in the sun
> that melted
> 15   the wings' wax
>
> unsignificantly
> off the coast
> there was
>
> a splash quite unnoticed
> 20   this was
> Icarus drowning

1 Brueghel (broi'gəl): Pieter Brueghel the Elder (1525?–1569), who painted *Landscape with the Fall of Icarus.*

6 pageantry: colorful, showy display.

LANDSCAPE WITH THE FALL OF ICARUS   **403**

Connect to the Literature

1. **What Do You Think?**
   What are your thoughts about what happens to Icarus?

   Comprehension Check
   - What does Daedalus use to make the wings for his son and himself?
   - What warning does Daedalus give his son about flying?

Think Critically

2. **ACTIVE READING: READING NARRATIVE POETRY** Look back at the sequence chain you created in your **READER'S NOTEBOOK**. How would you summarize the plot of this myth?

3. To what extent is Daedalus responsible for his son's death? Cite reasons to support your answer.

4. Why do you think Icarus does not heed his father's warning?

5. How would you describe the relationship between Daedalus and Icarus?

THINK ABOUT
- Daedalus' feelings as he fits the wings on his son
- Icarus' last words
- Daedalus' reaction when he sees "the wings on the waves"

Extend Interpretations

6. **The Writer's Style** A writer may use **foreshadowing** to hint at the outcome of a story. For example, in lines 14 and 15, the narrator says, "And Icarus, his son, stood by and watched him, / Not knowing he was dealing with his downfall." These lines foreshadow Icarus' death. Find other passages that foreshadow the end of the story.

7. **Comparing Texts** Reread the poem "Landscape with the Fall of Icarus" on page 403. How does the speaker's description of Icarus' death differ from Ovid's?

8. **Connect to Life** What situations in modern life do the events in this myth call to mind?

LITERARY ANALYSIS: MYTH

A **myth** is a traditional story, usually concerning some superhuman being or unlikely event, that was once widely believed to be true. Myths were passed down from one generation to the next. Though the original authors are unknown, myths reflect particular cultures' values and beliefs. Ovid's retellings of the classical myths still captivate and inspire. These timeless tales also explore issues that are relevant today.

Cooperative Learning Activity
Get together with a small group of classmates to discuss the following questions: What lessons does this myth teach about youth and age? about independence? about technology? about great talent? Record your responses, along with supporting examples, on a chart like the one shown below. Then share your chart with other groups.

Issues	Examples
youth and age	
independence	
technology	
great talent	

The Urge to Fly

For thousands of years, Ovid's story of Daedalus and Icarus has had a powerful hold on people's imagination. Perhaps the main reason for the story's appeal is that it deals with the fulfillment of one of mankind's oldest dreams—to fly like a bird. Have you ever pictured yourself flying like Icarus? What if you could soar through the air in a human-powered flying machine?

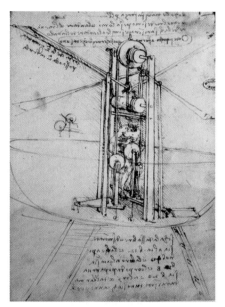

Leonardo da Vinci's drawing of a flying machine

In the 15th century, the Italian artist Leonardo da Vinci studied the flight of birds and drew sketches of flying machines. Thanks to recent advances in technology, this long-held dream is closer to reality. Take a look at the two photos of human-powered aircraft below.

A Modern Icarus At the time this book went to press, more than 100 human-powered flying machines had flown all over the world. The record for the longest distance flown in one of these machines was set in 1988 by Kanellos Kanellopoulos. Like Icarus, he flew from Crete. His destination was an island more than 70 miles away. Flying about 15 feet above the water, he stayed airborne for almost four hours. Only 35 feet short of the goal, his aircraft was damaged by a gust of wind and plunged into the sea. Unlike Icarus, however, Mr. Kanellopoulos was rescued.

Research Project Look up information about the latest advances in human-powered flight. Also find out who holds the current records for flying time and distance. Use the Internet as your main tool for research. (Be sure to check out the Raven Project site.) Present your findings to your classmates in a multimedia report.

RESEARCH STARTER
CLASSZONE.COM

Two human-powered flying machines: the *Gossamer Condor (top)* was the first such machine capable of sustained flight; the *Monarch B (bottom)* completed a 1,500-meter flight in just three minutes in 1984.

from the **ANNALS**

THE BURNING OF ROME

TACITUS • *Translated by* **MICHAEL GRANT**

Tacitus
C. A.D. 56–120

Living in Turbulent Times Tacitus, one of the greatest historians of ancient Rome, lived in troubled times. Plague and fire frequently ravaged Rome. An eruption of Mount Vesuvius buried the splendors of Pompeii under tons of volcanic ash. Even though the Roman Empire expanded to its utmost limits, tyrants, rebellions, and wars left a bloody mark on the times. No wonder Tacitus felt the need to set the written record straight.

Writer of History Tacitus is known mainly for two historical works. Unfortunately, only portions of these works have survived. The first, called the *Histories,* covers the years A.D. 69–96, a period dominated by the reigns of the emperors Vespasian, Titus, and Domitian. Tacitus' second important work is the *Annals.* It deals with events from the death of Augustus in A.D. 14 to the death of Nero in A.D. 68.

In your study of ancient Rome, you have read writings of the three greatest poets of the Augustan Age—Virgil, Horace, and Ovid. Now you will read an account written by an ancient Roman historian. This account will help you imagine what life was like in Rome during a crisis.

In this excerpt Tacitus tells about a terrible fire that swept through Rome in A.D. 64. The fire began in the Circus Maximus, an arena in which chariot races were held, and raged out of control for several days. At the time, Nero was emperor. At first wise and serious, he had by this time become unpredictable and brutal. Many Romans even believed that Nero himself had secretly set fire to the city. As you read this excerpt, ask yourself these questions:

1. What was Tacitus' purpose for writing?
2. What details are particularly interesting?
3. What does this account add to my understanding of ancient Rome?

Now started the most terrible and destructive fire which Rome had ever experienced. It began in the Circus, where it adjoins the hills. Breaking out in shops selling inflammable[1] goods, and fanned by the wind, the conflagration instantly grew and swept the whole length of the Circus. There were no walled mansions or temples, or any other obstructions which could arrest it. First, the fire swept violently over the level spaces. Then it climbed the hills—but returned to ravage the lower ground again. It outstripped every counter-measure. The ancient city's narrow winding streets and irregular blocks encouraged its progress.

Terrified, shrieking women, helpless old and young, people intent on their own safety, people unselfishly supporting invalids or waiting for them, fugitives and lingerers alike—all heightened the confusion. When people looked back, menacing flames sprang up before them or outflanked them. When they escaped to a neighboring quarter, the fire followed—even districts believed remote proved to be involved. Finally, with no idea where or what to flee, they crowded on to the country roads, or lay in the fields. Some who had lost everything—even their food for the day—could have escaped, but preferred to die. So did others, who had failed to rescue their loved ones. Nobody dared fight the flames. Attempts to do so were prevented by menacing gangs. Torches, too, were openly

HUMANITIES CONNECTION This bust of a laurel-crowned ruler may depict the emperor Nero. A moderate ruler at first, Nero later indulged in every kind of excess. Faced with plots against him, he took his own life.

thrown in, by men crying that they acted under orders. Perhaps they had received orders. Or they may just have wanted to plunder unhampered.

Nero was at Antium.[2] He only returned to the city when the fire was approaching the mansion he had built to link the Gardens of Maecenas to

---

1. **inflammable:** able to burn.

2. **Antium** (ăn'tē-əm): a resort city on the Italian coast, about 30 miles south of Rome.

the Palatine.[3] The flames could not be prevented from overwhelming the whole of the Palatine, including his palace. Nevertheless, for the relief of the homeless, fugitive masses he threw open the Field of Mars, including Agrippa's public buildings, and even his own Gardens. Nero also constructed emergency accommodation for the destitute[4] multitude. Food was brought from Ostia and neighboring towns, and the price of corn was cut. Yet these measures, for all their popular character, earned no gratitude. For a rumor had spread that, while the city was burning, Nero had gone to his private stage and, comparing modern calamities with ancient, had sung of the destruction of Troy.

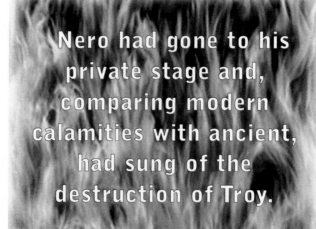

Nero had gone to his private stage and, comparing modern calamities with ancient, had sung of the destruction of Troy.

By the sixth day enormous demolitions had confronted the raging flames with bare ground and open sky, and the fire was finally stamped out. But before panic had subsided, or hope revived, flames broke out again in the more open regions of the city. Here there were fewer casualties; but the destruction of temples and pleasure arcades was even worse. This new conflagration caused additional ill-feeling because it started on Tigellinus' estate.[5] For people believed that Nero was ambitious to found a new city to be called after himself.

Of Rome's fourteen districts only four remained intact. Three were leveled to the ground. The other seven were reduced to a few scorched and mangled ruins. To count the mansions, blocks, and temples destroyed would be difficult. They included shrines of remote antiq-

uity, the precious spoils of countless victories, Greek artistic masterpieces, and authentic records of old Roman genius. All the splendor of the rebuilt city did not prevent the older generation from remembering these irreplaceable objects. It was noted that the fire had started on July 19th, the day on which the Senonian Gauls[6] had captured and burnt the city.

But Nero profited by his country's ruin to build a new palace. Its wonders were not so much customary and commonplace luxuries like gold and jewels, but lawns and lakes and faked rusticity—woods here, open spaces and views there. With their cunning, impudent artificialities, Nero's architects and contractors outbid Nature.

They also fooled away an emperor's riches. For they promised to dig a navigable canal from Lake Avernus[7] to the Tiber estuary, over the stony shore and mountain barriers. The only water to feed the canal was in the Pontine marshes.[8] Elsewhere, all was

---

3. **Palatine** (păl′ə-tīn′): a hill on which many Roman emperors built their palaces.

4. **destitute:** without money or possessions.

5. **Tigellinus'** (tĭj′ə-lī′nəs) **estate:** the property of one of Nero's closest advisers.

6. **Senonian** (sə-nō′nē-ən) **Gauls:** a barbarian tribe that sacked Rome about 390 B.C.

7. **Lake Avernus** (ə-vûr′nəs): a lake near Naples, about 120 miles southeast of Rome.

8. **Pontine** (pŏn′tēn) **marshes:** a swampy region between Rome and Naples.

precipitous[9] or waterless. Moreover, even if a passage could have been forced, the labor would have been unendurable and unjustified. But Nero was eager to perform the incredible; so he attempted to excavate the hills adjoining Lake Avernus. Traces of his frustrated hopes are visible today.

In parts of Rome unfilled by Nero's palace, construction was not—as after the burning by the Gauls—without plan or demarcation.[10] Street-fronts were of regulated dimensions and alignment, streets were broad, and houses spacious. Their height was restricted, and their frontages protected by colonnades. Nero undertook to erect these at his own expense, and also to clear debris from building-sites before transferring them to their owners. He announced bonuses, in proportion to rank and resources, for the completion of houses and blocks before a given date. Rubbish was to be dumped in the Ostian marshes by corn-ships returning down the Tiber.

A fixed proportion of every building had to be massive, untimbered stone from Gabii or Alba (these stones being fireproof). Furthermore, guards were to ensure a more abundant and extensive public water-supply, hitherto diminished by irregular private enterprise. Householders were obliged to keep fire-fighting apparatus in an accessible place; and semi-detached houses were forbidden—they must have their own walls. These measures were welcomed for their practicality, and they beautified the new city. Some, however, believed that the old town's configuration had been healthier, since its narrow streets and high houses had provided protection against the burning sun, whereas now the shadowless open spaces radiated a fiercer heat.

So much for human precautions. Next came attempts to appease heaven. After consultation of the Sibylline books,[11] prayers were addressed to Vulcan, Ceres, and Proserpina. Juno, too, was propitiated. But neither human resources, nor imperial munificence,[12] nor appeasement of the gods, eliminated sinister suspicions that the fire had been instigated. To suppress this rumor, Nero fabricated[13] scapegoats—and punished with every refinement the notoriously depraved Christians (as they were popularly called). Their originator, Christ, had been executed in Tiberius' reign by the governor of Judaea, Pontius Pilatus. But in spite of this temporary setback the deadly superstition had broken out afresh, not only in Judaea (where the mischief had started) but even in Rome. All degraded and shameful practices collect and flourish in the capital.

First, Nero had self-acknowledged Christians arrested. Then, on their information, large numbers of others were condemned—not so much for incendiarism[14] as for their anti-social tendencies. Their deaths were made farcical.[15] Dressed in wild animals' skins, they were torn to pieces by dogs, or crucified, or made into torches to be ignited after dark as substitutes for daylight. Nero provided his Gardens for the spectacle, and exhibited displays in the Circus, at which he mingled with the crowd—or stood in a chariot, dressed as a charioteer. Despite their guilt as Christians, and the ruthless punishment it deserved, the victims were pitied. For it was felt that they were being sacrificed to one man's brutality rather than to the national interest. ❖

---

9. **precipitous** (prĭ-sĭp′ĭ-təs): very steep.

10. **demarcation:** marking of boundaries.

11. **Sibylline** (sĭb′ə-līn′) **books:** collections of prophecies, kept in a temple at Rome.

12. **munificence** (myo͞o-nĭf′ĭ-səns): generosity.

13. **fabricated:** dreamed up.

14. **incendiarism** (ĭn-sĕn′dē-ə-rĭz′əm): deliberate setting of fires.

15. **farcical** (fär′sĭ-kəl): ridiculous.

Literature of Ancient Rome

Reflect and Assess

What did you learn about the literature of ancient Rome from reading the selections in Unit Two, Part 2? Why do you think it is important to learn about the ancient Romans and their literature? Use the following options to help you explore what you have learned.

Pasquius Proculus and his wife. Wall painting from Pompeii. Museo Archeologico Nazionale, Naples, Italy.

Reflecting on the Literature

Literature and Values The ancient Romans believed that literary works should serve a practical purpose—in Horace's words, "to teach and delight." In the selections in Part 2, the writers describe both conduct they favor and conduct they scorn. Think about the selections you've read, and identify the values each writer supports. Discuss whether these values are still important in today's world.

Reviewing Literary Concepts

Appreciating Imagery In this part of the book, you learned about a literary element known as **imagery.** What images in the selections still stand out in your mind? List each image, and write the sense or senses that it appeals to. Which of these images do you think best supports the writer's message?

🗁 Building Your Portfolio

Writing Options Look back at the various Writing Options you completed for the lessons in this part of the book. Which piece of writing represents you at your creative best? Add that assignment to your **Presentation Portfolio** 🗁, along with a cover note explaining your choice.

Self **ASSESSMENT**

📖 READER'S NOTEBOOK

You learned the following names and terms as you read the selections in this part. Write a sentence to describe or define each name or literary term. If you are unsure of a term, review its definition in Part 2 or check the **Glossary of Literary Terms** (page R91).

written epic	Emperor Augustus
epic simile	Roman Empire
culture hero	*Metamorphoses*
Helen of Troy	narrative poem
"Seize the day."	foreshadowing
odes	myth

Setting **GOALS**

The *Aeneid,* as you have learned, has had a profound influence on Western culture and still stirs readers today. In this part, you read a lengthy excerpt from Book 2 of this epic poem. Why not read more of Virgil's masterpiece? Ask your teacher or a librarian to help you locate a modern translation to read on your own.

Extend Your *Reading*

LITERATURE CONNECTIONS
Julius Caesar

WILLIAM SHAKESPEARE

This tragedy dramatizes the key events before and after Caesar's assassination. Shakespeare focuses on the conspirator Marcus Brutus, "the noblest Roman of them all." Loving Caesar yet fearing his growing power, Brutus decides to kill him for the good of Rome.

Here are just a few of the related readings that accompany *Julius Caesar:*

The Life of Caesar
BY SUETONIUS

Epitaph on a Tyrant
BY W. H. AUDEN

A Eulogy to Dr. Martin Luther King, Jr.
BY ROBERT F. KENNEDY

The Roman Way

EDITH HAMILTON

In this informal history, the author describes the Roman spirit as it is revealed in the works of the greatest authors of ancient Rome— including Virgil, Cicero, Caesar, and Horace. According to Hamilton, these authors were "Romans first, individual artists only second."

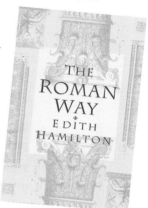

And Even *More* . . .

Books
Silver Pigs LINDSEY DAVIS
This mystery novel, set in A.D. 70, tells of the humorous adventures of Marcus Didius Falco, a dirt-poor detective. He shrewdly observes daily life in both Rome and Britain, giving the reader an inside view of political intrigue in the Roman Empire.

The Portable Roman Reader BASIL DAVENPORT, ED.
This anthology contains essential writings of many ancient Roman authors in fine English translations. Among the authors included are Terence, Plautus, Caesar, Cicero, Catullus, Virgil, Horace, Martial, Lucretius, Ovid, and Apuleius.

Other Media
Ancient Rome
Part of the History Through Art series, this video presents the story of Rome from the rule of the Etruscans through the decline of the Roman Empire. 40 minutes. Zenger Media. (VIDEOCASSETTE)

Spartacus
This film, directed by Stanley Kubrick, is based on the true story of a gladiator who led a slave revolt against the Roman Republic. Kirk Douglas, Laurence Olivier, and Jean Simmons star. 196 minutes. Zenger Media. (VIDEOCASSETTE)

Handbook to Life in Ancient Rome

LESLEY ADKINS AND ROY A. ADKINS

This handy reference, written by two professional archaeologists, contains a wealth of useful illustrations. The thematic chapters cover a variety of topics, including rulers, the legal system, and architectural feats.

Reading & Writing for Assessment

Throughout high school, you will be tested on your ability to read and understand different kinds of reading selections. The tests will assess your basic understanding of ideas and knowledge of vocabulary. They will also assess your ability to analyze and evaluate the messages of the selections, along with the techniques the writers use in getting their messages across.

Some useful test-taking strategies are presented in this lesson. Practice applying the strategies by working through each of the models provided.

PART 1 How to Read a Test Selection

Sometimes a test requires you to read a passage and then answer multiple-choice questions about it. Applying these test-taking strategies, taking notes, and marking important passages as you read can help you focus on information.

> **STRATEGIES** FOR READING A TEST SELECTION

> **Before you begin reading, skim the questions that follow the passage.** These can help focus your reading.

> **Think about the title.** What does it suggest about the overall message or theme of the selection?

> **Use active reading strategies, such as analyzing, predicting, and questioning.** Take notes in the margin or highlight important words and passages to help you focus your reading. (Do not do this, however, if the test directions forbid you to mark on the test.)

> **Look for main ideas.** You will often find them stated at the beginning or end of paragraphs. Sometimes they are implied rather than directly stated. After reading each paragraph, ask yourself, What was this passage about?

> **Note the literary elements and techniques used by the writer.** You might, for example, consider the writer's tone or use of comparison and contrast. Then ask yourself what effect is created by each element or technique.

> **Examine the sequence of ideas.** Are the ideas developed in chronological order, presented in order of importance, or organized in some other way—as causes and effects, for instance, or as problems and solutions?

> **Think about the writer's purpose and message.** What questions does the selection answer? What new questions does it raise? What generalizations can you make about the subject?

❶ Ancient Greece Revived in Rome; Colosseum Reopens as Theater with Staging of *Oedipus Rex*
by Sarah Delaney

1   ❷ More than 15 centuries after its last gladiators saluted Caesar, the Roman Colosseum reopened tonight as a place of public entertainment, this time for a small, cultured audience rather than tens of thousands of plebeians screaming for blood. The draw for tonight's 500 people . . . was a Greek-language performance of the ancient Greek drama *Oedipus Rex*. As spotlights illuminated chambers and walls of the giant ruin, actors played out the classic story of love and incest.

2   Costas Galanakis, cast as the old blind seer, Tiresias, declared it "a great, emotional moment to perform here."

3   ❸ Concetta Notardonato, 47, a Roman and an avid theatergoer, said from her standing position on the third tier of the arena that "it's a great idea, and the setting is fantastic." But she felt ticket prices, about $25, were too high. And, she objected to the language. "We don't all know Greek," she lamented. "A unique performance like this should be more accessible to everybody; the Colosseum is a symbolic place for the people."

4   Opened in the year 80 as a venue for Rome's beloved spectacles, the grand stone structure closed and descended into ruin in the centuries after the fall of the empire. But this evening, courtesy of government agencies here, it reopened for a show ❹ that could not have been less like the mayhem of Ridley Scott's film *Gladiator*.

5   A large helium balloon floated in balmy summer air over the arena; the chorus, loosely clad in white, chanted and sang amid ghostly white plaster statues set up as part of the scenery. From the distance came the sounds of sirens and streetcars.

6   The stage was a newly built wooden platform. It partly re-created the arena's long-lost oak floor that covered walkways and cells where exotic beasts and armored fighters waited to come up and entertain Romans of every sort. The show, put on by the Greek National Theater, was the first of eight performances of Sophocles' Oedipus trilogy, including *Antigone* and an opera based on *Oedipus at Colonus*. . . .

---

❶ **Look at the title.**

ONE STUDENT'S THOUGHTS

"The title tells me that this article deals with ancient Greek culture and the Roman Colosseum."

❷ **Look for main ideas.**
"This selection is about the reopening of the Roman Colosseum after more than 1,500 years."

YOUR TURN
Look at the end of the article for other stated main ideas.

❸ **Evaluate sources of information.**
"The person being quoted lives in Rome and goes to the theater often. She probably knows what she's talking about, and maybe her views are shared by other theatergoers."

❹ **Note the signal words indicating the writer's use of contrast.**
"The writer tells me what this show is *not* like. Even if I've never seen the film *Gladiator*, I know that this show is not violent or rowdy."

YOUR TURN
Find other instances of comparison and contrast.

7   The Colosseum was begun by the emperor Vespasian. Built to hold 75,000 people, it has the same basic form as present-day sports facilities. ❺ Even now, visitors can sense the awe that it commanded in its day.

8   A day at the Colosseum 20 centuries ago was a decidedly popular form of entertainment. Notices were placed around the city and entrance was free. Seating was determined by social standing and sex; the emperor and his family naturally got the best spot, near where today's politicians and selected guests were seated, at the east end of the elliptical arena.

9   Members of the ancient Roman Senate occupied the lowest section—the box seats—while choice places also went to priests, judges and ambassadors. Young men who had not yet reached adulthood had their own section, and their teachers were assigned places nearby. Women were ❻ relegated to the top tiers. White cloth awnings around the top of the open-air bowl shielded spectators from the sun.

10   The *venationes,* or beast hunts, in the arena took place amid elaborate scenery evoking the exotic lands from which the tigers, lions, hippopotamuses or even giraffes were taken. Gladiators fought against or among the animals, which had often been held in the dark without food for long periods before being loosed into the arena.

11   Gladiatorial games were abolished in 438, the *venationes* in 523. In the centuries that followed, the structure was reduced to a quarry site from which marble and limestone were pilfered. An entire side of the structure disappeared.

12   Still, the Colosseum by moonlight has enchanted visitors for centuries, including the German poet Goethe, who wrote in his *Italian Journey* that "The Colosseum looked especially beautiful. . . . This is the kind of illumination by which to see the Pantheon, the Capitol, the square in front of St. Peter's. . . . Like the human spirit, the sun and the moon have a quite different task to perform here than they have in other places, for here their glance is returned by gigantic, solid masses."

STRATEGIES IN ACTION

❺ Read actively by questioning.
"What was the Colosseum really like in 'its day'?"

❻ Use context clues to unlock word meanings.
"Women were given the worst seats. *Relegated* must mean 'assigned to an undesirable place.'"

Skim the questions that follow the passage.
"I see there's a question about the writer's purpose. What is her purpose? She seems fairly enthusiastic, but is she really trying to persuade me? I think she is informing me."

How to Answer Multiple-Choice Questions

Use the strategies in the box and the notes in the side column to help you answer the questions below and on the following pages.

On the basis of the selection you have just read, choose the best answer for each of the following questions.

1. After reading paragraph 1, what two things can you expect to find compared in this article?
   A. small audiences and large audiences
   B. ancient and modern entertainments in the Roman Colosseum
   C. life in the fifth century and life today
   D. people who are cultured and people who are bloodthirsty

2. According to one spectator, what is wrong with the performance of *Oedipus Rex?*
   A. The Colosseum is too crowded.
   B. The play is performed in Greek, which is unfamiliar to most of the Italian audience.
   C. The play is too old to be interesting.
   D. all of the above

3. Which of the following statements most closely paraphrases the quotation from Goethe?
   A. The Colosseum is like the human spirit.
   B. The Colosseum is the most beautiful building in Rome.
   C. The Colosseum and other Roman buildings are more massive than anything else lit by the sun and the moon.
   D. The Colosseum is so large that it blocks the light of the sun.

4. Which of the following statements best expresses the article's main idea?
   A. Greek plays are much better than beast hunts.
   B. Even after centuries of decay, the glory of the Colosseum lives on.
   C. The ancient Romans were unsophisticated.
   D. Everyone should see *Oedipus Rex.*

5. What was the writer's purpose for writing this article?
   A. to inform
   B. to persuade
   C. to entertain
   D. to remind

STRATEGIES FOR ANSWERING MULTIPLE-CHOICE QUESTIONS

▶ **Ask questions** that help you eliminate some of the choices.

▶ **Pay attention to choices** such as "all of the above" or "none of the above." To eliminate them, all you need to find is one answer that doesn't fit.

▶ **Skim your notes.** Details you noticed as you read may provide answers.

STRATEGIES IN ACTION

Pay attention to choices such as "all of the above."

ONE STUDENT'S THOUGHTS
"No one says anything at all about the Colosseum's being crowded, so I can eliminate choice A and, therefore, choice D as well."

YOUR TURN
Look at the quotations to see whether choice B or choice C makes more sense.

Skim your notes.

ONE STUDENT'S THOUGHTS
"I don't think a straightforward article like this is meant to entertain, and I really don't think the writer is trying to remind me of anything, so I can eliminate choices C and D."

YOUR TURN
What other choice can you eliminate?

TEST PRACTICE

PART 3

How to Respond in Writing

Sometimes, you may be asked to write answers to questions about a reading passage. **Short-answer questions** usually ask you to answer in a sentence or two. An **essay question** requires a fully developed piece of writing.

Short-Answer Question

STRATEGIES FOR RESPONDING TO SHORT-ANSWER QUESTIONS

▶ **Identify the key words** in the writing prompt that tell you the ideas to discuss. Make sure you know what is meant by each.
▶ **Make your response** direct and to the point.
▶ **Support your ideas** by using evidence from the selection.

> **Sample Question**
>
> Answer the following question in one or two sentences.
>
> Why do you think the writer has included the quotation from Goethe at the end of the article?

STRATEGIES IN ACTION

Support your ideas by using evidence from the selection.

ONE STUDENT'S THOUGHTS

"I should look at the text leading up to the quotation. I'll probably find a clue there about why the writer used it."

YOUR TURN

Find the text that precedes the quotation from Goethe. How does the quotation fit into its context?

Essay Question

STRATEGIES FOR ANSWERING ESSAY QUESTIONS

▶ **Look for direction words** in the writing prompt—for example, *essay, analyze, describe,* or *compare and contrast*—that tell you how to respond.
▶ **List the points** you want to make before beginning to write.
▶ **Write an interesting introduction** that presents your main point.
▶ **Develop your ideas** by using evidence from the selection to support your statements.
▶ **Present the ideas** in a logical order.
▶ **Write a conclusion** that summarizes your points.
▶ **Check your work** for correct grammar.

> **Sample Prompt**
>
> From this article, what conclusions can you draw about the differences between entertainments in ancient Rome and in present-day Rome? Write a short essay in which you compare and contrast the forms of entertainment, using evidence from the text to support your conclusions.

Look for direction words.

ONE STUDENT'S THOUGHTS

"The prompt is asking me to *compare and contrast* entertainments in ancient and contemporary Rome. I'll have to look for evidence about both kinds of entertainment and explain how they are alike and how they are different."

YOUR TURN

Make a list of similarities and differences between ancient and contemporary Roman entertainments. You might want to organize your thoughts in a Venn diagram.

PART 4

How to Revise and Edit Your Test Essay

Here is part of a student's first draft in response to the writing prompt at the bottom of page 416. Read it and answer the multiple-choice questions that follow.

1	Ancient and contemporary Romans chose very different kinds of
2	public entertainment based on this article. First of all, the
3	gladiator games and venationes were rowdy, violent spectacles
4	open to all social classes. In contrast, the modern performance of
5	*Oedipus Rex* was a much quieter, more civilized event. The cost of
6	admission, and the fact that the performance was in Greek, limited
7	the audience to educated people with some money to spend.
8	It seems that ancient Romans were more concerned with
9	showing everyone a noisy good time. Even if it involved
10	bloodshed. Contemporary Romans have always appeared to have
11	gentler tastes and to be more exclusive.

> **STRATEGIES** FOR
> REVISING, EDITING,
> AND PROOFREADING
>
> ▶ **Read the passage carefully.**
> ▶ **Note the parts that are confusing** or don't make sense. What kinds of errors would such problems signal?
> ▶ **Look for errors** in grammar, usage, spelling, and capitalization. Common errors include:
> • run-on sentences
> • sentence fragments
> • faulty subject-verb agreement
> • unclear pronoun reference

1. What is the BEST way to revise the first sentence of this essay?
   A. According to this article, the writer shows great differences between entertainment in ancient and contemporary Rome.
   B. Ancient and contemporary Romans are very different.
   C. According to this article, ancient and contemporary Romans chose very different kinds of public entertainment.
   D. There are two distinct differences between entertainment in ancient and contemporary Rome based on this article.

2. What is the BEST way to revise the beginning of the second paragraph?
   A. It seems that ancient Romans are more concerned with showing everyone a noisy good time. Even if it involved bloodshed.
   B. Ancient Romans were more concerned with showing everyone a noisy good time; even if it involved bloodshed.
   C. It seems that ancient Romans were more concerned with showing everyone a noisy good time, even if it involved bloodshed.
   D. Even if it involved bloodshed: it seems that ancient Romans were more concerned with showing everyone a noisy good time.

3. What is the BEST revision of the final sentence?
   A. Contemporary Romans appear to have gentler tastes and to be more exclusive.
   B. Contemporary Romans appeared to have gentler tastes and to be more exclusive.
   C. Contemporary Romans are appearing to have gentler tastes and to be more exclusive.
   D. Contemporary Romans will forever appear to have gentler tastes and to be more exclusive.

Traditions in Chinese and Japanese Literature 1600 B.C.–A.D. 1800

Moonlight on the River Seba, Andō Hiroshige. Musée Guimet, Paris. Giraudon/Art Resource, New York.

*"Everything has beauty
but not everyone sees it."*

—Confucius

PART 1
From Observation to Insight:
Literature of Ancient China 420–485

⸎

PART 2
Capturing the Moment:
Literature of Japan 486–561

Literature of Ancient China

Why It Matters

Everything about China is on a vast scale. It is the world's third-largest country in area and has the largest population. It also has the world's oldest continuing civilization, one that has been in existence for more than 3,500 years. The people of ancient China—philosophers, artists, writers, scientists— created a rich, brilliant culture. Their ideas, art, literature, and inventions command respect and wonder and still affect life today.

For Links to Ancient China, click on:

HUMANITIES
CLASSZONE.COM

Arabian Sea

	China, c. 220 B.C.
ᴎᴎᴎ	Great Wall
—	Silk Roads
▲	Mountain

1 The Development of Writing In 1936, archaeologists at an ancient site called An-yang discovered thousands of turtle shells covered with a form of writing called **pictographs**—simplified drawings of objects. These shells—as shown on the right—dated to about 1400 B.C. The writing system used in China today developed from this pictographic writing.

Taklimakan Desert

Kunlun Mountains

4

HIMALAYAS

TIBET

INDIA

Bay of Bengal

4 The Silk Trade Silk has been produced in China since about 3000 B.C. About 206 B.C., camel caravans loaded with silk and other luxury goods began to travel along what came to be called the **Silk Roads,** the long routes between China and Europe. Many Chinese merchants made fortunes carrying silk to the West. Trade along the Silk Roads also resulted in interaction among a wide variety of cultures.

0	250	500 miles
0	250	500 kilometers

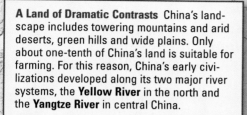

A Land of Dramatic Contrasts China's land-scape includes towering mountains and arid deserts, green hills and wide plains. Only about one-tenth of China's land is suitable for farming. For this reason, China's early civilizations developed along its two major river systems, the **Yellow River** in the north and the **Yangtze River** in central China.

ASIA

MONGOLIA

Gobi Desert

Great Wall

Yellow River

Great Wall

Great Wall

Yellow River

2

• Peking

Hao

An-yang

1

Yellow River

Ch'ang-an

• Lo-yang

3

Han River

CHINA

• Nanking

Wu Mountains

Three Gorges

Yangtze River

• Ch'ang-ming

Wu Mountains

▲ Lu Mountain

Yellow Sea

JAPAN

PACIFIC OCEAN

TAIWAN

VIETNAM

2 **Border Protection** In the third century B.C., the first **Great Wall** of China was completed. Winding along the long northern border of China, the wall was a defense against invading tribes. Made of stone and earth, each section of the wall rose to an average height of 23 to 26 feet and in places stretched wide enough for five horses to gallop side by side along the top.

3 **The Rule of Emperors** In the third century B.C., the leader of the state of Ch'in made himself the **first emperor** of China. He expanded China's borders and created a great empire that would set the course of China's future. As a testament to his impressive power, the emperor was buried in an enormous tomb guarded by an army of 6,000 life-size terra-cotta soldiers, like those seen to the right.

A dynasty consists of a series of rulers from a single family. Reading about some of the important dynasties in ancient China will help you understand the events that influenced and inspired Chinese writers and their culture.

Terra-cotta soldier

Shang
c. 1600–1050 B.C.

Chinese history is marked by a succession of dynasties, beginning with the great Shang dynasty. The Shang were warrior-nobles headed by a king. These rulers were known for their love of warfare and hunting. The people had great loyalty to their king, their families, and their ancestors, whom they honored with sacrifices.

The Shang dynasty produced a stunning culture. Shang artisans learned how to make cloth from **silk** and excelled in **bronze working.** Their beautiful weapons and ceremonial vessels are among the finest ever made. The Shang dynasty was also the first to leave written records.

Bronze wine vessel

Chou
c. 1050–221 B.C.

About 1050 B.C., a people called the Chou overthrew the Shang and established their own dynasty. It was to be the longest in Chinese history. The early years of the Chou dynasty saw great expansion and the establishment of **feudalism.** Under this system, different regions of the country were controlled by lords who were loyal to the king and protective of the local people. Confucius viewed the early Chou culture as a model society.

The strength of the Chou dynasty lessened as tribes invaded from the northern frontier. The feudal lords also began to fight one another. As a result, the decline of the dynasty was called the **Warring States** period.

Ch'in
221–207 B.C.

The state of Ch'in (from which the name China derives) defeated the Chou dynasty, and in 221 B.C. the Ch'in king declared himself Shih Huang Ti, or First Emperor. Determined to unify the country, he subdued internal conflicts and conquered invaders. He also centralized the **government,** built an extensive network of roads, and set uniform standards for weights and measures.

Although the First Emperor's achievements brought important changes, his methods were cruel. He forced vast numbers of peasants to build the **Great Wall.** Many of them died during construction. He murdered scholars and burned books. Revolt led to the fall of the dynasty three years after Shih Huang Ti's death.

History to Literature

EVENT IN HISTORY	EVENT IN LITERATURE
Rebellions and invasions during Chou dynasty	Ancient Chinese poets compose war poems in the *Book of Odes.*
Prosperity in T'ang dynasty	Li Po and Tu Fu write China's greatest poetry.

SHANG	CHOU
1600 B.C.	1050 B.C.

Han

206 B.C.–A.D. 220

Following the downfall of the Ch'in dynasty, the Han dynasty came to power. This dynasty, which ruled China for more than 400 years, had lasting influence on China's government, education, culture, and commerce. The Han is divided into two periods, Former and Later. The Former Han was a glorious period of innovation and prosperity. Chinese commerce expanded, opening up the **Silk Roads** to most of Asia and, via India, all the way to Rome. Chinese agriculture, technology, arts, and literature also flourished. Nevertheless, social and political unrest ended the Former Han about A.D. 9.

The Han were restored to power in A.D. 25, and the first decades of the Later Han were also prosperous. The religion of **Buddhism** spread from India to China, where it took root. Within a century, however, political, economic, and social problems began to weaken Han rule again. In A.D. 220, the last emperor abdicated, and the Later Han dynasty disintegrated into three rival kingdoms.

T'ang

A.D. 618–907

During the four centuries after the Han dynasty collapsed, many minor dynasties rose and fell before the T'ang dynasty came to power. The T'ang rulers again expanded the Chinese empire. They promoted foreign trade and improvements in agriculture, and they restored China's vast bureaucracy and civil service system.

The T'ang period was a **golden age,** especially in poetry and painting. The capital city, **Ch'ang-an,** grew in wealth and population to become the most sophisticated city of its time. Scholarship thrived. The powerful

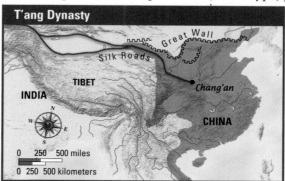

T'ang Dynasty

Great Wall · Silk Roads · TIBET · INDIA · Chang'an · CHINA

0 250 500 miles
0 250 500 kilometers

Chinese woman emperor **Empress Wu** ruled during this period.

The T'ang empire became subject to rebel attacks under the rule of later, weaker emperors. In 907, it fell to rebel forces.

Sung

A.D. 960–1279

After the T'ang dynasty ended, rival warlords divided China into separate kingdoms. In 960, one general reunited China and established himself as the first Sung emperor. Although the Sung empire was smaller than the Han or T'ang, it produced a thriving culture.

Education spread. Literature, calligraphy, and painting flourished. The Chinese carefully studied human anatomy and made charts and models of the body. Among the most significant **inventions** of this era were movable type, paper money, and the use of the magnetic compass for sailing. The position of women declined during this era, however. Foreign trade—especially ocean trade—expanded under the Sung emperors. Chinese culture spread throughout Southeast Asia, and China became a major sea power. Yet despite economic prosperity and technological advances, the Sung dynasty fell to the Mongols in 1279.

CH'IN ▼ 221–207 B.C.

HAN	T'ANG	SUNG

206 B.C.　　　　　　　　　A.D. 618　　　　A.D. 960　　　A.D. 1279

Chinese society in ancient times had a strict class structure, with the emperor at the top and the lowliest workers at the bottom. Each of the four main social classes—the rulers, peasants, artisans, and merchants—was ranked according to its contribution to society.

Rulers

The **emperor** was the central figure of authority in ancient China. Powerful and wealthy, he presided over political, social, and religious rituals. Below the emperor were members of the royal family, nobles, and **scholar-officials** in the imperial civil service.

Kuang Wu Ti, Han dynasty emperor

Chinese emperors often rewarded loyal followers with posts in the civil service. During the T'ang and Sung dynasties, however, a system of written examinations was developed to select officials. Applicants—primarily sons of wealthy landowners—studied and were tested on the Confucian classics. Successful scholars then joined the elite and privileged ranks of administrators and teachers.

Peasants

The mainstay of ancient Chinese society was the peasants, the **farmers** who raised the food for the empire. During the Chou dynasty, most peasants labored for wealthy feudal landowners, to whom they gave a large share of their harvest. As this system declined, peasants began to own their own land but still owed part of their yearly crops to the government.

Peasants ranked just below the ruling class because they performed an important role in Chinese society. However, they led difficult lives. Typically, they lived in simple, one-room houses with a dirt floor and little furniture. They had only a few tools. Every year, they faced devastating floods and droughts.

The peasants were often required to supply labor or military service to the government. Emperors built roads and canals with this source of labor and filled the ranks of China's vast armies.

Artisans

Artisans are craftspeople who work with their hands. Skilled artisans in ancient China made useful items such as tools for agriculture, weapons for war, furniture, and household goods. They also made luxury items—silk, porcelain, and carved jade—for the upper classes and for export. Artisans who produced the luxury items tended to be wealthy themselves, but those who produced everyday necessities were not.

Beginning in the Shang dynasty, Chinese emperors controlled the supply of raw materials that artisans used. Although some artisans worked independently, others labored in government-owned factories.

Artisans produced many of the works that were placed in the tombs of emperors and noblemen. These included eating utensils, jewelry, textiles, tools, and weapons. Archaeologists continue to discover rich treasures in ancient burial sites.

Rice farmers

Selling paper

Merchants

Merchants sold the goods that artisans made. Because they did not actually produce anything, they occupied a low place on China's social ladder. Strictly controlled by the government, merchants were allowed to sell only certain goods, such as silk, spices, tea, and porcelain. They were forced to pay heavy taxes but were prohibited from owning land. During Han times, a merchant even had to wear special clothing—a white turban bearing his name and trade and one white and one black shoe.

Although many merchants grew wealthy as a result of the growth of **trade** during the T'ang and Sung dynasties, they found it difficult to improve their social status. Traditionally, merchants were not allowed to take the civil service examination and so were excluded from government jobs. However, prosperous merchants sent their sons to schools that trained them for civil service jobs or arranged their daughters' marriages to civil servants.

Servants and Slaves

The people on the lowest rungs of Chinese society were not considered important or worthy enough to have a class of their own. Such people included servants, migrant laborers, professional soldiers, entertainers, butchers, and tanners. The Chinese also had slaves. During T'ang times, nomads from Mongolia and Central Asia who were captured in war were forced into slave labor. All these groups were regarded as inferior to the four main classes of society and thus were excluded from the civil service examination.

Female servant carrying lantern

Tomb figure of equestrienne on horse (eighth century). The Art Institute of Chicago.

Women in Ancient China

Women were subservient to men in ancient Chinese society. Boys alone attended school and took the civil service exam. Few girls were educated unless their fathers taught them how to read and write. Marriages were arranged, and a girl as young as 14 might leave home to live with her husband's family.

In the Han and T'ang periods, some privileged women had a few more freedoms than in other dynasties. In T'ang times, women rode horses, hunted, played polo, and participated in politics. By the Sung period, however, the status of women had declined again, especially among the upper classes in cities. There a woman's work was deemed less important to the family's prosperity and prestige.

One sign of women's changing status was the custom of binding the feet of upper-class girls to keep their feet from growing. The practice spread during the Sung period and continued into the 20th century. Women with bound feet could never walk normally. Their condition reflected the wealth and position of their families, since they were unsuited for manual labor.

The ancient Chinese developed one of the most advanced civilizations of their time. Their art and literature are unsurpassed in beauty and craftsmanship, and their philosophical classics continue to be read for their wisdom and insight.

Philosophy and Religion

From the sixth century B.C. to the first century A.D., three main systems of thought took hold in ancient China—Confucianism, Taoism, and Buddhism. The teachings of Confucius and of Taoism emerged during the sixth century B.C.

Confucianism focused on the importance of family relationships and order in society. The teachings emphasized virtue in all interactions between people and valued learning, respect, and duty.

Taoism was based on following the Way, or Tao, a universal force underlying all of life. Taoists sought humility, simplicity, and harmony with nature.

Buddhism, based on the teachings of Siddhartha Gautama, originated in India and reached China about the first century a.d. More a religion than a philosophy, Buddhism emphasized detachment from earthly life in order to attain spiritual enlightenment.

From earliest times, the ancient Chinese also practiced religious devotion to their ancestors. They believed that the dead live on as spirits and are closely tied to the living. Ancestors were honored through offerings, prayers, and elaborate ceremonies.

These various philosophical and religious teachings existed together in ancient China. Sometimes they were in opposition, but in general there was tolerance and even a blending of beliefs and practices.

Literature

China has one of the oldest continuous literary traditions in the world, dating back more than 3,000 years. It is a vast body of work, surpassing that of any other civilization. The earliest known major literary work is the *Book of Odes,* a collection of poems dating from the Shang and Chou dynasties. These poems have been revered, studied, and memorized throughout China's history.

In later dynasties, writing poetry was considered an essential accomplishment for scholars and gentlemen. The finest poems in all of China's literature were produced during the T'ang dynasty, when the lyric poets **Li Po** and **Tu Fu** were writing.

Prose was also a strong tradition. Important works include the *Analects* of Confucius, Taoist tales, philosophical essays, and *The Records of the Historian,* a main source of information about early China.

Confucius, a major Chinese philosopher

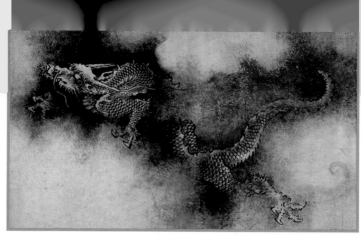

Detail of *Nine Dragons* (c. 1244), Chen Rong. Hand scroll, ink and touches of red on paper, 18¾₆″ × 431¹¹⁄₁₆″. Courtesy of the Museum of Fine Arts, Boston. Francis Gardner Curtis Fund, 1917.

The Arts

From Shang times, the ancient Chinese excelled in the arts. They distinguished themselves in the production of pottery, bronze work, sculpture, jade carvings, calligraphy, and painting. As early as 2000 B.C., Chinese artists used the potter's wheel to create beautiful vases and urns. They discovered how to make fine porcelain during later T'ang times. Chinese artists were known for their realistic sculpture. Examples of their skill include the lifelike terra-cotta figures buried in Shih Huang Ti's tomb and

Jade sculpture of dragon. National Museum of Oriental Art, Rome.

the thousands of stone Buddha statues carved into caves after Buddhism spread to China. Calligraphy, or "beautiful writing," was considered one of the fine arts. The best calligraphers became famous, and their work was much sought after.

During the Sung dynasty, Chinese painting reached its greatest glory. The focus shifted from the human figure to landscapes. Artists painted towering mountains, plunging waterfalls, and peaceful lakes. This attention to landscape, which reflects the Taoist love of nature, influenced painting in China for the next thousand years. The paintings were done on silk or paper scrolls, and the artists often preferred black ink. Said one Sung artist, "Black is ten colors." During the Sung dynasty, the combination of the "three perfections"—calligraphy, poetry, and landscape painting—was regarded as the highest achievement of the arts.

Turning Points in Literature

During the Han dynasty, the invention of **paper** changed forever the way words were recorded in China. Chinese paper was made from mulberry bark, silk rags, hemp, bamboo, and fishing nets, which were mixed together and soaked in water. The mixture was then boiled, mashed, and pounded into pulp. A fine screen was dipped into the pulp to scoop up a thin layer of fibers. After the layer of pulp was pressed to remove the water, it was dried on a heated wall. The sheet of paper was then carefully peeled away.

The invention of paper led to the creation of books and spurred the Chinese inventions of **woodblock printing** and **movable type.** The first Chinese books, which were hand written by scholars, were made of paper rolled into long scrolls.

The use of paper also created new possibilities in the art of **calligraphy.** To produce the delicate strokes, calligraphers practiced for years to master the thousands of characters in the Chinese writing system.

Time Line

c.   approximately
B.C.   before Christ
A.D.   after Christ

3000 B.C.   A.D. 1   PRESENT

EVENTS IN CHINESE LITERATURE

1200 B.C.	800 B.C.	400 B.C.

c. 1400–1100 B.C. Earliest evidence of Chinese writing is found on Shang oracle bones

c. 1000–600 B.C. Earliest known Chinese poems composed

551–479 B.C. Confucius teaches about ethical values such as honesty, loyalty, and respect for elders; his disciples later record his teachings in *Analects*

c. 500s B.C. Lao-tzu, legendary founder of Taoism, develops teachings of *Tao Te Ching*

c. 500 B.C. The *Shih Ching (Book of Odes),* the first anthology of Chinese poetry, is compiled

c. 330 B.C. Taoist philosopher Chuang Tzu writes the *Chuang Tzu*

c. 85 B.C. Ssu-ma Ch'ien writes *Records of the Historian,* a history of China through Wu Ti's reign

EVENTS IN CHINESE HISTORY

1200 B.C.	800 B.C.	400 B.C.

c. 1050 B.C. Chou dynasty is established and institutes feudalism

771 B.C. Nomads from the north capture and plunder Hao, the Chou dynasty capital, and local warlords battle one another

c. 500s B.C. The Chinese begin to cast iron

475 B.C. Warring States period begins

221 B.C. Shih Huang Ti becomes emperor of China

c. 214 B.C. First Great Wall is begun

206 B.C.–A.D. 220 Silk routes opened up for trade during the Han dynasty

EVENTS IN WORLD HISTORY

1200 B.C.	800 B.C.	400 B.C.

c. 1200 B.C. The Trojan War is fought

c. 1020 B.C. The Hebrews establish the kingdom of Israel

1000–500 B.C. Aryan communities begin to appear in the Ganges River basin in India

776 B.C. First recorded Olympic Games, founded in Greece to honor the god Zeus

c. 563 B.C. Birth of Siddhartha Gautama, founder of Buddhism

509 B.C. Roman Republic is created

c. 500 B.C. Nok in West Africa develop iron-making technology

331–330 B.C. Alexander the Great conquers Syria, Mesopotamia, and Persia

218 B.C. Hannibal crosses the Alps

44 B.C. Julius Caesar is assassinated

30 B.C. Rome conquers Egypt

A.D. 54 Pan Ku writes *History of the Former Han Dynasty*

C. A.D. 100 The first Chinese dictionary is compiled

A.D. 106 Pan Chao—a scholarly widow, sister of Pan Ku and imperial historian after his death—writes *Lessons for Women*

A.D. 365 Birth of T'ao Ch'ien, important early lyric poet

C. A.D. 690 Poetry writing is included in the civil service examination

A.D. 699 Birth of Wang Wei, painter and poet

A.D. 701 Birth of Li Po

A.D. 712 Birth of Tu Fu

A.D. 868 *Diamond Sutra*, the first book with a printed date, is published

C. A.D. 900–1200 Song lyrics, or *tz'u*, sung by women entertainers become a major poetic form; Li Ch'ing-chao masters the genre

A.D. 9 Period of the Former Han ends

A.D. 25 Period of Later Han begins under Kuang Wu Ti

C. A.D. 65 Buddhism reaches China

C. A.D. 105 The Chinese invent paper

A.D. 610 Grand Canal is completed, linking the Yangtze and Yellow rivers

A.D. 626–649 Civil service examination system is begun under T'ang emperor T'ai Tsung

A.D. 690–705 Reign of Empress Wu

A.D. 756 An Lu-shan's rebels capture T'ang capital city of Ch'ang-an

C. A.D. 850 Gunpowder is invented

A.D. 907 Last T'ang emperor is deposed

A.D. 1126 Northern China falls to the Chin, invaders from the northeast

A.D. 1279 Sung dynasty falls to Mongols

C. A.D. 29 Jesus is crucified

A.D. 100 Moche civilization develops in South America

C. A.D. 391 Christianity declared official religion of Roman Empire

A.D. 449 Anglo-Saxon tribes invade England

A.D. 476 Fall of Western Roman Empire

C. A.D. 570 Birth of Muhammad

A.D. 750 Ancient kingdom of Ghana becomes an empire

A.D. 794 Beginning of Japan's Heian period

A.D. 1054 The Christian Church divides

A.D. 1066 Norman conquest of England ➤

The Chinese have made numerous contributions to art, science, medicine, technology, agriculture, philosophy, and mathematics. Many of the important inventions and ideas that first developed in ancient China still have an impact on life in the 21st century. How many of these Chinese innovations affect your daily life?

Philosophy

Although Lao-tzu's *Tao Te Ching* dates from about the 6th century B.C., his ideas still influence thought and literature around the world. Many contemporary authors have very loosely applied the teachings of the Tao to such unlikely subjects as how to train cats and dogs and how to practice effective leadership. The **yin-yang** diagram, a popular image today, symbolizes the unity of the Tao.

Eating and Drinking

The art of making **porcelain** developed in China about 800. Made from a special clay and a mineral found only in China, this highly prized pottery became known as china. **Tea,** made from the leaves of the tea plant, was first popularized by the ancient Chinese.

Gingerroot

Medicine

As early as 2500 B.C. the Chinese developed the practice of **acupuncture.** Needles are inserted at specific points on the body to restore the balance of energy in the body. Acupuncture has been in continuous use in China and now is practiced in many parts of the world. Extensive use of herbs has also been part of Chinese medicine for centuries. Herbs have been used to treat and prevent conditions such as diabetes, high blood pressure, and lack of appetite. **Herbal medicine** is in wide use in the 21st century.

Entertainment

The Chinese invented the **kite** about 2,000 years ago. Kites were used for military purposes as well as for pleasure. The **yo-yo** and **playing cards** originated in China also. Gunpowder was invented by the Chinese about 850 and later was used to make **fireworks,** which were called fire trees, flame flowers, or peach blossoms.

Inventions

About the 1st century B.C., the Chinese invented the **wheelbarrow,** which they called the wooden ox. Other significant Chinese inventions include the **collar harness** for horses (3rd century B.C.); **paper** (2nd century A.D.); **matches** (6th century A.D.); the mechanical **clock** and movable **type** (11th century A.D.); and the magnetic **compass** (12th century A.D.).

Moral Teaching Through Literature

How would you convey an important message about right and wrong to your classmates? Would you print a slogan on a T-shirt? prepare a public-service announcement for radio or TV? design a button or a bumper sticker? In ancient civilizations around the world, such messages were often conveyed through **didactic literature**—literature that instructs its readers.

In didactic literature, writers teach lessons about how to live a moral life. They give their views about what is right and good, focusing on such qualities as honesty, courage, wisdom, and kindness. Sometimes they state their ideas directly, as in Horace's poem "Better to live, Licinius, . . ." At other times, they present their teachings by means of examples, as in the parable of the Prodigal Son in the New Testament.

Ancient Chinese and Japanese writers were among those who used literature to communicate their ideas about what they considered to be right and wrong. Philosophers and religious teachers in China and Japan recognized the power of literature to convey the moral ideals they followed and to persuade readers to act in certain ways. They and their followers expressed their teachings in various forms, including maxims, anecdotes, and parables.

Maxim

A **maxim** is a statement of a general truth about human behavior, perhaps offering some practical advice as well. Maxims vary in length from one or two brief sentences to a short paragraph. They are writers' attempts to put the spotlight on the right way to live—on what ideals to pursue and what actions and attitudes to avoid.

Some maxims are phrased in a particularly pointed and witty way. Because of their clever yet simple structure, such maxims—sometimes called **aphorisms**—are easy to recall and to memorize. An example is Confucius' statement "To study without thinking is futile. To think without studying is dangerous."

> Zigong asked: "Is there any single word that could guide one's entire life?" The Master said: "Should it not be *reciprocity?* What you do not wish for yourself, do not do to others."
>
> —Confucius, *Analects*

> If you look to others for fulfillment, you will never truly be fulfilled. If your happiness depends on money, you will never be happy with yourself.
>
> —Lao-tzu, *Tao Te Ching*

> If you make the acquisition and retention of goods or status your aim in life, this is a way to anxiety and sorrow.
>
> —Musō Soseki, *Dream Conversations*

On the T-shirt: **Practice Random Acts of Kindness**

Anecdote

An **anecdote** is a brief story that focuses on a single interesting event, sometimes taken from the life of a real person. The event is meant to illustrate a particular truth or teaching. The Taoist philosopher Chuang Tzu used many delightful anecdotes to convey his ideas and reflections about the nature of the world.

Chuang Tzu said, "Once upon a time I dreamed myself a butterfly, floating like petals in the air, happy to be doing as I pleased, no longer aware of myself! But soon enough I awoke and then, frantically clutching myself, Chuang Tzu I was! I wonder: Was Chuang Tzu dreaming himself the butterfly, or was the butterfly dreaming itself Chuang Tzu? Of course, if you take Chuang Tzu and the butterfly together, then there's a difference between them. But that difference is only due to their changing material forms."

—Chuang Tzu, *Chuang Tzu*

Parable

A **parable** is also a brief story, but its teaching is more pointed. Each plot detail is intended to illustrate an aspect of some moral truth. Early Japanese writers used parables to convey important concepts of Zen Buddhism.

"You are wise brothers," he told them. "You know what is right and what is not right. You may go somewhere else to study if you wish, but this poor brother does not even know right from wrong. Who will teach him if I do not? I am going to keep him here even if all the rest of you leave."

A torrent of tears cleansed the face of the brother who had stolen. All desire to steal had vanished.

—"Right and Wrong"

YOUR TURN What are some other examples of literature that you have read in which morals are taught? What standards of behavior are encouraged? Did the writers include maxims, anecdotes, or parables?

Strategies for Reading: Didactic Literature

1. Notice the form of the work you are reading. Is it a maxim? an anecdote? a parable?

2. Identify the writer's message. Is it stated directly, or is it implied? Write a paraphrase of it.

3. Look for patterns of repetition, figurative language, and imagery. How does the writer help you remember the main point he or she is trying to communicate?

4. Monitor your reading strategies, and modify them when your understanding breaks down. Remember to use the strategies for active reading: **predict, visualize, connect, question, clarify,** and **evaluate.**

from the

ANALECTS *Confucius*

Confucius
551–479 B.C.

Surprising Contrasts

Confucius did not write a book, he failed to gain the political reforms he longed for, and at times he endured poverty and threats on his life. Yet his ideas became the foundation of Chinese thought and society for more than 2,000 years. Born to poor parents of noble ancestry, he showed a great love of learning from an early age, and he viewed himself as a scholar by the time he was 15. He sought out instruction in the Chinese classical arts and traditions, including music, archery, math, charioteering, calligraphy, poetry, and history.

Failed Ambitions Confucius was born at a time of crisis and violence in China. He had an abiding passion to restore the order and moral living of earlier times to his society. For many years he hoped to develop enough political power to put his ideas into practice. But although he was active in politics, he was never able to gain the power he sought. At one point he went into self-imposed exile from his home state of Lu for almost 12 years, advising rulers in other states and spreading his ideas on education and moral order.

Wise Teacher Despite Confucius' failure to change the political structure of his time, his reputation as a teacher grew. He broke new ground by offering his teaching not only to the aristocracy but also to people of other classes. He taught that the authority to rule should come from moral commitment, not from hereditary status. He eventually gained a large group of disciples, or followers, who revered him for his ideas on the importance of good character and the need for order and authority in all areas of life. It was his disciples who preserved his ideas and sayings, which were written down in the form known today as the *Analects*.

For a humanities activity, click on:

Build Background

Lasting Legacy The *Analects* (*analect* means "a selection") is a collection of about 500 sayings, dialogues, and brief stories, which was put together over a period of many years following Confucius' death. The *Analects* presents Confucius' teachings on how people should live to create an orderly and just society. Over time, Confucian thought became the basis for the Chinese system of government and remained a part of Chinese life into the 20th century.

Confucius' view that true authority to rule comes from a commitment to moral living, not from an aristocratic birth, was revolutionary for his time. This view meant that rulers must have high standards for themselves and must care about what is best for their subjects. It also meant that all educated people had a responsibility to act with loyalty, courtesy, and respect. Three of the most important concepts in Confucius' teachings are humanity (*jen*), gentleman (*chün-tzu*), and ritual (*li*).

Key Confucian Concepts

- **Humanity** The concept of humanity represents the highest ideal for moral behavior in Confucian thought. Humanity is especially concerned with how a person behaves toward others. It is demonstrated in such attitudes as respect, truthfulness, generosity, and love. According to Confucius, humanity is the most important quality to have.

- **Gentleman** In Confucian thought, the word *gentleman* refers not to a man of aristocratic birth but to a person who is committed to an ethical life. An aristocrat could lose the right to be called a gentleman, and an ordinary person could become a gentleman. This shift in meaning reflects Confucius' teaching that the moral life is more important than social status.

- **Ritual** The term *ritual* covers all of what Confucius viewed as proper conduct. It includes everything from everyday manners to religious observances. Confucius thought that the observance of ritual was essential to a sense of order and respect in society.

Connect to Your Life

The *Analects* offers guidance about what is most important in life. What sources of wisdom and guidance are important to you in your life? family members? friends? books? teachers? Jot down three people or writings that you rely on, and note the reasons each one is important to you.

Focus Your Reading

LITERARY TERM: MAXIM

A **maxim** is a short, concise statement that expresses a general truth or rule of conduct. Maxims condense important ideas into memorable language that gets the reader's attention. The following section from the *Analects* is an example of a maxim:

> *Don't worry if people don't recognize your merits; worry that you may not recognize theirs.*

As you read Confucius' thoughts and advice, look for statements that could be considered maxims.

ACTIVE READING: ANALYZING MAXIMS

When reading a maxim, you need to decide if it is true to life and how it relates to your own experiences.

READER'S NOTEBOOK As you read the *Analects,* write down the maxims you find in a chart like the following. In one column, list maxims that are primarily concerned with individual behavior. In the second, list those that involve relationships with others.

Individual Behavior	Relationships with Others
"To study without thinking . . ." (2.15)	

from the
Analects
Confucius
Translated by Simon Leys

Confucius. China Confucius/ Chinakongzi.

The Master[1] said: "Don't worry if people don't recognize your merits; worry that you may not recognize theirs." (1.16)

The Master said: "He who rules by virtue is like the polestar,[2] which remains unmoving in its mansion while all the other stars revolve respectfully around it." (2.1)

Ziyou[3] asked about filial piety.[4] The Master said: "Nowadays people think they are dutiful sons when they feed their parents. Yet they also feed their dogs and horses. Unless there is respect, where is the difference?" (2.7)

The Master said: "To study without thinking is futile.[5] To think without studying is dangerous." (2.15)

Lord Ji Kang[6] asked: "What should I do in order to make the people respectful, loyal, and zealous?"[7] The Master said: "Approach them with dignity and they will be respectful. Be yourself a good son and a kind father, and they will be loyal. Raise the good and train the incompetent, and they will be zealous." (2.20)

The Master said: "Authority without generosity, ceremony without reverence, mourning without grief—these, I cannot bear to contemplate."[8] (3.26)

The Master said: "I have never seen a man who truly loved goodness and hated evil. Whoever truly loves goodness would put nothing above it; whoever truly hates evil would practice goodness in such a way that no evil could enter him. Has anyone ever devoted all his strength to goodness just for one day? No one ever has, and yet it is not for want of strength—there may be people who do not have even the small amount of strength it takes, but I have never seen any." (4.6)

---

1. **Master:** Confucius.
2. **polestar:** the North Star, which, unlike other stars, appears to remain in the same place in the sky as the earth rotates.
3. **Ziyou** (dzŭ′yoo′): a younger disciple of Confucius, known for his literary talent.
4. **filial piety** (fĭl′ē-əl pī′ĭ-tē): respect and reverence for one's parents and ancestors—an important concept in Confucianism.
5. **futile** (fyoot′l): useless.
6. **Lord Ji Kang** (jē′ käng′): a powerful official in Confucius' home state of Lu.
7. **zealous** (zĕl′əs): enthusiastic.
8. **contemplate:** think about; consider.

A Literary Gathering, Han Huang. Palace Museum, Beijing.

HUMANITIES CONNECTION This painting, done on silk, shows a group of scholars reading and writing. A mastery of literary skills was necessary for anyone wanting to hold a government position. The figure in the lower right is a servant grinding ink.

The Master said: "Do not worry if you are without a position; worry lest you do not deserve a position. Do not worry if you are not famous; worry lest you do not deserve to be famous." (4.14)

The Master said: "Set your heart upon the Way;[9] rely upon moral power; follow goodness; enjoy the arts." (7.6)

The Master said: "Without ritual,[10] courtesy is tiresome; without ritual, prudence[11] is timid; without ritual, bravery is quarrelsome; without ritual, frankness[12] is hurtful. When gentlemen treat their kin generously, common people are attracted to goodness; when old ties are not forgotten, common people are not fickle."[13] (8.2)

The Master said: "A gentleman abides by three principles which I am unable to follow: his humanity[14] knows no anxiety; his wisdom knows no hesitation; his courage knows no fear." Zigong[15] said: "Master, you have just drawn your own portrait." (14.28)

Zigong asked: "Is there any single word that could guide one's entire life?" The Master said: "Should it not be *reciprocity?* What you do not wish for yourself, do not do to others." (15.24)

---

9. **Way:** ideal pattern of behavior.

10. **ritual:** an important Confucian concept, as is "gentlemen" in the next sentence (see Building Background).

11. **prudence:** caution and forethought.

12. **frankness:** blunt, honest expression.

13. **fickle:** quick to change their mind or opinion.

14. **humanity:** virtuous behavior toward others (see Building Background).

15. **Zigong** (dzŭ′gŏŏng′): a diplomat and merchant who was one of Confucius' most dedicated disciples.

Thinking through the LITERATURE

Connect to the Literature

1. What Do You Think?
Were the teachings in the *Analects* surprising in any way? Discuss your thoughts with a classmate.

Comprehension Check
• What kinds of behavior does Confucius talk about in the *Analects*?
• What does Confucius mean by the word *reciprocity*?

Think Critically

2. What kind of person does Confucius seem to be?

THINK ABOUT

• the kinds of behavior he advises people to pursue
• his attitude toward the listener or reader
• how he views himself

3. Do you think Confucius views human nature in an optimistic or a pessimistic way? Explain your opinion.

4. ACTIVE READING: ANALYZING MAXIMS Look back at the chart you created in your 📖 **READER'S NOTEBOOK.** Does Confucius seem more concerned with individual behavior or with behavior toward others?

5. Do you agree with all of Confucius' teachings? Explain your opinion.

Extend Interpretations

6. Critic's Corner One critic suggests that reading the *Analects* is like being invited into a conversation with Confucius. Do you think this is a helpful way of approaching these excerpts? Explain your answer.

7. Connect to Life Choose one of Confucius' sayings that you think relates directly to life today. Explain your choice.

LITERARY ANALYSIS: MAXIM

A **maxim** offers insight into how life should be lived. Maxims can help you evaluate your own behavior and the values and goals of your society. They can be a gentle reminder of what is good, or they can be a sharp criticism of weakness or selfishness.

Paired Activity With a classmate, write three maxims about how you think people should live. Be as specific as you can. Try to make your maxims relate to attitudes and behavior in your family, school, and community. For example, try writing a maxim that relates to popular entertainment, to using the Internet, or to doing homework. Your maxims can be serious or humorous.

from the

Tao Te Ching

LAO-TZU

Lao-tzu
500s B.C.

Founder of Taoism Did Lao-tzu (lou′dzŭ′) really exist? No one knows. Although a person named Lao-tzu is credited with being the first philosopher of Taoism (dou′ĭz′əm), the details of his life are a mystery. Legend claims that Lao-tzu (which means "Old Master" or "Old Philosopher") had a miraculous birth and lived to be 160. The main source of information about his life is a biography written about 100 B.C. by the Chinese historian Ssu-ma Ch'ien (sŏŏ′mä′ chē-ĕn′). According to this work, Lao-tzu was the court archivist, or keeper of the sacred books, during the later years of the Chou dynasty. At one time he was supposedly visited by Confucius. The account says that Lao-tzu advised Confucius to get rid of his "air of pride and many desires." Confucius later told his students that Lao-tzu was like a dragon that "rides on the winds and clouds and ascends to heaven."

Tao Te Ching The biography describes Lao-tzu as a person who sought virtue and harmony with the universe rather than fame. When he realized that the Chou dynasty was on the decline, he set out for the western border of China. A border guard begged Lao-tzu to set down his teachings in a book. Lao-tzu then wrote the *Tao Te Ching* (dou′ dě jǐng′), the main expression of Taoist thought. Nothing more was ever heard of him.

Lasting Influence Most scholars now think that the *Tao Te Ching* was written in the third or fourth century B.C., probably by more than one author. It will never be known if Lao-tzu had anything to do with the writings. Nevertheless, he has been a revered figure in China through many centuries, seen as a philosopher by some and as a saint and even a god by others. The teachings of Taoism have been a prominent force in Chinese civilization. The Taoist emphasis on virtue, simplicity, and harmony with nature has been valued for more than 2,000 years.

Build Background

Small but Powerful The *Tao Te Ching*, a short book of about 81 pages, is probably the best-known work in Chinese literature. After the Bible, it is the most translated book in history. The *Tao Te Ching* is concerned with teaching what is referred to as the Way.

Confucian thought focuses on specific actions and emphasizes respect for authority and an orderly society. In contrast, Taoist thought focuses on the Way, or Tao, which is seen as the source and purpose of all existence. The Tao gives birth to all living things, but it also becomes part of every living thing. It is a force that moves all things toward being in harmony with their true nature.

To live according to the Tao, a person needs to be close to nature and live in simplicity and joy. An important idea in the *Tao Te Ching* is that of *wu-wei* (woō'wā'), or nonaction. This concept means that instead of being competitive, ambitious, and active, a person should just let things happen. A simple life and freedom from desires are said to help people discover the Way.

Because of the nature of Taoist thought, seemingly contradictory statements run throughout the *Tao Te Ching* and challenge most readers. For example, here is a teaching from passage 22:

> *If you want to be reborn,*
> *let yourself die.*
> *If you want to be given everything,*
> *give everything up.*

Each reader is invited to ponder these mysterious sayings and decide what they might mean in his or her own life.

Woman practicing tai chi, a form of movement that expresses the principles of the *Tao Te Ching*

Connect to Your Life

It is important to most people to find some meaning in their lives. Think of a person who seems to have a strong sense of meaning in his or her life. What does this person value? How does this person act toward others? Describe the person to your classmates.

Focus Your Reading

LITERARY ANALYSIS: PARADOX

A **paradox** is a statement that seems contradictory but is actually true. The reader has to solve the puzzle of the apparent contradiction in order to understand what is being said. An example of a paradox is this statement from the New Testament:

> *For whosoever will save his life shall lose it:*
> *. . . (Matthew 16:25)*

As you read the three excerpts from the *Tao Te Ching,* look for examples of paradox.

ACTIVE READING: INTERPRETING PARADOXES

When you come upon a paradox in your reading, you face the challenge of trying to figure out what it means. For example, in the biblical quotation above, the idea that if you want to save your life you will lose it doesn't seem to make sense. To understand the paradox, think about all the ways to interpret the words *save* and *lose.* In this case, saving one's life might mean being selfish. By not sharing your life with others, you lose meaning in life.

READER'S NOTEBOOK In a chart like the one below, write down any paradoxes that you identify as you read these excerpts. In each paradox, circle the words that seem contradictory. Then explain the paradox.

Paradox	Meaning

from the Tao Te Ching

Lao-tzu

Translated by Stephen Mitchell

The Tao never does anything,
yet through it all things are done.

If powerful men and women
could center themselves in it,
the whole world would be transformed
by itself, in its natural rhythms.
People would be content
with their simple, everyday lives,
in harmony, and free of desire.

When there is no desire,
all things are at peace.

Detail of *Lady with Fan* (mid 19th century), Ju Qing.
Album leaf, ink & color on silk, 27 cm × 36.5 cm.
Collection of the Art Museum of the Chinese University
of Hong Kong.

Fame or integrity:[1] which is more important?
Money or happiness: which is more valuable?
Success or failure: which is more destructive?

If you look to others for fulfillment,
you will never truly be fulfilled.
If your happiness depends on money,
you will never be happy with yourself.

Be content with what you have;
rejoice in the way things are.
When you realize there is nothing lacking,
the whole world belongs to you.

---

1. integrity (ĭn-tĕg′rĭ-tē): personal honesty
and uprightness.

Lao-tzu on an ox (early/middle 16th century), Zhang Lu. Hanging scroll, ink on paper, 101.5 cm × 55.3 cm. Collection of the National Palace Museum, Taipei, Taiwan, Republic of China. Bridgeman Art Library, London.

HUMANITIES CONNECTION This portrayal of Lao-tzu pictures the Taoist philosopher as a free spirit making a journey, following a fluttering butterfly. The scroll he is carrying represents the *Tao Te Ching*.

The best athlete
wants his opponent at his best.
The best general
enters the mind of his enemy.
The best businessman
serves the communal good.[2]
The best leader
follows the will of the people.

All of them embody
the virtue of non-competition.
Not that they don't love to compete,
but they do it in the spirit of play.
In this they are like children
and in harmony with the Tao.

2. **communal good:** welfare of the community.

from CHUANG TZU

The Fish Rejoice
Chuang Tzu

Translated by Moss Roberts

The writer Chuang Tzu[1] believed that all living things are equal. In this tale, the human and animal worlds connect as Chuang Tzu rejoices with the fish.

Chuang Tzu and his close friend Hui Tzu[2] were enjoying each other's company on the shores of the Hao.[3] Chuang Tzu said, "The flashing fish are out enjoying each other, too, swimming gracefully this way and that. Such is the joy of fish!"

"You're no fish," said Hui Tzu. "How could you know their joy?"

"You're no Chuang Tzu," said Chuang Tzu. "How could you know I don't know the joy of fish?"

"If 'I am no Chuang Tzu,'" said Hui Tzu, "means 'I don't know Chuang Tzu,' then to be consistent, you don't know the joy of fish if you aren't a fish!"

"Let's go back to the beginning," said Chuang Tzu. "Your own question, 'How could you know the joy of fish?' already made an assumption about my knowing it! I don't have to jump in the water to know!"

---

1. **Chuang Tzu** (jwäng′ dzŭ′): a Taoist philosopher of the fourth century B.C., author of a book (also called *Chuang Tzu*) that is one of the main works of Taoist literature.

2. **Hui Tzu** (hwē′ dzŭ′): a Confucian scholar and senior minister at the royal court, with whom Chuang Tzu had a friendly rivalry.

3. **Hao** (hou): a river in the province of Anhwei in eastern China.

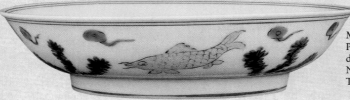

Ming dish (16th century). Porcelain with overglaze enamel decoration. Collection of the National Palace Museum, Taipei, Taiwan, Republic of China.

Connect to the Literature

1. **What Do You Think?**
   Which of the teachings do you most agree with? Explain your choice.

   Comprehension Check
   - Name one contrast that is presented in passage 37.
   - What seems to be the Taoist attitude toward money as expressed in passage 44?
   - What is identified as a virtue in passage 68?

Think Critically

2. In passage 37, the writer refers to "powerful men and women." What do you think is the Taoist attitude toward being a powerful person?

   THINK ABOUT
   - the Taoist emphasis on living a simple life in passage 37
   - the warning in passage 44 that "if you look to others for fulfillment, you will never truly be fulfilled"
   - the reference to competition in passage 68

3. According to your understanding of Taoist thought, what do you think are the correct answers to the questions posed in passage 44? Explain your ideas.

4. In passage 68, the writer speaks of competing in a "spirit of play." What do you think he means?

5. **ACTIVE READING: INTERPRETING PARADOXES** With a partner, compare the charts you created in your **READER'S NOTEBOOK**. Discuss the paradoxes you identified and their meanings. How similar were your interpretations?

Extend Interpretations

6. **Comparing Texts** Reread "The Fish Rejoice" on page 444. Which of the excerpts from the *Tao Te Ching* do you think relates most closely to this tale? Support your ideas with details from the selections.

7. **Comparing Texts** Compare the passages you have read from the *Tao Te Ching* with the selections from the *Analects* on pages 437–438. How do the two schools of thought differ in their teachings about conduct in everyday life? How do they compare in their attitudes toward leadership and authority?

8. **Connect to Life** How would life in modern American society change if people lived according to Taoist teachings? Do you think the change would be for the better? Explain.

LITERARY ANALYSIS: PARADOX

The Tao Te Ching contains many **paradoxes**—statements that seem contradictory but nevertheless express truths. The use of paradox forces the reader to interpret the meaning of the passages. Understanding the paradox brings the reader closer to an understanding of the Tao. Consider the paradox in the following lines from passage 44:

When you realize there is nothing lacking,
the whole world belongs to you.

To understand the paradox, you must think about what "the whole world" probably means in Taoist thought. The paradox helps teach the Taoist principle of being content with a simple life.

Paired Activity Read the following lines from passage 33 of the *Tao Te Ching*.

If you realize that you have enough,
you are truly rich.
If you stay in the center
and embrace death with your whole heart,
you will endure forever.

With a partner, identify the paradoxes in the passage. Discuss possible interpretations of each paradox. Then write a brief paraphrase of each one.

from the

BOOK OF ODES

Build Background

Ancient Masterpieces The *Book of Odes* is a group of 305 poems that are the most ancient works still in existence in Chinese literature. This collection was put together around the sixth century B.C., but some of the poems may date back to 1000 B.C. The poems were originally songs, set to music that has since been lost. The full history of how the poems first came to be and who collected them is not known. The glimpses they give of Chinese people in ancient times, however, make those people come to life.

The poems in the *Book of Odes* range from folk songs depicting everyday life to songs of court life and stately hymns. This is not a literature of heroes only. The voices of the common people, women as well as men, are heard. In the folk songs, they express their hopes and disappointments as they go about their daily tasks, as they search for love, and as they go to war. The court poems have many of the same subjects and concerns as the folk songs, but they reflect a more aristocratic lifestyle. The hymns, which include the oldest poems, were used in religious rituals.

In Chinese culture, the *Book of Odes* has been as important as national epics have been to the civilizations of Greece and Rome. The philosopher Confucius considered the poems an essential source of moral teaching. The *Book of Odes* has also been a model of poetic style in Chinese literature. The Chinese word for poetry, *shih* (shŭ), came from the original name of the work—*Shih Ching* ("Classic of Poetry"). These poems have, in fact, been so revered throughout the history of China that, until early in the 20th century, they had to be memorized in their entirety by all Chinese schoolchildren. Today the poems are appreciated for their beauty, freshness, and lyrical qualities.

Connect to Your Life

The two court poems that you are about to read express deep feelings about love and war. Think of a current popular song or type of music that conveys strong emotions. What features of the music appeal to the listener's experience and emotions? Compare your ideas with those of your classmates.

Focus Your Reading

LITERARY ANALYSIS: REPETITION
Poetry from an oral tradition that was sung usually uses **repetition**—sounds, words, and groups of words that are repeated for emphasis. As you read the poems, look for the repeated elements.

ACTIVE READING: READING POETRY ALOUD
Reading a poem aloud helps you hear the rhythms, repetition, and sound effects. Often, hearing the sounds of a poem allows you to better understand what it means.

READER'S NOTEBOOK After you have read these poems once or twice silently, read them aloud. Jot down one or two aspects of each poem that became clearer or more forceful to you. Use a chart like the one below to record your comments for each poem.

"Mulberry on the Lowland"	
Lines	**Comments on Reading Aloud**
4, 8, 12, and 16	*helps you feel the strength of the speaker's emotions*

from the Book of Odes
Mulberry on the Lowland
Translated by Arthur Waley

The mulberry on the lowland, how graceful!
Its leaves, how tender!
Now that I have seen my lord,
Ah, what delight!

5 The mulberry on the lowland, how graceful!
Its leaves, how glossy!
Now that I have seen my lord,
What joy indeed!

The mulberry on the lowland, how graceful,
10 Its leaves, how fresh!
Now I have seen my lord,
His high fame holds fast.

Love that is felt in the heart,
Why should it not be told in words?
15 To the core of my heart I treasure him,
Could not ever cease to love him.

1 mulberry: a tree valued in China because its leaves are the food of silkworms, the moth larvae that produce the fiber from which silk cloth is made.

Figure of sitting woman. Imperial Museum, Beijing. Robert Harding Picture Library, London.

HUMANITIES CONNECTION This figure of a woman was found in 1964 in a cotton field near the tomb of the first emperor of China. Rulers often had a variety of figures buried with them to help them in their afterlife. This piece would have represented an attendant or servant.

Horseman (second century A.D.). Bronze. National Museum, Beijing.
Photograph copyright © Erich Lessing/Art Resource, New York.

HUMANITIES CONNECTION This figure of an infantryman was one of three discovered in 1969 at the site of the tomb of a general. The figure is carrying a weapon called a halberd, which has both a blade and a spike.

from the Book of Odes

We Pick Ferns, We Pick Ferns

Translated by Burton Watson

We pick ferns, we pick ferns,
for the ferns are sprouting now:
oh to go home, to go home
before the year is over!
5 No rooms, no houses for us,
all because of the Hsien-yün,
no time to kneel or sit down,
all because of the Hsien-yün.

We pick ferns, we pick ferns,
10 the ferns now are tender:
oh to go home, to go home!
Our hearts are saddened,
our sad hearts smolder and burn.
We are hungry, we are thirsty,
15 no limit to our border duty,
no way to send home for news.

We pick ferns, we pick ferns,
now the ferns have grown tough:
oh to go home, to go home
20 in the closing months of the year!
The king's business allows no slacking,
no leisure to kneel or rest.
Our sad hearts are sick to death,
this journey of ours has no return!

6 Hsien-yün (shyŭn'yün'): fierce tribes who invaded China from the north and were finally driven back around 800 B.C.

Ink drawing. Collection of National Palace Museum, Taipei, Taiwan, Republic of China.

25 What splendor is here?
    The splendor of cherry flowers.
    What chariot is this?
    The chariot of our lord.
    The war chariot is yoked,
30 four stallions sturdy and strong.
    How would we dare to stop and rest?
    In one month, three engagements!

    We yoke those four stallions,
    four stallions stalwart and strong,
35 for our lord to ride behind,
    for lesser men to shield.
    Four stallions stately,
    ivory bow-ends, fish-skin quivers:
    could we drop our guard for a day?
40 The Hsien-yün are fearfully swift!

    Long ago we set out
    when willows were rich and green.
    Now we come back
    through thickly falling snow.
45 Slow slow our march,
    we are thirsty, we are hungry,
    our hearts worn with sorrow,
    no one knows our woe.

38 quivers: cases for carrying arrows.

Connect to the Literature

1. What Do You Think?
Which details from these poems were you able to visualize? Explain your response.

Comprehension Check
- What details about the mulberry tree does the speaker describe in "Mulberry on the Lowland"?
- How do the ferns change during the course of the poem "We Pick Ferns, We Pick Ferns"?

Think Critically

2. Do you think "Mulberry on the Lowland" tells more about the speaker or more about her lord? Explain your answer.

 THINK ABOUT
- what she tells you about her lord
- what she tells you about her feelings

3. How successful is the military campaign in "We Pick Ferns, We Pick Ferns"?

 THINK ABOUT
- how long the campaign seems to have lasted
- the conditions the soldiers face
- what the speaker says about the enemy

4. Why do you think the poet refers to ferns, cherry blossoms, and willows in a poem describing war?

5. ACTIVE READING READING POETRY ALOUD Look back at the notes you made in your 📖 **READER'S NOTEBOOK.** How was your understanding or appreciation of the poems helped by reading them aloud?

Extend Interpretations

6. Critic's Corner One critic has said that readers of the poems in the *Book of Odes* have found a "window into another person's heart, a person like themselves." Do you agree with this statement? Support your answer with details from the poems.

7. Comparing Texts These two poems portray different moods. Identify the mood in each poem, and list three words or phrases in each that help create this mood.

8. Connect to Life In "We Pick Ferns, We Pick Ferns," the speaker describes the loneliness and hardships of going to fight in a war. Do you think 21st-century soldiers face similar difficulties? Explain your answer.

LITERARY ANALYSIS: REPETITION

The **repetition** of various elements in a poem—sounds, words, phrases, or lines—helps to emphasize images or details, make connections between ideas, and create rhythmic patterns. Repetition can unify a poem by creating a clear structure.

Activity Find examples of repetition in "Mulberry on the Lowland" and "We Pick Ferns, We Pick Ferns," and record them in a chart like the one shown. For each example, explain what you think is the purpose of the repetition in the poem. Do you think repetition is more important in one of the poems than in the other? Discuss your conclusions with your classmates.

"Mulberry on the Lowland"	
Examples	**Purpose**
"The mulberry on the lowland, how graceful!" (lines 1, 5, 9)	emphasizes the main image in the poem

Selected Poems

Li Po

Li Po
701–762

Famous Nonconformist

Perhaps the best-known poet of China, Li Po (lē' pō') was a romantic nonconformist who spent most of his life traveling, writing poetry, and enjoying his friends. He was born in central Asia, where his ancestors had gone into exile. Although Li Po and his family returned to China when he was very young, he liked to emphasize his unusual beginnings and to appear as colorful a character as possible. He showed early literary talent, which might have led to a career in government. He never took the imperial civil-service examination, however. Instead, when he was about 19 years old, he began a series of journeys.

Wandering Poet

It is hard to trace exactly the events of Li Po's life. He spent some years as a Taoist recluse in the mountains. He also married at least twice and had children. As he traveled, he became well-known as an intriguing personality, a notorious drinker, and a brilliant poet. He was welcomed wherever he went. In 742, Li Po arrived in the splendid T'ang capital of Ch'ang-an, where he was appointed a court poet. However, he was dismissed two years later, possibly because of his outrageous behavior. In 744, he met the poet Tu Fu, who greatly admired him and wrote several poems to and about him.

Turmoil and Change

When rebellion broke out against the emperor in 755, Li Po became involved in political intrigue and suffered imprisonment and exile. He was later pardoned, but he had become sick, and political chaos was still erupting. He continued his travels, sometimes having to flee from rebel uprisings. He died from illness while visiting a relative in the winter of 762. A legend persists that Li Po drowned when he fell from a boat as he tried to embrace the moon's reflection. The whimsical quality of this story captures the hold that Li Po has had on the hearts and imagination of his readers through 13 centuries.

Build Background

Golden Age The T'ang dynasty, especially the years 713–765, saw a flourishing of poetry unequaled in all the history of China. This was brought about in part by the action of the Empress Wu, who made the writing of poetry part of the civil service examinations. More than 2,200 poets were writing at the height of the T'ang period, and the nearly 49,000 poems that have survived are only a portion of their total work.

The two major poets of this period were Li Po and Tu Fu. While Tu Fu tended to be serious and formal in his poetry, Li Po was freewheeling and exuberant. He preferred poetic forms that allowed for variations in rhythm to those requiring strict, regular lines and patterns. He wrote about friendship, drinking, nature, solitude, love, and his yearnings for other times and places.

Three Poems by Li Po

"The River-Merchant's Wife: A Letter" (page 454) belongs to a tradition of Chinese poems portraying women left alone by their lovers. Although the speaker in many Chinese poems is the poet, in this work it is the young woman who has been left behind by her husband.

Probably Li Po's most famous poem is the brief **"Still Night Thoughts"** (page 456), written in his later years. The moon, which is central to this poem, occurs as an image in more than a third of Li Po's poems. For centuries, Chinese schoolchildren were taught to memorize "Still Night Thoughts."

"Gazing at the Lu Mountain Waterfall" (page 457) was written during Li Po's early travels and reflects the Taoist emphasis on living in harmony with nature. The poem provides a clear example of the force and energy that characterize Li Po's poems celebrating the beauty, wonder, and grandeur of the natural world.

Connect to Your Life

In two of the poems you are about to read, the speakers seem to long for those they love, but the speaker of the third seems to prefer solitude. Is it important to have some times of solitude? Is there a difference between solitude and loneliness? Write some of your thoughts about solitude in your journal.

Focus Your Reading

LITERARY ANALYSIS: IMAGERY

The term **imagery** refers to words and phrases that create vivid sensory experiences for the reader. Poets use imagery to make such details as sights and sounds clear and immediate. For example, in line 1 of "The River-Merchant's Wife: A Letter," the poet creates a picture of the speaker as a little girl through her words "my hair was still cut straight across my forehead." This description shows that she had a child's simple haircut, not a more elaborate style appropriate to a young woman.

As you read these poems, note the imagery that makes the descriptions and experiences sharp and memorable.

ACTIVE READING: VISUALIZING

Forming a mental picture from a written description is called **visualizing.** For example, vivid details in a description of a scene from nature help you see that scene in your imagination. In his poems, Li Po provides many details that allow you to visualize the times, places, and people he is writing about.

READER'S NOTEBOOK As you read, fill in a chart like the one below for each poem.

"Still Night Thoughts"	
Detail	**What I Visualize**
"Moonlight in front of my bed" (line 1)	bright moonlight streaming through a window

The River-Merchant's Wife: A Letter

Li Po

Translated by Ezra Pound

While my hair was still cut straight across my forehead
I played about the front gate, pulling flowers.
You came by on bamboo stilts, playing horse,
You walked about my seat, playing with blue plums.
5   And we went on living in the village of Chōkan:
Two small people, without dislike or suspicion.

At fourteen I married My Lord you.
I never laughed, being bashful.
Lowering my head, I looked at the wall.
10   Called to, a thousand times, I never looked back.

At fifteen I stopped scowling,
I desired my dust to be mingled with yours
Forever and forever and forever.
Why should I climb the look out?

15   At sixteen you departed,
You went into far Ku-tō-en, by the river of swirling eddies,
And you have been gone five months.
The monkeys make sorrowful noise overhead.

5 Chōkan (chō′kän): a town near Nanking in eastern China, located on the Yangtze River, China's longest.

14 Why . . . look out?: a reference to the story of a young wife who spent years in a tower, watching for the return of her departed husband.

16 Ku-tō-en (kōō′tō-ĕn′): a narrow, dangerous section of the Yangtze, far upriver from Chōkan; **eddies:** whirlpools.

Woman writing a letter (1640), Min Qiji. From a 17th-century edition of the *Romance of the Western Chamber*. Museum für Ostasiatische Kunst, Cologne, Germany. Inv.-No. R 61.2 [No. 18]. Photograph copyright © Rheinisches Bildarchiv, Cologne.

You dragged your feet when you went out.
20 By the gate now, the moss is grown, the different mosses,
Too deep to clear them away!
The leaves fall early this autumn, in wind.
The paired butterflies are already yellow with August
Over the grass in the West garden;
25 They hurt me. I grow older.
If you are coming down through the narrows of the river
    Kiang,
Please let me know beforehand,
And I will come out to meet you
           As far as Chō-fū-Sa.

26 river Kiang (jyäng): that is, the Yangtze.

29 Chō-fū-Sa (chō′fōō-sä′): "Long Wind Beach," several hundred miles upriver from Chōkan.

Still Night Thoughts
Li Po
Translated by Burton Watson

Moonlight in front of my bed—
I took it for frost on the ground!
I lift my head, gaze at the bright moon,
lower it and dream of home.

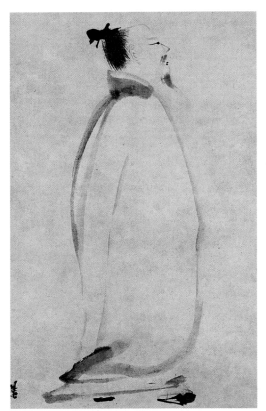

Li Po (Southern Song dynasty), Liang Kai. Hanging scroll,
ink on paper, 31⅔″ × 12⅛″ (80.4 cm × 30.7 cm).
Tokyo National Museum.

Gazing at the Lu Mountain Waterfall

Li Po

Translated by David Hinton

1

Climbing west toward Incense-Burner Peak,
I look south and see a falls of water, a cascade

hanging there, three thousand feet high,
then seething dozens of miles down canyons.

5 Sudden as lightning breaking into flight,
its white rainbow of mystery appears. Afraid

at first the celestial Star River is falling,
splitting and dissolving into cloud heavens,

I look up into force churning in strength,
10 all power, the very workings of Creation.

It keeps ocean winds blowing ceaselessly,
shines a mountain moon back into empty space,

empty space it tumbles and sprays through,
rinsing green cliffs clean on both sides,

15 sending pearls in flight scattering into mist
and whitewater seething down towering rock.

Here, after wandering among these renowned
mountains, the heart grows rich with repose.

Why talk of cleansing elixirs of immortality?
20 Here, the world's dust rinsed from my face,

I'll stay close to what I've always loved,
content to leave that peopled world forever.

1 Incense-Burner Peak: a peak of Lu Mountain in China's Kiangsi province. Seeking to escape a war in his home region, Li Po moved to a town near Lu Mountain for a time.

7 celestial Star River: the Milky Way.

18 repose: rest; calm.

19 elixirs of immortality: magic potions with the power to make people live forever.

2

Sunlight on Incense-Burner kindles violet smoke.
Watching the distant falls hang there, river

25 headwaters plummeting three thousand feet in flight,
I see Star River falling through nine heavens.

Early Spring, Kuo Hsi. Collection of the National Palace Museum, Taipei, Taiwan, Republic of China.

HUMANITIES CONNECTION Landscape painting flourished in the 11th and 12th centuries and is considered the finest of all Chinese painting. Its forms and styles continue to influence traditional painting in China to this day.

Thinking *through the* LITERATURE

Connect to the Literature

1. What Do You Think?
Which of these poems appealed to you the most?

Comprehension Check
- In "The River-Merchant's Wife: A Letter," why is the wife writing a letter?
- In "Still Night Thoughts," what does the speaker say the moonlight looks like?
- What kind of scene does the poet describe in "Gazing at the Lu Mountain Waterfall"?

Think Critically

2. How would you describe the relationship between the speaker of "The River-Merchant's Wife: A Letter" and her husband?

- how long they have known each other
- the description in line 19 of her husband's attitude when he left home
- how she feels about his absence

3. What do you think are the speaker's feelings in "Still Night Thoughts"?

4. In "Gazing at the Lu Mountain Waterfall," what effect does seeing the waterfall have on the speaker?

- his description of the waterfall in line 6
- what he means by "the heart grows rich with repose" (line 18)
- his statement in lines 21 and 22

5. ACTIVE READING: VISUALIZING Look back at the charts you completed in your ▌READER'S NOTEBOOK. How did visualizing the scenes in these poems help you understand the experiences being described?

Extend Interpretations

6. Comparing Texts Look again at "Mulberry on the Lowland" (page 447) from the *Book of Odes.* What similarities and differences are there between the feelings of the speaker in that poem and those of the speaker in "The River-Merchant's Wife: A Letter"?

7. Connect to Life In much of Li Po's poetry, nature is a source of renewal and serenity. How do people in today's world view nature?

LITERARY ANALYSIS: IMAGERY

One of the most important elements of any poem is its **imagery,** the words and phrases that create vivid sensory experiences for the reader. Most images are visual, but imagery may also appeal to the other four senses: hearing, smell, taste, and touch. In the following lines from "Gazing at the Lu Mountain Waterfall," the imagery appeals to sight, hearing, and touch:

empty space it tumbles and sprays through,
rinsing green cliffs clean on both sides,

Paired Activity With a classmate, list examples of imagery from Li Po's poems in a chart like the one below. Then discuss how the imagery helps convey particular emotions, scenes, and ideas.

Image	Poem/Line(s)	Sense(s) Appealed To
"empty space . . . on both sides"	"Gazing at the . . .," lines 13–14	sight, hearing, touch

Writing Options

1. Mood Poem Using "Still Night Thoughts" as a model, write a four-line poem that expresses a mood. Choose a central image that helps create that mood. Aim for simplicity. Place the poem in your

🗁 **Working Portfolio.**

2. Notes for a Plot Think of "The River-Merchant's Wife: A Letter" as the beginning of a short story. Write notes describing how the story might develop. Keep in mind the elements of character, setting, and conflict as you imagine possible details.

3. Descriptive Paragraph
Imagine that you are preparing a travel guidebook for the Lu Mountain area. For your guidebook, write a prose description of the scene Li Po portrays in "Gazing at the Lu Mountain Waterfall." Try to make your description appealing but accurate.

Writing Handbook
See page R27: Descriptive Writing.

Activities & Explorations

1. Film Score Suppose you have been asked to provide music for a short film based on "The River-Merchant's Wife: A Letter." Look for recordings of pieces of music that you think would help convey the events and emotions described in the poem. Play them in a sequence that matches them to the developments in the wife's story. ~ MUSIC

2. Landscape Painting Create a painting or drawing based on some detail of nature described in one of the poems. The subject of the painting can be a small detail or a wide view. ~ ART

3. Dramatic Reading Prepare a dramatic reading of one of the two long poems. You may want to do this with one or more other students. Consider using costumes or props to enhance your presentation. ~ SPEAKING AND LISTENING

Inquiry & Research

1. Cosmopolitan City
Ch'ang-an, the capital of the T'ang empire, was the largest, richest, and most sophisticated city of its day. It had a population of 2 million, and it was a center of learning, art, trade, religion, and government. Investigate what life in this city was like at its height in the T'ang period.

2. Powerful Empress
Investigate the rule of the Empress Wu, the only Chinese woman to reign in her own right. Find out how she came to power and what kind of leader she was.

RESEARCH STARTER
CLASSZONE.COM

Translating Chinese Poetry

Translators of poetry want to convey the meaning of the original poems as closely as possible. They also, however, wish to produce the most finely crafted poems possible, which may require them to take some liberties with the originals. Translators of Chinese poetry have additional challenges. Unlike English, Chinese does not have an alphabet. Instead, it has about 40,000 characters—symbols that represent words or parts of words. To read Chinese, a person must have memorized thousands of characters.

A further challenge in translating Chinese poetry involves the verbal structure of the poems. There are few conjunctions or pronouns. Verbs do not have tenses. Nouns do not show number. The subject of a sentence may be omitted. Not surprisingly, translators sometimes differ in how they interpret the same sequences of words.

The following are lines 25 and 26 of "The River-Merchant's Wife: A Letter." Under the Chinese characters is a character-by-character translation by Wai-lim Yip.

感	此	傷	妾	心
moved-by	*this*	*hurt*	*my*	*heart*

坐	愁	紅	顏	老
sit	*grieve*	*red*	*face*	*old*

In his verse translation below, Wai-lim Yip adds connecting words, replaces several words, and develops complete sentences to express his interpretation of the lines. (*These* refers to the butterflies described in the previous lines.)

These smite my heart.
I sit down worrying and youth passes away.

Now compare two more translations of the same lines.

They hurt me. I grow older.
    —Ezra Pound

And, because of all this, my heart is breaking
And I fear for my bright cheeks, lest they fade.
    —Witter Bynner

You can see that each translator makes different decisions about words and structure to convey the meaning of the original and to create a distinctive style.

Activity Look again at the character-by-character translation of the two lines from Li Po's poem, and reread the three verse translations. Then try writing your own translation of the lines. You can choose different words or combine words or phrases that the other translators have used.

SELECTED POEMS
Tu Fu

Tu Fu
712–770

Failed Political Career Tu Fu is considered by many readers and critics to be the greatest of all Chinese poets. Unfortunately, his poetic genius was not generally recognized during his own lifetime. He was also unlucky in his political career. Born into a poor scholarly family, Tu Fu received a classical education. Yet as a young man he repeatedly failed the examinations in prose and poetry that would have earned him a high position in the imperial government. Although he eventually held a series of minor posts, Tu Fu endured a life of poverty and uncertainty.

Witness to War In 755, Tu Fu was granted a position in the imperial court, in the capital city of Ch'ang-an. Before he could begin serving, however, the city was attacked by rebel forces. Fearful for his family's safety, Tu Fu moved his wife and children from their home in Feng-hsien, about 80 miles northeast of Ch'ang-an, to Fu-chou. He describes this journey in "Song of P'eng-ya" (page 468). The war and its aftermath continued to affect Tu Fu for many years. Constantly searching for government work, the poet wandered from place to place. He was often forced to hide from the rebels or flee before their advancing armies. Illnesses, including asthma and malaria, also began to plague Tu Fu during this time.

Productive Final Years By the end of 759, Tu Fu had become disillusioned with public life. Although the decision brought financial hardship on his family, Tu Fu chose to retire and concentrate on his poetry. As a result, the last 11 years of his life were very productive ones. His output as well as the quality and complexity of his work increased greatly. This accomplishment is particularly remarkable in light of the revolts and unrest that continued to afflict the region. It was, in fact, while fleeing by boat before a Tibetan invasion that Tu Fu died.

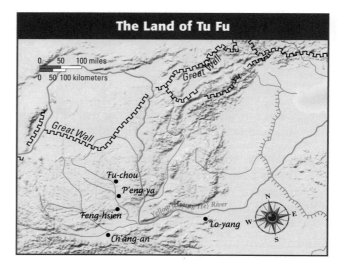

The Land of Tu Fu

Build Background

Poet-Historian Much of Tu Fu's poetry reflects the events of his time. Deeply affected by the political upheaval of the High T'ang period, Tu Fu wrote about the devastation of war, the decay of Chinese society, and the suffering of the common people. In later centuries, his accounts earned him a reputation as a poet-historian.

The major political event of Tu Fu's time was the An Lu-shan Rebellion of 755–757. An Lu-shan was a very powerful military governor whose armies stormed and captured the capital of Ch'ang-an. Tu Fu himself was held prisoner by the rebels for a time. As a result of his experiences, the poet wrote compassionately about the lives of those most affected by war—the poor.

Private Perspectives Tu Fu often wrote about public events. But he wrote about these events in terms of his own private experiences of them. In "Song of P'eng-ya," for example, a poem about the rebellion, Tu Fu wrote lovingly about his children. The intimate family details make the event personal and touching. Such scenes of domestic life are not found in Chinese poetry before Tu Fu but became more common after him.

Fellow Artists Tu Fu is most often compared to his friend and contemporary Li Po. However, the two poets couldn't have been more different. Li Po was a Taoist romantic whose style was original and bold. Tu Fu was a Confucian moralist who longed to be useful to society and wrote carefully crafted poems. It is said that Li Po is the people's poet, while Tu Fu is the poets' poet.

Tu Fu and Li Po met and traveled together briefly. Although they saw each other only once more after that early encounter, Tu Fu continued to admire Li Po. He wrote more than a dozen poems about his friend, including "Dreaming of Li Po." Li Po, on the other hand, is said to have made fun of Tu Fu for his painstaking approach to writing. In a poem addressed to Tu Fu, he gently teased his fellow-poet:

> *How is it you've gotten so thin since we parted?*
>
> *Must be all those poems you've been suffering over.*

Connect to Your Life

Think about a recent public event that had an impact on you. You might consider a natural disaster or a political incident. Get together with a partner to discuss the event. What private insight or perspective could you provide about the event that wouldn't appear in a newspaper account of it?

Focus Your Reading

LITERARY ANALYSIS: MOOD AND IMAGERY

Mood is the feeling or atmosphere that a writer creates for the reader. One element that contributes to the mood of a poem is **imagery**—the words and phrases that create sensory experiences. Notice the mood evoked in the following lines from "Jade Flower Palace":

> *The stream swirls. The wind moans in*
> *The pines.*

As you read the poems by Tu Fu, consider how words and images contribute to the mood.

ACTIVE READING: UNDERSTANDING AND APPRECIATING POETRY

A poem is made up of many elements working together. Rhythms, sounds, word choice, and imagery all contribute to the final form and meaning of a poem. It will help you to fully appreciate a poem if you read the poem several times. It will also help if you read the poem aloud. With each reading, you will discover new connections and insights that you missed earlier.

READER'S NOTEBOOK Read each of Tu Fu's poems three times, including once aloud. After each reading, use a chart like the one below to record your impressions and insights.

"Dreaming of Li Po"
First Reading
Second Reading
Third Reading

Dreaming of Li Po
Tu Fu

Translated by Burton Watson

Parting from the dead, I've stifled my sobs,
but this parting from the living brings me constant pain.
South of the Yangtze is a land of plague and fever;
no word comes from the exile.
5 Yet my old friend has entered my dreams,
proof of how long I've pined for him.
He didn't look the way he used to,
the road so far—farther than I can guess.
His spirit came from where the maple groves are green,
10 then went back, leaving me in borderland blackness.
Now you're caught in the meshes of the law—
how could you have wings to fly with?
The sinking moon floods the rafters of my room
and still I seem to see it lighting your face.
15 Where you go, waters are deep, the waves so wide—
don't let the dragons, the horned dragons harm you!

3–4 South of the Yangtze
(yäng′dzŭ′) . . . **exile:** Li Po had
been sent into exile in southwest
China for his involvement with a
prince who led a minor rebellion.

Ceramic jar with dragon (1426–1435).
The Metropolitan Museum of Art, New York.

Jade Flower Palace
Tu Fu

Translated by Kenneth Rexroth

The stream swirls. The wind moans in
The pines. Grey rats scurry over
Broken tiles. What prince, long ago,
Built this palace, standing in
5 Ruins beside the cliffs? There are
Green ghost fires in the black rooms.
The shattered pavements are all
Washed away. Ten thousand organ
Pipes whistle and roar. The storm
10 Scatters the red autumn leaves.
His dancing girls are yellow dust.
Their painted cheeks have crumbled
Away. His gold chariots
And courtiers are gone. Only
15 A stone horse is left of his
Glory. I sit on the grass and
Start a poem, but the pathos of
It overcomes me. The future
Slips imperceptibly away.
20 Who can say what the years will bring?

3–4 What prince . . . built this palace: The palace had been the summer home of T'ai-tsung, emperor of China from A.D. 626 to 649.

17 pathos (pā'thŏs'): sorrow.

19 imperceptibly (ĭm'pər-sĕp'tə-blē): in a barely noticeable way.

Running horse (Han Dynasty). Bronze. Imperial Museum, Beijing. Robert Harding Picture Library, London.

HUMANITIES CONNECTION This piece of sculpture depicts a so-called celestial horse, one of a tall breed of horses introduced into China in the first century B.C. This is the only known ancient Chinese sculpture of a galloping horse.

OZYMANDIAS

Percy Bysshe Shelley

I met a traveler from an antique land,
Who said—"Two vast and trunkless legs of stone
Stand in the desert. . . . Near them, on the sand,
Half sunk a shattered visage lies, whose frown,
5   And wrinkled lip, and sneer of cold command,
Tell that its sculptor well those passions read
Which yet survive, stamped on these lifeless things,
The hand that mocked them, and the heart that fed;
And on the pedestal, these words appear:
10   My name is Ozymandias, King of Kings,
Look on my Works, ye Mighty, and despair!
Nothing beside remains. Round the decay
Of that colossal Wreck, boundless and bare
The lone and level sands stretch far away."

2 trunkless legs: legs separated from the rest of the body.

4 visage (vĭz′ĭj): face.

6 those passions: that is, Ozymandias' passions.

8 This line may be paraphrased as "The sculptor's hand, which mocked the passions of the king, and the king's heart, which fed those passions."

10 Ozymandias (ŏz′ĭ-măn′dyəs): title of the Egyptian pharaoh Rameses II, who reigned from 1304 to 1237 B.C.

HUMANITIES CONNECTION This stone head is part of a massive set of sculptures at the burial site in Turkey of King Antiochus I, who ruled about 50 B.C. Few people know anything about him or his kingdom of Commagene now, despite the magnificent memorial he created for himself.

Song of P'eng-ya
Tu Fu

Translated by Burton Watson

I remember when we first fled the rebels,
hurrying north over dangerous trails;
night deepened on P'eng-ya Road,
the moon shone over White-water Hills.
5 A whole family endlessly trudging,
begging without shame from the people we met:
valley birds sang, a jangle of soft voices;
we didn't see a single traveler returning.
The baby girl in her hunger bit me;
10 fearful that tigers or wolves would hear her cries,
I hugged her to my chest, muffling her mouth,
but she squirmed and wailed louder than before.
The little boy pretended he knew what was happening;
importantly he searched for sour plums to eat.
15 Ten days, half in rain and thunder,
through mud and slime we pulled each other on.
There was no escaping from the rain,
trails slick, clothes wet and clammy;
getting past the hardest places,
20 a whole day advanced us no more than three or four li.
Mountain fruits served for rations,
low-hung branches were our rafter and roof.
Mornings we traveled by rock-bedded streams,
evenings camped in mists that closed in the sky.
25 We stopped a little while at the marsh of T'ung-chia,
thinking to go out by Lu-tzu Pass;
an old friend there, Sun Tsai,
ideals higher than the piled-up clouds;
he came out to meet us as dusk turned to darkness,

1 rebels: troops led by the traitorous general An Lu-shan, who attacked and captured the Chinese capital of Ch'ang-an in A.D. 756.

3 P'eng-ya (pŭng′yä′) **Road:** a road to the town of P'eng-ya, about 130 miles north of Ch'ang-an. Tu Fu and his family passed through P'eng-ya as they sought safety from the rebel forces.

20 three or four li: less than a mile and a half.

25 T'ung-chia (tŏong′jyä′).
26 Lu-tzu (lōō′dzŭ′).
27 Sun Tsai (sŏōn′ dzī′).

Circular box with garden scene, Yung Lo. Collection of the National Palace Museum, Taipei, Taiwan, Republic of China.

HUMANITIES CONNECTION Lacquer is made from the sap of a tree that is native to China. To create a piece of solid lacquer thick enough for carving this type of box, as many as 40 applications of thin lacquer had to be layered, a process that took many days.

30   called for torches, opening gate after gate,
    heated water to wash our feet,
    cut strips of paper to call back our souls.
    Then his wife and children came;
    seeing us, their tears fell in streams.
35   My little chicks had gone sound to sleep;
    he called them to wake up and eat from his plate,
    said he would make a vow with me,
    the two of us to be brothers forever.
    At last he cleared the room where we sat,
40   wished us goodnight, all he had at our command.
    Who is willing, in the hard, bleak times,
    to break open, lay bare his innermost heart?
    Parting from you, a year of months has rounded,
    Tartar tribes still plotting evil,
45   and I think how it would be to have strong wings
    that would carry me away, set me down before you.

32 cut strips of paper to call back our souls: It was believed that the soul could leave the body when a person was frightened. The ritual referred to here was intended to restore the souls of the frightened travelers.

44 Tartar tribes: the forces of An Lu-shan.

Connect to the Literature

1. **What Do You Think?**
Which poem do you think has the most vivid images? Explain why.

Comprehension Check
- In "Dreaming of Li Po," why is Tu Fu so worried about Li Po?
- What has apparently happened to the prince and the palace in "Jade Flower Palace"?
- In "Song of P'eng-ya," what act of kindness does Tu Fu's friend perform?

Think Critically

2. In "Dreaming of Li Po," what might each of the following refer to: "land of plague and fever," "wings to fly with," "waters," "horned dragons"?

3. How would you summarize the theme, or message, of "Jade Flower Palace"?

 THINK ABOUT
- the details used to describe the palace
- what is left of the palace
- what life was probably like in the palace

4. In "Song of P'eng-ya," what details about a family fleeing from a rebel army does Tu Fu provide that wouldn't appear in a factual historical account?

5. ACTIVE READING: UNDERSTANDING AND APPRECIATING POETRY Look at the charts you created in your 📖 **READER'S NOTEBOOK.** Did your impressions and reactions change during the second and third readings of the poems? Did you discover new connections or insights? Discuss your experience with a classmate.

Extend Interpretations

6. Comparing Texts Compare "Jade Flower Palace" with "Ozymandias" (pages 466–467). How do the narrators differ in their attitudes toward their subjects? What similar atmospheres and messages do the poems convey?

7. Critic's Corner One critic has said that Tu Fu's appeal may be due to "the way he documents his life, from the smallest details to the biggest dimensions of social context." Do the poems you have read support this statement? Explain your answer.

8. Connect to Life Although Tu Fu wrote in the eighth century, his poems are still enjoyed today. In what ways are his poems relevant to the modern world?

LITERARY ANALYSIS: MOOD AND IMAGERY

The **mood** of a poem is the feeling or atmosphere the writer creates for the reader. Many elements can contribute to the mood, including word choice, descriptive details, and even rhythm. One of the most important elements is **imagery,** words and phrases that create sensory experiences. Remember that imagery can appeal to any of the five senses—sight, smell, hearing, taste, and touch.

Paired Activity With a partner, come up with a word or phrase that captures the mood of each one of Tu Fu's poems. Write it in the center circle of a word web like the one below. Then, in the surrounding circles, add images from the poem that contribute to the overall mood. Share your word webs with the rest of the class.

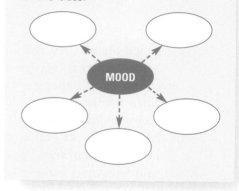

The Refugees: People Without a Country

Tu Fu and his family fled rebel armies in 756; but the anguish of the refugee was not new then, and it continues even today, in every country. In fact, one estimate places the number of refugees in the world today at over 12 million. But what causes thousands of people to suddenly leave their homes, livelihoods, and everything they know, only to live in overcrowded refugee camps, or worse?

What Makes a Refugee? Sometimes a country is torn by war or politics, the stronger faction terrorizing and forcing out its "enemies." Sometimes religious and ethnic differences cause one group to be persecuted by another, to the point where the victimized group has to flee. And sometimes a whole population of refugees can be created by the failure of an economy or by a sudden environmental disaster.

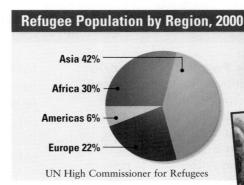

Refugee Population by Region, 2000

Asia 42%
Africa 30%
Americas 6%
Europe 22%

UN High Commissioner for Refugees

How many of the following refugee situations sound familiar to you, either because you've heard about them or because you or someone in your family lived through one?

- Soviet political and religious persecution
- conflict in Bosnia-Herzegovina
- Ethiopian famine
- the flight of the Vietnamese boat people
- the Palestinian situation
- ethnic cleansing in Kosovo
- the Irish potato famine
- the Chinese invasion of Tibet

Research Project It's one thing to hear about these situations. It's another to truly understand them—or to do something to help. Do some research on one of the situations above. Create a report or multimedia presentation that will help others understand it and that might even encourage someone to get involved. Your presentation may include information about

- the problem or conflict that caused the situation
- the number of people displaced
- the lives of the refugees in exile
- relief efforts
- the resolution of or recent developments in the crisis
- the future

RESEARCH STARTER
CLASSZONE.COM

The Kosovo refugees need your help.
Please call
1-800-USAID-RELIEF

Poems of Li Ch'ing-chao

TRANSLATED BY Kenneth Rexroth

Li Ch'ing-chao
1084?–1151?

Early Promise Li Ch'ing-chao (lē' chǐng'jou'), China's greatest woman poet, was one of the most accomplished and spirited women of her time. She was born to a distinguished family and was encouraged to write by her literary parents. When she was 18, Li Ch'ing-chao married a student in the Imperial Academy. Deeply happy in their marriage, the couple shared a passion for literature, art, and antiquities. Together they collected a vast number of paintings, sculptures, and manuscripts—enough to fill ten huge rooms.

Tragic Loss Calamity struck in 1126 when the Chin from Manchuria invaded China. In the chaos that followed, Li Ch'ing-chao was separated from her husband for many months. She eventually reached him, but in the meantime the Chin burned the couple's house, and much of their precious artwork went up in flames. A far worse tragedy occurred in 1129, when Li Ch'ing-chao's husband fell ill and died.

Enduring Legacy In the years that followed, Li Ch'ing-chao was often in flight from the Chin invaders. Despite the upheaval and loneliness, she continued to write. By the end of her life, she had written six volumes of poetry and seven of essays. Unfortunately, all of her work was lost except for about 50 poems. Little is known about her last years, but her poetry is a rare treasure that the world has held in high esteem for more than 800 years.

Lyric Poetry In this part of the book, you have read a number of lyric poems. **Lyric poems** are poems in which the speakers express personal thoughts and feelings. Such poems can have a variety of forms and cover a wide range of subjects and emotions.

The poetry of Li Ch'ing-chao is also in the lyric tradition. Her poems are known for the depth of feeling they express, from the joys of young love to the despair of grief. In addition, her work is praised for its clear imagery. Li Ch'ing-chao's poems were originally set to music, and she is considered a master of the song lyric of her time.

The two poems you are about to read are from two different periods of her life. The first was written when she was a young woman, probably in the early days of her marriage. The second poem was written after her husband had died. As you read the poems, ask yourself these questions:

1. *What images reflect the speakers' feelings most effectively?*

2. *Both poems are set in spring. What are the differences between them?*

3. *Are there any similarities, in theme or imagery, between these poems and the other ancient Chinese poems in this part of Unit Three?*

TWO SPRINGS

Spring has come to the women's quarter.
Once more the new grass is kingfisher green.
The cracked red buds of plum blossoms
Are still unopened little balls.
5   Blue-green clouds carve jade dragons.
The jade powder becomes fine dust.
I try to hold on to my morning dream.
I have already drained and broken
The cup of Spring.
10 Flower shadows lie heavy
On the garden gate.
In the orange twilight
Pale moonlight spreads
On the translucent curtain.
15 Three times in two years
My lord has gone away to the East.
Today he returns,
And my joy is already
Greater than the Spring.

1 women's quarter: In Li Ch'ing-chao's time, living spaces for men and women were generally separate.

2 kingfisher: a bright-colored crested bird.

14 translucent (trăns-lōō'sənt): letting light shine through.

Spring Morning in the Han Palace. Qui Ying. Collection of the National Palace Museum, Taipei, Taiwan, Republic of China.

HUMANITIES CONNECTION This scene from a silk scroll painting gives glimpses into the restricted inner sections of the palace. The artist may have painted himself in the figure of the portrait painter in the doorway.

ON PLUM BLOSSOMS

This morning I woke
In a bamboo bed with paper curtains.
I have no words for my weary sorrow,
No fine poetic thoughts.
5 The sandalwood incense smoke is stale,
The jade burner is cold.
I feel as though I were filled with quivering water.
To accompany my feelings
Someone plays three times on a flute
10 "Plum Blossoms Are Falling
in a Village by the River."
How bitter this Spring is.
Small wind, fine rain, *hsiao, hsiao,*
Falls like a thousand lines of tears.
15 The flute player is gone.
The jade tower is empty.
Broken hearted—we had relied on each other.
I pick a plum branch,
But my man has gone beyond the sky,
20 And there is no one to give it to.

13 *hsiao, hsiao* (shyou): words mimicking the sad sound of the rainfall.

Detail of *The Old Plum* (1647), attributed to Kano Sansetsu. The Metropolitan Museum of Art (New York).

Writing Workshop   Lyric Poetry

Painting with words . . .

From Reading to Writing Not everyone can explain what poetry is, but most people know it when they see it. **Poetry** is a form of creative writing that emphasizes language and imagery. In poetry, the sound of the words and their arrangement on the page work together with the meaning to create a strong impact— one of beauty, excitement, sadness, or even fear. Some poems, such as Li Ch'ing-chao's "Two Springs," express personal thoughts and feelings. Such poems are known as **lyric poems.** Often, a lyric poem will describe a single image or moment rather than tell a story.

For Your Portfolio

WRITING PROMPT Write a poem that describes an experience, an idea, a place, a person, or a feeling.

  Purpose: To express yourself in an original way

  Audience: Your classmates, friends, or family

Basics in a Box

Poetry at a Glance

rhythm

sensory words

rhyme

mood

figurative language

sound devices

free verse

stanzas

RUBRIC Standards for Writing

A successful poem should

- focus on a single experience, idea, place, person, or feeling

- use precise, sensory words in a fresh, interesting way

- incorporate figurative language, such as similes and metaphors

- include sound devices, such as alliteration, assonance, and rhyme, that support the mood and meaning of the poem

Analyzing Student Models

**Shakira Hightower
Dover High School**

Harlemite Easter

I take Daryl uptown to see the parade
marching on the Avenue

I watch his eyes
watching
little girls with Vaselined legs
white socks/gloves
hats atop ringlets and ribbons
pinks, yellows
dresses that rise when they spin and
feet that go tippity-tap in Sunday
patent leather

I follow him
following
smoothly shaven heads
of little boys and men
collars being tugged at
but under the mindful eyes of

Women
wearing flowers and pumps
that match
purses
that match
hats

I look at him
looking at them filing
into the churches along the corners
of the Avenue
on Easter

RUBRIC
IN ACTION

❶ Focuses on an experience

❷ Repetition creates rhythm and emphasis.

❸ Uses alliteration and assonance to create rhythm

❹ Repetition here is similar to repetition at number 2.

❺ Alliteration, repetition, and assonance combine with a vivid description of the women's appearance.

❻ Repetition similar to that at numbers 2 and 4

❼ Line breaks emphasize *Avenue* and *Easter*.

Susan Gray
Solomon Schechter High School

Revolution

When I water the plants I like to watch
the soil sponges darken in welcome,
feel the wet dirt yield to my finger.
I sniff the soft earth
as water dribbles out the bottom.
The violet whispers urgently from its
    plastic pot.
Shyly it shows me the veins under the
    leaves.
I take its pulse. I smooth its hair.
I scratch it behind the ears.
The old yellow leaves breathe tired
    thanks,
while the young ones at center bristle
    green
as they erupt in revolution.

RUBRIC
IN ACTION

❶ The sensory description involves sight, touch, and smell.

❷ The poet uses personification, characterizing the violet as a shy, whispering person.

Michael Brinker
James Madison High School

Yellow

Yellow;
the ideal sports car, not one but many,
bumper to bumper
in an infinite parking lot;

like a field of tulips
catching the sun
and throwing it around;

like the eager line
    of buses
waiting to take
the children home;

like a bold bee
riding atop the
speeding blur of
    a taxicab

❶ The entire poem springs from a single idea—the color yellow.

❷ A simile brings life to the idea of yellow by comparing the color to a sunny field of tulips.

❸ The poet uses a simile in each stanza. Each simile compares the color yellow to something new; the repetition of similes creates structure and rhythm.

Writing Your Poem

❶ Prewriting

Many poets start with a single phrase, image, or feeling. Find a quiet place to work and then reflect about moments, places, people, or ideas that strike you in some way. Jot down your thoughts and any interesting words that come to mind, especially those describing sensory experiences. See the **Idea Bank** in the margin for more suggestions. After choosing a topic, follow the steps below.

Planning Your Poem

1. **Write freely about your topic.** Review the notes you made while searching for a topic. Circle any interesting words, images, and details. Then make a concept web to explore ideas related to those items.

2. **Identify the mood you want to express.** Does your topic make you feel happy? sad? curious? angry? Think about images and details that will create or reinforce that mood.

3. **Choose a focus.** Which word, line, or image seems to lead to other good images and ideas? Look for one powerful phrase to begin your poem.

❷ Drafting

Writing freely, compose your poem, playing with ideas and language. Choose words for their meaning and their sound. Read your writing aloud and listen for its rhythm, or cadence. Consider using some of the following poetic devices.

DEVICE	EXAMPLE
Sound Devices	
alliteration	yelping and yammering
assonance	howling loudly
rhyme	bags of rags
repetition	into the cold, cold night
Figures of Speech	
simile	The park was as quiet as midnight.
metaphor	Winter was a blanket that covered the city.
personification	The clock tower guarded the citizens as they slept.

In general, use descriptive language that appeals to the five senses. Also experiment with stanzas, line breaks, and indented lines. When you're done with your draft, read it aloud and listen to the language. Think about how you might add shape to your poem by changing words, line breaks, and punctuation.

IDEABank

1. Your Working Portfolio
Build on the **Writing Option** you completed earlier in this unit:
- **Mood Poem,** p. 460

2. Personality Poem
Think about the most unusual person you know. How would you describe this person? What is unusual about him or her? Write a poem characterizing the person.

3. Found Photo
Look through newspapers, magazines, or books to find a photograph that suggests strong emotion or an unusual situation. Write a poem about what you see in the photo.

LANGUAGE SKILLS

Sound confusing?

For definitions of *alliteration, assonance, repetition, rhyme,* and *meter,* look in the **Glossary of Literary Terms,** p. R91

Need revising help?

Review the **Rubric,** p. 476

Consider **peer reader** comments

Check **revision guidelines,** p. R19

Puzzled by punctuation?

See the **Grammar Handbook,** pp. R77–R78

Publishing IDEAS

- Submit your poem to your school's literary magazine.
- Publish your poem in your own chapbook, or booklet.
- Read your poem aloud at a class poetry circle. Record the readings on videotape or audiotape.

PUBLISHING OPTIONS
CLASSZONE.COM

❸ Revising

TARGET SKILL ▶ USING SOUND DEVICES Sound and rhythm are important features of poetry. Add features such as alliteration, assonance, repetition, rhyme, or meter to your poem in order to create rhythm and emphasis.

Ask Your Peer Reader

- How does this poem make you feel?
- Which images are the strongest or most vivid?
- What is the most interesting aspect of the poem?

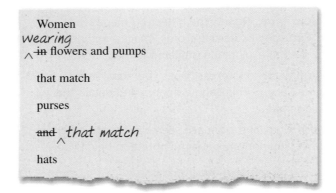

❹ Editing and Proofreading

TARGET SKILL ▶ USING PUNCTUATION When you write poetry, you are freed from certain prose conventions. Nonetheless, punctuation marks have the same meaning in poetry as they do in prose. In general, use standard rules for punctuating your poetry. Punctuation will clarify your ideas, helping you communicate your meaning.

I take its pulse, I smooth its hair.

I scratch it behind the ears.

the old yellow leaves breathe tired thanks,

While the young ones at center bristle green

as they erupt in revolution.

❺ Reflecting

FOR YOUR WORKING PORTFOLIO In writing your poem, what did you learn about your topic and about yourself? Did you come up with any surprising descriptions? What techniques would you like to try in your next poem? Attach your answers to your finished work. Save your poem in your **Working Portfolio.**

Read this paragraph from the first draft of an essay. The underlined sections may include the following kinds of errors:

- **incorrect end marks**
- **errors in comma usage**
- **incorrect quotation marks**
- **incorrect use of semicolons**

For each underlined section, choose the revision that most improves the writing.

> Every year I go to a great summer camp. <u>It's a poetry workshop; students from around the city come together to express themselves</u> in writing. <u>The Young Poets as the students are called work in classes of ten.</u> <u>We spend every morning writing, every afternoon we share our work.</u> Our counselor <u>calls out, 'Who wants to give us a poem?'</u> Every Friday afternoon is the Grand Jamboree, where we all <u>read recite, rap, or sing</u> our poems from the week. <u>What part do I enjoy the most.</u> I like meeting new people and hearing so many different voices.
>
> (1) ... (2) ... (3) ... (4) ... (5) ... (6)

1. A. It's a poetry workshop, students from around the city come together to express themselves

B. It's a poetry workshop, students from around the city come together; to express themselves

C. It's a poetry workshop; students from around the city, come together to express themselves

D. Correct as is

2. A. The Young Poets, as the students are called, work in classes of ten.

B. The Young Poets, as the students are called work in classes of ten.

C. The Young Poets as the students are called, work in classes of ten.

D. Correct as is

3. A. We spend every morning writing: every afternoon we share our work.

B. We spend every morning writing, every afternoon, we share our work.

C. We spend every morning writing; every afternoon we share our work.

D. Correct as is

4. A. calls out, "Who wants to give us a poem?"

B. calls out: 'Who wants to give us a poem?'

C. calls out—"Who wants to give us a poem?"

D. Correct as is

5. A. read, recite rap or sing

B. read recite rap or sing

C. read, recite, rap, or sing

D. Correct as is

6. A. What part do I enjoy the most!

B. What part do I enjoy the most?

C. What part do I enjoy the most.

D. Correct as is

Need extra help?

See the **Grammar Handbook**

Correcting Run-On Sentences, p. R73

Quick Reference: Capitalization, p. R79

Correcting Fragments, p. R73

Quick Reference: Punctuation, p. R77

TEST PRACTICE

Building Vocabulary — Homophones, Homonyms, and Homographs

Words with Similar Sounds and Spellings The English language contains many unrelated words that happen to have the same spelling and/or pronunciation. Many of these words have entirely different origins; the resemblance is only a coincidence. However, their similarity often confuses readers and writers. Read the excerpt on the right. If you didn't know that the verb *pine* means "to long for," you might think it had something to do with an evergreen tree.

Pine and *pine* are **homonyms**—words that have the same pronunciation and spelling but different meanings. One word comes from the Latin *pīnus*, meaning "pine tree," and the other comes from the Greek *poinē*, meaning "penalty."

> Parting from the dead, I've stifled my
> sobs, . . .
> Yet my old friend has entered my dreams,
> proof of how long I've pined for him.
>
> —Tu Fu, "Dreaming of Li Po"

Strategies for Building Vocabulary

In addition to homonyms, **homophones** and **homographs** may confuse readers and writers. Use the information below to help you distinguish these words from their confusing partners.

❶ Homophones The term *homophone* comes from two Greek words: *homos* ("same"), and *phōnē* ("sound"). Homophones are words that sound the same but are spelled differently and have different meanings. Practice will help you remember the different spellings and meanings of words like *foreword* and *forward*, *sight* and *site*, and *principal* and *principle*.

Homophones

Alike in	Different in	Example
pronunciation	spelling and meaning	*holy* and *wholly*

❷ Homonyms The term *homonym* comes from the Greek words *homos* ("same") and *onumos* ("name"). Although homonyms have the same spelling and pronunciation, they are actually different words with different derivations. The fact that they are spelled and pronounced alike is a coincidence. These words have separate entries in the dictionary. *Tire* ("to grow weary") and *tire* ("a wheel covering") are homonyms.

Homonyms

Alike in	Different in	Example
pronunciation and spelling	meaning	*loaf* ("a mass of bread") and *loaf* ("to be idle")

❸ Homographs The term *homograph* comes from the Greek words *homos* ("same") and *graphē* ("writing"). Homographs are spelled the same but have different meanings and pronunciations. *Content* (kŏn′tĕnt′), meaning "subject matter" and *content* (kən-tĕnt′), meaning "satisfied" are two examples. Like homonyms, homographs have separate dictionary entries.

Homographs

Alike in	Different in	Example
spelling	meaning and pronunciation	*invalid* ("not valid; faulty") and *invalid* ("one completely disabled by illness")

EXERCISE Look up each pair of words in a dictionary. Pronounce each word and identify its meanings and origins. Then classify the two words as homophones, homonyms, or homographs, and use each word in a sentence.

1. *mail* and *mail*
2. *compound* and *compound*
3. *wet* and *whet*
4. *bear* and *bear*
5. *miner* and *minor*

Sentence Crafting | Using Parallelism for Effect

Grammar from Literature When writers want to say something powerful or memorable, they sometimes use **parallelism** to create emphasis. Parallelism is the expression of related concepts in similar grammatical structures. You learned on page 157 that parallel construction is grammatically necessary for elements in a series. It is also a graceful and effective way to group similar ideas and to show contrasts between opposing or greatly different ideas. Look at the following model.

> Lord Ji Kang asked: "What should I do in order to make the people respectful, loyal, and zealous?" The Master said: "Approach them with dignity and they will be respectful. Be yourself a good son and a kind father, and they will be loyal. Raise the good and train the incompetent, and they will be zealous."
>
> —Confucius, *Analects*

In each of the three sentences, the Master gives a command (**approach, be, raise**) followed by a consequence (**and they will be . . .**). The repetition of this structure creates a strong rhythmic pattern, which is both graceful and memorable.

Notice how the parallel construction highlights the contrast in this second passage from Confucius' *Analects*.

> The Master said: "To study without thinking is futile. To think without studying is dangerous."

What if the Master had said, "To study without thinking is futile. The other way around is dangerous"? The statement would have had the same meaning, but it would not have had the same effect.

GRAMMAR EXERCISE You will find parallelism in the writings and speeches of many authors and orators. For each of the following quotations, write down the groups of words that have parallel form.

1. "The Master said: 'Authority without generosity, ceremony without reverence, mourning without grief—these, I cannot bear to contemplate.'" (*Analects*)
   (*Sample answer: authority without generosity, ceremony without reverence, and mourning without grief*)
2. "Truthful words do not flatter. Flattering words are not true." (*Tao Te Ching*, 81)
3. "A president's hardest task is not to *do* what is right, but to *know* what is right." (Lyndon B. Johnson, State of the Union Address, January 4, 1965)
4. "She handled her brushes with a certain ease and freedom which came, not from long and close acquaintance with them, but from a natural aptitude." (Kate Chopin, *The Awakening*)

WRITING EXERCISE Choose three of the six passages quoted on this page, including those in the Grammar Exercise. Then write three passages of your own, imitating the structure of the passages you chose. For example, if you chose to imitate the first quotation in the Grammar Exercise, you might write: "The baker said: 'Bread without yeast, cake without sugar, doughnuts without holes—these, I will not sell in my shop.'"

Literature of Ancient China

Reflect and Assess

What impressions of the people of ancient China did you have after reading the selections in this part of Unit Three? What joys, sorrows, and concerns did you discover in the literature? Use the activities below to help you think further about what you have read.

Detail of *Spring Morning in the Han Palace.*

Reflecting on the Literature

Thoughtful Observation Ancient Chinese literature touches on many aspects of life, from details of everyday experience to larger questions about the right way to live. The writers are careful observers of both beauty and human relationships. Think back over the selections you have read, and call to mind details that delighted you and thoughts that stirred you. Briefly summarize the view of life that you find in this literature.

Reviewing Literary Concepts

Lyric Poetry You have read lyric poems by several poets in this part of the book. These poems present a variety of emotions and situations. Which two poems especially appealed to you? For each one, identify the speaker and the experience the poem deals with. Then note the main emotion the speaker expresses. What makes each poem particularly moving to you?

Building Your Portfolio

Writing Workshop and Writing Options Look back at the lyric poem you wrote for the Writing Workshop on page 476 and your work for the Writing Options on page 460. Which piece are you most pleased with? Put that piece in your **Presentation Portfolio**, along with a note explaining why you think it works well.

Self **ASSESSMENT**

READER'S NOTEBOOK

The names and terms below are important in this part of the book. On a piece of paper, list the words. Then write a sentence or two explaining each one. If you are not certain about a term, review the lessons or check the **Glossary of Literary Terms** (page R91).

didactic literature	Taoism
Analects	*Book of Odes*
maxim	lyric poetry
Tao Te Ching	imagery
paradox	mood

Setting **GOALS**

Think about the works you have read in this part of Unit Three. Which author or selection would you like to investigate further? Look at the suggestions in Extend Your Reading, or ask your teacher or a librarian to help you find additional works or different translations.

Extend Your *Reading*

A Floating Life:
The Adventures of Li Po

SIMON ELEGANT

This historical novel conveys Li Po's genius as a poet as well as his appetite for adventure. The novel presents the poet's life in the form of a memoir told by Li Po to a young boy, who copies it down as a writing exercise. Li Po's spirit comes to life in a series of tales dealing with his experiences at the emperor's court and in exile. Based on historical accounts, Elegant's fiction captures the essence of Li Po while faithfully portraying life in eighth-century China.

In the Land of the Dragon:
Imperial China, A.D. 960–1368

This volume of Time-Life's What Life Was Like series traces the history of China from the beginning of the Sung dynasty through the rise and fall of the Mongol Empire. During much of this period, art and culture flourished and important inventions helped transform the world. Prosperity gave way to great upheaval, however, when the Mongols overran and conquered China. This tumultuous time is vividly brought to life through the book's engaging text and beautiful illustrations.

And Even *More* . . .

Books
The Essential Confucius THOMAS CLEARY, TRANS.
In this edition, the teachings of Confucius are grouped by subject to make them easier to understand. The format is easy to follow and helps make Confucian thought clear and direct.

The Terracotta Army of the First Emperor of China
WILLIAM LINDESAY AND GUO BAOFU
Photographs, diagrams, and informative text tell the story behind the incredible life-size pottery warriors discovered in China in 1974.

Other Media
The Tao of Pooh
Benjamin Hoff reads his best-selling book, in which he uses the beloved bear Winnie-the-Pooh and his friends to explain basic Taoist beliefs. Harper Audio.
(AUDIOCASSETTE)

China: Dynasties of Power
This film in the Lost Civilizations series examines the glory and might of ancient China's greatest rulers and re-creates the building of the Great Wall. Time-Life Video.
(VIDEOCASSETTE)

Chuang Tsu: Inner Chapters

JANE ENGLISH AND GIA-FU FENG, TRANS.

The wisdom and humor of the Taoist philosopher Chuang Tzu are evident in these fables and anecdotes. English's black-and-white photographs of nature enhance the text and help draw the reader into the spiritual world of Taoism.

Literature of Japan

Why It Matters

Simplicity. Discipline. Nature. These three words reflect the major themes of the literature selections that you will read in this part. The words also reflect the foundations of modern Japanese culture. As a result, the best way to understand Japan as it is today may be to study its history and traditional literature and art. You may even find interesting similarities between Japanese culture and your own.

For Links to Japan, click on:

HUMANITIES
CLASSZONE.COM

ASIA

CHINA

4

Religious Traditions A large red gate usually marks the entrance to a Shinto shrine. **Shinto** and **Buddhism,** the two main religions of Japan, are based on a respect for nature.

4 The Influence of China Around A.D. 500, Chinese ideas and customs began to influence the Japanese. Important influences included Buddhism and the Chinese system of writing.

KOREA

3 An Island Culture There are about 4,000 islands in the Japanese island group. Most Japanese live on the four largest islands— **Honshu, Hokkaido, Kyushu,** and **Shikoku.** Many people depend on the sea for food and industry.

Yellow Sea

1 **A Mountainous Terrain** About 70 percent of Japan is covered by mountains and hills. **Mount Fuji,** the country's highest and most famous mountain, is considered sacred. More than 100,000 people climb it each year.

2 **The Way of the Warrior** From the 12th century until 1867, Japan was controlled by powerful warlords, called **shoguns,** and their loyal warriors, called **samurai.** The first shoguns established their center of power in **Kamakura.**

Hokkaido

Sea of Japan

JAPAN

Honshu

● Edo (Tokyo)

● Kamakura

▲ Mt. Fuji

PACIFIC OCEAN

Heian ● (Kyoto)

Nara ●

Shikoku

Kyushu

0   100   200 miles

0   100   200 kilometers

Until the 7th century, Japan was ruled by strong local clans, or families. In the 700s, however, the Japanese established a centralized imperial government.

Heian Period
794–1185

Portrait of Emperor Saga, ruler from 809–823

The Heian period marked the high point of imperial rule in Japan. The imperial court and many noble families moved from the old capital, **Nara,** to the new one, **Heian** (now Kyoto), where a highly cultured court society arose. Gentlemen and ladies of the court filled their days with poetry writing, painting, and elaborate ritual.

During most of the Heian period, Japan's central government was controlled by the rich Fujiwara family. By the middle of the 11th century, however, their power began to be challenged by private landowners, who hired samurai to protect their land. In time, large military clans controlled armies of samurai. This marked the beginning of a **feudal system** of localized rule in Japan.

Kamakura Period
1185–1333

Japan's two most powerful clans—the Taira and the Minamoto—fought for power during the late 1100s. After almost 30 years of war, the Minamoto clan emerged victorious. In 1192, Minamoto Yoritomo became Japan's first shogun, or "great general." Though the emperor reigned from **Kyoto,** which had been built on the ruins of war-torn Heian, the real center of power was at Yoritomo's military headquarters in Kamakura.

Over time, the Kamakura shoguns strengthened their control by assigning **daimyo,** or military governors, to oversee particular regions. The daimyo also oversaw the samurai. By the late 1200s, victories over the Mongols had drained the shoguns' treasury. Loyal samurai became angry when the government could no longer pay them. As a result, the samurai attached themselves more closely to their daimyo.

Ashikaga Period
1338–1467

By the early 14th century, the political and social stability of Japan had weakened. In 1333, the Kamakura shogunate was overthrown by Emperor Go-Daigo, who sought to restore imperial authority. In 1336, Go-Daigo was himself ousted by a powerful military leader, **Ashikaga Takauji.** Go-Daigo set up court in Yoshino, and Takauji established a new military and imperial government in Kyoto in 1338. For the next 54 years, the two imperial courts were constantly at war.

In the early 15th century, the rival courts were briefly brought together when Ashikaga Yoshimitsu, the third Ashikaga shogun, established peace and gained control. However, conditions began to deteriorate once again as the central government's control of the noble landowners under its command gradually lessened. The bitter conflict and political unrest that had marked the Ashikaga period continued as nobles struggled for land and power.

Warring States Period
1467–1568

In 1467, civil war threw Japan into chaos. Daimyo in hundreds of separate regions took power away from the shogun, seizing control of old feudal estates and offering peasants and others protection in return for their loyalty. They also built fortified castles and created small armies of samurai. These warrior-chieftains became lords in a new kind of Japanese feudalism.

A number of ambitious daimyo sought to take control of the entire country. One of them, the ruthless **Oda Nobunaga,** defeated his rivals and seized the imperial capital of Kyoto in 1568. However, Nobunaga was not able to unify all of Japan.

After Nobunaga's death in 1582, one of his generals, **Toyotomi Hideyoshi,** attempted to complete the fallen leader's mission. By 1590, Hideyoshi controlled most of the country. His later efforts to extend his power by conquering Korea ended in failure.

Samurai sword

Detail of statue of Tokugawa Ieyasu at Toshogu Shrine in Nikko

Tokugawa Period
1603–1867

After Hideyoshi's death in 1598, **Tokugawa Ieyasu** completed the unification of Japan. In 1600, he defeated his rival daimyo at the Battle of Sekigahara. Three years later, Ieyasu became Japan's ruling shogun. He moved Japan's capital to **Edo,** a small fishing village that would later become the city of **Tokyo.**

Under the Tokugawa shogunate, Japan enjoyed relative stability and prosperity. Japanese culture, which began to reflect the tastes of a sophisticated urban population, also flourished. However, in an attempt to control foreign influence, Japan instituted a "closed country policy" for more than 200 years. The policy ended in 1854 when Japan established trade with the United States.

History to Literature

EVENT IN HISTORY	EVENT IN LITERATURE
Kana, a Japanese writing system based on Chinese characters, is introduced during the Heian period.	Sei Shōnagon *(The Pillow Book)* and Murasaki Shikibu *(The Tale of Genji),* ladies in waiting in the Heian court, write detailed accounts of court life in Japanese.
The Taira and Minamoto clans clash during the late 1100s.	An anonymous nobleman writes *The Tale of the Heike,* a war epic that chronicles the rise and fall of the Taira family.

ASHIKAGA PERIOD	WARRING STATES PERIOD	TOKUGAWA PERIOD	
1338	1467	1603	1867

During the Tokugawa period, Japanese society became rigidly ordered. The rulers were at the top of the social scale, followed by samurai, peasants, artisans, and merchants. Since a person's position was determined by birth, it was nearly impossible for Japanese to improve their social status.

Rulers

The emperor, who was believed to be descended from the Shinto sun goddess, held the highest rank in Japanese society. He lived in a vast palace with his family and other nobles and was never seen by the common people. He held no political power.

Emperor Go-Yōzei, who reigned from 1586 to 1611

Real control of the country was in the hands of the shogun. The shogun acted as a military dictator and ruled in the emperor's name. He oversaw the daimyo who governed at the local level. To keep the daimyo from rebelling, the shogun required that they spend every other year in the capital. When the daimyo returned to their lands, they had to leave their families behind, in Edo, as hostages.

Samurai

Samurai were an elite class of warriors who were loyal to the daimyo. They fought for their lords in exchange for pay and lived according to a demanding code of behavior called **Bushido,** or "the way of the warrior." A samurai warrior was expected to show reckless courage, reverence for the gods, fairness, and generosity toward those weaker than himself. Many samurai practiced **Zen Buddhism,** which stresses self-discipline and living in harmony with nature.

In battle, samurai wore elaborate armor made of metal and wood. The warriors carried richly crafted swords with fine steel blades. The blades of new swords were usually tested on iron sheets, but they were sometimes tested on condemned criminals. Only samurai were allowed to carry swords. More than just a weapon, the sword was symbolic of the samurai's courage and loyalty; in fact, it represented his soul. A true samurai would have died before giving up his sword.

During the Tokugawa period, special schools were established to instruct the sons of samurai. There boys learned such skills as sword fighting, martial arts, archery, and horsemanship. The schools also provided instruction in literature. For, in addition to being accomplished soldiers, samurai were expected to be well versed in the Confucian classics. Many samurai also wrote poetry.

Swordsmiths crafting samurai swords

Peasants

In Tokugawa Japan, peasant farmers made up about 80 percent of the population. In theory, these farmers were valued because, according to Confucian teaching, the ideal society depended on agriculture. In reality, however, the farmers bore a heavy tax burden—paying as much as half of their harvests. In order to pay their taxes, some peasants were forced to sell their family members into slavery.

The peasants' daily lives were also harshly regulated by the ruling class. They were not allowed to carry swords or use their family names. They were even told what crops to produce, when to work, what to eat, and what to wear. Fed up with their miserable lives, some peasants took part in uprisings against the ruling class. Others abandoned their farms and fled to the cities. There they mixed freely with samurai, artisans, and merchants.

Artisans and Merchants

Artisans played an important role in Japanese society because they produced the goods necessary for everyday life. In the 17th century, some of the most successful artisans in Japan were roofers, carpenters, and stonemasons. Swordsmiths who crafted samurai swords sometimes became close personal friends of the samurai.

Merchants held the lowest status in Tokugawa society because they did not produce anything. Nonetheless, many merchants enjoyed great prosperity. They sold rice, salt, paper, straw mats, noodles, and other goods. They also acted as bankers, lending money to nobles and samurai. Wealthy businessmen lived in lavish homes in the cities and patronized the arts. As urban areas grew, Japan's merchant class gradually became more powerful and respected.

Women in Early Japan

In the Heian period, aristocratic women produced the greatest literature of the time. **Sei Shōnagon** wrote *The Pillow Book,* a witty and revealing diary of court life, and **Murasaki Shikibu** wrote *The Tale of Genji,* considered by many to be the first novel ever written.

During the Kamakura period, samurai wives managed households alone if their husbands died or went to war. Some of these women even engaged in warfare.

By the Tokugawa period, however, the role of most women had become severely restricted. The supreme duty of a woman was to honor the men in her life. Although the rise of large commercial centers had increased employment opportunities for women by the mid-1700s, the typical Japanese woman was a peasant wife who led a sheltered and restricted life. She carried out her duties at home and in the fields and obeyed her husband without question.

Although Chinese cultural influence remained strong in Japan, distinctive styles of Japanese drama, art, literature, and architecture began to emerge.

Theater

Three very different drama traditions developed in Japan, and all three forms remain alive today. **Noh,** the oldest form, developed in 14th-century Japan as religious drama. Noh was perfected in the late 14th and early 15th centuries by **Kanami Kiyotsugu** and his son **Zeami Motokiyo.** Influenced by the simplicity and discipline of Zen Buddhism, Noh features actors who wear masks and use formal language, mime, and stylized gestures to convey the relation between the real and supernatural worlds.

Two other forms of drama—**Kabuki** and **Bunraku**— developed in the 17th century. Townspeople flocked to Kabuki performances in which troupes of actors in colorful costumes acted out dramas about historical events or contemporary urban life. Unlike Noh theater, Kabuki features elaborate sets, special effects such as trap doors and revolving stages, and melodramatic plots.

During the Tokugawa period, Bunraku, or puppet theater, rivaled Kabuki in popularity. In Bunraku, puppets about four feet tall are manipulated by two or three puppeteers each. The puppets are made to move in accompaniment to music and a tale told by a narrator. During the performance, the puppeteers, musician, and narrator are all visible to the audience.

Masked Noh actor

Painting

Moonlit Landscape (15th century), Saiyo. Ink and color on paper, 22³⁄₁₆″ × 8½″. Seattle (Washington) Art Museum, Eugene Fuller Memorial Collection.

Japanese art has always been characterized by an appreciation of beauty and tradition. Artists of the Heian period painted scrolls that combined images and calligraphy. During the Kamakura period, many artists used series of pictures on long scrolls to tell historical tales.

In the 14th century, ink painting began to flourish. Inspired by the art of Sung China, Japanese artists developed their own style of painting with black ink. The works of these artists, who captured scenes of nature with skillful brushwork, reflected the Zen Buddhist values of simplicity and beauty.

During the Tokugawa period, artists captured the sophisticated atmosphere of city life in colorful woodblock prints. The technique of woodblock printing allowed artists to produce many copies of popular pictures and sell them at reasonable prices.

Literature

Early Japanese writers excelled in poetry. The first Japanese poetry anthology was compiled in about 759. The collection contains more than 4,500 poems. Most of the poems are **tanka,** 31-syllable lyrical poems that deal mostly with nature and love. From the 700s until the 1500s, tanka was the most common form of poetry in Japan.

Literature—poetry and prose—flourished during the Heian period. Most writers at that time were members of the nobility. Two of the finest writers were Sei Shōnagon and Murasaki Shikibu, both of whom depicted Heian court life in their prose.

Toward the end of the Heian period, Japanese poets began to divide tanka into smaller parts. From this practice, Japanese poets created the **haiku,** a 17-syllable poem that presents images of nature. Great haiku masters, among them Matsuo Bashō, wrote their verse during the Tokugawa period.

Religion and Architecture

Shinto, meaning "way of the gods," was Japan's earliest—and only native— religion. Based on a reverence for nature, Shinto has no complex rituals or philosophy. Buddhism, which was introduced into Japan in the 6th century, is more complex. Buddhists believe that they can achieve peace by eliminating any attachment to material things. A form of Buddhism called Zen came to Japan in the 12th century. Zen followers try to achieve a state of spiritual enlightenment through both self-discipline and meditation.

Statue of the Great Buddha in Kamakura

Many architectural monuments in Japan are religious buildings. Buddhist temples are distinguished by their gracefully curved tile roofs. Shinto shrines are simple wooden structures designed to fit in with their natural surroundings. These temples and shrines and the modern buildings they have inspired reflect the Japanese desire to remain in harmony with nature.

The Golden Pavilion, a Buddhist temple in Kyoto

Time Line

3000 B.C.	A.D. 1	PRESENT

c.   approximately
B.C.   before Christ
A.D.   after Christ

EVENTS IN JAPANESE LITERATURE

700

712 *Records of Ancient Matters*, a history and one of the oldest surviving Japanese books, is completed

c. 759 *Collection of Ten Thousand Leaves*, an anthology of more than 4,500 poems, is compiled

900

900s *Tale of the Bamboo Cutter*, the first work of Japanese fiction, is written

905 Ki Tsurayuki and others compile the first of 20 imperial poetry anthologies

c. 996 Sei Shōnagon writes *The Pillow Book*

c. 1010 Murasaki Shikibu writes *The Tale of Genji*

1100

c. 1220 *The Tale of the Heike*, a chronicle of the rise and fall of Japan's Taira (Heike) family, is written

Detail of Japanese screen. Asian Art Museum of San Francisco. The Avery Brundage Collection, Chong-Moon Lee Center for Asian Art and Culture.

EVENTS IN JAPANESE HISTORY

700

752 The Great Buddha, a bronze statue standing more than 50 feet tall, is dedicated at Todaiji Temple in Nara

794 A new capital, Heian (site of present-day Kyoto), is established

800s Kana, a system for writing Japanese, is developed

838 The last Japanese mission to T'ang China is made

900

1100

1185 The Kamakura period begins as the Minamoto clan crushes the Taira clan

1191 Zen Buddhism is introduced from China

1192 Minamoto Yoritomo becomes the first shogun and rules from military headquarters in Kamakura

1274 & 1281 The Mongols attack Japan

EVENTS IN WORLD HISTORY

700

800 Charlemagne, who unites much of Europe, is crowned emperor

900

900s Anasazi civilization in North America enters classic Pueblo period

1095 Pope Urban II issues call for First Crusade

1100

1215 England's King John signs the Magna Carta

1235 Sundiata founds the Mali empire in Africa

1279 Kublai Khan conquers the Sung dynasty and establishes Mongol rule in China

1300	1500	1700

c. 1330 Buddhist priest Yoshida Kenkō writes *Essays in Idleness*

1439 The last imperial poetry anthology appears

1443 Zeami Motokiyo, who was instrumental in the development of Noh drama, dies

c. 1661 Asai Ryōi, a samurai and the first professional writer in Japan, publishes the novel *Tales of the Floating World*

1694 Haiku poet Matsuo Bashō writes *The Narrow Road to the Deep North,* a travel account interspersed with haiku

1776 Ueda Akinari writes *Tales of Moonlight and Rain,* a collection of supernatural tales

1300	1500	1700

1338 The Ashikaga period begins; two imperial courts are established, one at Kyoto and one at Yoshino

1467 The Warring States period begins

1543 The Portuguese arrive in Japan and introduce firearms

1549 St. Francis Xavier introduces Christianity in Japan

1603 Tokugawa Ieyasu unites Japan and moves the capital to Edo

1614 Christianity is banned in Japan

1630s The shogun bans Japanese travel abroad; most ports are closed to foreigners

1707 Mount Fuji erupts

1853 American commodore Matthew C. Perry arrives in Edo Bay

1854 The Treaty of Kanagawa is signed, granting the United States access to two Japanese ports

1868 After the Tokugawa shogunate is overthrown, a new imperial government is established, with its capital in Edo

1300	1500	1700

1325 Aztecs build the city of Tenochtitlán

1347 Bubonic plague spreads to Europe, eventually killing millions

1368 Chinese rebels overthrow the Mongols

1455 The Gutenberg Bible is produced on a printing press in Germany

1492 Christopher Columbus sails across the Atlantic Ocean

1607 Jamestown becomes the first permanent North American colony

1631 Shah Jahan orders the building of the Taj Mahal in India ⋎

1776 The American colonies declare their independence from Britain

1789 The French Revolution begins

1804 Haiti gains independence from France

1830 Greece gains independence from the Ottoman Turks

Food
Traditional Japanese foods have become a part of
the American diet. Sashimi (shown above) consists
of thin slices of raw fish. Sushi (shown below) consists of cold cooked rice dressed with vinegar and
wrapped in seaweed along with slices of raw or
cooked fish, vegetables, or egg.

Zen
Japanese tea gardens, such as this one
in San Francisco's Golden Gate Park, are
popular attractions in many American
cities. The Zen-inspired setting offers an
oasis of peace and tranquillity to ease
the stress of modern life.

Art
Origami, or the art of paper folding, originated in China but is traditionally associated with
Japanese culture. Both simple and intricate
designs can be created by folding a single sheet
of paper. One of the most popular origami shapes is
the crane, which symbolizes long life and happiness to
the Japanese. Origami associations around the world
attest to the art's continuing popularity.

Nature

Bonsai, the art of growing miniature trees or plants in pots, originated in China but was perfected in Japan. For the Japanese, bonsai represents the harmony among people, nature, and the divine. Today the miniature trees are cultivated throughout the world.

Fashion

In the 1970s, Japanese fashion designers Issey Miyake and Rei Kawakubo rocked the fashion world. They combined Western materials and styles with the traditional Japanese principles of beauty and simplicity to create an innovative look.

from

THE PILLOW BOOK

Sei Shōnagon

Sei Shōnagon
965?–1013?

Woman of Mystery Very little is known about the Japanese writer Sei Shōnagon (sā′ shō′nä-gōn′). She is widely believed to have been the daughter of Motosuke (mō′tō-soo′kĕ), a well-known scholar and poet. However, whether Shōnagon was Motosuke's natural or adopted daughter is uncertain. Even the writer's real name is unknown. *Shōnagon,* a name given her at the imperial court where she served, means "minor counselor"; *Sei* refers to her family name.

A Sharp Wit Most of what we do know about Shōnagon comes from *The Pillow Book,* a sort of diary she kept while serving as lady in waiting to Empress Sadako (sä-dä′kō) during the last decade of the 900s. *The Pillow Book* is a collection of character sketches, lists, anecdotes, and poems that provides a vivid glimpse into the lives of the Japanese nobility during the Heian (hā′än) period (794–1185). During this period, the capital was moved from Nara to Heian, on the site of present-day Kyoto, and a highly refined court society arose among the upper class. The book also reveals Shōnagon as an intelligent woman who enjoyed conversing and matching wits with men as an equal.

Literary Rivals Shōnagon worried about how her book would be received. She probably knew that it would not find favor with Murasaki Shikibu (moo′rä-sä′kē shē′kē-boo′), the author of *The Tale of Genji* (see page 508). Murasaki, a lady in waiting for another empress at the Heian court, had a reputation for finding fault with her contemporaries. In her diary, Murasaki predicted that Shōnagon's unconventional behavior would have terrible consequences: "Someone who makes such an effort to be different from others is bound to fall in people's esteem, and I can only think that her future will be a hard one." Actually, nothing is known of Shōnagon's life after she left the palace. The traditional belief is that she died alone and in poverty. However, that bleak end may have been imagined by those who, like Murasaki, believed that was what Shōnagon deserved.

Build Background

Random Notes *The Pillow Book* is the first and best example of a Japanese genre known as *zuihitsu* (zo͞o´ē-hē´tso͞o), which means "random notes" or "occasional writings." In addition to lists, character sketches, and notes, Sei Shōnagon's collection includes brief essays ranging from observations of nature to witty comments on her experiences at the imperial court. Scholar and translator Arthur Waley has called the collection of observations and anecdotes of Heian court life "the most important document of the period that we possess."

In an anecdote appearing in the book's epilogue, Shōnagon claims that she began writing her accounts when a court official brought Empress Sadako a bundle of notebooks.

> *"Let me make them into a pillow,"* I said.
> *"Very well," said Her Majesty. "You may have them."*

Pillow refers to an informal book of notes written by a nobleman or noblewoman at night, in the privacy of the bedroom. Such books may have been tucked away in the drawers of the wooden pillows on which the nobility rested their heads while they slept.

The Pillow Book was not actually printed until the 1600s. It was read, however, well before then. At some point in the process—perhaps after the first draft was completed about 996—the book apparently was circulated around the court. According to Shōnagon, it was well received. She wrote: "[S]trange as it may seem, people who have read it say such things as, 'You put us all in the shade!'" Shōnagon's wit and the beauty of her language continue to be admired and have inspired Japanese writers for more than a thousand years.

Connect to Your Life

In these writings, you will read lists of things that Shōnagon finds hateful, graceful, and embarrassing. List some of the items you would record under these categories. Then get together with a partner and share your lists.

Focus Your Reading

LITERARY ANALYSIS: DIARY

A **diary** is a writer's personal day-by-day account of his or her experiences and impressions. As you read the excerpts from Sei Shōnagon's diary, think about some of the differences between her account of the period in which she lived and what you might find in a traditional history text.

ACTIVE READING: EXAMINING POINT OF VIEW

Point of view refers to the method of narrating used in a piece of writing. Shōnagon's diary—like any diary—is written from the first-person point of view. That is, the author is an active participant in the events and situations she describes and comments on. While you learn about everyday court life, you also learn about Shōnagon. When you read the judgments she makes about others, you can draw conclusions about her personality.

📖 **READER'S NOTEBOOK** As you read the diary excerpts, create three different charts and list the things Shōnagon finds hateful, embarrassing, and graceful. After you list an item, write down what the observation reveals about the author.

WORDS TO KNOW Vocabulary Preview

ablution	basking	ignoramus
banish	clandestine	

from The Pillow Book

Sei Shōnagon

Translated by Ivan Morris

Woman and a Cat. Utagawa Kunimasa. Tokyo National Museum.

HUMANITIES CONNECTION The cat in this painting is perched on top of a foot warmer. In the extravagant Heian period, aristocrats were accustomed to luxury.

The cat who lived in the Palace had been awarded the headdress of nobility and was called Lady Myōbu.[1] She was a very pretty cat, and His Majesty saw to it that she was treated with the greatest care.

One day she wandered on to the veranda, and Lady Uma, the nurse in charge of her, called out, "Oh, you naughty thing! Please come inside at once." But the cat paid no attention and went on basking sleepily in the sun. Intending to give her a scare, the nurse called for the dog, Okinamaro.[2]

"Okinamaro, where are you?" she cried. "Come here and bite Lady Myōbu!" The foolish Okinamaro, believing that the nurse was in earnest, rushed at the cat, who, startled and terrified, ran behind the blind in the Imperial Dining Room, where the Emperor happened to be sitting. Greatly surprised, His Majesty picked up the cat and held her in his arms. He summoned his gentlemen-in-waiting. When Tadataka, the Chamberlain,[3] appeared, His Majesty ordered that Okinamaro be chastised and banished to Dog Island. The attendants all started to chase the dog amid great confusion. His Majesty also reproached Lady Uma. "We shall have to find a new nurse for our cat," he told her. "I no longer feel I can count on you to look after her." Lady Uma bowed; thereafter she no longer appeared in the Emperor's presence.

The Imperial Guards quickly succeeded in catching Okinamaro and drove him out of the Palace grounds. Poor dog! He used to swagger about so happily. Recently, on the third day of the Third Month,[4] when the Controller First Secretary paraded him through the Palace grounds, Okinamaro was adorned with garlands of willow leaves, peach blossoms on his head, and cherry blossoms round his body. How could the dog have imagined that this would be his fate? We all felt sorry for him. "When Her Majesty was having her meals," recalled one of the ladies-in-waiting, "Okinamaro always used to be in attendance and sit opposite us. How I miss him!"

It was about noon, a few days after Okinamaro's banishment, that we heard a dog howling fearfully. How could any dog possibly cry so long? All the other dogs rushed out in excitement to see what was happening. Meanwhile a woman who served as a cleaner in the Palace latrines ran up to us. "It's terrible," she said. "Two of the Chamberlains are flogging a dog. They'll surely kill him. He's being punished for having come back after he was banished. It's Tadataka and Sanefusa[5] who are beating him." Obviously the victim was Okinamaro. I was absolutely wretched and sent a servant to ask the men to stop; but just then the howling finally ceased. "He's dead," one of

---

1. **Lady Myōbu** (myō′bōo): a name formed from titles given to a high-ranking lady in waiting.

2. **Okinamaro** (ō-kē′nä-mä′rō).

3. **Tadataka** (tä′dä-tä′kä), **the Chamberlain:** one of the officials in the emperor's private office.

4. **third day of the Third Month:** the day of the annual Peach Festival, when palace dogs were often decorated with flowers and leaves.

5. **Sanefusa** (sä′nĕ-fōo′sä).

WORDS TO KNOW

basking (bǎs′kǐng) *n.* warming oneself pleasantly **bask** *v.*
banish (bǎn′ǐsh) *v.* to force to leave a place or country

THE PILLOW BOOK   **501**

Three Women Reading a Letter, Katsukawa Terushige. Tokyo National Museum.

the servants informed me. "They've thrown his body outside the gate."

That evening, while we were sitting in the Palace bemoaning Okinamaro's fate, a wretched-looking dog walked in; he was trembling all over, and his body was fearfully swollen.

"Oh dear," said one of the ladies-in-waiting. "Can this be Okinamaro? We haven't seen any other dog like him recently, have we?"

We called to him by name, but the dog did not respond. Some of us insisted that it was Okinamaro, others that it was not. "Please send for Lady Ukon,"[6] said the Empress, hearing our discussion. "She will certainly be able to tell." We immediately went to Ukon's room and told

her she was wanted on an urgent matter.

"Is this Okinamaro?" the Empress asked her, pointing to the dog.

"Well," said Ukon, "it certainly looks like him, but I cannot believe that this loathsome creature is really our Okinamaro. When I called Okinamaro, he always used to come to me, wagging his tail. But this dog does not react at all. No, it cannot be the same one. And besides, wasn't Okinamaro beaten to death and his body thrown away? How could any dog be alive after being flogged by two strong men?" Hearing this, Her Majesty was very unhappy.

---

6. **Ukon** ($\overline{oo}$′kōn).

When it got dark, we gave the dog something to eat; but he refused it, and we finally decided that this could not be Okinamaro.

On the following morning I went to attend the Empress while her hair was being dressed and she was performing her <u>ablutions</u>. I was holding up the mirror for her when the dog we had seen on the previous evening slunk into the room and crouched next to one of the pillars. "Poor Okinamaro!" I said. "He had such a dreadful beating yesterday. How sad to think he is dead! I wonder what body he has been born into this time.[7] Oh, how he must have suffered!"

At that moment the dog lying by the pillar started to shake and tremble, and shed a flood of tears. It was astounding. So this really was Okinamaro! On the previous night it was to avoid betraying himself that he had refused to answer to his name. We were immensely moved and pleased. "Well, well, Okinamaro!" I said, putting down the mirror. The dog stretched himself flat on the floor and yelped loudly, so that the Empress beamed with delight. All the ladies gathered round, and Her Majesty summoned Lady Ukon. When the Empress explained what had happened, everyone talked and laughed with great excitement.

The news reached His Majesty, and he too came to the Empress's room. "It's amazing," he said with a smile. "To think that even a dog has such deep feelings!" When the Emperor's ladies-in-waiting heard the story, they too came along in a great crowd. "Okinamaro!" we called, and this time the dog rose and limped about the room with his swollen face. "He must have a meal prepared for him," I said. "Yes," said the Empress, laughing happily, "now that Okinamaro has finally told us who he is."

The Chamberlain, Tadataka, was informed, and he hurried along from the Table Room. "Is it really true?" he asked. "Please let me see for myself." I sent a maid to him with the following reply: "Alas, I am afraid that this is not the same dog after all." "Well," answered Tadataka, "whatever you say, I shall sooner or later have occasion to see the animal. You won't be able to hide him from me indefinitely."

Before long, Okinamaro was granted an Imperial pardon and returned to his former happy state. Yet even now, when I remember how he whimpered and trembled in response to our sympathy, it strikes me as a strange and moving scene; when people talk to me about it, I start crying myself.

---

from **HATEFUL THINGS**

One is in a hurry to leave, but one's visitor keeps chattering away. If it is someone of no importance, one can get rid of him by saying, "You must tell me all about it next time"; but, should it be the sort of visitor whose presence commands one's best behavior, the situation is hateful indeed. . . .

A man who has nothing in particular to recommend him discusses all sorts of subjects at random as though he knew everything. . . .

To envy others and to complain about one's own lot; to speak badly about people; to be inquisitive about the most trivial matters and to resent and abuse people for not telling one, or, if one does manage to worm out some facts, to inform everyone in the most detailed fashion as if one had known all from the beginning—oh, how hateful!

---

7. **what body he has been born into this time:** Buddhism teaches that after death the soul or spirit is reborn in a new body.

One is just about to be told some interesting piece of news when a baby starts crying.

A flight of crows circle about with loud caws.

An admirer has come on a <u>clandestine</u> visit, but a dog catches sight of him and starts barking. One feels like killing the beast. . . .

One has gone to bed and is about to doze off when a mosquito appears, announcing himself in a reedy voice. One can actually feel the wind made by his wings and, slight though it is, one finds it hateful in the extreme.

A carriage passes with a nasty, creaking noise. Annoying to think that the passengers may not even be aware of this! If I am traveling in someone's carriage and I hear it creaking, I dislike not only the noise but also the owner of the carriage.

One is in the middle of a story when someone butts in and tries to show that he is the only clever person in the room. Such a person is hateful, and so, indeed, is anyone, child or adult, who tries to push himself forward.

One is telling a story about old times when someone breaks in with a little detail that he happens to know, implying that one's own version is inaccurate—disgusting behavior! . . .

A newcomer pushes ahead of the other members in a group; with a knowing look, this person starts laying down the law and forcing advice upon everyone—most hateful.

from GRACEFUL THINGS

A slim, handsome young nobleman in a Court cloak.

A pretty girl casually dressed in a trouser-skirt, over which she wears only a loosely sewn coat. Some herbal balls are attached to her sleeve by a long cord, and she is seated by the balustrade,[8] her face hidden behind a fan.

An attractive young woman raises the lower part of a white curtain of state[9] and attaches it to the cross-bar on top. Over her unlined robe of white damask she wears a coat of violet gauze. She is engaged in writing practice, and the fine, smooth sheets of her notebook are elegantly bound by threads of uneven shading.

A letter written on fine green paper is attached to a budding willow branch.

A bearded basket,[10] beautifully dyed, is attached to a five-needled pine branch.

A fan with three ribs. Five-ribbed fans are too thick and they look ugly in the middle.

An attractively designed cypress box.

Thin white braid.

A cypress-thatched roof, neither too new nor too old, is beautifully covered with iris.

Below a green bamboo blind one catches sight of a curtain of state whose bright, glossy material is decorated with a pattern of decaying wood. It is pretty too when the ornamental curtain-cord is allowed to flutter in the breeze.

One day by the balustrade before a set of thin head-blinds I saw a pretty cat with a red collar and a white name-tag. He looked very elegant as he walked along, pulling his anchor cord[11] and biting it.

EMBARRASSING THINGS

While entertaining a visitor, one hears some servants chatting without any restraint in one of the back rooms. It is embarrassing to know that one's visitor can overhear. But how to stop them?

---

8. **balustrade** (băl'ə-strād′): a railing supported by short posts or columns.

9. **curtain of state:** a portable frame hung with cloth strips, used to screen women from the view of men and strangers.

10. **bearded basket:** a bamboo basket with the loose ends of the bamboo wrapped around the outside, giving the basket a shaggy appearance.

11. **anchor cord:** a tether used to keep a cat from straying too far.

A man whom one loves gets drunk and keeps repeating himself.

To have spoken about someone not knowing that he could overhear. This is embarrassing even if it be a servant or some other completely insignificant person.

To hear one's servants making merry. This is equally annoying if one is on a journey and staying in cramped quarters or at home and hears the servants in a neighboring room.

Parents, convinced that their ugly child is adorable, pet him and repeat the things he has said, imitating his voice.

An ignoramus who in the presence of some learned person puts on a knowing air and converses about men of old.

A man recites his own poems (not especially good ones) and tells one about the praise they have received—most embarrassing.

Lying awake at night, one says something to one's companion, who simply goes on sleeping.

In the presence of a skilled musician, someone plays a zither[12] just for his own pleasure and without tuning it.

An adopted son-in-law who has long since stopped visiting his wife runs into his father-in-law in a public place.

distant province and one is worried about him, and then a letter suddenly arrives, one feels as though one were seeing him face to face. Again, it is a great comfort to have expressed one's feelings in a letter even though one knows it cannot yet have arrived. If letters did not exist, what dark depressions would come over one! When one has been worrying about something and wants to tell a certain person about it, what a relief it is to put it all down in a letter! Still greater is one's joy when a reply arrives. At that moment a letter really seems like an elixir of life.

I REMEMBER A CLEAR MORNING

I remember a clear morning in the Ninth Month[13] when it had been raining all night. Despite the bright sun, dew was still dripping from the chrysanthemums in the garden. On the bamboo fences and criss-cross hedges I saw tatters of spider webs; and where the threads were broken the raindrops hung on them like strings of white pearls. I was greatly moved and delighted.

As it became sunnier, the dew gradually vanished from the clover and the other plants where it had lain so heavily; the branches began to stir, then suddenly sprang up of their own accord. Later I described to people how beautiful it all was. What most impressed me was that they were not at all impressed. ❖

Detail of *Five Beautiful Women* (early 19th century), Katsushika Hokusai. Gouache and ink on silk. Seattle (Washington) Art Museum, Margaret E. Fuller Purchase Fund. Photograph by Susan Dirk.

12. **zither:** the koto, a Japanese instrument played by plucking its 13 strings.

13. **Ninth Month:** the autumn month in which the Chrysanthemum Festival was held.

LETTERS ARE COMMONPLACE

Letters are commonplace enough, yet what splendid things they are! When someone is in a

WORDS TO KNOW
ignoramus (ĭg′nə-rā′məs) *n.* a foolish or ignorant person

Connect to the Literature

1. What Do You Think? Which part of *The Pillow Book* did you think was the most interesting? Explain.

Comprehension Check
- Why doesn't Okinamaro answer to his name after his banishment from the court?
- What are some of the hateful things that Shōnagon lists?
- Why does Shōnagon consider letters "splendid things"?

Think Critically

2. After the ladies recognize the dog as Okinamaro, why do you think Shōnagon sends word to Tadataka that "this is not the same dog after all"?

THINK ABOUT
- what Tadataka does to Okinamaro when the dog is banished
- how the Empress and the ladies welcome Okinamaro back

3. ACTIVE READING: EXAMINING POINT OF VIEW Review the charts that you created in your ▢ **READER'S NOTEBOOK**. How would you describe the author, based on the things she finds hateful, graceful, and embarrassing?

4. Shōnagon says that when she described a beautiful morning to people, what most impressed her was "that they were not at all impressed." What do you think she means?

Extend Interpretations

5. Critic's Corner Murasaki Shikibu, the author of *The Tale of Genji* and a contemporary of Shōnagon's, wrote that Shōnagon had "the most extraordinary air of self-satisfaction." Based on what you have read of *The Pillow Book,* do you agree or disagree? Explain your answer.

6. Connect to Life Review the lists of hateful, graceful, and embarrassing things you created for the Connect to Your Life on page 499. Are any of the items you listed similar to those Shōnagon mentions? Which of her observations do you agree with? Considering that *The Pillow Book* was written over a thousand years ago, what generalizations can you make about human nature?

LITERARY ANALYSIS: DIARY

A **diary** contains a writer's personal day-by-day account of his or her experiences and impressions. In many ways, *The Pillow Book* isn't a typical diary. While most diaries are written in chronological order, Sei Shōnagon's book is randomly arranged. Also, diaries are usually not intended to be read by others. However, Shōnagon carefully crafted her writing with an eye to its eventual publication. Nonetheless, like other diaries, *The Pillow Book* provides an intimate glimpse into the life of its author. In the following passage, for example, notice the details that reveal Shōnagon's duties as a lady in waiting.

On the following morning I went to attend the Empress while her hair was being dressed and she was performing her ablutions. I was holding up the mirror for her when the dog we had seen on the previous evening slunk into the room and crouched next to one of the pillars.

Paired Activity Review the section titled "The Cat Who Lived in the Palace." From the descriptions and dialogue Shōnagon provides, what insights do you gain into life at the Heian court and the author's relationships with the people there? With a partner, list what you learned. Then think about the different kinds of details you might find in a more historical text on Heian court life. What are the advantages and disadvantages of each type of account?

Writing Options

1. Pillow Book Create a "pillow book" of your own. Record anecdotes about school events, and write down your impressions and observations about the students and teachers in your classes. Like Shōnagon, create a title for each group of notes. If you like, you can share some of your notes with the class. However, since a pillow book is meant to be a type of diary, you may choose to keep the contents to yourself.

Writing Handbook
See page R27: Descriptive Writing.

2. List of Distressing Things
Elsewhere in *The Pillow Book,* Shōnagon makes a list of "surprising and distressing things." Think about events that you find both unexpected and upsetting and compose your own list.

Activities & Explorations

1. Scene Illustration Create a drawing or painting that illustrates a description or scene from the selection. Share your work with classmates. ~ **ART**

2. Interview with Shōnagon
With a partner, take turns playing the role of Sei Shōnagon and conduct an interview about court life. Write a list of questions to prepare for the interview. For instance, you might ask Shōnagon's opinion of people in the court, including the Empress and the servants. You might also ask about Shōnagon's likes and dislikes. ~ **SPEAKING AND LISTENING**

Communication Handbook
See page R52: Conducting Interviews.

Inquiry & Research

Canine Communication In "The Cat Who Lived in the Palace," Okinamaro seems to express deep emotion when the ladies recognize him. Do you think dogs are really capable of expressing emotion, or do they just communicate their basic needs? Find out what researchers have discovered about how and what dogs communicate. Then share your findings with the rest of the class.

RESEARCH STARTER
CLASSZONE.COM

Vocabulary in Action

EXERCISE: ANALOGIES On your paper, write the word that best completes each analogy.

1. nervous : tense :: hidden : _____

2. brilliant : genius :: foolish : _____

3. lake : swimming :: sun : _____

4. liberate : enslave :: invite : _____

5. overweight : diet :: unclean : _____

WORDS TO KNOW

ablution	basking	ignoramus
banish	clandestine	

Building Vocabulary

For an in-depth study of analogies, see page 768.

Lady Murasaki Shikibu

The Tale of Genji

Yasunari Kawabata, a Japanese writer who won the Nobel Prize in literature in 1968, has called *The Tale of Genji* (gĕn'jē) "the highest pinnacle of Japanese literature." However, this 11th-century masterpiece, which is considered the world's first novel, was almost totally unfamiliar to Western readers until English translations of the work were published in the 20th century. To this day, little is known about the author of the work, Murasaki Shikibu.

Born around 978, Murasaki was the daughter of a provincial governor who was also a scholar of Chinese and a renowned poet. As a child, Murasaki eavesdropped on her brother's lessons and learned Chinese more quickly than he did. Murasaki's brilliance led her father to regret that she had not been born a boy. In 998, she married a middle-aged man with whom she had a daughter in the following year. Four years after her husband's death in 1001, Murasaki was appointed a lady in waiting to Empress Akiko. Many believe that she penned *The Tale of Genji* while she was in service at the imperial court.

Written at the height of the highly cultured Heian period, *The Tale of Genji* relates the many romances of its hero, Prince Genji, the handsome son of an emperor. Known as the Shining Prince, Genji embodies the high-

Phoenix Hall, built during the Heian period by the noble Fujiwara family

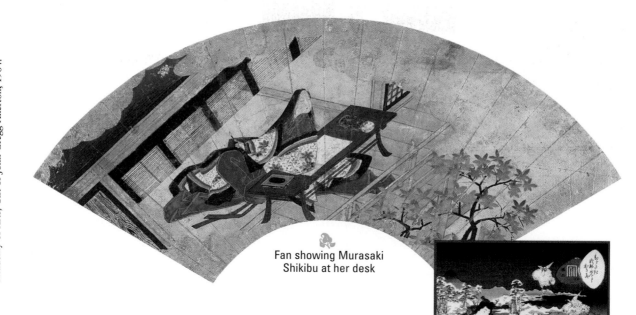

Fan showing Murasaki Shikibu at her desk

est ideals of Heian society—courtliness and sensitivity to nature. During the course of the novel, Genji marries three times and romances numerous women. Following his death, the tone of the novel grows more serious as it follows the next two generations of the prince's family.

The Tale of Genji offers a unique glimpse into Heian court society. The reader learns, for example, that aristocratic women blackened their teeth, covered their faces with white powder, shaved their eyebrows, and then painted brows high on their foreheads. Men used distinctive perfumes as a mark of identification. Both men and women were expected to be accomplished poets. To begin a romance, a man or woman composed a short poem that demonstrated his or her fine taste and artistry. The other person replied in kind. An error in poetic style could end the romance.

The novel does more than provide an account of Heian court life. It also reveals keen insight into the human heart because Murasaki created characters with emotional depth. Strikingly modern in its three-dimensional portrayal of characters, *The Tale of Genji* is often hailed as the first psychological novel.

With its compelling characters and dramatic events, *The Tale of Genji* has influenced Japanese culture for centuries. The novel has inspired painters and poets; passages from it have been incorporated into many Japanese Noh plays (see page 518). Japanese readers value the novel for its treatment of such traditional Japanese themes as nature, simplicity, and the impermanence of life. Yet, with its universal themes of love, loyalty, friendship, and family ties, the novel also has appeal for readers around the world.

Prince Genji with His Lover in a Boat Admiring the Snow in the Garden, woodblock print by Utagawa Hiroshige. Copyright © Bass Museum of Art/Corbis.

MILESTONE LINKS
CLASSZONE.COM

ZEN Teachings and Parables

Musō Soseki (1275–1351)

Pupil and Teacher From the time he was a young boy, Musō Soseki (mōō'sō sō-sĕk'ē) studied Shingon Buddhism. Soon after his teacher died, however, Musō converted to Zen Buddhism. He received instruction in Zen from both Chinese and Japanese masters but could not find the enlightenment he sought. Enlightenment is a state of spiritual awakening in which the individual rises above the desire for such earthly things as success and possessions. Musō's awakening finally occurred one day when he started to lean against a wall but lost his balance and fell. According to Musō's own account of the incident, his "wall of darkness" disappeared when he fell. In time, Musō himself became an influential Zen teacher with more than 50 disciples, an unusually high number.

Powerful Disciples In the 1330s, a powerful clan by the name of Ashikaga (ä'shē-kä'gä) established a new military government, with its capital at Kyoto. Members of this clan served as shoguns, or military leaders, of Japan. Two of Musō's most powerful disciples were Ashikaga shoguns. Influenced by Musō's Zen teachings, these shoguns instituted new policies affecting

commerce, religion, and culture. In this way, Zen teachings helped further the development of Japanese civilization. In addition to teaching the shoguns, Musō also instructed the emperor, from whom he received the title Kokushi (kō-kōō'shē), or National Teacher.

Lasting Legacy Under Musō's influence, Zen received official recognition from the imperial court and spread throughout Japan. Musō also helped shape monasteries into serious centers for Zen study. He served at several of these and supervised the building of new temples. Some time before his death, Musō left the following verse to his disciples. The lines reflect the Zen belief that we are merely transient, or temporary, and that our earthly life is a vehicle to a richer afterlife.

> *With one stroke I erase my delay in the transient world.*
> *What does this mean? Yasa!*

Build Background

Path to Enlightenment Zen is a form of Buddhism that originated in China, where it is called Ch'an. According to legend, Zen was first taught by a Buddhist monk named Bodhidharma (bō-dǐ-dûr'mə), who came to China from India in the A.D. 500s. By the 1100s, Zen had spread to Japan, where it quickly became a powerful religious and cultural force. During the 13th century, the samurai were drawn to Zen because of the importance it placed on discipline and simplicity. Zen also influenced the arts, inspiring the stylized structure of Noh drama and the conciseness of haiku.

Zen masters and their disciples aspire to achieve a state of spiritual enlightenment called satori (sä-tôr'ē). They believe that satori can be attained through meditation and by living a life of self-discipline and simplicity. Bodhidharma himself is said to have achieved satori only after gazing at a wall for nine years. Zen followers try to open their mind to new ways of thinking. They also try to control their ego.

The selections you are about to read include three Zen teachings and two Zen parables. The teachings are taken from a collection of Musō Soseki's replies to questions posed by one of the Ashikaga shoguns. The parables appear in a collection of stories drawn from a 13th-century book called the *Shaseki-shu* (shä-sĕk'ē-shōo') and from anecdotes of Zen monks. Both the teachings and the parables are intended to help others understand the spirit of Zen, which has been described as a door opening to insight.

Connect to Your Life

How would you sum up your own philosophy of life? Do you try to live by a certain set of rules, or do you have a more relaxed approach to life? Discuss your philosophy with a small group of classmates.

Focus Your Reading

LITERARY ANALYSIS: WISDOM LITERATURE

Wisdom literature is writing that teaches rules for living and conveys scholarly learning. Wisdom literature often takes the form of **parables,** brief stories that are meant to teach a lesson or illustrate a moral truth. The parables you are about to read contain paradoxes, or seeming contradictions, designed to make the reader question conventional logic. As you read the parables, think about the paradox each one contains.

ACTIVE READING: SUMMARIZING MAIN IDEAS

When you summarize the **main idea** of a piece of writing, you identify its main point. Sometimes the main point is clearly stated. At other times, however, you must "read between the lines" to figure out what point the writer is trying to get across.

📖 **READER'S NOTEBOOK** Keeping track of important details can help you identify and summarize a main idea. As you read the Zen teachings, record the details of each in a web diagram like the one below.

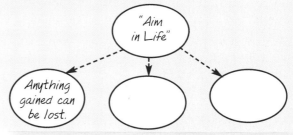

Zen Teachings

Musō Soseki

Translated by Thomas Cleary

Aim in Life

Read to find out what Zen followers think about earthly goods.

There is ultimately no means of safeguarding anything in this world; anything you gain can be lost, destroyed, or taken away. For this reason, if you make the acquisition and retention of goods or status your aim in life, this is a way to anxiety and sorrow.

HUMANITIES CONNECTION Every day the monks at Daisen-in, a famous Zen garden in Kyoto, rake the sand into furrows representing a calm ocean. Three mounds of sand are formed but only two are ever visible at one time, demonstrating that the world cannot be perceived in its entirety.

Contamination of Virtue

*What should be the motivation
for doing a good deed?*

Doing good seeking rewards is contaminated
virtue. Doing good without thought of reward,
dedicating it to enlightenment, is uncontaminated
virtue. Contamination and noncontamination
refer to the state of mind of the doer, not to the
good deed itself.

Hypocritical Scholars

Note the author's wisdom about teachers.

Many Buddhist scholars do not actually aspire to
enlightenment but really study to enhance their
own reputation and prestige and to feed their
personal pride. When they get some knowledge,
they set themselves up as teachers and fool the
ignorant. They tell people their bit of knowledge
and interpretation and give formal approval to
any scholars whose views correspond with their
own. This is a big mistake.

Zen Parables

Translated by Nyogen Senzaki and Paul Reps

Publishing the Sutras

*Why does Tetsugen give away
the money he collects for his books?*

Tetsugen,[1] a devotee of Zen in Japan, decided to publish the sutras,[2] which at that time were available only in Chinese. The books were to be printed with wood blocks in an edition of seven thousand copies, a tremendous undertaking.

Tetsugen began by traveling and collecting donations for this purpose. A few sympathizers would give him a hundred pieces of gold, but most of the time he received only small coins. He thanked each donor with equal gratitude. After ten years Tetsugen had enough money to begin his task.

It happened that at that time the Uji River[3] overflowed. Famine followed. Tetsugen took the funds he had collected for the books and spent them to save others from starvation. Then he began again his work of collecting.

Several years afterwards an epidemic spread over the country. Tetsugen again gave away what he had collected, to help his people.

For a third time he started his work, and after twenty years his wish was fulfilled. The printing blocks which produced the first edition of sutras can be seen today in the Obaku[4] monastery in Kyoto.[5]

The Japanese tell their children that Tetsugen made three sets of sutras, and that the first two invisible sets surpass even the last.

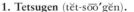

---

1. **Tetsugen** (tĕt-sōō′gĕn).
2. **sutras** (sōō′trəz): scriptures setting forth Buddhist doctrines.
3. **Uji** (ōō′jē).
4. **Obaku** (ō′bä-kōō′).
5. **Kyoto** (kyō′tō): Japan's imperial capital from A.D. 794 to 1869.

Right & Wrong

*Read to find out why students
are best taught by example.*

When Bankei[6] held his seclusion-weeks of meditation, pupils from many parts of Japan came to attend. During one of these gatherings a pupil was caught stealing. The matter was reported to Bankei with the request that the culprit be expelled. Bankei ignored the case.

Later the pupil was caught in a similar act, and again Bankei disregarded the matter. This angered the other pupils, who drew up a petition asking for the dismissal of the thief, stating that otherwise they would leave in a body.

When Bankei had read the petition he called everyone before him. "You are wise brothers," he told them. "You know what is right and what is not right. You may go somewhere else to study if you wish, but this poor brother does not even know right from wrong. Who will teach him if I do not? I am going to keep him here even if all the rest of you leave."

A torrent of tears cleansed the face of the brother who had stolen. All desire to steal had vanished.

●

Carving of Zen Priest Hoto Kokushi. Cleveland Museum of Art, Ohio/Superstock.

HUMANITIES CONNECTION During the Kamakura period, respected artists began creating realistic sculpted portraits of leading Zen priests. These sculptures were traditionally displayed only on special occasions. In this sculpture, the Zen master's hands are positioned in a characteristic meditative pose.

---

6. **Bankei** (bän′kā): a Zen master known as a realistic, down-to-earth teacher.

Connect to the Literature

1. **What Do You Think?**
   Which teaching or parable did you like the best? Why?

   Comprehension Check
   - According to Musō Soseki, what will happen to a person who cares only about possessions and status?
   - Why did Tetsugen take 20 years to publish the sutras?
   - Why did Bankei's pupils become angry and draw up a petition?

Think Critically

2. According to Musō Soseki, a good deed cannot be spoiled by the selfish intentions of the doer. Do you agree? Explain your answer.

3. Why might the state of mind of a hypocritical Buddhist scholar be considered "contaminated"?

4. What does the parable "Publishing the Sutras" suggest about what is important to Zen followers?

5. In the parable "Right & Wrong," the thief cries and loses his desire to steal after Bankei refuses to dismiss him. Why do you think Bankei's decision has such a powerful effect on the thief?

6. **ACTIVE READING: SUMMARIZING MAIN IDEAS**
   Compare the web diagram that you created in your 📖 **READER'S NOTEBOOK** with those of some of your classmates. Based on the details you recorded, how would you summarize the **main idea** in each Zen teaching?

Extend Interpretations

7. **Comparing Texts** Compare the Zen teachings and stories you have read with the teachings from the *Tao Te Ching* (page 440). What do both philosophies teach about worldly possessions? Which philosophy do you think would be more difficult to follow? Explain your answer.

8. **Connect to Life** Bankei refuses to give up trying to teach his student right from wrong. Think of a time when someone showed a great deal of patience while trying to teach you something. What did you learn? How did you feel toward your teacher? Do you think patience is a necessary characteristic of a teacher?

LITERARY ANALYSIS: WISDOM LITERATURE

Writing that teaches rules for living and conveys scholarly learning is called **wisdom literature.** One form of wisdom literature is the **parable**—a story that teaches a moral or lesson about life. The story told in a Zen parable often appears simple, but it contains a deep underlying message. A Zen parable may also contain a paradox, or seeming contradiction. For example, consider the paradox in the following sentence from "Publishing the Sutras":

The Japanese tell their children that Tetsugen made three sets of sutras, and that the first two invisible sets surpass even the last.

Thinking about a paradox presented in a story can help you infer the story's message, or moral.

Cooperative Learning Activity
With a group of classmates, analyze the two Zen parables you have read. Identify the paradox in each parable. Then use your understanding of the paradox to help you decide the parable's moral. Write down your ideas in a chart like the one shown below. Share your conclusions with the rest of the class.

Parable	Paradox	Moral
"Publishing the Sutras"		
"Right & Wrong"		

Writing Options

Zen Solutions Suppose someone in your class constantly cheats on tests. Imagine that this person copies others' answers and secretly uses detailed notes during tests. As a result of this cheating, the person receives high grades. Think about how you would apply what you have learned from the Zen teachings and parables to deal with this problem. Then write a paragraph explaining how you would handle the matter. Place the paragraph in your **Working Portfolio.**

Zen—Alive and Well

When Zen was introduced in the West in the 20th century, people found new ways to express and interpret its spirit. In the 1950s, for example, the Beats—a group of young, unconventional writers—interpreted Zen as a philosophy of living without restrictions or inhibitions. Beat writers such as Jack Kerouac and Allen Ginsberg tried to express their Zen spirit by producing works that were spontaneous, free of literary devices, and unrestricted by formal grammar.

Here are some other ways that the Zen spirit survives today.

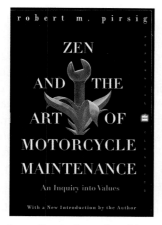

According to the author, "the Buddha . . . resides quite as comfortably in the circuits of a digital computer or the gears of a cycle transmission as he does at the top of a mountain or in the petals of a flower."

To reduce the stress of daily modern life and find meaning in a world dominated by possessions and status, many people have turned to Zen meditation.

In karate, a traditional Japanese martial art, students practice a sort of meditation in action. They are expected to perform all movements with an intense, Zenlike focus on the present.

Paired or Group Discussion Do you think Zen can be a part of everyday life as we live it today? If true Zen lies in being fully present in the here and now, how can you adapt Zen to taking a test? playing computer games? standing in line at the grocery store?

THE DESERTED CRONE

Zeami Motokiyo

Father and Son Born in 1363, Zeami Motokiyo (zā-ä′mē mō′tō-kē′yō) is known as the leading playwright of Japanese Noh (nō) drama. Noh began in 14th-century Japan as religious drama. Zeami, along with his father, Kanami Kiyotsugu (kän-ä′mē kē′yō-tsōō′gōō), developed Noh into one of the world's great dramatic forms. In 1374, when Zeami was only 11 years old, he and his father, both Noh actors, performed before the shogun Ashikaga Yoshimitsu (ä′shē-kä′gä yō′shē-mē′tsōō). The military leader was so impressed with the two actors that he offered their troupe his patronage. After Kanami died, Zeami took over the Noh acting school that his father had started. Zeami also began writing sophisticated new plays for his aristocratic audience. In 1422, Zeami became a Zen monk, and his son Motomasa (mō′tō-mä′sä) took his place as the leading figure in Noh theater.

Writer and Critic Zeami was the most prolific and talented of the Noh playwrights. In addition to plays, Zeami also wrote critical works on the Noh. His treatises were intended as manuals for his pupils, who began their training as children. In these works, Zeami identified the main principles of Noh acting. One of these he called *yūgen* (yōō′gĕn). According to Zeami, *yūgen* was "true beauty and gentleness." The term was also used to name the mysterious, indefinable quality underlying the text of the play and the actors' gestures. Zeami's own performances were said to convey this mysterious quality.

Exile and Death Zeami's charmed existence ended in 1429 when another member of the Ashikaga clan became shogun. The new military leader refused to allow Zeami's son Motomasa to perform at the imperial court in Kyoto. Motomasa died in 1432, and Zeami was exiled in 1434. He was allowed to return to Kyoto after the shogun's death in 1441. Zeami died just two years later. According to legend, the greatest playwright of Noh drama died alone in a Buddhist temple near Kyoto in 1443.

Build Background

The Magic of Noh Theater The curtain opens on a square stage with little scenery. A single note from a flute is played, and several characters appear in stylized masks and costumes. As the Noh play unfolds, the main character is revealed to be a ghost who is reluctant to leave the world. A long dance concludes the play.

Noh theater developed from dances performed at Shinto and Buddhist temples and shrines during harvest festivals and other celebrations. The dramatic form developed by Zeami retained its religious roots and appealed to Zen Buddhists because the plays were said to lead to spiritual enlightenment.

Every Noh play features certain principal roles. Here are the roles in *The Deserted Crone*.

shite (shē′tě): the main character, who performs the central dance

mae-jite (mī′jē′tě): the *shite* of the first part of the play

nochi-jite (nō′chē-jē′tě): the *shite* of the second part of the play

waki (wä′kē): a secondary character, who asks questions or introduces the story

wakizure (wä′kē-zōō′rě): a companion of the *waki*

kyōgen (kyō′gěn): a peasant or villager from the area in which the play is set

Noh and Greek Drama

In some ways, Noh is similar to Greek drama. In both forms, all the roles are performed by male actors who wear masks to convey character and emotion. Like a Greek tragedy, Noh drama is accompanied by dance, music, and a chorus. Plays in the two forms are often based on historical and legendary traditions.

Unlike a Greek tragedy, however, a Noh play involves little actual drama. The lines are spoken slowly, and Noh actors use gestures and movements to suggest meaning. Although a typical Noh play is only as long as a single act in a Greek play, the performance usually takes about an hour. The time is absorbed by the slow recitation of the lines and the concluding dance.

Connect to Your Life

Get together with a partner or small group and discuss a play you have seen performed recently, either live or on a movie or television screen. How does watching a play differ from watching a movie? What do you enjoy most about seeing a play? What do you like least? Jot down your thoughts.

Focus Your Reading

LITERARY ANALYSIS: SETTING AND CHARACTERS

The **setting** of a play is the time and place of the action. In Noh drama, often the only scenery on stage is a pine tree at the back. Thus, setting must be suggested by the play's dialogue and action. **Characters** are the people who participate in the action. Noh characters appear flat and one-dimensional. However, the words they speak help convey **mood,** or feeling. As you read the play, think about the relationship between the setting and the characters.

ACTIVE READING: QUESTIONING

When you read a challenging piece of writing, it is often helpful to stop occasionally and question what is happening. Searching for reasons behind events and characters' feelings can help you understand what you are reading.

READER'S NOTEBOOK As you read *The Deserted Crone,* write down any questions you have about the characters, setting, and action. Write down the answers, too, if you can figure them out from the text.

WORDS TO KNOW **Vocabulary Preview**

delusion	inhospitable	unimpeded
fleeting	solace	

The Deserted Crone

Zeami Motokiyo

Translated by **Stanleigh H. Jones, Jr.**

FOCUS In this play, a traveler journeys to Mount Obasute to view the full moon at the height of autumn. Read to find out whom he encounters at Obasute and what he learns there.

PERSONS A Traveler from the Capital (*waki*)
Two Companions to the traveler (*wakizure*)
An Old Woman (*mae-jite*)
The Ghost of the old woman (*nochi-jite*)
A Villager (*kyōgen*)

PLACE Mount Obasute (ō′bä-sōō′tě) in Shinano Province

TIME The fifteenth night of the eighth month
(midpoint of autumn, when the moon is full)

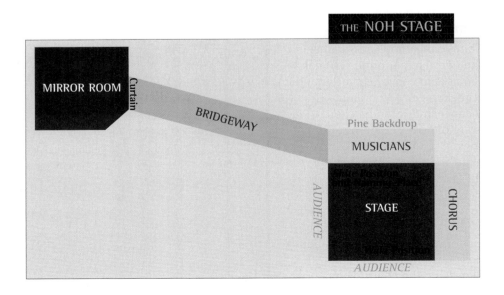

THE NOH STAGE

MIRROR ROOM

Curtain

BRIDGEWAY

Pine Backdrop

MUSICIANS

AUDIENCE

STAGE

CHORUS

AUDIENCE

Scene from a Noh play

(*A* Traveler *and two* Companions *from the Capital* [Kyoto] *enter and face each other at stage center. They wear short swords and conical* kasa *hats made of reeds.*)

Together. Autumn's height,
> The full moon's night is near,
> Soon the full moon's glory.
> Let us go and visit Mount Obasute.

(*The* Traveler *removes his hat and faces front.*)

5 **Traveler.** I am a man of the Capital. I have yet to see the moon of Sarashina and this autumn I have bestirred myself at last. I hurry now to Obasute Mountain.

(*He puts his hat back on and faces his* Companions.)

Together. On our journey—
> Fleeting are the dreams at inns along the way,
10 > Fleeting are the dreams at inns along the way,
> And once again we take our leave;
> Nights and days in lonely hostels
> Bring us here to famed Sarashina,

(*The* Traveler *faces front and takes a few steps forward, then returns to his place.*)

6 Sarashina (sä′rä-shē′nä): a locale in the mountains of central Japan—a popular place for viewing the moon.

Together. We have reached Obasute Mountain,
15   Reached Obasute Mountain.

(*His return indicates that he has arrived. He takes off his hat and faces front.*)

Traveler. We have traveled so swiftly that we are here already at Mount Obasute.

Companion. Indeed, that is so.

(*The* Companions *move to the* waki-*position. The* Traveler *goes to stage center.*)

Traveler. Now that I am here at Mount Obasute I see that
20   all is just as I imagined it—the level crest, the infinite sky, the <u>unimpeded</u> thousands of leagues of night flooded by the moon so clear. Yes, here I will rest and tonight gaze upon the moon.

(*The* Old Woman, *wearing the* fukai *mask, slowly starts down the bridgeway. The* Traveler *moves to the* waki-*position.*)

Old Woman. You there, traveler, what is it you were
25   saying?

(Traveler, *standing, goes downstage left.*)

Traveler. I have come from the Capital, and this is my first visit here. But tell me, where do you live?

Old Woman. In this village, Sarashina. Tonight is that mid-autumn night for which all have waited.

30   The moon has hurried the dusk of day,
        And now the high plain of heaven
        Glows in mounting brilliance—
        In all directions, the crystalline night.
        How wonderful the moon this evening!

35   **Traveler.** Oh, are you from Sarashina? Can you tell me then the spot where in ancient days the old woman was left to die?

(*The* Old Woman *has reached the* shite-*position.*)

Old Woman. You ask of the fate of the old woman of Obasute?—a thoughtless question. But if you mean the
40   remains of the woman who sang:

        "No <u>solace</u> for my heart at Sarashina
        When I see the moon
        Shining down on Mount Obasute,"

[Stage Direction] *fukai* (foo′kī) **mask**: a mask representing the face of a middle-aged woman.

Fukai mask (16th century). Painted Japanese cypress. The Tokugawa Art Museum, Nagoya, Japan.

WORDS TO KNOW
unimpeded (ŭn′ĭm-pē′dĭd) *adj.* not held back or obstructed
solace (sŏl′ĭs) *n.* comfort in sorrow or distress

They are here in the shadow of the little laurel tree—the
45   remains of an old woman long ago abandoned.

Traveler. Then here beneath this tree lie the woman's
    remains, the woman who was deserted?

Old Woman. Yes, deep in the loam,
    Buried in obscure grasses
50   Cut by the reaper.
    Short-lived, they say, as is this world,
    And already now . . .

Traveler. It is an ancient tale,
    Yet perhaps attachments still remain.

55 **Old Woman.** Yes, even after death . . . somehow . . .

Traveler. The dismal loneliness of this moor,

Old Woman. The penetrating wind,

Traveler. The lonely heart of autumn.

Chorus (*for the* Old Woman). Even now,
60   "No solace for my heart at Sarashina,
    No solace for my heart at Sarashina."
    At dusk of day on Mount Obasute
    The green lingers in the trees,
    The intermingled pines and laurels,
65   The autumn leaves so quickly tinged.
    Thin mists drift over One-Fold Mountain—
    Folds of faintly dyed cloth;
    In a cloudless sky a doleful wind.
    Lonely mountain vista,
70   Remote and friendless landscape.

68 doleful: very sad; full of grief.

Old Woman. Traveler, from where have you come?

Traveler. I am from the Capital, as I told you, but I have
    long heard of the beauties of the moon at Sarashina, and
    I come here now for the first time.

75 **Old Woman.** Are you indeed from the Capital? If that is so,
    then I will show myself with the moon tonight and
    entertain you here.

Traveler. Who are you that you should entertain me
    tonight?

80 **Old Woman.** In truth, I am from Sarashina . . .

Traveler. But where do you live now?

Old Woman. Where do I live? On this mountain . . .

Traveler. This famous mountain that bears the name . . .

Old Woman. Obasute Mountain of the Deserted Crone.

85 **Chorus** (*for the* Old Woman). Even to pronounce the
      name—
    How shameful!
    Long ago I was abandoned here.
    Alone on this mountainside
    I dwell, and every year
90   In the bright and full mid-autumn moon
    I try to clear away
    The dark confusion of my heart's attachment.
    That is why tonight I have come before you.

Chorus (*narrating*). Beneath the tree,
95   In the evening shadows,
    She vanished like a phantom,
    Like an apparition . . . disappeared . . .

(*She exits.*)

PAUSE & REFLECT What conclusion can you
draw about the old woman's identity? What evidence
supports your conclusion?

FOCUS Read to find out more about the old woman
and how she came to Mount Obasute.

(*The* Villager *enters and stands at the naming-
place. He wears a short sword.*)

Villager. I live at the foot of this mountain.
    Tonight the moon is full, and I think I will climb the
100   mountain and gaze at the moon.

(*He sees the* Traveler.)

    Ah! There's a gentleman I have never seen before. You
    sir, standing there in the moonlight, where are you from
    and where are you bound?

Traveler. I am from the Capital. I suppose you live in this
105   neighborhood?

Villager. Yes indeed, I do.

Traveler. Then come a bit closer. I have something to ask
    you.

Villager. Certainly.

(*He kneels at stage center.*)

91–92 I try . . . heart's attachment:
Following Buddhist teachings, the
woman tries to free herself from
worldly desires in order to achieve
enlightenment and final rest.

Lacquer writing box from the
Ashikaga period

Villager. You said you had something to ask. What might it be?

Traveler. You may be somewhat surprised at what I have to ask, but would you tell me anything you may know about the pleasures of moonviewing at Sarashina and the story of Obasute Mountain?

Villager. That is indeed a surprising request. I do live in this vicinity, it is true, but I have no detailed knowledge of such matters. Yet, would it not appear inhospitable if, the very first time we meet, I should say I know nothing of these things you ask? I will tell you, then, what in general I have heard.

Traveler. That is most kind of you.

Villager. Well then, here is the story of Mount Obasute: Long ago there lived at this place a man named Wada no Hikonaga. When he was still a child his parents died and he grew up under the care of an aunt. From the day of his marriage his wife hated his aunt and made many accusations against her. But Hikonaga would not listen to her. At length, however, his wife spoke out so strongly that he forgot his aunt's many years of kindness and bowing to his wife's demands, he said one day to the old woman: "Not far from this mountain is a holy image of the Buddha. Let us go there and make our offerings and prayers." So he brought her to this mountain and in a certain place he abandoned her. Later he looked back at the mountain where now the moon was bright and clear. He wanted to go back and fetch his aunt, but his wife was a crafty woman and she detained him until it was too late. The old woman died and her heart's attachment to this world turned her to stone. Hikonaga later went in search of her, and when he saw the stone he realized the dreadful thing he had done. He became a priest they say. Ever since then the mountain has been called Mount Obasute—Mountain of the Deserted Old Woman. Long ago it seems that the mountain was known as Sarashina Mountain. Well, that is what I know of the story. But why do you ask? It seems such an unusual request.

Traveler. How kind of you to tell me this story! I asked you for this reason: As I said a little while ago, I am from the Capital, but I had heard about Sarashina and so I made a special journey here to view the moon. A short while

124–125 Wada no Hikonaga (wä′dä nō hē′kō-nä′gä).

ago, as I was waiting for the moon to rise, an old
woman appeared to me from nowhere and recited to me
the poem about Obasute Mountain. She promised to
155 entertain me this night of the full moon, and I asked her
who she was. Long ago, she told me, her home was in
Sarashina, but now she dwelled on Mount Obasute. She
had come here this night in order to dispel the dark confusion of her heart's attachment. No sooner had she spoken
160 than here, in the shadows of this tree, she vanished.

Villager. Oh! Amazing! It must be the old woman's spirit,
still clinging to this world, who appeared and spoke with
you. If so, then stay awhile; recite the holy scriptures and
kindly pray for her soul's repose. I believe you will see
165 this strange apparition again.

Traveler. I think so too. I will gaze at the moon and cleanse
my heart. For somehow I feel certain I shall see this mysterious figure again.

Villager. If you have any further need of me, please call.

170 **Traveler.** I will.

Villager. I am at your service.

(*He exits.*)

PAUSE & REFLECT Why did Wada no Hikonaga bring
the old woman to Mount Obasute? What happened to her
there?

FOCUS As you continue reading, think about why the old
woman is drawn to Obasute and the real world.

Traveler and Companions. Evening twilight deepens,
And quickens on the moon which sheds
Its first light-shadows of the night.
175 How lovely:
Ten thousand miles of sky, every corner clear—
Autumn is everywhere the same.
Serene my heart, this night I shall spend in poetry.
"The color of the moon new-risen—
180 Remembrances of old friends
Two thousand leagues away."

HUMANITIES CONNECTION The *uba* mask was originally used in a play in which an old woman and an old man represent the spirits of two pine trees. It has since come to be used as well for the roles of ordinary old women.

Uba mask (Edo period).
Polychromed wood.
Tokyo National Museum.

(*The* Ghost *of the old woman enters, wearing the* uba *mask. She stands at the* shite-*position.*)

Ghost. How strange and wonderful this moment,
   Superb yet strange this moment out of time—
   Is my sadness only for the moon tonight?
185   With the dawn
   Half of autumn will have passed,
   And waiting for it seemed so long.
   The brilliant autumn moon of Mount Obasute,
   So matchless, flawless I cannot think
190   I have ever looked upon the moon before;
   Unbearably beautiful—
   Surely this is not the moon of long ago.

Traveler. Strange,
   In this moonlit night already grown so late
195   A woman robed in white appears—
   Do I dream?—Is it reality?

Ghost. Why do you speak of dreams?
   That aged figure who came to you by twilight
   In shame has come again.

200 **Traveler.** What need have you for apologies?

[Stage Direction] *uba* (o͞o′bä)
mask: a mask representing the face of an old woman who has once been beautiful.

Kariginu, Noh costume.
Eisei-Bunko Foundation,
Tokyo.

HUMANITIES CONNECTION The *kariginu* (hunting robe) is considered the most important outer garment for male actors in Noh plays. Originally worn by Heian aristocrats, such robes were later adopted by elite samurai as their most formal garment.

This place, as everybody knows is called . . .
Obasute—

Ghost. Mountain where an old hag dwells.

Traveler. The past returns,
205   An autumn night . . .

Ghost. Friends had gathered
To share the moon together . . .
Grass on the ground was our cushion . . .

Traveler. Waking, sleeping, among flowers,
210   The dew clinging to our sleeves.

Together. So many varied friends
Reveling in the moonlight . . .
When did we first come together?
Unreal—like a dream.

215 **Chorus** (for the Ghost). Like the lady-flower nipped
          by time,
The lady-flower past its season,
I wither in robes of grass;
Trying to forget that long ago
I was cast aside, abandoned,
220   I have come again to Mount Obasute.
How it shames me now to show my face
In Sarashina's moonlight, where all can see!
Ah, well, this world is all a dream—
Best I speak not, think not,
225   But in these grasses of remembrance
Delight in flowers, steep my heart in the moon.

(*She gazes upward, then advances a few steps during the following passage.*)

Chorus (*for the* Ghost). "When pleasure moved me,
          I came;
The pleasure ended, I returned."
Then, as now tonight, what beauty in the sky!

230 **Ghost.** Though many are the famous places
Where one may gaze upon the moon,
Transcending all—Sarashina.

Chorus (*for the* Ghost). A pure full disk of light,
Round, round, leaves the coastal range,
235   Cloudless over Mount Obasute.

Ghost. Even though the vows of the many Buddhas

227–228 "When pleasure . . . I returned": An allusion to the words of a nobleman in ancient China, who journeyed to see a friend but turned back as soon as he reached the friend's gate. When asked the reason for his action, the nobleman said, "Moved by pleasure, I came; the pleasure ended, I returned."

Chorus. Cannot be ranked in terms of high or low,
 None can match the light of Amida's Vow,
 Supreme and all-pervading in its mercy.

(*She dances.*)

240 And so it is, they say,
 The westward movement of the sun, the moon, and stars
 Serves but to guide all living things
 Unto the Paradise of the West.
 The moon, that guardian who stands on Amida's right,
245 Leads those with special bonds to Buddha:
 Great Seishi, "Power Supreme," he is called,
 For he holds the highest power to lighten heavy crimes.
 Within his heavenly crown a flower shines,
 And its jeweled calyx reveals with countless leaves
250 The pure lands of all the other worlds.
 The sounds of the wind in the jeweled tower,
 Tones of string and flute,
 Variously bewitch the heart.
 Trees by the Pond of Treasures,
255 Where the lotus blooms red and white,
 Scatter flowers along their avenues;
 On the water's little waves—
 A riot of sweet fragrances.

Ghost. The incomparable voices of the birds of paradise—

260 **Chorus** (*for the* Ghost). Peacocks and parrots call their
 notes
 In harmonies of imitation.
 Throughout that realm—unimpeded, all-pervading—
 The radiance that gives his name—"Light without
 limit."
 But here the moon through its rift of clouds,
265 Now full and bright, now dimly seen,
 Reveals the inconstancy of this world
 Where all is perpetual change.

Ghost. My sleeves move again in dances
 Of sweet remembered nights of long ago.

(*She continues to dance, her song alternating
back and forth between herself and the* Chorus.)

238 Amida's Vow: the promise made by the Buddha Amida to establish a paradise—known as the Western Paradise or Pure Land—into which the faithful would be reborn after death.

239 all-pervading: spreading throughout all things.

246 Seishi (sā'shē): one of Amida's two attendants, who offers wisdom to human beings.
249 calyx (kā'lĭks): a cuplike structure enclosing the base of a flower.
250 other worlds: the infinite Buddha paradises in the universe.

254 Pond of Treasures: a pool in the Western Paradise.

263 "Light without limit": another name for Seishi.

Chukei fan. Eisei-Bunko Foundation, Tokyo.

270 **Chorus.** "No solace for my heart at Sarashina
　　When I see the moon
　　Shining down on Mount Obasute"
　　When I see the shimmering moon.

Ghost. No stranger to the moon,
275　　I dally among the flowers
　　For these moments, brief as dew on autumn grasses . . .

Chorus. Fleeting as the dew indeed . . .
　　Why should I have come here?
　　A butterfly at play . . .

280 **Ghost.** Fluttering . . .
　　Dancing sleeves . . .

Chorus. Over and return, over and . . .

Ghost. . . . Return, return
　　Autumn of long ago.

285 **Chorus.** My heart is bound by memories,
　　Unshakable <u>delusions</u>.
　　In this piercing autumn wind tonight
　　I ache with longing for the past,
　　Hunger after the world I knew—
290　　Bitter world,
　　　Autumn,
　　　　Friends.
　　But even as I speak,
　　See how the night already pales,
295　　And daylight whitens into morning.
　　I shall vanish,
　　The traveler will return.

(*The* Traveler *exits.*)

Ghost. Now, alone,
　　Deserted,
300　　A moss-grown wintry hag.

(*She watches the* Traveler *depart, and weeps.*)

Chorus. Abandoned again as long ago.
　　And once again all that remains—
　　Desolate, forsaken crag,
　　Mountain of the Deserted Crone.

(*She spreads her arms and remains immobile at the*
shite-*position.*)

WORDS TO KNOW
delusion (dĭ-lōō′zhən) *n.* a false idea or belief

Connect to the Literature

1. **What Do You Think?**
   What is your reaction to the plight of the old woman in this play?

   Comprehension Check
   • Why was the woman abandoned on Mount Obasute?
   • Why does the ghost of the old woman return every year to dance in the full mid-autumn moon?

Think Critically

2. **ACTIVE READING: QUESTIONING** Get together in a small group and discuss the questions that you wrote in your **READER'S NOTEBOOK**. If you still have unanswered questions, see if others in the group can answer them. Then discuss the strategies you used to answer your questions, such as rereading or using a dictionary to define unfamiliar words. Which strategies were most helpful?

3. Why do you think the spirit of the old woman still clings to the real world?

   > **THINK ABOUT**
   > • the manner of her death
   > • her memories of viewing the moon with friends
   > • her appreciation of the beauty of nature

4. What does the moon that shines on Mount Obasute seem to represent? How does the light cast by the moon compare with the light shed by Amida and other Buddhist deities?

5. How would you describe the **mood,** or feeling, created by the play?

6. What does the play seem to suggest about the nature of life and the physical world?

Extend Interpretations

7. **Comparing Texts** In Sophocles' *Oedipus the King,* the chorus plays an active role, occasionally advising the main characters and voicing opinions. What different role does the chorus play in *The Deserted Crone?* In what way, if any, are the roles of the two choruses similar?

8. **Connect to Life** The old woman in the play is described as a crone, a wintry hag, and a withered flower. What do these descriptions suggest about how elderly women were regarded in Zeami's time? Do you think old women are viewed differently today? Explain your answer.

"lonely heart of autumn"
"remote and friendless landscape"

Choices & CHALLENGES

Writing Options

1. Name and Legend Think of a place, one that is famous or one that exists not far from your home. Create a new name for it, and then write a legend that explains how the place got its name. For example, you might rename a park in your community "Park of the Lazy Student" and write a story based on that name. You can write a humorous story or a sad one, similar to the legend of Mount Obasute.

2. Character Sketch Write a character sketch of the old woman in *The Deserted Crone.* Use figurative language and sensory details to describe the woman's appearance and how she feels when she sees the moon at mid-autumn. Also, explain how she came to be abandoned on the mountain and tell why she clings to the real

world. In your character sketch, try to create the melancholy mood that is conveyed in the play when the woman is described.

Writing Handbook
See page R27: Descriptive Writing.

Activities & Explorations

Noh Performance Work with a small group of classmates to perform *The Deserted Crone.* Assign roles and use the stage directions and diagram on page 520 to help you put on the play. Use understated gestures and actions to depict character. Also choose music to evoke the proper mood. If possible, design and create paper Noh masks for the actors to wear. After you have rehearsed the play, perform it for the rest of the class.
~ **PERFORMING**

Inquiry & Research

Shakespearean Noh Plays
Kuniyoshi Munakata Ueda, a Japanese scholar who has devoted his life to poetry, has adapted several Shakespearean plays for the Noh stage. Some of the plays he has written, staged, and directed are *Hamlet, Macbeth,* and *King Lear.* Munakata Ueda, who has performed the *shite* role in many productions, worked for six years before he felt fully capable of chanting English in the Noh style. Find out more about Munakata Ueda and his Noh Shakespeare Group or about other modern Noh theater companies. If possible, bring pictures or a video of a performance to share with the class.

RESEARCH STARTER
CLASSZONE.COM

Vocabulary in Action

EXERCISE: MEANING CLUES On your paper, write the word that is described by each clue.

1. A member of the clergy might offer this to console grieving relatives at a funeral.
2. This describes the progress of a car that does not have to stop at red lights.
3. A person who does not offer food or drink to a guest might be called this.
4. If you believe that the queen of England lives in your closet, you are probably laboring under this.
5. When time goes by quickly, it is often described in this way.

Building Vocabulary
For an in-depth study of context clues, see page 674.

tanka poetry

Tanka Poets

Ono Komachi (circa mid-800s) Because she is named in the preface to an important anthology of Japanese verse, Ono Komachi (ō′nō kō-mä′chē) is revered as one of the Six Immortals of Poetry. However, almost nothing is known about the poet's life. In fact, historical facts about Komachi have become obscured by the legends created about her. Perhaps because she wrote passionate love poetry, she is said to have been a matchless beauty who conquered many men's hearts. Other legends describe the poet's cruel treatment of her lovers and—perhaps as revenge—her loss of beauty in old age. As a result of these legends, Komachi became the subject of a series of Noh plays.

Lady Ise (875?–939) Born into a family of prominent scholars and poets, Lady Ise (ē′sě) served as a lady in waiting at the Heian court during the reigns of Emperors Uda (ōō′dä) and Daigo (dī′gō). Like Ono Komachi, Ise wrote passionate poetry. A woman of immense talent and reportedly a great beauty, Ise received much attention from men all her life. Some of these men tried to take advantage of her position at court, but she is said to have used her literary ability to outsmart them.

Ki Tsurayuki (868?–946?) Ki Tsurayuki (kē′ tsōō′rä-yōō′kē) was the most influential poet of his age. Many of his poems were combined with painting on Japanese screens. These screen poems were composed at the request of the emperor or another high official and publicly displayed. The poems were often technically brilliant, but they lacked depth of feeling. Tsurayuki's later work, however, revealed more personal feeling and demonstrated his considerable poetic gifts. He also pioneered the travel-diary form in his *Tosa Diary.* Written from the point of view of a fictional woman, the diary describes Tsurayuki's journey from Japan's Tosa province to Kyoto.

Saigyō (1118–1190) Saigyō (sī′gyō) is one of the three most beloved poets in Japanese literature. At the age of 23, he abandoned a promising military career to become a Buddhist monk. While living as a hermit, he composed poems about nature and the impermanence of life, a basic Buddhist belief. He also helped develop the meditative travel diary, a form later perfected by poet Matsuo Bashō (mä-tsōō′ō bä′shō).

Ono Komachi

Build Background

Short Songs Tanka (täng'kə) are Japanese lyrical poems that express a single thought or tell a brief story. Tanka means "short songs," and a traditional tanka poem consists of just 31 syllables divided among five lines. The first and third lines contain 5 syllables each; the remaining lines contain 7 syllables each. This rigid construction is usually not retained in English translations of the poems. Instead, translators try to preserve the mood and imagery of the poetry.

Tanka was the dominant form of Japanese verse from the 700s until the 1500s. It emerged shortly after Japan developed a system for writing Japanese. At this time, Japanese writers began to write in Japanese instead of Chinese. The earliest examples of tanka appeared in a collection of poetry written in the 700s. By the early 900s, tanka was thriving as a uniquely Japanese form. During the Heian period, aristocrats routinely composed and exchanged tanka with their loved ones.

Not surprisingly, love is a common theme in tanka. The beauty of nature and the passage of time are other frequent subjects. Tanka poets attempt to capture a moment and evoke a certain response through the use of imagery. Much of what the poets say, however, is implied rather than directly stated. The reader must read between the lines to understand the insight expressed.

Eventually, tanka inspired the more concise verse form known as haiku (hī'kōō), a three-line poem of 17 syllables. In time, haiku surpassed tanka as the major Japanese poetic form. Nonetheless, Japanese poets continue to write tanka today. Many take part in a tanka-writing contest held at the beginning of each year by the emperor of Japan.

Connect to Your Life

What's your favorite way to capture a moment in time? Would you prefer to write about the moment, draw a picture of it, photograph it, or talk about it? Get together with a partner and take turns recalling special moments that occurred recently in your lives. Discuss how you tried to hold on to the moments.

Focus Your Reading

LITERARY ANALYSIS: DICTION

Diction refers to a writer's choice of words. Diction includes both the words used and the way the writer arranges them. In the tanka poems you are about to read, the diction is **figurative** rather than **literal**. The words imply meaning; they don't state it directly. As you read the poems, be aware of the diction used by the poets.

ACTIVE READING: COMPARING MOODS

Mood is the feeling or atmosphere that a writer creates for the reader. The use of imagery can help set the mood. **Imagery** refers to words and phrases that create vivid sensory experiences for the reader by appealing to one of more of the senses of sight, smell, hearing, taste, and touch.

📖 **READER'S NOTEBOOK** As you read each tanka poem, list in a chart the words or phrases that contribute to the poem's feeling or atmosphere.

Poem	Words and Phrases
"I've gone to him"	
"Spring rains weaving"	
"In this world"	
"As I look at the moon"	

Tanka Poetry

Translated by Burton Watson

I've gone to him
by dream paths,
my feet never resting—
but it can never match
one glimpse of him in real life

—Ono Komachi

Spring rains weaving
eccentric brocades
across the face of the water—
will they dye all the hills green?

—Lady Ise

Japanese writing
box and tools

In this world
there are many kinds of longing,
but no longing to match
the longing for one's child

—Ki Tsurayuki

Detail of *Pastimes and Observances of Four Seasons,*
Maruyama Okyo. The Tokugawa Art Museum, Nagoya, Japan.

As I look at the moon
my mind goes roaming,
till I live again
the autumns that I
knew long ago.

—Saigyō

Poet Saigyō Viewing the Moon
(c.1637), Iwasa Katsumochi.
Gunma Prefectural Museum of
Modern Art, Gunma Prefecture,
Japan.

HUMANITIES CONNECTION
The inscription on this scroll
transcribes a poem by Saigyō,
in which he wrote: "I wonder
if the sleeves of those I left at
home / are wet with tears
tonight."

Connect to the Literature

1. What Do You Think?
Which of these tanka did you enjoy the most? Discuss with the class the reasons for your choice.

Think Critically

2. What impressions of nature do the tanka by Lady Ise and Saigyō convey?

3. In the tanka by Komachi and Tsurayuki, what can you infer about the subjects?

4. What do these poems suggest about time and change?

THINK ABOUT
- the glimpse of spring in Lady Ise's poem
- the longing expressed by Tsurayuki
- Saigyō's reflection on autumn

5. ACTIVE READING: COMPARING MOODS Review the chart that you created in your 📖 **READER'S NOTEBOOK.** How would you describe the mood in each one of the poems? Compare your ideas with a classmate. Decide if any of the tanka have similar moods.

Extend Interpretations

6. What If? If Lady Ise's poem were about winter rather than spring, what images might she have used?

7. Comparing Texts Which of the tanka have a dreamlike or otherworldly quality? According to Buddhist teaching, the soul lives on after death. How do some of the tanka reflect the Buddhist belief in an afterlife?

8. Connect to Life Although the tanka you have read were written hundreds of years ago, the emotions and insights they convey are still fresh today. Select one of the tanka and identify modern images that might evoke the same response.

LITERARY ANALYSIS: DICTION

Diction refers to a writer's choice of words. Diction includes both the vocabulary used by a writer and the way in which the chosen words are arranged. Diction can be described as **formal** or **informal** and as **literal** or **figurative.** The figurative diction in the four tanka fits the poems' moods and meanings. Consider the diction in these lines by Ono Komachi:

I've gone to him
by __dream paths__,
__my feet never resting__—

"Dream paths" implies a sleeping or unconscious state, while "my feet never resting" suggests that the speaker is unceasing in her desire to reach the "him" of the poem. The lines convey a yearning, dreamlike state.

Paired Activity Reread the following tanka by Lady Ise, paying particular attention to the underlined phrases. Then rewrite the phrases, using literal diction.

__Spring rains weaving__
__eccentric brocades__
__across the face of the water—__
__will they dye all the hills green?__

Get together with a partner and share your new versions. Discuss the differences between the literal and figurative versions.

Haiku Across the Centuries

OVERVIEW

Japanese Haiku   541

Haiku in the 20th Century   547

Standardized Test Practice:
Writing About Literature   551

One of the most popular forms of poetry is the haiku. This type of poetry originated in Japan hundreds of years ago. It's a form that has many rules, but they are relatively easy to follow.

This lesson contains haiku of three great Japanese masters. Also included are haiku of two famous 20th-century writers, one Mexican and one American, to show how poets continue to play with the form. In the pages that follow, you will be asked to compare and contrast various haiku. Comparing traditional haiku with haiku written in the 20th century will help you see which elements of the poems have changed and which have remained the same.

Points of Comparison

The following poem illustrates the basic rules of haiku. As you will later see, poets don't always follow these rules, but knowing the rules is a good way to start.

Traditional Haiku

Spun in high, dark clouds,
Snow forms vast webs of white flakes
And drifts lightly down.

One word or phrase suggests season.
• First line has 5 syllables.
• Second line has 7 syllables.
• Third line has 5 syllables.

Poem presents an image from nature—here, an image of snow falling.

Analyze the Poems Use a chart like the one shown to help you take notes about the poems. You will first choose two traditional haiku, each by a different Japanese poet, to analyze in depth. Later, you will choose a 20th-century haiku to compare with the other two.

	Traditional	Traditional	20th-Century
Author			
First line of poem			
Traditional form (5/7/5 syllables)? (yes/no)			
Season/season word (if present)			
Image(s)			
Mood suggested			

Standardized Test Practice: Comparison-and-Contrast Essay After you have finished reading all the poems, you will have the option of writing a comparison-and-contrast essay. Your notes will help you plan and write the essay.

Japanese
Haiku

Japanese Haiku Poets

Matsuo Bashō (1644–1694) Matsuo Bashō (mä-tsoō'ō bä'shō) is considered the greatest master of the haiku. Bashō led a contemplative life, seeking a deeper understanding of the world through his solitary travels and in the writing of haiku. In 1684, he began the first of many journeys that provided inspiration for much of his poetry and travel journals. By the time of his death, Bashō had more than 2,000 students.

Yosa Buson (1716–1784) Recognized as the second-greatest master of haiku, Yosa Buson (yō'sä boō'sōn) moved to the Japanese capital of Edo at the age of 20 to study painting and poetry. Although he made his living as a painter, Buson also wrote poetry full of vivid images.

Kobayashi Issa (1763–1828) Kobayashi Issa (kō'bä-yä'shē ēs'sä) dealt with tragedy all his life. His first four children died in infancy, and his wife died shortly after giving birth to the fourth child. Issa remarried, and a healthy daughter was born after his death. Issa's poetry often reflects the pain of his personal suffering.

Build Background

Precision, Economy, and Delicacy Haiku possess three qualities greatly valued in Japanese art: precision, economy, and delicacy. In just 17 syllables, a haiku must create a couple of vivid images that convey an emotion or an observation about nature.

Haiku poets frequently use a seasonal word or image, called a *kigo* (kē'gō), to bring a certain time of year to mind. For instance, "cherry blossoms" suggests of spring; "snowfall" indicates a wintry scene.

For a humanities activity, click on:

Connect to Your Life

Many of the poems you are about to read convey images of the seasons. With a partner, list images and emotions that come to mind when you think about each season. You might refer to these notes as you read the haiku.

Focus Your Reading

LITERARY ANALYSIS: ANALYZING IMAGERY
Imagery consists of words and phrases that appeal to the senses of a reader. These words help bring a piece of writing to life by creating vivid images in the reader's mind. A haiku usually contains two main images. For example, the poem on page 540 presents an image of dark clouds and one of vast webs of white flakes. Readers must draw a connection between the images to understand the poem's meaning. As you read the haiku, think about the images being presented in each one.

ACTIVE READING: INTERPRETING DETAILS
In order to fully appreciate haiku, you should read each poem slowly. Allow a mental picture to form, based on the details provided. Then read the poem a second time, stopping to think about the mood or emotion created by the details.

READER'S NOTEBOOK As you read the haiku by Bashō, Buson, and Issa, jot down the details from each poem in a chart. Try to picture the images suggested by the details, and think about how they make you feel. Then record your emotional response to the poem.

Haiku Poets

Matsuo Bashō

Translated by Sam Hamill

Pitifully—under
a great soldier's empty helmet,
a cricket sings

Withered winter grass—
waves of warm spring air
shimmering just above

After morning snow
onion shoots rise in the garden
like little signposts

Bashō's
Death Poem

Sick on my journey,
only my dreams will wander
these desolate moors

Yosa Buson

Translated by Robert Hass

Coolness—
the sound of the bell
    as it leaves the bell.

White blossoms of the pear
and a woman in moonlight
    reading a letter.

The old man
cutting barley—
    bent like a sickle.

It cried three times,
the deer,
    then silence.

Kobayashi Issa

Translated by Robert Hass

A huge frog and I,
staring at each other,
neither of us moves.

Asked how old he was,
the boy in the new kimono
stretched out all five fingers.

In a dream
my daughter lifts a melon
to her soft cheek.

The pheasant cries
as if it just noticed
the mountain.

from

The Spring of
My Life

KOBAYASHI ISSA

This excerpt from Kobayashi Issa's diary captures the love and delight he felt for his infant daughter. Though prose, this delicate portrait reflects the art of the great haiku master.

Last summer, around the day for bamboo planting, a daughter was born to us in this world so full of sad events. Though she may have been born stupid, we hoped she would grow up to be a clever girl, and decided to call her Sato.[1] This year, from around the day we celebrated her birthday, she began to laugh if we clapped our hands, and to nod her head if we patted it lightly.

Once, when she saw a child her age with what is called a pinwheel, she wanted it for herself badly and fussed so much that we hurriedly got one for her. But soon she was chewing on it noisily and then she threw it away. Without showing a drop of regret, she turned her attention to something else, and began breaking the bowls that happened to be at hand. Soon bored with that too, she started tearing the thin paper off the sliding door. We said, "Well done! well done!" as though praising her. She thought we meant it and, cackling, went on tearing away intently. Not a speck of dust in her heart, she seemed as bright and pure as the full moon of autumn. As if witnessing a superb actor, I felt the wrinkles being smoothed out of my heart.

Again, when someone came along and said to her, "Where's the bow-wow?" she'd point at a dog, and when asked, "Where's the caw-caw?" she'd point at a crow. From her mouth to the tips of her fingers she brimmed with charm and lovableness, and I thought she was gentler than the butterflies that play around the first spring herbs.

The child must have been protected by the buddhas. On the evening before the anniversary of someone's death, as soon as I lit a candle and tinkled the bell at our family altar, wherever she might be, she would busily crawl up beside me, press together the hands that were as small as sprouting ferns, and recite "Nammu, Nammu"[2]—her voice touching, elegant, stirring, admirable.

—Translated by Hiroaki Sato

---

1. **Sato** (sä′tō): a name related to the Japanese word *satoshi*, meaning "clever" or "bright."
2. **"Nammu, Nammu"**: a child's imitation of the phrase *Namu Amida Butsu,* "Praise to Amida Buddha."

Connect to the Literature

1. What Do You Think?
Which of these haiku do you think is the most powerful? Explain.

Think Critically

2. What impressions of nature do the three haiku poets seem to share?

3. ACTIVE READING: INTERPRETING DETAILS
Compare the charts that you recorded in your
📖 **READER'S NOTEBOOK** with those of a classmate. Were your emotional responses to the haiku similar? Discuss.

LITERARY ANALYSIS: ANALYZING IMAGERY

Imagery consists of words and phrases that appeal to the senses and create vivid images for the reader. In most haiku, two images are presented for the reader to connect. For example, the Bashō poem beginning "Pitifully . . ." presents a soldier's helmet and a singing cricket. Since the helmet is now empty, it may represent death. Because the cricket is singing, it may represent continuing life.

Cooperative Learning Activity
With a group of classmates, analyze the images in the other haiku. Identify the images in each poem, and determine how they might be related. Then discuss the meaning of each poem.

Points of Comparison

Review the haiku, and fill in your comparison-and-contrast chart. Focus on the two haiku you decided to analyze. The following questions may help focus your attention:
- Does the haiku follow the traditional syllable form?
- Is a specific season suggested by a word or phrase?
- Is there one main image or two? What is each an image of?
- What mood is created by each image? That is, what thoughts or feelings does the image evoke?

Paired Activity Share your chart with a classmate, and discuss the similarities and differences between the two haiku. Use the discussion to help you fill in your chart.

	Traditional	Traditional	20th-Century
Author	Bashō	Buson	
First line of poem	"Pitifully—under"		
Traditional form (5/7/5 syllables)? (yes/no)	no		
Season/season word (if present)	summer/ "cricket"		
Image(s)			
Mood suggested			

HAIKU
IN THE 20TH CENTURY

Now that you have read several examples of traditional Japanese haiku, it's time to turn your attention to modern haiku by authors far removed from Japan. Western writers have been interested in studying and writing haiku since early in the 20th century. As you will see, these 20th-century poems have much in common with traditional Japanese haiku, but they also differ in interesting ways.

José Juan Tablada
1871–1945

A Restless Spirit Born in Mexico City, José Juan Tablada (hô-sä' hwän' tä-blä'dä) was a respected journalist, poet, and art critic. Tablada had a restless spirit and a questioning mind. As a young man, he broke away from modernism, a literary movement that stressed innovation and the rejection of traditional forms. Instead, Tablada wrote in a lively, playful style about Mexico's ancient religions and heritage. After a trip to Japan in 1900, he also introduced the haiku form into the Spanish language. In 1914, during the Mexican Revolution, Tablada was forced to leave his country for political reasons. He fled to New York, where he lived in exile for four years. In 1918 the new president of Mexico pardoned Tablada and appointed him to a diplomatic position in South America, but the poet resigned after two years because of health problems. He returned to New York, where he remained until his death.

Richard Wright
1908–1960

A Social Commentator Richard Wright, the son of a poor sharecropper, was born in Mississippi. His childhood was marked by hunger, beatings, and a struggle against the religious and racial restrictions imposed on him by his family and his culture. He wrote later that it was only through books that he managed to stay alive, books that he got by borrowing a white man's library card. As a young man, Wright escaped to Chicago, where he embarked on his writing career. In 1940, he gained international fame for his novel *Native Son.* In his fiction and in his autobiographies, *Black Boy* and *American Hunger,* Wright exposed the brutal racism in American life. During the last 18 months of his life, however, the writer began constructing delicate, vivid images of nature in haiku. Ill and living in Paris, Wright worked intensely on these poems. Before his death he collected 817 of his haiku into a manuscript, but he did not live to witness its publication.

Haiku

José Juan Tablada

MEXICO

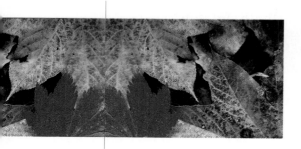

DRY LEAVES

The garden is full of dry leaves.
I never saw that many leaves
on the trees, when they were green, in the spring.

—TRANSLATED BY W. S. Merwin

FLYING FISH

Struck by the sun's gold
the pane of the sea bursts into splinters.

—TRANSLATED BY W. S. Merwin

WATERMELON

Red cold
guffaw of summer,
slice
of watermelon!

—TRANSLATED BY Samuel Beckett

Haiku
Richard Wright
UNITED STATES

A soft wind at dawn
Lifts one dry leaf and lays it
Upon another.

The metallic taste
Of a siren cutting through
The hot summer air.

Just enough of snow
To make you look carefully
At familiar streets.

The Rhythm of a Corner
(1957). Photo by W. Eugene
Smith. Copyright © The
Heirs of W. Eugene Smith,
courtesy Black Star, Inc.
New York. Collection,
Center for Creative Photo-
graphy, The University of
Arizona, Tucson.

Connect to the Literature

1. What Do You Think?
Which image in these haiku did you find most striking? Why?

Think Critically

2. In general, what seems to be the mood of Tablada's haiku?

3. Fall, summer, and winter are represented in the three haiku by Wright. What do these poems suggest about the speakers' reactions to the seasons?

4. Compare Tablada's "Watermelon" with Wright's haiku about summer. Based on these poems, what do you think summer represents to each poet?

- the mood and tone of each poem
- the sensory details used
- the images each poet uses to depict summer

Points of Comparison

Paired Activity Now that you have read and studied all of the poems, work with a partner to compare and contrast the haiku you have already analyzed with one by a 20th-century author. Together, respond to the Points of Comparison questions on page 546. Use your discussion to help you complete the comparison-and-contrast chart.

	Traditional	Traditional	20th-Century
Author	Bashō	Buson	Wright
First line of poem	"Pitifully—under"	"The old man"	"Just enough of snow"
Traditional form (5/7/5 syllables)? (yes/no)	no	no	yes
Season/season word (if present)	summer/ "cricket"		
Image(s)			
Mood suggested			

Writing About Literature

PART 1 **Reading the Prompt**

In writing assessments, you may be asked to compare and contrast works of literature that have a similar form, such as the haiku that you have analyzed. You are now going to practice writing an essay that involves this type of comparison.

> ### Writing Prompt
>
> Traditional Japanese haiku and haiku written in the 20th century have interesting similarities and differences. Choose three haiku— two by different Japanese poets and one by a 20th-century poet— and compare and contrast them. For each haiku, discuss the form (the pattern of syllables), the season (if known), the images, and the thoughts and feelings evoked by those images. Point out differences and similarities among the haiku. Give evidence from the poems to support your analysis.

STRATEGIES
IN ACTION

❶ I have to **compare and contrast** three haiku.

❷ For each poem, I need to discuss the **form, season, images,** and **thoughts and feelings** evoked.

❸ I need to include **details, examples,** or **quotations** from the poems to support my opinion.

PART 2 **Planning a Comparison-and-Contrast Essay**

• Review the comparison-and-contrast chart that you completed for the Points of Comparison features in this lesson.

• Using your chart, find examples of similarities and differences to point out in your essay.

• Create an outline to help organize your ideas.

PART 3 **Drafting Your Essay**

Introduction Begin by introducing your topic and identifying the basis of comparison. Briefly express your opinion about what the three haiku have in common. Then explain what you see as major differences.

Body You may wish to devote one paragraph to each poem. Within your paragraphs, you will need to discuss how each poem is different from the others and how it is similar. Pay the most attention to the feelings and ideas evoked by each poem. Use your comparison-and-contrast chart to help you identify details and examples.

Conclusion Wrap up your essay with a summary of the major differences and similarities.

Revision Check the use of signal words, such as *similarly, also, like, but, unlike,* and *while,* to show comparisons and contrasts.

TEST PRACTICE

Writing Workshop

Writing to solve problems . . .

From Reading to Writing In his Zen teachings, Musō Soseki tells a number of short morality tales. These tales are meant to serve as examples for readers, offering advice about how to handle life's troubles and problems. A good deal of nonfiction writing throughout history has been concerned with giving advice or solutions to problems. Even today, many people—such as journalists, businesspeople, and concerned citizens—write **problem-solution essays** as a way of exploring an issue and proposing a solution.

For Your Portfolio

WRITING PROMPT Write a problem-solution essay examining a problem that deeply interests you.

Purpose: To inform and to persuade

Audience: Anyone interested in the problem you are addressing

---

Basics in a Box

Problem-Solution Essay at a Glance

Introduction
Present and analyze the problem

Body
Present and explain possible solutions

Conclusion
Restate the problem and the benefits of the solution(s)

RUBRIC Standards for Writing

A successful problem-solution essay should

- clearly state a problem and explain its significance
- explore all aspects of the problem, including its causes and effects
- offer one or more reasonable solutions and explain how to put them into effect
- use anecdotes, examples, facts, or statistics to support the proposed solutions
- use logical reasoning to persuade the audience

Analyzing a Student Model

by Lucy Kinnear
Burr Oak High School

LANGUAGE SKILLS

The Need for Elder Care

Last week there was a fire in our apartment. My mom, my little brother, and I were standing outside when Mom suddenly shouted, "I smell smoke!" She turned and ran inside, just in time to put out a fire that started after my grandmother accidentally placed a newspaper on the lit stove. Grandma was sitting in the living room, reading a magazine and oblivious to the fire. If a similar fire had happened while Grandma was alone, she might not have been able to put out the flames before they spread.

My grandmother is a relatively strong, healthy woman. She moved in with us last year after my grandfather died. Since then she has become depressed, and six months ago she suffered a small stroke, which caused her to become forgetful and distracted. We love having her at home, but I do worry about her. Both of my parents work, and my grandmother is left alone every day until I get home from school. I fear that one day an accident will happen and we'll arrive too late.

This isn't just one family's problem; it's a problem faced by every American family with elderly members. Even active, healthy people in their 70s or 80s may need someone around the house. Otherwise, they may not be able to get help if they are injured, and they may not receive proper nutrition. In addition, the boredom and loneliness suffered by the elderly can cause mental and physical health problems.

Ironically, people who are too healthy and independent to enter nursing homes are the ones most likely to suffer from this problem. Most of them can't afford—or don't want—a full-time companion. For many independent elderly people, the last thing they want is to have some stranger come in and take charge of their lives.

Elder care has changed greatly over the centuries. For one thing, we now have more elderly people in our population. The life expectancy of Americans has almost doubled in the past two hundred years, rising from age 35 to age 75. Since 1990, the number of elderly people in the United States has grown quickly, and people age 85 and older are the fastest-growing group of elderly people. The U.S. Census Bureau predicts that by the year 2050, as many as 20 percent of Americans could be elderly, up from 12 percent in 1997.

❶ Introduces problem with an anecdote
Another Option:
• Begins with a direct explanation of the problem

❷ Describes the problem on a societal level

❸ Identifies one cause of the problem and elaborates with statistics

However, even as elderly people increase in number, fewer are living in nursing homes. Between 1985 and 1995, the number of nursing home residents age 85 and older decreased by 10 percent. More and more people are spending their later years at home, and many of them live alone.

In generations past, older people lived with their grown children. However, most Americans no longer live with their extended families. Today, the elderly still rely on their children or other relatives, but they most often live apart from them—sometimes even in a different state. While more people are relying on younger relatives for their care, there are fewer people with time to care for them.

Women have traditionally cared for the elderly, and women still make up the majority of caregivers. However, the majority of these women now hold paying jobs in addition to their family responsibilities. People in almost one-fourth of U.S. households provide some form of care to elderly relatives or friends. It's easy to see the financial, emotional, and physical strain that can result from these conditions.

We need day-care centers for senior citizens who live alone or who are home alone during the day. This is not to say that the elderly should be treated like children. They are adults with a lifetime of experience and individual needs. However, structured companionship and care can go a long way in meeting these needs. These centers should be warm, friendly, and professionally staffed. People would find companionship among their peers. There would be classes to take, books to read, food to eat, and a place to nap. No one would go hungry because he or she forgot to eat or felt too tired to prepare a meal.

Some object that such a center wouldn't really be all that happy, cheerful, or homey—that it would end up as a place to tuck away unwanted seniors. This must not happen. These centers must make it a priority to maintain an energetic and nurturing atmosphere, giving attention to individual needs. A caring staff and a wide range of activities could make the center comfortable for all.

It always takes people a while to adapt to new ideas, and day care for the elderly must be introduced in a caring and respectful manner. Its primary goal should be to provide services with dignity and compassion. With this goal in mind and community resources behind it, elder day care can fill a gap that we cannot afford to ignore.

❹ Explores other causes of the problem

❺ Proposes a solution to the problem, offering some detail about how it should work

❻ Anticipates and counters a possible objection to this solution

❼ Concludes by summing up the goals of the proposed solution and arguing for its necessity

Writing Your Problem-Solution Essay

❶ Prewriting

Begin by thinking of a meaningful problem that exists in a local, national, or international community. Brainstorm a list of problems that affect you directly or indirectly, or problems you've read about. Try to focus on problems that are specific enough to be reasonably addressed; for example, world hunger is a lot harder to tackle than hunger in your own community. See the **Idea Bank** in the margin for more suggestions. After you have selected a problem in need of a solution, follow the steps below.

Planning Your Problem-Solution Essay

▸ **1. Think about the problem.** Why do you think this is a serious problem? Whom does it affect and how? What are its causes?

▸ **2. Brainstorm possible solutions.** How might this problem be solved? Draw a cluster map to display possible solutions.

▸ **3. Consider each solution and eliminate impractical ones.** Does one solution stand out as the best? Would people support it? What kind of political and economic backing might it draw? What kind of opposition might it attract?

▸ **4. Identify your audience.** Who will read your essay? What do your readers already know and think about the problem? How can you address their concerns?

▸ **5. Research necessary supporting facts.** What kinds of data will help support the solution to the problem? Do you need to do research, consult experts, or examine your own thoughts?

---

❷ Drafting

At first, just write the essay from beginning to end, getting your thoughts on paper. Don't worry yet about form or completeness; that will come later. Consider using the following structure:

- **Identify** the problem and explain why it's important.

- **Explain** the problem's causes and effects, giving facts, statistics, examples, or quotations to support your points.

- **Explain** and support the proposed solution or solutions. Address any concerns or objections you anticipate from your audience.

- **Conclude** by summarizing your solution and describing how to achieve it.

IDEABank

1. Your Working Portfolio 📁
Build on the **Writing Option** you completed earlier in this unit:
Zen Solutions, p. 517

2. Talk of the Town
Read the front section of your local newspaper. What issues are causing problems? What solutions can you offer?

3. Community Beat
As you walk, bicycle, or otherwise travel through your community, make a mental note of any problems you see, such as a dangerous empty lot or unplowed streets. Think about what solutions you might propose.

LANGUAGE SKILLS

❸ Revising

TARGET SKILL ▶ ELABORATING WITH FACTS AND STATISTICS As you revise your essay, look for places where you can elaborate on your ideas by adding facts and statistics. A fact is a statement that can be proved or disproved by the use of reference materials or by firsthand observation. Statistics are facts expressed in numbers.

Need revising help?

Review the **Rubric,** p. 552

Consider **peer reader** comments

Check **revision guidelines,** p. R19

Review the **elaboration guidelines,** p. R25

Need help with verb forms?

See the **Grammar Handbook,** p. R59

Ask Your Peer Reader

- How would you define the problem I've described?
- Which information did you find most convincing? Which was the least convincing?
- What questions do you still have about the problem or the solution?
- What parts are unclear?

> *Since 1990*
> ~~In the last few years,~~ the number of elderly people in the United States has grown quickly, *and people age 85 and older are the fastest-growing group of elderly people.*

❹ Editing and Proofreading

TARGET SKILL ▶ INCORRECT VERB FORMS Verbs take different forms to show tense, mood, and voice. The use of incorrect verb forms can confuse your reader and make a bad impression in situations where standard English is expected, such as school essays. Read your work carefully and check for errors in verb forms. If you aren't sure whether a verb form is correct, check a grammar book that lists the principal parts of verbs.

> We loved having her at home, but I do worry about her.

Publishing IDEAS

- Send your essay as a letter to the editor of your local or school newspaper.
- Post your essay to a chat room or electronic bulletin board on the topic.

PUBLISHING OPTIONS
CLASSZONE.COM

❺ Reflecting

FOR YOUR WORKING PORTFOLIO How did writing your essay help you find a solution to the problem? Attach your answer to your finished work. Save your problem-solution essay in your **Working Portfolio.** 📁

Read this paragraph from the first draft of a letter to the editor. The underlined phrases may include the following kinds of errors:

- **incorrect verb forms**
- **weak use of the passive voice**
- **double negatives**
- **capitalization errors**

For each underlined phrase, choose the revision that most improves the writing.

Winter has come, and <u>it has brung a foot of snow.</u> Last Monday's blizzard
(1)
turned the streets of <u>hoagland falls into a disaster area.</u> Although the snowplows
(2)
came out early Monday morning, <u>only a few major streets were plowed by them.</u>
(3)
People spent hours on Monday and Tuesday shoveling out their cars on side
streets, only to have them <u>plown under</u> when the city finally sent out the plows
(4)
again <u>without telling no one they were coming.</u> Why doesn't the city plow
(5)
alternate sides of the streets on alternate days? If people know what to expect,
<u>their cars can be moved</u> in time to make room for the plows and to save their
(6)
own cars from being plowed in.

---

1. A. it has broughten a foot of snow.
   B. it has brought a foot of snow.
   C. it brang a foot of snow.
   D. Correct as is

2. A. Hoagland Falls into a disaster area.
   B. Hoagland Falls into a Disaster Area.
   C. Hoagland falls into a disaster area.
   D. Correct as is

3. A. only a few major streets were plowed.
   B. they plowed only a few major streets.
   C. plowing only a few major streets.
   D. Correct as is

4. A. plowed under
   B. plow under
   C. being plowed under
   D. Correct as is

5. A. without telling nobody they were coming.
   B. without telling.
   C. without telling anyone they were coming.
   D. Correct as is

6. A. their cars can always be moved
   B. they can move their cars
   C. their cars can be moved by them
   D. Correct as is

Need extra help?

See the **Grammar Handbook**

Verbs, p. R59

Active and Passive Voice, p. R61

Double Negatives, p. R64

Quick Reference: Capitalization, p. R79

TEST PRACTICE

Building Vocabulary | Using Reference Tools

In an age of information, when we have hundreds of reference tools to choose from, the dictionary and the thesaurus remain two of the most valuable and reliable. The following strategies can help you make the most of these trusty, familiar books.

Strategies for Building Vocabulary

❶ **Dictionary** A dictionary entry has many parts. By taking a few extra moments to study the entire entry, you can strengthen your understanding of that word and of related words.

> **ar•dor** (är′dər) *n.* Ⓐ 1. Fiery intensity of feeling. Ⓑ *He began to write songs with renewed ardor.* 2. Strong enthusiasm or devotion; zeal. 3. Intense heat or glow, as of fire. Ⓒ [ME *ardour*, from OF, from L *ārdor*, from *ārdēre*, to burn. Ⓓ See **ARSON**.]

Ⓐ **Numbered Definitions** Read every definition to be sure you've found the one you're looking for, and to get a more complete sense of the word.

Ⓑ **Sample Usage** Seeing a word used in context is often the fastest and easiest way to understand it.

Ⓒ **Etymology** This brief history shows the succession of a word's "ancestors" in other languages, starting with the most recent. Many dictionaries use standard abbreviations here, such as *ME* for *Middle English, OF* for *Old French,* and *L* for *Latin.* You can find a key to these abbreviations in the front of your dictionary. You can see here that *ardor* is descended from the Latin word *ārdēre,* which means "to burn."

Ⓓ **Related Words** Knowing other English words with the same root can shed light on a word's meaning.

All of this information should help you remember that *ardor* describes a fiery passion or heat and is descended from a Latin word meaning "burn." The next time you see this word or related words in print, or have reason to use them, you'll be on much firmer ground.

❷ **Thesaurus** Imagine that you want to think of another word for *stubborn* in this sentence: "Yoshi tried to convince his cousin to change his mind, but Hiro remained stubborn." Look at the following thesaurus entry for *stubborn.*

> **stubborn** *adjective* Firmly, often unreasonably resolved or determined: adamant, implacable, incompliant, obstinate.

Consider the synonyms listed. Each has a different **connotation,** or shade of meaning. For example, *adamant* means "stubbornly inflexible," while *implacable* means "impossible to pacify or satisfy." When you're unsure of a word's exact meaning, check the dictionary.

In this case, *adamant* is probably the best substitute for *stubborn.* Remember, though, that a fancy word is not necessarily better than a plain one, and sometimes you may wish to stick with your first choice. Nonetheless, a look in a thesaurus will always show you the range of words available to you.

EXERCISE For each of the words below, use a dictionary to find its meanings and etymology, along with any related words. Write down this information, choose one definition (if the word has more than one), and then use the word in a sentence. Finally, look up the word in a thesaurus and find a synonym to replace the word in your sentence.

1. earnest
2. adornment
3. loath
4. acquisition
5. contaminate

Grammar from Literature Skilled writers know how to construct sentences that express ideas concisely and effectively. Using a variety of sentence structures can strengthen your writing and add shape to your paragraphs.

A **simple sentence** contains a single independent clause, which can stand alone. A **compound sentence** consists of two independent clauses connected by a semicolon or by a comma and a coordinating conjunction, such as *and, but,* or *or.*

independent clause
He summoned his gentlemen-in-waiting.

coordinating conjunction
independent clause   independent clause
All the ladies gathered round, and Her Majesty summoned Lady Ukon.

—Sei Shōnagon, *The Pillow Book*

A **complex sentence** consists of one independent clause and at least one subordinate clause, which does not express a complete thought and cannot stand alone as a sentence. Subordinate clauses are introduced by subordinating conjunctions, such as *when, if, before,* and *where.*

subordinate clause
When the Empress explained what had happened,

independent clause
everyone talked and laughed with great excitement.
—*The Pillow Book*

Showing connections between ideas is an important feature of good writing. Look through your writing for related ideas and consider combining them in compound or complex sentences.

RELATED IDEAS
Lady Uma didn't like dogs. She found this one charming.

COMPOUND SENTENCE   coordinating conjunction
Lady Uma didn't like dogs, but she found this one charming.

COMPLEX SENTENCE
subordinating conjunction
Although Lady Uma didn't like dogs, she found this one charming.

Usage Tip A subordinate clause that stands alone is called a **fragment.** Complete sentence fragments by combining them with independent clauses or rewriting them as independent clauses.

WITH FRAGMENT
When Lady Uma picked up the dog. He started to growl.
CORRECT
When Lady Uma picked up the dog, he started to growl.

If you use a comma between the two independent clauses in a compound sentence, you must also include a coordinating conjunction. Leaving out the coordinating conjunction results in a type of run-on sentence known as a comma splice.

COMMA SPLICE
The dog snapped at her, she let him drop.
CORRECT
The dog snapped at her, so she let him drop.

WRITING EXERCISE Combine the following pairs of sentences, using the suggestion given in parentheses. Identify the new sentence as compound or complex.

1. The Emperor was given a cat. He was very fond of her. (semicolon)
2. She was only a cat. He awarded her a title of nobility. (although)
3. Okinamaro, one of the dogs at court, harassed the cat. He was banished to Dog Island. (when)
4. A dog from the island was beaten severely. He had tried to return to court. (because)
5. The people at court didn't recognize the dog at first. They finally realized it was Okinamaro. (but)

GRAMMAR EXERCISE Rewrite the following sentences, correcting any sentence fragments and comma splices.

1. Lady Myōbu was a very lovely cat. Who had the best of everything.
2. She ate the finest treats, she slept on a silken pillow.
3. Lady Uma fed the cat. Whenever she was hungry.
4. As long as she lived. The cat wanted for nothing.
5. The Empress loved her, the Emperor thought she could do no wrong.

Reflect and Assess

What did you learn about Japanese culture from reading the selections in Unit Three, Part Two? Did the literature give you a better understanding of traditional Japanese values? Use the following options to help you explore what you have learned.

Detail of *Five Beautiful Women* (early 19th century), Katsushika Hokusai. Gouache and ink on silk. Seattle (Washington) Art Museum, Margaret E. Fuller Purchase Fund. Photograph by Susan Dirk.

Reflecting on the Literature

Recurring Topics Nature, time, and duty are recurring topics in traditional Japanese literature. Think about the literature you have read in this part of the book. Then choose three selections: one that makes an observation about nature, one that deals with time, and one that comments on duty. In your own words, state the writer's message about each topic.

Reviewing Literary Concepts

Identifying Imagery and Mood Most of the selections in this part of the book use vivid images to help bring a character, a setting, or an object to life. Select three images found in the literature that you think are especially striking. What sensory details did the writer use to create each word picture? Then think about the mood the image conveys. In your opinion, which image most powerfully conveys a particular mood?

📁 Building Your Portfolio

Writing Workshop and Writing Options Review the problem-and-solution essay you wrote for the Writing Workshop on page 552 and the various Writing Options you completed for the lessons in this part of the book. Which piece would you consider sharing with others? Add the assignment to your **Presentation Portfolio** 📁, along with a cover note telling what obstacles you overcame to write it.

Self ASSESSMENT

📖 READER'S NOTEBOOK

The following list contains terms that you encountered as you learned about traditional Japanese literature. Copy the list on a piece of paper. Then work with a partner to write a sentence describing or defining each word or concept. If you don't remember the meaning of a term, review the lesson in which it appeared or consult the **Glossary of Literary Terms** (page R91).

haiku	simplicity
Noh drama	Zen
The Pillow Book	imagery
tanka	parable

Setting GOALS

Try your hand at writing some of the traditional Japanese literary forms you have learned about. You might write delicate haiku or tanka about nature, or you might keep a *Pillow Book*-style journal in which you record your observations and philosophy of life. If you prefer working in a group, collaborate with your classmates on writing a modern Noh play.

Extend Your *Reading*

As I Crossed a Bridge of Dreams

LADY SARASHINA; IVAN MORRIS, TRANS.

Enchanted by *The Tale of Genji,* Lady Sarashina spent her youth longing to go to Kyoto and visit the novel's setting. When she finally traveled to the capital, however, she spent most of her time reading. Her own "Prince Genji" appeared, but their love ended, and Lady Sarashina returned to her former quiet existence. As the author looks back over her life, a delicate portrait emerges of a woman who was not a scholar, like Murasaki Shikibu, or an amusing storyteller, like Sei Shōnagon, but a deeply sensitive writer who preferred fiction to real life.

Legends of the Samurai

HIROAKI SATO

In this collection of stories about the samurai, Hiroaki Sato presents legends ranging in origin from ancient times to the early 18th century. Through translations of original tales, laws, and eyewitness reports, the author traces the samurai's beginnings and rise to political power. The result is an authentic picture of the samurai warrior, who was as celebrated for his skill in battle as for his devotion to a code of duty, discipline, and artistry.

And Even *More* . . .

Books

The Spring of My Life and Selected Haiku
KOBAYASHI ISSA; SAM HAMILL, TRANS.
Issa's diary and poems to his daughter are moving and reveal his deep appreciation of nature and simplicity.

Essays in Idleness
YOSHIDA KENKŌ; DONALD KEENE, TRANS.
Similar to *The Pillow Book,* this collection of insights and observations by a 14th-century Buddhist priest reflects the culture and values of medieval Japan.

Other Media

Seven Samurai
Set in the 16th century, this classic film by the Japanese director Akira Kurosawa tells the story of a band of samurai hired to protect a small Japanese village. Home Vision Cinema. (VIDEOCASSETTE, DVD)

Sanctuary: Music from a Zen Garden
Gentle duets for Japanese versions of the flute and zither still the mind and soothe the spirit. EMD/Narada. (AUDIO CD)

Five Modern Nō Plays

YUKIO MISHIMA; DONALD KEENE, TRANS.

Yukio Mishima adapted traditional Noh plays, using contemporary settings and characters. While preserving the spirit and themes of the original works, Mishima has presented the plays in a form that can be easily understood by Western audiences.

Literature of the Middle East and Africa A.D. 300–1900

Gnawa musicians, descendants of West Africans enslaved in Morocco, play a form of Islamic religious music.

"Knowledge enables its possessor to distinguish right from wrong; it lights the way to Heaven; it is our friend in the desert, our society in solitude, our companion when friendless."

— MUHAMMAD

PART 1
Mysticism, Morals, Magic:
Persian and Arabic Literature . . . 564–611

PART 2
Giving Guidance, Praising Greatness:
West African Oral Literature 612–677

PART 1 Mysticism, Morals, Magic
Persian and Arabic Literature

Why It Matters

In the seventh century A.D., the cultures of Persia and Arabia began to flourish as never before. They advanced intellectually, socially, artistically, and technologically. Under the banner of a new religion—Islam—these cultural achievements were spread far and wide. Many have influenced us. Our mail service, banking, astronomy, navigation, medicine, mathematics, and literature owe a great debt to the Persian and Arabic cultures.

SPAIN
Córdoba

Granada

Tangier

For Links to Persia and Arabia, click on:

HUMANITIES
CLASSZONE.COM

Muslim world, A.D. 1200

A F R I C A

1 Persia Already an empire with over 1,000 years of rich history, Persia embraced **Islam** and became a major center of Islamic learning. Four famous Islamic poets—Ferdowsi, Omar Khayyám, Rumi, and Sadi—were Persian. Shown above is a Persian **illuminated manuscript.**

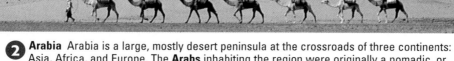

2 Arabia Arabia is a large, mostly desert peninsula at the crossroads of three continents: Asia, Africa, and Europe. The **Arabs** inhabiting the region were originally a nomadic, or wandering, people who herded camels and used them to cross the desert in long trains called **caravans.** In spreading Islam, the Arabs spread their language and culture far and wide.

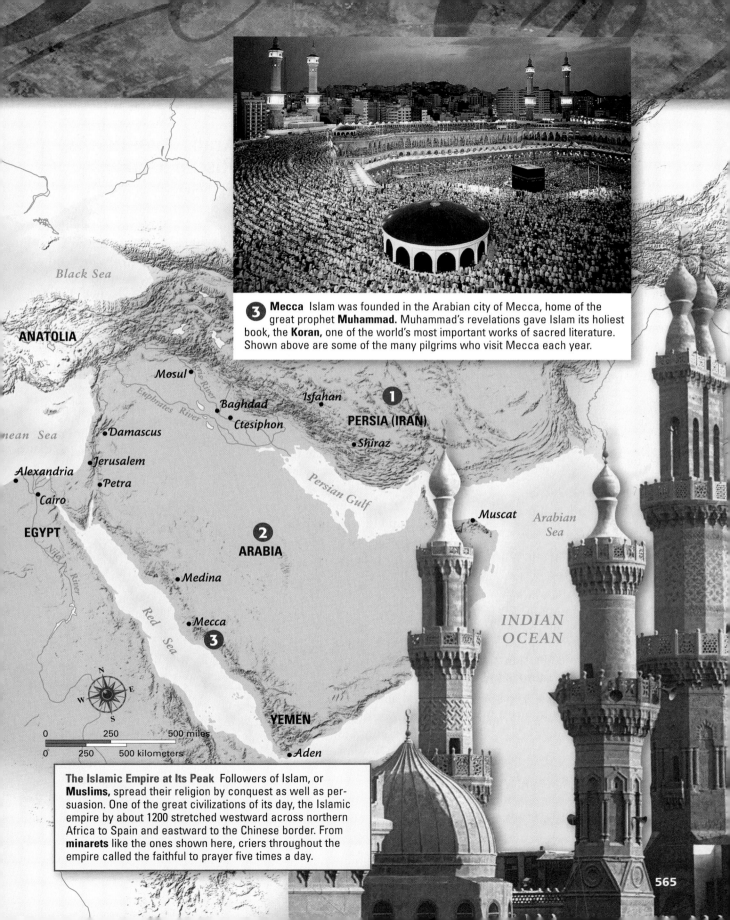

3 Mecca Islam was founded in the Arabian city of Mecca, home of the great prophet **Muhammad.** Muhammad's revelations gave Islam its holiest book, the **Koran,** one of the world's most important works of sacred literature. Shown above are some of the many pilgrims who visit Mecca each year.

The Islamic Empire at Its Peak Followers of Islam, or **Muslims,** spread their religion by conquest as well as persuasion. One of the great civilizations of its day, the Islamic empire by about 1200 stretched westward across northern Africa to Spain and eastward to the Chinese border. From **minarets** like the ones shown here, criers throughout the empire called the faithful to prayer five times a day.

The Persian Empire had existed for almost 1,200 years when it embraced a new religion, Islam, spreading outward from Arabia. The encounter between the two peoples was one that benefited both and led to major cultural advances.

Pre-Islamic Persia

1000 B.C.–A.D. 642

The Persians were originally **Aryan** nomads. Sometime around 1000 B.C., they settled in a plateau west of India that became known as Persia or **Iran**—"land of the Aryans."

Darius receiving his son Xerxes

Around 600 B.C., a prophet and religious reformer named **Zoroaster** founded a religion that would influence Persian culture for the next 1,200 years. Zoroastrianism saw the world and human morality in terms of a struggle between good and evil divinities.

Like other peoples of the region, the Persians evolved into a military power in order to survive. In 550 B.C., **Cyrus the Great** began to establish a Persian empire that would stretch from the Indus River to Anatolia (now Turkey). Unlike other conquerors, Cyrus did not loot and destroy conquered lands; instead, he treated the people mercifully, respecting their customs and beliefs. His successors **Cambyses II** and **Darius I** extended Cyrus' conquests. Darius built a system of roads to tie the empire together and introduced coinage and standardized weights and measures to promote trade. Eventually he was defeated by the Greeks at the Battle of Marathon in 490 B.C. In 331 B.C., **Alexander the Great** conquered the Persian Empire, making it part of his own. Then, in 224 B.C., a native Persian dynasty, the Sassanids, regained control of the region. They ruled until they were defeated by Muslim Arabs in A.D. 651.

Arabs and the Rise of Islam

A.D. 570–1258

In the early 600s, Persian culture was overshadowed by that of Arabia. Arabic tradition teaches that the Arabs descend from **Abraham,** the ancestor of the Hebrews. Originally desert nomads, some Arabs became farmers and traders. Towns arose at oases—desert watering holes—or along the coast, often near main trade routes. One such town was **Mecca,** where the prophet **Muhammad** was born about 570. According to tradition, the angel Gabriel visited Muhammad and revealed

PRE-ISLAMIC PERSIA

1000 B.C.

A.D. 1

to him the will of God, or Allah. Muhammad began to preach **Islam,** or "submission to Allah's will." The new faith alarmed the citizens of Mecca, who forced the prophet and his followers to flee to Medina. From there they launched successful military campaigns against the enemies of Islam. By 631, most of Arabia had sworn allegiance to the new faith, and by 640, so had much of Persia. After Muhammad's death, a series of **caliphs,** or successors, ruled the expanding empire. From 762 to 1258, the Abbasid dynasty ruled from the great capital **Baghdad.** By 1200, the empire had reached its greatest expansion. In 1258, the rise of independent Muslim states began to break it apart.

The great mosque commissioned by Malik Shah in Isfahan, Persia

Persian Rebirth
A.D. 819–1502

In the ninth century, a Persian dynasty called the **Samanids** gained power in the northeastern part of the Islamic empire, spearheading a renaissance, or rebirth, of Persian culture. The Persian city of **Bukhara** soon rivaled the Islamic capital of Baghdad as a center of learning, and in 945 the Persians took control of Baghdad itself. Although educated Persians then spoke and wrote Arabic, the language of Islamic ritual, now they began also writing in Persian. Persian culture continued to flourish even when the Persians lost political power to Turkish-speaking peoples from central

Asia like the **Seljuks,** who captured Baghdad in 1055. Great admirers of Persian learning, the Seljuk sultans, or shahs (Persian for kings), moved the capital to **Isfahan** in Persia and appointed Persians as prime ministers. The famous Seljuk sultan Malik Shah was a great patron of the arts and sciences as well as a powerful political leader. Persia remained under Turkish rule until 1502.

Islam spread by conquest as well as by persuasion.

History to Literature

EVENT IN HISTORY	EVENT IN LITERATURE
Muhammad becomes the prophet of Islam.	Allah's revelations to Muhammad are gathered in the Koran.
Trade and navigation flourish in the region.	*The Thousand and One Nights* tells the adventures of a sailor named Sindbad.
The Samanids support a revival of Persian culture.	The Samanids commission a Persian epic, the *Shahnameh.*
A mystical form of Islam called Sufism arises.	Rumi gives poetic expression to the ideas of Sufism.

ARABS AND THE RISE OF ISLAM		PERSIAN REBIRTH	
A.D. 570	A.D. 819	A.D. 1258	A.D. 1502

People and Society

In one way, the groups of people who made up the Islamic empire were very similar. They shared a common faith and a common set of guidelines for moral behavior. In other ways, they were quite different. Because of its size, the empire included a wide variety of cultural backgrounds. The spread of Islam also helped create new social roles and class distinctions.

Nomads

The Islamic empire included many Arabs who remained desert nomads, or wanderers, like their ancestors. Known as **Bedouins,** they were organized into tightly knit clans that were further grouped into tribes. The Bedouins prided themselves on their ability to survive in the rough desert terrain. They were also excellent warriors and made up the core of the Islamic armies.

Nomads in the desert

The Ruling Class

The Islamic empire was initially a **theocracy,** or government by religious authority. Religious

leaders held the political reins. However, by the 10th century, these leaders had become puppet rulers. Political power was held instead by military dictators or hereditary aristocrats such as **emirs** ("princes"), **sultans** ("rulers"), and **shahs** ("kings"), who often governed with the help of chief ministers known as **viziers.** Members of the ruling class were often strong supporters of learning and the arts.

The Lower Classes

Muhammad's moral perspective was influenced at least in part by the plight of the poor in Mecca. The lives of those in poverty was greatly improved under Islam, which stressed the

Breadmaker pounding grain to make flour

importance of helping the needy and giving charity to the poor. Islamic teaching also encouraged the freeing of slaves.

As the Islamic empire expanded, it welcomed conquered peoples into its fold and allowed them to enter Muslim society. However, society did make some distinctions between those who were born Muslim, those who converted, and those who practiced other religions. Converts to Islam paid higher taxes than born Muslims, and nonbelievers paid a still higher tax. Nevertheless, if they paid their tax and did not promote their religions, non-Muslims were treated reasonably well.

Scholars in the House of Wisdom

Merchants and Traders

Many Arabs grew wealthy as merchants and traders. Local merchants sold their wares in outdoor town and city markets, called **bazaars;** other traders traveled land and sea to obtain and sell their goods. Arabia and Persia were connected to the major ocean and land trade routes of the time, and many merchants and traders from other lands passed through these regions. Their presence, together with Arabs' and Persians' own travels abroad, made commerce not only a source of great wealth and abundance of goods, but also one of information and ideas.

The Learned Class

Scholars, scientists, writers, and artists were valued members of Islamic society. They often received financial support from powerful rulers who saw scientific and cultural achievements as an important part of their legacy. In the early 800s, Caliph al-Ma'mun dreamed that he spoke with the Greek philosopher Aristotle. Inspired by this dream, the caliph opened a combination academy and library in Baghdad called the **House of Wisdom.** There, scholars of different cultures and beliefs worked side by side translating texts from Greece, India, Persia, and elsewhere.

Islamic Mystics

Respect also went to religious leaders and **dervishes**—mystic monks who sought a close personal relationship with Allah. Many mystics were associated with **Sufism,** an Islamic movement that flourished in the 12th and 13th centuries. Sufi dervishes belonged to brotherhoods like those of European monks and often lived in schools or communities similar to monasteries. Traveling dervishes, called fakirs, lived by begging and were given charity in accordance with the teachings of Islam.

Sufi dervishes today continue to practice sacred dance as a form of worship.

Women in the Islamic World

The lives of women improved under Islam, which granted them important rights concerning marriage, family, and property. As believers in Islam, women were considered equal to men in the eyes of Allah, though over time they were forced to live increasingly secluded lives.

Arts and Culture

Because of Muslim tolerance of conquered peoples and the emphasis on learning, the Islamic empire blended a rich variety of cultures and traditions. At a time when Europe was in its Middle Ages, the Muslim world displayed great intellectual and artistic liveliness, producing many works of scholarship and art.

Islamic Architecture

Astrolabe

The Islamic empire is renowned for magnificent architecture, both religious and secular. Islamic houses of worship, called **mosques,** are typically domed, with beautiful arched or vaulted walkways. Often they are decorated with carved lacelike patterns called arabesques. Next to the central portion of the mosque is a graceful high tower, called a **minaret** (from the Arabic for a beacon), from which a crier known as a **muezzin** calls the faithful to pray five times a day. Palaces, too, are domed and vaulted. One of the most splendid Muslim palaces is the Alhambra in Granada, Spain; perhaps the most famous of the scores of classical mosques is the Great Mosque of Damascus, sometimes called the Umayyad Mosque because it was built in the era of the Umayyad caliphs. Shown below is the Dome of the Rock, built on the Temple Mount, site of Solomon's Temple in Jerusalem.

Scholarship and Science

A spirit of inquiry thrived in the Islamic world, spurred by Muhammad's own emphasis on study and learning as well as by the many new cultural contacts Muslims made as their empire expanded. Muslim cities from Spain to Central Asia flourished as centers of learning; great universities encouraged the study of religion, philosophy, law, and Arabic grammar. At the Baghdad academy and research library known as the House of Wisdom, major translations were undertaken and many new works of scholarship were written. In Muslim Spain, Averroës reconciled Islamic thinking with the ideas of the Greek philosopher Aristotle. In Egypt, the Spanish Jew Moses Ben Maimon (Maimonides) reconciled philosophy and Jewish law in a noted philosophical work, *Guide for the Perplexed.* Alhazen's book *Optics* aided in the development of the telescopic lens and led to advances in astronomy that benefited mapmaking and navigation.

Literature

Arabic Literature In pre-Islamic times, Arabic literature was composed mainly in the oral tradition. Elaborate odes, called *qasida*, were memorized and recited to celebrate important occasions; short lyrics expressed strong emotions such as love or grief. With the advent of Islam, such poetic traditions continued and were often put into writing. Also written down was the official text of Islam's sacred book, the Koran, in about 653. A century later, Arabic literature entered a golden age that saw the production of many types of literature, including works of history, philosophy, science, and biography.

Persian Literature Persia produced great literature before the advent of Islam, including the *Avesta*, the sacred text of the Zoroastrian religion. But afterward came a long period when virtually all literary and scholarly writing was in Arabic. Then, in the ninth century, the native Samanids gained power, fostering a cultural revival that produced major literary works in Persian. The blending of the Persian poetic tradition with the mystical brand of Islam known as Sufism resulted in some of the great lyric poetry of the world.

Decorative Arts

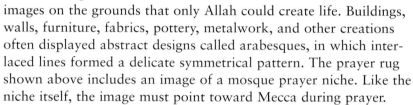

From elegantly carved swords of Damascus to the beautiful ceramic tiles and exquisitely woven carpets of Persia, the Islamic world produced a vast array of decorative art. Much of it was abstract, for although the representation of living creatures is not expressly banned in the Koran, Islamic thought condemned such images on the grounds that only Allah could create life. Buildings, walls, furniture, fabrics, pottery, metalwork, and other creations often displayed abstract designs called arabesques, in which interlaced lines formed a delicate symmetrical pattern. The prayer rug shown above includes an image of a mosque prayer niche. Like the niche itself, the image must point toward Mecca during prayer.

One type of Islamic art that was not abstract, Persian miniature paintings depicted people and animals in recognizable, often urban, scenes. Sometimes they were painted onto silk, but most often they were used as manuscript illustrations.

How Was Literature Presented ?

Because of the Islamic ban on the artistic representation of people and animals, words took on artistic importance, and a rich tradition of Islamic calligraphy—writing used as a form of visual art—developed. Using reed pens, Islamic calligraphers produced exquisite writing in the graceful vertical letters of the Arabic alphabet. Calligraphy was also an integral part of illuminated manuscripts, which were often decorated with gold and silver, brilliant colors, and intricate designs. Islamic rulers commissioned the creation of ornately bound illuminated manuscripts of treasured works like the Persian national epic the *Shahnameh* and, later, *The Thousand and One Nights*.

Time Line

c.   approximately
B.C.   before Christ
A.D.   after Christ

2500 B.C.   A.D. 1   PRESENT

EVENTS IN PERSIAN AND ARABIC LITERATURE

A.D. 500

c. 500 Pre-Islamic oral poetry flourishes in Arabic; translated Sanskrit tales, in Persia

610 Beginning of revelations to the prophet Muhammad that become the Koran

c. 622 First *ghazals,* or love lyrics, composed in Arabic

c. 653 Uthman, third caliph, authorizes the official text of the Koran

A.D. 700

c. 750 Golden age of Arabic literature begins; Ibn Ishaq composes definitive biography of Muhammad

c. 800 Arabic poet Abu Nuwas creates his famous poetry collection the *Khamriyyat*

c. 800 Tales later collected in *The Thousand and One Nights* start appearing in Arabic

A.D. 900

c. 920 Rudaki initiates revival of Persian-language poetry

1010 Ferdowsi completes his version of the Persian epic the *Shahnameh*

c. 1050 Arabic mystic Ibn Hazm composes his philosophical work *The Ring of the Dove*

c. 1075 Malik Shah becomes the patron of the astronomer and poet Omar Khayyám

EVENTS IN THE MIDDLE EAST

A.D. 500

c. 570 Birth of Muhammad

622 Muhammad's flight to Medina

632 Death of Muhammad; Abu-Bakr becomes first caliph

637–651 Arabs conquer Jerusalem, Alexandria, and Persia

661 Umayyad dynasty comes to power and makes Damascus the new Islamic capital

A.D. 700

786–809 Caliph Harun al-Rashid makes Baghdad the center of Arabic culture

c. 819–900 Samanid dynasty wields power in Persia and spurs a cultural revival

830 Caliph al-Ma'mun builds the House of Wisdom in Baghdad

c. 850 Al-Khwarizmi outlines the principles of algebra

A.D. 900

998 Mahmud, a Ghaznevid Turk, becomes sultan of the Persian province of Khorasan

1064 Seljuk Turks come to power in much of Islamic empire

1099 Crusaders capture Jerusalem and massacre Muslims and Jews

EVENTS IN WORLD HISTORY

A.D. 500

527 Justinian I becomes Byzantine emperor

618 Beginning of China's T'ang dynasty

A.D. 700

732 Battle of Tours in France stops Muslim incursions in Europe

794 Beginning of Japan's Heian period, known for its elegant imperial court life

800 Charlemagne crowned as emperor, uniting western Europe

c. 850 Empire of Ghana flourishes in western Africa

A.D. 900

900s Anasazi civilization in North America enters classic Pueblo period

1054 Christianity splits into Eastern Orthodoxy and Roman Catholicism

1066 Normans under William I invade and conquer England

1095 Pope Urban II begins the First Crusade to wrest the Holy Land from Muslims

c. 1177 Persian mystic Farid-ad-Din Attar completes allegoric poem *The Conference of the Birds*

1244 Rumi meets Shams ad-Din, inspiration for the poems in *Divan-e Shams*

1257–1258 Sadi composes his *Bustan* and *Gulistan*

c. 1360 Persian poet Hafiz composes his *Divan*

c. 1370 Persian poetry begins to decline

1375–1379 Ibn Khaldun writes the *Muqaddimah*, a monumental history of world civilization

c. 1500 *The Thousand and One Nights* is recorded in its present form

1187 Muslims under the Kurdish leader Saladin recapture Jerusalem

1218 Mongols under Genghis Khan invade Persia

c. 1300 Turkish chieftain Osman I founds the Ottoman state in what is now Turkey

1383–1385 Mongol rebel Timur the Lame (Tamerlane) briefly holds power in Persia

1453 Byzantine capital, Constantinople, falls to the Ottoman Turks

1502 Safavid dynasty comes to power in Persia

1520 Suleiman the Magnificent rules the Ottoman Empire

c. 1150 Angkor Wat, magnificent temple compound in what is now Cambodia, completed

1206 Genghis Khan begins Mongol conquests in Asia

1279 Mongol ruler Kublai Khan conquers China

1235 Sundiata founds Mali empire in Africa

c. 1300 Western Europe's Renaissance begins in Italy

c. 1450 Aztecs flourish in Mexico; Incas in Peru

c. 1455 German printer Johannes Gutenberg prints landmark Bible on his new press

1492 Muslims driven from Spain; Columbus makes voyage of discovery to the New World

1517 Martin Luther begins Reformation

1521 Cortés conquers Aztecs

Connect to Today: The Legacy of Persia and Arabia

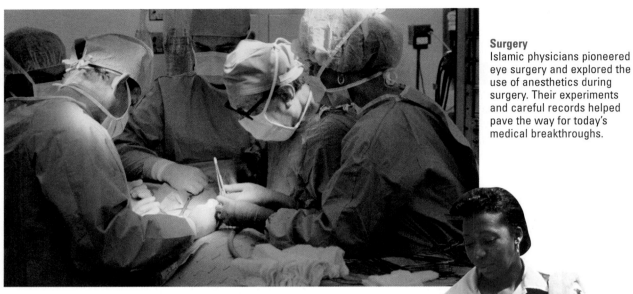

Surgery
Islamic physicians pioneered eye surgery and explored the use of anesthetics during surgery. Their experiments and careful records helped pave the way for today's medical breakthroughs.

The Mail System
Did you ever hear the famous postal service slogan "Neither snow, nor rain, nor heat, nor gloom of night stays these couriers from the swift completion of their appointed rounds"? The statement was first applied not to the U.S. mail but to the relay system of royal messengers that Darius I established in the ancient Persian Empire.

Modern Banking
To make it easier to conduct business, money handlers established banks throughout the Islamic empire. Using a letter of credit from a bank in one city, a merchant could get cash from a bank in another.

$$0 \ 1 \ 2 \ 3 \ 4 \ 5$$
$$6 \ 7 \ 8 \ 9$$

Mathematics

Though devised in India, our number system comes to us through the efforts of Arabic mathematicians—which is why we call *1, 2, 3,* and so on, Arabic numerals. Probably the most famous Arabic mathematician was al-Khwarizmi, who laid out most of the principles of algebra that we still use today. In fact, the mathematical term *algorithm* comes from the Latin pronunciation of al-Khwarizmi's name.

$$12x^2 - 3y^2$$

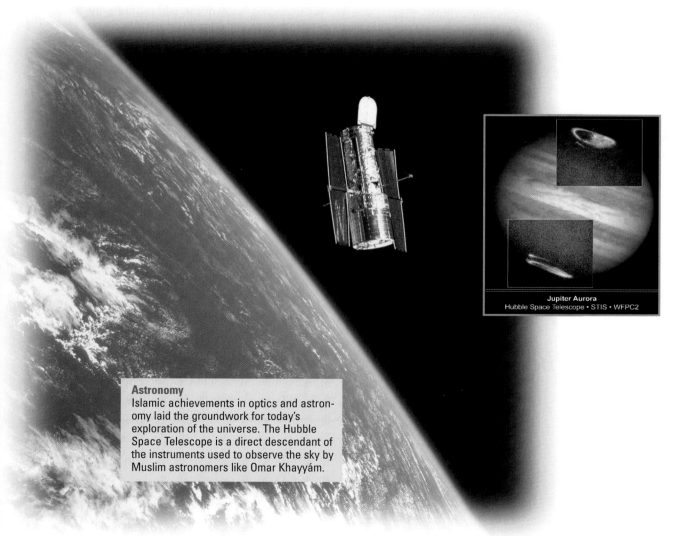

Jupiter Aurora
Hubble Space Telescope • STIS • WFPC2

Astronomy

Islamic achievements in optics and astronomy laid the groundwork for today's exploration of the universe. The Hubble Space Telescope is a direct descendant of the instruments used to observe the sky by Muslim astronomers like Omar Khayyám.

from the

KORAN

Build Background

The Birth of Islam About A.D. 610, when the prophet Muhammad was 40 years old, he is said to have received his first visit from the archangel Gabriel—the same Gabriel who appears in the Jewish and Christian Bible. According to tradition, during this visit Gabriel revealed the Word of God to Muhammad. This revelation was the first of many experienced by Muhammad throughout his life. Together, these revelations formed the basis of the faith called Islam, which literally means "submission to the will of Allah (God)." At first Muhammad reported God's revelations orally, and his followers memorized them and recited them in ritual prayers. Later the revelations were written down in a book called the Koran (also spelled Qur'an), which means "recitation."

> ## *"Seek knowledge from the cradle to the grave."*
> —Muhammad

What Is the Koran?

As the sacred book of the Islamic faith, the Koran is to followers of Islam what the Bible is to Jews and Christians. It is considered the true Word of God as revealed to Muhammad. In fact, followers of Islam—called Muslims—believe that the Koran they read is simply a copy of an eternal book found in heaven. To Muslims, the Koran is the world's most important book, the chief authority in all matters of Islamic life. It is a continuing source of inspiration to those who read or recite it.

The most important idea in the Koran is the principle of **monotheism,** the concept that there is only one God. God is the creator of the universe. Though merciful and compassionate, he still requires all human beings to submit to his will. Human beings are seen as the greatest of God's creations but also as creatures capable of evil as well as good. The Koran clearly states moral principles that should be followed in life, stressing the value of daily prayer, faith, work, charity, brotherly love, respect for elders, kindness to animals, honesty, humility, bravery, justice, cleanliness, and moderation, among other things. It indicates that people will one day stand before God and be judged on their earthly behavior.

Worship and the Koran In addition to following the moral principles expressed in the Koran, Muslims are expected to perform five formal acts of worship, called the Five Pillars of Islam:

1. Professing their faith

2. Praying five times a day

3. Giving charity to the poor

4. Fasting from sunrise to sundown during the holy month of Ramadan, the ninth month of the Islamic calendar

5. Making a pilgrimage to the holy city of Mecca, birthplace of Muhammad

In praying, Muslims recite passages from the Koran, including a short opening *sura,* or chapter, that is usually translated as "The Exordium," or "Introduction." (See page 578.)

Muslim women and children observe Ramadan.

For a humanities activity, click on:

Connect to Your Life

Each *sura* of the Koran opens with the same line: "In the name of God, the Compassionate, the Merciful." What do the words *compassionate* and *merciful* mean to you? Discuss your definitions of these words, along with some examples of merciful and compassionate behavior.

Focus Your Reading

LITERARY ANALYSIS: PARALLELISM
The use of similar grammatical constructions to express ideas that are related or equal in importance is called **parallelism.**

If not us, who? *If not now, when?*
<u>FIRST IDEA</u>   <u>SECOND IDEA</u>

Parallelism can also be used to contrast ideas.

Some soar like eagles. *Some crawl like bugs.*
<u>FIRST IDEA</u>   <u>SECOND IDEA</u>

As you read the excerpts from the Koran, look for examples of parallelism.

ACTIVE READING: QUESTIONING
In reading a challenging text, it can be helpful to keep track of questions as they come up and to actively look for answers.

READER'S NOTEBOOK As you read this selection, jot down any questions you have. These might concern who or what is being talked about, the meanings of particular words or phrases, or the connection between parts of sentences, for example. If you think you might know the answer, write that down too, even if you are not sure. Use a chart like the one shown to record your questions and answers. Write in pencil so that you can make revisions later on.

My Questions About the Koran	
Questions	**Answers**
Who is speaking?	

from the Koran

Translated by N. J. Dawood

 *the* Exordium

IN THE NAME OF GOD
THE COMPASSIONATE
THE MERCIFUL

Praise be to God, Lord of the Universe,
The Compassionate, the Merciful,
Sovereign of the Day of Judgment!
You alone we worship, and to You alone
we turn for help.
Guide us to the straight path,
The path of those whom You have favored,
Not of those who have incurred[1] Your wrath,
Nor of those who have gone astray.

Faith in God

In the Name of God, the Compassionate, the Merciful

All that is in the heavens and the earth gives glory to God. He is the Mighty, the Wise One.

It is He that has sovereignty[2] over the heavens and the earth. He ordains life and death, and has power over all things.

He is the First and the Last, the Visible and the Unseen. He has knowledge of all things.

---

1. **incurred:** brought upon oneself.
2. **sovereignty** (sŏv′ər-ĭn-tē): supremacy of authority or rule.

It was He who created the heavens and the earth in six days, and then mounted the throne. He knows all that goes into the earth and all that emerges from it, all that comes down from heaven and all that ascends to it. He is with you wherever you are. God is cognizant[3] of all your actions.

He has sovereignty over the heavens and the earth. To God shall all things return. He causes the night to pass into the day, and causes the day to pass into the night. He has knowledge of the inmost thoughts of men.

Have faith in God and His Apostle[4] and give in alms[5] of that which He has made your inheritance; for whoever of you believes and gives in alms shall be richly rewarded.

And what cause have you not to believe in God, when the Apostle calls on you to have faith in your Lord, who has made a covenant with you, if you are true believers?

Night

In the Name of God, the Compassionate, the Merciful

By the night, when she lets fall her darkness, and by the radiant day! By Him that created the male and the female, your endeavors have varied ends!

For him that gives in charity and guards himself against evil and believes in goodness, We[6] shall smooth the path of salvation; but for him that neither gives nor takes and disbelieves in goodness, We shall smooth the path of affliction. When he breathes his last, his riches will not avail him.

It is for Us to give guidance. Ours is the life to come, Ours the life of this world. I warn you, then, of the blazing fire, in which none shall burn save the hardened sinner, who denies the Truth and gives no heed. But the good man who purifies himself by almsgiving shall keep away from it: and so shall he that does good works for the sake of the Most High only, seeking no recompense. Such men shall be content.

---

3. **cognizant:** aware.

4. **Apostle:** Muhammad.

5. **alms:** money or goods given as charity to the poor.

6. **We:** God.

HUMANITIES CONNECTION Islamic belief discourages the use of images to represent living things. As a result, illuminations of the Koran, like the one here, often rely on the use of abstract designs and decorative lettering to achieve striking effects.

Daylight

In the Name of God, the Compassionate, the Merciful

By the light of day, and by the dark of night, your Lord has not forsaken you,[7] nor does He abhor[8] you.

The life to come holds a richer prize for you than this present life. You shall be gratified with what your Lord will give you.

Did He not find you an orphan and give you shelter?

Did He not find you in error and guide you?

Did He not find you poor and enrich you?

Therefore do not wrong the orphan, nor chide[9] away the beggar. But proclaim the goodness of your Lord.

---

7. **you:** Muhammad, Allah's prophet.

8. **abhor:** strongly reject; hate violently.

9. **chide:** scold; reprimand.

Connect to the Literature

1. **What Do You Think?** What image or images did you find most memorable in these excerpts? Explain your response.

Think Critically

2. **ACTIVE READING: QUESTIONING** With a small group of classmates, discuss the questions that you wrote in your **READER'S NOTEBOOK.** Together try to come up with answers to all of the questions. Make a note of any unanswered questions to bring up with the class as a whole.

3. According to the Koran, what qualities and actions make a person righteous?

4. How do the excerpts you read support the idea of "God, the Compassionate, the Merciful"?

> **THINK ABOUT**
> - the kind of behavior God wants from people
> - how God punishes sin
> - how God rewards goodness

Extend Interpretations

5. **Different Perspectives** How might the words of the Koran be applied not just to individuals but also to governments or social groups?

6. **The Writer's Style** Based on their tone, word choice, imagery, and other literary qualities, how do you think these excerpts from the Koran should be read aloud in order best to convey their meaning?

7. **Connect to Life** What kind of rules or guidelines for behavior do you think a person should follow in life? How do these compare with those set forth in the Koran?

LITERARY ANALYSIS: PARALLELISM

Parallelism is the use of similar grammatical forms or sentence structures to express ideas that are related or of equal importance.

Did He not find you in error and guide you?
Did He not find you poor and enrich you?

In some cases parallel constructions bring ideas together in a way that suggests they are opposites. This is sometimes referred to as **antithesis.**

For him that gives in charity . . . We shall smooth the path of salvation; but for him that neither gives nor takes . . . We shall smooth the path of affliction.

Parallelism gives writers a way to emphasize relationships and ideas while adding a kind of rhythm to their words.

Cooperative Learning Activity
With a group of classmates, find other examples of parallelism and antithesis in the excerpts from the Koran. Then discuss which example of parallelism or antithesis is the most powerful.

THE SECOND VOYAGE OF *Sindbad THE Sailor*

Build Background

A Famous Collection Have you ever heard of
Aladdin and the Magical Lamp, Sindbad the Sailor, or
Ali Baba and the Forty Thieves? All are characters from
The Thousand and One Nights, one of the world's
best-known story collections. Written in Arabic and
sometimes called *The Arabian Nights,* this famous
collection dates in its present form to about the 15th
century A.D. The stories themselves, however, had
been floating around the Middle East for many
centuries before that.

A Thousand and One Nights of Storytelling The
title *The Thousand and One Nights* refers to the loose
framework, called a **frame story,** that joins all the
stories together in one long narrative. This frame story
tells of Shahryar (shä-ryär'), the powerful ruler of a
Central Asian kingdom, who has come to hate all
women after having been betrayed by one. Each
day Shahryar weds a new wife, only to have her
executed the next day, before he weds another. Finally
Scheherezade (shə-hĕr'ə-zäd'), the clever daughter of
the king's vizier, or prime minister, concocts a plan to
put an end to the violence. She agrees to marry the
king, and on their wedding night she begins a gripping

story but leaves it unfinished. Fascinated by the tale,
the king spares her life so that she can complete the
story the next night. She does so but then moves on
to another story that she does not finish. Again he
spares her life the next day so that she can finish that
night, and again she leaves a new story unfinished.
This continues for a thousand and one nights, until
finally the king realizes that he loves Scheherezade
and does not want her killed.

Origins of the Tales The tradition of using a frame
story to hold together a collection of loosely related
stories seems to go back at least as far as ancient
India. The *Panchatantra* (see page 146), which is
about 1,000 years older than the Arabic collection,
is organized in this way, and many of the tales told
by Scheherezade can be found there in one version
or another. Other tales very likely come from other
traditions, some even older. Some scholars believe
that the basic plot of the Sindbad tales may go back
to an ancient Egyptian story called "The Tale of the
Shipwrecked Sailor," which predates *The Thousand
and One Nights* by more than 3,500 years.

Connect to Your Life

Recall an important project or trip that you undertook and the reasons you had for doing so. What did you hope to gain? What were some of the problems that you faced? What did you do to overcome them?

Focus Your Reading

LITERARY ANALYSIS: PLOT

The **plot** of a story is the chain of related events that take place in the story. Usually, the events of a plot progress because of a **conflict,** or struggle between a character and another person, nature, circumstances, or even himself or herself. For example, in the following selection the main character gets left behind by his ship while he is visiting a strange island. As a story progresses, new conflicts, or **complications,** arise. As you read "The Second Voyage of Sindbad the Sailor," take note of the complications that Sindbad must face.

ACTIVE READING: ANALYZING PROBLEMS AND SOLUTIONS

From the point of view of a character, a conflict is a problem that he or she must try to solve. A character's attempts to solve a problem may succeed, or they may fail. Either way, the attempted solution may lead to new complications.

📖 **READER'S NOTEBOOK** As you read about Sindbad's second voyage, look for the problems he faces, the solutions he comes up with, and the results that follow. Keep track of the problems and solutions in a chart like the one below.

Problem	Sindbad's Solution	Result
Sindbad has no shelter for the night.	Sindbad finds a cave to sleep in.	

WORDS TO KNOW **Vocabulary Preview**

confounded	oblivious	tumult
jubilant	sumptuous	

The Sindbad Tales

The excerpt you are about to read is one of several tales about a man named Sindbad (often spelled Sinbad). His story begins in Baghdad (in what is now Iraq) during its heyday as the commercial and cultural capital of the Islamic empire. At the beginning of the story, we are introduced to a poor Baghdad porter, or baggage carrier, who sits outside a palace and wonders why the rich man inside deserves such wealth. That rich man, Sindbad the Sailor, invites the porter in and proceeds to tell his story. Sindbad explains that as a merchant in the reign of Harun al-Rashid (A.D. 786–809), he made seven voyages to strange and distant lands, each voyage fraught with peril but leaving him wealthier than before. In the end, the porter agrees that Sindbad deserves his riches, and Sindbad shares some of them with the porter.

from The Thousand and One Nights

The Second Voyage of Sindbad the Sailor

Translated by N. J. Dawood

For some time after my return to Baghdad I continued to lead a joyful and carefree life, but it was not long before I felt an irresistible longing to travel again about the world and to visit distant cities and islands in quest of profit and adventure. So I bought a great store of merchandise and, after making preparations for departure, sailed down the Tigris to Basrah.[1] There I embarked, together with a band of merchants, in a fine new vessel, well-equipped and manned by a sturdy crew, which set sail the same day.

Aided by a favorable wind, we voyaged for many days and nights from port to port and from island to island, selling and bartering our goods, and haggling with merchants and officials wherever we cast anchor. At length Destiny carried our ship to the shores of an uninhabited island, rich in fruit and flowers, and jubilant with the singing of birds and the murmur of crystal streams.

Here passengers and crew went ashore, and we all set off to enjoy the delights of the island. I strolled through the green meadows, leaving my companions far behind, and sat down in a shady thicket to eat a simple meal by a spring of water. Lulled by the soft and fragrant breeze which blew around me, I lay upon the grass and presently fell asleep.

I cannot tell how long I slept, but when I awoke I saw none of my fellow-travelers, and soon realized that the ship had sailed away without anyone noticing my absence. I ran in frantic haste towards the sea, and on reaching the shore saw the vessel, a white speck upon the vast blue ocean, dissolving into the far horizon.

Broken with terror and despair, I threw myself upon the sand, wailing: "Now your end has come, Sindbad! The jar that drops a second time is sure to break!" I cursed the day I bade farewell to the joys of a contented life and bitterly repented my folly in venturing again upon the hazards and hardships of the sea, after having so narrowly escaped death in my first voyage.

At length, resigning myself to my doom, I rose and, after wandering about aimlessly for some time, climbed into a tall tree. From its top I gazed long in all directions, but could see nothing save the sky, the trees, the birds, the sands, and the boundless ocean. As I scanned the interior of the island more closely, however, I gradually became aware of some white object looming in the distance. At once I climbed down the tree and made my way towards it. Drawing nearer, I found to my astonishment that it was a white dome of extraordinary dimensions. I walked all round it, but could find no door or entrance of any kind; and so smooth and slippery was its surface that any attempt to climb it would have been fruitless. I walked round it again, and, making a mark in the sand near its base, found that its circumference measured more than fifty paces.

Whilst I was thus engaged the sun was suddenly hidden from my view as by a great cloud and the

---

1. **sailed down the Tigris to Basrah** (bäs′rə): The Tigris River runs south through Iraq to the port city of Basra.

jubilant (jōō′bə-lənt) *adj.* extremely joyful

hidden from my view as by a great cloud and the world grew dark around me. I lifted up my eyes towards the sky, and was <u>confounded</u> to see a gigantic bird with enormous wings which, as it flew through the air, screened the sun and hid it from the island.

The sight of this prodigy[2] instantly called to my mind a story I had heard in my youth from pilgrims and adventurers—how in a far island dwelt a bird of monstrous size called the roc, which fed its young on elephants; and at once I realized that the white dome was none other than a roc's egg. In a twinkling the bird alighted upon the egg, covering it completely with its wings and stretching out its legs behind it on the ground. And in this posture it went to sleep. (Glory to Him who never sleeps!)

Rising swiftly, I unwound my turban from my head, then doubled it and twisted it into a rope with which I securely bound myself by the waist to one of the great talons of the monster. "Perchance this bird," I thought, "will carry me away to a civilized land; wherever I am set down, it will surely be better than a solitary island."

I lay awake all night, fearing to close my eyes lest the bird should fly away with me while I slept. At daybreak the roc rose from the egg, and, spreading its wings, took to the air with a terrible cry. I clung fast to its talon as it winged its way through the void and soared higher and higher until it almost touched the heavens. After some time it began to drop, and sailing swiftly downwards came to earth on the brow of a steep hill.

Trembling with fear, I hastened to untie my turban before the roc became aware of my presence. Scarcely had I released myself when the monster darted off towards a great black object lying near and, clutching it in its fearful claws, took wing again. As it rose in the air I was astonished to see that this was a serpent of immeasurable length; and with its prey the bird vanished from sight.

"NO SOONER DO I ESCAPE FROM ONE PERIL THAN I FIND MYSELF IN ANOTHER MORE GRIEVOUS."

Looking around, I found myself on a precipitous hillside overlooking an exceedingly deep and vast valley. On all sides towered craggy mountains whose beetling[3] summits no man could ever scale. I was stricken with fear and repented my rashness. "Would that I had remained in that island!" I thought to myself. "There at least I lacked neither fruit nor water, while these barren steeps offer nothing to eat or drink. No sooner do I escape from one peril than I find myself in another more grievous. There is no strength or help save in Allah!"

When I had made my way down the hill I marveled to see the ground thickly covered with the rarest diamonds, so that the entire valley blazed with a glorious light. Here and there among the glittering stones, however, coiled deadly snakes and vipers, dread keepers of the fabulous treasure. Thicker and longer than giant palm-trees, they could have swallowed whole elephants at one gulp. They were crawling back into their sunless dens, for by day they hid themselves from their enemies the rocs and the eagles and moved about only at night.

Overwhelmed with horror, and <u>oblivious</u> of hunger and fatigue, I roamed the valley all day searching with infinite caution for a shelter where I might pass the night. At dusk I came

---

2. **prodigy:** a rare or extraordinary event.

3. **beetling:** overhanging.

WORDS TO KNOW

confounded (kən-foun′dĭd) *adj.* confused; befuddled
oblivious (ə-blĭv′ē-əs) *adj.* not aware; unmindful

upon a narrow-mouthed cave, into which I crawled, blocking its entrance from within by a great stone. I thought to myself: "Here I shall be safe tonight. When tomorrow comes, let Destiny do its worst."

Scarcely had I advanced a few steps, when I saw at the far end of the cave an enormous serpent coiled in a great knot round its eggs. My hair stood on end and I was transfixed with terror. Seeing no way of escape, however, I put my trust in Allah and kept vigil all night. At day break I rolled back the stone and staggered out of the cave, reeling like a drunken man.

As I thus stumbled along I noticed a great joint of flesh come tumbling down into the valley from rock to rock. Upon closer inspection I found this to be a whole sheep, skinned and drawn. I was deeply perplexed at the mystery, for there was not a soul in sight; but at that very moment there flashed across my mind the memory of a story I had once heard from travelers who had visited the Diamond Mountains—how men obtained the diamonds from this treacherous and inaccessible valley by a strange device. Before sunrise they would throw whole carcasses of sheep from the top of the mountains, so that the gems on which they fell penetrated the soft flesh and became embedded in it. At midday rocs and mighty vultures would swoop down upon the mutton and carry it away in their talons to their nests in the mountain heights. With a great clamor the merchants would then rush at the birds and force them to drop the meat and fly away, after which it would only remain to look through the carcasses and pick out the diamonds.

As I recalled this story a plan of escape formed in my mind. I selected a great quantity of priceless stones and hid them all about me, filling my pockets with them and pressing them into the folds of my belt and garments. Then I unrolled my turban, stuffed it with more diamonds, twisted it into a rope as I had done before, and, lying down below the carcass, bound it firmly to my chest. I had not remained long in that position when I suddenly felt myself lifted from the ground by the talons of a huge vulture which had tightly closed upon the meat. The bird climbed higher and higher and finally alighted upon the top of a mountain. As soon as it began to tear at the flesh there arose from behind the neighboring rocks a great <u>tumult</u>, at which the bird took fright and flew away. At once I freed myself and sprang to my feet, with face and clothes all bloody.

I saw a man come running to the spot and stop in alarm as he saw me. Without uttering a word he cautiously bent over the carcass to examine it, eyeing me suspiciously all the while; but finding no diamonds, he wrung his hands and lifted up his arms, crying: "O heavy loss! Allah, in whom alone dwell all power and majesty, defend us from the wiles of the Evil One!"

Before I could explain my presence the man, shaking with fear, turned to me and asked: "Who are you, and how came you here?"

"Do not be alarmed, sir," I replied, "I am no evil spirit, but an honest man, a merchant by profession. My story is an extraordinary one, and the adventure which has brought me to these mountains surpasses in wonder all the marvels that men have seen or heard of. But first pray accept some of these diamonds, which I myself gathered in the fearful valley below."

I took some splendid jewels from my pocket and offered them to him, saying: "These will bring you all the riches you can desire."

The owner of the bait was overjoyed at the unexpected gift; he warmly thanked me and called down blessings upon me. Whilst we were thus talking, several other merchants came up from the mountain-side. They crowded round us, listening in amazement to my story, and congratulated me, saying: "By Allah, your escape was a miracle; for no man has ever set foot in that valley and returned alive. Allah alone be praised for your salvation."

WORDS TO KNOW

tumult (to͞o′mŭlt′) *n.* a disorderly noisiness or disturbance

Illustration by Edmund Dulac. Copyright © 1998 by Ragnarok Press. Ragnarok Press reserves all rights not specifically granted to licensee.

HUMANITIES CONNECTION Edmund Dulac (1882–1953) was one of the most successful and best-loved book illustrators of all time. His works were among the first to be reproduced using the process of color separation, which yields colors faithful to the original.

FROM FAR AND NEAR MEN CAME TO HEAR ME SPEAK OF MY ADVENTURES AND TO LEARN THE NEWS OF FOREIGN LANDS FROM ME.

The merchants then led me to their tent. They gave me food and drink and there I slept soundly for many hours. Early next day we set out from our tent and, after journeying over a vast range of mountains, came at length to the seashore. After a short voyage we arrived in a pleasant, densely wooded island, covered with trees so huge that beneath one of them a hundred men could shelter from the sun. It is from these trees that the aromatic substance known as camphor is extracted. The trunks are hollowed out, and the sap oozes drop by drop into vessels which are placed beneath, soon curdling into a crystal gum.

In that island I saw a gigantic beast called the karkadan,[4] or rhinoceros, which grazes in the fields like a cow or buffalo. Taller than a camel, it has a single horn in the middle of its forehead, and upon this horn Nature has carved the likeness of a man. The karkadan attacks the elephant and, impaling it upon its horn, carries it aloft from place to place until its victim dies. Before long, however, the elephant's fat melts in the heat of the sun and, dripping down into the karkadan's eyes, puts out its sight, so that the beast blunders helplessly along and finally drops dead. Then the roc swoops down upon both animals and carries them off to its nest in the high mountains. I also saw many strange breeds of buffalo in that island.

I sold a part of my diamonds for a large sum and exchanged more for a vast quantity of merchandise. Then we set sail and, trading from port to port and from island to island, at length arrived safely in Basrah. After a few days' sojourn[5] there I set out upstream to Baghdad, the City of Peace.

Loaded with precious goods and the finest of my diamonds, I hastened to my old street and, entering my own house, rejoiced to see my friends and kinsfolk. I gave them gold and presents, and distributed alms among the poor of the city.

I soon forgot the perils and hardships of my travels and took again to <u>sumptuous</u> living. I ate well, dressed well, and kept open house for innumerable gallants and boon companions.[6]

From far and near men came to hear me speak of my adventures and to learn the news of foreign lands from me. All were astounded at the dangers I had escaped and wished me joy of my return. Such was my second voyage.

Tomorrow, my friends, if Allah wills, I shall relate to you the extraordinary tale of my third voyage. ❖

---

4. **karkadan** (kär′kə-dăn′).

5. **sojourn:** a brief stay or visit.

6. **gallants** (gə-lănts′) **and boon companions:** fashionably dressed men and pleasant, merry companions.

WORDS TO KNOW

sumptuous (sŭmp′choo-əs) *adj.* costly; magnificent

Connect to the Literature

1. What Do You Think? Based on this story, do you think Sindbad deserves his wealth? Explain your response.

Comprehension Check
- How does Sindbad escape the island?
- How does Sindbad escape the valley?

Think Critically

2. ACTIVE READING: ANALYZING PROBLEMS AND SOLUTIONS With a classmate, go over the problems, solutions, and results you each recorded in your **READER'S NOTEBOOK**. Based on your discussion, do you see Sindbad as a good problem solver?

3. Does Sindbad succeed more because he is lucky or because he is clever? Support your opinion with examples.

4. Judging from the story, do you think Sindbad deserves to be called a heroic character?

> THINK ABOUT
> - his motives in making the voyage
> - how he responds to danger and defeat
> - how he treats others

Extend Interpretations

5. Different Perspectives How do you think King Shahryar might respond to Scheherezade's story about Sindbad the Sailor?

6. Connect to Life In your opinion, does the greatest success belong to those who, like Sindbad, take the biggest risks? Explain.

LITERARY ANALYSIS: PLOT

Plot is the chain of related events that take place in a story. In most plots events are set in motion by **conflicts**—struggles between a character and external or internal forces. Most plots include the following stages:

Exposition This stage provides groundwork for the plot. Characters are introduced, the setting is described, and conflicts are identified.

Rising Action As the story progresses, complications usually arise, causing difficulties for the main characters.

Climax This is the turning point of the story, the moment when interest and intensity reach their peak. Usually, an important discovery or decision is made.

Falling Action This stage consists of events that occur after the climax. Often, the conflict is resolved.

Cooperative Learning Activity

With a group of classmates, identify the four elements of a plot in "The Second Voyage of Sindbad the Sailor." Create a diagram like the one below to illustrate your findings.

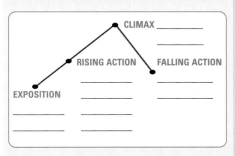

Writing Options

1. Sindbad Adventure

Imagine that Sindbad made eight voyages instead of seven. Write a story about his eighth voyage. Before you write, brainstorm answers to these questions:

- Where does Sindbad go?
- What difficulties does he encounter?
- How does he deal with them?
- What does he bring back from his journey?

Writing Handbook
See page R29: Narrative Writing.

2. Persuasive Essay

To a person who knew nothing of Sindbad's adventures, his wealth might seem undeserved. Think of a successful person you know who might appear simply lucky but who has earned his or her success in ways that are not apparent. Write a persuasive essay arguing that this person deserves his or her success.

Activities & Explorations

1. Art Discussion

Imagine that "The Second Voyage of Sindbad the Sailor" could have only one illustration. Decide what this should be. Then, with two or three classmates who have different ideas, stage a panel discussion in which you all present the reasons for your choices. ~ SPEAKING AND LISTENING

2. Sindbad Illustration

Decide what one illustration the story should have, as in the assignment above. Then create the illustration, adding a short quotation from the story as a caption. ~ ART, VIEWING AND REPRESENTING

Inquiry & Research

"Sindbad's World" Report

Sindbad's story unfolds against the backdrop of an Islamic empire that was at the center of major world-trade routes. Many people made or lost a fortune—or even their life—on voyages to acquire or trade goods. Find out more about these expeditions—the destinations they had, the routes they followed, the treasures they sought, the dangers they faced. Present your findings in an oral report that includes at least one visual aid, such as a map, a chart, or an illustration.

RESEARCH STARTER
CLASSZONE.COM

Vocabulary in Action

EXERCISE: CONTEXT CLUES Write the Word to Know that would best fill in the blank in each sentence.

1. When left behind on the island, Sindbad was at first _____; he did not know what to do.

2. It was too late to raise a _____ on the shore, for the boat was long gone.

3. He feared that the roc to which he tied himself would notice him, but the huge bird was _____.

4. Sindbad was _____ when he landed in the field of diamonds, for he could not believe his good luck.

5. He now envisioned a _____ life filled with every luxury.

WORDS TO KNOW

confounded	oblivious	tumult
jubilant	sumptuous	

Building Vocabulary

For an in-depth lesson on understanding context clues, see page 674.

Sindbad Yesterday, Today, and Tomorrow

A Perennial Favorite People don't seem to get tired of Sindbad (or Sinbad) the Sailor. Since 1935, this character and his exploits have been the subject of at least nineteen movies, three television series, and numerous books, plays, musicals, and video games.

Some of these productions are based on the actual Sindbad stories in *The Thousand and One Nights.* Others just borrow the main character and create entirely new adventures for him. Even when the names are unfamiliar, some influence may be perceived. The book *Robinson Crusoe* (1719) owes something to Sindbad, as does Jules Verne's *Mysterious Island* (1874).

In science fiction of the last century, outer space has replaced the sea as the passageway to the unknown. Such space travelers as Captain Kirk and Captain Picard of the *Star Trek* series can be thought of as modern-day versions of Sindbad.

Group Discussion Why do you think Sindbad and Sindbad-like stories continue to hold such fascination for us? Support your response to this question with examples from your own experience with books, movies, and television.

One of the earliest Sindbad films, *Sinbad the Sailor* (1947), starred Douglas Fairbanks, Jr., and Maureen O'Hara.

Jules Verne's *Mysterious Island* featured a giant bird much like Sindbad's roc. Here is a scene from the movie based on Verne's novel.

Sinbad: Beyond the Veil of Mists (2000) was the first film to be made entirely using 3-D animated motion capture, a technique that allows filmmakers to capture the natural movements of the human body in computer animation.

Ferdowsi

The Shahnameh
—Epic of Persia

The *Shahnameh,* or *Book of Kings,* is the national epic of Persia. It tells the story of the Persian people from the creation of the world to the Arab conquest. A long poem of some 60,000 couplets, or pairs of rhymed lines, the *Shahnameh* recounts the stories not only of kings but also of other great Persian heroes, real and mythical, from ancient times up through the 7th century.

The *Shahnameh* had special significance in 11th-century Persia. By that time, Persia had embraced Islam and become integrated into the Islamic empire. But the Persian historical and cultural tradition, which

Leaf from a manuscript of the *Shahnameh.*
The Metropolitan Museum of Art, New York.

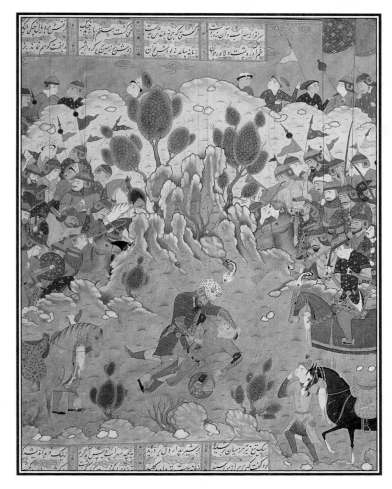

Rustam Stabs Suhrab, Garrett
Islamic manuscript, Mss. Third
Series, no. 310 Folio: 77:2.
Manuscripts Division,
Department of Rare Books and
Special Collections, Princeton
University Library.

extended back over 1,400 years, was becoming lost. Because Arabic
was the official tongue of religion, law, and education, even the Persian
language had begun to lose its identity.

In an effort to revive Persian culture and language, members of the
ruling Samanid dynasty of the 9th and 10th centuries commissioned a
national epic. Eventually this ambitious project was taken up by a man
now known as Ferdowsi, or "Heavenly One." For Ferdowsi, the
Shahnameh was a labor of love, and he kept at it for 35 years, finally
completing the work in 1010.

The history, mythology, and legends that make up the *Shahnameh*
had existed in oral and written versions long before Ferdowsi began
his project. But he incorporated them all into a single great work of
extraordinary artistry and beauty. Like those of Greece and Rome,
Persia's national epic not only embodies a culture but also represents a
great poetic achievement.

FROM THE **Rubáiyát of Omar Khayyám**

Translated by Edward FitzGerald

Omar Khayyám
1048–1131

The Early Years Omar Khayyám attended a good local school in his native city of Nishapur. There he received firm grounding in the sciences and philosophies of the day. He went on to study in Balkh and Samarkand, important Islamic cultural centers in central Asia.

The Ironies of Fame In Samarkand, Omar Khayyám published an important book on algebra, which brought him to the attention of the powerful sultan Malik Shah. So impressed was the sultan that he asked Omar to help develop a new calendar and to build an astronomical observatory.

Though Omar Khayyám wrote important works on astronomy, mathematics, medicine, and philosophy, he is today best known for his poetry. Yet during his lifetime and for centuries after his death, his achievements in science and mathematics overshadowed his literary accomplishments.

Build Background

Edward FitzGerald The British poet Edward FitzGerald (1809–1883) deserves credit for bringing Omar Khayyám's work to public attention. FitzGerald translated Omar's poems and published them in 1859. The *Rubáiyát* quickly captured the imagination of the English-speaking world, and it remains one of our best-known and most beloved works.

The *Rubáiyát* In Omar Khayyám's day, Persian poets expressed insights about life in four-line poems in which the first, second, and fourth lines rhymed. The Arabic word for such a poem is *rubái* (rōō'bī), and the plural *rubáiyát* (rōō'bī-yät').

Connect to Your Life

What is your philosophy of life? Try to answer this question in a single sentence that you would offer as advice to others.

Focus Your Reading

LITERARY ANALYSIS: METAPHOR AND THEME
A **metaphor** is a comparison that does not contain the word *like* or *as*. Such a comparison may be stated directly, as in "Life is a broken-winged bird," or it may be implied, as in "the Bird of Time." In literature, metaphors can be an effective means of conveying **theme**—a message or insight about life or human nature that the writer wishes to communicate. As you read these poems from the *Rubáiyát*, look for metaphors that are used to express theme.

ACTIVE READING: DRAWING CONCLUSIONS ABOUT TONE
Tone is an expression of the attitude—the thoughts or feelings—that a writer has about a subject. In speaking, tone can be communicated through the voice. A writer, however, establishes tone through choice of words and details.

📖 **READER'S NOTEBOOK** Jot down at least one thought or feeling that each poem seems to express. Then think of one or two adjectives that describe the tone.

Poem	Writer's Attitude	Tone
1	*Thought: Don't waste the day sleeping! Feelings: excitement, eagerness*	*Excited, optimistic*

1

Wake! For the Sun, who scatter'd into flight
The Stars before him from the Field of Night,
   Drives Night along with them from Heav'n,
     and strikes
The Sultan's Turret with a Shaft of Light.

7

5 Come, fill the Cup, and in the fire of Spring
Your Winter-garment of Repentance fling:
   The Bird of Time has but a little way
To flutter—and the Bird is on the Wing.

12

A Book of Verses underneath the Bough,
10 A Jug of Wine, a Loaf of Bread—and Thou
   Beside me singing in the Wilderness—
Oh, Wilderness were Paradise enow!

13

Some for the Glories of This World; and some
Sigh for the Prophet's Paradise to come;
15   Ah, take the Cash, and let the Credit go,
Nor heed the rumble of a distant Drum!

27

Myself when young did eagerly frequent
Doctor and Saint, and heard great argument
   About it and about: but evermore
20 Came out by the same door where in I went.

28

With them the seed of Wisdom did I sow,
And with mine own hand wrought to make it grow;
   And this was all the Harvest that I reap'd—
"I came like Water, and like Wind I go."

4 Sultan's (sŭl′tənz) **Turret:** a tower in the palace of a Muslim ruler.

6 Repentance: sorrow for having done wrong.

9 Bough: branch of a tree.

12 enow: enough.

14 the Prophet's Paradise: the paradise promised by Muhammad.

Detail of *Fête champêtre* [Picnic on the grass] (c. 1610–1615), Riza. The Keir Collection, England.

HUMANITIES CONNECTION Persian art is noted for its beautiful and detailed miniatures. Many of them were created as book illuminations, which had to be painted by hand and needed to be small.

29

25 Into this Universe, and *Why* not knowing
    Nor *Whence,* like Water willy-nilly flowing;
        And out of it, as Wind along the Waste,
    I know not *Whither,* willy-nilly blowing.

26 *Whence:* from what place.

28 *Whither:* to what place or condition.

46

    And fear not lest Existence closing your
30 Account, and mine, should know the like no more;
        The Eternal Sákí from that Bowl has pour'd
    Millions of Bubbles like us, and will pour.

31 the Eternal Sákí (sä′kē): the form of God who intoxicates the soul through the pouring of the wine of love.

63

Oh threats of Hell and Hopes of Paradise!
One thing at least is certain—*This* Life flies;
    One thing is certain and the rest is Lies;
The Flower that once has blown for ever dies.

64

Strange, is it not? that of the myriads who
Before us pass'd the door of Darkness through,
    Not one returns to tell us of the Road,
Which to discover we must travel too.

37 myriads (mĭr'ē-ədz): countless numbers (of people).

68

We are no other than a moving row
Of Magic Shadow-shapes that come and go
    Round with the Sun-illumined Lantern held
In Midnight by the Master of the Show;

69

But helpless Pieces of the Game He plays
Upon this Checker-board of Nights and Days;
    Hither and thither moves, and checks, and slays,
And one by one back in the Closet lays.

47 hither and thither: here and there.

71

The Moving Finger writes; and, having writ,
Moves on: nor all your Piety nor Wit
    Shall lure it back to cancel half a Line,
Nor all your Tears wash out a Word of it.

49 the Moving Finger: fate.

96

Yet Ah, that Spring should vanish with the Rose!
That Youth's sweet-scented manuscript should close!
    The Nightingale that in the branches sang,
Ah whence, and whither flown again, who knows!

99

Ah Love! could you and I with Him conspire
To grasp this sorry Scheme of Things entire,
    Would not we shatter it to bits—and then
Re-mold it nearer to the Heart's Desire!

57 with Him conspire: plot together with the recorder of everyone's fate (mentioned in stanza 98).

Connect to the Literature

1. **What Do You Think?** What did you find to be the most interesting image in these poems? Explain.

Think Critically

2. How would you describe the philosophy of life expressed by the **speaker?**

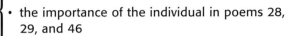

> THINK ABOUT
> - what he compares time to in poem 7
> - the actions he advocates in poems 1, 7, 12, and 13
> - the importance of the individual in poems 28, 29, and 46
> - his view of death in poems 63, 64, 68, 69, and 96

3. **ACTIVE READING: DRAWING CONCLUSIONS ABOUT TONE** Look back over the chart you created in your 📖 **READER'S NOTEBOOK.** What generalizations can you make about the overall tone of the *Rubáiyát?* How does the tone support the theme or themes of these poems?

4. What do we learn from these poems about the person they are addressed to?

Extend Interpretations

5. **Critic's Corner** Scholar and translator Peter Avery points out that Omar Khayyám lived in unstable times in northeastern Persia, "when there was occasion for pessimism and little room for a sense of security." In what way might the poems of the *Rubáiyát* be seen as a response to this?

6. **Comparing Texts** Compare these poems from the *Rubáiyát* with Horace's famous ode "Seize the Day" (page 394). How are the themes similar and how are they different?

7. **Connect to Life** The speaker suggests that happiness can be achieved very simply, with "A Book of Verses . . . , / A Jug of Wine, a Loaf of Bread—and Thou." Do you think most people can be satisfied with such simple pleasures? Give reasons for your opinion.

LITERARY ANALYSIS: METAPHOR AND THEME

In poetry, **metaphors**—comparisons made without the word *like* or *as*—often help convey **themes,** or insights, that writers wish to communicate. For example, in poem 7, time is compared to a bird that has already completed part of a short journey. This comparison helps convey the theme that time is limited and passes quickly.

Paired Activity With a partner, identify at least five other metaphors in these poems. Explain what two things are compared in each metaphor, and determine what theme or themes the metaphor helps convey. Create a chart like the one started below to record your findings.

Poem	Metaphor	Theme(s)
1	The sun is compared to a warrior on the attack.	
7		

FitzGerald's *Rubáiyát*

Many English-speaking readers know the work of Omar Khayyám only through the translations of Edward FitzGerald, a 19th-century British poet. FitzGerald's rendition of the *Rubáiyát* is admired by many as a literary treasure and has been reprinted in hundreds of editions since it was first published in 1859.

FitzGerald admitted that his versions were not absolutely faithful to Omar Khayyám's original poems. He translated only some of them, and these he arranged in a different order, to flow as one man's thoughts during a single day. Sometimes, to achieve the effect he wanted, FitzGerald "mashed" two verses into one, introduced new ideas, or left out unfamiliar references to Persian history. Critics view the result as a collaboration—the product of the hybrid poet "Omar-FitzGerald," in the words of Louis Untermeyer.

Because FitzGerald took so many liberties with the poems, other translators have attempted more faithful versions. They hoped to strip away FitzGerald's 19th-century quirks, such as overly romanticized language, and reveal to readers what Omar Khayyám actually said. Compare one of the best-known quatrains translated by FitzGerald with a more literal translation.

Edward FitzGerald
1809–1883

Edward FitzGerald

A Book of Verses underneath the Bough,
A Jug of Wine, a Loaf of Bread—and Thou
   Beside me singing in the Wilderness—
Oh, Wilderness were Paradise enow!

FitzGerald keeps the *aaba* rhyme scheme of the original but chooses archaic words to fill out the pattern.

FitzGerald introduces ideas not present in the original poem.

Robert Graves and Omar Ali-Shah

A gourd of red wine and a sheaf of poems—
A bare subsistence, half a loaf, not more—
Supplied us two alone in the free desert:
What Sultan could we envy on his throne?

This is an unrhymed translation. Notice that the language is simpler and more direct.

This line keeps the original comparison to a sultan's life.

Questions to Consider

1. What other differences do you notice in the translations? How much do they affect meaning?

2. Which translation do you prefer, and why?

POEMS BY Rumi

Rumi
1207–1273

The Road to Konya The poet Jalal ad-Din, known as Rumi (rōō′mē), was born in the Persian city of Balkh, in what is now Afghanistan. His father was a famous Muslim religious scholar, and Rumi was educated to follow in his footsteps. Fleeing from a Mongol attack on Balkh, the family eventually settled in Konya, capital of the Turkish sultanate of Rum (rōōm) in Anatolia. The name Rumi reflects the poet's ties to this region.

An Important Encounter Like his father, Rumi was a Muslim mystic, believing that spiritual awareness comes in flashes brought on by deep contemplation. The most influential event in his spiritual life occurred in 1244, when he met another mystic, Shams ad-Din, on the streets of Konya. The two became very close, devoting virtually all their time to mystical contemplation, until one day Shams disappeared— killed, it was proved much later, by one of Rumi's jealous followers. To ease his sense of loss, Rumi composed his *Divan-e-Shams,* a collection of poems in Shams's honor. He signed the poems with Shams's name instead of his own to show that he and Shams were spiritually one.

Lasting Fame The mystical form of Islam that Rumi and Shams practiced is known as **Sufism.** Rumi was one of Sufism's greatest thinkers, producing several volumes of prose explaining the Sufi philosophy. His most famous work, however, is a volume of poetry called the *Masnavi* (mäs-nä′vē). An epic of 26,000 couplets, or rhymed pairs of lines, the *Masnavi* offers guidance on how to live, behave, and practice Sufism. So important was the *Masnavi* to Persian-speaking people that it has been called the Persian Koran.

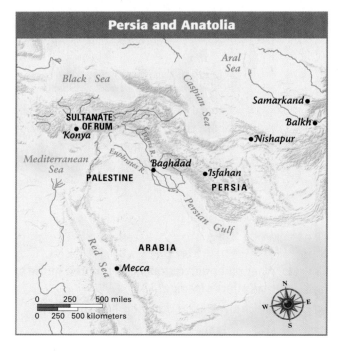

Persia and Anatolia

Build Background

What Is Sufism? Sufism is a mystical form of Islam in which Muslims seek spiritual love and wisdom through direct personal experience with God. An early form of Sufism arose in the 7th century as a reaction to the materialism of the Islamic world. However, the real flowering of Sufism took place in the 12th and 13th centuries, when Sufi brotherhoods were established in special communities, or schools. Like the monks of medieval Europe, Sufi mystics tried to avoid what they considered the lures and traps of the material world. In fact, they are often called dervishes, from the Persian word for a monk who lives in poverty. Rumi founded an order of Sufi mystics that embraced sacred dance as a form of worship. Because of this practice, these mystics acquired the nickname "whirling dervishes."

Prayer in the Mosque (19th century), Jean-Léon Gérôme. The Metropolitan Museum of Art, New York.

The Poetry of Love From the viewpoint of literature, Sufism is of great importance, for it inspired some of the finest mystical love poetry in the world. Most of that poetry was written in Arabic, Persian, Turkish, and Urdu (the chief language of Indian Muslims and today's Pakistan). Rumi, who wrote in Persian, is often named as the greatest of the Sufi poets.

Connect to Your Life

In these poems Rumi tries to convey experiences that are hard to put into words. What experiences or feelings might you find difficult to express? Why might this be difficult for you?

Focus Your Reading

LITERARY ANALYSIS: IMAGERY AND TONE
When writers use words and phrases to create vivid sensory experiences for the reader, they are making use of **imagery.** Although most imagery appeals to the sense of sight, imagery may also appeal to the senses of smell, hearing, taste, or touch. The title "Birdsong from Inside the Egg," for example, appeals to the senses of both sight and hearing. Often, a writer uses imagery to convey his or her **tone,** or attitude, toward a subject. The image of a bird's song coming from inside an egg expresses an attitude of amazement and joy. As you read Rumi's poems, notice the images that he uses and think about the kinds of tone they convey.

ACTIVE READING: READING DIFFICULT POETRY
Rumi's poetry presents difficulties for many readers because of his use of unusual images to convey abstract ideas. Even an experienced reader depends on strategies such as these:

- Read each poem slowly and deliberately.
- Read each poem several times. Read first to get an overall sense of the poem's meaning. Then focus on understanding individual parts.
- Write down notes about the stanzas and images that you think you understand.
- If you are still confused by certain sections of a poem, don't be too concerned. Use the parts of the poem that you do understand to help make sense of the ones that may still be unclear.

READER'S NOTEBOOK As you read each poem several times, jot down notes about specific stanzas or images that you think you understand. Allow yourself to make guesses at times about the ideas Rumi is expressing.

Birdsong from Inside the Egg

Rumi

Translated by **Coleman Barks**

Sometimes a lover of God may faint
in the presence. Then the beloved bends
and whispers in his ear, "Beggar, spread out
your robe. I'll fill it with gold.

5 I've come to protect your consciousness.
Where has it gone? Come back into awareness!"

This fainting is because
lovers want *so much*.

A chicken invites a camel into her henhouse,
10 and the whole structure is demolished.

A rabbit nestles down
with its eyes closed
in the arms of a lion.

There is an *excess*
15 in spiritual searching
that is profound ignorance.

Let that ignorance be our teacher!
The Friend breathes into one
who has no breath.

20 A deep silence revives the listening
and the speaking of those two
who meet on the riverbank.

18 the Friend: the form of God
who functions as a playful, happy
acquaintance.

20 revives: gives new spirit to;
renews in the mind.

Topkapi Saray Museum, Istanbul, Turkey.

HUMANITIES CONNECTION This detail from a 16th-century Turkish manuscript illustrates a miraculous story in which a cow bows down before Rumi.

Like the ground turning green in a spring wind.
Like birdsong beginning inside the egg.

25   Like this universe coming into existence,
the lover wakes, and whirls
in a dancing joy,

then kneels down
in praise.

The Grasses
Rumi

Translated by Coleman Barks

The same wind that uproots trees
makes the grasses shine.

The lordly wind loves the weakness
and the lowness of grasses.
5   Never brag of being strong.

The axe doesn't worry how thick the branches are.
It cuts them to pieces. But not the leaves.
It leaves the leaves alone.

A flame doesn't consider the size of the woodpile.
10   A butcher doesn't run from a flock of sheep.

What is form in the presence of reality?
Very feeble. Reality keeps the sky turned over
like a cup above us, revolving. Who turns
the sky wheel? The universal intelligence.

15   And the motion of the body comes
from the spirit like a waterwheel
that's held in a stream.

The inhaling-exhaling is from spirit,
now angry, now peaceful.
20   Wind destroys, and wind protects.

There is no reality but God,
says the completely surrendered sheikh,
who is an ocean for all beings.

The levels of creation are straws in that ocean.
25   The movement of the straws comes from an agitation
in the water. When the ocean wants the straws calm,
it sends them close to shore. When it wants them
back in the deep surge, it does with them
as the wind does with the grasses.

30   This never ends.

22 sheikh (shēk): a spiritual master
in the Islamic tradition.

Connect to the Literature

1. **What Do You Think?** Which image in these two poems did you find most memorable? Explain your choice.

Think Critically

2. **ACTIVE READING: READING DIFFICULT POETRY** Look back at the notes you made in your 📖**READER'S NOTEBOOK.** Are there any portions of the poems that you still find confusing? With a group of classmates, work at clarifying the overall meaning of each poem.

3. In "Birdsong from Inside the Egg," what advice does Rumi have for the lover of God?

THINK ABOUT

- God's response to the fainted lover
- the explanation of why the fainting occurs
- what Rumi says about ignorance in lines 14–17
- the comparisons in lines 23–29

4. In "The Grasses," what is being compared to the grasses? What message is the poet trying to communicate with this comparison?

5. Are different relationships between a person and God presented in the two poems? Support your response with examples from the poems.

Extend Interpretations

6. **Critic's Corner** According to the scholar Dick Davis, Rumi's work has the "reputation of being simultaneously both very simple and very difficult to understand properly." Do you agree? Cite examples from the poems to illustrate your opinion.

7. **Comparing Texts** Compare Rumi's poetry with the Zen teachings of Musō Soseki (page 512). What do the two writers' works have in common? Which do you find easier to comprehend, and why?

8. **Connect to Life** In your opinion, how relevant is Rumi's advice for people living in today's world?

LITERARY ANALYSIS: IMAGERY AND TONE

The use of words and phrases to create sensory experiences for readers is called **imagery.** Images not only bring a poem to life; they can also help a writer convey his or her **tone,** or attitude, toward a subject. Rumi's images are often unusual or surprising and frequently express a strong attitude.

Cooperative Learning Activity

With a group of classmates, identify images in these two poems that you think convey a particular tone. Then discuss how you think each poem's tone supports the meaning of the poem. Create charts like the one shown here to prepare for your discussion.

Image	Line(s)	Tone
"Birdsong" a camel going into a henhouse	9-10	

from the

Gulistan

SADI

Translated by Omar Ali-Shah

Sadi
1213–1292

A Sufi and a Wandering Dervish Like Rumi, Sadi (sä-dē') was a member of the mystical Sufi sect. As a Sufi, he had neither possessions nor a home, choosing instead to devote his life to wandering, study, meditation, and writing. During a long period of exile from his native Persia, Sadi traveled throughout the Middle East and beyond. He is said to have made several pilgrimages to Mecca and to have encountered on his travels a number of famous Sufi mystics, including perhaps Rumi himself. He eventually returned to Persia and in his later years wrote the works he is best known for, including the *Gulistan.*

The Gulistan, *or "Rose Garden," includes stories, poems, witty sayings, and personal anecdotes. Most of the stories are simple fables that attempt to teach something about life. Sadi brought to his writing not only his religious outlook but also his extensive experience of the world. The Gulistan is filled with the Sufi spririt, but it is also noted for its humor, worldly wisdom, and profound understanding of human nature.*

*Like several other works of literature you have read, Sadi's Gulistan contains short, simple stories intended to teach wisdom. Mixed in with these stories are **proverbs**, brief sayings that express general truths or give practical advice. The proverbs are meant to help the reader make sense of the stories. In each of the tales that follow, someone does something unusual or surprising. As you read, ask yourself,*

1. Why do the characters behave as they do?
2. How do the proverbs connect to the stories?
3. What wisdom does each story teach?

Tale 1

They tell of a king who gave the command that a captive should be executed. The unfortunate victim, in a state of despair, began to abuse the king with vile language, for it is said that he who washes his hands of life speaks all that he has in his heart.

> The tongue of a desperate man sheds
> its curb as the cornered cat springs
> at the dog.
> At the instant of necessity when
> flight is impossible the bare hand
> will grasp the keen blade of the sword.

The king asked: "What does he say?" One of his ministers, a man of kindly disposition, replied: "My Lord, he says: 'And those who restrain anger and pardon men, and Allah loves the doer of good,' a verse from the Holy Koran." The king was touched with pity and pardoned him, but another minister of contradictory character said: "It is not meet for those of our standing to speak aught but the truth in the presence of kings. The man abused His Majesty."

The king's face clouded at these words and he said: "That falsehood of his is more acceptable to me than the truth you have spoken, for it was a well-intentioned lie, whereas your truth was malicious. Have not the wise said: 'The well-intentioned lie is better than the truth which causes mischief'?"

> Whosoever advises the king as to his
> actions does ill if he advises aught
> but good.
> Over the vault of Feridun[1] was
> inscribed:

> "The world, O brother, remains with
> no one, attach your heart to the
> world's Creator—Enough!
> Lean not nor rely upon the world's
> promises for many have been reared
> by it and perished.
> When it is time for the pure soul
> to leave
> what matter if from a throne
> or from the naked earth?"

Tale 15

A Vizier,[2] who had been dismissed from office, entered a Sufi fraternity.[3] The blessing of their meditations communicated itself to him and gave him peace of mind. His former master became well-disposed to him again and bade him return to court. The Vizier demurred[4] and said: "Being out of office and close to wisdom is better than any occupation."

> Those who seat themselves in a
> safe corner
> are safe from the teeth of dogs
> and the tongues of men.
> They tear up the paper and
> break the pen and escape the
> hands and tongues of cavilers.[5]

---

1. **the vault of Feridun** (fĕr´ĭ-dōōn´): the tomb of a legendary Persian hero and ruler.

2. **vizier** (vĭ-zîr´): a high officer in a Muslim government.

3. **Sufi fraternity:** a group of members of a Muslim sect that values love of and devotion to God above all else.

4. **demurred** (dĭ-mûrd´): refused; objected.

5. **cavilers** (kăv´ə-lərz): individuals who find fault with others, especially about small things.

Said the king: "I need a man of wisdom to advise me on the government of the realm."

Replied the Vizier: "The sign of wisdom is not to engage in such activities: the *Huma* is superior to all other birds in that it eats bones and does not trouble any other bird."

They asked a lynx: "How was it that you became a servant of the lion?" He replied: "I eat the remains of his prey and live, safe from any enemies under the shadow of his authority."

They questioned: "Now that you have the protection of his might and have acknowledged your debt to him, why do you not approach nearer and enter the inner circle of his special servants and fellows?" The lynx replied: "However, at the same time I am not inapprehensive of[6] his strength."

> If a Zoroastrian feeds his fire[7] for
> a hundred years
> he has only to fall in once to
> be consumed.

Sometimes a courtier may be rewarded by gold, sometimes by the loss of his head.

As the sages say, it is as well to be on guard against the fickleness of monarchs, for they may take umbrage[8] at a salute or give a robe of honor in reply to abuse.

> Surely it is true when they say that
> great wit is a merit in a courtier but
> a fault in the wise.
> Conduct yourself with dignity;
> leave jesting to courtiers.

Tale 27

A certain man was skilled in the art of wrestling and had mastered three hundred and sixty excellent throws and sleights[9] and developed new stratagems every day. He had a favorite pupil to whom he taught three hundred and fifty-nine of these maneuvers, postponing the instruction of the last secret. Soon the youth reached such a standard of proficiency that no one could stand against him.

One day, in the presence of the king, the stripling[10] declared himself equal to his master in strength and skill. The king was displeased at such boastfulness and commanded that they should wrestle before him. A spacious place was chosen and the audience was composed of the lords and ladies of the realm and athletes from all over the world.

In the contest the young man charged, like a mad elephant, with such force that a mountain of iron would have been uprooted by the impact. The master, knowing his pupil to be stronger and as skilled as he himself, used the secret hold, overcame the youth and flung him to the ground. A great shout arose from the audience and the king bestowed a robe of honor and money on the winner.

---

6. **not inapprehensive of:** somewhat fearful of.
7. **Zoroastrian** (zôr′ō-ăs′trē-ən) **feeds his fire:** In the temples of Zoroastrianism (a religion founded by the Persian Prophet Zoroaster), a fire was kept burning constantly.
8. **umbrage** (ŭm′brĭj): offense.
9. **sleights** (slīts): tricks.
10. **stripling:** young man.

Said the master: "This hold I reserved for such a day, for have the wise not said: 'Do not give a friend so much power that should he wish to harm you, he will be able to do so'? Have you not heard of the teacher who suffered wrong from his pupil:

'Every day I instructed him in archery
until the day when his arm waxed strong,
and he shot me.
Perhaps fidelity[11] was a stranger
in the world or no one practiced
it in days of yore.
No one who has learned archery from me
has failed to make me his target!'"

Tale 30

A king ordered the execution of an innocent man. The condemned said: "O King, do not injure yourself on account of the anger that you feel for me." "What do you mean?" said the king. He replied: "My punishment will be over in a moment but the guilt of it will be with you forever.

As the wind sweeps over the desert
so does the term of life.
The suffering, the joy, the ugly and
the beautiful have passed away.
The tyrant thought to punish
yet that punishment I escaped
is now fixed on him."

This admonition impressed the king, who gave up the idea of shedding his blood. ❖

Sadi (in the striped robe) sitting with his patron. Page from a manuscript of the *Kulliyat* (collected works) of Sadi (c. 1600–1605), attributed to Aqa Riza. Opaque watercolor and gold on paper, 41.7 cm × 26.4 cm. Collection of Prince Sadruddin Aga Khan, Geneva (MS 35).

Rebuking the loser, the king said: "You presumed to overcome your teacher yet failed in your presumption." The youth replied: "My lord, my master withheld from me one hold and used it today, thus he triumphed not by strength."

---

11. **fidelity:** faithfulness; loyalty.

Persian and Arabic Literature

Reflect and Assess

What has reading the selections in Unit Four, Part 1, contributed to your understanding and appreciation of Persian and Arabic literature? What new discoveries did you make? Use the following activities to help you explore what you have learned.

Detail of *Fête champêtre* [Picnic on the grass] (c. 1610–1615), Riza. The Keir Collection, England.

Reflecting on the Literature

Human Fate Each of the selections in this part of the book explores how human beings are affected by fate. Fate might be understood as luck, as divine will, or simply as part of the general human condition. Fate might or might not be affected by human action or inaction. Think about the works you have read, and identify three different views of fate. Describe each view in your own words. Then choose the one you feel best applies to the world we live in, and explain why.

Reviewing Literary Concepts

Reflecting on Theme In different ways, the selections in this part of the book offer truths to live by. Choose three of these truths, each one from a different selection, and explain each briefly in your own words. For each truth, include at least one example of how a person might live by it. Which of the three do you think is most relevant to your own life? Explain your answer.

⬜ Building Your Portfolio

Writing Options Look back at the written assignment that you chose to complete for *The Thousand and One Nights.* If you feel that it is good enough, write a cover note explaining its strong points and add the piece to your **Presentation Portfolio.** ⬜

Self **ASSESSMENT**

📖 **READER'S NOTEBOOK**

Below are some important names and terms that you encountered in this part of the book. Go through the list and explain the meaning or significance of each one. If you have trouble with a term, go back to the place where it was first introduced and try to determine its meaning or significance in context, or look it up in the **Glossary of Literary Terms** (page R91).

Islam	Sindbad
antithesis	conflict
rubái	imagery
metaphor	Sufism
Scheherezade	frame story

Setting **GOALS**

Which of the major works excerpted in this part of the book would you like to continue reading? Write a paragraph explaining your choice, and make arrangements to carry out this reading sometime during the next month.

Extend Your *Reading*

Night & Horses & the Desert

An Anthology of Classical Arabic Literature

ROBERT IRWIN, ED.

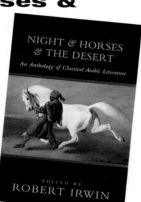

This anthology will help you delve more deeply into the Arabic literary tradition while still focusing on its highlights. Organized by historical period, the collection includes literature not only from the great age of Arabic literature, but also from pre-Islamic times.

The Essential Rumi

COLEMAN BARKS, TRANS.

That the work of a 13th-century Persian mystic should resonate so strongly with modern readers and make him one of the most widely read poets in America is an amazing tribute to the power of literature to bridge the gap between cultures. This collection contains some of Rumi's finest work in a translation that sparkles.

And Even *More* . . .

Books

The Gift: Poems by Hafiz, the Great Sufi Master
DANIEL LADINSKY, TRANS.
Hafiz is the other great Sufi mystic and poet, with a style uniquely his own.

Rumi Speaks Through Sufi Tales KRISH KHOSLA
This collection shows that Rumi excelled as a storyteller as well as a poet.

Other Media

Islam: 600–1200
This video focuses on the history, culture, and religion of the Islamic world during its golden age. Zenger Media. (VIDEOCASSETTE)

Rumi: Poet of the Heart
This documentary, featuring Coleman Barks, Robert Bly, and Deepak Chopra and narrated by Debra Winger, focuses on Rumi's life and work and their relevance in our own time. Magnolia Films. (VIDEOCASSETTE)

Scheherezade
In this symphonic tone poem, the 19th-century Russian composer Nikolai Rimski-Korsakov celebrates and brings to musical life several of the tales from *The Thousand and One Nights*. Nonesuch. (AUDIO CD)

Arabian Nights and Days

NAGUIB MAHFOUZ

In this spellbinding work, the renowned Nobel Prize–winning novelist Naguib Mahfouz retells many of the tales from *The Arabian Nights*. Set in medieval times but with a distinctly modern flavor, these versions bring new life to the classic stories.

West African Oral Literature

Why It Matters

West Africa has a rich cultural tradition, full of wisdom, grandeur, and humor. Much of the art, music, and oral literature of the area recalls the glories of its ancient kingdoms. These cultural forms traveled with West Africans when millions of them were brought to the Americas during the Atlantic slave trade. Today, distinctive parts of the U.S., Latin American, and Caribbean cultures show West African influence.

For Links to West Africa, click on:

HUMANITIES
CLASSZONE.COM

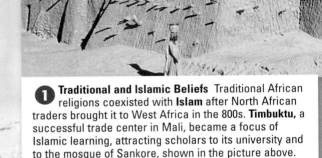

① Traditional and Islamic Beliefs Traditional African religions coexisted with **Islam** after North African traders brought it to West Africa in the 800s. **Timbuktu,** a successful trade center in Mali, became a focus of Islamic learning, attracting scholars to its university and to the mosque of Sankore, shown in the picture above.

SOUTH AMERICA

② Wealthy Cities and Empires Ancient cities such as Djenné-Djeno prospered through trade. North African caravans laden with blocks of salt and other goods would cross the Sahara to trade for gold, ivory, and other precious resources of West Africa. Centers of the **gold trade** expanded into the great empires of **Ghana** and **Mali.**

612

Many Ethnic Groups West Africa is home to many different groups with different languages and customs. In ancient times, their ways of life diverged even more than they do today. The **Soninke**, for example, were traders; the **Fulani** were cattle herders; and the **Yoruba** were yam farmers.

AFRICA

Sahara

GHANA EMPIRE,
c. 300–1200
(Soninke people)

❶ Timbuktu

MALI EMPIRE,
1235–1500
(Mandinka people)

Senegal R.

Niger R.

❷ Djenné-Djeno

OYO KINGDOM,
c. 1200–1800
(Yoruba people)

ASHANTI EMPIRE,
1695–1901
(Ashanti people)

❸

❹

BENIN KINGDOM,
c. 1170–1900
(Edo people)

Gulf of
Guinea

Congo R.

ATLANTIC
OCEAN

❸ The African Diaspora Over 300 years of the **slave trade** dispersed millions of West Africans and other Africans throughout the Americas. West African coastal cities were centers of the trade. Despite this violent disruption, many enslaved Africans managed to hold on to their traditions and pass them to their descendants.

❹ Rich Artistic Traditions Magnificently carved head-pieces and masks and stunning bronze sculptures, such as this leopard from **Benin,** are only some of the West African art treasures prized around the globe. West African music, too, has enriched the world and has given rise to other forms, such as American blues and jazz.

```
0        400      800 miles
0    400    800 kilometers
```

N
W   E
S

Historical Highlights

The history of West Africa is both exciting and tragic. The region was shaped by the rise and fall of mighty empires and city-states, the spread of a new religion, the wounds of the slave trade, and colonization by European powers.

This representation of Mansa Musa is from a 14th-century Spanish map.

Rise of Ghana
c. 300–1200

West Africa's first empire was ancient **Ghana,** founded by the **Soninke** people, merchants who lived just south of the Sahara. They named their state after their ruler, or *ghana* ("war chief").

Called the land of gold by early travelers, Ghana ironically produced no gold itself. Instead, the Soninke kings took advantage of their strategic location between northern and southern trade routes. The gold that draped these kings in splendor came from taxing traders. Eventually, Ghana was weakened by Islamic invasions.

Spread of Islam
c. 800–1900

Islam spread to West Africa both peacefully, through trade, and violently, through conquest. Members of the local ruling courts, who learned of the religion through contact with Muslim traders, were usually the first to convert. But many people in the countryside kept their traditional beliefs.

In 1076, Islamic reformers called **Almoravids** (or Moors) captured the capital of Ghana and converted its people. Later, **Fulani** converts to Islam spread the religion farther into West Africa through holy wars against non-Muslim rulers.

Rise of Mali
1235–1500

Mali succeeded Ghana to become the first great Muslim empire in West Africa. The epic *Sundiata* tells of Mali's founder, the **Mandinka** hero **Sundiata Keita.** In 1235, he defeated a rival, non-Muslim king to establish the empire.

Perhaps Mali's greatest ruler was Sundiata's grandnephew **Mansa Musa,** who brought the empire to the height of its size and power. Under him, the cities of Timbuktu and Djenné became great centers of Muslim education. During his famous pilgrimage to Mecca in 1324, he lavished so many gifts of gold on his hosts in Cairo that the price of gold dropped drastically throughout Egypt.

History to Literature

EVENT IN HISTORY	EVENT IN LITERATURE
Ancient Ghana, the empire of the Soninke, flourishes for hundreds of years.	The epic *Dausi* includes the earliest legends of the Soninke; the most famous episode is *Gassire's Lute.*
Sundiata Keita defeats a rival king and founds the empire of Mali.	The epic *Sundiata* of the Mandinka describes the life of Sundiata Keita and celebrates his great victory.

GHANA EMPIRE

300

Forest Kingdoms Prosper

c. 1170–1900

While Mali was at its height, smaller forest kingdoms to the south were prospering as well. One forest group was the **Yoruba**, a deeply religious people who composed eloquent praise songs to their gods. The Yoruba had a government of ruling families, each headed by a strong king called an *oba* or *alafin*, who was considered divine. One of the achievements of the Yoruba was the creation of city-states. The two biggest, **Ife** and **Oyo**, supported large populations of traders, craftspeople, and artists.

The **Edo** people of **Benin**, southwest of Ife near the coast, had a government and trading system similar to those of the Yoruba. Benin has become world-famous for the fine quality of its royal sculpture. Gleaming brass plaques commemorating the king's achievements adorned the palace walls, and elegantly cast bronze heads immortalized the royal family. In the 1470s, the first Portuguese trading ships sailed into Benin's port, making a contact that would open up West Africa to the **Atlantic slave trade**.

This painting depicts the tragedy of the Atlantic slave trade. Millions of Africans were captured, enslaved, and shipped to the Americas.

Atlantic Slave Trade

1518–1870

Traditionally, slavery in West Africa was small-scale. Africans regularly enslaved prisoners of war or minor criminals. The large-scale business of trading slaves first began with the Muslims in West Africa and continued with the Portuguese. Then, after 1625, Europeans increased their demand for slaves to work their mines and plantations in the Americas and the Caribbean islands. In exchange for slaves, Europeans offered guns. This led to local wars and raids designed to bring in prisoners, who would be sold as slaves for more guns. Even African kings who resisted the thriving trade couldn't stop it. As a result, West Africa lost between 10 and 15 million of its people.

Ashanti Empire

1695–1901

The **Ashanti** (or Asante) were one group involved in the slave trade. Originally small farmers, they banded together in 1695 to form a strong union. The symbol of their unity was the Golden Stool, which they believed was brought from heaven for their ruler to sit on.

The empire prospered until the 1870s, when it began a series of wars with the British that led to its **colonization**. The Ashanti experience was repeated throughout Africa during the period known as the "Scramble for Africa" (1880–1900). With superior weapons, the European powers colonized 90 percent of the African continent, imposing new governments, languages, and faiths.

	FOREST KINGDOMS		ASHANTI EMPIRE	
MALI EMPIRE				
1170	1235	1500	1695	1901

People and Society

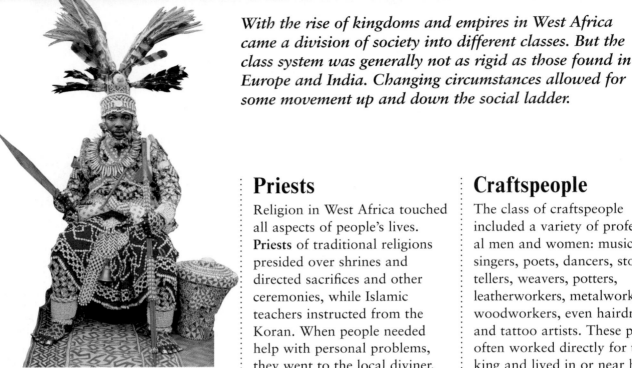

With the rise of kingdoms and empires in West Africa came a division of society into different classes. But the class system was generally not as rigid as those found in Europe and India. Changing circumstances allowed for some movement up and down the social ladder.

Rulers

At the top of the social ladder in West Africa were the **kings**, nobles, and **chiefs**. These members of high-ranking families controlled the government and the wealth. Rulers were also spiritual leaders of their people. Sometimes, groups of rulers shared power among themselves.

Since none of the early West African civilizations used money, rulers accumulated their wealth in goods and services. For example, traders paid taxes in gold, and fishermen gave a portion of their catch. In return, the people received the protection of the king's army.

Priests

Religion in West Africa touched all aspects of people's lives. **Priests** of traditional religions presided over shrines and directed sacrifices and other ceremonies, while Islamic teachers instructed from the Koran. When people needed help with personal problems, they went to the local diviner. **Diviners** were special religious figures who were thought to understand messages from the spirit world. After tracing the cause of a person's problem, they would recommend a solution. Diviners also acted as healers, treating people's physical problems with herbal medicines.

Craftspeople

The class of craftspeople included a variety of professional men and women: musicians, singers, poets, dancers, storytellers, weavers, potters, leatherworkers, metalworkers, woodworkers, even hairdressers and tattoo artists. These people often worked directly for the king and lived in or near his court. Such royal patronage usually required artists to celebrate the ruler in their art. This was especially true in the forest kingdoms. The Yoruba established one of the greatest schools of sculpture in the world at Ife. The Edo people of Benin developed their famous style of **royal sculpture** after learning from Ife artists.

This image of a Dahomean king was made by a court sculptor and based on a diviner's prophecies about the king's reign.

Used to measure gold, this weight from Ghana depicts a farming family.

Freeborn People

The designation *freeborn* is generally applied to the great mass of ordinary people who weren't slaves. Rich merchants, traders, and landowners, as well as humble farmers, fishermen, and miners, were freeborn. As time went on and kingdoms grew larger, there also emerged a group of appointed officials, usually freeborn, who helped run the government.

Still, *free* was a relative term in West Africa. Everyone owed something to the rulers—either a product or a service. Craftspeople, although technically free, lived under a variety of restrictions, depending on what king they worked for. And in wartime, a free man or woman could be captured and turned into a slave overnight.

Slaves

Slavery among early West Africans was looser than what later developed in the Americas. Enslaved war captives and law-breakers often had the same jobs as the freeborn, working on farms, in mines, and in homes. Unlike Greek and Roman rulers, who never trusted their slaves to fight for them, West African kings frequently used slaves as professional soldiers. Still, slaves had fewer rights than the freeborn, and they could be sold anytime.

Some slaves managed to gain their freedom through loyal service, hard work, or marriage into their owner's family. Those lucky enough to be court slaves working directly for the king often enjoyed greater power and privilege than the freeborn. In a few instances, freed slaves even became chiefs and kings.

Women in West Africa

According to an Ashanti proverb, "it's a woman who gave birth to a man; it's a woman who gave birth to a chief." This saying indicates the high status that women, especially mothers, enjoyed in West Africa. Most husbands and wives worked as equal economic partners. Women usually didn't hold political office, although a few warrior-queens existed. A more typical leadership role for a woman was that of queen mother. Often the mother or widow of a former king, a **queen mother** had to give consent before another man could be king. As adviser to the king, she attended political meetings and had veto power over the king's laws. Queen mothers sometimes acted as judges and even rode into battle on occasion.

Arts and Culture

West African culture has always been tied to the life of the community. Literature, religion, music, and art—like eating and drinking—are part of people's daily existence. For this reason, many of West Africa's cultural traditions remain as vital today as they were hundreds of years ago.

Literature

West Africa has an extremely rich and varied **oral tradition**, encompassing grand epics and humble proverbs; solemn praise poems and funny trickster tales; stories about people, animals, and supernatural forces; origin myths and riddles. In earlier times, as now, oral literature entertained the community and helped educate the young in the history and values of a people. Literary performance customarily brought people together, not only in the smallest villages but also in the biggest cities and at the king's palace. It culturally united large empires and gave the people cause for pride and celebration. All the ethnic groups of Mali could rejoice in the glorious life of their first empire builder, Sundiata. The Yoruba in the cities and the countryside alike could sing praises to the same *orishas,* or family of gods.

How Was Literature Presented?

The grand epics of the Soninke, Mandinka, and other groups were not read from books but were performed by professional bards called *dielis,* or griots. Griots recount the histories of prominent families, compose praise songs, play instruments, advise rulers, and perform many other functions. Griots belong to their own special caste and pass their knowledge to their children.

Religion

Traditional West African religions, although varied, shared common elements:

- the idea of one god who withdrew from human affairs after the creation
- worship of lesser gods and spirits who were more active in human affairs
- faith in the ability of **ancestral spirits** to influence the lives of living family members
- belief in witches and sorcerers who caused misfortune
- faith in the ability of diviners to solve problems both supernatural and natural

Fundamental to all these beliefs is the idea of a connection between the spirit world and the natural world. Rulers had the responsibility of maintaining harmony between these two worlds to ensure rain, good crops, and other life-sustaining conditions.

With the introduction of Islam, many of the old beliefs and practices died out. But some old ways persisted. For example, West African Muslim women often shocked Arab Muslim visitors by mixing freely with men in public and leaving their face unveiled—two things Arab women were forbidden to do.

In West Africa, musicianship is highly regarded, and children are encouraged to become skilled at a young age.

Music and Dance

In West Africa, music is generally a social activity—part of games, ceremonies, festivals, and work. African musicians favor melody over harmony, and **improvisation** over strict rules. They use the distinctive qualities of musical instruments and human voices to maximum effect. Xylophones, flutes, horns, and whistles combine with different stringed instruments, such as the *kora*, the 21-string harp, and the *xalam,* the ancestor of the banjo. And driving all the music is the rhythm of the drums. The sheer variety of African percussion instruments is mind-boggling, including drums, bells, and rattles of all shapes, sizes, and materials. In rhythmical sophistication African music is unsurpassed.

African dance is as rhythmic and energetic as the music. Dancing—in solo or group performances—accompanies the music at most social and religious functions. Like the music, it serves to reinforce the vitality of the community.

Art

West African art includes exquisite jewelry, pottery, and sculpture made from such materials as wood, clay, ivory, and metal. In ancient times, most art was religious and used to evoke spiritual power. For example, someone might carve a beautiful figurine to entice an ancestral or nature spirit to inhabit it. In a similar way, individuals wore elaborate masks and headpieces to attract different spirits. Typically, African ritual art aims to express a spirit's essence—its power to make crops grow, for example—rather than its outward appearance. The idea that art need not represent a thing realistically in order to express its essence is the founding principle of modern art. The **expressionistic** design of African ritual objects influenced a number of modern artists, notably the 20th-century Spanish artist Pablo Picasso.

African masks, such as these Ivory Coast examples, are collected worldwide.

619

Time Line

c.   approximately
B.C. before Christ
A.D. after Christ

WEST AFRICAN ORAL LITERATURE
(A.D. 300–1900)

2500 B.C.   A.D. 1   PRESENT

EVENTS IN WEST AFRICAN LITERATURE

300

c. 300–1100 Soninke epic poets compose the *Dausi*, which has survived only in fragments ➤

900

1068 Muslim scholar Abu Ubayd al-Bakri completes first written history of West Africa

The lute accompanies performances of epics.

EVENTS IN WEST AFRICAN HISTORY

300

c. 300 Ancient kingdom of Ghana founded by the Soninke people, according to legend

600

c. 670 Arab Muslims rule Egypt and large part of North African coast

c. 800 Muslim traders from North Africa increase travel across the Sahara to West Africa

c. 800 Kingdom of Ghana develops an empire from wealth gained in gold-salt trade

900

1050s Muslim Almoravids move from the western Sahara to conquer Morocco

1076 Almoravids overrun Ghana empire

c. 1100–1600 ➤ Walled city of Ife is center of most powerful Yoruba kingdom

Bronze head from Ife, depicting a king or god

EVENTS IN WORLD HISTORY

300

500–1500 Middle Ages in Europe

c. 570 Birth of Muhammad, prophet of Islam

600

618–907 T'ang dynasty expands Chinese empire

622 Beginning of the Muslim era

750 Islamic empire extends from Atlantic Ocean to Indus River

771–814 Charlemagne builds empire that includes all of France and parts of Spain, Italy, and Germany

c. 850 Chinese invent gunpowder

900

900s Anasazi civilization in North America enters classic Pueblo period

939 Vietnam gains independence from China

1054 Final split between Roman Catholic and Eastern Orthodox churches

1095 Beginning of the Crusades, a 200-year struggle between Christians and Muslims over the Holy Land

1200	1500	1800

c. 1250–1400 Mandinka poets compose Mali's epic, *Sundiata*

1352 North African historian Ibn Battuta visits Mali, later writes of his travels

1650 African scholar Abd al-Rahman as-Sadi writes a history of ancient Ghana and Mali

1789 Olaudah Equiano, a freed slave originally from Benin, publishes his autobiography, *The Interesting Narrative of the Life of Olaudah Equiano*

1200	1500	1800

1203–1235 Fulani people control former Ghana trade routes

1235 Sundiata Keita defeats Fulani army and founds Mali empire

1324–1325 Mali king Mansa Musa goes on pilgrimage to Mecca and brings back Arab architect to build mosques in Timbuktu and Gao

1400s Mali declines

1480s Kingdom of Benin begins trading with Portuguese

1518 Spanish carry first cargo of enslaved Africans directly from West Africa to Caribbean islands

1625 Atlantic slave trade expands

c. 1650–1789 City-state of Oyo replaces Ife as center of Yoruba power

1695–1717 Founding of Ashanti empire

mid-1700s British exchange more than 100,000 guns a year for enslaved Africans

c. 1800 Most West African kingdoms involved in Atlantic slave trade

1807–1826 Ashanti battle British over control of coast

1874 British burn Ashanti capital during Ashanti-British war

1884–1885 European powers divide Africa among themselves at Berlin Conference

1901 Ashanti empire becomes British colony

1200	1500	1800

1200–1521 Aztecs build empire in Mexico

1206–1227 Genghis Khan builds Mongol Empire

1345–1352 Epidemic of ➤ bubonic plague devastates large areas of China, the Middle East, and Europe

1492 Christopher Columbus reaches the Caribbean

1507 Spain conquers territory in the Caribbean and Central America

Plague victims in 14th-century Europe

c. 1800 Africans make up half the populations of Brazil and Venezuela

1804 Napoleon becomes emperor of France

1804 Haiti gains independence from France

1821 Mexico declares independence from Spain

1861–1865 Civil War ends slavery in the United States

Connect to Today: The Legacy of West Africa

Popular Dance
Many popular American dances have West African counterparts. Such dances were first performed in black communities and then spread to the general population. In the United States they include the shimmy, Charleston, snakehips, Lindy, and twist. In Latin America, they include the merengue, mambo, and samba. Today's hottest dances still borrow movements from traditional West African dances.

Personal Adornment
Since the 1960s, many African Americans in the United States have celebrated their West African heritage through their hair and clothing styles. West Africa has inspired more widespread fashion trends as well. Think of intricate braids, elaborate head wraps, bright dashikis and voluminous djellabas, fabrics such as kente and mud cloth, multilayered beads, and cowrie-shell decoration.

Musical Rhythms
One of West Africa's greatest gifts to the world has been its music, with its complex rhythms and exciting improvisations. Over centuries, African music styles blended with European styles to form new American genres, such as jazz. Today, similar cross-fertilization takes place on the African continent as well. New African artists fuse traditional and pop music and continue to excite audiences internationally.

Worship Styles

Traditional influences can be seen in the modern religious practices of many Americans descended from Africans. The call-and-response pattern of African-American church sermons is characteristically West African, as are emotional, animated expressions of devotion. Ancient African gods are still worshiped in the Americas—for example, by those Cubans who practice the religion known as *santería*.

ANANSI THE SPIDER
a tale from the Ashanti
by Gerald McDermott

Storytelling

Familiar folktales told about Brer Rabbit in the southern United States and about Anansi the spider in Jamaica are versions of traditional West African trickster tales. Today, illustrated picture books bring African stories to children of all backgrounds.

African-Based Music

Many styles of popular music show West African or other African influences.

Blues is similar to the music played and sung by West African griots.

Jazz, like African music, has syncopated, or shifting, rhythms and is improvised by musicians who respond to one another's signals.

Calypso, from Trinidad, uses rhythms from Yoruba and Fon religious music.

Salsa comes from the Cuban *son,* which has a syncopated beat and is played on African instruments.

Samba, played at Carnival in Brazil, is based on Angolan rhythms and is named for a navel-touching dance step.

HOW THE WORLD WAS CREATED FROM A DROP OF MILK

Build Background

Cattle-Herding People "How the World Was Created from a Drop of Milk" is a myth from the Fulani (foō-lä'nē) people, who live in a large territory that includes Senegal, Guinea, Mali, Niger, Nigeria, and Cameroon. The Fulani are set apart from other ethnic groups of West Africa by their cattle-herding way of life, their Fulfulde language, and their relatively fair skin and sharp features.

For hundreds of years, many Fulani were nomads, migrating in search of pasture for their livestock. Although they lived in their own isolated communities, they often cooperated with farmers in the areas they moved to. The farmers would allow Fulani cattle into harvested fields to graze on stubble. In turn, the cattle left behind manure, which fertilized the next season's crops. The Fulani also traded dairy products to their neighbors in exchange for grain, vegetables, and other goods.

Fulani Religion Because the Fulani depended so much on cattle, it is not surprising that cow and dairy images appear in many Fulani myths. The Fulani traditionally worshiped a supreme, all-powerful god, whom they called Gueno (gwā'nō), as well as lesser gods. Doondari (doōn-dä'rē), a creator god, is one of the forms Gueno takes. These gods are mentioned in the myth you are about to read, which dates from the Fulani's pre-Islamic past. Since the 18th century, most Fulani have adopted Islam as their religion, and they have played a major role in spreading Islam throughout West Africa.

Connect to Your Life

This myth explains, among other things, how death came into the world. What explanations have you heard for the existence of death?

Focus Your Reading

LITERARY ANALYSIS: MYTH

A **myth** is a traditional story that explains why the world is the way it is. A creation story is a particular kind of myth that tells how the earth and human beings were created. Note what this Fulani creation story explains about the world.

ACTIVE READING: ANALYZING RELATIONSHIPS

To understand the set of beliefs about the world presented in a myth, you must pay attention to the relationships in the story. Here are some important types of relationships to look for.

Chronological—X happened before Y happened.

Cause-and-effect—X caused Y to happen.

Hierarchical—X ranks above Y.

Constituent—X is made up of Y and Z.

📖 **READER'S NOTEBOOK** As you read this myth, notice the relationships among the beings and elements mentioned. Draw diagrams to show a few of these relationships. For example, a diagram putting one set of events in chronological order is shown below.

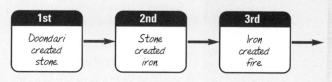

1st	2nd	3rd
Doondari created stone.	Stone created iron.	Iron created fire.

Fulani woman making butter. Chad. Copyright © Jacques Jangoux/Tony Stone Images.

At the beginning there was a huge drop of milk.
Then Doondari came and he created the stone.
Then the stone created iron;
And iron created fire;
5   And fire created water;
And water created air.
Then Doondari descended the second time. And he
   took the five elements

And he shaped them into man.
But man was proud.
10 Then Doondari created blindness and blindness defeated
        man.
But when blindness became too proud,
Doondari created sleep, and sleep defeated blindness;
But when sleep became too proud,
Doondari created worry, and worry defeated sleep;
15 But when worry became too proud,
Doondari created death, and death defeated worry.
But when death became too proud,
Doondari descended for the third time,
And he came as Gueno, the eternal one,
20 And Gueno defeated death.

Connect to the Literature

1. **What Do You Think?** What questions do you have about events in this myth?

Think Critically

2. How was the world created, according to the first part of the myth? Summarize events in your own words.

3. **ACTIVE READING: ANALYZING RELATIONSHIPS**
Look over the diagrams you created in your
READER'S NOTEBOOK. What relationships do you see presented in the myth?

4. How do you interpret the series of defeats in the myth? In what sense does blindness defeat man, sleep defeat blindness, and so on?

5. Why do you think Doondari returns as Gueno to defeat death?

6. What truths about human nature or life do you find in this myth?

Extend Interpretations

7. **What If?** If man had not been proud, how might the world have turned out?

8. **Comparing Texts** How would you compare this Fulani creation story with the creation stories from the Hebrew Bible (page 63) and the *Popol Vuh* (page 76)?

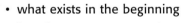

> THINK
> ABOUT
{ • what exists in the beginning
• how humans are created
• whether the creators are satisfied with their creations
• what the creators do in the end

9. **Connect to Life** How satisfying do you find this Fulani myth's explanation of why death exists?

LITERARY ANALYSIS: MYTH

A **myth** is a traditional story, passed down through generations, that explains why the world is the way it is. Myths are essentially religious, and in them, events usually result from the actions of gods. Myths have the following functions:

- **To explain features of the natural world.** For example, the Mayan *Popol Vuh* (page 76) explains that monkeys look like people because they are an earlier, failed version of human beings.
- **To support social customs.** According to a myth in the *Rig Veda*, the four social classes of India were created from the mouth, arms, thighs, and feet of Purusha, the first man.
- **To guide people through life.** Even today, the ancient Greek myth of Icarus, who died after flying too close to the sun, warns people not to overreach.

Cooperative Learning Activity
Think about these functions of myths as you reread "How the World Was Created from a Drop of Milk." Working in small groups, write down all that this myth explains about the natural world. When you have finished, discuss how the myth might also offer guidance for living.

The FIRST BARD AMONG the SONINKE

Retold by Ousmane Sako and Harold Courlander

Build Background

Soninke Society The Soninke people founded the ancient Ghana empire more than 1,000 years ago. This empire, located in what is now Mali and Mauritania, flourished as a center of trade across the Sahara. Soninke society was divided into several classes. At the bottom were slaves. At the top were ruling families and Islamic officials. Just below the nobility, enjoying high prestige and power, were bards.

The Role of the Bard In many traditional African societies, bards are responsible for preserving the history of their people. They are also storytellers, musicians, praise singers, advisers, and genealogists. The Soninke word for bard, *dieli* (jā'lē), means "singer of family history." In the world of the ancient Soninke, this function was especially important, since people were judged by the prestige of their ancestors as well as by their own accomplishments. Another meaning of *dieli* is "blood." Read this legend about the origin of the *dieli* to find out why.

Connect to Your Life

In this story, one person helps another. Think of a time when someone helped you. What would you have done if that person had been hurt in helping you?

Focus Your Reading

LITERARY ANALYSIS: LEGEND

A **legend** is a story that has been handed down from the past and that is popularly believed to be based on historical fact. Legends differ from myths in that they claim to tell about real people and are often set in a particular time and place. Like some myths, however, certain legends explain the origin of social customs and institutions. As you read this legend, note what it explains about Soninke society.

ACTIVE READING: IDENTIFYING CULTURAL VALUES

Legends can reveal much about the cultural values of an ethnic group or nation. For example, the legends of King Arthur and his knights show that bravery, chivalry, and loyalty were admired in medieval England.

📖 **READER'S NOTEBOOK** As you read the story, jot down actions or practices that are presented as good. Be prepared to infer from them what was valued in Soninke culture.

"Good"
Actions or Practices

I n ancient times there were two brothers who went hunting for game in the bush. They traveled far, but they did not find any game to kill. One, two, three days they were in the bush, hunting, hunting. They did not find anything. They became lost. They did not know how to return to their village. Hunger overtook them. Because it was the dry season, there was no fruit for them to eat. Because they could not find game, they had no meat to eat.

On the fourth day the younger brother said to the older: "My brother, I cannot go any farther. I am too hungry. I have no strength to go on. If I am to die, I will die here."

The older brother answered: "Yes, rest here. You are my younger brother and I do not want you to die. I will go on ahead and try to find a small animal of some kind. Then you will have something to eat. Wait for me. I will come back."

The older brother left the younger and went ahead. He did not find anything. There was no game of any kind. At last he took out his knife and cut a piece of meat from his thigh, and after that he returned to where his younger brother was waiting. He said: "Oh yes! I found a small animal and killed it. I will make a fire. I will cook the meat for you. When you have eaten it, you will feel strong again." He made a fire and cooked the meat. When it was ready, he gave it to the younger brother. The younger brother ate, and his strength returned.

After a while the older brother saw smoke in the distance and knew there must be a village out there. He said: "Oh younger brother, don't

Five terra-cotta horseback riders. Courtesy of Bernard de Grunne.

HUMANITIES CONNECTION These ancient terra-cotta horsemen have Soninke scarification marks on their temples. The Soninke and other groups traditionally adorned their bodies with patterns of raised scars.

Henceforth I will be your dieli—
the bard who sings of your great deeds and of the history of your family.

you see the smoke in the distance? There is a village at that place. Now we will be saved from starvation. I will go ahead to make certain, then I will come back for you."

The younger brother answered: "No, now I feel strong again. I will go with you."

So they started out. They traveled toward the place where the smoke was rising. The older brother kept his bloody thigh covered as best he could, but blood stained his clothing. When the younger brother saw that, he asked: "What is it? What happened to you?" He uncovered the older brother's wound. He touched it. Then he understood everything.

He said: "Yes, my older brother! Now I understand what you have done for me. You saved my life with flesh taken from your thigh. To give someone your own flesh and blood is the greatest expression of love. Henceforth I will be your dieli—the bard who sings of your great deeds and of the history of your family. Whatever you ask of me, I will do it. I will follow you and serve you. My family will follow your family. My grandson will follow your grandson. My descendants will follow your descendants forever. We will be as slaves to your people until the end of time and sing praises of your noble character."

The younger brother became the slave and bard of the older brother. His descendants became slaves and bards of the older brother's descendants. They were called dieli, meaning blood, because of the older brother's blood gift that had saved the younger brother's life. Because they wished to please their masters, the dieli became accomplished singers and musicians, and they sang stories of times that had passed, of great events and ancestor heroes. To this day the bards pass their knowledge and their songs on to their sons, and the sons become the bards and historians of the family descended from the older brother.

Of the two brothers who went hunting together in the bush, the younger brother became the first dieli, and ever since that day it has been the custom for noble families to have bards to recall the happenings of ancient days. ❖

Thinking through the LITERATURE

Connect to the Literature

1. What Do You Think?
How did you react to the older brother's sacrifice?

Comprehension Check
- What does the older brother do to feed the younger brother?
- How does the younger brother learn where the food came from?
- How does the younger brother reward the older brother?

Think Critically

2. Do you think that the younger brother responds appropriately after he learns how he was saved? Explain.

3. ACTIVE READING: IDENTIFYING CULTURAL VALUES Look over the notes you made in your 📖 **READER'S NOTEBOOK**. What can you infer about Soninke values from the things presented as good in this legend?

4. Imagine the storyteller and describe his **tone,** or attitude toward the events he relates.

Extend Interpretations

5. Comparing Texts Both "How the World Was Created from a Drop of Milk" and "The First Bard Among the Soninke" tell about origins, or beginnings. Compare the views of human nature in these selections.

6. Connect to Life In modern American culture, how might someone who saved a life be rewarded? Would the reward be comparable to the one in this legend?

LITERARY ANALYSIS: LEGEND

A **legend** is a story that has been handed down from the past and that is popularly believed to be based on historical events. Unlike myths, legends claim to tell of real human beings and are often set in a particular time and place. Still, events in legends may be exaggerated; legendary heroes are often larger than life. The stories of King Arthur and Robin Hood are examples of legends.

Some legends explain a tradition or social custom. What does "The First Bard Among the Soninke" explain about the profession of the bard?

Cooperative Learning Activity
Working in small groups, create a legend to explain a custom practiced at your school or in society. For example, you might explain why your school honors its particular mascot.

from

Sundiata
An Epic of Old Mali

Build Background

Mali's Lion King *Sundiata* is the most famous African epic. It tells the story of Sundiata Keita (sōōn-jä'tä kē'tä), who founded the Mali empire in the 13th century. Although loosely based on historical events, the epic transforms its hero into a legendary figure with extraordinary powers. Like the *Iliad* of Greece and the *Ramayana* of India, *Sundiata* played an important role in shaping a national identity.

The historical Sundiata was also known as Sogolon Djata, Mari Djata, and the Lion of Mali. He came from the royal family of the Mandinka (also called Malinké or Mandingo), who live in the western Sudan region. He rose to power about 1235, after defeating Soumaoro Kante (kän'tä), king of Sosso. Sundiata created a strong, centralized monarchy with a standing army, which allowed him to expand Mali's territory westward into large gold fields. The empire's capital was Niani, in what is now Guinea. Mali became the most powerful state in the Sudan, renowned for its prosperity and stable society.

Told by Griots There is no single author of this oral epic, nor is there any fixed version. Trained storytellers known as **griots** (grē-ōz') have adapted it to suit different audiences and occasions. Even today, *Sundiata* is performed frequently in West African villages. The version you will read is a prose adaptation by D. T. Niane, who based his work on the performances of Mamoudou Kouyaté (mä-mōō'dōō kōō-yä'-tä), a griot from Guinea. In this version, Niane attempts to capture some of the flavor of the griot's performance.

Recited with Music A performance of *Sundiata* has three components. In addition to reciting the narrative sections of the epic, the griot chants praise poems describing the greatness of the characters. He or she also sings songs to the accompaniment of the *kora* or *balafon* (instruments resembling a harp and a xylophone). Griots must be highly trained to memorize and perform a work as complex as *Sundiata*. In Mandinka society they are greatly respected for their vital role in linking past and present. Mamoudou Kouyaté described griots as "the memory of mankind."

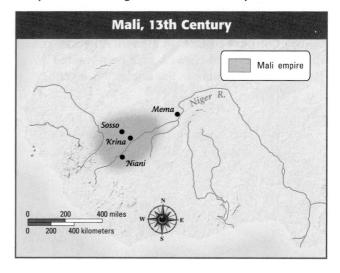

Mali, 13th Century

Mali empire

Niger R.

Mema

Sosso

Krina

Niani

0   200   400 miles
0   200   400 kilometers

The Story of Sundiata

Late-Blooming Hero As a literary character, Sundiata has much in common with other epic heroes. He is the son of King Naré Maghan. His mother is Sogolon Kedjou, the king's second wife. Sogolon is an ugly, hunchbacked "buffalo-woman" whom the king married because of a prophecy that she would give birth to a great ruler. Despite the prophecy, the child Sundiata lags far behind other children and seems destined for failure.

Sassouma Bérété is the king's first wife. She is an ambitious woman who wants to ensure that her own son, Dankaran, inherits the throne. After the king dies, she persuades Dankaran to send Sundiata and his mother into exile. Sundiata travels to various kingdoms and becomes a mighty warrior and adviser to the king of Mema.

Return from Exile After learning that the evil sorcerer Soumaoro Kante has conquered Mali and other kingdoms in the region, Sundiata returns home. He makes alliances with other rulers and attacks Soumaoro on the battlefield at Krina. He kills Soumaoro with a magic arrow tipped with the spur of a white rooster. He then unites the region's kingdoms into a powerful empire, which he rules wisely and justly.

In the following excerpt, you will read about a famous incident from Sundiata's youth, involving a baobab tree.

For a humanities activity, click on:

CLASSZONE.COM

Connect to Your Life

Have you ever had to prove you could do something when others thought you couldn't? What made you prove yourself? How did others respond to you afterward? Share your story with classmates.

Focus Your Reading

LITERARY ANALYSIS: CONFLICT

Conflict is the struggle between opposing forces. An **external conflict** pits a character against some outside force, such as a storm or an enemy soldier. An **internal conflict** occurs within a character. For example, a character may desire something but be afraid to pursue it. As you read, be aware of the conflicts involving Sundiata and note which ones are external and which are internal.

ACTIVE READING: PREDICTING

A **prediction** is a guess about what will happen next in a story. When making predictions, take the following things into account:

- details about characters, setting, and events
- **foreshadowing,** or hints about what is going to happen
- your own experience and your knowledge of human behavior

📖 **READER'S NOTEBOOK** As you read *Sundiata,* create a chart like this one to record your predictions, together with the information

I Predict . . .	Because . . .

WORDS TO KNOW **Vocabulary Preview**

affront	derisively	innuendo	malicious
blandly	heedless	intrigue	taciturn
condiment	imperceptibly		

from Sundiata:
An Epic of Old Mali

Recorded by D. T. Niane

Translated by G. D. Pickett

 *Childhood*

God has his mysteries which none can fathom. You, perhaps, will be a king. You can do nothing about it. You, on the other hand, will be unlucky, but you can do nothing about that either. Each man finds his way already marked out for him and he can change nothing of it.

Sogolon's son[1] had a slow and difficult childhood. At the age of three he still crawled along on all-fours while children of the same age were already walking. He had nothing of the great beauty of his father Naré Maghan.[2] He had a head so big that he seemed unable to support it; he also had large eyes which would open wide whenever anyone entered his mother's house. He was <u>taciturn</u> and used to spend the whole day just sitting in the middle of the house. Whenever his mother went out he would crawl on all-fours to rummage about in the calabashes[3] in search of food, for he was very greedy.

<u>Malicious</u> tongues began to blab. What three-year-old has not yet taken his first steps? What three-year-old is not the despair of his parents through his whims and shifts of mood? What three-year-old is not the joy of his circle through his backwardness in talking? Sogolon Djata[4] (for it was thus that they called him, prefixing his mother's name to his), Sogolon Djata, then, was very different from others of his own age. He spoke little and his severe face never relaxed into a smile. You would have thought that he was already thinking, and what amused children of his age bored him. Often Sogolon would make some of them come to him to keep him company. These children were already walking and she hoped that Djata, seeing his companions walking, would be tempted to do likewise. But nothing came of it. Besides, Sogolon Djata would brain the poor little things with his already strong arms and none of them would come near him any more.

The king's first wife[5] was the first to rejoice at Sogolon Djata's infirmity. Her own son, Dankaran Touman,[6] was already eleven. He was a fine and lively boy, who spent the day running about the village with those of his own age. He had even begun his initiation in the bush.[7] The king had had a bow made for him and he used to go behind the town to practice archery with his companions. Sassouma was quite happy and snapped her fingers at Sogolon, whose child was still crawling on the ground. Whenever the latter happened to pass by her house, she would say, "Come, my son, walk, jump, leap about. The

---

1. **Sogolon's son:** Sundiata. Sogolon is his mother.
2. **Naré Maghan** (nä-rä′ mä′gän): king of a large territory in Mali.
3. **calabashes** (kăl′ə-ˈbăsh′ĭz): dried gourd husks used as dishes and bottles.
4. **Sogolon Djata** (sō′gō-lôn′ jä′tä): This, along with "Mari Djata," is an alternative name for Sundiata.
5. **the king's first wife:** Sassouma Bérété (sä′sōō-mä bā′rā-tä).
6. **Dankaran Touman** (dän-kä′rän tōō′män).
7. **initiation in the bush:** preparation, through learning tribal history, for becoming a full-fledged member of the tribe.

WORDS TO KNOW

taciturn (tăs′ĭ-tûrn′) *adj.* not talkative
malicious (mə-lĭsh′əs) *adj.* evil; wicked

jinn[8] didn't promise you anything out of the ordinary, but I prefer a son who walks on his two legs to a lion that crawls on the ground." She spoke thus whenever Sogolon went by her door. The <u>innuendo</u> would go straight home and then she would burst into laughter, that diabolical laughter which a jealous woman knows how to use so well.

Her son's infirmity weighed heavily upon Sogolon Kedjou; she had resorted to all her talent as a sorceress to give strength to her son's legs, but the rarest herbs had been useless. The king himself lost hope.

How impatient man is! Naré Maghan became <u>imperceptibly</u> estranged[9] but Gnankouman Doua never ceased reminding him of the hunter's words.[10] Sogolon became pregnant again. The king hoped for a son, but it was a daughter called Kolonkan. She resembled her mother and had nothing of her father's beauty. The disheartened king debarred Sogolon from his house and she lived in semi-disgrace for a while. Naré Maghan married the daughter of one of his allies, the king of the Kamaras.[11] She was called Namandjé[12] and her beauty was legendary. A year later she brought a boy into the world. When the king consulted soothsayers on the destiny of this son he received the reply that Namandjé's child would be the right hand of some mighty king. The king gave the newly-born the name of Boukari. He was to be called Manding Boukari or Manding Bory later on.

Naré Maghan was very perplexed. Could it be that the stiff-jointed son of Sogolon was the one the hunter soothsayer had foretold?

"The Almighty has his mysteries," Gnankouman Doua would say and, taking up the hunter's words, added, "The silk-cotton tree emerges from a tiny seed."

One day Naré Maghan came along to the house of Nounfaïri,[13] the blacksmith seer of Niani. He was an old, blind man. He received

Terra-cotta seated figure. The Metropolitan Museum of Art, New York.

HUMANITIES CONNECTION Many sitting, kneeling, and sleeping figures have been found at ancient sites in Mali. Scholars think they might represent prisoners.

the king in the anteroom which served as his workshop. To the king's question he replied, "When the seed germinates growth is not always easy; great trees grow slowly but they plunge their roots deep into the ground."

"But has the seed really germinated?" said the king.

"Of course," replied the blind seer. "Only the growth is not as quick as you would like it; how impatient man is."

---

8. **jinn:** spirits that have supernatural influence over people.

9. **estranged:** unsympathetic or indifferent.

10. **Gnankouman Doua** (nyäɴʹko͞o-mäɴ do͞oʹä) . . . **the hunter's words:** Gnankouman Doua is the king's griot and chief counselor. A hunter had foretold that the king must marry the ugly Sogolon, who would bear him a great son.

11. **Kamaras** (käʹmä-räz): a clan related to that of Naré Maghan.

12. **Namandjé** (nä-mäɴʹjä).

13. **Nounfaïri** (no͞on-fäʹrē).

WORDS TO KNOW

innuendo (ĭnʹyo͞o-ĕnʹdō) *n.* an indirect hint or reference, usually negative
imperceptibly (ĭmʹpər-sĕpʹtə-blē) *adv.* in a barely noticeable way

This interview and Doua's confidence gave the king some assurance. To the great displeasure of Sassouma Bérété the king restored Sogolon to favor and soon another daughter was born to her. She was given the name of Djamarou.[14]

However, all Niani talked of nothing else but the stiff-legged son of Sogolon. He was now seven and he still crawled to get about. In spite of all the king's affection, Sogolon was in despair. Naré Maghan aged and he felt his time coming to an end. Dankaran Touman, the son of Sassouma Bérété, was now a fine youth.

One day Naré Maghan made Mari Djata come to him and he spoke to the child as one speaks to an adult. "Mari Djata, I am growing old and soon I shall be no more among you, but before death takes me off I am going to give you the present each king gives his successor. In Mali every prince has his own griot. Doua's father was my father's griot, Doua is mine and the son of Doua, Balla Fasséké[15] here, will be your griot. Be inseparable friends from this day forward. From his mouth you will hear the history of your ancestors, you will learn the art of governing Mali according to the principles which our ancestors have bequeathed to us. I have served my term and done my duty too. I have done everything which a king of Mali ought to do. I am handing an enlarged kingdom over to you and I leave you sure allies. May your destiny be accomplished, but never forget that Niani is your capital and Mali the cradle of your ancestors."

The child, as if he had understood the whole meaning of the king's words, beckoned Balla Fasséké to approach. He made room for him on the hide he was sitting on and then said, "Balla, you will be my griot."

"Yes, son of Sogolon, if it pleases God," replied Balla Fasséké.

The king and Doua exchanged glances that radiated confidence.

The Lion's Awakening

A short while after this interview between Naré Maghan and his son the king died. Sogolon's son was no more than seven years old. The council of elders met in the king's palace. It was no use Doua's defending the king's will which reserved the throne for Mari Djata, for the council took no account of Naré Maghan's wish. With the help of Sassouma Bérété's intrigues, Dankaran Touman was proclaimed king and a regency council[16] was formed in which the queen mother was all-powerful. A short time after, Doua died.

As men have short memories, Sogolon's son was spoken of with nothing but irony and scorn. People had seen one-eyed kings, one-armed kings, and lame kings, but a stiff-legged king had never been heard tell of. No matter how great the destiny promised for Mari Djata might be, the throne could not be given to someone who had no power in his legs; if the jinn loved him, let them begin by giving him the use of his legs. Such were the remarks that Sogolon heard every day. The queen mother, Sassouma Bérété, was the source of all this gossip.

Having become all-powerful, Sassouma Bérété persecuted Sogolon because the late Naré Maghan had preferred her. She banished Sogolon and her son to a back yard of the palace. Mari Djata's mother now occupied an old hut which had served as a lumber-room of Sassouma's.

The wicked queen mother allowed free passage to all those inquisitive people who wanted to see the child that still crawled at the age of

---

14. **Djamarou** (jä′mä-rōō).

15. **Balla Fasséké** (bä′lä fä-sä-kā′).

16. **regency council:** group chosen to rule in place of a monarch who is too young to assume control.

intrigue (ĭn′trēg′) *n.* a secret scheme; plot

seven. Nearly all the inhabitants of Niani filed into the palace and the poor Sogolon wept to see herself thus given over to public ridicule. Mari Djata took on a ferocious look in front of the crowd of sightseers. Sogolon found a little consolation only in the love of her eldest daughter, Kolonkan. She was four and she could walk. She seemed to understand all her mother's miseries and already she helped her with the housework. Sometimes, when Sogolon was attending to the chores, it was she who stayed beside her sister Djamarou, quite small as yet.

Sogolon Kedjou and her children lived on the queen mother's left-overs, but she kept a little garden in the open ground behind the village. It was there that she passed her brightest moments looking after her onions and gnougous. One day she happened to be short of condiments and went to the queen mother to beg a little baobab leaf.[17]

"Look you," said the malicious Sassouma, "I have a calabash full. Help yourself, you poor woman. As for me, my son knew how to walk at seven and it was he who went and picked these baobab leaves. Take them then, since your son is unequal to mine." Then she laughed derisively with that fierce laughter which cuts through your flesh and penetrates right to the bone.

Sogolon Kedjou was dumbfounded. She had never imagined that hate could be so strong in a human being. With a lump in her throat she left Sassouma's. Outside her hut Mari Djata, sitting on his useless legs, was blandly eating out of a calabash. Unable to contain herself any longer, Sogolon burst into sobs and seizing a piece of wood, hit her son.

"Oh son of misfortune, will you never walk? Through your fault I have just suffered the greatest affront of my life! What have I done, God, for you to punish me in this way?"

Mari Djata seized the piece of wood and, looking at his mother, said, "Mother, what's the matter?"

"Shut up, nothing can ever wash me clean of this insult."

"But what then?"

"Sassouma has just humiliated me over a matter of a baobab leaf. At your age her own son could walk and used to bring his mother baobab leaves."

"Cheer up, Mother, cheer up."

"No. It's too much. I can't."

"Very well then, I am going to walk today," said Mari Djata. "Go and tell my father's smiths to make me the heaviest possible iron rod. Mother, do you want just the leaves of the baobab or would you rather I brought you the whole tree?"

"Ah, my son, to wipe out this insult I want the tree and its roots at my feet outside my hut."

Balla Fasséké, who was present, ran to the master smith, Farakourou,[18] to order an iron rod.

Sogolon had sat down in front of her hut. She was weeping softly and holding her head between her two hands. Mari Djata went calmly back to his calabash of rice and began eating again as if nothing had happened. From time to time he looked up discreetly at his mother who was murmuring in a low voice, "I want the whole tree, in front of my hut, the whole tree."

All of a sudden a voice burst into laughter behind the hut. It was the wicked Sassouma telling one of her serving women about the scene of humiliation and she was laughing loudly so that Sogolon could hear. Sogolon fled into the hut

---

17. **gnougous** (nyo͞o′go͞oz) . . . **baobab** (bā′ō-bǎb) **leaf:** Gnougous are African food plants. The baobab is a tree whose leaves are used for seasoning.

18. **Farakourou** (fä-rä-ko͞o′ro͞o).

and hid her face under the blankets so as not to have before her eyes this <u>heedless</u> boy, who was more preoccupied with eating than with anything else. With her head buried in the bed-clothes Sogolon wept and her body shook violently. Her daughter, Sogolon Djamarou, had come and sat down beside her and she said, "Mother, Mother, don't cry. Why are you crying?"

Mari Djata had finished eating and, dragging himself along on his legs, he came and sat under the wall of the hut for the sun was scorching. What was he thinking about? He alone knew.

The royal forges were situated outside the walls and over a hundred smiths worked there. The bows, spears, arrows and shields of Niani's warriors came from there. When Balla Fasséké came to order the iron rod, Farakourou said to him, "The great day has arrived then?"

"Yes. Today is a day like any other, but it will see what no other day has seen."

The master of the forges, Farakourou, was the son of the old Nounfaïri, and he was a sooth-sayer like his father. In his workshops there was an enormous iron bar wrought by his father Nounfaïri. Everybody wondered what this bar was destined to be used for. Farakourou called six of his apprentices and told them to carry the iron bar to Sogolon's house.

When the smiths put the gigantic iron bar down in front of the hut the noise was so frightening that Sogolon, who was lying down, jumped up with a start. Then Balla Fasséké, son of Gnankouman Doua, spoke.

"Here is the great day, Mari Djata. I am speaking to you, Maghan,[19] son of Sogolon. The waters of the Niger can efface[20] the stain from the body, but they cannot wipe out an insult. Arise, young lion, roar, and may the bush know that from henceforth it has a master."

The apprentice smiths were still there, Sogolon had come out and everyone was watching Mari Djata. He crept on all-fours and came to the iron bar. Supporting himself on his knees and one hand, with the other hand he picked up the iron bar without any effort and stood it up vertically. Now he was resting on nothing but his knees and held the bar with both his hands. A deathly silence had gripped all those present. Sogolon Djata closed his eyes, held tight, the muscles in his arms tensed. With a violent jerk he threw his weight on to it and his knees left the ground. Sogolon Kedjou was all eyes and watched her son's legs which were trembling as though from an electric shock. Djata was sweating and the sweat ran from his brow. In a great effort he straightened up and was on his feet at one go— but the great bar of iron was twisted and had taken the form of a bow!

Then Balla Fasséké sang out the "Hymn to the Bow," striking up with his powerful voice:

> "Take your bow, Simbon,[21]
> Take your bow and let us go.
> Take your bow, Sogolon Djata."

When Sogolon saw her son standing she stood dumb for a moment, then suddenly she sang these words of thanks to God who had given her son the use of his legs:

> "Oh day, what a beautiful day,
> Oh day, day of joy;
> Allah Almighty, you never created a finer day.
> So my son is going to walk!"

Standing in the position of a soldier at ease, Sogolon Djata, supported by his enormous rod, was sweating great beads of sweat. Balla Fasséké's song had alerted the whole palace and people came running from all over to see what had happened, and each stood bewildered before

---

19. **Maghan:** a name relating Sundiata to his father.

20. **efface** (ĭ-fās′): rub out; erase.

21. **Simbon:** a title used for a great hunter.

Sogolon's son. The queen mother had rushed there and when she saw Mari Djata standing up she trembled from head to foot. After recovering his breath Sogolon's son dropped the bar and the crowd stood to one side. His first steps were those of a giant. Balla Fasséké fell into step and pointing his finger at Djata, he cried:

> "Room, room, make room!
> The lion has walked;
> Hide antelopes,
> Get out of his way."

Behind Niani there was a young baobab tree and it was there that the children of the town came to pick leaves for their mothers. With all his might the son of Sogolon tore up the tree and put it on his shoulders and went back to his mother. He threw the tree in front of the hut and said, "Mother, here are some baobab leaves for you. From henceforth it will be outside your hut that the women of Niani will come to stock up."

Sogolon Djata walked. From that day forward the queen mother had no more peace of mind. But what can one do against destiny? Nothing. Man, under the influence of certain illusions, thinks he can alter the course which God has mapped out, but everything he does falls into a higher order which he barely understands. That is why Sassouma's efforts were vain against Sogolon's son, everything she did lay in the child's destiny. Scorned the day before and the object of public ridicule, now Sogolon's son was as popular as he had been despised. The multitude loves and fears strength. All Niani talked of nothing but Djata; the mothers urged their sons to become hunting companions of Djata and to share his games, as if they wanted their offspring to profit from the nascent[22] glory of the buffalo-woman's son.[23] The words of Doua on the name-giving day[24] came back to men's minds and Sogolon was now surrounded with much respect; in conversation people were fond of contrasting Sogolon's modesty with the pride and malice of Sassouma

Terra-cotta horse and rider. Werner Forman Archive. Courtesy Entwistle Gallery, London.

Bérété. It was because the former had been an exemplary wife and mother that God had granted strength to her son's legs for, it was said, the more a wife loves and respects her husband and the more she suffers for her child, the more valorous will the child be one day. Each is the child of his mother; the child is worth no more than the mother is worth. It was not astonishing that the king Dankaran Touman was so colorless, for his mother had never shown the slightest respect to her husband and never, in the presence of the late king, did she show that humility which every wife should show before her husband. People recalled her scenes of jealousy and the spiteful remarks she circulated about her co-wife and her child. And people would conclude gravely, "Nobody knows God's mystery. The snake has no legs yet it is as swift as any other animal that has four." ❖

---

22. **nascent** (năs′ənt): emerging.

23. **buffalo-woman's son:** Sogolon, Sundiata's mother, had a buffalo for a totem (family emblem and protector).

24. **the words of Doua on the name-giving day:** Gnankouman Doua had stated that Sundiata would be the first of a great line of kings.

Thinking through the LITERATURE

Connect to the Literature

1. What Do You Think?
Were you surprised by Sundiata's actions after his mother is insulted? Why or why not?

Comprehension Check
- Why is Sundiata scorned as a young boy?
- How does Sassouma treat Sundiata and his mother after the king's death?
- How does Sundiata change the people's opinion of him?

Think Critically

2. ACTIVE READING: PREDICTING How accurate were the predictions you made in your 📖 **READER'S NOTEBOOK?** Discuss with classmates the details that either helped or misled you.

3. Describe how Sundiata changes from the beginning of the selection to the end. What do you think makes him change?

4. How would you compare Sogolon Kedjou and Sassouma?

THINK ABOUT	{	• their relationship with the king
		• their treatment of others
		• the narrator's comments about them

5. Based on what you have read in *Sundiata,* which qualities do you think were most admired in traditional Mandinka society? Support your answer with details from the story.

Extend Interpretations

6. The Writer's Style How well does the recorder, D. T. Niane, convey the sense that a griot is performing the epic for an audience? Discuss what an actual griot would be able to do that the written text cannot do.

7. Connect to Life Do you agree with the ideas about life expressed in this epic? For example, do you agree that a person cannot change his or her fate, or that a child is worth no more than its mother?

LITERARY ANALYSIS: CONFLICT

Conflict is the struggle between opposing forces. **External conflict** occurs when a character is pitted against an outside force, such as another character, a physical obstacle, or an aspect of nature or society. **Internal conflict** occurs when the struggle takes place within a character. In this excerpt from *Sundiata,* for example, Naré Maghan is torn between his wish to believe the prophecies about Sundiata's future greatness and doubts raised by Sundiata's appearance and behavior. The selection also has numerous examples of external conflict, such as the rivalry between Sogolon Kedjou and Sassouma.

Paired Activity With a classmate, review external and internal conflicts in the selection. Fill in a chart like the one below, indicating which opposing forces are involved in each conflict and how the conflict is resolved, if it is.

Conflict	External or Internal?	Resolution

REVIEW: EPIC HERO

An **epic hero** is usually someone of high social status who performs courageous and sometimes even superhuman deeds. Epic heroes generally reflect the ideals and values of their culture. With a small group of classmates, discuss Sundiata's heroic qualities. Compare his experiences and deeds with those of other epic heroes, such as Rama, Arjuna, and Aeneas. Refer to the background on page 633.

Choices & CHALLENGES

Writing Options

1. Character Analysis How can you tell, just from this brief excerpt, that Sundiata will grow up to be a great hero? In a short essay, describe the heroic characteristics that he shows. Place the essay in your **Working Portfolio.**

Writing Handbook
See page R33: Analysis.

2. Evaluation of Themes The griot Mamoudou Kouyaté stated, "I teach kings the history of the ancestors so that the lives of the ancients might serve them as an example." Write a few paragraphs explaining how this episode from *Sundiata* does or does not offer good lessons for modern people.

3. Biographical Article Perhaps Sundiata reminds you of someone else who proved his or her worth after being ridiculed. If so, write a biographical article recounting this person's triumph. Place the paper in your **Working Portfolio.**

Activities & Explorations

1. Griot's Performance Perform part of this selection as you think a griot might have performed it. Add appropriate music and gestures. Encourage your audience to respond with comments such as "That's true" and "Indeed." Look back at page 618 to see how griots look, and, if you like, dress the part.
~ SPEAKING AND LISTENING

2. Movie Review If possible, view *Keita: Heritage of the Griot,* a film by the West African director Dani Kouyaté that dramatizes the *Sundiata* epic. Afterward, discuss how closely the film conforms to what you imagined and how it presents the griot's role.
~ VIEWING AND REPRESENTING

Inquiry & Research

1. Modern Griots Do research on contemporary musicians from West Africa who perform in the griot tradition, such as Foday Musa Suso, Salif Keita, and Boubacar Traoré. Bring in recordings of their music to share with the class.

2. Ancient Mali Work in a small group to find out more about the ancient Mali empire. Give oral reports on various topics related to the empire—for example, the pilgrimage of the ruler Mansa Musa or the description of Mali given by the Berber traveler Ibn Battuta.

RESEARCH STARTER
CLASSZONE.COM

Vocabulary in Action

EXERCISE: RELATED WORDS Write the letter of the word in each set that is not related in meaning to the other words in the set.

1. (a) plot, (b) intrigue, (c) gathering, (d) scheme
2. (a) wicked, (b) confused, (c) malicious, (d) harmful
3. (a) salt, (b) potato, (c) ketchup, (d) condiment
4. (a) hurriedly, (b) blandly, (c) unworriedly, (d) casually
5. (a) compliment, (b) praise, (c) honor, (d) affront
6. (a) derisively, (b) mockingly, (c) simply, (d) sarcastically
7. (a) impossibly, (b) unnoticeably, (c) scarcely, (d) imperceptibly
8. (a) heedless, (b) unconcerned, (c) blameless, (d) unaware
9. (a) enthusiastic, (b) quiet, (c) taciturn, (d) withdrawn
10. (a) insinuation, (b) innuendo, (c) implication, (d) incompetence

Building Vocabulary

For an in-depth lesson on connotations and denotations, see page 1090.

PRAISE SONGS FOR ORISHAS

Build Background

Songs That Celebrate Praise songs are one of the most common forms of poetry in West Africa. Bards or griots perform them in public to honor gods, kings, and other important figures. Often the songs are composed spontaneously. Praise songs usually describe their subjects' deeds and qualities in glowing terms. The praise may be mixed with criticism, however, if the singer wants to challenge leaders to live up to their responsibilities. In the Yoruba (yôr′ə-bə) language, praise songs are called *oriki* (ō-rē′kē). Most Yoruba have a personal praise song, which on formal occasions is used to announce their arrival. The most poetic and complex oriki are those dedicated to the *orishas* (ō-rē′shäz), or gods.

Yoruba Religion Although many Yoruba are Christian or Muslim, the traditional Yoruba religion is still widely practiced. In the traditional Yoruba religion, Olorun (ō-lō-rŏŏn′) or Olodumare (ō-lō′dōō-mä-rä′) is the supreme being. Yet no shrines are dedicated to him, nor is he honored with offerings and other rituals. Because he is such a remote and incomprehensible figure, worshipers turn to the orishas, a group of lesser gods.

Yoruba myths about orishas vary. Some orishas are thought of as notable humans who were given divine status after death. The orishas personify forces of nature. Each one is associated with particular colors and materials. According to tradition, there are 401 orishas. Many are local gods; others are worshiped throughout Yoruba lands. Following are some of the principal orishas.

Orisha	Qualities
Obatala (ō-bä′tä-lä)	Creator god who formed the earth and human beings. People with hunchbacks and other deformities are sacred to him, because he made them while drunk.
Shango (shän′gō)	God of thunder. Quick-tempered, but generous to his followers.
Oshun (ō-sōōn′)	Beautiful river goddess and healer. Kind, gentle, and motherly, she can make women fertile.
Ogun (ō-gōōn′)	God of iron and war. Personifies creative and destructive forces.
Eshu (ä-sōō′)	Trickster god. Carries messages between the gods and humankind.

Methods of Worship Orishas are honored in different ways. They can be worshiped daily at shrines or temples dedicated to them. People can seek their advice through reading the pattern of palm nuts or cowrie shells tossed on a sacred tray. Through initiation, people can become priests or priestesses of a particular orisha, who "claims" them. At special ceremonies involving dance and sacred drumming, orishas are believed to come to earth and possess these followers, who wear clothing in the orishas' special colors and carry objects associated with them, such as Shango's double-headed ax. At these ceremonies, oriki are sung.

Shango priest

Connect to Your Life

In these songs, the speakers praise Yoruba gods. Think of poems, prayers, or songs from your own culture that praise God or great leaders. What qualities are glorified in these poems or songs?

Focus Your Reading

LITERARY ANALYSIS: CHARACTERIZATION

The term **characterization** refers to the techniques that writers use to develop characters. Characters may be portrayed through

- physical description
- their speech, thoughts, feelings, and actions
- other characters' reactions to them
- direct comments by the narrator or speaker

As you read each praise song, imagine that it is being recited aloud, about a character. Look for images in the song that give you a sense of the orisha's personality.

ACTIVE READING: SYNTHESIZING

When you put together ideas and information to reach a conclusion or achieve some kind of insight, you are **synthesizing.** For example, you might look for patterns in a literary work or connect something in the work with background information already learned. Synthesizing is necessary for you to truly understand what you read.

READER'S NOTEBOOK As you read each praise song, create a word web for the orisha it describes. Fill in the web with words or phrases from the song that offer clues to the orisha's character. Also include information from the Build Background section or the sidenotes that adds to your understanding of the orisha.

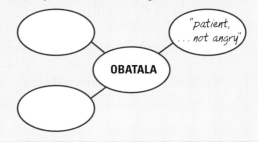

Praise Songs for Orishas

OBATALA
GOD OF CREATION

He is patient, he is not angry.
He sits in silence to pass judgment.
He sees you even when he is not looking.
He stays in a far place—but his eyes are on the town.

5   The granary of heaven can never be full.
The old man full of life force.

He kills the novice.
And wakens him to let him hear his words.
We leave the world to the owner of the world.
10 Death acts playfully till he carries away the child.
He rides on the hunchback.
He stretches out his right hand.
He stretches out his left hand.

He stands by his children and lets them succeed.
15 He causes them to laugh—and they laugh.
Ohoho—the father of laughter.
His eye is full of joy,
He rests in the sky like a swarm of bees.

We dance to our sixteen drums that sound jingin, jingin,
20 To eight of the drums we dance bending down,
To eight of the drums we dance erect.
We shake our shoulders, we shake our hips.
Munusi, munusi, munusi,
We dance to your sixteen drums.

5 granary: a place for storing grain.

7 He kills the novice: Persons being initiated into most orisha groups go through a ritual of symbolic death and resurrection.

11 He rides on the hunchback: Hunchbacks are sacred to Obatala.

15 He causes them to laugh: He gives them the breath of life after creating them.

25 Those who are rich owe their property to him.
    Those who are poor, owe their property to him.
    He takes from the rich and gives to the poor.
    Whenever you take from the rich—come and give it to me!

    Obatala—who turns blood into children.
30 I have only one cloth to dye with blue indigo.
    I have only one headtie to dye with red camwood.
    But I know that you keep twenty or thirty children for me
    Whom I shall bear.

30–31 indigo . . . camwood: plant sources of blue and red dye.

GOD OF THUNDER

    When the elephant wakes up in the morning
    He must pay his respects to his new wife.
    When the guinea fowl wakes up in the morning
    It must prostrate to the lord of the forest.
5   If it fails to greet him thus,
    It will be killed by the hunter.
    He will carry it home on his back.
    He will sell it in the market
    And use the money to make charms.
10 If the antelope wakes in the morning
    And does not bow to the lord of the forest
    The hunter will come and eat its head with pounded yam.
    Shango, I prostrate to you every morning,
    Before I set out to do anything.

15 The dog stays in the house of its master
    But it does not know his intentions.
    The sheep does not know the intentions
    Of the man who feeds it.
    We ourselves follow Shango
20 Although we do not know his intentions.
    It is not easy to live in Shango's company.
    Crabs' feet are confusion.
    The parrot's feet are crooked.

3 guinea fowl: a pheasantlike bird of Africa.

4 prostrate: to lie face down in worship.

When the crab leaves its hole
25 We do not know which direction it is taking.
Shango went to Ibadan and arrived at Ilorin.

Rain beats the Egungun mask, because he cannot find shelter.
He cries: "Help me, dead people in heaven, help me!"
But the rain cannot beat Shango.
30 They say that fire kills water.
He rides fire like a horse.
Lightning—with what kind of cloth do you cover your body?
With the cloth of death.
Shango is the death that drips to, to, to,
35 Like indigo dye dripping from a cloth. . . .

26 Ibadan (ē-bäd′n) . . . **Ilorin** (ē′lə-rēn′): Ibadan is a city in southwestern Nigeria. Ilorin is about 95 miles northeast of it.

27 Rain beats the Egungun (ā-gōōn′gōōn) **mask:** Egungun festivals, involving dancers wearing elaborate masks, are held to honor dead ancestors. If the dancers are not on good terms with Shango, the god of thunder, rain may spoil their ceremony.

Wood sculpture of Shango priest and fellow worshipers, Lamidi Fakeye.

HUMANITIES CONNECTION Lamidi Fakeye comes from four generations of master Yoruba woodcarvers. Although this sculpture is not meant for ritual use, it resembles carvings that adorn Shango shrines.

RIVER GODDESS

We call her and she replies with wisdom.
She can cure those whom the doctor has failed.
She cures the sick with cold water.
When she cures the child, she does not charge the father.
5   We can remain in the world without fear.
Iyalode who cures children—help me to have my own child.
Her medicines are free—she feeds honey to the children.
She is rich and her words are sweet.
Large forest with plenty of food.
10 Let a child embrace my body.
The touch of a child's hand is sweet.

Owner of brass.
Owner of parrots' feathers.
Owner of money.

15 My mother, you are beautiful, very beautiful.
Your eyes sparkle like brass.
Your skin is soft and smooth,
You are black like velvet.

Everybody greets you when you descend on the world.
20 Everybody sings your praises.

6 Iyalode (ē-yä'lō-dā): a title given to a woman chief in Yoruba communities, here used in reference to Oshun.

Thinking through the LITERATURE

Connect to the Literature

1. **What Do You Think?** What did you find most surprising or unusual in these praise songs?

Think Critically

2. **ACTIVE READING: SYNTHESIZING** Look over the word webs you created in your 📖 **READER'S NOTEBOOK.** What overall impression do you get of each orisha?

3. Describe the relationship between humans and gods found in the praise songs.

4. What seems to be the tone, or attitude, of the speakers in the praise songs?

5. Which of the orishas do you find most appealing? Explain why.

   | THINK
   | ABOUT } • what role each orisha plays in human affairs
   | • each orisha's personality traits

Extend Interpretations

6. **Critic's Corner** The Yoruba praise song has been described as "a collage of verbal images." A collage is an artwork made of different fragments joined together. Commentators also note that praise songs contain **allusions,** or references, to longer stories familiar in the culture. How do these characteristics of praise songs affect your reading of the songs?

7. **Connect to Life** Which ideas in the praise songs remind you of views expressed in other religious works familiar to you? Explain.

LITERARY ANALYSIS: CHARACTERIZATION

The composers of these praise songs rely on the same techniques of **characterization** that fiction writers use to develop characters. Following are the four basic means of characterization:

- description of the character's physical appearance
- presentation of the character's speech, thoughts, feelings, and actions
- presentation of other characters' reactions to the character
- the speaker's or narrator's direct comments about the character

Cooperative Learning Activity
With classmates, look again at the word webs you made in your 📖 **READER'S NOTEBOOK** for Obatala, Shango, and Oshun. Identify words from the songs that help create your impressions of these orishas. Which methods of characterization do these words represent? Use these same methods of characterization to write a praise song about your teacher or a classmate.

Orishas in the Americas

If you are a fan of Latin music, the names of Shango, Obatala, and other orishas may already be familiar to you. Artists as diverse as Mongo Santamaria, Celia Cruz, Carlos Santana, and Desi Arnaz have recorded songs related to the Yoruba gods. "Babalu," which you may have heard Arnaz sing on *I Love Lucy,* is addressed to the orisha Babalu Ayé, who gives smallpox to those who anger him. Many aspects of Latin American culture show the influence of Yoruba religion.

How Did the Yoruba Religion Spread? Yoruba who were captured during the Atlantic slave trade (1518–1870) brought their religion to Latin America and the Caribbean. In Cuba, the religion is practiced as *santería* (sän-tĕ-rē'ä) or *lucumí* (lōō-kōō-mē'). In Brazil, it is known as *candomblé* (kän-dōm-blā'), while in Trinidad, it is called *shangó.* The rituals remain very similar but have taken on new forms in a new setting. Because the religion was repressed by Christian slaveholders, enslaved Yoruba disguised their faith by identifying their orishas with Catholic saints. The orisha Shango, for example, became identified with Saint Barbara.

As Latin American and Caribbean immigrants have come to the United States, they have brought the Yoruba religion to this country, where it has gained more followers. According to a *Boston Globe* newspaper article, more than 100,000 people in the United States today practice some form of Yoruba-based religion.

Research Project Find out more about the Yoruba religion as it is practiced in the Americas or as it has influenced U.S. or Latin American culture. You might investigate and report on one of the following topics (or another of your choice):

- Sacred *bata* rhythms in Afro-Cuban music

- Yoruba-influenced visual artists, such as the Brazilian sculptor Mestre Didi

- Oyotunji Village in South Carolina, an African-American re-creation of a traditional Yoruba village

- The 1993 Supreme Court decision upholding religious freedom in *Church of the Lukumi Babalu Aye* v. *City of Hialeah*

RESEARCH STARTER
CLASSZONE.COM

Desi Arnaz and His Orchestra— *Babalu*

Santana—*Shangó*

Celia Cruz—*Tributo a los orishas*

Trickster Tales

OVERVIEW

Tales of Anansi the Spider   651

Tales of Iktomi the Spider   658

Standardized
Test Practice   663

The **trickster tale** is a genre of literature found in West Africa and all over the world. It is a humorous folktale in which an animal or person creates mischief by trying to outwit others. Usually a culture will have a whole cycle of stories about the same trickster character. Famous tricksters include the Native American Coyote, the African-American Brer Rabbit (who descended from a West African trickster hare), and even the cartoon character Bugs Bunny.

In the pages that follow, you will read trickster tales from West African and Native American cultures. You will compare and contrast Anansi the spider, a West African trickster, and the Native American spider known as Iktomi, and you will decide how well each character displays the qualities of a trickster. Through this comparison, you will decide if the two tricksters are basically the same character.

Points *of* Comparison

The trickster is a complex character with both admirable and terrible qualities. He can be a **culture hero** who brings good things to people and teaches them to live properly. He can be a **clever deceiver** who uses trickery to capture or humiliate others. He can also be a **fool** whose greed or arrogance leads to his own downfall. The chart below lists some common characteristics of tricksters.

Analyzing Trickster Tales
As you read the Anansi stories, keep track of the trickster characteristics you see in Anansi on a chart similar to this one. Later you will do the same for Iktomi.

Trickster Characteristics	Anansi (West African)	Iktomi (Native American)
clever		
heroic		
supernaturally powerful		
greedy, selfish		
lying, deceitful		
proud, self-important		
foolish		

Standardized Test Practice: Comparison-and-Contrast Essay After you have finished reading all the stories, you will have the information you need to write a comparison-and-contrast essay. Your notes will help you include details and examples from the stories.

Tales of *Anansi* the *Spider*

Build Background

West African Tricksters There are several tricksters in African folklore. In east, central, and southern Africa and the western Sudan, the trickster is the hare. Among the Yoruba, Edo, and Ibo of Nigeria, the trickster is the tortoise. Anansi the spider is the famous trickster of the Ashanti people, who live in Ghana. All Ashanti folk tales are referred to as *anansesem,* or "spider tales," whether Anansi appears in them or not.

Hundreds of stories have been told about Anansi; his wife, Aso; and his sons, Kweku Tsin and Intikuma. Traditionally, the stories are told only after dark. Anansi is a culture hero to the Ashanti, responsible for scattering wisdom throughout the world and otherwise making things as they are today. He is also a model for bad behavior, however. Through Anansi stories, the Ashanti make fun of human faults.

Anansi Abroad Anansi stories were brought to the Americas as a result of the slave trade. Many Ashanti slaves were transported to Jamaica, and Anansi stories are told there as Anancy or Aunt Nancy stories. Stories told in Jamaica are almost identical to the original West African stories, although modern writers such as Andrew Salkey have invented new Anansi stories to comment on today's world.

Connect to Your Life

How would you get someone to do what you wanted him or her to do, without that person's realizing what you were up to? Share a strategy that worked for you.

Focus Your Reading

LITERARY ANALYSIS: TRICKSTER TALE

A **trickster tale** involves a human or animal character who engages in clever deceit, physical harm, or magic to try to get what he or she desires. Sometimes the trickster fools others; sometimes he or she is fooled. Trickster tales are usually humorous, and often they explain how some feature of the world or society came to be. Look for these qualities in the Anansi tales you are about to read.

ACTIVE READING: INTERPRETING THEMES

Often, the beginning or end of a trickster tale will state outright what feature of the world the story explains. The first story, for example, tells you,

> *"In this way Anansi . . . became the owner of all stories that are told."*

The more important theme of a trickster tale is usually unstated, however. Frequently it is a moral lesson that can be inferred from what is rewarded or punished in the story. One unstated theme of the first story might be "If you let yourself be flattered, you might suffer."

READER'S NOTEBOOK. As you read each Anansi tale, take notes, following the model below.

_____ is rewarded for _____.

_____ is punished for _____.

Lesson:_____.

Tales of Anansi the Spider

Retold by Harold Courlander

All Stories Are Anansi's

In the beginning, all tales and stories belonged to Nyame, the Sky God. But Kwaku Anansi,[1] the spider, yearned to be the owner of all the stories known in the world, and he went to Nyame and offered to buy them.

The Sky God said: "I am willing to sell the stories, but the price is high. Many people have come to me offering to buy, but the price was too high for them. Rich and powerful families have not been able to pay. Do you think you can do it?"

Anansi replied to the Sky God: "I can do it. What is the price?"

"My price is three things," the Sky God said. "I must first have Mmoboro, the hornets. I must then have Onini, the great python. I must then have Osebo,[2] the leopard. For these things I will sell you the right to tell all stories."

Anansi said: "I will bring them."

He went home and made his plans. He first cut a gourd from a vine and made a small hole in it. He took a large calabash and filled it with water. He went to the tree where the hornets lived. He poured some of the water over himself, so that he was dripping. He threw some water over the hornets, so that they too were dripping. Then he put the calabash on his head, as though to protect himself from a storm, and called out to the hornets: "Are you foolish people? Why do you stay in the rain that is falling?"

The hornets answered: "Where shall we go?"

"Go here, in this dry gourd," Anansi told them. The hornets thanked him and flew into the gourd through the small hole. When the last of them had entered, Anansi plugged the hole with a ball of grass, saying: "Oh, yes, but you are really foolish people!"

He took his gourd full of hornets to Nyame, the Sky God. The Sky God accepted them. He said: "There are two more things."

Anansi returned to the forest and cut a long bamboo pole and some strong vines. Then he walked toward the house of Onini, the python, talking to himself. He said: "My wife is stupid. I say he is longer and stronger. My wife says he is shorter and weaker. I give him more respect. She gives him less respect. Is she right or am I right? I am right, he is longer. I am right, he is stronger."

When Onini, the python, heard Anansi talking to himself, he said: "Why are you arguing this way with yourself?"

The spider replied: "Ah, I have had a dispute with my wife. She says you are shorter and weaker than this bamboo pole. I say you are longer and stronger."

Onini said: "It's useless and silly to argue when you can find out the truth. Bring the pole and we will measure."

So Anansi laid the pole on the ground, and the python came and stretched himself out beside it.

---

1. **Nyame** (nyä´mě´) . . . **Kwaku Anansi** (kwä´ kōō ä-nän´sē). *Kwaku* means "Wednesday-born."
2. **Mmoboro** (mō-bō´rō) . . . **Onini** (ō-nē´nē) . . . **Osebo** (ō-sě´bô´).

"You seem a little short," Anansi said.

The python stretched further.

"A little more," Anansi said.

"I can stretch no more," Onini said.

"When you stretch at one end, you get shorter at the other end," Anansi said. "Let me tie you at the front so you don't slip."

> "Whenever a man tells a story, he must acknowledge that it is Anansi's tale."

He tied Onini's head to the pole. Then he went to the other end and tied the tail to the pole. He wrapped the vine all around Onini, until the python couldn't move.

"Onini," Anansi said, "it turns out that my wife was right and I was wrong. You are shorter than the pole and weaker. My opinion wasn't as good as my wife's. But you were even more foolish than I, and you are now my prisoner."

Anansi carried the python to Nyame, the Sky God, who said: "There is one thing more."

Osebo, the leopard, was next. Anansi went into the forest and dug a deep pit where the leopard was accustomed to walk. He covered it with small branches and leaves and put dust on it, so that it was impossible to tell where the pit was. Anansi went away and hid. When Osebo came prowling in the black of night, he stepped into the trap Anansi had prepared and fell to the bottom. Anansi heard the sound of the leopard falling, and he said: "Ah, Osebo, you are half-foolish!"

When morning came, Anansi went to the pit and saw the leopard there.

"Osebo," he asked, "what are you doing in this hole?"

"I have fallen into a trap," Osebo said. "Help me out."

"I would gladly help you," Anansi said. "But I'm sure that if I bring you out, I will have no thanks for it. You will get hungry, and later on you will be wanting to eat me and my children."

"I swear it won't happen!" Osebo said.

"Very well. Since you swear it, I will take you out," Anansi said.

He bent a tall green tree toward the ground, so that its top was over the pit, and he tied it that way. Then he tied a rope to the top of the tree and dropped the other end of it into the pit.

"Tie this to your tail," he said.

Osebo tied the rope to his tail.

"Is it well tied?" Anansi asked.

"Yes, it is well tied," the leopard said.

"In that case," Anansi said, "you are not merely half-foolish, you are all-foolish."

And he took his knife and cut the other rope, the one that held the tree bowed to the ground. The tree straightened up with a snap, pulling Osebo out of the hole. He hung in the air head downward, twisting and turning. And while he hung this way, Anansi killed him with his weapons.

Then he took the body of the leopard and carried it to Nyame, the Sky God, saying: "Here is the third thing. Now I have paid the price."

Nyame said to him: "Kwaku Anansi, great warriors and chiefs have tried, but they have been unable to do it. You have done it. Therefore, I will give you the stories. From this day onward, all stories belong to you. Whenever a man tells a story, he must acknowledge that it is Anansi's tale."

In this way Anansi, the spider, became the owner of all stories that are told. To Anansi all these tales belong.

Anansi Plays Dead

One year there was a famine in the land. But Anansi and his wife Aso[3] and his sons had a farm, and there was food enough for all of them. Still the thought of famine throughout the country made Anansi hungry. He began to plot how he could have the best part of the crops for himself. He devised a clever scheme.

One day he told his wife that he was not feeling well and that he was going to see a sorcerer. He went away and didn't return until night. Then he announced that he had received very bad news. The sorcerer had informed him, he said, that he was about to die. Also, Anansi said, the sorcerer had prescribed that he was to be buried at the far end of the farm, next to the yam patch. When they heard this news, Aso, Kwaku Tsin, and Intikuma[4] were very sad. But Anansi had more instructions. Aso was to place

> The sorcerer had informed him, he said, that he was about to die.

in his coffin a pestle and mortar,[5] dishes, spoons, and cooking pots, so that Anansi could take care of himself in the Other World.

In a few days, Anansi lay on his sleeping mat as though he were sick, and in a short time he pretended to be dead. So Aso had him buried at the far end of the farm, next to the yam patch, and they put in his coffin all of the cooking pots and other things he had asked for.

But Anansi stayed in the grave only while the sun shone. As soon as it grew dark, he came out of the coffin and dug up some yams and cooked them. He ate until he was stuffed. Then he returned to his place in the coffin. Every night he came out to select the best part of the crops and eat them, and during the day he hid in his grave.

Aso and her sons began to observe that their best yams and corn and cassava[6] were being stolen from the fields. So they went to Anansi's grave and held a special service there. They asked Anansi's soul to protect the farm from thieves.

That night Anansi again came out, and once more he took the best crops and ate them. When Aso and her sons found out that Anansi's soul

---

3. Aso (ä′sō′).

4. **Kwaku Tsin** (kwä′kōō chǐn′) . . . **Intikuma** (ǐn′tǐ-kōō′mə).

5. **pestle and mortar:** a small, club-shaped tool for grinding substances, and the container in which the grinding is done.

6. **cassava** (kə-sä′və): a large, starchy plant root eaten as a food.

Akunitam cloth (mid/late 20th century). Photograph copyright © Franko Khoury/National Museum of African Art, Smithsonian Institution, Washington, D.C.

HUMANITIES CONNECTION Important chiefs in Ghana wear embroidered *akunitam* cloth, or "cloth of the great." Some symbols on the cloth represent characters from folk tales. Anansi the spider is in the upper left corner.

was not protecting them, they devised a plan to catch the person who was stealing their food. They made a figure out of sticky gum. It looked like a man. They set it up in the yam patch.

That night Anansi crawled out of his coffin to eat. He saw the figure standing there in the moonlight.

"Why are you standing in my fields?" Anansi said.

The gum-man didn't answer.

"If you don't get out of my fields, I will give you a thrashing," Anansi said.

The gum-man was silent.

"If you don't go quickly, I will have to beat you," Anansi said.

There was no reply. The gum-man just stood there. Anansi lost his temper. He gave the gum-man a hard blow with his right hand. It stuck fast to the gum-man. Anansi couldn't take it away.

"Let go of my right hand," Anansi said. "You are making me angry!"

But the gum-man didn't let go.

"Perhaps you don't know my strength," Anansi said fiercely. "There is more power in my left hand than in my right. Do you want to try it?"

As there was no response from the gum-man, Anansi struck him with his left hand. Now both his hands were stuck.

"You miserable creature," Anansi said, "so you don't listen to me! Let go at once and get out of my fields or I will really give you something to remember! Have you ever heard of my right foot?"

There was no sound from the gum-man, so Anansi gave him a kick with his right foot. It, too, stuck.

"Oh, you like it, do you?" Anansi shouted. "Then try this one, too!"

He gave a tremendous kick with his left foot, and now he was stuck by both hands and both feet.

"Oh, are you the stubborn kind?" Anansi cried. "Have you ever heard of my head?"

And he butted the gum-man with his head, and that stuck as well.

"I'm giving you your last chance now," Anansi said sternly. "If you leave quietly, I won't complain to the chief. If you don't, I'll give you a squeeze you will remember!"

The gum-man was still silent. So Anansi took a deep breath and gave a mighty squeeze. Now he was completely stuck. He couldn't move this way or that. He couldn't move at all.

In the morning when Aso, Kweku Tsin, and Intikuma came out to the fields, they found Anansi stuck helplessly to the gum-man. They understood everything. They took him off the gum-man and led him toward the village to be judged by the chief. People came to the edge of the trail and saw Anansi all stuck up with gum. They laughed and jeered and sang songs about him. He was deeply shamed, and covered his face with his headcloth. And when Aso, Kweku Tsin, and Intikuma stopped at a spring to drink, Anansi broke away and fled. He ran into the nearest house, crawled into the rafters, and hid in the darkest corner he could find.

From that day until now, Anansi has not wanted to face people because of their scoffing and jeering, and that is why he is often found hiding in dark corners. ❖

Connect to the Literature

1. **What Do You Think?** What was your opinion of Anansi after reading the first story? Did it change after you read the second story?

Comprehension Check
- In the first tale, how did Anansi meet the three demands of the Sky God?
- In the second tale, why did Anansi pretend he was dead?
- How did Anansi's family find out that he was not really dead?

Think Critically

2. **ACTIVE READING: INTERPRETING THEMES** Look at the notes you took in your **READER'S NOTEBOOK.** Tell what these two stories explain about the natural world or society. What other, unstated lessons do they teach?

3. What do you think was the best example of trickery in these stories? Why?

4. What did you learn from these stories about the culture of the Ashanti people?

THINK ABOUT
- their source of food
- their natural surroundings
- their social groups
- their values and beliefs

Points of Comparison

Review the two Anansi stories and fill in the "Anansi" column of your comparison-and-contrast chart.

Paired Activity Compare your chart with that of a classmate and discuss the similarities and differences between them. On the basis of your discussion, decide whether you want to change any of your answers before going on to the next part of this lesson. An example is given for you.

Trickster Characteristics	Anansi (West African)	Iktomi (Native American)
clever	Traps hornets by persuading them to fly into a gourd	
heroic		
supernaturally powerful		
greedy, selfish		
lying, deceitful		
proud, self-important		
foolish		

Now that you have read two stories about Anansi, the Ashanti trickster, you will read two stories about Iktomi, a Native American trickster. Judge how similar the tales are.

Build Background

The Lakota The spider-man Iktomi is the trickster of the Lakota people, also known as the Teton Sioux. Originally from the woodlands of Minnesota, the Lakota migrated to the Great Plains in the late 1700s and dominated the area that is now South Dakota, North Dakota, and Nebraska. There they maintained a nomadic way of life, hunting buffalo on horseback. The Lakota were forced onto reservations with the coming of white settlers and the destruction of buffalo herds at the end of the 19th century. The following two stories were recorded on the Rosebud Sioux Reservation in South Dakota.

Iktomi the Spider Iktomi is a culture hero who, according to the Lakota, created time and space, invented language, named the animals, and foretold the coming of the white man. He is so sacred to the Lakota that they avoid squashing spiders. But even though Iktomi is sacred, he is not completely good. He has been called "the grandfather of lies" and "the imp of mischief whose delight is to make others ridiculous."

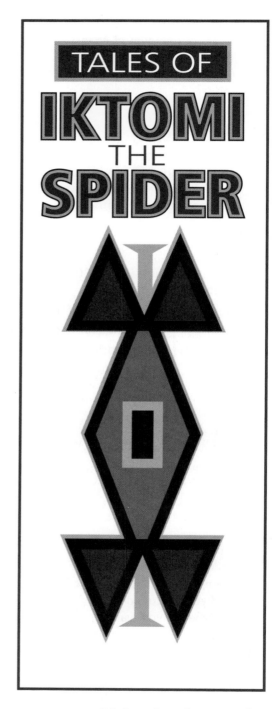

TALES OF
IKTOMI THE SPIDER

Retold by **Richard Erdoes and Alfonso Ortiz**

  Iktomi and the Wild Ducks

One day, Iktomi,[1] the spider fellow, was taking a walk to see what he could see. Tiptoeing through the woods, he saw water sparkling through the leaves. "I am coming to a lake," Iktomi said to himself. "There might be some fat ducks there. I shall creep up to this lake very carefully so that I cannot be seen. Maybe I shall catch something."

Iktomi crept up to the water's edge on all fours, hiding himself behind some bushes. Sure enough, the lake was full of nice, plump ducks. At the sight of them Iktomi's mouth began to water. But how was he to catch the birds? He had neither a net nor his bow and arrows. But he had a stick. He suddenly popped up from behind the bushes, capering[2] and dancing.

"Ho, cousins, come here and learn to dance. I have eight legs and I am the best dancer in the world."

All the ducks swam to the shore and lined up in a row, spellbound[3] by Iktomi's fancy dancing. After a while Iktomi stopped. "Cousins, come closer still," he cried. "I am the gentle, generous Spider-Man, the friend of all the birds, cousin to all fliers, and I shall teach you the duck song.

---

1. **Iktomi** (ēk'tō-mē).
2. **capering:** leaping and jumping playfully.
3. **spellbound:** fascinated; as if in a trance.

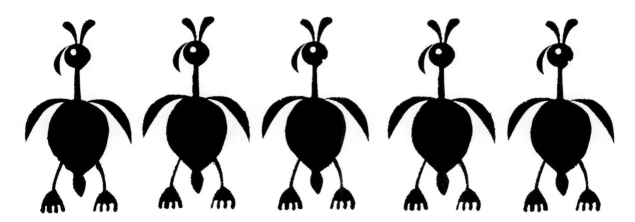

> **I don't quite trust that fellow with the eight legs. I'll risk one eye. One red eye isn't so bad.**

Now, when I start singing, you must all close your eyes in order to concentrate better. Do not peek while I sing, or you will be turned into ugly mud hens with red eyes. You don't want this to happen, do you? You have, no doubt, noticed my stick. It is a drumstick with which I will beat out the rhythm. Are you ready? then close your eyes."

Iktomi started to sing and the foolish ducks crowded around him, doing as he had told them, flapping their wings delightedly and swaying to and fro. And with his stick Iktomi began to club them dead—one after another.

Among the ducks was one young, smart one. "I better check on what's happening," this duck said to himself. "I don't quite trust that fellow with the eight legs. I'll risk one eye. One red eye isn't so bad." He opened his left eye and in a flash saw what Iktomi was up to. "Take off! Take off!" he cried to the other ducks. "Or we'll all wind up in this man's cooking pot!"

The ducks opened their eyes and flew away, quacking loudly.

Still, Iktomi had a fine breakfast of roast duck. The Spider-Man's power turned the smart young duck into a mud hen.

This is why, to this day, mud hens swim alone, away from other ducks, always on the lookout, diving beneath the water as soon as they see or hear anyone approaching, thinking it might be wicked Iktomi with a new bag of tricks. Better a live, ugly mud hen than a pretty, dead duck.

Iktomi Takes Back a Gift

Tunka, Inyan, the Rock, is the oldest divinity in the Lakota cosmology.[4] Everything dies; only the Rock is forever.

Iktomi, the tricky Spider-Man, was starving. There had been no game for a long time. Iktomi was just skin and bones. His empty stomach growled. He was desperate. Then it occurred to him to go for help to Inyan, the Rock, who has great powers, and who might answer his prayers.

Iktomi wrapped himself in his blanket, because it was late in the year and cold. Then he went to a place where a large upright rock was standing. This rock was *lila wakan*,[5] very sacred. Sometimes people came to pray to it.

When Iktomi arrived at that place he lifted up his hands to Inyan: *"Tunkashila, onshimalaye,*[6] grandfather, have pity on me. I am hungry. If you do not help me, I will starve to death. I need meat, grandfather."

Iktomi took his blanket from his shoulder and draped it around Inyan. "Here, grandfather, *tunkashila,* accept this gift. It is the only thing I have to give. It will keep you warm. Please let me find something good to eat."

After praying to Inyan for a long time, Iktomi went off to search for food. He had a feeling Inyan would answer his prayers, and he was right. Iktomi had not gone very far when he came upon a freshly killed deer. It had an arrow piercing its neck, the feathered nock sticking out on one side of the neck and the arrowhead on the other.

"Ohan,"[7] said Iktomi, "the deer has been able to run for a distance after being hit and the hunter has lost it. Inyan has arranged it that way. Well, that is only fair. Did I not give him my blanket? Well, anyhow, *pilamaya,*[8] *tunkashila*—thank you, grandfather!"

Iktomi took his sharp knife out of its beaded knife sheath and began to skin and dress the deer. Then he gathered wood and, with his strike-a-light and tinder, made a fire. There was not much wood and it was wet. It wasn't much of a fire. And it had grown very cold. Iktomi was shivering. His teeth were chattering. He was saying to himself: "What good is my blanket to Inyan? He is just a rock. He does not feel either cold or heat. He does not need it. And, anyway, I don't think Inyan had anything to do with my finding this deer. I am smart. I saw certain tracks. I smelled the deer. So there, I did it all by myself. I did not have to give Inyan anything. I shall take my blanket back!"

Iktomi went back to the sacred rock. He took the blanket off him. *"Tunkashila,"* he said, "this blanket is mine. I am freezing. You don't need this blanket; I do."

Iktomi wrapped the blanket tightly around his body. "Ah, that feels good," he said. "Imagine, giving a blanket to a rock!"

When Iktomi came back to the place where he had left the deer, he discovered that it had disappeared—vanished, gone! Only a heap of dry bones was left. There were no tracks or any signs that somebody had dragged the deer away. It had been transformed into dry bones by a powerful magic.

"How mean of Inyan," said Iktomi, "and how stupid of me. I should have eaten first and then taken the blanket back." ❖

---

4. **cosmology:** a concept of the universe and all its parts and laws.

5. *lila wakan* (lē′lä wä-kän′).

6. *tunkashila* (to͞on′kä-shē-lä) *onshimalaye* (o͞on′shē-mä-lä-yĕ).

7. *ohan* (ō-hŭn′): OK; all right.

8. *pilamaya* (pē-lä′mä-yä).

Connect to the Literature

1. **What Do You Think?** Which one of these stories did you enjoy more? Explain your choice.

Comprehension Check
- How does Iktomi catch the wild ducks?
- Why does Iktomi lose the deer he has found?

Think Critically

2. What feature of the natural world is explained by "Iktomi and the Wild Ducks"?

3. What do you think of Iktomi's statement at the end of "Iktomi Takes Back a Gift"?

4. What social rules does Iktomi violate in the two stories? Discuss the lessons the stories might present to children.

5. What do you learn about Lakota culture from these stories?

Points of Comparison

Paired Activity Now that you have read the last two stories, work with a partner to evaluate Iktomi as a trickster. Fill in the "Iktomi" column of your chart. Then compare and contrast Anansi and Iktomi. What characteristics of the trickster do they share?

Trickster Characteristics	Anansi (West African)	Iktomi (Native American)
clever	Traps hornets by persuading them to fly into a gourd	Catches ducks by saying he will teach them to dance
heroic		
supernaturally powerful		
greedy, selfish		
lying, deceitful		
proud, self-important		
foolish		

Standardized Test Practice

Writing About Literature

PART 1 **Reading the Prompt**

In writing assessments, you may be asked to compare and contrast characters. You are now going to practice writing an essay that involves this type of comparison.

> **Writing Prompt**
> The West African character Anansi and the Native American character Iktomi are two famous tricksters in world literature. Compare Anansi ❶ and Iktomi, discussing how well they show the characteristics of the ❷ trickster. Would you say that they are essentially the same character, or do they have important differences? Give evidence from the four ❸❹ stories you read to support your analysis.

STRATEGIES
IN ACTION

❶ I have to **compare** two **characters**.

❷ I have to evaluate how well each shows **characteristics of the trickster**.

❸ I have to conclude whether they are **more alike** or **more different.**

❹ I need to include **details, examples,** or **quotations** from the stories to support my opinion.

PART 2 **Planning a Comparison-and-Contrast Essay**

- Review the comparison-and-contrast chart that you filled out for the West African and Native American trickster tales.
- In your chart, look for examples of similarities and differences to point out in your essay.
- Create an outline to organize your ideas.

PART 3 **Drafting Your Essay**

Introduction Begin by introducing your topic, the trickster, and identifying the typical trickster's characteristics. Briefly state who Anansi and Iktomi are, and identify the cultures they come from.

Body You can organize in two ways: (1) You can discuss Anansi first, showing how he has characteristics of the trickster, and then discuss Iktomi. (2) Alternatively, you can organize by characteristic, discussing how Anansi and Iktomi are clever, then discussing how they are heroic. Use your comparison-and-contrast chart for details and examples.

Conclusion Wrap up your essay by drawing a conclusion about whether Anansi and Iktomi are alike enough to be thought of as basically the same character.

Revision Make sure that you have used signal words, such as *similarly, also, but, unlike,* and *while,* to make your comparisons and contrasts clear.

WEST AFRICAN PROVERBS

*West African oral literature is particularly rich in **proverbs**—short, well-known sayings that express widely held beliefs. Proverbs are used in every culture; some proverbs that may be familiar to you are "Look before you leap" and "The early bird catches the worm." Such sayings are not really about leaping or catching worms, of course; they are simple ways of making a point. The first statement warns a listener not to act too hastily, and the second encourages taking initiative.*

Proverbs have the same function in West Africa that they do all over the world. They warn, encourage, and console people. West Africans are especially proud of their proverbs, regarding their use as necessary for good conversation. As the Nigerian writer Chinua Achebe has said, "Proverbs are the palm oil with which words are eaten."

Look at the symbols on these pages. They are found stamped on Ghanaian adinkra *cloth, a fabric traditionally worn at funerals and other important rituals. Many of the* adinkra *symbols have proverbs associated with them. For example, the ram's-horn symbol ⚏ suggests the saying, "It is the heart and not the horns that leads a ram to charge." The symbol is linked to the idea of strength.*

The West African proverbs you will read are from a collection that identifies some by ethnic group and some only by nation. As you read each proverb, consider the following questions:

1. *What does the proverb mean? You may want to restate it in your own words.*

2. *What visual images does the proverb bring to mind?*

3. *To what kinds of situations might the proverb apply?*

One camel does not make fun of another camel's hump.   **Guinea**

It takes a whole village to raise one child.   **Yoruba**

Only when you have crossed the river, can you say the crocodile has a lump on his snout.   **Ashanti**

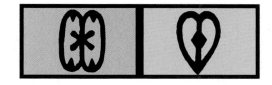

A wise man who knows proverbs reconciles difficulties.   **Yoruba**

To spend the night in anger is better than to spend it repenting.   **Senegal**

Ashes will always blow back into the face of the thrower.   **Yoruba**

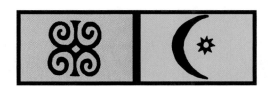

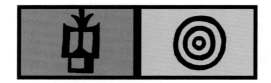

Don't look where you fell, but where you slipped.   **Liberia**

If familiarity were useful, water wouldn't cook fish.   **Fulani**

If something that was going to chop off your head only
knocked off your cap, you should be grateful.   **Yoruba**

If you are in hiding, don't light a fire.   **Ashanti**

No one can leave his character behind him when he
goes on a journey.   **Yoruba**

Love does not hear advice.   **Ghana**

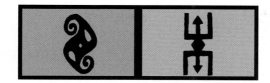

Money is sharper than a sword.

Ashanti

When you get older you keep warm with the wood you gathered as a youth.

Bambara

The one who is carried does not realize how far away the town is.

Nigeria

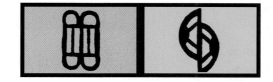

Lying will get you a wife, but it won't keep her.

Fulani

The wisdom of this year is the folly of the next.

Yoruba

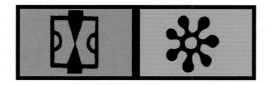

Writing Workshop

Describing an interesting individual . . .

From Reading to Writing The excerpt from D. T. Niane's version of the epic *Sundiata,* on page 634, contains a number of characters who repeatedly hurt, frustrate, and anger one another. Niane makes these characters seem real and believable by describing their actions, their words, and their physical appearance. Writers use the same techniques in creating the **personality profiles** that appear in newspapers and magazines. In a personality profile, compelling information and lively writing are used to present a detailed portrait of a real person.

For Your Portfolio

WRITING PROMPT Write a personality profile of a person you know or admire.

Purpose: To acquaint the reader with the person described

Audience: Your peers, family, or general readers

Basics in a Box

Personality Profile at a Glance

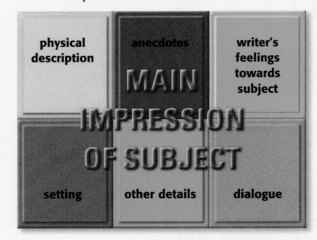

physical description	anecdotes	writer's feelings towards subject
	MAIN IMPRESSION OF SUBJECT	
setting	other details	dialogue

RUBRIC Standards for Writing

A successful personality profile should

- create a vivid impression of a person with lively description, details, anecdotes, and/or dialogue
- put the person in a context that reveals aspects of his or her personality
- make it clear why the person is important to the writer
- be a word portrait that shows the person's character
- have a unified tone and create a unified impression
- capture the reader's interest at the beginning and convey a sense of completeness at the end

Analyzing a Student Model

José Flores
Oak Park and River Forest
High School

Model Teacher, Model Person

She could not be a more normal-looking person. No taller than five feet, hair always tidy and pulled back in a ponytail, she is the very essence of normal—until she begins to talk. Her choice of words, her gestures, and the emotion with which she speaks make up a personality that is anything but ordinary. Respected by her peers, loved by her students, and confident in herself and her methods, she personifies her profession and sets an example for others who wish to do what she does.

At first glance the classroom, like the teacher, looks normal. Upon closer inspection, however, it becomes clear that very little is usual here. Visible immediately are two wooden shelves overflowing with tissue boxes, as well as books that could fill the history section of a library. There are pictures drawn by past students and a monstrous red structure just poking out from under a purple drop cloth. Students sit, somewhat frightened by now, waiting for her to speak, preparing to bolt out of their desks and run if necessary.

"Write down something that you want me to ask you about. If you don't, you may be sorry." With this warning she lets the class write and stands above them, like a hawk examining its prey. Eventually, she comes to the unfortunate victim she was looking for, the one with a blank sheet of paper.

"Justify your existence in this universe!" she tells him. The hapless student desperately searches his mind, looking for something satisfactory, wondering at the same time if she is serious. She eventually moves on, smiling as everyone who has blank paper scrambles to write. As the day begins, her system has already begun to work.

Day after day, students walk into the room to be introduced to something new. Bit by bit, they pick up information about what makes Mrs. Belle unique and what makes the room uniquely hers. The protruding object under the drop cloth turns out to be a *Fallbeil*, or miniature guillotine, painted deep red and fully workable. As she unveils it, the students gasp in disbelief. She calmly takes a pencil, sticks it in the hole, and drops the wooden blade. The blade falls with a sickening crack, and flying pencil shrapnel clears to reveal two halves of a pencil—the splintered remains of Mrs. Belle's latest victim. The lesson begins, and everyone's gaze is fixed on the short woman with the pencil shavings on her shirt.

❶ Captures reader's interest by contrasting the person's ordinary physical appearance with her unusual speaking manner; creates suspense by not immediately identifying her

❷ Places her in the context of her own classroom, which helps to reveal her personality

❸ Bit of dialogue shows how she relates to her students.

❹ Anecdote helps to reveal Mrs. Belle's methods of capturing her students' attention.

Mrs. Belle hands out papers, which turn out to be permission slips. She is doing what so few high school teachers do: a real-world field trip. Her field trips take the students to restaurants, and they happen after school. Three times a year, caravans of people unite in a migration that is so full of fun and laughter that it actually seems preferable to the various European adventures that she has talked about. At this point it becomes clear that through the field trips, the jokes, and the odd items in her room, she makes every moment in class keenly memorable. And as they remember the class, her students remember history. By being personal and unique, she has earned the trust of her students, and she can be sure that they know and appreciate the history that she is teaching.

Mrs. Belle is a woman who has realized that fun and teaching go together, and in that order. She is strict, one of the strictest teachers about homework, and she won't take excuses. Here, however, in sharp contrast to other classes, students feel that they *must* do their work, not for fear of a bad grade but for fear of disappointing her—a fear equal to that of diving off the ten-meter platform for the first time. Students know for certain that she will not disappoint, and they feel comforted by what she says whenever she assigns a report: "I won't let anything bad happen to you." As the class warms up, the lesson plan expands to include toy soldiers, paper clips, pencils, whiteout, and other things that ordinarily have nothing to do with history but here make perfect sense.

Mrs. Belle's room is always filled with kids; this is the risk she takes by making it clear that her door is always open for any kind of help. Her former and current students have a certain kinship, a sense that they have known one of the best that the educational system has to offer. They cherish the time they have spent in her class and wait like children in line at an ice-cream truck for the opportunity to be taught by her again. Her students love history, they love her class (if not the rest of school), and they treat their fellow students with courtesy and respect. She teaches not only that which her curriculum dictates but also that which her experience and morals dictate, that which life necessitates, making her the kind of teacher all educators should strive to be and the kind of person all people should try to emulate.

❺ Creates a strong impression of Mrs. Belle as a unique, creative individual

❻ Shows why she is important to the writer (who is presumably one of her students) as well as how other students feel about her

❼ Sums up her excellence as a teacher and a person

Writing Your Personality Profile

❶ Prewriting Whom do you want to describe? With a few classmates, discuss what kinds of people you find interesting and what is remarkable about them. Consider the people you know—neighbors, relatives, teachers, friends, community leaders. Who strikes you as particularly interesting or admirable? What comes to mind when you think about that person? See the **Idea Bank** in the margin for more suggestions. After you select a subject, follow the steps below.

Planning Your Personality Profile

▷ 1. **Explore your attitude toward the subject.** Why is the person important to you? What details or incidents can you present to show his or her importance to you?

▷ 2. **Set your goal for writing.** What impression of the person do you want to create in the reader's mind? Analyze your subject to find an angle—a dominant impression or theme that conveys the essence of the person.

▷ 3. **Consider the traits you would like to depict.** What stands out about the person? Use a chart like this one to record details.

Personality Characteristics			
How Person Looks	What Person Says	How Person Behaves	How Others React

▷ 4. **Plan your organizational structure.** There are several ways to organize a personality profile:

- **In Chronological Order** Narrate events in the order in which they occurred. You might want to focus on a series of events that reveals something special about the person, or on a day in his or her life.

- **By Category** One at a time, analyze different aspects of your subject's personality, such as interests, behaviors, or opinions.

- **In Order of Importance** Many writers place the most important event or detail at the very beginning or the very end of their piece.

❷ Drafting Start by simply getting your ideas down on paper. Keep your goal in mind as you try to get into the flow of your writing. Roughly following your organizational plan, get down everything you want to say. Later, you can cut unnecessary details or add things you've forgotten.

IDEABank

1. Your Working Portfolio 🗂
Build on one of the Writing Options you completed earlier in this unit:
- **Character Analysis,** p. 641
- **Biographical Article,** p. 641

2. Personal Heroes
Who are your role models? Think about people you admire—ones known to you personally and ones in public life. What traits of theirs do you wish to emulate?

3. And the Winner Is . . .
Imagine that you're going to give an award to the person who best exemplifies a certain trait—kindness, originality, honesty, or humor, for example. Whom would you honor, and why?

LANGUAGE SKILLS

Ask Your Peer Reader

- What dominant impression did you get of my subject?

- How would you describe my attitude toward the person?

- What details were particularly vivid or memorable?

- What details, if any, distracted you from the picture I was trying to present?

- What more would you like to know about the person?

Have a Question?

See the **Writing Handbook**
Introductions, p. R22
Descriptive Writing, pp. R27–R28

❸ Revising

TARGET SKILL ▶ ADDING DETAIL In descriptive writing, concrete details and examples help the reader envision a scene. With them, you can show a person's traits in action instead of just naming them. Remember, however, to select details carefully, so that they build a coherent impression.

> ‸*and flying pencil shrapnel clears to reveal two halves*
>   *of a pencil—*
> The blade falls with a sickening crack ~~and the pencil breaks in two,~~
>   ‸
>
> the splintered remains of Mrs. Belle's latest victim. The lesson
>   *the short woman with the pencil shavings on her shirt.*
> begins, and everyone's gaze is fixed on ~~her.~~
>   ‸

Need revising help?

Review the **Rubric,** p. 668

Consider **peer reader** comments

Check **revision guidelines,** p. R19

Confused by subject-verb agreement?

See the **Grammar Handbook,** p. R74

❹ Editing and Proofreading

TARGET SKILL ▶ ERRORS IN SUBJECT-VERB AGREEMENT A verb must agree with its subject in person and number. Sometimes it can be difficult to determine whether a verb's subject is singular or plural.

> Her choice of words, her gestures, and the emotion with which
>
> she speaks make~~s~~ up a personality that is anything but ordinary.

When reading the model above, you might think that the verb *makes* agrees with the subject *emotion.* However, the true subject is compound: *choice, gestures,* and *emotion.* A compound subject whose parts are joined by *and* takes a plural verb form, so *make* is correct. Review your writing for any errors in subject-verb agreement.

Publishing IDEAS

- Collect the class's profiles in a booklet titled *People to Know.* Distribute the booklet in your school or to local libraries, churches, or community centers.
- Submit your profile to a student-writing Web site.

PUBLISHING OPTIONS
CLASSZONE.COM

❺ Reflecting

FOR YOUR WORKING PORTFOLIO What did you discover about your subject while writing the personality profile? What did you learn about yourself or about life? Attach your answers to these questions to your finished personality profile. Save your personality profile in your **Working Portfolio.**

Read this paragraph from the first draft of a personality profile. The underlined sections may include the following kinds of errors:

- **errors in subject-verb agreement**
- **errors in pronoun agreement**
- **incorrect plurals**
- **errors in the use of *who* and *whom***

For each underlined section, choose the revision that most improves the writing.

I walk into a neighborhood café and see an elderly man standing next to the piano, singing his heart out. He sings with great passion, and <u>the crowd love him</u>. After a couple of songs, he asks, "<u>Whom in the audience can sing</u> the harmony for 'This Land Is Your Land'?" I raise my hand, and he invites me up to join him for a song. I've never had so much fun singing with anyone! After our duet, he sings a few more <u>solos</u> and then takes a bow. At the end of the show, <u>everyone in the house has a smile on their face</u> and <u>are clapping wildly</u>. Afterwards, over a cup of coffee, Leo asks me if I'd like to sing with him again. <u>Who knew</u> that I'd meet such a great person just by walking into a café?

1. A. the crowd loves him
   B. the crowd loved him
   C. the crowds love him
   D. Correct as is

2. A. Whomever in the audience can sing
   B. Who's in the audience can sing
   C. Who in the audience can sing
   D. Correct as is

3. A. soloes
   B. solo's
   C. soloe's
   D. Correct as is

4. A. everyone in the house has a smile on the face
   B. everyone in the house has a smile on his or her face
   C. everyone in the house has a smile on their faces
   D. Correct as is

5. A. was clapping wildly
   B. were clapping wildly
   C. is clapping wildly
   D. Correct as is

6. A. Whom knew
   B. Whomever knew
   C. Who's knew
   D. Correct as is

Need extra help?

Review the **Grammar Handbook**

Subject-Verb Agreement, p. R74

Pronoun Agreement, p. R57

Interrogative Pronouns, p. R58

TEST PRACTICE

Building Vocabulary | Using Context Clues

Reading is one of the best ways to improve vocabulary—better than studying word lists or dictionaries. Whenever you read, you are likely to encounter unfamiliar words. Often, you can infer the meanings of such words from clues in the surrounding passages—that is, from the words' **context**. For example, in the following sentence about *Sundiata*, the word *enigma* is immediately followed by a definition.

> In the end, the condition of Mari Djata remains an enigma—a deep and confounding mystery.

Being alert to context clues will help you absorb unfamiliar words as you read.

Strategies for Building Vocabulary

Here are a few types of context clues.

❶ Definition or Restatement Clues The model above shows that a writer sometimes provides a clue to a word's meaning by restating the meaning. In the example above, the restatement is in the form of an **appositive**—a phrase that explains a word or idea. An appositive follows the word it explains, separated from it by a comma or dash. Other restatements are signaled by such words as *that is, or, in other words,* and *also called.*

❷ Example Clues Sometimes an unfamiliar word is followed by one or more examples that illustrate its meaning. In the passage below, a king is talking to his son, and he gives examples of kings and their successors. These examples can help you determine that *successor* means "one who takes the place of another."

> ". . . before death takes me off I am going to give you the present each king gives his successor. In Mali every prince has his own griot. Doua's father was my father's griot, Doua is mine and the son of Doua, Balla Fasséké here, will be your griot."
>
> —*Sundiata*

❸ Comparison and Contrast Clues You may be able to infer a word's meaning if a writer compares or contrasts it with a more familiar idea. Comparisons are often signaled by words such as *like, as, similar to,* and *also.* Contrasts are signaled by words such as *although, but, unlike, rather than,* and *however.* For example, in the sentence "Far from being a kind friend to Sogolon, Sassouma was horribly **vindictive**," the words *far from* signal a contrast between *vindictive* and *kind*.

❹ Inference Clues The meaning of a word is often suggested by the general sense of the words and sentences that surround it.

> Her son's infirmity weighed heavily upon Sogolon Kedjou; she had resorted to all her talent as a sorceress to give strength to her son's legs, but the rarest herbs had been useless.
>
> —*Sundiata*

Sogolon is troubled by her son's infirmity and has been unable to "give strength to her son's legs." *Infirmity* must refer to the legs' lack of strength. One can infer from the context that an infirmity is a physical weakness or illness.

EXERCISE Explain the meaning of the boldfaced word in each sentence. Then identify the type of context clue and the details that helped you to define it.

1. Although Sogolon encouraged her son to speak, he remained **taciturn.**
2. While the other children walked with **agility,** Mari Djata could only crawl.
3. She overheard the **malicious** talk about her son; people said he was an ugly, stupid cripple.
4. The king was **perplexed;** he couldn't understand why his son had turned out this way.
5. Sassouma insulted Sogolon and laughed in her face. Sogolon had never been so **affronted.**

Sentence Crafting | Using Adverbs and Adverb Phrases

Grammar from Literature Look at the sentences from "Anansi Plays Dead" below. Notice the information that the highlighted adverbs and adverb phrases add to the sentences. (One-word adverbs appear in red type; adverb phrases appear in blue type.)

> when
> One day he told his wife that he was not feeling well and
> ⌐ how ⌐
> where   where
> that he was going to see a sorcerer. He went away and
> how   when
> didn't [not] return until night.

> how
> Anansi struck him with his left hand.

> when   to what extent   how
> Now he was completely stuck. He couldn't [not] move
> where   how   to what extent
> this way or that. He couldn't [not] move at all.

As you can see, adverbs and adverb phrases answer the questions *how, where, when, for what purpose,* and *to what extent.* They modify verbs, adjectives, and other adverbs.

Types of Adverb Phrases Prepositional phrases can function as adverb phrases. The following sentence contains a prepositional phrase modifying the verb *covered,* answering the question *how.*

> He was deeply shamed, and covered his face with his headcloth.
> —"Anansi Plays Dead"

Infinitive phrases can also function as adverb phrases. In the sentence below, the highlighted infinitive phrase modifies the verb *came,* answering the question *for what purpose.*

> Every night he came out to select the best part of the crops and eat them, and during the day he hid in his grave.
> —"Anansi Plays Dead"

Using Adverbs in Your Writing When you revise a piece of writing, examine the verbs and modifiers you have used. Would the addition of adverbs and adverb phrases telling *how, when, where, for what purpose,* and *to what extent* make your writing more precise or accurate? Notice how crucial the adverbs are in this synopsis of part of "Anansi Plays Dead."

> Every night, Anansi emerged silently from his grave to steal the best crops from the field and cook them for himself. He did this for days. Finally, his wife and son made a figure out of sticky gum and set it in the fields. Anansi confronted the gum-man angrily and attacked him with great confidence. He soon found himself stuck by every limb to the gum-man.

Try rereading the passage, mentally deleting all of the adverbs and adverb phrases. Without these modifiers, the passage makes little sense. Which of the adverbs and adverb phrases are essential to the expression of complete thoughts? Which are not essential but add useful or interesting information? In your own writing, look for places to include adverbs and adverb phrases that provide interesting details.

WRITING EXERCISE Rewrite the following sentences, adding adverbs and adverb phrases that modify the underlined words. Follow the instructions in parentheses, using your imagination to come up with suitable modifiers.

1. Anansi <u>visited</u> the hornets. (Tell where and when he visited the hornets.)
2. He <u>captured</u> them. (Tell how and where he captured them.)
3. Although the hornets <u>complained,</u> he <u>refused</u> to let them go. (Tell how and where they complained and to what extent he refused.)
4. He <u>presented</u> the gourd full of hornets to Nyame, the Sky God. (Tell when and how he presented the gourd.)
5. The Sky God <u>accepted</u> them. (Tell how the Sky God accepted them.)

West African Oral Literature

Reflect and Assess

Did you gain a better appreciation of oral literature after reading the West African selections in Unit 4, Part 2? What did you discover about West African societies? Use the following activities to pull together what you've learned.

Five terra-cotta horseback riders.
Courtesy of Bernard de Grunne.

Reflecting on the Literature

Cultural Values One important function of oral literature is to instill values. For each selection you have read in Part 2, identify one or two cultural values that you think are taught or supported. You might phrase these as do's or don'ts—for example, "Don't be too proud." Explain why you believe the selection expresses that particular value. After considering all the selections, try to make some generalizations about West African cultural values.

Reviewing Literary Concepts

Oral Genres In this part of the book, you read examples of several genres of oral literature: myth, legend, oral epic, praise song, trickster tale, and proverb. Tell what makes them different from one another. Which genres do you think lose the most in written translation?

📁 Building Your Portfolio

Writing Workshop and Writing Options Look again at the personality profile you wrote for the Writing Workshop and at any Writing Options you completed. Which was your most effective piece of writing? Add that assignment to your **Presentation Portfolio** 📁, along with a note identifying your favorite passage and telling what you were trying to accomplish in it.

Self **ASSESSMENT**

📖 **READER'S NOTEBOOK**

Following are important terms from this part of the book. Create groups of two or more related terms, then explain how they are connected. Different groupings are possible. If you are unclear about any term, go back through the unit or consult the **Glossary of Literary Terms** (page R91).

Sundiata	Mali
internal conflict	trickster tale
Yoruba	griot
orishas	praise song
Anansi	external conflict

Setting **GOALS**

Look back through your assignments and notebook to identify writing or critical-thinking skills that you would like to strengthen.

Extend Your *Reading*

The Hero with an African Face

CLYDE W. FORD

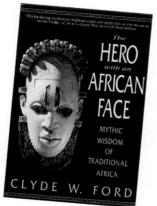

Ford, a psychotherapist, explores "the mythic wisdom of traditional Africa." He retells and interprets myths and epics from different parts of the continent, finding such universal themes as death and resurrection, the master animal, and the sacred circle. An especially interesting chapter covers the *Mwindo Epic,* from the Congo.

Jali Kunda

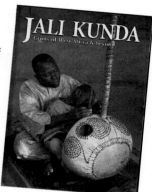

This book and companion music CD introduce the West African tradition of the jali (dieli), or griot. At the heart of the book is a memoir by the Mandinka griot Foday Musa Suso, who now lives and records in the United States. Many full-page color photographs of musicians are included, along with commentary on griots by the poet Amiri Baraka and the music critic Robert Palmer. The CD offers two different performances of *Sundiata.*

And Even *More . . .*

Books

Voices of the Ancestors: African Myth
Another impressive book in Time-Life's Myth and Mankind series, containing creation stories and other narratives illustrated with masterworks of African art.

Leaf and Bone: African Praise-Poems JUDITH GLEASON
Praise poems from all over Africa, addressed to orishas, rulers, common people, animals—even trains and bicycles.

West African Trickster Tales MARTIN BENNETT
More tales of Anansi the spider, as well as tales about the trickster hare and trickster tortoise.

Other Media

The Roots of African Civilization
This 25-minute film uses location footage, expert commentary, and photographs of art to introduce viewers to precolonial West Africa. Knowledge Unlimited. (VIDEOCASSETTE)

Encarta Africana
An absorbing multimedia encyclopedia of African and African-American cultures containing thousands of essays and photos, along with virtual tours, interactive maps, and music. Microsoft. (CD-ROM)

West Africa Before the Colonial Era

BASIL DAVIDSON

An easy-to-read survey of West African history before 1850. Among its topics are ancient Ghana and Mali, Yoruba kingdoms, the economy, religion, social groups, and the slave trade.

Standardized Test Practice

Reading & Writing for Assessment

When you studied strategies for reading a test selection on pages 412–417, you practiced techniques for success on reading and writing assessments. These kinds of tests are often important end-of-course examinations.

 The following pages will give you more test-taking strategies. You will have a chance to apply them in the practice activities that follow the selection.

PART 1 How to Read a Test Selection

In many tests, you will read a selection and then answer multiple-choice questions about it. Applying the basic strategies that follow can help you focus on the information you will need to know.

STRATEGIES FOR READING A TEST SELECTION

▶ **Before you begin reading, skim the questions that follow the selection.** These can help focus your reading.

▶ **Use active reading strategies, such as clarifying, evaluating, and questioning.** As you read, make notes in the margin or underline key words and passages, as long as the test directions allow you to do so.

▶ **Think about the title.** What does it suggest about the overall message or theme of the selection?

▶ **Look for main ideas.** You will often find a main idea stated at the beginning or end of a paragraph. Sometimes it is implied, not stated. After reading each paragraph, ask yourself, "What was this paragraph about?"

▶ **Note the literary elements and techniques used by the writer.** Look out for such elements as descriptive language and the use of quotations. Then ask yourself what effect the writer achieves with each one.

▶ **Examine the sequence of ideas.** Are the ideas developed in chronological order, presented in order of importance, or organized in some other way? What does the sequence of ideas suggest about the writer's message?

▶ **Unlock word meanings.** Use context clues and word parts to help you unlock the meaning of unfamiliar words.

▶ **Think about the message or theme.** What larger lesson can you draw from the selection? That is, can you infer anything or make generalizations about other similar situations, human beings, or life in general?

---

❶ Edison's Curse

by Stanley Coren

1 ❷ "Most people overeat 100 percent, and oversleep 100 percent, because they like it. That extra 100 percent makes them unhealthy and inefficient. The person who sleeps eight or ten hours a night is never fully asleep and never fully awake—they have only different degrees of doze through the twenty-four hours."

2 The man who wrote these words in his diary was not a psychologist, psychiatrist, or medical researcher. It was Thomas Alva Edison, the man who changed the world by creating over 1,300 inventions, including the phonograph, the electric typewriter, the first practical motion picture camera and projector, and the carbon microphone (which made the telephone possible). ❸ Yet it is not Edison the inventor who captures our interest at the moment, but Edison the social engineer who profoundly changed the psychology of the modern world. It was his desire to be known as the man who finally eradicated the waste of human potential represented by all those hours spent in "unproductive sleep."

3 Edison's reasoning was really quite simple: If sleep could be eliminated, it would add additional work hours to the day. This would improve productivity, bring prosperity to all of society, and hasten the progress of civilization. "Anything which tends to slow work down is a waste," he explained. "We are always hearing people talk about 'loss of sleep' as a calamity. They better call it loss of time, vitality, and opportunities."

4 His plan was fairly straightforward and involved an invention that he had worked on for many years—the electric lightbulb. This great boon to society would banish the darkness and thus make it possible for people to work continuously through the night hours. Edison believed, from personal experience, that sleep was merely a bad habit and could be done away with quite easily. "For myself I never found need of more than four or five hours sleep in the twenty-four," he claimed. His personal experience also convinced him that sleep was ❹ deleterious to health and made people lazy and stupid. "When by chance I have taken more [hours of sleep than usual]," he wrote, "I wake dull and indolent." Edison was later able to confirm his personal experiences with sleep and with the beneficial effects of the lightbulb using other observations: "When I went through Switzerland in a motor-car, so that I could visit little towns and villages, I noted the effect of artificial light on the inhabitants. Where water power and electric light had been developed, everyone seemed normally

STRATEGIES
IN ACTION

❶ **Think about the title; read actively by questioning.**

ONE STUDENT'S THOUGHTS

"Is this about Thomas Edison, inventor of the light bulb? What kind of curse could this be?"

❷ **Note the writer's technique of using a quotation for the introduction.**

"That's a pretty extreme statement. I wonder if this quotation reflects the writer's point of view."

❸ **Notice the article's main idea.**

"Now I see that this essay is going to be about Edison and how he influenced our sleep patterns."

❹ **Use context clues to determine word meanings.**

"Here, the writer is discussing the negative effects that Edison attributed to sleep. *Deleterious* must mean 'harmful.'"

YOUR TURN

Use context clues to determine the meanings of other words in the selection.

TEST PRACTICE

intelligent. ⑤ Where these appliances did not exist, and the natives went to bed with the chickens, staying there till daylight, they were far less intelligent." . . .

5   Did Edison have any effect on human sleep patterns as a result of his invention? I think he would be gratified to learn that ⑥ people regularly sleep less now than before the lightbulb was invented and that he is, at least partly, responsible for that. . . .

6   When Edison introduced the lightbulb, he was opening the door to a new technological era that had the potential to allow us to abandon sleep and work around the clock. However, the intended user of this new technology is a biological machine with a very long history of adaptive evolution. Technology has evolved at a speed that has far outstripped the rate of biological evolution. Our physiology cannot change with a flick of the switch. Human beings today are making demands on their bodies and their minds that are in conflict with their biological nature. . . .

7   ⑦ For some 4 million years man was basically a hunter and a gatherer. Gathering such foods as nuts, berries, and roots required light and could not be efficiently done in the dark. Hunting also required light. The end result was that man slept through the dark hours because it was too inefficient and too dangerous to do anything else. After all, if there were saber-toothed tigers out there in the dark, it was safer to be asleep in a nice, well-hidden cave. Given the average light cycles in the regions of the world where man is believed to have originally developed, human beings were probably dealing with up to 14 hours of darkness, or relative darkness, each day. Presumably, much of this time was spent sleeping. . . .

8   Unfortunately, we still have the physiology of the hunter-gatherer. . . . Evolution has not yet responded to the needs of the night shift worker or the hard-driving, ambitious stock manager monitoring the Tokyo exchange prices from his New York apartment in the middle of the night. No matter how wasteful sleep may seem to us today, it has probably evolved for a purpose.

9   Just how much flexibility do we have in terms of our sleep requirements? Is sleep really a worthless time-out period that merely squanders one-third of our lives? If so, can we find some way to go without it or at least reduce its wasteful impact? If not, are there any long-term or serious consequences of our modern proclivity to do without sleep or at least to cheat as much as possible on our sleep time? The answers to these questions are becoming more important because it is beginning to look like many current problems may have more to do with too little sleep rather than with time wasted sleeping. It seems that we have not evolved fast enough to keep pace with our present technological world.

STRATEGIES
IN ACTION

⑤ **Read actively by evaluating.**

"This can't be true. Perhaps Edison was noticing that people with electric lights were more cultured or sophisticated, which he mistook for intelligence."

⑥ **Note cause-and-effect relationships.**

"Edison's invention of the light bulb gave people the opportunity to work at night and thus sleep less."

⑦ **Note the sequence of ideas.**

"The writer has chosen to present his information not in chronological order but in another logical order. He begins with Edison's time and then takes us back in time in order to provide background about human sleep patterns."

Skim the questions that follow the selection.

"I see there's a question about the writer's viewpoint. I think he believes we should question the belief that we can sacrifice sleep for work without negative consequences."

How to Answer Multiple-Choice Questions

Use the strategies in the box at the right and the notes below them to help you answer the questions below.

Choose the best answer for each of the following questions about the selection you have just read.

1. What is "Edison's curse"?
   A. a tendency to overeat
   B. the modern tendency to sacrifice sleep for work
   C. lower levels of intelligence
   D. all of the above

2. Which of the following best describes Thomas Edison as presented in this essay?
   A. an innovator
   B. a social critic
   C. a hard worker
   D. all of the above

3. According to the writer, how did the introduction of the light bulb affect people's sleep habits?
   A. Electric light made it possible for people to work and be active after dark, and as a result, they slept less.
   B. Exposure to electric light changed the chemistry of the human brain in such a way that people required less sleep.
   C. The light bulb made people more intelligent and thus aware of the wastefulness of too much sleep.
   D. People were so excited by the light bulb that they simply could not sleep.

4. Human physiology hasn't changed much since humans were engaged in which of the following lifestyles?
   A. farming
   B. factory work
   C. hunting and gathering
   D. office work

5. Which statement best expresses the writer's point of view?
   A. It is time for human evolution to catch up with technology.
   B. People should better respect the biological need for sleep.
   C. Thomas Edison was ahead of his time.
   D. none of the above

STRATEGIES FOR ANSWERING MULTIPLE-CHOICE QUESTIONS

▸ **Ask questions** that help you eliminate some of the choices.
▸ **Pay attention to choices** such as "all of the above" or "none of the above." To eliminate them, all you need to find is one answer that doesn't fit.
▸ **Skim your notes and the text you've underlined.** Details you noticed as you read may provide answers.

STRATEGIES IN ACTION

Pay attention to choices such as "all of the above."

ONE STUDENT'S THOUGHTS

"Can I eliminate any of the first three choices? Actually, the essay depicts Edison as both an innovator and a social critic, and I don't have the option to choose only two answers: it's either all or one. When I think about it, the essay also conveys that he was a hard worker. The answer must be D."

Skim your notes.

ONE STUDENT'S THOUGHTS

"The writer makes it quite clear that human physiology (and therefore, human brain chemistry) has not changed to accommodate current lifestyles, so I can eliminate choice B."

YOUR TURN
What other choice can you eliminate?

TEST PRACTICE

PART 3

How to Respond in Writing

Sometimes you will be asked to write answers to questions about a reading selection. **Short-answer questions** usually ask you to answer in a sentence or two. **Essay questions** require a fully developed piece of writing.

STRATEGIES FOR RESPONDING TO SHORT-ANSWER QUESTIONS

▶ **Identify the key words** in the writing prompt—the words that tell you what ideas to discuss. Make sure you know what each word means.

▶ **Make your response** direct and to the point.

▶ **Support your ideas** with evidence from the selection.

▶ **Use correct grammar.**

> **Sample Prompt**
>
> Answer the following question in one or two sentences.
>
> How does the writer's use of quotations help to characterize Edison?

Essay Question

STRATEGIES FOR ANSWERING ESSAY QUESTIONS

▶ **Look for direction words** in the writing prompt—words such as *essay, analyze, describe,* or *compare and contrast* that tell you how to respond directly to the prompt.

▶ **List the points** you want to make before beginning to write.

▶ **Write an interesting introduction** that presents your main point.

▶ **Develop your ideas** by using evidence from the selection that supports the statements you make.

▶ **Present your ideas** in a logical order.

▶ **Write a conclusion** that summarizes your points.

▶ **Check your work** for correct grammar.

> **Sample Prompt**
>
> How has the development of technology caused a change in human sleep patterns? Write an essay in which you analyze this cause-and-effect relationship as it is presented in the selection.

STRATEGIES IN ACTION

Identify the key words in the writing prompt.

ONE STUDENT'S THOUGHTS

"The key words are *quotations* and *characterize.* I will have to find examples of quotations in the selection and then explain how the writer uses them to characterize Edison. Maybe I can find one quotation in particular to use as an example."

YOUR TURN

Go back to the selection and find a quotation that reveals something about Edison.

Look for direction words.

ONE STUDENT'S THOUGHTS

"The prompt is asking me to write an *essay* in which I *analyze* the *cause-and-effect relationship* between technology and sleep habits as presented in the selection. I'll have to look through the selection for statements about this relationship and write about the different parts of that relationship.

YOUR TURN

Make a list of statements from the selection that connect technology and sleep in some way. What are the different aspects of the relationship between the two?

Here is part of a student's first draft in response to the writing prompt at the bottom of page 682. Read the draft and then answer the multiple-choice questions that follow.

1	The writer of this essay makes it clear that the sleep habits
2	in our society have been strongly affected by developments in
3	technology—by the introduction of the electric light bulb.
4	Before electric light was available, humans had little reason
5	to stay up late, as they couldn't do much in the dark. When the
6	light bulb was introduced. People suddenly had the ability to
7	work late into the night. Since the invention of the light bulb
8	people sleep less, although their physical need for sleep had
9	not changed. This loss of sleep will surely have a great effect
10	on our society.

STRATEGIES FOR
REVISING, EDITING,
AND PROOFREADING

▶ **Read the text carefully.**

▶ **Note the parts that are confusing** or don't make sense. What kinds of errors would such problems signal?

▶ **Look for errors** in grammar, usage, spelling, and capitalization. Common errors include
• run-on sentences
• sentence fragments
• lack of subject-verb agreement
• unclear pronoun reference
• lack of transition words

1. What is the BEST modifier to add to the phrase following the dash in the first sentence?

   A. specifically,

   B. mostly,

   C. partly,

   D. also,

2. What is the BEST change, if any, to make to the sentences in lines 5–7 ("When the light bulb . . . late into the night.")?

   A. When the light bulb was introduced; people suddenly had the ability to work late into the night.

   B. When the light bulb was introduced, people suddenly had the ability to work late into the night.

   C. People suddenly had the ability to work late into the night when the light bulb was introduced.

   D. Make no change.

3. What is the BEST change, if any, to make to the sentence in lines 7–9 ("Since the invention . . . had not changed.")?

   A. Since the invention of the light bulb people sleep less, although their physical need for sleep did not change.

   B. Since the invention of the light bulb people sleep less, although their physical need for sleep has not changed.

   C. Since the invention of the light bulb people sleep less, although their physical need for sleep is not changed.

   D. Make no change.

Europe in Transition
400–1789

Primavera [Spring] (c. 1481), Sandro Botticelli. Uffizi, Florence, Italy. Photograph copyright © Scala/Art Resource, New York.

"We are such stuff as dreams are made on. . . ."

—William Shakespeare

PART 1
Heroic Quests:
Literature of the Middle Ages. . . 686–771

⟡

PART 2
Human Possibility:
Literature of the Renaissance and
Enlightenment 772–867

Literature of the Middle Ages

Why It Matters

Valiant knights, elegant damsels, towering cathedrals, moated castles—such associations have helped establish the Middle Ages as an era of magical romance and adventure. Learning about that fascinating time will help you explore its mysteries and understand its magnificent literature.

For Links to the Middle Ages, click on:

HUMANITIES
CLASSZONE.COM

To the Manor Born In the social and economic system called **feudalism,** lords granted land in exchange for loyalty and military service. A lord's estate, called a manor, was a self-sufficient small community that included workshops and a church as well as houses and farmland. Peasants called **serfs** worked the land belonging to the manor.

SCOTLAND

IRELAND

North Sea

ENGLAND

WALES

London • *Canterbury*

English Channel FLANDERS

ATLANTIC OCEAN

NORMANDY

BRITTANY *•Paris*

Chartres

ANJOU **1**

FRANCE BURGUNDY

AQUITAINE

3

Venice•

NAVARRE

•Bologna

Florence•

ARAGON

Adriatic Sea

Rome•

Naples•

Mediterranean Sea

3 **Towns and Cities** As farming improved and the population grew, small communities gradually evolved into towns and cities, where **guilds** —organizations of skilled workers—gained great influence. Cities like Paris and London became important trading centers; Italian ports like Venice and Naples prospered from trade with the East.

A F R I C A

1 Age of Faith During the Middle Ages, the church was a civilizing force in an otherwise unstable world. The church guided human conduct, and its ceremonies and sacraments were important to community life. As an expression of faith, people built huge **cathedrals** like the one at Chartres, France, pictured above, and made pilgrimages to sacred sites.

ASIA

Black Sea

• Constantinople

2 Age of Warfare Castles were built for protection in an era of almost constant warfare. Over time, pagan warriors gave way to Christian knights who followed (at least in theory) a code of conduct known as **chivalry.** Knights also took part in the **Crusades,** wars to free Jerusalem from Muslim rule.

2
Jerusalem

N
W   E
S

0   250   500 miles
0   250   500 kilometers

The fall of the Western Roman Empire ushered in a period of European history known as the Middle Ages. A new social order gradually emerged in this period, which lasted from 476 until about 1500.

The Beginnings
476–700

The European Middle Ages, or medieval period, began in A.D. 476, when the Western Roman Empire finally collapsed. Western Europe became a collection of tribal kingdoms, each with its own laws and customs. Trade and communications declined, roads deteriorated, and many cities died out. Learning also declined, except for what was preserved in the one major institution that survived the collapse—the **Roman Catholic Church.** After a time, religious communities sprang up in the countryside—monasteries for men and convents for women. Gradually, many of the Germanic tribes began to adopt Christianity, starting with the Franks (who occupied what is now France). The church itself began to wield political influence under **Gregory I,** who became pope in 590.

Charlemagne

The Early Middle Ages
700–1000

In the early 700s, Charles Martel came to power among the Franks, establishing a dynasty. His grandson **Charlemagne,** or Charles the Great, expanded the kingdom, uniting most of western Europe in an empire that was the forerunner of the Holy Roman Empire. After his death in 814, however, his heirs split the empire. In these violent times, there arose a system now called **feudalism,** in which landowners, or **lords,** gave out parcels of land, called **fiefs,** in exchange for military service. A person receiving a fief was known as a **vassal.** It was possible for one lord to have several vassals, some of whom might even live in a different country.

The High Middle Ages
1000–1300

As invasions subsided and farming improved, western Europe entered a period of prosperity often called the High Middle Ages. Feudalism dominated continental Europe and was introduced into Britain when **William of Normandy** invaded England in 1066. During this period trade resumed, towns again sprang up, and occupations became more diversified. Merchants and skilled workers banded together in organizations called **guilds.** They held trade fairs and traveled the roads, exchanging not only goods but new ideas. The spread of ideas led to the founding of new centers of learning—the first **universities.**

Throughout the feudal age, the church was a powerful force that bound the people of Europe together. Saint Dominic

and Saint Francis of Assisi founded new orders of traveling preachers who proclaimed the gospel and helped the needy. The new wealth in this age of faith found an outlet in the building of great cathedrals and the making of **pilgrimages,** or journeys to holy sites.

In 1095, Pope Urban II issued a call for a holy war, or **crusade,** to take Jerusalem from Muslim control. Over the next two centuries, several expeditions of knights set out on the Crusades. Though the effort ultimately failed, contact with Byzantine and Muslim cultures contributed to the rebirth of prosperity and learning in western Europe.

The Late Middle Ages

1300–1500

About 1300, medieval Europe entered a period of great change. The growth of banking was transforming the old economy into one based on trade and commerce. Since a strong central government was better for trade, city merchants began to support a strong monarchy. Towns grew into cities, offering a life free of feudal restrictions but also one in which crowded conditions helped spread fires and deadly diseases. Between 1347 and 1352, a terrible plague known as the **Black Death** devastated Europe.

It was a time of conflict within the church and between nations. In England, John Wycliffe began to question church authority. The French monarchy, too, came into conflict with the church during the Great Schism, in which rival popes ruled in Rome and France.

France's great rival of this period, however, was England, with its hereditary claims to French lands. In the **Hundred Years' War** (1337–1453) England gave up those claims but not before executing **Joan of Arc,** a girl who had rallied the French. Spain also saw much fighting until Ferdinand and Isabella succeeded in expelling the Muslims in 1492—the year in which Isabella agreed to finance Columbus's voyage across the Atlantic Ocean.

History to Literature

EVENT IN HISTORY	EVENT IN LITERATURE
Charlemagne's army is attacked in Spain.	The *Song of Roland* celebrates a hero who was killed in that attack.
Thomas à Becket is murdered at Canterbury Cathedral, which becomes a place of pilgrimage.	Geoffrey Chaucer's *Canterbury Tales* vividly portrays people from different walks of life on a pilgrimage to this cathedral.
Political feuds in the Italian city of Florence cause Dante to be banished.	While in exile, Dante is inspired to compose his masterpiece, *The Divine Comedy*.

The Wife of Bath from *The Canterbury Tales*

THE HIGH
MIDDLE AGES

1000

THE LATE
MIDDLE AGES

1300

1500

The Ruling Class

Under feudalism, the ruling class included kings, lords, ladies, and their families—all making up a hereditary nobility. Almost every noble was a vassal of someone above and a lord over those below. Though a king was an acknowledged leader, his real power extended only over his own land. Lords called **barons**, who had received land from a king, wielded great power. They, in turn, had the allegiance of lesser lords and knights.

The knights were expected to follow a code of conduct known as **chivalry**. This code stressed loyalty—to God, to one's feudal lord, and to one's chosen lady.

The Clergy

The church had its own hierarchy, at the top of which was the pope. The church owned much land, and those in charge of church lands—for example, bishops at cathedrals and abbots at monasteries—were often as powerful as feudal lords.

In monasteries and convents, monks and nuns devoted much of their time to study and prayer. Friars did not live in monasteries. Instead, they lived in the outside world, traveling and preaching. Priests serving lords might live comfortably, but many priests were poor and came from the peasant class.

Serfs

Many people in the Middle Ages were **serfs**, peasants who were bound to the land and not permitted to leave the manors where they were born. They farmed the land and did outdoor tasks. In exchange for their labor, their lords were expected to house and protect them.

Merchants and Artisans

After a time, towns and cities offered a more varied life outside the feudal structure. Skilled workers belonged to **guilds**, which regulated particular trades—baking, weaving, tailoring, carpentry, and so on. An apprentice worked for a master craftsman without pay for five to nine years. After learning the craft, he was promoted to journeyman and was paid for his work. To rise to master craftsman, a journeyman had to produce a "master piece" that met guild standards.

Women in the Middle Ages

In early feudal times, the wife of a lord could inherit his property and was even expected to defend the manor when her husband was away. Some women even dressed in armor and mounted warhorses. Other women had positions of authority in convents and abbeys. Most women, however, were still poor and powerless. They spent their lives bearing children, raising their families, and doing household tasks.

Religion and Medieval Culture

During the Middle Ages, the cultural life of western Europe centered on religion. Writers and artists expressed their faith in a variety of art forms. Scholars explored it in philosophical writings and at the new universities. Most people, though, could not read. For them, the arts served as teaching tools. From paintings, sculptures, stained-glass windows, and dramatic presentations of Bible stories, medieval people learned the truths of their faith.

Literature and Manuscripts

During the Middle Ages, scholarly works were written in **Latin,** which was regarded as the language of the educated in Europe. The Celtic and Germanic cultures, however, had oral traditions in which traveling poet-musicians sang in their native languages about heroic deeds and human joys and sorrows. In the

1100s, epics like the French *Song of Roland* and the Spanish *Song of My Cid* celebrated national heroes, and Celtic legends of a king named Arthur were retold in popular romances. Poet-musicians like the Provençal **troubadours** and the German **minnesingers** entertained at noble courts, singing of love and honor. Medieval monks working as scribes wrote down some of these oral compositions; they also copied the Bible and other works in beautiful **illuminated manuscripts**—decorated with gold, silver, and colorful designs and illustrations.

Scholarship and Universities

Medieval scholarship fell mainly to the clergy; in fact, many lords and ladies never even learned to read and write. At first, monasteries and cathedral schools were the centers of learning, but after the 11th century scholars founded important universities in Paris, Bologna, Oxford, and many other cities. The course of study included religion, philosophy, law, medicine, geometry, astronomy, music, grammar, and logic. Instruction was conducted in Latin.

Arts and Architecture

Medieval works of art were intended to glorify God. Nowhere was this religious purpose more evident than in the awe-inspiring **cathedrals,** which often took generations of devoted effort to complete.

Until about 1100, most cathedrals were built in the **Romanesque** style, with small windows and thick walls and columns. Then in the 1100s, the **Gothic** style replaced the Romanesque. Gothic cathedrals thrust upward as if reaching toward heaven. They had tall spires, vaulted ceilings, and huge stained-glass windows that let in light. Paintings, sculptures, and woodcarvings enhanced their interiors. Gothic cathedrals were magnificent temples of the human spirit.

Time Line

c.   approximately

A.D. 1   PRESENT

EVENTS IN EUROPEAN LITERATURE

A.D. 400	600	800

427 St. Augustine of Hippo completes his monumental Latin work *The City of God*

524 Roman scholar Boethius writes *The Consolation of Philosophy*

c. 550 Welsh poets Taliesin and Aneirin compose and sing oral verse

597 Irish poet Dallán Forgaill composes *Elegy of St. Columba*

c. 650 *Heldenlieder*, early oral Germanic verse in praise of heroes

731 The Venerable Bede completes his Latin history of the English people

c. 750 Earliest versions of Old English epic *Beowulf*

c. 850 Scandinavian skalds compose oral verse

c. 950 Beginnings of drama in medieval Europe

c. 950 Oldest surviving Provençal verse

EVENTS IN EUROPEAN HISTORY

A.D. 400	600	800

449 Traditional date of Britain's invasion by Angles, Saxons, and Jutes

476 Collapse of the Western Roman Empire

520 St. Benedict begins writing rules for monasteries

527 Justinian I becomes Byzantine emperor

711 Muslim forces take control of Spain

732 Charles Martel triumphs in Battle of Tours, stopping further Muslim advances in Europe

771 Charlemagne becomes king of the Franks

790–795 Danes (Vikings) attack Britain and Ireland

800 Charlemagne is crowned emperor

c. 860 Vikings under Prince Rurik found a Russian state

912 Abd ar-Rahman III takes power in Muslim Spain, making it a center of learning

962 Otto I, a German king, is crowned Holy Roman Emperor

EVENTS IN WORLD HISTORY

A.D. 400	600	800

400 Nazca civilization flourishing in Peru; Zapotec civilization, in Mexico

500 Empire of Aksum dominates northeastern Africa

c. 500 Indian mathematicians calculate the value of pi

c. 560 Buddhism is introduced in Japan

c. 610 Muhammad begins preaching the faith of Islam

618 Beginning of China's T'ang dynasty

650 Mayan ➤ civilization flourishing in Mexico

794 Beginning of Japan's Heian period

c. 850 Empire of Ghana flourishing in western Africa

900s Anasazi civilization in North America enters classic Pueblo period

935 Korea's Koryo dynasty begins

939 Vietnamese win independence from China

1000   **1200**   **1400**

c. 1100 "Kilhwch and Olwen," Welsh tale that makes early mention of King Arthur

c. 1100 *Song of Roland*, French epic

c. 1140 *Song of My Cid*, Spanish epic

c. 1160 Marie de France and Chrétien de Troyes write narrative verse

c. 1200 *Nibelungenlied*, German epic by an anonymous Austrian poet

c. 1225 Snorri Sturluson preserves Norse (Scandinavian) mythology in his *Prose Edda*

1321 Italian poet Dante Alighieri completes his allegorical epic *The Divine Comedy*

1386 England's Geoffrey Chaucer begins writing *The Canterbury Tales*

c. 1450 Medieval morality plays grow popular

1461 French poet François Villon writes his *Testament*

1485 Pioneer English printer William Caxton prints Sir Thomas Malory's famed retelling of Arthurian romances, *Le Morte d'Arthur*

1000   **1200**   **1400**

1054 Final split between Eastern Orthodox and Roman Catholic churches

1066 Norman conquest of England

1095 Pope Urban II initiates the Crusades to take the Holy Land from the Muslims

1152 Eleanor of Aquitaine marries Henry II of England

1260 Chartres Cathedral consecrated in France

1337 Start of Hundred Years' War between France and England

1347 Bubonic plague, called the Black Death, begins to sweep across Europe

1431 Joan of Arc is burned at the stake

1455 German printer Johann Gutenberg prints landmark Bible on his new press

1492 Muslims ousted from Spain; Columbus begins first voyage to the New World

---

1000   **1200**   **1400**

c. 1000 Viking explorer Leif Eriksson lands in North America

1064 Seljuk Turks come to power in eastern Islamic empire

1099 Knights of the First Crusade capture Jerusalem

1187 Muslims under Saladin retake Jerusalem from Christian crusaders

1206 Genghis Khan begins Mongol conquests in Asia

1235 Sundiata founds West Africa's Mali empire

1368 Chinese overthrow Mongols and establish Ming dynasty

1398 Timur the Lame (Tamerlane), central Asian invader, devastates India

1420 Mutota begins Mutapa empire in southern Africa

1438 Pachacutec becomes ruler of Incas

1453 Byzantine capital of Constantinople falls to the Ottoman Turks

1502 Montezuma II becomes ruler of Aztecs

Medieval Festivals
The age of chivalry lives again at medieval fairs. Modern audiences enjoy the pageantry and excitement of a joust as two "knights" on horseback charge at each other.

Courtly Love
The notion of love as a passionate relationship based on personal choice derives from the "courtly love" tradition of the Middle Ages. In this tradition, a lover was required to make sacrifices to prove himself worthy of his beloved. This tradition influences dating and courtship rituals today.

Knights
The Middle Ages continue to stir the imagination. With his skill in battle, his valor, and his moral code of behavior, what is a Jedi knight in *Star Wars* but an updated version of a medieval knight?

Monarchy
Prince William of Great Britain, the grandson of Elizabeth II, helped design his own coat of arms (shown above) to mark his 18th birthday. The design incorporates Elizabeth's coat of arms with the addition of a white label of three points with a red escallop shell on the central point. This shell is derived from the Spencer coat of arms, used by Prince William's mother—the late Diana, princess of Wales.

from

THE SONG OF
ROLAND

Build Background

The National Epic of France *The Song of Roland* is the earliest surviving French epic poem. It is a masterpiece of a form of medieval French poetry known as *chansons de geste,* or "songs of deeds." These poems—mixing fiction with fact—retell the legends of King Charlemagne (shär′lə-mān′) and his court. This particular poem focuses primarily on the noble deeds of Count Roland, a nephew of Charlemagne.

Charlemagne ruled the Franks (an early Germanic tribe) from 768 to 814. In 800, he was crowned emperor by Pope Leo III. A civilized king, he helped spread Christianity, art, and learning throughout western Europe. During the Middle Ages, he was regarded as the ideal of a Christian ruler.

The Song of Roland is loosely based on an incident that occurred during one of Charlemagne's wars. In 778, the king led a siege on the Spanish city of Saragossa. Unable to take the city, he retreated across the Pyrenees, the mountain range that divides Spain from France. In the narrow valley of Roncesvalles (rŏn′sə-vălz′), his rear guard was attacked and destroyed by local Basque (băsk) warriors. Among those slain was Roland, a leader of the rear guard.

In *The Song of Roland,* the skirmish against the Basques is changed to a battle against the Muslims—referred to as "Saracens" or "pagans." This change had deep meaning for Christians in the 12th century. Fresh in their minds were memories of the First Crusade. This "holy war" had been fought from 1096 to 1099 in an attempt to recover the Holy Land from the Muslims. By fighting the Muslims, Roland is thus depicted as a kind of crusader—a Christian warrior who fights to the death against the enemies of Christ.

Unknown Authorship With its stirring descriptions of battle, *The Song of Roland* was very popular during the Middle Ages. The earliest manuscript of the poem dates from the decades after 1100. No one knows who composed the poem or whether it was the work of a single author. Some scholars believe that the poem is the product of several oral poets, each of whom added something to the retelling before passing it down to the next generation. The poem was most likely performed as an entertainment at court by French poets called *trouvères* (trōō-věr′), who recited or sang such poems before French lords and ladies.

The Story of Roland

As the poem begins, Charlemagne has fought against the Saracens in Spain for seven years. He is supported by his vassals, or those knights who have sworn loyalty to him—including Roland, Oliver, and Archbishop Turpin. The Saracen leader, Marsilion, agrees to accept Charlemagne's demands if the Franks will leave Spain and return to France. Though Roland suspects foul play, he offers to deliver Charlemagne's reply to the Saracens. Charlemagne, however, refuses to send Roland or any of the other volunteers on this risky mission. Roland then nominates his stepfather, Ganelon (gän-lôn'), to serve as envoy to the Saracens. Angry with his stepson for endangering him, Ganelon stoops to treachery. He encourages the Saracens to attack Charlemagne's rear guard on the return to France. He then persuades Charlemagne to give Roland the command of this unit.

As this excerpt begins, Roland and his troops are trapped in a mountain pass in the Pyrenees, greatly outnumbered by the Saracens. Roland's companion Oliver has gone to scout the enemy.

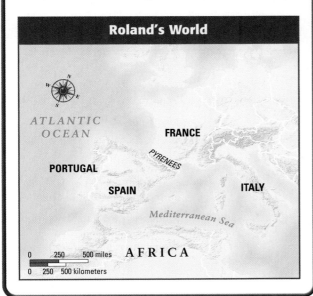

Roland's World

For a humanities activity, click on:

HUMANITIES
CLASSZONE.COM

Connect to Your Life

In this poem, Roland finds himself in a difficult situation. He must decide whether to fight the Saracens with only his own troops or to summon his king for reinforcements. How do you react when you find yourself in difficult situations? Do you usually rely on yourself, or do you seek help from someone you trust? Share your views with a small group of classmates.

Focus Your Reading

LITERARY ANALYSIS: EPIC HERO

In an epic poem, as you recall, the main character is the **epic hero,** a larger-than-life figure. In the Middle Ages, poets adapted the concept of the epic hero to reflect the values important to their culture. As you read this excerpt from *The Song of Roland,* consider Roland's decisions and actions. What do they reveal about his values?

ACTIVE READING: QUESTIONING

To understand Roland's function as the **epic hero,** ask yourself questions as you read. Try using the following tips:

- Pay attention to all questions that come to mind.
- Search for reasons behind events. Ask yourself why the characters act as they do.
- Be aware of your own response to what you read. Note any points that cause surprise, confusion, or other emotions.
- Jot down your questions, and supply the answers if and when you find them.

READER'S NOTEBOOK

As you read, record any questions that come to mind about the events or characters in the poem. Jot down the answers to your questions as they become clear.

Why does Roland decide to fight the Saracens on his own?

from The Song of Roland

Translated by Frederick Goldin

Illustration of Charlemagne's army setting off for Spain. Photograph by
Dagli Orti/Biblioteca Nazionale Marciana, Venice/The Art Archive.

81

Oliver has gone up upon a hill,
sees clearly now: the kingdom of Spain,
and the Saracens assembled in such numbers:
helmets blazing, bedecked with gems in gold,
5   those shields of theirs, those hauberks sewn with brass,
and all their spears, the gonfanons affixed;
cannot begin to count their battle corps,
there are too many, he cannot take their number.
And he is deeply troubled by what he sees.
10 He made his way quickly down from the hill,
came to the French, told them all he had seen. . . .

3 Saracens (săr′ə-sənz): Muslims
during the time of the Crusades.

5 hauberks (hô′bərks): long tunics
made of chain mail.
6 gonfanons (gän′fə-nänz′): banners.

83

Said Oliver: "The pagan force is great;
from what I see, our French here are too few.
Roland, my companion, sound your horn then,
15   Charles will hear it, the army will come back."
Roland replies: "I'd be a fool to do it.
I would lose my good name all through sweet France.
I will strike now, I'll strike with Durendal,
the blade will be bloody to the gold from striking!
20   These pagan traitors came to these passes doomed!
I promise you, they are marked men, they'll die." . . .

87

Roland is good, and Oliver is wise,
both these vassals men of amazing courage:
once they are armed and mounted on their horses,
25   they will not run, though they die for it, from battle.
Good men, these Counts, and their words full of spirit.
Traitor pagans are riding up in fury.
Said Oliver: "Roland, look—the first ones,
on top of us—and Charles is far away.
30   You did not think it right to sound your olifant:
if the King were here, we'd come out without losses.
Now look up there, toward the passes of Aspre—
you can see the rear-guard: it will suffer.
No man in that detail will be in another."
35   Roland replies: "Don't speak such foolishness—
shame on the heart gone coward in the chest.
We'll hold our ground, we'll stand firm—we're the ones!
We'll fight with spears, we'll fight them hand to hand!" . . .

91

Roland went forth into the Spanish passes
40   on Veillantif, his good swift-running horse.
He bears his arms—how they become this man!—
grips his lance now, hefting it, working it,
now swings the iron point up toward the sky,
the gonfanon all white laced on above—
45   the golden streamers beat down upon his hands:
a noble's body, the face aglow and smiling.
Close behind him his good companion follows;
the men of France hail him: their protector!

18 Durendal (dü-rən-däl′): the name of Roland's sword, said to be the same sword formerly used by the Trojan hero Hector.

30 olifant (äl′ə-fənt): Roland's horn.

32 the passes of Aspre (äs′prə): passages through the Pyrenees.

40 Veillantif (vā-yən-tēf′).

He looks wildly toward the Saracens,
50 and humbly and gently to the men of France;
and spoke a word to them, in all courtesy:
"Barons, my lords, easy now, keep at a walk.
These pagans are searching for martyrdom.
We'll get good spoils before this day is over,
55 no king of France ever got such treasure!"
And with these words, the hosts are at each other. . . .

54 spoils: the goods or property seized by the victors after a battle.

105

Roland the Count comes riding through the field,
holds Durendal, that sword! it carves its way!
and brings terrible slaughter down on the pagans.
60 To have seen him cast one man dead on another,
the bright red blood pouring out on the ground,
his hauberk, his two arms, running with blood,
his good horse—neck and shoulders running with blood!
And Oliver does not linger, he strikes!
65 and the Twelve Peers, no man could reproach them;
and the brave French, they fight with lance and sword.
The pagans die, some simply faint away!
Said the Archbishop: "Bless our band of brave men!"
Munjoie! he shouts—the war cry of King Charles. . . .

65 the Twelve Peers: Charlemagne's chief vassals.

68 the Archbishop: Archbishop Turpin, one of the Twelve Peers.

69 munjoie (mün-zhwä′): a medieval war cry of the Franks, meaning "mount joy."

110

70 The battle is fearful and full of grief.
Oliver and Roland strike like good men,
the Archbishop, more than a thousand blows,
and the Twelve Peers do not hang back, they strike!
the French fight side by side, all as one man.
75 The pagans die by hundreds, by thousands:
whoever does not flee finds no refuge from death,
like it or not, there he ends all his days.
And there the men of France lose their greatest arms;
they will not see their fathers, their kin again,
80 or Charlemagne, who looks for them in the passes.
Tremendous torment now comes forth in France,
a mighty whirlwind, tempests of wind and thunder,
rains and hailstones, great and immeasurable,
bolts of lightning hurtling and hurtling down:
85 it is, in truth, a trembling of the earth.
From Saint Michael-in-Peril to the Saints,

HUMANITIES CONNECTION Some of the finest art of the Middle Ages is found in the illuminations that decorate the pages of manuscripts. This one, which dates from about the year 1250, shows attacking knights being driven back from a well-defended town.

from Besançon to the port of Wissant,
there is no house whose veil of walls does not crumble.
A great darkness at noon falls on the land,
90   there is no light but when the heavens crack.
No man sees this who is not terrified,
and many say: "The Last Day! Judgment Day!
The end! The end of the world is upon us!"
They do not know, they do not speak the truth:
95   it is the worldwide grief for the death of Roland. . . .

130

And Roland says: "We are in a rough battle.
I'll sound the olifant, Charles will hear it."
Said Oliver: "No good vassal would do it.
When I urged it, friend, you did not think it right.
100   If Charles were here, we'd come out with no losses.
Those men down there—no blame can fall on them."
Oliver said: "Now by this beard of mine,
If I can see my noble sister, Aude,
once more, you will never lie in her arms!"

86–87 from Saint Michael-in-Peril . . . Wissant: Saint-Michael-in-Peril is a monastery on an island off the coast of France called Mont Saint Michel. Besançon (bĭ-zän-sŏn′) is a city of eastern France; Wissant (vē-säN′) is a port town in the northwest tip of France. The lines mean "throughout all of France."

103 Aude (ō′də) . . . **never lie in her arms:** Roland was to marry Oliver's sister, Aude.

131

105 And Roland said: "Why are you angry at me?"
Oliver answers: "Companion, it is your doing.
I will tell you what makes a vassal good:
        it is judgment, it is never madness;
restraint is worth more than the raw nerve of a fool.
110 Frenchmen are dead because of your wildness.
And what service will Charles ever have from us?
If you had trusted me, my lord would be here,
we would have fought this battle through to the end,
Marsilion would be dead, or our prisoner.
115 Roland, your prowess—had we never seen it!
        And now, dear friend, we've seen the last of it.
No more aid from us now for Charlemagne,
a man without equal till Judgment Day,
you will die here, and your death will shame France.
120 We kept faith, you and I, we were companions;
        and everything we were will end today.
We part before evening, and it will be hard."

112 If you had trusted . . . be here: Oliver earlier had asked Roland to blow his horn, but Roland had refused.
115 prowess (prou′ĭs): skill; ability.

132

Turpin the Archbishop hears their bitter words,
digs hard into his horse with golden spurs
125 and rides to them; begins to set them right:
"You, Lord Roland, and you, Lord Oliver,
I beg you in God's name do not quarrel.
To sound the horn could not help us now, true,
but still it is far better that you do it:
130 let the King come, he can avenge us then—
these men of Spain must not go home exulting!
Our French will come, they'll get down on their feet,
and find us here—we'll be dead, cut to pieces.
They will lift us into coffins on the backs of mules,
135 and weep for us, in rage and pain and grief,
and bury us in the courts of churches;
and we will not be eaten by wolves or pigs or dogs."
Roland replies, "Lord, you have spoken well."

131 exulting: rejoicing.

133

Roland has put the olifant to his mouth,
140 he sets it well, sounds it with all his strength.

The hills are high, and that voice ranges far,
they heard it echo thirty great leagues away.
King Charles heard it, and all his faithful men.
And the King says: "Our men are in a battle."

145 And Ganelon disputed him and said:
"Had someone else said that, I'd call him liar!"

145 **disputed**: disagreed with.

134

And now the mighty effort of Roland the Count:
he sounds his olifant; his pain is great,
and from his mouth the bright blood comes leaping out,

150 and the temple bursts in his forehead.
That horn, in Roland's hands, has a mighty voice:
King Charles hears it drawing through the passes.
Naimon heard it, the Franks listen to it.
And the King said: "I hear Count Roland's horn;

155 he'd never sound it unless he had a battle."
Says Ganelon: "Now no more talk of battles!
You are old now, your hair is white as snow,
the things you say make you sound like a child.
You know Roland and that wild pride of his—

160 what a wonder God has suffered it so long!
Remember? he took Noples without your command:
the Saracens rode out, to break the siege;
they fought with him, the great vassal Roland.
Afterwards he used the streams to wash the blood

165 from the meadows: so that nothing would show.
He blasts his horn all day to catch a rabbit,
he's strutting now before his peers and bragging—
who under heaven would dare meet him on the field?
So now: ride on! Why do you keep on stopping?

170 The Land of Fathers lies far ahead of us." . . .

153 **Naimon** (nā-môn´): an adviser to Charlemagne.

161 **Noples** (nô´plə): a city in Spain.

170 **the Land of Fathers**: France.

168

Now Roland feels that death is very near.
His brain comes spilling out through his two ears;
prays to God for his peers: let them be called;
and for himself, to the angel Gabriel;

175 took the olifant: there must be no reproach!
took Durendal his sword in his other hand,
and farther than a crossbow's farthest shot
he walks toward Spain, into a fallow land,

174 **the angel Gabriel**: an archangel who often serves as God's messenger.

178 **fallow**: plowed but left unseeded.

HUMANITIES CONNECTION Warfare in the Middle Ages was violent and chaotic, as this illumination from a French manuscript shows. Notice the armed knights on horseback and the people trampled underfoot.

and climbs a hill: there beneath two fine trees

180 stand four great blocks of stone, all are of marble;
and he fell back, to earth, on the green grass,
has fainted there, for death is very near.

(169)

High are the hills, and high, high are the trees;
there stand four blocks of stone, gleaming of marble.

185 Count Roland falls fainting on the green grass,
and is watched, all this time, by a Saracen:
who has feigned death and lies now with the others,   **187 feigned** (fānd): pretended.
has smeared blood on his face and on his body;
and quickly now gets to his feet and runs—

190 a handsome man, strong, brave, and so crazed with pride
that he does something mad and dies for it:
laid hands on Roland, and on the arms of Roland,
and cried: "Conquered! Charles's nephew conquered!
I'll carry this sword home to Arabia!"

195 As he draws it, the Count begins to come round.

(170)

Now Roland feels: *someone taking his sword!*
opened his eyes, and had one word for him:
"I don't know you, you aren't one of ours";

grasps that olifant that he will never lose,
200 strikes on the helm beset with gems in gold,
shatters the steel, and the head, and the bones,
sent his two eyes flying out of his head,
dumped him over stretched out at his feet dead;
and said: "You nobody! how could you dare
205 lay hands on me—rightly or wrongly: how?
Who'll hear of this and not call you a fool?
Ah! the bell-mouth of the olifant is smashed,
the crystal and the gold fallen away."

171

Now Roland the Count feels: his sight is gone;
210 gets on his feet, draws on his final strength,
the color on his face lost now for good.
Before him stands a rock; and on that dark rock
in rage and bitterness he strikes ten blows:
the steel blade grates, it will not break, it stands unmarked.
215 "Ah!" said the Count, "Blessed Mary, your help!
Ah Durendal, good sword, your unlucky day,
for I am lost and cannot keep you in my care.
The battles I have won, fighting with you,
the mighty lands that holding you I conquered,
220 that Charles rules now, our King, whose beard is white!
Now you fall to another: it must not be
              a man who'd run before another man!
For a long while a good vassal held you:
there'll never be the like in France's holy land." . . .

173

225 Roland the Count strikes down on a dark rock,
and the rock breaks, breaks more than I can tell,
and the blade grates, but Durendal will not break,
the sword leaped up, rebounded toward the sky.
The Count, when he sees that sword will not be broken,
230 softly, in his own presence, speaks the lament:
"Ah Durendal, beautiful, and most sacred,
the holy relics in this golden pommel!
Saint Peter's tooth and blood of Saint Basile,
a lock of hair of my lord Saint Denis,
235 and a fragment of blessed Mary's robe:
your power must not fall to the pagans,

207 bell-mouth: the flared end of a horn, through which the sound is emitted.

214 grates: makes a rasping noise.

232 pommel: the knob on the handle of a sword.
233–234 Saint Peter's . . . Saint Denis: Saint Peter was one of the twelve Apostles of Christ; Saint Basile was an early church leader; Saint Denis was the patron saint of France.

you must be served by Christian warriors.
May no coward ever come to hold you!
It was with you I conquered those great lands
240 that Charles has in his keeping, whose beard is white,
the Emperor's lands, that make him rich and strong."

174

Now Roland feels: death coming over him,
death descending from his temples to his heart.
He came running underneath a pine tree
245 and there stretched out, face down, on the green grass,
lays beneath him his sword and the olifant.
He turned his head toward the Saracen hosts,
and this is why: with all his heart he wants
King Charles the Great and all his men to say,
250 he died, that noble Count, a conqueror;
makes confession, beats his breast often, so feebly,
offers his glove, for all his sins, to God. . . .

252 offers his glove: a sign of submission to a lord.

176

Count Roland lay stretched out beneath a pine;
he turned his face toward the land of Spain,
255 began to remember many things now:
how many lands, brave man, he had conquered;
and he remembered: sweet France, the men of his line,
remembered Charles, his lord, who fostered him:
cannot keep, remembering, from weeping, sighing;
260 but would not be unmindful of himself:
he confesses his sins, prays God for mercy:
"Loyal Father, you who never failed us,
who resurrected Saint Lazarus from the dead,
and saved your servant Daniel from the lions:
265 now save the soul of me from every peril
for the sins I committed while I still lived."
Then he held out his right glove to his Lord:
Saint Gabriel took the glove from his hand.
He held his head bowed down upon his arm,
270 he is gone, his two hands joined, to his end.
Then God sent him his angel Cherubin
and Saint Michael, angel of the sea's Peril;
and with these two there came Saint Gabriel:
they bear Count Roland's soul to Paradise.

263–264 who resurrected . . . from the lions: In the New Testament, Jesus raised Lazarus from the dead. In the Old Testament, God tamed the lions into whose cage the prophet Daniel had been thrown.

271–272 his angel Cherubin and Saint Michael: *Cherubim* is a class of angels, but the word is used here to refer to one specific angel. Saint Michael is an archangel, known for his skill in battle.

Connect to the Literature

1. What Do You Think? How did you react to Roland's death?

Comprehension Check
- Why do Roland and his companion Oliver quarrel during the battle?
- What happens to Roland when he sounds the horn?

Think Critically

2. ACTIVE READING: QUESTIONING Review the questions you listed in your **READER'S NOTEBOOK.** Discuss with a classmate any questions you still have about this poem.

3. If you were in Roland's position, would you have summoned Charlemagne before the battle or not? Support your answer with details from the poem.

4. How would you evaluate Count Roland as a vassal, or loyal knight, of Charlemagne?

> **THINK ABOUT**
> - his attitude toward Charlemagne
> - his deeds in battle
> - his sense of honor
> - Oliver's view of Roland's key decision

Extend Interpretations

5. What If? While blowing his horn, Roland spits blood and bursts his temples. Eventually, he dies from his superhuman efforts. Imagine, instead, that he had died in battle, slain by a Saracen. How do you think your reaction to the poem might be different?

6. The Writer's Style Words and phrases that appeal to one or more of the five senses are called **imagery.** Reread one of your favorite passages in this poem, perhaps the description of Roland advancing toward the enemy (lines 39–46) or of the storm darkening France (lines 81–93). What images make the passage come alive for you?

7. Connect to Life Explain the meaning of the following **aphorism,** or wise saying, and discuss how it might apply to students today: "Restraint is worth more than the raw nerve of a fool" (line 109).

LITERARY ANALYSIS: EPIC HERO

The **hero,** or **protagonist,** is the central character in a literary work. A hero's good qualities help him or her to triumph over an enemy. **Epic heroes** are larger-than-life figures who do amazing deeds and display great courage. They provide examples of noble behavior that inspire and guide other members of their culture. Count Roland lives by certain values that were important in medieval society. Taken together, these noble values were referred to as the code of honor or code of chivalry.

Cooperative Learning Activity

With a small group of classmates, identify several contrasts between Roland, the hero, and Ganelon, the villain. In a chart like the one shown below, jot down your conclusions. Then use your chart as a starting point to discuss the values that make up Roland's code of chivalry.

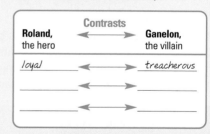

Roland, the hero	Contrasts	Ganelon, the villain
loyal	⟷	treacherous
	⟷	
	⟷	

FROM **Perceval:**

THE STORY OF THE GRAIL

‡ Chrétien de Troyes ‡

Medieval Poet Chrétien de Troyes (krā-tyăn′ də trwä′) was the author of five narrative poems, or **romances,** about King Arthur's knights. Little else is known of this poet's life. His name suggests a connection with Troyes, a city in northeastern France. His excellent education is reflected in his poems. From the dedication of one of them, it can be inferred that he served at the court of Marie, the countess of Champagne. Chrétien also may have served as a court poet to Philip, count of Flanders (in what is now Belgium).

Writer of Arthurian Legends It is believed that Chrétien (c. 1130–c. 1185) was the first to introduce the legends of King Arthur and his knights into French literature. These legends had been passed down orally from one generation to the next in Wales and in Brittany, a region in northwestern France. In composing his works, Chrétien adapted the legends to suit the times in which he lived. His characters are noble heroes inspired by love, honor, and loyalty to their king.

Down through the centuries, Chrétien's Arthurian romances have inspired many authors in different countries, including Sir Thomas Malory, who retold the Arthurian legends in English in *Le Morte d'Arthur* ("The Death of Arthur"), a work completed around 1470. It is from Malory's writings that most of the English-speaking world has come to know King Arthur.

Other Works
Cligés; Yvain; Lancelot

Illustration from medieval manuscript of Perceval at the castle of the wounded Fisher King. Bibliothèque Nationale de France, Paris.

Build Background

The Code of Chivalry Chrétien depicts Arthur as a great king who holds a magnificent court at Camelot. To this court flock the bravest warriors in the land, including Gawain and Lancelot. They form a special fellowship, the Knights of the Round Table. Arthur's knights live by the code of chivalry. This code stresses the highest standards—courage, loyalty, honor, and protection of the weak. One of the knights inspired by this code is Perceval, the hero of Chrétien's poem *Perceval: The Story of the Grail.*

The Holy Grail This poem introduced one of the most important elements of Arthurian literature: the quest for the Holy Grail. After Chrétien, other writers imagined the grail as the cup Jesus drank from at the Last Supper. This cup was also said to hold drops of Jesus' blood shed at the crucifixion. Supposedly, the grail lay hidden in a magic castle, and only a truly pure knight could find it. Many of Arthur's knights searched in vain for the Holy Grail. Perceval, however, was one of the few knights privileged to see it.

Perceval the Knight

When Perceval was a boy, his mother tried to shelter him from knightly adventures. She feared that he would be killed, as were her two other sons and her husband. However, after Perceval encountered several knights, his mother changed her mind. She realized that her son must be free to follow his destiny. She then sent him to King Arthur's court. As he rode off, Perceval saw his mother faint from grief. Nevertheless, he continued on his way. Later, filled with remorse, he tried to find her again. The excerpt you are about to read begins at this point in the story.

Connect to Your Life

In many popular movies, the main character goes on a **quest**, a journey to attain a particular goal. This quest involves a series of adventures that serve as tests or trials. Consider Dorothy in *The Wizard of Oz*. In order to return home to Kansas, she first must overcome many obstacles. Working with a small group, list books or other movies that feature quests. What tests or trials do the main characters face?

Focus Your Reading

LITERARY ANALYSIS: ROMANCE

A **romance** is an imaginative story that describes the deeds of noble heroes. The main character usually goes on a quest in which he faces difficult tests and trials. On this quest, magical or even supernatural events sometimes occur.

ACTIVE READING: STRATEGIES FOR READING A ROMANCE

Romances contain elements found in other narratives—for example, **setting, characters,** and **plot.** In romances, however, these elements create a sense of mystery and wonder. Read a romance the way you might read a fairy tale or a fantasy. Open your mind to the strange and the unusual. Try to visualize the wondrous characters and scenes. Step into the world of chivalry—a world of brave knights, glorious ladies, magical castles, and mysterious events.

READER'S NOTEBOOK This romance is composed of different episodes involving the hero Perceval, or, as he is called, "the boy." As you read, keep track of what happens to him. Create a flow chart like the one below. In each box describe an event and Perceval's reaction to it.

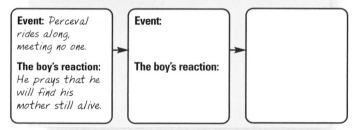

Event: Perceval rides along, meeting no one.

The boy's reaction: He prays that he will find his mother still alive.

Event:

The boy's reaction:

from Perceval: The Story of the Grail

Chrétien de Troyes

Translated by Nigel Bryant

Perceval in Quest of the Holy Grail, Ferdinand Leeke. Photograph copyright © Christie's Images, New York.

Manuscript illumination of Galahad, Boort, Perceval, and his sister arriving at an island, from the *Roman du Saint Graal* (15th century).

GUIDE FOR READING

FOCUS Searching for his mother, the boy finds his way blocked by a river. He calls to a stranger whom he sees fishing from a boat. Read to find out how this stranger treats him.

All day long he rode on, meeting no earthly being, neither Christian man nor Christian woman, who could guide him on his way. He constantly prayed to God the sovereign father to grant that he might find his mother full of life and health, if it were His will. He was still praying when he caught sight of a river flowing down a hill. He saw that the water was swift and deep and he did not dare to ride in; and he said:

"Oh! almighty Lord, if only I could cross this river I think I'd find my mother on the other side, if she's still alive."

He rode along the bank until he came near a rock, and the river washed all round it so that he could go no further. But suddenly he noticed a boat with two men on board, sailing down-stream. He stopped and waited, thinking that they would sail on down to him. But they stopped and stayed dead still in midstream, most securely anchored. The one at the front was fishing with a line, baiting his hook with a little fish slightly bigger than a minnow. The boy, not knowing what to do or where to find a crossing, greeted them and asked them:

"Tell me, my lords, is there a bridge across this river?"

And the one who was fishing replied:

"No indeed, brother, by my faith; nor is there any boat, I think, bigger than the one we're in, which wouldn't carry five men. You can't cross on horseback for twenty leagues upstream or down, for there's no ferry or bridge or ford."

"Then tell me, in God's name," he said, "where I could find lodging."

And the man replied:

"You've need of that and more besides, I think. I will give you lodging tonight. Ride up through the cleft[1] in that rock, and when you come to the top you'll see a house in a valley ahead of you where I live, near the river and the woods."

So he climbed up on to the rock; but when he reached the top he looked all around him and

---

1. **cleft:** an opening made by a crack or break.

saw nothing but sky and earth; and he said:

"What did I come up here to find? Foolishness and nonsense! God bring disgrace on the one who sent me here! What fine guidance he gave

---

BUT JUST THEN, in a valley nearby,
the top of a tower caught his eye.
From here to Beirut you would not
have found a more handsome
one or one more finely placed.

---

me, telling me I'd find a house when I reached the top! Fisherman who told me so, you did a most unworthy deed, if you said it to do me harm."

But just then, in a valley nearby, the top of a tower caught his eye. From here to Beirut you would not have found a more handsome one or one more finely placed. It was square and built of gray rock, flanked by two smaller towers. The hall stood before the tower, and lodges before the hall. The boy rode down towards it, saying that the one who had sent him there had guided him well, and he praised the fisherman, no longer calling him treacherous or dishonest or untruthful, now that he had found a place to lodge. He headed towards the gate; and before the gate he found a drawbridge, and it was lowered. He rode in over the bridge, and four boys came to meet him; two of them disarmed him, while the third led away his horse and gave it hay and oats; the fourth dressed him in a fresh and brand new mantle[2] of scarlet cloth. Then they led him to the lodges; and I tell you, a man could have searched as far as Limoges[3] without finding or seeing any so handsome. The boy stayed in the lodges until he was summoned to

go to the lord, who sent two servants to him. He returned with them to the hall, which was square, being as long as it was wide. In the middle of the hall he saw, sitting in a bed, a most handsome nobleman with graying hair; on his head he wore a hat of sable, dark as mulberry, covered in a deep rich cloth on top, and his whole gown was the same. He was leaning on his elbow, and before him was a huge fire of dry logs, blazing brightly, surrounded by four columns. Four hundred men could easily have sat around that fire and each would have had an excellent place. The columns were very strong, supporting a tall, wide chimney of heavy bronze. The two servants who were escorting the boy, one on each side of him, came before their lord. When the lord saw him coming he greeted him at once, and said:

"My friend, don't be upset if I don't get up to meet you, for I'm unable to."

"In God's name, sir," said the boy, "say no more about it; may God give me joy and health, it doesn't upset me at all."

But the worthy man so exerted himself for the boy's sake that he struggled up as much as he could; then he said:

"Come here, my friend. Don't be afraid of me: sit down here beside me, you're quite safe. I command you."

The boy sat down at his side, and the nobleman asked him:

"Where have you come from today, my friend?"

"Sir," he said, "I rode this morning from Beaurepaire[4]—that was its name."

"God help me," said the nobleman, "you've traveled a very long way today. You must have

---

2. **mantle:** a long, sleeveless coat or cloak.

3. **Limoges** (lē-mōzh'): a city in west-central France.

4. **Beaurepaire** (bō'rə-pâr'): a fortified town that the boy has just rescued from attackers.

HUMANITIES CONNECTION This illustration from a 13th-century manuscript depicts a medieval banquet like the one Perceval attends at the Fisher King's castle. The guests share goblets and dishes and eat with their fingers.

> THE SWORD'S POMMEL was made of
> the finest gold of Arabia or Greece,
> and the scabbard was of
> golden thread from Venice.

left before the watch blew the dawn signal this morning."

"No indeed," said the boy. "The first hour[5] had already been sounded, I promise you."

While they were talking thus, a boy came in through the door; he was carrying a sword hung round his neck, and presented it to the nobleman. He drew it half out of its scabbard, and saw clearly where it was made, for it was written on the sword. And he also learned from the writing that it was of such fine steel that there was only one way it could ever be broken, which no-one knew except the one who had forged and tempered it. The boy who had brought it to him said:

"Sir, the beautiful fair-haired girl, your niece, has sent you this present; you never saw a finer sword as long and as broad as this. You may give it to whoever you like, but my lady would be most happy if it were put to good use where it's bestowed.[6] The one who forged the sword has only ever made three, and he's about to die, so this is the last he'll ever make."

And straight away the lord girded his guest with the sword by its straps, which themselves were worth a fortune. The sword's pommel was made of the finest gold of Arabia or Greece, and the scabbard was of golden thread from Venice. With all its rich decoration, the lord presented it to the boy and said:

"Good brother, this sword was intended and

destined for you, and I very much want you to have it; come, gird it on and draw it."

The boy thanked him, and girded it on so that it was not restricting, and then drew it, naked, from the scabbard; and after gazing at it for a while, he slid it back into the sheath. And truly, it lay splendidly at his side, and even better in his hand, and it seemed indeed that in time of need he would wield it like a man of valor. Behind him he saw some boys standing around the brightly burning fire; he noticed the one who was looking after his arms, and he entrusted the sword to him, and he kept it for him. Then he sat down again beside the lord, who treated him with the greatest honor. And no house lit by candles could ever provide a brighter light than there was in that hall.

PAUSE & REFLECT The stranger turns out to be the lord of the castle. Why do you think he gives the boy the wondrous sword?

FOCUS The boy observes two marvelous objects carried from room to room in the castle. As you read, look for details that tell you about these objects.

While they were talking of one thing and another, a boy came from a chamber clutching a white lance[7] by the middle of the shaft, and passed between the fire and the two who were sitting on the bed. Everyone in the hall saw the white lance with its white head; and a drop of blood issued from the tip of the lance's head, and right down to the boy's hand this red drop ran. The lord's guest gazed at this marvel that had appeared there that night, but restrained himself from asking how it came to be, because he remembered the advice of

---

5. **the first hour:** six o'clock in the morning.

6. **bestowed** (bĭ-stōd′): presented as a gift or honor.

7. **lance:** a weapon with a long wooden handle and a sharp metal point.

Detail of *Mystery of the Holy Grail*, W. Hauschild. Neuschwanstein Castle, Germany.
Photograph by Dagli Orti/The Art Archive.

HUMANITIES CONNECTION This painting depicts the maiden as she carries the
Holy Grail. Notice the unearthly quality that the artist conveys through the maiden's
look of reverence and the light radiating from the chalice.

the nobleman who had made him a knight,[8] who had taught and instructed him to beware of talking too much; he feared it would be considered base[9] of him if he asked, so he did not. Just then two other boys appeared, and in their hands they held candlesticks of the finest gold, inlaid with black enamel. The boys who carried the candlesticks were handsome indeed. In each candlestick burned ten candles at the very least. A girl who came in with the boys, fair and comely[10] and beautifully adorned, was holding a grail between her hands. When she entered holding the grail, so brilliant a light appeared that the candles lost their brightness like the stars or the moon when the sun rises. After her came another girl, holding a silver trencher.[11] The grail, which went ahead, was made of fine, pure gold; and in it were set precious stones of many kinds, the richest and most precious in the earth or the sea: those in the grail surpassed all other jewels, without a doubt. They passed before the bed as the lance had done, and disappeared into another chamber. The boy saw them pass, but did not dare to ask who was served from the grail, for he had taken the words of the wise nobleman to heart. I fear he may suffer for doing so, for I have heard it said that in time of need a man can talk too little as well as too much. I don't know whether it will bring him good or ill, but he asked nothing.

The lord commanded the boys to bring them water and to lay the cloths. Those whose job it usually was did as they were bidden, and the lord and the boy washed their hands in warm water. Two boys brought in a wide table of ivory—according to my source-book it was all one solid piece—and they held it for a moment in front of their lord and the boy until two other boys came with two trestles. The wood of which the trestles were made had two fine qualities: they would last forever, for they were made of ebony, a wood which need never be expected to rot or burn—it is proof against both. The table was set upon these trestles and the cloth was laid. And what should I say about the cloth? No legate[12] or cardinal or pope ever dined at one so white. The first dish was a haunch of venison,[13] seasoned with hot pepper and cooked in fat. There was no shortage of clear, delicious wine to drink, from golden cups. Before them a boy carved pieces from the peppered haunch of venison, drawing the haunch

WHEN SHE ENTERED holding the grail,
so brilliant a light appeared
that the candles lost their brightness
like the stars or the moon
when the sun rises.

to him with the silver trencher, and presented the pieces to them on a slice of perfectly baked bread. And meanwhile the grail passed before them again, but the boy did not ask who was served from it: he refrained because of the nobleman's well-meaning warning not to talk too much—he had taken it to heart and remembered it constantly. But he held his tongue more than he should have done, for as each dish was served he saw the grail pass before him, right before his eyes, and he did not know who was served from it and he longed to know. But he said to himself that before he left he would

8. **the nobleman . . . a knight:** a noble knight had taught the boy the duties and responsibilities of knighthood. He advised the boy not to say too much because his speech would reveal his lack of education.

9. **base:** beneath his dignity.

10. **comely** (kŭm′lē): attractive.

11. **trencher:** a platter on which food is carved or served.

12. **legate** (lĕg′ĭt): an official messenger, often from the pope.

13. **venison:** meat from a deer.

certainly ask one of the boys of the court, but he would wait till the morning when he took his leave of the lord and the rest of the household. And so he put it off till a later time, and concentrated on eating and drinking.

They were not mean[14] with the wines and dishes, and they were delicious and most agreeable. The food was fine and good: the worthy man and the boy were served that night with all the dishes befitting a king or a count or an emperor. And after they had dined they stayed up together and talked, while the boys prepared the beds and provided fruit to eat—and there was fruit of the dearest kind: dates, figs and nutmegs, and cloves and pomegranates, and to finish there were electuaries and ginger from Alexandria, then pliris archonticum and digestive stomaticum.[15] Then there were many different drinks to taste: sweet, aromatic wine, made with neither honey nor pepper, and old mulberry wine and clear syrup. The boy, who had no knowledge of these, was filled with wonder. Then the nobleman said:

"Good friend, it's time to take to our beds for the night. I'll go now, if you don't mind, and sleep there in my chambers, and whenever you wish you can go to sleep in here. I have no strength in my body: I shall have to be carried."

Then four servants, strong and hearty, came from the chamber, and taking hold of the four corners of the blanket that was spread across the bed on which the nobleman was sitting, they carried him where they were told. Other boys stayed with his guest and served him and fulfilled his every need: when he wished they took off his shoes and clothes and bedded him in sheets of fine white linen.

He slept until the morning when day had broken and the household had risen; but he could see no-one as he looked about him, and he had to get up alone whether he liked it or not. Seeing that he had no choice he did the best he could, and put on his shoes without waiting for help;

then he went to don his arms again, finding that they had been brought and left at the head of a table. When he had fully armed his limbs he headed for the doors of the chambers which he had seen open the night before; but the move was fruitless,[16] for he found them shut tight. He called and beat and barged a good deal. Nobody opened up for him or said a word. After calling out for quite a while he turned back to the door of the hall. He found it open, and went down the steps to find his horse saddled, and saw his lance and shield leaning against a wall. He mounted and went looking everywhere, but did not find a living soul and could not see a squire or boy. So he came straight to the gate and found the drawbridge lowered: it had been left like that so that, at whatever time he came to leave, nothing should stop him passing straight across. Seeing that the bridge was down he thought the boys must all have gone into the woods to check their traps and snares. He had no wish to stay any longer, and decided to go after them to see if any of them would tell him why the lance bled, if perhaps there were something wrong, and where the grail was carried. And so he rode out through the gate; but before he had got across the bridge, he felt his horse's hooves rise high into the air. The horse made a great leap; and if he had not jumped so well both horse and rider would have been in a sorry plight. The boy looked back to see what had happened, and saw that the bridge had been raised. He called out, but no-one replied.

"Hey!" he cried. "Whoever raised the bridge, talk to me! Where are you? I can't see you.

---

14. **mean:** stingy.

15. **electuaries** (ĭ-lĕk′chōō-ĕr′-ēz) . . . **pliris archonticum** (plē′rĭs är-kôn′tĭ-kŏŏm) **and digestive stomaticum:** Electuaries were medicines mixed with sweet liquid into a pasty mass. Pliris archonticum and digestive stomaticum were digestive aids.

16. **fruitless** (frōōt′lĭs): unsuccessful.

Come out and let me look at you: there's something I want to ask you."

But he was wasting his time calling out like this, for nobody would answer him.

PAUSE & REFLECT What do you think the bleeding lance and the radiant grail might represent?

FOCUS The boy leaves the castle in a troubled state of mind. In the forest, he comes upon a weeping maiden. Read to find out what she tells him about the lord of the castle.

He headed towards the forest, and came upon a path where he found fresh tracks where horses had passed.

"I think," he said, "that the ones I'm looking for went this way."

So he went galloping through the wood as far as the tracks led him, until he chanced to see a girl beneath an oak tree weeping and crying and lamenting, filled with sorrow and misery.

"Alas!" she cried. "How unfortunate I am! I was born in an evil hour! Cursed be the hour I was conceived and the hour when I was born! Nothing has caused me such anguish before. Would to God my love were not dead in my arms: it would have been better by far if he had lived and I had died. Why did Death, who has brought me such grief, take his soul rather than mine? What's my life worth when I see the one I loved most lying dead? Truly, with him gone I care nothing for my life or my body. Come, Death, and take my soul! Let it be the chambermaid and companion of his, if he'll accept it."

Such was the girl's lament for a knight she was holding, whose head had been cut off. The boy rode straight up to her when he saw her, and as he came near he greeted her, and she greeted him, her head bowed, never ceasing to lament. And the boy asked her:

"Young lady, who killed this knight who is lying in your lap?"

"Good sir," she replied, "a knight killed him, this very morning. But there's something that quite amazes me: God save me, you could ride, so they say, forty leagues the way you've come, and you wouldn't find any good or honest or wholesome lodging, yet your horse is well fed and his coat smooth. If he'd been washed and groomed and given a manger of oats and hay he wouldn't have had a fuller belly or a sleeker coat. And it seems to me that you yourself had a comfortable and restful night."

"Truly, dear girl," he said, "I had all the comfort possible last night, and if it shows it's with good reason. But if you shouted loudly from where we are now, it would be heard quite clearly where I lodged last night. You don't know this country very well, and haven't explored it at all, for without a doubt I had the finest lodging I've ever had."

"Oh, sir! then you lodged at the house of the rich Fisher King!"

AND THE BOY ASKED HER:
"Young lady, who killed this knight who is lying in your lap?"

"By the Savior, girl, I don't know if he's a fisherman or a king, but he's very wise and courteous. I can't tell you anything more, except that I came across two men in a boat very late yesterday, sailing gently along. One of them was rowing, the other was fishing with a hook, and he told me the way to his house last night, and gave me lodging."

And the girl said:

"Good sir, he *is* a king, I can assure you. But he was wounded in a battle and completely crippled, so that he's helpless now, for he was

The Forest Crossed by Perceval to Liberate Amfortas at the Castle of the Grail, Christian Jank.
Neuschwanstein Castle, Germany. Photograph by Dagli Orti/The Art Archive.

struck by a javelin through both his thighs; and he still suffers from it so much that he can't mount a horse. But when he wants to engage in some pleasure and sport he has himself placed in a boat and goes fishing with a hook; that's why he's called the Fisher King. And he finds his enjoyment that way because he couldn't manage or cope with any other sport: he can't hunt in the woods or along the riverbanks and marshes. But he has men to hunt the wildfowl, and huntsmen and archers who go shooting with their bows in the forests. That's why he likes to live in this house just here; for in all the world he could never find a retreat so suited to his needs, and he's had a house built befitting a rich king."

"By my faith, young lady, it's true what you say, and I wondered at it when I came before him last night. I stood a little way from him, and he told me to come and sit beside him, and not to take it for haughtiness if he didn't get up to greet me, for he didn't have the strength or power; so I went and sat at his side."

"Truly, he did you a great honor when he seated you beside him. And tell me now: when you sat down at his side, did you see the lance whose point bleeds, though it has neither flesh nor veins?"

"Did I see it? Yes, in faith!"

"And did you ask why it bled?"

"God help me, I didn't say word."

"Then I tell you, you've done great wrong. And did you see the grail?"

"I saw it clearly."

"Who was holding it?"

"A girl."

"Where did she come from?"

"From a chamber."

"And where did she go?"

"She went into another chamber."

"Did anyone go ahead of the grail?'

"Yes."

"Who?"

"Two boys, that's all."

"What were they holding in their hands?"

"Candlesticks full of candles."

"And who came after the grail?"

"Another girl."

"What was she holding?"

"A small silver trencher."

"Did you ask them where they were going?"

"Not a word crossed my lips."

"God help me, so much the worse. What's your name, friend?"

And the boy, who did not know his name, guessed and said that his name was Perceval the Welshman, not knowing if it were true or not. But it was true, though he did not know it. And when the girl heard this she stood up before him and said angrily:

"Your name is changed, good friend."

"To what?"

"Perceval the wretched! Oh, luckless Perceval! How unfortunate you are to have failed to ask all this! You would have healed the good king who is crippled, and he would have regained the use of his limbs and the rule of his land—and you would have profited greatly! But know this now: many ills will befall both you and others. And know this, too: this has come upon you because of the sin against your mother,[17] for she has died of grief on your account. I know you better than you know me; you don't know who I am, but I was brought up with you at your mother's house for a very long time: I'm your cousin and you are mine. And I grieve no less for your misfortune in not learning what was done with the grail or where it's taken, than for your mother who has died, or for this knight whom I loved and adored because he called me his dear love and loved me like a noble, loyal knight."

"Oh, cousin!" cried Perceval. "If what you've told me is true, tell me how you know."

"I know it to be true," said the girl, "for I saw her laid in the earth." ❖

---

17. **the sin against your mother:** Perceval had left his mother to become a knight.

Lancelot and Guinevere: The Dawn of Love (1867), after Gustave Doré. Steel engraving.
The Granger Collection, New York.

Connect to the Literature

1. What Do You Think?
What was your reaction to the boy's missed opportunities?

Comprehension Check
- What is strange about the lance that is carried in the castle?
- What name does the boy's cousin give him in the forest? Why?

Think Critically

2. ACTIVE READING: STRATEGIES FOR READING A ROMANCE Review the flow chart you made in your **READER'S NOTEBOOK.** What do you think is the most important lesson that the boy learns from his adventures?

3. What do you **predict** the boy will do now that his cousin has told him about his mistake and its consequences?

4. To what extent is the boy to blame for not asking about the lance and the grail? Explain your answer.

> THINK ABOUT
> - the way the lord of the castle has treated him
> - the boy's reason for keeping silent

Extend Interpretations

5. Comparing Texts How does Perceval differ from Roland, the epic hero of *The Song of Roland*?

6. Connect to Life Perceval finds out from his cousin that he should have asked the Fisher King about the lance and the grail. In your own experience, when is it important to speak up? When is it important to remain silent?

LITERARY ANALYSIS: ROMANCE

A **romance** is an imaginative story that includes such elements as noble heroes, a chivalric code of honor, passionate love, and daring deeds. Popular in the Middle Ages, romances still appeal to readers today. One reason is that they transport readers from everyday life to a make-believe world. In this world, marvelous events—even supernatural ones—happen as a matter of course:

While they were talking of one thing and another, a boy came from a chamber clutching a white lance by the middle of the shaft. . . . Everyone in the hall saw the white lance with its white head; and a drop of blood issued from the tip of the lance's head, and right down to the boy's hand this red drop ran.

Moreover, the heroes of romances are suited to this make-believe world. Writers of romances tend to idealize their heroes, depicting them as larger than life.

Cooperative Learning Activity
With a small group of classmates, imagine that Perceval has been transported from the make-believe world of medieval romance to the everyday world of a modern high school. How might he handle real-life situations? Brainstorm a list of situations, and then improvise a skit in which Perceval deals with one or two of them. Perform your skit for other groups.

The Arthurian Legend in Film and Story

In 12th-century France, the legends about King Arthur and his knights inspired Chrétien de Troyes to write romances. Down through the centuries, these same legends have cast their spell on countless other authors. Today, they continue to entertain and thrill modern audiences and readers. Arthur and his knights still brandish sword and lance in books, movies, Broadway shows, comic strips, Web sites, and computer and video games. "Knights," clad in armor, gallop and joust at medieval fairs and restaurants.

Moreover, the ideals represented by King Arthur and his knights still exert their magical power. People still go on quests, embrace noble causes, and try to make the world a better place.

Books

T. H. White, *The Once and Future King* (1958)

John Steinbeck, *The Acts of King Arthur and His Noble Knights* (1976)

Mary Stewart, *The Last Enchantment* (1979)

Rosemary Sutcliff, *The Road to Camlann* (1982)

Marion Zimmer Bradley, *The Mists of Avalon* (1982)

Deepak Chopra, *The Return of Merlin* (1995)

Movies and Television

Camelot (1967)

Monty Python and the Holy Grail (1975)

Excalibur (1981)

Indiana Jones and the Last Crusade (1989)

First Knight (1995)

The TV miniseries *Merlin* (1998)

Computer and Video Games

The Quest: Interactive Game

Zelda

Warcraft

Group Discussion Where have you come upon traces of the Arthurian legend in the modern world? Why do you think people today still retell and enjoy stories about a legendary medieval king and his knights? Share your views with a small group of classmates.

THE LAY OF THE
WERE-WOLF

MARIE de FRANCE

Translated by **Eugene Mason**

Marie de France
(c. 1140–c. 1190)

Her Life Marie de France is the earliest known French woman poet. As with Chrétien de Troyes, little is known about her. In fact, she is known as Marie de France only because the epilogue to her collection of fables states, *"Marie ai nun, si sui de France"* ("Marie is my name; I come from France"). The dialect of Norman French in which she wrote suggests that she grew up in Brittany, a region in northwestern France just south of Normandy. She seems to have been well educated and to have spent time in England at the court of Eleanor of Aquitaine. Under Eleanor's influence, this court became a center of learning and literary activity.

Her Poetry Marie de France earned a place in literary history for a particular type of poem known as the *lai* (lā). A **lai** (or lay) is a brief narrative poem about love and adventure. In writing her *lais,* Marie de France mostly drew on Celtic legends from Brittany. She composed her *lais* to entertain an aristocratic audience, probably performing them to music. Like the romances of Chrétien de Troyes, her *lais* reflect 12th-century views about chivalry and courtly love. In all, she wrote twelve *lais.*

The lais of Marie de France often explore the problems faced by noble women and men who are in love. In "The Lay of the Were-Wolf," for example, the main character is a noble who suffers from a horrid affliction. Periodically, he flees to the woods where he changes from a human into a wolf. Out of his great love for his wife, he reveals this dark secret to her. You are about to read a prose translation of Marie de France's narrative poem. As you read, ask yourself these questions:

1. *How is the depiction of courtly life in this story similar to that in the excerpt from* Perceval: The Story of the Grail?

2. *How does the main character in this story compare with werewolves depicted in horror movies?*

Amongst the tales I tell you once again, I would not forget the Lay of the Were-Wolf. Such beasts as he are known in every land. Bisclavaret[1] he is named in Brittany; whilst the Norman[2] calls him Garwal.

It is a certain thing, and within the knowledge of all, that many a christened man has suffered this change, and ran wild in woods, as a Were-Wolf. The Were-Wolf is a fearsome beast. He lurks within the thick forest, mad and horrible to see. All the evil that he may, he does. He goeth to and fro, about the solitary place, seeking man, in order to devour him. Hearken, now, to the adventure of the Were-Wolf, that I have to tell.

---

1. Bisclavaret (bēs-klä-və-rā′).

2. Brittany . . . the Norman: Brittany is a region of north-western France. Normans are people from Normandy, the region just to the northeast of Brittany.

In Brittany there dwelt a baron who was marvelously esteemed of all his fellows. He was a stout knight, and a comely, and a man of office and repute. Right private was he to the mind of his lord, and dear to the counsel of his neighbors. This baron was wedded to a very worthy dame, right fair to see, and sweet of semblance.[3] All his love was set on her, and all her love was given again to him. One only grief had this lady. For three whole days in every week her lord was absent from her side. She knew not where he went, nor on what errand. Neither did any of his house know the business which called him forth.

On a day when this lord was come again to his house, altogether joyous and content, the lady took him to task, right sweetly, in this fashion,

"Husband," said she, "and fair, sweet friend, I have a certain thing to pray of you. Right willingly would I receive this gift, but I fear to anger you in the asking. It is better for me to have an empty hand, than to gain hard words."

When the lord heard this matter, he took the lady in his arms, very tenderly, and kissed her.

"Wife," he answered, "ask what you will. What would you have, for it is yours already?"

"By my faith," said the lady, "soon shall I be whole. Husband, right long and wearisome are the days that you spend away from your home. I rise from my bed in the morning, sick at heart, I know not why. So fearful am I, lest you do aught to your loss, that I may not find any comfort. Very quickly shall I die for reason of my dread. Tell me now, where you go, and on what business! How may the knowledge of one who loves so closely, bring you to harm?"

"Wife," made answer the lord, "nothing but evil can come if I tell you this secret. For the

> "NOTHING BUT EVIL CAN COME IF I TELL YOU THIS SECRET."

mercy of God do not require it of me. If you but knew, you would withdraw yourself from my love, and I should be lost indeed."

When the lady heard this, she was persuaded that her baron sought to put her by with jesting words.[4] Therefore she prayed and required him the more urgently, with tender looks and speech, till he was overborne, and told her all the story, hiding naught.

"Wife, I become Bisclavaret. I enter in the forest, and live on prey and roots, within the thickest of the wood."

After she had learned his secret, she prayed and entreated the more as to whether he ran in his raiment, or went spoiled of vesture.[5]

"Wife," said he, "I go naked as a beast."

"Tell me, for hope of grace, what you do with your clothing?"

"Fair wife, that will I never. If I should lose my raiment, or even be marked as I quit my vesture, then a Were-Wolf I must go for all the days of my life. Never again should I become man, save in that hour my clothing were given back to me. For this reason never will I show my lair."[6]

"Husband," replied the lady to him, "I love you better than all the world. The less cause have you for doubting my faith, or hiding any tittle[7] from me. What savor is here of friendship? How have I made forfeit of your love; for what sin do you mistrust my honor? Open now your heart, and tell what is good to be known."

---

3. **semblance:** outward appearance.

4. **put her by with jesting words:** put her off or distract her by joking with her.

5. **raiment . . . vesture:** Both words are old-fashioned terms for clothing.

6. **lair:** an animal's den.

7. **tittle:** very small bit or portion.

The Werewolf of Eschenbach, Germany (1685). Line engraving. The Granger Collection, New York.

So at the end, outwearied and overborne by her importunity,[8] he could no longer refrain, but told her all.

"Wife," said he, "within this wood, a little from the path, there is a hidden way, and at the end thereof an ancient chapel, where oftentimes I have bewailed my lot. Near by is a great hollow stone, concealed by a bush, and there is the secret place where I hide my raiment, till I would return to my own home."

On hearing this marvel the lady became sanguine of visage,[9] because of her exceeding fear. She dared no longer to lie at his side, and turned over in her mind, this way and that, how best she could get her from him. Now there was a certain knight of those parts, who, for a great while, had sought and required this lady for her love. This knight had spent long years in her service, but little enough had he got thereby, not even fair words, or a promise. To him the dame wrote a letter, and meeting, made her purpose plain.

"Fair friend," said she, "be happy. That which you have coveted so long a time, I will grant without delay. Never again will I deny your suit. My heart, and all I have to give, are yours, so take me now as love and dame."

Right sweetly the knight thanked her for her grace, and pledged her faith and fealty.[10] When she had confirmed him by an oath, then she told him all this business of her lord—why he went, and what he became, and of his ravening[11] within the wood. So she showed him of the chapel, and of the hollow stone, and of how to spoil the

---

8. **importunity** (ĭm′pôr-tōō′nĭ-tē): persistence in asking.

9. **sanguine** (săng′gwĭn) **of visage**: red in the face.

10. **fealty**: loyalty; allegiance.

11. **ravening**: seeking prey or plunder.

Were-Wolf of his vesture. Thus, by the kiss of his wife, was Bisclavaret betrayed. Often enough had he ravished[12] his prey in desolate places, but from this journey he never returned. His kinsfolk and acquaintance came together to ask of his tidings, when this absence was noised abroad. Many a man, on many a day, searched the woodland, but none might find him, nor learn where Bisclavaret was gone.

The lady was wedded to the knight who had cherished her for so long a space. More than a year had passed since Bisclavaret disappeared. Then it chanced that the King would hunt in that self-same wood where the Were-Wolf lurked. When the hounds were unleashed they ran this way and that, and swiftly came upon his scent. At the view the huntsman winded on his horn, and the whole pack were at his heels. They followed him from morn to eve, till he was torn and bleeding, and was all adread lest they should pull him down. Now the King was very close to the quarry, and when Bisclavaret looked upon his master, he ran to him for pity and for grace. He took the stirrup within his paws, and fawned upon the prince's foot. The King was very fearful at this sight, but presently he called his courtiers to his aid.

"Lords," cried he, "hasten hither, and see this marvelous thing. Here is a beast who has the sense of man. He abases[13] himself before his foe, and cries for mercy, although he cannot speak. Beat off the hounds, and let no man do

him harm. We will hunt no more to-day, but return to our own place, with the wonderful quarry we have taken."

The King turned him about, and rode to his hall, Bisclavaret following at his side. Very near to his master the Were-Wolf went, like any dog, and had no care to seek again the wood. When the King had brought him safely to his own castle, he rejoiced greatly, for the beast was fair and strong, no mightier had any man seen. Much pride had the King in his marvelous beast. He held him so dear, that he bade all those who wished for his love, to cross the Wolf in naught, neither to strike him with a rod, but ever to see that he was richly fed and kenneled warm. This commandment the Court observed willingly. So all the day the Wolf sported with the lords, and at night he lay within the chamber of the King. There was not a man who

---

12. **ravished:** seized and carried away by force.
13. **abases:** lowers or humbles.

did not make much of the beast, so frank was he and debonair.[14] None had reason to do him wrong, for ever was he about his master, and for his part did evil to none. Every day were these two companions together, and all perceived that the King loved him as his friend.

Hearken now to that which chanced.

The King held a high Court, and bade his great vassals and barons, and all the lords of his venery[15] to the feast. Never was there a goodlier feast, nor one set forth with sweeter show and pomp. Amongst those who were bidden, came that same knight who had the wife of Bisclavaret for dame. He came to the castle, richly gowned, with a fair company, but little he deemed whom he would find so near. Bisclavaret marked his foe the moment he stood within the hall. He ran towards him, and seized him with his fangs, in the King's very presence, and to the view of all. Doubtless he would have done him much mischief, had not the King called and chidden him, and threatened him with a rod. Once, and twice, again, the Wolf set upon the knight in the very light of day. All men marveled at his malice, for sweet and serviceable was the beast, and to that hour had shown hatred of none. With one consent the household deemed that this deed was done with full reason, and that the Wolf had suffered at the knight's hand some bitter wrong. Right wary of his foe was the knight until the feast had ended, and all the barons had taken farewell of their lord, and departed, each to his own house. With these, amongst the very first, went that lord whom Bisclavaret so fiercely had assailed.[16] Small was the wonder that he was glad to go.

No long while after this adventure it came to pass that the courteous King would hunt in that forest where Bisclavaret was found. With the prince came his wolf, and a fair company. Now at nightfall the King abode within a certain lodge of that country, and this was known of that dame who before was the wife of Bisclavaret. In the morning the lady clothed her in her most dainty apparel, and hastened to the lodge, since she desired to speak with the King, and to offer him a rich present. When the lady entered in the chamber, neither man nor leash might restrain the fury of the Wolf. He became as a mad dog in his hatred and malice. Breaking from his bonds he sprang at the lady's face, and bit the nose from her visage. From every side men ran to the succor[17] of the dame. They beat off the wolf from his prey, and for a little would have cut him in pieces with their swords. But a certain wise counselor said to the King, "Sire, hearken now to me. This beast is always with you, and there is not one of us all who has not known him for long. He goes in and out amongst us, nor has molested any man, neither done wrong or felony to any, save only to this dame, one only time as we have seen. He has done evil to this lady, and to that knight, who is now the husband of the dame. Sire, she was once the wife of that lord who was so close and private to your heart, but who went, and none might find where he had gone. Now, therefore, put the dame in a sure place, and question her straitly, so that she may tell—if perchance she knows thereof—for what reason this Beast holds her in such mortal hate. For many a strange deed has chanced, as well we know, in this marvelous land of Brittany."

> NEITHER MAN NOR LEASH MIGHT RESTRAIN THE FURY OF THE WOLF.

---

14. **debonair** (dĕb´ə-nâr´): pleasant; carefree and cheerful.

15. **the lords of his venery** (vĕn´ə-rē): the huntsmen of the king.

16. **assailed:** attacked repeatedly and violently.

17. **succor:** help; aid.

HUMANITIES CONNECTION This 15th-century woodcut from Germany shows a werewolf attacking its victim while a stunned companion looks on. The artist captures the fury of the werewolf, who has lost his humanity and descended to the level of a beast. Notice the contrast between the woods, where the beast dwells, and the house, where humans live.

The King listened to these words, and deemed the counsel good. He laid hands upon the knight, and put the dame in surety[18] in another place. He caused them to be questioned right straitly, so that their torment was very grievous. At the end, partly because of her distress, and partly by reason of her exceeding fear, the lady's lips were loosed, and she told her tale. She showed them of the betrayal of her lord, and how his raiment was stolen from the hollow stone. Since then she knew not where he went, nor what had befallen him, for he had never come again to his own land. Only, in her heart, well she deemed and was persuaded, that Bisclavaret was he.

Straightway the King demanded the vesture of his baron, whether this were to the wish of the lady, or whether it were against her wish. When the raiment was brought him, he caused it to be spread before Bisclavaret, but the Wolf made as though he had not seen. Then that cunning and crafty counselor took the King apart, that he might give him a fresh rede.[19]

"Sire," said he, "you do not wisely, nor well, to set this raiment before Bisclavaret, in the sight of all. In shame and much tribulation must he lay aside the beast, and again become man. Carry your wolf within your most secret chamber, and put his vestment therein. Then close the

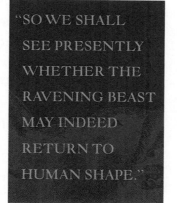

"SO WE SHALL SEE PRESENTLY WHETHER THE RAVENING BEAST MAY INDEED RETURN TO HUMAN SHAPE."

door upon him, and leave him alone for a space. So we shall see presently whether the ravening beast may indeed return to human shape."

The King carried the Wolf to his chamber, and shut the doors upon him fast. He delayed for a brief while, and taking two lords of his fellowship with him, came again to the room. Entering therein, all three, softly together, they found the knight sleeping in the King's bed, like a little child. The King ran swiftly to the bed and taking his friend in his arms, embraced and kissed him fondly, above a hundred times. When the man's speech returned once more, he told him of his adventure. Then the King restored to his friend the fief[20] that was stolen from him, and gave such rich gifts, moreover, as I cannot tell. As for the wife who had betrayed Bisclavaret, he bade her avoid his country, and chased her from the realm. So she went forth, she and her second lord together, to seek a more abiding city, and were no more seen.

The adventure that you have heard is no vain fable. Verily and indeed it chanced as I have said. The Lay of the Were-Wolf, truly, was written that it should ever be borne in mind. ❖

---

18. **surety:** custody.

19. **rede** (rēd): piece of advice or counsel.

20. **fief** (fēf): piece of land; estate.

Dante Alighieri

OVERVIEW

Life and Times	732
from the **Inferno** ~ EPIC POETRY	736
from **La Vita Nuova** ~ AUTOBIOGRAPHY	757
The Author's Style	760
Author Study Project	761

> *"More can be learned about how to write poetry from Dante than from any English poet."*
>
> —*T. S. Eliot*

Italy's Poetic Genius

Dante Alighieri (dän′tā ä′lē-gyĕ′rē) *is widely regarded as the world's greatest poet of ideas. He was not only a learned man but also a keen observer of everyday life. His poem* The Divine Comedy *is a monumental work—vast in scope, rich in meaning, and timeless in appeal. Like a medieval cathedral, it is a marvel of construction and detail. In this poem, Dante turned Christian ideas into great literature. One of Dante's countless admirers, the Irish poet William Butler Yeats, once called him "the chief imagination of Christendom."*

1265–1321

SCHOLAR AND PUBLIC SERVANT Dante was born in the city of Florence, in the west-central Italian region of Tuscany. His father provided him with a fine education in both classical and Christian literature. One of his teachers was Brunetto Latini, a Florentine scholar who stressed not only scholarship but the importance of participating in community life. By the age of 18, Dante had taught himself how to write verse. The Florentine poet Guido Cavalcanti, with whom Dante became

	1265 Is born in Florence, Italy	1274 Meets Beatrice for the first time

HIS LIFE HIS TIMES	1245	1250	1255	1260	1265	1270

	1248 King Louis IX of France (Saint Louis) leads the Seventh Crusade.		1260 Ghibellines defeat Guelphs, killing or exiling many of their leaders.	1273 St. Thomas Aquinas completes his Christian philosophical work *Summa theologiae.*

close friends, encouraged Dante's poetic efforts. Yet, true to Latini's teachings, Dante made writing and scholarship secondary to public service. After serving in the army, he pursued a career in politics and diplomacy.

FLORENCE AND ITS POLITICS By the time Dante was born, Florence had evolved into a largely independent city-state. Like many other Italian city-states, it had prospered greatly from trade with the Middle East and Asia and the equipping of soldiers for the Crusades. Moreover, Florence had become the banking center of a growing commercial economy that was replacing feudalism in western Europe.

As a city-state, Florence was basically self-governing and created its own foreign policy. Nevertheless, it suffered from political conflict that had arisen years earlier in the Holy Roman Empire. The conflict was between the Guelphs (gwĕlfs), or those who supported the authority of the pope in Rome, and the Ghibellines (gĭb′ə-lēnz′), or those who supported the authority of the emperor, usually a German-speaking monarch.

Medieval Florence

LITERARY *Contributions*

Works in Italian By showing the literary power of the Italian language, Dante inspired writers throughout western Europe to write in their native tongues instead of in Latin. Dante's Italian works include

La Vita Nuova [The New Life]
Il Convivio [The Banquet]
La Divina Commedia [The Divine Comedy], an epic poem in three parts:
• *Inferno* [Hell]
• *Purgatorio* [Purgatory]
• *Paradiso* [Paradise]

Works in Latin Like most other educated writers of his day, Dante also wrote in Latin, the language of Church scholarship. His Latin works include

De Vulgari Eloquentia [Concerning Vernacular Eloquence]
De Monarchia [On Monarchy]
Eclogae Latinae (poetry)

| 1277 Is betrothed to Gemma Donati | 1289 Fights against the Ghibellines in the Battle of Campaldino | 1290 Mourns Beatrice | c. 1293 Writes *La Vita Nuova* | 1302 Is exiled from Florence |

1275   1280   1285   1290   1295   1300   1305

| 1274 Edward I of England is crowned at Westminster Abbey. | 1279 Kublai Khan conquers China's Sung Dynasty. | 1291 Crusades end with Muslims maintaining control of Jerusalem. | 1295 Italian traveler Marco Polo returns to Venice from China. | c. 1301 The artist Cimabue creates his *St. John the Evangelist.* |

Dante, who supported the Guelphs, fought the Ghibellines in the Battle of Campaldino in 1289.

POLITICAL LIFE AND EXILE In 1295, Dante joined Florence's medical guild, which was open to all scholars, and used his membership as a springboard to public office. He rose from city councilman to prior, a high-ranking position, and also served as an occasional ambassador to other Italian city-states. Unfortunately, Florence was again in turmoil. The Guelphs had split into two factions—the Whites and the Blacks. Dante, a White Guelph, sided against the pope, instead of with him. In 1301, while Dante was away on a diplomatic mission, the Black Guelphs gained control of Florence. They banished Dante from the city. He spent the rest of his life in exile, mostly at the courts of those sympathetic to the White Guelphs.

DANTE'S INSPIRATION Most of Dante's early verse is courtly love poetry, in which the speaker expresses love for an ideal lady out of his reach. Though Dante married Gemma Donati, a woman to whom he had been betrothed when he was a boy, the object of his poetic devotions was a woman named Beatrice—probably Beatrice Portinari, daughter of a Florentine nobleman. According to *La Vita Nuova*—a collection of his early love poems to Beatrice and his accounts of how he came to write them—Dante met Beatrice only twice: once when he was nine and again nine years later. Yet in her he saw all that was virtuous, and her untimely death at age 24 broke his heart.

THE DIVINE COMEDY Dante wrote his masterpiece, the epic poem *The Divine Comedy*, during his exile. He began the poem around 1308 and finished it shortly before his death in 1321. It consists of three sections: *Inferno*, *Purgatorio*, and *Paradiso*. Each section is divided into parts called cantos (the Italian word *canto* comes from a Latin word meaning "song"). The cantos, 100 in all, are written in three-line stanzas in a verse form known as *terza rima*, which Dante himself created. To Dante, the number three had deep spiritual meaning. It suggested the divine mystery of the three persons in one God, which is central to Christian belief.

c. 1308
Begins *The Divine Comedy*

1319
Moves to the court of Guido Novello da Polenta in Ravenna

1321
Completes *The Divine Comedy*; dies in Ravenna

1310   1315   1320   1325

1312
Henry VII is crowned Holy Roman Emperor but dies a year later.

c. 1320
The artist Giotto paints frescoes in Florence's Santa Croce chapels.

1325
The Aztecs found their capital, Tenochtitlán, on the site of present-day Mexico City.

Dante with His Poem (1465), Domenico di Michelino. Duomo, Florence, Italy.
Photograph copyright © Scala/Art Resource, New York.

The Divine Comedy: Dante's Dream Vision

This painting by a 15th-century Italian artist was inspired by Dante's masterpiece, *The Divine Comedy*. In the center of the painting, Dante holds a book of his poetry. To his left is the city of Florence, with its domed cathedral. The other scenes show the places Dante visits in the three sections of *The Divine Comedy*: On his right, sinners descend into the terrible pit that is Hell. In the back, sinners try to climb the mountain of Purgatory, which leads to Paradise.

In *The Divine Comedy*, Dante himself is the main character, a traveler who stands for all of humanity. He first journeys down into the Inferno, or Hell, a hideous realm where sinners receive fitting eternal punishments. He then travels to Purgatory, a place of temporary punishment, and finally to Paradise, where he stands before the throne of God. On his journey, Dante encounters characters from mythology, from history, and from his own time—including some of his friends and enemies. The poem, therefore, is not only an imaginative vision of the afterlife but also a rich portrait of medieval times.

When Dante wrote his poem, he gave it the title *Commedia* [Comedy] because it ends happily. In time, it became known as *The Divine Comedy* because of its deeply spiritual content. To many readers, the poem suggests the soul's odyssey from the darkness of sin to a glimpse of eternal glory, beauty, and truth.

One of the greatest works in all of literature, Dante's poem was very popular in his own lifetime. According to one commentator, children ran after Dante in the streets to touch the garment of the man who had visited Hell. Down through the centuries, the poem has inspired a host of writers, artists, and musicians.

AUTHOR LINK
CLASSZONE.COM

NetActivities:
Author Exploration

FROM
THE

INFERNO
DANTE ALIGHIERI

Build Background

The *Inferno* is the first of the three sections of *The Divine Comedy.* Here, Dante describes the first stage of his journey through the afterlife. He and his guide, the Roman poet Virgil, travel through the different circles, or levels, of Hell.

Dante envisions Hell as a pit within the earth where sinners are punished in the afterlife for their evil deeds. This pit is shaped like a cone that funnels downward. It has nine levels: the lower the level, the worse the sinner—and the more terrible the punishment.

1. Limbo

2. The Lustful

3. The Gluttonous

4. The Greedy

5. The Wrathful

6. Heretics

7. The Violent

8. Frauds

9. Betrayers

Connect to Your Life

With a classmate, list several acts that you consider wrong—for example, forgery, theft, and murder. Debate the seriousness of the actions and rank them from least to most serious. What did you rank as the greatest wrong?

Focus Your Reading

LITERARY ANALYSIS: ALLEGORY

The Divine Comedy can be read as an **allegory,** a work with two layers of meaning. In an allegory, most of the characters, places, objects, and events stand for abstract ideas or qualities. For example, in the *Inferno*, a physical place—such as the "dark woods"—stands for Dante's spiritual condition.

ACTIVE READING: CLARIFYING MEANING

To explore meaning in this allegory, use these tips:
- Refer to the Guide for Reading, the Preview paragraphs, and the sidenotes for help in understanding difficult words and passages.
- Reread difficult passages slowly and carefully. Try to **paraphrase** them—that is, restate them in your own words.
- Ask yourself what the characters, places, objects, and events might represent.

📖 **READER'S NOTEBOOK** As you read, take notes about the characters and events. Write down the Pause & Reflect questions you encounter and provide an answer for each.

WORDS TO KNOW **Vocabulary Preview**

abject	discourse	hapless
avail	disdain	imbued
compulsion	fortitude	protrude
discern		

from the Inferno

Dante Alighieri

Translated by Robert Pinsky

GUIDE FOR READING

FOCUS Dante finds himself trapped in a dark forest. As you read, try to decide what the path, the woods, and the three beasts might represent.

Preview Halfway through life, Dante wanders off the right path and into dark, frightening woods. As he tries to climb a hill, he finds his way blocked by three beasts—a leopard, a lion, and a she-wolf. He later meets the spirit of the poet Virgil, who tells him he must take another path. Virgil offers to guide Dante on a journey through Hell and Purgatory.

CANTO 1

Midway on our life's journey, I found myself
   In dark woods, the right road lost. To tell
   About those woods is hard—so tangled and rough

And savage that thinking of it now, I feel
5   The old fear stirring: death is hardly more bitter.
   And yet, to treat the good I found there as well

I'll tell what I saw, though how I came to enter
   I cannot well say, being so full of sleep
   Whatever moment it was I began to blunder

10 Off the true path. But when I came to stop
   Below a hill that marked one end of the valley
   That had pierced my heart with terror, I looked up

The Granger Collection, New York.

HUMANITIES CONNECTION This illumination, from a 15th-century Italian manuscript, shows Virgil rescuing Dante from the three beasts. Leaving the dark woods, the two poets embark on their journey.

Toward the crest and saw its shoulders already
    Mantled in rays of that bright planet that shows
15   The road to everyone, whatever our journey.

Then I could feel the terror begin to ease
    That churned in my heart's lake all through the night.
    As one still panting, ashore from dangerous seas,

Looks back at the deep he has escaped, my thought
20   Returned, still fleeing, to regard that grim defile
    That never left any alive who stayed in it.

After I had rested my weary body awhile
    I started again across the wilderness,
    My left foot always lower on the hill,

25   And suddenly—a leopard, near the place
    The way grew steep: lithe, spotted, quick of foot.
    Blocking the path, she stayed before my face

13 crest: the top of the hill.

14 that bright planet: the sun, which in Dante's time was believed to be a planet that moved around the earth.

17 my heart's lake: This detail reflects the medieval belief that the heart was a reservoir for blood.

20 defile: a steep, narrow valley.

25–38 a leopard . . . a lion . . . a grim she-wolf: These three animals are generally believed to stand for lust, pride, and greed, the three general categories of sin treated in the poem.

And more than once she made me turn about
   To go back down. It was early morning still,
30   The fair sun rising with the stars attending it

As when Divine Love set those beautiful
   Lights into motion at creation's dawn,
   And the time of day and season combined to fill

My heart with hope of that beast with festive skin—
35   But not so much that the next sight wasn't fearful:
   A lion came at me, his head high as he ran,

Roaring with hunger so the air appeared to tremble.
   Then, a grim she-wolf—whose leanness seemed to compress
   All the world's cravings, that had made miserable

40   Such multitudes; she put such heaviness
   Into my spirit, I lost hope of the crest.
   Like someone eager to win, who tested by loss

Surrenders to gloom and weeps, so did that beast
   Make me feel, as harrying toward me at a lope
45   She forced me back toward where the sun is lost.

PAUSE & REFLECT How does Dante react to the she-wolf?

FOCUS Driven back into the dark woods, Dante meets
the spirit of Virgil. Read to find out why Virgil is a good
guide for the lost poet.

While I was ruining myself back down to the deep,
   Someone appeared—one who seemed nearly to fade
   As though from long silence. I cried to his human shape

In that great wasteland: "Living man or shade,
50   Have pity and help me, whichever you may be!"
   "No living man, though once I was," he replied.

"My parents both were Mantuans from Lombardy,
   And I was born *sub Julio*, the latter end.
   I lived in good Augustus's Rome, in the day

34 that beast with festive skin:
the leopard, whose coat is gaily
colored.

**38–39 whose leanness . . . crav-
ings:** whose thinness seemed to
squeeze together all the desires of
the world.

44 harrying: moving threateningly.

46 ruining: falling into ruin or disaster.

49 shade: a spirit of a dead person.

52 Mantuans from Lombardy:
Lombardy, a region in northern
Italy, is where the city of Mantua is
located.

53 *sub Julio*: during the reign of
Julius Caesar.

54 Augustus's Rome: Rome under
its first emperor, Augustus, grandnephew of Julius Caesar.

55   Of the false gods who lied. A poet, I hymned
          Anchises' noble son, who came from Troy
          When superb Ilium in its pride was burned.

      But you—why go back down to such misery?
          Why not ascend the delightful mountain, source
60   And principle that causes every joy?"

      "Then are you Virgil? Are you the font that pours
          So overwhelming a river of human speech?"
          I answered, shamefaced. "The glory and light are yours,

      That poets follow—may the love that made me search
65   Your book in patient study <u>avail</u> me, Master!
          You are my guide and author, whose verses teach

      The graceful style whose model has done me honor.
          See this beast driving me backward—help me resist,
          For she makes all my veins and pulses shudder."

70   "A different path from this one would be best
          For you to find your way from this feral place,"
          He answered, seeing how I wept. "This beast,

      The cause of your complaint, lets no one pass
          Her way—but harries all to death. Her nature
75   Is so malign and vicious she cannot appease

      Her voracity, for feeding makes her hungrier.
          Many are the beasts she mates: there will be more,
          Until the Hound comes who will give this creature

      A painful death. Not nourished by earthly fare,
80   He will be fed by wisdom, goodness and love.
          Born between Feltro and Feltro, he shall restore

      Low Italy, as Nisus fought to achieve.
          And Turnus, Euryalus, Camilla the maiden—
          All dead from wounds in war. He will remove

56 Anchises' (ăn-kī′sēz′) **noble son:** Aeneas (ĭ-nē′əs), who fled from Troy (Ilium) when it was burned and eventually founded Rome. His story is told in Virgil's *Aeneid* (see pages 356–381).

71 feral: wild; savage.

75–76 appease her voracity: satisfy her hunger.

78–81 the Hound . . . Feltro and Feltro: The Hound may be Cangrande della Scala, who supported Dante in exile and who was born in Verona, between the cities of Feltre and Montefeltro.

82–83 Nisus . . . Turnus, Euryalus (yŏŏ-rī′ə-ləs), **Camilla the maiden:** These are characters in Virgil's *Aeneid* who die in the war between the Trojans and the Latins.

WORDS TO KNOW

avail (ə-vāl′) *v.* to be of use to; help

85   This lean wolf, hunting her through every region
        Till he has thrust her back to Hell's abyss
        Where Envy first dispatched her on her mission.

    Therefore I judge it best that you should choose
        To follow me, and I will be your guide
90   Away from here and through an eternal place:

    To hear the cries of despair, and to behold
        Ancient tormented spirits as they lament
        In chorus the second death they must abide.

    Then you shall see those souls who are content
95   To dwell in fire because they hope some day
        To join the blessed: toward whom, if your ascent

    Continues, your guide will be one worthier than I—
        When I must leave you, you will be with her.
        For the Emperor who governs from on high

100   Wills I not enter His city, where none may appear
        Who lived like me in rebellion to His law.
        His empire is everything and everywhere,

    But that is His kingdom, His city, His seat of awe.
        Happy is the soul He chooses for that place!"
105   I: "Poet, please—by the God you did not know—

    Help me escape this evil that I face,
        And worse. Lead me to witness what you have said,
        Saint Peter's gate, and the multitude of woes—"

    Then he set out, and I followed where he led.

94–96 souls who are content . . . to join the blessed: souls in Purgatory, who know they will someday go to Heaven.

97 one worthier than I: Beatrice.

100–101 where none may appear . . . His law: Virgil, a pagan Roman, did not worship God and thus cannot enter Heaven.

Thinking Through the Literature

1. How does Dante feel about himself at the beginning of the story?

2. What is Dante's attitude toward Virgil?

3. What do you **predict** might happen to Dante on his journey through Hell?

FOCUS The two poets arrive at the gate of Hell and read the inscription above it. They then enter the vestibule and notice the souls confined there. Read to find out about these souls.

Preview In Canto 2, Virgil explains that Beatrice, the woman Dante had idealized and loved from afar when she was alive, descended from Heaven in order to ask him to guide Dante on his journey. In Canto 3, Virgil takes Dante through the gate of Hell into a dark, starless vestibule. They notice the souls of the unsure, those who chose neither good nor evil in life. When the two poets arrive at the shore of the river Acheron, Dante sees an old man gathering sinners to ferry across the river into Hell.

CANTO 3

THROUGH ME YOU ENTER INTO THE CITY OF WOES,
    THROUGH ME YOU ENTER INTO ETERNAL PAIN,
    THROUGH ME YOU ENTER THE POPULATION OF LOSS.

JUSTICE MOVED MY HIGH MAKER, IN POWER DIVINE,
5   WISDOM SUPREME, LOVE PRIMAL. NO THINGS WERE
    BEFORE ME NOT ETERNAL; ETERNAL I REMAIN.

ABANDON ALL HOPE, YOU WHO ENTER HERE.
    These words I saw inscribed in some dark color
    Over a portal. "Master," I said, "make clear

10 Their meaning, which I find too hard to gather."
    Then he, as one who understands: "All fear
    Must be left here, and cowardice die. Together,

We have arrived where I have told you: here
    You will behold the wretched souls who've lost
15   The good of intellect." Then, with good cheer

In his expression to encourage me, he placed
    His hand on mine: so, trusting to my guide,
    I followed him among things undisclosed.

5 primal: original; most important.

9 portal: doorway.

14–15 souls . . . intellect: those who have lost sight of God.

Inscription over the Gate
(1824–1827), William Blake.
Illustration to *Hell*, Canto 3, of
Dante's *The Divine Comedy*.
Watercolor, 52.7 cm × 37.4 cm.
Tate Gallery, London/Art
Resource, New York.

The sighs, groans and laments at first were so loud,
20   Resounding through starless air, I began to weep:
    Strange languages, horrible screams, words <u>imbued</u>

With rage or despair, cries as of troubled sleep
    Or of a tortured shrillness—they rose in a coil
    Of tumult, along with noises like the slap

25   Of beating hands, all fused in a ceaseless flail
    That churns and frenzies that dark and timeless air
    Like sand in a whirlwind. And I, my head in a swirl

Of error, cried: "Master, what is this I hear?
    What people are these, whom pain has overcome?"
30   He: "This is the sorrowful state of souls unsure,

Whose lives earned neither honor nor bad fame.
    And they are mingled with angels of that base sort
    Who, neither rebellious to God nor faithful to Him,

30–31 souls unsure, . . . bad fame:
those souls who in life acted neither for good nor evil.

WORDS TO KNOW

imbued (ĭm-byood') *adj.* filled or inspired **imbue** *v.*

Chose neither side, but kept themselves apart—
35 Now Heaven expels them, not to mar its splendor,
    And Hell rejects them, lest the wicked of heart

Take glory over them." And then I: "Master,
    What agony is it, that makes them keen their grief   **38 keen:** wail.
    With so much force?" He: "I will make brief answer:

40 They have no hope of death, but a blind life
    So abject, they envy any other fate.
    To all memory of them, the world is deaf.

Mercy and justice disdain them. Let us not
    Speak of them: look and pass on." I looked again:
45 A whirling banner sped at such a rate

It seemed it might never stop; behind it a train
    Of souls, so long that I would not have thought
    Death had undone so many. When more than one

I recognized had passed, I beheld the shade   **49–51 the shade . . . by cowardice:**
50 Of him who made the Great Refusal, impelled   probably a reference to Pope
    By cowardice: so at once I understood   Celestine V, who gave up the papa-
                                                         cy after only five months because
                                                         of political pressures on him.

Beyond all doubt that this was the dreary guild   **52–53 the dreary guild . . . enemies:**
    Repellent both to God and His enemies—   the unhappy group offensive to
    Hapless ones never alive, their bare skin galled   both God and demons.

                                                         54 galled: broken; made sore.

55 By wasps and flies, blood trickling down the face,
    Mingling with tears for harvest underfoot
    By writhing maggots. Then, when I turned my eyes   **57 maggots:** the larvae of flies,
                                                         often found in decaying matter.

Farther along our course, I could make out
    People upon the shore of some great river.
60 "Master," I said, "it seems by this dim light

That all of these are eager to cross over—
    Can you tell me by what law, and who they are?"
    He answered, "Those are things you will discover

When we have paused at Acheron's dismal shore."
65 I walked on with my head down after that,
    Fearful I had displeased him, and spoke no more.

PAUSE & REFLECT How are the souls of the unsure
punished in the afterlife?

FOCUS Dante notices an old man in a boat. Read to find
out who he is and what he does.

Then, at the river—an old man in a boat:
    White-haired, as he drew closer shouting at us,
    "Woe to you, wicked souls! Give up the thought

70 Of Heaven! I come to ferry you across
    Into eternal dark on the opposite side,
    Into fire and ice! And you there—leave this place,

You living soul, stand clear of these who are dead!"
    And then, when he saw that I did not obey:
75 "By other ports, in a lighter boat," he said,

"You will be brought to shore by another way."
    My master spoke then, "Charon, do not rage:
    Thus is it willed where everything may be

Simply if it is willed. Therefore, oblige,
80 And ask no more." That silenced the grizzled jaws
    Of the gray ferryman of the livid marsh,

Who had red wheels of flame about his eyes.
    But at his words the forlorn and naked souls
    Were changing color, cursing the human race,

85 God and their parents. Teeth chattering in their skulls,
    They called curses on the seed, the place, the hour
    Of their own begetting and their birth. With wails

And tears they gathered on the evil shore
    That waits for all who don't fear God. There demon
90 Charon beckons them, with his eyes of fire;

64 Acheron's (ăk′ə-rŏn′) **dismal
shore:** Acheron is the first river
Dante comes upon in Hell. Its
waters flow downward into the
frozen river at the lowest level of
Hell.

67–68 an old man: Charon
(kâr′ən), who, in classical mythology, ferries souls of the dead into
the underworld.

**83–85 the forlorn and naked souls
. . . their parents:** The souls of the
damned are without divine grace
and are not permitted to repent;
they can only curse.

Wood engraving
after Gustave Doré.
The Granger
Collection, New
York.

HUMANITIES CONNECTION This woodcut depicts Virgil and Dante observing the eternal punishment of greedy sinners who bought or sold religious offices. The sinners are set, heads down, in a perforated rock. Their protruding feet are scorched by flames.

Crowded in a herd, they obey if he should summon,
   And he strikes at any laggards with his oar.
   As leaves in quick succession sail down in autumn

Until the bough beholds its entire store
95   Fallen to the earth, so Adam's evil seed
   Swoop from the bank when each is called, as sure

As a trained falcon, to cross to the other side
   Of the dark water; and before one throng can land
   On the far shore, on this side new souls crowd.

100 "My son," said the gentle master, "here are joined
   The souls of all who die in the wrath of God,
   From every country, all of them eager to find

Their way across the water—for the goad
   Of Divine Justice spurs them so, their fear
105   Is transmuted to desire. Souls who are good

Never pass this way; therefore, if you hear
   Charon complaining at your presence, consider
   What that means." Then, the earth of that grim shore

Began to shake: so violently, I shudder
110   And sweat recalling it now. A wind burst up
   From the tear-soaked ground to erupt red light and batter

My senses—and so I fell, as though seized by sleep.

92 laggards: individuals who lag behind.

95 seed: descendants.

103 goad: something that prods.

104–105 their fear . . . desire: In life the sinners hardened their hearts against grace. They are now required by Divine Justice to wish for Hell.

Thinking Through the Literature

1. What are your impressions of Charon, the demon boatman?
2. Why does Charon complain about Dante's presence at the river?
3. In lines 93–96, the souls at the river are compared to leaves falling from a tree. Why is this simile effective?

FOCUS Dante and Virgil enter the second level of Hell. At its gate, sinners are judged by Minos. As you read, look for details that describe this character and how he passes judgment.

Preview Minos judges each sinner to determine his or her proper place in Hell. This level, dark and stormy, is home to the souls of Cleopatra, Helen of Troy, and other illicit lovers. Dante speaks with one of them, Francesca Malatesta, who tells him how she and her brother-in-law Paolo fell in love. Their torment fills Dante with pity, causing him to faint.

CANTO 5

So I descended from first to second circle—
    Which girdles a smaller space and greater pain,
    Which spurs more lamentation. Minos the dreadful

    Snarls at the gate. He examines each one's sin,
5   Judging and disposing as he curls his tail:
    That is, when an ill-begotten soul comes down,

It comes before him, and confesses all;
    Minos, great connoisseur of sin, <u>discerns</u>
    For every spirit its proper place in Hell,

10 And wraps himself in his tail with as many turns
    As levels down that shade will have to dwell.
    A crowd is always waiting: here each one learns

His judgment and is assigned a place in Hell.
    They tell; they hear—and down they all are cast.
15   "You, who have come to sorrow's hospice, think well,"

Said Minos, who at the sight of me had paused
    To interrupt his solemn task mid-deed:
    "Beware how you come in and whom you trust,

Don't be deceived because the gate is wide."
20   My leader answered, "Must you too scold this way?
    His destined path is not for you to impede:

3 Minos: In classical mythology, Minos was a wise king of Crete who, after his death, became a judge of the dead in the underworld. Here, Minos is a monster that assigns each soul its proper depth in Hell.

8 connoisseur: someone with great knowledge and discriminating taste.

15 hospice: inn.

WORDS TO KNOW

748

discern (dĭ-sûrn') *v.* to perceive with the eyes or intellect

Thus is it willed where every thing may be
    Because it has been willed. So ask no more."
    And now I can hear the notes of agony

25 In sad crescendo beginning to reach my ear;
    Now I am where the noise of lamentation
    Comes at me in blasts of sorrow. I am where

All light is mute, with a bellowing like the ocean
    Turbulent in a storm of warring winds,
30   The hurricane of Hell in perpetual motion

Sweeping the ravaged spirits as it rends,
    Twists, and torments them. Driven as if to land,
    They reach the ruin: groaning, tears, laments,

And cursing of the power of Heaven. I learned
35   They suffer here who sinned in carnal things—
    Their reason mastered by desire, suborned.

PAUSE & REFLECT How does Minos indicate each sinner's place in Hell?

FOCUS Dante and Virgil look at the spirits of the great lovers. As you read about Francesca and Paolo, try to picture the moment they fall in love.

As winter starlings riding on their wings
    Form crowded flocks, so spirits dip and veer
    Foundering in the wind's rough buffetings,

40 Upward or downward, driven here and there
    With never ease from pain nor hope of rest.
    As chanting cranes will form a line in air,

So I saw souls come uttering cries—wind-tossed,
    And lofted by the storm. "Master," I cried,
45   "Who are these people, by black air oppressed?"

"First among these you wish to know," he said,
    "Was empress of many tongues—she so embraced
    Lechery that she decreed it justified

25 crescendo: a gradual but steady increase in sound.

28 mute: dim.

35 carnal: having to do with the flesh.

36 suborned: led to commit evil acts.

Legally, to evade the scandal of her lust:
50   She is that Semiramis of whom we read,
        Successor and wife of Ninus, she possessed

The lands the Sultan rules. Next, she who died
        By her own hand for love, and broke her vow
        To Sychaeus's ashes. After her comes lewd

55   And wanton Cleopatra. See Helen, too,
        Who caused a cycle of many evil years;
        And great Achilles, the hero whom love slew

In his last battle. Paris and Tristan are here—"
        He pointed out by name a thousand souls
60   Whom love had parted from our life, or more.

When I had heard my teacher tell the rolls
        Of knights and ladies of antiquity,
        Pity overwhelmed me. Half-lost in its coils,

"Poet," I told him, "I would willingly
65   Speak with those two who move along together,
        And seem so light upon the wind." And he:

"When they drift closer—then entreat them hither,
        In the name of love that leads them: they will respond."
        Soon their course shifted, and the merciless weather

70   Battered them toward us. I called against the wind,
        "O wearied souls! If Another does not forbid,
        Come speak with us." As doves whom desire has
            summoned,

With raised wings steady against the current, glide
        Guided by will to the sweetness of their nest,
75   So leaving the flock where Dido was, the two sped

Through the malignant air till they had crossed
        To where we stood—so strong was the compulsion
        Of my loving call. They spoke across the blast:

50–51 Semiramis (sə-mĭr′ə-mĭs′) . . . **Ninus** (nī′nəs): Semiramis , an Assyrian queen known widely for her sexual excesses, took control after the death of her husband, Ninus.

52–54 she who died . . . Sychaeus's (sĭ-kē′ə-sĭz) **ashes:** Dido, the queen of Carthage who, according to the *Aeneid,* vowed to remain faithful to the memory of her dead husband, Sychaeus, but fell in love with Aeneas. When Aeneas left for Italy, the abandoned Dido committed suicide.

55–56 Cleopatra . . . Helen . . . evil years: Cleopatra was queen of Egypt and a mistress to Julius Caesar and Mark Antony. Helen, according to Greek mythology, was the most beautiful of women. She left her husband, Menelaus (mĕn′ə-lā′əs), to run off with Paris, a prince of Troy. This action set off the Trojan War.

57 Achilles: the hero of the Trojan War who, according to one legend, deserted the Greeks when he fell in love with Polyxena (pə-lĭk′sĕ-nə), daughter of King Priam of Troy. On his way to meet her in a temple, he was slain by Paris.

58 Paris and Tristan: Paris' love for Helen caused the Trojan War. Tristan, a hero from medieval romances, had a love affair with his uncle's bride.

71 Another: God.

WORDS TO KNOW

compulsion (kəm-pŭl′shən) *n.* an ability to force action; irresistible impulse

Dante's Dream (1871), Dante Gabriel Rossetti.
Board of Trustees of the National Museums and
Galleries on Merseyside, Walker Art Gallery,
Liverpool, England.

"O living soul, who with courtesy and compassion
80   Voyage through black air visiting us who stained
The world with blood: if heaven's King bore affection

For such as we are, suffering in this wind,
Then we would pray to Him to grant you peace
For pitying us in this, our evil end.

85 Now we will speak and hear as you may please
To speak and hear, while the wind, for our <u>discourse</u>,
Is still. My birthplace is a city that lies

Where the Po finds peace with all its followers.
Love, which in gentle hearts is quickly born,
90   Seized him for my fair body—which, in a fierce

Manner that still torments my soul, was torn
Untimely away from me. Love, which absolves
None who are loved from loving, made my heart burn

With joy so strong that as you see it cleaves
95   Still to him, here. Love gave us both one death.
Caina awaits the one who took our lives."

These words were borne across from them to us.
When I had heard those afflicted souls, I lowered
My head, and held it so till I heard the voice

100 Of the poet ask, "What are you thinking?" I answered,
"Alas—that sweet conceptions and passion so deep
Should bring them here!" Then, looking up toward

87–88 My birthplace . . . all its followers: The speaker is Francesca Malatesta (frän-chäs′kä mä′lä-tĕs′tä)—a real-life contemporary of Dante's—who was born in Ravenna, a city near the mouth of the Po River. She was married to Giovanni Malatesta in 1275 but fell in love with his younger brother, Paolo (pä′ō-lō). The affair continued for several years until Giovanni happened upon them and killed them both.

94 cleaves: clings.

96 Caina . . . our lives: Caina, part of the lowest circle of Hell, holds the spirits of those who betrayed their kin. Francesca expects that it will be her husband's fate to go there. When Dante wrote the *Inferno*, Giovanni Malatesta was still alive.

WORDS TO KNOW
discourse (dĭs′kôrs′) *n.* talk; conversation

The lovers: "Francesca, your suffering makes me weep
For sorrow and pity—but tell me, in the hours
105   Of sweetest sighing, how and in what shape

Or manner did Love first show you those desires
So hemmed by doubt?" And she to me: "No sadness
Is greater than in misery to rehearse

Memories of joy, as your teacher well can witness.
110   But if you have so great a craving to measure
Our love's first root, I'll tell it, with the fitness

Of one who weeps and tells. One day, for pleasure,
We read of Lancelot, by love constrained:
Alone, suspecting nothing, at our leisure.

> **113 Lancelot, by love constrained:**
> In the Arthurian legends, Lancelot
> was King Arthur's noblest knight.
> He could not resist falling in love
> with the king's wife, Guinevere.

115   Sometimes at what we read our glances joined,
Looking from the book each to the other's eyes,
And then the color in our faces drained.

But one particular moment alone it was
Defeated us: *the longed-for smile*, it said,
120   *Was kissed by that most noble lover:* at this,

This one, who now will never leave my side,
Kissed my mouth, trembling. A Galeotto, that book!
And so was he who wrote it; that day we read

> **122 Galeotto** (gä'lĕ-ō'tō): the go-
> between who passed messages
> from Lancelot to Guinevere.

No further." All the while the one shade spoke,
125   The other at her side was weeping; my pity
Overwhelmed me and I felt myself go slack:

> **126 go slack:** lose muscle tension
> or become unconscious.

Swooning as in death, I fell like a dying body.

Thinking Through the Literature

1. What was your reaction to Francesca and Paolo?

2. In his book *The Power of Myth,* the writer and scholar Joseph Campbell states that the lines describing how Francesca and Paolo fell in love are "the most famous lines in Dante." Why do you think these lines appeal to many readers?

3. All the lovers in this level of Hell are buffeted by strong, dark winds. What do you think the winds might represent?

FOCUS Dante and Virgil have reached the lowest level of Hell. As you read, look for details that help you visualize it.

Preview In Cantos 6–33, Dante and Virgil travel down through the successive levels of Hell. In Canto 34, they enter the final level, home to Dis, the ruler of Hell. The shades dwelling there are frozen in ice. Dis is a three-faced giant. His upper body protrudes from the ice of the river Cocytus. Each of his bloody mouths holds a sinner guilty of a terrible betrayal—Judas Iscariot, Brutus, and Cassius.

FROM
CANTO 34

"And now, *Vexilla regis prodeunt*
    Inferni—therefore, look," my master said
    As we continued on the long descent,

"And see if you can make him out, ahead."
5   As though, in the exhalation of heavy mist
    Or while night darkened our hemisphere, one spied

A mill—blades turning in the wind, half-lost
    Off in the distance—some structure of that kind
    I seemed to make out now. But at a gust

10 Of wind, there being no other shelter at hand,
    I drew behind my leader's back again.
    By now (and putting it in verse I find

Fear in myself still) I had journeyed down
    To where the shades were covered wholly by ice,
15   Showing like straw in glass—some lying prone,

And some erect, some with the head toward us,
    And others with the bottoms of the feet;
    Another like a bow, bent feet to face.

1–2 *Vexilla regis prodeunt Inferni* (vĕk-sĭl′ə rĕg′ĭs prō′dĕ-ŏŏnt ĭn-fĕr′nē): a Latin phrase meaning "The banners of the king of Hell advance" (an alteration of the first line of a famous Christian hymn).

15 prone: face downward.

Dante and Virgil in the Ninth Circle of the Inferno,
Gustave Doré. Photograph copyright © Christie's Images.

HUMANITIES CONNECTION This painting by the
French artist Gustave Doré (1832–1883) depicts
Virgil and Dante in the ninth circle of the Inferno,
where betrayers are fixed in ice. The poets
notice two heads in the same hole. One of the
heads gnaws on the nape of the other's neck.

When we had traveled forward to the spot
20   From which it pleased my master to have me see
        That creature whose beauty once had been so great,

He made me stop, and moved from in front of me.
        "Look: here is Dis," he said, "and here is the place
        Where you must arm yourself with the quality

25 Of <u>fortitude</u>." How chilled and faint I was
        On hearing that, you must not ask me, reader—
        I do not write it; words would not suffice:

I neither died, nor kept alive—consider
        With your own wits what I, alike denuded
30   Of death and life, became as I heard my leader.

PAUSE & REFLECT What covers the shades in the lowest level of Hell?

FOCUS At last, Dante views Dis, or Lucifer, the ruler of Hell. Look for details that describe this character.

The emperor of the realm of grief <u>protruded</u>
        From mid-breast up above the surrounding ice.
        A giant's height, and mine, would have provided

Closer comparison than would the size
35   Of his arm and a giant. Envision the whole
        That is proportionate to parts like these.

If he was truly once as beautiful
        As he is ugly now, and raised his brows
        Against his Maker—then all sorrow may well

40 Come out of him. How great a marvel it was
        For me to see three faces on his head:
        In front there was a red one; joined to this,

Each over the midpoint of a shoulder, he had
        Two others—all three joining at the crown.
45   That on the right appeared to be a shade

21–23 That creature whose beauty . . . Dis: Dis, or Lucifer, was the most beautiful of the angels until he rebelled against God and was cast from Heaven.

27 suffice: be enough; be sufficient.

29 denuded: stripped bare.

WORDS TO KNOW

fortitude (fôr′tǐ-tōōd′) *n.* courage
protrude (prō-trōōd′) *v.* to jut out; project

Of whitish yellow; the third had such a mien
    As those who come from where the Nile descends.
    Two wings spread forth from under each face's chin,

Strong, and befitting such a bird, immense—
50   I have never seen at sea so broad a sail—
    Unfeathered, batlike, and issuing three winds

That went forth as he beat them, to freeze the whole
    Realm of Cocytus that surrounded him.
    He wept with all six eyes, and the tears fell

55 Over his three chins mingled with bloody foam.
    The teeth of each mouth held a sinner, kept
    As by a flax rake: thus he held three of them

In agony. For the one the front mouth gripped,
    The teeth were as nothing to the claws, which sliced
60   And tore the skin until his back was stripped.

"That soul," my master said, "who suffers most,
    Is Judas Iscariot; head locked inside,
    He flails his legs. Of the other two, who twist

With their heads down, the black mouth holds the shade
65   Of Brutus: writhing, but not a word will he scream;
    Cassius is the sinewy one on the other side.

But night is rising again, and it is time
    That we depart, for we have seen the whole."
    As he requested, I put my arms round him . . .

46 mien (mēn): appearance.

53 Cocytus (kō-kī′təs): a river of Hell.

57 flax rake: a tool for separating the fibers of the flax plant so that cloth can be woven from them.

62 Judas Iscariot (jōō′dəs ĭ-skăr′ē-ət): the betrayer of Jesus Christ.

65–66 Brutus . . . Cassius (kăsh′əs): betrayers of Julius Caesar. In Dante's time, Caesar's assassination was considered to be a setback to the development of the Roman Empire.

66 sinewy: lean and muscular.

FROM
LA VITA NUOVA

TRANSLATED BY MARK MUSA

PREPARING to *Read*

Build Background *La Vita Nuova* [The New Life], a short work by Dante, contains sonnets and a prose narrative about his love for Beatrice. In this excerpt from the work (page 758), Dante tells of the moment he fell in love with her. His love for Beatrice—powerful and passionate—may remind you of the love between Francesca and Paolo, immortalized in Canto 5 of the *Inferno.*

Beata Beatrix (1863–1870), Dante Gabriel Rossetti. Photograph by John Webb. Tate Gallery, London/The Art Archive, London.

THE FIRST SIGHT OF BEATRICE

Nine times already since my birth the heaven of light had
circled back to almost the same point, when there appeared
before my eyes the now glorious lady of my mind, who
was called Beatrice even by those who did not know what
her name was. She had been in this life long enough for the
heaven of the fixed stars to be able to move a twelfth of a
degree to the East in her time; that is, she appeared to me
at about the beginning of her ninth year, and I first saw her
near the end of my ninth year. She appeared dressed in the
most patrician[1] of colors, a subdued and decorous crimson,
her robe bound round and adorned in a style suitable to
her years. At that very moment, and I speak the truth, the
vital spirit, the one that dwells in the most secret chamber
of the heart, began to tremble so violently that even the
most minute veins of my body were strangely affected; and
trembling, it spoke these words: *Ecce deus fortior me, qui
veniens dominabitur michi.*[2]

THE EFFECTS OF LOVE

After that vision my natural spirit was interfered with in its
functioning, because my soul had become wholly absorbed
in thinking about this most gracious lady; and in a short
time I became so weak and frail that many of my friends
were worried about the way I looked; others, full of malicious curiosity, were doing their best to discover things
about me, which, above all, I wished to keep secret from
everyone. I was aware of the maliciousness of their questioning and, guided by Love who commanded me
according to the counsel of reason, I would answer that it
was Love who had conquered me. I said that it was Love
because there were so many of his signs clearly marked on
my face that they were impossible to conceal. And when
people would ask: "Who is the person for whom you are
so destroyed by Love?" I would look at
them and smile and say nothing.

1. **patrician:** noble.
2. *Ecce deus . . . michi:* "Here is a god stronger than I who
   comes to rule over me."

Connect to the Literature

1. What Do You Think?
What was your reaction to Dante's vision of Hell?

Comprehension Check
- What type of sinner is found in the lowest level in Hell?
- Of all the sinners in Hell, who suffers the most?

Think Critically

2. ACTIVE READING: CLARIFYING MEANING Using your ▯READER'S NOTEBOOK, work with a partner and compare your answers to the Pause & Reflect questions. Also try to clarify any points of confusion that either of you might still have about what happens in these excerpts.

3. Think about Dante's portrayal of himself. What are his main qualities?

4. How would you describe the relationship between Dante and Virgil?

5. Are the punishments that Dante describes fair or not? Explain your opinion.

THINK ABOUT
- the punishment of the souls of the unsure
- the fact that illicit lovers are punished less severely than other sinners
- the fact that betrayers receive the most severe punishment of all
- the fact that all these punishments are eternal

Extend Interpretations

6. What If? At the lowest level of Hell, Virgil and Dante come upon Dis, who is said to be weeping. Imagine that Dis were portrayed in some other way—for example, as grinning or gloating. How do you think your reaction might differ?

7. Critic's Corner One famous admirer of Dante's work was Ralph Waldo Emerson, a 19th-century American poet and essayist. Emerson praised *The Divine Comedy* as "the best textbook" for teaching the art of writing. In the excerpt you read, identify three or more qualities of good writing—for example, the use of vivid details—that an aspiring writer should take notice of.

8. Connect to Life Judging by what you have read in these excerpts, to what extent do you think the *Inferno* is relevant to readers today? Explain.

LITERARY ANALYSIS: ALLEGORY

A **symbol** is a person, place, or object that has a concrete meaning in itself and stands for something beyond itself. For example, the American flag is a symbol of the United States. An **allegory** is a literary work filled with symbols. Dante's *Divine Comedy* can be read as an allegory. Here are some important points to keep in mind:

- It has two levels of meaning—a literal one and a symbolic one.
- To explore the symbolic meaning, pay attention to details about the characters, objects, events, and settings. For example, details describing the she-wolf in Canto 1 of the *Inferno* suggest that this animal represents greed:

> *Her nature*
> *Is so malign and vicious she cannot appease*
> *Her voracity, for feeding makes her hungrier.* (lines 74–76)

Paired Activity The chart below lists several details from the *Inferno*. Go back through the excerpts, and then write down what you think each detail might mean on a symbolic level. Compare your interpretations with a partner's.

Person, Object, Place, Event	Possible Meaning
The dark woods	The confusion and misery caused by sin
A whirling banner followed by many souls	
The character of Virgil	
The dark wind that tortures the lovers	
The ice at the lowest level of Hell	

Dante's Poetic Language

The **style** of a work of literature is the particular way in which it is written. A writer's style reflects his or her unique way of communicating with the reader. In the *Inferno*, for example, Dante used poetic language to convey his imaginative vision of eternal punishments in the afterlife.

Key Aspects of Dante's Style

- vivid details and images that convey ideas and feelings
- figurative language, including similes like those found in classical epics
- allusions to legendary or historical figures
- precise and sometimes lofty words

Analysis of Style

At the right are brief passages from the *Inferno*. Study the list of stylistic elements above, and read each excerpt carefully. Then complete the following activities:

- Find examples of each aspect of Dante's style in the excerpts.
- Find additional examples of each aspect in other passages from the *Inferno*.
- Find a passage from the *Inferno* that you think is especially moving. With a partner, discuss the stylistic techniques Dante used.

Applications

1. **Changing Style** Choose a passage from the *Inferno* that contains figurative language. Then write a **paraphrase** of the passage, expressing the same ideas in everyday prose. Read your paraphrase and Dante's original to a partner. Discuss what Dante has conveyed through his use of poetic language.

2. **Imitation of Style** Try imitating Dante's style as you write a few three-line stanzas about a fitting punishment for a notorious evildoer of the 20th century—for example, Hitler or Stalin.

3. **Speaking and Listening** Present an oral reading of one of the four passages to the right. Choose appropriate phrasings, pitches, and gestures to convey the emotion of the passage.

---

from the **Inferno, Canto 1**

Midway on our life's journey, I found myself
In dark woods, the right road lost. To tell
About those woods is hard—so tangled and rough
And savage that thinking of it now, I feel
The old fear stirring: death is hardly more bitter.

---

from the **Inferno, Canto 3**

As leaves in quick succession sail down in autumn
Until the bough beholds its entire store
Fallen to the earth, so Adam's evil seed
Swoop from the bank when each is called,

---

from the **Inferno, Canto 5**

         See Helen, too,
Who caused a cycle of many evil years;
And great Achilles, the hero whom love slew
In his last battle. Paris and Tristan are here—"

---

from the **Inferno, Canto 34**

He wept with all six eyes, and the tears fell
Over his three chins mingled with bloody foam.

Writing Option

Subject Analysis Write a brief essay in response to this prompt: Does Dante make his journey through Hell believable to the reader? Support your opinion with details from the poem. Place your analysis in your **Working Portfolio.**

Writing Handbook
See page R35: Persuasive Writing.

Activities & Explorations

Dramatic Reading With three or four classmates, rehearse and perform a dramatic reading of one of the cantos in the *Inferno.* Add background music or sound effects to accompany your performance.

~ **SPEAKING AND LISTENING**

Inquiry & Research

Character Profile Research one of the legendary or historical figures who appear in the *Inferno*—for example, Virgil, Charon, Cleopatra, Dido, Tristan, Francesca Malatesta, Brutus, or Judas Iscariot. Report your findings in a written profile.

Vocabulary in Action

EXERCISE: ANALOGIES Choose a word from the list of Words to Know to complete each analogy.

1. enjoyable : unpleasant :: lucky : _____
2. observe : detect :: examine : _____
3. speech : individual :: _____ : partners
4. notice : observe :: assist : _____
5. sports : strength :: crisis : _____
6. poor : _____ :: hungry : starving
7. created : made :: inspired : _____
8. _____ : outward :: withdraw : inward
9. shower : thunderstorm :: habit : _____
10. applause : enjoy :: ridicule : _____

Building Vocabulary

For an in-depth lesson on analogies, see page 768.

Where did Dante live after he was banished from Florence? What might his life have been like during those dark years? Working with a small group of classmates, research Dante's life during his exile from Florence. Then create an interactive map that shows Italy in Dante's time. On the map, identify several sites he visited during his exile. Each group member should choose one of these sites and look up information about Dante's connection with it. Then record the information so that users of the map can listen to it.

Biographical Sources Supplement the information on Dante provided on pages 732–735 with information from reference books, literary biographies, and reliable online sources. These sources might include Web sites maintained by university literature departments and reputable literary societies (including Dante societies).

Historical Sources Use reference books, historical atlases, and books or other sources on Italian history to help you map the Italian city-states in Dante's day. Again, consider reliable online Web sites, such as those maintained by Italian cities and by reputable historical or medieval societies.

RESEARCH STARTER
CLASSZONE.COM

Writing Workshop

Examining the parts of a subject . . .

From Reading to Writing In this unit you've read selections on topics ranging from werewolves to chivalry to the Holy Grail. You can explore such topics further by analyzing them in writing. In a **subject analysis,** a writer breaks a topic into parts and examines each one. For example, an analysis of werewolves might treat the history of werewolf folklore, the characteristics of werewolves, and the parts of the world where tales of these creatures are told. Analysis can be applied to a wide variety of topics. In the essay on the following page, the writer analyzes different aspects of school athletics.

For Your Portfolio

WRITING PROMPT Write an essay in which you present an analysis of a subject of your choice.

Purpose: To explain the parts of a subject and examine how they relate to one another

Audience: Readers interested in understanding the subject in depth

---

Basics in a Box

Subject Analysis at a Glance

Introduces Subject

Examines Parts of Subject

Draws a Conclusion

RUBRIC Standards for Writing

A successful subject analysis should

- introduce the subject in an interesting, informative manner
- identify the subject's principal parts
- examine each part thoroughly
- present information in a logical order
- show how the parts relate to the whole subject and how the discussion of them supports the analysis's main idea, or thesis
- include an effective conclusion

Analyzing a Student Model

Bryan Dobkin
Buffalo Grove High School

Going the Distance

What comes to mind when you hear the term *student athlete?* Perhaps you think of a swimmer getting up to practice at 5 A.M. every day or of football players performing drills like recruits at boot camp. On the other hand, maybe you think of exclusive social cliques or of jocks flunking their classes. Whatever mental picture you have of student athletes, one thing is true: school sports—from lacrosse to gymnastics to basketball—play a major part in the lives of many young people. Before becoming involved yourself, it's helpful to think about the many aspects of athletics in the school community.

First of all, being part of a team is a great gift for any kid to have. The team atmosphere can make a student feel safe and secure in what is sometimes a very scary environment. When a student enters high school and is surrounded by hundreds of new faces, joining a sports team is a great way to meet people with similar interests. A team can provide an athlete with a very close circle of friends to rely on and look to for guidance. Teammates often feel great respect for and pride in one another. Being on a sports team can also provide a student with a sense of self-worth, the positive feeling that comes from being part of the team.

Second, playing on a sports team teaches students many skills that are of great use in school and in life. Having a coach is a great way to learn respect and obedience. Many teachers have commented that students who are involved in sports have a greater respect for them and are much easier to teach. Sports also teach kids self-discipline, holding them back from dangerous or self-destructive behavior. By engaging in illegal activities, such as drinking or doing drugs, a student athlete jeopardizes not only his or her health and school career but also his or her spot on a team. This is a strong incentive to avoid such activities. Participating in a sport also increases an athlete's awareness of bodily health, so the athlete is likely to think twice before putting his or her health at risk.

RUBRIC
IN ACTION

❶ Writer introduces the subject by asking the reader a question and giving a reason for the analysis.

Other Options:
· Tell an interesting anecdote.
· Present a surprising fact.

❷ States the main idea

❸ Identifies and examines one positive element— athletic camaraderie

❹ Identifies other positive elements— respect and self-discipline— and gives supporting examples

LANGUAGE SKILLS

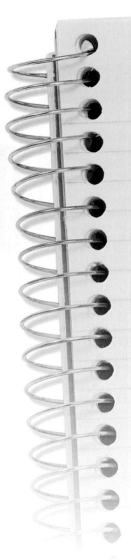

School sports are not without their problems, however. Some student athletes do not have enough time to thoroughly concentrate on their schoolwork. Most high school coaches require athletes to practice every school day and on many weekends and holidays. The athletic contests usually take place on the weekends, sometimes every week. After a full day of school, an athlete must attend practice, which in most cases does not end until the middle of the evening. He or she then has to return home, only to spend the rest of the evening on schoolwork. After such a physically and mentally tiring day, many students do not have the energy or the drive to complete their schoolwork. They sometimes end up with grades that do not fully reflect their abilities. Poor grades can be damaging to the future of any student, especially the college-bound. Even for those who intend to play sports in college, a strong academic record remains the most important factor in college admissions.

Another negative aspect of school sports is the effect they have on non-athletes. I mentioned that sports teams provide student athletes with circles of friends. Sometimes, however, these social circles can turn into exclusive cliques, creating an unpleasant or even threatening environment for other students. The members of a football team, for example, may feel a need to act macho and put down people that aren't like them. Many people feel that they are excluded or looked down upon by such a group because they do not participate in the same activity. The social atmosphere created by a strong sports culture may actually affect students' confidence and inhibit the learning process. How can students be expected to concentrate in class when they are being ridiculed outside of class?

School sports are obviously a strong force in shaping the lives of both student athletes and nonathletes. They bring kids together socially while teaching them things like discipline and respect. On the other hand, sports may take time away from more important academic work, and they may create an environment that makes it hard for some students to learn. No matter what view you take on the subject, sports in school will be with us for a long time. Being aware of sports' various influences will help us ensure that they remain a positive experience for everyone.

❺ Uses a transition to turn to negative aspects of school sports

❻ Examines one negative element—distraction from schoolwork

❼ Examines another negative element—sports' effect on a school's social environment

❽ Concludes by showing how the reader can use the information in the analysis
Other Options:
· Leave the reader with a question to consider.
· Draw a general conclusion from specific information presented.

Writing Your Subject Analysis

❶ Prewriting

Begin your search for a topic by listing issues or problems that you would like to understand better. You might consider matters of local or national importance, such as school security or high-tech innovations. See the **Idea Bank** for more suggestions. After you have chosen your topic, follow the steps below.

Planning Your Analysis

▷ **1. Explore the topic.** What do you already know about the topic? What do you want to know? Draft a list of questions on the subject. Consider what sources will be likely to provide you with answers to your questions—books, magazines, reference materials, experts, or on-line sources.

▷ **2. Think about your purpose and audience.** Do you simply want to inform your readers, or do you want your analysis to persuade them to accept a conclusion? What will they already know about the subject? What background information will they require? What terms will you need to define? What tone will be most appropriate?

▷ **3. Write a thesis statement.** What is the main point that you'd like to communicate? Write this idea in one or two sentences.

▷ **4. Break the subject into parts.** Analysis is the breakdown of a subject into its parts. Will your analysis involve steps in a process, stages of development, elements of a problem, pros and cons, or other characteristics?

Now think about how to **organize** your analysis. Although every topic will require a slightly different approach, the steps below can help you develop a solid structure.

- Provide a **provocative introduction** to quickly attract readers' interest.
- **Identify your subject** and the purpose of your analysis in a sentence or short paragraph.
- **Describe the parts** that make up your subject.
- **Examine each part** in relationship to other parts or to the subject as a whole.

Incorporate these features into an **outline** for your essay.

❷ Drafting

Using your outline as a guide, write your first draft. Try to write freely, without worrying about details or mistakes. You can take care of those things later. As you get your ideas down on paper, you may find that you want to change your thesis statement, or you may decide to rearrange your ideas.

IDEABank

1. Your Working Portfolio 📁
Build on the **Writing Options** you completed earlier in this unit:

- **Subject Analysis,** p. 761

2. Periodical Search
Read through several magazines and newspapers to find a topic that interests you. Take notes on any interesting articles, jotting down ideas for your analysis.

3. Web Hunt
Look through reputable Web sites for news and information on political, scientific, artistic, or social topics that appeal to you. You might start with general Web sites, then pursue links to more-specific sites that look interesting.

LANGUAGE SKILLS

Ask Your Peer Reader

- What are the key points of my analysis? Which terms, if any, should I define?
- Describe the structure of my analysis.
- What could I change or add to make my analysis clearer?

Need revising help?

Review the **Rubric**, p. 762

Consider **peer reader** comments

Check **Revision Guidelines**, p. R19

Confused by active and passive voice?

See the **Grammar Handbook**, p. R61

Publishing IDEAS

- Submit your work to your school or community newspaper.
- If you know of a local organization that is concerned with your topic, send it a copy of your analysis.

PUBLISHING OPTIONS
CLASSZONE.COM

❸ Revising

TARGET SKILL ▶ USING THE ACTIVE VOICE Writing sentences in the active voice can help you create a lively and engaging style. While the passive voice is sometimes necessary, its overuse can make your writing clumsy and dull.

Having a coach is a great way to learn respect and obedience. *Many teachers have commented* ~~It has been commented upon by many teachers~~ that students who are involved in sports have a greater respect for them and are much easier to teach. *Sports also teach kids self-discipline, holding them back* ~~Students are also taught self-discipline by sports and are held back~~ from dangerous or self-destructive behavior.

❹ Editing and Proofreading

TARGET SKILL ▶ AVOIDING REDUNDANCY Needless repetition will weaken your writing. When reviewing your work, keep an eye out for redundant words or phrases. These can easily slip into your work, especially during revision, when you might add a new word but forget to take out the word it was meant to replace.

School sports are not without their problems, however. Some student athletes do not have enough time to thoroughly concentrate on their schoolwork ~~properly.~~

❺ Reflecting

FOR YOUR WORKING PORTFOLIO How did writing your analysis affect your thinking about your topic? How might you pursue the topic further? Attach your answers to your finished work. Save your analysis in your **Working Portfolio.**

Read this paragraph from the first draft of a subject analysis. The underlined sections may include the following kinds of errors:

- **inconsistent use of verb tenses**
- **errors in parallelism**
- **redundant wording**
- **misplaced modifiers**

For each underlined section, choose the revision that most improves the writing.

The werewolf appears in folklore around the world, <u>in tales most prominently from Europe</u>. The term *werewolf* comes from the Old English *werwulf*, which means "man-wolf." This creature is a person who turns into a wolf, <u>usually at night and he often does this under a full moon</u>. The tales vary; some <u>werewolves have chosen their condition of being a werewolf</u>, <u>whereas others are bitten</u> by werewolves or transformed by magic spells. A werewolf usually preys on people. These people sometimes <u>try to protect themselves</u> by bringing the werewolf back to human form or by injuring him (the injury will appear on the werewolf's human form, allowing others to identify him or her). In 16th-century France there were many reports of werewolves. People suspected of being werewolves, <u>or *loups-garous*, were convicted and executed for being *loups-garous*</u>.

(1) (2) (3) (4) (5) (6)

---

1. A. in tales from most prominently Europe

   B. most prominently in tales from Europe

   C. in most prominently tales from Europe

   D. Correct as is

2. A. usually doing this at night and he often does it under a full moon

   B. usually at night and often doing this under a full moon

   C. usually at night and often under a full moon

   D. Correct as is

3. A. have chosen their condition of being a werewolf

   B. werewolves have chosen their werewolf-condition

   C. werewolves have chosen their condition

   D. Correct as is

4. A. whereas others were bitten

   B. whereas others have been bitten

   C. whereas others will be bitten

   D. Correct as is

5. A. tried to protect themselves

   B. have tried to protect themselves

   C. will try to protect themselves

   D. Correct as is

6. A. or *loups-garous,* were convicted and executed

   B. or *loups-garous,* were convicted and executed for being werewolves

   C. or *loups-garous,* were convicted and executed for this crime

   D. Correct as is

Need extra help?

See the **Grammar Handbook**

Verb Tense, p. R60

Modifiers, p. R62

Building Vocabulary | Understanding Analogies

Recognizing Relationships Good writers often help us notice connections between things, people, and experiences. Frequently, they do so by making comparisons. One type of comparison is called an **analogy**. In the following excerpt from Dante's *Inferno*, for example, the narrator asks a stranger whether he is the Roman poet Virgil.

> "Then are you Virgil? Are you the font that pours
> So overwhelming a river of human speech?"

In his inquiry, the narrator compares Virgil and his speech to a font (spring) and the water flowing from it.

As you can see, the analogy involves two pairs of things that are related to each other in the same way. A spring pours forth water, and a poet pours forth human speech.

Strategies for Building Vocabulary

Analogies are at the heart of literary metaphors, but they can also be used to test your ability to make logical connections. When used for this purpose, they are often presented as formulas. The analogy discussed above, for example, could be expressed as follows:

FONT : WATER :: poet : speech

To read this, you would say, "A font is to water as a poet is to speech."

❶ Determine Word Relationships The first step in analyzing an analogy is to determine the relationship between the first pair of words in it. What do you think is the relationship between these two words?

DOZE : SLEEP

When trying to complete an analogy, it's often helpful to formulate a sentence that expresses the relationship between the first pair of words. In this case you could say, "To doze is to sleep lightly." Now try to fit the following word pairs into the sentence "To x is to y lightly." Which pair makes the best sense?

(A) whisper : talk   (C) rotate : revolve
(B) scorch : heat   (D) sing : shout

Although the words in each pair are related in some way, pair A best parallels the relationship between *doze* and *sleep*: "To whisper is to talk lightly."

❷ Distinguish Different Types of Analogies Many standardized tests require you to complete analogies. This chart will help you to become familiar with some of the more common types of analogies.

Common Relationships in Analogies		
Type	**Example**	**Relationship**
Degree of intensity	WHISPER : SHOUT	x is a less (or more) intense form of y.
Synonyms	MIRTH : HUMOR	x is the same as y.
Antonyms	RIDICULOUS : SERIOUS	x is the opposite of y.
Classification	GRASS : PLANT	x is a type of y.
Description	FUNNY : COMEDIAN	x is a characteristic of y.
Part to whole	ERASER : PENCIL	x is a part of y.
Cause to effect	POVERTY : HUNGER	x leads to y.
Worker to creation	CARPENTER : HOUSE	x is one who makes y.
Location	FLOWERS : GARDEN	x is found in y.

EXERCISE Complete each analogy, identifying the relationship that the word pairs exemplify.

1. SPANIARD : EUROPEAN :: oak : _____
2. DEFINITION : DICTIONARY :: recipe : _____
3. AMIABLE : HOSTILE :: charming : _____
4. FEAR : HESITATION :: hunger : _____
5. CREATIVE : COMPOSER :: strict : _____

Grammar from Literature In both poetry and prose, writers vary the structure of their sentences. They do this for a number of reasons:

- to emphasize certain ideas
- to create poetic effects
- to add variety to paragraphs

One way to change a sentence's structure is to invert, or reverse the order of, the subject and the verb. In an inverted sentence, the verb precedes the subject.

> INVERTED   verb   subject
> "Husband, right long and wearisome **are** the days that you spend away from your home."
>   —Marie de France, "The Lay of the Were-Wolf"
>
> SUBJECT FIRST   subject
> "Husband, the days that you spend away from your
>   verb
> home **are** right long and wearisome."

Besides inverting the subject and the verb, you can also place other sentence parts in unusual places.

>   adverbs   subject   verb
> **Right sweetly** the knight **thanked** her for her grace, and pledged her faith and fealty.
>   —Marie de France, "The Lay of the Were-Wolf"
>
>   prepositional phrase   subject   verb
> and **from his mouth** the bright blood **comes** leaping out,
>   —*The Song of Roland*
>
>   subject
>   direct object   verb
> **What fine guidance** he **gave** me, . . .
>   —Chrétien de Troyes, *Perceval*

As you look at your own writing, ask yourself these questions to see whether you should consider using unusual word orders:

- Are my sentences too similar in structure or length?
- Do I want to emphasize certain words or ideas?
- Would changing the order of sentence elements create an interesting rhythm?

Usage Tip When you place a verb before its subject, make sure you use a verb form that agrees with the subject. Plural subjects need plural verbs; singular subjects need singular verbs. This issue also arises in sentences beginning with *here* or *there*. In such sentences, the introductory word does not function as a subject.

> INCORRECT
> **Deep in the woods lurk a great beast.**
>
> CORRECT
> **Deep in the woods lurks a great beast.**

Punctuation Tip When you move more than one prepositional phrase to the beginning of a sentence, remember to put a comma after the last of the prepositional phrases.

> prep. phrase   prep. phrase
> **On the last day of the festival, the werewolf died.**
>
> prep. phrase   prep. phrase
> **After all of their hard work, the farm still failed.**

WRITING EXERCISE Change the structure of each sentence by moving the underlined words to a different position. (You may have to make other adjustments to the wording.) Remember to punctuate the revised sentence correctly.

1. A baron lived in Brittany <u>long ago.</u>
2. He had <u>a beautiful young wife.</u>
3. He left her alone <u>for three days out of every week.</u>
4. He wandered the countryside as a werewolf <u>when he was away from her.</u>
5. His young wife was <u>so curious</u> about his secret that she begged him to tell her where he went.

PROOFREADING EXERCISE Rewrite the sentences below, correcting any errors in punctuation or usage.

1. "There come a time each week when I must leave home and go into the woods," he told his wife.
2. "During this part of the week I run about as a werewolf."
3. "In that form I hunt for my food just as a wolf does."
4. "Beneath this hollow rock lie my clothing."
5. "There has been many times I have wished my life could be different."

Literature of the Middle Ages

Reflect and Assess

What did you learn about the Middle Ages from reading the selections in Unit Five, Part 1? Why do you think medieval literature is still valued and enjoyed? Use the following options to help you explore what you have learned.

Detail of French manuscript illustration of warfare in the Middle Ages—the siege of a fortified town (1250). The Granger Collection, New York.

Reflecting on the Literature

The Literature of Honor The literature of the Middle Ages often paints idealized portraits of aristocratic society. In many of the tales, the main characters are noble figures, inspired by the highest motives. Think about the selections you've read, and identify the main character in each one. What values does each character hold dear?

Reviewing Literary Concepts

Romance In this part of the book, you learned about a type of imaginative story known as a **romance.** In a romance, some of the events described are far removed from those of ordinary life. Recall the plots of the excerpt from *Perceval: The Story of the Grail* and "The Lay of the Were-Wolf." What mysterious events in these stories impressed you the most? How important are these events to the plot of the story?

☐ Building Your Portfolio

Writing Workshop and Writing Options Look back at the subject analysis you wrote for the Writing Workshop on page 762 and at the Writing Option you completed for the Author Study on Dante Alighieri. Which writing assignment did you find most challenging? Add that assignment to your **Presentation Portfolio** ☐ , along with a cover note explaining your choice.

Self ASSESSMENT

📖 READER'S NOTEBOOK

In this part you learned the following names and terms as you read the selections. Write a sentence to describe or define each one. If you have trouble recalling a name or a term, review the lesson where it is introduced.

Charlemagne	courtly love
epic hero	*lai*
Crusades	allegory
feudalism	*The Divine Comedy*
romance	quest
Arthurian legend	Holy Grail
chivalry	

Setting GOALS

The stories of King Arthur and his knights have greatly influenced Western culture and are still popular today. Look back at the titles of books about King Arthur listed in the Connect to Today on page 723. Choose one of these books to read.

Extend Your *Reading*

The Canterbury Tales: Selected Works

GEOFFREY CHAUCER

People from different classes and walks of life set forth on a pilgrimage to the shrine of Thomas à Becket in Canterbury, England. Along the way, they tell tales—tales that vividly portray life in the Middle Ages. This rich sample contains the complete Prologue and seven of the tales.

Here are just a few of the related readings that accompany *The Canterbury Tales:*

***from* The Life and Times of Chaucer**
BY JOHN GARDNER

Laüstic (The Nightingale)
BY MARIE DE FRANCE

***from* The Autobiography of Malcolm X**
BY MALCOLM X

A Distant Mirror: The Calamitous 14th Century

BARBARA W. TUCHMAN

In this acclaimed work, the author explores the stark contrasts of life in the 14th century. It was a splendid era of castles, cathedrals, and chivalry. It was also a tortured century racked with war and plague. Through these pages gallops the knight, a figure of bravery and folly.

And Even *More* . . .

Books

Joan of Arc MARY GORDON
In this brief biography, the author, a best-selling novelist, draws upon her understanding of character and eye for detail. She probes the mystery of the peasant girl who led the armies of France to glory, only to die a terrible death at the stake.

The Medieval Reader NORMAN F. CANTOR, ED.
This rich collection of almost 100 first-hand accounts of medieval life includes letters, essays, and documents as well as excerpts from literary works. Among the writers represented are prominent women such as Christine de Pisan and Hildegard von Bingen.

Other Media

Becket
This film traces the friendship and later the feud between Henry II of England and Thomas à Becket, the Archbishop of Canterbury. Richard Burton, Peter O'Toole, and Sir John Gielgud star. 151 minutes. Zenger Media. (VIDEOCASSETTE)

The Medieval World

PHILIP STEELE

This account, easy-to-read and richly illustrated, provides a good introduction to the age of chivalry. It gives the reader an inside look at castle life, providing details about topics such as food and drink, and hunting and hawking.

Literature of the Renaissance and Enlightenment

Why It Matters

The era between 1300 and 1798 produced a revolution in thought. The Renaissance, whose name means "rebirth" in French, ushered in a return to the classical learning of ancient Greece and Rome and a flowering of the arts. Its focus on human potential led to the Enlightenment, or Age of Reason. New ideas about government, science, and the arts paved the way for the modern world.

For Links to the Renaissance and Enlightenment, click on:

HUMANITIES
CLASSZONE.COM

Europe in 1648

1 Power of Monarchs Renaissance thinkers revived many classical ideas, but they also created a new concept—the **nation**. Powerful European monarchs, such as **Elizabeth I** of England (shown here), arose to lead these new nations. Reigning from 1558 to 1603, she was so influential that the Renaissance in England is often called the Elizabethan age.

4 Age of Discovery From the Strait of Magellan to the Arctic Ocean, from India to the Americas, curious **explorers** were drawn to unknown shores. The symbol of this pioneering spirit, **Christopher Columbus,** sailed westward from Spain toward Asia in 1492. He never reached that continent, but he opened a new world to European settlement.

SWEDEN

SCOTLAND

IRELAND

ENGLAND

North Sea

Baltic

London

1

ATLANTIC OCEAN

Paris

FRANCE

PORTUGAL

4

SPAIN

Madrid

REPUBLIC OF GENOA

Florence PAPAL STATES

TUSCANY **2**

Rome

VENETIAN REPUBLIC

Adriatic Sea

3

KINGDOM OF THE TWO SICILIES

Mediterranean Sea

AFRICA

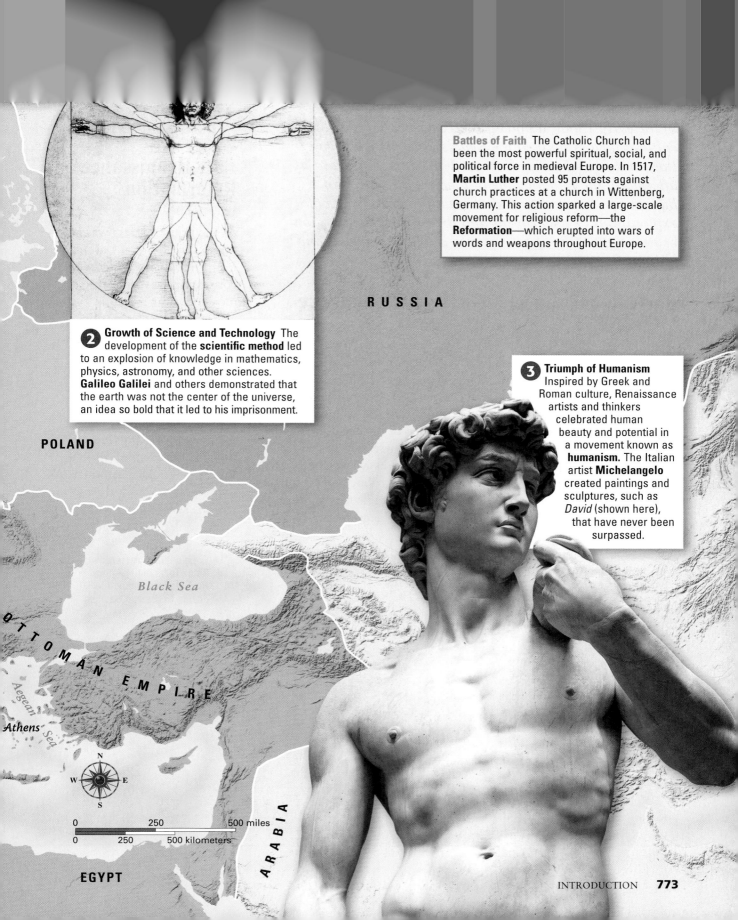

Battles of Faith The Catholic Church had been the most powerful spiritual, social, and political force in medieval Europe. In 1517, **Martin Luther** posted 95 protests against church practices at a church in Wittenberg, Germany. This action sparked a large-scale movement for religious reform—the **Reformation**—which erupted into wars of words and weapons throughout Europe.

RUSSIA

2 **Growth of Science and Technology** The development of the **scientific method** led to an explosion of knowledge in mathematics, physics, astronomy, and other sciences. **Galileo Galilei** and others demonstrated that the earth was not the center of the universe, an idea so bold that it led to his imprisonment.

3 **Triumph of Humanism** Inspired by Greek and Roman culture, Renaissance artists and thinkers celebrated human beauty and potential in a movement known as **humanism.** The Italian artist **Michelangelo** created paintings and sculptures, such as *David* (shown here), that have never been surpassed.

POLAND

Black Sea

OTTOMAN EMPIRE

Aegean Sea

Athens

N
W E
S

| 0 | 250 | 500 miles |
| 0 | 250 | 500 kilometers |

ARABIA

EGYPT

In the early 1300s, a powerful mix of social, political, and cultural factors sparked the Renaissance, which began in Italy and spread across Europe. The Renaissance and its aftermath, the Enlightenment, touched all aspects of human life. It was a period of great progress, from bold explorations of the heavens and the earth to the creation of stunning works of art, yet also a time of violence and poverty for many.

Early Renaissance
1300–1495

Several conditions in early-14th-century Italy made it fertile ground for a cultural revolution: (1) Cities grew and became powerful. (2) Extensive trade promoted a lively exchange of ideas. (3) A successful merchant class had the time and money to support art and literature. (4) The heritage of ancient Greece and Rome inspired artists and thinkers.

Philosophers and scholars who knew the ancient Latin and Greek masters often challenged traditional ways of thinking. New ideas spread like wildfire from city to city.

Along with the factors that encouraged change, there was a powerful force opposing it—the Catholic Church. The church expected its members to be more concerned with heavenly than with worldly matters.

High Renaissance
1495–1530

When the Renaissance was at its height in Italy, citizens of Florence and Rome viewed their cities as rivals of ancient Athens. Princes, church leaders, and men of fortune dominated politics. These men sponsored artists such as **Michelangelo, Leonardo da Vinci,** and **Raphael,** who gave people new ways of looking at themselves.

Late Renaissance and Reformation
1530–1600

As the printing press was helping to spread literacy and new ideas, impatience with church corruption was triggering a movement for religious reform—the **Reformation.** Beginning with the public protest of a German monk named **Martin Luther** in 1517, the movement spread across Europe. For decades, **Protestants**—led by Luther in Germany, **John Calvin** in France, and **Henry VIII** in England—fought Catholics. As the pope's power declined, nations such as England and Spain took center stage.

Pope Julius II restored Rome to its old splendor. Michelangelo helped to design St. Peter's Basilica.

EARLY RENAISSANCE	HIGH RENAISSANCE	
1300	1495	1530

This painting of France's King Louis XIV shows his splendor and pride.

Age of Kings
1600–1700

Convinced that they had a divine right to rule, monarchs sought and achieved absolute power. **Philip II** of Spain created a wealthy empire that stretched from Africa to the New World. **Louis XIV** made France the most powerful nation in Europe, but his lavish lifestyle and continual wars led to great suffering among his people. In Russia, **Peter the Great** turned what had been an isolated territory into a power competitive with other European nations.

In England, the government, after a bloodless revolution, limited the power of the monarch. England created a **constitutional monarchy,** a form of government still used today.

Age of Enlightenment
1700–1789

During the Enlightenment, human concerns, from government to personal happiness, became subjects of wide-reaching philosophical thought. One English political thinker, **Thomas Hobbes,** concluded that a strong government was needed to control people's basically evil nature. His countryman **John Locke,** on the other hand, found people to be essentially good and able to govern themselves. **Mary Wollstonecraft** argued that women had as much potential as men. In France, thinkers such as **Voltaire, Jean Jacques Rousseau,** and **Baron de Montesquieu** challenged long-held assumptions about the privileges of the upper class, the divine right of kings, and the authority of the church. Toward the end of the era, a new belief in the rights of the individual inspired revolutions in America and France and helped change the course of Western civilization.

History to Literature

EVENT IN HISTORY	EVENT IN LITERATURE
Exploration around the world expands Europe's horizons during the 1400s and 1500s.	In 1516, Thomas More publishes *Utopia,* a fictional account of a perfect society in the New World.
Puritan religious reformers seek power and influence in England in the late 1500s.	Shakespeare satirizes Puritans around 1600 in *Twelfth Night.*
In 1749, Voltaire serves as adviser to the Prussian king Frederick the Great, an ambitious reformer.	In 1759, Voltaire publishes *Candide,* in which he satirizes people who seek to create a perfect society.

LATE RENAISSANCE AND REFORMATION	AGE OF KINGS		AGE OF ENLIGHTENMENT	
	1600		1700	1789

The revolution in ways of thinking about the world that took place in the Renaissance and Enlightenment eventually produced revolutionary changes in people's day-to-day lives. The rigid class distinctions of feudalism gradually gave way to new roles, rights, and responsibilities.

Lorenzo de Medici (1449–1492) was a ruler of Florence.

Aristocrats

Membership in the aristocracy in this period was not simply a matter of birth. Merchants who made their own fortunes could be awarded titles and enjoy all the accompanying power. Many bankers and merchants, like the powerful **Medici** family of Florence, used their riches to promote culture rather than just their own welfare. Without their influence, the great artist **Michelangelo** might have remained a poor stonecutter.

Clergy

Although the clergy had wielded much power during the Middle Ages, their role began to change as the winds of reform gathered force. Some clergymen, such as **Martin Luther** in Germany, brought about social change as they broke from the church. Others, such as the Dutch scholar **Desiderius Erasmus,** criticized the church from within. Still others, such as **Cardinal Richelieu** in France, aligned themselves with the established powers. All, however, were forced to reexamine their roles in a changing world.

Soldiers

The life of a soldier in the Renaissance and Enlightenment, as in other periods of history, was hard and often short. Although the Republic of Venice was employing 30,000 soldiers by 1509, the occupation was no longer a passport to wealth and influence, as it had been in the Middle Ages. The growth of professional armies—groups of soldiers who would work for the highest bidder—made the work less prestigious. As power shifted from the battlefield to the marketplace and the bank vault, making war became just another dangerous job.

The Middle Class

A business boom in the 16th century created not only a merchant aristocracy but also a thriving middle class of people who made their livings in a variety of occupations. Crafts, shopkeeping, manufacturing, banking, and trade offered ways for people to earn more money with less backbreaking effort than working the land. For the first time, even art and literature could provide their practitioners a living wage.

Martin Luther in 1533

Peasants and Farmers

Despite the social and economic changes during the Renaissance and Enlightenment, four out of every five people were still farmers. These peasants labored long hours on land they didn't own for the privilege of paying taxes to their lords. Even death was no release, since half their money often went to their masters when they died. Although some peasants became tenant farmers, laborers, or artisans, they seldom could escape the cycle of hard work and hardship that kept them in poverty.

Women in the Renaissance and Enlightenment

While powerful monarchs such as England's **Elizabeth I** and Russia's **Catherine the Great** were shaping history and Spain's **Teresa of Avila** was helping to reform the Catholic Church, the majority of women led less remarkable lives. Often working in the fields, women seldom had any voice in their own lives, let alone in religion, philosophy, or politics.

One notable woman who devoted her life to the advancement of equality between the sexes was **Mary Wollstonecraft** (1759–1797). A self-taught British citizen, Wollstonecraft argued that the rights of man must be extended to include the rights of women. She urged that women be educated in the same manner as men to achieve their full potential.

Mary Wollstonecraft

This painting by an unknown 16th-century artist shows a marketplace in Antwerp, a city in what is now Belgium.

177

The period of renewed interest in classical ideas and culture was also marked by a spirit of exploration and expansion of human horizons. This rebirth led to radically new approaches and achievements in almost every artistic and cultural activity.

Sir Isaac Newton

Philosophy and Science

The development of the scientific method led to a totally new way of thinking about the natural world. The Polish scientist Nicolaus Copernicus challenged perhaps the most basic idea about the universe—that the earth was at its center. His sun-centered model was later proved true by the German astronomer Johannes Kepler. The Italian Galileo Galilei made observations of the planets that also supported Copernicus's theory. In the global spirit of the Renaissance, the English scientist Isaac Newton later combined these discoveries into a unified set of laws describing motion. During the Enlightenment, also known as the Age of Reason, philosophers shone the light of reason on everything from individual rights to government and social responsibilities.

Enlightenment Thinkers at a Glance

Person	Idea	Impact
Jean Jacques Rousseau (1712–1778)	"Man is born free and everywhere he is in chains."	Democratic governments worldwide are based on the consent of the governed.
Baron de Montesquieu (1689–1755)	"Power should be a check to power."	Constitutions in France, the United States, and Latin America guarantee separation of powers.
Voltaire (1694–1778)	"Each individual [has] his natural rights. . . ."	Bills of rights in England, France, and the United States guarantee individual freedoms.

Literature

Writers increasingly relied on their native languages, such as English, Spanish, and Italian, instead of the Latin favored by the Middle Ages to express their ideas. A spirit of experimentation greatly influenced the literature of the era.

Tales written by the Italian Giovanni Boccaccio in the 14th century paved the way for the new genre of the **novel.** This literary form was refined by the 16th-century French writer François Rabelais, the 17th-century Spaniard Miguel de Cervantes, and the 18th-century Englishmen Daniel Defoe and Henry Fielding.

Another genre, **lyric poetry,** was practiced by writers throughout Europe, from Francesco Petrarch in Italy to Pierre de Ronsard in France to William Shakespeare in England.

Dramatists such as Shakespeare and Oliver Goldsmith in England, Molière and Jean Racine in France, and Lope de Vega in Spain provided popular entertainment to an increasingly literate public.

The literature of the late 17th and 18th centuries is sometimes called **neoclassical** because it reflects the order and restraint that marked the literature of ancient Rome.

In this painting, the Dutch artist Jan Vermeer (1632–1675) shows himself at work.

Painting, Sculpture, and Architecture

The new way of looking at the world that developed in the Renaissance drastically affected the way visual artists portrayed it. They devised new techniques based on classical Greek and Roman ideals of proportion. Leonardo da Vinci and Michelangelo did anatomical studies that helped artists create realistic figures. The use of perspective, a technique in which lines converge at a vanishing point, gave an illusion of depth and distance in the paintings of the Italians Raphael and Titian, the Dutchman Rembrandt, and the German Albrecht Dürer. As sculptors and architects, da Vinci, Donatello, and Michelangelo brought technical mastery of proportion to near perfection.

Music

Music also experienced a rebirth in three distinct periods—Renaissance, baroque, and classical. In the **Renaissance** period (1450–1600), sacred music was joined by new forms reflecting national tastes. New types of instrumental music also developed, often for the lute.

Baroque music (1600–1750) showed experimentation, complex melodies, and dance rhythms. Prominent composers included Johann Sebastian Bach and Antonio Vivaldi. Drama and music were blended in **opera,** a new form.

In the **classical** period (1750–1825), composers made use of tightly structured rhythms and melodies. Franz Joseph Haydn and Wolfgang Amadeus Mozart were two of the leading composers; the leading instrument was the piano.

Turning Points in Literature

The Printing Press

Although the Chinese had invented movable type around 1045, it didn't come into common use until Johann Gutenberg (1400?–1468?) recreated it in Germany four centuries later. With this invention, hundreds of identical copies could be produced quickly and cheaply; works no longer had to be copied by hand, as scribes had done for centuries. Mass-produced books, newspapers, and magazines dealt with both religious and secular topics.

Time Line

A.D. 1   PRESENT

EVENTS IN EUROPEAN LITERATURE

1300	1400	1500
1341 Francesco Petrarch is crowned poet laureate in Rome	**1455** Gutenberg Bible is produced on a printing press in Germany	**1523** Hans Sachs writes a poetic allegory honoring Martin Luther
1348 Boccaccio begins writing *The Decameron*	**1477** Chaucer's *Canterbury Tales* is printed in England	**1532** French writer François Rabelais publishes the first book of *Gargantua and Pantagruel*
1375 Robin Hood appears in popular English literature	**1498** Comedies of the ancient Greek playwright Aristophanes are published in Venice	**1543** Polish scientist Nicolaus Copernicus publishes his work on the solar system

A pilgrim in Chaucer's
Canterbury Tales

EVENTS IN EUROPEAN HISTORY

1300	1400	1500
1337 Hundred Years' War between England and France begins	**1428** Joan of Arc leads a French army against the English	**1508** Michelangelo begins painting the ceiling of the Sistine Chapel in Rome
1347–1350 Bubonic plague kills a third of Europe's population	**1497** Italian Leonardo da Vinci paints *The Last Supper*	**1517** Martin Luther posts protests of church practices on a church door in Wittenberg, Germany, starting the Reformation
1389 Truce signed by England, Scotland, and France		**1522** Magellan's expedition sails around the world
		1534 Henry VIII of England breaks with the Catholic Church

EVENTS IN WORLD HISTORY

1300	1400	1500
c. 1300 Osman establishes the Ottoman Empire in Anatolia	**1400** Iroquois League is formed in North America	**1502** Ismail I founds the Safavid dynasty and establishes Islam as the state religion in Persia
1325 Aztecs build their capital, Tenochtitlán, in Mexico	**1438** Pachacutec becomes ruler of the Incas in Peru	**1521** Cortés conquers the Aztecs in Mexico
1325 Noh drama develops in Japan	**1453** Ottomans conquer Constantinople	**1532** Pizarro conquers the Incas in Peru
1368 Hung-wu founds the Ming dynasty in China	**1464** Sunni Ali founds the Songhai empire in West Africa	
	1492 Christopher Columbus reaches Hispaniola in North America	

1551 Thomas More's *Utopia* translated into English from Latin

1580 Michel Eyquem de Montaigne publishes his first essays

1601 William Shakespeare completes *Hamlet*

1605 Miguel de Cervantes publishes the first part of *Don Quixote*

1667 John Milton publishes the first version of *Paradise Lost*

1670 Molière writes the ballet-comedy *Le Bourgeois Gentilhomme*

1726 Jonathan Swift publishes *Gulliver's Travels*

1759 Voltaire publishes *Candide*

1773 Johann Wolfgang von Goethe writes the earliest version of *Faust*

1781 Jean Jacques Rousseau publishes *Confessions*

1558 Elizabeth I is crowned queen of England

1588 Spanish Armada is defeated by England

1640 Portugal gains independence

1649 England declared a commonwealth

1669 Venice loses its last colony, Crete, to the Turks

1697 France attempts to colonize West Africa

1707 England and Scotland unite as Great Britain

1762 Catherine the Great of Russia begins her reign as empress

1789 French Revolution begins with establishment of National Assembly

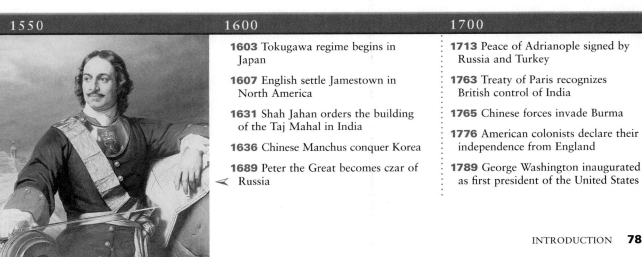

1603 Tokugawa regime begins in Japan

1607 English settle Jamestown in North America

1631 Shah Jahan orders the building of the Taj Mahal in India

1636 Chinese Manchus conquer Korea

1689 Peter the Great becomes czar of Russia

1713 Peace of Adrianople signed by Russia and Turkey

1763 Treaty of Paris recognizes British control of India

1765 Chinese forces invade Burma

1776 American colonists declare their independence from England

1789 George Washington inaugurated as first president of the United States

Mass Communication

The beginnings of the communication explosion in our contemporary world can be traced to the Renaissance and Enlightenment. The printing press made books affordable, and the resulting increase in literacy helped to usher in mass communication. Magazines and newspapers informed the masses and helped shape public opinion.

Human Rights

The term *human rights* originated in the 20th century, but the concept has roots in the Renaissance and Enlightenment. Bills of rights in England (1689), France (1789), and the United States (1791) were intended to protect individual rights and freedoms. These important documents influence today's activists who seek to protect the safety and liberty of peoples around the world.

Science and Medicine

Modern science and medicine owe a great deal to the scientific discoveries of the Renaissance and Enlightenment. In the 17th century, for example, the British physician William Harvey discovered the secrets of the circulation of blood.

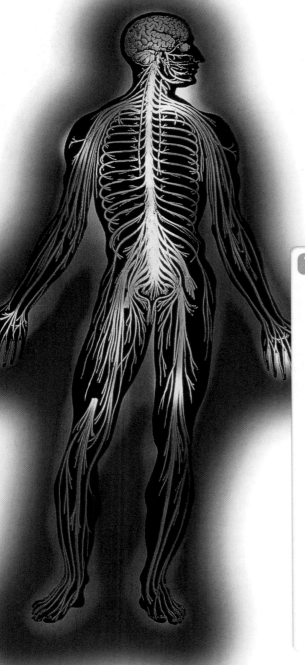

Mathematics and Engineering

The electronic world that we know today, with its graphing calculators, DVDs, computers, and the Internet, has its origins in the Renaissance and Enlightenment. The French philosopher and mathematician Blaise Pascal created a calculating machine in 1642.

The Legacy of Language

Words and phrases from the Renaissance and Enlightenment still influence our language today. Here's just a sample of expressions that have their origins in this time period.

Renaissance Man An educated man in the Renaissance was expected to develop knowledge and skills in many areas. The term was first applied to Leon Battista Alberti, an Italian writer, musician, mathematician, and artist. Today, the term is applied to any person notable for a broad range of achievements and interests.

Utopian This word comes from Utopia, the name of an imaginary island where life is nearly perfect—the subject of a book by the English scholar and statesman Thomas More. Now, the term *utopian* means "based on hopelessly impractical ideals."

Quixotic This word also comes from a literary work, the comic novel *Don Quixote* by the Spanish writer Miguel de Cervantes. Its hero, Don Quixote, is a dreamer who pursues his ideals without regard to their practicality. The word *quixotic* now describes any idealistic effort that has little chance of success.

"Liberty! Equality! Fraternity!" This phrase helped to start the French Revolution in 1789. It became not only a declaration of rights for all people but also a call to arms. Echoes of this phrase still spur people to political action.

from THE DECAMERON

federigo's falcon

GIOVANNI BOCCACCIO

An Overbearing Father

Giovanni Boccaccio
1313–1375

Giovanni Boccaccio (jō-vän'nē bō-kä'chĕ-ō') began writing poetry as a youth, but his early talent was not rewarded. Instead, his father, a merchant from Florence, demanded that Boccaccio forget about writing and learn business. While still a teenager, Boccaccio was sent from his home in Florence to Naples, where he was apprenticed to a banker for 6 years. He disliked commerce, so his father arranged for him to study religious law, a pursuit he also found disagreeable. After about 12 years in Naples, Boccaccio was recalled home to seek other employment. Although he later held several government and diplomatic positions, none of his jobs were very satisfactory, and he often lived on the brink of poverty.

A Source of Inspiration

Fortunately, despite his father's objections, Boccaccio had continued to write. In Naples, he produced an abundance of prose and poetry. It was also in Naples that he may have met his beloved "Fiammetta," a young woman who became the subject of much of his early writing and who appears as a narrator in *The Decameron.* The real identity of this woman, who probably died in the plague of 1348, has never been established.

An Influential Poet and Scholar

Boccaccio complained that because his father "strove to bend" his talent, he was unable to become "a distinguished poet." Eventually, however, he did achieve greatness as a poet, storyteller, and scholar. He completed his long work *The Decameron* in 1353. He then turned to writing scholarly works in Latin, including a biography of Dante Alighieri. Along with his lifelong friend Petrarch (see page 806), Boccaccio helped to set new directions for Italian literature and for the study of classical Greek and Latin texts.

Build Background

Boccaccio's Classic Tales

The Decameron is the first great work of prose fiction in Italian. Its 100 tales are set within a **frame story,** or outer story, about ten young friends who leave Florence to escape the plague. While passing time in the countryside, they amuse themselves by telling stories over a period of ten days (the word *decameron* means "work of ten days"). Each day a different "king" or "queen" is appointed to direct the entertainment of the group. Fiammetta, the queen of the fifth day, asks everyone to provide tales about rocky love affairs that end happily.

Fiammetta's own story, "Federigo's Falcon," involves a frustrated lover whose most precious possession is a falcon. During the Middle Ages, many noblemen in western Europe practiced the sport of falconry. Trainers would catch falcons, other types of hawks, or eagles and teach them to hunt prey.

Love, however, not hunting, is the subject of "Federigo's Falcon." Federigo will do anything to gain the affection of a married noblewoman with whom he has fallen in love. His dilemma is a typical one in the literature of **courtly love.** This philosophy of love takes its name from the royal courts of the Middle Ages. Under the rules of courtly love, a man had to dedicate his life to his lady, whom he idealized in word and deed. During this time in Europe, most upper-class marriages were arranged for reasons of wealth or family reputation, so writers did not consider marriage fertile ground for such romance. Many tales of courtly love tell about the love between one man and the wife of another, an arrangement that was permitted as long as the passion remained idealized.

Connect to Your Life

In this story, a man sacrifices everything for the woman he loves. Share examples of sacrifices for love that you have heard of or read about. What were the results of these sacrifices?

Focus Your Reading

LITERARY ANALYSIS: SITUATIONAL IRONY

Irony is a contrast between expectation and reality. **Situational irony** occurs when a character or the reader expects one thing to happen but something entirely different happens. A famous story by O. Henry illustrates such irony: a young married man buys his wife combs for her beautiful hair, only to learn that she has cut her hair and sold it to pay for a present for him. As you read Boccaccio's story, look for examples of situational irony.

ACTIVE READING: PREDICTING

A **prediction** is an attempt to determine what will happen next in a story. When you predict, you combine information from the text with your own prior knowledge to make guesses about how the **plot** will advance. As you read further, you will often come across new information that may cause you to adjust your prediction.

📖 **READER'S NOTEBOOK** After reading the first five paragraphs of "Federigo's Falcon," make a prediction about what will happen. Then adjust your prediction or make new predictions every time you encounter important new information. Record your predictions and adjustments.

WORDS TO KNOW **Vocabulary Preview**

anguish	discretion	inevitably
commend	donor	meagerly
compel	illustrious	presumption
diminish		

from The Decameron

Federigo's Falcon

Giovanni Boccaccio

Translated by Mark Musa and Peter Bondanella

ilomena had already finished speaking, and when the Queen saw there was no one left to speak except for Dioneo, who was exempted because of his special privilege,[1] she herself with a cheerful face said:

It is now my turn to tell a story and, dearest ladies, I shall do so most willingly with a tale similar in some respects to the preceding one, its purpose being not only to show you how much power your beauty has over the gentle heart, but also so that you yourselves may learn, whenever it is fitting, to be the <u>donors</u> of your favors instead of always leaving this act to the whim of Fortune,[2] who, as it happens, on most occasions bestows such favors with more abundance than <u>discretion</u>.

You should know, then, that Coppo di Borghese Domenichi,[3] who once lived in our city and perhaps still does, a man of great and respected authority in our times, one most <u>illustrious</u> and worthy of eternal fame both for his way of life and his ability much more than for the nobility of his blood, often took delight, when he was an old man, in discussing things from the past with his neighbors and with others. He knew how to do this well, for he was more logical and had a better memory and a more eloquent style of speaking than any other man. Among the many beautiful tales he told, there was one he would often tell about a young man who once lived in Florence named Federigo, the son of Messer Filippo Alberighi,[4] renowned above all other men in Tuscany for his prowess in arms and for his courtliness.[5]

As often happens to most men of gentle breeding, he fell in love, with a noble lady named Monna Giovanna,[6] in her day considered to be one of the most beautiful and most charming ladies that ever there was in Florence; and in order to win her love, he participated in jousts[7] and tournaments, organized and gave banquets, spending his money without restraint; but she, no less virtuous than beautiful, cared little for these things he did on her behalf, nor did she care for the one who did them. Now, as Federigo was spending far beyond his means and getting nowhere, as can easily happen, he lost his wealth and was reduced to poverty, and was left with nothing to his name but his little farm (from whose revenues he lived very <u>meagerly</u>) and one falcon, which was among the finest of its kind in the world.

---

1. **Dioneo** (dē′ô-nä′ō) **. . . privilege:** Dioneo had been given permission always to tell the last story of the day.

2. **Fortune:** the power, personified, that supposedly distributes good and bad luck to people.

3. **Coppo di Borghese Domenichi** (kôp′pō dē bôr-gä′zě dô-mě′nē-kē).

4. **Messer Filippo Alberighi** (mās′sěr fē-lēp′pō äl-bě-rē′gē).

5. **courtliness:** elegance and refinement.

6. **Monna Giovanna** (môn′nä jō-vän′nä).

7. **jousts:** combats between two men on horseback.

La Pia de Tolommei (1868-1880), Dante Gabriel Rossetti. Oil on canvas, 104.8 cm × 120.6 cm. Spencer Museum of Art, University of Kansas.

More in love than ever, but knowing that he would never be able to live the way he wished to in the city, he went to live at Campi, where his farm was. There he passed his time hawking whenever he could, imposing on no one, and enduring his poverty patiently. Now one day, during the time that Federigo was reduced to these extremes, it happened that the husband of Monna Giovanna fell ill, and realizing death was near, he made his last will: he was very rich, and he left everything to his son, who was just growing up, and since he had also loved Monna Giovanna very much, he made her his heir should his son die without any legitimate[8] children; and then he died.

Monna Giovanna was now a widow, and every summer, as our women usually do, she would go to the country with her son to one of their estates very close by to Federigo's farm. Now this young boy of hers happened to become more and more friendly with Federigo and he began to enjoy birds and dogs; and after seeing Federigo's falcon fly many times, it made him so happy that he very much wished it were his own, but he did not dare to ask for it, for he could see how precious it was to Federigo. During this time, it happened that the young boy took ill, and his mother was much grieved, for he was her only child and she loved him dearly; she would spend the entire day by his side, never ceasing to comfort him, asking him time and again if there was anything he wished, begging him to tell her what it might be, for if it was possible to obtain

8. **legitimate** (lə-jĭt′ə-mĭt): born of parents who are legally married to each other.

She knew that Federigo had been in love with her for some time now. . . .

it, she would certainly do everything in her power to get it. After the young boy had heard her make this offer many times, he said:

"Mother, if you can arrange for me to have Federigo's falcon, I think I would get well quickly."

When the lady heard this, she was taken aback for a moment, and then she began thinking what she could do about it. She knew that Federigo had been in love with her for some time now, but she had never deigned[9] to give him a second look; so, she said to herself:

"How can I go to him, or even send someone, and ask for this falcon of his, which is, as I have heard tell, the finest that ever flew, and furthermore, his only means of support? And how can I be so insensitive as to wish to take away from this nobleman the only pleasure which is left to him?"

And involved in these thoughts, knowing that she was certain to have the bird if she asked for it, but not knowing what to say to her son, she stood there without answering him. Finally the love she bore her son persuaded her that she should make him happy, and no matter what the consequences might be, she would not send for the bird, but rather go herself to fetch it and bring it back to him; so she answered her son:

"My son, cheer up and think only of getting well, for I promise you that first thing tomorrow morning I shall go and fetch it for you."

The child was so happy that he showed some improvement that very day. The following morning, the lady, accompanied by another woman, as if they were out for a stroll, went to Federigo's modest little house and asked for him. Since the weather for the past few days had not been right for hawking, Federigo happened to be in his orchard attending to certain tasks, and when he heard that Monna Giovanna was asking for him

at the door, he was so surprised and happy that he rushed there; as she saw him coming, she rose to greet him with womanly grace, and once Federigo had welcomed her most courteously, she said:

"How do you do, Federigo?" Then she continued, "I have come to make amends[10] for the harm you have suffered on my account by loving me more than you should have, and in token of this, I intend to have a simple meal with you and this companion of mine this very day."

To this Federigo humbly replied: "Madonna,[11] I have no recollection of ever suffering any harm because of you; on the contrary: so much good have I received from you that if ever I was worth anything, it was because of your worth and the love I bore for you; and your generous visit is certainly so very dear to me that I would spend all over again all that I spent in the past, but you have come to a poor host."

And having said this, he humbly led her through the house and into his garden, and because he had no one there to keep her company, he said:

"My lady, since there is no one else, this good woman, who is the wife of the farmer here, will keep you company while I see to the table."

though he was very poor, Federigo until now had never realized to what extent he had wasted his wealth; but this morning, the fact that he had nothing in the house with which he could honor the lady for the love of whom he had in the past entertained countless people, gave him cause to reflect: in great <u>anguish</u>, he cursed himself and his fortune, and like someone out of his senses he started running here and there through-

---

9. **deigned** (dānd): considered worthy of one's dignity.

10. **make amends:** make payment of some sort for a loss or injury.

11. **Madonna:** Italian for "my lady," a polite way to address a married woman. "Monna" is a contraction of this term.

out the house, but unable to find either money or anything he might be able to pawn,[12] and since it was getting late and he was still very much set on serving this noble lady some sort of meal, but unwilling to turn for help to even his own farmer (not to mention anyone else), he set his eyes upon his good falcon, which was sitting on its perch in a small room, and since he had nowhere else to turn, he took the bird, and finding it plump, he decided that it would be a worthy food for such a lady. So, without giving the matter a second thought, he wrung its neck and quickly gave it to his servant girl to pluck, prepare, and place on a spit to be roasted with care; and when he had set the table with the whitest of tablecloths (a few of which he still had left), he returned, with a cheerful face, to the lady in his garden and announced that the meal, such as he was able to prepare, was ready.

The lady and her companion rose and went to the table together with Federigo, who waited upon them with the greatest devotion, and they ate the good falcon without knowing what it was they were eating. Then, having left the table and spent some time in pleasant conversation, the lady thought it time now to say what she had come to say, and so she spoke these kind words to Federigo:

"Federigo, if you recall your former way of life and my virtue, which you perhaps mistook for harshness and cruelty, I have no doubt at all that you will be amazed by my <u>presumption</u> when you hear what my main reason for coming here is; but if you had children, through whom you might have experienced the power of parental love, I feel certain that you would, at least in part, forgive me. But, just as you have no child, I do have one, and I cannot escape the laws common to all mothers; the force of such laws <u>compels</u> me to follow them, against my own will and against good manners and duty, and to ask of you a gift which I know is most

Peregrine falcon. Raja Serfogee of Tanjore Collection, by permission of the British Library.

precious to you; and it is naturally so, since your extreme condition has left you no other delight, no other pleasure, no other consolation; and this gift is your falcon, which my son is so taken by that if I do not bring it to him, I fear his sickness will grow so much worse that I may lose him. And therefore I beg you, not because of the love that you bear for me, which does not oblige you in the least, but because of your own nobleness, which you have shown to be greater than that of all others in practicing courtliness, that you be pleased to give it to me, so that I may say that I have saved the life of my son by means of this gift, and because of it I have placed him in your debt forever."

---

12. **pawn:** borrow money against.

When he heard what the lady requested and knew that he could not oblige her because he had given her the falcon to eat, Federigo began to weep in her presence, for he could not utter a word in reply. The lady at first thought his tears were caused more by the sorrow of having to part with the good falcon than by anything else, and she was on the verge of telling him she no longer wished it, but she held back and waited for Federigo's reply once he stopped weeping. And he said:

"My lady, ever since it pleased God for me to place my love in you, I have felt that Fortune has been hostile to me in many ways, and I have complained of her, but all this is nothing compared to what she has just done to me, and I shall never be at peace with her again, when I think how you have come here to my poor home, where, when it was rich, you never deigned to come, and how you requested but a small gift, and Fortune worked to make it impossible for me to give it to you; and why this is so I shall tell you in a few words. When I heard that you, out of your kindness, wished to dine with me, I considered it only fitting and proper, taking into account your excellence and your worthiness, that I should honor you, according to my possibilities, with a more precious food than that which I usually serve to other people. So I thought of the falcon for which you have just asked me and of its value and I judged it a food worthy of you, and this very day I had it roasted and served to you as best I could. But seeing now that you desired it another way, my sorrow in not being able to serve you is so great that never shall I be able to console myself again."

And after he had said this, he laid the feathers, the feet, and the beak of the bird before her as proof. When the lady heard and saw this, she first reproached him for having killed a falcon such as this to serve as a meal to a woman. But then to herself she commended the greatness of his spirit, which no poverty was able, or would be able, to diminish; then, having lost all hope of getting the falcon and thus, perhaps, of improving the health of her son, she thanked Federigo both for the honor paid to her and for his good intentions, and then left in grief to return to her son. To his mother's extreme sorrow, whether in disappointment in not having the falcon or because his illness inevitably led to it, the boy passed from this life only a few days later.

After the period of her mourning and her bitterness had passed, the lady was repeatedly urged by her brothers to remarry, since she was very rich and still young; and although she did not wish to do so, they became so insistent that remembering the worthiness of Federigo and his last act of generosity—that is, to have killed such a falcon to do her honor—she said to her brothers:

"I would prefer to remain a widow, if only that would be pleasing to you, but since you wish me to take a husband, you may be sure that I shall take no man other than Federigo degli Alberighi."

In answer to this, her brothers, making fun of her, replied:

"You foolish woman, what are you saying? How can you want him? He hasn't a penny to his name."

To this she replied: "My brothers, I am well aware of what you say, but I would much rather have a man who lacks money than money that lacks a man."

Her brothers, seeing that she was determined and knowing Federigo to be of noble birth, no matter how poor he was, accepted her wishes and gave her with all her riches in marriage to him; when he found himself the husband of such a great lady, whom he had loved so much and who was so wealthy besides, he managed his financial affairs with more prudence than in the past and lived with her happily the rest of his days. ❖

WORDS TO KNOW

commend (kə-mĕnd′) *v.* to express approval of; praise
diminish (dĭ-mĭn′ĭsh) *v.* to lessen
inevitably (ĭn-ĕv′ĭ-tə-blē) *adv.* unavoidably

FROM

the art of *courtly* love

ANDREAS CAPELLANUS

Translated by John Jay Parry

Andreas Capellanus lived in the 1100s and is thought to have been a chaplain at a French court. Around 1185, he wrote The Art of Courtly Love, *which established a set of rules for love among the nobility. The following excerpt comes from the beginning of his work, where he defines love as a type of suffering.*

ove is a certain inborn suffering derived from the sight of and excessive meditation upon the beauty of the opposite sex, which causes each one to wish above all things the embraces of the other and by common desire to carry out all of love's precepts[1] in the other's embrace.

That love is suffering is easy to see, for before the love becomes equally balanced on both sides there is no torment greater, since the lover is always in fear that his love may not gain its desire and that he is wasting his efforts. He fears, too, that rumors of it may get abroad, and he fears everything that might harm it in any way, for before things are perfected a slight disturbance often spoils them. If he is a poor man, he also fears that the woman may scorn his poverty; if he is ugly, he fears that she may despise his lack of beauty or may give her love to a more handsome man; if he is rich, he fears that his parsimony[2] in the past may stand in his way. To tell the truth, no one can number the fears of one single lover. This kind of love, then, is a suffering which is felt by only one of the persons and may be called "single love." But even after both are in love the fears that arise are just as great, for each of the lovers fears that what he has acquired with so much effort may be lost through the effort of someone else, which is certainly much worse for a man than if, having no hope, he sees that his efforts are accomplishing nothing, for it is worse to lose the things you are seeking than to be deprived of a gain you merely hope for. The lover fears, too, that he may offend his loved one in some way; indeed he fears so many things that it would be difficult to tell them.

---

1. **precepts:** rules that dictate a particular course of conduct.
2. **parsimony:** extreme stinginess.

Connect to the Literature

1. What Do You Think?
Were you surprised by the turn of events in this story? Why or why not?

Comprehension Check
- How does Federigo lose his wealth?
- Why does Monna Giovanna want Federigo's falcon?
- What happens when she goes to visit him?

Think Critically

2. ACTIVE READING: PREDICTING Look again at the initial prediction you recorded in your 📖 READER'S NOTEBOOK. How accurate was it? What adjustments or new predictions did you make as you read the story?

3. Do you think the actions of Federigo illustrate the beauty of love or the foolishness of love? Explain your reasoning.

4. What is your opinion of Monna Giovanna?

THINK ABOUT
- her response to Federigo's lavish spending
- the promise she makes to her son
- her behavior at Federigo's house
- her decision to marry Federigo

5. Fiammetta explains that her story shows females the power that their beauty has "over the gentle heart." What other lessons does the story offer? Explain.

Extend Interpretations

6. What If? Suppose that Monna Giovanna had explained the purpose of her visit before Federigo killed the falcon. Do you think she still would have married him? Why or why not?

7. Comparing Texts In *The Art of Courtly Love,* Andreas Capellanus suggests that love always involves suffering. Compare his view of love with the way Boccaccio portrays love in "Federigo's Falcon."

8. Connect to Life Monna Giovanna's decision to remarry is influenced by her brothers. What sort of pressures today influence a person's decision to marry? Are these pressures as strong as the ones that Monna Giovanna faced?

LITERARY ANALYSIS: SITUATIONAL IRONY

Irony is a contrast between what is expected and what actually exists or happens. **Situational irony** occurs when a character or the reader expects one thing to happen but something entirely different happens. For example, in Boccaccio's tale, Federigo spends lavishly in the hope of winning Monna Giovanna's favor, but she visits him only after he is impoverished.

Paired Activity With a partner, create a chart like the one below and list the ironic situations that occur in the story. Then discuss what the irony suggests about the nature of love.

What's Expected	What Actually Happens
Federigo expects to impress his lady with his wealth.	She finally visits him when he is too poor to feed her.

REVIEW: PLOT As you know, the **plot** of a story usually includes the following stages: **exposition, rising action, climax,** and **falling action.** Create a diagram in which you identify these stages in "Federigo's Falcon." (See page 589 for an example of such a diagram.)

Writing Options

1. Dramatic Scene Write a dialogue in which Monna Giovanna explains to her brothers why Federigo is the only man she will marry. Start by reviewing the last few paragraphs of the story.

2. Comparing Portrayals of Love Write a brief essay comparing the portrayals of love in Boccaccio's story and another work you have read, such as a poem by Sappho. Include specific examples from both works.

Writing Handbook
See page R31: Compare and Contrast.

Activities & Explorations

1. Storytelling Festival With a small group of classmates, create some stories about great sacrifices made for love. The stories can be original creations or retellings of well-known stories. Rehearse your stories, and then present them orally to the rest of the class.
~ SPEAKING AND LISTENING

2. Booklet of Quotations With a group of classmates, prepare a booklet of famous quotations about love. Illustrate your booklet with drawings, photographs, or copies of art. ~ ART

Inquiry & Research

Report on Courtly Love
Prepare an oral report on the history of courtly love. When did courtly love begin? How were gentlemen supposed to woo ladies, and how were the ladies supposed to respond?

RESEARCH STARTER
CLASSZONE.COM

Vocabulary in Action

EXERCISE: CONTEXT CLUES Write the vocabulary word that is closest in meaning to the italicized word or phrase in each sentence.

1. Nothing could *reduce* Federigo's love for Monna Giovanna.

2. Federigo did not show *good judgment* when he spent all his money trying to impress her.

3. Federigo's overspending led *in an inescapable manner* to the loss of his fortune.

4. Only a request from her sick son could *irresistibly drive* Monna Giovanna to ask a favor.

5. Because Federigo lived *with a lack of abundant resources,* Monna Giovanna was reluctant to ask for his last precious possession.

6. After Monna Giovanna apologized for her *daring and insulting request,* Federigo wept.

7. Federigo thought Monna Giovanna would *speak highly of* the excellent meal.

8. The boy wanted Federigo to be a *patron or supporter* by making a gift of his falcon.

9. After the meal, Federigo could not disguise his *suffering* over having served the bird.

10. Perhaps Federigo eventually became *noted* for his faithfulness in love.

Building Vocabulary

For an in-depth lesson on denotation and connotation, see page 1090.

Sir Thomas More

from Utopia

Sir Thomas More
1477–1535

A Privileged Childhood Born in London, Thomas More was the son of a prominent English lawyer and judge. As a boy, he attended a prestigious school and served as a page in the home of the archbishop of Canterbury. The archbishop took an interest in the boy, whom he said would grow to be a "marvellous man," and later supported More's attendance at Oxford University. While studying at Oxford, More became friends with some of England's most influential humanist scholars (see page 773 for a discussion of Renaissance humanism).

Brilliant Lawyer, Statesman, and Scholar A devoutly religious man, More seriously considered becoming a monk but instead pursued a career in law and politics. In 1504, around the time of his first marriage, he became a member of Parliament. With exacting self-discipline, More also continued his literary and scholarly pursuits. His household became famous for its hospitality to scholars. While More was serving on a diplomatic mission, he began to write his famous book *Utopia,* an account of an ideal society. More coined the name *Utopia* from two Greek words meaning "no place." In 1518, the highly respected More was appointed by King Henry VIII to act as an ambassador. More was knighted in 1521 and eight years later became lord chancellor—the highest position next to the king in the English government.

A Violent Death In 1532, More resigned as lord chancellor because he opposed Henry VIII's plan to divorce the queen and marry Anne Boleyn in defiance of the Roman Catholic Church. In 1534, after the king had broken away from the church and married Boleyn, More refused to take the Oath of Supremacy, which recognized Henry as the head of the English church. As a result, More was imprisoned in the Tower of London. At his trial for treason, he was found guilty and sentenced to die. Before his beheading, More uttered the conviction that he was "the king's good servant, but God's first." Because he put his religious beliefs ahead of his duties to the government, More was eventually made a saint. Widely admired for his intelligence and his devotion to his faith, More inspired the play *A Man for All Seasons* (1960), by Robert Bolt.

Build Background

WORDS TO KNOW **Vocabulary Preview**

benevolent	hinder	insatiable	prevalent
compulsory	incessantly	novice	superfluous
grave	indigent		

Connect to Your Life

What comes to mind when you hear the word *utopia?* Do you have your own mental image of a perfect society, or do you recall books or films that deal with the effort to create a perfect world? With a small group of classmates, discuss your ideas and images of utopias.

Focus Your Reading

LITERARY ANALYSIS: AUTHOR'S PURPOSE
Authors typically write for one or more of the following purposes: to entertain, to inform, to express opinions, or to persuade. As you read the excerpts from *Utopia,* consider what purpose or purposes More might have had when he wrote the book.

ACTIVE READING: DRAWING CONCLUSIONS
To identify More's purpose for writing, you will need to draw conclusions based upon the text. A conclusion is a logical statement that combines what you already know with what you learn from your reading. Consider the following passage from More's text:

> *Agriculture is the one pursuit which is common to all, both men and women, without exception.*

You know that in most societies only some people are farmers. You might conclude from this passage that More believes that farming is so important that everyone should share in the work.

📖 **READER'S NOTEBOOK** Make a chart, like the one shown below, to keep track of how, according to these excerpts, Utopia differs from other countries. The differences will help you to draw conclusions about More's values and purpose for writing.

	In Utopia	In Other Countries
Farming		
Other occupations		
Money		

from Utopia
Sir Thomas More
Translated by G. C. Richards

The Land and Its People

The island contains fifty-four city-states, all spacious and magnificent, identical in language, traditions, customs, and laws. They are similar also in layout and everywhere, as far as the nature of the ground permits, similar even in appearance. None of them is separated by less than twenty-four miles from the nearest, but none is so isolated that a person cannot go from it to another in a day's journey on foot. From each city three old and experienced citizens meet to discuss the affairs of common interest to the island once a year at Amaurotum,[1] for this city, being in the very center of the country, is situated most conveniently for the representatives of all sections. It is considered the chief as well as the capital city.

The lands are so well assigned to the cities that each has at least twelve miles of country on every side, and on some sides even much more, to wit, the side on which the cities are farther apart. No city has any desire to extend its territory, for they consider themselves the tenants rather than the masters of what they hold.

Everywhere in the rural districts they have, at suitable distances from one another, farmhouses well equipped with agricultural implements. They are inhabited by citizens who come in succession[2] to live there. No rural household numbers less than forty men and women, besides two serfs attached to the soil. Over them are set a master and a mistress, serious in mind and ripe in years. Over every group of thirty households rules a phylarch.[3]

Twenty from each household return every year to the city, namely, those having completed two years in the country. As substitutes in their place, the same number are sent from the city. They are to be trained by those who have been there a year and who therefore are more expert in farming; they themselves will teach others in the following years. There is thus no danger of anything going wrong with the annual food supply through want of skill, as might happen if all at one time were newcomers and <u>novices</u> at farming. Though this system of changing farmers is the rule, to prevent any individual's being forced against his will to continue too long in a life of rather hard work, yet many men who take a natural pleasure in agricultural pursuits obtain leave to stay several years.

The occupation of the farmers is to cultivate the soil, to feed the animals, and to get wood and convey it to the city either by land or by water, whichever way is more convenient. They breed a vast quantity of poultry by a wonderful contrivance. The hens do not brood over the eggs, but the farmers, by keeping a great number of them at a uniform heat, bring them to life and hatch them.[4] As soon as they come out of the shell, the chicks follow and acknowledge humans as their mothers! . . .

---

1. **Amaurotum** (ä-mô-rō′tōŏm).
2. **in succession:** by turns; one after another.
3. **phylarch** (fī′lärk′): an officer in charge of 30 rural households.
4. **the farmers . . . hatch them:** The device described is similar to the incubators used today for hatching eggs.

WORDS TO KNOW

novice (nŏv′ĭs) *n.* a beginner in a job or activity

How Utopians Breed Chickens by Incubation, François van Bleyswyck.
Bibliothèque Nationale de France, Paris.

Occupations

Agriculture is the one pursuit which is common to all, both men and women, without exception. They are all instructed in it from childhood, partly by principles taught in school, partly by field trips to the farms closer to the city as if for recreation. Here they do not merely look on, but, as opportunity arises for bodily exercise, they do the actual work.

Besides agriculture (which is, as I said, common to all), each is taught one particular craft as his own. This is generally either wool-working or linen-making or masonry[5] or metal-working or carpentry. There is no other pursuit which occupies any number worth mentioning. As for clothes, these are of one and the same pattern throughout the island and down the centuries, though there is a distinction between the sexes and between the single and married. The garments are comely to the eye, convenient for bodily movement, and fit for wear in heat and cold. Each family, I say, does its own tailoring.

Of the other crafts, one is learned by each person, and not the men only, but the women too. The latter as the weaker sex have the lighter occupations and generally work wool and flax. To the men are committed the remaining more laborious crafts. For the most part, each is brought up in his father's craft, for which most have a natural inclination. But if anyone is attracted to another occupation, he is transferred by adoption to a family pursuing that craft for which he has a liking. Care is taken not only by his father but by the authorities, too, that he will be assigned to a grave and honorable householder. Moreover, if anyone after being thoroughly taught one craft desires another also, the same permission is given. Having acquired both, he practices his choice unless the city has more need of the one than of the other.

The chief and almost the only function of the syphogrants[6] is to manage and provide that no one sit idle, but that each apply himself industriously to his trade, and yet that he be not wearied like a beast of burden with constant toil from early morning till late at night. Such wretchedness is worse than the lot of slaves, and yet it is almost everywhere the life of workingmen— except for the Utopians. The latter divide the day and night into twenty-four equal hours and assign only six to work. There are three before noon, after which they go to dinner. After dinner, when they have rested for two hours in the afternoon, they again give three to work and finish up with supper. Counting one o'clock as beginning from midday, they go to bed about eight o'clock, and sleep claims eight hours.

The intervals between the hours of work, sleep, and food are left to every man's discretion, not to waste in revelry[7] or idleness, but to devote the time free from work to some other occupation according to taste. These periods are commonly devoted to intellectual pursuits. For it is their custom that public lectures are daily delivered in the hours before daybreak. Attendance is compulsory only for those who have been specially chosen to devote themselves to learning. A great number of all classes, however, both males and females, flock to hear the lectures, some to one and some to another, according to their natural inclination. But if anyone should prefer to devote this time to his trade, as is the case with many minds which do not reach the level for any of the higher intellectual disciplines, he is not hindered; in fact, he is even praised as useful to the commonwealth.[8] . . .

But here, lest you be mistaken, there is one

---

5. **masonry:** stonework or brickwork.

6. **syphogrants** (sĭf'ə-grănts'): another name for a phylarch.

7. **revelry** (rĕv'əl-rē): loud partying or merrymaking.

8. **commonwealth:** a nation or state governed by its people.

How the Island of Utopia Is Shaped like a Crescent,
François van Bleyswyck. Bibliothèque Nationale de
France, Paris.

point you must examine more closely. Since they devote but six hours to work, you might possibly think the consequence to be some scarcity of necessities. But so far is this from being the case that the aforesaid[9] time is not only enough but more than enough for a supply of all that is requisite[10] for either the necessity or the convenience of living. This phenomenon you too will understand if you consider how large a part of the population in other countries exists without working. First, there are almost all the women, who constitute half the whole; or, where the women are busy, there as a rule the men are snoring in their stead.[11] Besides, how great and how lazy is the crowd of priests and so-called religious! Add to them all the rich, especially the masters of estates, who are commonly termed gentlemen and noblemen. Reckon with them their retainers[12]—I mean, that whole rabble of good-for-nothing swashbucklers.[13] Finally, join in the lusty[14] and sturdy beggars who make some disease an excuse for idleness. You will certainly find far less numerous than you had supposed those whose labor produces all the articles that mortals require for daily use.

Now estimate how few of those who do work are occupied in essential trades. For, in a society where we make money the standard of everything, it is necessary to practice many crafts which are quite vain and superfluous, ministering only to luxury and licentiousness.[15] Suppose the host of those who now toil were distributed over only as few crafts as the few needs and conveniences demanded by nature. In the great abundance of commodities which must then arise, the prices set on them would be too low for the craftsmen to earn their livelihood by their work. But suppose all those fellows who are now busied with unprofitable crafts, as well as all the lazy and idle throng, any one of whom now consumes as much of the fruits of other men's labors as any two of the workingmen, were all set to work and indeed to useful work. You can easily see how small an allowance of time would be enough and to spare for the production of all that is required by necessity or comfort (or even pleasure, provided it be genuine and natural). . . .

---

9. **aforesaid:** spoken of earlier.

10. **requisite** (rĕk′wĭ-zĭt): required; essential.

11. **stead:** place.

12. **retainers:** servants or attendants of people with money or high rank.

13. **swashbucklers:** adventurers; in this case, probably a reference to those who seek personal gain.

14. **lusty:** strong; vigorous.

15. **licentiousness** (lī-sĕn′shəs-nĭs): immoral behavior, especially of a sexual nature.

The Commonwealth Outside Utopia

Now I have described to you, as exactly as I could, the structure of that commonwealth which I judge not merely the best but the only one which can rightly claim the name of a commonwealth. Outside Utopia, to be sure, men talk freely of the public welfare—but look after their private interests only. In Utopia, where nothing is private, they seriously concern themselves with public affairs. Assuredly in both cases they act reasonably. For, outside Utopia, how many are there who do not realize that, unless they make some separate provision for themselves, however flourishing the commonwealth, they will themselves starve? For this reason, necessity compels them to hold that they must take account of themselves rather than of the people, that is, of others.

On the other hand, in Utopia, where everything belongs to everybody, no one doubts, provided only that the public granaries[16] are well filled, that the individual will lack nothing for his private use. The reason is that the distribution of goods is not niggardly.[17] In Utopia there is no poor man and no beggar. Though no man has anything, yet all are rich.

For what can be greater riches for a man than to live with a joyful and peaceful mind, free of all worries—not troubled about his food or harassed by the querulous[18] demands of his wife or fearing poverty for his son or worrying about his daughter's dowry, but feeling secure about the livelihood and happiness of himself and his family: wife, sons, grandsons, great-grandsons, great-great-grandsons, and all the long line of their descendants that gentlefolk anticipate? Then take into account the fact that there is no less provision for those who are now helpless but once worked than for those who are still working.

At this point I should like anyone to be so bold as to compare this fairness with the so-called justice prevalent in other nations, among which, upon my soul, I cannot discover the slightest trace of justice and fairness. What brand of justice is it that any nobleman whatsoever or goldsmith-banker or moneylender or, in fact, anyone else from among those who either do no work at all or whose work is of a kind not very essential to the commonwealth, should attain a life of luxury and grandeur on the basis of his idleness or his nonessential work? In the meantime, the common laborer, the carter, the carpenter, and the farmer perform work so hard and continuous that beasts of burden could scarcely endure it and work so essential that no commonwealth could last even one year without it. Yet they earn such scanty fare and lead such a miserable life that the condition of beasts of burden might seem far preferable. The latter do not have to work so incessantly nor is their food much worse (in fact, sweeter to their taste) nor do they entertain any fear for the future. The workmen, on the other hand, not only have to toil and suffer without return or profit in the present but agonize over the thought of an indigent old age. Their daily wage is too scanty to suffice even for the day: much less is there an excess and surplus that daily can be laid by for their needs in old age.

Now is not this an unjust and ungrateful commonwealth? It lavishes great rewards on so-called gentlefolk and banking goldsmiths and the rest of that kind, who are either idle or mere

---

16. **granaries** (grăn′ə-rēz): storage houses for grain.

17. **niggardly**: stingy.

18. **querulous** (kwĕr′ə-ləs): complaining; grumbling.

parasites[19] and purveyors[20] of empty pleasures. On the contrary, it makes no <u>benevolent</u> provision for farmers, colliers, common laborers, carters, and carpenters without whom there would be no commonwealth at all. After it has misused the labor of their prime[21] and after they are weighed down with age and disease and are in utter want, it forgets all their sleepless nights and all the great benefits received at their hands and most ungratefully requites them[22] with a most miserable death.

What is worse, the rich every day extort a part of their daily allowance from the poor not only by private fraud but by public law. Even before they did so it seemed unjust that persons deserving best of the commonwealth should have the worst return. Now they have further distorted and debased the right[23] and, finally, by making laws, have palmed it off as justice. Consequently, when I consider and turn over in my mind the state of all commonwealths flourishing anywhere today, so help me God, I can see nothing else than a kind of conspiracy of the rich, who are aiming at their own interests under the name and title of the commonwealth. They invent and devise all ways and means by which, first, they may keep without fear of loss all that they have amassed by evil practices and, secondly, they may then purchase as cheaply as possible and abuse the toil and labor of all the poor. These devices become law as soon as the rich have once decreed their observance in the name of the public—that is, of the poor also!

Yet when these evil men with <u>insatiable</u> greed have divided up among themselves all the goods which would have been enough for all the people, how far they are from the happiness of the Utopian commonwealth! In Utopia all greed for money was entirely removed with the use of money. What a mass of troubles was then cut away! What a crop of crimes was then pulled up by the roots! Who does not know that fraud, theft, rapine,[24] quarrels, disorders, brawls, seditions, murders, treasons, poisonings, which are avenged rather than restrained by daily executions, die out with the destruction of money? Who does not know that fear, anxiety, worries, toils, and sleepless nights will also perish at the same time as money? What is more, poverty, which alone money seemed to make poor, forthwith[25] would itself dwindle and disappear if money were entirely done away with everywhere. ❖

19. **parasites:** people who live off the generosity of others.

20. **purveyors:** suppliers.

21. **prime:** a period or phase of peak condition.

22. **requites them:** pays them back.

23. **debased the right:** corrupted what is right, lowering its value.

24. **rapine:** forcible seizure of another's property.

25. **forthwith:** immediately.

WORDS TO KNOW

benevolent (bə-něv′ə-lənt) *adj.* intended to promote the happiness of others; kindly
insatiable (ĭn-sā′shə-bəl) *adj.* impossible to satisfy

UTOPIA **801**

Connect to the Literature

1. What Do You Think?
Do you think that you would like to live in Utopia? Cite details in the text to support your response.

Comprehension Check
- About how many people live in a rural household: 5, 10, or 40?
- Why don't Utopians have to work long hours?
- How would you describe Utopian fashions?

Think Critically

2. Most Utopian men learn their father's craft, and most workers follow the same daily schedule. What are the benefits of such a system, and what are the drawbacks? Support your opinion with details from the text.

3. Why have the Utopians done away with money? What do you think of this idea?

4. ACTIVE READING: DRAWING CONCLUSIONS Get together with a classmate and compare the charts you made in your **READER'S NOTEBOOK**. What are the main differences between Utopia and other countries? What conclusions can you draw about those differences?

5. All aspects of life in Utopia are meant to promote "the public welfare." Do you think that Utopia is truly an ideal society?

> **THINK ABOUT**
> - how Utopians achieve equality
> - the duties that Utopian individuals have to society
> - the amount of personal freedom in Utopian society

Extend Interpretations

6. Critic's Corner The writer Anatole France made the following comment about the human desire for a perfect society: "Without the Utopias of other times, men would still live in caves, miserable and naked. . . . Utopia is the principle of all progress." What do you think France meant? Explain.

7. Connect to Life Suppose that Raphael Hythloday were transported to the present time. Do you think he would consider our economy "a kind of conspiracy of the rich"?

Vocabulary in Action

EXERCISE: ANTONYMS Match each word in the first column with the word in the second column that is most nearly opposite in meaning. Use each word only once.

1. novice	**a.** cruel		
2. prevalent	**b.** encourage		
3. indigent	**c.** optional		
4. compulsory	**d.** carefree		
5. insatiable	**e.** satisfiable		
6. superfluous	**f.** master		
7. benevolent	**g.** wealthy		
8. hinder	**h.** occasionally		
9. incessantly	**i.** unusual		
10. grave	**j.** essential		

Building Vocabulary

For an in-depth lesson on using a dictionary and a thesaurus, see page 558.

Connect to Today

Searching for Utopia

The longing for an ideal society began long before Thomas More's day, and people have never stopped imagining such a place. Plato described an ideal state in his *Republic,* and Jonathan Swift portrayed a rational and "humane" world of intelligent horses in *Gulliver's Travels.* In modern times, some political leaders have tried to create utopias in their countries, often with disastrous results. To enforce the equal sharing of property, for example, various communist governments have treated citizens with shocking brutality. Books and movies like *The Giver, Brave New World,* and *Animal Farm* show how the "perfect" society can go horribly wrong.

Group Activity With a small group of classmates, devise your own ideal community. Give it a name. Where will it be? Who can live there? Decide on the government, the housing, the community's work ethic, and its social rules. Then give an oral or written report describing your ideal place.

RESEARCH STARTER
CLASSZONE.COM

KAT KINKADE
By

IS IT Utopia YET?

An Insider's View of Twin Oaks Community In Its *26*th Year

From a book about Twin Oaks, a utopian community in rural Virginia established by the author in 1967.

The Sonnet

The Ever-Popular Sonnet

The sonnet became one of the most popular literary forms of the Renaissance, and its popularity continues today. Because Renaissance sonnets so often deal with love, they appealed especially to the young. As a new art form, the sonnet represented a break with the past because Renaissance poets typically wrote sonnets in their own language instead of in Latin, the literary language of the Middle Ages.

Reasons for Popularity The sonnet became popular because it caught the spirit of the age. Poets used the sonnet to express deeply personal feelings about love and life. Readers enjoyed the sonnet partly because they found their own thoughts and feelings reflected there. The sonnet also provided a feast for the ears because poets created beautiful sound patterns that made the poems a pleasure to read aloud.

Sonnet Structure A sonnet is a highly structured form of poetry. Renaissance writers and readers knew the "rules" of that structure. Knowing the basic elements of sonnet structure will help you become a better reader of sonnets.

What Is a Sonnet?

Length A sonnet is 14 lines long.

Rhyme Scheme A sonnet typically follows a **rhyme scheme,** or pattern of end rhyme, which makes the poem pleasing to the ear and easier to memorize. To identify a poem's rhyme scheme, you assign a letter of the alphabet to each line according to the rhymed sound at the end of the line, as illustrated by the example on the next page.

The Petrarchan Sonnet One type of sonnet, the Petrarchan sonnet, takes its name from Petrarch, the Italian poet who perfected the form. Petrarchan sonnets are often divided into two major sections. The first section, called an **octave,** is eight lines, and the second, a **sestet,** is six lines.

The Shakespearean Sonnet When the sonnet form reached England, poets modified its form somewhat. Shakespeare became such a master of the English form that eventually it took his name: the Shakespearean sonnet. Study his "Sonnet 73" on the next page.

The Sonnet Through the Ages

1300s	Francesco Petrarch *1304–1374*	ITALY
1500s	Pierre de Ronsard *1524–1585*	FRANCE
	William Shakespeare *1564–1616*	ENGLAND
1600s	Sor Juana Inés de la Cruz *1651?–1695*	MEXICO
1800s	William Wordsworth *1770–1850*	ENGLAND
1900s	Jorge Luis Borges *1899–1986*	ARGENTINA
	Gwendolyn Brooks *1917–2000*	UNITED STATES

A Sonnet Analyzed

The following poem illustrates the structure of the Shakespearean sonnet. Note that the poem consists of three groups of four rhymed lines, called **quatrains,** and a rhymed pair of lines, called a **couplet.**

Generally, the first quatrain introduces a situation or problem. Here, the speaker says that another person ("thou") can notice that he is in decline, like the autumn.

In this quatrain, the speaker compares himself to the day fading at twilight.

Here, the speaker compares himself to a fire, which must die out.

> That time of year thou mayst in me behold *a*
> When yellow leaves, or none, or few, do hang *b*
> Upon those boughs which shake against the cold, *a*
> Bare ruined choirs, where late the sweet birds sang. *b*
>
> In me thou see'st the twilight of such day *c*
> As after sunset fadeth in the west; *d*
> Which by and by black night doth take away, *c*
> Death's second self, that seals up all in rest. *d*
>
> In me thou see'st the glowing of such fire, *e*
> That on the ashes of his youth doth lie, *f*
> As the deathbed whereon it must expire, *e*
> Consumed with that which it was nourished by. *f*
>
> This thou perceiv'st, which makes thy love more strong, *g*
> To love that well which thou must leave ere long. *g*

—Shakespeare, "Sonnet 73"

The rhyme pattern *abab* marks this group of four lines as a quatrain.

Often, a turn, or shift in thought, occurs in the third quatrain or in the couplet. Here, the couplet provides a new twist on the subject developed in the previous quatrains: Because everything in life is subject to decline and death, we must love while we can.

Strategies for Reading: The Sonnet

1. Read the sonnet several times, at least once aloud.

2. Use letters to label like-sounding words or syllables at the ends of lines. The labeling will allow you to identify the **rhyme scheme**. Then use the rhyme scheme and end punctuation marks to identify major units of thought or feeling.

3. In your own words, describe the situation introduced in the first part of the sonnet. Continue through each of the major units of thought, stating in your own words the ideas or feelings expressed by the speaker.

4. Look for a **turn,** if there is one.

5. Study the **imagery** and **figurative language** for clues to the emotions expressed.

THE SONNET POETS

Francesco Petrarch
1304–1374

Renaissance Man Francesco Petrarch's life reflects the spirit of the Renaissance. As a scholar, Petrarch (pē'trärk') promoted interest in the literature of ancient Greece and Rome, even helping to recover lost texts. As a poet writing in his native Italian, he perfected the sonnet form. Because of his influence, the sonnet spread to all corners of Europe. He also had a deep interest in religious studies, which led him to join the clergy. In 1340, Petrarch received invitations from both Paris and Rome to become poet laureate. He chose Rome and in 1341 was honored for being that city's first poet laureate since ancient times.

Build Background

The Mysterious Laura Like his friend Giovanni Boccaccio, Petrarch was inspired by a mysterious woman who probably died in the plague of 1348. Most of the 366 sonnets and odes in the *Canzoniere* ("Book of Songs"), Petrarch's poetic masterpiece, are about his love for this woman, known as Laura. Most of what we know about Laura comes from the poems. "Sonnet 3" describes the first time Petrarch sees Laura, reportedly in a church during Good Friday services on April 6, 1327. Although Laura did not return his love, Petrarch remained devoted to her, and his poems explore the conflicting emotions she aroused in him.

Connect to Your Life

In the two sonnets that follow, the speakers address women whom they love but who do not return their love. Discuss examples of books and films featuring characters who try to get others to fall in love with them. What tactics do they use? Which of the tactics are most effective?

Focus Your Reading

LITERARY ANALYSIS: EXTENDED METAPHOR
A **metaphor** is a comparison between two things that are basically unlike but have something in common. In an **extended metaphor,** two things are compared at length and in various ways. As you read the sonnets, look for metaphors that make simple comparisons and for extended metaphors.

ACTIVE READING: COMPARING AND CONTRASTING SPEAKERS
As you will see, the speakers in the following two poems express very different ideas about love. These different ideas may reflect the personalities of the poets.

READER'S NOTEBOOK As you read each sonnet, pay close attention to the feelings and attitudes of the speaker. Look for evidence of each speaker's "personality" in clues provided in the poems. Record your findings in your notebook.

Sonnet 3

Francesco Petrarch

Translated by Joseph Auslander

It was the morning of that blessèd day
Whereon the Sun in pity veiled his glare
For the Lord's agony, that, unaware,
I fell a captive, Lady, to the sway
5 Of your swift eyes: that seemed no time to stay
The strokes of Love: I stepped into the snare
Secure, with no suspicion: then and there
I found my cue in man's most tragic play.
Love caught me naked to his shaft, his sheaf,
10 The entrance for his ambush and surprise
Against the heart wide open through the eyes,
The constant gate and fountain of my grief:
How craven so to strike me stricken so,
Yet from you fully armed conceal his bow!

4 sway: influence; control.

5 stay: hold back; stop.

8 man's most tragic play: the crucifixion of Christ, remembered on Good Friday.

9 Love . . . his sheaf: Love is often personified by a young boy shooting an arrow (shaft). A sheaf is a case for carrying arrows.

13 craven: cowardly.

Pierre de Ronsard
1524–1585

Early Years Pierre de Ronsard (rôn-sär′) was born in a French castle. His father, a soldier, planned for Ronsard to pursue a military and diplomatic career. As a youth, Ronsard served as a page and a squire at the French court, but his career abruptly ended after a serious illness left him partially deaf. He then devoted himself to a classical education and studied Greek and Latin poets.

Prince of Poets In the 1550s, Ronsard published a number of poetry collections, which established his reputation. Ambitious and often arrogant, he claimed to be the first French lyrical poet and set out to prove himself the literary equal of Horace and Petrarch. As a result of his success, Ronsard was called the Prince of French Poets and was honored in 1558 by being named the official court poet of King Henry II.

Years of Obscurity Toward the end of his life, however, Ronsard experienced another serious illness as well as the failure of *La Franciade* (1572), his sprawling epic about France. He also lost favor with the French king, Henry III, who preferred another poet. During this time, he wrote a series of sonnets about Hélène de Surgères, a young lady-in-waiting at the French court. These sonnets reflect the sufferings and disappointments of an aging poet. Ronsard was largely ignored for two centuries after his death in 1585.

Old Woman Reading (1665), Rembrandt Harmensz van Rijn. Private collection/The Bridgeman Art Library, London.

TO HÉLÈNE

PIERRE DE RONSARD

Translated by Humbert Wolfe

When you are old, at evening candle-lit
    beside the fire bending to your wool,
read out my verse and murmur, "Ronsard writ
    this praise for me when I was beautiful."

5 And not a maid but, at the sound of it,
    though nodding at the stitch on broidered stool,
will start awake, and bless love's benefit
    whose long fidelities bring Time to school.
I shall be thin and ghost beneath the earth
10   by myrtle shade in quiet after pain,
but you, a crone, will crouch beside the hearth
    mourning my love and all your proud disdain.
And since what comes to-morrow who can say?
Live, pluck the roses of the world to-day.

6 broidered: embroidered.

10 by myrtle shade: under the shade of a myrtle tree.

11 crone: old woman.

Connect to the Literature

1. **What Do You Think?**
Which images remain in your mind after reading these sonnets?

Comprehension Check
- In "Sonnet 3," who has been struck by the arrows of love?
- What future event is imagined in "To Hélène"?

Think Critically

2. What do you learn about the speaker in "Sonnet 3" and about the woman he loves?

3. Review the closing **couplet,** the last two lines, of "To Hélène." What do these lines reveal about what the speaker desires?

4. In your judgment, why does each poem include references to death?

- why the speaker in "Sonnet 3" takes his "cue" from the Crucifixion
- how the speaker in "To Hélène" imagines his own death

5. **ACTIVE READING: COMPARING AND CONTRASTING SPEAKERS** Look over the information you recorded in your **READER'S NOTEBOOK.** What similarities and differences do you see between the speaker of Petrarch's "Sonnet 3" and the speaker in Ronsard's "To Hélène"?

Extend Interpretations

6. **The Writer's Style** The term **tone** refers to a writer's attitude toward his or her subject. How would you describe the **tone** of each sonnet? How does the tone help convey each sonnet's meaning?

7. **Connect to Life** Which of these poems offers a more realistic portrayal of love? Explain your reasoning.

Extended Metaphor:
—"fell a captive"
—"strokes"

Dealing with the Sonnet

As you might imagine, translating a sonnet from one language to another is no easy task. To translate a sonnet by Petrarch, for example, a translator must decide whether to try to follow the Italian rhyme scheme in English. The translator also must work hard to find English words and phrases that suggest the meaning of the original Italian. At the same time, the English itself has to sound like a poem.

The following examples, using the first four lines of Petrarch's "Sonnet 3," illustrate some of the choices that translators make.

Petrarch's Original Italian

Era il giorno ch'al sol si scoloraro
Per la pietà del suo fattore i rai,
Quando i' fui preso, e non me ne guardai,
Ché i be' vostr'occhi, donna, mi legaro.

Note that each line ends with a vowel, forming an *abba* rhyming pattern. As you can see, many Italian words end in vowels, which makes rhyming easy.

Translation by Joseph Auslander

It was the morning of that blessèd day
Whereon the Sun in pity veiled his glare
For the Lord's agony, that, unaware,
I fell a captive, Lady, to the sway

Auslander followed Petrarch's *abba* rhyme pattern. To find a rhyme for "day," however, Auslander chose "sway," which meant that he could not complete the sentence at the end of line 4.

Auslander established rhythm by using iambic pentameter. Each line has ten syllables, which follow a regular pattern of emphasis. See page 817 for more information about meter.

Auslander took some liberties. He made his reference to the Good Friday setting more obvious than Petrarch's: Auslander's translation refers directly to "the Lord's agony," while Petrarch's reference is more subtle.

Paired Activity With a partner, study the following translation of the same four lines from Petrarch's sonnet. Compare and contrast this version with Auslander's version. Which one do you prefer? Explain.

Translation by Mark Musa

It was the day the sun's ray had turned pale
with pity for the suffering of his Maker
when I was caught, and I put up no fight,
my lady, for your lovely eyes had bound me.

Shakespeare
Sonnets

William Shakespeare
1564–1616

Ordinary Beginnings William Shakespeare, considered by many to be the greatest writer of the Western world, was the son of a merchant of Stratford-upon-Avon, England. Little is known about his youth. Although never educated at a university, he most likely attended his local grammar school, where he would have studied Latin and classical literature. In 1582, at the age of 18, he married Anne Hathaway, with whom he had two daughters and a son. Probably during the 1580s, he moved to London, where he launched his career as an actor and playwright for the Lord Chamberlain's Men (later known as the King's Men), London's leading theater company.

Popular Bard Shakespeare quickly became one of London's most prominent and successful playwrights. During his lifetime, he composed more than 35 plays, as well as 154 sonnets and two narrative poems. No other playwright of the period could match his range, and audiences responded strongly to his memorable and recognizably human characters. Shakespeare's plays appealed to everyone, from refined aristocrats to uneducated laborers.

Lasting Fame Shakespeare's success as a writer made him a wealthy, important citizen. He was one of seven shareholders who financed the construction of the Globe Theater in 1599. His plays were performed before Queen Elizabeth I and King James I. He was a welcome visitor in the homes of some of the finest families in London, a respected figure in the literary establishment, a loyal friend to fellow actors, and apparently a shrewd investor, because he was able to live in comfortable retirement after he left the theater. Today, Shakespeare's plays are performed more frequently, and in more countries, than the works of any other playwright.

Build Background

Shakespeare's Sonnets Though Shakespeare is best known as a playwright, his sonnets alone would have made him an important author. In 1609, a collection of the sonnets appeared in print. He probably wrote most of them in the 1590s, when it was fashionable for English poets to create sonnet sequences—groups of sonnets arranged to form narratives. As the chart below illustrates, Shakespeare's sonnets go beyond the conventions of the typical sonnet sequence.

Typical Sonnet Sequence	Shakespeare's Sonnets
Addressed to Beautiful, unattainable woman	• Some written to a handsome young man, a friend of the speaker • Some written to a mysterious "dark lady" • Some not addressed to anyone in particular
Subject Matter • The lady's coldness and beauty • The speaker's contradictory feelings • The immortality of poetry	The typical subjects, plus a broader range of issues, such as • friendship • fame • moral responsibility • the inevitability of death

Connect to Your Life

With a classmate, share examples of songs about love. Do your examples show that love makes people feel more secure, or do they portray people who are made anxious by love? Why do you think love can have both of these effects?

Focus Your Reading

LITERARY ANALYSIS: METER

One of the distinctive characteristics of a sonnet is the **meter,** or predictable **rhythm.** The meter of a poem is like the beat of a song. The **Shakespearean sonnet** relies on the most commonly used type of meter in English poetry— **iambic pentameter.** In simple terms, that means that each ten-syllable line has five major stresses, with alternating unstressed and stressed syllables—a "da DUM, da DUM" rhythm. Note the five stresses in these lines from "Sonnet 29":

> When in disgrace with Fortune and men's eyes
> I all alone beweep my outcast state

When you read the sonnets that follow, try reading them aloud so that you can catch the beat.

ACTIVE READING: CLARIFYING MEANING IN SONNETS

Shakespeare's sonnets may be difficult to understand because he arranged words to fit the meter and rhyme scheme of the sonnet form. You can often clarify the meaning of a line or lines by following these two steps:

1. Rearrange the word order. Rearrange a line so that the subject comes closer to the verb: "When [I am] in disgrace."
2. **Paraphrase** certain lines by putting them in your own words. For example, the lines displayed above might be paraphrased as follows: "In those times when I have fallen out of favor because of misfortune or other people's bad opinion of me, I feel so completely alone that I cry."

📖 **READER'S NOTEBOOK** As you read the sonnets, try paraphrasing some of their lines in your notebook.

Sonnet 29
William Shakespeare

When in disgrace with Fortune and men's eyes
I all alone beweep my outcast state,
And trouble deaf heaven with my bootless cries,
And look upon myself and curse my fate,
5   Wishing me like to one more rich in hope,
Featur'd like him, like him with friends possess'd,
Desiring this man's art, and that man's scope,
With what I most enjoy contented least;
Yet in these thoughts myself almost despising,
10 Haply I think on thee, and then my state
(Like to the lark at break of day arising
From sullen earth) sings hymns at heaven's gate,
    For thy sweet love rememb'red such wealth brings,
    That then I scorn to change my state with kings.

2 state: condition.

3 bootless: useless.

6 featured like him, . . . possess'd: attractive-looking like one man, having friends like another.

7 scope: knowledge or intellectual powers.

10 haply: by chance or accident; **state:** mood.

12 sullen: dark; gloomy.

Love Among the Ruins (1894), Sir Edward Burne-Jones. Wightwick Manor, Wolverhampton, England.

Sonnet 30
William Shakespeare

Sir Henry Percy, Nicolas Hilliard. Rijksmuseum, Amsterdam, The Netherlands.

When to the sessions of sweet silent thought
I summon up remembrance of things past,
I sigh the lack of many a thing I sought,
And with old woes new wail my dear time's waste;
5 Then can I drown an eye (unus'd to flow)
For precious friends hid in death's dateless night,
And weep afresh love's long since cancell'd woe,
And moan th' expense of many a vanish'd sight;
Then can I grieve at grievances foregone,
10 And heavily from woe to woe tell o'er
The sad account of fore-bemoaned moan,
Which I new pay as if not paid before:
　　But if the while I think on thee, dear friend,
　　All losses are restor'd, and sorrows end.

3 sigh: sigh for.

4 new . . . waste: express new sorrow for the waste of precious time.

6 dateless: never-ending.

7 cancell'd: paid in full with sadness.

8 expense: loss.

9 foregone: past.

10 heavily: sadly; **tell:** count.

11 sad . . . moan: the upsetting total of previously expressed sorrows.

Sonnet 64

William Shakespeare

When I have seen by Time's fell hand defaced
The rich proud cost of outworn buried age;
When sometime lofty towers I see down rased,
And brass eternal slave to mortal rage;
5   When I have seen the hungry ocean gain
Advantage on the kingdom of the shore,
And the firm soil win of the wat'ry main,
Increasing store with loss, and loss with store;
When I have seen such interchange of state,
10   Or state itself confounded to decay,
Ruin hath taught me thus to ruminate,
That Time will come and take my love away.
     This thought is as a death, which cannot choose
     But weep to have that which it fears to lose.

1 fell: cruel.

2 The rich . . . age: The monuments of old that were produced by great wealth and pride.

3 sometime: formerly.

4 brass . . . rage: long-lasting brass damaged by the destructive power of decay.

7 win of: gain at the expense of.

8 Increasing store . . . store: One gaining as the other loses, and vice versa.

9 state: condition.

10 state itself confounded: greatness itself reduced.

11 ruminate: to think about for a long time.

Connect to the Literature

1. **What Do You Think?**
Which sonnet made the most sense to you? Which sonnet left you with the most questions? Share your initial reactions with a classmate.

Comprehension Check
- What changes the speaker's mood in "Sonnet 29"?
- In "Sonnet 30," how does the speaker feel about the past?
- Which word best describes time in "Sonnet 64": *destructive, creative,* or *powerless?*

Think Critically

2. The last six lines of "Sonnet 29" express a very different mood from the first eight lines. Such a shift in thought is called a **turn.** Describe both moods and explain what causes them.

- why the speaker compares himself with others
- how the speaker views himself
- how the speaker feels about "thy sweet love"

3. In "Sonnet 30," what does the speaker feel that he has lost, and how can such losses be "restor'd" (line 14)?

4. In "Sonnet 64," what are the powers of time, and how does the speaker feel about such powers?

5. **ACTIVE READING: CLARIFYING MEANING IN SONNETS** Get together with a classmate and compare what you each recorded in your 📖 **READER'S NOTEBOOK.** Then choose a particularly challenging passage (two to four lines) and restate that passage in your own words. Explain how the passage contributes to your understanding of the poem.

Extend Interpretations

6. **Critic's Corner** The critic Edward Dowden says that Shakespeare's sonnets "tell more of Shakespeare's sensitiveness than of Shakespeare's strength." Judging by your readings, do you agree with this statement? Why or why not?

7. **Comparing Texts** Compare and contrast the speakers in two of the sonnets. What are the similarities and differences in their attitudes toward love?

8. **Connect to Life** Which of the three sonnets comes closest to your own views of love? Explain.

Meter is the rhythmical pattern of poetry. Like the beat of a song, meter establishes a predictable emphasis on certain syllables in the poem. A technique called **scanning** will enable you to determine the meter of a poem. To scan a poem, you need to mark the stressed and unstressed syllables, as in this example:

> Whĕn Í|hăve seén|bў Time's|fĕll
>   hand|dĕfaćed
> Thĕ rich|prŏud cóst|ŏf oút|wŏrn
>   bŭr|ĭed aǵe

When reading these lines aloud, you stress the syllables marked by the slanted lines. The syllables are grouped in units called **feet,** marked off by vertical lines. The pattern illustrated above—the basic pattern of Shakespeare's poetry—is called **iambic pentameter.** *Pentameter* means that there are five feet in each line. An **iamb** is a foot that consists of an unstressed syllable followed by a stressed one.

Paired Activity Work with a partner to scan one of the three sonnets. Be aware that Shakespeare sometimes varies the pattern by adding an extra syllable to a foot or by using a foot that is not an iamb. For example, some critics believe that line 2 of "Sonnet 29" begins with two accented syllables:

> Í aĺl ălońe

The Plays of Shakespeare

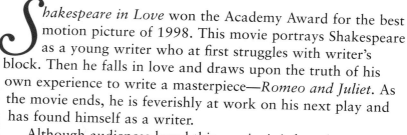

LOVE IS THE ONLY INSPIRATION

GWYNETH
PALTROW
JOSEPH
FIENNES
GEOFFREY
RUSH
COLIN
FIRTH
BEN
AFFLECK
JUDI
DENCH

SHAKESPEARE IN LOVE

*S*hakespeare in Love won the Academy Award for the best motion picture of 1998. This movie portrays Shakespeare as a young writer who at first struggles with writer's block. Then he falls in love and draws upon the truth of his own experience to write a masterpiece—*Romeo and Juliet*. As the movie ends, he is feverishly at work on his next play and has found himself as a writer.

Although audiences loved this movie, it is based more on fiction than fact. Most of the details of Shakespeare's life are unknown. What is certain is that he became one of the greatest dramatists who ever lived. From about 1590 to 1613, he wrote approximately 37 plays. Most of them were very popular in his time. Today, almost 400 years after his death, his plays still are widely read and performed all over the world. Their timeless appeal supports what Ben Jonson—a rival playwright—wrote of Shakespeare: "He was not of an age, but for all time."

❊ Selected Plays by William Shakespeare ❊

Histories   *Richard II, Richard III, Henry IV (Parts 1 and 2), Henry V*

Comedies   *The Comedy of Errors, The Taming of the Shrew, A Midsummer Night's Dream, The Merchant of Venice, As You Like It, Much Ado About Nothing, Twelfth Night*

Tragedies   *Romeo and Juliet, Julius Caesar, Hamlet, Othello, King Lear, Macbeth, Antony and Cleopatra*

Romances   *The Winter's Tale, The Tempest*

Most of these plays were first performed at the Globe Theater in London, England. This open-air theater could hold about 3,000 spectators. Its stage jutted out into a courtyard, allowing the actors to perform very close to the audience.

Like people today, this audience went to the theater to be entertained. Shakespeare gave them what they wanted—powerful speeches, sword fights, humor, and supernatural events. But Shakespeare did much more than write crowd pleasers. He also created characters who lived and breathed—characters as complex as real people—and put them in thrilling scenes. As the audience looked on, Romeo and Juliet expressed their doomed love, Hamlet held up a skull and looked death in the face, Mark Antony in *Julius Caesar* turned the citizens of Rome into a raging mob, and Macbeth met three witches who recognized his guilty soul.

These characters and many others spoke some of the most beautiful language ever written for the theater. Shakespeare's language is marked by vivid imagery, an incredibly rich vocabulary, and subtle rhythms. Shakespeare used words in new ways to forge fresh comparisons and convey profound insights. For example, consider the following metaphor in *As You Like It*:

> **All the world's a stage,**
> **And all the men and women merely players;**
> **They have their exits and their entrances,**
> **And one man in his time plays many parts,**
> **His acts being seven ages.**

Notice the insight about human life that the following lines from *The Tempest* convey:

> **We are such stuff**
> **As dreams are made on, and our little life**
> **Is rounded with a sleep.**

Shakespeare's plays are treasures of the English language. They continue to stir the imagination, expand the mind, and engage the feelings. They invite readers and audiences to experience what it means to be human.

MILESTONE LINKS
CLASSZONE.COM

Sonnets by Women

OVERVIEW

Sonnet 23	821
Sonnet 165	824
Standardized Test Practice: Writing About Literature	827

As you know, the sonnet became popular in many different countries during the Renaissance. This lesson includes sonnets by two extraordinary women of the Renaissance, the French writer Louise Labé and the Mexican writer Sor Juana Inés de la Cruz. In order to write, both women had to break down barriers created by prejudice and social custom, for women were not expected to become authors.

In the pages that follow, you will be asked to compare and contrast two sonnets, both of which are about women who have been badly treated in love. Your comparisons should help you to appreciate the sonnet form and the perspective of two fascinating Renaissance writers.

Points of Comparison

Because the great majority of writers in the Renaissance period were male, most sonnets about love expressed a man's point of view. In this lesson, you will see love expressed from another perspective—a woman's. As you will see, both sonnets express various complaints about the man's role in love.

Analyzing Love Sonnets

As you read the two sonnets, use a chart like the one shown to make notes about each sonnet.

	Sonnet 23 Louise Labé	Sonnet 165 Sor Juana Inés de la Cruz
What do you learn about the speaker's past relationship with the man being addressed?		
How does the speaker now feel about the man? What is the speaker's tone, or attitude, toward the subject of love?		
Does the speaker take any pleasure in her memories of love?		
How would you describe the personality of the speaker?		

Standardized Test Practice: Comparison-and-Contrast Essay After you finish reading the two sonnets, you will have the opportunity to write a comparison-and-contrast essay. Your notes will help you plan and write the essay.

SONNET 23

Louise Labé

Louise Labé
1524?–1566

A Courtly Education Louise Labé (lä-bā') was born in Lyon, France. Her father was a prosperous ropemaker who could neither read nor write, yet he prepared his daughter for entrance into polite society by giving her an education. She studied Latin, Italian, music, and horsemanship, becoming an accomplished lute player, singer, and rider. In about 1543, she married a much older widower who was a successful ropemaker like her father. Before her husband's death in 1560, Labé fell in love with the poet Olivier de Magny, the subject of many of her love poems.

Literary Success In 1555, Labé published her only book, *Works*, which included 24 love sonnets and a prose "debate" between Folly and Love. In the book's preface, Labé called on women to set aside their chores and frivolous pastimes to pursue literature and other cultural activities.

Build Background

As you will see, the man who is addressed in "Sonnet 23" was well schooled in the ways of courtly love. According to the "rules" of such love, the male was supposed to be extravagant in his praise of the woman's beauty, comparing her physical qualities to the wonders of the natural world and swearing an eternal love.

Connect to Your Life

People in love often make it seem as if they have no power to resist. Think of phrases drawn from poetry, popular music, or your own experience that suggest love's power. Is it healthy or wise to think of love in such terms?

Focus Your Reading

LITERARY ANALYSIS: TONE
In oral communication, tone is usually easy to identify because the speaker's voice expresses the speaker's attitude and emotion. In writing, the tone is often more difficult to identify because the reader must make inferences about the writer's attitude. As you read "Sonnet 23," try to identify the tone, or attitude, expressed by the speaker about the man being described.

ACTIVE READING: ANALYZING DICTION
In poetry, the writer's **diction,** or word choice, often provides clues to the tone. In the first eight lines of "Sonnet 23," we learn how the man once described the speaker and his love for her. Beginning with line 9 the speaker expresses her own feelings about their relationship.

📖 **READER'S NOTEBOOK** As you read, jot down key phrases from lines 1–8 and lines 9–14. You will analyze these phrases later.

Sonnet 23

Louise Labé

Translated by **Willis Barnstone**

Mary Magdalen (c. 1540), Jan van Scorel. Oil on panel, 67 cm × 76.5 cm. Rijksmuseum, Amsterdam, Netherlands.

What good is it to me if long ago
you eloquently praised my golden hair,
compared my eyes and beauty to the flare
of two suns where, you say, love bent the bow,
5   sending the darts that needled you with grief?
Where are your tears that faded in the ground?
Your death? by which your constant love is bound
in oaths and honor now beyond belief?
Your brutal goal was to make *me* a slave
10   beneath the ruse of being served by you.
Pardon me, friend, and for once hear me through:
I am outraged with anger and I rave.
Yet I am sure, wherever you have gone,
your martyrdom is hard as my black dawn.

2 eloquently: with powerful, persuasive words.

5 needled: pierced.

12 rave: speak wildly.

14 martyrdom: great suffering or death for one's beliefs.

Connect to the Literature

1. **What Do You Think?** Based on your reading of the poem, what is your first impression of the speaker? Explain.

Think Critically

2. What do the first eight lines of the poem reveal about the past relationship between the speaker and the man being addressed?

   THINK ABOUT
   - the language that he used to praise her beauty
   - the promises that he made
   - why the speaker says, "What good is it to me"

3. **ACTIVE READING: ANALYZING DICTION** Working with a partner, review the key phrases that you recorded in your ▥ **READER'S NOTEBOOK**. What do these phrases tell you about the speaker's attitude toward the man?

4. Why do you think the speaker accuses the man of wanting to make her "a slave / beneath the ruse of being served by you" (lines 9–10)?

5. The couplet at the end of the poem is puzzling to many readers. What do you think the speaker means by referring to the man's "martyrdom"? Explain.

Points of Comparison

Activity Review "Sonnet 23" and answer the questions in your comparison-and-contrast chart that pertain to it. An example has been done for you.

	Sonnet 23 Louise Labé	Sonnet 165 Sor Juana Inés de la Cruz
What do you learn about the speaker's past relationship with the man being addressed?	The man promised to love her always.	
How does the speaker now feel about the man? What is the speaker's tone, or attitude, toward the subject of love?		
Does the speaker take any pleasure in her memories of love?		
How would you describe the personality of the speaker?		

PREPARING to *Read*

The Louise Labé poem has given you one woman's perspective on love gone wrong. The following poem offers another woman's perspective on this topic, though the feelings expressed are different.

Noble Beginnings Juana Inés de la Cruz (hwä'nä ē-něs' dě lä krōōs') was born into a noble Mexican family. By the time she was 6 years old, she was able to read every book in her grandfather's library. At about the age of 15, she became a lady in waiting to the marquise of Mancera, the wife of Mexico's governor. For several years, she lived in the palace, where she wrote, studied, and served the marquise.

A Religious Calling When she was about 19, Juana Inés decided to become a nun. This decision gave her an opportunity to pursue her writing and education. While living in a convent, she accumulated thousands of books, acquired scientific instruments, and corresponded with friends in Spain and the United States. Because she was not burdened with household responsibilities, she had time to write songs, poetry, and plays. However, in 1690, Sor Juana faced a crisis when she published a highly critical letter about the ideas of a well-known Jesuit priest. Persecuted by the archbishop of Mexico as a result of writing this letter, she was forced to stop writing altogether and had to turn over her books and scientific equipment to charity. After Sor Juana died in an epidemic in 1695, the archbishop's representatives confiscated her remaining possessions—except one carefully hidden poem.

Build Background

Some scholars believe that Sor Juana's sonnets are about previous relationships in her life. Others believe that the sonnets are not biographical but simply a product of her rich imagination. In "Sonnet 165," the speaker addresses a man who seems to have broken off his romantic relationship with her.

Sister Juana Inés de la Cruz (1750), Miguel Cabrera. Museo National de Historia, Castillo de Chapultepec, Mexico City, D.F., Mexico. Photograph copyright © Schalkwijk/Art Resource, New York.

SONNET 165

Sor Juana Inés de la Cruz

TRANSLATED BY Octavio Paz

Stay, shadow of contentment too short-lived,
illusion of enchantment I most prize,
fair image for whom happily I die,
sweet fiction for whom painfully I live.
5   If to your charms attracted I submit,
obedient, like steel to magnet fly,
by what logic do you flatter and entice,
only to flee, a taunting fugitive?
'Tis no triumph that you so smugly boast
10   that I fell victim to your tyranny;
though from encircling bonds that held you fast
your elusive form too readily slipped free,
and though to my arms you are forever lost,
you are a prisoner in my fantasy.

2 illusion: something that misleads because it is not real.

7 entice: to attract by arousing hopes; tempt.

8 a taunting fugitive: one who runs away, mocking or making fun as he goes.

12 elusive: hard to catch or pin down.

Connect to the Literature

1. **What Do You Think?** In analyzing poetry, you should begin by focusing on what you understand. With a partner, write down two statements about this poem that you believe are true. Compare your statements with those of your classmates.

Think Critically

2. In the poem's first four lines, the speaker refers to the man being addressed as a "shadow of contentment," an "illusion of enchantment," and a "sweet fiction." What does such language suggest about the speaker's feelings toward the man?

3. In lines 5–6, the speaker admits to her romantic attraction to the man. According to lines 7–8, how does the man respond to her attraction?

4. On the basis of lines 9–14, what do you think happened to the relationship between the speaker and the man?

5. What might the speaker mean when she concludes that "you are a prisoner in my fantasy" (line 14)?

Extend Interpretations

6. **Connect to Life** Why do you think reality and fantasy so often become blended in the experience of romantic love?

Points *of* Comparison

Activity Now that you have read both poems, complete the rest of your comparison-and-contrast chart. If you are still uncertain about the meanings of certain lines, discuss them with your classmates. An additional example has been filled in.

	Sonnet 23 Louise Labé	Sonnet 165 Sor Juana Inés de la Cruz
What do you learn about the speaker's past relationship with the man being addressed?	*The man promised to love her always.*	*He left her.*
How does the speaker now feel about the man? What is the speaker's tone, or attitude, toward the subject of love?		
Does the speaker take any pleasure in her memories of love?		
How would you describe the personality of the speaker?		

Standardized Test Practice

Writing About Literature

PART 1 Reading the Prompt

In writing assessments, you may be asked to compare and contrast works of literature with a common subject, such as the two poems that you have just read. You are now going to write an essay that involves this type of comparison.

> **Writing Prompt**
>
> Throughout the centuries, poets have praised the experience of love. Yet love can also go wrong. Compare and contrast the two poems by ❶ Louise Labé and Sor Juana Inés de la Cruz. How do the speakers in these poems view their romantic relationships? Consider what you ❷ learn about the men involved and each speaker's tone, or attitude, toward love. In your opinion, which speaker seems to have the healthier or more sensible attitude toward the loss of love? Support ❸ your analysis with details and quotations from the poems. ❹

STRATEGIES
IN ACTION

❶ I have to **compare and contrast** two poems.

❷ For each poem, I have to discuss the speaker's **view of the romance** and the speaker's **tone**.

❸ I have to decide which speaker has **a healthier attitude** toward the loss of love.

❹ I have to include **details** and **quotations** from the poems to support my analysis.

PART 2 Planning a Comparison-and-Contrast Essay

- Review the comparison-and-contrast chart that you completed for "Sonnet 23" and "Sonnet 165."
- Using your chart, find examples of similarities and differences to point out in your essay. If necessary, review the poems again to find more evidence.
- Create an outline to organize your ideas.

PART 3 Drafting Your Essay

Introduction You might begin by offering your own thoughts about why poets write about the loss of love. Introduce the two poems and briefly explain what they have in common. Describe interesting differences between the poems.

Body The questions in your comparison-and-contrast chart may help you identify the key points you want to make. In one paragraph, for example, you might discuss the romantic relationships described in the sonnets. Use examples and details.

Conclusion Wrap up your essay with a summary of the poems' major similarities and differences.

Revision Look for places where you may not have explained your ideas fully. Also, see if more examples or quotations are needed.

TEST PRACTICE

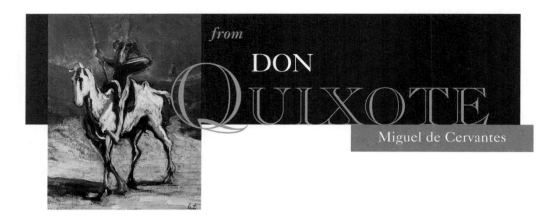

from

DON
QUIXOTE

Miguel de Cervantes

Miguel de Cervantes
1547–1616

From Soldier to Slave Little is known about the early years of the Spanish writer Miguel de Cervantes. The son of a barber-surgeon—in those days, barbers set bones and performed other medical duties—he was born in a small town near Madrid. As a young man, he enlisted as a soldier and, in 1571, fought against the Turks in the Battle of Lepanto, where he was severely wounded. Cervantes proved to be a worthy soldier, showing great courage in battle and advancing to the rank of captain. On his return voyage to Spain in 1575, he was captured by pirates and taken to Algiers as a slave. Despite his repeated efforts to escape, he remained in captivity for five years, until he was freed following the payment of a ransom.

Disappointment and Failure In the 25 years after his return to Spain, Cervantes suffered a series of disappointments. He expected to be rewarded with an important position but instead struggled to earn a living in various jobs, including royal messenger, tax collector, and commissary for the navy. Cervantes also tried his hand at writing fiction, drama, and poetry. Though he met with some success, he could not support himself by writing. Twice he was imprisoned over monetary matters. By his own account, he came up with the idea for *Don Quixote* while in prison.

Success and Acclaim In 1605, Cervantes published the first part of *Don Quixote*, the novel that turned his life around. This satire about the adventures of an elderly, idealistic "knight" was an immediate success, bringing Cervantes international fame and at least some financial stability. In 1615, he published a second part to the novel, which became another great success.

Build Background

The Tale of Don Quixote

First Modern Novel *Don Quixote* is generally considered the first modern novel. Its hero, Don Quixote, is a poor, elderly gentleman who loses his mind from reading too many tales about the daring deeds of heroic knights. Don Quixote decides to win fame as a knight, assisted by a peasant "squire" named Sancho Panza. Cervantes devoted over 100 chapters to their comically ill-fated adventures.

A Parody of Romances In the novel's prologue, Cervantes declares that his intention is to parody romances, the most popular form of literature in Spain for much of the 16th century. A **parody** imitates or mocks another work or type of literature. There was certainly plenty to mock in the romance genre. These rambling narratives told of knights who performed incredible deeds of valor without ever feeling any fear or doubt. Cervantes exposed the absurdity of romances by placing his hero in a realistic setting. Instead of encountering brave knights and evil sorcerers, Don Quixote attempts to fulfill chivalric ideals in a world of barbers, innkeepers, and farmers. He mistakes windmills for giants and country inns for castles.

A Quixotic Hero Cervantes achieved something more than parody in *Don Quixote*. The novel is a fascinating exploration of the relationship between fantasy and reality. Although Don Quixote is clearly mad, he does achieve a kind of nobility through his idealism and persistence. From his name comes the term *quixotic,* which describes an impractical idealist, someone who gallantly tries to pursue unreachable goals.

For a humanities activity, click on:

HUMANITIES
CLASSZONE.COM

Connect to Your Life

Don Quixote mistakes his fantasies for reality. What is your attitude toward fantasy and imagination? Do you think that such activities should be left to children, or do they serve a useful purpose in adult life? Give examples.

Focus Your Reading

LITERARY ANALYSIS: CHARACTERIZATION

Characterization refers to the techniques used to develop characters. Writers can portray a character through a combination of physical description; the speech, thoughts, feelings, or actions of the character; what other characters do, say, or think in response to that character; and direct commentary by the narrator. The following quotation illustrates a physical description:

> *This gentleman of ours was close on to fifty, of a robust constitution but with little flesh on his bones and a face that was lean and gaunt.*

As you read, notice how the various techniques are used to develop the main character.

ACTIVE READING: ANALYZING EXPOSITION

Exposition is the stage of a plot that provides background information. The first chapter of *Don Quixote* serves as an exposition that introduces the main character.

📖 **READER'S NOTEBOOK** As you read the first chapter, record information about Don Quixote, using a chart like the one shown.

Don Quixote	
What He Reads	**Image of Himself**
Imaginative Way of Seeing	
sees cardboard, imagines a helmet's visor	

WORDS TO KNOW **Vocabulary Preview**

affable	incongruous	ingenuity	lucid
conjecture	indolent	interminable	scrutinizing
haughty	infatuation		

from Don Quixote

Miguel de Cervantes

Translated by Samuel Putnam

CHAPTER 1

Part 1

In a village of La Mancha[1] the name of which I have no desire to recall, there lived not so long ago one of those gentlemen who always have a lance in the rack, an ancient buckler,[2] a skinny nag, and a greyhound for the chase. A stew with more beef than mutton in it, chopped meat for his evening meal, scraps for a Saturday, lentils on Friday, and a young pigeon as a special delicacy for Sunday, went to account for three-quarters of his income.

---

1. **La Mancha:** a high, flat, barren region in central Spain.
2. **buckler:** a small, round shield carried or worn on the arm.

The rest of it he laid out on a broadcloth greatcoat[3] and velvet stockings for feast days, with slippers to match, while the other days of the week he cut a figure in a suit of the finest homespun. Living with him were a housekeeper in her forties, a niece who was not yet twenty, and a lad of the field and market place who saddled his horse for him and wielded the pruning knife.

This gentleman of ours was close on to fifty, of a robust constitution[4] but with little flesh on his bones and a face that was lean and gaunt. He was noted for his early rising, being very fond of the hunt. They will try to tell you that his surname was Quijada or Quesada[5]—there is some difference of opinion among those who have written on the subject—but according to the most likely <u>conjectures</u> we are to understand that it was really Quejana.[6] But all this means very little so far as our story is concerned, providing that in the telling of it we do not depart one iota from the truth.

You may know, then, that the aforesaid gentleman, on those occasions when he was at leisure, which was most of the year around, was in the habit of reading books of chivalry with such pleasure and devotion as to lead him almost wholly to forget the life of a hunter and even the administration of his estate. So great was his curiosity and <u>infatuation</u> in this regard that he even sold many acres of tillable land in order to be able to buy and read the books that he loved, and he would carry home with him as many of them as he could obtain.

Don Quixote on Horseback, Honoré Daumier. Neue Pinakothek, Munich, Germany. Giraudon/ Art Resource, New York.

Of all those that he thus devoured none pleased him so well as the ones that had been composed by the famous Feliciano de Silva,[7] whose <u>lucid</u> prose style and involved conceits[8] were as precious to him as pearls; especially when he came to read those tales of love and amorous challenges that are to be met with in many places, such a passage as the following, for example: "The reason of the unreason that afflicts my reason, in such a manner weakens my reason that I with reason lament me of your comeliness." And he was similarly affected when his eyes fell upon such lines as these: ". . . the high Heaven of your divinity divinely fortifies you with the stars and renders you deserving of that desert your greatness doth deserve."

---

3. **broadcloth greatcoat:** heavy wool overcoat.

4. **robust constitution:** vigorous, healthy physical nature.

5. **Quijada** (kē-hä′dä) or **Quesada** (kě-sä′dä): last names mistakenly given to the main character.

6. **Quejana** (kě-hä′nä).

7. **Feliciano de Silva** (fě-lē-syä′nô dě sēl′vä): a Spanish author of fictional books about knights.

8. **conceits:** lengthy, exaggerated comparisons.

WORDS TO KNOW

conjecture (kən-jěk′chər) *n.* a conclusion based on guesswork
infatuation (ĭn-făch′oo-ā′shən) *n.* a foolish, unreasonable attraction
lucid (loo′sĭd) *adj.* clear; easily understood

The poor fellow used to lie awake nights in an effort to disentangle the meaning and make sense out of passages such as these, although Aristotle[9] himself would not have been able to understand them, even if he had been resurrected for that sole purpose. He was not at ease in his mind over those wounds that Don Belianís[10] gave and received; for no matter how great the surgeons who treated him, the poor fellow must have been left with his face and his entire body covered with marks and scars. Nevertheless, he was grateful to the author for closing the book with the promise of an <u>interminable</u> adventure to come; many a time he was tempted to take up his pen and literally finish the tale as had been promised, and he undoubtedly would have done so, and would have succeeded at it very well, if his thoughts had not been constantly occupied with other things of greater moment.

He often talked it over with the village curate,[11] who was a learned man, a graduate of Sigüenza,[12] and they would hold long discussions as to who had been the better knight, Palmerin of England or Amadis of Gaul;[13] but Master Nicholas, the barber of the same village, was in the habit of saying that no one could come up to the Knight of Phoebus,[14] and that if anyone *could* compare with him it was Don Galaor,[15] brother of Amadis of Gaul, for Galaor was ready for anything—he was none of your finical[16] knights, who went around whimpering as his brother did, and in point of valor he did not lag behind him.

In short, our gentleman became so immersed in his reading that he spent whole nights from sundown to sunup and his days from dawn to dusk in poring over his books, until, finally, from so little sleeping and so much reading, his brain dried up and he went completely out of his mind. He had filled his imagination with everything that he had read, with enchantments, knightly encounters, battles, challenges, wounds, with tales of love and its torments, and all sorts of impossible things, and as a result had come to believe that all these fictitious happenings were true; they were more real to him than anything else in the world. He would remark that the Cid Ruy Díaz[17] had been a very good knight, but there was no comparison between him and the Knight of the Flaming Sword,[18] who with a single backward stroke had cut in half two fierce and monstrous giants. He preferred Bernardo del

---

9. **Aristotle:** a Greek philosopher (384–322 B.C.) widely known for his wisdom.

10. **Don Belianís** (dôn bĕ-lyä-nēs'): the hero of a chivalric romance.

11. **curate** (kyŏŏr'ĭt): a priest in charge of a parish.

12. **Sigüenza** (sē-gwĕn'sä): a "minor" university of Spain, whose graduates were often mocked.

13. **Palmerin of England or Amadis** (ä'mə-dĭs) **of Gaul:** two legendary knights known for bravery and unbelievably heroic deeds.

14. **Knight of Phoebus** (fē'bəs): the hero of a romance called *Knight of the Sun, Mirror of Princes and Knights.*

15. **Galaor** (gä-lä-ôr').

16. **finical:** finicky; picky.

17. **Cid Ruy Díaz** (sēd' rwē' dē'äs): Rodrigo Díaz de Vivar, known as the Cid, was an actual Spanish military leader and national hero about whom an epic poem was written.

18. **Knight of the Flaming Sword:** Amadis of Greece, a hero of romances who had a red sword stamped on his shield.

WORDS TO KNOW

interminable (ĭn-tûr'mə-nə-bəl) *adj.* unending

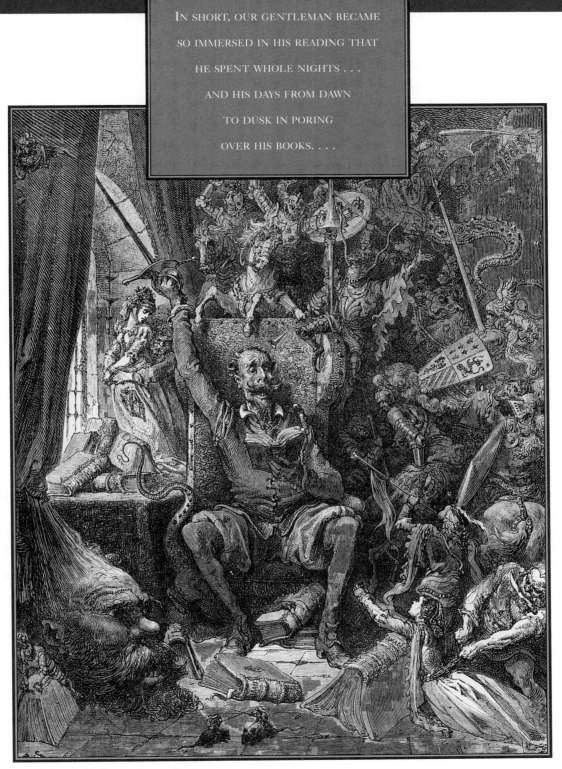

IN SHORT, OUR GENTLEMAN BECAME

SO IMMERSED IN HIS READING THAT

HE SPENT WHOLE NIGHTS . . .

AND HIS DAYS FROM DAWN

TO DUSK IN PORING

OVER HIS BOOKS. . . .

Don Quixote in his library, Gustave Doré.

HUMANITIES CONNECTION For centuries, artists have been drawn to the story of *Don Quixote*. This woodcut provides a humorous portrayal of Don Quixote's crowded imagination. Note the many knights, the dragon, and the damsels in distress.

Carpio,[19] who at Roncesvalles had slain Roland despite the charm the latter bore, availing himself of the stratagem which Hercules employed when he strangled Antaeus, the son of Earth, in his arms.

He had much good to say for Morgante[20] who, though he belonged to the haughty, overbearing race of giants, was of an affable disposition and well brought up. But, above all, he cherished an admiration for Rinaldo of Montalbán,[21] especially as he beheld him sallying forth from his castle to rob all those that crossed his path, or when he thought of him overseas stealing the image of Mohammed which, so the story has it, was all of gold. And he would have liked very well to have had his fill of kicking that traitor Galalón,[22] a privilege for which he would have given his housekeeper with his niece thrown into the bargain.

At last, when his wits were gone beyond repair, he came to conceive the strangest idea that ever occurred to any madman in this world. It now appeared to him fitting and necessary, in order to win a greater amount of honor for himself and serve his country at the same time, to become a knight-errant[23] and roam the world on horseback, in a suit of armor; he would go in quest of adventures, by way of putting into practice all that he had read in his books; he would right every manner of wrong, placing himself in situations of the greatest peril such as would redound[24] to the eternal glory of his name. As a reward for his valor and the might of his arm, the poor fellow could already see himself

> AT LAST, WHEN HIS WITS WERE GONE BEYOND REPAIR, HE CAME TO CONCEIVE THE STRANGEST IDEA THAT EVER OCCURRED TO ANY MADMAN IN THIS WORLD.

crowned Emperor of Trebizond[25] at the very least; and so, carried away by the strange pleasure that he found in such thoughts as these, he at once set about putting his plan into effect.

The first thing he did was to burnish up some old pieces of armor, left him by his great-grandfather, which for ages had lain in a corner, moldering and forgotten. He polished and adjusted them as best he could, and then he noticed that one very important thing was lacking: there was no closed helmet, but only a morion, or visorless headpiece, with turned up brim of the kind foot soldiers wore. His ingenuity, however, enabled him to remedy this, and he proceeded to fashion out of cardboard a kind of half-helmet, which, when attached to the morion, gave the appearance of a whole one. True, when he went to see if it was strong enough to withstand a good slashing blow, he was somewhat disappointed; for when he drew his sword and gave it a couple of thrusts, he succeeded

---

19. **Bernardo del Carpio:** another hero of Spanish epic poetry. The story referred to here puts him at the battle portrayed in the French epic *The Song of Roland* and claims he killed Roland by lifting him up into the air until Roland was dead, as Hercules did to the giant Antaeus.

20. **Morgante** (môr-gän′tě): a ferocious giant in an Italian romantic poem, who later became sweet and loving.

21. **Rinaldo of Montalbán** (môn-täl-bän′): the hero of a series of French epic poems.

22. **Galalón** (gä-lä-lôn′): Ganelon, the stepfather and betrayer of Roland, the French epic hero.

23. **knight-errant:** a knight who wanders the countryside in search of adventure to prove his chivalry.

24. **redound:** contribute.

25. **Trebizond:** a former Greek empire, often referred to in stories of knighthood.

834

only in undoing a whole week's labor. The ease with which he had hewed it to bits disturbed him no little, and he decided to make it over. This time he placed a few strips of iron on the inside, and then, convinced that it was strong enough, refrained from putting it to any further test; instead, he adopted it then and there as the finest helmet ever made.

After this, he went out to have a look at his nag; and although the animal had more *cuartos,* or cracks, in its hoof than there are quarters in a real,[26] and more blemishes than Gonela's steed[27] which *tantum pellis et ossa fuit,*[28] it nonetheless looked to its master like a far better horse than Alexander's Bucephalus or the Babieca of the Cid.[29] He spent all of four days in trying to think up a name for his mount; for—so he told himself—seeing that it belonged to so famous and worthy a knight, there was no reason why it should not have a name of equal renown. The kind of name he wanted was one that would at once indicate what the nag had been before it came to belong to a knight-errant and what its present status was; for it stood to reason that, when the master's worldly condition changed, his horse also ought to have a famous, high-sounding appellation, one suited to the new order of things and the new profession that it was to follow.

After he in his memory and imagination had made up, struck out, and discarded many names, now adding to and now subtracting from the list, he finally hit upon "Rocinante,"[30] a name that impressed him as being sonorous[31] and at the same time indicative of what the steed had been when it was but a hack, whereas now it was nothing other than the first and foremost of all the hacks[32] in the world.

Having found a name for his horse that pleased his fancy, he then desired to do as much for himself, and this required another week, and by the end of that period he had made up his mind that he was henceforth to be known as Don Quixote,[33] which, as has been stated, has led the authors of this veracious[34] history to assume that his real name must undoubtedly have been Quijada, and not Quesada as others would have it. But remembering that the valiant Amadis was not content to call himself that and nothing more, but added the name of his kingdom and fatherland that he might make it famous also, and thus came to take the name

> . . . AND BY THE END OF THAT PERIOD
>
> HE HAD MADE UP HIS MIND
>
> THAT HE WAS HENCEFORTH
>
> TO BE KNOWN AS DON QUIXOTE. . . .

Amadis of Gaul, so our good knight chose to add his place of origin and become "Don Quixote de la Mancha"; for by this means, as he saw it, he was making very plain his lineage and was conferring honor upon his country by taking its name as his own.

---

26. **quarters in a real** (rā-äl'): A real was a coin worth about five cents.

27. **Gonela's steed:** the horse of the Italian court comedian Pietro Gonela, which was famous for having gas.

28. *tantum pellis et ossa fuit:* a Latin phrase meaning "was only skin and bones."

29. **Alexander's Bucephalus** (byōō-sĕf'ə-ləs) **or the Babieca** (bä-byĕ'kä) **of the Cid:** famous horses. Alexander is Alexander the Great, the early conqueror of Asia.

30. **Rocinante** (rô-sē-nän'tĕ).

31. **sonorous** (sŏn'ər-əs): having a full, rich sound.

32. **foremost of all the hacks:** *Rocin* means "nag" or "hack" in Spanish; *ante* means "before" or "first." So the name Rocinante indicates that it is the first, or premier, nag.

33. **Quixote** (kē-hô'tĕ): The literal meaning is "a piece of armor that protects the thigh."

34. **veracious:** truthful.

And so, having polished up his armor and made the morion over into a closed helmet, and having given himself and his horse a name, he naturally found but one thing lacking still: he must seek out a lady of whom he could become enamored; for a knight-errant without a ladylove was like a tree without leaves or fruit, a body without a soul.

"If," he said to himself, "as a punishment for my sins or by a stroke of fortune I should come upon some giant hereabouts, a thing that very commonly happens to knights-errant, and if I should slay him in a hand-to-hand encounter or perhaps cut him in two, or, finally, if I should vanquish and subdue him, would it not be well to have someone to whom I may send him as a present, in order that he, if he is living, may come in, fall upon his knees in front of my sweet lady, and say in a humble and submissive tone of voice, 'I, lady, am the giant Caraculiambro,[35] lord of the island Malindrania, who has been overcome in single combat by that knight who never can be praised enough, Don Quixote de la Mancha, the same who sent me to present myself before your Grace that your Highness may dispose of me as you see fit'?"

Oh, how our good knight reveled in this speech, and more than ever when he came to think of the name that he should give his lady! As the story goes, there was a very good-looking farm girl who lived near by, with whom he had once been smitten,[36] although it is generally believed that she never knew or suspected it. Her name was Aldonza Lorenzo,[37] and it seemed to him that she was the one upon whom he should bestow the title of mistress of his thoughts. For her he wished a name that should not be <u>incongruous</u> with his own and that would convey the suggestion of a princess or a great lady; and, accordingly, he resolved to call her "Dulcinea del Toboso,"[38] she being a native of that place. A musical name to his ears, out of the ordinary and significant, like the others he had chosen for himself and his appurtenances.[39]

---

35. **Caraculiambro** (kä-rä-kōō-lyäm′brô).
36. **smitten:** entranced; in love.
37. **Aldonza Lorenzo** (äl-dôn′sä lô-rĕn′sô).
38. **Dulcinea del Toboso** (dōōl-sē-nĕ′ä dĕl tô-bô′sô).
39. **appurtenances:** accessories.

WORDS TO KNOW

incongruous (ĭn-kŏng′grōō-əs) *adj.* not appropriate; out of place

After completing his preparations, Don Quixote sets off on his first adventure. During his three days of travel, he persuades an innkeeper to dub him a knight. Then he "rescues" a servant boy from his master's beating, but as soon as "our knight" leaves, the master beats the boy even harder. Don Quixote next mistakes a traveling group of merchants for hostile knights. After insulting the merchants for failing to swear to the beauty of Dulcinea del Toboso, he is badly beaten. A neighbor finds him on the road and carries him home, to the great relief of his family and friends. They blame Don Quixote's mad behavior on his reading habits, so for his own good they decide to burn his books.

FROM
CHAPTER 7
Part 1

That night the housekeeper burned all the books there were in the stable yard and in all the house; and there must have been some that went up in smoke which should have been preserved in everlasting archives,[40] if the one who did the <u>scrutinizing</u> had not been so <u>indolent</u>. Thus we see the truth of the old saying, to the effect that the innocent must sometimes pay for the sins of the guilty.

One of the things that the curate and the barber advised as a remedy for their friend's sickness was to wall up the room where the books had been, so that, when he arose, he would not find them missing—it might be that the cause being removed, the effect would cease—and they could tell him that a magician had made away with them, room and all. This they proceeded to do as quickly as possible. Two days later, when Don Quixote rose from his bed, the first thing he did was to go have a look at his library, and, not finding it where he had left it, he went from one part of the house to another searching for it. Going up to where the door had been, he ran his hands over the wall and rolled his eyes in every direction without saying a word; but after some little while he asked the housekeeper where his study was with all his books.

She had been well instructed in what to answer him. "Whatever study is your Grace talking about?" she said. "There is no study, and no books, in this house; the devil took them all away."

"No," said the niece, "it was not the devil but an enchanter who came upon a cloud one night, the day after your Grace left here; dismounting from a serpent that he rode, he entered your study, and I don't know what all he did there, but after a bit he went flying off through the roof, leaving the house full of smoke; and when we went to see what he had done, there was no study and not a book in sight. There is one thing, though, that the housekeeper and I remember very well: at the time that wicked old fellow left, he cried out in a loud voice that it was all on account of a secret enmity that he bore the owner of those books and that study,

---

40. **archives:** places where records and other documents are stored.

WORDS TO KNOW

scrutinizing (skrōōt′n-ī′zĭng) *n.* observing or inspecting with great care **scrutinize** *v.*
indolent (ĭn′də-lənt) *adj.* lazy

DON QUIXOTE **837**

and that was why he had done the mischief in this house which we would discover. He also said that he was called Muñatón[41] the Magician."

"Frestón, he should have said," remarked Don Quixote.

"I can't say as to that," replied the housekeeper, "whether he was called Frestón or Fritón;[42] all I know is that his name ended in a *tón*."

"So it does," said Don Quixote. "He is a wise enchanter, a great enemy of mine, who has a grudge against me because he knows by his arts and learning that in the course of time I am to fight in single combat with a knight whom he favors, and that I am to be the victor and he can do nothing to prevent it. For this reason he seeks to cause me all the trouble that he can, but I am warning him that it will be hard to gainsay or shun that which Heaven has ordained." . . .

In the meanwhile Don Quixote was bringing his powers of persuasion to bear upon a farmer who lived near by, a good man—if this title may be applied to one who is poor—but with very few wits in his head. The short of it is, by pleas and promises, he got the hapless rustic to agree to ride forth with him and serve him as his squire. Among other things, Don Quixote told him that he ought to be more than willing to go, because no telling what adventure might occur which would win them an island, and then he (the farmer) would be left to be the governor of it. As a result of these and other similar assurances, Sancho Panza forsook his wife and children and consented to take upon himself the duties of squire to his neighbor.

Next, Don Quixote set out to raise some money, and by selling this thing and pawning that and getting the worst of the bargain always, he finally scraped together a reasonable amount. He also asked a friend of his for the loan of a buckler and patched up his broken helmet as well as he could. He advised his squire, Sancho, of the day and hour when they were to take the road and told him to see to laying in a supply of those things that were most necessary, and, above all, not to forget the saddlebags. Sancho replied that he would see to all this and added that he was also thinking of taking along with him a very good ass that he had, as he was not much used to going on foot.

With regard to the ass, Don Quixote had to do a little thinking, trying to recall if any knight-errant had ever had a squire thus asininely[43] mounted. He could not think of any, but nevertheless he decided to take Sancho with the intention of providing him with a nobler steed as soon as occasion offered; he had but to appropriate the horse of the first discourteous knight he met. Having furnished himself with shirts and all the other things that the innkeeper had recommended, he and Panza rode forth one night unseen by anyone and without taking leave of wife and children, housekeeper or niece. They went so far that by the time morning came they were safe from discovery had a hunt been started for them.

> THE SHORT OF IT IS, BY PLEAS AND PROMISES,
> HE GOT THE HAPLESS RUSTIC
> TO AGREE TO RIDE FORTH WITH HIM
> AND SERVE HIM AS HIS SQUIRE.

---

41. **Muñatón** (mōō-nyä-tôn′).

42. **Frestón** (frĕs-tôn′) **or Fritón** (frē-tôn′): Frestón, a magician, was thought to be the author of *History of Belianís of Greece.*

43. **asininely:** foolishly; ridiculously. The word is derived from the name of the animal.

Detail of *Don Quixote and the Dead Mule* (1867), Honoré Daumier. Musée d'Orsay, Paris.
Photograph copyright © Erich Lessing/Art Resource, New York.

FROM CHAPTER 8

Part 1

At this point they caught sight of thirty or forty windmills which were standing on the plain there, and no sooner had Don Quixote laid eyes upon them than he turned to his squire and said, "Fortune is guiding our affairs better than we could have wished; for you see there before you, friend Sancho Panza, some thirty or more lawless giants with whom I mean to do battle. I shall deprive them of their lives, and with the spoils from this encounter we shall begin to enrich ourselves; for this is righteous warfare, and it is a great service to God to remove so accursed a breed from the face of the earth."

"What giants?" said Sancho Panza.

"Those that you see there," replied his master, "those with the long arms some of which are as much as two leagues in length."

"But look, your Grace, those are not giants but windmills, and what appear to be arms are their wings which, when whirled in the breeze, cause the millstone to go."

"It is plain to be seen," said Don Quixote, "that you have had little experience in this matter of adventures. If you are afraid, go off to one side and say your prayers while I am engaging them in fierce, unequal combat."

Saying this, he gave spurs to his steed Rocinante, without paying any heed to Sancho's warning that these were truly windmills and not giants that he was riding forth to attack. Nor even when he was close upon them did he perceive what they really were, but shouted at the top of his lungs, "Do not seek to flee, cowards and vile creatures that you are, for it is but a single knight with whom you have to deal!"

At that moment a little wind came up and the big wings began turning.

"Though you flourish as many arms as did the giant Briareus,"[44] said Don Quixote when he perceived this, "you still shall have to answer to me."

He thereupon commended himself with all his heart to his lady Dulcinea, beseeching her to succor[45] him in this peril; and, being well covered with his shield and with his lance at rest, he bore down upon them at a full gallop and fell upon the first mill that stood in his way, giving a thrust at the wing, which was whirling at such a speed that his lance was broken into bits and

---

44. **Briareus** (brē-âr′yŏŏs): a mythological giant with 100 arms.

45. **succor:** to provide aid; help.

Don Quixote and the Windmill, after Gustave Doré. Engraving by Heliodore Joseph Pisan.
Bibliothèque Nationale de France, Paris. Giraudon/Art Resource, New York.

both horse and horseman went rolling over the plain, very much battered indeed. Sancho upon his donkey came hurrying to his master's assistance as fast as he could, but when he reached the spot, the knight was unable to move, so great was the shock with which he and Rocinante had hit the ground.

"God help us!" exclaimed Sancho, "did I not tell your Grace to look well, that those were nothing but windmills, a fact which no one could fail to see unless he had other mills of the same sort in his head?"

"Be quiet, friend Sancho," said Don Quixote. "Such are the fortunes of war, which more than any other are subject to constant change. What is more, when I come to think of it, I am sure that this must be the work of that magician Frestón, the one who robbed me of my study and my books, and who has thus changed the giants into windmills in order to deprive me of the glory of overcoming them, so great is the enmity that he bears me; but in the end his evil arts shall not prevail against this trusty sword of mine."

"May God's will be done," was Sancho Panza's response. And with the aid of his squire the knight was once more mounted on Rocinante, who stood there with one shoulder half out of joint. And so, speaking of the adventure that had just befallen them, they continued along the Puerto Lápice[46] highway; for there, Don Quixote said, they could not fail to find many and varied adventures, this being a much traveled thoroughfare. ❖

---

46. **Puerto Lápice** (pwĕr′tô lä′pē-sĕ).

A SOLDIER OF URBINA[1]

Jorge Luis Borges

Translated by ALASTAIR REID

Beginning to fear his own unworthiness
for campaigns like the last he fought, at sea,
this soldier, resigning himself to minor duty,
wandered unknown in Spain, his own harsh country.

5 To get rid of or to mitigate[2] the cruel
weight of reality, he hid his head in dream.
The magic past of Roland and the cycles
of Ancient Britain[3] warmed him, made him welcome.

Sprawled in the sun, he would gaze on the widening
10 plain, its coppery glow going on and on;
he felt himself at the end, poor and alone,

unaware of the music he was hiding;
plunging deep in a dream of his own,
he came on Sancho and Don Quixote, riding.

---

1. **Urbina:** Cervantes served as a soldier under Captain
Diego Urbina.

2. **mitigate:** to moderate; lessen in intensity.

3. **cycles of Ancient Britain:** stories and poems about King
Arthur and knights of his era.

Connect to the Literature

1. What Do You Think?
Do you like the character of Don Quixote? Explain why or why not.

Comprehension Check
- What causes Don Quixote's madness?
- Why does Sancho Panza agree to become Don Quixote's squire?
- Why does Don Quixote attack the windmill?

Think Critically

2. ACTIVE READING: ANALYZING EXPOSITION Look over the chart you made in your █ **READER'S NOTEBOOK**. What details in the exposition help you understand why Don Quixote "went completely out of his mind"?

3. The knights' code of honor, or **chivalry,** idealized qualities such as bravery, courtesy, and gallantry toward women. Contrast the ideal image of a knight with Don Quixote's actual life. Do you find the contrast amusing or sad? Explain.

THINK ABOUT
- Don Quixote's fragile helmet and his "skinny nag" Rocinante
- his "great lady," the farm girl Dulcinea del Toboso
- his quest for heroic adventures

4. A **foil** is a character who provides a striking contrast to another character. How does Sancho Panza serve as a foil to Don Quixote? Give examples to support your opinion.

5. What does Don Quixote's encounter with the windmill illustrate about his character?

6. Do you predict that Don Quixote's fantasies will turn out to be dangerous to himself and others? Why or why not?

Extend Interpretations

7. Compare Texts In "A Soldier of Urbina" on page 843, the poet imagines how Cervantes came to create his major characters. According to the poem, what do Cervantes and Don Quixote have in common?

8. Connect to Life Don Quixote's fantasies lead him into ridiculous situations and sometimes even cause injury. Is fantasy in adults always harmful, or are there times when it can be healthy and useful? Explain.

LITERARY ANALYSIS: CHARACTERIZATION

Characterization refers to the techniques that writers use to develop characters. There are four basic methods of characterization:
1. A writer may describe the physical appearance of the character. For example, Cervantes tells us that Don Quixote has "little flesh on his bones."
2. A character's nature may be revealed through his or her own speech, thoughts, feelings, or actions. Don Quixote's sale of land to pay for books reveals his lack of practicality.
3. The speech, thoughts, feelings, and actions of other characters may be used to develop a character. Sancho Panza's willingness to go along on the journey suggests that Don Quixote is persuasive.
4. The narrator may make direct comments about the character's nature. In this excerpt, the narrator tells us that Don Quixote's "wits were gone beyond repair."

Paired Activity With a partner, identify five short passages in these excerpts that help create a strong impression of either Don Quixote or Sancho Panza. Use a chart like the one shown to record your findings.

Don Quixote		
Passage	**Method of Characterization**	**Qualities Revealed**
"his wits were gone beyond repair"	4	

Writing Options

1. Speech About Chivalry

Does the concept of chivalry have any value in the modern world? Write a persuasive speech on the topic. Before you begin, review the information about chivalry on pages 690 and 709. Begin the speech with a clear statement of your opinion. Then present your supporting points clearly and logically. Finish up with a summation of your argument. Place the speech in your **Working Portfolio.**

2. Letter from Sancho

Pretend you are Sancho Panza and write a letter to your wife after the windmill incident. Describe what happened to Don Quixote and reveal your thoughts about him.

Explain whether the incident raised any doubts in your mind about the journey.

Writing Handbook
See page R27: Descriptive Writing.

Activities & Explorations

Quixote Improv With a small group, create an improvised dramatization in which Don Quixote and Sancho Panza take part in an adventure in your community. Imagine, for example, how Don Quixote might respond to a football game or a car wash.
~ SPEAKING AND LISTENING

Inquiry & Research

1. Chivalrous Knights

Find out more about one of the famous knights mentioned in *Don Quixote.* Which romance does the knight appear in? What adventures does he have? Is this character based on a real person or is he entirely fictional? Report your findings to the class.

2. Fantasy and Reality

Theories of mental health have changed considerably since Cervantes's time. With a partner, research mental disorders that involve mistaking fantasy for reality. How might a psychologist diagnose Don Quixote? Do you think Don Quixote would be happier if his disorder were brought under control?

RESEARCH STARTER
CLASSZONE.COM

Vocabulary in Action

EXERCISE: CONTEXT CLUES On your paper, complete each of the following sentences.

1. A(n) _____ story about a knight's adventure would not confuse its readers.

2. Some romances were _____ tales that piled one adventure on another.

3. In coming up with Rocinante's unusual name, Don Quixote showed considerable _____.

4. Don Quixote's _____ with books about knights kept him reading and reading.

5. As a landowner, Don Quixote was _____ and impractical because all he did was read.

6. Sancho Panza was a(n) _____ fellow who got along easily with his master.

7. Some knights could be _____ in their treatment of their inferiors.

8. After _____ the windmills, Sancho Panza realized that they were not giants after all.

9. The _____ scene of an old man fighting the windmills is a famous one.

10. Readers might _____ that Don Quixote will someday become an honored knight.

WORDS TO KNOW

affable	incongruous	ingenuity	lucid
conjecture	indolent	interminable	scrutinizing
haughty	infatuation		

Building Vocabulary
For an in-depth lesson on context clues, see page 674.

The Plays of Molière

Molière (mōl-yâr′) is considered by many to be the greatest French playwright of all time. Today, more than three centuries after his death, his comedies are still popular in France. In translation, they still delight and instruct people throughout the world. Several of his works rank as masterpieces of world literature.

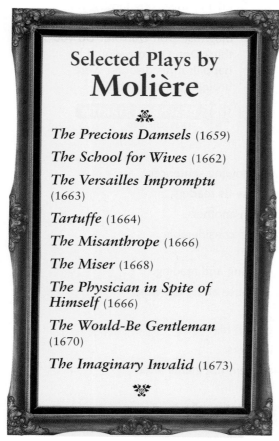

Selected Plays by
Molière

❧

The Precious Damsels (1659)

The School for Wives (1662)

The Versailles Impromptu (1663)

Tartuffe (1664)

The Misanthrope (1666)

The Miser (1668)

The Physician in Spite of Himself (1666)

The Would-Be Gentleman (1670)

The Imaginary Invalid (1673)

❧

"Molière" was the stage name of Jean Baptiste Poquelin (zhän′ bä-tēst′ pô-klăɴ′). Molière, whose lifelong love of the theater made him excel at his craft, began his career as an actor and a director. Later, he would perform the lead role in several of his own plays. He kept both the stage and his audience in mind when he wrote his comedies—about 32 in all.

To Molière, the main function of comedy was to "correct men's vices." Often he would base a play on a particular vice or failing and then exaggerate his selected trait in one of the characters. These characters are universal types—fanatics and flirts, quacks and misers, hypocrites and hypochondriacs. Molière pokes fun at their extreme conduct, which is contrary to moderation and good sense. Believing that the universe is ruled by reason, he sought to teach in his comedies that human life should be rational too.

Molière's first great comedy was *The School for Wives* (1662). The main character is a middle-aged man who wants to marry his ward, a young lady. He is convinced that he has reared her to be the ideal wife by limiting her education. She, however, chooses to follow

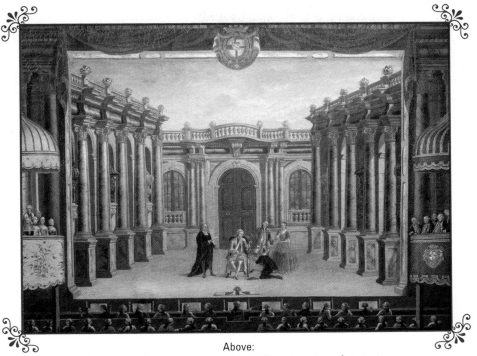

Above:
Scene from The Imaginary Invalid. *18th century French painting.*

Below:
*A print of Molière in
the lead role in his play*
The School for Husbands

her own heart and rejects him. Love conquers all—even the best-laid schemes of the controlling protagonist. This play, like many others by Molière, triggered heated protests.

By far, the bitterest attacks were directed at Molière's play *Tartuffe* (tär-t̄ōōf'). In this play, the title character pretends to be pious in order to deceive the gullible and fill his own pockets. He tricks a religious fanatic and nearly ruins the man's family. The play shows the folly of too much trust and too little sense. It was perceived, however, as an attack on religion, and banned for several years.

The Misanthrope is generally considered Molière's greatest play. The title, which means "hater of humankind," applies to its main character, Alceste. He takes sincerity to ridiculous extremes, scornful of telling even a white lie. Though Alceste is an idealist with some admirable traits, his extreme reactions make him comic. Still, at the end of this play, the audience is left to ponder the need for more truth in everyday life.

Molière's comedies target human folly. They make audiences and readers laugh and think—and look within. One translator of Molière's plays describes their effect this way: "Again and again he leads us from the enjoyable but shallow reaction of laughing at a fool to recognizing in that fool others whom we know, and ultimately ourselves." Perhaps this is why his plays are still enjoyed today.

FROM

Candide

VOLTAIRE

Voltaire
1694–1778

Early Success Philosopher, poet, playwright, historian, and rebel—Voltaire (vōl-târ′) was all of these. Born François Marie Arouet, he was imprisoned early in his literary career for insulting the regent, or acting ruler, of France. Shortly after his release from prison in 1718, his first major play, *Oedipe* (œ-dēp′), achieved international success, and he chose the pen name Voltaire. Other successes quickly followed. By his early 30s, Voltaire had become independently wealthy through wise investments and enjoyed the status of an honored celebrity at the court of King Louis XV.

English Influence Circumstances changed abruptly when Voltaire insulted a young nobleman in 1726. Given the option of imprisonment or exile, Voltaire chose exile in England, where he befriended many writers and political leaders. After Voltaire returned to Paris in 1729, he wrote a book praising England's political liberties and traditions of tolerance. However, the book was thought to be critical of the French government. In 1734, fearing another unpleasant jail term, Voltaire was forced to flee Paris again.

Exile and Return For the next four decades, Voltaire spent most of the time away from Paris, living as far away as Berlin and Geneva. He produced a steady flow of essays, books, plays, poems, pamphlets, and letters. Many of his works criticized religious intolerance and persecution and advocated the use of reason. In his most famous work, *Candide* (1759), he used satire to attack optimism and simple-minded idealism. Although Voltaire enjoyed a triumphant return to Paris at age 83, the excitement of his return proved too much for him, and he died shortly thereafter. Always a controversial figure in his lifetime, Voltaire was later regarded as a kind of "saint of reason." During the French Revolution, his remains were removed to the Panthéon in Paris, where many of France's most famous citizens are buried.

Build Background

A Comic Masterpiece

Candide is Voltaire's most widely read work of fiction. This philosophical tale tells about the comic misadventures of an innocent young man who has grown up in the household of a powerful baron. From his tutor, Dr. Pangloss, Candide learns that all is for the best in "this best of all possible worlds." After he is cast out of this "paradise," Candide travels the world in an effort to reunite with his beloved Cunegonde, the baron's daughter. He wanders through Europe and the Americas, occasionally meeting up with members of his former household, who also endure great misfortune. At each turn, Candide learns more about the flaws of humanity, realizing that all is not for the best. Although the novel ends on a relatively happy note, Candide realizes that the world is not the paradise he had once imagined.

The Best of All Possible Worlds Voltaire wrote *Candide* in reaction to a way of looking at the world known as **optimism.** An optimist is a person who looks for the best in every situation and person. According to the philosopher most associated with optimism, Gottfried Wilhelm Leibniz (līp'nĭts), our world is "the best of all possible worlds." The English poet Alexander Pope put it another way: "Whatever is, is right." Voltaire was attracted to such ideas in his youth. However, he came to reject optimism because he felt it did not do justice to the tragedies and suffering of human life. Also, he feared that optimism discouraged people from trying to remedy injustices and social problems.

Connect to Your Life

For some people, the glass is always half full; others see it as half empty. Do you prefer to be in the company of optimists or their opposites, pessimists? What are the advantages and disadvantages of each of these outlooks on life?

Focus Your Reading

LITERARY ANALYSIS: SATIRE AND HUMOR

Satire is a literary technique in which ideas, customs, behaviors, or institutions are ridiculed for the purpose of improving society. In satire, **humor** and exaggeration are used as weapons of mockery, intended to provoke the reader's laughter and thought. For example, the baron in *Candide* is "one of the most powerful lords" in his kingdom because "his castle possessed a door and windows."

ACTIVE READING: MAKING JUDGMENTS

To appreciate the intended meaning of a satirical work, readers must make judgments about the characters. For example, readers might begin judging Pangloss when Voltaire introduces him as a teacher of "metaphysico-theologo-cosmolonigology." By exaggerating Pangloss's area of study, Voltaire encourages us to be skeptical of his ideas.

📖 **READER'S NOTEBOOK** As you read this excerpt from *Candide*, record key information about the main characters in a chart like the one shown.

Character	Trait(s)
Dr. Pangloss	Pretentious, spends his time studying ridiculous subjects
The Baron	
Candide	
Cunegonde	

WORDS TO KNOW **Vocabulary Preview**

candor	pensive	vivacity
docile	reiterated	

from Candide
Voltaire
Translated by Richard Aldington

Uniforms of imperial cavalry (18th century). Watercolor. Heeresgeschichtliches Museum, Vienna, Austria. Photograph copyright © Erich Lessing/Art Resource, New York.

Chapter I

How Candide was brought up in a noble castle, and how he was expelled from the same

In the castle of Baron Thunder-ten-tronckh in Westphalia[1] there lived a youth, endowed by Nature with the most gentle character. His face was the expression of his soul. His judgment was quite honest and he was extremely simple-minded; and this was the reason, I think, that he was named Candide.[2] Old servants in the house suspected that he was the son of the Baron's sister and a decent honest gentleman of the neighborhood, whom this young lady would never marry because he could only prove seventy-one quarterings,[3] and the rest of his genealogical tree[4] was lost, owing to the injuries of time.

The Baron was one of the most powerful lords in Westphalia, for his castle possessed a door and windows. His Great Hall was even decorated with a piece of tapestry. The dogs in his stableyards formed a pack of hounds when necessary; his grooms were his huntsmen; the village curate was his Grand Almoner.[5] They all called him "My Lord," and laughed heartily at his stories.

The Baroness weighed about three hundred and fifty pounds, was therefore greatly respected, and did the honors of the house with a dignity which rendered her still more respectable. Her daughter Cunegonde,[6] aged seventeen, was rosy-cheeked, fresh, plump and tempting. The Baron's son appeared in every respect worthy of his father. The tutor Pangloss[7] was the oracle of the house, and little Candide followed his lessons with all the <u>candor</u> of his age and character.

Pangloss taught metaphysico-theologo-cosmolonigology.[8] He proved admirably that there is no effect without a cause and that in this best of all possible worlds, My Lord the Baron's castle was the best of castles and his wife the best of all possible Baronesses.

"'Tis demonstrated," said he, "that things cannot be otherwise; for, since everything is made for an end, everything is necessarily for the best end. Observe that noses were made to wear spectacles; and so we have spectacles. Legs were visibly instituted to be breeched, and we have breeches. Stones were formed to be quarried and to build castles; and My Lord has a very noble castle; the greatest Baron in the province should have the best house; and as pigs were made to be

---

1. **Baron Thunder-ten-tronckh** (thŭn′dər-tĕn-trônk′) **in Westphalia** (wĕst-fāl′yə): Westphalia is a region of west-central Germany.
2. **Candide** (kän-dēd′): a French word meaning "innocent" or "without sophistication."
3. **seventy-one quarterings:** Quarterings are divisions in coats of arms that indicate connections with other noble families; 71 of these is a ridiculous number.
4. **genealogical tree:** a diagram showing ancestry in a family.
5. **Grand Almoner:** a person in charge of distributing charity, or alms, to the poor.
6. **Cunegonde** (kün-gônd′).
7. **Pangloss:** a combination of Greek words meaning "all" and "tongue."
8. **metaphysico-theologo-cosmolonigology** (mĕt′ə-fĭz′ĭ-kō-thē-ŏl′ə-gō-kŏz-mŏl′ə-nĭ-gŏl′ə-jē): a made-up field of study. The ending *-nigology* comes from a French word meaning "foolish."

WORDS TO KNOW
candor (kan′dər) *n.* frankness; openness

The Stolen Kiss (late 1780s), Jean-Honoré Fragonard. Oil on canvas, 45 cm × 55 cm. The Hermitage, St. Petersburg, Russia.

her every day; and the fourth to listen to Doctor Pangloss, the greatest philosopher of the province and therefore of the whole world.

One day when Cunegonde was walking near the castle, in a little wood which was called The Park, she observed Doctor Pangloss in the bushes, giving a lesson in experimental physics to her mother's waiting-maid, a very pretty and docile brunette. Mademoiselle Cunegonde had a great inclination for science and watched breathlessly the reiterated experiments she witnessed; she observed clearly the Doctor's sufficient reason, the effects and the causes, and returned home very much excited, pensive, filled with the desire of learning, reflecting that she might be the sufficient reason of young Candide and that he might be hers.

eaten, we eat pork all the year round; consequently, those who have asserted that all is well talk nonsense; they ought to have said that all is for the best."

Candide listened attentively and believed innocently; for he thought Mademoiselle Cunegonde extremely beautiful, although he was never bold enough to tell her so. He decided that after the happiness of being born Baron of Thunder-ten-tronckh, the second degree of happiness was to be Mademoiselle Cunegonde; the third, to see

On her way back to the castle she met Candide and blushed; Candide also blushed. She bade him good-morning in a hesitating voice; Candide replied without knowing what he was saying. Next day, when they left the table after dinner, Cunegonde and Candide found themselves behind a screen; Cunegonde dropped her handkerchief, Candide picked it up; she innocently held his hand; the young man innocently kissed the young lady's hand with remarkable vivacity, tenderness and grace; their lips met,

WORDS TO KNOW

docile (dŏs'əl) *adj.* obedient; easily led or managed
reiterated (rē-ĭt'ə-rā'tĭd) *adj.* repeated **reiterate** *v.*
pensive (pĕn'sĭv) *adj.* thoughtful; moody
vivacity (vĭ-văs'ĭ-tē) *n.* liveliness

their eyes sparkled, their knees trembled, their hands wandered. Baron Thunder-ten-tronckh passed near the screen, and, observing this cause and effect, expelled Candide from the castle by kicking him in the backside frequently and hard. Cunegonde swooned;[9] when she recovered her senses, the Baroness slapped her in the face; and all was in consternation[10] in the noblest and most agreeable of all possible castles.

. . . FOR HE THOUGHT Mademoiselle Cunegonde EXTREMELY BEAUTIFUL, ALTHOUGH HE WAS NEVER BOLD ENOUGH TO TELL HER SO.

Chapter II

What happened to Candide among the Bulgarians

Candide, expelled from the earthly paradise, wandered for a long time without knowing where he was going, turning up his eyes to Heaven, gazing back frequently at the noblest of castles which held the most beautiful of young Baronesses; he lay down to sleep supperless between two furrows in the open fields; it snowed heavily in large flakes. The next morning the shivering Candide, penniless, dying of cold and exhaustion, dragged himself towards the neighboring town, which was called Waldberghofftrarbk-dikdorff. He halted sadly at the door of an inn. Two men dressed in blue noticed him.

"Comrade," said one, "there's a well-built young man of the right height."

They went up to Candide and very civilly invited him to dinner.

"Gentlemen," said Candide with charming modesty, "you do me a great honor, but I have no money to pay my share."

"Ah, sir," said one of the men in blue, "persons of your figure and merit never pay anything; are you not five feet five tall?"

"Yes, gentlemen," said he, bowing, "that is my height."

"Ah, sir, come to table; we will not only pay your expenses, we will never allow a man like you to be short of money; men were only made to help each other."

"You are in the right," said Candide, "that is what Doctor Pangloss was always telling me, and I see that everything is for the best."

They begged him to accept a few crowns, he took them and wished to give them an IOU; they refused to take it and all sat down to table.

"Do you not love tenderly . . ."

"Oh, yes," said he. "I love Mademoiselle Cunegonde tenderly."

"No," said one of the gentlemen. "We were asking if you do not tenderly love the King of the Bulgarians."

---

9. **swooned:** fainted.
10. **consternation:** condition of being greatly upset.

"Not a bit," said he, "for I have never seen him."

"What! He is the most charming of Kings, and you must drink his health."

"Oh, gladly, gentlemen." And he drank.

"That is sufficient," he was told. "You are now the support, the aid, the defender, the hero of the Bulgarians; your fortune is made and your glory assured."

They immediately put irons on his legs and took him to a regiment.[11] He was made to turn to the right and left, to raise the ramrod[12] and return the ramrod, to take aim, to fire, to double up, and he was given thirty strokes with a stick; the next day he drilled not quite so badly, and received only twenty strokes; the day after, he only had ten and was looked on as a prodigy[13] by his comrades.

Candide was completely mystified and could not make out how he was a hero. One fine spring day he thought he would take a walk, going straight ahead, in the belief that to use his legs as he pleased was a privilege of the human species as well as of animals. He had not gone two leagues when four other heroes, each six feet tall, fell upon him, bound him and dragged him back to a cell.

> "YOU ARE NOW THE SUPPORT, THE AID, THE DEFENDER, *the hero of the Bulgarians;* YOUR FORTUNE IS MADE AND YOUR GLORY ASSURED."

He was asked by his judges whether he would rather be thrashed thirty-six times by the whole regiment or receive a dozen lead bullets at once in his brain. Although he protested that men's wills are free and that he wanted neither one nor the other, he had to make a choice; by virtue of that gift of God which is called *liberty,* he determined to run the gauntlet[14] thirty-six times and actually did so twice. There were two thousand men in the regiment. That made four thousand strokes which laid bare the muscles and nerves from his neck to his backside. As they were about to proceed to a third turn, Candide, utterly exhausted, begged as a favor that they would be so kind as to smash his head; he obtained this favor; they bound his eyes and he was made to kneel down. At that moment the King of the Bulgarians came by and inquired the victim's crime; and as this King was possessed of a

---

11. **put irons . . . regiment:** Voltaire is mocking the military recruiting practices of Frederick the Great, the Prussian king whom Voltaire served for three years.

12. **ramrod:** a rod used to ram gunpowder and bullets into a musket.

13. **prodigy:** person of remarkable skill or intelligence.

14. **run the gauntlet:** endure a military punishment in which a person is forced to run between two lines of soldiers who beat the person as he passes.

Assassination of Albrecht Wallenstein, Duke of Friedland (18th century). Watercolor. Heeresgeschichtliches Museum, Vienna, Austria. Photograph © Erich Lessing/Art Resource, New York.

HUMANITIES CONNECTION This 18th-century watercolor painting shows soldiers in the midst of carrying out an assassination. Note the bright colors and elegant tailoring of the uniforms.

vast genius, he perceived from what he learned about Candide that he was a young metaphysician[15] very ignorant in worldly matters, and therefore pardoned him with a clemency[16] which will be praised in all newspapers and all ages. An honest surgeon healed Candide in three weeks with the ointments recommended by Dioscorides.[17] He had already regained a little skin and could walk when the King of the Bulgarians went to war with the King of the Abares. ❖

15. **metaphysician** (mĕt′ə-fĭ-zĭsh′-ən): philosopher who studies the nature of reality.
16. **clemency:** mercy.
17. **Dioscorides** (dī′əs-kôr′ĭ-dēz′): a Greek physician of the first century A.D.

Connect to the Literature

1. **What Do You Think?**
   What mental image of Candide did you form as you were reading? What details in the text contribute to that image?

   Comprehension Check
   • Why does the baron expel Candide from his castle?
   • Why does the Bulgarian army give Candide a beating?

Think Critically

2. **ACTIVE READING: MAKING JUDGMENTS** With a classmate, compare the charts you created in your **READER'S NOTEBOOK**. What judgments can you make about the main characters, based on the information you recorded?

3. What types of behaviors or institutions does Voltaire ridicule in this selection?

   > **THINK ABOUT**
   > • why the baron's sister would never marry the "honest gentleman"
   > • the baron's reason for expelling Candide from his castle
   > • Pangloss's teaching methods, both in the castle and in the woods
   > • Candide's treatment in the Bulgarian army

4. Why do you think the baron approves of Pangloss's philosophy? Do you think the people who are the baron's subjects would have the same opinion? Explain.

5. Much of the humor in *Candide* comes from the **narrator.** How would you describe the narrator's attitude? Read aloud passages from the selection in a way that expresses his attitude.

Extend Interpretations

6. **Comparing Texts** Compare Candide's experiences with those of Don Quixote. What similarities and differences do you see between them?

7. **Different Perspectives** How would this selection be different if it were narrated by Candide? Why might Voltaire have decided against using a first-person narrator?

8. **Connect to Life** If Voltaire were writing today, what philosophies or ways of thinking do you think he would mock? Give reasons to support your opinion.

LITERARY ANALYSIS: SATIRE AND HUMOR

Humor is always an important element in satire, in which mockery is used as a tool for the purpose of improving society. The three basic types of humor all involve exaggeration and/or irony. (For a definition of *irony,* see page R98.)

• **Humor of situation** usually involves exaggerated events. For example, Candide innocently expects to be helped by the men dressed in blue, but they end up forcing him into the army.

• **Humor of character** often involves exaggerated personality traits or characters who fail to recognize their own flaws. Pangloss's exaggerated self-satisfaction is an example of this type of humor.

• **Humor of language** may include sarcasm, exaggeration, word play, or absurdity. The name Pangloss, which means "all tongue" or "all words" in Greek, is an example of this type of humor.

Cooperative Learning Activity
With a small group, find six more examples of Voltaire's humor in the selection. For each example, decide which type of humor it is and what is being mocked. Use a chart like the one shown to record your findings.

Passage	Type of Humor	What Is Mocked
"They all called him 'My Lord,' and laughed heartily at his	humor of situation j857	People laugh at the Baron's stories only because of his power.

Choices & CHALLENGES

Writing Options

1. Satirical Writing Write a brief satirical tale. First, choose a behavior or institution that you want to ridicule in order to improve society. Then imagine characters and a plot that will convey your message. In your satire, use exaggeration and irony to create humor.
Writing Handbook
See page R29: Narrative Writing.

2. War Diary At the end of the selection, Candide has barely survived his punishment. Pretend you are Candide and write a diary entry in which you express your thoughts and feelings about the army's treatment of you.

Activities and Explorations

1. Candide's Song With a partner, create song lyrics based on Candide's experiences or philosophy of life. If you are bold enough, put your lyrics to music and perform it before your classmates. ~ **MUSIC**

2. Voltaire News Working with a small group, create a television news report in the mocking style of Voltaire. First, find news items that are worthy of ridicule. Then write your news report in a way that shows your mockery of the events or people involved. Present your report to the class. ~ **SPEAKING AND LISTENING**

Inquiry & Research

1. The Lisbon Earthquake In 1755, a terrible earthquake struck Lisbon, Portugal. Find out more about this earthquake and the effect it had on Voltaire. If possible, also review Voltaire's poem *The Lisbon Disaster.* Give an oral report on your findings.
Communication Handbook
See page R47: Skimming and Scanning.

2. Voltaire's World With a small group of classmates, do research to find out what daily life was like for the average European during the 18th century. Each student should focus on a particular aspect of daily life, such as work or nutrition. After you report your findings to the group, discuss whether this information contradicts or supports Leibniz's view that this is "the best of all possible worlds."

RESEARCH STARTER
CLASSZONE.COM

Vocabulary in Action

EXERCISE: SYNONYMS Write on your paper the letter of the word that is the best synonym for the boldfaced word.

1. Voltaire's outraged **candor** about the failings of French leaders frequently got him into trouble.

   (a) unfairness, (b) honesty, (c) ignorance, (d) forgetfulness

2. The outspoken French philosopher was never known as a **docile** personality.

   (a) bold, (b) aggressive, (c) mild, (d) irritating

3. His prose style is famous for its wit, sarcasm, and **vivacity.**

   (a) vitality, (b) viciousness, (c) vanity, (d) vagueness

4. He frequently **reiterated** his strong criticisms of authorities.

   (a) rejected, (b) restated, (c) softened, (d) regretted

5. Despite his bold and daring humor, Voltaire also had his quietly **pensive** moments.

   (a) carefree, (b) angry, (c) cheerful, (d) reflective

Building Vocabulary

For an in-depth lesson on context clues, see page 674.

Communication Workshop
Persuasive Speech

Speaking your mind . . .

From Reading to Writing In *Utopia,* Sir Thomas More wrote persuasively about the benefits of life in his imaginary society. While More presented his ideas in a book, many people choose to persuade others through speech. In a **persuasive speech,** a speaker tries to convince his or her audience to adopt a certain point of view or take a certain action. Whether addressing a student council meeting or an international peace summit, a speaker uses certain basic strategies to persuade his or her audience.

For Your Portfolio

WRITING PROMPT Write and deliver a persuasive speech about an issue that is important to you.

Purpose: To convince others to agree with you

Audience: Anyone who can help you achieve your goal or whose views you want to change

Basics in a Box

RUBRIC Writing and Delivering a Speech

Content

A successful persuasive speech should

- open with an example, an anecdote, or a thesis statement
- clearly state the issue and the writer's position on it
- be geared to its audience
- include facts, examples, statistics, and reasons that support the writer's position

- answer opposing views
- show clear reasoning
- include features, such as frequent summaries, that help listeners remember the message and the reasons for the position
- end with a strong restatement of the position or a call to action

Delivery

An effective speaker should

- convey enthusiasm and confidence
- stand with straight, relaxed posture and make eye contact with the audience

- use gestures and body language to enhance the presentation
- incorporate visual aids effectively

Analyzing a Student Model

Leahruth Jemilo
Walter Payton High School

Do You Buy It?

I was watching TV when an eye-catching commercial came on. A pretty woman got her cute boyfriend to buy her something in a store, apparently because her silky, smooth hair was irresistible to him; the ad was promoting a shampoo. But really—if I used this shampoo, would it help me attract cute guys and get them to run errands for me? I think not. The ad appealed to me, though, because I wanted to be as beautiful as the woman in it, and I wanted boys to react to me in the same way. So I bought the shampoo. Why was I so strongly influenced by advertising? We teenagers must resist these tempting but false advertisements. They do not portray the real world, and they make us feel bad about ourselves.

Americans experience a daily onslaught of advertising images. According to one estimate, the average adult is exposed to more than 250 ads every day on television and radio and in magazines and newspapers. This constant exposure to ads can't help but affect the way we view the world and the way we see ourselves. I know it affects me. I remember seeing another TV commercial, one for tight leather pants. The girl modeling the pants was very thin and attractive. As I sat on my couch wishing that I had her pants and could look as good in them as she, I suddenly regretted the food that I was nibbling on. How did this commercial have the power to make me regret what I ate and how I looked? This experience is widespread. In a Canadian study of female university students, subjects in an experimental group became depressed and hostile when asked about their mood, body satisfaction, and eating patterns after viewing magazine ads featuring female fashion models.

The fact is, fashion models serve as role models for us. As teenagers, we are still developing our own identities, constantly looking for examples and ideas of how to look or act or think. Unfortunately, the look we admire is not a healthy one. You don't have to look very far to see that most teen fashion models fit the same mold—thin, with a few variations in hair length or skin color. Many magazines, newspapers, and responsible adults tell us that these skinny girls are unattractive and not good role models for growing teenage girls. Yet, the advertisements

---

RUBRIC IN ACTION

❶ Opens with a personal anecdote

❷ Clearly states the issue

❸ Gestures can add emphasis to a personal anecdote.

❹ Cites university study as supporting evidence

❺ Connects with audience

❻ Visual aids can provide examples of skinny fashion models.

LANGUAGE SKILLS

continue to showcase only skinny models. These ads affect how teens feel about themselves and contribute to the forces that push teens toward unhealthy diets, depression, and eating disorders.

Eating disorders affect more than 5 million Americans—men and women—each year. Of those 5 million people, 95 percent are women between the ages of 12 and 25. About a thousand women die every year from anorexia nervosa, an eating disorder marked by severe weight loss and a persistent unwillingness to eat, partly in response to a distorted body image. It is also estimated that 15 percent of young women have substantially disordered eating attitudes and behavior, which can lead to actual eating disorders.

7 Gives statistics as supporting evidence

Can we really blame the advertisers? After all, they're just trying to sell their products. Of course they are going to portray their products in an attractive light. What else would they do? If teenagers have self-image problems, they just have to toughen up a little. You won't get very far in life if you're going to be pushed around by a TV commercial!

8 Presents and answers opposing viewpoint

This is all true, of course. Advertisers are not in the business of making us feel better about ourselves or expanding our narrow notions of beauty, and we're not likely to change that. What we can change is the way we perceive advertising messages. Teens must be able to distinguish between healthy fitness and the unusually perfect and uniform images of teen models in the media.

So whenever you read a magazine, watch TV, or drive by a billboard, remember that the people in the ads are models. They were hired because they look a certain way. Ads are designed to make you feel that you are missing something, that you need something. If you suddenly feel too fat or too plain or too boring, the advertisers have done their job. And if you suddenly begin to think that a PRODUCT is your key to feeling thin or glamorous or exciting, remember that personal transformations don't come in snazzy, colorful packages. You can't buy happiness, no matter how many people claim to sell it.

9 Ends by calling on audience to think critically about advertisements

Writing and Delivering Your Persuasive Speech

❶ Planning and Drafting

To find a topic for your speech, make a list of issues you feel strongly about. Also, with your classmates, **brainstorm** a list of issues you like to debate. See the **Idea Bank** in the margin for more suggestions. After you've chosen a topic that you'd like to cover in a speech, follow the steps below.

Planning Your Speech

▶ **1. Clarify your position.** How do you feel about the issue, and why?

▶ **2. Find support for your position.** What research will you have to do to back up your case? Where can you find the necessary information? What evidence will help you make your point most effectively?

▶ **3. Identify your audience.** What do your listeners already know about the issue? What is their position on it?

▶ **4. Consider how to grab your listeners' attention.** What startling statistic, amusing anecdote, or intriguing question can you use to hook your audience at the beginning of your speech?

▶ **5. Decide how to present your arguments.** How can you organize your arguments so that they have the greatest impact? Do you want to begin with an argument your audience will probably agree with and then move to more controversial points? Would it be better to put your strongest argument at the beginning or at the end?

Think about how to present your speech. Would your listeners respond best to a straightforward, scholarly approach, or would humor be more effective? Might they respond to a dramatic presentation, or is it best to be low-key? What verbal and nonverbal techniques will work best to capture and hold your audience's interest and attention?

When you have finished planning, draft your speech. As you are writing and revising, you might want to read parts of it out loud. If something is hard to say, it probably sounds awkward, and you should think of another way to say it.

❷ Practicing and Delivering

The best way to practice your speech is to present it aloud over and over again. Try speaking in front of a mirror or videotaping your speech so that you can evaluate and improve your posture, gestures, eye contact, and use of visual aids. You might tape-record a practice session so that you can critique your voice quality and effectiveness.

IDEABank

1. Your Working Portfolio 🗂
Look for ideas in the **Writing Option** you completed earlier in this unit:

- **Speech About Chivalry,** p. 845

2. Media Watch
Keep your eyes and ears open for discussions in the media of topics you feel strongly about.

3. Community Concerns
Make a list of problems or needs in your community. What can be done about them? Choose one of these issues to write your speech about.

LANGUAGE SKILLS

Need revising help?

Review the **Rubric**, p. 858

Consider **peer reviewer** comments

Check **revision guidelines**, p. R19

Publishing IDEAS

- Record the delivery of your speech on videotape or audiotape.
- Set up a soapbox event with several other classmates, delivering your speeches in turn.
- If there is a community organization concerned with your topic, write the organization and offer to speak at one of its meetings.
- Deliver your speech to your family.

PUBLISHING OPTIONS
CLASSZONE.COM

Ask Your Peer Reviewer

- What part of my argument was most convincing?
- Which points do you disagree with, and why?
- What aspects of my delivery were most effective? Which could use improvement?

Steps for Delivering Your Speech

1. Breathe deeply. Deep, steady breaths will help you remain calm and collected. Deep breathing is also very important to good speaking; it helps you speak loudly enough to be heard and helps you avoid tiring your voice.

2. Use your voice effectively. Speak out and be sure to enunciate clearly. If your audience can't easily hear and understand what you're saying, all of your hard work will be lost. Speak more loudly and clearly than you would in conversation, but try to maintain a natural tone of voice.

3. Maintain eye contact. Look directly at different members of the audience while you speak.

4. Incorporate gestures and facial expressions. Remember, your listeners are more likely to be interested in your topic if they can see that you are interested.

5. Use visual aids. Organize your information in charts, graphs, or drawings that will reinforce your message. Make sure your materials are large enough and clear enough that everyone in the audience can read them.

❸ Refining Your Delivery

TARGET SKILL ► RESPONDING TO AUDIENCE FEEDBACK A persuasive speech is successful only if it convinces an audience. Here are some comments your peer reviewers might make, along with ways you can change your speech or delivery in response to the comments.

- **I couldn't hear/understand you.** This is a common complaint. Speak loudly and pronounce your words carefully. Remember that most people speak too fast, so watch your speed too.

- **It seemed as if you were reading your speech rather than saying it.** Learn your speech well enough that you don't have to keep your eyes glued to the paper. Then you will have the freedom to look around and speak naturally.

- **I didn't always know what you were talking about.** As you make a transition, include a summary, such as the following: "I've just explained that X is true for these reasons. Now let's think for a moment about Y."

- **Your evidence didn't convince me.** Anticipate arguments from listeners with opposing views and gather additional expert opinions, facts, statistics, and examples.

❹ Reflecting

FOR YOUR WORKING PORTFOLIO What did you learn about your topic from writing and delivering your speech? Write your response and attach it to your speech. Save your speech in your **Working Portfolio.**

Read this paragraph from the first draft of a persuasive speech. The underlined sections may include the following kinds of errors:

- **incorrect pronoun case**
- **correctly written sentences that should be combined**
- **lack of pronoun-antecedent agreement**
- **lack of subject-verb agreement**

For each underlined section, choose the revision that most improves the writing.

There is a proposal before the school board that would require students to wear school uniforms. Although <u>many students want the right to wear his or her own clothing</u> (1) to school every day, <u>there is great advantages</u> (2) to school uniforms. Many students are obsessed with <u>appearances. They pay great attention to clothing, hair, jewelry, and makeup</u> (3). Some students are very critical of others <u>who don't dress as well as them</u> (4), and <u>students that can't afford designer clothing</u> (5) are branded as outcasts. Besides easing these problems, school uniforms create a sense of order and discipline in a school. <u>Some of the schools that have instituted the wearing of uniforms has noticed</u> (6) improved student behavior.

1. **A.** every student wants the right to wear their own clothing
    B. many students want the right to wear their own clothing
    C. many students want the right to wear one's own clothing
    D. Correct as is

2. **A.** there are great advantages
    B. there is great advantage
    C. there is great advantages
    D. Correct as is

3. **A.** appearances. They really pay great attention to clothing, hair, jewelry, and makeup
    B. appearances, paying great attention to clothing, hair, jewelry, and makeup
    C. appearances, they pay great attention to clothing, hair, jewelry, and makeup
    D. Correct as is

4. **A.** who don't dress as well as they do
    B. who don't dress as well as her
    C. who don't dress as well as themselves
    D. Correct as is

5. **A.** students what can't afford designer clothing
    B. students whom can't afford designer clothing
    C. students which can't afford designer clothing
    D. Correct as is

6. **A.** Some of the schools that has instituted the wearing of uniforms have noticed
    B. Some of the schools that has instituted the wearing of uniforms has noticed
    C. Some of the schools that have instituted the wearing of uniforms have noticed
    D. Correct as is

Need extra help?

See the **Grammar Handbook**

Pronoun Case, p. R57

Pronoun Agreement, p. R57

Relative Pronouns,, p. R59

Subject-Verb Agreement, p. R74

TEST PRACTICE

Building Vocabulary

What's in a Word? One way to determine the meaning of an unfamiliar word is to break it down into parts. There are three kinds of word parts: **base words,** which by themselves are complete words; **roots,** which are the core parts of words; and **affixes,** which can be added (or affixed) to roots or base words. Look at the words in the passage on the right. Which words seem to consist of more than one part?

Two examples are the nouns *curiosity* and *infatuation.* The first consists of the Latin root *curios* and the affix *-ity;* the second consists of the Latin root

fatu and the affixes *in-* and *-ation.* Another word in the passage, the adjective *tillable,* consists of the base word *till* and the affix *-able.*

> So great was his curiosity and infatuation in this regard that he even sold many acres of tillable land in order to be able to buy and read the books that he loved, and he would carry home with him as many of them as he could obtain.
>
> —Miguel de Cervantes, *Don Quixote*

Strategies for Building Vocabulary

Affixes can be added to the beginning or end of roots and base words. Affixes added to the beginning of words and roots are called **prefixes;** affixes added to the end are called **suffixes.** The word *infatuation,* for example, consists of a prefix, a root, and a suffix.

Prefix		Root		Suffix
in-	+	*fatu*	+	*-ation*
"in"		"foolish"		"condition"

The parts come together to mean, literally, "in a foolish condition." This is very close to the proper definition, "a foolish passion or attraction." The following strategies can help you recognize common affixes.

❶ **Look for Prefixes** The prefix *in-* is part of many words. For example, the word *ingrate,* meaning "a person who is not thankful," is formed by adding the prefix *in-,* here meaning "not," to the Latin root *grat,* meaning "pleasing" or "thankful." Some prefixes have more than one meaning—for example, the prefix *in-* can also mean "in" or "into." The table on the right shows the meanings of several common prefixes.

❷ **Identify Suffixes** Adding or changing a suffix often changes a word from one part of speech to another. For example, the suffix *-ion* changes the verb *illustrate* into the noun *illustration.* You can find more examples of suffixes in the table at right. Note that some suffixes have more than one meaning.

Prefix	Meaning	Words
auto-	self	autobiography, autonomy
dis-	not, opposite of	disgust, displeasure
ex-	former *or* out of	ex-husband *or* expel
hyper-	excessive, excessively	hyperactive, hyperconscious
im-	not *or* into	imbalance *or* immigrate
pan-	all	panorama, pan-American

Suffix	Meaning	Words
-arium, -ary	a place for	aquarium, mortuary
-ion	action, process, state, quality of	caution, hesitation
-fy, -ify, -efy	cause to become, make	quantify, purify, liquefy
-ment	action, process *or* result of action or process	development *or* amazement
-ous	full of, characterized by	porous, fabulous, envious
-tude	state or condition	gratitude, servitude

EXERCISE Identify the word parts that make up each word below. Use the meanings of the word parts to help you define the word. Check your definition in a dictionary, and then use the word in a sentence.

1. signify   3. aviary   5. disquieting
2. expatriate   4. implode

Grammar from Literature A noun clause is a subordinate clause that is used as a noun in a sentence. It can serve any of the functions of a single-word noun, including subject, direct object, or object of a preposition. Notice the noun clauses, printed in blue, in the following passages from *Don Quixote*.

> "But look, your Grace, those are not giants but windmills,
> noun clause as subject   verb
> and what appear to be arms are their wings which, when whirled in the breeze, cause the millstone to go."

> verb   noun clause as direct object
> ". . . I don't know what all he did there, but after a bit he went flying off through the roof, leaving the house full of smoke. . . ."

> preposition   noun clause as object of preposition
> Going up to where the door had been, he ran his hands over the wall and rolled his eyes in every direction without saying a word. . . .

A noun clause can be introduced by a pronoun (such as *what, whatever, who, whoever, whom,* or *whomever*) or by a subordinating conjunction (such as *how, that, when, where, whether,* or *why*). One common type of noun clause begins with *that* and follows a verb such as *tell, say, see,* or *know.*

> Among other things, Don Quixote told him that he ought to be more than willing to go, because no telling what adventure might occur which would win them an island. . . .
> —*Don Quixote*

In this type of clause, it is common for *that* to be understood rather than stated directly: "Don Quixote told him (that) he ought to be more than willing to go."

Using Noun Clauses in Your Writing Noun clauses allow you to express ideas efficiently and gracefully. Most people use noun clauses without even knowing what they are. Imagine how you might rewrite the following sentence without a noun clause.

> WITH NOUN CLAUSE
> **Candide was completely mystified and could not make out** how he was a hero.
> —*Candide*

Usage Tip People are often puzzled about whether to use *who* or *whom* in a noun clause. The choice depends on how the pronoun functions within the clause. Use *who* (or *whoever*) when the word functions as a subject or a predicate nominative. Use *whom* (or *whomever*) when it functions as a direct object, an indirect object, or the object of a preposition.

> **I don't know** whom **you mean.**
> (*YOU* IS THE SUBJECT OF THE CLAUSE, AND *WHOM* IS THE DIRECT OBJECT OF *MEAN.*)

> **Feel free to invite** whomever **you like.**
> (*YOU* IS THE SUBJECT OF THE CLAUSE, AND *WHOMEVER* IS THE DIRECT OBJECT OF *LIKE.*)

> Whoever **wants to come is welcome.**
> (*WHOEVER* IS THE SUBJECT OF THE CLAUSE.)

WRITING EXERCISE Rewrite each sentence or pair of sentences, changing the underlined words to a noun clause. Add introductory words or switch the order of sentence elements if necessary. Eliminate the words in italics.

1. Don Quixote loved to read *books. He read any books* he could get his hands on.
2. Books on chivalry were *something that* he really loved.
3. *Somehow* he decided to become a knight. *It* was a mystery.
4. Would he be a good knight? He did not worry about *that.*
5. You never know *the kinds of things* people will decide to do.

GRAMMAR EXERCISE Rewrite the sentences below, correcting errors in pronoun usage. If a sentence contains no error, write *Correct.*

1. Don Quixote wondered who he should love and honor.
2. He also had to decide whom he should choose as a trusted companion.
3. In his search for foes, Don Quixote would fight whoever came along.
4. It's hard to imagine whom would be afraid of such a silly knight.
5. Whoever had the slightest strength or skill could surely beat him.

Literature of the Renaissance and Enlightenment

Reflect and Assess

What have you learned about the Renaissance and Enlightenment as a result of your readings? What are you likely to remember about this literature and the ways of thinking it represents? Use the following options to review what you have learned.

Mary Magdalen (c. 1540), Jan van Scorel. Oil on panel, 67 cm × 76.5 cm. Rinksmuseum, Amsterdam, Netherlands.

Reflecting on the Literature

In Pursuit of an Ideal In the Renaissance and Enlightenment, many people pursued ideals, from a perfect romance to a just society. Review the selections in this part, and identify three different types of ideals that are presented in them. Explain each ideal in your own words and discuss whether it is an ideal that can be reached by human beings. Do you think that these ideals continue to influence people's beliefs and behavior today?

Reviewing Literary Concepts

Sonnet Review the explanation of the sonnet form on pages 804 and 805. Then find a modern poem, one written after 1900, that is a sonnet. Write a brief essay that compares and contrasts your modern sonnet with one of the sonnets in Unit Five, Part 2. Pay attention to both the form and the content of the poems.

Building Your Portfolio

Communication Workshop and Writing Options Review the persuasive speech that you wrote for the Communication Workshop on page 858 and the various Writing Options you completed in this part of the book. What do these pieces reveal about your strengths and weaknesses as a writer? On a piece of paper, make one list that identifies your strengths as a writer and one list that identifies your weaknesses. Attach the paper to the assignment that best illustrates your strengths, and add them both to your **Presentation Portfolio.**

Self ASSESSMENT

📖 READER'S NOTEBOOK

The following list consists of important names and terms from this part of Unit Five. Copy the terms in your notebook. Next to each term, jot down a brief explanation of what it means. For additional help, make use of the index or the **Glossary of Literary Terms** (on page R91).

Renaissance	courtly love
situational irony	*Utopia*
extended metaphor	tone
Petrarchan sonnet	satire
Enlightenment	
Shakespearean sonnet	

Setting GOALS

Are you a good reader of poetry? Make a list of your strengths and weaknesses as a reader of poetry. Then circle those weaknesses that you would like to work on. In Unit Six, Part 1, you will have many opportunities to work on your poetry skills.

Extend Your *Reading*

LITERATURE CONNECTIONS
The Tempest

WILLIAM SHAKESPEARE

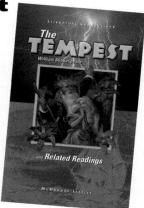

For 12 years, Prospero, the former duke of Milan, Italy, has lived on a remote island with his daughter, Miranda. His life changes abruptly when survivors of a recent shipwreck arrive—including his hated brother, Antonio, the man who stole Prospero's throne. Prospero's magical powers are put to the test as he battles with his brother and contends with his daughter's new love, his enemy's son.

Here are just a few of the related readings that accompany *The Tempest*:

Rappaccini's Daughter
BY NATHANIEL HAWTHORNE

Caliban
BY NORRIE EPSTEIN

LITERATURE CONNECTIONS
Macbeth

WILLIAM SHAKESPEARE

On a bloody battlefield, Macbeth, a young Scottish nobleman, wins a great victory. After meeting three witches who hail him as king of Scotland, Macbeth's ambitions are stirred. Only the good king Duncan stands between Macbeth and the throne of Scotland. How far will Macbeth go to achieve his ambition? And, once the crimes begin, where will they end?

Here are just a few of the related readings that accompany *Macbeth*:

Insomniac
BY OCTAVIO PAZ

Like a Bad Dream
BY HEINRICH BÖLL

How Many Children Had Lady Macbeth?
BY DON NIGRO

And Even *More* . . .

Books
The House of Medici: Its Rise and Fall CHRISTOPHER HIBBERT
The Medicis were perhaps the richest family of the European Renaissance. They were patrons of great artists and scientists, including Leonardo da Vinci and Galileo, yet they also committed great crimes.

Renaissance Lives: Portraits of an Age THEODORE K. RABB
The author tells the story of the Renaissance through short biographies of writers, scientists, merchants, artists, and saints.

Other Media
History Through Literature: Renaissance and Reformation
This half-hour video makes history come alive through dramatic readings and insightful commentary by America's poet laureate Robert Pinsky. Clearvue. (VIDEO)

Molière: The Misanthrope
An acclaimed production of one of Molière's most popular plays. Films for the Humanities & Sciences. (VIDEO)

Age of Exuberance
DONALD JOHNSON GREENE

In this spirited and humorous account of life in 18th-century England, Greene examines some of the stereotypes about Enlightenment culture. As the author shows, life had much more to offer than the calm pursuit of rational pleasures.

19th-Century European Literature
1798–1899

Dance at the Moulin de la Galette, Montmartre (1876), Pierre Auguste Renoir. Oil on canvas, 131 cm × 175 cm. Musée d'Orsay, Paris. Réunion des Musées Nationaux/Art Resource, New York.

"We have all of us one human heart."

—WILLIAM WORDSWORTH

PART 1
Expressions of the Heart:
The Age of Romanticism 870–933

PART 2
Life's Lessons:
The Emergence of Realism 934–1093

PART 1 Expressions of the Heart
The Age of Romanticism

Why It Matters

At the end of the 18th century, a movement called **Romanticism** began to influence the social and political life of Europe. The Romantics rejected science and reason and instead embraced nature, emotion, and individual experience. These rebellious ideas inspired the Romantics to champion the rights of the common people. Eventually, Romanticism's revolutionary spirit inspired a desperate struggle for freedom and reform.

For Links to Romanticism, click on:

HUMANITIES
CLASSZONE.COM

1 **Enlightened Ideas** France was the birthplace of Romanticism's spiritual father, **Jean Jacques Rousseau** (shown here). His ideas echoed those expressed earlier by England's **John Locke,** who declared that all humans are created equal.

A Time of Upheaval The Romantic period was a time of rebellion and revolution. As many Europeans tried to bring about political and social changes, the boundaries of countries were torn apart and redrawn.

KINGDOM OF DENMARK AND NORWAY

UNITED KINGDOM OF GREAT BRITAIN AND IRELAND

4

•*London*

Berlin •

2

CONFEDERATION OF THE RHINE

•*Paris*

1

FRENCH EMPIRE

SWITZERLAND

ITALY

ILLYRIAN

ATLANTIC OCEAN

PORTUGAL

•*Madrid*

SPAIN

CORSICA

Rome •

SARDINIA

KIN N

Mediterranean Sea

SICILY

AFRICA

4 **Idealized Nature** Romantic artist **John Constable** drew inspiration for many of his paintings from his homeland, the countryside of southeastern England. Like many other Romantic artists, Constable idealized nature, creating landscapes that glorified its tranquillity and beauty.

2 Revolutionary Fervor
Defending equality and human rights, the **French Revolution** inspired revolutions across Europe. The French Revolution began in Paris in 1789, after peasants stormed the Bastille, a prison and a hated symbol of royal oppression.

• Moscow

RUSSIAN EMPIRE

UCHY
SAW

IAN
RE

3 The Spread of Nationalism
Feelings of **nationalism**—devotion to one's nation rather than to a ruler—were stirred throughout Europe when **Napoleon Bonaparte** attempted to impose French rule on the continent. Eventually this nationalistic spirit inspired the people of Greece to wage a successful struggle for their independence.

Black Sea

OTTOMAN EMPIRE

• Constantinople

3

• Athens

N W E S

| 0 | 250 | 500 miles |
| 0 | 250 | 500 kilometers |

Historical Highlights

To understand the enormous impact of Romanticism on the social and political life of Europe, it is important to know about the events that led up to and occurred during the movement.

Roots in the Enlightenment

Romanticism is rooted in the **Enlightenment,** a movement of the 18th century that championed science and reason. Enlightenment philosophers believed that the power to reason was equal in all people and defended human dignity and worth.

In the 17th-century, English philosopher John Locke had declared that people had rights to life, liberty, and happiness. In the 18th century, Locke's ideas were echoed by Jean Jacques Rousseau. The French philosopher believed that laws and government should reflect the people's will. Rousseau's ideas influenced the leaders of the French Revolution. With his belief in people's natural goodness and in the value of the individual, Rousseau also foreshadowed Romanticism.

Revolution in France

Although Rousseau's ideas helped inspire the French Revolution, outrage at the social and economic conditions in France in the second half of the 1700s actually ignited the conflict. In 1788, taxes on the poor were raised just when wages dropped and food supplies were scarce. Tensions finally exploded on July 14, 1789, when a mob of Parisians seized the Bastille. The French Revolution had begun.

At first, the revolution brought about positive change. Feudalism in France was ended, the country was declared a republic, and a new constitution was drafted. Tragically, the revolution also produced the **Reign of Terror,** led by a group of revolutionaries. From 1793 to 1794, this group executed anyone judged to be an enemy of the new French republic. Tens of thousands of people were executed by guillotine.

Rise and Fall of Napoleon

Beginning in 1792, the new republic engaged in a series of wars to defend and spread the ideas of the French Revolution. With all citizens involved in the war effort, a sense of nationalism arose throughout the French republic. Leading the battles was the young, heroic general Napoleon Bonaparte, who would crown himself emperor of France in 1804.

In time, it became clear that Napoleon's ambitions extended well beyond the borders of France. He wanted to conquer all of Europe. To prevent French domination, European allies mobilized forces against Napoleon. Fearful that Russia would join the alliance, Napoleon invaded that country in 1812. The decision proved disastrous. Napoleon lost more than 500,000 men. His losses encouraged his enemies to attack. In 1815, Napoleon suffered a decisive defeat at the **Battle of Waterloo** in Belgium.

Napoleon's army retreats from Russia.

Struggles for Independence

Inspired first by the French Revolution's ideals of freedom and later by opposition to the Napoleonic invasions, national movements gained momentum in 19th-century Europe. These movements often led to revolutions for independence.

Greece waged the first successful revolution in 1830. That same year, Belgium also gained its independence. Not all of the bids for freedom were successful, however. When a group of young Russian aristocrats called the Decembrists led a rebellion against Czar Nicholas I in December 1825, the uprising was quickly crushed.

Revolutionary fervor was rekindled in 1848, when France once again rose up against its king. Soon, ethnic uprisings had swept across Europe, sparking revolts in Austria, Hungary, and Germany. Although these uprisings were suppressed by the ruling powers, people's dreams of freedom were not crushed.

Revolution in Industry

While political and social revolutions erupted in France and swept across Europe, rebellion was repressed in Great Britain. Those in power had moved decisively to keep Britain from falling victim to the violence and anarchy they saw in France. Instead, Great Britain was involved in a different kind of revolution that had begun in the 1700s—an industrial revolution, which changed the economy from one mainly centered on agriculture to one driven by industry.

Industrialization would eventually greatly improve people's standards of living and opportunities. In the early 1800s, however, the rapid pace of industrialization caused many serious problems, including unsafe working conditions, child labor, and unhealthy urban living conditions. Reformers sought to correct the labor and social problems caused by industrialization, but their efforts were often equated with revolution and crushed. Largely as a result of these reformist efforts, Romanticism faded in England, and a new movement called **realism** began to emerge. Realists focused on everyday life, often bringing social problems to public attention.

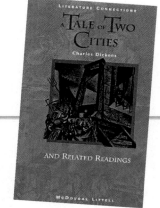

History to Literature

Events that occurred during the Romantic age inspired writers of the time as well as writers throughout the 19th century.

EVENT IN HISTORY	EVENT IN LITERATURE
French Revolution	English novelist Charles Dickens uses the French Revolution as the background of his 1859 novel *A Tale of Two Cities,* which is set in London and Paris.
Napoleon's invasion of Russia	In a narrative poem called "The Expiation," about the career of Napoleon Bonaparte, French writer Victor Hugo vividly describes the French army's retreat from Moscow.

Arts and Culture

Romanticism dominated European intellectual and artistic life in the first half of the 19th century. The Romantics created a new movement of individual freedom and self-expression in literature, art, and music.

Philosophy

Before the Romantic movement, most philosophers emphasized intellect and reason over instincts and emotion. This philosophical tradition began to change with Jean Jacques Rousseau, whose ideas about the individual and the power of the imagination inspired Romantic philosophers in the 19th century.

One of these was the German philosopher **Arthur Schopenhauer,** who rejected the idea that reason could be used to explain the world. Instead, he believed that people experience the world through their senses. As a result, Schopenhauer claimed, people experience the world not as it is, but as their senses perceive it. Such ideas inspired Romantic artists, writers, and composers to use their senses and emotions to describe the world and to convey a poetic wonder about nature and life.

In this painting, Delacroix represents a Moroccan chief greeting members of his tribe.

Painting

Romantic artists broke with conventional subject matter to paint subjects that were dramatic and imaginative. These artists were united by their desire to express their individual feelings and beliefs.

Many Romantic artists painted landscapes to convey their feelings about nature. The two most important English landscape artists were John Constable and **J. M. W. Turner.** Constable expressed his love for the English countryside by portraying its beauty and harmony. Turner, on the other hand, emphasized the energy and destructive force of the natural world. **Caspar David Friedrich,** considered the greatest German Romantic painter, also focused on the power of nature. The otherworldly quality of Friedrich's work inspires the viewer with a sense of mystery and awe. (See page 878 for an example of Friedrich's work.)

The greatest French Romantic painter, **Eugène Delacroix,** broke away from the landscape artists to depict more exotic subject matter. Many of his paintings reflect his fascination with the people and history of other cultures. Delacroix created a sense of mood and mystery in these works through the use of rich color and deep shadow.

Turner used color and indistinct shapes to convey the power and energy of nature.

Literature

Romanticism deeply influenced the literature of England, France, and Germany. While the Romantic movement and literature of each country had unique features, they also shared many defining characteristics, such as an emphasis on emotion, imagination, the individual, and nature.

In England, critics traditionally mark the beginning of the Romantic movement with the publication in 1798 of the poetry collection *Lyrical Ballads* by **William Wordsworth** and **Samuel Taylor Coleridge.** In France, Romanticism began around the time of the French Revolution. **Victor Hugo** eventually emerged as the leading Romantic writer in France. One of the leaders of the early Romantic movement in Germany was **Johann Wolfgang von Goethe.** In their poetry, all of these Romantic writers explored the intricate workings of their own minds and the complexities of their emotions.

You can learn more about Romantic literature in Learning the Language of Literature on pages 878–879.

Music

In the early years of the 19th century, composers began to experiment with classical musical forms, adding intense personal feeling. Their music reflected the Romantic emphasis on originality, individuality, and emotion. The German composer **Ludwig van Beethoven** helped bridge the classical and Romantic periods in music. Although his formal musical techniques were classical, the passion and dramatic expressiveness of his music made it a model for Romantic composers.

Strongly sympathetic to the ideals of the French Revolution, Beethoven composed his Symphony no. 3, the *Eroica* ("Heroic"), and dedicated it to Napoleon with these words: "a grand symphony dedicated to Bonaparte." However, after hearing that Napoleon had declared himself emperor, Beethoven tore up the original inscription and replaced it with the words "composed to celebrate the memory of a great man."

Ludwig van Beethoven

Time Line

EVENTS IN EUROPEAN ROMANTICISM

1790	1800	1810

1793 French painter Jacques Louis David paints *The Murder of Marat*

1794 William Blake publishes *Songs of Experience*

1797 Samuel Taylor Coleridge writes "Kubla Khan" (published in 1816)

1798 William Wordsworth and Samuel Taylor Coleridge publish *Lyrical Ballads*

1800 Dorothy Wordsworth begins keeping her *Grasmere Journals*

1804 Ludwig van Beethoven completes Symphony no. 3, *Eroica*

1805 J. M. W. Turner paints *The Shipwreck*

1808 Goethe publishes *Faust, Part 1*

1818 Mary Shelley's *Frankenstein* published anonymously

1819 Percy Bysshe Shelley writes "Ode to the West Wind"; John Keats writes "Ode on a Grecian Urn"

EVENTS IN EUROPEAN HISTORY

1790	1800	1810

1792 France declared a republic

1793 Mass executions carried out in France as the Reign of Terror begins; French king Louis XVI executed by guillotine

1796 Spain declares war on Britain

1799 Coup d'état establishes Napoleon as dictator of France

1800 Act of Union passed, creating United Kingdom of Great Britain and Ireland

1804 Napoleon crowns himself emperor of France

1805 Napoleon begins conquering most of Europe

1807 British slave trade abolished

1812 Napoleon invades Russia; Britain fights United States in War of 1812

1814 Congress of Vienna opens, seeking to remake Europe after Napoleon's downfall

1815 Allied armies under British leader Wellington defeat Napoleon at Waterloo; Napoleon banished to St. Helena

EVENTS IN WORLD HISTORY

1790	1800	1810

1790 Philadelphia becomes capital of the United States

1794 Eli Whitney patents cotton gin, paving the way for increasing slavery by making it more profitable

1799 George Washington dies

1801 Thomas Jefferson becomes president of the United States

1803 United States buys Louisiana Territory from France; Robert Fulton powers boat by steam

1804 Haiti gains independence from France

1810 Revolts in New Granada, Rio de la Plata, and Mexico

c. 1816 Zulu chief Shaka begins rule over large kingdom in southeastern Africa

1820	1830	1840

1820 Blake illustrates the Book of Job

1821 Keats, aged 25, dies of tuberculosis

1822 Percy Shelley, aged 32, drowns off coast of Italy

1824 Lord Byron, aged 38, dies of fever

1827 Heine publishes *The Book of Songs*; Beethoven dies; Blake dies

1831 Victor Hugo publishes *The Hunchback of Notre Dame* to great popular acclaim

1832 Goethe publishes *Faust, Part 2*; Goethe dies; French writer George Sand publishes *Indiana*

1833 Russian poet and novelist Aleksandr Pushkin publishes *Eugene Onegin*

1834 Coleridge dies

1843 William Wordsworth appointed poet laureate of England

1844 French writer Alexandre Dumas publishes best-selling novel *The Count of Monte Cristo*

1845 Hugo begins writing *Les Misérables* (published in 1862)

1820	1830	1840

1821 Greeks begin war for independence

1825 Decembrist revolt in Russia crushed

1830 Greece wins full independence from Ottoman Turks; Belgium declares independence from the Netherlands; Charles X of France is removed from power by revolution and is succeeded by Louis Philippe

1834 Spanish Inquisition finally suppressed after six centuries

1837 Victoria becomes queen of Great Britain

1842 Riots and strikes break out in industrial regions of England

1843 Military revolt in Spain

1848 Revolution in France leads to establishment of Second Republic; Louis Napoleon elected president of France; revolutions sweep across Europe

1820	1830	1840

1821 Spain's Latin American empire begins to collapse as Mexico, several Central American states, and Venezuela win independence

1823 U.S. president Monroe issues Monroe Doctrine to keep Europe out of Latin America

1824 Simón Bolívar liberates last Spanish colonies in Latin America

1831 Nat Turner leads Virginia slave revolt

1836 Texas gains independence from Mexico and becomes a republic

1839 First Opium War between Britain and China begins

1842 First Opium War between Britain and China ends

1847 Liberia becomes independent republic

1848 First U.S. women's rights convention meets in Seneca Falls, New York; gold discovered in California

Romanticism

Have you ever been surprised by the power of emotions expressed in a literary work? Maybe you've tried to convey your own feelings in a poem or story. Writing that emphasizes the expression of intense emotion is called **Romantic.** Romantic writing is also marked by an intense interest in nature, individual experience, and the imagination.

Romanticism was an artistic and intellectual movement that began in Europe in the late 18th century and continued well into the mid-19th century. The movement revolutionized ideas regarding artistic creation and forms of expression in Germany, England, and France. In fact, many of the intensely emotional and imaginative qualities of Romantic writing are evident in literature today.

Romanticism often emphasized the individual's experience with nature. *The Wanderer Above the Sea of Clouds.* (1818). Caspar David Friedrich. Hamburg Kunsthalle, Germany. The Bridgeman Art Library.

Revolt Against Neoclassicism

Romantic writers rebelled against the neoclassical ideals of the 18th century. While the neoclassicists valued reason, form, and order, the Romantics celebrated spontaneous feeling and freedom from rules and conventions. While the neoclassicists wrote tightly controlled poetry in the classical mold and witty satiric essays, the Romantics wrote serious lyric poems about their own experiences. The chart below identifies some of the differences between neoclassical and Romantic writers.

Neoclassical Writers	Romantic Writers
▶ Stressed reason and intellect	▶ Stressed emotions and imagination
▶ Wrote about objective issues that concerned society as a whole, such as politics and religion	▶ Wrote about subjective experiences of the individual, such as desires, hopes, and dreams
▶ Respected the man-made institutions of church and state	▶ Appreciated nature in all its creative and destructive forces
▶ Believed in order in all things	▶ Believed in spontaneity in thought and action
▶ Maintained traditional standards	▶ Believed in experimentation
▶ Focused on adult concerns, primarily those of the ruling class	▶ Reflected on the experiences of childhood, unsophisticated societies, and common people
▶ Controlled emotion, which was often expressed in the form of wit	▶ Celebrated intense passion and vision
▶ Followed formal rules and diction in poetry	▶ Sought a more natural poetic form and diction

Romantic Movements Across Europe

German Romanticism Romanticism in Germany developed as a series of separate movements. Some of the defining characteristics of German Romanticism first appeared in the late-18th-century movement called *Sturm und Drang* (shtŏŏrm′ ŏŏnt dräng′), meaning "storm and stress." Among the leading figures in this movement, which glorified nature, emotion, and originality, was the writer Johann Wolfgang von Goethe. The handsome, brooding main character of Goethe's popular first novel, *The Sorrows of Young Werther* (1774), came to represent the model young **Romantic hero**. Later movements in German Romanticism emphasized an interest in folklore and an exploration of the supernatural.

YOUR TURN Why do you think many Romantics were attracted to the supernatural?

English Romanticism Critics often mark the beginning of the English Romantic age with the publication of the poetry collection *Lyrical Ballads* by William Wordsworth and Samuel Taylor Coleridge in 1798. In his famous preface to *Lyrical Ballads*, Wordsworth described poetry as "the spontaneous overflow of powerful feelings."

In addition to Wordsworth and Coleridge, the poets William Blake, Lord Byron, Percy Bysshe Shelley, and John Keats dominated the English Romantic movement. These poets deliberately chose language and subjects from common life instead of upper-class life. They also turned to nature to stimulate their own thinking and reflected on the relationship between the real and the ideal.

YOUR TURN Why do you think the Romantics found such strong inspiration in the natural world?

French Romanticism The Romantic movement did not emerge in France until 1820. Profoundly influenced by the events and ideas of the French Revolution, the French people called for "a new society, a new literature." They found a literary leader in Victor Hugo, whose highly personal and emotional poetry, novels, and dramas reflected Romanticism's independence from the rules of neoclassicism. Among his best-known works are *The Hunchback of Notre Dame* (1831) and *Les Misérables* (1862), both of which reveal Hugo's interest in the suffering of common people. Other major French Romantics were the novelists George Sand and Stendhal.

Strategies for Reading: Romantic Literature

1. Notice how the Romantic writers freely embraced such subjects as life, death, love, and nature.

2. Read each poem aloud several times and identify its sound devices. Think about what mood these devices help create.

3. Pay attention to the extensive use of imagery and figurative language and try to visualize the images and comparisons being made.

4. Watch for elements of the exotic and supernatural and think about what these might represent.

5. **Monitor** your reading strategies and modify them when your understanding breaks down. Remember to use your strategies for active reading: **predict, visualize, connect, question, clarify,** and **evaluate.**

FROM

Faust

Johann Wolfgang von Goethe

**Johann Wolfgang
von Goethe**
1749–1832

Literary Giant Considered one of the giants of world literature, the German poet, playwright, and novelist Johann Wolfgang von Goethe (yō'hän vôlf'gäng fôn gœ'tə) inspired literary movements and influenced the novel form. He was also a scientist and a statesman. Born in Frankfurt am Main, Goethe was groomed by his father to study law. The young man, however, had other ideas. At the University of Leipzig and later at the university in Strasbourg, Goethe neglected his law courses to study music, art, and architecture and to write poetry and plays. During a long recovery from an illness, he pursued an interest in magic and the occult. All of these early interests are evident in Goethe's important works. One of his first, the novel *The Sorrows of Young Werther* (1774), achieved great success and helped initiate the *Sturm und Drang* literary movement, the forerunner of the Romantic movement in Germany.

Years at Weimar Goethe's fame brought him to the attention of Duke Charles Augustus, who in 1775 invited the writer to move to his court at Weimar. Goethe accepted the invitation, and Weimar became his home for the rest of his life. During his first ten years there, Goethe largely abandoned his literary aspirations. Made a minister of state, he dedicated himself to his duties. In 1786, however, Goethe embarked on a two-year trip to Italy, and it was during this period that he "found himself again as an artist." His subsequent friendship with the German poet and playwright Friedrich von Schiller strengthened his resolve to return to literature.

The Writing of *Faust* In particular, Goethe resumed his work of dramatizing the Faust (foust) legend. The poet's fascination with Faust had begun in his boyhood, when he saw a puppet show about the legendary magician. In the 1770s, he had started to write a verse drama about Faust. In 1790, a fragment of the work was published. By 1797, Goethe had begun working in earnest on the drama and decided to present the story in two parts. *Faust, Part 1,* published in 1808, was well received. Goethe did not return to work on the second part until 1824. It was finally completed in 1832, shortly before his death.

Build Background

The Faust Legend The Faust legend was based on a real person named Johann Faust, who died around 1540. The real Faust was a German astrologer and magician. Legend has it that he performed such magical feats as producing wine from thin air. People also said that he had sold his soul to the devil to gain knowledge. In 1587, an anonymous collection of legends about Faust appeared in print, and it was widely read. The story of Faust was retold over the next two centuries in German popular dramas and puppet shows.

All of these works portrayed Faust as a sinner who deserved damnation. Goethe, however, portrayed him as a much more sympathetic character. He chose to present Faust as a Romantic hero, emphasizing his tormented emotions and his restless search for knowledge. Although Goethe called his drama a **tragedy,** it ends with Faust's salvation.

Drama, Epic, or Poetry? It is difficult to determine what **genre,** or literary form, Goethe's *Faust* belongs to. With its dialogue and stage directions, *Faust* is certainly a drama. However, because of its great length and many scene changes, it is rarely performed on stage. The work contains elements of an **epic,** but epics are narratives, not dramas. Even the poetry Goethe wrote for the two-part *Faust* is difficult to categorize, since he used such a wide variety of poetic styles. All in all, *Faust* might be said to transcend genre.

The Story of *Faust*

Have you ever heard the phrase "to make a deal with the devil" or "to sell your soul to the devil"? These phrases originated with the Faust legend. In Goethe's version, Doctor Faust, a university professor, is dissatisfied with his own academic studies. He makes a deal with the devil Mephisto (mə-fĭs′tō), who promises to help Faust discover real knowledge. They agree that if Faust ever becomes contented, the devil will seize his soul.

For a humanities activity, click on:

HUMANITIES
CLASSZONE.COM

Connect to Your Life

In Goethe's play, Faust is willing to give up his soul to attain a godlike knowledge and experience of the world. What would you give up to achieve your dream? Health? Love? Your soul? The respect of others? Share your thoughts with a classmate.

Focus Your Reading

LITERARY ANALYSIS: DIALOGUE
Written conversation between two or more people, in either fiction or nonfiction, is called **dialogue.** In fiction, dialogue is used to bring characters to life and to give readers insights into the characters' personalities. As you read these excerpts from *Faust,* think about how the dialogue reveals the characters' personalities.

ACTIVE READING: CLARIFYING MEANING
The elevated language and the way in which words are arranged in Goethe's *Faust* can pose real challenges for readers. Here are some suggestions for **clarifying meaning** as you read:

- **Read sidenotes and Words to Know** Use the notes in the margins and the Words to Know at the bottom of the pages to learn the meanings of unfamiliar words.

- **Reorder words** Unusual word order is often used in poetry to maintain **meter** or a **rhyme scheme.** Reorder the words so that they sound more natural and make sense to you.

- **Paraphrase** Restate difficult lines and speeches in your own words.

- **Summarize** Clarify the speeches in *Faust* by summarizing the most important ideas being expressed.

📖 **READER'S NOTEBOOK** As you read the excerpts, write down particularly difficult passages and use the strategies listed above to clarify their meaning.

WORDS TO KNOW **Vocabulary Preview**

abate	genial	resolute	waive
connive	humanely	sloth	
despair	repose	stature	

from Faust

Johann Wolfgang von Goethe

Translated by Walter Kaufmann

FOCUS In this verse drama, the devil Mephisto proposes a bet to win Faust's soul. Read to find out what the Lord thinks of the devil's bet.

The "Prologue in Heaven" introduces the devil Mephisto, one of the drama's main characters. In Heaven, surrounded by the archangels Raphael, Gabriel, and Michael, the Lord allows Mephisto to appear before him. After the three archangels praise God's glorious works on earth, Mephisto addresses the Lord.

Prologue in Heaven

Mephisto:

> Since you, oh Lord, have once again drawn near,
> And ask how we have been, and are so <u>genial</u>,
> And since you used to like to see me here,
> You see me, too, as if I were a menial.
> 5 I cannot speak as nobly as your staff,
> Though by this circle here I shall be spurned:
> My pathos would be sure to make you laugh,
> Were laughing not a habit you've unlearned.
> Of suns and worlds I know nothing to say;
> 10 I only see how men live in dismay.
> The small god of the world will never change his ways
> And is as whimsical—as on the first of days.
> His life might be a bit more fun,
> Had you not given him that spark of heaven's sun;
> 15 He calls it reason and employs it, <u>resolute</u>
> To be more brutish than is any brute.

4 menial (mē′nē-əl): servant.

7 pathos (pā′thŏs): pitiable condition.

11 the small god of the world: humankind.

WORDS TO KNOW

genial (jēn′yəl) *adj.* pleasant; agreeable
resolute (rĕz′ə-lōōt′) *adj.* resolved; determined

You'll lose him yet to me . . .

Copyright © 1989 Ron Scherl/StageImage.

HUMANITIES CONNECTION Several operas have been based on Goethe's *Faust*. In *Mefistofele,* by Italian composer Arrigo Boito, the devil is the central character. Samuel Ramey, pictured here, has received worldwide accolades for his performance of this role.

He seems to me, if you don't mind, Your Grace,
Like a cicada of the long-legged race,
That always flies, and, flying, springs,
And in the grass the same old ditty sings;
If only it were grass he could <u>repose</u> in!
There is no trash he will not poke his nose in.

The Lord:

Can you not speak but to abuse?
Do you come only to accuse?
Does nothing on the earth seem to you right?

Mephisto:

No, Lord. I find it still a rather sorry sight.
Man moves me to compassion, so wretched is his plight.
I have no wish to cause him further woe.

20

25

WORDS TO KNOW

repose (rĭ-pōz′) *v.* to rest

The Lord:

   Do you know Faust?

Mephisto:

                                     The doctor?

The Lord:

                                          Aye, my servant.

Mephisto:

                                                              Lo!

30   He serves you most peculiarly, I think.
     Not earthly are the poor fool's meat and drink.
     His spirit's ferment drives him far,
     And he half knows how foolish is his quest:
     From heaven he demands the fairest star,
35   And from the earth all joys that he thinks best;
     And all that's near and all that's far
     Cannot soothe the upheaval in his breast.

The Lord:

     Though now he serves me but confusedly,
     I shall soon lead him where the vapor clears.
40   The gardener knows, however small the tree,
     That bloom and fruit adorn its later years.

Mephisto:

     What will you bet? You'll lose him yet to me,
     If you will graciously <u>connive</u>
     That I may lead him carefully.

The Lord:

45   As long as he may be alive,
     So long you shall not be prevented.
     Man errs as long as he will strive.

Mephisto:

     Be thanked for that; I've never been contented
     To waste my time upon the dead.
50   I far prefer full cheeks, a youthful curly-head.
     When corpses come, I have just left the house—
     I feel as does the cat about the mouse.

The Lord:

     Enough—I grant that you may try to clasp him,
     Withdraw this spirit from his primal source
55   And lead him down, if you can grasp him,

31–32 Not earthly . . . drives him far: Faust is not interested in food and drink; he is driven by the agitation in his soul.

39 I shall soon . . . where the vapor clears: The Lord will help Faust think clearly.

54 his primal source: God, or the desire for good.

<u>WORDS TO KNOW</u>

884   **connive** (kə-nīv′) *v.* to fail to take action; secretly cooperate

Upon your own abysmal course—
And stand abashed when you have to attest:
A good man in his darkling aspiration
Remembers the right road throughout his quest.

Mephisto:

60   Enough—he will soon reach his station;
About my bet I have no hesitation,
And when I win, concede your stake
And let me triumph with a swelling breast:
Dust he shall eat, and that with zest,
65   As my relation does, the famous snake.

The Lord:

Appear quite free on that day, too;
I never hated those who were like you:
Of all the spirits that negate,
The knavish jester gives me least to do.
70   For man's activity can easily <u>abate</u>,
He soon prefers uninterrupted rest;
To give him this companion hence seems best
Who roils and must as Devil help create.
But you, God's rightful sons, give voice
75   To all the beauty in which you rejoice;
And that which ever works and lives and grows
Enfold you with fair bonds that love has wrought,
And what in wavering apparition flows
That fortify with everlasting thought.
(*The heavens close, the Archangels disperse.*)

Mephisto (*alone*):

80   I like to see the Old Man now and then
And try to be not too uncivil.
It's charming in a noble squire when
He speaks <u>humanely</u> with the very Devil.

> **PAUSE & REFLECT** Why does the Lord allow Mephisto to strive for Faust's soul?

57 And stand . . . attest: and be ashamed when you must admit.

58 darkling: dim; confused.

65 the famous snake: Satan, who, disguised as a serpent, tempted Eve in the Garden of Eden.

69 knavish jester: foolish joker.

71–72 He soon . . . seems best: People need a challenge to keep them from becoming lazy and complacent.

73 roils (roilz): disturbs; vexes.

74 But you, God's rightful sons: The Lord is now addressing the archangels.

WORDS TO KNOW
abate (ə-bāt′) *v.* to lessen in intensity
humanely (hyōō-mān′lē) *adv.* in a compassionate or sympathetic way

*Frustrated by the limits of human knowledge, Faust employs magic to
summon the Spirit of the Earth. The Spirit, however, is too powerful for
Faust and vanishes. Desperate to escape his earthbound life, Faust is about
to take poison when he hears a choir of angels. Their song momentarily
recalls him to life, but his dissatisfaction quickly resurfaces. Faust seeks to
lift his spirits by walking in the countryside. There he sees a strange
poodle. The dog follows Faust to his study, where the animal reveals himself to be Mephisto. Faust tries to hold the devil but in vain. Mephisto
soon returns, however, and offers a remedy for Faust's unhappiness.*

Faust's Study

Mephisto:
      Stop playing with your melancholy
85   That, like a vulture, ravages your breast;
      The worst of company still cures this folly,
      For you are human with the rest.
      Yet that is surely not to say
      That you should join the herd you hate.
90   I'm not one of the great,
      But if you want to make your way
      Through the world with me united,
      I should surely be delighted
      To be yours, as of now,
95   Your companion, if you allow;
      And if you like the way I behave,
      I shall be your servant, or your slave.

Faust:
      And in return, what do you hope to take?

Mephisto:
      There's so much time—so why insist?

Faust:
100   No, no! The Devil is an egoist
      And would not just for heaven's sake

Christian Nickel as Faust in 2000 stage production of Goethe's *Faust*. Staged in Berlin by Peter Stein. Photograph copyright © Ruth Walz.

Turn into a philanthropist.
Make your conditions very clear;
Where such a servant lives, danger is near.

Mephisto:

105   *Here* you shall be the master, I be bond,
And at your nod I'll work incessantly;
But when we meet again *beyond,*
Then you shall do the same for me.

Faust:

Of the beyond I have no thought;
110   When you reduce this world to nought,
The other one may have its turn.
My joys come from this earth, and there,
That sun has burnt on my <u>despair</u>:

102 philanthropist (fĭ-lăn'thrə-pĭst): person who promotes human well-being through charitable donations or activities.

105 bond: servant or slave.

110 nought: nothing.

<u>WORDS TO KNOW</u>
despair (dĭ-spâr') *n.* complete loss of hope

Once I have left those, I don't care:
115 What happens is of no concern.
I do not even wish to hear
Whether beyond they hate and love,
And whether in that other sphere
One realm's below and one above.

Mephisto:
120 So minded, dare it cheerfully.
Commit yourself and you shall see
My arts with joy. I'll give you more
Than any man has seen before.

Faust:
What would you, wretched Devil, offer?
125 Was ever a man's spirit in its noble striving
Grasped by your like, devilish scoffer?   126 **grasped:** understood.
But have you food that is not satisfying,
Red gold that rolls off without rest,
Quicksilver-like, over your skin—
130 A game in which no man can win—
A girl who, lying at my breast,
Ogles already to entice my neighbor,
And honor—that perhaps seems best—
Though like a comet it will turn to vapor?
135 Show me fruit that, before we pluck them, rot,
And trees whose foliage every day makes new!

Mephisto:
Such a commission scares me not,
With such things I can wait on you.
But, worthy friend, the time comes when we would
140 Recline in peace and feast on something good.

Faust:
If ever I recline, calmed, on a bed of <u>sloth</u>,
You may destroy me then and there.
If ever flattering you should wile me
That in myself I find delight,   144 **that in myself I find delight:**
145 If with enjoyment you beguile me,   so that I become too pleased with
Then break on me, eternal night!   myself.
This bet I offer.

Mephisto:
                    I accept it.

WORDS TO KNOW
sloth (slôth) *n.* laziness

888

Faust:

                                    Right.

If to the moment I should say:
Abide, you are so fair—
150　Put me in fetters on that day,
I *wish* to perish then, I swear.
Then let the death bell ever toll,
Your service done, you shall be free,
The clock may stop, the hand may fall,
155　As time comes to an end for me.

Mephisto:

Consider it, for we shall not forget it.

Faust:

That is a right you need not <u>waive</u>.
I did not boast, and I shall not regret it.
As I grow stagnant I shall be a slave,
160　Whether or not to anyone indebted.

159 As I grow stagnant: if I stay as I am now.

Mephisto:

At the doctor's banquet tonight I shall do
My duties as a servant without fail.
But for life's sake, or death's—just one detail:
Could you give me a line or two?

161 the doctor's banquet: an awards dinner for professors that Faust would be attending.

Faust:

165　You pedant need it black on white?
Are man and a man's word indeed new to your sight?
Is not my spoken word sufficient warrant
When it commits my life eternally?
Does not the world rush on in every torrent,
170　And a mere promise should hold me?
Yet this illusion our heart inherits,
And who would want to shirk his debt?
Blessed who counts loyalty among his merits.
No sacrifice will he regret.
175　And yet a parchment, signed and sealed, is an abhorrent
Specter that haunts us, and it makes us fret.
The word dies when we seize the pen,
And wax and leather lord it then.
What, evil spirit, do you ask?
180　Paper or parchment, stone or brass?
Should I use chisel, style, or quill?
It is completely up to you.

165 You pedant . . . white?: Are you so narrow-minded that you need it in writing?

175–176 abhorrent (ăb-hôr′ənt) **specter:** hateful ghost or spirit.

181 style: slender, pointed writing instrument once used on wax tablets.

WORDS TO KNOW

waive (wāv) *v.* to voluntarily give up; abandon

Mephisto:

> Why get so hot and overdo
> Your rhetoric? Why must you shrill?
> 185   Use any sheet, it is the same;
> And with a drop of blood you sign your name.

Faust:

> If you are sure you like this game,
> Let it be done to humor you.

Mephisto:

> Blood is a very special juice.

PAUSE & REFLECT According to Faust's own terms, under what conditions will he lose his soul? Why do you suppose the devil wants him to sign the pact in blood?

FOCUS As you continue reading, think about what types of knowledge and experience Faust hopes to gain from the bargain with Mephisto.

Faust:

> 190   You need not fear that someday I retract.
> That all my striving I unloose
> Is the whole purpose of the pact.
> Oh, I was puffed up all too boldly,
> At your rank only is my place.
> 195   The lofty spirit spurned me coldly,
> And nature hides from me her face.
> Torn is the subtle thread of thought,
> I loathe the knowledge I once sought.
> In sensuality's abysmal land
> 200   Let our passions drink their fill!
> In magic veils, not pierced by skill,
> Let every wonder be at hand!
> Plunge into time's whirl that dazes my sense,
> Into the torrent of events!
> 205   And let enjoyment, distress,
> Annoyance and success
> Succeed each other as best they can;
> For restless activity proves a man.

Mephisto:

> You are not bound by goal or measure.
> 210   If you would nibble everything

191 unloose: unleash; give free rein to.

194 at your rank . . . place: Faust suggests that his pride places him on a level with the devil.

You need
not fear
that
someday
I retract.

Bruno Ganz as Faust and Johann Adam Oest as Mephisto in 2000 stage production of Goethe's *Faust.*
Staged in Berlin by Peter Stein. Photograph copyright © Ruth Walz.

HUMANITIES CONNECTION This photograph is of a rare live production of both parts of
Faust, staged in Berlin. The marathon presentation of the drama took 21 hours—15 for the
performance itself, 6 for intermissions.

> Or snatch up something on the wing,
> You're welcome to what gives you pleasure.
> But help yourself and don't be coy!

213 coy: shy in a false way.

Faust:
> Do you not hear, I have no thought of joy!
> 215   The reeling whirl I seek, the most painful excess,
> Enamored hate and quickening distress.
> Cured from the craving to know all, my mind
> Shall not henceforth be closed to any pain,
> And what is portioned out to all mankind,
> 220   I shall enjoy deep in my self, contain
> Within my spirit summit and abyss,
> Pile on my breast their agony and bliss,
> And thus let my own self grow into theirs, unfettered,
> Till as they are, at last I, too, am shattered.

Mephisto:

225   Believe me who for many a thousand year
     Has chewed this cud and never rested,
     That from the cradle to the bier
     The ancient leaven cannot be digested.
     Trust one like me, this whole array
230   Is for a God—there's no contender:
     He dwells in his eternal splendor,
     To darkness we had to surrender,
     And you need night as well as day.

Faust:

     And yet it is my will.

Mephisto:

                 It does sound bold.
235   But I'm afraid, though you are clever,
     Time is too brief, though art's forever.
     Perhaps you're willing to be told.
     Why don't you find yourself a poet,
     And let the gentleman ransack his dreams:
240   And when he finds a noble trait, let him bestow it
     Upon your worthy head in reams and reams:
     The lion's daring,
     The swiftness of the hind,
     The northerner's forbearing
245   And the Italian's fiery mind,
     Let him resolve the mystery
     How craft can be combined with magnanimity,
     Or how a passion-crazed young man
     Might fall in love after a plan.
250   If there were such a man, I'd like to meet him,
     As Mr. Microcosm I would greet him.

Faust:

     Alas, what am I, if I can
     Not reach for mankind's crown which merely mocks
     Our senses' craving like a star?

Mephisto:

255   You're in the end—just what you are!
     Put wigs on with a million locks
     And put your foot on ell-high socks,
     You still remain just what you are.

228 the ancient leaven: all the experience and sensation that the world has to offer.

241 reams and reams: very large amounts.

247 how craft . . . magnanimity (măg′nə-nĭm′ĭ-tē): how cunning can be combined with a noble heart.

251 Mr. Microcosm (mī′krə-kŏz′əm): a person who would embody all aspects of the universe.

257 ell-high socks: An ell is a measurement 45 inches long.

Copyright © Ruth Walz.

Faust:

    I feel, I gathered up and piled up high
260   In vain the treasures of the human mind:
    When I sit down at last, I cannot find
    New strength within—it is all dry.
    My <u>stature</u> has not grown a whit,
    No closer to the Infinite.

Mephisto:

265   Well, my good sir, to put it crudely,
    You see matters just as they lie;
    We have to look at them more shrewdly,
    Or all life's pleasures pass us by.
    Your hands and feet—indeed that's trite—
270   And head and seat are yours alone;
    Yet all in which I find delight,
    Should they be less my own?

271–272 Yet all . . . less my own?: Shouldn't I possess all the things that give me pleasure?

WORDS TO KNOW

stature (stăch′ər) *n.* status or importance gained by growth or achievement

FAUST   **893**

Suppose I buy myself six steeds:
I buy their strength; while I recline
275   I dash along at whirlwind speeds,
For their two dozen legs are mine.
Come on! Let your reflections rest
And plunge into the world with zest!
I say, the man that speculates
280   Is like a beast that in the sand,
Led by an evil spirit, round and round gyrates,
And all about lies gorgeous pasture land.

Faust:
How shall we set about it?

Mephisto:

Simply leave. . . .

*A student appears outside Faust's study. When Faust exclaims that
he doesn't want to see the student, Mephisto dons the doctor's cap
and gown. After the soliloquy that appears here, Mephisto will
pretend to be Faust while the doctor prepares for their trip.*

Some fifteen minutes should be all I need;
285   Meanwhile get ready for our trip, and speed!
     (Faust *exit.*)

Mephisto (*in* Faust's *long robe*):
Have but contempt for reason and for science,
Man's noblest force spurn with defiance,
Subscribe to magic and illusion,
The Lord of Lies aids your confusion,
290   And, pact or no, I hold you tight.—
The spirit which he has received from fate
Sweeps ever onward with unbridled might,
Its hasty striving is so great
It leaps over the earth's delights.
295   Through life I'll drag him at a rate,
Through shallow triviality,
That he shall writhe and suffocate;
And his insatiability,
With greedy lips, shall see the choicest plate
300   And ask in vain for all that he would cherish—
And were he not the Devil's mate
And had not signed, he still must perish.

279 the man that speculates: someone who thinks too much.

281 gyrates (jī′rāts′): spins.

289 The Lord of Lies: the devil.

296 shallow triviality: all that is of no importance or consequence.

FROM
Letter to His Friends

Johann Wolfgang von Goethe

Johann Wolfgang von Goethe (1828), J. K. Stieler. Oil on canvas. The Granger Collection, New York.

Goethe wrote this letter to a friend near the end of his two-year stay in Italy. The letter reveals his eagerness to resume writing as well as his reawakened interest in the Faust legend.

March 1, 1788

It has been a week of rich experience for me, and seems like a month in my memory. First I drew up a plan for "Faust,"[1] and I trust it will be a successful one. To write this play now is, of course, a very different thing from what it was fifteen years ago. I think it will lose nothing by its long suspension, especially as I now believe I have recovered the thread. Also in respect to the tone in general I feel content. I have already written out a new scene, and if I fumigate[2] the paper, nobody, I should think, would recognize it from the old.

—*Translated by Berthold Biermann*

---

1. **drew up a plan for "Faust":** At this time, Goethe was revising his first version of the play, which would be published as *Faust, ein Fragment* in 1790.

2. **fumigate:** use smoke or fumes to disinfect. Goethe is saying that he could use smoke to make the new paper appear old.

Connect to the Literature

1. What Do You Think?
What is your reaction to the deal Faust makes with Mephisto? Share your response in a classroom discussion.

Comprehension Check
- What are some of the things Faust challenges Mephisto to show him?
- Why is Faust dissatisfied with the knowledge he has gained from his academic studies?

Think Critically

2. ACTIVE READING: CLARIFYING MEANING Get together with a classmate and discuss the passages you recorded in your 📖 **READER'S NOTEBOOK**. Work together to clarify the meaning of any passages that still confuse you. Then use paraphrasing to restate lines 105–108 in your own words.

3. What seems to be Faust's opinion of Mephisto? What does the devil think of Faust? Provide details that support your answer.

4. Based on what you have learned about the Romantic hero, what characteristics of this type of hero does Faust display?

> **THINK ABOUT**
> - Mephisto's remark to Faust "Stop playing with your melancholy" (line 84)
> - the desire Faust expresses when he says, "I shall . . . contain / Within my spirit summit and abyss" (lines 220–221)
> - Faust's lament "Alas, what am I, if I can / Not reach for mankind's crown" (lines 252–253)

5. What do you think is the most important **theme,** or message about human nature, conveyed by this selection?

Extend Interpretations

6. What If? Suppose that the Lord had not allowed Mephisto to strike his bargain with Faust. Do you think that the devil would have pursued his plan anyway and challenged Faust? Why or why not?

7. Critic's Corner According to the critic Irmgard Wagner, "against Faust's emotional and spiritual nature," Mephisto is "cool intelligence." What evidence in the excerpts you've read supports this characterization of the devil?

8. Connect to Life Faust claims that "restless activity proves a man." In today's world, do you think this is true? Is constant action necessary to achieve success? Explain your answer.

LITERARY ANALYSIS: DIALOGUE

Dialogue—the written conversation between two or more people—helps bring characters in a drama to life by providing insight into their personalities. It also reveals the relationships between the characters. Read the following lines of dialogue between the Lord and Mephisto:

The Lord: *Can you not speak but to abuse? / Do you come only to accuse? / Does nothing on the earth seem to you right?*

Mephisto: *No, Lord. I find it still a rather sorry sight. / Man moves me to compassion, so wretched is his plight. / I have no wish to cause him further woe.*

The conversation reveals Mephisto's ironic wit and his teasing relationship with the Lord.

Cooperative Learning Activity
With a small group of classmates, choose two or three examples of dialogue from the excerpts. Then use a chart like the one below to list the personality traits revealed by the dialogue. Also indicate what the dialogue suggests about the relationships between the characters.

Dialogue	Traits Revealed	Relationships Revealed

SOLILOQUY A **soliloquy** is a speech in a dramatic work that a character makes while alone on stage. In the speech, the character reveals his or her thoughts to the audience. Reread Mephisto's soliloquy at the end of the excerpts from *Faust.* What does the speech reveal about Mephisto's motives?

Choices & CHALLENGES

Writing Options

1. Divine Dialogue Write a dialogue between Faust and the Lord after Faust signs his pact with Mephisto. Have Faust explain what he hopes to gain from the bargain, and have the Lord offer some advice. Make sure the dialogue reveals each character's personality.

2. Story of Ambition A "Faustian bargain" is a decision to betray one's values in order to gain power, wealth, or some other advantage. Write a story about someone who makes a Faustian bargain. First, decide what your main character wishes to gain and what values he or she will betray. Then plan other story elements, including setting, plot, and additional characters. You might want to create an events chart to help you organize the story's action.

Writing Handbook
See page R29: Narrative Writing.

Activities & Explorations

1. Character Portrait Draw a picture of what you think Faust or Mephisto might look like. Your portrait should convey the character's personality as it is revealed by the dialogue in the excerpt you just read. ~ **ART**

2. Dramatic Reading With a classmate, prepare a dramatic reading of one of the scenes in *Faust*. First, rehearse your lines and discuss what tones and gestures you should use in delivering them. Then present the scene to the class. If you like, play background music during the performance that reflects the mood of the scene. ~ **PERFORMING**

Inquiry & Research

Who Was Faust? Find out more about the real Faust and share your discoveries with the class.

RESEARCH STARTER
CLASSZONE.COM

Vocabulary in Action

EXERCISE: CONTEXT CLUES Write the word that best completes each sentence.

1. Mephisto seemed a _____ fellow, pleasant and agreeable to talk to.

2. Yet his mind was firmly made up: he was _____ in his desire to ensnare Faust.

3. Mephisto thought that to succeed, he needed the Lord to plot, or _____, with him.

4. Though he spoke to Faust _____, Mephisto would show him no kindness.

5. He simply wanted to win over someone of Faust's importance and _____.

6. Faust knew the shortcomings of the world: hate instead of love, _____ rather than hard work.

7. Still, his desire to experience the world did not _____; instead, it increased in intensity.

8. He was willing to _____ all chance for salvation to get what he wanted.

9. Would Faust ever regret his decision and feel _____ over his terrible bargain?

10. When his life was over, would he not want to cease his activity and _____ with the Lord?

WORDS TO KNOW

abate	genial	resolute	waive
connive	humanely	sloth	
despair	repose	stature	

Building Vocabulary

For an in-depth study of context clues, see page 674.

Romantic Poetry

OVERVIEW

Poems by
William Wordsworth   899

Romantic Poetry
from Other Cultures   905

Standardized Test Practice:
Writing About Literature   909

Poets of the Romantic period celebrated strong emotions, the imagination, and above all, nature. In fact, Romantic poetry is often called nature poetry. However, Romantic poets did not merely describe the natural world they saw around them. They looked to nature for inspiration and spiritual comfort.

In this lesson you will read two poems by the well-known British Romantic poet William Wordsworth. You will also read a poem by the Cuban poet José Martí and one by the Inuk (Eskimo) poet Uvavnuk. Martí and Uvavnuk composed their poems after the Romantic period had ended in Europe. Although Wordsworth, Martí, and Uvavnuk lived in different times and places, they are connected by their love of nature. In the pages that follow, you will be asked to compare and contrast the works of all three poets. Comparing poems of the Romantic period with two written outside of the period will help you identify similarities and differences in Romantic poetry across cultures.

Points of Comparison

Analyzing the Poem Create a chart like the one shown to help you take notes about the poems. First you will analyze the two Wordsworth poems in depth. Later you will compare them with the poems by Martí and Uvavnuk.

	"The World Is Too Much With Us" (Wordsworth)	"My Heart Leaps Up" (Wordsworth)	from *Simple Verses* (Martí)	"Shaman Song" (Uvavnuk)
Speaker's Point of View				
Images of Nature				
Mood Suggested by the Images				
Poet's Tone				
Comparisons Made				
Poet's View of Nature				

Standardized Test Practice: Comparison-and-Contrast Essay After you have finished reading all the poems, you will be asked to write a comparison-and-contrast essay. Your notes will help you plan and write the essay.

POEMS BY

WILLIAM WORDSWORTH

William Wordsworth
1770–1850

A Romantic Legend William Wordsworth is considered one of the great English poets. Powerfully imaginative and inspired by the beauty of nature, he became a leader of the Romantic movement in England. He was born in the beautiful Lake District of northern England. There he stored up images and emotions that would later find their way into his writing. In 1795, Wordsworth and his sister, Dorothy, settled in the county of Dorset, not far from where the poet Samuel Taylor Coleridge was living. The remarkable friendship that developed between the poets eventually led to the publication of *Lyrical Ballads* (1798), Wordsworth and Coleridge's famous collection of poetry, which signaled the beginning of Romanticism in England. Wordsworth was named Britain's poet laureate in 1843.

Build Background

The Importance of Nature Wordsworth claimed that people could understand their own feelings only by living a simple life, one close to nature. Drawing on images from nature and common experience and allowing his imagination free play, he made fresh observations about life and the world around him. In "The World Is Too Much With Us," for instance, the sea inspires the poet to think about mighty Greek gods.

Connect to Your Life

Think about a favorite natural setting, such as a prairie, a beach, or a mountain cliff. With a partner, discuss the setting and the images and feelings it inspires.

Focus Your Reading

LITERARY ANALYSIS: FIGURATIVE LANGUAGE
Language that communicates meaning beyond the literal meaning of the words is called **figurative language.** Similes, metaphors, and personification are types of figurative language. In a **simile** the word *like* or *as* is used to make a comparison. A **metaphor** makes a comparison without *like* or *as.* In **personification,** human qualities are attributed to an object, animal, or idea. As you read the following poems by Wordsworth, look for examples of these types of figurative language.

ACTIVE READING: DRAWING CONCLUSIONS ABOUT MEANING
When you **draw conclusions** about the meaning of a text, you make logical judgments based on information you already know and details in the work. For instance, in Wordsworth's "The World Is Too Much With Us," details such as "getting and spending" might lead you to conclude that "the world" refers to the world of money and possessions.

READER'S NOTEBOOK As you read Wordsworth's poems, record the conclusions you draw about meaning from details and your own knowledge.

The World Is Too Much With Us
William Wordsworth

The world is too much with us; late and soon,
Getting and spending, we lay waste our powers:
Little we see in Nature that is ours;
We have given our hearts away, a sordid boon!
5   This Sea that bares her bosom to the moon;
The winds that will be howling at all hours,
And are up-gathered now like sleeping flowers;
For this, for every thing, we are out of tune;
It moves us not.—Great God! I'd rather be
10 A Pagan suckled in a creed outworn;
So might I, standing on this pleasant lea,
Have glimpses that would make me less forlorn;
Have sight of Proteus rising from the sea;
Or hear old Triton blow his wreathèd horn.

4 sordid boon: degrading gift.

10 a Pagan: a non-Christian (in this case, a worshiper of the gods of ancient Greece).

11 lea (lē): meadow.

13–14 Proteus (prō′tē-əs) . . . **Triton** (trīt′n): sea gods of Greek mythology.

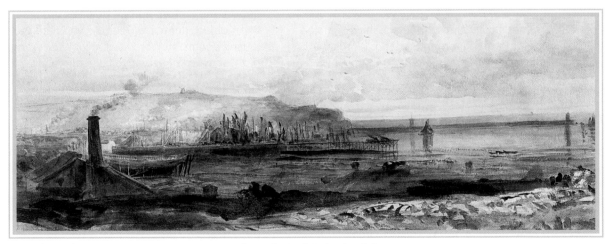

View of a Harbour (c. 1830), Peter De Wint. Watercolor, 10″ × 25½″. Laing Art Gallery. Tyne and Wear Museums Service. Newcastle upon Tyne, England.

HUMANITIES CONNECTION This painting reflects the development of the Industrial Revolution. Wordsworth believed that industrialization would destroy communities and the countryside. The poet particularly criticized child labor, which he felt would deny children an education through nature.

My Heart Leaps Up
William Wordsworth

The Passing Shower (1868), George Inness. Courtesy of the Canajoharie Library and Art Gallery,
Canajoharie, New York.

My heart leaps up when I behold
   A rainbow in the sky:
So was it when my life began;
So is it now I am a man;
5 So be it when I shall grow old,
   Or let me die!
The Child is father of the Man;
And I could wish my days to be
Bound each to each by natural piety.

9 piety (pī′ĭ-tē): religious feeling
and devotion.

from the

GRASMERE JOURNALS
Dorothy Wordsworth

FRIDAY 16 APRIL, 1802 (GOOD FRIDAY)

When I undrew my curtains in the morning, I was much affected by the beauty of the prospect and the change. The sun shone, the wind had passed away, the hills looked cheerful, the river was very bright as it flowed into the lake. The church rises up behind a little knot of rocks, the steeple not so high as an ordinary three storey house. Trees, in a row in the garden under the wall. After Wm had shaved we set forward. The valley is at first broken by little rocky woody knolls that make retiring places, fairy valleys in the vale, the river winds along under these hills travelling not in a bustle but not slowly to the lake. . . . As we go on the vale opens out more into one vale with somewhat of a cradle bed. Cottages with groups of trees on the side of the hills. We passed a pair of twin children two years old sat on the next bridge which we crossed a single arch. We rested again upon the turf and looked at the same bridge. We observed arches in the water occasioned by the large stones sending it down in two streams. . . . Primroses by the roadside, pile wort that shone like stars of gold in the sun, violets, strawberries, retired and half buried among the grass. When we came to the foot of Brothers Water I left William sitting on the bridge and went along the path on the right side of the lake through the wood. I was delighted with what I saw. The water under the boughs of the bare old trees, the simplicity of the mountains and the exquisite beauty of the path. There was one grey cottage. . . . I hung over the gate, and thought I could have stayed for ever. When I returned I found William writing a poem descriptive of the sights and sounds we saw and heard. There was the gentle flowing of the stream, the glittering lively lake, green fields without a living creature to be seen on them. . . .

Connect to the Literature

1. **What Do You Think?** What images remain in your mind after reading "The World Is Too Much With Us" and "My Heart Leaps Up"?

Think Critically

2. In "The World Is Too Much With Us," what does the speaker think we have lost? How?

3. In "My Heart Leaps Up," what is the speaker hoping for in line 5?

4. What do you think the speaker of "My Heart Leaps Up" means by "The Child is father of the Man" (line 7)? How does this belief reflect Romantic ideals?

5. **ACTIVE READING: DRAWING CONCLUSIONS ABOUT MEANING** Get together with a partner and compare the notes you recorded in your 📖 **READER'S NOTEBOOK**. Did you draw similar conclusions about meaning in the poems?

6. Determine Wordsworth's **tone,** or attitude toward the subject, in each poem, and then compare and contrast the tones. Cite examples in your response.

Extend Interpretations

7. **Comparing Texts** How does Dorothy Wordsworth's response to nature compare with her brother's? What similarities do you see in the imagery and the feelings expressed?

8. **Critic's Corner** Samuel Taylor Coleridge praised Wordsworth for capturing "the perfect truth of nature in his images and descriptions." Do you agree with this assessment of Wordsworth's writing? Support your answer with examples from the two poems.

9. **Connect to Life** If Wordsworth were alive today, what do you think he would say about the state of the environment and our relationship to nature? Explain.

LITERARY ANALYSIS: FIGURATIVE LANGUAGE

Figurative language is language that conveys meaning beyond the literal meanings of the words. Writers use figurative language to create effects, to emphasize ideas, and to evoke emotions. Types of figurative language include **simile, metaphor,** and **personification.** Notice the metaphor in the fourth line of "The World Is Too Much With Us":

We have given our hearts away, a sordid boon!

In this metaphor, hearts given away are compared to a "sordid boon," or foul gift. This comparison emphasizes the idea that our inability to appreciate nature has corrupted us.

Paired Activity Reread "The World Is Too Much With Us" with a partner, and work together to find an example of a simile and one of personification. Then discuss the effect created by this figurative language.

REVIEW: THEME

Theme in a work of literature is a message or idea about life or human nature. In poetry, **imagery**—words and phrases that create vivid sensory experiences for the reader—often conveys theme. Use the nature imagery in the Wordsworth poems to help you identify the theme of each one.

Writing Options

1. Nature Poem Write a poem about the natural setting you discussed for the Connect to Your Life activity on page 899. Describe the setting and your thoughts and feelings about it.

2. Cause-and-Effect Paragraph In "The World Is Too Much With Us," Wordsworth expresses sorrow over the fact that people have lost touch with nature. Think about what may cause people today to become alienated from the natural world. What do you think are the results of such alienation? Organize your thoughts in a cause-and-effect paragraph and place it in your **Working Portfolio.**

Writing Handbook
See page R32: Cause and Effect.

Activities & Explorations

Poem Illustration Illustrate a scene from one of Wordsworth's poems. Use the poet's descriptive imagery to help you capture the scene in a drawing, a collage, or even a large mural to decorate your classroom. ~ **ART**

Inquiry & Research

Failed Friendship Wordsworth and Coleridge collaborated on *Lyrical Ballads,* which heralded the beginning of the Romantic movement in Britain. The close friends also lived for a time as neighbors. However, by 1810 their friendship had soured. For the rest of their lives, the two famous poets rarely met or spoke to each other. Do research to find out what caused the rift between Wordsworth and Coleridge. Share your findings in an oral report.

RESEARCH STARTER
CLASSZONE.COM

Points of Comparison

Review the poems, and fill in the first two columns of your comparison-and-contrast chart. The following questions may help you focus your ideas:

- What is the speaker's point of view (first-person, second-person, or third-person)?
- What images of nature does the poem contain?
- What mood, or feeling, is created by these images?
- How would you describe the poet's tone?
- To whom or what is the subject compared?
- How do you think the poet views nature?

Cooperative Learning Activity Share your chart with a small group of classmates, and discuss the similarities and differences between the two Wordsworth poems.

	"The World Is Too Much With Us" (Wordsworth)	"My Heart Leaps Up" (Wordsworth)	from *Simple Verses* (Martí)	"Shaman Song" (Uvavnuk)
Speaker's Point of View	first-person			
Images of Nature	sea beneath the moon			
Mood Suggested by the Images				
Poet's Tone				
Comparisons Made				
Poet's View of Nature				

*R*OMANTIC POETRY
FROM OTHER CULTURES

Romantic literature is not limited to a particular time in Europe. Themes dealing with individual experience, strong emotions, and nature appear in works from other cultures and times as well. As you read the poems by José Martí and Uvavnuk, compare the poets' impressions of nature with those of the Romantic poet William Wordsworth.

José Martí
1853–1895

Writer and Revolutionary
Born in Havana, Cuba, José Martí (hō-sā′ mär-tē′) was a political activist, journalist, and leader in the Modernist movement in Spanish literature. He began his political career at the age of 16, when he first spoke out for Cuban independence. In 1871 Martí was deported to Spain and sentenced to hard labor for his activities, but he was released after six months. Once freed, Martí remained in Spain, where he received his university education. Over the next several years, Martí traveled a great deal, finally moving to New York City in 1881. There he worked as a journalist and as a poet, writing his most influential collection, *Simple Verses.*

Though an exile, Martí never abandoned the struggle for Cuban independence. In 1892 he helped form the Cuban Revolutionary Party; three years later, he arrived in Cuba with a small army of supporters. Martí died in the first battle he fought, but the seeds of revolution had been sown. Cuba eventually gained its independence, and Martí became celebrated as a great revolutionary hero.

Joyous Shaman Details about Uvavnuk (ōō-vav′nŏŏk), an Inuk (Eskimo) woman who probably lived in the 19th century, come largely from legends that were retold to Danish explorer Knud Rasmussen in the early 20th century. Rasmussen recorded the stories and published them in 1927. According to his reports, Uvavnuk, an ordinary woman, was suddenly struck by a ball of light from either a meteor or a bolt of lightning. The strike filled her with spiritual enlightenment. From that day on, she was a shaman—a medium between the physical world and the spirit world. Uvavnuk began to receive messages and songs from the spirit world. It was said that everyone who heard her sing the "Shaman Song" was filled with joy

and cleansed of evil. As legend has it, because of Uvavnuk's enlightenment her people enjoyed many years of great happiness and good fortune.

Eskimo shaman figure

from Simple Verses

José Martí

Cuba

Translated by Manuel A. Tellechea

I know of Egypt and Niger,
Of Persia and Xenophon, no less,
But more than these I prefer
The fresh mountain air's caress.

5 I know the ancient histories
Of man and his struggles for power,
But I prefer the buzzing bees
That hover round the bellflower.

I know the sound the wind made
10 When through the boughs it was flying:
Let no one tell me I'm lying,
There is no song as well played.

I know of a frightened fawn
That seeks the fold to expire,
15 And of a heart weary-worn
That dies hidden without ire.

1 Egypt and Niger: The African countries of Egypt and Niger were sites of important ancient civilizations.

2 Persia and Xenophon (zĕn′ə-fən): Persia is the former name of Iran; Xenophon was a Greek commander who led a troop of soldiers in the service of a Persian prince.

14 seeks the fold to expire: returns home to die.

16 ire: anger.

Shaman Song

Uvavnuk

Inuk (Eskimo)

Translated by Jane Hirshfield

The great sea
frees me, moves me,
as a strong river carries a weed.
Earth and her strong winds
5 move me, take me away,
and my soul is swept up in joy.

Foggy River (1990), Florence Brown Eden.
Gallery Contemporanea, Jacksonville, Florida/SuperStock.

Connect to the Literature

1. **What Do You Think?** Which poem do you prefer? Give reasons for your choice.

Think Critically

2. How would you describe the speaker's relationship to nature in "Shaman Song"?

3. Compare the first three stanzas of Martí's poem with the last stanza. How does the content of this stanza differ from the others?

4. Review the poems and note the **sensory details** that each contains. What ideas about nature do these details convey?

 THINK ABOUT
- Martí's comparison of nature with human achievements
- Uvavnuk's images of a strong river and strong winds
- the **moods** these images convey

Points of Comparison

Cooperative Learning Activity Now work with a small group of students to compare and contrast the Wordsworth poems you have already analyzed with those by Martí and Uvavnuk. Respond to the Points of Comparison questions on page 904. Use your answers to help you complete your chart.

	"The World Is Too Much With Us" (Wordsworth)	"My Heart Leaps Up" (Wordsworth)	from *Simple Verses* (Martí)	"Shaman Song" (Uvavnuk)
Speaker's Point of View	first-person		first-person	
Images of Nature	sea beneath the moon		fresh mountain air's caress	
Mood Suggested by the Images				
Poet's Tone				
Comparisons Made				
Poet's View of Nature				

Writing About Literature

PART 1 Reading the Prompt

In writing assessments you may be asked to compare and contrast works of literature that, like the poems you have analyzed, have similar themes. You are now going to practice writing an essay that involves this type of comparison.

> **Writing Prompt**
>
> Poetry from different cultures and time periods can have interesting thematic similarities and differences. You will compare and contrast four Romantic poems—two by William Wordsworth, one by José ❶ Martí, and one by Uvavnuk. For each poem, discuss the point of view, ❷ nature images, mood, tone, comparisons made, and view of nature expressed. Point out differences and similarities among the poems. Be ❸ sure to provide evidence from the poems to support your analysis.

STRATEGIES
IN ACTION

❶ I have to **compare and contrast** four Romantic poems that deal with nature.

❷ For each poem, I need to discuss the **point of view, nature images, mood, tone, comparisons made,** and **view of nature expressed.**

❸ I need to include **details, examples,** or **quotations** from the poems to support my ideas.

PART 2 Planning a Comparison-and-Contrast Essay

- Review the comparison-and-contrast chart that you completed for all four poems.
- Using your chart, find examples of similarities and differences to point out in your essay.
- Create an outline to organize your ideas.

PART 3 Drafting Your Essay

Introduction Begin by introducing your topic and identifying the basis of comparison. Briefly express your opinion about what the four poems have in common. Then explain what you see as major differences.

Body You may wish to devote one paragraph to each poem. Within your paragraphs, you will need to discuss how each poem is different from the others and how it is similar to them. Pay the most attention to the images and mood in each poem. Use your comparison-and-contrast chart to identify details and examples.

Conclusion Wrap up your essay with a summary of the major differences and similarities.

Revision Check that you have used signal words, such as *similarly, also, like, but, unlike,* and *while,* to indicate comparisons and contrasts.

THE *Lorelei*

HEINRICH HEINE   *Translated by* Aaron Kramer

Heinrich Heine
1797–1856

A Controversial Figure Born in Düsseldorf, Germany (then Prussia), to Jewish parents, Heinrich Heine (hīn'rĭĸн hī'nə) was a controversial figure in his homeland. Heine converted to Protestantism because government positions were not open to Jews at the time. His conversion was in vain, however, for he was never offered any of the jobs he desired. Instead, Heine turned to writing. His reputation as a poet was established with *The Book of Songs,* published in 1827. Besides poems, Heine's writings also included expressions of his political views. After settling in Paris in 1831, he wrote essays against the governments of both France and Germany. As a result, the German government eventually banned all of his works. In 1848, a serious illness permanently confined the poet to what he called his "mattress grave." Although in tremendous pain, Heine continued to write until his death.

Build Background

Legend of the Lorelei The Lorelei is a cliff overlooking the Rhine River. The echo heard at the cliff inspired a legend about a maiden who drowned herself after a lover betrayed her. According to the legend, the spirit of the maiden sits upon a rock, combing her hair in the moonlight and singing a haunting song that lures boatmen to their death. Heine had his own Lorelei, a cousin who rejected him and married another man. Her rejection was the inspiration for the poem you are about to read and for many of Heine's other ballads.

Connect to Your Life

With a classmate, discuss stories you have read about a love that dooms the lover. What do you think accounts for people's interest in such stories?

Focus Your Reading

LITERARY ANALYSIS: LITERARY BALLAD

A **folk ballad** is a narrative poem that was originally intended to be sung. Traditional folk ballads were composed by unknown authors and passed down orally. A **literary ballad** is written by a single author in conscious imitation of the folk-ballad style. Literary ballads became popular during the Romantic period. As you read "The Lorelei," listen for its musical qualities.

ACTIVE READING: INTERPRETING SYMBOLS

A **symbol** is a person, place, object, or activity that stands for something beyond itself. When you interpret symbols in a literary work, you look beyond the work's literal meaning to gain a deeper understanding.

READER'S NOTEBOOK As you read "The Lorelei," write down your interpretation of the symbols in the poem.

Loreley (1864), Eduard Jakob von Steinle.
213.5 cm × 135.4 cm. Schack-Galerie,
Munich, Germany/Bayer & Mitko/Artothek.

I cannot explain the sadness
That's fallen on my breast.
An old, old fable haunts me,
And will not let me rest.

5   The air grows cool in the twilight,
And softly the Rhine flows on;
The peak of a mountain sparkles
Beneath the setting sun.

More lovely than a vision,
10   A girl sits high up there;
     Her golden jewelry glistens,
     She combs her golden hair.

     With a comb of gold she combs it,
     And sings an evensong;
15   The wonderful melody reaches
     A boat, as it sails along.

     The boatman hears, with an anguish
     More wild than was ever known;
     He's blind to the rocks around him;
20   His eyes are for her alone.

     —At last the waves devoured
     The boat, and the boatman's cry;
     And this she did with her singing,
     The golden Lorelei.

Die Lorelei, music. Copyright © 1987 by Curtis Music Press. All rights reserved.

Connect to the Literature

1. What Do You Think?
Which image in this poem did you find most striking? Explain.

Comprehension Check
- What old story does the speaker recall?
- What effect does the girl's singing have on the boatman?

Think Critically

2. ACTIVE READING: INTERPRETING SYMBOLS With a classmate, discuss the interpretation of **symbols** you wrote down in your READER'S NOTEBOOK. What do you think the Lorelei represents? Her song? The destroyed boat?

3. What does this poem suggest about the nature of love?

> **THINK ABOUT**
> - how the speaker feels as he recalls the "old, old fable" (line 3)
> - the description of the girl
> - the fate of the boatman

4. How would you describe the **mood** of "The Lorelei"? How does the mood reflect the Romantic spirit?

Extend Interpretations

5. The Writer's Style There are four images involving gold in "The Lorelei." What effect does this repeated image have on the portrayal of the girl?

6. Comparing Texts In what way is the representation of the sea in Wordsworth's "The World Is Too Much With Us" similar to that of the Rhine in "The Lorelei"? How do the images differ?

7. Connect to Life "The Lorelei" depicts a man who is overwhelmed by a song. Think of a time when you have had a strong emotional response to a song. Why do you think music has such a powerful effect on people?

LITERARY ANALYSIS: LITERARY BALLAD

"The Lorelei" is an example of a **literary ballad,** a poem that the writer has composed in the style of anonymous folk ballads. Typically, a **folk ballad**

- is a brief narrative poem originally intended to be sung
- is made up of four-line stanzas
- contains repetitions of lines or stanzas, sometimes with the wording slightly varied
- recounts a single dramatic, often tragic, episode
- contains supernatural elements
- includes dialogue
- implies more than it actually tells

Cooperative Learning Activity With a group of classmates, determine which typical characteristics of a folk ballad are contained in "The Lorelei." Refer to the list above for help. Compare your findings with those of other groups.

REVIEW: IMAGERY The term **imagery** refers to words and phrases that create vivid sensory experiences for the reader. Reread "The Lorelei" and identify several examples of imagery. To which sense or senses does each image appeal?

from THE EXPIATION

RUSSIA 1812

VICTOR HUGO

Victor Hugo
1802–1885

Early Years Victor Hugo was a poet, novelist, and dramatist whose talent was only matched by his larger-than-life personality. His early years were unsettled. The son of a general who served under Napoleon Bonaparte, Hugo spent much of his childhood traveling with his father to Italy and Spain during the Napoleonic Wars.

Artistic Success Hugo achieved early success as a writer, and he tackled his work with great energy. In 1826, he began an intense, 17-year period of writing and publishing plays, poems, and novels. In 1827, he established himself as the leader of the Romantic movement in France with the preface to his epic play *Cromwell.* In the preface Hugo spoke out against the restrictions of classical literature and called for writing that explored emotions and personal experience. He gained wider fame with the publication in 1831 of the Romantic historical novel *The Hunchback of Notre Dame.* Hugo's creative activity temporarily came to a halt in 1843, following the death of his daughter Léopoldine. Overwhelmed by grief, he published nothing during the next 10 years.

A Hero's Goodbye Eventually Hugo turned to politics, accepting an important post in the French government in 1845. However, six years later he was driven into exile when Louis Napoleon—later Napoleon III—seized power. While in exile, Hugo resumed writing and completed the protest novel *Les Misérables.* Published in 1862, the novel was a huge success in France and abroad. Soon after Napoleon III fell from power in 1870, Hugo returned to France. He resumed his political career for a time, but illness soon forced him to retire. Upon his death, Hugo was given a hero's funeral. European leaders, cavalry regiments, and as many as three million other people wound through the streets of Paris to honor him.

Hugo's funeral procession

Build Background

Napoleon's Crime and Punishment Victor Hugo wrote "The Expiation" while living in exile. The poem appeared in a collection of satiric poetry directed at Napoleon's nephew Louis Napoleon, whom Hugo despised for abolishing the French republic and reestablishing the empire.

In "The Expiation" Hugo portrays Napoleon Bonaparte as a flawed leader. The poem opens with Napoleon's ill-fated campaign against Russia. It moves to his defeat at the Battle of Waterloo and his subsequent exile on the island of Saint Helena, where he dies. The poem then recounts Napoleon's elevation as a hero after his death, but in the last part Hugo reveals the crime that in his view has to be expiated, or atoned for: Napoleon's seizure of power in France in 1799.

The excerpt you are about to read describes the result of Napoleon's disastrous invasion of Russia. The emperor set out in June 1812 with about 600,000 soldiers from all over his empire. By the time the troops reached Moscow in September, the Russians had abandoned and set fire to the city. With no place to spend the winter, Napoleon ordered his army to withdraw. As the troops trudged westward, a cold, early winter set in. The temperature fell as low as 22 degrees below zero. The soldiers were also plagued by attacks from Russian Cossacks. By the time the troops reached Poland, only about 10,000 men remained.

In "The Expiation," after each major defeat suffered by Napoleon, the emperor asks whether this is the penance, or punishment, he must pay for his crime. Each time a voice replies, "No." Finally the punishment becomes clear: Thirty years after Napoleon's death, the emperor in his tomb hears the voice of Napoleon III. The disgrace that the nephew has brought on the name of Napoleon is his uncle's punishment.

A STOPPAGE to a STRIDE over the GLOBE

Political cartoon, 1803

Connect to Your Life

Think about a hero of yours who has suffered some kind of defeat. The hero may be a political or community leader, an artist, or an athlete. How did you feel about your hero after the loss? Did you still support him or her? Did your attitude toward your hero change in any way? Share your experiences with a classmate.

Focus Your Reading

LITERARY ANALYSIS: SETTING IN NARRATIVE POETRY

A **narrative poem** is a poem that tells a story. Thus it contains many of the basic elements of a story, including characters, plot, and setting. The **setting** is the time and place of the action. Setting may play an important role in what happens. As you read "Russia 1812," think about how the setting affects the poem's plot, characters, and theme.

ACTIVE READING: VISUALIZING SETTING

When you read you probably **visualize,** or form mental pictures using details from the piece. Visualizing setting will help you understand what's happening. For example, by visualizing the setting of "Russia 1812" from the details that Hugo provides, you can gain insight into what Napoleon and his soldiers endured as they marched through Russia.

📖 **READER'S NOTEBOOK** As you read the poem, use a chart like the one below to record the images that help you visualize the setting. Jot down specific lines from the poem and descriptions of the pictures they bring to mind.

Lines	Images of Setting

Russia 1812

from The Expiation
Victor Hugo
Translated by Robert Lowell

The snow fell, and its power was multiplied.
For the first time the Eagle bowed its head—
dark days! Slowly the Emperor returned—
behind him Moscow! Its onion domes still burned.
5 The snow rained down in blizzards—rained and froze.
Past each white waste a further white waste rose.
None recognized the captains or the flags.
Yesterday the Grand Army, today its dregs!
No one could tell the vanguard from the flanks.
10 The snow! The hurt men struggled from the ranks,
hid in the bellies of dead horse, in stacks
of shattered caissons. By the bivouacs,
one saw the picket dying at his post,
still standing in his saddle, white with frost,
15 the stone lips frozen to the bugle's mouth!
Bullets and grapeshot mingled with the snow,
that hailed . . . The Guard, surprised at shivering, march
in a dream now; ice rimes the gray mustache.
The snow falls, always snow! The driving mire
20 submerges; men, trapped in that white empire,
have no more bread and march on barefoot—gaps!
They were no longer living men and troops,
but a dream drifting in a fog, a mystery,
mourners parading under the black sky.
25 The solitude, vast, terrible to the eye,
was like a mute avenger everywhere,
as snowfall, floating through the quiet air,
buried the huge army in a huge shroud.
Could anyone leave this kingdom? A crowd—

2 the Eagle: Napoleon; also, the standard on his coat of arms.

4 onion domes: The domes on Russian Orthodox churches are traditionally onion shaped.

9 the vanguard . . . the flanks: The vanguard is the troops leading an army; the flanks are those troops composing the sides of a military formation.

12 caissons (kā′sŏnz′) **. . . bivouacs** (bĭv′ōō-ăks′): Caissons are vehicles used to carry ammunition; bivouacs are temporary encampments.

13 picket: soldier on the alert to warn of an enemy's approach.

16 grapeshot: a cluster of small iron balls shot from a cannon.

18 rimes: covers with frost.

19 mire: deep, heavy mud or slush.

26 mute: silent; unable to speak.

On the March from Moscow (19th century), John Laslett Pott.
Forbes Magazine Collection, New York/The Bridgeman Art Library, London.

HUMANITIES CONNECTION Hunger was another hardship faced by Napoleon's soldiers. Thousands of horses died during the homeward march, and the hungry soldiers fought over the animals.

30   each man, obsessed with dying, was alone.
     Men slept—and died! The beaten mob sludged on,
     ditching the guns to burn their carriages.
     Two foes. The North, the Czar. The North was worse.
     In hollows where the snow was piling up,
35   one saw whole regiments fallen asleep.
     Attila's dawn, Cannaes of Hannibal!
     The army marching to its funeral!
     Litters, wounded, the dead, deserters—swarm,
     crushing the bridges down to cross a stream.
40   They went to sleep ten thousand, woke up four.
     Ney, bringing up the former army's rear,

36 Attila's . . . Hannibal: In A.D. 451 Attila, king of the Huns, engaged in the fierce and bloody Battle of Châlons but withdrew his troops once dawn revealed tens of thousands of soldiers on both sides lying dead. In 216 B.C. the Carthaginian general Hannibal defeated a Roman army larger than his own at Cannae (kăn′ē), by drawing the Romans into a trap.

41 Ney: Michel Ney (1769–1815), one of Napoleon's most famous commanders, was in charge of the troops defending the rear of the retreating French army.

Napoleon Bonaparte During Campaign in France (1864), Ernest Meissonier. Photograph by Dagli Orti/The Art Archive/Musée d'Orsay, Paris.

HUMANITIES CONNECTION
To ensure that he would not be captured alive by the enemy during the Russian campaign, Napoleon wore a vial of poison around his neck in a small leather bag.

hacked his horse loose from three disputing Cossacks . . .
All night, the *qui vive?* The alert! Attacks;
retreats! White ghosts would wrench away our guns,
45   or we would see dim, terrible squadrons,
circles of steel, whirlpools of savages,
rush sabering through the camp like dervishes.
And in this way, whole armies died at night.

The Emperor was there, standing—he saw.
50   This oak already trembling from the axe,
watched his glories drop from him branch by branch:
chiefs, soldiers. Each one had his turn and chance—
they died! Some lived. These still believed his star,
and kept their watch. They loved the man of war,
55   this small man with his hands behind his back,
whose shadow, moving to and fro, was black
behind the lighted tent. Still believing, they
accused their destiny of *lèse-majesté.*
His misfortune had mounted on their back.
60   The man of glory shook. Cold stupefied
him, then suddenly he felt terrified.
Being without belief, he turned to God:
"God of armies, is this the end?" he cried.

42 Cossacks: mounted Russian soldiers.

43 *qui vive?* (kē vēv´): a French phrase (meaning literally "Who lives?") used by sentries to determine the allegiance of those entering a military camp. It is equivalent to "Who goes there?"

47 dervishes: members of a Muslim religious sect whose devotions involve whirling dances.

58 *lèse-majesté* (lĕz´mä-zhĕs-tā´): a crime committed against a ruler.

60–61 stupefied him: dulled his senses.

And then at last the expiation came,
65 as he heard some one call him by his name,
some one half-lost in shadow, who said, "No,
Napoleon." Napoleon understood,
restless, bareheaded, leaden, as he stood
before his butchered legions in the snow.

The alert! Attacks; retreats! White ghosts would wrench away our guns . . .

Thinking through the LITERATURE

Connect to the Literature

1. What Do You Think?
What is your reaction to the description of the suffering endured by Napoleon's army?

Comprehension Check
- What dangers does the army face as it retreats from Moscow?
- How does Napoleon feel as he watches his troops die?

Think Critically

2. ACTIVE READING: VISUALIZING SETTING With a partner, discuss the chart you each created in your READER'S NOTEBOOK. Choose three images that contributed the most to your visualizing of the setting.

3. Irony is a surprising contrast between expectation and reality. What is ironic about the description of the picket in lines 13–15? What other examples of irony can you find in the poem?

4. Identify the metaphor in lines 49–52. Who is the oak? What do the branches represent?

5. What do you think is the speaker's attitude toward Napoleon?

THINK ABOUT
- the way in which Napoleon is described
- how the soldiers feel about him
- how Napoleon reacts after turning to God

Extend Interpretations

6. The Writer's Style Notice the repetition of the word *snow* in the first 19 lines of "Russia 1812." Why do you think Hugo chose to repeat this word? How does the repetition affect your reading of the poem?

7. Comparing Texts Compare the depiction of nature in "Russia 1812" with that in Heine's "The Lorelei." What similar view of nature is presented in these poems? How does this view correspond with the Romantic idea of nature?

8. Connect to Life How has climate or terrain affected soldiers or battles in modern wars you've heard or read about? In what wars have physical conditions helped determine the outcome?

LITERARY ANALYSIS: SETTING IN NARRATIVE POETRY

Like all literary works that tell a story, a **narrative poem** has characters, a plot, and a setting. **Setting,** the time and place of the action, often plays an important role in helping the reader understand the story's plot and characters. Setting can also support or enhance a story's theme. In the following lines from "Russia 1812," notice what the frozen setting suggests about Napoleon, the "Eagle" of the second line:

The snow fell, and its power was multiplied.
For the first time the Eagle bowed its head—
dark days!

Paired Activity With a classmate, complete a diagram like the one shown below. Briefly describe the setting of "Russia 1812." Then note ways in which the setting connects to the plot, characters, and theme of the narrative.

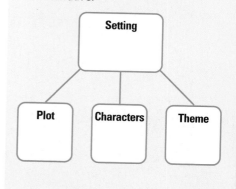

Victor Hugo on Stage and Screen

An individual's struggle against a cruel society, hopeless love, grand passions—such Romantic elements appeal to modern audiences. So it's probably not too surprising that many of Victor Hugo's best-known novels and plays have been translated to the stage and screen. Taking his subjects from common life, Hugo wrote about the hopes and dreams of ordinary people. Audiences identify with these characters, whose emotions and struggles reflect their own.

It's not every day that a 19th-century French novel is turned into a long-running Broadway play. During performances of *Les Misérables*, the musical adaptation of Hugo's novel, audiences cheered as Jean Valjean repeatedly escaped the clutches of the relentless policeman Javert.

Hugo's novel *The Hunchback of Notre Dame* tells the story of Quasimodo, the deformed bell ringer who loves the beautiful gypsy Esmeralda. The many films based on the novel capture the sadness and even the nobility of Quasimodo's situation.

Paired Discussion Discuss the Romantic elements in movies and other productions you have seen. You might recall dramas featuring dashing heroes, acts of individual courage, or strong emotions.

Giuseppe Verdi's opera *Rigoletto* is based on Hugo's play *The King Has Fun*. Rigoletto, a hunchbacked jester, tries to protect his daughter from the powerful Duke—with tragic consequences. The characters' intense feelings are well suited to opera.

POEMS BY

Charles BAUDELAIRE

Charles Baudelaire
1821–1867

Wild Youth Charles Baudelaire (bōd-lâr′), possibly the most influential French poet of the 19th century, is almost as well-known for his extravagant lifestyle as for his writing. His stepfather, a strict disciplinarian, tried to tame the young Baudelaire by sending him to a military boarding school. Later, the boy was sent to a high school in Paris from which he was expelled for his outrageous behavior. Baudelaire further displeased his family when he announced his intention to become a writer. He enrolled in law school but rarely attended. Instead, he fell in with a radical crowd and began leading an unconventional existence. Alarmed, Baudelaire's stepfather sent the young man on a voyage to India in 1841. Although Baudelaire returned to France before completing the trip, the voyage had a powerful influence on his writing.

Rich Man, Poor Man Shortly after his return, Baudelaire received his inheritance and began living a life of leisure. However, within two years he had spent nearly half of the money. His family consequently took control of his finances, and Baudelaire was forced to earn a living as an art critic. From 1852 to 1865, he also translated the works of American writer Edgar Allan Poe. Baudelaire's translations established Poe's reputation in France. They also helped Baudelaire clarify his own ideas about poetry.

Last Years Baudelaire's fame grew as a result of his translations, and some of his own poetry began to appear in print. In 1857 he published *The Flowers of Evil,* a collection of poems about love and the role of the artist. The collection caused a scandal. Baudelaire and his publisher were both charged with and found guilty of obscenity and blasphemy. Six of the poems were banned. Although Baudelaire continued to write, he never recovered from the failure of *The Flowers of Evil.* During an unsuccessful lecture tour in Belgium, Baudelaire became severely ill. In 1866 he returned to Paris, where he died the next year in his mother's arms, at the age of 46. At his funeral, already calling themselves his followers, were the writers who would become the leaders of the Symbolist movement.

The Absinthe Drinker (c. 1875–76), Edgar Degas. Oil on canvas, 36¼″ × 26¾″. Copyright © Francis G. Mayer/Corbis.

Build Background

Beauty in Evil Although Baudelaire's poetry contains elements of Romanticism, his themes helped pave the way for the **Symbolists,** poets who used symbols to suggest meaning and mood. Like the Romantics, Baudelaire wrote with great passion. Unlike the Romantics, however, he was passionate about depicting what he saw as the ugliness of city life and the cruelty of existence.

In *The Flowers of Evil,* Baudelaire described the human condition. According to the poet, good and evil existed side by side within people. Left to their own devices, Baudelaire believed, people would be inclined toward evil. They could only be saved through art.

"The Albatross" and "Invitation to the Voyage" both appear in the first section of *The Flowers of Evil.* "The Albatross" is based on an incident Baudelaire witnessed during his uncompleted voyage to India. Some sailors on the ship had captured an albatross and were amusing themselves by watching its futile efforts to escape. Albatross are large sea birds whose long, narrow wings allow them to glide gracefully over water but hamper them from taking flight except from the open sea. "Invitation to the Voyage" is one of several poems that Baudelaire wrote for Marie Daubrun, an actress he fell in love with.

Cover of French edition of *Les Fleurs du Mal* [The flowers of evil]. New York University Libraries.

Connect to Your Life

In "Invitation to the Voyage," the speaker describes an ideal land where he and his love would be happy together. Describe a place—real or imaginary—where you think you would be perfectly happy. Compare your description with those of a small group of classmates.

Focus Your Reading

LITERARY ANALYSIS: SOUND DEVICES

Poets use a variety of **sound devices** to produce special qualities of sound. These include the following:

- **repetition**—repeated words and phrases
- **alliteration**—the repetition of consonant sounds at the beginnings of words
- **rhyme scheme**—the pattern of rhymes at the ends of lines

As you read the poems, be aware of the sound devices used by Baudelaire.

ACTIVE READING: INTERPRETING SENSORY DETAILS

Sensory details are words and phrases that appeal to the reader's senses of sight, hearing, touch, smell, and taste. The images created by sensory details help bring a piece of writing to life. Notice how the following sensory details from "Invitation to the Voyage" appeal to the sense of smell:

> *Flowers of rarest bloom*
> *Proffering their perfume*
> *Mixed with the vague fragrances of amber;*

📖 **READER'S NOTEBOOK** As you read the poems by Baudelaire, use a chart like the one below to record sensory details. Then indicate which sense or senses each detail appeals to.

Poem	Sensory Details	Sense(s) Appealed To
"Invitation to the Voyage"		
"The Albatross"		

Invitation to the Voyage

Charles Baudelaire

Translated by Richard Wilbur

My child, my sister,
            dream
  How sweet all things would seem
Were we in that kind land to live together,
  And there love slow and long,
5   There love and die among
Those scenes that image you, that sumptuous weather.
  Drowned suns that glimmer there
  Through cloud-disheveled air
Move me with such a mystery as appears
10   Within those other skies
  Of your treacherous eyes
When I behold them shining through their tears.

There, there is nothing else but grace and measure,
Richness, quietness, and pleasure.

8 cloud-disheveled (dĭ-shĕv′əld) **air:** sky streaked with clouds.

13 grace and measure: beauty and a sense of proportion.

On Board a Sailing Ship (1818–1819), Caspar David Friedrich. Oil on canvas, 71 cm × 56 cm. The Hermitage, St. Petersburg, Russia/Giraudon/Art Resource, New York.

15   Furniture that wears
        The luster of the years
Softly would glow within our glowing chamber,
        Flowers of rarest bloom
        Proffering their perfume

19 proffering: offering.

20 Mixed with the vague fragrances of amber;
        Gold ceilings would there be,
        Mirrors deep as the sea,
The walls all in an Eastern splendor hung—
        Nothing but should address

23 in an Eastern splendor hung: covered with rich cloths and wall hangings from the Orient.

25   The soul's loneliness,
Speaking her sweet and secret native tongue.

There, there is nothing else but grace and measure,
Richness, quietness, and pleasure.

        See, sheltered from the swells

29 swells: large waves.

30   There in the still canals
Those drowsy ships that dream of sailing forth;
        It is to satisfy
        Your least desire, they ply

33 ply: travel a course regularly.

Hither through all the waters of the earth.
35   The sun at close of day
        Clothes the fields of hay,
Then the canals, at last the town entire
        In hyacinth and gold:
        Slowly the land is rolled
40 Sleepward under a sea of gentle fire.

There, there is nothing else but grace and measure,
Richness, quietness, and pleasure.

The Albatross
Charles Baudelaire
Translated by James McGowan

La Grande famille [The Great family] (1963), Réne Magritte.
Private collection/Lauros-Giraudon, Paris/SuperStock.

Often, when bored, the sailors of the crew
Trap albatross, the great birds of the seas,
Mild travelers escorting in the blue
Ships gliding on the ocean's mysteries.

5   And when the sailors have them on the planks,
Hurt and distraught, these kings of all outdoors
Piteously let trail along their flanks
Their great white wings, dragging like useless oars.

This voyager, how comical and weak!
10 Once handsome, how unseemly and inept!
One sailor pokes a pipe into his beak,
Another mocks the flier's hobbled step.

The Poet is a kinsman in the clouds
Who scoffs at archers, loves a stormy day;
15 But on the ground, among the hooting crowds,
He cannot walk, his wings are in the way.

6 distraught: confused and upset.

10 unseemly and inept: inappropriate and clumsy.

Connect to the Literature

1. What Do You Think? Which of these poems do you prefer? Explain why.

Think Critically

2. ACTIVE READING: INTERPRETING SENSORY DETAILS
The stanzas in "Invitation to the Voyage" contain images of richness, quietness, and pleasure—the three qualities mentioned in the **refrain.** Get together with a partner and review the sensory-detail chart you created in your **READER'S NOTEBOOK**. Use the chart to determine which stanza evokes which quality. What sensory details helped you make your determinations?

3. What does "Invitation to the Voyage" suggest about love?

> **THINK ABOUT**
> - the speaker's reference to his beloved's "treacherous eyes" in the first stanza
> - the speaker's reference to "the soul's loneliness" in the second stanza

4. In "The Albatross," the speaker compares the bird to the poet in society. Through this comparison, what do you think Baudelaire is expressing about both poetry and society?

5. How would you describe the **mood** of each poem?

Extend Interpretations

6. Comparing Texts Compare the view of women and love in "Invitation to the Voyage" with that presented in Heine's "The Lorelei." What words do you think the speakers of these poems would use to describe the characters of the women they love?

7. Critic's Corner Some critics maintain that the poems in *The Flowers of Evil* contain both Romantic and classical elements. Refer to the chart on page 878, then identify some of these elements in the two poems you've read.

8. Connect to Life Think again about your answer to question 4. Do you think poets and artists are seen or treated differently today? Explain your opinion.

LITERARY ANALYSIS: SOUND DEVICES

Like many poets, Baudelaire used **sound devices** to help emphasize certain words, create moods, and unify works. Such devices include **repetition** (repeated words and phrases), **alliteration** (the repetition of consonant sounds at the beginnings of words), and **rhyme scheme** (the pattern of rhymes at the ends of lines). Notice the use of repetition (*how*), alliteration (*p*), and rhyme scheme (*weak/beak* and *inept/step*) in the following lines from "The Albatross":

This voyager, __how comical and weak!__
Once handsome, __how unseemly and inept!__
One sailor __pokes__ a __pipe__ into his __beak,__
Another mocks the flier's hobbled __step.__

Paired Activity With a partner, identify at least one example of repetition, alliteration, and rhyme scheme in each of the poems. Then discuss how the sound devices affect the mood and meaning of the poems.

SYMBOL A **symbol** is a person, a place, an object, or an activity that stands for something beyond itself. In "The Albatross," for example, the sea bird is used as a symbol representing the poet. Several other symbols are named in the last stanza of the poem, including "archers," "stormy day," and "wings." Reread the poem and then discuss with a group of classmates what these symbols might represent.

ARTHUR RIMBAUD

The SLEEPER in the VALLEY

AUTUMN SONG

PAUL VERLAINE

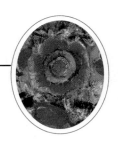

Paul Verlaine
1844–1896
Arthur Rimbaud
1854–1891

Baudelaire's Followers Arthur Rimbaud (răm-bō′) and Paul Verlaine (vĕr-lān′) belonged to the Symbolist movement in France. The Symbolists were a group of writers and artists who used symbols to evoke ideas and emotions. The leaders of the Symbolist movement were chiefly inspired by Charles Baudelaire, whose exploration of controversial subject matter contrasted with Romanticism's emphasis on nature and emotion.

A Troubled Friendship When Rimbaud and Verlaine met in 1871, the two poets began an intense friendship. After a couple of years, however, the pair had a violent falling-out. Verlaine shot his friend, wounding him in the wrist. As a result, Verlaine was given a two-year jail sentence.

After their split, Rimbaud published a collection of poetry called *A Season in Hell.* Unfortunately, the book was not well received. Deeply hurt and disillusioned with literature, Rimbaud apparently never wrote another poem. He was only 19 years old.

Verlaine, on the other hand, achieved some success with the publication of *Wisdom* in 1880. He also published Rimbaud's *Illuminations* in 1886, which made its author famous.

Although Rimbaud and Verlaine sought to break away from the emotion and self-indulgence (as they regarded it) of Romantic poetry, their work is not entirely free of Romantic elements. The view of nature expressed in the poems you are about to read, for example, has much in common with the Romantic view. As you read the poems, ask yourself:

1. *How do the images of nature in the poems compare with those you've observed in Romantic poetry?*
2. *What other Romantic elements do the poems contain?*
3. *What symbols can you identify? Whom or what do they represent?*

The Sleeper in the Valley

Arthur Rimbaud

Translated by William Jay Smith

This is the green wherein a river chants
Whose waters on the grasses wildly toss
Its silver tatters, where proud sunlight slants
Within a valley thick with beams like moss.

5 A youthful soldier, mouth agape, head bare,
And nape where fresh blue water cresses drain
Sleeps stretched in grass, beneath the cloud, where
On abundant green the light descends like rain.

His feet on iris roots, smiling perhaps
10 As would some tiny sickly child, he naps.
O nature, he is cold: make warm his bed.

This quiver of perfume will not break his rest;
In sun he sleeps, his hand on quiet breast.
Upon one side there are two spots of red.

5 agape: wide open.

6 nape: the back of the neck.

Autumn Song

Paul Verlaine

Translated by **Louis Simpson**

*V*iolins complain
Of autumn again,
⠀⠀⠀They sob and moan.
And my heartstrings ache
5⠀Like the song they make,
⠀⠀⠀A monotone.

Suffocating, drowned,
And hollowly, sound
⠀⠀⠀The midnight chimes.
10⠀Then the days return
I knew, and I mourn
⠀⠀⠀For bygone times.

And I fall and drift
With the winds that lift
15⠀⠀⠀My heavy grief.
Here and there they blow,
And I rise and go
⠀⠀⠀Like a dead leaf.

6 monotone: sound or song with
one note.

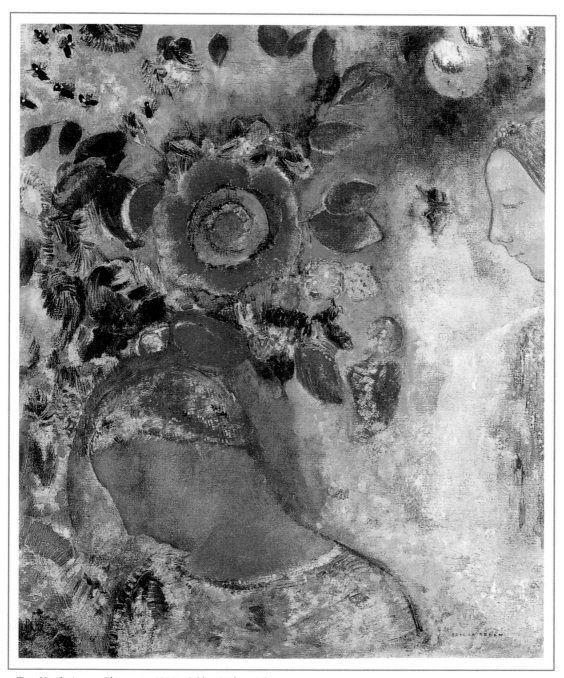

Two Heads Among Flowers (c. 1905), Odilon Redon. Oil on canvas,
24″ × 19¾″. Private collection, Cambridge, Massachusetts.

HUMANITIES CONNECTION Odilon Redon was one of the greatest
French Symbolist artists. Like the writers of the Symbolist movement,
Redon tried to give form to his thoughts, emotions, and dreams.

The Age of Romanticism

Reflect and Assess

What did you learn about Romanticism from reading the selections in Unit Six, Part 1? Did the literature stimulate your own imagination and feelings? Use the following options to help you explore what you have learned.

Detail of *On Board a Sailing Ship* (1818–1819), Caspar David Friedrich. Oil on canvas, 71 cm × 56 cm. The Hermitage, St. Petersburg, Russia/Giraudon/Art Resource, New York.

Reflecting on the Literature

Romantic Subjects Life, death, love, and nature are favorite subjects of Romantic writers. Think about how the literature in this part of the book deals with these subjects. Then choose four selections: one that reveals a perception about life, one that comments on death, one that makes an observation about love, and one that conveys an impression of nature. State what the selection suggests about the subject, and indicate whether you agree with the writer's ideas.

Reviewing Literary Concepts

Figurative Language Romantic poets used figurative language, such as similes, metaphors, and personification, to create effects, emphasize ideas, and evoke emotions. Look back over the literature in this part of the book and choose an example of a simile, a metaphor, and personification. Identify the type of figurative language used, and explain its effect.

Building Your Portfolio

Writing Options Review the various Writing Options you completed for the lessons in this part of the book. Which piece would you consider reading aloud to your classmates? Add the assignment to your **Presentation Portfolio**, and include a note with ideas on the speaking rate, tone, facial expressions, and gestures you might use for an effective delivery.

Self ASSESSMENT

READER'S NOTEBOOK

The following list contains concepts and terms that you encountered as you learned about European Romantic writers. Copy the list on a separate piece of paper. Then work with a small group of classmates to write a sentence describing or defining each word or term. If you don't remember the meaning of a term, review the lesson in which it appeared or consult the **Glossary of Literary Terms** (page R91).

the natural world	imagery
Faust	"Russia 1812"
setting	sound devices
literary ballad	Symbolists

Setting GOALS

Look over the list of books in **Extend Your Reading** on the following page. Select one of the books and read it. After you finish reading, write a paragraph or two identifying some of the Romantic elements in the book.

Extend Your *Reading*

Les Misérables

VICTOR HUGO; LEE FAHNESTOCK, TRANS.

Set in Paris during the political upheaval of the 1820s and 1830s, Hugo's romantic epic tells the story of the outcast Jean Valjean. After being unjustly imprisoned, Valjean struggles to make a new life for himself. His dreams of a normal life, however, are threatened by the police inspector Javert, who is bent on tracking down Valjean and returning him to prison. This sweeping tale is at once a suspenseful thriller and a perceptive study of human nature. Hugo brings his characters to vibrant life as they fight—and die—for their personal and political freedom.

The Sorrows of Young Werther

JOHANN WOLFGANG VON GOETHE; MICHAEL HULSE, TRANS.

This novella created such a stir when it was published that it became fashionable for young German men to imitate Werther's manner of dress, as well as his most desperate acts. The young hero's hopeless passion for the unattainable Charlotte is described largely through letters written to a friend. In the best Romantic tradition, Werther meditates on beauty, art, and nature as he longs for his beloved. With its tragic ending, the story paints a heart-rending portrait of those who become obsessed with love.

And Even *More . . .*

Books

Songs of Love & Grief HEINRICH HEINE; WALTER W. ARNDT, TRANS.
Full of anguish and irony, the German songs in this collection convey the Romantic spirit through Heine's use of mood and imagery.

The Grasmere Journals DOROTHY WORDSWORTH; PAMELA WOOF, ED.
Observations on walks, weather, friends, and poetry provide an intimate glimpse into life at Dove Cottage for Dorothy Wordsworth and her famous brother.

Other Media

Napoleon
From his humble upbringing in Corsica to his glorious days as emperor, Napoleon's life holds the viewer spellbound in this dramatic four-hour documentary. PBS Home Video. (VIDEOCASSETTE)

The Hunchback of Notre Dame
In this 1939 film—widely considered the best screen adaptation of Hugo's classic novel—Charles Laughton creates a touching portrait of the hunchback Quasimodo. Turner Home Video. (VIDEOCASSETTE, DVD)

Frankenstein

MARY WOLLSTONECRAFT SHELLEY

This gothic novel about the monster created by Dr. Frankenstein has little in common with the popular horror films of the same name. The monster of Shelley's masterpiece is a tragic hero whose very human search for love and companionship contrasts with the actions of the scientist who has overthrown the laws of nature.

The Emergence of Realism

Why It Matters

About 1840, a movement called **realism** began taking hold in literature and the arts in Europe. The realists wanted their art to show life as it was really lived. To some extent, they were reacting to the idealism and sentimentality of the Romantics. But they were also concerned with the new realities brought about by the Industrial Revolution.

For Links to Realism, click on:

HUMANITIES
CLASSZONE.COM

1 Ideas, Discoveries, and Inventions The Industrial Revolution sparked an explosion of scientific discoveries and inventions—electric power, the light bulb, X-rays, anesthesia, and aspirin, just to name a few. In England, Charles Darwin's theory of evolution ignited a storm of controversy. The invention of photography, with its real-life images, had a direct influence on the realists.

UNITED KINGDOM OF GREAT BRITAIN AND IRELAND

London **1**

NETHERLANDS   *Berlin* .

English Channel

BELGIUM   **2**

Paris

3   **4**

GERMANY

Vienna

FRANCE   *Bern*
SWITZERLAND   **AUSTRIA–HU**

ATLANTIC OCEAN

PORTUGAL

ITALY   **BOSNIA–HERZEGOVINA**

Lisbon .   *Madrid* .   SER

SPAIN   *Rome* .   MONTENEGRO

Adriatic Sea

Mediterranean Sea

4 Railroad Networks Railroads were essential to the industrialization of Europe. Trains carried manufactured goods from the factories to the cities and brought raw materials into the factories. Rail lines also cut travel time across long distances. By connecting isolated areas of Germany, railroads united the nation and contributed to its rise as an industrial giant.

2 Rich and Poor The Industrial Revolution brought great advances but had a dark side as well. **Middle-class** businessmen profited from the growth of **factories.** But those in the **working class,** which included women and children as well as men, were overworked and underpaid. They toiled 12 to 14 hours a day, sometimes under dangerous conditions, as shown in this 1875 painting of a German steel factory.

R U S S I A

Black Sea

Attempts at Reform Injustice and harsh conditions in the 19th century prompted calls for reform. Some of the resulting efforts met with success. **Suffrage**, or the right to vote, was extended to men outside the aristocracy in Britain, France, and Germany. The British abolished slavery throughout their empire in 1833, and the French freed the slaves in their colonies in 1848. Russian serfs—peasants who labored in the fields under conditions very similar to those of slavery—gained their freedom in 1861.

O M A N   E M P I R E

3 Monument to Progress The French government had the Eiffel Tower built to celebrate the 100th anniversary of the French Revolution and to symbolize industrial progress. Though light and airy in appearance, the 984-foot iron tower is extremely strong. Considered an engineering marvel when it opened in 1889, the Eiffel Tower still amazes tourists visiting Paris.

0	250	500 miles
0	250	500 kilometers

Historical Highlights

The second half of the 19th century in Europe has been called the Second Industrial Revolution, the Age of Imperialism, and the Age of Reform. Regardless of the title, the events of this time period had a global impact and far-reaching consequences. We are still feeling the effects today.

Children living in poverty in London, about 1860

Development of Nations

One of the ideas unleashed by the French Revolution was **nationalism,** the belief that people who share a common culture and history make up a nation. After Napoleon's defeat at Waterloo in 1815, three major empires remained on the European continent: the Austrian Empire, the Russian Empire, and the Ottoman Empire. In the mid-1800s, ethnic groups within these empires demanded nationhood and democratic reforms in an outburst of revolts. During this same period, independent German and Italian states also unified into two nations. But the eventual cost of German unification was dictatorship and two world wars. Though tattered, the Russian Empire remained intact until the Communist revolution of 1917.

Flags of Germany and Italy, 1848

Imperialism

To improve their economies, the industrialized nations of Europe began to look for new sources of raw materials. The Europeans descended on resource-rich Africa and expanded their holdings in Asia. By the turn of the century, they had carved up Africa into colonies, with Britain and France having the largest share. In addition, the British controlled India and joined the French, Dutch, and Americans in dividing Southeast Asia. This process of taking over and then dominating other countries is called **imperialism.** Its effect in the 19th century, for the most part, was to increase the wealth of the imperialist nations at the expense of the colonies.

Queen Victoria

Mass Production

The Industrial Revolution changed the nature of work. What used to be made by hand could now be produced faster and cheaper by machines. The operation of the machines was divided among the factory workers, who each specialized in some detail of the production process. Mass production of textiles and pottery made inexpensive clothes and dishes available for the first time.

Mass production, and industrialization in general, benefited people of the middle class more than anyone else. Many factory owners, merchants, and bankers got rich. The standard of living also rose for shop owners, accountants, factory managers, architects, office workers, and carpenters.

Need for Reform

The working class lived and worked under terrible conditions. Children as young as five often had to work. The British Parliament did pass some laws restricting the age of child laborers and limiting the workday in factories to ten hours for women and children. Workers also formed unions to negotiate for improved working conditions. One successful reform effort was the spread of **free public education** in most European nations by the late 1800s.

As more men won voting rights, women started organizing to get the vote as well, especially in Britain. Despite women's protests, however, no European countries gave women the vote at this time.

Scientific Breakthroughs

The amazing scientific and technological achievements of the 19th century would eventually revolutionize people's lives. Experiments with electricity introduced a new kind of power and made electric inventions such as the light bulb possible. The full impact of such inventions as the telephone and the automobile wouldn't be felt until the next century, but discoveries in the field of biology had more immediate effects. Working in the mid-1800s, the French chemist **Louis Pasteur** discovered that bacteria cause disease. This discovery led not only to the development of pasteurization, a process for killing harmful bacteria in milk and other foods, but also to the use of germ-killing antiseptics in hospitals. New vaccines for many serious diseases, such as typhoid fever, were also developed during this time.

Louis Pasteur

History to Literature

EVENT IN HISTORY

Czar Alexander II frees Russian serfs.

The Industrial Revolution causes changes among the social classes.

EVENT IN LITERATURE

Novelist Leo Tolstoy portrays peasant life in *Anna Karenina*.

Short-story writer Guy de Maupassant examines moral conflicts of the French middle class and peasantry.

Arts and Culture

With people crowding into industrial cities and more voices calling for reform, troubling social and political realities became impossible to ignore. Artists and intellectuals faced the issues directly. Scientists, meanwhile, tried to better understand the physical world.

Visual Arts

When a 19th-century French painter examined early photographs, he boldly declared: "From today painting is dead." He was wrong. The camera's factual accuracy actually inspired realist art.

Realism began in France with the work of three painters: Gustave Courbet, Honoré Daumier, and Camille Corot. Courbet headed the movement away from idealized Romantic painting and toward an accurate record of contemporary life. One of his greatest works, *The Stone Breakers,* shows two men laboring in a stark rural landscape. The raw honesty of Courbet's painting shocked the French art world, who expected to see pictures of smiling peasants in clean clothes. Daumier, a painter and sculptor, also drew cartoons. These cartoons ruthlessly satirized French politicians, business-men, lawyers, and other rising middle-class professionals who took themselves too seriously. Corot was a landscape painter whose small, naturalistic sketches captured the basic truth the realists aimed for.

The French sculptor Auguste Rodin can be considered a realist, although he wasn't officially part of the movement. His portrayals of the human figure were so lifelike they caused scandals.

Rodin's *The Thinker*

Literature

Realist writers also rebelled against Romanticism as too emotional and idealistic. Influenced by the real-world emphasis of photography and science, they took a hard look at the people around them—such as peasants, coal miners, clerks, middle-class wives, orphans, and thieves.

Novels were particularly well suited to examining contem-porary life because they could show development over time and extensive interaction among characters. Many great novelists were writing during this period: Honoré de Balzac, Gustave Flaubert, and Émile Zola in France; George Eliot in Britain; and Leo Tolstoy and Fyodor Dostoyevsky in Russia. Guy de Maupassant and Anton Chekhov mastered the **short story** form to capture brief but meaningful glimpses into characters' everyday lives.

Drama also underwent drastic changes. Scandinavian playwrights August Strindberg and Henrik Ibsen produced brutally insightful plays about class conflict, women's roles, and middle-class hypocrisy. Such issues unsettled middle-class audiences, who were used to happy endings in the theater.

Karl Marx

Political Thought

One response to the economic inequities and harsh working conditions of the 19th century was *The Communist Manifesto*, a pamphlet published in 1848 by **Karl Marx** and his friend **Friedrich Engels.** In it, Marx argued that the workers, whom he called the proletariat, should overthrow the greedy business owners, or capitalists, and take control of the industries. The ultimate goal Marx set was the establishment of justice and equality in a classless society with no private property and no government. Marx's ideas led to major revolutions in the 20th century before declining in influence late in the century.

Scientific Theories

The development of science and scientific theory, with its focus on the physical world, was one of the important influences on realism in the 19th century. One of the most controversial scientific ideas was proposed in 1859 by **Charles Darwin** in his book *On the Origin of Species.* Darwin theorized that the great diversity of species on earth resulted from what he called natural selection: as members of a species compete for food, only those whose traits give them an advantage will survive long enough to reproduce. These survivors in turn pass the traits on to their offspring. Darwin's theory came to be known as the theory of evolution.

During the same period, an Austrian botanist, **Gregor Mendel,** was exploring the question of how physical traits are passed on from one generation to another. In his work, Mendel studied the differences in pea plants. He theorized that traits are passed from the parent plants to their descendants in paired hereditary units, now called **genes.** Mendel's experiments established the laws of heredity and began the science of genetics.

Connect to Today

In the 21st century, we are still living with ideas and perspectives generated in the latter half of the 19th century.

- Realism has had a direct influence on film. This influence is seen in the use of realistic settings and true-to-life portrayals of people and situations.

- Although weakened, communism is still a revolutionary force in parts of Latin America, Africa, and Southeast Asia.

- Refinements of Mendel's original discoveries have made further genetic research possible. Breakthroughs are leading to new treatments for diseases such as cancer.

Time Line

A.D. 1   PRESENT

EVENTS IN EUROPEAN REALISM

1840	1850	1860

1829–1847 Honoré de Balzac writes *The Human Comedy,* a collection of novels and short stories about French society

1848 Karl Marx and Friedrich Engels publish *The Communist Manifesto*

1849 French painter Gustave Courbet ushers in the realist movement in art

1857 Publication in France of Gustave Flaubert's realistic novel *Madame Bovary*

1859 Charles Darwin publishes *On the Origin of Species by Means of Natural Selection*

1860 George Eliot's novel *The Mill on the Floss* analyzes the impact of mechanization on a rural family

1865–1869 Publication of Leo Tolstoy's great novel *War and Peace,* set during the Napoleonic Wars

1866 Fyodor Dostoyevsky publishes *Crime and Punishment*, a novel about the moral and psychological consequences of a murder

EVENTS IN EUROPEAN HISTORY

1840	1850	1860

1842 Ether is first used as an anesthesia in surgery

1847 British Parliament passes a law limiting the workday to ten hours for women and children

1848 Revolutions erupt in France, Italy, Austrian Empire, and Germany

1850s Early development of modern photography

1852 Napoleon III proclaims himself emperor of France

1858 Completion of the first successful trans-Atlantic telegraph cable

1860 In London, Florence Nightingale opens the first school to train nurses

1860s French chemist Louis Pasteur discovers the germ origin of disease and invents the process of pasteurization

1860s Liberal reforms in Britain and France extend voting rights and allow more freedom of the press

1861 Alexander II frees Russia's 20 million serfs

EVENTS IN WORLD HISTORY

1840	1850	1860

1842 Hong Kong given to Britain after the Chinese are defeated in the First Opium War (1839–1842)

1844 Samuel Morse sends first long-distance telegraph message between Baltimore and Washington, D.C.

1853 Commodore Matthew Perry opens U.S. relations with Japan

1867 The last Japanese shogun steps down, ending over 700 years of military rule

1867 Mexican reformer Benito Juárez reelected president after defeating the French

1869 Elizabeth Cady Stanton and Susan B. Anthony found the National Woman Suffrage Association

Susan B. Anthony dollar

1875–1877 Tolstoy's novel *Anna Karenina* examines romantic love and family life

1879 Henrik Ibsen produces *A Doll's House,* which shocks audiences with its uncompromising portrayal of a middle-class marriage

1880 French sculptor Auguste Rodin casts the bronze statue *The Thinker*

1880–1890 Guy de Maupassant writes most of his famous short stories

1885 Émile Zola uses an extreme form of realism called naturalism in his novel *Germinal,* about a coal miners' strike

1892–1898 Anton Chekhov writes short stories about Russian peasants, intellectuals, and factory owners

1896 Chekhov's play *The Seagull* is performed in St. Petersburg

1871 Otto von Bismarck completes the unification of the German Empire, making it one of the most powerful European nations

1871 Trade-Union Act of 1871 makes British labor unions legal

1884 Invention of the automatic machine gun

1885 German engineer Karl Benz invents the first automobile with an internal combustion engine

1895 Discovery of X-rays

1895 Guglielmo Marconi invents wireless telegraphy, or radio

1898 French physicists Marie and Pierre Curie discover radium

1899 The medicinal value of aspirin is recognized

1873–1874 The Ashanti of West Africa fight a war with the British

1876 Alexander Graham Bell patents the telephone

1877 Thomas A. Edison invents the phonograph

1879 Edison invents the light bulb

1884 Congo Basin in Africa falls under control of King Leopold II of Belgium

1883 Brooklyn Bridge completed in New York

1887 Land of Zulus in southern Africa falls under British control

1888 Easy-to-use Kodak box camera first produced

1893 Laos becomes part of French Indochina, which already included Vietnam and Cambodia

1894–1895 Japan and China fight over Korea in the Sino-Japanese War

1898 With help from the United States, Cuba gains independence from Spain

1899–1902 Boers—descendants of Dutch and German settlers in southern Africa—rebel against British rule

Realism

Realism refers to the accurate—or realistic—portrayal of life in literature and the arts. In fiction and drama, the term is often used to describe works that deal with the daily struggles and disappointments of ordinary people.

Realism was a product of the new realities that took hold in Europe in the 19th century. These included the ups and downs of democratic reform, the social and economic changes brought about by the Industrial Revolution, and new methods of observation opened up by science and photography.

Characteristics of Realism

Realist writers were a varied group, but they shared certain ideas about their writing.

A New Kind of Subject Matter Romantic writers of the early 19th century had glorified the individual. Realists weren't looking for glory or grandeur or heroism, however; they were looking for an understanding of their time. And understanding for them lay in the facts of an individual's life. Therefore, the characters they wrote about were often peasants, businessmen, and housewives. Upper-class characters were portrayed with faults rather than idealized. Instead of creating elaborate plots, the realists focused on everyday occurrences. The result was a closer examination of character, especially as it related to moral behavior.

A New View The realistic writers took the view that life doesn't always work out for the best. As a result, their works often did not have happy endings.

A Change in Method The writing of the Romantics tended to be emotional and highly imaginative. The realists, however, adopted the scientific method of detached observation and recording of facts to describe their characters. Much of their writing has the clarity and precision of a black-and-white photograph. To better understand how these two methods differ, compare the following descriptions:

Major Writers of Realism

Honoré de Balzac
1799–1850
- *Old Goriot*
- *Cousin Bette*

George Eliot
1819–1880
- *Adam Bede*
- *The Mill on the Floss*

Gustave Flaubert
1821–1880
- *Madame Bovary*
- *Sentimental Education*

Leo Tolstoy
1828–1910
- *War and Peace*
- *Anna Karenina*

Henrik Ibsen
1828–1906
- *An Enemy of the People*
- *The Wild Duck*

Guy de Maupassant
1850–1893
- "The Necklace"
- "Two Friends"

Anton Chekhov
1860–1904
- "Gooseberries"
- *The Cherry Orchard*

> They were no longer living men and troops,
> but a dream drifting in a fog, a mystery,
> mourners parading under the black sky.
> —Victor Hugo, "Russia 1812"

> Then a wagon passed at the jerky trot of a nag, shaking strangely,
> two men seated side by side and a woman in the bottom of the
> vehicle, the latter holding on to the sides to lessen the hard jolts.
> —Guy de Maupassant, "A Piece of String"

YOUR TURN Which passage is more emotional and which is more informational? Describe the kinds of details the writers use to achieve such opposite effects.

Realism in Drama

There was little serious drama being written in the mid-19th century. Most productions were light entertainment—melodrama and farce. When realism burst upon the stage with Ibsen's *A Doll's House* in 1879, it brought energy and creativity back to the theater. Although attacked by critics and the public alike, Ibsen had opened the door to a new era in drama.

Beyond Realism to Naturalism

Naturalism developed out of realism and was more concerned with plot than character. Coming later in the century and heavily influenced by new scientific theories, naturalists portrayed human life as determined by outside forces of heredity and environment. In the works of the French novelist Émile Zola, the foremost writer of the naturalistic movement, the characters are trapped in a world they can't control; only the strong survive.

Three Ways of Looking at a Sparrow

To understand the different points of view of a Romantic, a realist, and a naturalist, consider how each might write about a sparrow.

Romantic Point of View:

> Behold the lowly sparrow—
> So small, so innocent!
> Such gifts that nature brings
> Make me glad to see
> tomorrow.

Realist Point of View:

The sparrow searches for food. He hops around, looking under leaves, picking at twigs, cocking his head to listen for danger.

Naturalist Point of View:

The sparrow is quick, but not quick enough. The hawk swoops, capturing its prey in its strong talons.

Strategies for Reading: Realistic Literature

1. Pay attention to concrete details for information about characters and setting.

2. Notice the values of the characters and whether any characters have conflicting values.

3. Determine what causes a character's downfall.

4. Look for truths about ordinary life.

5. **Monitor** your reading strategies and modify them when your understanding breaks down. Remember to use the strategies for active reading: **predict, visualize, connect, question, clarify,** and **evaluate.**

A Piece of STRING

Guy de Maupassant

Guy de Maupassant
1850–1893

The Well-Crafted Story

Guy de Maupassant (gē′ də mō-pă-sän′) is considered by many to be the greatest French short story writer, and he has been an inspiration to generations of European and American writers. He always presented his characters objectively—not judging them but simply recording their actions. And with remarkable precision, he focused on the exact gesture, feeling, or word that defined each character's personality. The effect was to make his perfectly crafted stories seem, in his words, "to be pieces of human existence torn from reality."

Unremarkable Beginnings Maupassant was born to upper-middle-class parents in the French province of Normandy. After high school, he served in the French army and studied law in Paris. In his early 20s, he took a clerical position with the French government, a job he disliked but apparently succeeded at.

Becoming a Writer When he was a young writer, Maupassant's inspiration and guide was Gustave Flaubert (gōō-stäv′ flō-bâr′), the author of *Madame Bovary* (1857) and other realistic works. Flaubert was a friend of Maupassant's mother and invited the young Maupassant regularly to his house in Paris for lunch and conversation. At these lunches, Flaubert discussed writing style and technique, and he critiqued pieces that Maupassant had written. Flaubert also introduced the young writer to leading literary figures, such as the naturalistic writer Émile Zola (ā-mēl′ zō-lä′). Though Maupassant disliked being labeled, he did develop a naturalistic tone in his own work.

Rich and Famous Maupassant's first short story, "Ball of Fat," appeared in 1880 in an anthology compiled by Émile Zola. This story, considered to be one of his best, made Maupassant famous. Over the next 10 years, he produced an enormous amount of work: more than 300 short stories, six novels, three travel books, and one book of poetry. He sold his stories to magazines and newspapers, published them in collections, and eventually grew quite rich. But Maupassant enjoyed his success only a short time before his deteriorating health overcame him. He died in an asylum from complications of an incurable disease a month before his 43rd birthday.

Other Works
"The Necklace"
"The Jewelry"
"The Umbrella"
A Life
Good Friend

Build Background

Maupassant's Norman Roots "A Piece of String" is set in Normandy, a farming region of northern France. A beautiful area of low hills, fields, and hedges, Normandy is famous for its butter, cheeses, and apple cider. When Maupassant was a boy, he had many opportunities to observe Norman peasants. These small-scale farmers generally led difficult lives. Peasant families consumed most of what they raised and sold the rest in open-air markets. Some traditional Norman markets are still in existence today.

Maupassant once wrote of Normandy:

> *I love this land, and I love to live in it because my roots are here, those deep and delicate roots that attach a man to the land where his fathers were born and died, attach him to the thoughts men think, the food they eat, the words they use, their peasant drawl; to the odors that rise from the soil and the villages and linger in the very air itself.*

Despite this deep attachment, he avoided sentimentality in his Norman stories. The peasants he portrays are sometimes stingy, coarse, and cruel. Maupassant wanted his fiction to be true to life, even if that life was unpleasant. Like other realist writers associated with naturalism, he was especially interested in how people's social circumstances and natural drives can determine their fates.

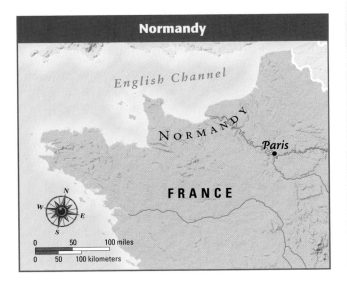

Normandy

English Channel

NORMANDY

Paris

FRANCE

```
0        50        100 miles
0     50     100 kilometers
```

Connect to Your Life

How do you think you would feel if you were falsely accused of wrongdoing? How might such an experience affect the way you interact with people? Share your thoughts with the class.

Focus Your Reading

LITERARY ANALYSIS: CHARACTERIZATION IN REALISM

Characterization refers to the techniques used to develop characters. Writers can portray characters through physical description, characters' words and actions, the words and actions of other characters, and direct commentary by the narrator.

Because realist writers are concerned with examination of character, characterization is an important element in their works. As you read this story, notice which techniques Maupassant uses.

ACTIVE READING: INTERPRETING DETAILS

"A Piece of String" is filled with **details** that help create a realistic impression of the people and way of life described in the story. Interpreting these details will help you draw conclusions about Maupassant's characters and themes.

📖 **READER'S NOTEBOOK** As you read the story, create cluster diagrams like the one below to help you organize descriptive details. Create one diagram for the setting; another for the main character, Maître Hauchecome; and a third for the peasants in general.

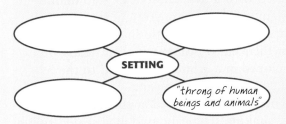

SETTING

"throng of human beings and animals"

WORDS TO KNOW **Vocabulary Preview**

credence	impassive	indignation
din	indifferent	

A Piece of String

Guy de Maupassant

Along all the roads around Goderville[1] the peasants and their wives were coming toward the burgh[2] because it was market day. The men were proceeding with slow steps, the whole body bent forward at each movement of their long twisted legs, deformed by their hard work, by the weight on the plow which, at the same time, raised the left shoulder and swerved the figure, by the reaping of the wheat which made the knees spread to make a firm "purchase,"[3] by all the slow and painful labors of the country. Their blouses, blue, "stiff-starched," shining as if varnished, ornamented with a little design in white at the neck and wrists, puffed about their bony bodies, seemed like balloons ready to carry them off. From each of them a head, two arms, and two feet protruded.

Some led a cow or a calf by a cord, and their wives, walking behind the animal, whipped its haunches with a leafy branch to hasten its progress. They carried large baskets on their arms from which, in some cases, chickens and, in others, ducks thrust out their heads. And they walked with a quicker, livelier step than their husbands. Their spare straight figures were wrapped in a scanty little shawl, pinned over their flat bosoms, and their heads were enveloped in a white cloth glued to the hair and surmounted[4] by a cap.

Then a wagon passed at the jerky trot of a nag, shaking strangely, two men seated side by side and a woman in the bottom of the vehicle, the latter holding on to the sides to lessen the hard jolts.

In the public square of Goderville there was a crowd, a throng of human beings and animals mixed together. The horns of the cattle, the tall hats with long nap of the rich peasant, and the headgear of the peasant women rose above the surface of the assembly. And the clamorous, shrill, screaming voices made a continuous and savage <u>din</u> which sometimes was dominated by the robust lungs of some countryman's laugh, or the long lowing of a cow tied to the wall of a house.

All that smacked of the stable, the dairy and the dirt heap, hay and sweat, giving forth that unpleasant odor, human and animal, peculiar to the people of the field.

Maître Hauchecome, of Breaute,[5] had just arrived at Goderville, and he was directing his steps toward the public square, when he perceived upon the ground a little piece of string. Maître Hauchecome, economical like a true Norman, thought that everything useful ought to be picked up, and he bent painfully, for he suffered from rheumatism. He took the bit of thin cord from the ground and began to roll it carefully when he noticed Maître Malandain,[6] the

---

1. **Goderville** (gôd-ər-vēl′): a town in Normandy (a region of northwest France), about ten miles inland from the English Channel.
2. **burgh** (bûrg): town.
3. **purchase:** a position of the body necessary in order to move a large weight.
4. **surmounted** (sər-moun′tĭd): topped.
5. **Maître Hauchecome** (mě′trə ōsh-côm′), **of Breaute** (brōt): *Maître* is French for *master*. Breaute, like most of the other places mentioned in the story, was a small farming community within a few miles of Goderville.
6. **Malandain** (mä-län-dăn′).

WORDS TO KNOW

din (dĭn) *n.* a loud, confused noise

> **" . . . they were on bad terms, being both good haters. Maître Hauchecome was seized with a sort of shame to be seen thus by his enemy, picking a bit of string out of the dirt."**

harness-maker, on the threshold of his door, looking at him. They had heretofore had business together on the subject of a halter,[7] and they were on bad terms, being both good haters. Maître Hauchecome was seized with a sort of shame to be seen thus by his enemy, picking a bit of string out of the dirt. He concealed his "find" quickly under his blouse, then in his trousers' pocket; then he pretended to be still looking on the ground for something which he did not find, and he went toward the market, his head forward, bent double by his pains.

He was soon lost in the noisy and slowly moving crowd, which was busy with interminable bargainings. The peasants milked, went and came, perplexed, always in fear of being cheated, not daring to decide, watching the vender's eye, ever trying to find the trick in the man and the flaw in the beast.

The women, having placed their great baskets at their feet, had taken out the poultry which lay upon the ground, tied together by the feet, with terrified eyes and scarlet crests.

They heard offers, stated their prices with a dry air and impassive face, or perhaps, suddenly deciding on some proposed reduction, shouted to the customer who was slowly going away: "All right, Maître Authirne,[8] I'll give it to you for that."

Then little by little the square was deserted, and the Angelus[9] ringing at noon, those who had stayed too long, scattered to their shops.

At Jourdain's[10] the great room was full of people eating, as the big court was full of vehicles of all kinds, carts, gigs, wagons, dump carts, yellow with dirt, mended and patched, raising their shafts to the sky like two arms, or perhaps with their shafts in the ground and their backs in the air.

Just opposite the diners seated at the table, the immense fireplace, filled with bright flames, cast a lively heat on the backs of the row on the right. Three spits were turning on which were chickens, pigeons, and legs of mutton; and an appetizing odor of roast beef and gravy dripping over the nicely browned skin rose from the hearth, increased the jovialness,[11] and made everybody's mouth water.

All the aristocracy of the plow[12] ate there, at Maître Jourdain's, tavern keeper and horse dealer, a rascal who had money.

The dishes were passed and emptied, as were the jugs of yellow cider. Everyone told his affairs, his purchases, and sales. They discussed the crops. The weather was favorable for the green things but not for the wheat.

---

7. **halter:** strap with a noose by which horses are tied or led.

8. **Maître Authirne** (ō-tûrn′).

9. **Angelus** (ăn′jə-ləs): the church bells that ring to announce the Angelus prayer, which is recited at morning, noon, and evening.

10. **Jourdain's** (zhoor-dănz′).

11. **jovialness:** state of heartiness and good cheer.

12. **aristocracy of the plow:** humorous way of referring to farmers.

WORDS TO KNOW

impassive (ĭm-păs′ĭv) *adj.* revealing no emotion; expressionless

Suddenly the drum beat in the court, before the house. Everybody rose except a few <u>indifferent</u> persons, and ran to the door, or to the windows, their mouths still full and napkins in their hands.

After the public crier had ceased his drum-beating, he called out in a jerky voice, speaking his phrases irregularly:

"It is hereby made known to the inhabitants of Goderville, and in general to all persons present at the market, that there was lost this morning, on the road to Benzeville,[13] between nine and ten o'clock, a black leather pocketbook containing five hundred francs[14] and some business papers. The finder is requested to return same with all haste to the mayor's office or to Maître Fortune Houlbreque of Manneville,[15] there will be twenty francs reward."

Then the man went away. The heavy roll of the drum and the crier's voice were again heard at a distance.

Then they began to talk of this event, discussing the chances that Maître Houlbreque had of finding or not finding his pocketbook.

And the meal concluded. They were finishing their coffee when a chief of the gendarmes[16] appeared upon the threshold.

He inquired:

"Is Maître Hauchecome, of Breaute, here?"

Maître Hauchecome, seated at the other end of the table, replied:

"Here I am."

And the officer resumed:

"Maître Hauchecome, will you have the goodness to accompany me to the mayor's office? The mayor would like to talk to you."

The peasant, surprised and disturbed, swallowed at a draft his tiny glass of brandy, rose, and, even more bent than in the morning, for the first steps after each rest were specially difficult, set out, repeating: "Here I am, here I am."

The mayor was awaiting him, seated on an armchair. He was the notary[17] of the vicinity, a stout, serious man, with pompous[18] phrases.

"Maître Hauchecome," said he, "you were seen this morning to pick up, on the road to Benzeville, the pocketbook lost by Maître Houlbreque, of Manneville."

The countryman, astounded, looked at the mayor, already terrified, by this suspicion resting on him without his knowing why.

"Me? Me? Me pick up the pocketbook?"

"Yes, you, yourself."

"Word of honor, I never heard of it."

"But you were seen."

"I was seen, me? Who says he saw me?"

"Monsieur Malandain, the harness-maker."

The old man remembered, understood, and flushed with anger.

"Ah, he saw me, the clodhopper, he saw me pick up this string, here, M'sieu'[19] the Mayor." And rummaging in his pocket he drew out the little piece of string.

But the mayor, incredulous, shook his head.

"You will not make me believe, Maître Hauchecome, that Monsieur Malandain, who is a man worthy of <u>credence</u>, mistook this cord for a pocketbook."

The peasant, furious, lifted his hand, spat at one side to attest[20] his honor, repeating:

"It is nevertheless the truth of the good God, the sacred truth, M'sieu' the Mayor. I repeat it

---

13. **Benzeville** (băNz-vēl′).

14. **francs:** The franc is the basic monetary unit of France.

15. **Fortune Houlbreque** (fôr-tün′ ōōl-brĕk′) **of Manneville** (män-vēl′).

16. **gendarmes** (zhän′därmz′): armed police.

17. **notary:** a person with the legal authority to witness and certify documents.

18. **pompous** (pŏm′pəs): full of self-importance.

19. **M'sieu'** (mə-syœ′): a shortened form of *monsieur*, French for *mister* or *sir*.

20. **attest** (ə-tĕst′): testify to; affirm.

The Peasants of Flagey Returning from the Fair, Ornans (1850–1855), Gustave Courbet.
Musée des Beaux-Arts, Besançon, France/Giraudon/Art Resource, New York.

HUMANITIES CONNECTION This painting caused a stir in the Paris art world of the 1850s because it showed peasants as they really were rather than in some romanticized, sentimental way. The critics did not think that Courbet's realistic portrayal of such people was fitting in a work of art.

on my soul and my salvation."

The mayor resumed:

"After picking up the object, you stood like a stilt, looking a long while in the mud to see if any piece of money had fallen out."

The good, old man choked with indignation and fear.

"How anyone can tell—how anyone can tell—such lies to take away an honest man's reputation! How can anyone—"

There was no use in his protesting, nobody believed him. He was confronted with Monsieur Malandain, who repeated and maintained his affirmation.[21] They abused each other for an hour. At his own request, Maître Hauchecome was searched, nothing was found on him.

Finally the mayor, very much perplexed, discharged him with the warning that he would consult the public prosecutor and ask for further orders.

The news had spread. As he left the mayor's office, the old man was surrounded and questioned with a serious or bantering[22] curiosity, in which there was no indignation. He began to tell the story of the string. No one believed him. They laughed at him.

He went along, stopping his friends, beginning endlessly his statement and his protestations, showing his pockets turned inside out, to prove that he had nothing.

They said:

"Old rascal, get out!"

And he grew angry, becoming exasperated, hot, and distressed at not being believed, not knowing what to do and always repeating himself.

Night came. He must depart. He started on his way with three neighbors to whom he pointed out the place where he had picked up the bit of string; and all along the road he spoke of his adventure.

In the evening he took a turn in the village of Breaute, in order to tell it to everybody. He only met with incredulity.[23]

It made him ill at night.

The next day about one o'clock in the afternoon, Marius Paumelle, a hired man in the employ of Maître Breton, husbandman at Ymanville,[24] returned the pocketbook and its contents to Maître Houlbreque of Manneville.

This man claimed to have found the object in the road; but not knowing how to read, he had carried it to the house and given it to his employer.

The news spread through the neighborhood. Maître Hauchecome was informed of it. He immediately went the circuit and began to recount his story completed by the happy climax. He was in triumph.

"What grieved me so much was not the thing itself, as the lying. There is nothing so shameful as to be placed under a cloud on account of a lie."

He talked of his adventure all day long, he told it on the highway to people who were passing by, in the wineshop to people who were drinking there, and to persons coming out of church the following Sunday. He stopped strangers to tell them about it. He was calm now, and yet something disturbed him without his knowing exactly what it was. People had the air of joking while they listened. They did not seem convinced. He seemed to feel that remarks were being made behind his back.

On Tuesday of the next week he went to the market at Goderville, urged solely by the necessity he felt of discussing the case.

Malandain, standing at his door, began to laugh on seeing him pass. Why?

---

21. **affirmation:** something declared to be true.

22. **bantering:** spoken in a teasing or playful way.

23. **incredulity** (ĭn′krĭ-dōō′lĭ-tē): unwillingness or inability to believe; doubt.

24. **Paumelle** (pō-mĕl′) . . . **Breton** (brĕ-tôN′), **husbandman at Ymanville** (ü-män-vēl′): *Husbandman* means "farmer."

WORDS TO KNOW

indignation (ĭn′dĭg-nā′shən) *n.* anger caused by something mean or unjust

> **"A piece of string, a piece of string—look—here it is, M'sieu' the Mayor."**

He approached a farmer from Crequetot,[25] who did not let him finish, and giving him a thump in the stomach said to his face:

"You big rascal."

Then he turned his back on him.

Maître Hauchecome was confused, why was he called a big rascal?

When he was seated at the table, in Jourdain's tavern he commenced to explain "the affair."

A horse dealer from Monvilliers[26] called to him:

"Come, come, old sharper, that's an old trick; I know all about your piece of string!"

Hauchecome stammered:

"But since the pocketbook was found."

But the other man replied:

"Shut up, papa, there is one that finds, and there is one that reports. At any rate you are mixed with it."

The peasant stood choking. He understood. They accused him of having had the pocketbook returned by a confederate, by an accomplice.

He tried to protest. All the table began to laugh.

He could not finish his dinner and went away, in the midst of jeers.

He went home ashamed and indignant, choking with anger and confusion, the more dejected that he was capable with his Norman cunning of doing what they had accused him of, and even boasting of it as of a good turn. His innocence to him, in a confused way, was impossible to prove, as his sharpness was known. And he was stricken to the heart by the injustice of the suspicion.

Then he began to recount the adventures again, prolonging his history every day, adding each time, new reasons, more energetic protestations, more solemn oaths which he imagined and prepared in his hours of solitude, his whole mind given up to the story of the string. He was believed so much the less as his defense was more complicated and his arguing more subtle.

"Those are lying excuses," they said behind his back.

He felt it, consumed his heart over it, and wore himself out with useless efforts. He wasted away before their very eyes.

The wags[27] now made him tell about the string to amuse them, as they make a soldier who has been on a campaign tell about his battles. His mind, touched to the depth, began to weaken.

Toward the end of December he took to his bed.

He died in the first days of January, and in the delirium of his death struggles he kept claiming his innocence, reiterating:

"A piece of string, a piece of string—look—here it is, M'sieu' the Mayor." ❖

---

25. **Crequetot** (krĕk-tō′).

26. **Monvilliers** (môN-vē-yĕr′). Also spelled *Montivilliers*.

27. **wags:** people who like to make jokes.

Thinking through the LITERATURE

Connect to the Literature

1. What Do You Think?
What were your thoughts about Maître Hauchecome as you finished reading this story?

Comprehension Check
• Why is Maître Hauchecome accused of taking the pocketbook?
• What happens after the pocketbook is returned by someone else?

Think Critically

2. ACTIVE READING: INTERPRETING DETAILS Get together with a classmate and compare the cluster diagrams you created in your 📖 **READER'S NOTEBOOK**. How would you describe the attitude of the other peasants toward Maître Hauchecome's suspected misbehavior? What details give you this impression?

3. In your opinion, to what extent is Maître Hauchecome responsible for his downfall?

 THINK ABOUT
{ • his relationship with Maître Malandain
• his dealings with people in the past
• his behavior when no one believes him innocent

4. Why do you think Maître Hauchecome tries so hard to persuade others of his innocence?

5. Maître Hauchecome tries to camouflage his stinginess when he takes the piece of string, but ironically his action leads to a much more serious misunderstanding. What message does Maupassant seem to be giving about how much control human beings have over their lives?

Extend Interpretations

6. What If? Suppose that Maître Hauchecome had not kept insisting that he was innocent. How might the story have turned out differently?

7. Critic's Corner The great Russian novelist Leo Tolstoy wrote that Maupassant had the "gift of seeing what others have not seen." Based on your reading of "A Piece of String," do you agree with Tolstoy? Why or why not?

8. Connect to Life The peasants of Goderville made assumptions about Maître Hauchecome based on their experience with him. Their assumptions led to the wrong conclusion, however. What does this story have to say about making judgments concerning other people's behavior?

LITERARY ANALYSIS: CHARACTERIZATION IN REALISM

Characterization refers to the techniques that writers use to develop characters. There are four basic methods of characterization:
• A writer may describe the physical appearance of the character.
• A character's nature may be revealed through his or her own speech, thoughts, feelings, or actions.
• The speech, thoughts, feelings, or actions of other characters in response to a character can be used to develop that character.
• The narrator can make direct comments about the character's nature.

Most realistic writers use the fourth method sparingly, preferring to let readers form their own judgments of characters. However, sometimes the best way to convey information is through direct comments. For example, Maupassant's narrator tells us that Maître Hauchecome is "economical like a true Norman."

Cooperative Learning Activity
With a group of classmates, identify four details in the story that reveal aspects of Maître Hauchecome's character. For each detail, identify the characterization method that Maupassant used and what the detail reveals about the character. Fill in a chart such as the one below.

Detail	Characterization Method	What It Reveals
peasants' bent backs	description of physical appearance	the difficulty of their lives

Choices & CHALLENGES

Writing Options

1. Speech for the Defense
Suppose that Maître Hauchecome does go to trial for theft. Imagine that you are a provincial official assigned to defend him at the trial. Write your opening speech in which you explain how Maître Hauchecome himself is the victim in this situation.

2. Cause-and-Effect Essay
Write a brief essay in which you discuss the chain of events that leads to Maître Hauchecome's death. Before you begin, create a diagram showing how events are related. In your essay, present causes and effects in a logical order. Keep in mind that an action can have more than one effect and an outcome can have several causes. Place your draft in your **Working Portfolio.**

Writing Handbook
See pages R32–R33: Cause and Effect.

Activities & Explorations

1. Character Interviews
With two other classmates, stage interviews with Maître Hauchecome and Monsieur Malandain, first with one and then with the other. Ask each to explain his relationship with the other person and the reasons for his own behavior. Then bring the two together and have the rest of the class offer brief opinions about how they might have changed their behavior.
~ SPEAKING AND LISTENING

Communications Handbook
See page R52: Conducting Interviews.

2. Town Banner
Create a design for a banner to be displayed in the public square of Goderville. The design should reflect some interesting aspect of town life, such as wares for sale at the market or a lively gathering at the Jourdain tavern. Base your design on specific details in the story. ~ ART

Inquiry & Research

Peasant Life Find out more about the lives of the peasants in 19th-century France. Explore such topics as whether they were educated, what kinds of work they did, whether they owned land, what their family structure was like, and what their celebrations and festivals were. Summarize what you learn in a written report.

Vocabulary in Action

EXERCISE: RELATED WORDS Write the letter of the word in each set that has a meaning different from the other words in the set.

1. (a) laughter, (b) fun, (c) amusement, (d) indignation
2. (a) impassive, (b) handicapped, (c) expressionless, (d) emotionless
3. (a) din, (b) den, (c) noise, (d) blare
4. (a) contrasting, (b) unmatching, (c) unalike, (d) indifferent
5. (a) faith, (b) credence, (c) belief, (d) church

1828–1910

OVERVIEW

Life and Times	954
How Much Land Does a Man Need? ~ FICTION	958
Letter from Leo Tolstoy to N. A. Nekrasov	974
What Men Live By ~ FICTION	976
from **Sonya Tolstoy's Diary**	993
The Author's Style	996
Author Study Project	997

"The hero of my tale . . . is Truth."

Leo Tolstoy

The Great Novelist and Moralist

Leo Tolstoy has been hailed not only as one of the world's greatest novelists but also as a great thinker and reformer. The author of the epic novel War and Peace *was a man of contradictions, however. Tolstoy was a wealthy aristocrat who dressed as a peasant, a famous novelist who later condemned his great works, and a stern moralist who ultimately failed to live up to his own high standards.*

A HAPPY CHILDHOOD Tolstoy did not have the easiest childhood, but he remembered it as being a happy time. Both of his parents died before he was 10 years old, and in the next few years he lost his grandmother and an aunt, both of whom had cared for him. The love and care of another aunt and in particular a favorite cousin gave him abundant security and affection, however. As a boy, he was like a ray of light, said his sister, full of passion and charm.

Tolstoy was educated at home by private tutors and then attended a university for a few years without obtaining a degree.

1828
Born
August 28
at his
family's
estate

1844
**Enters
Kazan
University**

HIS LIFE
HIS TIMES

1825   1830   1835   1840

1825
**Decembrist
uprising
crushed by
czar's troops**

1837
**Victoria becomes
Queen of the
United Kingdom
of Great Britain
and Ireland**

At age 19, he inherited his family's 2,000-acre estate, Yasnaya Polyana, about 130 miles from Moscow. His weakness for gambling and late-night parties never seemed to hurt the handsome young count, for he always had plenty of money. In 1851, Tolstoy joined his brother in the army and later was wounded and almost killed by an exploding bomb.

THE MAKING OF A WRITER Tolstoy's writing began with his diary, which he started when he was 18 and continued, with interruptions, throughout his long life. His first published work, *Childhood*, was a short fictionalized account of his "blissful" early life and won him instant success. Over the next years, he published several stories based on his experiences in the army.

In his early fiction, Tolstoy refined his considerable talent by experimenting with narrative techniques and characterization. As a realist, he was careful to portray authentic characters and situations. And although he made radical changes in his life, Tolstoy never abandoned his realist principles. "An artist is an artist because he sees things not as he wishes to see them but as they really are," he declared in 1894. Truth was always his hero.

Tolstoy wearing the uniform of an artillery officer

LITERARY *Contributions*

Short Fiction Tolstoy began and ended his career writing short stories and short novels. In between, he completed his two great novels. Here are some titles from each period of Tolstoy's career.

Early Works
Childhood
"The Raid"
"Sevastopol in May"

Later Works
"Where Love Is, God Is"
"What Men Live By"
"How Much Land Does a Man Need?"
The Death of Ivan Ilyich

Novels Tolstoy's genius can be seen in his two masterpieces:
War and Peace
Anna Karenina

Nonfiction Tolstoy wrote a number of works detailing his beliefs.
A Confession
What I Believe
The Kingdom of God Is Within You
What Is Art?

1851 Fights in Caucasus with Russian army

1852 *Childhood* first published

1859 Starts school for children of serfs on his family estate

1862 Marries Sofya (Sonya) Bers

1869 Publishes *War and Peace*

1875–1877 Publishes *Anna Karenina*

1878 Spiritual crisis

1845   1850   1855   1860   1865   1870   1875

1853–1856 Russia loses to France, England, and Turkey in Crimean War; Sevastopol under siege for 11 months.

1861 Czar Alexander II frees Russian serfs, who can now own land.

1863 Abraham Lincoln issues Emancipation Proclamation.

1866 Publication of Fyodor Dostoyevsky's *Crime and Punishment*

1872 Karl Marx's *Das Kapital* translated into Russian

THE GREAT AUTHOR In 1862, the 34-year-old Tolstoy, a literary hero by this time, married Sofya Bers, the spirited 18-year-old daughter of family friends. Sonya, as she was called, provided Tolstoy with the large family he wanted and the support he needed as a writer. For the next 15 years, Tolstoy prospered emotionally and creatively. He worked steadily on the 3,000-page manuscript of *War and Peace,* which was published in its final form in 1869 to international acclaim. The novel's epic sweep allowed Tolstoy to explore ideas and to exercise his profound powers of observation and analysis. He narrowed his focus to family life in his next novel, *Anna Karenina,* which begins with the often-quoted line "Happy families are all alike; every unhappy family is unhappy in its own way."

THE CRISIS After the publication of *Anna Karenina,* Tolstoy experienced a moral and spiritual crisis that completely changed the direction of his life. He had achieved everything: happiness, wealth, fame, and artistic excellence. Even his health was good. But for Tolstoy, it wasn't enough. What's the point of all this success, he asked himself, if I'm just going to die anyway? At first, he turned to the Russian Orthodox Church to find an answer to the meaning of life. However, he soon rejected the church and all institutions as corrupt and gradually developed a personal faith based on the teachings of Jesus. Tolstoy analyzed his crisis in *A Confession* and explained his newfound purpose in life: to locate the goodness within and promote that goodness in the world.

Tolstoy tried to practice what he preached. He worked among the poor, helped with famine relief, and simplified his life so as not to participate in what he considered an evil social, economic, and political system. He also became a pacifist, a vegetarian, and a strong supporter of nonviolent civil disobedience.

To continue promoting his vision of the kingdom of God, Tolstoy wrote essays and religious tracts explaining his ideas. These writings disturbed many people. The government considered him a dangerous threat, and most of his nonfiction was banned in Russia. Tolstoy's most controversial work was his last novel, *Resurrection,* in which he attacked both the church and the state. The church responded by excommunicating him.

1882
Completes *A Confession,* which is banned in Russia; publishes "What Men Live By"

1886
Publishes *The Death of Ivan Ilyich* and "How Much Land Does a Man Need?"

1891–1892
Organizes famine relief

1901
Excommunicated from Russian Orthodox Church; meets Anton Chekhov

1910
Dies at Astapovo railway station

1880   **1885**   **1890**   **1895**   **1900**   **1905**   **1910**

1881
Terrorist group assassinates Alexander II.

1898
Anton Chekhov's *The Seagull* performed in Moscow

1899
Sigmund Freud publishes *The Interpretation of Dreams.*

1905–1906
Revolutionary strikes, peasant uprisings, mutinies, and violent clashes disrupt Russian Empire.

1914
Beginning of World War I

A CHANGE IN STYLE In the fiction Tolstoy wrote after 1880, his style as well as his purpose for writing had changed. He dismissed his two great novels as frivolous and appealing only to the upper classes. Art for him now had to be simple and direct; it had to be accessible to the common people; and it had to have a clear moral. Tolstoy's new style and purpose drove all of his later fiction, including "How Much Land Does a Man Need?" (page 958) and "What Men Live By" (page 976).

Tolstoy writing

UNHAPPY ENDING Although Tolstoy attracted devoted followers after his conversion, he alienated most of his family. His son Ilya wrote: "From the fun-loving, lively head of our family he was transformed before our eyes into a stern, accusatory prophet." Tolstoy became increasingly disturbed by the gap between his strict moral values and his comfortable aristocratic life, which his wife wanted to maintain for their children's future.

In a desperate effort to escape the complications of his life, Tolstoy fled his ancestral home in secret on October 28, 1910. A few days later, he lay dying of pneumonia in the stationmaster's house at a railway station. Just a few feet away was a crush of photographers and reporters eager to record the great man's last moments. Surrounded by his closest followers and several of his children, Tolstoy whispered his final words, "To seek, always to seek . . ."

AUTHOR LINK
CLASSZONE.COM

 NetActivities: **Author Exploration**

What's So Great About *War and Peace*?

War and Peace is acclaimed by many modern writers as the world's greatest novel. Set in the years 1805 to 1820, it tells the stories of five aristocratic families during the time of Napoleon's war against Russia. With its vast scope and hundreds of characters, *War and Peace* has everything—heroism and villainy, history and philosophy, innocence and maturity, battle scenes and love stories. And all is woven together in Tolstoy's flawless narrative style—as though life were writing itself, according to one critic.

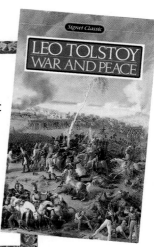

How **Much** Land Does a **Man** Need?

Leo Tolstoy
Translated by Louise and Aylmer Maude

Build Background

Searching for Solutions As a social reformer, Tolstoy strongly supported the freeing of the serfs in 1861. Before that time, Russian serfs were like slaves in that they were considered the property of large landowners, such as Tolstoy himself. After gaining their freedom, some serfs bought land and even grew wealthy, but most remained dirt poor.

Tolstoy felt a deep affection for humble peasants, whose work on the land he thought gave them a deep understanding of life's meaning. He frequently labored alongside the serfs on his own estate and tried to improve their lot through education. But the longer Tolstoy worked among the poor, the more he believed that material solutions—money or land, for instance—were not the answer to society's basic problems, which he considered to be moral rather than economic. One of Tolstoy's most popular and compelling stories, "How Much Land Does a Man Need?" dramatizes these ideas.

Connect to Your Life

"If only I had . . . " Sound familiar? Name one thing you really want and one thing you absolutely need. Discuss with your classmates the difference between the two. Then think about how your life might change if you could get exactly what you want.

Focus Your Reading

LITERARY ANALYSIS: THEME IN FICTION
The **theme** of a short story is its central idea, insight, or observation. Most themes in fiction are not stated directly but must be inferred. For example, the theme of Maupassant's "A Piece of String" might be stated this way: Once a man is accused, people automatically think he's guilty, even if he's later proved innocent.

The title of Tolstoy's story gives a clue to its theme. As you read, think about Tolstoy's answer to the question of need.

ACTIVE READING: DRAWING CONCLUSIONS
Drawing conclusions from details in a story can help you determine the theme. In Tolstoy's story, watch for small things—scraps of dialogue, brief thoughts, and descriptions—that subtly build up to a big revelation at the end.

READER'S NOTEBOOK This story is divided into nine sections. As you read, stop at the end of each section and jot down notes about important details. For example, you might note the dialogue between the two sisters in section I.

An elder sister came to visit her younger sister in the country. The elder was married to a tradesman in town, the younger to a peasant in the village. As the sisters sat over their tea talking, the elder began to boast of the advantages of town life: saying how comfortably they lived there, how well they dressed, what fine clothes her children wore, what good things they ate and drank, and how she went to the theater, promenades, and entertainments.

The younger sister was piqued,[1] and in turn disparaged[2] the life of a tradesman, and stood up for that of a peasant.

"I would not change my way of life for yours," said she. "We may live roughly, but at least we are free from anxiety. You live in better style than we do, but though you often earn more than you need, you are very likely to lose all you have. You know the proverb, 'Loss and gain are brothers twain.'[3] It often happens that people who are wealthy one day are begging their bread the next. Our way is safer. Though a peasant's life is not a fat one, it is a long one. We shall never grow rich, but we shall always have enough to eat."

The elder sister said sneeringly:

"Enough? Yes, if you like to share with the pigs and the calves! What do you know of elegance or manners! However much your goodman may slave, you will die as you are living—on a dung heap—and your children the same."

"Well, what of that?" replied the younger. "Of course our work is rough and coarse. But, on the other hand, it is sure, and we need not bow to any one. But you, in your towns, are surrounded by temptations; today all may be right, but tomorrow the Evil One may tempt your husband with cards, wine, or women, and all will go to ruin. Don't such things happen often enough?"

Pakhom, the master of the house, was lying on the top of the stove[4] and he listened to the women's chatter.

"It is perfectly true," thought he. "Busy as we are from childhood tilling[5] mother earth, we peasants have no time to let any nonsense settle in our heads. Our only trouble is that we haven't land enough. If I had plenty of land, I shouldn't fear the Devil himself!"

The women finished their tea, chatted a while about dress, and then cleared away the tea-things and lay down to sleep.

But the Devil had been sitting behind the stove, and had heard all that was said. He was pleased that the peasant's wife had led her husband into boasting, and that he had said that if he had plenty of land he would not fear the Devil himself.

"All right," thought the Devil. "We will have a tussle. I'll give you land enough; and by means of that land I will get you into my power."

Close to the village there lived a lady, a small landowner who had an estate of about three hundred acres. She had always lived on good terms with the peasants until she engaged as her steward[6] an old soldier, who took to burdening

---

1. **piqued** (pēkt): irritated; angry.
2. **disparaged** (dĭ-spăr′ĭjd): belittled; put down.
3. **twain:** two.
4. **Pakhom** (pä′ĸнōm) . . . **lying on top of the stove:** The stoves and ovens in Russian peasant homes had large tops that were often used for sleeping because they provided extra warmth.
5. **tilling:** plowing land to prepare it for planting.
6. **steward:** a person in charge of the household affairs of a large estate.

Tolstoy in the Field of Labour (1889), after Ilya Yefimovich Repin. Photograph copyright © Gianni Dagli Orti/Corbis.

HUMANITIES CONNECTION Tolstoy came to believe that the peasants' way of life had more truth and value than the aristocracy's. Tolstoy dressed like the peasants and joined them in their work. This painting shows Tolstoy plowing on one of his estates.

the people with fines. However careful Pakhom tried to be, it happened again and again that now a horse of his got among the lady's oats, now a cow strayed into her garden, now his calves found their way into her meadows—and he always had to pay a fine.

Pakhom paid up, but grumbled, and going home in a temper, was rough with his family. All through that summer, Pakhom had much trouble because of this steward, and he was even glad when winter came and the cattle had to be stabled. Though he grudged the fodder⁷ when they

could no longer graze on the pasture-land, at least he was free from anxiety about them.

In the winter the news got about that the lady was going to sell her land and that the keeper of the inn on the high road was bargaining for it. When the peasants heard this they were very much alarmed.

"Well," thought they, "if the innkeeper gets the land, he will worry us with fines worse than the

---

7. **fodder:** food for livestock, such as hay or straw.

lady's steward. We all depend on that estate."

So the peasants went on behalf of their commune,[8] and asked the lady not to sell the land to the innkeeper, offering her a better price for it themselves. The lady agreed to let them have it. Then the peasants tried to arrange for the commune to buy the whole estate, so that it might be held by them all in common. They met twice to discuss it, but could not settle the matter; the Evil One sowed discord among them and they could not agree. So they decided to buy the land individually, each according to his means; and the lady agreed to this plan as she had to the other.

Presently Pakhom heard that a neighbor of his was buying fifty acres, and that the lady had consented to accept one half in cash and to wait a year for the other half. Pakhom felt envious.

"Look at that," thought he, "the land is all being sold, and I shall get none of it." So he spoke to his wife.

"Other people are buying," said he, "and we must also buy twenty acres or so. Life is becoming impossible. That steward is simply crushing us with his fines."

So they put their heads together and considered how they could manage to buy it. They had one hundred rubles[9] laid by. They sold a colt and one half of their bees, hired out one of their sons as a laborer and took his wages in advance; borrowed the rest from a brother-in-law, and so scraped together half the purchase money.

Having done this, Pakhom chose out a farm of forty acres, some of it wooded, and went to the lady to bargain for it. They came to an agreement, and he shook hands with her upon it and paid her a deposit in advance. Then they went to town and signed the deeds; he paying half the price down, and undertaking to pay the remainder within two years.

So now Pakhom had land of his own. He borrowed seed, and sowed it on the land he had bought. The harvest was a good one, and within a year he had managed to pay off his debts both to the lady and to his brother-in-law. So he became a landowner, plowing and sowing his own land, making hay on his own land, cutting his own trees, and feeding his cattle on his own pasture. When he went out to plow his fields, or to look at his growing corn, or at his grass-meadows, his heart would fill with joy. The grass that grew and the flowers that bloomed there seemed to him unlike any that grew elsewhere. Formerly, when he had passed by that land, it had appeared the same as any other land, but now it seemed quite different.

So Pakhom was well-contented, and everything would have been right if the neighboring peasants would only not have trespassed on his corn-fields and meadows. He appealed to them most civilly, but they still went on: now the communal herdsmen would let the village cows stray into his meadows, then horses from the night pasture would get among his corn. Pakhom turned them out again and again, and forgave their owners, and for a long time he forbore to prosecute any one. But at last he lost patience and complained to the district court. He knew it was the peasants' want of land, and no evil intent on their part, that caused the trouble, but he thought:

"I cannot go on overlooking it or they will destroy all I have. They must be taught a lesson."

So he had them up, gave them one lesson, and

---

8. **commune:** in late 19th-century Russia, a local organization of peasants that held land in common for its members. A peasant could also own land individually while still belonging to the commune.

9. **rubles:** The ruble is the basic monetary unit of Russia.

then another, and two or three of the peasants were fined. After a time Pakhom's neighbors began to bear him a grudge for this, and would now and then let their cattle on to his land on purpose. One peasant even got into Pakhom's wood at night and cut down five young lime trees for their bark. Pakhom passing through the wood one day noticed something white. He came nearer and saw the stripped trunks lying on the ground, and close by stood the stumps where the trees had been. Pakhom was furious.

"If he had only cut one here and there it would have been bad enough," thought Pakhom, "but the rascal has actually cut down a whole clump. If I could only find out who did this, I would pay him out."[10]

He racked his brains as to who it could be. Finally he decided: "It must be Simon—no one else could have done it." So he went to Simon's homestead to have a look round, but he found nothing, and only had an angry scene. However, he now felt more certain than ever that Simon had done it, and he lodged a complaint. Simon was summoned. The case was tried, and retried, and at the end of it all Simon was acquitted, there being no evidence against him. Pakhom felt still more aggrieved, and let his anger loose upon the elder and the judges.

"You let thieves grease your palms,"[11] said he. "If you were honest folk yourselves you would not let a thief go free."

So Pakhom quarreled with the judges and with his neighbors. Threats to burn his building began to be uttered. So though Pakhom had more land, his place in the commune was much worse than before.

About this time a rumor got about that many people were moving to new parts.

"There's no need for me to leave my land," thought Pakhom. "But some of the others might leave our village and then there would be more room for us. I would take over their land myself and make my estate a bit bigger. I could then live

"I WOULD TAKE OVER THEIR LAND MYSELF AND MAKE MY ESTATE A BIT BIGGER."

more at ease. As it is, I am still too cramped to be comfortable."

One day Pakhom was sitting at home when a peasant, passing through the village, happened to call in. He was allowed to stay the night, and supper was given him. Pakhom had a talk with this peasant and asked him where he came from. The stranger answered that he came from beyond the Volga,[12] where he had been working. One word led to another, and the man went on to say that many people were settling in those parts. He told how some people from his village had settled there. They had joined the commune, and had had twenty-five acres per man granted them. The land was so good, he said, that the rye sown on it grew as high as a horse, and so thick that five cuts of a sickle made a sheaf. One peasant, he said, had brought nothing with him but his bare hands, and now he had six horses and two cows of his own.

---

10. **pay him out:** get even with him.

11. **grease your palms:** bribe you.

12. **Volga:** The longest river in Russia, the Volga flows from north of Moscow to the Caspian Sea.

Pakhom's heart kindled with desire. He thought:

"Why should I suffer in this narrow hole, if one can live so well elsewhere? I will sell my land and my homestead here, and with the money I will start afresh over there and get everything new. In this crowded place one is always having trouble. But I must first go and find out all about it myself."

Towards summer he got ready and started. He went down the Volga on a steamer to Samara,[13] then walked another three hundred miles on foot, and at last reached the place. It was just as the stranger had said. The peasants had plenty of land: every man had twenty-five acres of communal land given him for his use, and any one who had money could buy, besides, at two shillings an acre as much good freehold land[14] as he wanted.

Having found out all he wished to know, Pakhom returned home as autumn came on, and began selling off his belongings. He sold his land at a profit, sold his homestead and all his cattle, and withdrew from membership of the commune. He only waited till the spring, and then started with his family for the new settlement.

IV

As soon as Pakhom and his family reached their new abode, he applied for admission into the commune of a large village. He stood treat[15] to the elders and obtained the necessary documents. Five shares of communal land were given him for his own and his sons' use: that is to say—125 acres (not all together, but in different fields) besides the use of the communal pasture. Pakhom put up the buildings he needed, and bought cattle. Of the communal land alone he had three times as much as at his former home, and the land was good corn-land. He was ten times better off than he had been. He had plenty of arable[16] land and pasturage, and could keep as many head of cattle as he liked.

At first, in the bustle of building and settling down, Pakhom was pleased with it all, but when he got used to it he began to think that even here he had not enough land. The first year, he sowed wheat on his share of the communal land and had a good crop. He wanted to go on sowing wheat, but had not enough communal land for the purpose, and what he had already used was not available; for in those parts wheat is only sown on virgin soil or on fallow[17] land. It is sown for one or two years, and then the land lies fallow till it is again overgrown with prairie grass. There were many who wanted such land and there was not enough for all; so that people quarreled about it. Those who were better off wanted it for growing wheat, and those who were poor wanted it to let to dealers, so that they might raise money to pay their taxes. Pakhom wanted to sow more wheat, so he rented land from a dealer for a year. He sowed much wheat and had a fine crop, but the land was too far from the village—the wheat had to be carted more than ten miles. After a time Pakhom noticed that some peasant-dealers were living on separate farms and were growing wealthy; and he thought:

"If I were to buy some freehold land and have a homestead on it, it would be a different thing altogether. Then it would all be nice and compact."

The question of buying freehold land recurred to him again and again.

---

13. **Samara** (sə-mâr′ə): a city in southern Russia, on the Volga River.
14. **freehold land:** land held for life with the right to pass it along to one's heirs.
15. **stood treat:** paid for the cost of drinks or entertainment.
16. **arable** (ăr′ə-bəl): fit for plowing and planting.
17. **fallow:** plowed but left unplanted during a growing season.

He went on in the same way for three years, renting land and sowing wheat. The seasons turned out well and the crops were good, so that he began to lay money by. He might have gone on living contentedly, but he grew tired of having to rent other people's land every year, and having to scramble for it. Wherever there was good land to be had, the peasants would rush for it and it was taken up at once, so that unless you were sharp about it you got none. It happened in the third year that he and a dealer together rented a piece of pasture land from some peasants; and they had already plowed it up, when there was some dispute and the peasants went to law about it, and things fell out so that the labor was all lost.

"If it were my own land," thought Pakhom, "I should be independent, and there would not be all this unpleasantness."

So Pakhom began looking out for land which he could buy; and he came across a peasant who had bought thirteen hundred acres, but having got into difficulties was willing to sell again cheap. Pakhom bargained and haggled with him, and at last they settled the price at 1,500 rubles, part in cash and part to be paid later. They had all but clinched the matter when a passing dealer happened to stop at Pakhom's one day to get a feed for his horses. He drank tea with Pakhom and they had a talk. The dealer said that he was just returning from the land of the Bashkirs,[18] far away, where he had bought thirteen thousand acres of land, all for 1,000 rubles. Pakhom questioned him further, and the tradesman said:

"All one need do is to make friends with the chiefs. I gave away about one hundred rubles worth of silk robes and carpets, besides a case of tea, and I gave wine to those who would drink it; and I got the land for less than a penny an acre." And he showed Pakhom the title-deeds, saying:

"The land lies near a river, and the whole prairie is virgin soil."

Pakhom plied him with questions, and the tradesman said:

"There is more land there than you could cover if you walked a year, and it all belongs to the Bashkirs. They are as simple as sheep, and land can be got almost for nothing."

"There now," thought Pakhom, "with my one thousand rubles, why should I get only thirteen hundred acres, and saddle myself with a debt besides? If I take it out there, I can get more than ten times as much for the money."

Pakhom inquired how to get to the place, and as soon as the tradesman had left him, he prepared to go there himself. He left his wife to look after the homestead, and started on his journey taking his man with him. They stopped at a town on their way and bought a case of tea, some wine, and other presents, as the tradesman had advised. On and on they went until they had gone more than three hundred miles, and on the seventh day they came to a place where the Bashkirs had pitched their tents. It was all just as the tradesman had said. The people lived on the steppes,[19] by a river, in felt-covered tents. They neither tilled the ground, nor ate bread. Their cattle and horses grazed in herds on the steppe. The colts were tethered[20] behind the tents, and the mares were driven to them twice a day. The mares were milked, and from the milk kumiss[21] was made. It was the women who prepared kumiss, and they also made cheese. As far as the

---

18. **Bashkirs** (băsh-kîrz'): a group of people of Asiatic origin who lived in southwestern Russia.

19. **steppes** (stĕps): vast semidry, grass-covered plains.

20. **tethered** (tĕth'ərd): tied up with a rope or chain.

21. **kumiss** (kōō-mĭs'): an intoxicating beverage made from mare's or camel's milk.

The Harvest, Paul Serusier. Musée des Beaux-Arts, Nantes, France.
Photograph copyright © Giraudon/Art Resource, New York.

"HOW CAN I TAKE AS MUCH AS I LIKE?" THOUGHT PAKHOM.

men were concerned, drinking kumiss and tea, eating mutton, and playing on their pipes, was all they cared about. They were all stout and merry, and all the summer long they never thought of doing any work. They were quite ignorant, and knew no Russian, but were good-natured enough.

As soon as they saw Pakhom, they came out of their tents and gathered round their visitor. An interpreter was found, and Pakhom told them he had come about some land. The Bashkirs seemed very glad; they took Pakhom and led him into one of the best tents, where they made him sit on some down cushions placed on a carpet, while they sat round him. They gave him some tea and kumiss, and had a sheep killed, and gave him mutton to eat. Pakhom took presents out of his cart and distributed them among the Bashkirs, and divided the tea amongst them. The Bashkirs were delighted. They talked a great deal among themselves, and then told the interpreter to translate.

"They wish to tell you," said the interpreter, "that they like you, and that it is our custom to do all we can to please a guest and to repay him for his gifts. You have given us presents, now tell us which of the things we possess please you best, that we may present them to you."

"What pleases me best here," answered Pakhom, "is your land. Our land is crowded and the soil is exhausted; but you have plenty of land and it is good land. I never saw the like of it."

The interpreter translated. The Bashkirs talked among themselves for a while. Pakhom could not understand what they were saying, but saw that they were much amused and that they shouted and laughed. Then they were silent and looked at Pakhom while the interpreter said:

"They wish me to tell you that in return for your presents they will gladly give you as much land as you want. You have only to point it out with your hand and it is yours."

The Bashkirs talked again for a while and began to dispute. Pakhom asked what they were disputing about, and the interpreter told him that some of them thought they ought to ask their chief about the land and not act in his absence, while others thought there was no need to wait for his return.

While the Bashkirs were disputing, a man in a large fox-fur cap appeared on the scene. They all became silent and rose to their feet. The interpreter said, "This is our chief himself."

Pakhom immediately fetched the best dressing-gown and five pounds of tea, and offered these to the chief. The chief accepted them, and seated himself in the place of honor. The Bashkirs at once began telling him something. The chief listened for a while, then made a sign with his head for them to be silent, and addressing himself to Pakhom, said in Russian:

"Well, let it be so. Choose whatever piece of land you like; we have plenty of it."

"How can I take as much as I like?" thought Pakhom. "I must get a deed to make it secure, or else they may say, 'It is yours,' and afterwards may take it away again."

"Thank you for your kind words," he said aloud. "You have much land, and I only want a little. But I should like to be sure which bit is mine. Could it not be measured and made over to me? Life and death are in God's hands. You good people give it to me, but your children might wish to take it away again."

"You are quite right," said the chief. "We will make it over to you."

"I heard that a dealer had been here," continued Pakhom, "and that you gave him a little land, too, and signed title-deeds to that effect. I should like to have it done in the same way."

The chief understood.

"Yes," replied he, "that can be done quite easily. We have a scribe, and we will go to town with you and have the deed properly sealed."

"And what will be the price?" asked Pakhom.

"Our price is always the same: one thousand rubles a day."

Pakhom did not understand.

"A day? What measure is that? How many acres would that be?"

"We do not know how to reckon it out," said the chief. "We sell it by the day. As much as you can go round on your feet in a day is yours, and the price is one thousand rubles a day."

Pakhom was surprised.

"But in a day you can get round a large tract of land," he said.

The chief laughed.

"It will all be yours!" said he. "But there is one condition: If you don't return on the same day to the spot whence you started, your money is lost."

"But how am I to mark the way that I have gone?"

"Why, we shall go to any spot you like, and stay there. You must start from that spot and make your round, taking a spade with you. Wherever you think necessary, make a mark. At every turning, dig a hole and pile up the turf; then afterwards we will go round with a plow from hole to hole. You may make as large a circuit as you please, but before the sun sets you must return to the place you started from. All the land you cover will be yours."

Pakhom was delighted. It was decided to start early next morning. They talked a while, and after drinking some more kumiss and eating some more mutton, they had tea again, and then the night came on. They gave Pakhom a feather-bed to sleep on, and the Bashkirs dispersed for the night, promising to assemble the next morning at day-break and ride out before sunrise to the appointed spot.

VII

Pakhom lay on the feather-bed, but could not sleep. He kept thinking about the land.

"What a large tract I will mark off!" thought he. "I can easily do thirty-five miles in a day. The days are long now, and within a circuit of thirty-five miles what a lot of land there will be! I will sell the poorer land, or let it to peasants, but I'll pick out the best and farm it. I will buy two ox-teams, and hire two more laborers. About a hundred and fifty acres shall be plow-land, and I will pasture cattle on the rest."

Pakhom lay awake all night, and dozed off only just before dawn. Hardly were his eyes closed when he had a dream. He thought he was lying in that same tent and heard somebody chuckling outside. He wondered who it could be, and rose and went out, and he saw the Bashkir chief sitting in front of the tent holding his sides and rolling about with laughter. Going nearer to the chief, Pakhom asked: "What are you laughing at?" But he saw that it was no longer the chief, but the dealer who had recently stopped at his house and had told him about the land. Just as Pakhom was going to ask, "Have you been here long?" he saw that it was not the dealer, but the peasant who had come up from the Volga, long ago, to Pakhom's old home. Then he saw that it was not the peasant either, but the Devil himself with hoofs and horns, sitting there and chuckling, and before him lay a man barefoot, prostrate on the ground, with only trousers and a shirt on. And Pakhom dreamt that he looked more attentively to see what sort of man it was that was lying there, and he saw that the man was dead, and that it was himself! He awoke horror-struck.

"What things one does dream," thought he.

Looking round he saw through the open door that the dawn was breaking.

"It's time to wake them up," thought he. "We ought to be starting."

He got up, roused his man (who was sleeping in his cart), bade him harness; and went to call the Bashkirs.

"It's time to go to the steppe to measure the land," he said.

The Bashkirs rose and assembled, and the chief came too. Then they began drinking kumiss again, and offered Pakhom some tea, but he would not wait.

"If we are to go, let us go. It is high time," said he.

VIII

The Bashkirs got ready and they all started: some mounted on horses, and some in carts. Pakhom drove in his own small cart with his servant and took a spade with him. When they reached the steppe, the morning red was beginning to kindle. They ascended a hillock (called by the Bashkirs a *shikhan*[22]) and dismounting from their carts and their horses, gathered in one spot. The chief came up to Pakhom and stretching out his arm toward the plain:

"See," said he, "all this, as far as your eye can reach, is ours. You may have any part of it you like."

Pakhom's eyes glistened: it was all virgin soil, as flat as the palm of your hand, as black as the seed of a poppy, and in the hollows different kinds of grasses grew breast high.

The chief took off his fox-fur cap, placed it on the ground and said:

"This will be the mark. Start from here, and return here again. All the land you go round shall be yours."

Pakhom took out his money and put it on the cap. Then he took off his outer coat, remaining in his sleeveless under-coat. He unfastened his girdle[23] and tied it tight below his stomach, put a little bag of bread into the breast of his coat, and tying a flask of water to his girdle, he drew up the tops of his boots, took the spade from his man, and stood ready to start. He considered for some moments which way he had better go—it was tempting everywhere.

"No matter," he concluded, "I will go towards the rising sun."

He turned his face to the east, stretched himself, and waited for the sun to appear above the rim.

"I must lose no time," he thought, "and it is

---

22. *shikhan* (shē′KHän).

23. **girdle:** a belt or sash that fastens around the waist.

Motherland (1886), Apollinarii Mikhailovich Vasnetsov. Oil on canvas.
The State Tretyakov Gallery, Moscow.

easier walking while it is still cool."

The sun's rays had hardly flashed above the horizon, before Pakhom, carrying the spade over his shoulder, went down into the steppe.

Pakhom started walking neither slowly nor quickly. After having gone a thousand yards he stopped, dug a hole, and placed pieces of turf one on another to make it more visible. Then he went on; and now that he had walked off his stiffness he quickened his pace. After a while he dug another hole.

Pakhom looked back. The hillock could be distinctly seen in the sunlight, with the people on it, and the glittering tires of the cart-wheels. At a rough guess Pakhom concluded that he had walked three miles. It was growing warmer; he took off his under-coat, flung it across his shoulder, and went on again. It had grown quite warm now; he looked at the sun, it was time to think of breakfast.

"The first shift is done, but there are four in a day, and it is too soon yet to turn. But I will just take off my boots," said he to himself.

He sat down, took off his boots, stuck them into his girdle, and went on. It was easy walking now.

"I will go on for another three miles," thought he, "and then turn to the left. This spot is so fine, that it would be a pity to lose it. The further one goes, the better the land seems."

He went straight on for a while, and when he looked round, the hillock was scarcely visible and the people on it looked like black ants, and he could just see something glistening there in the sun.

"Ah," thought Pakhom, "I have gone far enough in this direction, it is time to turn. Besides I am in a regular sweat, and very thirsty."

He stopped, dug a large hole, and heaped up pieces of turf. Next he untied his flask, had a drink, and then turned sharply to the left. He went on and on; the grass was high, and it was very hot.

Pakhom began to grow tired: he looked at the sun and saw that it was noon.

"Well," he thought, "I must have a rest."

He sat down, and ate some bread and drank some water; but he did not lie down, thinking that if he did he might fall asleep. After sitting a little while, he went on again. At first he walked easily: the food had strengthened him; but it had become terribly hot and he felt sleepy, still he went on, thinking: "An hour to suffer, a life-time to live."

He went a long way in this direction also, and was about to turn to the left again, when he perceived a damp hollow: "It would be a pity to

"IT WOULD BE A PITY TO LEAVE THAT OUT," HE THOUGHT.

leave that out," he thought. "Flax[24] would do well there." So he went on past the hollow, and dug a hole on the other side of it before he turned the corner. Pakhom looked towards the hillock. The heat made the air hazy: it seemed to be quivering, and through the haze the people on the hillock could scarcely be seen.

"Ah!" thought Pakhom, "I have made the sides too long; I must make this one shorter." And he went along the third side, stepping faster. He looked at the sun: it was nearly half-way to the horizon, and he had not yet done two miles of the third side of the square. He was still ten miles from the goal.

"No," he thought, "though it will make my land lop-sided, I must hurry back in a straight line now. I might go too far, and as it is I have a great deal of land."

So Pakhom hurriedly dug a hole, and turned straight towards the hillock.

IX

Pakhom went straight towards the hillock, but he now walked with difficulty. He was done up with the heat, his bare feet were cut and bruised, and his legs began to fail. He longed to rest, but it was impossible if he meant to get back before sunset. The sun waits for no man, and it was sinking lower and lower.

"Oh dear," he thought, "if only I have not blundered trying for too much! What if I am too late?"

He looked towards the hillock and at the sun. He was still far from his goal, and the sun was already near the rim.

24. **flax:** a plant grown for its seed and for its fine fibers.

Pakhom walked on and on; it was very hard walking but he went quicker and quicker. He pressed on, but was still far from the place. He began running, threw away his coat, his boots, his flask, and his cap, and kept only the spade which he used as a support.

"What shall I do?" he thought again, "I have grasped too much and ruined the whole affair. I can't get there before the sun sets."

And this fear made him still more breathless. Pakhom went on running, his soaking shirt and trousers stuck to him and his mouth was parched. His breast was working like a blacksmith's bellows, his heart was beating like a hammer, and his legs were giving way as if they did not belong to him. Pakhom was seized with terror lest he should die of the strain.

Though afraid of death, he could not stop. "After having run all that way they will call me a fool if I stop now," thought he. And he ran on and on, and drew near and heard the Bashkirs yelling and shouting to him, and their cries inflamed his heart still more. He gathered his last strength and ran on.

The sun was close to the rim, and cloaked in mist looked large, and red as blood. Now, yes now, it was about to set! The sun was quite low, but he was also quite near his aim. Pakhom could already see the people on the hillock waving their arms to hurry him up. He could see the fox-fur cap on the ground and the money on it, and the chief sitting on the ground holding his sides. And Pakhom remembered his dream.

"There is plenty of land," thought he, "but will God let me live on it? I have lost my life, I have lost my life! I shall never reach that spot!"

Pakhom looked at the sun, which had reached the earth: one side of it had already disappeared. With all his remaining strength he rushed on, bending his body forward so that his legs could hardly follow fast enough to keep him from falling. Just as he reached the hillock it suddenly grew dark. He looked up—the sun had already set! He gave a cry: "All my labor has been in vain," thought he, and was about to stop, but he heard the Bashkirs still shouting, and remembered that though to him, from below, the sun seemed to have set, they on the hillock could still see it. He took a long breath and ran up the hillock. It was still light there. He reached the top and saw the cap. Before it sat the chief laughing and holding his sides. Again Pakhom remembered his dream, and he uttered a cry: his legs gave way beneath him, he fell forward and reached the cap with his hands.

"Ah, that's a fine fellow!" exclaimed the chief. "He has gained much land!"

Pakhom's servant came running up and tried to raise him, but he saw that blood was flowing from his mouth. Pakhom was dead!

The Bashkirs clicked their tongues to show their pity.

His servant picked up the spade and dug a grave long enough for Pakhom to lie in, and buried him in it. Six feet from his head to his heels was all he needed. ❖

Connect to the Literature

1. What Do You Think?
Did you feel sorry for Pakhom at the end of the story? Why or why not?

Comprehension Check
- After buying his first farm, what conflicts does Pakhom have?
- Why does he want to buy land from the Bashkirs?
- What happens at the end of the story?

Think Critically

2. What causes Pakhom's downfall?

THINK ABOUT

- how his motivation for wanting land changes in the story
- what part the Devil plays
- what the last line implies about wants and needs

3. ACTIVE READING: DRAWING CONCLUSIONS
Look back at the details you recorded in your READER'S NOTEBOOK. Do you think Pakhom's fate is inevitable? If so, why? If not, at what point could he have avoided what happened?

4. This story is full of **ironies,** surprising twists and reversals that are the opposite of what you'd expect. Name one or two ironies that you found.

5. Contrast the Bashkirs and their way of life with Pakhom and the other peasants. Which group, if any, do you think Tolstoy admires more? Explain your answer.

Extend Interpretations

6. What If? What if Pakhom had succeeded in getting back to the hilltop alive and received his land? Would he have been satisfied? Explain why or why not.

7. Connect to Life How is Tolstoy's 19th-century story about a Russian peasant's drive for land relevant to people living in the United States in the 21st century?

LITERARY ANALYSIS: THEME IN FICTION

In a story, a **theme** is a main idea about life or human nature conveyed by the characters and events. Clues to theme can sometimes be found in a story's title and also in what a reader may already know about the author's life or beliefs.

Cooperative Learning Activity
Get together with a small group of classmates to determine the theme of Tolstoy's story. In your discussion, consider these points:
- what you know about Tolstoy's moral principles
- Pakhom's motivation and behavior
- how the opening dialogue between the sisters relates to Pakhom's fate
- what central issue the title of the story points to
- what is considered wrong or evil in the story

Then write a statement of the theme as your group understands it. Compare your thematic statement with those of other groups.

Writing Options

1. News Coverage Write a news item reporting on Pakhom's death. Try to imitate Tolstoy's own unbiased tone in relating events.

Writing Handbook
See page R29: Narrative Writing.

2. Family Letter Suppose you are Pakhom's wife. Write a letter to your sister after you learn of Pakhom's death, telling her what your life has been like since your earlier conversation. Take into account the difference of opinion that existed between you and your sister at that time.

3. Children's Version Rewrite this story as a tale for kindergarten children. Be sure to simplify the plot and the language and to state the moral clearly at the end.

Activities & Explorations

1. Imaginary Dialogue Imagine that Tolstoy is a character in his story. What might he tell Pakhom to help him, and how might Pakhom respond? Working with a partner, create a dialogue between Tolstoy and Pakhom and perform it for the class. ~ **PERFORMING**

2. Pakhom on Trial In a court of law, Pakhom could not be charged with doing anything illegal. But what about in Tolstoy's moral court? With a group of classmates, create a trial in which Pakhom can be judged morally. Divide your group into a prosecution team and a defense team. After the prosecution team comes up with at least one charge of wrongdoing and the defense team pleads guilty or not guilty to the charge, the two teams should present their cases to the rest of the class, serving as the jury. After the cases have been presented, the jury should discuss the merits of the cases and decide on the verdict and the sentence. ~ **SPEAKING AND LISTENING**

Communication Handbook
See page R49: Critical Thinking.

Inquiry & Research

1. Peasant Communes Research peasant communes in Russia before and after serfdom was abolished in 1861. What was the purpose of the communes, and how were they organized? Was the communal system economically efficient? Report your findings to the class.

RESEARCH STARTER
CLASSZONE.COM

2. Tolstoy and Gandhi Following his spiritual crisis, Tolstoy explored many new ideas and eventually became a pacifist. His views on nonviolence were an important influence on the Indian leader Mohandas Gandhi. Research biographies of Tolstoy, as well as his diaries and letters, to learn more about his views and his relationship to Gandhi. Write a brief summary of what you learn.

Letter from Leo Tolstoy
to N. A. Nekrasov

Translated by R. F. Christian

PREPARING to *Read*

Build Background

When Nikolay Nekrasov, editor of the Russian journal *The Contemporary*, accepted Tolstoy's novel *Childhood* for publication, Tolstoy admitted in his diary that it "made me absurdly happy." This was Tolstoy's first published work, so naturally he was nervous about the public's reaction to it. At first, he didn't even sign his name, only the initials L. N. (for Lev Nikolayevich, his first and middle names). But when he read the piece as it was first printed, Tolstoy was furious at the changes made to the original. In a fit of anger, he dashed off the following letter. He never sent it, however, and later, when he had calmed down, he wrote a milder version.

Starogladovskaya, 18 November 1852

Dear Sir,

I was extremely displeased to read in *The Contemporary*, No. IX, a *story* entitled *A History of My Childhood*, and to recognize it as the *novel Childhood* which I sent to you. I made it the first condition of publication that you should *first evaluate the manuscript and send me what you think it is worth*. This condition has not been fulfilled. The second condition was that nothing should be altered in it. Still less has that condition been fulfilled: you have altered everything, starting with the title. Having read this pathetic, mutilated story with the saddest of feelings, I tried to discover the reasons which prompted the editors to behave so ruthlessly towards it. Either the editors set themselves the task of mutilating this novel as much as possible, or else they entrusted the proof-reading, without any checking, to a completely illiterate employee. The title *Childhood* and the few words of the introduction explained the idea of the work; but the title *A History of My Childhood* contradicts the idea of the work. Who is interested in the history of *my* childhood? . . . It is not possible or necessary to list all the alterations of this sort; but not to speak of the innumerable scraps of meaningless phrases, the misprints, the incorrectly transposed punctuation marks, the bad spelling or the unfortunate word alterations such as *to breathe* for *to pant* (of dogs), or *dropped to the ground in tears* for *fell* (cattle drop), which prove ignorance of the language, I would mention one alteration which is incomprehensible to me. Why has the whole story of Natalya Savishna's love been omitted, a story which depicted her and the old way of life and which imparted significance and humanity to the character? . . . It's incomprehensible. I will only say that when I read the work in print I experienced the unpleasant feeling which a father experiences at the sight of his beloved son whose hair has been cut in an ugly and uneven way by a self-taught hairdresser. "Where did those bare patches and forelocks come from, when he was a fine-looking boy before?" My child was not very handsome to start with, but to make matters worse he has been cropped and mutilated. I can only console myself with the fact that I have the opportunity to publish the whole novel separately under my own name, and to renounce completely the story of *A History of My Childhood*, which by rights belongs not to me, but to an unknown employee of your editorial staff.

I have the honor to be, Sir,
Your most obedient servant,
L.N.

What **Men** Live By

Leo Tolstoy

Translated by Louise and Aylmer Maude

Build Background

A Tale Retold In his later years, Tolstoy was very attracted to folk literature because of its wide appeal and the deep truths it expresses. He felt that this literature spoke to the most basic feelings and yearnings shared by all people. He chose a number of tales and legends from the Russian tradition to retell, using them as a way of conveying his beliefs about the meaning of life. In an article called "On Truth in Art," which was published in 1887, Tolstoy wrote:

> *. . . there are fairy tales, parables, fables, legends, in which marvelous things are described which never happened or ever could happen, and these legends, fairy tales, and fables are true, because they show wherein the will of God has always been, and is, and will be.*

Based on a folk tale Tolstoy heard from a traveling storyteller, "What Men Live By" tells what happens when a poor peasant encounters a stranger in need. In retelling the tale, Tolstoy wanted to retain the simplicity and moral force of the original, while at the same time creating a good short story. As you read it, you can decide whether he succeeded.

Connect to Your Life

Would you give your last dollar to a friend? to a stranger? Discuss the idea of giving with your classmates. Then create a few moral guidelines that people could use when making decisions about giving.

Focus Your Reading

LITERARY ANALYSIS: FORESHADOWING

Foreshadowing is a writer's use of hints or clues to suggest what will happen later. For example, in "How Much Land Does a Man Need?" Pakhom's dream in section VII foreshadows his fate at the end. As you read, look for clues that foreshadow what's to come.

ACTIVE READING: PREDICTING

Predicting what will happen next in a story can alert you to foreshadowing. Keep in mind what you know about Tolstoy, and always use your own ability to figure things out in making your predictions.

READER'S NOTEBOOK "What Men Live By" has many strange events that are not explained until the end of the story. As you come across each event in your reading, write a question about it and then a brief **prediction** that might answer the question. Use a chart like this one to keep track of your predictions.

Question	Prediction
1. Who's the stranger that appears in section I?	**1.**

I

A shoemaker named Simon, who had neither house nor land of his own, lived with his wife and children in a peasant's hut and earned his living by his work. Work was cheap but bread was dear, and what he earned he spent for food. The man and his wife had but one sheep-skin coat between them for winter wear, and even that was worn to tatters, and this was the second year he had been wanting to buy sheep-skins for a new coat. Before winter Simon saved up a little money: a three-ruble note lay hidden in his wife's box, and five rubles and twenty kopeks[1] were owed him by customers in the village.

So one morning he prepared to go to the village to buy the sheep-skins. He put on over his shirt his wife's wadded nankeen[2] jacket, and over that he put his own cloth coat. He took the three-ruble note in his pocket, cut himself a stick to serve as a staff, and started off after breakfast. "I'll collect the five rubles that are due to me," thought he, "add the three I have got, and that will be enough to buy sheep-skins for the winter coat."

He came to the village and called at a peasant's hut, but the man was not at home. The peasant's wife promised that the money should be paid next week, but she would not pay it herself. Then Simon called on another peasant, but this one swore he had no money, and would only pay twenty kopeks which he owed for a pair of boots Simon had mended. Simon then tried to buy the sheep-skins on credit, but the dealer would not trust him.

"Bring your money," said he, "then you may have your pick of the skins. We know what debt-collecting is like."

So all the business the shoemaker did was to get the twenty kopeks for boots he had mended and to take a pair of felt boots a peasant gave him to sole with leather.

Simon felt downhearted. He spent the twenty kopeks on vodka and started homewards without having bought any skins. In the morning he had felt the frost; but now, after drinking the vodka, he felt warm even without a sheep-skin coat. He trudged along, striking his stick on the frozen earth with one hand, swinging the felt boots with the other, and talking to himself.

"I'm quite warm," said he, "though I have no sheep-skin coat. I've had a drop and it runs through my veins. I need no sheep-skins. I go along and don't worry about anything. That's the sort of man I am! What do I care? I can live without sheep-skins. I don't need them. My wife will fret, to be sure. And, true enough, it *is* a shame; one works all day long and then does not get paid. Stop a bit! If you don't bring that money along, sure enough I'll skin you, blessed if I don't. How's that? He pays twenty kopeks at a time! What can I do with twenty kopeks? Drink it—that's all one can do! Hard up, he says he is! So he may be—but what about me? You have house, and cattle, and everything; I've only what I stand up in! You have corn of your own growing, I have to buy every grain. Do what I will, I must spend three rubles every week for bread alone. I come home and find the bread all used up and I have to work out another ruble and a half. So just you pay up what you owe, and no nonsense about it!"

By this time he had nearly reached the shrine[3] at the bend of the road. Looking up, he saw something whitish behind the shrine. The daylight was fading, and the shoemaker peered at the thing without being able to make out what it was. "There was no white stone here before. Can it be an ox? It's not like an ox. It has a head like a man, but it's too white; and what could a man be doing there?"

---

1. **kopeks** (kō′pĕks): A kopek is one hundredth of a ruble.
2. **nankeen:** a sturdy cotton cloth.
3. **shrine:** a place at which devotion is paid to God or a holy person.

The House in Gray (1917), Marc Chagall. Oil on canvas, 68 cm × 74 cm.
Photograph copyright © Museo Thyssen-Bornemisza, Madrid.

He came closer, so that it was clearly visible. To his surprise it really was a man, alive or dead, sitting naked, leaning motionless against the shrine. Terror seized the shoemaker, and he thought, "Some one has killed him, stripped him, and left him here. If I meddle I shall surely get into trouble."

So the shoemaker went on. He passed in front of the shrine so that he could not see the man. When he had gone some way he looked back, and saw that the man was no longer leaning against the shrine but was moving as if looking towards him. The shoemaker felt more frightened than before, and thought, "Shall I go back to him or shall I go on? If I go near him something dreadful may happen. Who knows who the fellow is? He has not come here for any good. If I go near him he may jump up and throttle me, and there will be no getting away. Or if not, he'd still be a burden on one's hands. What could I do with a naked man? I couldn't give him my last clothes. Heaven only help me to get away!"

So the shoemaker hurried on, leaving the shrine behind him—when suddenly his conscience smote him and he stopped in the road.

"What are you doing, Simon?" said he to

himself. "The man may be dying of want, and you slip past afraid. Have you grown so rich as to be afraid of robbers? Ah, Simon, shame on you!"

So he turned back and went up to the man.

II

Simon approached the stranger, looked at him and saw that he was a young man, fit, with no bruises on his body, but evidently freezing and frightened, and he sat there leaning back without looking up at Simon, as if too faint to lift his eyes. Simon went close to him and then the man seemed to wake up. Turning his head, he opened his eyes and looked into Simon's face. That one look was enough to make Simon fond of the man. He threw the felt boots on the ground, undid his sash, laid it on the boots, and took off his cloth coat.

"It's not a time for talking," said he. "Come, put this coat on at once!" And Simon took the man by the elbows and helped him to rise. As he stood there, Simon saw that his body was clean and in good condition, his hands and feet shapely, and his face good and kind. He threw his coat over the man's shoulders, but the latter could not find the sleeves. Simon guided his arms into them, and drawing the coat on well, wrapped it closely about him, tying the sash round the man's waist.

Simon even took off his cap to put it on the man's head, but then his own head felt cold and he thought: "I'm quite bald, while he has long curly hair." So he put his cap on his own head again. "It will be better to give him something for his feet," thought he; and he made the man sit down and helped him to put on the felt boots, saying, "There, friend, now move about and warm yourself. Other matters can be settled later on. Can you walk?"

The man stood up and looked kindly at Simon but could not say a word.

"Why don't you speak?" said Simon. "It's too cold to stay here, we must be getting home. There now, take my stick, and if you're feeling weak lean on that. Now step out!"

The man started walking and moved easily, not lagging behind.

As they went along, Simon asked him, "And where do you belong to?"

"I'm not from these parts."

"I thought as much. I know the folks hereabouts. But how did you come to be there by the shrine?"

"I cannot tell."

"Has some one been ill-treating you?"

"No one has ill-treated me. God has punished me."

"Of course God rules all. Still, you'll have to find food and shelter somewhere. Where do you want to go to?"

"It is all the same to me."

Simon was amazed. The man did not look like a rogue, and he spoke gently, but yet he gave no account of himself. Still Simon thought, "Who knows what may have happened?" And he said to the stranger: "Well then, come home with me and at least warm yourself awhile."

So Simon walked towards his home, and the stranger kept up with him, walking at his side. The wind had risen and Simon felt it cold under his shirt. He was getting over his tipsiness by now and began to feel the frost. He went along sniffling and wrapping his wife's coat round him, and he thought to himself: "There now—talk about sheep-skins! I went out for sheep-skins and come home without even a coat to my back, and what is more, I'm bringing a naked man along with me. Matrëna[4] won't be pleased!" And when he thought of his wife he felt sad, but when he looked at the stranger and remembered

---

4. Matrëna (mä-trō′nä).

how he had looked up at him at the shrine, his heart was glad.

III

Simon's wife had everything ready early that day. She had cut wood, brought water, fed the children, eaten her own meal, and now she sat thinking. She wondered when she ought to make bread: now or tomorrow? There was still a large piece left.

"If Simon has had some dinner in town," thought she, "and does not eat much for supper, the bread will last out another day."

She weighed the piece of bread in her hand again and again and thought: "I won't make any more today. We have only enough flour left to bake one batch. We can manage to make this last out till Friday."

So Matrëna put away the bread and sat down at the table to patch her husband's shirt. While she worked she thought how her husband was buying skins for a winter coat.

"If only the dealer does not cheat him. My good man is much too simple; he cheats nobody, but any child can take him in. Eight rubles is a lot of money—he should get a good coat at that price. Not tanned skins, but still a proper winter coat. How difficult it was last winter to get on without a warm coat. I could neither get down to the river nor go out anywhere. When he went out he put on all we had, and there was nothing left for me. He did not start very early today, but still it's time he was back. I only hope he has not gone on the spree!"[5]

Hardly had Matrëna thought this than steps were heard on the threshold and some one entered. Matrëna stuck her needle into her work and went out into the passage. There she saw two men: Simon, and with him a man without a hat and wearing felt boots.

Matrëna noticed at once that her husband smelt of spirits. "There now, he has been drinking," thought she. And when she saw that he was coatless, had only her jacket on, brought no parcel, stood there silent, and seemed ashamed, her heart was ready to break with disappointment. "He has drunk the money," thought she, "and has been on the spree with some good-for-nothing fellow whom he has brought home with him."

Matrëna let them pass into the hut, followed them in, and saw that the stranger was a young, slight man, wearing her husband's coat. There was no shirt to be seen under it, and he had no hat. Having entered, he stood neither moving nor raising his eyes, and Matrëna thought: "He must be a bad man—he's afraid."

Matrëna frowned, and stood beside the stove looking to see what they would do.

Simon took off his cap and sat down on the bench as if things were all right.

"Come, Matrëna; if supper is ready, let us have some."

Matrëna muttered something to herself and did not move but stayed where she was, by the stove. She looked first at the one and then at the other of them and only shook her head. Simon saw that his wife was annoyed, but tried to pass it off. Pretending not to notice anything, he took the stranger by the arm.

"Sit down, friend," said he, "and let us have some supper."

The stranger sat down on the bench.

"Haven't you cooked anything for us?" said Simon.

Matrëna's anger boiled over. "I've cooked, but not for you. It seems to me you have drunk your wits away. You went to buy a sheep-skin coat but come home without so much as the coat you had on and bring a naked vagabond home with

---

5. **on the spree:** on a wild or carefree outing.

"HE HAS DRUNK THE MONEY," THOUGHT SHE, "AND HAS BEEN ON THE SPREE WITH SOME GOOD-FOR-NOTHING FELLOW WHOM HE HAS BROUGHT HOME WITH HIM."

you. I have no supper for drunkards like you."

"That's enough, Matrëna. Don't wag your tongue without reason! You had better ask what sort of man—"

"And you tell me what you've done with the money?"

Simon found the pocket of the jacket, drew out the three-ruble note, and unfolded it.

"Here is the money. Trifonov did not pay, but promises to pay soon."

Matrëna got still more angry; he had bought no sheep-skins but had put his only coat on some naked fellow and had even brought him to their house.

She snatched up the note from the table, took it to put away in safety, and said: "I have no supper for you. We can't feed all the naked drunkards in the world."

"There now, Matrëna, hold your tongue a bit. First hear what a man has to say—!"

"Much wisdom I shall hear from a drunken fool. I was right in not wanting to marry you—a drunkard. The linen my mother gave me you drank; and now you've been to buy a coat—and have drunk it too!"

Simon tried to explain to his wife that he had only spent twenty kopeks; tried to tell how he

had found the man—but Matrëna would not let him get a word in. She talked nineteen to the dozen[6] and dragged in things that had happened ten years before.

Matrëna talked and talked, and at last she flew at Simon and seized him by the sleeve.

"Give me my jacket. It is the only one I have, and you must needs take it from me and wear it yourself. Give it here, you mangy dog, and may the devil take you."

Simon began to pull off the jacket, and turned a sleeve of it inside out; Matrëna seized the jacket and it burst its seams. She snatched it up, threw it over her head, and went to the door. She meant to go out, but stopped undecided—she wanted to work off her anger, but she also wanted to learn what sort of a man the stranger was.

IV

Matrëna stopped and said: "If he were a good man he would not be naked. Why, he hasn't even a shirt on him. If he were all right, you would say where you came across the fellow."

"That's just what I am trying to tell you," said Simon. "As I came to the shrine I saw him sitting all naked and frozen. It isn't quite the weather to sit about naked! God sent me to him or he would have perished. What was I to do? How do we know what may have happened to him? So I took him, clothed him, and brought him along. Don't be so angry, Matrëna. It is a sin. Remember, we must all die one day."

Angry words rose to Matrëna's lips, but she looked at the stranger and was silent. He sat on the edge of the bench, motionless, his hands folded on his knees, his head drooping on his breast, his eyes closed, and his brows knit as if in

---

6. **nineteen to the dozen:** quickly and excessively.

pain. Matrëna was silent, and Simon said: "Matrëna, have you no love of God?"

Matrëna heard these words, and as she looked at the stranger, suddenly her heart softened towards him. She came back from the door, and going to the stove she got out the supper. Setting a cup on the table, she poured out some kvas.[7] Then she brought out the last piece of bread and set out a knife and spoons.

"Eat, if you want to," said she.

Simon drew the stranger to the table.

"Take your place, young man," said he.

Simon cut the bread, crumbled it into the broth, and they began to eat. Matrëna sat at the corner of the table, resting her head on her hand and looking at the stranger.

And Matrëna was touched with pity for the stranger and began to feel fond of him. And at once the stranger's face lit up; his brows were no longer bent, he raised his eyes and smiled at Matrëna.

When they had finished supper, the woman cleared away the things and began questioning the stranger. "Where are you from?" said she.

"I am not from these parts."

"But how did you come to be on the road?"

"I may not tell."

"Did some one rob you?"

"God punished me."

"And you were lying there naked?"

"Yes, naked and freezing. Simon saw me and had pity on me. He took off his coat, put it on me, and brought me here. And you have fed me, given me drink, and shown pity on me. God will reward you!"

Matrëna rose, took from the window Simon's old shirt she had been patching, and gave it to the stranger. She also brought out a pair of trousers for him.

"There," said she, "I see you have no shirt. Put this on, and lie down where you please, in the loft or on the stove."

The stranger took off the coat, put on the shirt, and lay down in the loft. Matrëna put out the candle, took the coat, and climbed to where her husband lay on the stove.

Matrëna drew the skirts of the coat over her and lay down but could not sleep; she could not get the stranger out of her mind.

When she remembered that he had eaten their last piece of bread and that there was none for tomorrow and thought of the shirt and trousers she had given away, she felt grieved; but when she remembered how he had smiled, her heart was glad.

Long did Matrëna lie awake, and she noticed that Simon also was awake—he drew the coat towards him.

"Simon!"

"Well?"

"You have had the last of the bread and I have not put any to rise. I don't know what we shall do tomorrow. Perhaps I can borrow some of the neighbor Martha."

"If we're alive we shall find something to eat."

The woman lay still awhile, and then said, "He seems a good man, but why does he not tell us who he is?"

"I suppose he has his reasons."

"Simon!"

"Well?"

"We give; but why does nobody give us anything?"

Simon did not know what to say; so he only said, "Let us stop talking" and turned over and went to sleep.

---

7. **kvas** (kväs): a Russian drink, similar to beer, made from fermented grains.

Still-Life with Lamp (1910), Marc Chagall. Oil on canvas, 70 cm × 45 cm. Private collection. Courtesy Galerie Rosengart, Lucerne, Switzerland.

V

In the morning Simon awoke. The children were still asleep; his wife had gone to the neighbor's to borrow some bread. The stranger alone was sitting on the bench, dressed in the old shirt and trousers, and looking upwards. His face was brighter than it had been the day before.

Simon said to him, "Well, friend; the belly wants bread and the naked body clothes. One has to work for a living. What work do you know?"

"I do not know any."

This surprised Simon, but he said, "Men who want to learn can learn anything."

"Men work and I will work also."

"What is your name?"

"Michael."

"Well, Michael, if you don't wish to talk about yourself, that is your own affair; but you'll have to earn a living for yourself. If you will work as I tell you, I will give you food and shelter."

"May God reward you! I will learn. Show me what to do."

Simon took yarn, put it round his thumb and began to twist it.

"It is easy enough—see!"

Michael watched him, put some yarn round his own thumb in the same way, caught the knack,[8] and twisted the yarn also.

Then Simon showed him how to wax the thread. This also Michael mastered. Next Simon showed him how to twist the bristle in, and how to sew, and this, too, Michael learned at once.

Whatever Simon showed him he understood at once, and after three days he worked as if he had sewn boots all his life. He worked without stopping and ate little. When work was over he sat silently, looking upwards. He hardly went into the street, spoke only when necessary, and neither joked nor laughed. They never saw him smile, except that first evening when Matrëna gave him supper.

VI

Day by day and week by week the year went round. Michael lived and worked with Simon. His fame spread till people said that no one sewed boots so neatly and strongly as Simon's workman, Michael; from all the district round people came to Simon for their boots, and he began to be well off.

One winter day, as Simon and Michael sat working, a carriage on sledge-runners, with three horses and with bells, drove up to the hut. They looked out of the window; the carriage stopped at their door; a fine servant jumped down from the box and opened the door. A gentleman in a fur coat got out and walked up to Simon's hut. Up jumped Matrëna and opened the door wide. The gentleman stooped to enter the hut, and when he drew himself up again his head nearly reached the ceiling and he seemed quite to fill his end of the room.

Simon rose, bowed, and looked at the gentleman with astonishment. He had never seen any one like him. Simon himself was lean, Michael was thin, and Matrëna was dry as a bone, but this man was like some one from another world: red-faced, burly, with a neck like a bull's, and looking altogether as if he were cast in iron.

The gentleman puffed, threw off his fur coat, sat down on the bench, and said, "Which of you is the master bootmaker?"

"I am, your Excellency," said Simon, coming forward.

Then the gentleman shouted to his lad, "Hey, Fédka,[9] bring the leather!"

The servant ran in, bringing a parcel. The gentleman took the parcel and put it on the table.

"Untie it," said he. The lad untied it.

The gentleman pointed to the leather.

"Look here, shoemaker," said he, "do you see this leather?"

"Yes, your honor."

"But do you know what sort of leather it is?"

Simon felt the leather and said, "It is good leather."

"Good, indeed! Why, you fool, you never saw such leather before in your life. It's German and cost twenty rubles."

Simon was frightened and said, "Where should I ever see leather like that?"

"Just so! Now, can you make it into boots for me?"

"Yes, your Excellency, I can."

Then the gentleman shouted at him: "You *can*, can you? Well, remember whom you are to make them for, and what the leather is. You must make me boots that will wear for a year, neither losing shape nor coming unsewn. If you can do it, take the leather and cut it up; but if you can't, say so. I warn you now, if your boots come

---

8. **knack:** the exact way of doing something.

9. **Fédka** (fyĕd′kă).

LEO TOLSTOY

unsewn or lose shape within a year I will have you put in prison. If they don't burst or lose shape for a year, I will pay you ten rubles for your work."

Simon was frightened and did not know what to say. He glanced at Michael and nudging him with his elbow, whispered: "Shall I take the work?"

Michael nodded his head as if to say, "Yes, take it."

Simon did as Michael advised and undertook to make boots that would not lose shape or split for a whole year.

Calling his servant, the gentleman told him to pull the boot off his left leg, which he stretched out.

"Take my measure!" said he.

Simon stitched a paper measure seventeen inches long, smoothed it out, knelt down, wiped his hands well on his apron so as not to soil the gentleman's sock, and began to measure. He measured the sole, and round the instep, and began to measure the calf of the leg, but the paper was too short. The calf of the leg was as thick as a beam.

"Mind you don't make it too tight in the leg."

Simon stitched on another strip of paper. The gentleman twitched his toes about in his sock looking round at those in the hut, and as he did so he noticed Michael.

"Whom have you there?" asked he.

"That is my workman. He will sew the boots."

"Mind," said the gentleman to Michael, "remember to make them so that they will last me a year."

Simon also looked at Michael and saw that Michael was not looking at the gentleman, but was gazing into the corner behind the gentleman, as if he saw some one there. Michael looked and looked, and suddenly he smiled, and his face became brighter.

"What are you grinning at, you fool?" thundered the gentleman. "You had better look to it that the boots are ready in time."

"They shall be ready in good time," said Michael.

"Mind it is so," said the gentleman, and he put on his boots and his fur coat, wrapped the latter round him, and went to the door. But he forgot to stoop, and struck his head against the lintel.[10]

He swore and rubbed his head. Then he took his seat in the carriage and drove away.

When he had gone, Simon said: "There's a figure of a man for you! You could not kill him with a mallet. He almost knocked out the lintel, but little harm it did him."

And Matrëna said: "Living as he does, how should he not have grown strong? Death itself can't touch such a rock as that."

VII

Then Simon said to Michael: "Well, we have taken the work, but we must see we don't get into trouble over it. The leather is dear, and the gentleman hot-tempered. We must make no mistakes. Come, your eye is truer and your hands have become nimbler than mine, so you take this measure and cut out the boots. I will finish off the sewing of the vamps."[11]

Michael did as he was told. He took the leather, spread it out on the table, folded it in two, took a knife and began to cut out.

Matrëna came and watched him cutting and was surprised to see how he was doing it. Matrëna was accustomed to seeing boots made, and she looked and saw that Michael was not cutting the leather for boots, but was cutting it round.

She wished to say something, but she thought to herself: "Perhaps I do not understand how

---

10. **lintel:** horizontal beam at the top of a door frame.

11. **vamps:** upper parts of shoes or boots, covering the instep or the instep and the toes.

gentlemen's boots should be made. I suppose Michael knows more about it—and I won't interfere."

When Michael had cut up the leather he took a thread and began to sew not with two ends, as boots are sewn, but with a single end, as for soft slippers.

Again Matrëna wondered, but again she did not interfere. Michael sewed on steadily till noon. Then Simon rose for dinner, looked around, and saw that Michael had made slippers out of the gentleman's leather.

"Ah!" groaned Simon, and he thought, "How is it that Michael, who has been with me a whole year and never made a mistake before, should do such a dreadful thing? The gentleman ordered high boots, welted,[12] with whole fronts, and Michael has made soft slippers with single soles and has wasted the leather. What am I to say to the gentleman? I can never replace leather such as this."

And he said to Michael, "What are you doing, friend? You have ruined me! You know the gentleman ordered high boots, but see what you have made!"

Hardly had he begun to rebuke[13] Michael, when "rat-tat" went the iron ring hung at the door. Some one was knocking. They looked out of the window; a man had come on horseback and was fastening his horse. They opened the door, and the servant who had been with the gentleman came in.

"Good day," said he.

"Good day," replied Simon. "What can we do for you?"

"My mistress has sent me about the boots."

"What about the boots?"

"Why, my master no longer needs them. He is dead."

"Is it possible?"

"He did not live to get home after leaving you but died in the carriage. When we reached home and the servants came to help him alight, he rolled over like a sack. He was dead already, and so stiff that he could hardly be got out of the carriage. My mistress sent me here, saying: 'Tell the bootmaker that the gentleman who ordered boots of him and left the leather for them no longer needs the boots, but that he must quickly make soft slippers for the corpse. Wait till they are ready and bring them back with you.' That is why I have come."

Michael gathered up the remnants of the leather; rolled them up, took the soft slippers he had made, slapped them together, wiped them down with his apron, and handed them and the roll of leather to the servant, who took them and said: "Good-bye, masters, and good day to you!"

VIII

Another year passed, and another, and Michael was now living his sixth year with Simon. He lived as before. He went nowhere, only spoke when necessary, and had only smiled twice in all those years—one when Matrëna gave him food, and a second time when the gentleman was in their hut. Simon was more than pleased with his workman. He never now asked him where he came from and only feared lest Michael should go away.

They were all at home one day. Matrëna was putting iron pots in the oven; the children were running along the benches and looking out of the window; Simon was sewing at one window and Michael was fastening on a heel at the other.

One of the boys ran along the bench to Michael, leant on his shoulder, and looked out of the window.

"Look, Uncle Michael! There is a lady with

---

12. **welted:** made with a leather strip stitched between the shoe sole and the vamp.

13. **rebuke:** to criticize; express disapproval of.

Grain Harvest (1908), Natalya Sergeyevna Goncharova. Oil on canvas, 96 cm × 103 cm.
The State Russian Museum, St. Petersburg, Russia.

little girls! She seems to be coming here. And one of the girls is lame."

When the boy said that, Michael dropped his work, turned to the window, and looked out into the street.

Simon was surprised. Michael never used to look out into the street, but now he pressed against the window, staring at something. Simon also looked out and saw that a well-dressed woman was really coming to his hut, leading by the hand two little girls in fur coats and woolen shawls. The girls could hardly be told one from the other, except that one of them was crippled in her left leg and walked with a limp.

The woman stepped into the porch and entered the passage. Feeling about for the entrance she found the latch, which she lifted and opened the door. She let the two girls go in first, and followed them into the hut.

"Good day, good folk!"

"Pray come in," said Simon. "What can we do for you?"

THEY ALL LOOKED TOWARDS HIM AND SAW HIM SITTING, HIS HANDS FOLDED ON HIS KNEES, GAZING UPWARDS AND SMILING.

The woman sat down by the table. The two little girls pressed close to her knees, afraid of the people in the hut.

"I want leather shoes made for these two little girls, for spring."

"We can do that. We never have made such small shoes, but we can make them; either welted or turnover shoes,[14] linen lined. My man, Michael, is a master at the work."

Simon glanced at Michael and saw that he had left his work and was sitting with his eyes fixed on the little girls. Simon was surprised. It was true the girls were pretty, with black eyes, plump, and rosy-cheeked, and they wore nice kerchiefs and fur coats, but still Simon could not understand why Michael should look at them like that—just as if he had known them before. He was puzzled but went on talking with the woman and arranging the price. Having fixed it, he prepared the measure. The woman lifted the lame girl on to her lap and said: "Take two measures from this little girl. Make one shoe for the lame foot and three for the sound one. They both have the same-sized feet. They are twins."

Simon took the measure and, speaking of the lame girl, said: "How did it happen to her? She is such a pretty girl. Was she born so?"

"No, her mother crushed her leg."

Then Matrëna joined in. She wondered who this woman was and whose the children were, so she said: "Are not you their mother, then?"

"No, my good woman; I am neither their mother nor any relation to them. They were quite strangers to me, but I adopted them."

"They are not your children and yet you are so fond of them?"

"How can I help being fond of them? I fed them both at my own breasts. I had a child of my own, but God took him. I was not so fond of him as I now am of these."

"Then whose children are they?"

IX

The woman, having begun talking, told them the whole story.

"It is about six years since their parents died, both in one week: their father was buried on the Tuesday, and their mother died on the Friday. These orphans were born three days after their father's death, and their mother did not live another day. My husband and I were then living as peasants in the village. We were neighbors of theirs, our yard being next to theirs. Their father was a lonely man, a wood-cutter in the forest. When felling trees one day they let one fall on him. It fell across his body and crushed his bowels out. They hardly got him home before his soul went to God; and that same week his wife gave birth to twins—these little girls. She was poor and alone; she had no one, young or old, with her. Alone she gave them birth, and alone she met her death.

---

14. **turnover shoes:** shoes made with a piece of leather folded over.

"The next morning I went to see her, but when I entered the hut, she, poor thing, was already stark and cold. In dying she had rolled on to this child and crushed her leg. The village folk came to the hut, washed the body, laid her out, made a coffin, and buried her. They were good folk. The babies were left alone. What was to be done with them? I was the only woman there who had a baby at the time. I was nursing my first-born—eight weeks old. So I took them for a time. The peasants came together, and thought and thought what to do with them; and at last they said to me: 'For the present, Mary, you had better keep the girls, and later on we will arrange what to do for them.' So I nursed the sound one at my breast, but at first I did not feed this crippled one. I did not suppose she would live. But then I thought to myself, why should the poor innocent suffer? I pitied her and began to feed her. And so I fed my own boy and these two—the three of them—at my own breast. I was young and strong and had good food, and God gave me so much milk that at times it even overflowed. I used sometimes to feed two at a time, while the third was waiting. When one had had enough I nursed the third. And God so ordered it that these grew up, while my own was buried before he was two years old. And I had no more children, though we prospered. Now my husband is working for the corn merchant at the mill. The pay is good and we are well off. But I have no children of my own, and how lonely I should be without these little girls! How can I help loving them! They are the joy of my life!"

She pressed the lame little girl to her with one hand, while with the other she wiped the tears from her cheeks.

And Matrёna sighed, and said: "The proverb is true that says, 'One may live without father or mother, but one cannot live without God.'"

So they talked together, when suddenly the whole hut was lighted up as though by summer lightning from the corner where Michael sat.

They all looked towards him and saw him sitting, his hands folded on his knees, gazing upwards and smiling.

X

The woman went away with the girls. Michael rose from the bench, put down his work, and took off his apron. Then, bowing low to Simon and his wife, he said: "Farewell, masters. God has forgiven me. I ask your forgiveness, too, for anything done amiss."

And they saw that a light shone from Michael. And Simon rose, bowed down to Michael, and said: "I see, Michael, that you are no common man, and I can neither keep you nor question you. Only tell me this: how is it that when I found you and brought you home, you were gloomy, and when my wife gave you food you smiled at her and became brighter? Then when the gentleman came to order the boots, you smiled again and became brighter still? And now, when this woman brought the little girls, you smiled a third time and have become as bright as day? Tell me, Michael, why does your face shine so, and why did you smile those three times?"

And Michael answered: "Light shines from me because I have been punished, but now God has pardoned me. And I smiled three times, because God sent me to learn three truths, and I have learnt them. One I learnt when your wife pitied me, and that is why I smiled the first time. The second I learnt when the rich man ordered the boots, and then I smiled again. And now, when I saw those little girls, I learnt the third and last, and I smiled the third time."

And Simon said: "Tell me, Michael, what did God punish you for? and what were the three truths? that I, too, may know them."

And Michael answered: "God punished me for

disobeying him. I was an angel in heaven and disobeyed God. God sent me to fetch a woman's soul. I flew to earth and saw a sick woman lying alone who had just given birth to twin girls. They moved feebly at their mother's side but she could not lift them to her breast. When she saw me, she understood that God had sent me for her soul, and she wept and said: 'Angel of God! My husband has just been buried, killed by a falling tree. I have neither sister, nor aunt, nor mother: no one to care for my orphans. Do not take my soul! Let me nurse my babes, feed them, and set them on their feet before I die. Children cannot live without father or mother.' And I hearkened[15] to her. I placed one child at her breast and gave the other into her arms, and returned to the Lord in heaven. I flew to the Lord, and said: 'I could not take the soul of the mother. Her husband was killed by a tree; the woman has twins and prays that her soul may not be taken. She says: "Let me nurse and feed my children, and set them on their feet. Children cannot live without father or mother." I have not taken her soul.' And God said: 'Go—take the mother's soul, and learn three truths: Learn *What dwells in man,* *What is not given to man,* and *What men live by.* When thou hast learnt these things, thou shalt return to heaven.' So I flew again to earth and took the mother's soul. The babes dropped from her breasts. Her body rolled over on the bed and crushed one babe, twisting its leg. I rose above the village, wishing to take her soul to God, but a wind seized me and my wings drooped and dropped off. Her soul rose alone to God, while I fell to earth by the roadside."

XI

And Simon and Matrëna understood who it was that had lived with them and whom they had clothed and fed. And they wept with awe and with joy. And the angel said: "I was alone in the field, naked. I had never known human needs, cold and hunger, till I became a man. I was famished, frozen, and did not know what to do. I saw, near the field I was in, a shrine built for God, and I went to it hoping to find shelter. But the shrine was locked and I could not enter. So I sat down behind the shrine to shelter myself at least from the wind. Evening drew on, I was hungry, frozen, and in pain. Suddenly I heard a man coming along the road. He carried a pair of boots and was talking to himself. For the first time since I became a man I saw the mortal face of a man, and his face seemed terrible to me and I turned from it. And I heard the man talking to himself of how to cover his body from the cold in winter, and how to feed his wife and children. And I thought: 'I am perishing of cold and hunger and here is a man thinking only of how to clothe himself and his wife, and how to get bread for themselves. He cannot help me.' When the man saw me he frowned and became still more terrible and passed me by on the other side. I despaired; but suddenly I heard him coming back. I looked up and did not recognize the same man: before, I had seen death in his face; but now he was alive and I recognized in him the presence of God. He came up to me, clothed me, took me with him, and brought me to his home. I entered the house; a woman came to meet us and began to speak. The woman was still more terrible than the man had been; the spirit of death came from her mouth; I could not breathe for the stench[16] of

---

15. hearkened: paid attention to; listened.
16. stench: foul smell.

The Dream (1939), Marc Chagall. Gouache on paper, 20⁹⁄₁₆″ × 26¾″. The Phillips Collection, Washington, D.C.

HUMANITIES CONNECTION The word *dream* occurs in the titles of a number of Marc Chagall's works, and many of his paintings have a magical, unreal quality. People, animals, and buildings appear to float in the air, and details are combined in such unexpected ways that it seems possible for anything to happen.

death that spread around her. She wished to drive me out into the cold, and I knew that if she did so she would die. Suddenly her husband spoke to her of God, and the woman changed at once. And when she brought me food and looked at me, I glanced at her and saw that death no longer dwelt in her; she had become alive, and in her too I saw God.

"Then I remembered the first lesson God had set me: *'Learn what dwells in man.'* And I understood that in man dwells Love! I was glad that God had already begun to show me what He had promised, and I smiled for the first time. But

I had not yet learnt all. I did not yet know *What is not given to man*, and *What men live by.*

"I lived with you and a year passed. A man came to order boots that should wear for a year without losing shape or cracking. I looked at him, and suddenly, behind his shoulder, I saw my comrade—the angel of death. None but me saw that angel; but I knew him, and knew that before the sun set he would take the rich man's soul. And I thought to myself, 'The man is making preparation for a year and does not know that he will die before evening.' And I remembered God's second saying, *'Learn what is not given to man.'*

"What dwells in man I already knew. Now I learnt what is not given him. It is not given to man to know his own needs. And I smiled for the second time. I was glad to have seen my comrade angel—glad also that God had revealed to me the second saying.

"But I still did not know all. I did not know *What men live by.* And I lived on, waiting till God should reveal to me the last lesson. In the sixth year came the girl-twins with the woman; and I recognized the girls and heard how they had been kept alive. Having heard the story, I thought, 'Their mother besought[17] me for the children's sake, and I believed her when she said that children cannot live without father or mother; but a stranger has nursed them and has brought them up.' And when the woman showed her love for the children that were not her own and wept over them, I saw in her the living God, and understood *What men live by.* And I knew that God had revealed to me the last lesson and had forgiven my sin. And then I smiled for the third time."

XII

And the angel's body was bared, and he was clothed in light so that eye could not look on him; and his voice grew louder, as though it came not from him but from heaven above. And the angel said: "I have learnt that all men live not by care for themselves, but by love.

"It was not given to the mother to know what her children needed for their life. Nor was it given to the rich man to know what he himself needed. Nor is it given to any man to know whether, when evening comes, he will need boots for his body or slippers for his corpse.

"I remained alive when I was a man, not by care of myself but because love was present in a passer-by and because he and his wife pitied and loved me. The orphans remained alive not because of their mother's care, but because there was love in the heart of a woman, a stranger to them, who pitied and loved them. And all men live not by the thought they spend on their own welfare, but because love exists in man.

"I knew before that God gave life to men and desires that they should live; now I understood more than that.

"I understood that God does not wish men to live apart, and therefore he does not reveal to them what each one needs for himself; but he wishes them to live united, and therefore reveals to each of them what is necessary for all.

"I have now understood that though it seems to men that they live by care for themselves, in truth it is love alone by which they live. He who has love, is in God, and God is in him, for God is love."

And the angel sang praise to God, so that the hut trembled at his voice. The roof opened, and a column of fire rose from earth to heaven. Simon and his wife and children fell to the ground. Wings appeared upon the angel's shoulders and he rose into the heavens.

And when Simon came to himself the hut stood as before, and there was no one in it but his own family. ❖

---

17. **besought:** begged.

from Sonya Tolstoy's Diary

Translated by Alexander Werth

PREPARING to *Read*

Build Background

Sonya Tolstoy, Tolstoy's dutiful wife for 48 years, was a competent, independent woman with extraordinary mental and physical stamina. Not only did she give birth to 13 children and manage Tolstoy's large estate, but she also read, copied, and commented on all of his manuscripts. Sonya was an able and intelligent critic, and Tolstoy took her observations and insights seriously. Their son Ilya recalled her diligence: "Leaning over the manuscript and trying to decipher my Father's scrawl with her short-sighted eyes, she used to spend whole evenings at work, and often stayed up late at night after everyone else had gone to bed." Her contributions were indispensable to Tolstoy's work.

Like her famous husband, Sonya Tolstoy kept a diary when she could find the time. The first entry printed here (in which she refers to Tolstoy by his nickname, Lyova) concerns the novel *War and Peace*, which Sonya eventually copied seven times. The second entry is about *Anna Karenina*. Read these excerpts for insights into both husband and wife.

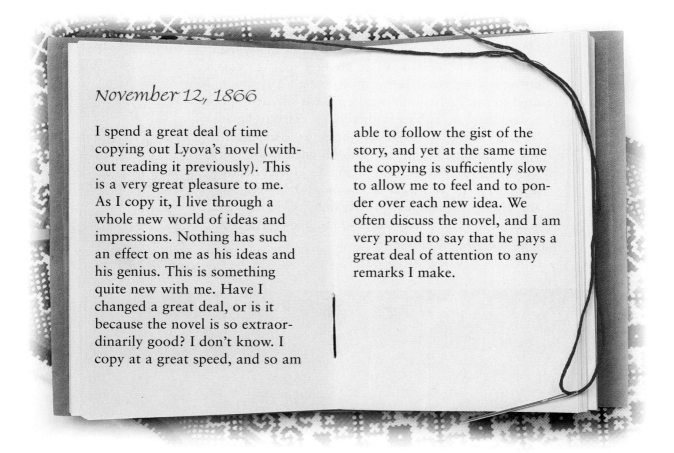

November 12, 1866

I spend a great deal of time copying out Lyova's novel (without reading it previously). This is a very great pleasure to me. As I copy it, I live through a whole new world of ideas and impressions. Nothing has such an effect on me as his ideas and his genius. This is something quite new with me. Have I changed a great deal, or is it because the novel is so extraordinarily good? I don't know. I copy at a great speed, and so am able to follow the gist of the story, and yet at the same time the copying is sufficiently slow to allow me to feel and to ponder over each new idea. We often discuss the novel, and I am very proud to say that he pays a great deal of attention to any remarks I make.

November 20, 1876

L. N. has just been telling me how the ideas for
his novel came to him:

"I was sitting alone in my study and looking at
the fine white silk embroidery on the sleeve of my
dressing-gown. This made me wonder how people
came to think of all this sewing and stitching and
embroidery, and I realized that it represented a whole
world of women's daily cares and interests; that it
must all be very fascinating and that it was no wonder
that women went in for it. And my thoughts naturally
turned to Anna Karenina, and in the end this bit of
embroidery on my sleeve suggested a whole chapter to
me. Anna is cut off from this joyful side of a woman's
existence, for she is alone, abandoned by all women,
and she has no one to talk to about a subject of such
universal, everyday interest to women." All autumn he
used to say: "My brain is asleep"; but suddenly, about
a week ago, something within him seemed to have
burst forth into blossom: he started to work cheerfully
and is thoroughly satisfied with his energy and work.
This morning, before even taking his coffee, he sat
down to write and went on for more than an hour,
and altered the chapter on Alexander Alexandrovich's
relation to Lydia Ivanovna, and the one on Anna's
arrival in St. Petersburg.

Connect to the Literature

1. What Do You Think?
What is your reaction to Michael's explanation of what men live by?

Comprehension Check
- Why does Simon take the stranger home?
- What happens to the man who ordered the boots?
- How did the twin babies survive after their mother's death?

Think Critically

2. ACTIVE READING: PREDICTING Review the chart you made in your 📖 READER'S NOTEBOOK. How accurate were your predictions? Which explanation of a mystery took you most by surprise? Discuss your responses with your classmates.

3. In your own words, explain what the three lessons are that Michael learns and how they are related.

4. Besides love, what are some other virtues illustrated by the characters in this story? Support your answer with evidence from the story.

THINK ABOUT

- why Simon and Matrëna rethink their initial reactions to Michael
- how Michael acts during his punishment
- what the woman says about caring for the twins

5. Do you think Michael deserved to be punished by God? Give reasons for your opinion.

Extend Interpretations

6. Different Perspectives Suppose you lived in the same village as Simon and Matrëna. How do you think you would view the events that occur in their household?

7. Connect to Life Taking in a stranger can be dangerous in our society today. What do you think would happen if Michael appeared in your neighborhood in need of food, clothing, and shelter? Do you think it would be possible for him to learn the same lessons? Give reasons for your answers.

LITERARY ANALYSIS: FORESHADOWING

In a story, hints or clues about what will happen later are called **foreshadowing.** In this story, Tolstoy uses foreshadowing not only to suggest later events but also to point toward a fuller understanding of events. For example, when Simon takes in Michael, the reader doesn't know the true significance of this act until Michael's identity is revealed. Still, clues that Michael is an angel come in section I when Simon first sees "something whitish behind the shrine." As a master storyteller, Tolstoy uses foreshadowing selectively, giving just enough hints to keep his reader guessing.

Paired Activity Working with a partner, go back through the story to look for four other clues that point to the moment when Michael reveals his identity. Use a chart like the one below to list the clues and to briefly explain the significance of each one in foreshadowing Michael's revelation that he is an angel.

Event: Michael Reveals His Identity	
Clue	**Significance of Clue**
1. Simon sees "something whitish behind the shrine"	1. suggests something out of the ordinary is going on
2.	
3.	
4.	

Tolstoy's Contrasting Styles

The style of Tolstoy's early fiction and his great novels has been called saturated realism because these works so fully absorb the reality of life. In his later fiction, however, he was concerned primarily with conveying a clear and simple moral message.

Key Aspects of Tolstoy's Styles

Realism
- An impartial, or unbiased, **tone** that carries no judgment
- Vivid **characterization** that reveals complex emotions
- Carefully selected **details** to render a scene, reveal an emotion, or express a thought with absolute clarity
- A smooth **narration** that seems to flow naturally

Moral Tales
- Clear messages, or **themes,** that convey moral truth
- Simple, direct **word choice** that all can understand
- Uncomplicated **characters** and **plot** that appeal to a wide range of readers

Analysis of Styles

The first excerpt on the right details a young man's first combat experience, and the second portrays Matrëna and the stranger. After studying the aspects of Tolstoy's two styles above, read the excerpts. Then complete these activities:

- Find an example of each aspect of Tolstoy's realist style in the first excerpt. Do the same for the moral-tales style in the second excerpt.

- Identify two stylistic differences between the two excerpts.

- Look for any aspects of realism that are present in the excerpt from "What Men Live By."

Applications

1. **Changing Styles** Try rewriting a brief passage from "How Much Land Does a Man Need?" or "What Men Live By" in the realist style of the excerpt from *War and Peace.*

2. **Speaking and Listening** How do you suppose Simon and Matrëna in their later years would describe their life with Michael? Pretend to be one of them and tell your story, using the style of the original tale or a more realistic style.

---

from **War and Peace**

Rostov . . . stepped on the bridge, not knowing what he had to do. There was no one to slash at with his sword (that was how he always pictured a battle to himself). . . . He stood and looked about him, when suddenly there was a rattle on the bridge, like a lot of nuts being scattered, and one of the hussars, the one standing nearest him, fell with a groan on the railing. Rostov ran up to him with the others. Again some one shouted. "Stretchers!" Four men took hold of the hussar and began lifting him up. . . . Nikolay Rostov turned away, and began staring into the distance, at the waters of the Danube, at the sky, at the sun, as though he were searching for something. . . . "Here is *it, it,* death hanging over me, all round me. . . . One instant, and I shall never see that sunshine, that water, that mountain gorge again. . . ." At that moment the sun went behind the clouds; more stretchers came into view ahead of Rostov. And the terror of death and of the stretchers, and the loss of the sunshine and life, all blended into one sensation of sickening fear.

---

from **"What Men Live By"**

Simon cut the bread, crumbled it into the broth, and they began to eat. Matrëna sat at the corner of the table, resting her head on her hand and looking at the stranger.

And Matrëna was touched with pity for the stranger and began to feel fond of him. And at once the stranger's face lit up; his brows were no longer bent, he raised his eyes and smiled at Matrëna.

Writing Options

1. Folk Tale Rewrite "What Men Live By" as the folk tale that you imagine Tolstoy first heard. What details would you omit to shorten and simplify the tale?

2. Maxims for Living Write three maxims, or rules of conduct, that could help people lead more meaningful and rewarding lives. You can use the guidelines for giving that you created in the Connect to Your Life activity on page 976.

3. Explanatory Essay Draw conclusions about Tolstoy's values from "How Much Land Does a Man Need?" and "What Men Live By." First, go back through the stories, listing virtues and vices and citing examples that illustrate them. Then write your conclusions, using selective examples as your support. Use a chart like the one below to organize your ideas.

Virtues	Vices
Generosity: Simon gives Michael his coat.	Envy: Pakhom envies a neighbor who buys land.

Writing Handbook
See page R25: Elaboration.

Activities & Explorations

1. News Display With your classmates, create a display of newspaper and magazine articles and photos that illustrate the theme of "What Men Live By." ~ **VIEWING AND REPRESENTING**

2. Story Dramatization With a small group of classmates, choose an excerpt from "What Men Live By" to dramatize in front of the class. ~ **PERFORMING**

Inquiry & Research

Biography Find out more about Sonya Tolstoy. A fascinating account of her relationship with her husband can be found in the second chapter of *The Hidden Writer: Diaries and the Creative Life* (1997) by Alexandra Johnson.

Leo Tolstoy

Author Study Project

CREATING A PHOTO BIOGRAPHY

Tolstoy's long, interesting life is well documented in both words and photographs. Work with a small group of classmates to create a photo biography of Tolstoy that highlights important stages in his life and shows the changes he went through. Use photos of Tolstoy to focus your research and guide you to the information to be included in the captions. For example, an image of Tolstoy as a young army cadet could lead you to information on his war experience and his writing about that experience. Your group could then decide on the kind of information to put in the caption—a quotation of Tolstoy's about war, an excerpt from one of his war stories, or a brief summary of biographical facts, for example. Whatever you choose to write for the captions, make sure they provide important insights into the man himself. Your aim should be to portray Tolstoy as a person as well as to show him as a "great man."

Primary Print Sources Tolstoy's diaries, letters, and many writings are good places to look for quotations. You might also try Sonya Tolstoy's diary.

Secondary Print Sources There are several biographies of Tolstoy. Some include a variety of good photos. Tolstoy had a number of followers who recorded his words in books of their own, such as A. B. Goldenweizer's *Talks with Tolstoy*.

Computer Resources Many images of Tolstoy are available on the Web, including a photo tour of his estate, Yasnaya Polyana. Online encyclopedias and reliable Web sites can also give you some basic information.

RESEARCH STARTER
CLASSZONE.COM

Realism in Fiction

OVERVIEW

A Problem   999

The Artist   1008

Standardized Test Practice:
Writing About Literature   1015

Realistic fiction focuses on the here and now, on the everyday experiences of people. It reflects life as it is. Realistic fiction often does not have a complicated plot. Instead, it concentrates on characters' behavior and reactions.

In this lesson you will read two stories that represent the realist tradition. One is by a 19th-century Russian master of realism, Anton Chekhov. The other is by a famous Indian writer of the 19th and 20th centuries, Rabindranath Tagore. The stories are set in different cultures and portray different kinds of characters and situations. In the pages that follow, you will be given the chance to compare some of the characteristics of realism that are present in each story. You will also be able to see how different realists create fictional worlds.

Points *of* Comparison

Important characteristics of realism include the following:
- Reflects what life is like—includes details of everyday activities
- Portrays characters who are ordinary people, not heroes or villains
- Focuses on characters' motivations, circumstances, and actions, not on plot
- Is concerned with social problems and struggles that characters face
- Is not idealistic or sentimental
- Often avoids clear resolutions

Analyze the Stories
Create a chart like the one shown to help you in taking notes about the stories. Add any additional questions that you think would help a reader understand the realism of the two works.

Questions for Analysis	"A Problem"	"The Artist"
What real-life situations are portrayed?		
What everyday details are described?		
What are the concerns and struggles of the main characters?		
What motivates their actions and responses?		
How does the story end?		

Standardized Test Practice: Comparison-and-Contrast Essay After you have finished reading the stories, you will have the opportunity to write a comparison-and-contrast essay. Your notes will help you in planning and writing the essay.

A Problem

ANTON CHEKHOV

Anton Chekhov
1860–1904

Doctor or Writer? The Russian realist Anton Chekhov (ən-tôn′ chĕk′ôf) found fame early in life. The son of a grocer and the grandson of a serf, Chekhov put himself through medical school and supported his family by selling his short stories to popular newspapers and magazines. By the time he graduated in 1884, he was well-known. Chekhov's work drew increasing attention, and although he did practice medicine, writing became the central focus of his life.

Literary Contribution Chekhov is considered a master of the modern short story and, along with Guy de Maupassant, had a major impact on its development. Chekhov's stories are known for their sensitive characterization and use of mood and symbolism. When Chekhov turned to writing drama, he brought the same sensitivity and insight that had graced his stories. Although failures at first, his plays soon found an eager audience at the Moscow Art Theater. In the years following the success of *The Seagull* in 1898, Chekhov established his reputation as Russia's great playwright.

Build Background

In 19th-century Europe, the upper classes had strict codes of behavior. Breaking those codes was to be avoided at all cost, and disgrace followed if a person did violate them. In "A Problem," a young man from a wealthy family has gotten into debt and forged a loan document. When he cannot pay the loan, his family finds out and faces certain scandal if the episode becomes known in society.

Connect to Your Life

In this story some of the characters are concerned with preserving their family's honor. What does the word *honor* mean to you? Can it have different meanings in different situations? Compare your ideas with those of some of your classmates.

Focus Your Reading

LITERARY ANALYSIS: IRONY

Irony exists when there is a difference between what is expected and what actually happens. For example, it is ironic that a young man from a rich family runs out of money. As you read "A Problem," look for other examples of irony.

ACTIVE READING: UNDERSTANDING CHARACTERS' VALUES

A character's values are the qualities that he or she thinks are most important in life. Examples of such qualities would be bravery, kindness, responsibility, love of money, ambition, or desire for power. Understanding a character's values helps the reader interpret the character's words and actions.

📖 **READER'S NOTEBOOK** As you read "A Problem," try to identify the values that are most important to the Colonel, Ivan Markovitch, and Sasha. For each of the three characters, write down the values and then note the words and actions that reflect those values.

WORDS TO KNOW **Vocabulary Preview**

assert	dissipated	inextricably	tranquilly
candid	edifying	paltry	
convention	indulgence	reprehensible	

A Problem

Anton Chekhov

Translated by Constance Garnett

he strictest measures were taken that the Uskovs'[1] family secret might not leak out and become generally known. Half of the servants were sent off to the theater or the circus; the other half were sitting in the kitchen and not allowed to leave it. Orders were given that no one was to be admitted. The wife of the Colonel, her sister, and the governess, though they had been initiated into the secret, kept up a pretense of knowing nothing; they sat in the dining-room and did not show themselves in the drawing-room or the hall.

Sasha Uskov, the young man of twenty-five who was the cause of all the commotion, had arrived some time before, and by the advice of kind-hearted Ivan Markovitch, his uncle, who was taking his part, he sat meekly in the hall by the door leading to the study, and prepared himself to make an open, candid explanation.

The other side of the door, in the study, a family council was being held. The subject under discussion was an exceedingly disagreeable and delicate one. Sasha Uskov had cashed at one of the banks a false promissory note,[2] and it had become due for payment three days before, and now his two paternal uncles[3] and Ivan Markovitch, the brother of his dead mother, were deciding the question whether they should pay the money and save the family honor, or wash their hands of it and leave the case to go for trial.

To outsiders who have no personal interest in the matter such questions seem simple; for those who are so unfortunate as to have to decide them in earnest they are extremely difficult. The uncles had been talking for a long time, but the problem seemed no nearer decision.

"My friends!" said the uncle who was a colonel, and there was a note of exhaustion and bitterness in his voice. "Who says that family honor is a mere convention? I don't say that at all. I am only warning you against a false view; I am pointing out the possibility of an unpardonable mistake. How can you fail to see it? I am not speaking Chinese; I am speaking Russian!"

"My dear fellow, we do understand," Ivan Markovitch protested mildly.

"How can you understand if you say that I don't believe in family honor? I repeat once more: fa-mil-y ho-nor false-ly un-der-stood is a prejudice! Falsely understood! That's what I say: whatever may be the motives for screening a scoundrel, whoever he may be, and helping him to escape punishment, it is contrary to law and unworthy of a gentleman. It's not saving the family honor; it's civic cowardice! Take the army, for instance. . . . The honor of the army is more precious to us than any other honor, yet we don't screen our guilty members, but condemn them. And does the honor of the army suffer in

---

1. **Uskovs** (o͞o'skôfs).

2. **promissory note:** a written promise, or IOU, to pay a specific amount of money to a certain person by a certain date. In the 19th century, a person could have a bank cash an IOU made out to him or her by another person. Sasha had forged an IOU and cashed it at a bank but did not have the money to repay the bank when the note came due.

3. **paternal uncles:** uncles who are brothers of one's father.

WORDS TO KNOW

candid (kăn'dĭd) *adj.* frank; blunt; straightforward
convention (kən-vĕn'shən) *n.* a social custom

Doppelbildnis Benesch [Double portrait of Otto and Heinrich Benesch] (1913),
Egon Schiele. Neue Galerie/Linz, Austria/Art Resource, New York.

consequence? Quite the opposite!"

The other paternal uncle, an official in the Treasury, a taciturn, dull-witted, and rheumatic man, sat silent, or spoke only of the fact that the Uskovs' name would get into the newspapers if the case went for trial. His opinion was that the case ought to be hushed up from the first and not become public property; but, apart from publicity in the newspapers, he advanced no other argument in support of this opinion.

The maternal uncle, kind-hearted Ivan Markovitch, spoke smoothly, softly, and with a tremor in his voice. He began with saying that youth has its rights and its peculiar temptations. Which of us has not been young, and who has not been led astray? To say nothing of ordinary mortals, even great men have not escaped errors and mistakes in their youth. Take, for instance, the biography of great writers. Did not every one of them gamble, drink, and draw down upon himself the anger of right-thinking people in his young days? If Sasha's error bordered upon crime, they must remember that Sasha had received practically no education; he had been expelled from the high school in the fifth class; he had lost his parents in early childhood, and so had been left at the tenderest age without guidance and good, benevolent influences. He was nervous, excitable, had no firm ground under his feet, and, above all, he had been unlucky. Even if he were guilty, anyway he deserved indulgence and the sympathy of all compassionate souls. He ought, of course, to be punished, but he was punished as it was by his conscience and the agonies he was enduring now while awaiting the sentence of his relations. The comparison with the army made by the Colonel was delightful, and did credit to his lofty intelligence; his appeal to their feeling of public duty spoke for the chivalry of his soul, but they must not forget that in each individual the citizen is closely linked with the Christian. . . .

"Shall we be false to civic duty," Ivan Markovitch exclaimed passionately, "if instead of punishing an erring boy we hold out to him a helping hand?"

Ivan Markovitch talked further of family honor. He had not the honor to belong to the Uskov family himself, but he knew their distinguished family went back to the thirteenth century; he did not forget for a minute, either, that his precious, beloved sister had been the wife of one of the representatives of that name. In short, the family was dear to him for many reasons, and he refused to admit the idea that, for the sake of a paltry fifteen hundred rubles, a blot should be cast on the escutcheon[4] that was beyond all price. If all the motives he had brought forward were not sufficiently convincing, he, Ivan Markovitch, in conclusion, begged his listeners to ask themselves what was meant by crime? Crime is an immoral act founded upon ill-will. But is the will of man free? Philosophy has not yet given a positive answer to that question. Different views were held by the learned. The latest school of Lombroso, for instance, denies the freedom of the will, and considers every crime as the product of the purely anatomical peculiarities of the individual.[5]

"Ivan Markovitch," said the Colonel, in a voice of entreaty, "we are talking seriously about an important matter, and you bring in Lombroso, you clever fellow. Think a little, what are you saying all this for? Can you imagine that all your thunderings and rhetoric will furnish an answer to the question?"

Sasha Uskov sat at the door and listened. He felt neither terror, shame, nor depression, but

---

4. **escutcheon** (ĭ-skŭch′ən): a shield-shaped emblem with a family's coat of arms.

5. **Lombroso** (lŏm-brō′sō) . . . **of the individual:** Cesare Lombroso, an Italian criminologist of the era, tried unsuccessfully to prove a relationship between criminal behavior and an individual's physical and mental defects.

WORDS TO KNOW
indulgence (ĭn-dŭl′jəns) *n.* a giving in to someone's wishes or desires
paltry (pôl′trē) *adj.* insignificant; almost worthless

only weariness and inward emptiness. It seemed to him that it made absolutely no difference to him whether they forgave him or not; he had come here to hear his sentence and to explain himself simply because kind-hearted Ivan Markovitch had begged him to do so. He was not afraid of the future. It made no difference to him where he was: here in the hall, in prison, or in Siberia.[6]

"If Siberia, then let it be Siberia . . . !"

He was sick of life and found it insufferably hard. He was <u>inextricably</u> involved in debt; he had not a farthing[7] in his pocket; his family had become detestable to him; he would have to part from his friends and his women sooner or later, as they had begun to be too contemptuous of his sponging on them. The future looked black.

Sasha was indifferent, and was only disturbed by one circumstance; the other side of the door they were calling him a scoundrel and a criminal. Every minute he was on the point of jumping up, bursting into the study and shouting in answer to the detestable metallic voice of the Colonel:

"You are lying!"

"Criminal" is a dreadful word—that is what murderers, thieves, robbers are; in fact, wicked and morally hopeless people. And Sasha was very far from being all that. . . . It was true he owed a great deal and did not pay his debts. But debt is not a crime, and it is unusual for a man not to be in debt. The Colonel and Ivan Markovitch were both in debt. . . .

"What have I done wrong besides?" Sasha wondered.

He had discounted a forged note. But all the young men he knew did the same. Handrikov and Von Burst always forged IOU's from their parents or friends when their allowances were not paid at the regular time, and then when they got their money from home they redeemed[8] them before they became due. Sasha had done the same, but had not redeemed the IOU because he had not

"And it's not in my character to bring myself to commit a crime. I am soft, emotional. . . . When I have the money I help the poor. . . ."

got the money which Handrikov had promised to lend him. He was not to blame; it was the fault of circumstances. It was true that the use of another person's signature was considered <u>reprehensible</u>; but, still, it was not a crime but a generally accepted dodge, an ugly formality which injured no one and was quite harmless, for in forging the Colonel's signature Sasha had had no intention of causing anybody damage or loss.

"No, it doesn't mean that I am a criminal . . ." thought Sasha. "And it's not in my character to bring myself to commit a crime. I am soft, emotional. . . . When I have the money I help the poor. . . ."

Sasha was musing after this fashion while they went on talking the other side of the door.

"But, my friends, this is endless," the Colonel

---

6. **Siberia:** a region in north-central Russia where criminals and political prisoners were sent.

7. **farthing:** a coin worth less than a penny.

8. **redeemed:** paid off.

WORDS TO KNOW

inextricably (ĭn-ĕk′strĭ-kə-blē) *adv.* in a way that one cannot get out of

reprehensible (rĕp′rĭ-hĕn′sə-bəl) *adj.* deserving of blame

declared, getting excited. "Suppose we were to forgive him and pay the money. You know he would not give up leading a dissipated life, squandering money, making debts, going to our tailors and ordering suits in our names! Can you guarantee that this will be his last prank? As far as I am concerned, I have no faith whatever in his reforming!"

The official of the Treasury muttered something in reply; after him Ivan Markovitch began talking blandly and suavely[9] again. The Colonel moved his chair impatiently and drowned the other's words with his detestable metallic voice. At last the door opened and Ivan Markovitch came out of the study; there were patches of red on his lean shaven face.

"Come along," he said, taking Sasha by the hand. "Come and speak frankly from your heart. Without pride, my dear boy, humbly and from your heart."

Sasha went into the study. The official of the Treasury was sitting down; the Colonel was standing before the table with one hand in his pocket and one knee on a chair. It was smoky and stifling in the study. Sasha did not look at the official or the Colonel; he felt suddenly ashamed and uncomfortable. He looked uneasily at Ivan Markovitch and muttered:

"I'll pay it . . . I'll give it back. . . ."

"What did you expect when you discounted the IOU?" he heard a metallic voice.

"I . . . Handrikov promised to lend me the money before now."

Sasha could say no more. He went out of the study and sat down again on the chair near the door. He would have been glad to go away altogether at once, but he was choking with hatred and he awfully wanted to remain, to tear the Colonel to pieces, to say something rude to him. He sat trying to think of something violent and effective to say to his hated uncle, and at that moment a woman's figure, shrouded[10] in the twilight, appeared at the drawing-room door. It was the Colonel's wife. She beckoned Sasha to her, and wringing her hands, said, weeping: "*Alexandre*,[11] I know you don't like me, but . . . listen to me; listen, I beg you. . . . But, my dear, how can this have happened? Why, it's awful, awful! For goodness' sake, beg them, defend yourself, entreat them."

Sasha looked at her quivering shoulders, at the big tears that were rolling down her cheeks, heard behind his back the hollow, nervous voices of worried and exhausted people, and shrugged his shoulders. He had not in the least expected that his aristocratic relations would raise such a tempest over a paltry fifteen hundred rubles! He could not understand her tears nor the quiver of their voices.

An hour later he heard that the Colonel was getting the best of it; the uncles were finally inclining to let the case go for trial.

"The matter's settled," said the Colonel, sighing. "Enough."

After this decision all the uncles, even the emphatic Colonel, became noticeably depressed. A silence followed.

"Merciful Heavens!" sighed Ivan Markovitch. "My poor sister!"

And he began saying in a subdued voice that most likely his sister, Sasha's mother, was present unseen in the study at that moment. He felt in his soul how the unhappy, saintly woman was weeping, grieving, and begging for her boy. For the sake of her peace beyond the grave, they ought to spare Sasha.

The sound of a muffled sob was heard. Ivan Markovitch was weeping and muttering something which it was impossible to catch through the door. The Colonel got up and paced from

---

9. **suavely** (swäv′lē): in a smoothly agreeable way.

10. **shrouded**: hidden from sight.

11. *Alexandre* (ä-lĕk-säN′drə): "Sasha" is short for the Russian name Aleksandr, of which "Alexandre" is the French form.

dissipated (dĭs′ə-pā′tĭd) *adj.* participating excessively in sensual or foolish pleasures

corner to corner. The long conversation began over again.

But then the clock in the drawing-room struck two. The family council was over. To avoid seeing the person who had moved him to such wrath, the Colonel went from the study, not into the hall, but into the vestibule. . . . Ivan Markovitch came out into the hall. . . . He was agitated and rubbing his hands joyfully. His tear-stained eyes looked good-humored and his mouth was twisted into a smile.

"Capital,"[12] he said to Sasha. "Thank God! You can go home, my dear, and sleep <u>tranquilly</u>. We have decided to pay the sum, but on condition that you repent and come with me tomorrow into the country and set to work."

A minute later Ivan Markovitch and Sasha in their great-coats and caps were going down the stairs. The uncle was muttering something <u>edifying</u>. Sasha did not listen, but felt as though some uneasy weight were gradually slipping off his shoulders. They had forgiven him; he was free! A gust of joy sprang up within him and sent a sweet chill to his heart. He longed to breathe, to move swiftly, to live! Glancing at the street lamps and the black sky, he remembered that Von Burst was celebrating his name-day[13] that evening at the "Bear," and again a rush of joy flooded his soul. . . .

"I am going!" he decided.

But then he remembered he had not a farthing, that the companions he was going to would despise him at once for his empty pockets. He must get hold of some money, come what may!

"Uncle, lend me a hundred rubles," he said to Ivan Markovitch.

His uncle, surprised, looked into his face and backed against a lamp-post.

"Give it to me," said Sasha, shifting impatiently from one foot to the other and beginning to pant.

He longed to breathe, to move swiftly, to live!

"Uncle, I entreat you, give me a hundred rubles."

His face worked; he trembled, and seemed on the point of attacking his uncle. . . .

"Won't you?" he kept asking, seeing that his uncle was still amazed and did not understand. "Listen. If you don't, I'll give myself up tomorrow! I won't let you pay the IOU! I'll present another false note tomorrow!"

Petrified, muttering something incoherent in his horror, Ivan Markovitch took a hundred-ruble note out of his pocket-book and gave it to Sasha. The young man took it and walked rapidly away from him. . . .

Taking a sledge,[14] Sasha grew calmer, and felt a rush of joy within him again. The "rights of youth" of which kind-hearted Ivan Markovitch had spoken at the family council woke up and <u>asserted</u> themselves. Sasha pictured the drinking-party before him, and, among the bottles, the women, and his friends, the thought flashed through his mind:

"Now I see that I am a criminal; yes, I am a criminal." ❖

---

12. **capital:** very good; excellent.
13. **name-day:** the feast day of the saint after whom one is named.
14. **sledge:** a sled drawn by animals.

WORDS TO KNOW

tranquilly (trăng′kwə-lē) *adv.* calmly; peacefully
edifying (ĕd′ə-fī′ĭng) *adj.* intended to improve morally; instructing **edify** *v.*
assert (ə-sûrt′) *v.* to express forcefully and positively

Connect to the Literature

1. What Do You Think?
How do you think Ivan Markovitch feels at the end of the story? Explain your answer.

Comprehension Check
• What is the "problem"?
• Who will make the decision about Sasha's fate?
• At the end of the story, what does Sasha threaten to do if his uncle won't give him money?

Think Critically

2. ACTIVE READING: UNDERSTANDING CHARACTERS' VALUES Review the notes you made in your READER'S NOTEBOOK. What are the most important values for the Colonel, for Ivan Markovitch, and for Sasha? What is your opinion of each character's values?

3. What kind of person is Sasha?

> THINK ABOUT
>
> • the kind of life he lives
> • what his uncles say about him
> • what he thinks as he listens to the uncles discuss his situation

4. How well does Ivan Markovitch understand Sasha? Explain your answer.

5. What do you think Sasha means when at the end he says, "I see that I am a criminal"?

6. How do you interpret the meaning of *honor* in this story?

Extend Interpretations

7. What If? Suppose that the uncles had decided not to pay Sasha's debts but rather to let his case go to trial. What do you think might have happened to him?

8. Connect to Life Because Sasha wants to do as he pleases, he accumulates debts and even resorts to forgery. What circumstances and expectations pressure people today to go into debt and become desperate about money?

LITERARY ANALYSIS: IRONY

Irony is the contrast between expectation and reality. Irony can surprise the reader, and it can be subtle. It can also reveal the truth about a character or situation. Irony is found in many works of realism.

Situational irony occurs when a character or the reader expects one thing to happen but something else actually does. Sometimes it springs from unexpected twists and reversals. For example, in Tolstoy's story "How Much Land Does a Man Need?" it is ironic that Pakhom dies just as he is about to get his land.

Paired Activity With a partner, find two examples of situational irony from "A Problem." Explain why each situation is ironic and what the irony reveals. Use a diagram like the one shown below to organize your ideas. Then discuss the following questions: How does irony contribute to the overall effect of the story? In what way does the title of the story prove ironic?

Example of Irony:
Uncles argue about the problem, while Sasha says almost nothing.

Why Ironic:
The person most affected by the situation is least involved.

What Irony Reveals:
Sasha is self-centered and doesn't care about the consequences of his actions.

EXERCISE: CONTEXT CLUES Write the word that would best fill in the blank in each sentence.

1. Considering the parties, drinking, and clothes that Sasha spent all his money on, a good word to describe his life would be _____.

2. He knew that he gave in to any _____ that appealed to him.

3. He also realized that he was _____ bogged down in spending and borrowing.

4. But Sasha viewed his forgery as a harmless incident, not something _____.

5. He considered the amount he owed to be _____, too insignificant to be worth such a fuss.

6. The Colonel thought that being put on trial would be a(n) _____ experience for a young man with so little self-control.

7. The Colonel was _____ in his statements, making no attempt to hide his disapproval.

8. He felt that Sasha's behavior involved family honor and reputation, not just a trivial _____.

9. As the uncles argued, Sasha became so resigned to his fate that he felt he would go _____ wherever he was sent.

10. After he heard their decision, however, his true nature began to _____ itself.

WORDS TO KNOW

assert	dissipated	inextricably	tranquilly
candid	edifying	paltry	
convention	indulgence	reprehensible	

Building Vocabulary

For an in-depth study of context clues, see page 674.

Points _of_ Comparison

Review the story and fill in the second column of your comparison-and-contrast chart. An example is given below.

Paired Activity Get together with a classmate and discuss the similarities and differences in your charts. Based on your discussion, you may want to make some changes in your chart.

Questions for Analysis	"A Problem"	"The Artist"
What real-life situations are portrayed?	young man gets himself in trouble	
What everyday details are described?		
What are the concerns and struggles of the main characters?		
What motivates their actions and responses?		
How does the story end?		

PREPARING to *Read*

Now that you have read Chekhov's story, it's time to turn your attention to a story by the Indian writer Tagore. You will see some of the same characteristics of realism in his work, but look for differences as well.

Rabindranath Tagore
1861–1941

A Many-Sided Genius It is hard to imagine anyone as multitalented as Rabindranath Tagore (rə-bēn'drə-nät' tə-gôr'), one of India's greatest modern writers. A prolific poet, he also wrote novels, short stories, plays, essays, and over 2,000 popular songs. Tagore almost single-handedly brought Indian literature into the modern era. Influenced by the European realists, he introduced new ways of writing poetry and fiction, and he used everyday language rather than the traditional Sanskrit (săn'skrĭt'). He took as his subject matter the great variety of Indian life as experienced by everyone from humble villagers to intellectuals. Because Tagore traveled widely, reading from his works and arguing eloquently for Indian independence, he essentially taught the rest of the world what India was really like. He was the first Asian writer to win the Nobel Prize in Literature (1913).

Build Background

Conflicting Values People with different goals and interests may disagree strongly about what is most important in life. These people often have great difficulty understanding each other. In this story, the two main characters—one an artist and the other a businessman—come into conflict.

The Artist

Rabindranath Tagore

Translated by Mary Lago, Tarun Gupta, and Amiya Chakravarty

Govinda came to Calcutta after graduation from high school in Mymensingh.[1] His widowed mother's savings were meager, but his own unwavering determination was his greatest resource. "I *will* make money," he vowed, "even if I have to give my whole life to it." In his terminology, wealth was always referred to as *pice*.[2] In other words he had in mind a very concrete image of something that could be seen, touched, and smelled; he was not greatly fascinated with fame, only with the very ordinary *pice,* eroded by circulation from market to market, from hand to hand, the tarnished *pice,* the *pice* that smells of copper, the original form of Kuvera,[3] who assumes the assorted guises[4] of silver, gold, securities, and wills, and keeps men's minds in a turmoil.

After traveling many tortuous roads and getting muddied repeatedly in the process, Govinda had now arrived upon the solidly paved embankment of his wide and free-flowing stream of money. He was firmly seated in the manager's chair at the MacDougal Gunnysack Company. Everyone called him MacDulal.[5]

When Govinda's lawyer-brother, Mukunda, died, he left behind a wife, a four-year-old son, a house in Calcutta, and some cash savings. In addition to this property there was some debt; therefore, provision for his family's needs depended upon frugality. Thus his son, Chunilal,[6] was brought up in circumstances that were undistinguished in comparison with those of the neighbors.

Mukunda's will gave Govinda entire responsibility for this family. Ever since Chunilal was a baby, Govinda had bestowed spiritual initiation upon his nephew with the sacred words: "Make money."

The main obstacle to the boy's initiation was his mother, Satyabati.[7] She said nothing outright; her opposition showed in her behavior. Art had always been her hobby. There was no limit to her enthusiasm for creating all sorts of original and decorative things from flowers, fruits and leaves, even foodstuffs, from paper and cloth cutouts, from clay and flour, from berry juices and the juices of other fruits, from *jaba-* and *shiuli*-flower[8] stems. This activity brought her considerable grief, because anything unessential or irrational has the character of flash floods in July: it has considerable mobility,

1. **Mymensingh** (mī′mən-sǐng′): a city about 200 miles northeast of Calcutta.
2. *pice* (pīs): a very small unit of money, formerly used in India.
3. **Kuvera** (ko͞o-vě′rə): the Hindu god of wealth.
4. **guises** (gī′zǐz): outward appearances.
5. **MacDulal** (măk′do͞o-läl′): The name is a play on the word *dulal,* which can mean "darling or spoiled child."
6. **Chunilal** (cho͞o′nē-läl′).
7. **Satyabati** (sät′yə-bə-tē′).
8. *jaba-* (jä′bə-) and *shiuli-* (shyo͞o′lē-) **flower:** The jaba flower is red. The shiuli flower is white and has a sweet scent.

but in relation to the utilitarian[9] concerns of life it is like a stalled ferry. Sometimes there were invitations to visit relatives; Satyabati forgot them and spent the time in her bedroom with the door shut, kneading a lump of clay. The relatives said, "She's terribly stuck-up." There was no satisfactory reply to this. Mukunda had known, even on the basis of his bookish knowledge, that value judgments can be made about art too. He had been thrilled by the noble connotations of the word "art," but he could not conceive of its having any connection with the work of his own wife.

This man's nature had been very equable.[10] When his wife squandered time on unessential whims, he had smiled at it with affectionate delight. If anyone in the household made a slighting remark, he had protested immediately. There had been a singular self-contradiction in Mukunda's makeup; he had been an expert in the practice of law, but it must be conceded that he had had no worldly wisdom with regard to his household affairs. Plenty of money had passed through his hands, but since it had not preoccupied his thoughts, it had left his mind free. Nor could he have tyrannized over his dependents in order to get his own way. His living habits had been very simple; he had never made any unreasonable demands for the attention or services of his relatives.

Mukunda had immediately silenced anyone in the household who cast an aspersion[11] upon Satyabati's disinterest in housework. Now and then, on his way home from court, he would stop at Radhabazar[12] to buy some paints, some colored silk and colored pencils, and stealthily he would go and arrange them on the wooden chest in his wife's bedroom. Sometimes, picking up one of Satyabati's drawings, he would say, "Well, this one is certainly very beautiful."

One day he had held up a picture of a man, and since he had it upside down, he had decided that the legs must be a bird's head. He had said, "Satu, this should be framed—what a marvelous picture

of a stork!" Mukunda had gotten a certain delight out of thinking of his wife's art work as child's play, and the wife had taken a similar pleasure in her husband's judgment of art. Satyabati had known perfectly well that she could not hope for so much patience, so much indulgence, from any other family in Bengal. No other family would have made way so lovingly for her overpowering devotion to art. So, whenever her husband had made extravagant remarks about her painting, Satyabati could scarcely restrain her tears.

One day Satyabati lost even this rare good fortune. Before his death her husband had realized one thing quite clearly: the responsibility for his debt-ridden property must be left in the hands of someone astute[13] enough to skillfully steer even a leaky boat to the other shore. This is how Satyabati and her son came to be placed completely under Govinda's care. From the very first day Govinda made it plain to her that the *pice* was the first and foremost thing in life. There was such profound degradation[14] in his advice that Satyabati would shrink with shame.

Nevertheless, the worship of money continued in diverse forms in their daily life. If there had been some modesty about it, instead of such constant discussion, it wouldn't have been so bad. Satyabati knew in her heart that all of this lowered her son's standard of values, but there was nothing to do but endure it. Since those delicate emotions endowed[15] with uncommon dignity are

---

9. **utilitarian** (yōō′tĭl′ĭ-târ′ē-ən): practical.

10. **equable** (ĕk′wə-bəl): calm; not easily disturbed.

11. **cast an aspersion** (ə-spûr′zhən): made an unfavorable or damaging remark.

12. **Radhabazar** (rä′tə-bə-zär′): a shopping area of Calcutta.

13. **astute** (ə-stōōt′): shrewd; crafty.

14. **degradation** (dĕg′rə-dā′shən): disgrace or dishonor.

15. **endowed**: equipped; supplied.

The Summer Elephant (mid-18th century), unknown artist. Miniature painting on paper,
25.7 cm × 34 cm. Courtesy of the Trustees of the Prince of Wales Museum of Western India, Mumbai.

HUMANITIES CONNECTION According to Hindu mythology, elephants once had wings
and were friendly with the clouds. After the elephants lost their wings, they were still
able to call upon the clouds to bring rain. These beasts are honored today in India for
their association with rainfall and good crops, and they are considered good luck.

the most vulnerable, they are very easily hurt or ridiculed by rude or insensitive people.

The study of art requires all sorts of supplies. Satyabati had received these for so long without even asking that she had felt no reticence[16] with regard to them. Amid the new circumstances in the family she felt terribly ashamed to charge all these unessential items to the housekeeping budget. So she would save money by economizing on her own food and have the supplies purchased and brought in secretly. Whatever work she did was done furtively,[17] behind closed doors. She was not afraid of a scolding, but the stares of insensitive observers embarrassed her.

Now Chuni was the only spectator and critic of her artistic activity. Gradually he became a participant. He began to feel its intoxication. The child's offense could not be concealed, since it overflowed the pages of his notebook onto the walls of the house. There were stains on his face, on his hands, on the cuffs of his shirt. Indra, the king of the gods,[18] does not spare even the soul of a little boy in the effort to tempt him away from the worship of money.

On the one hand the restraint increased, on the other hand the mother collaborated in the violations. Occasionally the head of the company would take his office manager, Govinda, along on business trips out of town. Then the mother and son would get together in unrestrained joy. This was the absolute extreme of childishness! They drew pictures of animals that God has yet to create. The likeness of the dog would get mixed up with that of the cat. It was difficult to distinguish between fish and fowl. There was no way to preserve all these creations; their traces had to be thoroughly obliterated before the head of the house returned. Only Brahma, the Creator, and Rudra, the Destroyer, witnessed the creative delight of these two persons; Vishnu,[19] the heavenly Preserver, never arrived.

The compulsion for artistic creation ran strong in Satyabati's family. There was an older nephew, Rangalal,[20] who rose overnight to fame as an artist. That is to say, the connoisseurs of the land roared with laughter at the unorthodoxy of his art.[21] Since their stamp of imagination did not coincide with his, they had a violent scorn for his talent. But curiously enough, his reputation thrived upon disdain and flourished in this atmosphere of opposition and mockery. Those who imitated him most took it upon themselves to prove that the man was a hoax as an artist, that there were obvious defects even in his technique.

This much maligned[22] artist came to his aunt's home one day, at a time when the office manager was absent. After persistent knocking and shoving at the door he finally got inside and found that there was nowhere to set foot on the floor. The cat was out of the bag.

"It is obvious," said Rangalal, "that the image of creation has emerged anew from the soul of the artist; this is not random scribbling. He and that god who creates form[23] are the same age. Get out all the drawings and show them to me."

Where should they get the drawings? That artist who draws pictures all over the sky in myriad[24] colors, in light and shadow, calmly discards his mists and mirages. Their creations had gone the same way. With an oath Rangalal said

---

16. **reticence** (rĕt′ĭ-səns): hesitancy to speak.

17. **furtively:** secretly.

18. **Indra, the king of the gods:** one of the chief gods of early Hinduism.

19. **Brahma** (brä′mə) . . . **Rudra** (rŏŏ′drə) . . . **Vishnu** (vĭsh′nŏŏ): the three major gods of Hinduism. "Rudra" is another name for Shiva.

20. **Rangalal** (rän′gə-läl′).

21. **connoisseurs** (kŏn′ə-sûrz′) . . . **unorthodoxy of his art:** Those with expert knowledge in art laughed at the untraditional style of his work.

22. **maligned** (mə-līnd′): spoken about in a harmful, misleading way meant to injure.

23. **that god who creates form:** probably Brahma, understood by Tagore as the originator of all art.

24. **myriad** (mĭr′ē-əd): many; innumerable.

Now Chuni was the only spectator and critic of her artistic activity. Gradually he became a participant. He began to feel its intoxication.

to his aunt, "From now on, I'll come and get whatever you make."

There came another day when the office manager had not returned. Since morning the sky had brooded in the shadows of July; it was raining. No one monitored the hands of the clock and no one wanted to know about them. Today Chuni began to draw a picture of a sailing boat while his mother was in the prayer room. The waves of the river looked like a flock of hungry seals just on the point of swallowing the boat. The clouds seemed to cheer them on and float their shawls overhead, but the seals were not conventional seals, and it would be no exaggeration to say of the clouds: "Light and mist merge in the watery waste." In the interests of truth it must be said that if boats were built like this one, insurance companies would never assume such risks. Thus the painting continued; the sky-artist drew fanciful pictures, and inside the room the wide-eyed boy did the same.

No one realized that the door was open. The office manager appeared. He roared in a thunderous voice, "What's going on?"

The boy's heart jumped and his face grew pale. Now Govinda perceived the real reason for Chunilal's examination errors in historical dates. Meanwhile the crime became all the more evident as Chunilal tried unsuccessfully to hide the drawing under his shirt. As Govinda snatched the picture away, the design he saw on it further astonished him. Errors in historical dates would be preferable to this. He tore the picture to pieces. Chunilal burst out crying.

From the prayer room Satyabati heard the boy's weeping, and she came running. Both Chunilal and the torn pieces of the picture were on the floor. Govinda went on enumerating the reasons for his nephew's failure in the history examination and suggesting dire remedies.

Satyabati had never said a word about Govinda's behavior toward them. She had quietly endured everything, remembering that this was the person on whom her husband had relied. Now her eyes were wet with tears, and shaking with anger, she said hoarsely, "Why did you tear up Chuni's picture?"

Govinda said, "Doesn't he have to study? What will become of him in the future?"

"Even if he becomes a beggar in the street," answered Satyabati, "he'll be better off in the future. But I hope he'll never be like you. May his pride in his God-given talent be more than your pride in *pices*. This is my blessing for him, a mother's blessing."

"I can't neglect my responsibility," said Govinda. "I will not tolerate this. Tomorrow I'll send him to a boarding school; otherwise, you'll ruin him."

The office manager returned to the office. The rain fell in torrents and the streets flowed with water.

Holding her son's hand, Satyabati said, "Let's go, dear."

Chuni said, "Go where, Mother?"

"Let's get out of this place."

The water was knee-deep at Rangalal's door. Satyabati came in with Chunilal. She said, "My dear boy, you take charge of him. Keep him from the worship of money." ❖

Connect to the Literature

1. **What Do You Think?** What was your reaction to Satyabati's decision to leave Chunilal with Rangalal?

Comprehension Check
- How did Mukunda treat Satyabati?
- Why is Govinda in charge of the affairs of Satyabati and Chunilal?
- What do Satyabati and Chunilal love to do?

Think Critically

2. In what ways are Mukunda and Govinda different?

3. What kind of mother is Satyabati?

4. What idea does Tagore convey about art and the worship of money?

Points *of* Comparison

Paired Activity Now that you have read and studied both stories, work with a partner to compare and contrast them. First, review the answers for "A Problem" in your comparison-and-contrast charts. Then, together, fill out the last column of your charts. An example is given at the right.

Questions for Analysis	"A Problem"	"The Artist"
What real-life situations are portrayed?	young man gets himself in trouble	mother and uncle disagree on how to raise a child
What everyday details are described?		
What are the concerns and struggles of the main characters?		
What motivates their actions and responses?		
How does the story end?		

Standardized Test Practice

Writing About Literature

PART 1 — Reading the Prompt

In writing assessments you may be asked to compare and contrast works of literature that share certain characteristics, such as the two examples of realism that you have just read. You are now going to practice writing an essay that involves this type of comparison.

> **Writing Prompt**
> Compare and contrast the stories "A Problem" and "The Artist" ❶ as works of realism. For each story consider what the characters ❷ are like, what conflicts they face, how circumstances and situations are portrayed, and how the story ends. Point out how the two stories share aspects of realism and how they differ as examples of ❸ realism. Support your analysis with examples from the stories. ❹

STRATEGIES
IN ACTION

❶ I have to **compare and contrast** two works of realism.

❷ For each story I need to discuss the **characters,** their **conflicts,** the **circumstances** and **situations,** and the **ending.**

❸ I need to explain how the stories are **similar** and **different** as works of realism.

❹ I have to support my discussion with **examples.**

PART 2 — Planning a Comparison-and-Contrast Essay

- Review the comparison-and-contrast chart that you filled out for "A Problem" and "The Artist."

- Referring to your chart, find examples of similarities and differences to point out in your essay. Review the stories for other examples.

- Create an outline to help you organize your ideas.

PART 3 — Drafting Your Essay

Introduction Begin by introducing both stories as works of realism. Explain that they share important characteristics of realism but also differ in some ways.

Body Present each story's treatment of characters, conflicts, situations, and so on. You can discuss each characteristic in a different paragraph, or you can first discuss the characteristics in one story and then those in the other. Point out the similarities and differences that emerge from your analysis. Consult your comparison-and-contrast chart for specific ideas and examples.

Conclusion Briefly summarize the major similarities and differences between the two stories. You might want to finish with a statement about any new understanding of realism you have gained.

Revision Check the use of signal words, such as *similarly, also, like, but,* and *while,* to make sure that your comparisons and contrasts are clear.

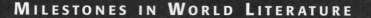

THE NOVELS OF

Fyodor Dostoyevsky

Imagine entering the mind of a murderer as he plots his crime against a defenseless old woman. Picture yourself as a bystander at a scandalous trial where a son is accused of murdering his father. When you open the pages of a Dostoyevsky (dŏs'tə-yĕf' skē) novel, you enter a strange and darkly fascinating world.

Both Fyodor Dostoyevsky (1821–1881) and his contemporary Leo Tolstoy have been praised as great realists. Where Tolstoy is famous for the scope of his novels, representing every level of Russian society, Dostoyevsky is known for portraying disturbed minds from the lower fringes of society. He said of his work, "I am only a realist in the highest sense. . . . I depict all the depths of the human soul."

Though Dostoyevsky was born into a respectable middle-class family, his life was marked by the very extremes that he wrote about. In his youth he was a political rebel, perhaps even a revolutionary. Later he fell prey to gambling sprees so serious that he lost his wife's dowry. For much of his adult life, he was burdened by huge debts and subject to agonizing epileptic fits. Yet he was also a doting father, a loyal brother and husband, a patriot, and at his death a national hero.

A street in St. Petersburg, 1886

As a young man in 1849, Dostoyevsky was imprisoned and sentenced to death for associating with political radicals. Just minutes before the prisoners' execution, a messenger announced that their lives had been spared by the czar. Dostoyevsky spent the next four years in a Siberian labor camp.

When Dostoyevsky returned from his Siberian exile, he was a changed man. His four greatest novels explore profound questions about the existence of God, the nature of freedom, and the origins of evil.

Crime and Punishment (1866). What happens to a poor young student who believes he is superior to everyone else? The student, Raskolnikov (rə-skôl′nĭ-kôf′), hatches a plan to kill a rich pawnbroker for money to support his family. After his crime he realizes that his motives were far more complex.

The Idiot (1868–1869). In this novel Dostoyevsky portrays "a positively beautiful person," the saintly Prince Myshkin (mĭsh′kĭn). The prince's virtue, however, proves no match for the grimy world of St. Petersburg, with all its greed, lust, and cruel ambition.

Scene from a 1998 film of Crime and Punishment, *with Ben Kingsley and Patrick Dempsey*

Demons (1872). In the Bible, Jesus casts out devils from a sick person, which then possess a herd of swine and proceed to drown themselves. In this political novel, inspired by the biblical story, various characters are "possessed" by the heartless ideas of revolution and atheism. The title is also translated as *The Possessed* and *Devils*.

The Brothers Karamazov (1880). What do a monk, an atheist, and a spendthrift drinker have in common? They are the Karamazov brothers, and their father is an embarrassment to everyone. When the father is murdered, one son stands accused and is put on trial. Yet all the major characters face personal trials as they search for life's meaning.

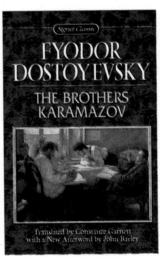

Dostoyevsky's influence continues to be felt today. His explorations into the dark recesses of the mind have influenced novelists, psychologists, artists, philosophers, and theologians. As one critic notes, "The major questions of modernity can all be traced to Dostoyevsky."

MILESTONE LINKS
CLASSZONE.COM

A Doll's House

HENRIK IBSEN

Henrik Ibsen
1828–1906

Early Life Hailed today as the father of modern drama, Henrik Ibsen (hĕn′rēk ĭb′sən) began life in a small Norwegian town. When he was seven, his father, who had been a respected merchant, went bankrupt, disgracing the family. In addition to poverty, the young Ibsen had to endure being socially outcast by the same people who used to come to his house for dinner parties. Ibsen never forgot the small-minded snobbishness that caused him such pain.

At the Theater Along with Shakespeare, Ibsen is one of very few playwrights who have had practical experience working in the theater. Starting at the age of 23, Ibsen spent approximately 11 years as a stage manager, director, and resident playwright. He eventually grew disgusted with the low-quality melodramas and silly comedies that dominated most European stages in the mid-1800s. With his wife and young son, he left Norway and began a 27-year period of wandering, mainly in Italy and Germany. During this crucial time, his genius matured as he experimented with several plays, some of them in verse. Two of them, *Brand* and *Peer Gynt* (pâr gĭnt), were popular successes. However, it was in *A Doll's House,* produced in 1879, that Ibsen found his true voice. The play caused an uproar, and conventional viewers were scandalized. A small but significant audience, however, was attracted to Ibsen's work and took it seriously. As he continued to write plays that broke new ground, his audience grew, and Ibsen became established as one of the foremost dramatists of his time.

Ibsen's Art According to one biographer, Ibsen was a "man who thought romantically, but wrote realistically." Ibsen resisted being called a realist. He didn't like what he called "photographic art." Yet Ibsen shared with the realists a desire to explore the truth, for better or worse. He set out to reveal the secret inner life of his characters, where he believed the truth really lay. Audiences who watched Ibsen's characters expose their true selves were forced to reexamine their own values and moral conduct. With his searing insight, Ibsen foreshadowed the shifts in thought that were to come in the next century.

Other Works
Ghosts
An Enemy of the People
Hedda Gabler
When We Dead Awaken

Build Background

Ibsen's Revolutionary Play *A Doll's House* caused a sensation after its initial performance in 1879. Critics debated Ibsen's social views in newspapers and magazines. Ministers even delivered sermons on the play. Although Ibsen was sensitive to criticism, he recognized that the controversy would benefit his career: "My enemies," he declared, "have been a great help to me—their attacks have been so vicious that people come flocking to see what all the shouting was about." By the late 1880s, *A Doll's House* had been produced throughout Europe, and Ibsen had become internationally famous.

Women and Society The "shouting" mainly concerned Ibsen's portrayal of a housewife who revolts against society's restrictions on women. In 19th-century Europe, husbands still had full legal authority over their wives. Married women could not carry out transactions such as taking out a loan, and they were expected to be obedient to their husbands. There was a growing movement to win political and economic rights for women. Ibsen was widely seen as a champion of women's rights after he wrote *A Doll's House.* However, he denied that he had intended the play as a political statement. "I have been more the poet and less the social philosopher than people generally seem inclined to believe," Ibsen said. "My task has been the *description of humanity."*

Realistic Drama Ibsen's exploration of women's issues wasn't the only controversial aspect of *A Doll's House.* Nineteenth-century theatergoers were used to plays with fanciful plots that led to happy endings. Ibsen revolted against this tradition by presenting a simple but powerful story drawn from everyday life. Instead of creating dialogue that used formal, elevated language, he let his characters speak as ordinary people do. His prose appears to be plain and straightforward, yet he used poetic elements such as symbolism to suggest ideas. Many critics have called *A Doll's House* the first modern drama.

For a humanities activity, click on:

HUMANITIES
CLASSZONE.COM

Connect to Your Life

Think of a time when a friend or relative wasn't taking you seriously or respecting your opinion. How did this person's attitude make you feel? What steps did you take to resolve the problem? Share your experience with a classmate.

Focus Your Reading

LITERARY ANALYSIS: REALISTIC DRAMA
A Doll's House is one of the first examples of **realistic drama.** As you read, notice how Ibsen develops **characters, setting,** and **themes** that reflect real life.

ACTIVE READING: STRATEGIES FOR READING REALISTIC DRAMA
The printed text of *A Doll's House* consists mainly of **dialogue** spoken by the characters and **stage directions.** To better understand the play, follow these strategies.

- Read the **cast of characters** to familiarize yourself with the names and relationships.

- Pay careful attention to the stage directions. Like many realist playwrights, Ibsen offers detailed descriptions.

- **Visualize** what the characters look like.

- Use the Guide for Reading for help in keeping track of developments in the play.

- To get a better sense of what the dialogue might sound like, try reading some of it aloud.

READER'S NOTEBOOK As you read, jot down the answers to the Guide for Reading questions that occur in each act. Also note any additional strategies you used, such as visualizing characters or setting, or reading dialogue aloud.

WORDS TO KNOW **Vocabulary Preview**

calculating	inane	rash
capricious	jauntily	tactless
chronic	petty	warily
desolate		

A Doll's House

Henrik Ibsen

Translated by Rolf Fjelde

THE CHARACTERS

TORVALD HELMER, a lawyer
NORA, his wife
DR. RANK
MRS. LINDE
NILS KROGSTAD, a bank clerk

THE HELMERS' THREE SMALL CHILDREN
ANNE-MARIE, their nurse
HELENE, a maid
A DELIVERY BOY

The action takes place in Helmer's *residence.*

Act One

A comfortable room, tastefully but not expensively furnished. A door to the right in the back wall leads to the entryway; another to the left leads to Helmer's study. Between these doors, a piano. Midway in the left-hand wall a door, and further back a window. Near the window a round table with an armchair and a small sofa. In the right-hand wall, toward the rear, a door, and nearer the foreground a porcelain stove with two armchairs and a rocking chair beside it. Between the stove and the side door, a small table. Engravings on the walls. An etagère[1] *with china figures and other small art objects; a small bookcase with richly bound books; the floor carpeted; a fire burning in the stove. It is a winter day.*

 A bell rings in the entryway; shortly after we hear the door being unlocked. Nora *comes into the room, humming happily to herself; she is wearing street clothes and carries an armload of packages, which she puts down on the table to the right. She has left the hall door open; and through it a* Delivery Boy *is seen, holding a Christmas tree and a basket, which he gives to the* Maid *who let them in.*

---

1. etagère (ā′tä-zhâr′): a piece of furniture with open shelves for displaying small objects.

FOCUS In this part you will be introduced to the play's two main characters. As you read, look for suggestions of misunderstanding and lack of communication between them.

Nora. Hide the tree well, Helene. The children mustn't get a glimpse of it till this evening, after it's trimmed. (*To the* Delivery Boy, *taking out her purse.*) How much?

Delivery Boy. Fifty, ma'am.

Nora. There's a crown.[2] No, keep the change. (*The* Boy *thanks her and leaves.* Nora *shuts the door. She laughs softly to herself while taking off her street things. Drawing a bag of macaroons[3] from her pocket, she eats a couple, then steals over and listens at her husband's study door.*) Yes, he's home. (*Hums again as she moves to the table right.*)

Helmer (*from the study*). Is that my little lark twittering out there?

Nora (*busy opening some packages*). Yes, it is.

Helmer. Is that my squirrel rummaging around?

Nora. Yes!

Helmer. When did my squirrel get in?

Nora. Just now. (*Putting the macaroon bag in her pocket and wiping her mouth.*) Do come in, Torvald, and see what I've bought.

Helmer. Can't be disturbed. (*After a moment he opens the door and peers in, pen in hand.*) Bought, you say? All that there? Has the little spendthrift been out throwing money around again?

Nora. Oh, but Torvald, this year we really should let ourselves go a bit. It's the first Christmas we haven't had to economize.

Helmer. But you know we can't go squandering.

Nora. Oh yes, Torvald, we can squander a little now. Can't we? Just a tiny, wee bit. Now that you've got a big salary and are going to make piles and piles of money.

Helmer. Yes—starting New Year's. But then it's a full three months till the raise comes through.

Nora. Pooh! We can borrow that long.

Helmer. Nora! (*Goes over and playfully takes her by the ear.*) Are your scatterbrains off again? What if today I borrowed a thousand crowns, and you squandered them over Christmas week, and then on New Year's Eve a roof tile fell on my head, and I lay there—

Nora (*putting her hand on his mouth*). Oh! Don't say such things!

Helmer. Yes, but what if it happened—then what?

Nora. If anything so awful happened, then it just wouldn't matter if I had debts or not.

Helmer. Well, but the people I'd borrowed from?

Nora. Them? Who cares about them! They're strangers.

Helmer. Nora, Nora, how like a woman! No, but seriously, Nora, you know what I think about that. No debts! Never borrow! Something of freedom's lost—and something of beauty, too—from a home that's founded on borrowing and debt. We've made a brave stand up to now, the two of us; and we'll go right on like that the little while we have to.

Nora (*going toward the stove*). Yes, whatever you say, Torvald.

Helmer (*following her*). Now, now, the little lark's wings mustn't droop. Come on, don't be a sulky squirrel. (*Taking out his wallet.*) Nora, guess what I have here.

Nora (*turning quickly*). Money!

Helmer. There, see. (*Hands her some notes.*) Good grief, I know how costs go up in a house at Christmastime.

Nora. Ten—twenty—thirty—forty. Oh, thank you,

---

2. **crown:** The crown, or krone, is the basic unit of currency in Norway.

3. **macaroons** (măk'ə-rōōnz'): sweet, chewy cookies.

Torvald; I can manage no end on this.

Helmer. You really will have to.

Nora. Oh yes, I promise I will! But come here so I can show you everything I bought. And so cheap! Look, new clothes for Ivar[4] here—and a sword. Here a horse and a trumpet for Bob. And a doll and a doll's bed here for Emmy; they're nothing much, but she'll tear them to bits in no time anyway. And here I have dress material and handkerchiefs for the maids. Old Anne-Marie really deserves something more.

Helmer. And what's in that package there?

Nora (*with a cry*). Torvald, no! You can't see that till tonight!

Helmer. I see. But tell me now, you little prodigal,[5] what have you thought of for yourself?

Nora. For myself? Oh, I don't want anything at all.

Helmer. Of course you do. Tell me just what—within reason—you'd most like to have.

Nora. I honestly don't know. Oh, listen, Torvald—

Helmer. Well?

Nora (*fumbling at his coat buttons, without looking at him*). If you want to give me something, then maybe you could—you could—

Helmer. Come on, out with it.

Nora (*hurriedly*). You could give me money, Torvald. No more than you think you can spare; then one of these days I'll buy something with it.

Helmer. But Nora—

Nora. Oh, please, Torvald darling, do that! I beg you, please. Then I could hang the bills in pretty gilt paper on the Christmas tree. Wouldn't that be fun?

Helmer. What are those little birds called that always fly through their fortunes?

Nora. Oh yes, spendthrifts; I know all that. But let's do as I say, Torvald; then I'll have time to decide what I really need most. That's very sensible, isn't it?

Helmer (*smiling*). Yes, very—that is, if you actually hung onto the money I give you, and you actually used it to buy yourself something. But it goes for the house and for all sorts of foolish things, and then I only have to lay out some more.

Nora. Oh, but Torvald—

Helmer. Don't deny it, my dear little Nora. (*Putting his arm around her waist.*) Spendthrifts are sweet, but they use up a frightful amount of money. It's incredible what it costs a man to feed such birds.

Nora. Oh, how can you say that! Really, I save everything I can.

Helmer (*laughing*). Yes, that's the truth. Everything you can. But that's nothing at all.

Nora (*humming, with a smile of quiet satisfaction*). Hm, if you only knew what expenses we larks and squirrels have, Torvald.

Helmer. You're an odd little one. Exactly the way your father was. You're never at a loss for scaring up money; but the moment you have it, it runs right out through your fingers; you never know what you've done with it. Well, one takes you as you are. It's deep in your blood. Yes, these things are hereditary, Nora.

Nora. Ah, I could wish I'd inherited many of Papa's qualities.

Helmer. And I couldn't wish you anything but just what you are, my sweet little lark. But wait; it seems to me you have a very—what should I call it?—a very suspicious look today—

Nora. I do?

---

4. **Ivar** (ē'vär).

5. **prodigal** (prŏd'ĭ-gəl): a person who is foolishly extravagant.

For myself?
Oh, I don't want anything at all.

Claire Bloom as Nora and Anthony Hopkins as Torvald in a 1973 film of *A Doll's House,*
directed by Patrick Garland

Helmer. You certainly do. Look me straight in the eye.

Nora (*looking at him*). Well?

Helmer (*shaking an admonitory[6] finger*). Surely my sweet tooth hasn't been running riot in town today, has she?

Nora. No. Why do you imagine that?

Helmer. My sweet tooth really didn't make a little detour through the confectioner's?[7]

Nora. No, I assure you, Torvald—

Helmer. Hasn't nibbled some pastry?

Nora. No, not at all.

Helmer. Not even munched a macaroon or two?

Nora. No, Torvald, I assure you, really—

Helmer. There, there now. Of course I'm only joking.

Nora (*going to the table, right*). You know I could never think of going against you.

Helmer. No, I understand that; and you *have* given me your word. (*Going over to her.*) Well, you keep your little Christmas secrets to yourself, Nora darling. I expect they'll come to light this evening, when the tree is lit.

Nora. Did you remember to ask Dr. Rank?

Helmer. No. But there's no need for that; it's assumed he'll be dining with us. All the same, I'll ask him when he stops by here this morning. I've ordered some fine wine. Nora, you can't imagine how I'm looking forward to this evening.

Nora. So am I. And what fun for the children, Torvald!

Helmer. Ah, it's so gratifying to know that one's gotten a safe, secure job, and with a comfortable salary. It's a great satisfaction, isn't it?

Nora. Oh, it's wonderful!

Helmer. Remember last Christmas? Three whole weeks before, you shut yourself in every evening till long after midnight, making flowers for the Christmas tree, and all the other decorations to surprise us. Ugh, that was the dullest time I've ever lived through.

Nora. It wasn't at all dull for me.

Helmer (*smiling*). But the outcome *was* pretty sorry, Nora.

Nora. Oh, don't tease me with that again. How could I help it that the cat came in and tore everything to shreds.

Helmer. No, poor thing, you certainly couldn't. You wanted so much to please us all, and that's what counts. But it's just as well that the hard times are past.

Nora. Yes, it's really wonderful.

Helmer. Now I don't have to sit here alone, boring myself, and you don't have to tire your precious eyes and your fair little delicate hands—

Nora (*clapping her hands*). No, is it really true, Torvald, I don't have to? Oh, how wonderfully lovely to hear! (*Taking his arm.*) Now I'll tell you just how I've thought we should plan things. Right after Christmas—(*The doorbell rings.*) Oh, the bell. (*Straightening the room up a bit.*) Somebody would have to come. What a bore!

Helmer. I'm not at home to visitors, don't forget.

Maid (*from the hall doorway*). Ma'am, a lady to see you—

Nora. All right, let her come in.

Maid (*to Helmer*). And the doctor's just come too.

Helmer. Did he go right to my study?

Maid. Yes, he did.

(Helmer *goes into his room. The* Maid *shows in* Mrs. Linde, *dressed in traveling clothes, and shuts the door after her.*)

---

6. **admonitory** (ăd-mŏn′ĭ-tôr′ē): expressing advice or warning.

7. **confectioner's:** a store where candy and other sweets are sold.

Mrs. Linde (*in a dispirited and somewhat hesitant voice*). Hello, Nora.

Nora (*uncertain*). Hello—

Mrs. Linde. You don't recognize me.

Nora. No, I don't know—but wait, I think— (*Exclaiming.*) What! Kristine! Is it really you?

Mrs. Linde. Yes, it's me.

Nora. Kristine! To think I didn't recognize you. But then, how could I? (*More quietly.*) How you've changed, Kristine!

Mrs. Linde. Yes, no doubt I have. In nine—ten long years.

Nora. Is it so long since we met! Yes, it's all of that. Oh, these last eight years have been a happy time, believe me. And so now you've come in to town, too. Made the long trip in the winter. That took courage.

Mrs. Linde. I just got here by ship this morning.

Nora. To enjoy yourself over Christmas, of course. Oh, how lovely! Yes, enjoy ourselves, we'll do that. But take your coat off. You're not still cold? (*Helping her.*) There now, let's get cozy here by the stove. No, the easy chair there! I'll take the rocker here. (*Seizing her hands.*) Yes, now you have your old look again; it was only in that first moment. You're a bit more pale, Kristine—and maybe a bit thinner.

Mrs. Linde. And much, much older, Nora.

Nora. Yes, perhaps a bit older; a tiny, tiny bit; not much at all. (*Stopping short; suddenly serious.*) Oh, but thoughtless me, to sit here, chattering away. Sweet, good Kristine, can you forgive me?

Mrs. Linde. What do you mean, Nora?

Nora (*softly*). Poor Kristine, you've become a widow.

Mrs. Linde. Yes, three years ago.

Nora. Oh, I knew it, of course; I read it in the papers. Oh, Kristine, you must believe me; I often thought of writing you then, but I kept postponing it, and something always interfered.

Mrs. Linde. Nora dear, I understand completely.

Nora. No, it was awful of me, Kristine. You poor thing, how much you must have gone through. And he left you nothing?

Mrs. Linde. No.

Nora. And no children?

Mrs. Linde. No.

Nora. Nothing at all, then?

Mrs. Linde. Not even a sense of loss to feed on.

Nora (*looking incredulously at her*). But Kristine, how could that be?

Mrs. Linde (*smiling wearily and smoothing her hair*). Oh, sometimes it happens, Nora.

Nora. So completely alone. How terribly hard that must be for you. I have three lovely children. You can't see them now; they're out with the maid. But now you must tell me everything—

Mrs. Linde. No, no, no, tell me about yourself.

Nora. No, you begin. Today I don't want to be selfish. I want to think only of you today. But there *is* something I must tell you. Did you hear of the wonderful luck we had recently?

Mrs. Linde. No, what's that?

Nora. My husband's been made manager in the bank, just think!

Mrs. Linde. Your husband? How marvelous!

Nora. Isn't it? Being a lawyer is such an uncertain living, you know, especially if one won't touch any cases that aren't clean and decent. And of course Torvald would never do that, and I'm with him completely there. Oh, we're simply delighted, believe me! He'll join the bank right after New Year's and start getting a huge salary and lots of commissions. From now on we can live quite differently—just as we want. Oh, Kristine, I feel so light and happy! Won't it be lovely to have stacks of money and not a care in the world?

Mrs. Linde. Well, anyway, it would be lovely to have enough for necessities.

Nora. No, not just for necessities, but stacks and stacks of money!

Mrs. Linde (*smiling*). Nora, Nora, aren't you sensible yet? Back in school you were such a free spender.

Nora (*with a quiet laugh*). Yes, that's what Torvald still says. (*Shaking her finger.*) But "Nora, Nora" isn't as silly as you all think. Really, we've been in no position for me to go squandering. We've had to work, both of us.

Mrs. Linde. You too?

Nora. Yes, at odd jobs—needlework, crocheting, embroidery, and such—(*Casually.*) and other things too. You remember that Torvald left the department when we were married? There was no chance of promotion in his office, and of course he needed to earn more money. But that first year he drove himself terribly. He took on all kinds of extra work that kept him going morning and night. It wore him down, and then he fell deathly ill. The doctors said it was essential for him to travel south.

Mrs. Linde. Yes, didn't you spend a whole year in Italy?

Nora. That's right. It wasn't easy to get away, you know. Ivar had just been born. But of course we had to go. Oh, that was a beautiful trip, and it saved Torvald's life. But it cost a frightful sum, Kristine.

Mrs. Linde. I can well imagine.

Nora. Four thousand, eight hundred crowns it cost. That's really a lot of money.

Mrs. Linde. But it's lucky you had it when you needed it.

Nora. Well, as it was, we got it from Papa.

Mrs. Linde. I see. It was just about the time your father died.

Nora. Yes, just about then. And, you know, I couldn't make that trip out to nurse him. I had to stay here, expecting Ivar any moment, and with my poor sick Torvald to care for. Dearest Papa, I never saw him again, Kristine. Oh, that was the worst time I've known in all my marriage.

Mrs. Linde. I know how you loved him. And then you went off to Italy?

Nora. Yes. We had the means now, and the doctors urged us. So we left a month after.

Mrs. Linde. And your husband came back completely cured?

Nora. Sound as a drum!

Mrs. Linde. But—the doctor?

Nora. Who?

Mrs. Linde. I thought the maid said he was a doctor, the man who came in with me.

Nora. Yes, that was Dr. Rank—but he's not making a sick call. He's our closest friend, and he stops by at least once a day. No, Torvald hasn't had a sick moment since, and the children are fit and strong, and I am, too. (*Jumping up and clapping her hands.*) Oh, dear God, Kristine, what a lovely thing to live and be happy! But how disgusting of me—I'm talking of nothing but my own affairs. (*Sits on a stool close by* Kristine, *arms resting across her knees.*) Oh, don't be angry with me! Tell me, is it really true that you weren't in love with your husband? Why did you marry him, then?

Mrs. Linde. My mother was still alive, but bedridden and helpless—and I had my two younger brothers to look after. In all conscience, I didn't think I could turn him down.

Nora. No, you were right there. But was he rich at the time?

Mrs. Linde. He was very well off, I'd say. But the business was shaky, Nora. When he died, it all fell apart, and nothing was left.

Nora. And then—?

Mrs. Linde. Yes, so I had to scrape up a living with a little shop and a little teaching and whatever else I could find. The last three years have been like one endless workday without a rest for me. Now it's over, Nora. My poor mother doesn't need me, for she's passed on. Nor the boys, either; they're working now and can take care of themselves.

Nora. How free you must feel—

Mrs. Linde. No—only unspeakably empty. Nothing to live for now. (*Standing up anxiously.*) That's why I couldn't take it any longer out in that <u>desolate</u> hole. Maybe here it'll be easier to find something to do and keep my mind occupied. If I could only be lucky enough to get a steady job, some office work—

Nora. Oh, but Kristine, that's so dreadfully tiring, and you already look so tired. It would be much better for you if you could go off to a bathing resort.

Mrs. Linde (*going toward the window*). I have no father to give me travel money, Nora.

Nora (*rising*). Oh, don't be angry with me.

Mrs. Linde (*going to her*). Nora dear, don't you be angry with me. The worst of my kind of situation is all the bitterness that's stored away. No one to work for, and yet you're always having to snap up your opportunities. You have to live; and so you grow selfish. When you told me the happy change in your lot, do you know I was delighted less for your sakes than for mine?

Nora. How so? Oh, I see. You think maybe Torvald could do something for you.

Mrs. Linde. Yes, that's what I thought.

Nora. And he will, Kristine! Just leave it to me; I'll bring it up so delicately—find something attractive to humor him with. Oh, I'm so eager to help you.

Mrs. Linde. How very kind of you, Nora, to be so concerned over me—doubly kind, considering you really know so little of life's burdens yourself.

Nora. I—? I know so little—?

Mrs. Linde (*smiling*). Well, my heavens—a little needlework and such—Nora, you're just a child.

Nora (*tossing her head and pacing the floor*). You don't have to act so superior.

Mrs. Linde. Oh?

Nora. You're just like the others. You all think I'm incapable of anything serious—

Mrs. Linde. Come now—

Nora. That I've never had to face the raw world.

Mrs. Linde. Nora dear, you've just been telling me all your troubles.

Nora. Hm! Trivia! (*Quietly.*) I haven't told you the big thing.

Mrs. Linde. Big thing? What do you mean?

Nora. You look down on me so, Kristine, but you shouldn't. You're proud that you worked so long and hard for your mother.

Mrs. Linde. I don't look down on a soul. But it *is* true: I'm proud—and happy, too—to think it was given to me to make my mother's last days almost free of care.

Nora. And you're also proud thinking of what you've done for your brothers.

Mrs. Linde. I feel I've a right to be.

Nora. I agree. But listen to this, Kristine—I've also got something to be proud and happy for.

I'll bet you're eaten up
with curiosity, Kristine.

Anna Massey as Mrs. Linde

Mrs. Linde. I don't doubt it. But whatever do you mean?

Nora. Not so loud. What if Torvald heard! He mustn't, not for anything in the world. Nobody must know, Kristine. No one but you.

Mrs. Linde. But what is it, then?

Nora. Come here. (*Drawing her down beside her on the sofa.*) It's true—I've also got something to be proud and happy for. I'm the one who saved Torvald's life.

Mrs. Linde. Saved—? Saved how?

Nora. I told you about the trip to Italy. Torvald never would have lived if he hadn't gone south—

Mrs. Linde. Of course; your father gave you the means—

Nora (*smiling*). That's what Torvald and all the rest think, but—

Mrs. Linde. But—?

Nora. Papa didn't give us a pin. I was the one who raised the money.

Mrs. Linde. You? That whole amount?

Nora. Four thousand, eight hundred crowns. What do you say to that?

Mrs. Linde. But Nora, how was it possible? Did you win the lottery?

Nora (*disdainfully*). The lottery? Pooh! No art to that.

Mrs. Linde. But where did you get it from then?

Nora (*humming, with a mysterious smile*). Hmm, tra-la-la-la.

Mrs. Linde. Because you couldn't have borrowed it.

Nora. No? Why not?

Mrs. Linde. A wife can't borrow without her husband's consent.

Nora (*tossing her head*). Oh, but a wife with a little business sense, a wife who knows how to manage—

Mrs. Linde. Nora, I simply don't understand—

Nora. You don't have to. Whoever said I *borrowed* the money? I could have gotten it other ways. (*Throwing herself back on the sofa.*) I could have gotten it from some admirer or other. After all, a girl with my ravishing[8] appeal—

Mrs. Linde. You lunatic.

Nora. I'll bet you're eaten up with curiosity, Kristine.

Mrs. Linde. Now listen here, Nora—you haven't done something indiscreet?[9]

Nora (*sitting up again*). Is it indiscreet to save your husband's life?

Mrs. Linde. I think it's indiscreet that without his knowledge you—

Nora. But that's the point: he mustn't know! My Lord, can't you understand? He mustn't ever know the close call he had. It was to *me* the doctors came to say his life was in danger—that nothing could save him but a stay in the south. Didn't I try strategy then! I began talking about how lovely it would be for me to travel abroad like other young wives; I begged and I cried; I told him please to remember my condition, to be kind and indulge me; and then I dropped a hint that he could easily take out a loan. But at that, Kristine, he nearly exploded. He said I was frivolous, and it was his duty as man of the house not to indulge me in whims and fancies—as I think he called them. Aha, I thought, now you'll just have to be saved—and that's when I saw my chance.

Mrs. Linde. And your father never told Torvald the money wasn't from him?

Nora. No, never. Papa died right about then. I'd considered bringing him into my secret and

---

8. **ravishing:** extremely attractive.

9. **indiscreet:** not showing self-restraint or good judgment; unwise.

begging him never to tell. But he was too sick at the time—and then, sadly, it didn't matter.

Mrs. Linde. And you've never confided in your husband since?

Nora. For heaven's sake, no! Are you serious? He's so strict on that subject. Besides— Torvald, with all his masculine pride—how painfully humiliating for him if he ever found out he was in debt to me. That would just ruin our relationship. Our beautiful, happy home would never be the same.

Mrs. Linde. Won't you ever tell him?

Nora (*thoughtfully, half smiling*). Yes—maybe sometime, years from now, when I'm no longer so attractive. Don't laugh! I only mean when Torvald loves me less than now, when he stops enjoying my dancing and dressing up and reciting for him. Then it might be wise to have something in reserve—(*Breaking off.*) How ridiculous! That'll never happen— Well, Kristine, what do you think of my big secret? I'm capable of something too, hm? You can imagine, of course, how this thing hangs over me. It really hasn't been easy meeting the payments on time. In the business world there's what they call quarterly interest and what they call amortization,[10] and these are always so terribly hard to manage. I've had to skimp a little here and there, wherever I could, you know. I could hardly spare anything from my house allowance, because Torvald has to live well. I couldn't let the children go poorly dressed; whatever I got for them, I felt I had to use up completely—the darlings!

Mrs. Linde. Poor Nora, so it had to come out of your own budget, then?

Nora. Yes, of course. But I was the one most responsible, too. Every time Torvald gave me money for new clothes and such, I never used more than half; always bought the simplest, cheapest outfits. It was a godsend that every-thing looks so well on me that Torvald never noticed. But it did weigh me down at times, Kristine. It *is* such a joy to wear fine things. You understand.

Mrs. Linde. Oh, of course.

Nora. And then I found other ways of making money. Last winter I was lucky enough to get a lot of copying to do. I locked myself in and sat writing every evening till late in the night. Ah, I was tired so often, dead tired. But still it was wonderful fun, sitting and working like that, earning money. It was almost like being a man.

Mrs. Linde. But how much have you paid off this way so far?

Nora. That's hard to say, exactly. These accounts, you know, aren't easy to figure. I only know that I've paid out all I could scrape together. Time and again I haven't known where to turn. (*Smiling.*) Then I'd sit here dreaming of a rich old gentleman who had fallen in love with me—

Mrs. Linde. What! Who is he?

Nora. Oh, really! And that he'd died, and when his will was opened, there in big letters it said, "All my fortune shall be paid over in cash, immediately, to that enchanting Mrs. Nora Helmer."

Mrs. Linde. But Nora dear—who *was* this gentleman?

Nora. Good grief, can't you understand? The old man never existed; that was only something I'd dream up time and again whenever I was at my wits' end for money. But it makes no difference now; the old fossil can go where he pleases for all I care; I don't need him or his will—because now I'm free. (*Jumping up.*)

---

10. **amortization** (ămʹər-tĭ-zāʹshən): the repayment of a debt by installments, with the interest on the debt decreasing from payment to payment.

Oh, how lovely to think of that, Kristine! Carefree! To know you're carefree, utterly carefree; to be able to romp and play with the children, and to keep up a beautiful, charming home—everything just the way Torvald likes it! And think, spring is coming, with big blue skies. Maybe we can travel a little then. Maybe I'll see the ocean again. Oh yes, it *is* so marvelous to live and be happy!

(*The front doorbell rings.*)

Mrs. Linde. (*rising*). There's the bell. It's probably best that I go.

Nora. No, stay. No one's expected. It must be for Torvald.

Maid (*from the hall doorway*). Excuse me, ma'am—there's a gentleman here to see Mr. Helmer, but I didn't know—since the doctor's with him—

Nora. Who is the gentleman?

Krogstad (*from the doorway*). It's me, Mrs. Helmer.

(Mrs. Linde *starts and turns away toward the window.*)

Nora (*stepping toward him, tense, her voice a whisper*). You? What is it? Why do you want to speak to my husband?

Krogstad. Bank business—after a fashion. I have a small job in the investment bank, and I hear now your husband is going to be our chief—

Nora. In other words, it's—

Krogstad. Just dry business, Mrs. Helmer. Nothing but that.

Nora. Yes, then please be good enough to step into the study. (*She nods indifferently as she sees him out by the hall door, then returns and begins stirring up the stove.*)

Mrs. Linde. Nora—who was that man?

Nora. That was a Mr. Krogstad—a lawyer.

Mrs. Linde. Then it really was him.

Nora. Do you know that person?

Mrs. Linde. I did once—many years ago. For a time he was a law clerk in our town.

Nora. Yes, he's been that.

Mrs. Linde. How he's changed.

Nora. I understand he had a very unhappy marriage.

Mrs. Linde. He's a widower now.

Nora. With a number of children. There now, it's burning. (*She closes the stove door and moves the rocker a bit to one side.*)

Mrs. Linde. They say he has a hand in all kinds of business.

Nora. Oh? That may be true; I wouldn't know. But let's not think about business. It's so dull.

(Dr. Rank *enters from* Helmer's *study.*)

Rank (*still in the doorway*). No, no, really—I don't want to intrude, I'd just as soon talk a little while with your wife. (*Shuts the door, then notices* Mrs. Linde.) Oh, beg pardon. I'm intruding here too.

Nora. No, not at all. (*Introducing him.*) Dr. Rank, Mrs. Linde.

Rank. Well now, that's a name much heard in this house. I believe I passed the lady on the stairs as I came.

Mrs. Linde. Yes, I take the stairs very slowly. They're rather hard on me.

Rank. Uh-hm, some touch of internal weakness?

Mrs. Linde. More overexertion,[11] I'd say.

Rank. Nothing else? Then you're probably here in town to rest up in a round of parties?

Mrs. Linde. I'm here to look for work.

Rank. Is that the best cure for overexertion?

Mrs. Linde. One has to live, Doctor.

---

11. **overexertion:** putting out too much strenuous effort; working or exercising too hard.

Rank. Yes, there's a common prejudice to that effect.

Nora. Oh, come on, Dr. Rank—you really do want to live yourself.

Rank. Yes, I really do. Wretched as I am, I'll gladly prolong my torment indefinitely. All my patients feel like that. And it's quite the same, too, with the morally sick. Right at this moment there's one of those moral invalids in there with Helmer—

Mrs. Linde (*softly*). Ah!

Nora. Who do you mean?

Rank. Oh, it's a lawyer, Krogstad, a type you wouldn't know. His character is rotten to the root—but even he began chattering all-importantly about how he had to *live*.

Nora. Oh? What did he want to talk to Torvald about?

Rank. I really don't know. I only heard something about the bank.

Nora. I didn't know that Krog—that this man Krogstad had anything to do with the bank.

Rank. Yes, he's gotten some kind of berth down there. (*To Mrs. Linde.*) I don't know if you also have, in your neck of the woods, a type of person who scuttles about breathlessly, sniffing out hints of moral corruption, and then maneuvers his victim into some sort of key position where he can keep an eye on him. It's the healthy these days that are out in the cold.

Mrs. Linde. All the same, it's the sick who most need to be taken in.

Rank (*with a shrug*). Yes, there we have it. That's the concept that's turning society into a sanatorium.[12]

(Nora, *lost in her thoughts, breaks out into quiet laughter and claps her hands.*)

Rank. Why do you laugh at that? Do you have any real idea of what society is?

Nora. What do I care about dreary old society? I was laughing at something quite different— something terribly funny. Tell me, Doctor—is everyone who works in the bank dependent now on Torvald?

Rank. Is that what you find so terribly funny?

Nora (*smiling and humming*). Never mind, never mind! (*Pacing the floor.*) Yes, that's really immensely amusing: that we—that Torvald has so much power now over all those people. (*Taking the bag out of her pocket.*) Dr. Rank, a little macaroon on that?

Rank. See here, macaroons! I thought they were contraband[13] here.

Nora. Yes, but these are some that Kristine gave me.

Mrs. Linde. What? I—?

Nora. Now, now, don't be afraid. You couldn't possibly know that Torvald had forbidden them. You see, he's worried they'll ruin my teeth. But hmp! Just this once! Isn't that so, Dr. Rank? Help yourself! (*Puts a macaroon in his mouth.*) And you too, Kristine. And I'll also have one, only a little one—or two, at the most. (*Walking about again.*) Now I'm really tremendously happy. Now there's just one last thing in the world that I have an enormous desire to do.

Rank. Well! And what's that?

Nora. It's something I have such a consuming desire to say so Torvald could hear.

Rank. And why can't you say it?

Nora. I don't dare. It's quite shocking.

Mrs. Linde. Shocking?

Rank. Well, then it isn't advisable. But in front of us you certainly can. What do you have such a desire to say so Torvald could hear?

---

12. **sanatorium:** an institution for the treatment of long-term diseases.

13. **contraband:** not allowed.

Nora. I have such a huge desire to say—to hell and be damned!

Rank. Are you crazy?

Mrs. Linde. My goodness, Nora!

Rank. Go on, say it. Here he is.

Nora (*hiding the macaroon bag*). Shh, shh, shh!

(Helmer *comes in from his study, hat in hand, overcoat over his arm.*)

Nora (*going toward him*). Well, Torvald dear, are you through with him?

Helmer. Yes, he just left.

Nora. Let me introduce you—this is Kristine, who's arrived here in town.

Helmer. Kristine—? I'm sorry, but I don't know—

Nora. Mrs. Linde, Torvald dear. Mrs. Kristine Linde.

Helmer. Of course. A childhood friend of my wife's, no doubt?

Mrs. Linde. Yes, we knew each other in those days.

Nora. And just think, she made the long trip down here in order to talk with you.

Helmer. What's this?

Mrs. Linde. Well, not exactly—

Nora. You see, Kristine is remarkably clever in office work, and so she's terribly eager to come under a capable man's supervision and add more to what she already knows—

Helmer. Very wise, Mrs. Linde.

Nora. And then when she heard that you'd become a bank manager—the story was wired out to the papers—then she came in as fast as she could and—Really, Torvald, for my sake you can do a little something for Kristine, can't you?

Helmer. Yes, it's not at all impossible. Mrs. Linde, I suppose you're a widow?

Mrs. Linde. Yes.

Helmer. Any experience in office work?

Mrs. Linde. Yes, a good deal.

Helmer. Well, it's quite likely that I can make an opening for you—

Nora (*clapping her hands*). You see, you see!

Helmer. You've come at a lucky moment, Mrs. Linde.

Mrs. Linde. Oh, how can I thank you?

Helmer. Not necessary. (*Putting his overcoat on.*) But today you'll have to excuse me—

Rank. Wait, I'll go with you. (*He fetches his coat from the hall and warms it at the stove.*)

Nora. Don't stay out long, dear.

Helmer. An hour; no more.

Nora. Are you going too, Kristine?

Mrs. Linde (*putting on her winter garments*). Yes, I have to see about a room now.

Helmer. Then perhaps we can all walk together.

Nora (*helping her*). What a shame we're so cramped here, but it's quite impossible for us to—

Mrs. Linde. Oh, don't even think of it! Good-bye, Nora dear, and thanks for everything.

Nora. Good-bye for now. Of course you'll be back this evening. And you too, Dr. Rank. What? If you're well enough? Oh, you've got to be! Wrap up tight now.

(*In a ripple of small talk the company moves out into the hall; children's voices are heard outside on the steps.*)

Nora. There they are! There they are! (*She runs to open the door. The children come in with their nurse,* Anne-Marie.) Come in, come in! (*Bends down and kisses them.*) Oh, you darlings—! Look at them, Kristine. Aren't they lovely!

Rank. No loitering in the draft here.

Helmer. Come, Mrs. Linde—this place is unbearable now for anyone but mothers.

PAUSE & REFLECT Nora has told her secret to Mrs. Linde. How has Torvald misunderstood Nora? Why has she avoided revealing her secret to him?

FOCUS Read to find out how Nora's plans will be complicated by another visitor.

(*Dr. Rank, Helmer, and* Mrs. Linde *go down the stairs.* Anne-Marie *goes into the living room with the children.* Nora *follows, after closing the hall door.*)

Nora. How fresh and strong you look. Oh, such red cheeks you have! Like apples and roses. (*The children interrupt her throughout the following.*) And it was so much fun? That's wonderful. Really? You pulled both Emmy and Bob on the sled? Imagine, all together! Yes, you're a clever boy, Ivar. Oh, let me hold her a bit, Anne-Marie. My sweet little doll baby! (*Takes the smallest from the nurse and dances with her.*) Yes, yes, Mama will dance with Bob as well. What? Did you throw snowballs? Oh, if I'd only been there! No, don't bother, Anne-Marie—I'll undress them myself. Oh yes, let me. It's such fun. Go in and rest; you look half frozen. There's hot coffee waiting for you on the stove. (*The nurse goes into the room to the left.* Nora *takes the children's winter things off, throwing them about, while the children talk to her all at once.*) Is that so? A big dog chased you? But it didn't bite? No, dogs never bite little, lovely doll babies. Don't peek in the packages, Ivar! What is it? Yes, wouldn't you like to know. No, no, it's an ugly something. Well? Shall we play? What shall we play? Hide-and-seek? Yes, let's play hide-and-seek. Bob must hide first. I must? Yes, let me hide first. (*Laughing and shouting, she and the children play in and out of the living room and the adjoining room to the right. At last* Nora *hides under the table. The children come storming in, search, but cannot find her, then hear her muffled laughter, dash over to the table, lift the cloth up and find her. Wild shouting. She creeps forward as if to scare them. More shouts. Meanwhile, a knock at the hall door; no one has noticed it. Now the door half opens, and* Krogstad *appears. He waits a moment; the game goes on.*)

Krogstad. Beg pardon, Mrs. Helmer—

Nora (*with a strangled cry, turning and scrambling to her knees*). Oh! What do you want?

Krogstad. Excuse me. The outer door was ajar; it must be someone forgot to shut it—

Nora (*rising*). My husband isn't home, Mr. Krogstad.

Krogstad. I know that.

Nora. Yes—then what do you want here?

Krogstad. A word with you.

Nora. With—? (*To the children, quietly.*) Go in to Anne-Marie. What? No, the strange man won't hurt Mama. When he's gone, we'll play some more. (*She leads the children into the room to the left and shuts the door after them. Then, tense and nervous:*) You want to speak to me?

Krogstad. Yes, I want to.

Nora. Today? But it's not yet the first of the month—

Krogstad. No, it's Christmas Eve. It's going to be up to you how merry a Christmas you have.

Nora. What is it you want? Today I absolutely can't—

Krogstad. We won't talk about that till later. This is something else. You do have a moment to spare, I suppose?

Nora. Oh yes, of course—I do, except—

Krogstad. Good. I was sitting over at Olsen's

Restaurant when I saw your husband go down the street—

Nora. Yes?

Krogstad. With a lady.

Nora. Yes. So?

Krogstad. If you'll pardon my asking: wasn't that lady a Mrs. Linde?

Nora. Yes.

Krogstad. Just now come into town?

Nora. Yes, today.

Krogstad. She's a good friend of yours?

Nora. Yes, she is. But I don't see—

Krogstad. I also knew her once.

Nora. I'm aware of that.

Krogstad. Oh? You know all about it. I thought so. Well, then let me ask you short and sweet: is Mrs. Linde getting a job in the bank?

Nora. What makes you think you can cross-examine me, Mr. Krogstad—you, one of my husband's employees? But since you ask, you might as well know—yes, Mrs. Linde's going to be taken on at the bank. And I'm the one who spoke for her, Mr. Krogstad. Now you know.

Krogstad. So I guessed right.

Nora (*pacing up and down*). Oh, one does have a tiny bit of influence, I should hope. Just because I am a woman, don't think it means that— When one has a subordinate[14] position, Mr. Krogstad, one really ought to be careful about pushing somebody who—hm—

Krogstad. Who has influence?

Nora. That's right.

Krogstad (*in a different tone*). Mrs. Helmer, would you be good enough to use your influence on my behalf?

Nora. What? What do you mean?

Krogstad. Would you please make sure that I keep my subordinate position in the bank?

Nora. What does that mean? Who's thinking of taking away your position?

Krogstad. Oh, don't play the innocent with me. I'm quite aware that your friend would hardly relish the chance of running into me again; and I'm also aware now whom I can thank for being turned out.

Nora. But I promise you—

Krogstad. Yes, yes, yes, to the point: there's still time, and I'm advising you to use your influence to prevent it.

Nora. But Mr. Krogstad, I have absolutely no influence.

Krogstad. You haven't? I thought you were just saying—

Nora. You shouldn't take me so literally. I! How can you believe that I have any such influence over my husband?

Krogstad. Oh, I've known your husband from our student days. I don't think the great bank manager's more steadfast[15] than any other married man.

Nora. You speak insolently[16] about my husband, and I'll show you the door.

Krogstad. The lady has spirit.

Nora. I'm not afraid of you any longer. After New Year's, I'll soon be done with the whole business.

Krogstad (*restraining himself*). Now listen to me, Mrs. Helmer. If necessary, I'll fight for my little job in the bank as if it were life itself.

Nora. Yes, so it seems.

Krogstad. It's not just a matter of income; that's the least of it. It's something else— All right, out with it! Look, this is the thing. You know,

---

14. **subordinate:** subject to the authority or control of another.

15. **steadfast:** firmly loyal.

16. **insolently** (ĭn'sə-lənt-lē): in an insulting, rude way.

That job in the bank
      was like the first rung in my ladder.
And now your husband wants to kick me
   right back down in the mud again.

Denholm Elliott as Krogstad

just like all the others, of course, that once, a good many years ago, I did something rather <u>rash</u>.

Nora. I've heard rumors to that effect.

Krogstad. The case never got into court; but all the same, every door was closed in my face from then on. So I took up those various activities you know about. I had to grab hold somewhere; and I dare say I haven't been among the worst. But now I want to drop all that. My boys are growing up. For their sakes, I'll have to win back as much respect as possible here in town. That job in the bank was like the first rung in my ladder. And now your husband wants to kick me right back down in the mud again.

Nora. But for heaven's sake, Mr. Krogstad, it's simply not in my power to help you.

Krogstad. That's because you haven't the will to—but I have the means to make you.

Nora. You certainly won't tell my husband that I owe you money?

Krogstad. Hm—what if I told him that?

Nora. That would be shameful of you. (*Nearly in tears.*) This secret—my joy and my pride—that he should learn it in such a crude and disgusting way—learn it from you. You'd expose me to the most horrible unpleasantness—

Krogstad. Only unpleasantness?

Nora (*vehemently*). But go on and try. It'll turn out the worse for you, because then my husband will really see what a crook you are, and then you'll *never* be able to hold your job.

Krogstad. I asked if it was just domestic[17] unpleasantness you were afraid of?

Nora. If my husband finds out, then of course he'll pay what I owe at once, and then we'd be through with you for good.

Krogstad (*a step closer*). Listen, Mrs. Helmer—you've either got a very bad memory, or else

no head at all for business. I'd better put you a little more in touch with the facts.

Nora. What do you mean?

Krogstad. When your husband was sick, you came to me for a loan of four thousand, eight hundred crowns.

Nora. Where else could I go?

Krogstad. I promised to get you that sum—

Nora. And you got it.

Krogstad. I promised to get you that sum, on certain conditions. You were so involved in your husband's illness, and so eager to finance your trip, that I guess you didn't think out all the details. It might just be a good idea to remind you. I promised you the money on the strength of a note I drew up.

Nora. Yes, and that I signed.

Krogstad. Right. But at the bottom I added some lines for your father to guarantee the loan. He was supposed to sign down there.

Nora. Supposed to? He did sign.

Krogstad. I left the date blank. In other words, your father would have dated his signature himself. Do you remember that?

Nora. Yes, I think—

Krogstad. Then I gave you the note for you to mail to your father. Isn't that so?

Nora. Yes.

Krogstad. And naturally you sent it at once—because only some five, six days later you brought me the note, properly signed. And with that, the money was yours.

Nora. Well, then; I've made my payments regularly, haven't I?

Krogstad. More or less. But—getting back to the point—those were hard times for you then, Mrs. Helmer.

---

17. **domestic:** having to do with the family.

Nora. Yes, they were.

Krogstad. Your father was very ill, I believe.

Nora. He was near the end.

Krogstad. He died soon after?

Nora. Yes.

Krogstad. Tell me, Mrs. Helmer, do you happen to recall the date of your father's death? The day of the month, I mean.

Nora. Papa died the twenty-ninth of September.

Krogstad. That's quite correct; I've already looked into that. And now we come to a curious thing—(*Taking out a paper.*) which I simply cannot comprehend.

Nora. Curious thing? I don't know—

Krogstad. This is the curious thing: that your father co-signed the note for your loan three days after his death.

Nora. How—? I don't understand.

Krogstad. Your father died the twenty-ninth of September. But look. Here your father dated his signature October second. Isn't that curious, Mrs. Helmer? (Nora *is silent.*) Can you explain it to me? (Nora *remains silent.*) It's also remarkable that the words "October second" and the year aren't written in your father's hand, but rather in one that I think I know. Well, it's easy to understand. Your father forgot perhaps to date his signature, and then someone or other added it, a bit sloppily, before anyone knew of his death. There's nothing wrong in that. It all comes down to the signature. And there's no question about *that*, Mrs. Helmer. It really *was* your father who signed his own name here, wasn't it?

Nora (*after a short silence, throwing her head back and looking squarely at him*). No, it wasn't. *I* signed Papa's name.

Krogstad. Wait, now—are you fully aware that this is a dangerous confession?

Nora. Why? You'll soon get your money.

Krogstad. Let me ask you a question—why didn't you send the paper to your father?

Nora. That was impossible. Papa was so sick. If I'd asked him for his signature, I also would have had to tell him what the money was for. But I couldn't tell him, sick as he was, that my husband's life was in danger. That was just impossible.

Krogstad. Then it would have been better if you'd given up the trip abroad.

Nora. I couldn't possibly. The trip was to save my husband's life. I couldn't give that up.

Krogstad. But didn't you ever consider that this was a fraud against me?

Nora. I couldn't let myself be bothered by that. You weren't any concern of mine. I couldn't stand you, with all those cold complications you made, even though you knew how badly off my husband was.

Krogstad. Mrs. Helmer, obviously you haven't the vaguest idea of what you've involved yourself in. But I can tell you this: it was nothing more and nothing worse that I once did—and it wrecked my whole reputation.

Nora. You? Do you expect me to believe that you ever acted bravely to save your wife's life?

Krogstad. Laws don't inquire into motives.

Nora. Then they must be very poor laws.

Krogstad. Poor or not—if I introduce this paper in court, you'll be judged according to law.

Nora. This I refuse to believe. A daughter hasn't a right to protect her dying father from anxiety and care? A wife hasn't a right to save her husband's life? I don't know much about laws, but I'm sure that somewhere in the books these things are allowed. And you don't know anything about it—you who practice the law? You must be an awful lawyer, Mr. Krogstad.

Krogstad. Could be. But business—the kind of business we two are mixed up in—don't you think I know about that? All right. Do what you want now. But I'm telling you *this:* if I get shoved down a second time, you're going to keep me company. (*He bows and goes out through the hall.*)

Nora (*pensive for a moment, then tossing her head*). Oh, really! Trying to frighten me! I'm not so silly as all that. (*Begins gathering up the children's clothes, but soon stops.*) But—? No, but that's impossible! I did it out of love.

The Children (*in the doorway, left*). Mama, that strange man's gone out the door.

Nora. Yes, yes, I know it. But don't tell anyone about the strange man. Do you hear? Not even Papa!

The Children. No, Mama. But now will you play again?

Nora. No, not now.

Maid. Oh, but Mama, you promised.

Nora. Yes, but I can't now. Go inside; I have too much to do. Go in, go in, my sweet darlings. (*She herds them gently back in the room and shuts the door after them. Settling on the sofa, she takes up a piece of embroidery and makes some stitches, but soon stops abruptly.*) No! (*Throws the work aside, rises, goes to the hall door and calls out.*) Helene! Let me have the tree in here. (*Goes to the table, left, opens the table drawer, and stops again.*) No, but that's utterly impossible!

Maid (*with the Christmas tree*). Where should I put it, ma'am?

Nora. There. The middle of the floor.

Maid. Should I bring anything else?

Nora. No, thanks. I have what I need.

(*The* Maid, *who has set the tree down, goes out.*)

Nora (*absorbed in trimming the tree*). Candles here—and flowers here. That terrible creature!

Talk, talk, talk! There's nothing to it at all. The tree's going to be lovely. I'll do anything to please you, Torvald. I'll sing for you, dance for you—

(Helmer *comes in from the hall, with a sheaf of papers under his arm.*)

Nora. Oh! You're back so soon?

Helmer. Yes. Has anyone been here?

Nora. Here? No.

Helmer. That's odd. I saw Krogstad leaving the front door.

Nora. So? Oh yes, that's true. Krogstad was here a moment.

Helmer. Nora, I can see by your face that he's been here, begging you to put in a good word for him.

Nora. Yes.

Helmer. And it was supposed to seem like your own idea? You were to hide it from me that he'd been here. He asked you that, too, didn't he?

Nora. Yes, Torvald, but—

Helmer. Nora, Nora, and you could fall for that? Talk with that sort of person and promise him anything? And then in the bargain, tell me an untruth.

Nora. An untruth—?

Helmer. Didn't you say that no one had been here? (*Wagging his finger.*) My little songbird must never do that again. A songbird needs a clean beak to warble with. No false notes. (*Putting his arm about her waist.*) That's the way it should be, isn't it? Yes, I'm sure of it. (*Releasing her.*) And so, enough of that. (*Sitting by the stove.*) Ah, how snug and cozy it is here. (*Leafing among his papers.*)

Nora (*busy with the tree, after a short pause*). Torvald!

Helmer. Yes.

Nora. I'm so much looking forward to the Stenborgs' costume party, day after tomorrow.

Helmer. And I can't wait to see what you'll surprise me with.

Nora. Oh, that stupid business!

Helmer. What?

Nora. I can't find anything that's right. Everything seems so ridiculous, so <u>inane</u>.

Helmer. So my little Nora's come to *that* recognition?

Nora (*going behind his chair, her arms resting on its back*). Are you very busy, Torvald?

Helmer. Oh—

Nora. What papers are those?

Helmer. Bank matters.

Nora. Already?

Helmer. I've gotten full authority from the retiring management to make all necessary changes in personnel and procedure. I'll need Christmas week for that. I want to have everything in order by New Year's.

Nora. So that was the reason this poor Krogstad—

Helmer. Hm.

Nora (*still leaning on the chair and slowly stroking the nape of his neck*). If you weren't so very busy, I would have asked you an enormous favor, Torvald.

Helmer. Let's hear. What is it?

Nora. You know, there isn't anyone who has your good taste—and I want so much to look well at the costume party. Torvald, couldn't you take over and decide what I should be and plan my costume?

Helmer. Ah, is my stubborn little creature calling for a lifeguard?

Nora. Yes, Torvald, I can't get anywhere without your help.

Helmer. All right—I'll think it over. We'll hit on something.

Nora. Oh, how sweet of you. (*Goes to the tree again. Pause.*) Aren't the red flowers pretty—? But tell me, was it really such a crime that this Krogstad committed?

Helmer. Forgery. Do you have any idea what that means?

Nora. Couldn't he have done it out of need?

Helmer. Yes, or thoughtlessness, like so many others. I'm not so heartless that I'd condemn a man categorically[18] for just one mistake.

Nora. No, of course not, Torvald!

Helmer. Plenty of men have redeemed themselves by openly confessing their crimes and taking their punishment.

Nora. Punishment—?

Helmer. But now Krogstad didn't go that way. He got himself out by sharp practices, and that's the real cause of his moral breakdown.

Nora. Do you really think that would—?

Helmer. Just imagine how a man with that sort of guilt in him has to lie and cheat and deceive on all sides, has to wear a mask even with the nearest and dearest he has, even with his own wife and children. And with the children, Nora—that's where it's most horrible.

Nora. Why?

Helmer. Because that kind of atmosphere of lies infects the whole life of a home. Every breath the children take in is filled with the germs of something degenerate.[19]

Nora (*coming closer behind him*). Are you sure of that?

---

18. **categorically** (kăt′ĭ-gôr′ĭ-klē): absolutely.

19. **degenerate** (dĭ-jĕn′ər-ĭt): having inferior or undesirable moral qualities.

WORDS TO KNOW
inane (ĭn-ān′) *adj.* pointless; silly

Helmer. Oh, I've seen it often enough as a lawyer. Almost everyone who goes bad early in life has a mother who's a <u>chronic</u> liar.

Nora. Why just—the mother?

Helmer. It's usually the mother's influence that's dominant, but the father's works in the same way, of course. Every lawyer is quite familiar with it. And still this Krogstad's been going home year in, year out, poisoning his own children with lies and pretense; that's why I call him morally lost. (*Reaching his hands out toward her.*) So my sweet little Nora must promise me never to plead his cause. Your hand on it. Come, come, what's this? Give me your hand. There, now. All settled. I can tell you it'd be impossible for me to work alongside of him. I literally feel physically revolted when I'm anywhere near such a person.

Nora (*withdraws her hand and goes to the other side of the Christmas tree*). How hot it is here! And I've got so much to do.

Helmer (*getting up and gathering his papers*). Yes, and I have to think about getting some of these read through before dinner. I'll think about your costume, too. And something to hang on the tree in gilt paper, I may even see about that. (*Putting his hand on her head.*) Oh you, my darling little songbird. (*He goes into his study and closes the door after him.*)

Nora (*softly, after a silence*). Oh, really! it isn't so. It's impossible. It must be impossible.

Anne-Marie (*in the doorway, left*). The children are begging so hard to come in to Mama.

Nora. No, no, no, don't let them in to me! You stay with them, Anne-Marie.

Anne-Marie. Of course, ma'am. (*Closes the door.*)

Nora (*pale with terror*). Hurt my children—! Poison my home? (*A moment's pause; then she tosses her head.*) That's not true. Never. Never in all the world.

What characteristics of Nora are revealed in each of these portrayals?

Alla Nazimova, silent film, 1922

Ruth Gordon,
Morosco Theater,
New York City, 1937

Janet McTeer, Belasco Theatre, New York City, 1997

Jane Fonda, film, 1973

Connect to the Literature

1. **What Do You Think?**
   What thoughts were in your mind as you finished reading Act One?

   Comprehension Check
   • What good news have Torvald and Nora recently received?
   • How did Nora raise money for the trip to Italy?
   • Why does Krogstad threaten Nora?

Think Critically

2. **ACTIVE READING: STRATEGIES FOR READING REALISTIC DRAMA** Look over what you recorded in your **READER'S NOTEBOOK**. Which strategies helped bring Act One to life for you?

3. How would you characterize Nora's and Torvald's attitudes toward each other?

   THINK ABOUT
   { • Torvald's pet names for Nora
   • Torvald's remarks about spending money
   • how Nora behaves when Torvald is not present }

4. What do you think are Nora's strengths and weaknesses?

5. A **foil** is a character who provides a striking contrast to another character. Why might Mrs. Linde be considered a foil for Nora?

Extend Interpretations

6. **Critic's Corner** According to the critic Harold Clurman, "Torvald owes his blissful domestic life to his thoughtlessness." What evidence in the play so far would support this statement?

7. **Connect to Life** Nora does not seem to have clear insight into herself or her relationships at this point in the play. What are some of the obstacles that prevent people from understanding what is going on in their own lives?

LITERARY ANALYSIS: CHARACTERS IN REALISTIC DRAMA

Characters are the individuals who take part in the action of a drama or narrative work. The most important ones are called **main characters.** In most realistic dramas the main characters are fully developed and possess many traits, mirroring the psychological complexity of real people. Less important figures, or **minor characters,** sometimes have only one or two dominant traits. In *A Doll's House,* Anne-Marie is a minor character. In realistic drama the characters usually belong to the middle or lower class. They tend to be ordinary people dealing with everyday problems.

Paired Activity With a partner, use a chart such as the one below to record information that you learn about the five main characters. In addition, write down one or more personality traits, or qualities, that you have observed in each character.

Character	Background Information	Personality Traits
Nora	*borrowed money and forged signature*	*willing to make sacrifices for others*
Torvald		
Mrs. Linde		
Dr. Rank		
Krogstad		

Act Two

GUIDE FOR READING

FOCUS In this act Nora tries to keep Torvald from finding out her secret. As you read, look for clues about her feelings for him.

Same room. Beside the piano the Christmas tree now stands stripped of ornament, burned-down candle stubs on its ragged branches. Nora's street clothes lie on the sofa. Nora, alone in the room, moves restlessly about; at last she stops at the sofa and picks up her coat.

Nora (*dropping the coat again*). Someone's coming! (*Goes toward the door, listens.*) No—there's no one. Of course—nobody's coming today, Christmas Day—or tomorrow, either. But maybe— (*Opens the door and looks out.*) No, nothing in the mailbox. Quite empty. (*Coming forward.*) What nonsense! He won't do anything serious. Nothing terrible could happen. It's impossible. Why, I have three small children.

(Anne-Marie, *with a large carton, comes in from the room to the left.*)

Anne-Marie. Well, at last I found the box with the masquerade clothes.

Nora. Thanks. Put it on the table.

Anne-Marie (*does so*). But they're all pretty much of a mess.

Nora. Ahh! I'd love to rip them in a million pieces!

Anne-Marie. Oh, mercy, they can be fixed right up. Just a little patience.

Nora. Yes, I'll go get Mrs. Linde to help me.

Anne-Marie. Out again now? In this nasty weather? Miss Nora will catch cold—get sick.

Nora. Oh, worse things could happen— How are the children?

Anne-Marie. The poor mites are playing with their Christmas presents, but—

Nora. Do they ask for me much?

Anne-Marie. They're so used to having Mama around, you know.

Nora. Yes, but Anne-Marie, I *can't* be together with them as much as I was.

Anne-Marie. Well, small children get used to anything.

Nora. You think so? Do you think they'd forget their mother if she was gone for good?

Anne-Marie. Oh, mercy—gone for good!

Nora. Wait, tell me, Anne-Marie—I've wondered so often—how could you ever have the heart to give your child over to strangers?

Anne-Marie. But I had to, you know, to become little Nora's nurse.

Do you think they'd forget their mother
if she was gone for good?

Dame Edith Evans as Anne-Marie

Nora. Yes, but how could you *do* it?

Anne-Marie. When I could get such a good place? A girl who's poor and who's gotten in trouble is glad enough for that. Because that slippery fish, he didn't do a thing for me, you know.

Nora. But your daughter's surely forgotten you.

Anne-Marie. Oh, she certainly has not. She's written to me, both when she was confirmed and when she was married.

Nora (*clasping her about the neck*). You old Anne-Marie, you were a good mother for me when I was little.

Anne-Marie. Poor little Nora, with no other mother but me.

Nora. And if the babies didn't have one, then I know that you'd— What silly talk! (*Opening the carton.*) Go in to them. Now I'll have to— Tomorrow you can see how lovely I'll look.

Anne-Marie. Oh, there won't be anyone at the party as lovely as Miss Nora. (*She goes off into the room, left.*)

Nora (*begins unpacking the box, but soon throws it aside*). Oh, if I dared to go out. If only nobody would come. If only nothing would happen here while I'm out. What craziness—nobody's coming. Just don't think. This muff—needs a brushing. Beautiful gloves, beautiful gloves. Let it go. Let it go! One, two, three, four, five, six— (*With a cry.*) Oh, there they are! (*Poises to move toward the door, but remains irresolutely standing.* Mrs. Linde *enters from the hall, where she has removed her street clothes.*)

Nora. Oh, it's you, Kristine. There's no one else out there? How good that you've come.

Mrs. Linde. I hear you were up asking for me.

Nora. Yes, I just stopped by. There's something you really can help me with. Let's get settled on the sofa. Look, there's going to be a costume party tomorrow evening at the Stenborgs' right above us, and now Torvald wants me to go as a Neapolitan peasant girl and dance the tarantella that I learned in Capri.[1]

Mrs. Linde. Really, are you giving a whole performance?

Nora. Torvald says yes, I should. See, here's the dress. Torvald had it made for me down there; but now it's all so tattered that I just don't know—

Mrs. Linde. Oh, we'll fix that up in no time. It's nothing more than the trimmings—they're a bit loose here and there. Needle and thread? Good, now we have what we need.

Nora. Oh, how sweet of you!

Mrs. Linde (*sewing*). So you'll be in disguise tomorrow, Nora. You know what? I'll stop by then for a moment and have a look at you all dressed up. But listen, I've absolutely forgotten to thank you for that pleasant evening yesterday.

Nora (*getting up and walking about*). I don't think it was as pleasant as usual yesterday. You should have come to town a bit sooner, Kristine— Yes, Torvald really knows how to give a home elegance and charm.

Mrs. Linde. And you do, too, if you ask me. You're not your father's daughter for nothing. But tell me, is Dr. Rank always so down in the mouth as yesterday?

Nora. No, that was quite an exception. But he goes around critically ill all the time—tuberculosis of the spine, poor man. You know, his father was a disgusting thing who kept mistresses and so on—and that's why the son's been sickly from birth.

---

1. **Neapolitan** (nē′ə-pŏl′ĭ-tən) . . . **tarantella** (tăr′ən-tĕl′ə) . . . **Capri** (kə-prē′): A Neapolitan is a person from Naples, Italy. The tarantella is a lively, whirling Italian dance. Capri is an island near Naples.

Mrs. Linde (*lets her sewing fall to her lap*). But my dearest Nora, how do you know about such things?

Nora (*walking more jauntily*). Hmp! When you've had three children, then you've had a few visits from—from women who know something of medicine, and they tell you this and that.

Mrs. Linde (*resumes sewing; a short pause*). Does Dr. Rank come here every day?

Nora. Every blessed day. He's Torvald's best friend from childhood, and *my* good friend, too. Dr. Rank almost belongs to this house.

Mrs. Linde. But tell me—is he quite sincere? I mean, doesn't he rather enjoy flattering people?

Nora. Just the opposite. Why do you think that?

Mrs. Linde. When you introduced us yesterday, he was proclaiming that he'd often heard my name in this house; but later I noticed that your husband hadn't the slightest idea who I really was. So how could Dr. Rank—?

Nora. But it's all true, Kristine. You see, Torvald loves me beyond words, and, as he puts it, he'd like to keep me all to himself. For a long time he'd almost be jealous if I even mentioned any of my old friends back home. So of course I dropped that. But with Dr. Rank I talk a lot about such things, because he likes hearing about them.

Mrs. Linde. Now listen, Nora; in many ways you're still like a child. I'm a good deal older than you, with a little more experience. I'll tell you something: you ought to put an end to all this with Dr. Rank.

Nora. What should I put an end to?

Mrs. Linde. Both parts of it, I think. Yesterday you said something about a rich admirer who'd provide you with money—

Nora. Yes, one who doesn't exist—worse luck. So?

Mrs. Linde. Is Dr. Rank well off?

Nora. Yes, he is.

Mrs. Linde. With no dependents?[2]

Nora. No, no one. But—

Mrs. Linde. And he's over here every day?

Nora. Yes, I told you that.

Mrs. Linde. How can a man of such refinement be so grasping?

Nora. I don't follow you at all.

Mrs. Linde. Now don't try to hide it, Nora. You think I can't guess who loaned you the forty-eight hundred crowns?

Nora. Are you out of your mind? How could you think such a thing! A friend of ours, who comes here every single day. What an intolerable situation that would have been!

Mrs. Linde. Then it really wasn't him.

Nora. No, absolutely not. It never even crossed my mind for a moment— And he had nothing to lend in those days; his inheritance came later.

Mrs. Linde. Well, I think that was a stroke of luck for you, Nora dear.

Nora. No, it never would have occurred to me to ask Dr. Rank— Still, I'm quite sure that if I had asked him—

Mrs. Linde. Which you won't, of course.

Nora. No, of course not. I can't see that I'd ever need to. But I'm quite positive that if I talked to Dr. Rank—

Mrs. Linde. Behind your husband's back?

Nora. I've got to clear up this other thing; *that's* also behind his back. I've *got* to clear it all up.

Mrs. Linde. Yes, I was saying that yesterday, but—

---

2. **dependents:** people whom one supports, such as a spouse or children.

Nora (*pacing up and down*). A man handles these problems so much better than a woman—

Mrs. Linde. One's husband does, yes.

Nora. Nonsense. (*Stopping.*) When you pay everything you owe, then you get your note back, right?

Mrs. Linde. Yes, naturally.

Nora. And can rip it into a million pieces and burn it up—that filthy scrap of paper!

Mrs. Linde (*looking hard at her, laying her sewing aside, and rising slowly*). Nora, you're hiding something from me.

Nora. You can see it in my face?

Mrs. Linde. Something's happened to you since yesterday morning. Nora, what is it?

Nora (*hurrying toward her*). Kristine! (*Listening.*) Shh! Torvald's home. Look, go in with the children a while. Torvald can't bear all this snipping and stitching. Let Anne-Marie help you.

Mrs. Linde (*gathering up some of the things*). All right, but I'm not leaving here until we've talked this out. (*She disappears into the room, left, as* Torvald *enters from the hall.*)

Nora. Oh, how I've been waiting for you, Torvald dear.

Helmer. Was that the dressmaker?

Nora. No, that was Kristine. She's helping me fix up my costume. You know, it's going to be quite attractive.

Helmer. Yes, wasn't that a bright idea I had?

Nora. Brilliant! But then wasn't I good as well to give in to you?

Helmer. Good—because you give in to your husband's judgment? All right, you little goose, I know you didn't mean it like that. But I won't disturb you. You'll want to have a fitting, I suppose.

Nora. And you'll be working?

Helmer. Yes. (*Indicating a bundle of papers.*) See. I've been down to the bank. (*Starts toward his study.*)

Nora. Torvald.

Helmer (*Stops*). Yes.

Nora. If your little squirrel begged you, with all her heart and soul, for something—?

Helmer. What's that?

Nora. Then would you do it?

Helmer. First, naturally, I'd have to know what it was.

Nora. Your squirrel would scamper about and do tricks, if you'd only be sweet and give in.

Helmer. Out with it.

Nora. Your lark would be singing high and low in every room—

Helmer. Come on, she does that anyway.

Nora. I'd be a wood nymph and dance for you in the moonlight.

Helmer. Nora—don't tell me it's that same business from this morning?

Nora (*coming closer*). Yes, Torvald, I beg you, please!

Helmer. And you actually have the nerve to drag that up again?

Nora. Yes, yes, you've got to give in to me; you *have* to let Krogstad keep his job in the bank.

Helmer. My dear Nora, I've slated his job for Mrs. Linde.

Nora. That's awfully kind of you. But you could just fire another clerk instead of Krogstad.

Helmer. This is the most incredible stubbornness! Because you go and give an impulsive promise to speak up for him, I'm expected to—

Nora. That's not the reason, Torvald. It's for your own sake. That man does writing for the worst papers; you said it yourself. He could do you any amount of harm. I'm scared to death of him—

Helmer. Ah, I understand. It's the old memories haunting you.

Nora. What do you mean by that?

Helmer. Of course, you're thinking about your father.

Nora. Yes, all right. Just remember how those nasty gossips wrote in the papers about Papa and slandered him so cruelly. I think they'd have had him dismissed if the department hadn't sent you up to investigate, and if you hadn't been so kind and open-minded toward him.

Helmer. My dear Nora, there's a notable difference between your father and me. Your father's official career was hardly above reproach. But mine is; and I hope it'll stay that way as long as I hold my position.

Nora. Oh, who can ever tell what vicious minds can invent? We could be so snug and happy now in our quiet, carefree home—you and I and the children, Torvald! That's why I'm pleading with you so—

Helmer. And just by pleading for him you make it impossible for me to keep him on. It's already known at the bank that I'm firing Krogstad. What if it's rumored around now that the new bank manager was vetoed by his wife—

Nora. Yes, what then—?

Helmer. Oh yes—as long as our little bundle of stubbornness gets her way—! I should go and make myself ridiculous in front of the whole office—give people the idea I can be swayed by all kinds of outside pressure. Oh, you can bet I'd feel the effects of that soon enough! Besides—there's something that rules Krogstad right out at the bank as long as I'm the manager.

Nora. What's that?

Helmer. His moral failings I could maybe over-look if I had to—

Nora. Yes, Torvald, why not?

Helmer. And I hear he's quite efficient on the job. But he was a crony of mine back in my teens—one of those rash friendships that crop up again and again to embarrass you later in life. Well, I might as well say it straight out: we're on a first-name basis. And that <u>tactless</u> fool makes no effort at all to hide it in front of others. Quite the contrary—he thinks that entitles him to take a familiar air around me, and so every other second he comes booming out with his "Yes, Torvald!" and "Sure thing, Torvald!" I tell you, it's been excruciating[3] for me. He's out to make my place in the bank unbearable.

Nora. Torvald, you can't be serious about all this.

Helmer. Oh no? Why not?

Nora. Because these are such <u>petty</u> considerations.

Helmer. What are you saying? Petty? You think I'm petty!

Nora. No, just the opposite, Torvald dear. That's exactly why—

Helmer. Never mind. You call my motives petty; then I might as well be just that. Petty! All right! We'll put a stop to this for good. (*Goes to the hall door and calls.*) Helene!

Nora. What do you want?

Helmer (*searching among his papers*). A decision. (*The* Maid *comes in.*) Look here; take this letter; go out with it at once. Get hold of a messenger and have him deliver it. Quick now. It's already addressed. Wait, here's some money.

Maid. Yes, sir. (*She leaves with the letter.*)

---

3. **excruciating** (ĭk-skrōō'shē-ā'tĭng): intensely painful.

Helmer (*straightening his papers*). There, now, little Miss Willful.

Nora (*breathlessly*). Torvald, what was that letter?

Helmer. Krogstad's notice.

Nora. Call it back, Torvald! There's still time. Oh, Torvald, call it back! Do it for my sake— for your sake, for the children's sake! Do you hear, Torvald; do it! You don't know how this can harm us.

Helmer. Too late.

Nora. Yes, too late.

Helmer. Nora dear, I can forgive you this panic, even though basically you're insulting me. Yes, you are! Or isn't it an insult to think that *I* should be afraid of a courtroom hack's revenge? But I forgive you anyway, because this shows so beautifully how much you love me. (*Takes her in his arms.*) This is the way it should be, my darling Nora. Whatever comes, you'll see: when it really counts, I have strength and courage enough as a man to take on the whole weight myself.

Nora (*terrified*). What do you mean by that?

Helmer. The whole weight, I said.

Nora (*resolutely*). No, never in all the world.

Helmer. Good. So we'll share it, Nora, as man and wife. That's as it should be. (*Fondling her.*) Are you happy now? There, there, there—not these frightened dove's eyes. It's nothing at all but empty fantasies— Now you should run through your tarantella and practice your tambourine. I'll go to the inner office and shut both doors, so I won't hear a thing; you can make all the noise you like. (*Turning in the doorway.*) And when Rank comes, just tell him where he can find me. (*He nods to her and goes with his papers into the study, closing the door.*)

Nora (*standing as though rooted, dazed with fright, in a whisper*). He really could do it. He will do it. He'll do it in spite of everything. No, not that, never, never! Anything but that! Escape! A way out— (*The doorbell rings.*) Dr. Rank! Anything but that! *Anything*, whatever it is! (*Her hands pass over her face, smoothing it; she pulls herself together, goes over and opens the hall door. Dr. Rank stands outside, hanging his fur coat up. During the following scene, it begins getting dark.*)

Nora. Hello, Dr. Rank. I recognized your ring. But you mustn't go in to Torvald yet; I believe he's working.

Rank. And you?

Nora. For you, I always have an hour to spare— you know that. (*He has entered, and she shuts the door after him.*)

Rank. Many thanks. I'll make use of these hours while I can.

Nora. What do you mean by that? While you can?

Rank. Does that disturb you?

Nora. Well, it's such an odd phrase. Is anything going to happen?

Rank. What's going to happen is what I've been expecting so long—but I honestly didn't think it would come so soon.

Nora (*gripping his arm*). What is it you've found out? Dr. Rank, you have to tell me!

Rank (*sitting by the stove*). It's all over with me. There's nothing to be done about it.

Nora (*breathing easier*). Is it you—then—?

Rank. Who else? There's no point in lying to one's self. I'm the most miserable of all my patients, Mrs. Helmer. These past few days I've been auditing my internal accounts.[4] Bankrupt! Within a month I'll probably be

---

4. **auditing my internal accounts:** checking over my physical health.

There's no point in lying to one's self.
I'm the most miserable
of all my patients, Mrs. Helmer.

Sir Ralph Richardson as Dr. Rank

laid out and rotting in the churchyard.

Nora. Oh, what a horrible thing to say.

Rank. The thing itself is horrible. But the worst of it is all the other horror before it's over. There's only one final examination left; when I'm finished with that, I'll know about when my disintegration will begin. There's something I want to say. Helmer with his sensitivity has such a sharp distaste for anything ugly. I don't want him near my sickroom.

Nora. Oh, but Dr. Rank—

Rank. I won't have him in there. Under no condition. I'll lock my door to him— As soon as I'm completely sure of the worst, I'll send you my calling card marked with a black cross, and you'll know then the wreck has started to come apart.

Nora. No, today you're completely unreasonable. And I wanted you so much to be in a really good humor.

Rank. With death up my sleeve? And then to suffer this way for somebody else's sins. Is there any justice in that? And in every single family, in some way or another, this inevitable retribution[5] of nature goes on—

Nora (*her hands pressed over her ears*). Oh, stuff! Cheer up! Please—be gay!

Rank. Yes, I'd just as soon laugh at it all. My poor, innocent spine, serving time for my father's gay army days.

Nora (*by the table, left*). He was so infatuated with asparagus tips and *pâté de foie gras,* wasn't that it?

Rank. Yes—and with truffles.[6]

Nora. Truffles, yes. And then with oysters, I suppose?

Rank. Yes, tons of oysters, naturally.

Nora. And then the port and champagne to go with it. It's so sad that all these delectable things have to strike at our bones.

Rank. Especially when they strike at the unhappy bones that never shared in the fun.

Nora. Ah, that's the saddest of all.

Rank (*looks searchingly at her*). Hm.

Nora (*after a moment*). Why did you smile?

Rank. No, it was you who laughed.

Nora. No, it was you who smiled, Dr. Rank!

Rank (*getting up*). You're even a bigger tease than I'd thought.

Nora. I'm full of wild ideas today.

Rank. That's obvious.

Nora (*putting both hands on his shoulders*). Dear, dear Dr. Rank, you'll never die for Torvald and me.

Rank. Oh, that loss you'll easily get over. Those who go away are soon forgotten.

Nora (*looks fearfully at him*). You believe that?

Rank. One makes new connections, and then—

Nora. Who makes new connections?

Rank. Both you and Torvald will when I'm gone. I'd say you're well under way already. What was that Mrs. Linde doing here last evening?

Nora. Oh, come—you can't be jealous of poor Kristine?

Rank. Oh yes, I am. She'll be my successor here in the house. When I'm down under, that woman will probably—

Nora. Shh! Not so loud. She's right in there.

Rank. Today as well. So you see.

Nora. Only to sew on my dress. Good gracious, how unreasonable you are. (*Sitting on the sofa.*) Be nice now, Dr. Rank. Tomorrow you'll see how beautifully I'll dance; and you can

---

5. **retribution:** punishment or return for wrongdoing.

6. *pâté de foie gras* (pä-tā′ də fwä grä′) . . . **truffles:** Pâté de foie gras is a rich meat paste made of duck or goose liver. Truffles are hard-to-find fungi that grow near certain trees and are eaten as delicacies.

imagine then that I'm dancing only for you—
yes, and of course for Torvald, too—that's
understood. (*Takes various items out of the
carton.*) Dr. Rank, sit over here and I'll show
you something.

Rank (*sitting*). What's that?

Nora. Look here. Look.

Rank. Silk stockings.

Nora. Flesh-colored. Aren't they lovely? Now it's
so dark here, but tomorrow— No, no, no, just
look at the feet. Oh well, you might as well
look at the rest.

Rank. Hm—

Nora. Why do you look so critical? Don't you
believe they'll fit?

Rank. I've never had any chance to form an opinion on that.

Nora (*glancing at him a moment*). Shame on you.
(*Hits him lightly on the ear with the
stockings.*) That's for you. (*Puts them away
again.*)

Rank. And what other splendors am I going to
see now?

Nora. Not the least bit more, because you've been
naughty. (*She hums a little and rummages
among her things.*)

Rank (*after a short silence*). When I sit here
together with you like this, completely easy
and open, then I don't know—I simply can't
imagine—whatever would have become of me
if I'd never come into this house.

Nora (*smiling*). Yes, I really think you feel completely at ease with us.

Rank (*more quietly, staring straight ahead*). And
then to have to go away from it all—

Nora. Nonsense, you're not going away.

Rank (*his voice unchanged*). —and not even be
able to leave some poor show of gratitude
behind, scarcely a fleeting regret—no more

than a vacant place that anyone can fill.

Nora. And if I asked you now for—? No—

Rank. For what?

Nora. For a great proof of your friendship—

Rank. Yes, yes?

Nora. No, I mean—for an exceptionally big
favor—

Rank. Would you really, for once, make me so
happy?

Nora. Oh, you haven't the vaguest idea what it is.

Rank. All right, then tell me.

Nora. No, but I can't, Dr. Rank—it's all out of
reason. It's advice and help, too—and a
favor—

Rank. So much the better. I can't fathom what
you're hinting at. Just speak out. Don't you
trust me?

Nora. Of course. More than anyone else. You're
my best and truest friend, I'm sure. That's why
I want to talk to you. All right, then, Dr.
Rank: there's something you can help me
prevent. You know how deeply, how inex-
pressibly dearly Torvald loves me; he'd never
hesitate a second to give up his life for me.

Rank (*leaning close to her*). Nora—do you think
he's the only one—

Nora (*with a slight start*). Who—?

Rank. Who'd gladly give up his life for you.

Nora (*heavily*). I see.

Rank. I swore to myself you should know this
before I'm gone. I'll never find a better chance.
Yes, Nora, now you know. And also you
know now that you can trust me beyond anyone else.

Nora (*rising, natural and calm*). Let me by.

Rank (*making room for her, but still sitting*).
Nora—

Nora (*in the hall doorway*). Helene, bring the

lamp in. (*Goes over to the stove.*) Ah, dear Dr. Rank, that was really mean of you.

Rank (*getting up*). That I've loved you just as deeply as somebody else? Was *that* mean?

Nora. No, but that you came out and told me. That was quite unnecessary—

Rank. What do you mean? Have you known—?

(*The* Maid *comes in with the lamp, sets it on the table, and goes out again.*)

Rank. Nora—Mrs. Helmer—I'm asking you: have you known about it?

Nora. Oh, how can I tell what I know or don't know? Really, I don't know what to say—Why did you have to be so clumsy, Dr. Rank! Everything was so good.

Rank. Well, in any case, you now have the knowledge that my body and soul are at your command. So won't you speak out?

Nora (*looking at him*). After that?

Rank. Please, just let me know what it is.

Nora. You can't know anything now.

Rank. I have to. You mustn't punish me like this. Give me the chance to do whatever is humanly possible for you.

Nora. Now there's nothing you can do for me. Besides, actually, I don't need any help. You'll see—it's only my fantasies. That's what it is. Of course! (*Sits in the rocker, looks at him, and smiles.*) What a nice one you are, Dr. Rank. Aren't you a little bit ashamed, now that the lamp is here?

Rank. No, not exactly. But perhaps I'd better go—for good?

Nora. No, you certainly can't do that. You must come here just as you always have. You know Torvald can't do without you.

Rank. Yes, but *you?*

Nora. You know how much I enjoy it when you're here.

Rank. That's precisely what threw me off. You're a mystery to me. So many times I've felt you'd almost rather be with me than with Helmer.

Nora. Yes—you see, there are some people that one loves most and other people that one would almost prefer being with.

Rank. Yes, there's something to that.

Nora. When I was back home, of course I loved Papa most. But I always thought it was so much fun when I could sneak down to the maids' quarters, because they never tried to improve me, and it was always so amusing, the way they talked to each other.

Rank. Aha, so it's *their* place that I've filled.

Nora (*jumping up and going to him*). Oh, dear, sweet Dr. Rank, that's not what I meant at all. But you can understand that with Torvald it's just the same as with Papa—

(*The* Maid *enters from the hall.*)

Maid. Ma'am—please! (*She whispers to* Nora *and hands her a calling card.*)

Nora (*glancing at the card*). Ah! (*Slips it into her pocket.*)

Rank. Anything wrong?

Nora. No, no, not at all. It's only some—it's my new dress—

Rank. Really? But—there's your dress.

Nora. Oh, that. But this is another one—I ordered it—Torvald mustn't know—

Rank. Ah, now we have the big secret.

Nora. That's right. Just go in with him—he's back in the inner study. Keep him there as long as—

Rank. Don't worry. He won't get away. (*Goes into the study.*)

PAUSE & REFLECT Why does Nora enjoy spending time with Dr. Rank? What does this suggest about her relationship with Torvald?

FOCUS Nora still hasn't found a solution to her problem. As you read, notice the ways in which she shows her desperation.

Nora (*to the* Maid). And he's standing waiting in the kitchen?

Maid. Yes, he came up by the back stairs.

Nora. But didn't you tell him somebody was here?

Maid. Yes, but that didn't do any good.

Nora. He won't leave?

Maid. No, he won't go till he's talked with you, ma'am.

Nora. Let him come in, then—but quietly. Helene, don't breathe a word about this. It's a surprise for my husband.

Maid. Yes, yes, I understand— (*Goes out.*)

Nora. This horror—it's going to happen. No, no, no, it can't happen, it mustn't. (*She goes and bolts* Helmer's door. *The* Maid *opens the hall door for* Krogstad *and shuts it behind him. He is dressed for travel in a fur coat, boots, and a fur cap.*)

Nora (*going toward him*). Talk softly. My husband's home.

Krogstad. Well, good for him.

Nora. What do you want?

Krogstad. Some information.

Nora. Hurry up, then. What is it?

Krogstad. You know, of course, that I got my notice.

Nora. I couldn't prevent it, Mr. Krogstad. I fought for you to the bitter end, but nothing worked.

Krogstad. Does your husband's love for you run so thin? He knows everything I can expose you to, and all the same he dares to—

Nora. How can you imagine he knows anything about this?

Krogstad. Ah, no—I can't imagine it either, now. It's not at all like my fine Torvald Helmer to have so much guts—

Nora. Mr. Krogstad, I demand respect for my husband!

Krogstad. Why, of course—all due respect. But since the lady's keeping it so carefully hidden, may I presume to ask if you're also a bit better informed than yesterday about what you've actually done?

Nora. More than you ever could teach me.

Krogstad. Yes, I *am* such an awful lawyer.

Nora. What is it you want from me?

Krogstad. Just a glimpse of how you are, Mrs. Helmer. I've been thinking about you all day long. A cashier, a night-court scribbler, a—well, a type like me also has a little of what they call a heart, you know.

Nora. Then show it. Think of my children.

Krogstad. Did you or your husband ever think of mine? But never mind. I simply wanted to tell you that you don't need to take this thing too seriously. For the present, I'm not proceeding with any action.

Nora. Oh no, really! Well—I knew that.

Krogstad. Everything can be settled in a friendly spirit. It doesn't have to get around town at all; it can stay just among us three.

Nora. My husband must never know anything of this.

Krogstad. How can you manage that? Perhaps you can pay me the balance?

Nora. No, not right now.

Krogstad. Or you know some way of raising the money in a day or two?

Nora. No way that I'm willing to use.

Krogstad. Well, it wouldn't have done you any good, anyway. If you stood in front of me with a fistful of bills, you still couldn't buy your signature back.

Nora. Then tell me what you're going to do with it.

Krogstad. I'll just hold onto it—keep it on file. There's no outsider who'll even get wind of it. So if you've been thinking of taking some desperate step—

Nora. I have.

Krogstad. Been thinking of running away from home—

Nora. I have!

Krogstad. Or even of something worse—

Nora. How could you guess that?

Krogstad. You can drop those thoughts.

Nora. How could you guess I was thinking of *that*?

Krogstad. Most of us think about *that* at first. I thought about it too, but I discovered I hadn't the courage—

Nora (*lifelessly*). I don't either.

Krogstad (*relieved*). That's true, you haven't the courage? You too?

Nora. I don't have it—I don't have it.

Krogstad. It would be terribly stupid, anyway. After that first storm at home blows out, why, then— I have here in my pocket a letter for your husband—

Nora. Telling everything?

Krogstad. As charitably as possible.

Nora (*quickly*). He mustn't ever get that letter. Tear it up. I'll find some way to get money.

Krogstad. Beg pardon, Mrs. Helmer, but I think I just told you—

Nora. Oh, I don't mean the money I owe you. Let me know how much you want from my husband, and I'll manage it.

Krogstad. I don't want any money from your husband.

Nora. What do you want, then?

Krogstad. I'll tell you what. I want to recoup,[7] Mrs. Helmer; I want to get on in the world— and there's where your husband can help me. For a year and a half I've kept myself clean of anything disreputable—all that time struggling with the worst conditions; but I was satisfied, working my way up step by step. Now I've been written right off, and I'm just not in the mood to come crawling back. I tell you, I want to move on. I want to get back in the bank—in a better position. Your husband can set up a job for me—

Nora. He'll never do that!

Krogstad. He'll do it. I know him. He won't dare breathe a word of protest. And once I'm in there together with him, you just wait and see! Inside of a year, I'll be the manager's right-hand man. It'll be Nils Krogstad, not Torvald Helmer, who runs the bank.

Nora. You'll never see the day!

Krogstad. Maybe you think you can—

Nora. I have the courage now—for *that*.

Krogstad. Oh, you don't scare me. A smart, spoiled lady like you—

Nora. You'll see; you'll see!

Krogstad. Under the ice, maybe? Down in the freezing, coal-black water? There, till you float up in the spring, ugly, unrecognizable, with your hair falling out—

Nora. You don't frighten me.

Krogstad. Nor do you frighten me. One doesn't do these things, Mrs. Helmer. Besides, what good would it be? I'd still have him safe in my pocket.

Nora. Afterwards? When I'm no longer—?

Krogstad. Are you forgetting that *I'll* be in control then over your final reputation? (Nora

---

7. **recoup** (rǐ-kōōp′): to regain a former favorable position.

stands speechless, staring at him.) Good; now I've warned you. Don't do anything stupid. When Helmer's read my letter, I'll be waiting for his reply. And bear in mind that it's your husband himself who's forced me back to my old ways. I'll never forgive him for that. Good-bye, Mrs. Helmer. (*He goes out through the hall.*)

Nora (*goes to the hall door, opens it a crack, and listens*). He's gone. Didn't leave the letter. Oh no, no, that's impossible too! (*Opening the door more and more.*) What's that? He's standing outside—not going downstairs. He's thinking it over? Maybe he'll—? (*A letter falls in the mailbox; then Krogstad's footsteps are heard, dying away down a flight of stairs. Nora gives a muffled cry and runs over toward the sofa table. A short pause.*) In the mailbox. (*Slips warily over to the hall door.*) It's lying there. Torvald, Torvald—now we're lost!

Mrs. Linde (*entering with the costume from the room, left*). There now, I can't see anything else to mend. Perhaps you'd like to try—

Nora (*in a hoarse whisper*). Kristine, come here.

Mrs. Linde (*tossing the dress on the sofa*). What's wrong? You look upset.

Nora. Come here. See that letter? *There!* Look—through the glass in the mailbox.

Mrs. Linde. Yes, yes, I see it.

Nora. That letter's from Krogstad—

Mrs. Linde. Nora—it's Krogstad who loaned you the money!

Nora. Yes, and now Torvald will find out everything.

Mrs. Linde. Believe me, Nora, it's best for both of you.

Nora. There's more you don't know. I forged a name.

Mrs. Linde. But for heaven's sake—?

Nora. I only want to tell you that, Kristine, so that you can be my witness.

Mrs. Linde. Witness? Why should I—?

Nora. If I should go out of my mind—it could easily happen—

Mrs. Linde. Nora!

Nora. Or anything else occurred—so I couldn't be present here—

Mrs. Linde. Nora, Nora, you aren't yourself at all!

Nora. And someone should try to take on the whole weight, all of the guilt, you follow me—

Mrs. Linde. Yes, of course, but why do you think—?

Nora. Then you're the witness that it isn't true, Kristine. I'm very much myself; my mind right now is perfectly clear; and I'm telling you: nobody else has known about this; I alone did everything. Remember that.

Mrs. Linde. I will. But I don't understand all this.

Nora. Oh, how could you ever understand it? It's the miracle now that's going to take place.

Mrs. Linde. The miracle?

Nora. Yes, the miracle. But it's so awful, Kristine. It mustn't take place, not for anything in the world.

Mrs. Linde. I'm going right over and talk with Krogstad.

Nora. Don't go near him; he'll do you some terrible harm!

Mrs. Linde. There was a time once when he'd gladly have done anything for me.

Nora. He?

Mrs. Linde. Where does he live?

Nora. Oh, how do I know? Yes. (*Searches in her pocket.*) Here's his card. But the letter, the letter—!

Helmer (*from the study, knocking on the door*). Nora!

You must give up everything this
evening for me. No business
    —don't even touch your pen.

Nora (*with a cry of fear*). Oh! What is it? What do you want?

Helmer. Now, now, don't be so frightened. We're not coming in. You locked the door—are you trying on the dress?

Nora. Yes, I'm trying it. I'll look just beautiful, Torvald.

Mrs. Linde (*who has read the card*). He's living right around the corner.

Nora. Yes, but what's the use? We're lost. The letter's in the box.

Mrs. Linde. And your husband has the key?

Nora. Yes, always.

Mrs. Linde. Krogstad can ask for his letter back unread; he can find some excuse—

Nora. But it's just this time that Torvald usually—

Mrs. Linde. Stall him. Keep him in there. I'll be back as quick as I can. (*She hurries out through the hall entrance.*)

Nora (*goes to* Helmer's *door, opens it, and peers in*). Torvald!

Helmer (*from the inner study*). Well—does one dare set foot in one's own living room at last? Come on, Rank, now we'll get a look— (*In the doorway.*) But what's this?

Nora. What, Torvald dear?

Helmer. Rank had me expecting some grand masquerade.

Rank (*in the doorway*). That was my impression, but I must have been wrong.

Nora. No one can admire me in my splendor—not till tomorrow.

Helmer. But Nora dear, you look so exhausted. Have you practiced too hard?

Nora. No, I haven't practiced at all yet.

Helmer. You know, it's necessary—

Nora. Oh, it's absolutely necessary, Torvald. But I can't get anywhere without your help. I've forgotten the whole thing completely.

Helmer. Ah, we'll soon take care of that.

Nora. Yes, take care of me, Torvald, please! Promise me that? Oh, I'm so nervous. That big party— You must give up everything this evening for me. No business—don't even touch your pen. Yes? Dear Torvald, promise?

Helmer. It's a promise. Tonight I'm totally at your service—you little helpless thing. Hm—but first there's one thing I want to— (*Goes toward the hall door.*)

Nora. What are you looking for?

Helmer. Just to see if there's any mail.

Nora. No, no, don't do that, Torvald!

Helmer. Now what?

Nora. Torvald, please. There isn't any.

Helmer. Let me look, though. (*Starts out. Nora, at the piano, strikes the first notes of the tarantella. Helmer, at the door, stops.*) Aha!

Nora. I can't dance tomorrow if I don't practice with you.

Helmer (*going over to her*). Nora dear, are you really so frightened?

Nora. Yes, so terribly frightened. Let me practice right now; there's still time before dinner. Oh, sit down and play for me, Torvald. Direct me. Teach me, the way you always have.

Helmer. Gladly, if it's what you want. (*Sits at the piano.*)

Nora (*snatches the tambourine up from the box, then a long, varicolored shawl, which she throws around herself, whereupon she springs forward and cries out:*) Play for me now! Now I'll dance!

(Helmer *plays and* Nora *dances.* Rank *stands behind* Helmer *at the piano and looks on.*)

Helmer (*as he plays*). Slower. Slow down.

Nora. Can't change it.

Helmer. Not so violent, Nora!

Nora. Has to be just like this.

Helmer (*stopping*). No, no, that won't do at all.

Nora (*laughing and swinging her tambourine*). Isn't that what I told you?

Rank. Let me play for her.

Helmer (*getting up*). Yes, go on. I can teach her more easily then.

(Rank *sits at the piano and plays;* Nora *dances more and more wildly.* Helmer *has stationed himself by the stove and repeatedly gives her directions; she seems not to hear them; her hair loosens and falls over her shoulders; she does not notice, but goes on dancing.* Mrs. Linde *enters.*)

Mrs. Linde (*standing dumbfounded at the door*). Ah—!

Nora (*still dancing*). See what fun, Kristine!

Helmer. But Nora darling, you dance as if your life were at stake.

Nora. And it is.

Helmer. Rank, stop! This is pure madness. Stop it, I say!

(Rank *breaks off playing, and* Nora *halts abruptly.*)

Helmer (*going over to her*). I never would have believed it. You've forgotten everything I taught you.

Nora (*throwing away the tambourine*). You see for yourself.

Helmer. Well, there's certainly room for instruction here.

Nora. Yes, you see how important it is. You've got to teach me to the very last minute. Promise me that, Torvald?

Helmer. You can bet on it.

Nora. You mustn't, either today or tomorrow, think about anything else but me; you mustn't open any letters—or the mailbox—

Helmer. Ah, it's still the fear of that man—

Nora. Oh yes, yes, that too.

Helmer. Nora, it's written all over you—there's already a letter from him out there.

Nora. I don't know. I guess so. But you mustn't read such things now; there mustn't be anything ugly between us before it's all over.

Rank (*quietly to* Helmer). You shouldn't deny her.

Helmer (*putting his arm around her*). The child can have her way. But tomorrow night, after you've danced—

Nora. Then you'll be free.

Maid (*in the doorway, right*). Ma'am, dinner is served.

Nora. We'll be wanting champagne, Helene.

Maid. Very good, ma'am. (*Goes out.*)

Helmer. So—a regular banquet, hm?

Nora. Yes, a banquet—champagne till daybreak! (*Calling out.*) And some macaroons, Helene. Heaps of them—just this once.

Helmer (*taking her hands*). Now, now, now—no hysterics. Be my own little lark again.

Nora. Oh, I will soon enough. But go on in—and you, Dr. Rank. Kristine, help me put up my hair.

Rank (*whispering, as they go*). There's nothing wrong—really wrong, is there?

Helmer. Oh, of course not. It's nothing more than this childish anxiety I was telling you about.

(*They go out, right.*)

Nora. Well?

Mrs. Linde. Left town.

Nora. I could see by your face.

Mrs. Linde. He'll be home tomorrow evening. I wrote him a note.

Nora. You shouldn't have. Don't try to stop anything now. After all, it's a wonderful joy, this waiting here for the miracle.

Mrs. Linde. What is it you're waiting for?

Nora. Oh, you can't understand that. Go in to them; I'll be along in a moment.

(Mrs. Linde goes into the dining room. Nora stands a short while as if composing herself; then she looks at her watch.)

Nora. Five. Seven hours to midnight. Twenty-four hours to the midnight after, and then the tarantella's done. Seven and twenty-four? Thirty-one hours to live.

Helmer *(in the doorway, right)*. What's become of the little lark?

Nora *(going toward him with open arms)*. Here's your lark!

> Seven hours to midnight. Twenty-four hours to the midnight after, and then the tarantella's done.

Connect to the Literature

1. What Do You Think?

How has your impression of Nora changed in Act Two?

Comprehension Check

- What steps does Nora take to try to prevent Torvald from finding out her secret?
- What does Krogstad want his letter to accomplish?
- How does Mrs. Linde think she can help Nora?

Think Critically

2. ACTIVE READING: STRATEGIES FOR READING REALISTIC DRAMA Which stage directions give you insight into Nora's state of mind in Act Two? Explain what they suggest to you in your 📖 READER'S NOTEBOOK.

3. What do you think the "miracle" might be? Support your answer with evidence from the text.

4. Krogstad says that Torvald has "forced me back to my old ways" (page 1057, col. 1). How responsible is Torvald for Krogstad's actions? Explain your answer.

THINK ABOUT

- Krogstad's past
- Krogstad's behavior in Act Two
- Torvald's attitude and actions with regard to Krogstad

5. A **symbol** is a person, a place, an object, or an activity that stands for something beyond itself. In what way are the references to disguise (page 1046, col. 2) and masquerade (page 1058, col. 1) symbolic?

Extend Interpretations

6. What If? Imagine that Nora does accept help from Rank. How might this affect the outcome of the play?

7. Comparing Texts Monna Giovanna in "Federigo's Falcon" (page 784) and Nora both take unusual measures to save the life of someone they love. What similarities and differences do you see between the two characters?

8. Connect to Life Good communication in marriage and in other important relationships continues to be of great concern in today's society. What do you think people can learn from Ibsen's portrayal of Nora and Torvald's relationship?

Translating Drama

Translators of drama have a complicated job. They are translating literary works that will be read, but they are also translating scripts that actors will use to create performances. Of course, it is important that the translation of a play convey the meaning of the original as closely as possible. In addition, however, its language must free the actors to interpret the actions, mood, personalities, and ideas of the work.

Below are two translations of a passage from Act One of *A Doll's House*. One is from the version you have read, and the other is from another recent translation. Each is attempting to convey the freshness and naturalness of the original Norwegian; but note the differences in wording and sentence structure.

Helmer. You're an odd little one. Exactly the way your father was. You're never at a loss for scaring up money; but the moment you have it, it runs right out through your fingers; you never know what you've done with it. Well, one takes you as you are. It's deep in your blood. Yes, these things are hereditary, Nora.

Nora. Ah, I could wish I'd inherited many of Papa's qualities.

—*Rolf Fjelde*

Helmer. What a funny little one you are! Just like your father. Always on the look-out for money, wherever you can lay your hands on it; but as soon as you've got it, it just seems to slip through your fingers. You never seem to know what you've done with it. Well, one must accept you as you are. It's in the blood. Oh yes, it is, Nora. That sort of thing is hereditary.

Nora. Oh, I only wish I'd inherited a few more of Daddy's qualities.

—*James McFarlane*

Activity Imagine that you are an actor getting ready to audition for a part in *A Doll's House*. Get together with a classmate and prepare readings of each of the passages above. As you work with the two translations, think about the differences between them and how those differences might affect the performance. Then tell whether you prefer one over the other and, if so, why.

Act Three

GUIDE FOR READING

FOCUS In this part Mrs. Linde finally has a chance to speak with Krogstad. As you read, notice how her plans have changed since she last spoke to Nora.

Same scene. The table, with chairs around it, has been moved to the center of the room. A lamp on the table is lit. The hall door stands open. Dance music drifts down from the floor above. Mrs. Linde sits at the table, absently paging through a book, trying to read, but apparently unable to focus her thoughts. Once or twice she pauses, tensely listening for a sound at the outer entrance.

Mrs. Linde (*glancing at her watch*). Not yet—and there's hardly any time left. If only he's not— (*Listening again.*) Ah, there he is. (*She goes out in the hall and cautiously opens the outer door. Quiet footsteps are heard on the stairs. She whispers:*) Come in. Nobody's here.

Krogstad (*in the doorway*). I found a note from you at home. What's back of all this?

Mrs. Linde. I just *had* to talk to you.

Krogstad. Oh? And it just *had* to be here in this house?

Mrs. Linde. At my place it was impossible; my room hasn't a private entrance. Come in; we're all alone. The maid's asleep, and the Helmers are at the dance upstairs.

Krogstad (*entering the room*). Well, well, the Helmers are dancing tonight? Really?

Mrs. Linde. Yes, why not?

Krogstad. How true—why not?

Mrs. Linde. All right, Krogstad, let's talk.

Krogstad. Do we two have anything more to talk about?

Mrs. Linde. We have a great deal to talk about.

Krogstad. I wouldn't have thought so.

Mrs. Linde. No, because you've never understood me, really.

Krogstad. Was there anything more to understand—except what's all too common in life? A calculating woman throws over a man the moment a better catch comes by.

Mrs. Linde. You think I'm so thoroughly calculating? You think I broke it off lightly?

Krogstad. Didn't you?

Mrs. Linde. Nils—is that what you really thought?

Krogstad. If you cared, then why did you write me the way you did?

Mrs. Linde. What else could I do? If I had to break off with you, then it was my job as well to root out everything you felt for me.

WORDS TO KNOW

1064   **calculating** (kăl′kyə-lā′tĭng) *adj.* crafty; scheming

Krogstad (*wringing his hands*). So that was it. And this—all this, simply for money!

Mrs. Linde. Don't forget I had a helpless mother and two small brothers. We couldn't wait for you, Nils; you had such a long road ahead of you then.

Krogstad. That may be; but you still hadn't the right to abandon me for somebody else's sake.

Mrs. Linde. Yes—I don't know. So many, many times I've asked myself if I did have that right.

Krogstad (*more softly*). When I lost you, it was as if all the solid ground dissolved from under my feet. Look at me; I'm a half-drowned man now, hanging onto a wreck.

Mrs. Linde. Help may be near.

Krogstad. It was near—but then you came and blocked it off.

Mrs. Linde. Without my knowing it, Nils. Today for the first time I learned that it's you I'm replacing at the bank.

Krogstad. All right—I believe you. But now that you know, will you step aside?

Mrs. Linde. No, because that wouldn't benefit you in the slightest.

Krogstad. Not "benefit" me, hm! I'd step aside anyway.

Mrs. Linde. I've learned to be realistic. Life and hard, bitter necessity have taught me that.

Krogstad. And life's taught me never to trust fine phrases.

Mrs. Linde. Then life's taught you a very sound thing. But you do have to trust in actions, don't you?

Krogstad. What does that mean?

Mrs. Linde. You said you were hanging on like a half-drowned man to a wreck.

Krogstad. I've good reason to say that.

Mrs. Linde. I'm also like a half-drowned woman on a wreck. No one to suffer with; no one to care for.

Krogstad. You made your choice.

Mrs. Linde. There wasn't any choice then.

Krogstad. So—what of it?

Mrs. Linde. Nils, if only we two shipwrecked people could reach across to each other.

Krogstad. What are you saying?

Mrs. Linde. Two on one wreck are at least better off than each on his own.

Krogstad. Kristine!

Mrs. Linde. Why do you think I came into town?

Krogstad. Did you really have some thought of me?

Mrs. Linde. I have to work to go on living. All my born days, as long as I can remember, I've worked, and it's been my best and my only joy. But now I'm completely alone in the world; it frightens me to be so empty and lost. To work for yourself—there's no joy in that. Nils, give me something—someone to work for.

Krogstad. I don't believe all this. It's just some hysterical feminine urge to go out and make a noble sacrifice.

Mrs. Linde. Have you ever found me to be hysterical?

Krogstad. Can you honestly mean this? Tell me—do you know everything about my past?

Mrs. Linde. Yes.

Krogstad. And you know what they think I'm worth around here.

Mrs. Linde. From what you were saying before, it would seem that with me you could have been another person.

Krogstad. I'm positive of that.

Mrs. Linde. Couldn't it happen still?

Krogstad. Kristine—you're saying this in all seriousness? Yes, you are! I can see it in you. And do you really have the courage, then—?

Mrs. Linde. I need to have someone to care for; and your children need a mother. We both need each other. Nils, I have faith that you're good at heart—I'll risk everything together with you.

Krogstad (*gripping her hands*). Kristine, thank you, thank you— Now I know I can win back a place in their eyes. Yes—but I forgot—

Mrs. Linde. (*listening*). Shh! The tarantella. Go now! Go on!

Krogstad. Why? What is it?

Mrs. Linde. Hear the dance up there? When that's over, they'll be coming down.

Krogstad. Oh, then I'll go. But—it's all pointless. Of course, you don't know the move I made against the Helmers.

Mrs. Linde. Yes, Nils, I know.

Krogstad. And all the same, you have the courage to—?

Mrs. Linde. I know how far despair can drive a man like you.

Krogstad. Oh, if I only could take it all back.

Mrs. Linde. You easily could—your letter's still lying in the mailbox.

Krogstad. Are you sure of that?

Mrs. Linde. Positive. But—

Krogstad (*looks at her searchingly*). Is that the meaning of it, then? You'll save your friend at any price. Tell me straight out. Is that it?

Mrs. Linde. Nils—anyone who's sold herself for somebody else once isn't going to do it again.

Krogstad. I'll demand my letter back.

Mrs. Linde. No, no.

Krogstad. Yes, of course. I'll stay here till Helmer comes down; I'll tell him to give me my letter again—that it only involves my dismissal—that he shouldn't read it—

Mrs. Linde. No, Nils, don't call the letter back.

Krogstad. But wasn't that exactly why you wrote me to come here?

Mrs. Linde. Yes, in that first panic. But it's been a whole day and night since then, and in that time I've seen such incredible things in this house. Helmer's got to learn everything; this dreadful secret has to be aired; those two have to come to a full understanding; all these lies and evasions[1] can't go on.

Krogstad. Well, then, if you want to chance it. But at least there's one thing I can do, and do right away—

Mrs. Linde (*listening*). Go now, go, quick! The dance is over. We're not safe another second.

Krogstad. I'll wait for you downstairs.

Mrs. Linde. Yes, please do; take me home.

Krogstad. I can't believe it; I've never been so happy.

(*He leaves by way of the outer door; the door between the room and the hall stays open.*)

PAUSE & REFLECT Why does Mrs. Linde no longer want Krogstad to demand his letter back? How might her own experiences have influenced this change of mind?

FOCUS As you continue reading, look for signs of change in other characters.

Mrs. Linde (*straightening up a bit and getting together her street clothes*). How different now! How different! Someone to work for, to live for—a home to build. Well, it is worth the try! Oh, if they'd only come! (*Listening.*) Ah, there they are. Bundle up. (*She picks up her hat and coat.* Nora's *and* Helmer's *voices can be heard outside; a key turns in the lock, and* Helmer *brings* Nora *into the hall almost by force. She is wearing the Italian costume with a large black shawl about her; he has on evening dress, with a black domino[2] open over it.*)

---

1. **evasions:** avoidances.
2. **domino:** a hooded robe, usually worn at a masquerade.

Nora (*struggling in the doorway*). No, no, no, not inside! I'm going up again. I don't want to leave so soon.

Helmer. But Nora dear—

Nora. Oh, I beg you, please, Torvald. From the bottom of my heart, *please*—only an hour more!

Helmer. Not a single minute, Nora darling. You know our agreement. Come on, in we go; you'll catch cold out here. (*In spite of her resistance, he gently draws her into the room.*)

Mrs. Linde. Good evening.

Nora. Kristine!

Helmer. Why, Mrs. Linde—are you here so late?

Mrs. Linde. Yes, I'm sorry, but I did want to see Nora in costume.

Nora. Have you been sitting here, waiting for me?

Mrs. Linde. Yes. I didn't come early enough; you were all upstairs; and then I thought I really couldn't leave without seeing you.

Helmer (*removing* Nora's *shawl*). Yes, take a good look. She's worth looking at, I can tell you that, Mrs. Linde. Isn't she lovely?

Mrs. Linde. Yes, I should say—

Helmer. A dream of loveliness, isn't she? That's what everyone thought at the party, too. But she's horribly stubborn—this sweet little thing. What's to be done with her? Can you imagine, I almost had to use force to pry her away.

Nora. Oh, Torvald, you're going to regret you didn't indulge me, even for just a half hour more.

Helmer. There, you see. She danced her tarantella and got a tumultuous hand—which was well earned, although the performance may have been a bit too naturalistic—I mean it rather overstepped the proprieties[3] of art. But never mind—what's important is, she made a success, an overwhelming success. You think I

could let her stay on after that and spoil the effect? Oh no; I took my lovely little Capri girl—my <u>capricious</u> little Capri girl, I should say—took her under my arm; one quick tour of the ballroom, a curtsy to every side, and then—as they say in novels—the beautiful vision disappeared. An exit should always be effective, Mrs. Linde, but that's what I can't get Nora to grasp. Phew, it's hot in here. (*Flings the domino on a chair and opens the door to his room.*) Why's it dark in here? Oh yes, of course. Excuse me. (*He goes in and lights a couple of candles.*)

Nora (*in a sharp, breathless whisper*). So?

Mrs. Linde (*quietly*). I talked with him.

Nora. And—?

Mrs. Linde. Nora—you must tell your husband everything.

Nora (*dully*). I knew it.

Mrs. Linde. You've got nothing to fear from Krogstad, but you have to speak out.

Nora. I won't tell.

Mrs. Linde. Then the letter will.

Nora. Thanks, Kristine. I know now what's to be done. Shh!

Helmer (*reentering*). Well, then, Mrs. Linde—have you admired her?

Mrs. Linde. Yes, and now I'll say good night.

Helmer. Oh, come, so soon? Is this yours, this knitting?

Mrs. Linde. Yes, thanks. I nearly forgot it.

Helmer. Do you knit, then?

Mrs. Linde. Oh yes.

Helmer. You know what? You should embroider instead.

Mrs. Linde. Really? Why?

---

3. **proprieties:** the customs of polite society.

Helmer. Yes, because it's a lot prettier. See here, one holds the embroidery so, in the left hand, and then one guides the needle with the right—so—in an easy, sweeping curve—right?

Mrs. Linde. Yes, I guess that's—

Helmer. But, on the other hand, knitting—it can never be anything but ugly. Look, see here, the arms tucked in, the knitting needles going up and down—there's something Chinese about it. Ah, that was really a glorious champagne they served.

Mrs. Linde. Yes, good night, Nora, and don't be stubborn anymore.

Helmer. Well put, Mrs. Linde!

Mrs. Linde. Good night, Mr. Helmer.

Helmer (*accompanying her to the door*). Good night, good night. I hope you get home all right. I'd be very happy to—but you don't have far to go. Good night, good night. (*She leaves. He shuts the door after her and returns.*) There, now, at last we got her out the door. She's a deadly bore, that creature.

Nora. Aren't you pretty tired, Torvald?

Helmer. No, not a bit.

Nora. You're not sleepy?

Helmer. Not at all. On the contrary, I'm feeling quite exhilarated. But you? Yes, you really look tired and sleepy.

Nora. Yes, I'm very tired. Soon now I'll sleep.

Helmer. See! You see! I was right all along that we shouldn't stay longer.

Nora. Whatever you do is always right.

Helmer (*kissing her brow*). Now my little lark talks sense. Say, did you notice what a time Rank was having tonight?

Nora. Oh, was he? I didn't get to speak with him.

Helmer. I scarcely did either, but it's a long time since I've seen him in such high spirits. (*Gazes at her a moment, then comes nearer her.*)

Hm—it's marvelous, though, to be back home again—to be completely alone with you. Oh, you bewitchingly lovely young woman!

Nora. Torvald, don't took at me like that!

Helmer. Can't I look at my richest treasure? At all that beauty that's mine, mine alone—completely and utterly.

Nora (*moving around to the other side of the table*). You mustn't talk to me that way tonight.

Helmer (*following her*). The tarantella is still in your blood, I can see—and it makes you even more enticing. Listen. The guests are beginning to go. (*Dropping his voice.*) Nora—it'll soon be quiet through this whole house.

Nora. Yes, I hope so.

Helmer. You do, don't you, my love? Do you realize—when I'm out at a party like this with you—do you know why I talk to you so little and keep such a distance away; just send you a stolen look now and then—you know why I do it? It's because I'm imagining then that you're my secret darling, my secret young bride-to-be, and that no one suspects there's anything between us.

Nora. Yes, yes; oh, yes, I know you're always thinking of me.

Helmer. And then when we leave and I place the shawl over those fine young rounded shoulders—over that wonderful curving neck—then I pretend that you're my young bride, that we're just coming from the wedding, that for the first time I'm bringing you into my house—that for the first time I'm alone with you—completely alone with you, your trembling young beauty! All this evening I've longed for nothing but you. When I saw you turn and sway in the tarantella—my blood was pounding till I couldn't stand it—that's why I brought you down here so early—

Nora. Go away, Torvald! Leave me alone. I don't want all this.

Helmer. What do you mean? Nora, you're teasing me. You will, won't you? Aren't I your husband—?

(*A knock at the outside door.*)

Nora (*startled*). What's that?

Helmer (*going toward the hall*). Who is it?

Rank (*outside*). It's me. May I come in a moment?

Helmer (*with quiet irritation*). Oh, what does he want now? (*Aloud.*) Hold on. (*Goes and opens the door.*) Oh, how nice that you didn't just pass us by!

Rank. I thought I heard your voice, and then I wanted so badly to have a look in. (*Lightly glancing about.*) Ah, me, these old familiar haunts. You have it snug and cozy in here, you two.

Helmer. You seemed to be having it pretty cozy upstairs, too.

Rank. Absolutely. Why shouldn't I? Why not take in everything in life? As much as you can, anyway, and as long as you can. The wine was superb—

Helmer. The champagne especially.

Rank. You noticed that too? It's amazing how much I could guzzle down.

Nora. Torvald also drank a lot of champagne this evening.

Rank. Oh?

Nora. Yes, and that always makes him so entertaining.

Rank. Well, why shouldn't one have a pleasant evening after a well-spent day?

Helmer. Well spent? I'm afraid I can't claim that.

Rank (*slapping him on the back*). But I can, you see!

Nora. Dr. Rank, you must have done some scientific research today.

Rank. Quite so.

Helmer. Come now—little Nora talking about scientific research!

Nora. And can I congratulate you on the results?

Rank. Indeed you may.

Nora. Then they were good?

Rank. The best possible for both doctor and patient—certainty.

Nora (*quickly and searchingly*). Certainty?

Rank. Complete certainty. So don't I owe myself a gay evening afterwards?

Nora. Yes, you're right, Dr. Rank.

Helmer. I'm with you—just so long as you don't have to suffer for it in the morning.

Rank. Well, one never gets something for nothing in life.

Nora. Dr. Rank—are you very fond of masquerade parties?

Rank. Yes, if there's a good array of odd disguises—

Nora. Tell me, what should we two go as at the next masquerade?

Helmer. You little featherhead—already thinking of the next!

Rank. We two? I'll tell you what: you must go as Charmed Life—

Helmer. Yes, but find a costume for *that!*

Rank. Your wife can appear just as she looks every day.

Helmer. That was nicely put. But don't you know what you're going to be?

Rank. Yes, Helmer, I've made up my mind.

Helmer. Well?

Rank. At the next masquerade I'm going to be invisible.

Helmer. That's a funny idea.

Rank. They say there's a hat—black, huge—have you never heard of the hat that makes you invisible? You put it on, and then no one on earth can see you.

Helmer (*suppressing a smile*). Ah, of course.

Rank. But I'm quite forgetting what I came for. Helmer, give me a cigar, one of the dark Havanas.

Helmer. With the greatest pleasure. (*Holds out his case.*)

Rank. Thanks. (*Takes one and cuts off the tip.*)

Nora (*striking a match*). Let me give you a light.

Rank. Thank you. (*She holds the match for him; he lights the cigar.*) And now good-bye.

Helmer. Good-bye, good-bye, old friend.

Nora. Sleep well, Doctor.

Rank. Thanks for that wish.

Nora. Wish me the same.

Rank. You? All right, if you like— Sleep well. And thanks for the light. (*He nods to them both and leaves.*)

Helmer (*his voice subdued*). He's been drinking heavily.

Nora (*absently*). Could be. (Helmer *takes his keys from his pocket and goes out in the hall.*) Torvald—what are you after?

Helmer. Got to empty the mailbox; it's nearly full. There won't be room for the morning papers.

Nora. Are you working tonight?

Helmer. You know I'm not. Why—what's this? Someone's been at the lock.

Nora. At the lock—?

Helmer. Yes, I'm positive. What do you suppose—? I can't imagine one of the maids—? Here's a broken hairpin. Nora, it's yours—

Nora (*quickly*). Then it must be the children—

Helmer. You'd better break them of that. Hm, hm—well, opened it after all. (*Takes the contents out and calls into the kitchen.*) Helene! Helene, would you put out the lamp in the hall. (*He returns to the room, shutting the hall door, then displays the handful of mail.*) Look how it's piled up. (*Sorting through them.*) Now what's this?

Nora (*at the window*). The letter! Oh, Torvald, no!

Helmer. Two calling cards—from Rank.

Nora. From Dr. Rank?

Helmer (*examining them*). "Dr. Rank, Consulting Physician." They were on top. He must have dropped them in as he left.

Nora. Is there anything on them?

Helmer. There's a black cross over the name. See? That's a gruesome notion. He could almost be announcing his own death.

Nora. That's just what he's doing.

Helmer. What! You've heard something? Something he's told you?

Nora. Yes. That when those cards came, he'd be taking his leave of us. He'll shut himself in now and die.

Helmer. Ah, my poor friend! Of course I knew he wouldn't be here much longer. But so soon— And then to hide himself away like a wounded animal.

Nora. If it has to happen, then it's best it happens in silence—don't you think so, Torvald?

Helmer (*pacing up and down*). He'd grown right into our lives. I simply can't imagine him gone. He with his suffering and loneliness— like a dark cloud setting off our sunlit happiness. Well, maybe it's best this way. For him, at least. (*Standing still.*) And maybe for us too, Nora. Now we're thrown back on each other, completely. (*Embracing her.*) Oh you, my darling wife, how can I hold you close enough? You know what, Nora—time and again I've wished you were in some terrible danger, just so I could stake my life and soul and everything, for your sake.

Nora (*tearing herself away, her voice firm and decisive*). Now you must read your mail, Torvald.

Helmer. No, no, not tonight. I want to stay with you, dearest.

Nora. With a dying friend on your mind?

Helmer. You're right. We've both had a shock. There's ugliness between us—these thoughts of death and corruption. We'll have to get free of them first. Until then—we'll stay apart.

Nora (*clinging about his neck*). Torvald—good night! Good night!

Helmer (*kissing her on the cheek*). Good night, little songbird. Sleep well, Nora. I'll be reading my mail now. (*He takes the letters into his room and shuts the door after him.*)

Nora (*with bewildered glances, groping about, seizing* Helmer's *domino, throwing it around her, and speaking in short, hoarse, broken whispers*). Never see him again. Never, never. (*Putting her shawl over her head.*) Never see the children either—them, too. Never, never. Oh, the freezing black water! The depths— down— Oh, I wish it were over— He has it now; he's reading it—now. Oh no, no, not yet. Torvald, good-bye, you and the children— (*She starts for the hall, as she does,* Helmer *throws open his door and stands with an open letter in his hand.*)

Helmer. Nora!

Nora (*screams*). Oh—!

Helmer. What is this? You know what's in this letter?

Nora. Yes, I know. Let me go! Let me out!

Helmer (*holding her back*). Where are you going?

Nora (*struggling to break loose*). You can't save

me, Torvald!

Helmer (*slumping back*). True! Then it's true what he writes? How horrible! No, no, it's impossible—it can't be true.

Nora. It *is* true. I've loved you more than all this world.

Helmer. Ah, none of your slippery tricks.

Nora (*taking one step toward him*). Torvald—!

Helmer. What *is* this you've blundered into!

Nora. Just let me loose. You're not going to suffer for my sake. You're not going to take on my guilt.

Helmer. No more playacting. (*Locks the hall door.*) You stay right here and give me a reckoning. You understand what you've done? Answer! You understand?

Nora (*looking squarely at him, her face hardening*). Yes. I'm beginning to understand everything now.

Helmer (*striding about*). Oh, what an awful awakening! In all these eight years—she who was my pride and joy—a hypocrite, a liar— worse, worse—a criminal! How infinitely disgusting it all is! The shame! (*Nora* says nothing and goes on looking straight at him. He stops in front of her.*) I should have suspected something of the kind. I should have known. All your father's flimsy values— Be still! All your father's flimsy values have come out in you. No religion, no morals, no sense of duty— Oh, how I'm punished for letting him off! I did it for your sake, and you repay me like this.

Nora. Yes, like this.

Helmer. Now you've wrecked all my happiness— ruined my whole future. Oh, it's awful to think of. I'm in a cheap little grafter's[4] hands;

---

4. **grafter's:** A grafter is a person who uses his or her position dishonestly to gain something.

You stay right here
and give me a reckoning.
You understand what you've done?

he can do anything he wants with me, ask for anything, play with me like a puppet—and I can't breathe a word. I'll be swept down miserably into the depths on account of a featherbrained woman.

Nora. When I'm gone from this world, you'll be free.

Helmer. Oh, quit posing. Your father had a mess of those speeches too. What good would that ever do me if you were gone from this world, as you say? Not the slightest. He can still make the whole thing known; and if he does, I could be falsely suspected as your accomplice. They might even think that I was behind it— that I put you up to it. And all that I can thank you for—you that I've coddled the whole of our marriage. Can you see now what you've done to me?

Nora (*icily calm*). Yes.

Helmer. It's so incredible, I just can't grasp it. But we'll have to patch up whatever we can. Take off the shawl. I said, take it off! I've got to appease him somehow or other. The thing has to be hushed up at any cost. And as for you and me, it's got to seem like everything between us is just as it was—to the outside world, that is. You'll go right on living in this house, of course. But you can't be allowed to bring up the children; I don't dare trust you with them— Oh, to have to say this to someone I've loved so much! Well, that's done with. From now on happiness doesn't matter; all that matters is saving the bits and pieces, the appearance— (*The doorbell rings. Helmer starts.*) What's that? And so late. Maybe the worst—? You think he'd—? Hide, Nora! Say you're sick. (Nora *remains standing motionless. Helmer goes and opens the door.*)

Maid (*half dressed, in the hall*). A letter for Mrs. Helmer.

Helmer. I'll take it. (*Snatches the letter and shuts the door.*) Yes, it's from him. You don't get it; I'm reading it myself.

Nora. Then read it.

Helmer (*by the lamp*). I hardly dare. We may be ruined, you and I. But—I've got to know. (*Rips open the letter, skims through a few lines, glances at an enclosure, then cries out joyfully.*) Nora! (Nora *looks inquiringly at him.*) Nora! Wait—better check it again— Yes, yes, it's true. I'm saved. Nora, I'm saved!

Nora. And I?

Helmer. You too, of course. We're both saved, both of us. Look. He's sent back your note. He says he's sorry and ashamed—that a happy development in his life—oh, who cares what he says! Nora, we're saved! No one can hurt you. Oh, Nora, Nora—but first, this ugliness all has to go. Let me see— (*Takes a look at the note.*) No, I don't want to see it; I want the whole thing to fade like a dream. (*Tears the note and both letters to pieces, throws them into the stove and watches them burn.*) There—now there's nothing left— He wrote that since Christmas Eve you— Oh, they must have been three terrible days for you, Nora.

Nora. I fought a hard fight.

Helmer. And suffered pain and saw no escape but— No, we're not going to dwell on anything unpleasant. We'll just be grateful and keep on repeating: it's over now, it's over! You hear me, Nora? You don't seem to realize—it's over. What's it mean—that frozen look? Oh, poor little Nora, I understand. You can't believe I've forgiven you. But I have, Nora; I swear I have. I know that what you did, you did out of love for me.

Nora. That's true.

Helmer. You loved me the way a wife ought to love her husband. It's simply the means that you couldn't judge. But you think I love you any the less for not knowing how to handle your affairs? No, no—just lean on me; I'll guide you and teach you. I wouldn't be a man if this feminine helplessness didn't make you twice as attractive to me. You mustn't mind those sharp words I said—that was all in the first confusion of thinking my world had collapsed. I've forgiven you, Nora; I swear I've forgiven you.

Nora. My thanks for your forgiveness. (*She goes out through the door, right.*)

Helmer. No, wait— (*Peers in.*) What are you doing in there?

Nora (*inside*). Getting out of my costume.

Helmer (*by the open door*). Yes, do that. Try to calm yourself and collect your thoughts again, my frightened little songbird. You can rest easy now; I've got wide wings to shelter you with. (*Walking about close by the door.*) How snug and nice our home is, Nora. You're safe here; I'll keep you like a hunted dove I've rescued out of a hawk's claws. I'll bring peace to your poor, shuddering heart. Gradually it'll happen, Nora; you'll see. Tomorrow all this will look different to you; then everything will be as it was. I won't have to go on repeating I forgive you; you'll feel it for yourself. How can you imagine I'd ever conceivably want to disown you—or even blame you in any way? Ah, you don't know a man's heart, Nora. For a man there's something indescribably sweet and satisfying in knowing he's forgiven his wife—and forgiven her out of a full and open heart. It's as if she belongs to him in two ways now; in a sense he's given her fresh into the world again, and she's become his wife and his child as well. From now on that's what you'll be to me—you little, bewildered, helpless thing. Don't be afraid of anything, Nora; just open your heart to me, and I'll be conscience and will to you both— (Nora *enters in her regular clothes.*) What's this? Not in bed? You've changed your dress?

Nora. Yes, Torvald, I've changed my dress.

Helmer. But why now, so late?

Nora. Tonight I'm not sleeping.

Helmer. But Nora dear—

Nora (*looking at her watch*). It's still not so very late. Sit down, Torvald; we have a lot to talk over. (*She sits at one side of the table.*)

Helmer. Nora—what is this? That hard expression—

Nora. Sit down. This'll take some time. I have a lot to say.

Helmer (*sitting at the table directly opposite her*). You worry me, Nora. And I don't understand you.

Nora. No, that's exactly it. You don't understand me. And I've never understood you either—until tonight. No, don't interrupt. You can just listen to what I say. We're closing out accounts, Torvald.

Helmer. How do you mean that?

Nora (*after a short pause*). Doesn't anything strike you about our sitting here like this?

Helmer. What's that?

Nora. We've been married now eight years. Doesn't it occur to you that this is the first time we two, you and I, man and wife, have ever talked seriously together?

Helmer. What do you mean—seriously?

Nora. In eight whole years—longer even—right from our first acquaintance, we've never exchanged a serious word on any serious thing.

Helmer. You mean I should constantly go and involve you in problems you couldn't possibly help me with?

Nora. I'm not talking of problems. I'm saying that we've never sat down seriously together and tried to get to the bottom of anything.

Helmer. But dearest, what good would that ever do you?

Nora. That's the point right there: you've never understood me. I've been wronged greatly, Torvald—first by Papa, and then by you.

Helmer. What! By us—the two people who've loved you more than anyone else?

Nora (*shaking her head*). You never loved me. You've thought it fun to be in love with me, that's all.

Helmer. Nora, what a thing to say!

Nora. Yes, it's true now, Torvald. When I lived at home with Papa, he told me all his opinions, so I had the same ones too; or if they were different I hid them, since he wouldn't have cared for that. He used to call me his doll-child, and he played with me the way I played with my dolls. Then I came into your house—

Helmer. How can you speak of our marriage like that?

Nora (*unperturbed*).[5] I mean, then I went from Papa's hands into yours. You arranged everything to your own taste, and so I got the same taste as you—or I pretended to; I can't remember. I guess a little of both, first one, then the other. Now when I look back, it seems as if I'd lived here like a beggar—just from hand to mouth. I've lived by doing tricks for you, Torvald. But that's the way you wanted it. It's a great sin what you and Papa did to me. You're to blame that nothing's become of me.

Helmer. Nora, how unfair and ungrateful you are! Haven't you been happy here?

Nora. No, never. I thought so—but I never have.

Helmer. Not—not happy!

Nora. No, only lighthearted. And you've always been so kind to me. But our home's been nothing but a playpen. I've been your doll-wife here, just as at home I was Papa's doll-child. And in turn the children have been my dolls. I thought it was fun when you played with me, just as they thought it fun when I played with them. That's been our marriage, Torvald.

Helmer. There's some truth in what you're saying—under all the raving exaggeration. But it'll all be different after this. Playtime's over; now for the schooling.

Nora. Whose schooling—mine or the children's?

Helmer. Both yours and the children's, dearest.

Nora. Oh, Torvald, you're not the man to teach me to be a good wife to you.

Helmer. And you can say that?

Nora. And I—how am I equipped to bring up children?

Helmer. Nora!

Nora. Didn't you say a moment ago that that was no job to trust me with?

Helmer. In a flare of temper! Why fasten on that?

Nora. Yes, but you were so very right. I'm not up to the job. There's another job I have to do first. I have to try to educate myself. You can't help me with that. I've got to do it alone. And that's why I'm leaving you now.

Helmer (*jumping up*). What's that?

Nora. I have to stand completely alone, if I'm ever going to discover myself and the world out there. So I can't go on living with you.

Helmer. Nora, Nora!

Nora. I want to leave right away. Kristine should put me up for the night—

Helmer. You're insane! You've no right! I forbid you!

Nora. From here on, there's no use forbidding me anything. I'll take with me whatever is mine. I don't want a thing from you, either now or later.

Helmer. What kind of madness is this!

Nora. Tomorrow I'm going home—I mean, home where I came from. It'll be easier up there to find something to do.

---

5. **unperturbed:** undisturbed; calm.

Helmer. Oh, you blind, incompetent child!

Nora. I must learn to be competent, Torvald.

Helmer. Abandon your home, your husband, your children! And you're not even thinking what people will say.

Nora. I can't be concerned about that. I only know how essential this is.

Helmer. Oh, it's outrageous. So you'll run out like this on your most sacred vows.

Nora. What do you think are my most sacred vows?

Helmer. And I have to tell you that! Aren't they your duties to your husband and children?

Nora. I have other duties equally sacred.

Helmer. That isn't true. What duties are they?

Nora. Duties to myself.

Helmer. Before all else, you're a wife and a mother.

Nora. I don't believe in that anymore. I believe that, before all else, I'm a human being, no less than you—or anyway, I ought to try to become one. I know the majority thinks you're right, Torvald, and plenty of books agree with you, too. But I can't go on believing what the majority says, or what's written in books. I have to think over these things myself and try to understand them.

Helmer. Why can't you understand your place in your own home? On a point like that, isn't there one everlasting guide you can turn to? Where's your religion?

Nora. Oh, Torvald, I'm really not sure what religion is.

Helmer. What—?

Nora. I only know what the minister said when I was confirmed. He told me religion was this thing and that. When I get clear and away by myself, I'll go into that problem too. I'll see if what the minister said was right, or, in any case, if it's right for me.

Helmer. A young woman your age shouldn't talk like that. If religion can't move you, I can try to rouse[6] your conscience. You do have some moral feeling? Or, tell me—has that gone too?

Nora. It's not easy to answer that, Torvald. I simply don't know. I'm all confused about these things. I just know I see them so differently from you. I find out, for one thing, that the law's not at all what I'd thought—but I can't get it through my head that the law is fair. A woman hasn't a right to protect her dying father or save her husband's life! I can't believe that.

Helmer. You talk like a child. You don't know anything of the world you live in.

Nora. No, I don't. But now I'll begin to learn for myself. I'll try to discover who's right, the world or I.

Helmer. Nora, you're sick; you've got a fever. I almost think you're out of your head.

Nora. I've never felt more clearheaded and sure in my life.

Helmer. And—clearheaded and sure—you're leaving your husband and children?

Nora. Yes.

Helmer. Then there's only one possible reason.

Nora. What?

Helmer. You no longer love me.

Nora. No. That's exactly it.

Helmer. Nora! You can't be serious!

Nora. Oh, this is so hard, Torvald—you've been so kind to me always. But I can't help it. I don't love you anymore.

Helmer (*struggling for composure*).[7] Are you also clearheaded and sure about that?

---

6. **rouse:** awaken.

7. **composure:** calmness; self-control.

Nora. Yes, completely. That's why I can't go on staying here.

Helmer. Can you tell me what I did to lose your love?

Nora. Yes, I can tell you. It was this evening when the miraculous thing didn't come—then I knew you weren't the man I'd imagined.

Helmer. Be more explicit; I don't follow you.

Nora. I've waited now so patiently eight long years—for, my Lord, I know miracles don't come every day. Then this crisis broke over me, and such a certainty filled me: *now* the miraculous event would occur. While Krogstad's letter was lying out there, I never for an instant dreamed that you could give in to his terms. I was so utterly sure you'd say to him: go on, tell your tale to the whole wide world. And when he'd done that—

Helmer. Yes, what then? When I'd delivered my own wife into shame and disgrace—!

Nora. When he'd done that, I was so utterly sure that you'd step forward, take the blame on yourself and say: I am the guilty one.

Helmer. Nora—!

Nora. You're thinking I'd never accept such a sacrifice from you? No, of course not. But what good would my protests be against you? That was the miracle I was waiting for, in terror and hope. And to stave that off,[8] I would have taken my life.

Helmer. I'd gladly work for you day and night, Nora—and take on pain and deprivation. But there's no one who gives up honor for love.

Nora. Millions of women have done just that.

Helmer. Oh, you think and talk like a silly child.

Nora. Perhaps. But you neither think nor talk like the man I could join myself to. When your big fright was over—and it wasn't from any threat against me, only for what might damage you—when all the danger was past, for you it

was just as if nothing had happened. I was exactly the same, your little lark, your doll, that you'd have to handle with double care now that I'd turned out so brittle and frail. (*Gets up.*) Torvald—in that instant it dawned on me that for eight years I've been living here with a stranger, and that I'd even conceived three children—oh, I can't stand the thought of it! I could tear myself to bits.

Helmer (*heavily*). I see. There's a gulf that's opened between us—that's clear. Oh, but Nora, can't we bridge it somehow?

Nora. The way I am now, I'm no wife for you.

Helmer. I have the strength to make myself over.

Nora. Maybe—if your doll gets taken away.

Helmer. But to part! To part from you! No, Nora, no—I can't imagine it.

Nora (*going out, right*). All the more reason why it has to be. (*She reenters with her coat and a small overnight bag, which she puts on a chair by the table.*)

Helmer. Nora, Nora, not now! Wait till tomorrow.

Nora. I can't spend the night in a strange man's room.

Helmer. But couldn't we live here like brother and sister—

Nora. You know very well how long that would last. (*Throws her shawl about her.*) Good-bye, Torvald. I won't look in on the children. I know they're in better hands than mine. The way I am now, I'm no use to them.

Helmer. But someday, Nora—someday—?

Nora. How can I tell? I haven't the least idea what'll become of me.

Helmer. But you're my wife, now and wherever you go.

---

8. **stave that off:** prevent that.

Oh, Torvald,
I've stopped believing in miracles.

Nora. Listen, Torvald—I've heard that when a wife deserts her husband's house just as I'm doing, then the law frees him from all responsibility. In any case, I'm freeing you from being responsible. Don't feel yourself bound, any more than I will. There has to be absolute freedom for us both. Here, take your ring back. Give me mine.

Helmer. That too?

Nora. That too.

Helmer. There it is.

Nora. Good. Well, now it's all over. I'm putting the keys here. The maids know all about keeping up the house—better than I do. Tomorrow, after I've left town, Kristine will stop by to pack up everything that's mine from home. I'd like those things shipped up to me.

Helmer. Over! All over! Nora, won't you ever think about me?

Nora. I'm sure I'll think of you often, and about the children and the house here.

Helmer. May I write you?

Nora. No—never. You're not to do that.

Helmer. Oh, but let me send you—

Nora. Nothing. Nothing.

Helmer. Or help you if you need it.

Nora. No. I accept nothing from strangers.

Helmer. Nora—can I never be more than a stranger to you?

Nora (*picking up the overnight bag*). Ah, Torvald—it would take the greatest miracle of all—

Helmer. Tell me the greatest miracle!

Nora. You and I both would have to transform ourselves to the point that— Oh, Torvald, I've stopped believing in miracles.

Helmer. But I'll believe. Tell me! Transform ourselves to the point that—?

Nora. That our living together could be a true marriage. (*She goes out down the hall.*)

Helmer (*sinks down on a chair by the door, face buried in his hands*). Nora! Nora! (*Looking about and rising.*) Empty. She's gone. (*A sudden hope leaps in him.*) The greatest miracle —?

(*From below, the sound of a door slamming shut.*) ❖

What aspects of the relationship between Nora and Torvald are shown in these scenes?

Alla Nazimova and Alan Hale, silent film, 1922

Liv Strømsted and Lars Nordrum, National Theatre, Oslo, Norway, 1957

Peter Donat and Marsha Mason, American Conservatory Theatre, San Francisco, 1972–1973

Christopher Plummer, Julie Harris, and Jason Robards, Jr., Hallmark Production, 1959

Liv Ullmann and Sam Waterston, New York Shakespeare Festival, 1975

Connect to the Literature

1. What Do You Think?
How did you react to Nora's decision to leave Torvald? Explain.

Comprehension Check
- What plans does Mrs. Linde make with Krogstad?
- How does Torvald react to the first letter from Krogstad?
- What does Torvald expect to happen after he reads the second letter?

Think Critically

2. ACTIVE READING: STRATEGIES FOR READING REALISTIC DRAMA Look over the stage directions in this act. Which sights and sounds do you think would have the greatest impact on the audience? How do they reinforce the play's meaning?

3. Do you find Nora's actions at the end of the play to be believable?

THINK ABOUT
- what strengths she has shown earlier in the play
- Torvald's reactions to Krogstad's letters
- what Nora means when she says she's "beginning to understand everything now" (page 1071, col. 2)
- what she means by "the greatest miracle of all" (page 1079, col. 2)

4. What is your opinion of Torvald?

THINK ABOUT
- the position of men in his society
- his actions and responses
- what happens at the end of the play

5. Irony is a contrast between what happens and what is expected. In what way is the frequent use of letters ironic in this play?

Extend Interpretations

6. The Writer's Style Ibsen is known for his use of **symbolism** in his plays. What do you think are the most important symbols in *A Doll's House?*

7. Different Perspectives Suppose Torvald were the central character in the play instead of Nora. In what ways do you think the play would be different?

LITERARY ANALYSIS: THEME IN REALISTIC DRAMA

A **theme** is a central idea or message conveyed by a literary work. It is a perception about life or human nature that the writer shares with the reader. Longer works usually have more than one theme. In realistic dramas, themes usually are not stated directly. Rather, they are suggested by the action or through literary techniques such as irony and symbolism.

Paired Activity With a classmate, discuss the themes that *A Doll's House* conveys about the following topics. Write a sentence stating each theme, and cite evidence from the play to support it.

- true love
- social obligations
- secrecy and deception in marriage
- women's role in society
- rigid moral views
- how the past influences people's lives

REVIEW: FORESHADOWING

Remember that **foreshadowing** is a writer's use of hints or clues to suggest what will happen later. What moments in the play are examples of foreshadowing?

Writing Options

1. Torvald's Response

Krogstad's letters to Torvald play a crucial role in Act Three. Write a letter from Torvald to Krogstad after Nora has left him. Model the style of your letter on the tone of Torvald's dialogue throughout the play.

2. Nora's Diary

Imagine that you are Nora. Write a diary entry describing an important moment in the play, such as when you decide to leave Torvald. Discuss your feelings about what happened and your concerns about the future.

3. Cause Analysis

Write an essay in which you explain the causes that lead to Nora's decision at the end of the play. Begin by listing important incidents and conversations from each act that have an effect on Nora. Decide which details are most critical to Nora's development. Present your ideas in a clear sequence that shows why Nora decides to leave Torvald. Place the essay in your **Working Portfolio.**

Writing Handbook
See page R32: Cause and Effect.

Activities & Explorations

1. Ibsen Improvisation

With a classmate, create an improvised scene in which Nora and Torvald meet by accident several years later. Before you begin, discuss how each character's life might have changed and how each might feel toward the other.

~ PERFORMING

2. Set Design

Sketch a design for the set of *A Doll's House*. Before you begin, review Ibsen's descriptions of the set in his stage directions. Decide which act of the play you wish to represent in your sketch.

~ VIEWING AND REPRESENTING

Inquiry & Research

Seeking Equality

With a classmate, prepare an oral report on the history of women's rights in a particular country. Find out if women may conduct business transactions, vote, and hold office, and, if so, when they gained these rights. You might also research topics such as job opportunities and marriage laws.

RESEARCH STARTER
CLASSZONE.COM

Vocabulary in Action

EXERCISE: WORD MEANINGS Match each situation described in the left column with the word in the right column that best fits it.

1. Quitting your job without having a new job lined up
2. The ruins of a building after a fire
3. Walking carefully on an icy sidewalk
4. A child skipping home from school
5. Talking a lot about your big hiking trip to a friend who has a broken leg
6. Noise and pollution problems that never get cleaned up
7. Criticizing someone for being two minutes late to a meeting
8. Doing things on the spur of the moment
9. Figuring out how to turn a hobby into a money-making scheme
10. Participating in a silly prank that you didn't even enjoy

a. chronic
b. calculating
c. rash
d. capricious
e. desolate
f. tactless
g. inane
h. warily
i. petty
j. jauntily

Women in Society

In the years since Nora shocked her husband and conventional 19th-century society by slamming the door on her marriage, there have been changes in the status of women. Today, many women lead independent lives and pursue their own interests. During the 20th century, events occurred that laid the groundwork for this freedom. In the early part of the century, suffragists in the United States fought for and won the right to vote. In the later part, many women struggled to achieve many more social, political, and economic rights.

There has also been resistance to changes in women's status. Different cultures have varying views and expectations of women. People within a society may have different viewpoints about the kinds of lives women should lead. There continues to be discussion about what women's roles should be.

In sports such as basketball, soccer, and softball, women now play in professional leagues of their own in a number of countries. Interest in watching women's sports teams has reached an all-time high, with the 1999 Women's World Cup soccer matches playing to record crowds.

Some women today combine raising their children with building a career. Others choose to stay at home, often pursuing interests in volunteer activities. Still others return to school or work after their children are grown.

Paired or Group Discussion On balance, women have made important changes, but many people would like to see more accomplished. Do you think there are certain rights that all women should have? If so, how do you think this could be achieved? If not, explain your opinion.

Writing Workshop

Looking at consequences . . .

From Reading to Writing Several of the stories in this unit describe characters who suffer dramatic consequences for their actions. Every event has consequences, great or small; one way to examine the relationship between an event and its consequences is to write a **cause-and-effect essay.** You can use this type of writing to show why something happens, what its consequences are, or how events are linked.

For Your Portfolio

WRITING PROMPT Write an essay that explains the causes or effects of an event or analyzes a series of events that are linked by cause and effect.

Purpose: To inform and explain

Audience: Your classmates or other interested readers

Basics in a Box

Cause-and-Effect Essay at a Glance

Introduction
Introduce the subject

Body
Describe the cause and its effects*

cause

effect   effect   effect

Conclusion
Summarize the cause-and-effect relationship

* or
• present an effect and then analyze its causes
• present and analyze a chain of events related as causes and effects

RUBRIC Standards for Writing

A successful cause-and-effect essay should

• clearly state the cause-and-effect relationship being examined

• provide any necessary background information

• present details in a logical order and include transitions to show relationships between effects and causes

• summarize the cause-and-effect relationship in the conclusion

Analyzing a Student Model

Nicholas Lilly
Oak Park and River Forest High School

Pressure to Produce in High School

This is a stressful time for college-bound high school students, who feel increasing pressure to get good grades, impress colleges, and do well in an ever more competitive college-application process. This pressure has numerous effects on students, their quality of life, and even the quality of their education. With its emphasis on end results—grades, test scores, and high school "résumés"—this pressure ultimately causes students to pay more attention to the impression they make on colleges and less attention to what they're actually learning.

A 97 percent growth rate in the last eight years . . . a record-breaking year, yielding a 23 percent increase . . . a second record-breaking year, showing a 16.5 percent annual growth rate . . . These statistics from USNews.com refer to the record increases in applications that colleges received from high school students. As the generation of Baby Boomers' children grows up and reaches the end of high school, greater numbers of students are preparing to go to college.

This increased competition causes students to become anxious about their futures. This apprehension, shared by parents, is due to the belief that being a success in life and having a good job rests on a quality college education. High school students really see it as a make-or-break point in their life. No longer content to focus on the learning process, students focus on their grades and their college-entrance-test scores. They pay thousands of dollars on classes guaranteed to improve their scores. The whole process is developing into quite a business.

In addition to the push for high grades and test scores, students feel a great drive to take part in sports, clubs, volunteer work, and other extracurricular activities. While many students certainly enjoy these activities, they are also keenly aware that a full "résumé" of high school activities will make them more attractive to colleges. The student's motivation is now slightly altered: rather than doing something purely for its own sake, he or she is also doing it for the sake of appearances. Students are cramming their schedules fuller than ever. Where is the time to relax, digest, or reflect? There is none.

As a result of these pressures, students live and work in an atmosphere with an undercurrent of general unpleasantness and forced rivalry. Some students, desperate for a way to escape the dominance of competition and pressure in their lives, look for

❶ Clearly states the cause-and-effect relationship being examined

❷ Provides background information on the topic

❸ Shows the relationship between the cause (competition) and the effect (pressure)

shortcuts. Tired of the pressure, or maybe just tired, some students choose to slack off, but just slightly. They do as little as possible while still getting by with the necessary grades. Others take easier classes—if they can do it without adversely impacting their grade point average—rather than facing the challenge of the school's most difficult classes.

Finally, to various degrees, students cheat. According to USNews.com, only 20 percent of college students in 1950 said they had cheated in high school; today, surveys show that number to be between 75 percent and 98 percent. When a student first cheats—maybe by copying part of a homework assignment—it seems almost benign. Unfortunately, it soon becomes a habit, a way around time constraints. Students begin to develop a similarly lax attitude toward tests. Again, in the beginning, students convince themselves that it is fairly harmless. Perhaps, in the hallway, they ask a simple question: "So what was on the test?" For some, this behavior may progress to sharing test questions, creating "cheat sheets," or even stealing tests before exam day.

❹ Shows a logical progression of events, from mild to extreme cheating

This cheating has a damaging effect on education. When students resort to these methods as a way to achieve success, they have given up on learning the material and have reached the point where they only care about grades. Moreover, students who refuse to resort to shortcuts often do not get the grades they deserve, because they are overworked; they are left to doubt their choice to be honest. What both groups have in common, however, is that the pressure exerted on them produces a poor high school experience. There is no passion, no joy in the process of learning. There is only an obsession with an end product: grades.

❺ Having shown the causes of cheating, uses a transition to introduce the effects of cheating

It's a destructive chain of events: the increased numbers of college applications, the anxiety of added competition, the pressure for grades, the academic shortcuts, and finally the cheating. These elements together produce a considerable strain on students and can only serve to detract from their education. It may be difficult to feel sympathy for the students who engage in unethical behavior, but their behavior is a symptom of a greater problem. There is no way to decrease the number of students applying to colleges or the number of applications submitted by each student—nor should that be the goal. However, we should acknowledge the effects of this increased competition and work to keep those factors under control.

❻ Concludes by summarizing the cause-and-effect relationships and stating the importance of recognizing these relationships

Writing Your Cause-and-Effect Essay

❶ Prewriting

Begin by thinking about topics for your essay. Consider events with causes or effects you don't understand. For example, perhaps you wonder why a business goes bankrupt or what happens to an ecosystem when a species becomes extinct. Any question that interests you and that has an answer of some complexity could be a suitable topic. **Brainstorm** a list of topics and then consider each one carefully, deciding which would yield the most interesting essay. See the **Idea Bank** in the margin for more suggestions. Once you have decided on a topic, follow the steps below.

Planning Your Cause-and-Effect Essay

1. **Think about the relationships between events.** Ask yourself whether these are really cause-and-effect relationships. Just because one event follows another doesn't necessarily mean that the first event caused the second. Also ask yourself whether a cause has one effect or more than one and whether an effect is the result of a single or multiple causes.

2. **Identify your audience.** What does your audience already know about your subject? What background information will you need to provide?

3. **Gather supporting information.** What will you need to learn about your topic? What sources of information can you draw on—personal observation and reflection, library research, interviews with experts?

4. **Map out your ideas.** How does the information you have collected fit together? You might create a graphic organizer to help you arrange what you already know and discover what you still need to find out.

❷ Drafting

Use drafting to explore the relationships between the events you have decided to write about. Write freely, leaving finer points and revisions for later. Be sure to clearly state the cause-and-effect relationship you're discussing. If at some point during drafting you find that you need more information, set aside your draft and conduct further research.

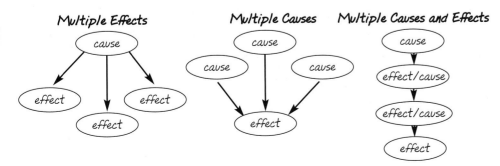

IDEABank

1. Your Working Portfolio
Look for ideas in the **Writing Option** you completed earlier in this unit:

- **Cause-and-Effect Paragraph,** p. 904

2. Acts of Nature
Make a list of natural phenomena (weather, environmental changes, natural disasters) you have experienced or heard about. Brainstorm about the causes and effects of these events.

3. Then and Now
Look through a newspaper or magazine, and make a list of current situations or events that interest or puzzle you. For each of these things, consider the various historical events that led to it.

Have questions?

See the **Writing Handbook**
Cause and Effect,
pp. R32–R33

LANGUAGE SKILLS

❸ Revising

TARGET SKILL ▸ USING TRANSITIONAL WORDS AND PHRASES Transitional words and phrases play an important role in showing the relationships between causes and effects. Choose from words and phrases such as *therefore, because, as a result, in response,* and *consequently.*

Need revising help?

Review the **Rubric**, p. 1084
Consider **peer reader** comments
Check **revision guidelines**, p. R19

Ask Your Peer Reader

- How would you summarize the main cause-and-effect relationship that I wrote about?
- What parts were unclear?
- What do you disagree with or want to know more about?

> *As a result of these   live and work in*
> ~~There are~~ pressures ~~on~~ students ~~and~~ an atmosphere with an undercurrent of general unpleasantness and forced rivalry. Some students, desperate for a way to escape the dominance of competition and pressure in their lives, look for shortcuts.

❹ Editing and Proofreading

TARGET SKILL ▸ MISSPELLED HOMOPHONES English is full of words that sound alike but are spelled differently and have different meanings. One very common example of near homophones is that of the words *effect* and *affect.* Their pronunciations differ only slightly, and they are commonly confused. Most of the time, *effect* is used as a noun meaning "result," and *affect* is used as a verb meaning "to have an impact on." Pay special attention to these spellings when writing about causes and effects. Misspelled homophones can confuse your readers and make a bad impression.

Publishing IDEAS

- Submit your essay to your school or community newspaper.
- Submit your essay to an academic journal—such as a history journal—for high school students.
- Present your essay orally to your history or science class.

> *stakes*
> This competition raises the ~~steaks~~, causing an increasing
> *their*
> pressure on students not only to excel with ~~there~~ grade point
> averages but also to make themselves peerless in the eyes of
> college admissions offices. This pressure, in many cases,
> *effect*
> has a negative ~~affect~~ on a student's high school experience.

PUBLISHING OPTIONS
CLASSZONE.COM

❺ Reflecting

FOR YOUR WORKING PORTFOLIO What did you learn about the cause-and-effect relationship you wrote about? What techniques did you learn that you can apply to other writing exercises? Attach your reflections to your finished essay. Save your essay in your **Working Portfolio.**

Read this paragraph from the first draft of a cause-and-effect essay. The underlined sections may include the following kinds of errors:

- **misspelled homophones**
- **sentence fragments**
- **run-on sentences**
- **comma errors**

For each underlined section, choose the revision that most improves the writing.

> When we think about technology responsible for our modern <u>lifestyle. We often think</u> (1) of <u>factories automobiles and the telephone.</u> (2) Household appliances such as the washing machine, the clothes dryer, and the refrigerator don't get that much attention these <u>days. Although their invention had a tremendous effect on the way we live.</u> (3) Before these labor-saving devices, laundry was an all-day chore: clothes had to be boiled, stirred, and <u>rung</u> (4) out by hand, then hung out to dry. Groceries had to be bought fresh daily or pulled in from the garden or the cellar. <u>There was no such thing as a microwave or a refrigerator, people couldn't even save</u> (5) a cooked meal for more than a few days, especially in hot weather. The people most directly <u>effected</u> (6) by these inventions, of course, were women. Relief from some of the most time-consuming household chores made it possible, eventually, for women to seek work outside the home.

1. **A.** lifestyle; we often think
   B. lifestyle, we often think
   C. lifestyle—we often think
   D. Correct as is

2. **A.** factories automobiles, and the telephone.
   B. factories, automobiles; and the telephone.
   C. factories, automobiles, and the telephone.
   D. Correct as is

3. **A.** days, although their invention had a tremendous effect on the way we live.
   B. days—although their invention had a tremendous effect on the way we live.
   C. days, but—although their invention had a tremendous effect on the way we live.
   D. Correct as is

4. **A.** wringed
   B. wrung
   C. rang
   D. Correct as is

5. **A.** Because there was no such thing as a microwave or a refrigerator. People couldn't even save
   B. There was no such thing as a microwave or a refrigerator; people couldn't even save
   C. There was no such thing as a microwave or a refrigerator people couldn't even save
   D. Correct as is

6. **A.** afflicted
   B. affected
   C. effecting
   D. Correct as is

Need extra help?

See the **Grammar Handbook**

Correcting Fragments, p. R73

Correcting Run-On Sentences, p. R73

Quick Reference: Punctuation, p. R77

TEST PRACTICE

Building Vocabulary

Recognizing Denotations and Connotations

> Then the mother and son would get together in unrestrained joy. This was the absolute extreme of childishness! They drew pictures of animals that God has yet to create. . . . There was no way to preserve all these creations; their traces had to be thoroughly obliterated before the head of the house returned.
>
> —Rabindranath Tagore, "The Artist"

Good writers choose their words very carefully, knowing that different words—even ones with similar meanings—can produce different impressions. Often, words that have the same **denotation,** or literal meaning, have very different **connotations,** or implied meanings. Notice the word *obliterated* in the passage at left. What comes to mind when you hear this word?

The dictionary definition of *obliterate* is "to do away with completely, so as to leave no trace." Why didn't Tagore use the word *removed, erased,* or *destroyed?*

The word *obliterate* carries a connotation of great destructive force. For example, one often hears it used in describing the destruction of a city by bombing. Although Tagore is only describing the destruction of some drawings, his choice of the word *obliterated* lends great power and a sense of violence to what might otherwise seem a minor act.

Strategies for Building Vocabulary

The following strategies can help you become aware of subtle differences in meaning.

❶ **Watch for Words That Create a Mood** As you read, look out for words that make a particular impression on you or create a certain mood. For example, you may find words that seem funny, sad, angry, or delicate. Look for meanings that are implied but not directly stated. For example, the word *clan* denotes a large family, but it connotes a sprawling, tight-knit family, sometimes even a powerful one.

❷ **Identify the Author's Purpose** Consider the author's purpose and intended audience. What feelings is he or she trying to convey? How does the choice of words affect the work's tone? For example, in the excerpt below, the word *meager,* which means "scanty," implies weakness and a lack of nourishment. By describing the widow's savings with this word, Tagore creates an image of her as a poor, frail creature.

> Govinda came to Calcutta after graduation from high school in Mymensingh. His widowed mother's savings were meager, but his own unwavering determination was his greatest resource.
>
> —Rabindranath Tagore, "The Artist"

❸ **Choose Words Carefully** When writing, remember that synonyms are not always interchangeable. They frequently have different connotations, and sometimes even slightly different denotations. For example, the words *sing* and *conduct* are both synonyms of *perform.* Of the two, however, only the first can replace *perform* in "to perform a song," and only the second will work in "to perform surgery."

Think about the meanings implied by each of the synonyms in the following examples.

1. Lalitha can be quite **firm** in an argument. (implies simply that she holds her ground)
2. Lalitha can be quite **tenacious** in an argument. (implies that she is strong, perhaps even fierce)
3. Lalitha can be quite **obstinate** in an argument. (implies that she is unwilling to listen to reason)

EXERCISE For each word, write a sentence containing that word. Then rewrite the sentence, replacing the word with a synonym. Explain how the meaning of the sentence changes when you use the synonym.

1. weep
2. innocent
3. fragile
4. curious
5. humid

Sentence Crafting — Using Adverb Clauses

Grammar from Literature Look at the following sentences from Guy de Maupassant's "A Piece of String." Notice the clauses highlighted in red. What kinds of information do they add to the sentences?

> Along all the roads around Goderville the peasants and their wives were coming toward the burgh because it was market day.
>
> After the public crier had ceased his drum-beating, he called out in a jerky voice, speaking his phrases irregularly.

The words in red are **adverb clauses.** Like adverbs, such clauses modify verbs, adjectives, and other adverbs. Adverb clauses answer such questions as *where, why, when*, and *to what extent.* In the sentences above, the adverb clauses modify the verbs *were coming* and *called.*

An adverb clause is a **subordinate clause**—it cannot stand alone but must be attached to an **independent clause** (also called a **main clause**). Adverb clauses are introduced by **subordinating conjunctions,** which can be classified according to the kinds of relationships they express.

Cause: *because, since, so that*
Condition: *although, as if, if, though, unless*
Place: *where, wherever*
Time: *after, as, before, since, until, when, while*

Using Adverb Clauses in Your Writing As you revise, examine how you have shown relationships between ideas. Use adverb clauses to combine sentences and make these relationships clearer.

> Maître Hauchecome looked around. He saw accusing faces.
>
> Wherever Maître Hauchecome looked, he saw accusing faces.

Usage Tip When you use a pronoun in a subordinate clause that follows an independent clause, make sure the antecedent of the pronoun is clear.

> UNCLEAR
> Maître Malandain saw Maître Hauchecome when he picked up the string.

In the sentence above, it is not clear who picked up the string. The problem can be solved by restructuring the sentence.

> CLEAR
> As Maître Hauchecome picked up the string, Maître Malandain saw him do it.

WRITING EXERCISE Combine each of the following pairs of sentences. Using a subordinating conjunction that expresses the relationship shown in parentheses, change one of the sentences into an adverb clause.

1. Maître Hauchecome was walking along the road. He saw a piece of string lying there. (time)
2. He was a frugal man. He took the string and began to roll it up. (cause)
3. He saw Maître Malandain watching him. He quickly put the string in his pocket. (time)
4. He continued to look at the ground. He was looking for something else. (condition)
5. He thought no more about it. The police questioned him. (time)

GRAMMAR EXERCISE Rewrite the sentences below so that there are no unclear pronoun antecedents.

1. When Maître Hauchecome met with the mayor, he had a very stern talk with him.
2. The mayor wanted to speak with him because of his suspicions about a theft.
3. As Pakhom's wife and her sister were talking, Pakhom overheard what she said.
4. The peasants and landlords had an agreement in which they were allowed to graze their cattle.
5. When Pakhom bought some land and another peasant wanted to pasture cattle on his land, he ran into trouble.

Reflect and Assess

What understanding of realism did you gain from reading the selections in Unit Six, Part 2? Did the literature challenge you in new ways? Use the following activities to explore further what you have read.

The Peasants of Flagey Returning from the Fair, Ornans (1850–1855), Gustave Courbet. Musée des Beaux-Arts, Besançon, France/Giraudon/Art Resource, New York.

Reflecting on the Literature

Exploring Realism Realistic fiction and drama portray ordinary people in real-life settings and struggles. In these works the writers try to reveal the motivations that underly characters' actions and conflicts. Think back over the selections you have read. Choose two passages that represent some aspect of realistic writing. Briefly explain how each one shows some characteristic of realism.

Reviewing Literary Concepts

Interpreting Irony Irony is often an element in realistic literature. In this part of the book, several of the writers use irony to give insight into characters or situations. Pick three examples of irony from the selections you have read. Explain why each example is ironic. Then tell how it contributes to the development of character, plot, or theme in the selection.

🗀 Building Your Portfolio

Writing Workshop and Writing Options Look back at the cause-and-effect essay you wrote for the Writing Workshop on page 1084 and at the Writing Options you completed for this part of the book. Which piece are you most satisfied with? Put that assignment in your **Presentation Portfolio** 🗀, along with a note explaining why you think it works well.

Self ASSESSMENT

📖 **READER'S NOTEBOOK**

The following list contains names and terms that relate to realism. List the words on a separate piece of paper. Next to each one, write a sentence describing or defining it. If you are uncertain about any word, review the places in this part of the book in which it is discussed or check the **Glossary of Literary Terms** (page R91).

realists	Anton Chekhov
naturalism	Fyodor Dostoyevsky
irony	Henrik Ibsen
A Doll's House	Guy de Maupassant
Leo Tolstoy	realistic drama

Setting GOALS

Several of the realist writers in this part of the book had an important influence on the writing of fiction and drama in the 20th century. As you read the literature in the next unit, look for connections to the realist works you have just read.

Extend Your *Reading*

Tess of the d'Urbervilles

THOMAS HARDY

The values of 19th-century society collide head-on with the personal life of Tess Durbeyfield, a 16-year-old girl from a poor English family. In this tragic tale of love and betrayal, a shiftless father's discovery of his aristocratic ancestry sets in motion a chain of events that spells disaster.

Here are just a few of the related readings that accompany *Tess of the d'Urbervilles*:

Life's Tragedy
BY PAUL LAURENCE DUNBAR

Disappointment Is the Lot of Woman
BY LUCY STONE

A Complaint
BY LADY CHWANG KËANG

Five Plays

ANTON CHEKHOV; RONALD HINGLEY, TRANS.

This collection features the Russian dramatist's five greatest plays: *Ivanov, The Seagull, Uncle Vanya, The Three Sisters,* and *The Cherry Orchard.* Using simple but powerful dialogue, Chekhov deals with such themes as love, death, jealousy, and despair. His fully drawn characters try to improve their lives and relationships with others but fail, often as a result of their own sense of helplessness. Writing from a realist perspective, Chekhov exposes the resistance to change evident in Russian society in the late 1800s.

And Even *More* . . .

Books

Adam Bede GEORGE ELIOT
In this tale of destructive love, Eliot combines a deep compassion for her characters with a condemnation of a society that judges young women without helping them.

The Overcoat and Other Tales of Good and Evil
NIKOLAI V. GOGOL; DAVID MAGARSHACK, TRANS.
Mixing realism and the supernatural, Gogol expresses in these stories his frustration with the Russian government and his compassion for the poor.

Other Media

A Doll's House
The thoughtful performances in this 1973 film help bring to life Ibsen's play about a woman stifled by 19th-century society. MGM/UA Studios. (VIDEOCASSETTE)

War and Peace
Tolstoy's epic novel about family and Napoleon's invasion of Russia in 1812 is faithfully re-created in this six-part series. BBC Video. (VIDEOCASSETTE)

Great Short Works of Leo Tolstoy

LOUISE AND AYLMER MAUDE, TRANS.

The eight short novels in this volume include *The Death of Ivan Ilyich* and *The Cossacks.* In these works, Tolstoy tackles such issues as death, war, and religion.

Modern and Contemporary Literature 1900–PRESENT

Photo of Earth from the Moon. Lyndon B. Johnson Space Center/NASA.

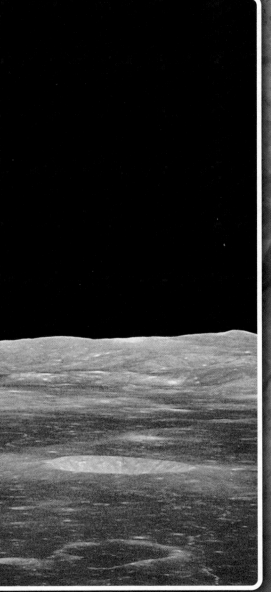

*"I feel that writing is an act of hope. . . .
The writer of good will carries a lamp to
illuminate the dark corners."*

—ISABEL ALLENDE

PART 1
Worlds of Change:
Expressions of Modernism 1102–1199

❦

PART 2
When Worlds Collide:
Responses to War
and Conflict 1200–1319

❦

PART 3
Critics and Dreamers:
Contemporary Nobel
Prize Winners 1320–1379

UNIT SEVEN
The Changing World

Perhaps no century in human history has experienced the degree of change that took place in the 1900s. At its best, the 20th century saw the spread of democracy, great scientific achievements, and marvels of technology. At its worst, it was the most violent, most destructive century in human history. Writers had no shortage of subjects.

An American astronaut stands on the surface of the moon.

Struggles for Power

The century was defined by its conflicts. In two world wars, great powers collided in struggles for economic and political domination. In the Cold War,

Indian leader Mahatma Gandhi, a key figure in India's successful revolt against British rule

competing systems—democratic capitalism and communism—fought for supremacy.

During the second half of the century, independence movements against European rule sprang up throughout Africa and Asia, resulting in bloody conflicts. More recently, power struggles became more localized, with terrorism and civil war taking high civilian casualties.

Triumphs—and Tragedies—of Science and Technology

In the 20th century, advances in science and technology changed life dramatically. The automobile, high-speed trains, and jet planes enabled us to travel faster and farther than ever before. A revolution in communication allowed us to send and receive information across the world in the blink of an eye. Radio, television, film, computers, cell phones, and the Internet—all were invented or flourished in the 20th century. With the flick of a switch, we can cool a house, light up a skyscraper, or heat an entire city. The same know-how has made it possible to send fresh foods across continents and oceans.

Perhaps the most beneficial achievements of the century occurred in medicine. Antibiotics, vaccines, surgery, and an arsenal of medicines can now fight disease and extend life. A more nutritious diet, thanks primarily to improved methods of farming and distribution, is now available to many. Life expectancy has climbed steadily, especially in developed countries.

Yet science and technology have also been put to destructive uses. In World War I, for example, advanced biological and chemical weapons killed thousands. The technology of war became even more powerful in the 1940s with the invention of the atom bomb, the most powerful means of destruction ever created. More recently, our great appetite for energy has depleted precious natural resources, while the pollution of air, soil, and water has posed a worldwide threat to health and safety. To a degree, we are victims of our own successes.

Soldier wearing gas mask (1942)

Family and friends watching their new cable television in the isolated Asian country of Bhutan

New Ways of Living

Over the century, everyday life changed at an ever-quickening pace. Industrialization, which had begun in Europe in the 18th century, gradually spread around the world. As a result, consumer goods became widely available, personal wealth increased, and cities grew rapidly. At the start of the 20th century, the vast majority of the world's population lived in rural areas. By century's end, more than 40 percent of that population lived in urban areas. In the cities, new economic opportunities opened, cultures mingled, and new ideas challenged traditional ways of life.

Throughout the world, many people have benefited from economic growth and progress in science, medicine, and agriculture. However, the gap between rich and poor nations is widening, and many still live in grinding poverty.

Global Interdependence

Advances in trade, technology, and communications have made the world a "smaller" place. In the first decades of the 20th century, Western countries seemed to control the fate of the world because of their power and colonial rule of nations in Asia and Africa. In recent decades, nations have become more interdependent. Former colonies welcome trade with and investment from the West, while businesses in developed countries, such as Japan, Germany, and the United States, depend on international markets.

As national economies blend into one global economy, some positive and negative effects have emerged. On the one hand, cultural exchanges can enrich individual nations. On the other hand, some countries fear losing their native cultures because of the influence of popular Western culture, with its rock music, jeans, and television shows.

Democracy and Education

In the last century, democracy and education became more widespread across the world.

In 1902, for example, only Australia and New Zealand allowed all adult citizens to vote. Over the next hundred years, citizen participation in government increased dramatically, especially for women and minorities. Democratic governments can now be found on every continent. Women now vote in nearly every country where men have the right to vote, and women, such as Margaret Thatcher (Great Britain) and Golda Meir (Israel), have served as elected heads of state.

The 20th century also witnessed dramatic changes in education. At the beginning of the century, widespread formal education was common only in the West and often limited to elementary levels. By the end of the century, nearly every country of the world provided free elementary education to its young people. The number of students receiving secondary and higher education has also increased significantly worldwide. In Africa, for example, more than 40 percent of the secondary–school-age population is enrolled in secondary school.

EVENTS IN WORLD LITERATURE AND ART

1900

1900 Austrian doctor Sigmund Freud publishes his theory of the unconscious in *The Interpretation of Dreams*

1907 Pablo Picasso and Georges Braque start artistic movement called cubism in Paris

1913 Russian composer Igor Stravinsky's *The Rite of Spring* marks beginning of modernism in music

1915 Franz Kafka publishes "Metamorphosis"

1916–1924 Dadaism, an artistic protest movement, attacks established values and ideas

1919 In Germany, Walter Gropius founds influential Bauhaus school of design that produces International style of functional, boxy architecture

1920

1920s In Jazz Age, Europeans dance to rhythms of American jazz

1921 Luigi Pirandello's innovative play *Six Characters in Search of an Author* performed

1922 James Joyce publishes his novel *Ulysses* in Paris

c. 1924–1937 Influenced by Freud's ideas, surrealist painters Max Ernst and Salvador Dali depict odd dream-worlds

1928 Federico García Lorca publishes his popular *Gypsy Ballads*

1929 Virginia Woolf publishes groundbreaking feminist work *A Room of One's Own*

1930s Léopold Senghor and Aimé Césaire found the Negritude movement

1940

1942 Albert Camus publishes classic novel of alienation, *The Stranger*

1944 U.S. composer Aaron Copland uses folk-song melodies and jazz rhythms in *Appalachian Spring*

1945–1960 Abstract expressionism, led by New York artist Jackson Pollock, gains respect of international art world

1948–1952 Pablo Neruda exiled from his native Chile for publicly criticizing the president

1948 Yasunari Kawabata publishes his novel *Snow Country*

1949 French writer Simone de Beauvoir publishes *The Second Sex*, arguing for an end to women's second-class status

EVENTS IN WORLD HISTORY

1900

1903 In U.S., Wright brothers make first successful airplane flight

1914–1918 World War I between Allies (Russia, France, Britain and later U.S.) and Central Powers (Germany and Austria-Hungary)

1917–1920 Russian Revolution topples czar and brings in communist government

1918 Women over 30 gain right to vote in Britain

1920

1920 World's first commercial radio station broadcasts in U.S.

1922 Benito Mussolini and Fascist Party gain control of Italy

1928 Scottish doctor Alexander Fleming discovers penicillin

1929 Stock market crash in New York soon plunges world into Great Depression

1933 Adolf Hitler and Nazi Party come to power in Germany

1937 Japan invades China

1939 Hitler invades Poland; France and Britain declare war on Germany, beginning World War II

1940

1941 Japan bombs U.S. fleet at Pearl Harbor, causing U.S. to enter war

1942 Hitler begins mass extermination of Jews

1945 Germany surrenders; Europe divided into Communist east and capitalist west

1945 U.S. drops two atomic bombs on Japan, causing Japanese surrender

1947 Muslim Pakistan splits from Hindu India after independence from Britain, resulting in thousands of deaths

1948 State of Israel formed, angering resident Palestinians and neighboring Arab countries

1949 Mao Zedong leads Communists to victory in Chinese civil war

Gil Mayers,
The Jazz Singer

Skyscrapers dominate skylines in cities across the world.

1950 — 1960 — 1980

1950s Theater of the absurd thrives with works by Samuel Beckett, Eugène Ionesco, and Edward Albee

1956 French philosopher and writer Jean-Paul Sartre explains existentialism in *Being and Nothingness*

1956–1957 Naguib Mahfouz publishes novels in his great *Cairo Trilogy*

1952 Pioneering French photojournalist Henri Cartier-Bresson publishes photo collection *The Decisive Moment*

1958 Elie Wiesel publishes *Night*, about his experiences in a Nazi death camp

1962 Aleksandr Solzhenitsyn publishes *One Day in the Life of Ivan Denisovich*, based on his experiences in a Soviet prison camp

1963 Anna Akhmatova publishes her long poem *Requiem*, a moving account of Stalin's abuses

1966 Wole Soyinka's play *Kongi's Harvest* opens the first Festival of Negro Arts in Dakar, Senegal

1967 Colombian novelist Gabriel García Márquez publishes his masterpiece of magical realism, *One Hundred Years of Solitude*

1974 Nadine Gordimer wins Booker Prize for her novel *The Conservationist*

1980s Wislawa Szymborska writes under a pseudonym for an underground press in Poland

1982 Isabel Allende publishes her first novel, *The House of the Spirits*

1987 Octavio Paz publishes his collected poems from a 30-year period

1995 Writer Ken Saro-Wiwa and eight other environmental activists executed by military dictatorship in Nigeria

1950 — 1960 — 1980

1950–1953 War in Korea between Communist and UN forces results in division of country

1951 U.S. engineers invent first commercial digital computer, UNIVAC

1953 Scientists discover the double-helix structure of DNA

1953 Cold War escalates after U.S. and Soviet Union test the hydrogen bomb

1954 In Vietnam, French troops surrender to Ho Chi Minh's Communist forces; country is divided

1957 Ghana is first African country to win independence from British rule

1959 Fidel Castro leads Cuban Revolution

1960 Nigeria wins independence from Britain

1962 Algeria gains independence from France after years of violent conflict

1965–1973 U.S. troops unsuccessfully battle Communist guerrillas in South Vietnam

1966–1976 Cultural Revolution in China stamps out intellectual and artistic activity

1971 On International Women's Day in London, women march for job opportunities and other issues

1974 First personal computer introduced in U.S.

1983 Scientists discover virus that causes AIDS

1987 Palestinians in Israel begin intifada, or uprising, against Israeli rule

1989 Chinese crackdown of pro-democracy movement in Beijing's Tiananmen Square

1989 Demolition of Berlin Wall signals fall of communism in Europe

1990 Reform begins in South Africa with repeal of apartheid laws

2000 Mexico's ruling party defeated after 71 years in power; Vicente Fox elected president

Nelson Mandela,
South African leader

UNIT SEVEN
Literary Map of the World

As you will see, writers in the 20th century often drew inspiration from other cultures and reached an international audience. Japanese writers studied Russian novelists. African writers drew inspiration from African-American writers in the United States. This map shows you where writers featured in this unit were born or, in some cases, the countries in which they made their fame.

Other Writers from Europe

Czech Republic
Rainer Maria Rilke

England
Virginia Woolf

Germany
Bertolt Brecht, Nelly Sachs

Italy
Luigi Pirandello

Ireland
James Joyce

Poland
Wislawa Szymborska

Russia
Aleksandr Solzhenitsyn

Romania
Elie Wiesel

Spain
Federico García Lorca

Mexico

Octavio Paz

Chile

Isabel Allende

Other Writers from South America

Chile
Gabriela Mistral
Pablo Neruda

Colombia
Gabriel García Márquez

Czech Republic

Franz Kafka

Russia

Anna Akhmatova

Writers from Middle East

Israel
Yehuda Amichai

Palestine
Mahmud Darwish

Japan

Yasunari Kawabata

Nigeria

Chinua Achebe

Others Writers from Africa

Algeria
Albert Camus

Egypt
Naguib Mahfouz

Nigeria
Wole Soyinka

Senegal
Léopold Sédar Senghor

South Africa
Nadine Gordimer

Australia

Judith Wright

PART 1 Worlds of Change
Expressions of Modernism

Why It Matters As a general term, *modernism* describes much of the art, literature, and thought of the first half of the 20th century. To be a modernist is to be someone in love with what is new and provocative. As a group, modernists typically fought against traditions of all kinds and set out to create innovative works, whether in art, literature, philosophy, or other forms of expression. The next few pages will help you to understand the cultural movement that gave birth to modern literature.

For Links to Modernism, click on:

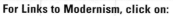
HUMANITIES
CLASSZONE.COM

Family Group

Art and Design

Many artists rebelled against earlier realistic styles. The founders of **cubism,** Pablo Picasso of Spain and Georges Braque of France, transformed natural shapes into fragmented geometric forms. **Expressionist** painters like the Russian Wassily Kandinsky used bold colors and distorted shapes to express emotion. Sculptors experimented with new ways of portraying the human body, as shown at right by a 1947 work of the British sculptor Henry Moore.

Even ordinary objects, such as chairs and dinnerware, became the province of art. The chair shown above was designed in 1928 by the Swiss-born French architect and designer Le Corbusier.

Movies and Photography

From the silent films of the early decades to the extravagant productions of the 1930s and 1940s, **movies** defined the 20th century. Early filmmakers such as the American D. W. Griffith and the Russian Sergei Eisenstein helped turned popular entertainment into works of art. Charlie Chaplin's silent films made him an international star. A scene from his 1936 *Modern Times* is shown here.

Photography also evolved into an art form, thanks to the efforts of such masters as the Americans Alfred Stieglitz, Edward Steichen, and Man Ray. Like painters before them, photographers held exhibitions of their work and sold photographs to bidders.

Architecture

Architects rejected traditional styles for new forms. The **International style,** popularized by the German Walter Gropius and his **Bauhaus** design school, was characterized by clean lines, open interiors, and the use of materials such as glass, steel, and concrete. The American Frank Lloyd Wright experimented with new materials and designs. Above is his Guggenheim Museum in New York City.

Music and Dance

Composers also rebelled against traditional styles. The Austrian composer Arnold Schönberg rejected traditional harmonies and musical scales. The Russian composer Igor Stravinsky relied on irregular rhythms and new sound combinations.

Modern dance reacted against the highly structured ballet of the late 19th century. The American Isadora Duncan danced barefoot in a loose tunic to express her personality. Martha Graham, shown at right, developed dance techniques to express complex emotions.

Cultural Highlights of Modernism

As a cultural movement, modernism began in Europe, though its influence soon spread internationally. For artists, writers, and thinkers, the world of the first half of the 20th century was both an exciting and dreadful place. Wars of furious destruction, dizzying changes in everyday life, new ideas everywhere—to modernists and ordinary people alike, the world seemed to be reinventing itself.

Sigmund Freud

Social Change in Europe

The changes begun during the Industrial Revolution continued into the 20th century. Millions of people crowded into cities, talked on telephones, and read by electric lights. The old aristocracy, although still rich, steadily lost power, while the middle classes gained both wealth and power. Then came a war and a revolution that completely knocked Europe off its 19th-century foundations. The massive slaughter of young men in World War I—nearly half a generation—horrified people, shaking their faith in their leaders and even in civilization itself. The Russian Revolution ushered in a new social, political, and economic order, called communism, that threatened the capitalist society built by industrialization.

In the 1920s, cars and radios helped speed up social change, as people—especially women—gained more freedom. But by the 1930s, unresolved political and economic problems boosted the rise of dictators. Mussolini (Italy), Hitler (Germany), and Stalin (Russia) unleashed the chaos and violence that led to another world war.

In Europe and the United States, women took to the streets, protesting laws that prohibited women from voting.

Breakdown of Traditional Beliefs

World War I shook many people's belief in the traditional virtues of reason, order, and obedience. But new ideas had begun hammering at traditional beliefs even earlier. Charles Darwin had dealt a major blow to traditional views of human nature with his theory of evolution, published in *On the Origin of Species* in 1859. In 1900, Sigmund Freud published his theory that unconscious, irrational desires rule human lives as much as reason. Soon after, the physicist Albert Einstein upset the idea of an orderly, predictable universe with his theory of relativity. To some, the breakdown of tradition created what T. S. Eliot called "the waste land." To others, it meant freedom.

Alienation of the Artist

Modernists sought a total break from the past and experimented constantly with new forms and ideas. But with liberation also came alienation. Modernists felt distant from society, often expressing hostility toward the very people who bought their art and read their works. In response, many heaped scorn upon the modernists, mocking what they could not understand. To advance the cause of art, artists and writers often banded together in various movements. A number of these groups published manifestos, or public statements of their views.

Search for the New

If there was one rallying cry that united the various modernists, it would have to be "Make it new!" This provocative phrase, uttered by the poet Ezra Pound, was understood by all. Sometimes "new" meant shocking, like the dislocated features in a Picasso portrait; sometimes it meant complicated, like the experimental fiction of Virginia Woolf, James Joyce, and Marcel Proust. In music, the new might be Stravinsky's dissonance, or clash of sounds, rather than a harmonious blend. In short, "new" meant anything that disrupted a reader's or audience's expectations. This constant search for the new resulted in the fragmentation of the art and literary worlds, producing many different movements and styles.

Pablo Picasso in his Paris studio

Man Leaning on a Table (1916), Pablo Picasso

Modernism as an International Movement

Like Romanticism in the 19th century, modernism was an international movement. Modernist artists and writers traveled widely and were subject to influences from many different countries, as shown

Artist	Born in	Also resided in	Influenced by
Le Corbusier *architect*	Switzerland	Paris	Italian Renaissance architecture
Pablo Picasso *painter, sculptor*	Spain	Paris, the south of France	African masks
René Magritte *painter*	Belgium	Paris	French 19th-century symbolist poetry
Rainer Maria Rilke *poet*	Czech Republic	Paris, Munich, Berlin, Russia, Spain, Austria	Russian landscape
James Joyce *writer*	Ireland	Trieste, Paris, Zurich	French novelists
Léopold Sédar Senghor *poet*	Senegal	Paris	African tribal culture

Modernism

The British writer Virginia Woolf (1882–1941) once declared that "in or about December, 1910, human character changed." Woolf picked that date to mark the enormous changes that occurred in her lifetime. Her bold statement sets the context for **modernism,** a literary and artistic movement that developed in the early decades of the 20th century. Woolf and other modernist writers shared a belief that their world was radically different from that of previous eras. The modernists felt disconnected from the social, religious, and artistic traditions of the past. To reflect their new and unsettling world, modernist writers experimented with daringly original literary styles and forms.

The Modernist Movement

In literature, modernism was a diverse movement that spanned Europe, the Americas, and even parts of Africa and Asia. While no two modernist writers employed the same style, the works of modernist writers do share some defining features.

The Mind as Subject Modernist writers often set out to explore the depths of the human mind. In fact, unlike the realistic novels of the 19th century, which involved many characters and settings, modernist novels often focused on the thought processes of a few main characters. Writers such as James Joyce and Virginia Woolf employed a new technique called **stream of consciousness,** in which the rapid and jumbled flow of a character's thoughts and feelings is presented as it occurs.

Innovative Styles and Forms Modernist writers typically broke new ground in style and form, following the advice of the American poet Ezra Pound to "make it new." For example, in T. S. Eliot's long poem *The Waste Land* (1922), the poet blended various styles and even languages, creating a collage of fragments. Eliot and other modern poets abandoned traditional stanza forms and meter for the more natural flow of **free verse.** In his novel *Ulysses* (1922), James Joyce tells an ingenious story modeled on Homer's *Odyssey*. Joyce's ordinary hero, Leopold Bloom, wanders the streets of Dublin on a June day in 1904. With breathtaking inventiveness, Joyce portrays the random thoughts of Bloom and others while making use of an array of styles of writing.

Writers and Artists: Modernist Allies

This painting by the French artist Marcel Duchamp caused a scandal when it was shown at the International Exhibition of Modern Art held in New York City in 1913. By throwing away the old conventions of realism, modern artists such as Duchamp and Pablo Picasso inspired writers to search for new forms of expression. In fact, Virginia Woolf's statement about the change in human character "in or about December, 1910" may have been inspired by a controversial exhibition of modern art that she viewed in London in that month and year.

Nude Descending a Staircase (No. 2) (1912), Marcel Duchamp. Oil on canvas, 57⅞″ × 35⅛″.

Anxiety and Alienation In many modernist works, the world is portrayed as a wasteland marked by violence and anxiety. The characters in these works are often alienated, or emotionally withdrawn, from society and sometimes even from themselves. In Joseph Conrad's short novel *Heart of Darkness* (1902), a main character, Kurtz, becomes corrupted, and he abandons civilization for a life of isolation. In the opening line of Franz Kafka's "Metamorphosis" (page 1108), we are introduced to a character so alienated from his world that he is transformed into a bug.

> As Gregor Samsa awoke one morning from uneasy dreams he found himself transformed in his bed into a gigantic insect.

Modernists in Their Own Words

Joseph Conrad: "My task which I am trying to achieve is, by the power of the written word, to make you hear, to make you feel—it is, before all, to make you *see*."

Virginia Woolf: "Let us record the atoms as they fall upon the mind in the order in which they fall, let us trace the pattern, however disconnected and incoherent in appearance."

Rainer Maria Rilke: "Works of art always spring from those who have faced the danger, gone to the very end of an experience, to the point beyond which no human being can go."

Marcel Proust: "If a little dreaming is dangerous, the cure for it is not to dream less but to dream more, to dream all the time."

Strategies for Reading: Modernist Literature

1. Visualize as you read. Modernist writers often present details and images that will help you "see" the characters and setting.

2. Notice what is "modern" about both the subject and the style. Think about what makes the work original or distinctive.

3. Be alert to anything in the work that seems contradictory to or inconsistent with your expectations. In "Metamorphosis," you will meet a man who turns into an insect yet is worried about being late for work. Often, the **theme** or the **tone** (the writer's attitude toward his or her subject) is revealed through such surprising turns.

4. Be patient with complexity. Give yourself time to understand what you are reading. Because modernist literature relies so heavily on suggestion, you shouldn't expect everything to make sense all at once.

5. Ask yourself about the writer's view of the modern world. Is it a bleak view or an optimistic one? Why?

6. **Monitor** your reading strategies and modify them when your understanding breaks down. Remember to use the strategies for active reading: **predict, visualize, connect, question, clarify,** and **evaluate.**

METAMORPHOSIS

FRANZ KAFKA

Franz Kafka
1883–1924

A Tortured Soul "I have the true feeling of myself only when I am unbearably unhappy." Franz Kafka wrote these words in a 1913 diary entry. A lonely and brooding man, Kafka suffered in body and spirit throughout his adult life. His physical ailments included insomnia, severe headaches, and tuberculosis, which eventually killed him at age 41. Although he loved writing, it exhausted him and caused him great frustration and self-doubt.

A Double Life Despite Kafka's inner torment, outwardly he led a successful and respectable life. He was born into a German-speaking, middle-class Jewish family in Prague, a city in what is now the Czech Republic, and trained as a lawyer. From 1907 to 1922, he worked steadily in the insurance business. His friends and fellow workers knew him as charming, intelligent, kind, industrious, and even humorous. Although he was engaged three times—twice to the same woman—he could never commit to marriage. He devoted himself fiercely to the literary life, however, pursuing it after work hours. Still, only a handful of his stories were published in his lifetime.

Fear of the Father Scholars have traced many of Kafka's problems to his tyrannical father. Hermann Kafka used to bully his timid, sensitive son to be more like himself—strong, powerful, self-assured, and self-satisfied. Fear of his father haunted Kafka all his life, and he believed that it even caused his avoidance of marriage and his inability to find happiness. Yet Kafka made creative use of his fear. In many of his stories, innocent people are menaced by cruel and unreasonable authorities.

A German Jew in Prague Kafka's lifelong feeling of being an outcast can be partially explained by his position in society. Although he grew up in the Czech city of Prague, Kafka considered himself German, and he always wrote in German. Because he was Jewish, however, the German community in Prague would have nothing to do with him. Two years before his death, Kafka became involved with a small Jewish community in Berlin. Had he lived, he would probably have been killed by the Nazis. His three sisters all died in concentration camps.

Other Works
In the Penal Colony
The Castle
The Trial

Build Background

A Famous Story of Transformation

Kafka's story draws upon the traditions of mythology and folklore, which are filled with stories of metamorphosis. A **metamorphosis** is a transformation from one state to another: a Greek god becomes a swan; a man becomes a donkey. In this story, which is Kafka's most famous one, the author blends the fantastic elements of mythology with the convincing details of realism. A mild-mannered salesperson named Gregor Samsa wakes up one morning mysteriously transformed into a giant bug. As you will see, this is only the beginning of his troubles. Although Gregor's transformation may be magical, his experience is made painfully real to the reader.

A Challenge to Readers Ever since the story was first published, readers have been challenged and puzzled by it. Many different interpretations have been offered to explain the story's message. As you read, try to build your own interpretation of what Kafka may have been trying to say.

WORDS TO KNOW **Vocabulary Preview**

amiably	imminent	omission
chagrin	intervene	refuge
dissuade	lavishly	unintelligible
equilibrium		

Connect to Your Life

"As Gregor Samsa awoke one morning from uneasy dreams he found himself transformed in his bed into a gigantic insect." So begins Kafka's story. Imagine yourself in Gregor's situation. Write a brief description of how you would react and how your family might respond. As you read, compare the reactions of Gregor and his family to the responses that you imagined.

Focus Your Reading

LITERARY ANALYSIS: POINT OF VIEW
Point of view is the narrative method used in a story. In a story told from the **first-person point of view,** a character in the story narrates what happens in his or her own words. Such a narrator uses a first-person pronoun, such as *I* or *me,* to refer to himself or herself. In a story told from the **third-person point of view,** a narrator outside the action of the story describes events and characters. Such a narrator uses third-person pronouns, such as *he, she,* and *they,* to refer to the characters. Furthermore, the narrator never refers to himself or herself. In "Metamorphosis," Kafka primarily uses what's known as a **third-person limited point of view.** The narrator is "limited" to the thoughts and feelings of only one character, the bug Gregor Samsa. Though Gregor does not tell the story himself, we see the events through his eyes.

ACTIVE READING: VISUALIZING DETAILS
Visualizing is the act of forming mental pictures based upon what you are reading. By paying close attention to the details given by the narrator, you will be able to visualize Gregor's experiences.

📖 **READER'S NOTEBOOK** As you read about the changes in Gregor's life, pause from time to time to "see" the scene being described. Form your own mental pictures from the many realistic details of Gregor's world. Make a list of the images that you can most easily visualize.

Metamorphosis

Franz Kafka

Translated by Willa and Edwin Muir

GUIDE FOR READING

FOCUS Gregor Samsa awakens to find that he has become a giant insect. Read to find out how he reacts to his situation and what he worries about.

As Gregor Samsa awoke one morning from uneasy dreams he found himself transformed in his bed into a gigantic insect. He was lying on his hard, as it were armor-plated, back and when he lifted his head a little he could see his domelike brown belly divided into stiff arched segments on top of which the bed quilt could hardly keep in position and was about to slide off completely. His numerous legs, which were pitifully thin compared to the rest of his bulk, waved helplessly before his eyes.

What has happened to me? he thought. It was no dream. His room, a regular human bedroom, only rather too small, lay quiet between the four familiar walls. Above the table on which a collection of cloth samples was unpacked and spread out—Samsa was a commercial traveler[1]—hung the picture which he had recently cut out of an illustrated magazine and put into a pretty gilt frame. It showed a lady, with a fur cap on and a fur stole, sitting upright and holding out to the spectator a huge fur muff into which the whole of her forearm had vanished!

Gregor's eyes turned next to the window, and the overcast sky—one could hear raindrops beating on the window gutter—made him quite melancholy.[2] What about sleeping a little longer and forgetting all this nonsense, he thought, but it could not be done, for he was accustomed to sleep on his right side and in his present condition he could not turn himself over. However violently he forced himself toward his right side he always rolled onto his back again. He tried it at least a hundred times, shutting his eyes to keep from seeing his struggling legs, and only desisted when he began to feel in his side a faint dull ache he had never experienced before.

Oh God, he thought, what an exhausting job I've picked on! Traveling about day in, day out. It's much more irritating work than doing the actual business in the office, and on top of that there's the trouble of constant traveling, of worrying about train connections, the bed and

---

1. **commercial traveler:** traveling salesperson.
2. **melancholy** (mĕl′ən-kŏl′ē): sad or depressed.

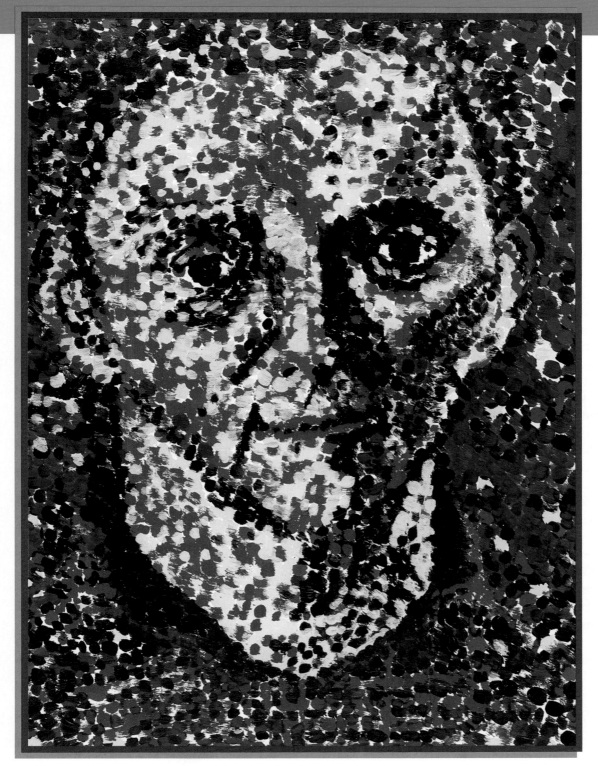

Hidden Resemblance (1991), Elizabeth Barakah Hodges. Copyright © SuperStock, Inc.

HUMANITIES CONNECTION American artist Elizabeth Barakah Hodges describes her work as magical realism. The face in this painting is drawn in a realistic manner, but the vibrant splotches of color give the image mysterious, dreamlike qualities.

irregular meals, casual acquaintances that are always new and never become intimate friends. The devil take it all! He felt a slight itching up on his belly; slowly pushed himself on his back nearer to the top of the bed so that he could lift his head more easily; identified the itching place which was surrounded by many small white spots the nature of which he could not understand and made to touch it with a leg, but drew the leg back immediately, for the contact made a cold shiver run through him.

He slid down again into his former position. This getting up early, he thought, makes one quite stupid. A man needs his sleep. Other commercials live like harem women. For instance, when I come back to the hotel of a morning to write up the orders I've got, these others are only sitting down to the breakfast. Let me just try that with my chief; I'd be sacked on the spot. Anyhow, that might be quite a good thing for me, who can tell? If I didn't have to hold my hand[3] because of my parents I'd have given notice long ago, I'd have gone to the chief and told him exactly what I think of him. That would knock him endways from his desk! It's a queer way of doing, too, this sitting on high at a desk and talking down to employees, especially when they have to come quite near because the chief is hard of hearing. Well, there's still hope; once I've saved enough money to pay back my parents' debts to him— that should take another five or six years—I'll do it without fail. I'll cut myself completely loose then. For the moment, though, I'd better get up, since my train goes at five.

He looked at the alarm clock ticking on the chest. Heavenly Father! he thought. It was half-past six o'clock and the hands were quietly moving on, it was even past the half-hour, it was getting on toward a quarter to seven. Had the alarm clock not gone off? From the bed one could see that it had been properly set for four o'clock; of course it must have gone off. Yes, but was it possible to sleep quietly through that ear-splitting noise? Well, he had not slept quietly, yet apparently all the more soundly for that. But what was he to do now? The next train went at seven o'clock; to catch that he would need to hurry like mad and his samples weren't even packed up, and he himself wasn't feeling particularly fresh and active. And even if he did catch the train he wouldn't avoid a row[4] with the chief, since the firm's porter would have been waiting for the five o'clock train and would have long since reported his failure to turn up. The porter was a creature of the chief's, spineless and stupid. Well, supposing he were to say he was sick? But that would be most unpleasant and would look suspicious, since during his five years' employment he had not been ill once. The chief himself would be sure to come with the sick-insurance doctor, would reproach his parents with their son's laziness, and would cut all excuses short by referring to the insurance doctor, who of course regarded all mankind as perfectly healthy malingerers.[5] And would he be so far wrong on this occasion? Gregor really felt quite well, apart from a drowsiness that was utterly superfluous after such a long sleep, and he was even unusually hungry.

PAUSE & REFLECT For a man who has awakened as a bug, Gregor's worries are surprising. What does he worry about?

FOCUS Read to find out what happens when Gregor's family comes to his door and he tries to leave his bed.

As all this was running through his mind at top speed without his being able to decide to leave his bed—the alarm clock had just struck a quarter to seven—there came a cautious tap at

---

3. **hold my hand:** hold back.
4. **row** (rou): disagreement; fight.
5. **malingerers** (mə-lĭng′gər-ərz): people who pretend to be sick in order to avoid work.

"GREGOR, GREGOR," HE CALLED, "WHAT'S THE MATTER WITH YOU?" AND AFTER A LITTLE WHILE HE CALLED AGAIN IN A DEEPER VOICE: "GREGOR! GREGOR!"

the door behind the head of his bed. "Gregor," said a voice—it was his mother's—"it's a quarter to seven. Hadn't you a train to catch?" That gentle voice! Gregor had a shock as he heard his own voice answering hers, unmistakably his own voice, it was true, but with a persistent horrible twittering squeak behind it like an undertone, which left the words in their clear shape only for the first moment and then rose up reverberating around them to destroy their sense, so that one could not be sure one had heard them rightly. Gregor wanted to answer at length and explain everything, but in the circumstances he confined himself to saying: "Yes, yes, thank you, Mother, I'm getting up now." The wooden door between them must have kept the change in his voice from being noticeable outside, for his mother contented herself with this statement and shuffled away. Yet this brief exchange of words had made the other members of the family aware that Gregor was still in the house, as they had not expected, and at one of the side doors his father was already knocking, gently, yet with his fist. "Gregor, Gregor," he called, "What's the matter with you?" And after a little while he called again in a deeper voice: "Gregor! Gregor!" At the other side door his sister was saying in a low, plaintive[6] tone: "Gregor? Aren't you well? Are you needing anything?" He answered them both at once: "I'm just ready," and did his best to make his voice sound as normal as possible by enunciating the words very clearly and leaving long pauses between them. So his father went back to his breakfast, but his sister whispered: "Gregor, open the door, do." However, he was not thinking of opening the door, and felt thankful for the prudent habit he had acquired in traveling of locking all doors during the night, even at home.

His immediate intention was to get up quietly without being disturbed, to put on his clothes, and above all eat his breakfast, and only then consider what else was to be done, since in bed, he was well aware, his meditations would come to no sensible conclusion. He remembered that often enough in bed he had felt small aches and pains, probably caused by awkward postures, which had proved purely imaginary once he got up, and he looked forward eagerly to seeing this morning's delusions gradually fall away. That the change in his voice was nothing but the precursor[7] of a severe chill, a standing ailment of commercial travelers, he had not the least possible doubt.

To get rid of the quilt was quite easy; he had only to inflate himself a little and it fell off by itself. But the next move was difficult, especially because he was so uncommonly broad. He would have needed arms and hands to hoist himself up; instead he had only the numerous little legs which never stopped waving in all directions and which he could not control in the least. When he tried to bend one of them it was the first to stretch itself straight; and did he succeed at last in making it do what he wanted, all the other legs meanwhile waved the more wildly in a high degree of unpleasant agitation. "But what's the use of lying idle in bed," said Gregor to himself.

---

6. **plaintive** (plān′tĭv): sorrowful; sad.

7. **precursor:** something that comes before; forerunner.

He thought that he might get out of bed with the lower part of his body first, but this lower part, which he had not yet seen and of which he could form no clear conception, proved too difficult to move; it shifted so slowly; and when finally, almost wild with annoyance, he gathered his forces together and thrust out recklessly, he had miscalculated the direction and bumped heavily against the lower end of the bed, and the stinging pain he felt informed him that precisely this lower part of his body was at the moment probably the most sensitive.

So he tried to get the top part of himself out first, and cautiously moved his head toward the edge of the bed. That proved easy enough, and despite its breadth and mass the bulk of his body at last slowly followed the movement of his head. Still, when he finally got his head free over the edge of the bed he felt too scared to go on advancing, for after all if he let himself fall in this way it would take a miracle to keep his head from being injured. And at all costs he must not lose consciousness now, precisely now; he would rather stay in bed.

But when after a repetition of the same efforts he lay in his former position again, sighing, and watched his little legs struggling against each other more wildly than ever, if that were possible, and saw no way of bringing any order into this arbitrary confusion, he told himself again that it was impossible to stay in bed and that the most sensible course was to risk everything for the smallest hope of getting away from it. At the same time he did not forget to remind himself occasionally that cool reflection, the coolest possible, was much better than desperate resolves. In such moments he focused his eyes as sharply as possible on the window, but, unfortunately, the prospect of the morning fog, which muffled even the other side of the narrow street, brought him little encouragement and comfort. "Seven o'clock already," he said to himself when the alarm clock chimed again, "seven o'clock already and still such a thick fog." And for a little while he lay quiet, breathing lightly, as if perhaps expecting such complete repose to restore all things to their real and normal condition.

But then he said to himself: "Before it strikes a quarter past seven I must be quite out of this bed, without fail. Anyhow, by that time someone will have come from the office to ask for me, since it opens before seven." And he set himself to rocking his whole body at once in a regular rhythm, with the idea of swinging it out of the bed. If he tipped himself out in that way he could keep his head from injury by lifting it at an acute angle when he fell. His back seemed to be hard and was not likely to suffer from a fall on the carpet. His biggest worry was the loud crash he would not be able to help making, which would probably cause anxiety, if not terror, behind all the doors. Still, he must take the risk.

When he was already half out of the bed—the new method was more a game than an effort, for he needed only to hitch himself across by rocking to and fro—it struck him how simple it would be if he could get help. Two strong people—he thought of his father and the servant girl—would be amply sufficient; they would only have to thrust their arms under his convex[8] back, lever him out of the bed, bend down with their burden, and then be patient enough to let him turn himself right over onto the floor, where it was to

---

8. **convex:** curved outward.

be hoped his legs would then find their proper function. Well, ignoring the fact that the doors were all locked, ought he really to call for help? In spite of his misery he could not suppress a smile at the very idea of it.

He had got so far that he could barely keep his equilibrium when he rocked himself strongly, and he would have to nerve himself very soon for the final decision since in five minutes' time it would be quarter past seven—when the front doorbell rang. "That's someone from the office," he said to himself, and grew almost rigid, while his little legs only jigged about all the faster. For a moment everything stayed quiet. "They're not going to open the door," said Gregor to himself, catching at some kind of irrational hope. But then of course the servant girl went as usual to the door with her heavy tread and opened it. Gregor needed only to hear the first good morning of the visitor to know immediately who it was—the chief clerk himself. What a fate, to be condemned to work for a firm where the smallest omission at once gave rise to the gravest suspicion! Were all employees in a body nothing but scoundrels, was there not among them one single loyal devoted man who, had he wasted only an hour or so of the firm's time in a morning, was so tormented by conscience as to be driven out of his mind and actually incapable of leaving his bed? Wouldn't it really have been sufficient to send an apprentice to inquire—if any inquiry were necessary at all—did the chief clerk himself have to come and thus indicate to the entire family, an innocent family, that this suspicious circumstance could be investigated by no one less versed in affairs than himself? And more through the agitation caused by these reflections than through any act of will Gregor swung himself out of bed with all his strength. There was a loud thump, but it was not really a crash. His fall was broken to some extent by the carpet, his back, too, was less stiff than he thought, and so there was merely a dull thud, not so very startling. Only he had not lifted his head carefully enough and had hit it; he turned it and rubbed it on the carpet in pain and irritation.

PAUSE & REFLECT Why is it so hard for Gregor to get out of bed?

FOCUS Gregor has finally managed to fall out of bed. Now read about his conversation with the chief clerk.

"That was something falling down in there," said the chief clerk in the next room to the left. Gregor tried to suppose to himself that something like what had happened to him today might someday happen to the chief clerk; one really could not deny that it was possible. But as if in brusque reply to this supposition the chief clerk took a couple of firm steps in the next-door room and his patent leather boots creaked. From the right-hand room his sister was whispering to inform him of the situation: "Gregor, the chief clerk's here." "I know," muttered Gregor to himself; but he didn't dare to make his voice loud enough for his sister to hear it.

"Gregor," said his father now from the left-hand room, "the chief clerk has come and wants to know why you didn't catch the early train. We don't know what to say to him. Besides, he wants to talk to you in person. So open the door, please. He will be good enough to excuse the untidiness of your room." "Good morning, Mr. Samsa," the chief clerk was calling amiably meanwhile. "He's not well," said his mother to the visitor, while his father was still speaking through the door, "he's not well, sir, believe me. What else would make him miss a train! The boy thinks about nothing but his work. It makes me almost cross the way he never goes out in the evenings; he's been here the last eight days and

WORDS TO KNOW

equilibrium (ē′kwə-lĭb′rē-əm) *n.* a stable or balanced condition
omission (ō-mĭsh′ən) *n.* an act of leaving out, passing over, or neglecting
amiably (ā′mē-ə-blē) *adv.* in a friendly manner; pleasantly

has stayed at home every single evening. He just sits there quietly at the table reading a newspaper or looking through railway timetables. The only amusement he gets is doing fretwork.[9] For instance, he spent two or three evenings cutting out a little picture frame; you would be surprised to see how pretty it is; it's hanging in his room; you'll see it in a minute when Gregor opens the door. I must say I'm glad you've come, sir; we should never have got him to unlock the door by ourselves; he's so obstinate; and I'm sure he's unwell, though he wouldn't have it to be so this morning." "I'm just coming," said Gregor slowly and carefully, not moving an inch for fear of losing one word of the conversation. "I can't think of any other explanation, madame," said the chief clerk, "I hope it's nothing serious. Although on the other hand I must say that we men of business—fortunately or unfortunately—very often simply have to ignore any slight indisposition,[10] since business must be attended to." "Well, can the chief clerk come in now?" asked Gregor's father impatiently, again knocking on the door. "No," said Gregor. In the left-hand room a painful silence followed this refusal, in the right-hand room his sister began to sob.

Why didn't his sister join the others? She was probably newly out of bed and hadn't even begun to put on her clothes yet. Well, why was she crying? Because he wouldn't get up and let the chief clerk in, because he was in danger of losing his job, and because the chief would begin dunning[11] his parents again for the old debts? Surely these were things one didn't need to worry about for the present. Gregor was still at home and not in the least thinking of deserting the family. At the moment, true, he was lying on the carpet and no one who knew the condition he was in could seriously expect him to admit the chief clerk. But for such a small discourtesy, which could plausibly be explained away somehow later on, Gregor could hardly be dismissed on the spot. And it seemed to Gregor that it would be much more

sensible to leave him in peace for the present than to trouble him with tears and entreaties. Still, of course, their uncertainty bewildered them all and excused their behavior.

"Mr. Samsa," the chief clerk called now in a louder voice, "what's the matter with you? Here you are, barricading yourself in your room, giving only 'yes' and 'no' for answers, causing your parents a lot of unnecessary trouble and neglecting—I mention this only in passing—neglecting your business duties in an incredible fashion. I am speaking here in the name of your parents and of your chief, and I beg you quite seriously to give me an immediate and precise explanation. You amaze me, you amaze me. I thought you were a quiet, dependable person, and now all at once you seem bent on making a disgraceful exhibition of yourself. The chief did hint to me early this morning a possible explanation for your disappearance—with reference to the cash payments that were entrusted to you recently—but I almost pledged my solemn word of honor that this could not be so. But now that I see how incredibly obstinate you are, I no longer have the slightest desire to take your part at all. And your position in the firm is not so unassailable.[12] I came with the intention of telling you all this in private, but since you are wasting my time so needlessly I don't see why your parents shouldn't hear it too. For some time past your work has been most unsatisfactory; this is not the season of the year for a business boom, of course, we admit that, but a season of the year for doing no business at all, that does not exist, Mr. Samsa, must not exist."

"But, sir," cried Gregor, beside himself and in his agitation forgetting everything else, "I'm just going to open the door this very minute. A slight

---

9. **fretwork:** ornamental woodworking.

10. **indisposition:** minor illness.

11. **dunning:** pestering for payment.

12. **unassailable** (ŭn′ə-sā′lə-bəl): safe from question or attack.

illness, an attack of giddiness, has kept me from getting up. I'm still lying in bed. But I feel all right again. I'm getting out of bed now. Just give me a moment or two longer! I'm not quite so well as I thought. But I'm all right, really. How a thing like that can suddenly strike me down! Only last night I was quite well, my parents can tell you, or rather I did have a slight presentiment.[13] I must have showed some sign of it. Why didn't I report it at the office! But one always thinks that an indisposition can be got over without staying in the house. Oh sir, do spare my parents! All that you're reproaching me with now has no foundation; no one has ever said a word to me about it. Perhaps you haven't looked at the last orders I sent in. Anyhow, I can still catch the eight o'clock train, I'm much better for my few hours' rest. Don't let me detain you here, sir; I'll be attending to business very soon, and do be good enough to tell the chief so and to make my excuses to him!"

And while all this was tumbling out pell-mell and Gregor hardly knew what he was saying, he had reached the chest quite easily, perhaps because of the practice he had had in bed, and was now trying to lever himself upright by means of it. He meant actually to open the door, actually to show himself and speak to the chief clerk; he was eager to find out what the others, after all their insistence, would say at the sight of him. If they were horrified then the responsibility was no longer his and he could stay quiet. But if they took it calmly, then he had no reason either to be upset, and could really get to the station for the eight o'clock train if he hurried. At first he slipped down a few times from the polished surface of the chest, but at length with a last heave he stood upright; he paid no more attention to the pains in the lower part of his body, however they smarted. Then he let himself fall against the back of a nearby chair, and clung with his little legs to the edges of it. That brought him into control of himself again and he stopped speaking, for now he could listen to what the chief clerk was saying.

"Did you understand a word of it?" the chief clerk was asking; "surely he can't be trying to make fools of us?" "Oh dear," cried his mother, in tears, "perhaps he's terribly ill and we're tormenting him. Grete! Grete!" she called out then. "Yes Mother?" called his sister from the other side. They were calling to each other across Gregor's room. "You must go this minute for the doctor. Gregor is ill. Go for the doctor, quick. Did you hear how he was speaking?" "That was no human voice," said the chief clerk in a voice noticeably low beside the shrillness of the mother's. "Anna! Anna!" his father was calling through the hall to the kitchen, clapping his hands, "get a locksmith at once!" And the two girls were already running through the hall with a swish of skirts—how could his sister have got dressed so quickly?—and were tearing the front door open. There was no sound of its closing again; they had evidently left it open, as one does in houses where some great misfortune has happened.

PAUSE & REFLECT When Gregor responds to the chief clerk's criticisms, everyone panics. Why are people so horrified by his voice?

FOCUS Read to find out what happens when Gregor leaves his room.

But Gregor was now much calmer. The words he uttered were no longer understandable, apparently, although they seemed clear enough to him, even clearer than before, perhaps because his ear had grown accustomed to the sound of them. Yet at any rate people now believed that something was wrong with him, and were ready to help him.

---

13. **presentiment** (prĭ-zĕn′tə-mənt): feeling that something is going to happen.

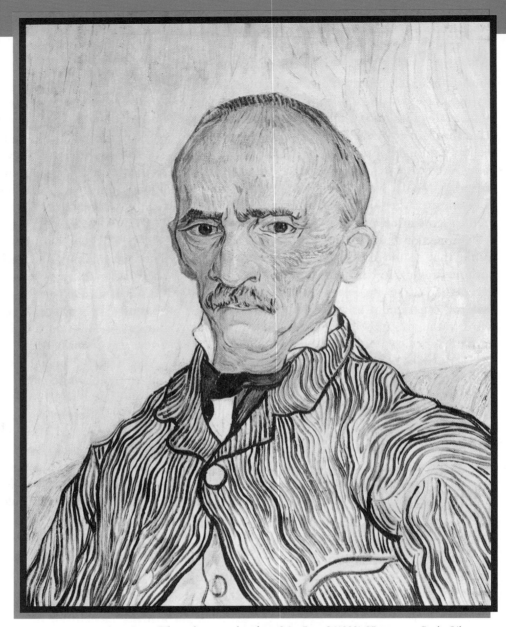

Der Irrenwarter von Saint-Remy [The asylum attendant from Saint-Remy] (1889), Vincent van Gogh. Oil on canvas, 61 cm × 46 cm. Dübi-Müller Foundation, Kunstmuseum Solothurn, Solothurn, Switzerland.

The positive certainty with which these first measures had been taken comforted him. He felt himself drawn once more into the human circle and hoped for great and remarkable results from both the doctor and the locksmith, without really distinguishing precisely between them. To make his voice as clear as possible for the decisive conversation that was now <u>imminent</u> he coughed a little, as quietly as he could, of course, since this noise too might not sound like a human cough for all he was able to judge. In the next room meanwhile there was complete silence. Perhaps his parents were sitting at the table with the chief clerk, whispering, perhaps they were all leaning against the door and listening.

Slowly Gregor pushed the chair toward the door, then let go of it, caught hold of the door for support—the soles at the end of his little legs were somewhat sticky—and rested against it for a

imminent (ĭm′ə-nənt) *adj.* about to happen

moment after his efforts. Then he set himself to turning the key in the lock with his mouth. It seemed, unhappily, that he hadn't really any teeth—what could he grip the key with?—but on the other hand his jaws were certainly very strong; with their help he did manage to set the key in motion, heedless of the fact that he was undoubtedly damaging them somewhere, since a brown fluid issued from his mouth, flowed over the key, and dripped on the floor. "Just listen to that," said the chief clerk next door; "he's turning the key." That was a great encouragement to Gregor; but they should all have shouted encouragement to him, his father and mother too: "Go on, Gregor," they should have called out, "keep going, hold on to that key!" And in the belief that they were all following his efforts intently, he clenched his jaws recklessly on the key with all the force at his command. As the turning of the key progressed he circled around the lock, holding on now only with his mouth, pushing on the key, as required, or pulling it down again with all the weight of his body. The louder click of the finally yielding lock literally quickened Gregor. With a deep breath of relief he said to himself: "So I didn't need the locksmith," and laid his head on the handle to open the door wide.

Since he had to pull the door toward him, he was still invisible when it was really wide open. He had to edge himself slowly around the near half of the double door, and to do it very carefully if he was not to fall plump upon his back just on the threshold. He was still carrying out this difficult maneuver, with no time to observe anything else, when he heard the chief clerk utter a loud "Oh!"—it seemed like a gust of wind—and now he could see the man, standing as he was nearest to the door, clapping one hand before his open mouth and slowly backing

away as if driven by some invisible steady pressure. His mother—in spite of the chief clerk's being there her hair was still undone and sticking up in all directions—first clasped her hands and looked at his father, then took two steps toward Gregor and fell on the floor among her outspread skirts, her face quite hidden on her breast. His father knotted his fist with a fierce expression on his face as if he meant to knock Gregor back into his room, then looked uncertainly around the living room, covered his eyes with his hands, and wept till his great chest heaved.

Gregor did not go now into the living room, but leaned against the inside of the firmly shut wing of the door, so that only half his body was visible and his head above it bending sideways to look at the others. The light had meanwhile strengthened; on the other side of the street one could see clearly a section of the endless long, dark gray building opposite—it was a hospital—abruptly punctuated by its row of regular windows; the rain was still falling, but only in large singly discernible and literally singly splashing drops. The breakfast dishes were set out on the table lavishly, for breakfast was the most important meal of the day to Gregor's father, who lingered it out for hours over various newspapers. Right opposite Gregor on the wall hung a photograph of himself in military service, as a lieutenant, hand on sword, a carefree smile on his face, inviting one to respect his uniform and military bearing. The door leading to the hall was open, and one could see that the front

> HIS FATHER **KNOTTED** HIS **FIST** WITH A FIERCE EXPRESSION ON HIS FACE AS IF HE MEANT TO KNOCK **GREGOR** BACK INTO HIS ROOM....

WORDS TO KNOW

lavishly (lăv′ĭsh-lē) *adv.* very freely and abundantly

door stood open too, showing the landing beyond and the beginning of the stairs going down.

"Well," said Gregor, knowing perfectly that he was the only one who had retained any composure, "I'll put my clothes on at once, pack up my samples, and start off. Will you only let me go? You see, sir, I'm not obstinate, and I'm willing to work; traveling is a hard life, but I couldn't live without it. Where are you going, sir? To the office? Yes? Will you give a true account of all this? One can be temporarily incapacitated, but that's just the moment for remembering former services and bearing in mind that later on, when the incapacity has been got over, one will certainly work with all the more industry and concentration. I'm loyally bound to serve the chief, you know that very well. Besides, I have to provide for my parents and my sister. I'm in great difficulties, but I'll get out of them again. Don't make things any worse for me than they are. Stand up for me in the firm. Travelers are not popular there, I know. People think they earn sacks of money and just have a good time. A prejudice there's no particular reason for revising. But you, sir, have a more comprehensive view of affairs than the rest of the staff, yes, let me tell you in confidence, a more comprehensive view of affairs than the chief himself, who, being the owner, lets his judgment easily be swayed against one of his employees. And you know very well that the traveler, who is never seen in the office almost the whole year around, can so easily fall a victim to gossip and ill luck and unfounded complaints, which he mostly knows nothing about, except when he comes back exhausted from his rounds, and only then suffers in person from their evil consequences, which he can no longer trace back to the original causes. Sir, sir, don't go away without a word to me to show that you think me in the right at least to some extent!"

But at Gregor's very first words the chief clerk had already backed away and only stared at him

with parted lips over one twitching shoulder. And while Gregor was speaking he did not stand still one moment but stole away toward the door, without taking his eyes off Gregor, yet only an inch at a time, as if obeying some secret injunction to leave the room. He was already at the hall, and the suddenness with which he took his last step out of the living room would have made one believe he had burned the sole of his foot. Once in the hall he stretched his right arm before him toward the staircase, as if some supernatural power were waiting there to deliver him.

PAUSE & REFLECT How do people respond to the sight of Gregor?

FOCUS Read to find out how Gregor is forced back into his room.

Gregor perceived that the chief clerk must on no account be allowed to go away in this frame of mind if his position in the firm were not to be endangered to the utmost. His parents did not understand this so well; they had convinced themselves in the course of years that Gregor was settled for life in this firm, and besides they were so preoccupied with their immediate troubles that all foresight had forsaken them. Yet Gregor had this foresight. The chief clerk must be detained, soothed, persuaded, and finally won over; the whole future of Gregor and his family depended on it! If only his sister had been there! She was intelligent; she had begun to cry while Gregor was still lying quietly on his back. And no doubt the chief clerk, so partial to[14] ladies, would have been guided by her; she would have shut the door of the flat and in the hall talked him out of his horror. But she was not there, and

14. **partial to:** having a special liking for.

Gregor would have to handle the situation himself. And without remembering that he was still unaware what powers of movement he possessed, without even remembering that his words in all possibility, indeed in all likelihood, would again be unintelligible, he let go the wing of the door, pushed himself through the opening, started to walk toward the chief clerk, who was already ridiculously clinging with both hands to the railing on the landing; but immediately, as he was feeling for a support, he fell down with a little cry upon all his numerous legs. Hardly was he down when he experienced for the first time this morning a sense of physical comfort; his legs had firm ground under them; they were completely obedient, as he noted with joy; they even strove to carry him forward in whatever direction he chose; and he was inclined to believe that a final relief from all his sufferings was at hand. But in the same moment as he found himself on the floor, rocking with suppressed eagerness to move, not far from his mother, indeed just in front of her, she, who had seemed so completely crushed, sprang all at once to her feet, her arms and fingers outspread, cried: "Help, for God's sake, help!" bent her head down as if to see Gregor better, yet on the contrary kept backing senselessly away; had quite forgotten that the laden table stood behind her; sat upon it hastily, as if in absence of mind, when she bumped into it; and seemed altogether unaware that the big coffeepot beside her was upset and pouring coffee in a flood over the carpet.

"Mother, Mother," said Gregor in a low voice, and looked up at her. The chief clerk, for the moment, had quite slipped from his mind; instead, he could not resist snapping his jaws together at the sight of the streaming coffee. That made his mother scream again, she fled from the table and fell

into the arms of his father, who hastened to catch her. But Gregor had now no time to spare for his parents; the chief clerk was already on the stairs; with his chin on the banisters he was taking one last backward look. Gregor made a spring, to be as sure as possible of overtaking him; the chief clerk must have divined his intention, for he leaped down several steps and vanished; he was still yelling "Ugh!" and it echoed throughout the whole staircase.

Unfortunately, the flight of the chief clerk seemed completely to upset Gregor's father, who had remained relatively calm until now, for instead of running after the man himself, or at least not hindering Gregor in his pursuit, he seized in his right hand the walking stick that the chief clerk had left behind on a chair, together with a hat and greatcoat, snatched in his left hand a large newspaper from the table, and began stamping his feet and flourishing the stick and the newspaper to drive Gregor back into his room. No entreaty of Gregor's availed, indeed no entreaty was even understood, however humbly he bent his head his father only stamped on the floor the more loudly. Behind his father his mother had torn open a window, despite the cold weather, and was leaning far out of it with her face in her hands. A strong draught set in from the street to the staircase, the window curtains blew in, the newspapers on the table fluttered, stray pages whisked over the floor. Pitilessly Gregor's father drove him back, hissing and crying "Shoo!" like a savage. But Gregor was quite unpracticed in walking backwards, it really was a slow business. If he only had a chance to turn around he could get back to his room at once, but he was afraid of exasperating his father by the slowness of such a rotation and at any moment the stick in his father's hand might hit him a fatal blow on the back or on the head. In the end, however, nothing else was left for him to do since to his horror he observed that in moving backwards he could not even control the direction he took; and so, keeping an anxious eye on his father all the time over his shoulder, he began to turn around as quickly as he could, which was in reality very slowly. Perhaps his father noted his good intentions, for he did not interfere except every now and then to help him in the maneuver from a distance with the point of the stick. If only he would have stopped making that unbearable hissing noise! It made Gregor quite lose his head. He had turned almost completely around when the hissing noise so distracted him that he even turned a little the wrong way again. But when at last his head was fortunately right in front of the doorway, it appeared that his body was too broad simply to get through the opening. His father, of course, in his present mood was far from thinking of such a thing as opening the other half of the door, to let Gregor have enough space. He had merely the fixed idea of driving Gregor back into his room as quickly as possible. He would never have suffered Gregor to make the circumstantial preparations for standing up on end and perhaps slipping his way through the door. Maybe he was now making more noise than ever to urge Gregor forward, as if no obstacle impeded him; to Gregor, anyhow, the noise in his rear sounded no longer like the voice of one single father; this was really no joke, and Gregor thrust himself—come what might—into the doorway. One side of his body rose up, he was tilted at an angle in the doorway, his flank was quite bruised, horrid blotches stained the white door, soon he was stuck fast and, left to himself, could not have moved at all, his legs on one side fluttered trembling in the air, those on the other were crushed painfully to the floor—when from behind his father gave him a strong push which was literally a deliverance and he flew far into the room, bleeding freely. The door was slammed behind him with the stick, and then at last there was silence.

PAUSE & REFLECT How is Gregor forced back into his room?

FOCUS Read to find out how the entire household settles into a new routine and how Gregor's sister takes care of him.

Not until it was twilight did Gregor awake out of a deep sleep, more like a swoon than a sleep. He would certainly have waked up of his own accord not much later, for he felt himself sufficiently rested and well slept, but it seemed to him as if a fleeting step and a cautious shutting of the door leading into the hall had aroused him. The electric lights in the street cast a pale sheen here and there on the ceiling and the upper surfaces of the furniture, but down below, where he lay, it was dark. Slowly, awkwardly trying out his feelers, which he now first learned to appreciate, he pushed his way to the door to see what had been happening there. His left side felt like one single long, unpleasantly tense scar, and he had actually to limp on his two rows of legs. One little leg, moreover, had been severely damaged in the course of that morning's events—it was almost a miracle that only one had been damaged—and trailed uselessly behind him.

He had reached the door before he discovered what had really drawn him to it: the smell of food. For there stood a basin filled with fresh milk in which floated little sops of white bread. He could almost have laughed with joy, since he was now still hungrier than in the morning, and he dipped his head almost over the eyes straight into the milk. But soon in disappointment he withdrew it again; not only did he find it difficult to feed because of his tender left side—and he could only feed with the palpitating collaboration[15] of his whole body—he did not like the

---

15. **palpitating collaboration:** working together of all the parts in a trembling way.

Dad getting Gregor into his room

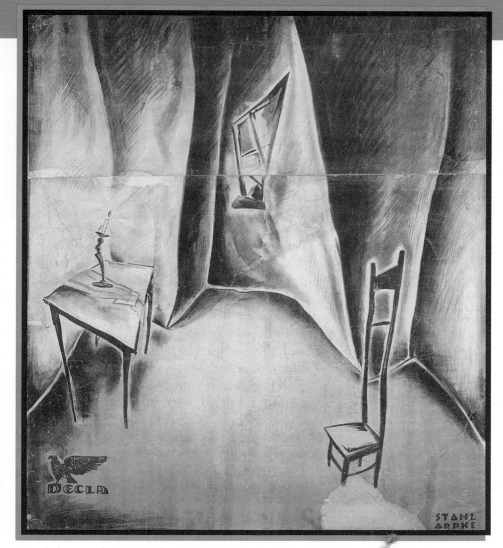

Detail of a poster for the 1920 film *Das Kabinett des Dr. Caligari* [The cabinet of Dr. Caligari].

although the flat was certainly not empty of occupants. "What a quiet life our family has been leading," said Gregor to himself, and as he sat there motionless staring into the darkness he felt great pride in the fact that he had been able to provide such a life for his parents and sister in such a fine flat. But what if all the quiet, the comfort, the contentment were now to end in horror? To keep himself from being lost in such thoughts Gregor took refuge in movement and crawled up and down the room.

Once during the long evening one of the side doors was opened a little and quickly shut again, later the other side door too; someone had apparently wanted to come in and then thought better of it. Gregor now stationed himself immediately before the living-room door, determined to persuade any hesitating visitor to come in or at least to discover who it might be; but the door was not opened again and he waited in vain. In the early morning, when the doors were locked, they had all wanted to come in, now that he had opened one door and the other had apparently been opened during the day, no one came in and even the keys were on the other side of the doors.

It was late at night before the gas went out in the living room, and Gregor could easily tell that his parents and his sister had all stayed awake milk either, although milk had been his favorite drink and that was certainly why his sister had set it there for him, indeed it was almost with repulsion that he turned away from the basin and crawled back to the middle of the room.

He could see through the crack of the door that the gas was turned on in the living room, but while usually at this time his father made a habit of reading the afternoon newspaper in a loud voice to his mother and occasionally to his sister as well, not a sound was now to be heard. Well, perhaps his father had recently given up this habit of reading aloud, which his sister had mentioned so often in conversation and in her letters. But there was the same silence all around,

WORDS TO KNOW

refuge (rĕf′yŏŏj) *n.* protection; comfort

> BUT THE LOFTY, **EMPTY** ROOM IN WHICH HE HAD TO LIE FLAT ON THE FLOOR FILLED HIM WITH AN APPREHENSION HE COULD NOT ACCOUNT FOR, SINCE IT HAD BEEN HIS VERY OWN ROOM FOR THE PAST FIVE YEARS....

until then, for he could clearly hear the three of them stealing away on tiptoe. No one was likely to visit him, not until the morning, that was certain; so he had plenty of time to meditate at his leisure on how he was to arrange his life afresh. But the lofty, empty room in which he had to lie flat on the floor filled him with an apprehension he could not account for, since it had been his very own room for the past five years—and with a half-unconscious action, not without a slight feeling of shame, he scuttled under the sofa, where he felt comfortable at once, although his back was a little cramped and he could not lift his head up, and his only regret was that his body was too broad to get the whole of it under the sofa.

He stayed there all night, spending the time partly in a light slumber, from which his hunger kept waking him up with a start, and partly in worrying and sketching vague hopes, which all led to the same conclusion, that he must lie low for the present and, by exercising patience and the utmost consideration, help the family to bear the inconvenience he was bound to cause them in his present condition.

Very early in the morning, it was still almost night, Gregor had the chance to test the strength of his new resolutions, for his sister, nearly fully dressed, opened the door from the hall and peered in. She did not see him at once, yet when she caught sight of him under the sofa—well, he had to be somewhere, he couldn't have flown away, could he?—she was so startled that without being able to help it she slammed the door shut again. But as if regretting her behavior she opened the door again immediately and came in on tiptoe, as if she were visiting an invalid or even a stranger. Gregor had pushed his head for-

ward to the very edge of the sofa and watched her. Would she notice that he had left the milk standing, and not for lack of hunger, and would she bring in some other kind of food more to his taste? If she did not do it of her own accord, he would rather starve than draw her attention to the fact, although he felt a wild impulse to dart out from under the sofa, throw himself at her feet, and beg her for something to eat. But his sister at once noticed, with surprise, that the basin was still full, except for a little milk that had been spilled all around it, she lifted it immediately, not with her bare hands, true, but with a cloth and carried it away. Gregor was wildly curious to know what she would bring instead, and made various speculations about it. Yet what she actually did next, in the goodness of her heart, he could never have guessed at. To find out what he liked she brought him a whole selection of food, all set out on an old newspaper. There were old, half-decayed vegetables, bones from last night's supper covered with a white sauce that had thickened; some raisins and almonds; a piece of cheese Gregor would have called uneatable two days ago; a dry roll of bread, a buttered roll, and a roll both buttered and salted. Besides all that, she set down again the same basin, into which she had poured some water, and which was apparently to be reserved for his exclusive use. And with fine tact, knowing that Gregor would not eat in her presence, she withdrew quickly and even turned the key, to let him understand that he could take his ease as much as he liked. Gregor's legs all whizzed toward the food. His wounds must have healed completely, moreover, for he felt no disability, which amazed him and made him reflect how more than a month ago he had cut one finger a little with a knife and had still suffered pain from the wound only the day before yesterday. Am I less sensitive now? he thought, and sucked greedily at the cheese, which above all the other edibles attracted him at once and strongly. One after another and with tears of satisfaction in his eyes he quickly devoured the cheese, the vegetables, and the sauce; the fresh food, on the other hand, had no charms for him, he could not even stand the smell of it and actually dragged away to some little distance the things he could eat. He had long finished his meal and was only lying lazily on the same spot when his sister turned the key slowly as a sign for him to retreat. That roused him at once, although he was nearly asleep, and he hurried under the sofa again. But it took considerable self-control for him to stay under the sofa, even for the short time his sister was in the room, since the large meal had swollen his body somewhat and he was so cramped he could hardly breathe. Slight attacks of breathlessness afflicted him and his eyes were starting a little out of his head as he watched his unsuspecting sister sweeping together with a broom not only the remains of what he had eaten but even the things he had not touched, as if these were now of no use to anyone, and hastily shoveling it all into a bucket, which she covered with a wooden lid and carried away. Hardly had she turned her back when Gregor came from under the sofa and stretched and puffed himself out.

In this manner Gregor was fed, once in the early morning while his parents and the servant girl were still asleep, and a second time after they had all had their midday dinner, for then his parents took a short nap and the servant girl could be sent out on some errand or other by his sister. Not that they would have

wanted him to starve, of course, but perhaps they could not have borne to know more about his feeding than from hearsay, perhaps too his sister wanted to spare them such little anxieties whenever possible, since they had quite enough to bear as it was.

Under what pretext the doctor and the locksmith had been got rid of on that first morning Gregor could not discover, for since what he said was not understood by the others it never struck any of them, not even his sister, that he could understand what they said, and so whenever his sister came into his room he had to content himself with hearing her utter only a sigh now and then and an occasional appeal to the saints. Later on, when she had got a little used to the situation—of course she could never get completely used to it—she sometimes threw out a remark which was kindly meant or could be so interpreted. "Well, he liked his dinner today," she would say when Gregor had made a good clearance of his food; and when he had not eaten, which gradually happened more and more often, she would say almost sadly: "Everything's been left standing again."

But although Gregor could get no news directly, he overheard a lot from the neighboring rooms, and as soon as voices were audible, he would run to the door of the room concerned and press his whole body against it. In the first few days especially there was no conversation that did not refer to him somehow, even if only indirectly. For two whole days there were family consultations at every mealtime about what should be done; but also between meals the same subject was discussed, for there were always at least two members of the family at home, since no one wanted to be alone in the flat and to leave it quite empty was unthinkable. And on the very first of these days the household cook—it was not quite clear what and how much she knew of the situation—went down on her knees to his mother and begged leave to go, and when she departed, a quarter of an hour later, gave thanks for her dismissal with tears in her eyes as if for the greatest benefit that could have been conferred on her, and without any prompting swore a solemn oath that she would never say a single word to anyone about what had happened.

Now Gregor's sister had to cook too, helping her mother; true, the cooking did not amount to much, for they ate scarcely anything. Gregor was always hearing one of the family vainly urging another to eat and getting no answer but: "Thanks, I've had all I want," or something similar. Perhaps they drank nothing either. Time and again his sister kept asking his father if he wouldn't like some beer and offered kindly to go and fetch it herself, and when he made no answer suggested that she could ask the concierge[16] to fetch it, so that he need feel no sense of obligation, but then a round "No" came from his father and no more was said about it.

In the course of that very first day Gregor's father explained the family's financial position and prospects to both his mother and his sister. Now and then he rose from the table to get some voucher or memorandum out of the small safe he had rescued from the collapse of his business five years earlier. One could hear him opening the complicated lock and rustling papers out and shutting it again. This statement made by his father was the first cheerful information Gregor had heard since his imprisonment. He had been of the opinion that nothing at all was left over from his father's business, at least his father had never said anything to the contrary, and of course he had not asked him directly. At that time Gregor's sole desire was to do his utmost to help the family to forget as soon as possible the catastrophe that had overwhelmed the business and thrown them all into a state of complete despair. And so he had set to work with unusual ardor[17] and almost overnight had become a commercial traveler instead of a little clerk, with of course much greater chances of earning money, and his success was immediately translated into good round coin which he could lay on the table for his amazed and happy family. These had been fine times, and they had never recurred, at least not with the same sense of glory, although later on Gregor had earned so much money that he was able to meet the expenses of the whole household and did so. They had simply got used to it, both the family and Gregor; the money was gratefully accepted and gladly given, but there was no special uprush of warm feeling. With his sister alone had he remained intimate, and it was a secret plan of his that she, who loved music, unlike himself, and could play movingly on the violin, should be sent next year to study at the Conservatorium,[18] despite the great expense that would entail, which must be made up in some other way. During his brief visits home the Conservatorium was often mentioned in the talks he had with his sister, but always merely as a beautiful dream which could never come true, and his parents discouraged even these innocent references to it; yet Gregor had made up his mind firmly about it and meant to announce the fact with due solemnity on Christmas Day.

Such were the thoughts, completely futile in his present condition, that went through his head as he stood clinging upright to the door and listening. Sometimes out of sheer weariness he had to give up listening and let his head fall negligently against the door, but he always had to pull himself together again at once, for even the slight sound his head made was audible next door and brought all conversation to a stop. "What can he be doing now?" his father would say after a while, obviously turning toward the door, and only then would the interrupted con-

---

16. **concierge** (kôn-syârzh'): a person who serves as a doorkeeper and janitor in an apartment complex.

17. **ardor:** eagerness; enthusiasm.

18. **Conservatorium:** school of music.

versation gradually be set going again.

Gregor was now informed as amply as he could wish—for his father tended to repeat himself in his explanations, partly because it was a long time since he had handled such matters and partly because his mother could not always grasp things at once—that a certain amount of investments, a very small amount it was true, had survived the wreck of their fortunes and had even increased a little because the dividends had not been touched meanwhile. And besides that, the money Gregor brought home every month—he had kept only a few dollars for himself—had never been quite used up and now amounted to a small capital sum. Behind the door Gregor nodded his head eagerly, rejoiced at this evidence of unexpected thrift and foresight. True, he could really have paid off some more of his father's debts to the chief with this extra money, and so brought much nearer the day on which he could quit his job, but doubtless it was better the way his father had arranged it.

Yet this capital was by no means sufficient to let the family live on the interest of it; for one year, perhaps, or at the most two, they could live on the principal, that was all. It was simply a sum that ought not to be touched and should be kept for a rainy day; money for living expenses would have to be earned. Now his father was still hale enough but an old man, and he had done no work for the past five years and could not be expected to do much; during these five years, the first years of leisure in his laborious though unsuccessful life, he had grown rather fat and become sluggish. And Gregor's old mother, how was she to earn a living with her asthma, which troubled her even when she walked through the flat and kept her lying on a sofa every other day panting for breath beside an open window? And was his sister to earn her bread, she who was still a child of seventeen and whose life hitherto had been so pleasant, consisting as it did in dressing herself nicely, sleeping long, helping in the housekeeping, going out to a few modest entertainments, and above all playing the violin? At first whenever the need for earning money was mentioned Gregor let go his hold on the door and threw himself down on the cool leather sofa beside it, he felt so hot with shame and grief.

Often he just lay there the long nights through without sleeping at all, scrabbling for hours on the leather. Or he nerved himself to the great effort of pushing an armchair to the window, then crawled up over the window sill and, braced against the chair, leaned against the windowpanes, obviously in some recollection of the sense of freedom that looking out of a window always used to give him. For in reality day by day things that were even a little way off were growing dimmer to his sight; the hospital across the street, which he used to execrate[19] for being all too often before his eyes, was now quite beyond his range of vision, and if he had not known that he lived in Charlotte Street, a quiet street but still a city street, he might have believed that his window gave on a desert waste where gray sky and gray land blended indistinguishably into each other. His quick-witted sister only needed to observe twice that the armchair stood by the window; after that whenever she had tidied the room she always pushed the chair back to the same place at the window and even left the inner casements open.

If he could have spoken to her and thanked her for all she had to do for him, he could have borne her ministrations better; as it was, they oppressed him. She certainly tried to make as light as possible of whatever was disagreeable in her task, and as time went on she succeeded, of course, more and more, but time brought more

---

19. **execrate** (ĕk'sĭ-krāt'): declare to be hateful.

Portrait of Mlle Ravoux (late-19th century), Vincent van Gogh. Photograph copyright © Christie's Images, London/SuperStock, Inc.

HUMANITIES CONNECTION Dutch artist Vincent van Gogh (1853–1890) used precise brushwork and strong colors to convey intense emotion. The dark, somber background of this portrait may be a reflection of the artist's deteriorating condition near the end of his life.

> ...HE OFTEN HEARD THEM EXPRESSING THEIR APPRECIATION OF HIS SISTER'S ACTIVITIES, WHEREAS FORMERLY THEY HAD FREQUENTLY SCOLDED HER FOR BEING AS THEY THOUGHT A SOMEWHAT **USELESS** DAUGHTER.

enlightenment to Gregor too. The very way she came in distressed him. Hardly was she in the room when she rushed to the window, without even taking time to shut the door, careful as she was usually to shield the sight of Gregor's room from the others, and as if she were almost suffocating tore the casements open with hasty fingers, standing then in the open draught for a while even in the bitterest cold and drawing deep breaths. This noisy scurry of hers upset Gregor twice a day; he would crouch trembling under the sofa all the time, knowing quite well that she would certainly have spared him such a disturbance had she found it at all possible to stay in his presence without opening the window.

On one occasion, about a month after Gregor's metamorphosis, when there was surely no reason for her to be still startled at his appearance, she came a little earlier than usual and found him gazing out of the window, quite motionless, and thus well placed to look like a bogey. Gregor would not have been surprised had she not come in at all, for she could not immediately open the window while he was there, but not only did she retreat, she jumped back as if in alarm and banged the door shut; a stranger might well have thought that he had been lying in wait for her there meaning to bite her. Of course he hid himself under the sofa at once, but he had to wait until midday before she came again, and she seemed more ill at ease than usual. This made him realize how repulsive the sight of him still was to her, and that it was bound to go on being repulsive, and what an effort it must cost her not to run away even from the sight of the small portion of his body that stuck out from under the sofa. In order to spare her that, therefore, one day he carried a sheet on his back to the sofa—it cost him four hours' labor—and arranged it there in such a way as to hide him completely, so that even if she were to bend down she could not see him. Had she considered the sheet unnecessary, she would certainly have stripped it off the sofa again, for it was clear enough that this curtaining and confining of himself was not likely to conduce to Gregor's comfort, but she left it where it was, and Gregor even fancied that he caught a thankful glance from her eye when he lifted the sheet carefully a very little with his head to see how she was taking the new arrangement.

For the first fortnight[20] his parents could not bring themselves to the point of entering his room, and he often heard them expressing their appreciation of his sister's activities, whereas formerly they had frequently scolded her for being as they thought a somewhat useless daughter. But now, both of them often waited outside the door, his father and his mother, while his sister tidied his room, and as soon as she came out she had to tell them exactly how things were in the room, what Gregor had eaten, how he had conducted himself this time, and whether there was not perhaps some slight improvement in his condition. His mother, moreover, began relatively soon to want to visit him, but his father and sister dissuaded her at first with arguments which Gregor listened to very attentively and altogether

---

20. **fortnight:** two weeks.

approved. Later, however, she had to be held back by main force, and when she cried out: "Do let me in to Gregor, he is my unfortunate son! Can't you understand that I must go to him?" Gregor thought that it might be well to have her come in, not every day, of course, but perhaps once a week; she understood things, after all, much better than his sister, who was only a child despite the efforts she was making and had perhaps taken on so difficult a task merely out of childish thoughtlessness.

PAUSE & REFLECT How has daily life changed for Gregor and the rest of his family? What do the actions of Gregor's sister reveal about her?

FOCUS To give Gregor more room for crawling, his mother and sister decide to move his furniture out. Read to find out what happens.

Gregor's desire to see his mother was soon fulfilled. During the daytime he did not want to show himself at the window, out of consideration for his parents, but he could not crawl very far around the few square yards of floor space he had, nor could he bear lying quietly at rest all during the night, while he was fast losing any interest he had ever taken in food, so that for mere recreation he had formed the habit of crawling crisscross over the walls and ceiling. He especially enjoyed hanging suspended from the ceiling; it was much better than lying on the floor; one could breathe more freely; one's body swung and rocked lightly; and in the almost blissful absorption induced by this suspension it could happen to his own surprise that he let go and fell plump on the floor. Yet he now had his body much better under control than formerly, and even such a big fall did him no harm. His sister at once remarked the new distraction Gregor had found for himself—he left traces behind him of the sticky stuff on his soles wherever he crawled—and she got the idea in her head

of giving him as wide a field as possible to crawl in and of removing the pieces of furniture that hindered him, above all the chest of drawers and the writing desk. But that was more than she could manage all by herself; she did not dare ask her father to help her; and as for the servant girl, a young creature of sixteen who had had the courage to stay on after the cook's departure, she could not be asked to help, for she had begged as a special favor that she might keep the kitchen door locked and open it only on a definite summons; so there was nothing left but to apply to her mother at an hour when her father was out. And the old lady did come, with exclamations of joyful eagerness, which, however, died away at the door of Gregor's room. Gregor's sister, of course, went in first, to see that everything was in order before letting his mother enter. In great haste Gregor pulled the sheet lower and rucked it more in folds so that it really looked as if it had been thrown accidentally over the sofa. And this time he did not peer out from under it; he renounced the pleasure of seeing his mother on this occasion and was only glad that she had come at all. "Come in, he's out of sight," said his sister, obviously leading her mother in by the hand. Gregor could now hear the two women struggling to shift the heavy old chest from its place, and his sister claiming the greater part of the labor for herself, without listening to the admonitions of her mother, who feared she might overstrain herself. It took a long time. After at least a quarter of an hour's tugging his mother objected that the chest had better be left where it was, for in the first place it was too heavy and could never be got out before his father came home, and standing in the middle of the room like that it would only hamper Gregor's movements, while in the second place it was not at all certain that moving the furniture would be doing a service to Gregor. She was inclined to think to the contrary; the sight of the naked walls made her own heart heavy, and why shouldn't

Gregor have the same feeling, considering that he had been used to his furniture for so long and might feel forlorn without it. "And doesn't it look," she concluded in a low voice—in fact she had been almost whispering all the time as if to avoid letting Gregor, whose exact whereabouts she did not know, hear even the tones of her voice, for she was convinced that he could not understand her words—"doesn't it look as if we were showing him, by taking away his furniture, that we have given up hope of his ever getting better and are just leaving him coldly to himself? I think it would be best to keep his room exactly as it has always been, so that when he comes back to us he will find everything unchanged and be able all the more easily to forget what has happened in between."

On hearing these words from his mother Gregor realized that the lack of all direct human speech for the past two months together with the monotony of family life must have confused his mind, otherwise he could not account for the fact that he had quite earnestly looked forward to having his room emptied of furnishing. Did he really want his warm room, so comfortably fitted with old family furniture, to be turned into a naked den in which he would certainly be able to crawl unhampered in all directions but at the price of shedding simultaneously all recollection of his human background? He had indeed been so near the brink of forgetfulness that only the voice of his mother, which he had not heard for so long, had drawn him back from it. Nothing should be taken out of his room; everything must stay as it was; he could not dispense with the good influence of the furniture on his state of mind; and even if the furniture did hamper him in his senseless crawling around and around, that was no drawback but a great advantage.

Unfortunately his sister was of the contrary opinion; she had grown accustomed, and not without reason, to consider herself an expert in Gregor's affairs as against her parents, and so her mother's advice was now enough to make her determined on the removal not only of the chest and the writing desk, which had been her first intention, but of all the furniture except the indispensable sofa. This determination was not, of course, merely the outcome of childish recalcitrance[21] and of the self-confidence she had recently developed so unexpectedly and at such cost; she had in fact perceived that Gregor needed a lot of space to crawl about in, while on the other hand he never used the furniture at all, so far as could be seen. Another factor might also have been the enthusiastic temperament of an adolescent girl, which seeks to indulge itself on every opportunity and which now tempted Grete to exaggerate the horror of her brother's circumstances in order that she might do all the more for him. In a room where Gregor lorded it all alone over empty walls no one save herself was likely ever to set foot.

And so she was not to be moved from her resolve by her mother, who seemed moreover to be ill at ease in Gregor's room and therefore unsure of herself, was soon reduced to silence, and helped her daughter as best she could to push the chest outside. Now, Gregor could do without the chest, if need be, but the writing desk he must retain. As soon as the two women had got the chest out of his room, groaning as they pushed it, Gregor stuck his head out from under the sofa to see how he might <u>intervene</u> as kindly and cautiously as possible. But as bad luck would have it, his mother was the first to return, leaving Grete clasping the chest in the room next door where she was trying to shift it all by herself, without of course moving it from the spot. His mother however was not accustomed to the sight of him, it might sicken her and so in alarm

---

21. **recalcitrance** (rĭ-kăl′sĭ-trəns): stubborn resistance to authority.

WORDS TO KNOW

intervene (ĭn′tər-vēn′) v. to come between; get involved in order to help

Gregor backed quickly to the other end of the sofa, yet could not prevent the sheet from swaying a little in front. That was enough to put her on the alert. She paused, stood still for a moment, and then went back to Grete.

Although Gregor kept reassuring himself that nothing out of the way was happening, but only a few bits of furniture were being changed around, he soon had to admit that all this trotting to and fro of the two women, their little ejaculations,[22] and the scraping of furniture along the floor affected him like a vast disturbance coming from all sides at once, and however much he tucked in his head and legs and cowered to the very floor he was bound to confess that he would not be able to stand it for long. They were clearing his room out; taking away everything he loved; the chest in which he kept his fret saw and other tools was already dragged off; they were now loosening the writing desk which had almost sunk into the floor, the desk at which he had done all his homework when he was at the commercial academy, at the grammar school before that, and, yes, even at the primary school—he had no more time to waste in weighing the good intentions of the two women, whose existence he had by now almost forgotten, for they were so exhausted that they were laboring in silence and nothing could be heard but the heavy scuffling of their feet.

And so he rushed out—the women were just leaning against the writing desk in the next room to give themselves a breather—and four times changed his direction, since he really did not know what to rescue first, then on the wall opposite, which was already otherwise cleared, he was struck by the picture of the lady muffled in so much fur and quickly crawled up to it and pressed himself to the glass, which was a good surface to hold on to and comforted his hot belly. This picture at least, which was entirely hidden beneath him, was going to be removed by nobody. He turned his head toward the door of the living room so as to observe the women when they came back.

They had not allowed themselves much of a rest and were already coming; Grete had twined her arm around her mother and was almost supporting her. "Well, what shall we take now?" said Grete, looking around. Her eyes met Gregor's from the wall. She kept her composure, presumably because of her mother, bent her head down to her mother, to keep her from looking up, and said, although in a fluttering, unpremeditated voice: "Come, hadn't we better go back to the living room for a moment?" Her intentions were clear enough to Gregor, she wanted to bestow her mother in safety and then chase him down from the wall. Well, just let her try it! He clung to his picture and would not give it up. He would rather fly in Grete's face.

But Grete's words had succeeded in disquieting her mother, who took a step to one side, caught sight of the huge brown mass on the flowered wallpaper, and before she was really conscious that what she saw was Gregor, screamed in a loud, hoarse voice: "Oh God, oh God!" fell with outspread arms over the sofa as if giving up, and did not move. "Gregor!" cried his sister, shaking her fist and glaring at him. This was the first time she had directly addressed him since his metamorphosis. She ran into the next room for some aromatic essence[23] with which to rouse her mother from her fainting fit. Gregor wanted to help too—there was still time to rescue the picture—but he was stuck fast to the glass and had to tear himself loose; he then ran after his sister into the next room as if he could advise her, as he used to do; but then had to stand helplessly behind her;

22. **ejaculations:** sudden, brief statements or exclamations.
23. **aromatic essence:** strong-smelling solution.

Nächtlicher Lärm [Nightly noise] (1919), Georg Scholz. Oil on canvas, 56.8 cm × 50.9 cm.
The Marvin and Janet Fishman Collection, Milwaukee, Wisconsin.

she meanwhile searched among various small bottles and when she turned around started in alarm at the sight of him; one bottle fell on the floor and broke; a splinter of glass cut Gregor's face and some kind of corrosive[24] medicine splashed him; without pausing a moment longer Grete gathered up all the bottles she could carry and ran to her mother with them; she banged the door shut with her foot. Gregor was now cut off from his mother, who was perhaps nearly dying because of him; he dared not open the door for fear of frightening away his sister, who had to stay with her mother; there was nothing he could do but wait; and harassed by self-reproach and worry he began now to crawl to and fro, over everything, walls, furniture, and ceiling, and finally in his despair, when the whole room seemed to be reeling around him, fell down onto the middle of the big table.

---

24. corrosive (kə-rō′sĭv): capable of eating away solid substances.

A little while elapsed, Gregor was still lying there feebly and all around was quiet, perhaps that was a good omen. Then the doorbell rang. The servant girl was of course locked in her kitchen, and Grete would have to open the door. It was his father. "What's been happening?" were his first words; Grete's face must have told him everything. Grete answered in a muffled voice, apparently hiding her head on his breast: "Mother has been fainting, but she's better now. Gregor's broken loose." "Just what I expected," said his father, "just what I've been telling you, but you women would never listen." It was clear to Gregor that his father had taken the worst interpretation of Grete's all too brief statement and was assuming that Gregor had been guilty of some violent act. Therefore Gregor must now try to propitiate[25] his father, since he had neither time nor means for an explanation. And so he fled to the door of his own room and crouched against it, to let his father see as soon as he came in from the hall that his son had the good intention of getting back into his room immediately and that it was not necessary to drive him there, but that if only the door were opened he would disappear at once.

Yet his father was not in the mood to perceive such fine[26] distinctions. "Ah!" he cried as soon as he appeared, in a tone that sounded at once angry and exultant. Gregor drew his head back from the door and lifted it to look at his father. Truly, this was not the father he had imagined to himself; admittedly he had been too absorbed of late in his new recreation of crawling over the ceiling to take the same interest as before in what was happening elsewhere in the flat, and he ought really to be prepared for some changes. And yet, and yet, could that be his father? The man who used to lie wearily sunk in bed whenever Gregor set out on a business journey; who welcomed him back of an evening lying in a long chair in a dressing gown; who could not really rise to his feet but only lifted his arms in greeting, and on the rare occasions when he did go out with his family, on one or two Sundays a year and on highest holidays,[27] walked between Gregor and his mother, who were slow walkers anyhow, even more slowly than they did, muffled in his old greatcoat, shuffling laboriously forward with the help of his crook-handled stick which he set down most cautiously at every step and, whenever he wanted to say anything, nearly always came to a full stop and gathered his escort around him? Now he was standing there in fine shape; dressed in a smart blue uniform with gold buttons, such as bank messengers wear; his strong double chin bulged over the stiff high collar of his jacket; from under his bushy eyebrows his black eyes darted fresh and penetrating glances; his onetime tangled white hair had been combed flat on either side of a shining and carefully exact parting.[28] He pitched his cap, which bore a gold monogram, probably the badge of some bank, in a wide sweep across the whole room onto a sofa and with the tail-ends of his jacket thrown back, his hands in his trouser pockets, advanced with a grim visage[29] toward Gregor. Likely enough he did not himself know what he meant to do; at any rate he lifted his feet uncommonly high, and Gregor was dumbfounded at the enormous size of his shoe soles. But Gregor could not risk standing up to him, aware as he had been from the very first day of his new life that his father believed only the severest measures suitable for dealing with him. And so he ran before his father, stopping when he stopped and scuttling forward again when his

---

25. **propitiate** (prō-pĭsh´ē-āt´): calm; soothe.

26. **fine:** subtle; precise.

27. **highest holidays:** probably a reference to major Christian holidays, such as Christmas and Easter.

28. **parting:** part.

29. **visage:** face.

father made any kind of move. In this way they circled the room several times without anything decisive happening, indeed the whole operation did not even look like a pursuit because it was carried out so slowly. And so Gregor did not leave the floor, for he feared that his father might take as a piece of peculiar wickedness any excursion of his over the walls or the ceiling. All the same, he could not stay this course much longer, for while his father took one step he had to carry out a whole series of movements. He was already beginning to feel breathless, just as in his former life his lungs had not been very dependable. As he was staggering along, trying to concentrate his energy on running, hardly keeping his eyes open; in his dazed state never even thinking of any other escape than simply going forward; and having almost forgotten that the walls were free to him, which in this room were well provided with finely carved pieces of furniture full of knobs and crevices—suddenly something lightly flung landed close behind him and rolled before him. It was an apple; a second apple followed immediately; Gregor came to a stop in alarm; there was no point in running on, for his father was determined to bombard him. He had filled his pockets with fruit from the dish on the sideboard and was now shying apple after apple, without taking particularly good aim for the moment. The small red apples rolled about the floor as if magnetized and cannoned into each other. An apple thrown without much force grazed Gregor's back and glanced off harmlessly. But another following immediately landed right on his back and sank in; Gregor wanted to drag himself forward, as if this startling, incredible pain could be left behind him; but he felt as if nailed to the spot and flattened himself out in a complete derangement of all his senses. With his last conscious look he saw the door of his room being torn open and his mother rushing out ahead of his screaming sister, in her underbodice, for her daughter had loosened her clothing to let her breathe more freely and recover from her swoon, he saw his mother rushing toward his father, leaving one after another behind her on the floor her loosened petticoats, stumbling over her petticoats straight to his father and embracing him, in complete union with him—but here Gregor's sight began to fail—with her hands clasped around his father's neck as she begged for her son's life.

PAUSE & REFLECT Why does the furniture-moving episode lead to the father's attack on Gregor?

FOCUS Gregor has been seriously wounded by the apple. Read to find out how Gregor and his family respond to his decline.

The serious injury done to Gregor, which disabled him for more than a month— the apple went on sticking in his body as a visible reminder, since no one ventured to remove it—seemed to have made even his father recollect that Gregor was a member of the family, despite his present unfortunate and repulsive shape, and ought not to be treated as an enemy, that, on the contrary, family duty required the suppression[30] of disgust and the exercise of patience, nothing but patience.

And though his injury had impaired, probably forever, his powers of movement, and for the time being it took him long, long minutes to creep across his room like an old invalid—there was no question now of crawling up the wall— yet in his own opinion he was sufficiently compensated for this worsening of his condition by the fact that toward evening the living-room

---

30. **suppression** (sə-prĕsh'ən): holding back or keeping in.

door, which he used to watch intently for an hour or two beforehand, was always thrown open, so that lying in the darkness of his room, invisible to the family, he could see them all at the lamp-lit table and listen to their talk, by general consent as it were, very different from his earlier eavesdropping.

True, their intercourse lacked the lively character of former times, which he had always called to mind with a certain wistfulness in the small hotel bedrooms where he had been wont to throw himself down, tired out, on damp bedding. They were now mostly very silent. Soon after supper his father would fall asleep in his armchair; his mother and sister would admonish each other to be silent; his mother, bending low over the lamp, stitched at fine sewing for an underwear firm; his sister, who had taken a job as a salesgirl, was learning shorthand and French in the evenings on the chance of bettering herself. Sometimes his father woke up, and as if quite unaware that he had been sleeping said to his mother: "What a lot of sewing you're doing today!" and at once fell asleep again, while the two women exchanged a tired smile.

With a kind of mulishness his father persisted in keeping his uniform on even in the house; his dressing gown hung uselessly on its peg and he slept fully dressed where he sat, as if he were ready for service at any moment and even here only at the beck and call of his superior. As a result, his uniform, which was not brand-new to start with, began to look dirty, despite all the loving care of the mother and sister to keep it clean, and Gregor often spent whole evenings gazing at the many greasy spots on the garment, gleaming with gold buttons always in a high state of polish, in which the old man sat sleeping in extreme discomfort and yet quite peacefully.

As soon as the clock struck ten his mother tried to rouse his father with gentle words and to persuade him after that to get into bed, for sitting there he could not have a proper sleep and

Le lessive [The wash] (early-20th century), Maria Blanchard. Copyright © Musée d'Art Moderne de la Ville de Paris/Lauros-Giraudon, Paris/SuperStock, Inc.

that was what he needed most, since he had to go on duty at six. But with the mulishness that had obsessed him since he became a bank messenger he always insisted on staying longer at the table, although he regularly fell asleep again and in the end only with the greatest trouble could be got out of his armchair and into his bed. However insistently Gregor's mother and sister kept urging him with gentle reminders, he would go on slowly shaking his head for a quarter of an hour, keeping his eyes shut, and refuse to get to his feet. The mother plucked at his sleeve, whispering endearments in his ear, the sister left her lessons to come to her mother's help, but Gregor's father was not to be caught. He would only sink down deeper in his chair. Not until the two women hoisted him up by the armpits did he open his eyes and look at them both, one after the other, usually with the remark: "This is a life. This is the peace and quiet of my old age." And leaning on the two of them he would heave himself up, with difficulty, as if he were a great burden to himself, suffer them to lead him as far as the door and then wave them off and go on alone, while the mother abandoned her needlework and the sister her pen in order to run after him and help him farther.

Who could find time, in this overworked and tired-out family, to bother about Gregor more than was absolutely needful? The household was reduced more and more; the servant girl was turned off; a gigantic bony charwoman[31] with white hair flying around her head came in morning and evening to do the rough work; everything else was done by Gregor's mother, as well as great piles of sewing. Even various family ornaments, which his mother and sister used to wear with pride at parties and celebrations, had to be sold, as Gregor discovered of an evening from hearing them all discuss the prices obtained. But what they lamented most was the fact that they could not leave the flat which was much too big for their present circumstances, because they could not think of any way to shift Gregor. Yet Gregor saw well enough that consideration for

...A GIGANTIC BONY CHARWOMAN WITH WHITE HAIR FLYING AROUND HER HEAD CAME IN MORNING AND EVENING TO DO THE ROUGH WORK....

him was not the main difficulty preventing the removal, for they could have easily shifted him in some suitable box with a few air holes in it; what really kept them from moving into another flat was rather their own complete hopelessness and the belief that they had been singled out for a misfortune such as had never happened to any of their relations or acquaintances. They fulfilled to the uttermost all that the world demands of poor people, the father fetched breakfast for the small clerks in the bank, the mother devoted her energy to making underwear for strangers, the sister trotted to and fro behind the counter at the behest of customers, but more than this they had not the strength to do. And the wound in Gregor's back began to nag at him afresh when his mother and sister, after getting his father into bed, came back again, left their work lying, drew close to each other, and sat cheek by cheek; when his mother, pointing toward his room, said: "Shut that door now, Grete," and he was left again in the darkness, while next door the women mingled their tears or perhaps sat dry-eyed staring at the table.

Gregor hardly slept at all by night or by day. He was often haunted by the idea that next time the door opened he would take the family's affairs in hand again just as he used to do; once more, after this long interval, there appeared in his thoughts the figures of the chief and the chief clerk, the commercial travelers

31. **charwoman:** cleaning woman.

and the apprentices, the porter who was so dull-witted, two or three friends in other firms, a chambermaid in one of the rural hotels, a sweet and fleeting memory, a cashier in a milliner's[32] shop, whom he had wooed earnestly but too slowly—they all appeared, together with strangers or people he had quite forgotten, but instead of helping him and his family they were one and all unapproachable, and he was glad when they vanished. At other times he would not be in the mood to bother about his family, he was only filled with rage at the way they were neglecting him, and although he had no clear idea of what he might care to eat he would make plans for getting into the larder to take the food that was after all his due, even if he were not hungry. His sister no longer took thought to bring him what might especially please him; but in the morning and at noon before she went to business hurriedly pushed into his room with her foot any food that was available, and in the evening cleared it out again with one sweep of the broom, heedless of whether it had been merely tasted, or—as most frequently happened—left untouched. The cleaning of his room, which she now did always in the evenings, could not have been more hastily done. Streaks of dirt stretched along the walls, here and there lay balls of dust and filth. At first Gregor used to station himself in some particularly filthy corner when his sister arrived, in order to reproach her with it, so to speak. But he could have sat there for weeks without getting her to make any improvement; she could see the dirt as well as he did, but she had simply made up her mind to leave it alone. And yet, with a touchiness that was new to her, which seemed anyhow to have infected the whole family, she jealously guarded her claim to be the sole caretaker of Gregor's room. His mother once subjected his room to a thorough cleaning, which was achieved only by means of several buckets of water—all this dampness of course upset Gregor too and he lay widespread, sulky, and motionless on the sofa—but she was well punished for it. Hardly had his sister noticed the changed aspect of his room that evening than she rushed in high dudgeon[33] into the living room and, despite the imploringly raised hands of her mother, burst into a storm of weeping, while her parents—her father had of course been startled out of his chair—looked on at first in helpless amazement; then they too began to go into action; the father reproached the mother on his right for not having left the cleaning of Gregor's room to his sister; shrieked at the sister on his left that never again was she to be allowed to clean Gregor's room; while the mother tried to pull the father into his bedroom, since he was beyond himself with agitation; the sister, shaken with sobs, then beat upon the table with her small fists; and Gregor hissed loudly with rage because not one of them thought of shutting the door to spare him such a spectacle and so much noise.

Still, even if the sister, exhausted by her daily work, had grown tired of looking after Gregor as she did formerly, there was no need for his mother's intervention or for Gregor's being neglected at all. The charwoman was there. This old widow, whose strong bony frame had enabled her to survive the worst a long life could offer, by no means recoiled from Gregor. Without being in the least curious she had once by chance opened the door of his room and at the sight of Gregor, who, taken by surprise, began to rush to and fro although no one was chasing him, merely stood there with her arms folded. From that time she never failed to open his door a little for a moment, morning and evening, to have a look at him. At first she even used to call him to her,

---

32. **milliner's:** hat maker's.
33. **in high dudgeon:** very angrily.

with words which apparently she took to be friendly, such as: "Come along, then, you old dung beetle!" or "Look at the old dung beetle, then!" To such allocutions[34] Gregor made no answer, but stayed motionless where he was, as if the door had never been opened. Instead of being allowed to disturb him so senselessly whenever the whim took her, she should rather have been ordered to clean out his room daily, that charwoman! Once, early in the morning—heavy rain was lashing on the window-panes, perhaps a sign that spring was on the way—Gregor was so exasperated when she began addressing him again that he ran at her, as if to attack her, although slowly and feebly enough. But the charwoman instead of showing fright merely lifted high a chair that happened to be beside the door, and as she stood there with her mouth wide open it was clear that she meant to shut it only when she brought the chair down on Gregor's back. "So you're not coming any nearer?" she asked, as Gregor turned away again, and quietly put the chair back into the corner.

Gregor was now eating hardly anything. Only when he happened to pass the food laid out for him did he take a bit of something in his mouth as a pastime, kept it there for an hour at a time, and usually spat it out again. At first he thought it was <u>chagrin</u> over the state of his room that prevented him from eating, yet he soon got used to the various changes in his room. It had become a habit in the family to push into his room things there was no room for elsewhere, and there were plenty of these now, since one of the rooms had been let to three lodgers. These serious gentlemen—all three of them with full beards, as Gregor once observed through a crack in the door—had a passion for order, not only in their own room but, since they were now members of the household, in all its arrangements, especially in the kitchen. Superfluous, not to say dirty, objects they could not bear. Besides, they had brought with them most of the furnishings they needed. For this reason many things could be dispensed with that it was no use trying to sell but that should not be thrown away either. All of them found their way into Gregor's room. The ash can likewise and the kitchen garbage can. Anything that was not needed for the moment was simply flung into Gregor's room by the charwoman, who did everything in a hurry; fortunately Gregor usually saw only the object, whatever it was, and the hand that held it. Perhaps she intended to take the things away again as time and opportunity offered, or to collect them until she could throw them all out in a heap, but in fact they just lay wherever she happened to throw them, except when Gregor pushed his way through the junk heap and shifted it somewhat, at first out of necessity, because he had not room enough to crawl, but later with increasing enjoyment, although after such excursions, being sad and weary to death, he would lie motionless for hours. And since the lodgers often ate their supper at home in the common living room, the living-room door stayed shut many an evening, yet Gregor reconciled himself quite easily to the shutting of the door, for often enough on evenings when it was opened he had disregarded it entirely and lain in the darkest corner of his room, quite unnoticed by the family. But on one occasion the charwoman left the door open a little and it stayed ajar even when the lodgers came in for supper and the lamp was lit. They set themselves at the top end of the table where formerly Gregor and his father and mother had eaten their meals, unfolded their napkins, and took knife and fork in hand. At once his mother appeared in the other doorway with a dish of meat and close behind her his sister with a dish of potatoes piled high. The food steamed with a thick vapor. The lodgers bent over the food set before them as if to scrutinize it before

34. **allocutions** (ăl′ə-kyōō′shənz): formal speeches. (The word is meant ironically here.)

WORDS TO KNOW
chagrin (shə-grĭn′) *n.* a feeling of disappointment or humiliation

METAMORPHOSIS   **1139**

Die Skatspieler [Skat players] (1920), Otto Dix. Oil on canvas and collage, 110 cm × 87 cm. Nationalgalerie, Staatliche Museen zu Berlin.

eating, in fact the man in the middle, who seemed to pass for an authority with the other two, cut a piece of meat as it lay on the dish, obviously to discover if it were tender or should be sent back to the kitchen. He showed satisfaction, and Gregor's mother and sister, who had been watching anxiously, breathed freely and began to smile.

The family itself took its meals in the kitchen. Nonetheless, Gregor's father came into the living room before going into the kitchen and with one prolonged bow, cap in hand, made a round of the table. The lodgers all stood up and murmured something in their beards. When they were alone again they ate their food in almost complete silence. It seemed remarkable to Gregor that among the various noises coming from the table he could always distinguish the sound of their masticating[35] teeth, as if this were a sign to Gregor that one needed teeth in order to eat, and that with toothless jaws even of the finest make

one could do nothing. "I'm hungry enough," said Gregor sadly to himself, "but not for that kind of food. How these lodgers are stuffing themselves, and here I am dying of starvation!"

On that very evening—during the whole of his time there Gregor could not remember ever having heard the violin—the sound of violin-playing came from the kitchen. The lodgers had already finished their supper, the one in the middle had brought out a newspaper and given the other two a page apiece, and now they were leaning back at ease reading and smoking. When the violin began to play they pricked up their ears, got to their feet, and went on tiptoe to the hall door where they stood huddled together. Their movements must have been heard in the kitchen, for Gregor's father called out: "Is the violin-playing disturbing you, gentlemen? It can be stopped at once." "On the contrary," said the middle lodger, "could not Fräulein[36] Samsa come and play in this room, beside us, where it is much more convenient and comfortable?" "Oh certainly," cried Gregor's father, as if he were the violin-player. The lodgers came back into the living room and waited. Presently Gregor's father arrived with the music stand, his mother carrying the music and his sister with the violin. His sister quietly made everything ready to start playing; his parents, who had never let rooms before and so had an exaggerated idea of the courtesy due to lodgers, did not venture to sit down on their own chairs; his father leaned against the door, the right hand thrust between two buttons of his livery coat, which was formally buttoned up; but his mother was offered a chair by one of the lodgers and, since she left the chair just where he had happened to put it, sat down in a corner to one side.

---

35. **masticating:** chewing.

36. **Fräulein** (froi′līn′): the German equivalent of "Miss."

Gregor's sister began to play; the father and mother, from either side, intently watched the movements of her hands. Gregor, attracted by the playing, ventured to move forward a little until his head was actually inside the living room. He felt hardly any surprise at his growing lack of consideration for the others; there had been a time when he prided himself on being considerate. And yet just on this occasion he had more reason than ever to hide himself, since, owing to the amount of dust that lay thick in his room and rose into the air at the slightest movement, he too was covered with dust; fluff and hair and remnants of food trailed with him, caught on his back and along his sides; his indifference to everything was much too great for him to turn on his back and scrape himself clean on the carpet, as once he had done several times a day. And in spite of his condition, no shame deterred him from advancing a little over the spotless floor of the living room.

To be sure, no one was aware of him. The family was entirely absorbed in the violin-playing; the lodgers, however, who first of all had stationed themselves, hands in pockets, much too close behind the music stand so that they could all have read the music, which must have bothered his sister, had soon retreated to the window, half whispering with downbent heads, and stayed there while his father turned an anxious eye on them. Indeed, they were making it more than obvious that they had been disappointed in their expectation of hearing good or enjoyable violin-playing, that they had had more than enough of the performance and only out of courtesy suffered a continued disturbance of their peace. From the way they all kept blowing the smoke of their cigars high in the air through nose and mouth one could divine their irritation. And yet Gregor's sister was playing so beautifully. Her face leaned

sideways, intently and sadly her eyes followed the notes of music. Gregor crawled a little farther forward and lowered his head to the ground so that it might be possible for his eyes to meet hers. Was he an animal, that music had such an effect upon him? He felt as if the way were opening before him to the unknown nourishment he craved. He was determined to push forward till he reached his sister, to pull at her skirt and so let her know that she was to come into his room with her violin, for no one here appreciated her playing as he would appreciate it. He would never let her out of his room, at least, not so long as he lived; his frightful appearance would become, for the first time, useful to him; he would watch all the doors of his room at once and spit at intruders; but his sister should need no constraint, she should stay with him out of her own free will; she should sit beside him on the sofa, bend down her ear to him, and hear him confide that he had had the firm intention of sending her to the Conservatorium, and that, but for his mishap, last Christmas—surely Christmas was long past?—he would have announced it to everybody without allowing a single objection. After this confession his sister would be so touched that she would burst into tears, and Gregor would then raise himself to her shoulder and kiss her on the neck, which, now that she went to business, she kept free of any ribbon or collar.

"Mr. Samsa!" cried the middle lodger to Gregor's father, and pointed, without wasting any more words, at Gregor, now working himself slowly forward. The violin fell silent, the middle lodger first smiled to his friends with a shake of the head and then looked at Gregor again. Instead of driving Gregor out, his father seemed to think it more needful to begin by soothing down the lodgers, although they were not at all agitated and apparently found Gregor more entertaining than the violin-playing. He hurried toward them and, spreading out his arms, tried to urge them back into their own room and at the same time to block their view of Gregor. They now began to be really a little angry, one could not tell whether because of the old man's behavior or because it had just dawned on them that all unwittingly they had such a neighbor as Gregor next door. They demanded explanations of his father, they waved their arms like him, tugged uneasily at their beards, and only with reluctance backed toward their room. Meanwhile, Gregor's sister, who stood there as if lost when her playing was so abruptly broken off, came to life again, pulled herself together all at once after standing for a while holding violin and bow in nervelessly hanging hands and staring at her music, pushed her violin into the lap of her mother, who was still sitting in her chair fighting asthmatically for breath, and ran into the lodgers' room to which they were now being shepherded by her father rather more quickly than before. One could see the pillows and blankets on the beds flying under her accustomed fingers and being laid in order. Before the lodgers had actually reached their room she had finished making the beds and slipped out.

The old man seemed once more to be so possessed by his mulish self-assertiveness that he was forgetting all the respect he should show to his lodgers. He kept driving them on and driving them on until in the very door of the bedroom the middle lodger stamped his foot loudly on the floor and so brought him to a halt. "I beg to announce," said

the lodger, lifting one hand and looking also at Gregor's mother and sister, "that because of the disgusting conditions prevailing in this household and family"—here he spat on the floor with emphatic brevity[37]—"I give you notice on the spot. Naturally I won't pay you a penny for the days I have lived here, on the contrary I shall consider bringing an action for damages against you, based on claims—believe me—that will be easily susceptible of[38] proof." He ceased and stared straight in front of him, as if he expected something. In fact his two friends at once rushed into the breach[39] with these words: "And we too give notice on the spot." On that he seized the door handle and shut the door with a slam.

Gregor's father, groping with his hands, staggered forward and fell into his chair; it looked as if he were stretching himself there for his ordinary evening nap, but the marked jerkings of his head, which were as if uncontrollable, showed that he was far from asleep. Gregor had simply stayed quietly all the time on the spot where the lodgers had espied him. Disappointment at the failure of his plan, perhaps also the weakness arising from extreme hunger, made it impossible for him to move. He feared, with a fair degree of certainty, that at any moment the general tension would discharge itself in a combined attack upon him, and he lay waiting. He did not react even to the noise made by the violin as it fell off his mother's lap from under her trembling fingers and gave out a resonant note.

"My dear parents," said his sister, slapping her hand on the table by way of introduction, "things can't go on like this. Perhaps you don't realize that, but I do. I won't utter my brother's name in the presence of this creature, and so all I say is: we must try to get rid of it. We've tried to look after it and to put up with it as far as is

---

37. **brevity:** briefness; abruptness.
38. **susceptible of:** open to.
39. **breach:** gap; opening.

humanly possible, and I don't think anyone could reproach us in the slightest."

"She is more than right," said Gregor's father to himself. His mother, who was still choking for lack of breath, began to cough hollowly into her hand with a wild look in her eyes.

His sister rushed over to her and held her forehead. His father's thoughts seemed to have lost their vagueness at Grete's words, he sat more upright, fingering his service cap that lay among the plates still lying on the table from the lodgers' supper, and from time to time looked at the still form of Gregor.

"We must try to get rid of it," his sister now said explicitly to her father, since her mother was coughing too much to hear a word, "it will be the death of both of you, I can see that coming. When one has to work as hard as we do, all of us, one can't stand this continual torment at home on top of it. At least I can't stand it any longer." And she burst into such a passion of sobbing that her tears dropped on her mother's face, where she wiped them off mechanically.

"My dear," said the old man sympathetically, and with evident understanding, "but what can we do?"

Gregor's sister merely shrugged her shoulders to indicate the feeling of helplessness that had now overmastered her during her weeping fit, in contrast to her former confidence.

"If he could understand us," said her father, half questioningly; Grete, still sobbing, vehemently waved a hand to show how unthinkable that was.

"If he could understand us," repeated the old man, shutting his eyes to consider his daughter's conviction that understanding was impossible, "then perhaps we might come to some agreement with him. But as it is—"

"He must go," cried Gregor's sister, "that's the only solution, Father. You must just try to get rid of the idea that this is Gregor. The fact that we've believed it for so long is the root of all our trouble. But how can it be Gregor? If this were Gregor, he would have realized long ago that human beings can't live with such a creature, and he'd have gone away on his own accord. Then we wouldn't have any brother, but we'd be able to go on living and keep his memory in honor. As it is, this creature persecutes us, drives away our lodgers, obviously wants the whole apartment to himself, and would have us all sleep in the gutter. Just look, Father," she shrieked all at once, "he's at it again!" And in an access[40] of panic that was quite incomprehensible to Gregor she even quitted her mother, literally thrusting the chair from her as if she would rather sacrifice her mother than stay so near to Gregor, and rushed behind her father, who also rose up, being simply upset by her agitation, and half spread his arms out as if to protect her.

Yet Gregor had not the slightest intention of frightening anyone, far less his sister. He had only begun to turn around in order to crawl back to his room, but it was certainly a startling operation to watch, since because of his disabled condition he could not execute the difficult turning movements except by lifting his head and then bracing it against the floor over and over again. He paused and looked around. His good

---

40. **access:** outburst.

> "AND **WHAT NOW?**" SAID GREGOR TO HIMSELF, LOOKING AROUND IN THE DARKNESS. SOON HE MADE THE DISCOVERY THAT HE WAS NOW UNABLE TO STIR A **LIMB.**

intentions seemed to have been recognized; the alarm had only been momentary. Now they were all watching him in melancholy silence. His mother lay in her chair, her legs stiffly outstretched and pressed together, her eyes almost closing for sheer weariness; his father and his sister were sitting beside each other, his sister's arm around the old man's neck.

Perhaps I can go on turning around now, thought Gregor, and began his labors again. He could not stop himself from panting with the effort, and had to pause now and then to take breath. Nor did anyone harass him, he was left entirely to himself. When he had completed the turn-around he began at once to crawl straight back. He was amazed at the distance separating him from his room and could not understand how in his weak state he had managed to accomplish the same journey so recently, almost without remarking it. Intent on crawling as fast as possible, he barely noticed that not a single word, not an ejaculation from his family, interfered with his progress. Only when he was already in the doorway did he turn his head around, not completely, for his neck muscles were getting stiff, but enough to see that nothing had changed behind him except that his sister had risen to her feet. His last glance fell on his mother, who was not quite overcome by sleep.

Hardly was he well inside his room when the door was hastily pushed shut, bolted, and locked. The sudden noise in his rear startled him so much that his little legs gave beneath him. It was his sister who had shown such haste. She had been standing ready waiting and had made a light spring forward, Gregor had not even heard her coming, and she cried "At last!" to her parents as she turned the key in the lock.

"And what now?" said Gregor to himself, looking around in the darkness. Soon he made the discovery that he was now unable to stir a limb. This did not surprise him, rather it seemed unnatural that he should ever actually have been able to move on these feeble little legs. Otherwise he felt relatively comfortable. True, his whole body was aching, but it seemed that the pain was gradually growing less and would finally pass away. The rotting apple in his back and the inflamed area around it, all covered with soft dust, already hardly troubled him. He thought of his family with tenderness and love. The decision that he must disappear was one that he held to even more strongly than his sister, if that were possible. In this state of vacant and peaceful meditation he remained until the tower clock struck three in the morning. The first broadening of light in the world outside the window entered his consciousness once more. Then his head sank to the floor of its own accord and from his nostrils came the last faint flicker of his breath.

When the charwoman arrived early in the morning—what between her strength and her impatience she slammed all the doors so loudly, never mind how often she had been begged not to do so, that no one in the whole apartment could enjoy any quiet sleep after her arrival—she noticed nothing unusual as she took her customary peep into Gregor's room. She thought he was lying motionless on purpose, pretending to be in the sulks; she credited him with every kind of intelligence. Since she happened to have the long-handled broom in her hand she tried to tickle him up with it from the doorway. When that too produced no reaction she felt provoked and poked at him a little harder, and only when she had pushed him along the floor without meeting any resistance was her attention aroused. It did not take her long to establish the truth of the matter, and her eyes widened, she let out a whistle, yet did not waste much time over it but tore open the door of the Samsas' bedroom and yelled into the darkness at the top of her voice: "Just look at this, it's dead; it's lying here dead and done for!"

Mr. and Mrs. Samsa started up in their double bed and before they realized the nature of the charwoman's announcement had some difficulty in overcoming the shock of it. But then they got out of bed quickly, one on either side, Mr. Samsa throwing a blanket over his shoulders, Mrs. Samsa in nothing but her nightgown; in this array they entered Gregor's room. Meanwhile the door of the living room opened, too, where Grete had been sleeping since the advent of the lodgers; she was completely dressed as if she had not been to bed, which seemed to be confirmed also by the paleness of her face. "Dead?" said Mrs. Samsa, looking questioningly at the charwoman, although she would have investigated for herself, and the fact was obvious enough without investigation. "I should say so," said the charwoman, proving her words by pushing Gregor's corpse a long way to one side with her broomstick. Mrs. Samsa made a movement as if to stop her, but checked it. "Well," said Mr. Samsa, "now thanks be to God." He crossed himself, and the three women followed his

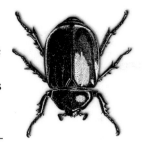

example. Grete, whose eyes never left the corpse, said: "Just see how thin he was. It's such a long time since he's eaten anything. The food came out again just as it went in." Indeed Gregor's body was completely flat and dry, as could only now be seen when it was no longer supported by the legs and nothing prevented one from looking closely at it.

"Come in beside us, Grete, for a little while," said Mrs. Samsa with a tremulous[41] smile, and Grete, not without looking back at the corpse, followed her parents into their bedroom. The charwoman shut the door and opened the window wide. Although it was so early in the morning a certain softness was perceptible in the fresh air. After all, it was already the end of March.

The three lodgers emerged from their room and were surprised to see no breakfast; they had been forgotten. "Where's our breakfast?" said the middle lodger peevishly to the charwoman. But she put her finger to her lips and hastily, without a word, indicated by gestures that they should go into Gregor's room. They did so and stood, their hands in the pockets of their somewhat shabby coats, around Gregor's corpse in the room where it was now fully light.

At that the door of the Samsas' bedroom opened and Mr. Samsa appeared in his uniform, his wife on one arm, his daughter on the other. They all looked a little as if they had been crying; from time to time Grete hid her face on her father's arm.

"Leave my house at once!" said Mr. Samsa, and pointed to the door without disengaging himself from the women. "What do you mean by that?" said the middle lodger, taken somewhat aback, with a feeble smile. The two others put their hands behind them and kept rubbing them

---

41. tremulous (trĕm′yə-ləs): timid or fearful.

together, as if in gleeful expectation of a fine set-to in which they were bound to come off the winners. "I mean just what I say," answered Mr. Samsa, and advanced in a straight line with his two companions toward the lodger. He stood his ground at first quietly, looking at the floor as if his thoughts were taking a new pattern in his head. "Then let us go, by all means," he said, and looked up at Mr. Samsa as if in a sudden access of humility he were expecting some renewed sanction[42] for this decision. Mr. Samsa merely nodded briefly once or twice with meaning eyes. Upon that the lodger really did go with long strides into the hall, his two friends had been listening and had quite stopped rubbing their hands for some moments and now went scuttling after him as if afraid that Mr. Samsa might get into the hall before them and cut them off from their leader. In the hall they all three took their hats from the rack, their sticks from the umbrella stand, bowed in silence, and quitted the apartment. With a suspiciousness that proved quite unfounded Mr. Samsa and the two women followed them out to the landing; leaning over the banister they watched the three figures slowly but surely going down the long stairs, vanishing from sight at a certain turn of the staircase on every floor and coming into view again after a moment or so; the more they dwindled,[43] the more the Samsa family's interest in them dwindled, and when a butcher's boy met them and passed them on the stairs coming up proudly with a tray on his head, Mr. Samsa and the two women soon left the landing and as if a burden had been lifted from them went back into their apartment.

They decided to spend this day in resting and going for a stroll; they had not only deserved such a respite from work, but absolutely needed it. And so they sat down at the table and wrote three notes of excuse, Mr. Samsa to his board of management, Mrs. Samsa to her employer, and Grete to the head of her firm. While they were writing,

the charwoman came in to say that she was going now, since her morning's work was finished. At first they only nodded without looking up, but as she kept hovering there they eyed her irritably. "Well?" said Mr. Samsa. The charwoman stood grinning in the doorway as if she had good news to impart to the family but meant not to say a word unless properly questioned. The small ostrich feather standing upright on her hat, which had annoyed Mr. Samsa ever since she was engaged, was waving gaily in all directions. "Well, what is it then?" asked Mrs. Samsa, who obtained more respect from the charwoman than the others. "Oh," said the charwoman, giggling so amiably that she could not at once continue, "just this, you don't need to bother about how to get rid of the thing next door. It's been seen to already." Mrs. Samsa and Grete bent over their letters again, as if preoccupied; Mr. Samsa, who perceived that she was eager to begin describing it all in detail, stopped her with a decisive hand. But since she was not allowed to tell her story, she remembered the great hurry she was in, obviously deeply huffed: "Bye, everybody," she said, whirling off violently, and departed with a frightful slamming of doors.

"She'll be given notice tonight," said Mr. Samsa, but neither from his wife nor his daughter did he get any answer, for the charwoman seemed to have shattered again the composure they had barely achieved. They rose, went to the window and stayed there, clasping each other tight. Mr. Samsa turned in his chair to look at them and quietly observed them for a little. Then he called out: "Come along, now, do. Let bygones be bygones. And you might have some consideration for me." The two of them complied at once, hastened to him, caressed him, and quickly finished their letters.

---

42. **sanction** (săngk′shən): authorization.
43. **dwindled**: became smaller.

Then they all three left the apartment together, which was more than they had done for months, and went by train into the open country outside the town. The tram, in which they were the only passengers, was filled with warm sunshine. Leaning comfortably back in their seats they canvassed[44] their prospects for the future, and it appeared on closer inspection that these were not at all bad, for the jobs they had got, which so far they had never really discussed with each other, were all three admirable and likely to lead to better things later on. The greatest immediate improvement in their condition would of course arise from moving to another house; they wanted to take a smaller and cheaper but also better situated and more easily run apartment than the one they had, which Gregor had selected. While they were thus conversing, it struck both Mr. and Mrs. Samsa, almost at the same moment, as they became aware of their daughter's increasing vivacity, that in spite of all the sorrow of recent times, which had made her cheeks pale, she had bloomed into a pretty girl with a good figure. They grew quieter and half unconsciously exchanged glances of complete agreement, having come to the conclusion that it would soon be time to find a good husband for her. And it was like a confirmation of their new dreams and excellent intentions that at the end of their journey their daughter sprang to her feet first and stretched her young body. ❖

---

44. **canvassed:** carefully examined or discussed.

Connect to the Literature

1. What Do You Think?
What is your reaction to the way the story ends? Explain.

Comprehension Check
- Who takes care of Gregor?
- Why is the furniture moved out of Gregor's room?
- What happens to his body after he dies?

Think Critically

2. For which character do you have the most sympathy? For which character do you have the least sympathy? Use examples from the story to support your opinion.

3. Consider the ways in which Gregor and the other members of his family respond to his transformation. What do you learn about each of these characters as a result of his or her response?

- why Gregor's mother won't enter his room
- what his father does to injure Gregor
- the change in his sister's treatment of Gregor
- how Gregor feels about his family

4. Compare the problems of Gregor's life as an insect to his problems before his change. Are his problems as an insect completely different from his earlier problems? Explain.

5. Why do you think Kafka chose to have Gregor transformed into an insect instead of another type of creature? Think about the characteristics of this bug, and how others react to it.

6. ACTIVE READING: VISUALIZING DETAILS Review the list of images recorded in your ▥ **READER'S NOTEBOOK.** Which image do you feel best captures the emotional atmosphere, or mood, of the story? Describe that mood.

Extend Interpretations

7. Critic's Corner When a publisher intended to illustrate "Metamorphosis," Kafka insisted that "the insect itself cannot be drawn." What do you think were Kafka's reasons?

8. The Writer's Style Kafka writes in a dry, matter-of-fact manner. Read aloud a passage that illustrates this style, then describe the effects of such a style.

9. Connect to Life Many other stories and films are about the transformation of a human being into another creature. Why do you think people find such stories interesting? Explain.

LITERARY ANALYSIS: POINT OF VIEW

The narrative method, or **point of view,** that Kafka chose for "Metamorphosis" is mainly **third-person limited.** Though Gregor is not the narrator, the reader learns about the events from Gregor's perspective, as if seeing through his eyes. Other characters are described only as they appear to Gregor, as in this passage about his mother:

As all this was running through his mind at top speed . . . there came a cautious tap at the door behind the head of his bed. "Gregor," said a voice—it was his mother's—"it's a quarter to seven. Hadn't you a train to catch?"

After Gregor dies, the story's point of view shifts to **third-person omniscient,** a perspective in which the narrator is all-knowing and can reveal the thoughts of all the characters.

Paired Activity Working with a partner, look through the story to find two particularly striking examples that illustrate the third-person limited point of view and two that illustrate the third-person omniscient point of view. How would the story be different if it were told completely from a third-person omniscient point of view?

Choices & CHALLENGES

Writing Options

1. Diary Entries Imagine that you are one of the characters other than Gregor. Write three diary entries from this character's point of view, describing key events in the story.

Writing Handbook
See page R27: Descriptive Writing.

2. Literary Analysis What is a central **theme,** or message, of this story? Does the story offer a lesson about the problems of modern life, a reflection about the disappointments of family relationships, or something else? Begin by completing the following sentence: "Metamorphosis" can be interpreted as a story that _____. Use that sentence as a working draft of your thesis statement. Then review the story and arrive at three or four ideas that support your thesis. Each of these ideas can be the basis of a paragraph or two that helps to advance your thesis. Place your essay in your **Working Portfolio.**

Activities & Explorations

1. Cover Illustration Draw a cover illustration for an edition of "Metamorphosis." Keep in mind Kafka's insistence that the insect not be portrayed. ~ **ART**

2. Dramatic Scene Get together with some of your classmates to dramatize a major scene from the story. Act out your scene or do a dramatic reading in front of the class. ~ **PERFORMANCE**

Inquiry & Research

1. Story Comparison Read another story by Kafka, such as "The Judgment" or "A Hunger Artist." Compare that story with "Metamorphosis" in terms of point of view and symbolic meaning.

2. Annotated Bibliography Research print and online sources to find five books or articles about Kafka's life. Then draw up a list of your resources and write a sentence or two summarizing the contents of each one. Include the author, title, publisher, and date of publication for each book and the Web address for each online site.

RESEARCH STARTER
CLASSZONE.COM

Vocabulary in Action

EXERCISE: CONTEXT CLUES Write the Word to Know that best completes each sentence.

1. When Gregor first awoke, he had no sense that _____ disaster was about to overtake him.

2. He worried that he might neglect his duty at work or be guilty of some small _____.

3. As he tried to arise from bed, it proved hard for him to establish his _____.

4. Was he surprised that his speech was _____ and that the clerk could not understand it?

5. The stingy owner of Gregor's firm did not treat his employees _____.

6. Gregor's family might have eased his anxiety if they had talked to him _____.

7. Gregor hoped that his sister might _____ with his parents and make peace.

8. Did he think she could understand his sense of humiliation and _____?

9. Gregor felt that his only place of _____ was under the sofa.

10. Did he think that remaining out of sight would _____ the family from hating him?

WORDS TO KNOW

amiably	imminent	omission
chagrin	intervene	refuge
dissuade	lavishly	unintelligible
equilibrium		

Building Vocabulary
For an in-depth lesson on context clues, see page 674.

P O E M S   B Y

R A I N E R   M A R I A   R I L K E   *AND*

F E D E R I C O   G A R C Í A   L O R C A

Rainer Maria Rilke
1875–1926

A Restless Poet Restlessness defines the life and career of Rainer Maria Rilke (rīn′ər mä-rē′ä rĭl′kə), considered one of the greatest poets of the 20th century. In his poetry he constantly experimented with new styles. Rilke moved frequently in search of places to sustain and inspire his art. After leaving his native Prague, he lived in Russia, France, Spain, Italy, Austria, and Switzerland.

Object Poetry While living in Paris in the early 1900s, Rilke became close friends with the famous sculptor Auguste Rodin (ô-güst′ rō-dăn′). Inspired by Rodin and the great art collections in Paris, Rilke developed a new poetic style called object poetry. In writing an object poem, such as "The Panther," Rilke approached his subject as a visual artist would and tried to translate his precise observations into words. Rilke wrote "The Panther" after Rodin had advised him to go to the Paris zoo and look at an animal long enough to see it truly.

Modernist Experiments Rilke continued to experiment with new ways of writing. In 1910 he wrote a modernist novel about a young poet searching for his identity in Paris. After serving briefly in World War I, Rilke moved to Switzerland, where he wrote two major books of poetry—*Duino Elegies* and *Sonnets to Orpheus*. In these collections of complex and daringly original poetry, Rilke expresses his belief in the spiritual unity of all things.

Connect to Your Life

The following poems portray two different scenes that convey strong emotions. Recall a brief scene in your life that produced strong feelings of pity or sadness. Write down a list of vivid phrases to describe that scene.

Focus Your Reading

LITERARY ANALYSIS: SOUND DEVICES
When a poem is translated into another language, some of its musical qualities are lost. However, translators still use **sound devices** to appeal to the ear. If you read the following poems aloud, you should be able to hear these sound devices.

- **Alliteration** is a repetition of consonant sounds at the beginning of words, as in "the <u>s</u>oft <u>s</u>ounds of the <u>s</u>ea."

- **Assonance** is a repetition of vowel sounds in syllables that do not rhyme, as in "It <u>i</u>s <u>i</u>mpossible."

- **Consonance** is a repetition of consonant sounds within or at the end of words, as in "constantly pa<u>ss</u>ing bar<u>s</u>."

ACTIVE READING: CONNECTING TO POETRY
When you read poetry, try to connect personally with what you are reading about. When you read "The Panther," for example, consider your own feelings about seeing caged animals at a zoo.

READER'S NOTEBOOK As you read these poems, jot down any thoughts, feelings, or memories that help to connect you to each poem.

The Panther
Rainer Maria Rilke
Translated by Stephen Mitchell

IN THE JARDIN DES PLANTES, PARIS

His vision, from the constantly passing bars,
has grown so weary that it cannot hold
anything else. It seems to him there are
a thousand bars; and behind the bars, no world.

5 As he paces in cramped circles, over and over,
the movement of his powerful soft strides
is like a ritual dance around a center
in which a mighty will stands paralyzed.

Only at times, the curtain of the pupils
10 lifts, quietly—. An image enters in,
rushes down through the tensed, arrested muscles,
plunges into the heart and is gone.

Federico García Lorca
1898–1936

Spain's Beloved Poet

Federico García Lorca (fĕ-dĕ-rē′kô gär-sē′ə lôr′kä) became one of Spain's most revered and deeply loved poets. Also a gifted pianist and successful playwright, he counted among his friends the leading talents of his generation, such as the surrealist painter Salvador Dali and the filmmaker Luis Buñuel (lōō-ēs′ bōō-nyōō-ĕl′).

International Fame

García Lorca believed that "verse is made to be recited." He began his career by giving oral readings of his poetry, often mixed with his piano performances of folk songs. His most popular collection of poetry, *Gypsy Ballads,* was inspired by folk music, stories of gypsies, and the rural life he had known as a child. His poem "The Guitar," from that collection, describes a flamenco performance. Flamenco guitar music is marked by forceful and improvised rhythms; it accompanies an equally forceful style of dance.

Violent Death

Violence and death haunt much of García Lorca's work. Even though he was never very politically active, his association with socialists was considered to mark him as a leftist in Spain's bloody civil war. At the war's outbreak, he was kidnapped and brutally executed by Nationalist soldiers. His body was never found.

Other Works
Lament for the Death of a Bullfighter and Other Poems
Poet in New York
Blood Wedding

THE GUITAR

FEDERICO GARCÍA LORCA

TRANSLATED BY ROBERT BLY

The crying of the guitar
starts.
The goblets
of the dawn break.
5 The crying of the guitar
starts.
No use to stop it.
It is impossible
to stop it.
10 It cries repeating itself
as the water cries,
as the wind cries
over the snow.
It is impossible
15 to stop it.
It is crying for things
far off.
The warm sand of the South
that asks for white camellias.
20 For the arrow with nothing to hit,
the evening with no dawn coming,
and the first bird of all dead
on the branch.
Guitar!
25 Heart wounded, gravely,
by five swords.

19 camellias (kə-mēl′yəz): roselike flowers that grow on small trees.

25 gravely: very seriously.

Connect to the Literature

1. **What Do You Think?**
   What mental images did you form while reading these poems? Describe those images.

   Comprehension Check
   - What does the panther do in his cage?
   - What kind of sound does the guitar make?

Think Critically

2. **ACTIVE READING: CONNECTING TO POETRY** How did you connect personally with these poems? Share what you wrote about in your 📖 READER'S NOTEBOOK.

3. From the panther's point of view, what do you think is the worst thing about being locked up?

4. The last stanza of "The Panther" tells about an image that "plunges into the [panther's] heart and is gone." What do you think the panther sees, and why does the image disappear?

5. In García Lorca's poem, why do you think the crying of the guitar cannot be stopped?

6. How would you describe the kinds of things the guitar cries for?

7. What might the guitar with its constant crying **symbolize,** or represent?

Extend Interpretations

8. **Connect to Life** Some animal-rights activists believe it is wrong to keep animals in captivity at a zoo. Does your reading of "The Panther" make you sympathetic to those views? Explain.

LITERARY ANALYSIS: SOUND DEVICES

Sound devices help make poetry pleasing to the ear. Poets use sound devices for the following purposes:
- to create musical sounds
- to emphasize certain words
- to heighten moods
- to unify passages
- to help create meaning

Three common sound devices are alliteration, assonance, and consonance.

Alliteration is a repetition of consonant sounds at the beginnings of words, **assonance** is a repetition of vowel sounds in syllables that do not rhyme, and **consonance** is a repetition of consonant sounds within or at the ends of words.

When looking for these sound devices in poetry, be sure to focus on sounds, not just letters. For example, "cramped circles" in the fifth line of "The Panther" is not an example of alliteration, because the initial *c* sounds are not the same. Likewise, "cannot hold" in the second line is not an example of assonance, because the *o* in *cannot* has a short sound, whereas the *o* in *hold* has a long sound.

Paired Activity Working with a partner, look through "The Panther" and "The Guitar" to find two examples of each sound device. Then review the list above, which identifies reasons for using sound devices. Which reasons seem to apply in the two poems? Compare your findings with those of your classmates.

Translating Modern Poetry

All poetry is difficult to translate, but modern poetry poses special challenges. Rilke's poetry, for example, relies so much on suggestion that the poet did not even use the German words for a cage and a panther in his poem "The Panther." At the same time, he created complex sound patterns, which are often lost in translation, as illustrated in the following examples.

Rilke's Original German, from "Der Panther"

Sein Blick **ist** vom Vorübergehn der Stäbe
so müd geworden, da**ss** er nicht**s** mehr hält.
Ihm i**st**, al**s** ob e**s** tausend Stäbe gäbe,
und hinter tau**s**end Stäben keine Welt.

The German word for bars, **Stäbe**, is repeated three times.

Rilke makes use of an *abab* rhyme scheme. **Stäbe** (shtā′bə) rhymes with **gäbe** (gā′bə), and **hält** (hĕlt) rhymes with **Welt** (vĕlt).

The underlined *s*'s in Rilke's German illustrate his use of consonance and alliteration (the repetition of *s* and *z* sounds).

Robert Bly's Translation

From seeing the bars, his seeing is so exhausted
that it no longer holds anything anymore.
To him the world is bars, a hundred thousand
bars, and behind the bars, nothing.

Bly repeats the word **bars** to echo the repetition in the original. He actually repeats the word more than Rilke does.

Note that Bly does not make use of rhyme. He does repeat some sounds, such as *b* and *s,* but he makes a more sparing use of sound devices than Rilke.

Paired Activity

With a partner, compare and contrast Bly's translation of the first stanza with the Mitchell translation of the same stanza on page 1151. What differences do you notice between the two translations? In your opinion, which version best expresses the emotions associated with the captivity of the panther?

PROFESSIONS FOR WOMEN

VIRGINIA WOOLF

Virginia Woolf
1882–1941

An Unlikely Rebel "Something had to be done. . . . And so the smashing and the crashing began." These words of Virginia Woolf describe a revolution—the new literary art created by modernist writers. As a leader of "the moderns," Woolf believed that the old forms of writing had outlived their usefulness; new techniques had to be invented that would capture life's complexity. Woolf was born in London into a prominent Victorian family, an unlikely setting for a rebel. Her father, Sir Leslie Stephen, was a distinguished intellectual who raised his children to appreciate the life of the mind. Like most Victorians, however, he expected more of his boys than of his girls, giving his sons a university education so that they could assume leadership roles in society.

The Bloomsbury Group After the death of both her parents, Woolf moved with her sister, Vanessa, and her two brothers to a house in an area of London called Bloomsbury. Her brothers regularly invited their friends from Cambridge University for spirited discussions of art, philosophy, and literature. Woolf and her artist sister eventually joined these social gatherings, which helped them achieve an intellectual freedom and equality with men rarely available to women at the time. Before long, those regularly attending the gatherings had become known as the Bloomsbury group. They included some of the leading writers, artists, and thinkers of Woolf's generation.

Breaking Traditions Woolf's most famous novels, *Mrs. Dalloway* (1925), *To the Lighthouse* (1927), and *The Waves* (1931), broke new ground in narrative technique and style. Woolf does not really report events as they happen but, rather, describes how those events are perceived and filtered through the minds of the characters. Her novels are made even more distinctive by her original style, which has the qualities of poetry. Besides novels, she wrote numerous reviews and critical essays. Her landmark essay *A Room of One's Own* (1929) argues that women need to be given the same freedom as men to develop their creative potential.

A Crippling Illness Throughout her life, Woolf struggled with manic-depressive illness. Her first breakdown occurred in 1895, shortly after her beloved mother died. The second one came after her father's death nine years later. Although Woolf recovered from both episodes, the illness returned periodically. In 1941, feeling another serious episode coming on, she walked to a nearby river, put stones in her pockets, and drowned herself.

Other Works
Orlando
The Common Reader
A Writer's Diary

Build Background

Victorian Inequality To Virginia Woolf's father, and to most men in Victorian England, women's subservience to men was considered "natural." It never occurred to them that women should have equal rights, such as the rights to own property, obtain a university education, and have a career. The ideal woman was a nurturing caregiver to her husband as well as her children—a self-sacrificing "Angel in the House," according to a famous poem of the time.

Advances for Women By Woolf's generation, women's condition had improved somewhat. When Woolf wrote her speech "Professions for Women" in 1931, women in Great Britain could vote, and a few, like Woolf herself, had professional careers. But the Angel in the House proved to be a difficult stereotype to overcome, both in society at large and in a woman's self-perception.

Connect to Your Life

In your judgment, what is most necessary for personal fulfillment? List the following items in the order of their importance to your life. Feel free to include additional items in your list.

- professional career
- family
- friends
- social service
- personal pleasure

Focus Your Reading

LITERARY ANALYSIS: DICTION AND AUDIENCE

Diction is a writer's choice of words. In many cases, a writer's diction is influenced by his or her awareness of the **audience,** the people who will read or listen to the message. Woolf originally wrote "Professions for Women" as a speech to be delivered to an organization of professional women. Like Woolf, many of these women were pioneers in their respective fields. As you read, pay attention to the words Woolf uses. Think about how her word choice might be related to her awareness of her audience.

ACTIVE READING: RECOGNIZING MAIN IDEAS

Virginia Woolf tells stories about her own professional experience to express her ideas. As a result, some of her main points are not stated directly; instead, a reader must infer them from her stories.

📖 **READER'S NOTEBOOK** As you read, make two lists like the ones started at right. These lists will help you to identify Woolf's main ideas.

WORDS TO KNOW
Vocabulary Preview

acute   perpetual
lethargy   reputable
nominally

Obstacles to a Woman's Writing
1. the Angel in the House
2.
3.

Rewards of Writing
1. money
2.
3.

Professions for Women

Virginia Woolf

When your secretary invited me to come here, she told me that your Society is concerned with the employment of women and she suggested that I might tell you something about my own professional experiences. It is true I am a woman; it is true I am employed; but what professional experiences have I had? It is difficult to say. My profession is literature; and in that profession there are fewer experiences for women than in any other, with the exception of the stage—fewer, I mean, that are peculiar to women. For the road was cut many years ago—by Fanny Burney,[1] by Aphra Behn,[2] by Harriet Martineau,[3] by Jane Austen,[4] by George Eliot[5]—many famous women, and many more unknown and forgotten, have been before me, making the path smooth, and regulating my steps. Thus, when I came to write, there were very few material[6] obstacles in my way. Writing was a <u>reputable</u> and harmless occupation. The family peace was not broken by the scratching of a pen. No demand was made upon the family purse. For ten and sixpence one can buy paper enough to write all the plays of Shakespeare—if one has a mind that way. Pianos and models, Paris, Vienna and Berlin, masters and mistresses, are not needed by a writer. The cheapness of writing paper is, of course, the reason why women have succeeded as writers before they have succeeded in the other professions.

But to tell you my story—it is a simple one. You have only got to figure to yourselves a girl in a bedroom with a pen in her hand. She had only to move that pen from left to right—from ten o'clock to one. Then it occurred to her to do what is simple and cheap enough after all—to slip a few of those pages into an envelope, fix a penny stamp in the corner, and drop the envelope into the red box[7] at the corner. It was thus that I became a journalist; and my effort was rewarded on the first day of the following month—a very glorious day it was for me—by a letter from an editor containing a check for one

---

1. **Fanny Burney:** English novelist (1752–1840).
2. **Aphra Behn:** English playwright, poet, and novelist (1640–1689); the first Englishwoman known to earn her living by writing.
3. **Harriet Martineau:** English novelist and writer on economics and history (1802–1876).
4. **Jane Austen:** English novelist (1775–1817), whose works include *Pride and Prejudice* and *Emma*.
5. **George Eliot:** pen name of Mary Ann Evans (1819–1880), English author of *Adam Bede, Silas Marner,* and *Middlemarch*.
6. **material:** significant; relevant.
7. **red box:** Mailboxes in England are characteristically red.

<u>WORDS TO KNOW</u>

reputable (rĕp′yə-tə-bəl) *adj.* of good reputation; honorable

pound ten shillings and sixpence.[8] But to show you how little I deserve to be called a professional woman, how little I know of the struggles and difficulties of such lives, I have to admit that instead of spending that sum upon bread and butter, rent, shoes and stockings, or butcher's bills, I went out and bought a cat—a beautiful cat, a Persian cat, which very soon involved me in bitter disputes with my neighbors.

What could be easier than to write articles and to buy Persian cats with the profits? But wait a moment. Articles have to be about something. Mine, I seem to remember, was about a novel by a famous man. And while I was writing this review, I discovered that if I were going to review books I should need to do battle with a certain phantom. And the phantom was a woman, and when I came to know her better I called her after the heroine of a famous poem, *The Angel in the House.*[9] It was she who used to come between me and my paper when I was writing reviews. It was she who bothered me and wasted my time and so tormented me that at last I killed her. You who come of a younger and happier generation may not have heard of her—you may not know what I mean by the Angel in the House. I will describe her as shortly as I can. She was intensely sympathetic. She was immensely charming. She was utterly unselfish. She excelled in the difficult arts of family life. She sacrificed herself daily. If there was chicken, she took the leg; if there was a

Virginia Woolf. Copyright © Bettmann/Corbis.

draught she sat in it—in short she was so constituted that she never had a mind or a wish of her own, but preferred to sympathize always with the minds and wishes of others. Above all—I need not say it—she was pure. Her purity was supposed to be her chief beauty—her blushes, her great grace. In those days—the last of Queen Victoria[10]— every house had its Angel. And when I came to write I encountered her with the very first words. The shadow of her wings fell on my page; I heard the rustling of her skirts in the room. Directly, that is to say, I took my pen in hand to review that novel by a famous man, she slipped behind me and whispered: "My dear, you are a young woman. You are writing about a book that has been written by a man. Be sympathetic; be tender; flatter; deceive, use all the arts and wiles[11] of our sex. Never let anybody guess that

---

8. **one pound . . . sixpence:** Pounds, shillings, and pence are denominations of British money.

9. ***The Angel in the House:*** a long verse novel, published by the British writer Coventry Patmore in segments in the 1850s and 1860s. It presents an idealized view of a woman's role in the family.

10. **Queen Victoria:** monarch of Britain from 1837 to 1901.

11. **wiles:** tricks intended to deceive.

you have a mind of your own. Above all, be pure." And she made as if to guide my pen. I now record the one act for which I take some credit to myself, though the credit rightly belongs to some excellent ancestors of mine who left me

> FOR, AS I FOUND, DIRECTLY I PUT PEN TO PAPER, YOU CANNOT REVIEW EVEN A NOVEL WITHOUT HAVING A MIND OF YOUR OWN, WITHOUT EXPRESSING WHAT YOU THINK TO BE THE TRUTH ABOUT HUMAN RELATIONS, MORALITY, SEX.

a certain sum of money—shall we say five hundred pounds a year?—so that it was not necessary for me to depend solely on charm for my living. I turned upon her and caught her by the throat. I did my best to kill her. My excuse, if I were to be had up in a court of law, would be that I acted in self-defense. Had I not killed her she would have killed me. She would have plucked the heart out of my writing. For, as I found, directly I put pen to paper, you cannot review even a novel without having a mind of your own, without expressing what you think to be the truth about human relations, morality, sex. And all these questions, according to the Angel in the House, cannot be dealt with freely and openly by women; they must charm, they must conciliate,[12] they must—to put it bluntly—tell lies if they are to succeed. Thus, whenever I felt the shadow of her wing or the radiance of her halo upon my page, I took up the inkpot and flung it at her. She died hard. Her fictitious nature was of great assistance to her. It is far harder to kill a phantom than a reality. She was always creeping back when I thought I had dis-

patched[13] her. Though I flatter myself that I killed her in the end, the struggle was severe; it took much time that had better have been spent upon learning Greek grammar; or in roaming the world in search of adventures. But it was a real experience; it was an experience that was bound to befall all women writers at that time. Killing the Angel in the House was part of the occupation of a woman writer. But to continue my story. The Angel was dead; what then remained? You may say that what remained was a simple and common object—a young woman in a bedroom with an inkpot. In other words, now that she had rid herself of falsehood, that young woman had only to be herself. Ah, but what is "herself"? I mean, what is a woman? I assure you, I do not know. I do not believe that you know. I do not believe that anybody can know until she has expressed herself in all the arts and professions open to human skill. That indeed is one of the reasons why I have come here—out of respect for you, who are in process of showing us by your experiments what a woman is, who are in process of providing us, by your failures and successes, with that extremely important piece of information.

But to continue the story of my professional experiences. I made one pound ten and six by my first review; and I bought a Persian cat with the proceeds. Then I grew ambitious. A Persian cat is all very well, I said; but a Persian cat is not enough. I must have a motor car. And it was thus that I became a novelist—for it is a very

---

12. **conciliate:** try to gain friendship by pleasant behavior.
13. **dispatched:** put to death.

La reve II [The dream], Balthus. Copyright © 2002 Artists Rights Society (ARS), New York/ ADAGP, Paris.

HUMANITIES CONNECTION The French artist known as Balthus (1908–2001) often used realistic techniques to portray dreamlike subjects. Note the differences in the two faces portrayed here.

strange thing that people will give you a motor car if you will tell them a story. It is a still stranger thing that there is nothing so delightful in the world as telling stories. It is far pleasanter than writing reviews of famous novels. And yet, if I am to obey your secretary and tell you my professional experiences as a novelist, I must tell you about a very strange experience that befell me as a novelist. And to understand it you must try first to imagine a novelist's state of mind. I hope I am not giving away professional secrets if I say that a novelist's chief desire is to be as unconscious as possible. He has to induce in himself a state of <u>perpetual</u> <u>lethargy</u>. He wants life to proceed with the utmost quiet and regularity. He wants to see the same faces, to read the same books, to do the same things day after day, month after month, while he is writing, so that nothing may break the illusion in which he is living—so that nothing may disturb or disquiet the mysterious nosings about, feelings round, darts, dashes and sudden discoveries of that very shy and illusive spirit, the imagination. I suspect that this state is the same both for men and women. Be that as it may, I want you to imagine me writing a novel in a state of trance. I want you to figure to yourselves a girl sitting with a pen in her hand, which for minutes, and indeed for hours, she never dips into the inkpot. The image that comes to my mind when I think of this girl is the image of a fisherman lying sunk in dreams on the verge[14] of a deep lake with a rod held out over the water. She was letting her imagination sweep unchecked round every rock and cranny of the world that lies submerged in the depths of our unconscious being.[15] Now came the experience, the experience that I believe

to be far commoner with women writers than with men. The line raced through the girl's fingers. Her imagination had rushed away. It had sought the pools, the depths, the dark places where the largest fish slumber. And then there was a smash. There was an explosion. There was foam and confusion. The imagination had dashed itself against something hard. The girl was roused from her dream. She was indeed in a state of the most <u>acute</u> and difficult distress. To speak without figure she had thought of some-

> INDEED IT WILL BE A LONG TIME STILL, I THINK, BEFORE A WOMAN CAN SIT DOWN TO WRITE A BOOK WITHOUT FINDING A PHANTOM TO BE slain, A ROCK TO BE DASHED AGAINST.

thing, something about the body, about the passions which it was unfitting for her as a woman to say. Men, her reason told her, would be shocked. The consciousness of what men will say of a woman who speaks the truth about her passions had roused her from her artist's state of unconsciousness. She could write no more. The trance was over. Her imagination could work no longer. This I believe to be a very common experience with women writers—they are impeded by the extreme conventionality[16] of the other sex.

---

14. **verge:** edge.

15. **the depths of our unconscious being:** Woolf is referring to that part of the mind that lies beyond our perception or control.

16. **conventionality:** a strong belief in traditional ways of thought and action.

For though men sensibly allow themselves great freedom in these respects, I doubt that they realize or can control the extreme severity with which they condemn such freedom in women.

These then were two very genuine experiences of my own. These were two of the adventures of my professional life. The first—killing the Angel in the House—I think I solved. She died. But the second, telling the truth about my own experiences as a body, I do not think I solved. I doubt that any woman has solved it yet. The obstacles against her are still immensely powerful—and yet they are very difficult to define. Outwardly, what is simpler than to write books? Outwardly, what obstacles are there for a woman rather than for a man? Inwardly, I think, the case is very different; she has still many ghosts to fight, many prejudices to overcome. Indeed it will be a long time still, I think, before a woman can sit down to write a book without finding a phantom to be slain, a rock to be dashed against. And if this is so in literature, the freest of all professions for women, how is it in the new professions which you are now for the first time entering?

Those are the questions that I should like, had I time, to ask you. And indeed, if I have laid stress upon these professional experiences of mine, it is because I believe that they are, though in different forms, yours also. Even when the path is <u>nominally</u> open—when there is nothing to prevent a woman from being a doctor, a lawyer, a civil servant—there are many phantoms and obstacles, as I believe, looming in her way. To discuss and define them is I think of great value and importance; for thus only can the labor be shared, the difficulties be solved. But besides this, it is necessary also to discuss the ends and the aims for which we are fighting, for which we are doing battle with these formidable obstacles. Those aims cannot be taken for granted; they must be perpetually questioned and examined. The whole position, as I see it—here in this hall surrounded by women practicing for the first time in history I know not how many different professions—is one of extraordinary interest and importance. You have won rooms of your own in the house hitherto exclusively owned by men. You are able, though not without great labor and effort, to pay the rent. You are earning your five hundred pounds a year. But this freedom is only a beginning; the room is your own, but it is still bare. It has to be furnished; it has to be decorated; it has to be shared. How are you going to furnish it, how are you going to decorate it? With whom are you going to share it, and upon what terms? These, I think are questions of the utmost importance and interest. For the first time in history you are able to ask them; for the first time you are able to decide for yourselves what the answers should be. Willingly would I stay and discuss those questions and answers—but not tonight. My time is up; and I must cease. ❖

WORDS TO KNOW

nominally (nŏm′ə-nə-lē) *adv.* apparently (but usually not in reality); seemingly

Thinking through the LITERATURE

Connect to the Literature

1. What Do You Think?
What impression did you form of Virginia Woolf as you were reading? Explain.

Comprehension Check
- Why did Woolf have trouble reviewing a male author's novel?
- What did Woolf have to do to the Angel in the House in order to write?
- Did Woolf feel that she could tell the truth about her "experiences as a body"?

Think Critically

2. What do you think Woolf meant by the phrase "the Angel in the House," and why did this angel have such power?

> THINK ABOUT
> - the personal qualities associated with this angel
> - the expectations that Victorian men had for women
> - how the Angel got in the way of writing

3. Why did Woolf believe that "killing the Angel in the House was part of the occupation of a woman writer"?

4. ACTIVE READING: RECOGNIZING MAIN IDEAS
Review the lists that you recorded in your
READER'S NOTEBOOK. Based on your lists, what do you think are the main ideas in Woolf's speech?

5. According to Woolf, women had to learn more about their possibilities in "the arts and professions" before any woman could truly "be herself." What do you think she meant? Do you agree with her?

6. Why did Woolf believe that she had been unable to tell the complete truth about her experiences?

7. Woolf tells her audience, "You have won rooms of your own in the house hitherto exclusively owned by men. . . . But this freedom is only a beginning. . . ." What remained to be done?

Extend Interpretations

8. Critic's Corner According to feminist critic Jane Marcus, "Writing, for Virginia Woolf, was a revolutionary act. . . . an act of aggression against the powerful." Does "Professions for Women" illustrate Marcus's point? Explain why or why not.

9. Connect to Life Do you think the Angel in the House has been permanently destroyed as an image of women? If so, what image, if any, has replaced it? Explain your opinion.

LITERARY ANALYSIS: DICTION AND AUDIENCE

Diction is a writer's choice of words. Diction can be described by the following sets of terms:
- **formal** (*an attractive sweater*) or **informal** (*an awesome sweater*)
- **technical** (*a 90-degree turn*) or **commonly understood** (*a right turn*)
- **abstract** (*justice*) or **concrete** (*a judge's gown*)
- **literal** (*running clumsily*) or **figurative** (*running like a gazelle on crutches*)

In writing her speech for a group of pathbreaking professional women, Woolf tailored her diction to suit her **audience.**

Cooperative Learning Activity

With a small group of classmates, analyze Woolf's diction. Use a chart like the one below to identify characteristics of her diction. For each pair of terms shown, circle the one that best describes Woolf's diction. Then find two examples—words, phrases, or sentences—to illustrate each term that you have circled.

Characteristics of Diction	Examples
formal / (informal)	*"But to tell you my story—it is a simple one."*
commonly understood/ technical	
abstract / concrete	
literal / figurative	

Writing Options

1. Personal Response Write a personal essay in which you identify Woolf's main ideas and judge whether they are still relevant today. First, make a list of her main ideas and find quotations that support those ideas. Then consider whether women continue to face the obstacles that Woolf identified.

2. Description of Male Ideal What ideal of manhood do men have to struggle with today? Using as a model Woolf's description of the Angel in the House, write a paragraph describing the stereotype of the ideal male. Try to think of an interesting image that captures the essence of the stereotype.

Activities & Explorations

1. Photo Essay Create a photo essay about the roles of women in today's society. Clip photos from magazines or download images from the Internet that show those roles. Find quotations from Woolf's essay to use as captions. ~ **VIEWING AND REPRESENTING**

2. Words of Wisdom Choose a topic that your own experience qualifies you to speak about, such as competing in sports or meeting some other challenge. Then compose and deliver a speech that explains how you dealt with obstacles in your way. ~ **SPEAKING AND LISTENING**

Communication Handbook
See page R50: Giving a Speech.

Inquiry & Research

Time Line of Women's History Research the history of the women's movement in England. Then create an annotated time line of important events, such as the passage of the Married Women's Property Act of 1882, giving a brief description of each event. Also include landmark publications, such as that of John Stuart Mill's *The Subjection of Women* (1869).

RESEARCH STARTER
CLASSZONE.COM

Vocabulary in Action

EXERCISE: CONTEXT CLUES Choose the Word to Know that best completes each sentence.

1. Woolf's father was extremely industrious; he had little patience with _____.

2. With her husband, Leonard, Woolf founded the Hogarth Press, which became a(n) _____ and influential publishing house.

3. Woolf is _____ listed as a translator of some books by Russians, but scholars doubt that she truly knew Russian.

4. After completing each of her novels, Woolf's mental anguish became _____.

5. Woolf doubted her own abilities, not realizing that her greatest books would bring her _____ fame.

WORDS TO KNOW

acute   perpetual
lethargy   reputable
nominally

Building Vocabulary

For an in-depth lesson on context clues, see page 674.

Eveline

JAMES JOYCE

James Joyce
1882–1941

Writer's Writer James Joyce has been called a writer's writer because of the bold originality and artistry of his fiction. According to one critic, Joyce "published nothing but masterpieces."

Son of Ireland Joyce was born to a large family in Dublin, in an Ireland dominated by England and the Roman Catholic Church. His mother was deeply religious, and his father was a talented singer, a reckless drinker, and an indifferent worker. Though the Joyce family gradually sank into poverty, James, the oldest child, received an excellent education. As a young man, he felt stifled by the Catholic Church and the bitter divisions of Irish politics. In 1904 he left Ireland, accompanied by the woman who would become his wife, Nora Barnacle.

Life in Exile Joyce settled in Trieste (a city now in Italy) from 1905 to 1915, teaching English to support Nora and their two children. By all accounts, Joyce's family life was a happy one. His troubles came primarily from publishers who, because of the author's frank treatment of his subjects, were unwilling to print his books for fear of violating censorship laws. Joyce had better luck publishing sections of his first novel, *A Portrait of the Artist as a Young Man,* in the *Egoist* magazine. The novel was later published in book form in 1916.

Critical Success The novel became an immediate critical success. It reveals the innermost thoughts of the young writer Stephen Dedalus, ending with his decision to leave Ireland and dedicate himself to art. The work attracted the attention of the American poet Ezra Pound, who convinced Joyce to move to Paris in 1920. By the time Joyce published his second novel, *Ulysses,* in Paris two years later, it had already become infamous for censorship troubles. The novel chronicles a single day in Dublin in 1904, making bold use of a technique called stream of consciousness, which tries to duplicate the rapid twists and turns of the mind in thought. *Ulysses* has been widely praised as the greatest novel of the 20th century.

Last Years For much of his later life, Joyce suffered from serious eye diseases. He had 25 operations and at times was completely blind. In Paris he had to rely on his increasing number of friends and followers to proofread his work. For 17 years, Joyce worked on his long final novel, *Finnegans Wake,* a complex, experimental, dreamlike work about a Dublin innkeeper and his family.

Build Background

Dubliners

A Break with the Past "Eveline" is one of 15 interrelated stories collected in *Dubliners.* Although the story is one of Joyce's earliest works—it was first published in 1904—it still shows a clear break with the artificial coincidences and surprises of stories by earlier masters, such as the French writer Guy de Maupassant (gē′ də mō-pä-sän′). Very little happens in Joyce's short stories. What matters instead is the richly suggestive portraits of the main characters and the close observation of everyday life.

A "Moral History" of Irish Life In Joyce's view, these stories present a "moral history" of Ireland. Joyce was sharply critical of Irish life because he felt that it restricted the human spirit. He set his stories in Dublin because he considered it "the center of paralysis."

Art as Revelation When Joyce was working on these stories, he called them epiphanies. The word *epiphany* usually refers to an experience of religious revelation. Joyce thought that art, like religion, possessed the power to reveal deep truths. He used the term *epiphany* to describe a sudden insight into the real truth of a situation or character.

Connect to Your Life

"Eveline" tells about a woman in her late teens who considers leaving home. What are some reasons that young adults might have for contemplating such an action?

LITERARY ANALYSIS: INTERNAL CONFLICT

An **internal conflict** is a struggle between opposing forces within a person or a character. In "Professions for Women," Virginia Woolf explains a professional woman's internal conflict between the freedom she wants and the social expectations she feels obligated to fulfill. In "Eveline," the main character undergoes a similar internal struggle as she considers a major decision in her life.

ACTIVE READING: ANALYZING MOTIVATION

Motivation is the reason someone does something—the "why" behind a person's action, thought, or feeling. Since this story is about Eveline, understanding her motivation is key to understanding the entire story.

READER'S NOTEBOOK As you read, make a chart similar to the one below to help you understand Eveline's internal conflict, as well as what motivates her final decision.

Decision to Be Made: _____	
Motivations to Go	**Motivations to Stay**

Eveline

James Joyce

She sat at the window watching the evening invade the avenue. Her head was leaned against the window curtains and in her nostrils was the odor of dusty cretonne.[1] She was tired.

Few people passed. The man out of the last house passed on his way home; she heard his footsteps clacking along the concrete pavement and afterwards crunching on the cinder path before the new red houses. One time there used to be a field there in which they used to play every evening with other people's children. Then a man from Belfast[2] bought the field and built houses in it—not like their little brown houses but bright brick houses with shining roofs. The children of the avenue used to play together in that field—the Devines, the Waters, the Dunns, little Keogh[3] the cripple, she and her brothers and sisters. Ernest, however, never played: he was too grown up. Her father used often to hunt them in out of the field with his blackthorn stick;[4] but usually little Keogh used to keep nix[5] and call out when he saw her father coming. Still they seemed to have been rather happy then. Her father was not so bad then; and besides, her mother was alive. That was a long time ago; she and her brothers and sisters were all grown up; her mother was dead. Tizzie Dunn was dead, too, and the Waters had gone back to England. Everything changes. Now she was going to go away like the others, to leave her home.

Home! She looked round the room, reviewing all its familiar objects which she had dusted once a week for so many years, wondering where on earth all the dust came from. Perhaps she would never see again those familiar objects from which she had never dreamed of being divided. And yet during all those years she had never found out the name of the priest whose yellowing photograph hung on the wall above the broken harmonium[6] beside the colored print of the promises made to Blessed Margaret Mary Alacoque.[7] He had been a school friend of her father. Whenever he showed the photograph to a visitor her father used to pass it with a casual word:

—He is in Melbourne[8] now.

She had consented to go away, to leave her home. Was that wise? She tried to weigh each side of the question. In her home anyway she had shelter and food; she had those whom she had known all her life about her. Of course she had to work hard both in the house and at business. What would they say of her in the Stores when they found out that she had run away with a fellow? Say she was a fool, perhaps, and her place would be filled up by advertisement. Miss Gavan would be glad. She had always had an edge on her, especially whenever there were people listening.

---

1. **cretonne** (krĭ-tŏn'): a heavy, colorfully printed cotton or linen fabric, often used for curtains.
2. **Belfast:** a city in Northern Ireland.
3. **Keogh** (kē'ō).
4. **blackthorn stick:** a walking stick made from the wood of the blackthorn, a type of thorny shrub.
5. **nix:** watch.
6. **harmonium:** an organlike keyboard instrument.
7. **promises made to Blessed Margaret Mary Alacoque** (ä-lä-kôk'): Many Irish Catholic households featured prints showing the Sacred Heart of Jesus and listing the promises made by God to Margaret Mary Alacoque (1647–1690), in which God vowed to honor and bless those who were faithful to the Sacred Heart.
8. **Melbourne:** a city in Australia.

Fishergirl, Newlyn, Alexander Stanhope Forbes. Copyright © Christie's Images.

—Miss Hill, don't you see these ladies are waiting?

—Look lively, Miss Hill, please.

She would not cry many tears at leaving the Stores.

But in her new home, in a distant unknown country, it would not be like that. Then she would be married—she, Eveline. People would treat her with respect then. She would not be treated as her mother had been. Even now, though she was over nineteen, she sometimes felt herself in danger of her father's violence. She knew it was that that had given her the palpitations.[9] When they were growing up he had never gone for her, like he used to go for Harry and Ernest, because she was a girl; but latterly he had begun to threaten her and say what he would do to her only for her dead mother's sake. And now she had nobody to protect her. Ernest was dead and Harry, who was in the church decorating business, was nearly always down somewhere in the country. Besides, the invariable squabble for money on Saturday nights had begun to weary her unspeakably. She always gave her entire wages—seven shillings[10]—and Harry always sent up what he could but the trouble was to get any money from her father. He said she used to squander the money, that she had no head, that he wasn't going to give her his hard-earned money to throw about the streets, and much more, for he was usually fairly bad of a Saturday night. In the end he would give her the money and ask her had she any intention of buying Sunday's dinner. Then she had to rush out as quickly as she could and do her marketing, holding her black leather purse tightly in her hand as she elbowed her way through the crowds and returning home late under her load of provisions. She had hard work to keep the house together and to see that the two young children who had been left to her charge went to school regularly and got their meals regularly. It was hard work—a hard life—but now that she was about to leave it she did not find it a wholly undesirable life.

---

9. **palpitations:** rapid or irregular heartbeats.

10. **seven shillings:** a very small amount of money. Eveline's wages place her at poverty level.

St. Patrick's Close, Dublin, Walter Osborne.
Copyright © The National Gallery of Ireland.

She was about to explore another life with Frank. Frank was very kind, manly, open-hearted. She was to go away with him by the night-boat to be his wife and to live with him in Buenos Ayres[11] where he had a home waiting for her. How well she remembered the first time she had seen him; he was lodging in a house on the main road where she used to visit. It seemed a few weeks ago. He was standing at the gate, his peaked cap pushed back on his head and his hair tumbled forward over a face of bronze. Then they had come to know each other. He used to meet her outside the Stores every evening and see her home. He took her to see *The Bohemian Girl*[12] and she felt elated as she sat in an unaccustomed part of the theater with him. He was awfully fond of music and sang a little. People knew that they were courting and, when he sang about the lass that loves a sailor, she always felt

pleasantly confused. He used to call her Poppens out of fun. First of all it had been an excitement for her to have a fellow and then she had begun to like him. He had tales of distant countries. He had started as a deck boy at a pound a month on a ship of the Allan Line going out to Canada. He told her the names of the ships he had been on and the names of the different services. He had sailed through the Straits of Magellan[13] and he told her stories of the terrible Patagonians.[14] He had fallen on his feet in Buenos Ayres, he said, and had come over to the old country just for a holiday. Of course, her father had found out the affair and had forbidden her to have anything to say to him.

—I know these sailor chaps, he said.

One day he had quarreled with Frank and after that she had to meet her lover secretly.

The evening deepened in the avenue. The white of two letters in her lap grew indistinct. One was to Harry; the other was to her father. Ernest had been her favorite but she liked Harry too. Her father was becoming old lately, she noticed; he would miss her. Sometimes he could be very nice. Not long before, when she had been laid up for a day, he had read her out a ghost story and made toast for her at the fire. Another day, when their mother was alive, they had all gone for a picnic to the Hill of Howth.[15] She remembered her father putting on her mother's bonnet to make the children laugh.

Her time was running out but she continued to sit by the window, leaning her head against the window curtain, inhaling the odor of dusty

11. **Buenos Ayres** (bwā′nəs âr′ēz): a city in Argentina (now spelled Buenos Aires).

12. *The Bohemian Girl:* a popular opera by the Irish composer Michael Balfe.

13. **Straits of Magellan:** a narrow water passage at the southern tip of South America, connecting the Atlantic and Pacific Oceans.

14. **Patagonians** (păt′ə-gō′nē-ənz): native inhabitants of Patagonia, a region in southern South America. They were traditionally thought to be of gigantic stature.

15. **Hill of Howth:** a landmark near Dublin, facing the Bay of Dublin.

cretonne. Down far in the avenue she could hear a street organ playing. She knew the air.[16] Strange that it should come that very night to remind her of the promise to her mother, her promise to keep the home together as long as she could. She remembered the last night of her mother's illness; she was again in the close dark room at the other side of the hall and outside she heard a melancholy air of Italy. The organ-player had been ordered to go away and given sixpence. She remembered her father strutting back into the sickroom saying:

—Damned Italians! coming over here!

As she mused the pitiful vision of her mother's life laid its spell on the very quick[17] of her being—that life of commonplace sacrifices closing in final craziness. She trembled as she heard again her mother's voice saying constantly with foolish insistence:

—Derevaun Seraun![18] Derevaun Seraun!

She stood up in a sudden impulse of terror. Escape! She must escape! Frank would save her. He would give her life, perhaps love, too. But she wanted to live. Why should she be unhappy? She had a right to happiness. Frank would take her in his arms, fold her in his arms. He would save her.

She stood among the swaying crowd in the station at the North Wall.[19] He held her hand and she knew that he was speaking to her, saying something about the passage over and over again. The station was full of soldiers with brown baggages. Through the wide doors of the sheds she caught a glimpse of the black mass of the boat, lying in beside the quay[20] wall, with illumined portholes. She answered nothing. She felt her cheek pale and cold and, out of a maze of distress, she prayed to God to direct her, to show her what was her duty. The boat blew a long mournful whistle into the mist. If she went, tomorrow she would be on the sea with

> *Her time was running out but she continued to sit by the window, leaning her head against the window curtain, inhaling the odor of dusty cretonne.*

Frank, steaming towards Buenos Ayres. Their passage had been booked. Could she still draw back after all he had done for her? Her distress awoke a nausea in her body and she kept moving her lips in silent fervent prayer.

A bell clanged upon her heart. She felt him seize her hand:

—Come!

All the seas of the world tumbled about her heart. He was drawing her into them: he would drown her. She gripped with both hands at the iron railing.

—Come!

No! No! No! It was impossible. Her hands clutched the iron in frenzy. Amid the seas she sent a cry of anguish!

—Eveline! Evvy!

He rushed beyond the barrier and called to her to follow. He was shouted at to go on but he still called to her. She set her white face to him, passive, like a helpless animal. Her eyes gave him no sign of love or farewell or recognition. ❖

---

16. **air:** melody; song.

17. **quick:** the most personal and sensitive part of the emotions.

18. **Derevaun Seraun:** seemingly, a misspoken phrase in Gaelic (the original language of Ireland), sometimes interpreted to mean "The end of pleasure is pain."

19. **North Wall:** a dock on the River Liffey, where passengers could board a "night-boat" to Liverpool, England. Apparently, Frank and Eveline have planned to travel to Liverpool, where they could then board a ship to Argentina.

20. **quay** (kē): a place where ships are loaded and unloaded; wharf.

Connect to the Literature

1. What Do You Think?
What did you think of Eveline by the end of the story?

Comprehension Check
• What decision does Eveline have to make?
• Why is Eveline's life difficult?
• What happens at the end of the story?

Think Critically

2. Why do you think Eveline refuses to go with Frank? Use examples from the story to support your opinion.

3. ACTIVE READING: ANALYZING MOTIVATION Review the chart you made in your 📖 **READER'S NOTEBOOK**. Compare Eveline's reasons for going with her reasons for staying. Do you think she made the right decision? Why or why not?

4. Joyce described his stories as epiphanies, but his readers do not always agree about what is revealed in them. In your opinion, what epiphany, or revelation, takes place at the end of this story?

5. What kind of life can Eveline expect to have now that she has decided to stay in Dublin?

THINK ABOUT
• her mother's life and death
• the way her father treats her
• the kind of job she has

Extend Interpretations

6. What If? What if Eveline had gone with Frank to Buenos Aires? Do you think she could have been happy? Explain your opinion.

7. Critic's Corner Joyce said that he chose Dublin as his setting because it was "the center of paralysis." How might this story illustrate that paralysis?

8. Comparing Texts How do you think Virginia Woolf would explain Eveline's problem? Apply Woolf's analysis of women's problems in "Professions for Women" to Eveline's situation.

9. Connect to Life When making an important decision, such as the one Eveline faced, which is more important to you, ensuring your freedom or fulfilling your responsibilities?

LITERARY ANALYSIS: INTERNAL CONFLICT

The struggle of opposing forces within a character is known as **internal conflict.** In "Eveline," the reader gets to see what's going on in Eveline's mind as she struggles with whether to leave with Frank or stay home.

Cooperative Learning Activity
Working with three classmates, review the story for evidence of what causes Eveline's internal conflict. One person should focus on how Eveline's father contributes to her internal conflict; another person should focus on the role of Eveline's dead mother. A third person should study how Frank influences Eveline's internal conflict, and a fourth person should analyze Eveline's own personality. Discuss your group's findings, then give a summary of the analysis to the rest of the class.

REVIEW: POINT OF VIEW
What is the narrative method, or **point of view,** in this story? Is it told from a **first-person,** a **third-person limited,** or a **third-person omniscient** point of view? What are the advantages of using this point of view in this story?

Writing Options

1. Literary Analysis Write a character sketch of Eveline based on what you know about her and her family life. In your analysis of her situation, explain why she ends up staying in Dublin. Use quotations from the story to support your views. Place your analysis in your **Working Portfolio.**

2. Advice Column What if Eveline had asked for help from an advice columnist? Write the letter that you imagine she would have written, and then answer the letter as you think an advice columnist would.

Activities & Explorations

1. Father-Daughter Dialogue Working with a partner, stage a dialogue between Eveline and her father that reveals not only their individual characters but also the kind of relationship they have. You may write out the dialogue ahead of time or stage an impromptu conversation.
~ SPEAKING AND LISTENING

2. Story Illustration If you had to choose one picture to accompany this story, what would it show? Look through art books to find a work of art that you think best captures the essence of the story. Show your illustration to the class and explain why you chose it.
~ VIEWING AND REPRESENTING

Inquiry & Research

1. Joyce vs. the Publishers Find out why Joyce had so much trouble getting publishers to print *Dubliners.* What did the Irish and British publishers object to? Try looking through the index of a biography of Joyce to narrow your search. Then tell the class what you found out.

2. Eveline's Prospects What prospects did young women in Dublin have at the beginning of the 20th century? What jobs could they get? What were their chances of getting married? What kind of life did single women have? The book *Joyce Annotated* by Don Gifford is a good resource for answering these questions. Report your findings to the class.

THE JAY

yasunari **kawabata**

Yasunari Kawabata
1899–1972

Childhood Losses The Nobel Prize-winning novelist Yasunari Kawabata (yä′sōō-nä′rē kä′wə-bä′tə) knew sadness and loss at an early age. His parents died shortly after his birth in Osaka, Japan. His grandmother, who helped raise him, died when he was seven, and his only sister died two years later. After the death of his grandfather, Kawabata found himself alone in the world at the age of 14. Many scholars have traced the sense of isolation and loneliness evident in much of Kawabata's work to these early childhood losses.

Literary Career By the time Kawabata graduated from Tokyo Imperial University in 1924, he had established a literary career. His first success was the semiautobiographical novel *The Izu Dancer*, about his youthful crush on a dancer. Kawabata's period of greatest creativity began after World War II, with the publication of his best-known novel, *Snow Country,* in 1948. In the 1950s he published two or three major works a year, including his masterpieces, *Thousand Cranes* and *The Sound of the Mountain.*

Traditional Influences Although Kawabata was well versed in modern European literature, his primary influences were Japanese. His choice of images, his use of paradoxical language, and his poetic way of telling a story all have links to traditional Buddhist thought and Japanese literary forms.

A Solitary Life Kawabata accepted his international fame with great humility and grace. Although in his later years he gave public lectures, spoke out on political issues, and actively supported aspiring writers, he always prized his solitude. For most of his life, he lived quietly with his wife in the ancient city of Kamakura, near Yokohama.

Other Works
"Of Birds and Beasts"
Beauty and Sadness
The Master of Go

Build Background

The Japanese Family Traditionally, the family has held an even more important place in Japanese society than in that of the United States. Before World War II, the typical Japanese family was an extended farm family with three or more generations living together. Individual desires often took second place to family responsibilities. Marriages were arranged by parents, and the eldest son customarily brought his wife home to live with his family. A married woman's duty was not only to have children and obey her husband but also to obey her husband's parents and take care of them as they aged. Divorce was possible but rare, and children of divorced parents always stayed with their father.

After Japan's defeat in World War II, many of these extended families broke apart. Postwar Japan's rapid economic growth and urbanization contributed to an increase in smaller families consisting only of married couples and their children. By 1955, extended families made up only 44 percent of all households. In addition, the new Japanese constitution gave women rights equal to men's for the first time in Japanese history.

Kawabata's "The Jay," published in 1949, does not explicitly deal with the changes in postwar Japanese society, but it illustrates their effects in a very personal way. The story gives us a close look at a family that has been broken apart by divorce and remarriage. It also shows the difficulty individual family members have in dealing with these changes.

Connect to Your Life

Consider how much you would be willing to give up for the sake of your family. For example, would you give up your boyfriend or girlfriend if your parents didn't approve? How about giving up your free afternoons to care for a younger sibling or an elderly grandparent? Discuss these questions with your classmates.

Focus Your Reading

LITERARY ANALYSIS: SYMBOL

A **symbol** is a person, place, or thing that stands for something beyond itself. For example, a trophy might stand for a particular victory or for a person's success in general. In "The Jay," the author uses a mother jay and her chick as symbols. As you read, think about how the jays are related to people and events in the story.

ACTIVE READING: CLARIFYING SEQUENCE

The events that have occurred in Yoshiko's family and the relationships between its various members may seem confusing at times. It will help your understanding of the story to have a clear picture of the family's history.

READER'S NOTEBOOK

As you read, create a chronology like the one started at the right, showing the key events in the life of the family.

Yoshiko's Family Chronology

1. Yoshiko's mother and father divorce.

2. Yoshiko and her younger brother live with their father.

3.

4.

5.

The Jay

Yasunari Kawabata

Translated by Lane Dunlop

Since daybreak, the jay had been singing noisily. When they'd slid open the rain shutters, it had flown up before their eyes from a lower branch of the pine, but it seemed to have come back. During breakfast, there was the sound of whirring wings.

"That bird's a nuisance." The younger brother started to get to his feet.

"It's all right. It's all right." The grandmother stopped him. "It's looking for its child. Apparently the chick fell out of the nest yesterday. It was flying around until late in the evening. Doesn't she know where it is? But what a good mother. This morning she came right back to look."

"Grandmother understands well," Yoshiko[1] said.

Her grandmother's eyes were bad. Aside from a bout with nephritis[2] about ten years ago, she had never been ill in her life. But, because of her cataracts,[3] which she'd had since girlhood, she could only see dimly out of her left eye. One had to hand her the rice bowl and the chopsticks. Although she could grope her way around the familiar interior of the house, she could not go into the garden by herself.

Sometimes, standing or sitting in front of the sliding-glass door, she would spread out her hands, fanning out her fingers against the sunlight that came through the glass, and gaze out. She was concentrating all the life that was left to her into that many-angled gaze.

At such times, Yoshiko was frightened by her grandmother. Though she wanted to call out to her from behind, she would furtively steal away.

This nearly blind grandmother, simply from having heard the jay's voice, spoke as if she had seen everything. Yoshiko was filled with wonder.

When, clearing away the breakfast things, Yoshiko went into the kitchen, the jay was singing from the roof of the neighbor's house.

In the back garden, there was a chestnut tree and two or three persimmon trees. When she looked at the trees, she saw that a light rain was falling. It was the sort of rain that you could not tell was falling unless you saw it against the dense foliage.

The jay, shifting its perch to the chestnut tree, then flying low and skimming the ground, returned again to its branch, singing all the while.

The mother bird could not fly away. Was it because her chick was somewhere around there?

Worrying about it, Yoshiko went to her room. She had to get herself ready before the morning was over.

In the afternoon, her father and mother were coming with the mother of Yoshiko's fiancé.

Sitting at her mirror, Yoshiko glanced at the white stars under her fingernails. It was said that, when stars came out under your nails, it was a sign that you would receive something, but Yoshiko remembered having read in the newspaper that it meant a deficiency of vitamin C or

---

1. **Yoshiko** (yō′shē-kō′).
2. **nephritis** (nə-frī′tĭs): an inflammation of the kidneys.
3. **cataracts:** cloudiness in the lenses of the eyes, causing impairment of vision.

something. The job of putting on her makeup went fairly pleasantly. Her eyebrows and lips all became unbearably winsome.[4] Her kimono,[5] too, went on easily.

She'd thought of waiting for her mother to come and help with her clothes, but it was better to dress by herself, she decided.

Her father lived away from them. This was her second mother.

When her father had divorced her first mother, Yoshiko had been four and her younger brother two. The reasons given for the divorce were that her mother went around dressed in flashy clothes and spent money wildly, but Yoshiko sensed

dimly that it was more than that, that the real cause lay deeper down.

Her brother, as a child, had come across a photograph of their mother and shown it to their father. The father hadn't said anything but, with a face of terrible anger, had suddenly torn the photograph to bits.

When Yoshiko was thirteen, she had welcomed the new mother to the house. Later, Yoshiko had come to think that her father had endured his loneliness for ten years for her sake.

---

4. **winsome** (wĭn′səm): charming (often in a childlike way).

5. **kimono** (kə-mō′nə): a long, wide-sleeved robe, worn with a sash.

The second mother was a good person. A peaceful home life continued.

When the younger brother, entering upper school, began living away from home in a dormitory, his attitude toward his stepmother changed noticeably.

"Elder sister, I've met our mother. She's married and lives in Azabu.[6] She's really beautiful. She was happy to see me."

Hearing this suddenly, Yoshiko could not say a word. Her face paled, and she began to tremble.

From the next room, her stepmother came in and sat down.

"It's a good thing, a good thing. It's not bad to meet your own mother. It's only natural. I've known for some time that this day would come. I don't think anything particular of it."

But the strength seemed to have gone out of her stepmother's body. To Yoshiko, her <u>emaciated</u> stepmother seemed pathetically frail and small.

Her brother abruptly got up and left. Yoshiko felt like smacking him.

"Yoshiko, don't say anything to him. Speaking to him will only make that boy go bad." Her stepmother spoke in a low voice.

Tears came to Yoshiko's eyes.

Her father summoned her brother back home from the dormitory. Although Yoshiko had thought that would settle the matter, her father had then gone off to live elsewhere with her stepmother.

It had frightened Yoshiko. It was as if she had been crushed by the power of masculine indignation and resentment. Did their father dislike even them because of their tie to their first mother? It seemed to her that her brother, who'd gotten to his feet so abruptly, had inherited the frightening male <u>intransigence</u> of his father.

And yet it also seemed to Yoshiko that she could now understand her father's sadness and pain during those ten years between his divorce and remarriage.

And so, when her father, who had moved away from her, came back bringing a marriage proposal, Yoshiko had been surprised.

"I've caused you a great deal of trouble. I told the young man's mother that you're a girl with these circumstances and that, rather than treating you like a bride, she should try to bring back the happy days of your childhood."

When her father said this kind of thing to her, Yoshiko wept.

If Yoshiko married, there would be no woman's hand to take care of her brother and grandmother. It had been decided that the two households would become one. With that, Yoshiko had made up her mind. She had dreaded marriage on her father's account, but, when it came down to the actual talks, it was not that dreadful after all.

When her preparations were completed, Yoshiko went to her grandmother's room.

"Grandmother, can you see the red in this kimono?"[7]

"I can faintly make out some red over there. Which is it, now?" Pulling Yoshiko to her, the grandmother put her eyes close to the kimono and the sash.

"I've already forgotten your face, Yoshiko. I wish I could see what you look like now."

Yoshiko <u>stifled</u> a desire to giggle. She rested her hand lightly on her grandmother's head.

Wanting to go out and meet her father and the others, Yoshiko was unable just to sit there,

---

6. **Azabu** (ä′zä-bōō′): an area of Tokyo.

7. **the red in this kimono:** Red, a traditional color of happiness in Japan, is often included in wedding attire.

WORDS TO KNOW

emaciated (ĭ-mā′shē-ā′tĭd) *adj.* unnaturally thin **emaciate** *v.*

intransigence (ĭn-trăn′sĭ-jəns) *n.* a condition of being stubborn and uncompromising

1178 **stifle** (stī′fəl) *v.* to hold back; repress

IF Yoshiko married, there would be no woman's hand to take care of her brother and grandmother. It had been decided that the two households would become one.

vaguely waiting. She went out into the garden. She held out her hand, palm upward, but the rain was so fine that it didn't wet the palm. Gathering up the skirts of her kimono, Yoshiko <u>assiduously</u> searched among the little trees and in the bear-grass bamboo thicket. And there, in the tall grass under the bush clover, was the baby bird.

Her heart beating fast, Yoshiko crept nearer. The baby jay, drawing its head into its neck feathers, did not stir. It was easy to take it up into her hand. It seemed to have lost its energy. Yoshiko looked around her, but the mother bird was nowhere in sight.

Running into the house, Yoshiko called out, "Grandmother! I've found the baby bird. I have it in my hand. It's very weak."

"Oh, is that so? Try giving it some water."

Her grandmother was calm.

When she ladled some water into a rice bowl and dipped the baby jay's beak in it, it drank, its little throat swelling out in an appealing way. Then—had it recovered?—it sang out, "Ki-ki-ki, Ki-ki-ki . . ."

The mother bird, evidently hearing its cry, came flying. Perching on the telephone wire, it sang. The baby bird, struggling in Yoshiko's hand, sang out again, "Ki-ki-ki . . ."

"Ah, how good that she came! Give it back to its mother, quick," her grandmother said.

Yoshiko went back out into the garden. The mother bird flew up from the telephone wire but kept her distance, looking fixedly toward Yoshiko from the top of a cherry tree.

As if to show her the baby jay in her palm, Yoshiko raised her hand, then quietly placed the chick on the ground.

As Yoshiko watched from behind the glass door, the mother bird, guided by the voice of its child singing plaintively and looking up at the sky, gradually came closer. When she'd come down to the low branch of a nearby pine, the chick flapped its wings, trying to fly up to her. Stumbling forward in its efforts, falling all over itself, it kept singing.

Still the mother bird cautiously held off from hopping down to the ground.

Soon, however, it flew in a straight line to the side of its child. The chick's joy was <u>boundless</u>. Turning and turning its head, its outspread wings trembling, it made up to its mother. Evidently the mother had brought it something to eat.

Yoshiko wished that her father and stepmother would come soon. She would like to show them this, she thought. ❖

WORDS TO KNOW
assiduously (ə-sĭj′ōō-əs-lē) *adv.* diligently
boundless (bound′lĭs) *adj.* without limits; infinite

Thinking through the LITERATURE

Connect to the Literature

1. What Do You Think?
How did you feel about Yoshiko as you read this story? Did your feelings change? Give reasons for your responses.

Comprehension Check
- Why is Yoshiko's mother not living with the family?
- What big change is about to occur in Yoshiko's life?
- What happens to the jay chick at the end of the story?

Think Critically

2. ACTIVE READING: CLARIFYING SEQUENCE Get together with a small group of classmates and compare the chronologies they wrote with the one in your own ▌READER'S NOTEBOOK. Make revisions as needed. Then discuss the question, How do these events affect relationships within the family?

3. Why is Yoshiko closer to her grandmother than to any other member of the family?

4. Why is Yoshiko overcome with emotion when she learns that her father has asked her future mother-in-law to "try to bring back the happy days" of Yoshiko's childhood?

> THINK ABOUT
> - how Yoshiko feels about her parents' divorce and the loss of her mother
> - why Yoshiko doesn't visit her mother, as her brother did
> - how Yoshiko reacts when her father moves away from her

5. At the end of the story, why does Yoshiko want to show her father and stepmother the mother jay reunited with her chick?

Extend Interpretations

6. What If? How might the story have been different if Yoshiko, like her brother, had gone to visit their mother?

7. Connect to Life Arranged marriages are uncommon in our society, but they still occur, particularly in ethnic groups where the custom has a long tradition. What might be some advantages and disadvantages of this way of obtaining a spouse?

LITERARY ANALYSIS: SYMBOL

A **symbol** is a person, place, or thing that stands for something beyond itself. In literature, symbols often communicate complicated, emotionally rich ideas more effectively than direct language. In "The Jay," for example, the mother jay looking for her lost chick helps the reader to understand and respond to Yoshiko's situation of being separated from her mother.

Cooperative Learning Activity
With a group of classmates, brainstorm various ways the jay and her chick are related to the story of Yoshiko and her family. Then discuss this question: What ideas and feelings does Kawabata convey to the reader through the symbol of the jays? Use a chart like the one shown to record your thoughts.

How Jays Are Related to Story	Ideas Communicated	Feelings Communicated

REVIEW: MOOD
A **mood** is a feeling or atmosphere that a writer conveys in a story. How would you describe the mood of Kawabata's story?

1180   UNIT SEVEN   PART 1: EXPRESSIONS OF MODERNISM

Choices & CHALLENGES

Writing Options

1. Character Analysis
Consider the thoughts, feelings, and actions of Yoshiko in "The Jay," and write an essay analyzing her character. Begin by describing your first impressions of Yoshiko. Then explain her inner qualities and the way they are revealed in the story. Conclude by making a general statement about what kind of person you think Yoshiko is. Place your character analysis in your **Working Portfolio**. 📁

2. Problem-Solution Essay
Yoshiko believes that her relationships with her father and brother are made more difficult by "male intransigence." What do you see as the biggest obstacle to good communication between men and women? Why does this obstacle exist? What problems does it create? What can be done to overcome it? Answer these questions in a short essay.

Writing Handbook
See page R33: Problem-Solution.

Activities & Explorations

1. Family Tree
Because of her parents' divorce and her own forthcoming marriage, Yoshiko will end up with a large and complex family. A family group that includes members other than a married couple and their children is often called an extended family. Investigate some extended families that you are familiar with, and create a poster-board presentation showing a few of the many combinations of people that can make up such groups. ~ **VIEWING AND REPRESENTING**

2. Reunion Dialogue
Imagine that Yoshiko and her mother are reunited. With a classmate, brainstorm the dialogue that might take place between them. Then perform your dialogue for the class. Be ready to explain why you think Yoshiko and her mother might interact in the way you have presented. ~ **SPEAKING AND LISTENING**

Inquiry & Research

Multimedia Display: The Japanese Family Find out more about how the Japanese family has changed since World War II and what it is like today. Use reference books, magazine or newspaper articles, literary works, and the Internet to find words and images that document these changes. Present your findings in the form of a multimedia display.

Communication Handbook
See page R54: Making Multimedia Presentations.

Vocabulary in Action

EXERCISE: CONTEXT CLUES On your paper, write the Word to Know that best completes each sentence.

1. Yoshiko's stepmother doesn't want to _____ her brother's desire to get to know his biological mother.

2. Yoshiko is glad to see that the baby jay has not been separated from its mother long enough to become _____.

3. The mother jay searches _____ for her chick until at last she finds it.

4. Yoshiko hopes that her father might someday forgive her mother, but she does not reckon with his _____.

5. Yoshiko feels _____ happiness when she learns that her brother and grandmother can live with her after her marriage.

WORDS TO KNOW

assiduously   emaciated   stifle
boundless   intransigence

Building Vocabulary
For an in-depth lesson on context clues, see page 674.

POEMS BY

LÉOPOLD SÉDAR SENGHOR

**Léopold Sédar
Senghor**
1906–2001

The Kingdom of Childhood

Léopold Sédar Senghor (lā-ô-pôl′ sā-där′ sän-gôr′) was born in a coastal village in French West Africa (now Senegal). As a child, he listened to folk tales and to songs of the local griots, or storytellers. He also took part in the traditions of his people, including seasonal rites and dances and visits to holy sites. Later, Senghor referred to this happy time as "the kingdom of my childhood." When Senghor was seven, his father sent him to a missionary school run by French priests. So began the Western education that eventually drew him out of Africa to Paris.

Between Two Cultures Senghor began studying in Paris in 1928 and eventually became the first black African to receive France's highest teaching certification. During his student days, he met black students from other French colonies and learned about the awakening of black awareness, both in the United States and in France. Yet, despite France's official policy of racial tolerance, he felt he was not accepted as an equal by most white Europeans.

Senghor taught at prep schools in France until he was drafted at the beginning of World War II. Although he fought bravely for France, the experience of war and his imprisonment in several German concentration camps increased his feeling of displacement.

African Identity When Senghor had begun to write poetry in the prewar years, his imagination had returned to the "kingdom" of his childhood for inspiration and subject matter. By the time his first book of poems, *Chants d'ombre* [Songs of shadow], was published in 1945, Senghor's sense of himself as an African had become fully developed.

Mr. President Senghor eventually gave up teaching to be the political leader of his people. After the war, he represented Senegal in the French government and helped draft a new constitution that gave more power to the colonies. When Senegal gained independence in 1960, Senghor served as its first president. He won reelection four times before retiring in 1980.

For a humanities activity, click on:

HUMANITIES
CLASSZONE.COM

Build Background

The Negritude Movement Léopold Senghor's writing reflects a philosophy called Negritude that Senghor developed with writers Aimé Césaire (ä-mä' sä-zâr') of Martinique and Léon Damas (lä-ôn' dä-mä') of French Guiana during their student days in Paris in the 1930s. Césaire coined the French term *negritude,* which literally means "blackness," to designate the investigation by French-speaking black intellectuals of their African heritage, culture, and identity. The Negritude movement sought to embrace a common African heritage, to promote African cultures and values in literature and art, and to assert the dignity and freedom of all people of African descent. Negritude writers were influenced by writers of the Harlem Renaissance in the United States, especially Langston Hughes and Claude McKay.

"And We Shall Be Steeped" In this poem, the speaker imagines a setting that is completely African, from the furniture in the room to the singing heard in the distance. To enhance this setting, Senghor specified that a recitation of the poem be accompanied by music played on a *khalam,* an African guitar often used in oral performance.

"Prayer to Masks" In African culture, masks have religious significance and are considered sacred. They may even possess supernatural powers. In this poem, the masks represent the spirits of ancestors, which can take an active role in contemporary life.

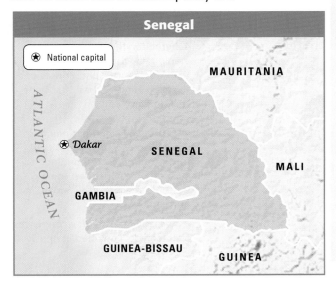

Senegal

★ National capital

MAURITANIA

ATLANTIC OCEAN

★ Dakar

SENEGAL

MALI

GAMBIA

GUINEA-BISSAU

GUINEA

Connect to Your Life

What associations or images come to mind when you hear the word *Africa*? Do you think of wild animals, ancient traditions, modern politics, or something else? Compare your responses with those of your classmates.

Focus Your Reading

LITERARY ANALYSIS: DENOTATION AND CONNOTATION

Poets choose their words with great care, paying close attention to what is suggested by each word. The **connotation** of a word is the set of associations, images, or feelings that the word conjures up. By contrast, the **denotation** of a word is its literal meaning, a definition you would find in the dictionary. For example, a denotative meaning of *Africa* is "the second-largest continent." However, as revealed in the Connect to Your Life activity above, the word *Africa* is also rich in connotative meanings. As you read these two poems, pay attention to the connotations as well as the denotations of particular words and phrases.

ACTIVE READING: PARAPHRASING

One strategy that can help you understand a poem more fully is paraphrasing. This means that you restate parts or all of the poem in your own words. When you paraphrase, you will often need to use more words than the poet uses.

📖 **READER'S NOTEBOOK** As you read each poem, identify lines that seem particularly significant or whose meaning is not completely clear to you. Try paraphrasing those lines, and record your results in a chart like the one shown.

Line	Paraphrase
And we shall be steeped my dear in the presence of Africa.	We will be surrounded by things that remind us of Africa and give us a strong feeling of its presence.

And we shall be steeped . . .

Léopold Sédar Senghor

Translated by John Reed and Clive Wake

Mask (20th century), Zaire-Angola. Wood, 9″ (22.8 cm). From Zaire River coastal region.

And we shall be steeped my dear in the presence
   of Africa.
Furniture from Guinea and Congo, heavy and
   polished, somber and serene.
On the walls, pure primordial masks distant and
   yet present.
Stools of honor for hereditary guests, for the
   Princes of the High Lands.
5 Wild perfumes, thick mats of silence
Cushions of shade and leisure, the noise of a
   wellspring of peace.
Classic words. In a distance, antiphonal singing like
   Soudanese cloths
And then, friendly lamp, your kindness to soothe
   this obsessive presence
White black and red, oh red as the African soil.

2 Guinea and Congo: countries in western Africa.

4 hereditary guests: people who would be welcome because of their noble birthright; **Princes of the High Lands:** rulers of ancient African empires.

7 antiphonal singing: singing in which two or more groups take turns singing or "responding" to each other; **Soudanese:** coming from the region of the Sudan, in northern Africa.

8 obsessive presence: a reference to the masks described in line 3.

Prayer to Masks

Léopold Sédar Senghor

Translated by Gerald Moore and Ulli Beier

Black mask, red mask, you black and white masks,
Rectangular masks through whom the spirit breathes,
I greet you in silence!
And you too, my lionheaded ancestor
5   You guard this place, that is closed to any feminine
    laughter, to any mortal smile.
You purify the air of eternity, here where I breathe the
    air of my fathers.
Masks of markless faces, free from dimples and wrinkles,
You have composed this image, this my face that bends
    over the altar of white paper.
In the name of your image, listen to me!
10   Now while the Africa of despotism is dying—it is the
    agony of a pitiable princess
Like that of Europe to whom she is connected through
    the navel—
Now fix your immobile eyes upon your children who
    have been called
And who sacrifice their lives like the poor man his last
    garment
So that hereafter we may cry "here" at the rebirth of the
    world being the leaven that the white flour needs.
15   For who else would teach rhythm to the world that has
    died of machines and cannons?
For who else should ejaculate the cry of joy, that arouses
    the dead and the wise in a new dawn?
Say, who else could return the memory of life to men
    with a torn hope?
They call us cotton heads, and coffee men, and
    oily men,
They call us men of death.
20   But we are the men of the dance whose feet only gain
    power when they beat the hard soil.

4 lionheaded: having a lion as a totem, or guardian, animal.

9 your image: the speaker himself, who carries on the traditions and values of his ancestors.

10 despotism: government rule based on tyranny or oppression.

12 immobile: unmoving.

14 leaven: a substance, like yeast, that causes bread dough to rise.

Thinking through the LITERATURE

Connect to the Literature

1. What Do You Think? What impressions of Africa and African culture do you get from these two poems?

Think Critically

2. ACTIVE READING: PARAPHRASING Review the paraphrases that you recorded in your READER'S NOTEBOOK. With a group of classmates, put together a paraphrase of each poem in its entirety. Discuss any lines that still seem unclear.

3. What mental picture do you form of the scene described by the speaker in "And We Shall Be Steeped"? What feelings about African culture are suggested by that picture?

4. In lines 1–14 of "Prayer to Masks," the speaker addresses the masks and asks for their help. What kind of help do you think the speaker wants from the masks?

5. In lines 10–12 of "Prayer to Masks," the speaker refers to the decline of European power in Africa, the "dying" of "the Africa of despotism." How do you think the speaker feels about the effects of colonialism on Africa? Support your opinion.

6. Reread lines 15–20 of "Prayer to Masks." How would you describe the speaker's vision of Africa's role in the future?

> THINK ABOUT
> - why Africans are "the leaven that the white flour needs"
> - what Africans can teach the rest of the world
> - why some people don't appreciate Africans (lines 18–19)

Extend Interpretations

7. Critic's Corner According to one scholar, Senghor's preferred English equivalent of the term *negritude* was "black personality." On the basis of these two poems, how would you describe that personality?

8. Connect to Life Think of a culture, either your own or one you admire, that you'd like to be "steeped in." How would you experience the "presence" of this culture, and what effect would it have on you?

LITERARY ANALYSIS: DENOTATION AND CONNOTATION

The literal, dictionary definition of a word is its **denotation.** A word may also have one or more **connotations**—particular associations, images, or feelings the word calls to mind. Connotations often make an important contribution to the meaning of a poem. The connotations of the words and phrases Senghor chose for his descriptions of African culture in the two poems convey his attitude toward and feelings about the culture.

Cooperative Learning Activity
With a group of classmates, identify in the poems particular words and phrases that have strong or important connotations, and record these words and phrases in a list. Then use the list to create a word portrait of Africa like the one started here.

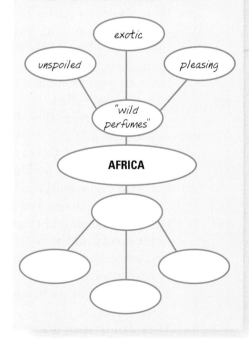

Appreciating Cultural Roots

As you have seen, the African heritage of Léopold Sédar Senghor influenced his development as a writer. When Senghor was a student in Senegal, however, his heritage was not appreciated by his teachers, who were Europeans. He recalled one teacher in particular "who told me we were savages, that we had no traditions, no civilization." According to Senghor, that incident established his direction in life: "All this made me want to defend the civilization [my teacher] was denying us, made me want to demonstrate and illustrate it."

Diversity in U.S. Schools Most classrooms in the United States today have a very different atmosphere than the one experienced by Senghor. Yet, it is no easy task for students in schools with an increasingly diverse student body to appreciate one another's culture.

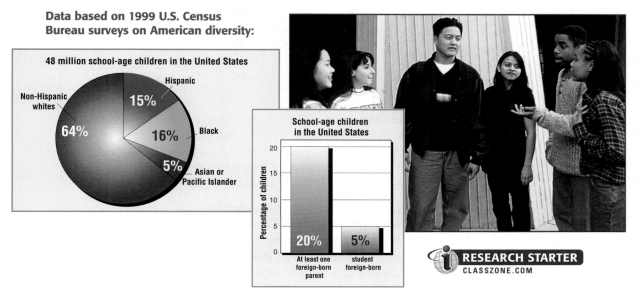

Data based on 1999 U.S. Census Bureau surveys on American diversity:

48 million school-age children in the United States

Hispanic 15%
Non-Hispanic whites 64%
Black 16%
Asian or Pacific Islander 5%

School-age children in the United States

Percentage of children

At least one foreign-born parent 20%
student foreign-born 5%

RESEARCH STARTER
CLASSZONE.COM

Research Project

To increase your appreciation of cultural diversity, choose one of the following projects. You can work either independently or in a small group.

- Create a statistical profile of students in your class. You may use the Census Bureau categories (see diagrams) or create your own categories to reflect the cultural, ethnic, and racial backgrounds of students. You may also investigate languages besides English that are spoken in students' homes. After you gather your statistics, prepare and then present an oral report on your findings, with visuals or handouts to communicate the statistics.

- Find out more about a culture that you are not familiar with that is represented in your school. Use reference works to learn more about that culture, including its art, customs, and traditions. Interview students or other people who are members of that culture. Report your findings orally or in a multimedia presentation.

TIME

GABRIELA MISTRAL   TRANSLATED BY **DORIS DANA**

Gabriela Mistral
1889–1957

Nobel Laureate A beloved Spanish-language poet, Gabriela Mistral (gä-brē-ĕ′lä mē-sträl′) became, in 1945, the first Latin American woman to win the Nobel Prize in literature. Mistral was born Lucila Godoy Alcayaga in a village in northern Chile. When she became a poet, she crafted a pseudonym from the names of her two favorite poets.

Multiple Careers Mistral combined her life as a poet with successful careers as a teacher, cultural minister, and diplomat. She became a teacher at the age of 15, advanced to the position of school principal, and eventually became a college professor. As a principal, she encouraged the poetic dreams of a shy but gifted boy who went on to publish his poems under the pseudonym Pablo Neruda and to win, in 1971, the Nobel Prize for literature.

Tragic Love Mistral's poetry is known for its emotional intensity and expression of tenderness for the weak and downtrodden. One of her early poems, "Dolor," describes the tragic suicide of a young man whom she deeply loved. This devastating loss may explain why Mistral never married. Many of her poems convey a love of children and a maternal longing that remained unsatisfied.

In this poem, Mistral describes the cycle of the day, from sunrise to nightfall. As you read, notice the emotions associated with each phase of the day. Form your own impression of the speaker—of her personality and her values.

DAYBREAK

My heart swells that the Universe
like a fiery cascade[1] may enter.
The new day comes. Its coming
leaves me breathless.
5 I sing. Like a cavern brimming
I sing my new day.

For grace[2] lost and recovered
I stand humble. Not giving. Receiving.
Until the Gorgon[3] night,
10 vanquished, flees.

MORNING

She has returned! She has returned!
Each morning the same and new.
Awaited every yesterday,
she must return this morning.

15 Mornings of empty hands
that promised and betrayed.
Behold this new morning unfold,
leap like a deer from the East,
awake, happy and new,
20 alert, eager and rich with deeds.

Brother, raise up your head
fallen to your breast. Receive her.
Be worthy of her who leaps up,
soars and darts like a halcyon,[4]
25 golden halcyon plunging earthward
    singing
Alleluia,[5] alleluia, alleluia!

AFTERNOON

I feel my heart melt like wax
in this sweetness:
slow oil, not wine,
30 my veins,
I feel my life fleeting
silent and sweet as a gazelle.[6]

NIGHT

Mountain ranges dissolve,
cattle wander astray,
35 the sun returns to its forge,[7]
all the world slips away.

Orchard and garden are fading,
the farmhouse already immersed.
My mountains submerge their crests
40 and their living cry.

All creatures are sliding aslant
down toward forgetfulness and sleep.
You and I, also, my baby,
tumble down toward night's keep.

---

1. **cascade:** waterfall (or something in the shape of a
   waterfall).
2. **grace:** love and mercy shown toward a person without
   that person's having earned or deserved it.
3. **Gorgon:** a mythological creature, with snakes for hair,
   who turned into stone anyone who looked into her eyes.
4. **halcyon** (hăl′sē-ən): bird that, according to legend, nested
   on the sea and calmed the water.
5. **alleluia** (ăl′ə-lōō′yə): an exclamation of praise for God.
6. **gazelle:** a small antelope of Africa and Asia.
7. **forge:** blacksmith's furnace.

Writing Workshop

Literary Interpretation

Making sense of it all . . .

From Reading to Writing Stories like Franz Kafka's "Metamorphosis" or James Joyce's "Eveline" and poems like Federico García Lorca's "The Guitar" may leave you a little confused and wondering what to think. One way to explore a puzzling piece of literature is by writing a **literary interpretation** in which you analyze the elements that contribute to the work's meaning.

For Your Portfolio

WRITING PROMPT Write an interpretive essay about a work of literature, in which you explore the work's meaning.

> **Purpose:** To explain your interpretation of the work
> **Audience:** Your teacher and classmates, others who are familiar with the work

Basics in a Box

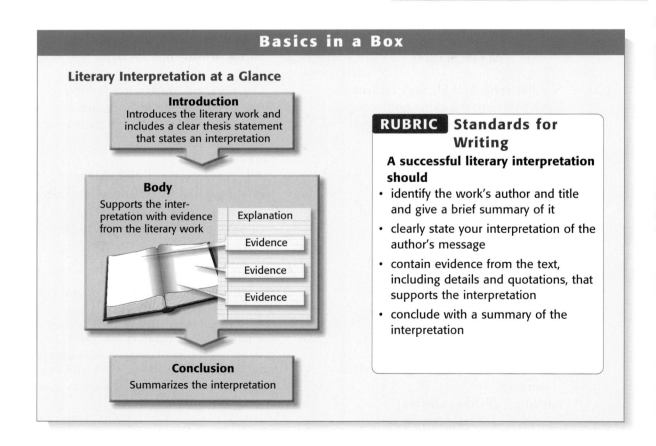

Literary Interpretation at a Glance

Introduction
Introduces the literary work and includes a clear thesis statement that states an interpretation

Body
Supports the interpretation with evidence from the literary work

Explanation

Evidence

Evidence

Evidence

Conclusion
Summarizes the interpretation

RUBRIC **Standards for Writing**

A successful literary interpretation should

- identify the work's author and title and give a brief summary of it
- clearly state your interpretation of the author's message
- contain evidence from the text, including details and quotations, that supports the interpretation
- conclude with a summary of the interpretation

Analyzing Student Models

Hannah Barker
Evanston Township
High School

LANGUAGE SKILLS

Futility and Indecision in James Joyce's "Eveline"

In his short story "Eveline," James Joyce tells a story of deep and paralyzing indecision. Eveline, a poor Irish girl, must make a choice. Should she follow her boyfriend, Frank, to Argentina, where they will be married and live a life of adventure? Or should she stay in Ireland and care for her family, as she promised her dying mother? She is torn; at the last moment she finds herself unable to act or decide, and the ship sails without her. Ultimately, Eveline's inability to decide determines her fate, keeping her at home in familiar, if bleak, surroundings. Upon first reading, it may seem that she has made a mistake—that she lets Frank go simply because she is afraid of change. However, a closer look at the story shows that Eveline's decision is far from simple. No matter what path she chooses, she'll be making a great sacrifice.

Certainly, her life in Ireland is miserable. She is only a little over 19, but she already has responsibility for running the household. Since her mother and her brother Ernest are dead and her brother Harry is away working, she receives little help in caring for the family. Eveline holds a job in a shop, under an unpleasant boss, but also takes responsibility for shopping, housekeeping, cooking, raising two young children, and caring for her elderly father. Her father is a curmudgeon who used to beat her brothers and now threatens to abuse her as well. He collects all of her wages and argues with her about how much she can spend on food for the family. Between work and family, Eveline lives a life of grinding struggle and boredom. If this were a fairy tale, she would be Cinderella. The reader feels sorry for Eveline and is relieved to think that she might find happiness with Frank, her Prince Charming.

Frank is a sailor and not a prince, but he does promise to rescue Eveline from her dreary existence. He takes her to the opera, walks her home from work, sings to her, and tells her stories about foreign countries and his exploits at sea. She enjoys it: "People knew that they were courting and, when he sang about the lass that loves a sailor, she always felt pleasantly confused." Instead of abandoning her when his vacation in Ireland is over, Frank offers to take her back to Buenos Aires and marry her. Eveline dreams of her new life in Buenos Aires. There, she imagines, she will find love, respect, and adventure, escaping the drudgery and unhappiness that she saw in her mother's life, which was a "life of commonplace sacrifices closing in final craziness." Frank is her best hope of escaping her mother's dismal fate.

❶ In the introduction, identifies the work's author and title and provides a brief summary of it

❷ Presents the thesis statement

❸ Describes the difficulty of Eveline's life, providing supporting details from the story

❹ Discusses the lure of life with Frank

However, as her departure draws near, Eveline begins to have second thoughts: "It was hard work—a hard life—but now that she was about to leave it she did not find it a wholly undesirable life." She calls up a few pleasant memories of her childhood, before her mother died and her friends moved away. She feels attached to her surroundings. Even her father is not entirely a burden; every now and then he can be sweet to her. Although many aspects of her daily life are grim, there is some comfort in being at home. After all, she's never known anything else.

And comfort or no, Eveline feels a tremendous obligation to support her family. As her mother lay dying, Eveline promised "to keep the home together as long as she could." In addition to caring for her father, she is raising two young children. If not for her, who would raise them? Her drunken father or absent brother? There is no one else who is responsible enough to run the household. Despite her terror at the thought of living a life of drudgery and dying insane like her mother, Eveline still feels bound by her familial duty, which is no small thing. Can she really desert her family, dishonor her dearly-departed mother, and leave behind the only home she's ever known? All this in pursuit of life abroad with a sailor, a man she hardly knows?

❺ Shows her strong and legitimate ties to home

At first it seems that she will. Eveline goes to the boat to meet Frank, prepared to make a new life for herself. However, she thinks twice before actually stepping on board. What seemed like a sea of opportunities has become a sea of uncertainty that threatens to overwhelm her: "All the seas of the world tumbled about her heart. He was drawing her into them: he would drown her." Eveline is paralyzed with fear. Unable to decide, she does not decide. She stands rooted to the spot, allowing Frank, her rescuer, to be swept onto the boat with the other passengers.

It would be a simple story, and sad enough, if the reader knew for certain that Eveline has made a terrible mistake. As it is, one can't be so sure. What if she did climb aboard and leave Ireland forever? She would have no guarantees of a better life. She would be facing a dangerous journey, at the end of which she would spend the rest of her life in a foreign land with a strange language and culture. She would be married to a sailor who might very well spend most of his days at sea.

❻ Concludes by summarizing the interpretation

Eveline is in an incredibly difficult position. Whatever she chooses, she will suffer a deep loss. In the end, she opts for the loss of her unknown future—a heartbreaking decision, but perhaps no worse than the alternative. In light of this futility, her paralysis seems natural and easy to understand. She really has no good way out.

Writing Your Literary Interpretation

❶ Prewriting

Think about stories and poems that have surprised, moved, or puzzled you. What work has really stayed with you? A work that you find especially troubling is often a good one to write about. See the **Idea Bank** in the margin for more suggestions. After you choose a story or poem to discuss, follow the steps below.

Planning Your Literary Interpretation

▶ 1. **Reread the work several times.** As you read, take notes in your Reader's Notebook. Which passages, ideas, or events confuse or trouble you? Do they become clearer when you reread the work? What questions do you still have about the work?

▶ 2. **Develop an interpretation.** Review your notes and write freely for 20 minutes or so about the literary elements of the work. What is the central conflict or image? What happens to the main character? Write a tentative thesis statement expressing your interpretation of the work.

▶ 3. **Gather evidence to support your interpretation.** In a chart, list significant passages of the text and explain how they support your interpretation.

Evidence from the Text	How It Supports Interpretation

▶ 4. **Test your interpretation.** Discuss your interpretation with others who have read the work. Are they convinced of your conclusion? Does anything in the work contradict your interpretation? How can you revise your interpretation to be more consistent with the evidence in the story or poem?

❷ Drafting

Start by introducing the work and the author, briefly telling what the work is about. Then include a thesis statement in which you present the main point of your interpretation—the idea that the rest of your essay will support. From there, write freely about the ideas and evidence that you have gathered to support your interpretation. After you have completed the first draft, you can begin to look at how your ideas are organized.

In the main body of your essay, you will need to provide **supporting evidence** for your interpretation in the form of **details** and **quotations** from the work. You may want to explain key passages in your own words. Sum up your interpretation in the **conclusion.**

IDEABank

1. Your Working Portfolio 🗂
Look for ideas in the **Writing Options** you completed earlier in this unit:
- **Literary Analysis,** p. 1149
- **Literary Analysis,** p. 1173

2. Literary Chat
Talk with your classmates about works you particularly liked or disliked or didn't understand. Which would you like to write about?

3. Author Search
Look through this book and write down the names of authors whose work you enjoyed. Then go to the library and find some other short works by those authors.

LANGUAGE SKILLS

Ask Your Peer Reader

- What is the main point of my interpretation?

- What evidence did I present to support my interpretation?

- Are you convinced that my interpretation is reasonable? Why or why not?

- What other points should I include to clarify my interpretation?

Need revising help?

Review the **Rubric**, p. 1190

Consider **peer reader** comments

Check **revision guidelines**, p. R19

Confused about the active voice?

See the **Grammar Handbook**, p. R61

Wondering about verb tense?

See the **Grammar Handbook**, p. R60

Publishing IDEAS

- Submit your work to a literary magazine that publishes student essays.
- Post your essay on a class Web site or another Web site for student work.

PUBLISHING OPTIONS
CLASSZONE.COM

❸ Revising

TARGET SKILL ▶ **USING THE ACTIVE VOICE** The active voice generally makes writing clearer and more graceful, so use it whenever possible. In a sentence with a verb in the active voice, the subject performs the action: *Eveline made dinner at four o'clock.* In a sentence written in the passive voice, the subject receives the action, or is acted upon: *Dinner was made at four o'clock.* Excessive or unconscious use of the passive voice may make your writing wordy, unclear, and awkward. It is, however, appropriate to use the passive voice when you don't know who performed an action or want to emphasize the action itself rather than the one performing it.

> And comfort or no, Eveline feels a tremendous obligation to support her family. As her mother lay dying, Eveline promised "to keep the home together as long as she could." ∧ *There is no one else who is responsible enough to run* The household ⊙ ~~cannot be run by anyone else.~~

❹ Editing and Proofreading

TARGET SKILL ▶ **VERB TENSE** When referring to events narrated in a literary work, use the present tense. (Such a usage is called the historical present.) In other words, write about the event as if it were happening now. Do not, however, change the tenses of verbs in quotations.

> *takes* *walks* *sings*
> He ~~took~~ her to the opera, ~~walked~~ her home from work, ~~sang~~
> ∧ ∧ ∧
> *tells*
> to her, and ~~told~~ her stories about foreign countries and his exploits at
> ∧
> sea. She enjoys it: "People knew that they were courting and, when he sang about the lass that loves a sailor, she always felt pleasantly confused."

❺ Reflecting

FOR YOUR WORKING PORTFOLIO How did writing about a work of literature help you understand it? How did your interpretation change as you wrote? Attach your reflections to your finished essay and save it in your **Working Portfolio.**

Read this passage from the first draft of a literary interpretation. The underlined sections may include the following kinds of errors:

- **ineffective use of passive voice**
- **errors in verb tenses**
- **incorrect verb forms**
- **capitalization errors**

For each underlined section, choose the revision that most improves the writing.

In "Metamorphosis," a story of alienation and bewilderment is told by Franz
 (1)   (2)
Kafka. At the beginning of the story, Gregor Samsa woke up in the morning to
                                                           (3)
find that he had turned into a large insect. He is puzzled by this fact, but he is

mostly troubled because he has overslept and is about to miss the train. With

great effort he manages to slide out of bed; by this time, his parents have growed
          (4)   (5)
very worried and someone from his workplace has come to the house, looking for

him. They couldn't imagine what could be keeping him. The odd thing is that
     (6)
despite his horrible transformation, Gregor is primarily worried about the

inconvenience and the trouble it will cause him in getting to work.

---

1. **A.** in "Metamorphosis,"
    B. In "metamorphosis,"
    C. in "metamorphosis,"
    D Correct as is

2. **A.** a story by Franz Kafka, a tale is told of alienation and bewilderment
    B. a tale of alienation and bewilderment by Franz Kafka is told
    C. Franz Kafka tells a story of alienation and bewilderment
    D. Correct as is

3. **A.** Gregor Samsa wakes up in the morning to find that he had turned into a large insect
    B. Gregor Samsa wakes up in the morning to find that he has turned into a large insect
    C. Gregor Samsa woke up in the morning to find that he has turned into a large insect
    D. Correct as is

4. **A.** he manages to slide out of bed: by this time
    B. he manages to slide out of bed, by this time
    C. he manages to slide out of bed . . . by this time
    D. Correct as is

5. **A.** grew
    B. grow
    C. have grown
    D. Correct as is

6. **A.** They won't be able to imagine
    B. They can't imagine
    C. They had not been able to imagine
    D. Correct as is

Need extra help?

See the **Grammar Handbook**

Active and Passive Voice, p. R61

Verbs, p. R59

Quick Reference: The Sentence and Its Parts, p. R66

TEST PRACTICE

Building Vocabulary

On pages 340 and 864 you learned about some of the Greek and Latin roots and affixes that can be found in English words. A group of words that have the same linguistic "ancestor" is called a **word family**. Knowing the etymology of a word will often help you identify and understand other words in the same family. For example, in the passage on the right from "Professions for Women," Virginia Woolf used the word *conciliate*. *Conciliate* contains *concil*, the root of the Latin word *concilium*, "a meeting or gathering of people." *Reconcile* contains the same root, and the word *council* is also descended from *concilium*. Knowing that these words are related will help you understand

that *conciliate* has something to do with people coming together. Sure enough, if you look in a dictionary, you will find that *conciliate* means "to overcome the distrust of" or "to appease."

> And all these questions, according to the Angel in the House, cannot be dealt with freely and openly by women; they must charm, they must *conciliate*, they must—to put it bluntly—tell lies if they are to succeed.

Strategies for Building Vocabulary

The strategies that follow can help you use information about words' etymologies—their origins and histories—as a tool for recognizing word families, inferring meanings, and improving spelling.

❶ **Break Words into Parts** Many complex words are combinations of roots and affixes. When you see an unfamiliar word, try to break the word into its parts and then determine the meanings of the parts, as in this example:

> *tenacious*
>
> word parts: *ten* + *-acious*

❷ **Build Word Families** The following table shows some members of the English family of words that contain the root *ten* and are derived from the Latin verb *tenēre*, "to hold." Notice how the meanings of the words are related. Knowing the meaning of one word in a family can help you predict the meanings of related words. If you know the meaning of *detention*, for example, you may be able to guess the meaning of *tenacious*.

English Words Derived from Latin *Tenēre*

English Word	Meaning
detention	the act of **holding** in custody or temporary confinement
contents	material that is **held** or contained
tenable	capable of being maintained or **held** in an argument
tenant	one that pays rent to occupy, or **hold**, land or a building
tenure	the status of **holding** one's position (as on a faculty) on a permanent basis

❸ **Spelling** In many cases, a knowledge of word families can help you spell more accurately. The word *tributary*, for example, contains *tribut*, a Latin root meaning "give" or "grant." This root is also found in *contribute, retribution, attribute,* and *distribute*. Notice that the root's spelling is the same in all of the words, even though the emphasis in pronunciation varies.

EXERCISE List and define as many words as you can that contain the following roots.

1. *bibl* (book)
2. *psych* (mind, soul)
3. *ben, bene* (good)
4. *vis, vid* (see)
5. *poli* (city)
6. *dont* (tooth)
7. *pod* (foot)
8. *cred* (believe)

Grammar from Literature Writers use adjectives to make their writing more accurate and colorful. Adjectives modify nouns and pronouns, answering the questions *what kind*, *which one*, *how many*, and *how much*. In addition to single-word adjectives, writers also use **adjective phrases and clauses,** which have similar functions.

Prepositional phrases, participial phrases, and infinitive phrases can all be used as adjectives. Read the following sentences from James Joyce's "Eveline," noting the adjective phrases that modify the nouns *sign* and *footsteps*.

> prepositional phrase
> **Her eyes gave him no sign** of love or farewell or recognition.

> **The man out of the last house passed on his way home;**
> participial phrase
> **she heard his footsteps** clacking along the concrete pavement . . .

An adjective clause also modifies a noun or pronoun, but unlike a phrase, it contains a subject and a verb. Adjective clauses are subordinate clauses, so they cannot stand alone. They begin with relative pronouns (*who, whose, that, which*) or with relative adverbs (*after, before, when, where, why*). The clauses in the following sentences from "Eveline" modify *those* and *Harry*.

> **In her home anyway she had shelter and food; she had**
> adjective clause
> **those** whom she had known all her life **about her.**

> adjective clause
> **Ernest was dead and Harry,** who was in the church decorating business, **was nearly always down somewhere in the country.**

Punctuation Tip An adjective clause can be **essential** or **nonessential**. An essential clause provides information that is necessary to complete the meaning of the sentence. A nonessential clause provides extra information that may be helpful but is not necessary.

> essential clause
> **Eveline headed for the ship** that was about to sail.
> *(Which ship? The one about to sail.)*

> nonessential clause
> **Eveline headed for the ship,** which was about to sail.
> *(There's only one ship; by the way, it's about to sail.)*

Nonessential clauses are always set off with commas; essential clauses are not. When faced with a choice between *that* and *which,* use *that* if the clause you're introducing is essential, *which* if it is nonessential. Most other relative pronouns and adverbs can be used to introduce both essential and nonessential clauses.

WRITING EXERCISE Rewrite each sentence, adding an adjective phrase or clause that modifies the underlined word. Use at least two adjective phrases and two adjective clauses. Sample answers are given for the first two sentences.

1. Eveline is planning to run away with Frank, a <u>sailor</u>.
   Sample answer: Eveline is planning to run away with Frank, a sailor *who lives in Buenos Aires.*
2. She is eager to leave behind her <u>job</u>.
   Sample answer: She is eager to leave behind her job *with Miss Gavan.*
3. Her <u>father</u> doesn't treat her very well.
4. She is looking forward to a new <u>life</u>.
5. Frank is waiting for her at the <u>ship</u>.

GRAMMAR EXERCISE For each sentence, determine whether the boldface adjective clause is essential or nonessential. Correct any errors in punctuation and in the use of *that* and *which.*

1. Eveline thinks about her mother, **who died some years before.**
2. On the day **that her mother died,** Eveline promised to take care of the children.
3. Her father **who has a very bad temper** is difficult to live with.
4. The one thing, **that gives her hope,** is the thought of a new life with Frank.
5. She is reluctant to leave her home, **which is so familiar.**

Expressions of Modernism

Reflect and Assess

As you have seen, the first half of the 20th century was marked by tremendous changes in the arts and literature, which can be loosely summed up by the term *modernism*. The following options will help you to review what you have learned about this fascinating period and the literature it produced.

Reflecting on the Literature

A Changing World Modernist literature often portrays people who are struggling with great changes in the world and in their lives. Choose three selections in this part that focus on change. For each selection, consider the following questions:

- What major changes are described in the selection?
- Do these changes mainly affect individuals or an entire society?
- Are such changes positive or negative or a mixture of both? Why?
- What can you infer about the author's attitude toward such changes?

Compare the views of change presented in the three selections.

Reviewing Literary Concepts

Point of View Compare and contrast the points of view used in two works of fiction in this part. How does each author's use of point of view influence your reaction to the story and the judgments that you make about the characters? How would each story change if told from another point of view?

Style Compare and contrast the styles of two selections in this part. What is distinctive about each author's style? Consider elements such as word choice, imagery, figurative language, sentence length, and tone.

Building Your Portfolio

Writing Workshop and Writing Options Look over the literary interpretation that you wrote for the Writing Workshop beginning on page 1190, as well as the Writing Options that you completed in this part of the book. Choose two pieces of your writing that show the most insight into the literature. Write a note explaining your choices, then add the note and both pieces of writing to your **Presentation Portfolio**.

Self ASSESSMENT

READER'S NOTEBOOK

As a way of reviewing your own knowledge of the terms below, work with a partner to create a two-column matching test. In one column, list each term from the list below; in the next column provide a phrase that defines or illustrates the term. For additional help, make use of the index or the **Glossary of Literary Terms** (beginning on page R91).

modernism	point of view
connotation	symbol
sound devices	Negritude
diction	stream of
epiphany	consciousness

Setting GOALS

Make a list of your strengths and weaknesses as a reader and writer. Circle those weaknesses that you think are the easiest to correct or improve upon in the near future. Use those items that you circled as goals for your work.

Extend Your *Reading*

LITERATURE CONNECTIONS
1984
GEORGE ORWELL

In this novel Orwell portrays a world in which a totalitarian government controls individual thought and even reality itself. Privacy has been outlawed, and Big Brother (the government) is everywhere, spying. This classic remains timely and continues to stir the imagination while asking important questions about human nature.

Here are just a few of the related readings that accompany *1984:*

End Game
J. G. BALLARD

***from* Politics and the English Language**
GEORGE ORWELL

No One Died in Tiananmen Square
WILLIAM LUTZ

Siddhartha
HERMANN HESSE

This 1922 novel, based upon the early life of Buddha, portrays a young man's search for meaning. Born into a life of privilege in India, the man, Siddhartha, abandons his comfortable home. As he wanders throughout the land, he tries living out various answers to the problems of life, such as wealth and romance, only to realize that the truth lies deeper.

And Even *More . . .*

Books
Dubliners JAMES JOYCE
This collection of related stories, first published in 1914, asks probing questions about the Irish experience and culture.

A Room Of One's Own VIRGINIA WOOLF
In this long essay, the author eloquently makes her case for female equality.

Other Media
The Trial
A black-and-white film adaptation of Kafka's nightmarish novel, directed by Orson Welles. Zenger Media. (VIDEO)

The Shock of the New
This series of eight hour-long videos is written and hosted by the distinguished art critic Robert Hughes. He explains the revolution in art that took place during the 20th century. Time-Life. (VIDEOCASSETTE)

The Trial
FRANZ KAFKA

In this novel, a respectable bank officer, Josef K., is arrested one day for no apparent reason. Many regard his subsequent nightmare experience as a parable about modern life.

Responses to War and Conflict

Why It Matters

Two world wars, regional and ethnic strife, bloody battles for independence— for all its achievements, the 20th century was one of the most violent times in history. Deeply troubled by these terrible struggles, writers often served as society's conscience. They explored the nature of war and its effects on people.

For Links to War and Conflict, click on:

HUMANITIES
CLASSZONE.COM

The Russian Revolution and the Cold War

Torn apart by revolution in 1917, Russia had by 1922 become part of a Communist dictatorship called the Soviet Union. It was led first by **Lenin** and later by **Stalin,** who are pictured at right. After World War II, the Soviet Union and the United States squared off as rival superpowers.

The Great War

Until a second world war came along, World War I (1914–1918) was known as the Great War, for its scope was far broader and its death toll far higher than those of any previous war. In the **Battle of the Somme** in 1916, for example, more than a million soldiers were killed in four months of trench warfare.

Italian soldiers in a trench. Imperial War Museum, London.

An Even Greater War
World War II (1939–1945) surpassed World War I as history's bloodiest conflict. It was fought on land, on the sea, and in the air in many parts of the world. This war came to an end after the United States dropped atomic bombs on the cities of **Hiroshima** and **Nagasaki** in Japan.

Struggles for Independence
In the aftermath of World War II, Britain, France, and other European nations lost most of their overseas colonies. The movements for independence were often violent. By 1970, many African and Asian nations had gained their independence.

Fighting for Freedom
While many nations were throwing off the yoke of communism in the late 1980s, China remained a Communist dictatorship. In 1989, the government brutally cracked down on students demanding democracy in **Tiananmen Square** in Beijing.

In the first half of the 20th century, two global wars and a political revolution changed the world forever. Tens of millions of soldiers and civilians lost their lives in these terrible upheavals.

Allied troops in battle in 1918

World War I

On June 28, 1914, a Serbian nationalist assassinated Archduke Franz Ferdinand, heir to the Austro-Hungarian throne, who was visiting the Bosnian capital of Sarajevo. This event ignited a war that had been smoldering for some time. On one side were the **Allied Powers** of Russia, France, and Great Britain, which were soon joined by Italy and other nations. The Allied Powers were opposed by the **Central Powers**—Germany, Austria-Hungary, Bulgaria, and the Ottoman Empire.

Stubborn leaders, patriotic propaganda, and new tools of war—poison gas, armored tanks, machine guns, and airplanes—helped make this war a horrendous struggle. It was known as "the war to end all wars." On the western front in Belgium and France, the opposing armies dug themselves into trenches and fought to a virtual stalemate, despite terrible loss of life. Only the late U.S. entry into the war tipped the scale in the Allies' favor, so that Germany was forced to sign an **armistice** on November 11, 1918.

The Russian Revolution and Its Aftermath

In 1917, the Russian people drove their ruler, Czar Nicholas II, from power. He was replaced by a provisional government that in November 1917 fell to the **Bolsheviks,** a small group of revolutionaries led by Vladimir Lenin. He soon ended his country's involvement in World War I, signing the Treaty of Brest-Litovsk with Germany in 1918.

The former Russian empire was later renamed the Union of Soviet Socialist Republics (USSR), or Soviet Union, in 1922, and the Bolsheviks became the Communist Party. After Lenin died in 1924, a power struggle brought forth an even harsher dictator, **Joseph Stalin.** Under Stalin, the government took total control of Soviet citizens' lives. People were forced to work on collective farms and in government-owned factories. Millions of people were executed or exiled to the frigid regions of Siberia.

The USS *West Virginia* in flames at Pearl Harbor

World War II

After World War I, economic problems in several nations led to the rise of dictators. In Italy, Benito Mussolini, who took charge in 1922, led a militant political movement called **fascism.** It stressed loyalty to the state and obedience to its leader. In Japan, a military dictatorship also came to power, though the emperor remained in nominal control. In Germany, where the Great Depression had crippled the economy, **Adolf Hitler** took control of the government in 1933.

Adolf Hitler

He led the Nazi party, which held that the "Aryan" race—Germans and certain other northern Europeans—should rule the world. In the mid-1930s, these three nations formed an alliance referred to as the **Axis.** On September 1, 1939,

Germany invaded Poland, and World War II began.

With his blitzkriegs, or "lightning wars," Hitler rapidly conquered most of continental Europe, including France. In each conquered nation, the Nazis set up a dictatorship, virtually enslaved the people, and killed millions of Jews and other "non-Aryans" in a ruthless campaign now known as the Holocaust. In June 1941, Germany invaded the Soviet Union. Six months later, Japan launched a surprise attack on an American naval base at **Pearl Harbor,** Hawaii, and the United States joined the conflict.

With the Soviets and Americans joining Britain in the fighting, the tide of war began to turn. After battling the Germans in North Africa, Allied troops moved north into Italy, where the Italians surrendered in September 1943. The Allies then mounted a massive invasion against Nazi forces in Normandy on June 6, 1944, known as **D-day.** In the following months, the Allies liberated France, Belgium, and Luxembourg and defeated the Nazis in the **Battle of the Bulge.** Germany surrendered on May 7, 1945. After the United States dropped atomic bombs on Hiroshima and Nagasaki, Japan surrendered on September 2, 1945, thus ending the war.

History to Literature

EVENT IN HISTORY	EVENT IN LITERATURE
Millions of soldiers die fighting in Europe in World War I.	Erich Maria Remarque's novel *All Quiet on the Western Front* describes the horror of war through a German soldier's eyes.
Nazi dictator Adolf Hitler institutes a policy of genocide against the Jewish people.	Anne Frank, Elie Wiesel, Primo Levi, and other writers provide eyewitness accounts of the horror of the Holocaust.
Soviet dictator Joseph Stalin exiles many to prison camps in Siberia.	Aleksandr Solzhenitsyn portrays the ordeal of Soviet prisoners in his novel *One Day in the Life of Ivan Denisovich.*

Historical Highlights: After World War II

No global wars occurred after World War II. Still, in the second half of the 20th century, armed conflicts raged like wildfires in several regions of the world.

In 1956, the Soviets crushed a rebellion in Hungary.

Mao Zedong

Revolution in China

China's last imperial dynasty fell in 1912, but the new Chinese republic was unstable, and civil war broke out. Within China's Nationalist Party, organized by **Sun Yat-sen**, were Communists with ties to the new Soviet Union. In 1928, **Chiang Kai-shek** took control of China's government. He forced the Communists to retreat north on the 6,000-mile Long March of 1934–1935, during which **Mao Zedong** became their leader. After World War II, there was a civil war in China. Chiang fled with his followers to the island of Taiwan, and in 1949 China became a Communist nation under Mao's control. In 1966, Mao launched the **Cultural Revolution,** a movement to establish a society of peasants and workers. It was led by students who formed militia units called **Red Guards** and targeted those who seemed to have special privileges. Thousands were executed or died in prison.

The Collapse of Colonial Empires

After World War II, struggles for independence occurred in many of the colonies ruled by Britain and France. In India, **Mohandas Gandhi,** a spiritual leader and activist, led nonviolent protests against British rule and helped India gain its independence in 1947. The West African nation of Nigeria achieved its independence from Great Britain in 1960. Algeria won its independence from France in 1962 after a long and bloody conflict.

South Africa left the British Commonwealth in 1961. After decades of pressure, **apartheid,** a policy of racial separation that denied civil rights to the nation's black majority, ended in 1991.

Crowds in Nigeria cheer election results in 1959, shortly before independence was achieved.

The Cold War

The United States and the Soviet Union emerged as superpowers after World War II. They then faced off in a rivalry known as the Cold War that lasted more than 40 years. It began when the Soviet Union set up Communist governments in Eastern Europe. The British leader Winston Churchill said that an **"iron curtain"** now separated the nations of Western Europe and Eastern Europe.

To halt the spread of communism, the United States sent troops to Korea in the early 1950s and to Vietnam in the 1960s and the early 1970s. Meanwhile, the superpowers waged a nuclear-arms race and a "space race" to see which nation would land someone on the moon first (the United States did, in 1969).

In 1985, Mikhail Gorbachev became the leader of the Soviet Union. His policy of **glasnost,** or "openness," gave the Soviet people more freedom. One by one, the nations of Eastern Europe cast off communism. The Soviet Union itself collapsed in 1991.

Palestinian and
Israeli flags

Conflicts in Latin America

Throughout the 20th century, many Latin American countries were plagued with political violence. In Argentina, **Juan Perón,** a military leader, won the presidency in 1946. He and his popular wife, Eva, ruled together, setting up a dictatorship. Driven from office in 1955, Perón was again elected president in 1973, shortly before his death.

In neighboring Chile, economic troubles led many to turn to **Salvador Allende,** a Marxist who was elected president in 1970. When economic woes continued, military leaders overthrew Allende in 1973 and, in the violent aftermath, many of his supporters fled or were killed.

One of the most enduring of Latin America's leaders has been **Fidel Castro.** He took control of Cuba after a revolution in 1959 and has ruled as a dictator for more than four decades. In 1961, he easily repulsed a group of anti-Castro exiles who invaded Cuba at a remote beach on the Bay of Pigs.

Conflicts in the Middle East

The Middle East also has seen terrible conflicts since World War II. In the 19th century, a movement known as **Zionism** sought a Jewish homeland in **Palestine.** After the horrors of the Holocaust, the call for such a homeland grew even stronger. Then, in 1947, the United Nations voted to partition Palestine to establish a Jewish homeland. On May 14, 1948, the Jews declared their portion of Palestine the independent nation of Israel; the next day, Israel's Arab neighbors attacked. Since then, relations between Israel and its neighbors have remained tense.

Elsewhere in the Middle East, about 1,000,000 people died in a war between Iran and Iraq before a cease-fire was declared in 1988. Two years later, **Saddam Hussein,** dictator of Iraq, invaded Kuwait. A coalition of troops led by the U.S. defeated Iraq in the **Persian Gulf War** of 1991.

Other Ethnic Conflicts

Ethnic conflicts erupted in Eastern Europe after Communist governments collapsed in the early 1990s. In Yugoslavia, several republics wished for an independent future. Slovenia, Croatia, Macedonia, and Bosnia-Herzegovina all voted for independence. Ethnic Serbs living in Croatia and Bosnia, however, fought to retain a portion of the land and to remain united with Serbia in a "greater Yugoslavia."

In the conflict that followed, people living in regions dominated by other ethnic groups were driven from their homes or killed. When the violence in **Bosnia** increased, the U.S. and its allies stepped in, and a peace agreement was reached in 1995. Four years later, Western nations again intervened to protect ethnic Albanians in Kosovo.

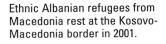

Ethnic Albanian refugees from Macedonia rest at the Kosovo-Macedonia border in 2001.

★ WAR ★

LUIGI PIRANDELLO

Luigi Pirandello
1867–1936

Dashed Dreams Luigi Pirandello (lōō-ē′jē pîr′ən-děl′ō) was one of the most important dramatists of the 20th century. He was born in Sicily to a family of mineral merchants and studied at universities in Rome and Germany. Upon completing his studies, he settled in Rome and applied himself to writing. When a landslide in 1903 shut down the sulfur mines from which his family derived its wealth, he was left nearly penniless. To support his young family, he supplemented his writing income by teaching Italian. His wife's mental illness added to his burdens. From 1919 until her death in 1959, Antonietta Pirandello had to be kept in an institution.

From Realism to Experimentation Pirandello's early writing was realistic fiction, often wryly humorous and set in his native Sicily. In time his interest in psychology, spurred by his wife's illness, led him to focus on his characters' inner conflicts. Increasingly, he turned to drama to explore the subconscious mind. By the early 1920s, he was writing experimental plays: *Henry IV*, which examines the relation between madness and truth, and *Six Characters in Search of an Author*, which explores the boundary between fantasy and reality.

International Acclaim Later in the 1920s, Pirandello toured the world with his own theater company. In 1934 he received the Nobel Prize for Literature. One of the great innovators in modern drama, he influenced several important playwrights, including Jean Anouilh, Jean-Paul Sartre, Eugene Ionesco, Samuel Beckett, and Edward Albee.

Other Works
The Oil Jar and Other Stories
The Late Mattia Pascal
Right You Are If You Think You Are

Build Background

Wartime Italy Pirandello's short story "War" is set in Italy during World War I. At that time, Italian patriotism was put to a severe test. Italy had become a unified nation only recently, in the second half of the 19th century. Before then, it was made up of separate city-states, kingdoms, and principalities. Many Italians, therefore, continued to feel a stronger loyalty to their local region than to the nation as a whole.

In 1915, Italy declared war against its neighbor Austria-Hungary. The Italian government hoped to conquer Austrian territory where Italians lived. However, the army suffered from low morale and a lack of modern equipment. Many of those drafted were peasants who did not understand why they had to fight. The war also stirred deep resentment among civilians, who experienced severe shortages of fuel and food.

The Italian Front stretched along the frontier between Italy and Austria-Hungary. The cold weather and the mountainous terrain made it difficult for either side to launch offensives. Usually, the opposing armies were bogged down in trench warfare. Though Italy ended up on the winning side, it paid a terrible price. About 600,000 Italian soldiers died—almost 2 percent of the country's population.

WORDS TO KNOW **Vocabulary Preview**

harrowing	retort	vitality
plight	stoically	

Connect to Your Life

In Unit Two, Part 2, you studied the ancient Roman poet Horace. One of his most famous sayings is "It is a great and beautiful thing to die for one's country." How do you think a young soldier going off to war might react to this statement? How might his or her parents react? Share your views with a group of classmates.

Focus Your Reading

LITERARY ANALYSIS: SETTING IN MODERN FICTION

The **setting** is the time and place in which the events of a story occur. In the opening paragraphs of this story, Pirandello uses details to establish the time and place of this story: it occurs at dawn in a second-class carriage of a local train bound for Sulmona, Italy. A story's setting may also include the historical context in which the story takes place. In this story, the historical context—World War I—is of great importance. As you read, consider how the setting affects the characters in the story.

ACTIVE READING: COMPARING AND CONTRASTING CHARACTERS

In "War," Pirandello portrays the conflicts that arise when characters respond differently to a stressful situation. To understand these conflicts, you must compare and contrast the characters' attitudes toward the war and the personal sacrifices they must make.

📖 **READER'S NOTEBOOK** As you read, use a chart like the one below to take notes about the characters' attitudes.

Character	Attitude Toward War and Personal Sacrifice
Wife	*is inconsolable because her only son has gone to the front*
Husband	
First passenger	
Second passenger	
Old man	

War

Luigi Pirandello

Translated by Samuel Putnam

The passengers who had left Rome by the night express had had to stop until dawn at the small station of Fabriano[1] in order to continue their journey by the small old-fashioned "local" joining the main line with Sulmona.[2]

At dawn, in a stuffy and smoky second-class carriage in which five people had already spent the night, a bulky woman in deep mourning was hoisted in—almost like a shapeless bundle. Behind her—puffing and moaning, followed her husband—a tiny man, thin and weakly, his face death-white, his eyes small and bright and looking shy and uneasy.

Having at last taken a seat he politely thanked the passengers who had helped his wife and who had made room for her; then he turned round to the woman trying to pull down the collar of her coat and politely inquired:

"Are you all right, dear?"

The wife, instead of answering, pulled up her collar again to her eyes, so as to hide her face.

"Nasty world," muttered the husband with a sad smile.

And he felt it his duty to explain to his traveling companions that the poor woman was to be pitied for the war was taking away from her her only son, a boy of twenty to whom both had devoted their entire life, even breaking up their home at Sulmona to follow him to Rome where he had to go as a student, then allowing him to volunteer for war with an assurance, however, that at least for six months he would not be sent to the front and now, all of a sudden, receiving a wire saying that he was due to leave in three days' time and asking them to go and see him off.

The woman under the big coat was twisting and wriggling, at times growling like a wild animal, feeling certain that all those explanations would not have aroused even a shadow of sympathy from those people who—most likely—were in the same plight as herself. One of them, who had been listening with particular attention, said:

"You should thank God that your son is only leaving now for the front. Mine has been sent there the first day of the war. He has already come back twice wounded and been sent back again to the front."

"What about me? I have two sons and three nephews at the front," said another passenger.

"Maybe, but in our case it is our only son," ventured the husband.

"What difference can it make? You may spoil your only son with excessive attentions, but you cannot love him more than you would all your other children if you had any. Paternal love is not like bread that can be broken into pieces and split amongst the children in equal shares. A father gives all his love to each one of his children without discrimination, whether it be one or ten, and if I am suffering now for my two sons, I am not suffering half for each of them but double. . . ."

"True . . . true . . ." sighed the embarrassed husband, "but suppose (of course we all hope it will never be your case) a father has two sons at

---

1. **Fabriano** (fä′brē-ä′nō): a city in eastern Italy, about 100 miles northeast of Rome.
2. **Sulmona** (sōōl-mō′nä): a city in eastern Italy, about 75 miles east of Rome.

WORDS TO KNOW

plight (plīt) *n.* a bad or unfortunate situation; predicament

Self Portrait, Käthe Kollwitz. Copyright © 2002 Artists Rights Society (ARS), New York/VG Bild-Kunst, Bonn, Germany.

AT DAWN, IN A STUFFY AND SMOKY SECOND-CLASS CARRIAGE IN WHICH FIVE PEOPLE HAD ALREADY SPENT THE NIGHT, A BULKY WOMAN IN DEEP MOURNING WAS HOISTED IN —ALMOST LIKE A SHAPELESS BUNDLE.

the front and he loses one of them, there is still one left to console him . . . while . . ."

"Yes," answered the other, getting cross, "a son left to console him but also a son left for whom he must survive, while in the case of the father of an only son if the son dies the father can die too and put an end to his distress. Which of the two positions is the worse? Don't you see how my case would be worse than yours?"

"Nonsense," interrupted another traveler, a fat, red-faced man with bloodshot eyes of the palest grey.

He was panting. From his bulging eyes seemed to spurt inner violence of an uncontrolled vitality which his weakened body could hardly contain.

"Nonsense," he repeated, trying to cover his mouth with his hand so as to hide the two missing front teeth. "Nonsense. Do we give life to our children for our own benefit?"

The other travelers stared at him in distress. The one who had had his son at the front since the first day of the war sighed: "You are right. Our children do not belong to us, they belong to the Country. . . ."

"Bosh," <u>retorted</u> the fat traveler. "Do we think of the Country when we give life to our children? Our sons are born because . . . well, because they must be born and when they come to life they take our own life with them. This is the truth. We belong to them but they never belong to us. And when they reach twenty they are exactly what we were at their age. We too had a father and mother, but there were so many other things as well . . . girls, cigarettes, illusions, new ties . . . and the Country, of course, whose call we would have answered—when we were twenty—even if father and mother had said no. Now, at our age, the love of our Country is still great, of course, but stronger than it is the love for our children. Is there any one of us here who wouldn't gladly take his son's place at the front if he could?"

World War I – *Fate tutti il vostro dovere!"* ["Everyone do your duty!"] Advertisement by Credito Italiano (an Italian Bank) for war bonds. Copyright © Jack Novak/SuperStock, Inc.

There was a silence all round, everybody nodding as to approve.

"Why then," continued the fat man, "shouldn't we consider the feelings of our children when

WORDS TO KNOW

retort (rĭ-tôrt') *v.* to reply quickly or sharply

they are twenty? Isn't it natural that at their age they should consider the love for their Country (I am speaking of decent boys, of course) even greater than the love for us? Isn't it natural that it should be so, as after all they must look upon us as upon old boys who cannot move any more and must stay at home? If Country exists, if Country is a natural necessity like bread, of which each of us must eat in order not to die of hunger, somebody must go to defend it. And our sons go, when they are twenty, and they don't want tears, because if they die, they die inflamed and happy (I am speaking, of course, of decent boys). Now, if one dies young and happy, without having the ugly sides of life, the boredom of it, the pettiness, the bitterness of disillusion . . . what more can we ask for him? Everyone should stop crying: everyone should laugh, as I do . . . or at least thank God—as I do—because my son, before dying, sent me a message saying that he was dying satisfied at having ended his life in the best way he could have wished. That is why, as you see, I do not even wear mourning. . . ."

He shook his light fawn[3] coat as to show it; his livid[4] lip over his missing teeth was trembling, his eyes were watery and motionless and soon after he ended with a shrill laugh which might well have been a sob.

"Quite so . . . quite so . . ." agreed the others.

The woman who, bundled in a corner under her coat, had been sitting and listening had—for the last three months—tried to find in the words of her husband and her friends something to console her in her deep sorrow, something that might show her how a mother should resign herself to send her son not even to death but to a probable danger of life. Yet not a word had she found amongst the many which had been said . . . and her grief had been greater in seeing that

nobody—as she thought—could share her feelings.

But now the words of the traveler amazed and almost stunned her. She suddenly realized that it wasn't the others who were wrong and could not understand her but herself who could not rise up to the same height of those fathers and mothers willing to resign themselves, without crying, not only to the departure of their sons but even to their death.

She lifted her head, she bent over from her corner trying to listen with great attention to the details which the fat man was giving to his companions about the way his son had fallen as a hero, for his King and his Country, happy and without regrets. It seemed to her that she had stumbled into a world she had never dreamt of, a world so far unknown to her and she was so pleased to hear everyone joining in congratulating that brave father who could so <u>stoically</u> speak of his child's death.

Then suddenly, just as if she had heard nothing of what had been said and almost as if waking up from a dream, she turned to the old man, asking him:

"Then . . . is your son really dead?"

Everybody stared at her. The old man, too, turned to look at her, fixing his great, bulging, horribly watery light grey eyes, deep in her face. For some little time he tried to answer, but words failed him. He looked and looked at her, almost as if only then—at that silly, incongruous question— he had suddenly realized at last that his son was really dead . . . gone for ever . . . for ever. His face contracted, became horribly distorted, then he snatched in haste a handkerchief from his pocket and, to the amazement of everyone, broke into <u>harrowing</u>, heart-rending, uncontrollable sobs. ❖

---

3. **fawn:** light yellowish brown.
4. **livid:** discolored, as from a bruise.

stoically (stō′ĭ-klē) *adv.* in a manner showing no emotion
harrowing (hăr′ō-ĭng) *adj.* extremely distressing

Connect to the Literature

1. **What Do You Think?** How did you react to the old man's fit of grief at the end of the story?

   Comprehension Check
   - Why does the husband feel that the other passengers should pity his wife?
   - According to the old man, how should parents react to the death of a son in the war?

Think Critically

2. **ACTIVE READING: COMPARING AND CONTRASTING CHARACTERS** Review the chart you made in your **READER'S NOTEBOOK**. Which attitudes do you find reasonable? Which do you find extreme? Share your views with a classmate.

3. Why does the wife's question cause the old man to lose his composure?

4. How would you contrast the wife and the old man?

5. What do you think is the author's **theme**—his message about war and the sacrifices it entails?

   THINK ABOUT
   - the wife's inability to put her grief into words
   - the old man's statement about the loss of his son
   - the old man's breakdown

Extend Interpretations

6. **The Writer's Style** A writer's use of hints or clues to indicate later events in a story is known as **foreshadowing**. What details in the story foreshadow the old man's breakdown?

7. **Connect to Life** For most of the story, the old man hides what he really feels. Why do people sometimes try to hide their true feelings from themselves and others?

LITERARY ANALYSIS: SETTING IN MODERN FICTION

Setting is the time and place of the action of a short story, a novel, a play, a narrative poem, or a work of narrative nonfiction. In addition to place and time frame, setting may include the larger historical and cultural contexts that form the background of a narrative. In some stories, setting can be a driving force, influencing events or affecting how the characters act and feel. In Pirandello's story the setting plays a central role.

Cooperative Learning Activity
With a small group of classmates, discuss the following questions:
- How does the historical context— wartime in Italy—affect the characters in this story?
- Why do you think the author set this story in a train rather than in a hotel, a restaurant, a stadium, or some other place?

Have one member of the group write a brief summary of the discussion. Then share your summary with other groups.

Writing Options

1. Different Ending What do you think might happen on the train after the old man suffers his emotional collapse? How might the other characters respond to his breakdown? Write a few paragraphs to extend the story.

Writing Handbook
See page R29: Narrative Writing.

2. Character Analysis In a brief essay, analyze the character of the old man. Begin by discussing the techniques that Pirandello uses to develop this character. Then discuss the old man's personality traits. Use details and quotations from the story to support your analysis.

3. Personal Response How did this story affect your views about the sacrifices war exacts of parents? Write a personal-response essay exploring your opinions.

Activities & Explorations

1. Story Illustration Create a portrait of one of the characters in the story "War." Base your drawing or painting on specific details in the story. ~ **ART**

2. Readers Theater In a Readers Theater presentation, performers read aloud, using a work of literature as a script. With a small group of classmates, prepare a dramatic reading of this story. Use the pitch, volume, and expression of your voice to suggest your character's attitudes and emotions. ~ **SPEAKING AND LISTENING**

Inquiry & Research

1. The Grieving Process Find out more about the process of grieving. What theories do psychologists use to explain this process? What stages do grieving people go through? What can help someone cope with extreme grief?

2. World War I Prepare an oral report about the fighting at the Italian Front during World War I. Include information about trench warfare and the state of military technology. Use photographs, maps, and other visual aids in your report.

RESEARCH STARTER
CLASSZONE.COM

Vocabulary in Action

EXERCISE: CONTEXT CLUES Choose the correct word to complete each sentence.

1. At first, the husband believed that his wife's _____ was worse than anyone else's.

2. The husband and the wife were weak and tired because their son's situation had drained much of their _____.

3. The wife in particular was so grief-stricken that she found it impossible to act _____.

4. The passengers didn't expect the old man to _____ angrily to their debate.

5. His troubles, it turned out, were more _____ than theirs.

Building Vocabulary
For an in-depth lesson on context clues, see page 674.

All Quiet on the Western Front

What if you were forced to leave your family and friends to stand face to face with death on the battlefield? As you struggled to control your emotions, questions might eat at your mind. Will I survive? If I do, can I ever return to the life I once knew? Will my memories of the war haunt me forever?

These are some of the disturbing questions that Erich Maria Remarque (ā′rĭкн mä-rē′ä rə-märk′) raises in *All Quiet on the Western Front,* one of the most famous novels of the 20th century. First published in 1929, this novel portrays the horrors of war as they appear to a young German soldier in World War I. Throughout the novel, the author's simple yet lyrical style creates vivid scenes.

> One morning two butterflies play in front of our trench. They are brimstone-butterflies, with red spots on their yellow wings. What can they be looking for here? There is not a plant nor a flower for miles. They settle on the teeth of a skull.

Below:
*German soldiers
on the attack*

ERICH MARIA REMARQUE

ALL QUIET ON THE WESTERN FRONT

THE ILLUSTRATED EDITION

The narrator of the novel is Paul Bäumer, a young recruit. Behind the lines, he endures the endless drills and mindless discipline of army life. At the front, he witnesses the horrors of trench warfare—the attacks and counterattacks, the barrages of shells and rockets, the swirl of poison gas, the senseless killings, the painful wounds that bring slow death. In one gripping scene, Paul dives into a shell hole and is forced to stab a French soldier. He then dresses the soldier's wounds and watches him slowly die. In the dead man's wallet, Paul finds pictures of his wife and little girl. He is overcome by feelings of pity and guilt.

Again and again, Paul shares his deepest thoughts and feelings with the reader. To survive on the front, he realizes, he must descend to the level of an animal—relying on instinct and trusting in blind luck. He worries that he and others like him have been ruined by their experiences at the front.

> We . . . do not know what the end may be. We know only that in some strange way we have become a waste land.

Yet amid the swirl of blood and death, Paul realizes that one value is stronger than bombs, bayonets, and bullets. That value is comradeship, "the finest thing that arose out of the war."

No wonder this book has become a modern classic. In 1933, the Nazis, outraged at the author's realistic depiction of war, burned copies of the book in Berlin—an ironic tribute to the power of Remarque's story of a common soldier's simple heroism. Written by one who had fought as a German soldier in World War I, the novel was translated into English by an ex-soldier who had fought on the other side.

MILESTONE LINKS
CLASSZONE.COM

Left:
Lew Ayres in the 1930 film version

Above:
Book cover for the illustrated edition, and poster for the 1930 film

I Am Not One of Those Who Left the Land

Anna Akhmatova

Translated by Stanley Kunitz with Max Hayward

Anna Akhmatova
1889–1966

Persecuted Poet "Anna Akhmatova" (ăкн-mä′tə-və) was the pen name of Anna Gorenko, one of Russia's greatest poets. By 1914, she had published two books of poetry, both widely read. Her world came apart, however, after the Russian Revolution of 1917. Civil war, famine, brutal repression, and strict censorship drove many writers into exile. In 1921, her former husband was executed for conspiracy, and Akhmatova came under suspicion. Though urged by friends to leave Russia, Akhmatova refused to do so. She wrote the following poem in 1922, when many writers had left Russia to escape its atrocities.

During the 1930s and 1940s, Akhmatova watched in horror as her friends and fellow writers were jailed and sometimes executed under the Soviet dictator Joseph Stalin.

Lasting Recognition Stalin's death in 1953 brought about an easing of government censorship, which enabled Akhmatova to publish a few volumes of her poetry. Her work earned her a place in literary history as a poet who captured the suffering of her people.

Connect to Your Life

Imagine that your own community is suddenly torn apart by violence. Buildings are damaged, the streets are unsafe, and people fear for their lives. Why might some people choose to stay in the community despite the violence?

Focus Your Reading

LITERARY ANALYSIS: SPEAKER AND TONE
The **speaker** of a poem is the voice that "talks" to the reader. This voice helps to convey the **tone,** or the writer's attitude toward his or her subject.

ACTIVE READING: DRAWING CONCLUSIONS
To **draw conclusions**, you combine what you read with what you already know in order to make logical guesses about some element in a literary work. As you read this poem, try to draw conclusions about the **speaker.** Consider the following:

• how she defines herself
• what she has endured

In your 📖 **READER'S NOTEBOOK**, list your conclusions about the speaker and record the evidence you used to reach them.

Mujer de la tierra [Woman from the earth] (1995), Maria Eugenia Terrazas.
Photograph copyright © Kactus Foto, Santiago, Chile/SuperStock, Inc.

I am not one of those who left the land
to the mercy of its enemies.
Their flattery leaves me cold,
my songs are not for them to praise.

5   But I pity the exile's lot.
Like a felon, like a man half-dead,
dark is your path, wanderer;
wormwood infects your foreign bread.

But here, in the murk of conflagration,
10 where scarcely a friend is left to know,
we, the survivors, do not flinch
from anything, not from a single blow.

Surely the reckoning will be made
after the passing of this cloud.
15 We are the people without tears,
straighter than you . . . more proud . . .

8 **wormwood:** something bitter or extremely unpleasant.

9 **conflagration:** a large destructive fire.

13 **reckoning:** settlement of accounts.

Thinking through the LITERATURE

Connect to the Literature

1. **What Do You Think?** What are your thoughts about the last two lines of this poem?

Think Critically

2. **ACTIVE READING: DRAWING CONCLUSIONS** Review the conclusions you listed in your 📖 **READER'S NOTEBOOK**. What values do you think are important to the speaker?

3. Why does the speaker feel that it was better to stay in Russia than to go into exile?

THINK ABOUT
- the comparisons that describe the exiles
- the suffering endured by the survivors
- the qualities that the survivors developed

4. In line 13, the speaker mentions a "reckoning" that will be made. What do you **predict** might happen when this reckoning occurs?

Extend Interpretations

5. **The Writer's Style** Akhmatova's poetry has been praised for its precise and concrete language. Point out words in this poem that are particularly effective in conveying the poet's meaning.

6. **Connect to Life** The speaker of this poem has survived a terrible ordeal. Do you think great suffering tends to strengthen a person or break his or her spirit? Explain your opinion.

LITERARY ANALYSIS: SPEAKER AND TONE

The **speaker** of a poem, like the narrator of a story, is the voice that "talks" to the reader. The speaker of "I Am Not One of Those Who Left the Land" may be closely identified with the poet herself, who refused to leave Russia after the Communists took control. Notice that in line 11, the pronoun *we* replaces *I*. This change suggests that the speaker is the voice of an entire group—all those who remained in Russia despite the terrible suffering.

The speaker helps to convey the tone of a poem, or the writer's attitude toward his or her subject. The **tone** might be described in one or more ways—for example, as serious, bitter, playful, or detached. To identify the tone, consider the writer's diction (word choice), any revealing details, and any direct statements of his or her position.

Cooperative Learning Activity

With a small group of students, create a chart like the one below. Fill in the boxes and then write down one or more words to describe the tone of "I Am Not One of Those Who Left the Land." Share your chart with other groups.

Diction	*"like a felon"*	Tone
Details		
Statements		

Living Dangerously: Writers in the 20th Century

As Anna Akhmatova learned, the 20th century was a dangerous time to be a writer. From 1923 to 1940, the Soviet government silenced Akhmatova, allowing no volumes of her poetry to be published. During those years, many Russian writers were imprisoned, exiled, or executed, including Osip Mandelstam, perhaps the greatest Russian poet of the 20th century, who died in a Siberian prison camp.

Although Akhmatova was allowed to publish some poetry during World War II, she fell again into disfavor. In 1946, the Central Committee of the Communist Party denounced her poetry, and a government official publicly called her a "harlot-nun." In 1949, her son was arrested and exiled to Siberia. To help gain her son's release, Akhmatova had to compromise her principles and publish a poem praising the Soviet dictator, Joseph Stalin.

The following time line gives examples of some of the ordeals faced by modern writers.

Iranian leader Ayatollah Khomeini issues a *fatwa* (legal opinion) against the Anglo-Indian writer Salman Rushdie for allegedly blaspheming Islam in a novel. A bounty is offered to anyone who executes Rushdie, who goes into hiding under the protection of Scotland Yard.

Chilean writer Pablo Neruda leaves Chile by crossing the Andes Mountains on horseback at night. Neruda had published a letter critical of Chile's president and went into exile to avoid arrest.

1956

Nigerian playwright Wole Soyinka is imprisoned for two years, allegedly for conspiring to support independence for Biafra, a region of Nigeria that formed a separate state from 1967 to 1970.

1974

2000

1948

African-raised British writer Doris Lessing is declared a "prohibited immigrant" by Southern Rhodesia (now Zimbabwe) because her fiction criticizes government policies of racial separation.

1967

Russian writer Aleksandr Solzhenitsyn is arrested and charged with treason for criticizing the Soviet Union. He is exiled from the Soviet Union a day later.

1989

Chinese poet and editor Bei Ling is arrested and imprisoned. Copies of Bei's literary magazine are confiscated and destroyed by the government.

Group Discussion Why do you think so many governments have felt threatened by writers? Do you think a government ever has the right to limit or restrict a writer's creative work? Explain why or why not.

The Spy

Bertolt Brecht

From Medicine to Writing

Bertolt Brecht (brĕkt), a major playwright of the 20th century, grew up in Augsburg, a city in Bavaria. He studied medicine in Munich from 1917 to 1921, with time spent in wartime service as an orderly in an army hospital in 1918. Disillusioned with his society for the part it played in the horrors of World War I, Brecht gave up medicine and turned to writing—poetry, nonfiction, and especially drama. In all, he wrote about 35 plays.

Bertolt Brecht
1898–1956

Fame and Flight

These plays, for the most part, were critical of society. For example, *Drums in the Night* (1922), Brecht's first successful play, tells of a soldier who rejects the violence of modern warfare. *The Threepenny Opera* (1928), his most popular work, explores serious issues such as poverty and crime and attacks the middle class. As a dramatist, Brecht sought to make his audience think deeply about his ideas. Many of his ideas, however, offended the Nazis. Brecht, therefore, had to flee from Germany when Adolf Hitler took control in 1933.

Exile and Return

During his exile, Brecht lived first in Scandinavia and then in the United States, where he worked for a brief time on films in Hollywood. Meanwhile, in Germany, his writings were burned and his citizenship was revoked. While in exile, Brecht wrote some of the finest plays in the German language—including *Mother Courage and Her Children* (1941) and *The Life of Galileo* (1943). After World War II, he lived in Switzerland for a time before returning to Germany. There he established the Berliner Ensemble, one of the world's finest acting troupes.

Other Works

The Good Woman of Setzuan
The Caucasian Chalk Circle
The Resistible Rise of Arturo Ui

Build Background

An Education in Hatred In Brecht's play *The Spy*, a man and his wife mistrust their only son because of his involvement with the Hitler Youth. This organization, set up by Hitler himself, promoted Nazi values and trained German youths for war. "Look at these young men and boys. What material! With them I can make a new world," Hitler thundered once in a speech. "A violently active, dominating, intrepid, brutal youth—that is what I am after."

Within a few years after Hitler's rise to power, about 60 percent of Germany's boys belonged to the Hitler Youth. They joined at age 10 and remained members until they turned 19. Their main activities included marching, playing sports and war games, and absorbing Nazi propaganda. Intellectual training was discouraged because the Nazis believed it would lead youths to question Hitler's ideas. At the same time young men were being trained in the Hitler Youth, a sister organization, the League of German Girls, sought to develop a generation of loyal Nazi women.

In 1936, participation in these youth organizations became mandatory in Germany. Any parents who failed to register their children were subject to fine or imprisonment. After a time, the Hitler Youth took on a more sinister role. Members were expected to spy on their own families in order to evaluate their parents' loyalty to the Nazis. This responsibility sometimes led boys to inform on their parents.

Hitler Youth

Connect to Your Life

What do you know about life in Germany under the Nazis? What beliefs did Adolf Hitler spread among the German people? Discuss these questions with a small group of classmates.

Focus Your Reading

LITERARY ANALYSIS: DIALOGUE AND MOOD

Dialogue is written conversation between two or more characters in a literary work. In drama, the story that unfolds is told almost exclusively through dialogue. The dialogue moves the plot forward, reveals character, and helps establish the **mood**—the feeling or atmosphere that a writer creates for the reader. As you read *The Spy,* notice the feeling that the dialogue stirs in you.

ACTIVE READING: UNDERSTANDING HISTORICAL CONTEXT

To make sense of the dialogue in this play, you must have some knowledge of the play's historical context. **Historical context** refers to the period in history in which a literary work is set. *The Spy* is set in Germany after the Nazis have taken over the government and established organizations to try to influence the young.

READER'S NOTEBOOK As you read the play, record in a chart two or more incidents or references that you are able to clarify by using your knowledge of the play's historical context.

Incident or Reference	Explanation
The man's criticism of the Brown House	The Brown House was Hitler's headquarters, so the man is criticizing Hitler and his government.

WORDS TO KNOW **Vocabulary Preview**

confiscate	jocular	wittingly
demoralizing	vindictive	

The Spy

Bertolt Brecht

Translated by John Willett

Cologne[1] 1935. A wet Sunday afternoon. The Man, *the* Wife *and the* Boy *have finished lunch. The* Maidservant *enters.*

The Maidservant. Mr. and Mrs. Klimbtsch[2] are asking if you are at home.

The Man (*snarls*). No.

(*The* Maidservant *goes out.*)

The Wife. You should have gone to the phone yourself. They must know we couldn't possibly have gone out yet.

The Man. Why couldn't we?

The Wife. Because it's raining.

The Man. That's no reason.

The Wife. Where could we have gone to? That's the first thing they'll ask.

The Man. Oh, masses of places.

The Wife. Let's go then.

The Man. Where to?

The Wife. If only it wasn't raining.

The Man. And where'd we go if it wasn't raining?

The Wife. At least in the old days you could go and meet someone.

(*pause*)

The Wife. It was a mistake you not going to the phone. Now they'll realize we don't want to have them.

The Man. Suppose they do?

The Wife. Then it wouldn't look very nice, our dropping them just when everyone else does.

The Man. We're not dropping them.

The Wife. Why shouldn't they come here in that case?

The Man. Because Klimbtsch bores me to tears.

The Wife. He never bored you in the old days.

The Man. In the old days . . . All this talk of the old days gets me down.

The Wife. Well anyhow you'd never have cut him just because the school inspectors are after him.

The Man. Are you telling me I'm a coward?

(*pause*)

The Man. All right, ring up and tell them we've just come back on account of the rain.

---

1. **Cologne** (kə-lōn′): a city in western Germany.
2. **Klimbtsch** (klĭmptsh).

Femme á la robe noir [Woman in a black dress], Tamara de Lempicka. Copyright © 2002 Artist Rights Society (ARS), New York/ADAGP, Paris.

(*The* Wife *remains seated.*)

The Wife. What about asking the Lemkes[3] to come over?

The Man. And have them go on telling us we're slack[4] about civil defense?

The Wife (*to the* Boy). Klaus-Heinrich, stop fiddling with the wireless.[5]

(*The* Boy *turns his attention to the newspapers.*)

The Man. It's a disaster, its raining like this. It's quite intolerable, living in a country where it's a disaster when it rains.

The Wife. Do you really think it's sensible to go round making remarks like that?

The Man. I can make what remarks I like between my own four walls. This is my home, and I shall damn well say . . .

(*He is interrupted. The* Maidservant *enters with coffee things. So long as she is present they remain silent.*)

The Man. Have we got to have a maid whose father is the block warden?[6]

The Wife. We've been over that again and again. The last thing you said was that it had its advantages.

The Man. What aren't I supposed to have said? If you mentioned anything of the sort to your mother we could land in a proper mess.

The Wife. The things I talk about to my mother . . .

---

3. Lemkes (lĕm′kəz).

4. **slack:** lacking in diligence; careless.

5. **Klaus-Heinrich** (klous′ hīn′rĭкн) . . . **wireless:** *Wireless* is an old term for radio.

6. **block warden:** someone appointed to oversee what goes on in a particular area.

(*Enter the* Maidservant *with the coffee.*)

The Wife. That's all right, Erna. You can go now, I'll see to it.

The Maidservant. Thank you very much, ma'am.

The Boy (*looking up from his paper*). Is that how vicars[7] always behave, dad?

The Man. How do you mean?

The Boy. Like it says here.

The Man. What's that you're reading?

(*snatches the paper from his hands*)

The Boy. Hey, our group leader[8] said it was all right for us to know about anything in that paper.

The Man. I don't have to go by what your group leader says. It's for me to decide what you can or can't read.

The Wife. There's ten pfennigs,[9] Klaus-Heinrich, run over and get yourself something.

The Boy. But it's raining.

(*He hangs round the window, trying to make up his mind.*)

The Man. If they go on reporting these cases against priests I shall cancel the paper altogether.

The Wife. Which are you going to take, then? They're all reporting them.

The Man. If all the papers are full of this kind of filth I'd sooner not read a paper at all. And I wouldn't be any worse informed about what's going on in the world.

The Wife. There's something to be said for a bit of a clean-up.

The Man. Clean-up indeed. The whole thing's politics.

The Wife. Well, it's none of our business anyway. After all, we're protestants.

The Man. It matters to our people all right if it can't hear the word vestry[10] without being reminded of dirt like this.

The Wife. But what do you want them to do when this kind of thing happens?

The Man. What do I want them to do? Suppose they looked into their own back yard. I'm told it isn't all so snowy white in that Brown House[11] of theirs.

The Wife. But that only goes to show how far our people's recovery has gone, Karl.

The Man. Recovery! A nice kind of recovery. If that's what recovery looks like, I'd sooner have the disease any day.

The Wife. You're so on edge today. Did something happen at the school?

The Man. What on earth could have happened at school? And for God's sake don't keep saying I'm on edge, it makes me feel on edge.

The Wife. We oughtn't to keep on quarreling so, Karl. In the old days . . .

The Man. Just what I was waiting for. In the old days. Neither in the old days nor now did I wish to have my son's imagination perverted[12] for him.

The Wife. Where has he got to, anyway?

The Man. How am I to know?

The Wife. Did you see him go?

The Man. No.

The Wife. I can't think where he can have gone. (*She calls.*) Klaus-Heinrich!

(*She hurries out of the room, and is heard calling. She returns.*)

The Wife. He really has left.

---

7. **vicars:** priests; pastors of parishes.

8. **group leader:** a local leader in the Hitler Youth.

9. **pfennigs** (fĕn´ĭgz): A pfennig is a small unit of German money.

10. **vestry:** a room in a church where priests' robes and other sacred objects are kept.

11. **Brown House:** Hitler's headquarters in Munich.

12. **perverted:** turned away from what is true or right.

The Man. Why shouldn't he?

The Wife. But it's raining buckets.

The Man. Why are you so on edge at the boy's having left?

The Wife. You remember what we were talking about?

The Man. What's that got to do with it?

Just what I was waiting for. In the old days. Neither in the old days nor now did I wish to have my son's imagination perverted for him.

The Wife. You've been so careless lately.

The Man. I have certainly not been careless, but even if I had what's that got to do with the boy's having left?

The Wife. You know how they listen to everything.

The Man. Well?

The Wife. Well. Suppose he goes round telling people? You know how they're always dinning[13] it into them in the Hitler Youth. They deliberately encourage the kids to repeat everything. It's so odd his going off so quietly.

The Man. Rubbish.

The Wife. Didn't you see when he went?

The Man. He was hanging round the window for quite a time.

The Wife. I'd like to know how much he heard.

The Man. But he must know what happens to people who get reported.

The Wife. What about that boy the Schmulkes[14] were telling us about? They say his father's still in a concentration camp.[15] I wish we knew how long he was in the room.

The Man. The whole thing's a load of rubbish.

(*He hastens to the other rooms and calls the Boy.*)

The Wife. I just can't see him going off somewhere without saying a word. It wouldn't be like him.

The Man. Mightn't he be with a school friend?

The Wife. Then he'd have to be at the Mummermanns'. I'll give them a ring. (*She telephones.*)

The Man. It's all a false alarm, if you ask me.

The Wife (*telephoning*). Is that Mrs. Mummermann? It's Mrs. Furcke[16] here. Good afternoon. Is Klaus-Heinrich with you? He isn't?—Then where on earth can the boy be?—Mrs. Mummermann do you happen to know if the Hitler Youth place is open on Sunday afternoons?—It is?—Thanks a lot, I'll ask them.

(*She hangs up. They sit in silence.*)

The Man. What do you think he overheard?

The Wife. You were talking about the paper. You shouldn't have said what you did about the Brown House. He's so patriotic about that kind of thing.

The Man. What am I supposed to have said about the Brown House?

---

13. **dinning:** instilling through constant repetition.

14. **Schmulkes** (shmo͞ol′kəz).

15. **concentration camp:** prison camp where individuals are subjected to brutal treatment—including starvation and torture—and often are killed.

16. **Furcke** (fo͞or′kə).

The Wife. You remember perfectly well. That things weren't all snowy white in there.

The Man. Well, nobody can take that as an attack, can they? Saying things aren't all white, or snowy white rather, as I qualified it—which makes a difference, quite a substantial one at that—well, it's more a kind of jocular remark like the man in the street makes in the vernacular,[17] sort of, and all it really means is that probably not absolutely everything even there is always exactly as the Führer[18] would like it to be. I quite deliberately emphasized that this was only "probably" so by using the phrase, as I very well remember, "I'm *told*" things aren't *all*—and that's another obvious qualification—so snowy white there. "I'm told"; that doesn't mean it's necessarily so. How could I say things aren't snowy white? I haven't any proof. Wherever there are human beings there are imperfections. That's all I was suggesting, and in very qualified form. And in any case there was a certain occasion when the Führer himself expressed the same kind of criticisms a great deal more strongly.

The Wife. I don't understand you. You don't need to talk to me in that way.

The Man. I'd like to think I don't. I wish I knew to what extent you gossip about all that's liable to be said between these four walls in the heat of the moment. Of course I wouldn't dream of accusing you of casting ill-considered aspersions on your husband, any more than I'd think my boy capable for one moment of doing anything to harm his own father. But doing harm and doing it wittingly are unfortunately two very different matters.

The Wife. You can stop that right now! What about the kind of things you say yourself? Here am I worrying myself silly whether you

Portrait of Prince Eristoff (1925), Tamara de Lempicka. Copyright © 2002 Artists Rights Society (ARS), New York/ADAGP, Paris.

made that remark about life in Nazi Germany being intolerable before or after the one about the Brown House.

The Man. I never said anything of the sort.

The Wife. You're acting absolutely as if I were the police. All I'm doing is racking my brains about what the boy may have overheard.

The Man. The term Nazi Germany just isn't in my vocabulary.

The Wife. And that stuff about the warden of our block and how the papers print nothing but lies, and what you were saying about civil defense the other day—when does the boy hear a single constructive remark? That just doesn't do any good to a child's attitude of mind, it's simply demoralizing, and at a time when the Führer keeps stressing that Germany's future lies in Germany's youth. He really isn't the kind of boy to rush off and denounce one just like that. It makes me feel quite ill.

---

17. **vernacular:** everyday spoken language.
18. **the Führer:** Hitler. *Führer* is German for a leader.

The Man. He's <u>vindictive</u>, though.

The Wife. What on earth has he got to be vindictive about?

The Man. God knows, but there's bound to be something. The time I confiscated his tree-frog perhaps.

The Wife. But that was a week ago.

The Man. It's that kind of thing that sticks in his mind, though.

The Wife. What did you <u>confiscate</u> it for, anyway?

The Man. Because he wouldn't catch any flies for it. He was letting the creature starve.

The Wife. He really is run off his feet, you know.

The Man. There's not much the frog can do about that.

The Wife. But he never came back to the subject, and I gave him ten pfennigs only a moment ago. He only has to want something and he gets it.

The Man. Exactly. I call that bribery.

The Wife. What do you mean by that?

The Man. They'll simply say we were trying to bribe him to keep his mouth shut.

The Wife. What do you imagine they could do to you?

The Man. Absolutely anything. There's no limit. My God! And to think I'm supposed to be a teacher. An educator of our youth. Our youth scares me stiff.

The Wife. But they've nothing against you.

The Man. They've something against everyone. Everyone's suspect. Once the suspicion's there, one's suspect.

The Wife. But a child's not a reliable witness. A child hasn't the faintest idea what it's talking about.

The Man. So you say. But when did they start having to have witnesses for things?

The Wife. Couldn't we work out what you could have meant by your remarks? Then he could just have misunderstood you.

The Man. Well, what did I say? I can't even remember. It's all the fault of that damned rain. It puts one in a bad mood. Actually I'm the last person to say anything against the moral resurgence[19] the German people is going through these days. I foresaw the whole thing as early as the winter of 1932.

The Wife. Karl, there just isn't time to discuss that now. We must straighten everything out right away. There's not a minute to spare.

The Man. I don't believe Klaus-Heinrich's capable of it.

The Wife. Let's start with the Brown House and all the filth.

The Man. I never said a word about filth.

The Wife. You said the paper's full of filth and you want to cancel it.

The Man. Right, the paper. But not the Brown House.

The Wife. Couldn't you have been saying that you won't stand for such filth in the churches? And that you think the people now being tried could quite well be the same as used to spread malicious rumors about the Brown House suggesting things weren't all that snowy white there? And that they ought to have started looking into their own place instead? And what you were telling the boy was that he should stop fiddling with the wireless and read the paper because you're firmly of the opinion that the youth of the Third Reich should have a clear view of what's happening round about them.

The Man. It wouldn't be any use.

---

19. **resurgence:** renewal; revival.

WORDS TO KNOW

vindictive (vĭn-dĭk′tĭv) *adj.* having a strong tendency toward revenge
confiscate (kŏn′fĭ-skāt′) *v.* to seize by authority

The Wife. Karl, you're not to give up now. You should be strong, like the Führer keeps on . . .

The Man. I'm not going to be brought before the law and have my own flesh and blood standing in the witness box and giving evidence against me.

The Wife. There's no need to take it like that.

The Man. It was a great mistake our seeing so much of the Klimbtsches.

The Wife. But nothing whatever has happened to him.

The Man. Yes, but there's talk of an inquiry.

The Wife. What would it be like if everybody got in such a panic as soon as there was talk of an inquiry?

The Man. Do you think our block warden has anything against us?

The Wife. You mean, supposing they asked him? He got a box of cigars for his birthday the other day and his Christmas box was ample.

The Man. The Gauffs gave him fifteen marks.

The Wife. Yes, but they were still taking a social-ist paper in 1932, and as late as May 1933 they were hanging out the old nationalist flag.[20]

(*The phone rings.*)

The Man. That's the phone.

The Wife. Shall I answer it?

The Man. I don't know.

The Wife. Who could be ringing us?

The Man. Wait a moment. If it rings again, answer it.

(*They wait. It doesn't ring again.*)

The Man. We can't go on living like this!

The Wife. Karl!

The Man. A Judas,[21] that's what you've borne me. Sitting at the table listening, gulping down the

---

20. **socialist paper . . . nationalist flag:** A socialist paper would reflect a leftist point of view, opposite to that held by the Nazis. Though not the official flag of Germany until 1935, the Nazi flag, which featured a swastika, had been in existence since about 1920.

21. **a Judas:** a traitor, such as Judas Iscariot, the betrayer of Jesus.

HUMANITIES CONNECTION Hitler set up organizations to train young people in Nazi teachings. This photograph shows children in Austria saluting the Nazi leader.

soup we've given him and noting down whatever his father says, the little spy.

The Wife. That's a dreadful thing to say.

(pause)

The Wife. Do you think we ought to make any kind of preparations?

The Man. Do you think he'll bring them straight back with him?

The Wife. Could he really?

The Man. Perhaps I'd better put on my Iron Cross.[22]

The Wife. Of course you must, Karl.

(He gets it and puts it on with shaking hands.)

The Wife. But they've nothing against you at school, have they?

The Man. How's one to tell? I'm prepared to teach whatever they want taught; but what's that? If only I could tell . . . How am I to know what they want Bismarck[23] to have been like? When they're taking so long to publish the new text books. Couldn't you give the maid another ten marks? She's another who's always listening.

The Wife *(nodding).* And what about the picture of Hitler; shouldn't we hang it above your desk? It'd look better.

The Man. Yes, do that.

(The Wife starts taking down the picture.)

The Man. Suppose the boy goes and says we deliberately rehung it, though, it might look as if we had a bad conscience.

(The Wife puts the picture back on its old hook.)

The Man. Wasn't that the door?

The Wife. I didn't hear anything.

The Man. It was.

The Wife. Karl!

(She embraces him.)

The Man. Keep a grip on yourself. Pack some things for me.

(The door of the flat opens. Man and Wife stand rigidly side by side in the corner of the room. The door opens and enter the Boy, a paper bag in his hand. Pause.)

The Boy. What's the matter with you people?

The Wife. Where have you been?

(The Boy shows her the bag, which contains chocolate.)

The Wife. Did you simply go out to buy chocolate?

The Boy. Wherever else? Obvious, isn't it?

(He crosses the room munching, and goes out. His parents look inquiringly after him.)

The Man. Do you suppose he's telling the truth?

(The Wife shrugs her shoulders.)

---

22. **Iron Cross:** a German medal awarded for bravery during wartime.

23. **Bismarck:** Otto von Bismarck (1815–1898), a German statesman who united the German states into an empire in 1871.

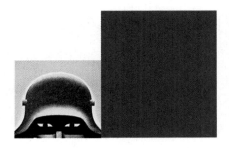

Connect to the Literature

1. **What Do You Think?**
   What did you expect to happen when the door opened near the end of the play?

   Comprehension Check
   - What are the boy's parents talking about before he leaves?
   - Why are the parents so fearful after their son goes out?

Think Critically

2. How would you describe family life under the Nazis?

   THINK ABOUT {
   - the wife's concern over her husband's remarks
   - the husband's reaction to his wife's gossiping
   - their attitude toward their son

3. Do you think the boy has informed on his parents? Cite details from the play to support your opinion.

4. Explain whether the title *The Spy* is an appropriate **title** for this play.

5. **ACTIVE READING: UNDERSTANDING HISTORICAL CONTEXT** Review the chart you made in your ▥ **READER'S NOTEBOOK**. With a partner, discuss any incidents or references that you still have questions about.

Extend Interpretations

6. **What If?** Imagine that the play had ended with the parents' arrest. How would your reaction be different?

7. **Connect to Life** In this play, the loss of privacy is a key issue. Do you think privacy is at risk in our world today? Explain your opinion.

LITERARY ANALYSIS: DIALOGUE AND MOOD

Playwrights rely heavily on **dialogue**—written conversation between two or more characters—to develop both character and plot. For example, consider what the following lines reveal about the husband and the wife in *The Spy:*

THE MAN: *It's a disaster, its raining like this. It's quite intolerable, living in a country where it's a disaster when it rains.*

THE WIFE: *Do you really think it's sensible to go round making remarks like that?*

You might infer that the husband feels tense, threatened, and frustrated. The wife's response suggests that she feels it is better to hide one's discontent than to vent it.

The dialogue also helps to establish the **mood**—the feeling or atmosphere that a writer creates for the reader. You might describe the mood in one of several ways— for example, as romantic, gloomy, or suspenseful.

Paired Activity Draw a web and in the center write down one or more words to describe the feeling you get from the play. Then, in the surrounding circles, write down lines from the play that help create this feeling. Share your diagram with a partner.

Writing Options

1. Research Plan Write an outline for a research paper about family life in Nazi Germany. Begin by reviewing a few sources in order to acquire a basic understanding of the subject. Then choose a topic that is limited enough to explore in a five-to-ten-page paper. Finally, write an outline of the paper, using a standard outline format. Place the outline in your **Writing Portfolio.**

Writing Handbook
See page R39: Options for Organization.

2. Top-Secret Memo Imagine that you are in a position to spy on the family portrayed in this play. Write a memo to your superiors, describing your observations. Explain whether you think the parents pose a threat to the state.

Activities & Explorations

1. Play Poster Suppose that a troupe of actors will visit your school to perform *The Spy.* How would you interest other students in the play? Design a poster that suggests the play's mood. Include a powerful line or two from the play as a caption. ~ **ART**

2. Improvisational Performance With a classmate, improvise a scene between the husband and the wife after their son goes into his bedroom with the bag of chocolates. Consider whether his return home might have altered the opinions the parents expressed earlier in the play. ~ **PERFORMING**

Inquiry & Research

1. Controlling Youths The Nazi regime wasn't the only one in history to use its nation's youth in the service of the state. Find out how young people were used in other totalitarian states, such as China during Mao Zedong's Cultural Revolution (1966–1976) and Cambodia under Pol Pot's Khmer Rouge (1975–1979).

 RESEARCH STARTER
CLASSZONE.COM

2. Brecht's Drama *The Spy* is part of a collection of 24 short plays by Brecht, called *Fear and Misery of the Third Reich.* Read another play from this collection, and summarize its plot for the class.

Vocabulary in Action

EXERCISE: WORD MEANINGS For each sentence, write *T* if the statement is true or *F* if it is false.

1. Klaus-Heinrich showed he was **vindictive** by going out and spending his money.

2. The father felt that it was **demoralizing** to be spied on all the time.

3. He hated the rain and spoke in a **jocular** way about it.

4. The father quite **wittingly** took away his son's tree frog.

5. The mother **confiscated** her son by calling friends to see if he was visiting them.

Building Vocabulary

For an in-depth lesson on context clues, see page 674.

FROM

THE WORLD WAS SILENT

ELIE WIESEL

Elie Wiesel
1928–

His Mission For decades, Elie Wiesel (ā'lē vē'səl) has been one of the world's most eloquent writers about the Holocaust. He himself survived the Nazi concentration camps. His mission as a writer is to keep alive the memory of the Holocaust in the hope that people will learn from the past.

Early Years Wiesel grew up in the orthodox Jewish community of Sighet (sē'gĕt), a small town in Romania. Isolated from the rest of Europe, the Jews of Sighet—about 15,000 in all—had no idea what lay in store when the Nazis rounded them up in 1944. They were shipped on a cattle train to Auschwitz (oush'vĭts'), a concentration camp in Poland. There young Elie was separated from his mother and sister, never to see them again. Later he and his father were transported to Buchenwald (bōō'ĸнən-vält'), a concentration camp in Germany. His father died in that camp shortly before the Allies set it free.

Telling the World After the war, Wiesel lived in France. He studied philosophy at the University of Paris and began a career in journalism. At first he wrote nothing about his concentration-camp experiences. Then, recognizing the need to tell the world what had happened, he drew upon his terrible ordeal to write *Night,* which appeared in French in 1958 and in English two years later. Since then, Wiesel has continued to give voice to the multitudes who perished in the Holocaust. He has also called attention to more recent human-rights violations, in countries such as South Africa, Bangladesh, and Bosnia. For his humanitarian efforts, he was awarded the Nobel Peace Prize in 1986.

Other Works
Dawn
The Accident
The Town Beyond the Wall
All Rivers Run to the Sea
And the Sea Is Never Full

For a humanities activity, click on:

HUMANITIES
CLASSZONE.COM

Build Background

Hitler's "Final Solution" The Holocaust was the Nazis' systematic murder of millions of Jews and non-Aryans during World War II (1939–1945). The literal meaning of the word *holocaust* is "a sacrificial offering that is completely burned."

As a young man, Adolf Hitler developed a fierce hatred of the Jews. After he came to power in 1933, he targeted the Jewish people for extermination. The Nazis gradually stripped Germany's Jews of their rights, boycotted and vandalized Jewish businesses, and fired Jews from government and university posts. Within a few years Jews were barred from public facilities.

This persecution increased during World War II. As Nazi troops swept through Poland and the Soviet Union, they massacred whole populations of Jews. Then in 1942, the Nazis devised their so-called "final solution of the Jewish question": a systematic policy to murder every Jewish man, woman, and child under German rule. Multitudes of Jews were arrested, herded onto railroad cars, and transported to concentration camps. Upon arrival, some prisoners were killed immediately in gas chambers and then cremated. Others were forced to become slave laborers.

For a prisoner, the journey by train to one of the death camps was a horrendous experience. In the excerpt you are about to read, the author describes his journey. He was only 15 at the time.

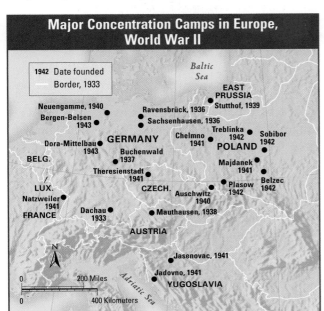

Major Concentration Camps in Europe, World War II

Connect to Your Life

Why do you think some Holocaust survivors feel the need to speak or write about their experiences in the concentration camps? What good might they accomplish by telling their stories? Discuss these questions with a small group of classmates.

Focus Your Reading

LITERARY ANALYSIS: AUTHOR'S PURPOSE
Authors write for one or more of the following purposes: to inform, to express an opinion, to entertain, and to persuade. As you read this excerpt, think about Wiesel's purpose for writing it.

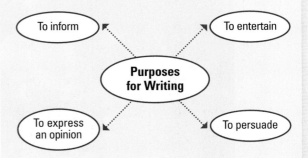

ACTIVE READING: CONNECTING TO THE AUTHOR'S EXPERIENCE
Literature that deals with disturbing events, such as Wiesel's memoir of the Holocaust, may stir intense feelings in you and lead you to reflect deeply about the world you live in. You may find yourself comparing the events retold in this excerpt with other events you have read about, heard about, or experienced. You may get so caught up as you read that you imagine yourself in the narrator's situation. These responses are ways of **connecting** with what you are reading.

📖**READER'S NOTEBOOK** As you read this excerpt, try to connect to the experiences Wiesel describes. Write down the ideas and feelings these events stir in you.

from The World Was Silent

Elie Wiesel

Translated by Moshe Spiegel

Copyright © Hulton-Deutsch Collection.

Indescribable confusion reigned.

Parents searched for their children, children for their parents, and lonely captives for their friends. The people were beset[1] by loneliness. Everyone feared that the outcome of the journey would be tragic and would claim its toll of lives. And so one yearned to have the companionship of someone who would stand by with a word, with a loving glance.

Afterward, an ominous silence fell upon us. We squatted on the soft snow that covered the floor of the railroad car like a carpet, and tried to keep warm by drawing closer to our neighbors.

When the train started to move, no one paid any attention to it. Careworn and burdened with conflicting thoughts, each of us wondered if he was wise to continue on the journey. But in our weari-

---

1. beset: continually troubled.

ness, whether one died today, tomorrow, a week or a generation later, hardly seemed to matter.

The night dragged on interminably, as though it were to go on to the end of time. When the gray dawn appeared in the east, I felt as though I had spent a night in a tomb haunted by evil spirits. Human beings, defeated and broken, sat like dusty tombstones in the dim light of early dawn. I looked about the subdued throng and tried to distinguish one from another. And, indeed, perhaps there was no distinction.

My gaze fell on one who stared blankly ahead. A wry[2] smile seemed to play on his ice-encrusted face. Those glazed eyes, whether living or dead, seemed to ensnare my gaze. A hundred and twenty captives, shadows of human lives, extinguished flames of burned-out candles lit on the anniversaries of the deaths of their loved ones.

Wrapped in a drenched blanket, his black cap pulled down over his ears, a layer of snow on his shoulders, my father sat beside me. Could it be that he, too, was dead? The thought flashed across my mind. I tried to talk to him. I wanted to shout, but all I could do was mutter. He did not reply, he did not utter a sound. I was certain that from then on I was to be all alone, all alone. Then I was filled with a numbing sense of indifference to everyone and to myself. Well, the Lord giveth and the Lord taketh away. The struggle was over. There was nothing and no one for whom to fight now.

The train ground to an abrupt halt in a snow-covered field. Awakened by the jolt, a few curious captives struggled to their feet to look out. The scene was reminiscent[3] of cattle staring stupidly from a livestock car.

German S.S. guards surrounded the human cargo, shouting, "All the dead are to be thrown out! All the dead are to be thrown out!"

The living were pleased; there would be more

Careworn and burdened with conflicting thoughts, each of us wondered if he was wise to continue on the journey.

space. It would not be as crowded now.

Strong men appeared and examined each one who could not stand up, and rapped out, "Here's one! Get hold of him!"

Whereupon two men would pick the corpse by the shoulders and feet and fling it out of the car like a sack of flour.

From various parts of the car came such cries as, "Here's another—my neighbor! He doesn't move. Help me get rid of him!"

Two deportees[4] stepped forward and tried to lift a form beside me. It was only then that I was aroused from my stupor, and realized the seriousness of the situation. And to this day I cannot understand how I summoned the strength and courage to save my father from the lurking[5] death. I kneeled over him, tearing at his clothes, slapping his face, kissing him and screaming, "Daddy, Daddy—wake up! Get up, Daddy! Don't let them throw you out of the car. . . ."

As he failed to respond, the two men said to me, "There's no use your screaming, little fellow. He's dead! Your father is dead, do you understand?"

"No! He is not dead! He's not dead!" I wailed, repeating the words over and over indefinitely. For some reason, I seemed to fear the death of my

---

2. **wry:** twisted.

3. **reminiscent:** awakening memories of something past.

4. **deportees:** people being deported, or sent out of a country.

5. **lurking:** waiting just out of sight.

father more than my own. I tried again and again to release him from the embrace of the angels of death, and I succeeded at last.

My father opened his glazed, ice-encrusted eyes, and regarded me in a dazed way, unable to understand what I was trying to convey to him or the commotion that was being made over him.

"See for yourselves, you murderers. He's alive, he's living!"

The two men eyed my father for a moment, then shrugged their shoulders and muttered, "Not for long," and turned to other silent forms.

There were some twenty-odd dead in our one car, and after they were stripped of their clothes, which the living snatched up, they were flung out of the car.

This task took several hours. Then the train chugged along, and as icy gusts shrieked about it, it seemed that through the accursed world about us could be heard the far-away, muffled wail of the naked bodies that had been abandoned on Polish snow-covered fields.

The journey was insufferable;[6] and every one who lived through it later questioned the natural laws that their survival seemed to disprove.

We were deprived of even bread and water, and snow was our only source of water. Cramped for space and thoroughly chilled, we were very weak by the third day of the journey. Days were turned into nights, and the nights cast a shadow of doom over our very souls.

The train plodded along for what seemed countless days, and the snow fell, fell, fell incessantly. And the exhausted, travel-weary unfortunates lay huddled for days on end, without uttering a word, eyes closed, waiting for one thing only—the next station, where the new yield of corpses would be got rid of. That was what we looked forward to.

The journey lasted ten interminable days and nights. Each day claimed its toll of victims and each night paid its homage[7] to the Angel of Death.

We passed through German settlements, generally in the early morning hours, only in a few instances. Sometimes men on their way to work would halt in their tracks to glare at us as though we were animals in a kind of demonic circus. Once a German hurled a chunk of bread into our car and caused pandemonium to break out as scores of famished men fought each other in an effort to pounce upon it. And the German workers eyed the spectacle with sneering amusement.

Years later, I chanced to land in the Oriental port of Aden.[8] Some of the ship's passengers, looking for excitement and exotic thrills, tossed coins into the water to be retrieved by native boys who arrived on the scene to entertain the pleasure-seeking travelers by diving into the deep waters for the coins. At times the young divers would remain underwater for several minutes, and the passengers cheered the novel sport that could be enjoyed for a mere sixpence. . . .

I had once before witnessed such a scene. An elderly aristocratic woman from Paris, holding a handful of coins, stood on the deck amusing herself by throwing them one at a time to a dozen young dark-skinned swimmers. Each time she tossed a coin into the stream, a fierce fight ensued among the divers—a fact that seemed to delight her no end, judging by her peals of laughter. Revolted[9] by the scene of children trying to choke each other under water for the possession of a coin, I pleaded with the woman not to throw any more coins.

"Why not?" she replied. "I love to give charity."

She loved almsgiving—and to see six- and seven-year-old children fighting each other for a worthless coin.

Then I looked back upon that morning when

---

6. **insufferable:** unbearable.

7. **homage:** respect; tribute.

8. **Aden** (äd'n): a former British colony in Arabia, now part of Yemen.

9. **revolted:** disgusted.

> **Once a German hurled a chunk of bread into our car and caused pandemonium to break out as scores of famished men fought each other in an effort to pounce upon it.**

our train, carrying its human cargo, had halted near the German city and the worker had thrown a piece of bread into our car, perhaps in compassion, although that is hard to believe. At any rate, the morsel of food caused the death of a number of men. The scramble for bread! The fight for life! The chunk of bread brought about its own kind of war to the death. The wildest instincts of the primeval[10] jungle had seized all of us, and we pounced upon the bread with all the savagery of enraged beasts. An atavistic[11] throw-back?

Unfortunately, the Torah does not relate how the children of Israel received the first manna in the wilderness.[12] Did they fight over it, and were there any casualties? And did scenes like the one in our car take place there? The German workers tarried a while, gazing at the amusing spectacle, and perhaps assuaging[13] their conscience at the same time with the thought of their benevolence in giving bread to the hungry.

All the other German workers soon followed the example of their kindhearted townsmen. Pieces of bread were cast into all the cars. Bread and victims. And they—the good, gallant[14] Germans— were pleased with themselves and smiled.

Strange, even while jotting down these words, the event seems incredible to me. I seem to be writing a horror novel—a novel that should not be read at night. It is hard to believe that what I set down in writing is really true, has actually happened to me.

And—only ten years ago!

I think to myself: if all that is alive in my memory, and that is seething in my heart, is really true, how am I able to sleep at night? How can I eat my food in peace? I can still see the scenes I experienced that early morning when the bits of bread fell from heaven.

Unfortunately, the bread also fell into our car. Though I was very hungry, my exhaustion was stronger. So I didn't budge from my spot, refusing to take part in what was going on. Let bread drop down—even from heaven. I would not risk my life to get it. I lacked the strength not only to fight for the hard crusts, but even to eat them. So I squatted in my corner, watching how human beings turned into animals as they attempted to snatch the morsels of food from each others' mouths.

A piece of the heavenly bread fell in a corner of the car; the next moment another corner was emptied of its occupants. Not far from me a young lad bit the ear of someone standing in front of him, in order to get to the priceless bread first. The injured person, bent only upon reaching the bread, was oblivious to the pain. I suddenly beheld a frail, elderly Jew crawling along the floor, one hand

---

10. **primeval:** from the first or earliest times.

11. **atavistic:** returning to a primitive type of behavior.

12. **the Torah . . . wilderness:** The Torah is the first five books of the Hebrew scriptures (that is, the first five books of the Old Testament in Christian Bibles). The Book of Exodus contains the story of how the Israelites were given manna, a miraculous food from heaven, during their flight from Egypt.

13. **assuaging:** soothing; relieving.

14. **gallant:** noble.

Zydowski Instytut Historyczny Instytut Naukowo-Badawczy, Warsaw, Poland. Courtesy of USHMM Photo Archives.

clutching his chest. At first I thought that he had been hurt in the fight. But then I saw him take a handful of crumbs from his bosom and devour them almost with ecstasy.

A sly smile played upon his deathly pale face for a moment, and disappeared. Then someone pounced on the old man like a phantom, and the two engaged in a death struggle, clawing, biting, trampling, kicking one another. The old man managed to raise his head, a glint of joy in his bloodshot eyes.

"Little Meyer! Meyer, my son," the graybeard mumbled. "Didn't you recognize me? You have hurt me so much. . . ."

Meyer still struggled to retrieve a piece of bread from his father's bosom. Then the dying old man groaned, "Meyer, you're beating your own father . . . I brought bread for you, too. I had risked my life . . . and you're hitting, beating me—your old father. . . ."

The old man seemed on the verge of death, he no longer made any sound. Meyer had triumphed: his right hand clutched the small piece of bread, and his left wiped the blood trickling from one of his eyes. The old man held a piece of bread in his clenched fist and tried to bring it up to his mouth—to die with the taste of food in his mouth. His eyes were alert now; he was clearly aware of the situation. He was at the portals[15] of death—a condition in which one comprehends all that goes on about him. As he brought the hand with the bread closer to his half-opened mouth, his face glowed with lust for the bread. . . . It seemed as though the old man was holding back the bread intentionally, so that the pleasure of the anticipated[16] feast should last longer. The eyes seemed about to burst from their sockets. And as the old man was about to bite into the bread with his darkened, broken teeth, Meyer once

15. **portals:** doorways.
16. **anticipated:** looked forward to.

more pounced upon him and snatched the bread from him.

The old man muttered, "What? A last will and testament?" But, except for me, neither his son nor anyone else heard him. At last he breathed his last; and his orphaned son ate the bread. He was sprawled on the floor of the car, his right hand stretched out as though protesting to God, who had transformed Meyer into a murderer.

I could not bear to look at the old man for long. The son soon found himself engaged in a new struggle. Catching sight of the bread in his hand, others then pounced upon him. He tried to defend himself, but the furious throng, thirsting for blood in their frenzy, killed him. And so the two of them, father and son, victims of the struggle for bread, were trampled upon. Both perished, starved and alone.

Suddenly, I had the feeling that someone was laughing behind me, and I wondered who it was. But I was afraid to look around for fear of learning that the laughter was not coming from behind me, but from myself. I was fifteen years old then. Do you understand—fifteen? Is it any wonder that I, along with my generation, do not believe either in God or in man; in the feelings of a son, in the love of a father. Is it any wonder that I cannot realize that I myself experienced this thing, that my childish eyes had witnessed it?

Meir[17] Katz, a robust, energetic Jew with a thundering voice, an old friend of my father, was with us in the car. He worked as a gardener in Buna.[18] He conducted himself gallantly, both physically and morally. He was placed in command of the human cargo in our car because of his strength. It was thanks to him that I finally arrived alive in the Buchenwald concentration camp.[19]

It was during the third night of our journey—or was it some other?—we lost track of time. We squatted, trying to doze off, when I was suddenly awakened by someone choking me. With superhuman effort, I managed to shout one word—

"Father!" That was all I managed to get out, as the unknown attacker was choking off my breath. Fortunately, my father awakened and tried to free me from the stranglehold. Unable to do so, however, he appealed to Meir Katz for help, whereupon the latter came to my rescue.

I didn't know the strangler or the reason for his violent act. After all, I had carried no bread with me. It may have been a sudden fit of insanity, or—just a case of mistaken identity.

Meir Katz also died during that journey. A few days before we reached Buchenwald, he said to my father, "Shloime,[20] I'm on my way out. I can't stand it any longer."

"Meir, don't give up!" my father tried to hearten him. "Bear up! You've got to! Try to have courage!"

"Shloime, it's no use—I'm washed-out," Meir muttered. "I can't go on."

Then the sturdy Meir Katz broke down and sobbed, mourning his son, who was killed in the early days of the Hitler terror.

On the last day of the journey, bitter cold, accompanied by a heavy snowfall, aggravated the situation even more. The end seemed to be near. Then someone warned, "Fellow Jews, in such weather, we've got to move about; we must not sit motionless—or we'll all freeze to death!"

So we all got up—even those who seemed to be dying—and wrapped our drenched blankets about our bodies. The scene was reminiscent of a congregation wrapped in prayer shawls,[21] swaying to and fro in prayer. The snow, the car, even the sky

---

17. **Meir** (mĕ-îr′).

18. **Buna:** a small town in eastern Germany, not far from the current Czech Republic border.

19. **Buchenwald concentration camp:** Located in eastern Germany near the city of Weimar, this camp held about 20,000 prisoners.

20. **Shloime** (shloi′mə).

21. **prayer shawls:** shawls with knotted fringe at the corners, traditionally worn by Jewish males, especially for morning prayers.

HUMANITIES CONNECTION This photograph was taken after the Allied troops liberated Buchenwald concentration camp. Wiesel is on the second bunk from the floor, the seventh person from the left.

gusts of wind and amid the swirling snow soared to heaven, but, echoing from the closed gates there, reverberated back to earth.

Before long, twenty-five cars crowded with deportees joined us in the hysterical song of death. Everyone had reached the breaking point. The end was drawing near. The train was struggling up the hill of the Thyring[23] forest. The divine tragi-comedy was approaching its finale. There were no longer any illusions about surviving; the thousands of deportees were aware of their doom.

"Why don't they mow us down on the spot?" Meir Katz asked through tears. "We could at least be spared further agony."

"Reb[24] Meir, we'll soon arrive at our destination," I tried to comfort him. But the wind drowned out my words. We stood in the open car, under the falling snow, screaming hysterically.

We arrived at the Buchenwald concentration camp late at night.

"Security police" of the camp came forward to unload the human cargo. The dead were left in the cars. Only those who were able to drag their feet got out. Meir Katz was left in the car; like so many others, he had frozen to death a short time before we reached our destination. The journey itself was the worst part of the ordeal. About forty of the deportees were claimed by death on that one day alone. Our car had originally started out with a hundred and twenty souls; twelve—among them my father and I—had survived the ordeal. ❖

(heaven?)—everything and everybody seemed to be swaying, worshiping, communing[22] with God, uttering the prayer of life, the prayer of death. The sword of the Angel of Death was suspended above. A congregation of corpses at prayer.

A shout, an outcry like that of a wounded animal, suddenly rent the air in the car. The effect was terrifying and some of the people could not endure it silently, and themselves began to scream. Their outcries seemed to come from another world. Soon the rest of us joined in the uproar; screaming and shrieking filled the air. The deafening roar rode the

22. **communing:** talking intimately.
23. **Thyring** (tü′rĭng).
24. **Reb:** a Jewish title of respect for a man.

When in early summer . . .

Nelly Sachs

**Translated by
Ruth and Matthew Mead**

*The sketch above was drawn by a young girl in Terezin
Concentration Camp. She died in captivity when she was
only 11. Nelly Sachs nearly became a Holocaust victim, too,
before escaping from Germany in 1940. Her poem opens
with images of the beauty of awakening nature. A voice,
however, discloses other realities—horrors perpetrated in
the midst of loveliness.*

When in early summer the moon sends out secret signs,
the chalices of lilies scent of heaven,
some ear opens to listen
beneath the chirp of the cricket
5 to earth turning and the language of spirits set free.

2 chalices: cup-shaped blossoms.

But in dreams fish fly in the air
and a forest takes firm root in the floor of the room.

But in the midst of enchantment a voice speaks clearly
   and amazed:
World, how can you go on playing your games
10 and cheating time—
World, the little children were thrown like butterflies,
wings beating into the flames—

and your earth has not been thrown like a rotten apple
into the terror-roused abyss—

15 And sun and moon have gone on walking—
two cross-eyed witnesses who have seen nothing.

Connect to the Literature

1. What Do You Think?
What thoughts did you
have after reading the
last sentence of this
selection?

Comprehension Check
• What were some specific
hardships endured by the
prisoners on the train?
• How did the prisoners react when
bread was thrown onto the train?

Think Critically

**2. ACTIVE READING: CONNECTING TO THE AUTHOR'S
EXPERIENCE** Review the notes you made in your
READER'S NOTEBOOK. Which details in this memoir
had the strongest effect on you?

3. How do you account for the prisoners' mental state?

> THINK
> ABOUT

- the fights to the death for bits of bread
- the attempt to strangle young Wiesel
- the terrible screaming

4. How would you contrast Meyer's and young Wiesel's
treatment of their fathers?

5. In your opinion, has Wiesel come to terms with his past, or
is he still haunted by it? Cite details from the selection to
support your opinion.

Extend Interpretations

6. What If? What might have happened to young Wiesel if he
had failed to save his father from being tossed off the train?

7. Compare Texts What connection do you see between
Wiesel's choice of title, *The World Was Silent,* and the poem
"When in Early Summer" (page 1241)?

8. Connect to Life The author writes about some of the
darkest moments of his life. If you had survived a terrible
ordeal, do you think you would choose to share it with
others in some way? Give reasons for your response.

LITERARY ANALYSIS: AUTHOR'S PURPOSE

Authors write for one or more of
these purposes: to inform, to
entertain, to express opinions, and
to persuade. For example, writers of
editorials seek to persuade readers
to do or believe something. Though
an author may have several
purposes, usually one is the most
important. To help you in
determining an author's purpose or
purposes, look for the following
features as you read. The purpose
that each feature might signal is
noted in parentheses.
- facts or explanations about
  people, places, or events (to inform
  or analyze)
- comments about facts (to express
  ideas, opinions, or emotions)
- statements that seem intended to
  convince you of something
  (to persuade)
- passages that you find particularly
  enjoyable or moving (to entertain)

Paired Activity With a classmate,
go back through the excerpt and
identify passages that provide clues
about Wiesel's purposes for writing.
Then in your notebook, list the
purposes you think Wiesel had, and
star the purpose
you think was his
most important
one. Share your
list with other
pairs of
students.

> Purposes for
> Writing
> 1. to inform readers
> about what
> happened on the
> transport trains
>
> 2.
>
> 3.

The Holocaust and Human Rights

"Wherever men or women are persecuted because of their race, religion, or political views, that place must—at that moment—become the center of the universe."

—Elie Wiesel

In the years since his liberation from Buchenwald, Elie Wiesel has devoted his life to preserving the memory of the Holocaust. Besides writing and speaking about his own experiences in concentration camps, Wiesel has sponsored various memorial activities and promoted the cause of human rights, as shown by the following:

• Served as Founding Chairman of the United States Holocaust Memorial Council, which built the United States Holocaust Memorial Museum in Washington, D.C.

• Worked tirelessly as a spokesperson for human rights, defending Cambodian refugees, victims of famine in Africa, victims of apartheid in South Africa, and victims of war in the former Yugoslavia.

• Established The Elie Wiesel Foundation for Humanity to advance the cause of human rights throughout the world.

Research Project and Group Discussion People can choose different ways to commemorate the Holocaust. With a partner, investigate one of the following projects or commemorations. Give an oral report about your findings and discuss with the class the best ways of commemorating the Holocaust.

• Steven Spielberg's Survivors of the Shoah Visual History Foundation

• Holocaust Memorial Day (Europe, January 27)

• The Elie Wiesel Foundation for Humanity

• Museum of Jewish Heritage: A Living Memorial to the Holocaust

• United States Holocaust Memorial Museum

• Holocaust memorial in Berlin, Germany (not yet built as of press date)

COULD THE HOLOCAUST HAVE BEEN PREVENTED?

If governments and leaders had spoken out . . .
If individuals had raised their voices . . .
If conscience had prevailed . . .
Millions of lives could have been saved.

Within weeks after this March 1944 photograph was taken of Emanuel and Avram Rosenthal in the Kovno ghetto, they were deported and killed by the Nazis.

NATIONAL DAYS OF REMEMBRANCE
Remembering the past for the sake of the future
April 15–22, 2001

REMEMBRANCE • EDUCATION • CONSCIENCE

For additional information on Days of Remembrance, visit the Museum's website: www. ushmm.org
100 Raoul Wallenberg Place, SW • Washington, DC 20024-2126 • (202) 488-0400

UNITED STATES HOLOCAUST MEMORIAL MUSEUM

Above, National Days of Remembrance poster. *At left,* photos of U.S. Holocaust Memorial Museum in Washington, D.C.

RESEARCH STARTER
CLASSZONE.COM

THE Guest

ALBERT CAMUS

Albert Camus
1913–1960

Early Years Albert Camus (äl-bĕr′ kä-mōō′), a French writer, is considered one of the most important literary figures of the 20th century. He grew up in Algeria, a country in northwestern Africa, when it was still a colony of France. Several of his novels and stories are set in this region.

When Camus was only an infant, his father died in action in World War I (1914–1918), leaving his family impoverished. The young Camus was an excellent student and won a scholarship that enabled him to attend high school. There he developed a love of sports, particularly swimming, boxing, and soccer. Unfortunately, his athletic career was cut short by the onset of tuberculosis, which was to trouble him for the rest of his life. He went on to earn a degree in philosophy from the University of Algiers.

Philosophical Writer After college, Camus began working for a French-language newspaper in Algiers. Soon he was publishing personal essays, novels, and stories. Many of them show the influence of a philosophy known as existentialism (ĕg′zĭ-stĕn′shə-lĭz′əm). According to this philosophy, there is no universal meaning to life. In his writings, Camus stressed the importance of personal choice and responsibility as a way to create meaning in an otherwise absurd world.

Social Commitment Both personally and professionally, Camus took a stand against oppression. He criticized French colonialism in Africa. Moreover, after moving to Paris in 1942, he joined the French resistance against the Nazi occupation in France. He edited the underground newspaper *Combat* and narrowly escaped arrest by the Gestapo, the Nazi secret police.

Postwar Fame After Paris was freed from the Nazis, Camus continued to edit *Combat* and to win acclaim for his own fiction and nonfiction. In 1957 he was awarded the Nobel Prize for literature. Three years later, he was killed in an automobile accident.

Other Works
The Stranger
The Plague
The Rebel

Build Background

The French in Algeria In 1830, France invaded Algeria. After an easy conquest, the French set up a repressive colonial government. Large tracts of fertile land were taken from the Algerians and handed over to European settlers. The settlers strongly opposed granting rights to the native population, Arab Muslims. As a result, the vast majority of Algerians suffered political, social, and economic injustice.

After World War II, Algerian Muslims grew increasingly frustrated as efforts at reform failed to bring about needed change. In 1954 a group called the National Liberation Front launched a guerrilla war against France, which responded by sending a large army to Algeria. Roughly 10,000 French troops and as many as 250,000 Muslims died in the six years of fighting that ensued. When Algeria finally gained its independence from France in 1962, most Europeans fled the country.

The conflict in Algeria caused Albert Camus much anguish. He knew that the Muslim Algerians had suffered terribly under colonial rule. "In Algeria, as elsewhere," he said, "terrorism can be explained by a lack of hope." Yet he also feared for the safety of the European Algerians, including members of his own family. Camus argued for a peaceful solution to the conflict—one that would allow both Muslims and Europeans to live in harmony. The story you are about to read takes place in Algeria shortly before the fighting breaks out.

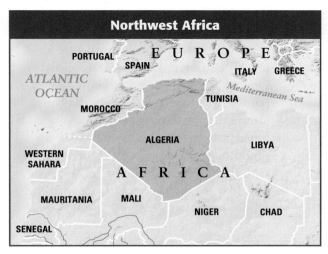

Northwest Africa

Connect to Your Life

In this story the characters are forced to make important decisions. Think about some important decisions you have made, perhaps about whether to stand up for a personal belief or to go along with the crowd. Why are some decisions so difficult to make? Share your ideas with a group of classmates.

Focus Your Reading

LITERARY ANALYSIS: THEME
A **theme** of a literary work is a central idea that the writer shares with the reader. It may be a lesson about life or human nature. Although some themes are stated directly, most must be inferred by the reader.

ACTIVE READING: MAKING INFERENCES
When you read a story, you often **make inferences** about such elements as theme, plot, and characters. That is, you "read between the lines," making logical guesses based on clues in the story. Consider, for example, what the following sentence suggests about Daru, the main character in "The Guest":

> *Daru felt a sudden wrath against the man, against all men with their rotten spite, their tireless hates, their blood lust.*

From this sentence, you might infer that Daru has lost faith in human nature.

📖 **READER'S NOTEBOOK** Make three charts like the one shown below—one for each character in the story. As you read the story, write down several actions of each character and the inferences that those actions lead you to make.

Daru	
Actions	**Inferences**
unties the Arab's hands →	has sympathy for a stranger in pain

WORDS TO KNOW **Vocabulary Preview**

adversary	chaotic	obstinate
avidly	disconcerted	

The Guest

Albert Camus

Translated by Justin O'Brien

Detail of *Portrait of a Man* (1942), Mario Mafai.
Photograph copyright © Araldo de Luca/Corbis.

FOCUS As the story begins, Daru, the schoolmaster, watches two travelers approaching in the distance. As you read, look for details that help you form impressions of Daru and the place where he lives.

The schoolmaster was watching the two men climb toward him. One was on horseback, the other on foot. They had not yet tackled the abrupt rise leading to the schoolhouse built on the hillside. They were toiling onward, making slow progress in the snow, among the stones, on the vast expanse of the high, deserted plateau.[1] From time to time the horse stumbled. Without hearing anything yet, he could see the breath issuing from the horse's nostrils. One of the men, at least, knew the region. They were following the trail although it had disappeared days ago under a layer of dirty white snow. The schoolmaster calculated that it would take them half an hour to get onto the hill. It was cold; he went back into the school to get a sweater.

---

1. **plateau:** an elevated, relatively level expanse of land.

He crossed the empty, frigid classroom. On the blackboard the four rivers of France, drawn with four different colored chalks, had been flowing toward their estuaries[2] for the past three days. Snow had suddenly fallen in mid-October after eight months of drought without the transition of rain, and the twenty pupils, more or less, who lived in the villages scattered over the plateau had stopped coming. With fair weather they would return. Daru now heated only the single room that was his lodging, adjoining the classroom and giving also onto the plateau to the east. Like the class windows, his window looked to the south too. On that side the school was a few kilometers from the point where the plateau began to slope toward the south. In clear weather could be seen the purple mass of the mountain range where the gap opened onto the desert.

Somewhat warmed, Daru returned to the window from which he had first seen the two men. They were no longer visible. Hence they must have tackled the rise. The sky was not so dark, for the snow had stopped falling during the night. The morning had opened with a dirty light which had scarcely become brighter as the ceiling of clouds lifted. At two in the afternoon it seemed as if the day were merely beginning. But still this was better than those three days when the thick snow was falling amidst unbroken darkness with little gusts of wind that rattled the double door of the classroom. Then Daru had spent long hours in his room, leaving it only to go to the shed and feed the chickens or get some coal. Fortunately the delivery truck from Tadjid, the nearest village to the north, had brought his supplies two days before the blizzard. It would return in forty-eight hours.

Besides, he had enough to resist a siege, for the little room was cluttered with bags of wheat that the administration left as a stock to distribute to those of his pupils whose families had suffered from the drought. Actually they had all been victims because they were all poor. Every day Daru would distribute a ration to the children. They had missed it, he knew, during these bad days. Possibly one of the fathers or big brothers would come this afternoon and he could supply them with grain. It was just a matter of carrying them over to the next harvest. Now shiploads of wheat were arriving from France and the worst was over. But it would be hard to forget that poverty, that army of ragged ghosts wandering in the sunlight, the plateaus burned to a cinder month after month, the earth shriveled up little by little, literally scorched, every stone bursting into dust under one's foot. The sheep had died then by thousands and even a few men, here and there, sometimes without anyone's knowing.

In contrast with such poverty, he who lived almost like a monk in his remote schoolhouse, nonetheless satisfied with the little he had and with the rough life, had felt like a lord with his whitewashed walls, his narrow couch, his unpainted shelves, his well, and his weekly provision of water and food. And suddenly this snow, without warning, without the foretaste of rain. This is the way the region was, cruel to live in, even without men—who didn't help matters either. But Daru had been born here. Everywhere else, he felt exiled.

PAUSE & REFLECT Why is life so difficult for Daru's pupils and their families?

---

2. **the four rivers of France . . . estuaries:** France's four major rivers are the Loire (lwär), the Seine (sān), the Marne (märn), and the Rhone (rōn). Their estuaries are the stretches near their mouths, into which ocean tides flow.

FOCUS In this part you meet the two travelers: Balducci, a police officer, and his prisoner. Read to find out how Daru reacts to Balducci.

He stepped out onto the terrace in front of the schoolhouse. The two men were now halfway up the slope. He recognized the horseman as Balducci,[3] the old gendarme he had known for a long time. Balducci was holding on the end of a rope an Arab who was walking behind him with hands bound and head lowered. The gendarme waved a greeting to which Daru did not reply, lost as he was in contemplation of the Arab dressed in a faded blue jellaba,[4] his feet in sandals but covered with socks of heavy raw

wool, his head surmounted by a narrow, short *chèche*.[5] They were approaching. Balducci was holding back his horse in order not to hurt the Arab, and the group was advancing slowly.

Within earshot, Balducci shouted: "One hour to do the three kilometers from El Ameur!"[6] Daru did not answer. Short and square in his thick sweater, he watched them climb. Not once had the Arab raised his head. "Hello," said Daru

---

3. **Balducci** (bäl-dōō′chē).

4. **jellaba** (jə-lä′bə): a long, loose, hooded cloak worn by Arab men (usually spelled *djellaba*).

5. *chèche* (shĕsh) *French*: scarf (here, a type of scarf worn by French troops in Africa).

6. **El Ameur** (ĕl ə-mœr′): a town in northern Algeria, about 150 miles southwest of Algiers.

when they got up onto the terrace. "Come in and warm up." Balducci painfully got down from his horse without letting go the rope. From under his bristling mustache he smiled at the schoolmaster. His little dark eyes, deep-set under a tanned forehead, and his mouth surrounded with wrinkles made him look attentive and studious. Daru took the bridle, led the horse to the shed, and came back to the two men, who were now waiting for him in the school. He led them into his room. "I am going to heat up the classroom," he said. "We'll be more comfortable there." When he entered the room again, Balducci was on the couch. He had undone the rope tying him to the Arab, who had squatted near the stove. His hands still bound, the *chèche* pushed back on his head, he was looking toward the window. At first Daru noticed only his huge lips, fat, smooth, almost Negroid; yet his nose was straight, his eyes were dark and full of fever. The *chèche* revealed an <u>obstinate</u> forehead and, under the weathered skin now rather discolored by the cold, the whole face had a restless and rebellious look that struck Daru when the Arab, turning his face toward him, looked him straight in the eyes. "Go into the other room," said the schoolmaster, "and I'll make you some mint tea." "Thanks," Balducci said. "What a chore! How I long for retirement." And addressing his prisoner in Arabic: "Come on, you." The Arab got up and, slowly, holding his bound wrists in front of him, went into the classroom.

With the tea, Daru brought a chair. But Balducci was already enthroned on the nearest pupil's desk and the Arab had squatted against the teacher's platform facing the stove, which stood between the desk and the window. When he held out the glass of tea to the prisoner, Daru hesitated at the sight of his bound hands. "He might perhaps be untied." "Sure," said Balducci. "That was for the trip." He started to get to his feet. But Daru, setting the glass on the floor, had knelt beside the Arab. Without saying anything,

The gendarme waved a greeting to which Daru did not reply.

the Arab watched him with his feverish eyes. Once his hands were free, he rubbed his swollen wrists against each other, took the glass of tea, and sucked up the burning liquid in swift little sips.

"Good," said Daru. "And where are you headed?"

Balducci withdrew his mustache from the tea. "Here, son."

"Odd pupils! And you're spending the night?"

"No. I'm going back to El Ameur. And you will deliver this fellow to Tinguit. He is expected at police headquarters."

Balducci was looking at Daru with a friendly little smile.

"What's this story?" asked the schoolmaster. "Are you pulling my leg?"

"No, son. Those are the orders."

"The orders? I'm not . . ." Daru hesitated, not wanting to hurt the old Corsican.[7] "I mean, that's not my job."

"What! What's the meaning of that? In wartime people do all kinds of jobs."

"Then I'll wait for the declaration of war!" Balducci nodded.

"O.K. But the orders exist and they concern you too. Things are brewing, it appears. There is talk of a forthcoming revolt.[8] We are mobilized,[9] in a way."

Daru still had his obstinate look.

---

7. **Corsican** (kôr′sĭ-kən): a person from Corsica, an island to the west of Italy.

8. **forthcoming revolt:** The Arabs are preparing to fight the French in order to win their independence.

9. **mobilized:** ready for war.

"Listen, son," Balducci said. "I like you and you must understand. There's only a dozen of us at El Ameur to patrol throughout the whole territory of a small department and I must get back in a hurry. I was told to hand this guy over to you and return without delay. He couldn't be kept there. His village was beginning to stir; they wanted to take him back. You must take him to Tinguit tomorrow before the day is over. Twenty kilometers shouldn't faze a husky fellow like you. After that, all will be over. You'll come back to your pupils and your comfortable life."

Behind the wall the horse could be heard snorting and pawing the earth. Daru was looking out the window. Decidedly, the weather was clearing and the light was increasing over the snowy plateau. When all the snow was melted, the sun would take over again and once more would burn the fields of stone. For days, still, the unchanging sky would shed its dry light on the solitary expanse where nothing had any connection with man.

"After all," he said, turning around toward Balducci, "what did he do?" And, before the gendarme had opened his mouth, he asked: "Does he speak French?"

"No, not a word. We had been looking for him for a month, but they were hiding him. He killed his cousin."

"Is he against us?"

"I don't think so. But you can never be sure."

"Why did he kill?"

"A family squabble, I think. One owed the other grain, it seems. It's not at all clear. In short, he killed his cousin with a billhook.[10] You know, like a sheep, *kreezk!*"

Balducci made the gesture of drawing a blade across his throat and the Arab, his attention attracted, watched him with a sort of anxiety. Daru felt a sudden wrath against the man, against all men with their rotten spite, their tireless hates, their blood lust.

> ✳ **D**aru felt a sudden wrath against the man, against all men with their rotten spite, their tireless hates, their blood lust.

But the kettle was singing on the stove. He served Balducci more tea, hesitated, then served the Arab again, who, a second time, drank avidly. His raised arms made the jellaba fall open and the schoolmaster saw his thin, muscular chest.

"Thanks, kid," Balducci said. "And now, I'm off."

He got up and went toward the Arab, taking a small rope from his pocket.

"What are you doing?" Daru asked dryly.

Balducci, disconcerted, showed him the rope. "Don't bother."

The old gendarme hesitated. "It's up to you. Of course, you are armed?"

"I have my shotgun."

"Where?"

"In the trunk."

"You ought to have it near your bed."

"Why? I have nothing to fear."

"You're crazy, son. If there's an uprising, no one is safe, we're all in the same boat."

"I'll defend myself. I'll have time to see them coming."

Balducci began to laugh, then suddenly the mustache covered the white teeth.

"You'll have time? O.K. That's just what I was saying. You have always been a little cracked. That's why I like you, my son was like that."

---

10. **billhook:** an implement consisting of a curved blade attached to a handle.

WORDS TO KNOW

avidly (ăv′ĭd-lē) *adv.* eagerly
1250   **disconcerted** (dĭs′kən-sûr′tĭd) *adj.* embarrassed or confused   **disconcert** *v.*

At the same time he took out his revolver and put it on the desk.

"Keep it; I don't need two weapons from here to El Ameur."

The revolver shone against the black paint of the table. When the gendarme turned toward him, the schoolmaster caught the smell of leather and horseflesh.

"Listen, Balducci," Daru said suddenly, "every bit of this disgusts me, and first of all your fellow here. But I won't hand him over. Fight, yes, if I have to. But not that."

The old gendarme stood in front of him and looked at him severely.

"You're being a fool," he said slowly. "I don't like it either. You don't get used to putting a rope on a man even after years of it, and you're even ashamed—yes, ashamed. But you can't let them have their way."

"I won't hand him over," Daru said again.

"It's an order, son, and I repeat it."

"That's right. Repeat to them what I've said to you: I won't hand him over."

Balducci made a visible effort to reflect. He looked at the Arab and at Daru. At last he decided.

"No, I won't tell them anything. If you want to drop us, go ahead; I'll not denounce you. I have an order to deliver the prisoner and I'm doing so. And now you'll just sign this paper for me."

"There's no need. I'll not deny that you left him with me."

"Don't be mean with me. I know you'll tell the truth. You're from hereabouts and you are a man. But you must sign, that's the rule."

Daru opened his drawer, took out a little square bottle of purple ink, the red wooden penholder with the "sergeant-major" pen he used for making models of penmanship, and signed. The gendarme carefully folded the paper and put it into his wallet. Then he moved toward the door.

"I'll see you off," Daru said.

"No," said Balducci. "There's no use being polite. You insulted me."

He looked at the Arab, motionless in the same spot, sniffed peevishly, and turned away toward the door. "Good-by, son," he said. The door shut behind him. Balducci appeared suddenly outside the window and then disappeared. His footsteps were muffled by the snow. The horse stirred on the other side of the wall and several chickens fluttered in fright. A moment later Balducci reappeared outside the window leading the horse by the bridle. He walked toward the little rise without turning around and disappeared from sight with the horse following him. A big stone could be heard bouncing down. Daru walked back toward the prisoner, who, without stirring, never took his eyes off him. "Wait," the schoolmaster said in Arabic and went toward the bedroom. As he was going through the door, he had a second thought, went to the desk, took the revolver, and stuck it in his pocket. Then, without looking back, he went into his room.

PAUSE & REFLECT Why does Balducci feel insulted by Daru?

FOCUS The Arab now becomes Daru's "guest" for the night. As you read, look for details that show how Daru treats him.

For some time he lay on his couch watching the sky gradually close over, listening to the silence. It was this silence that had seemed painful to him during the first days here, after the war. He had requested a post in the little town at the base of the foothills separating the upper plateaus from the desert. There, rocky walls, green and black to the north, pink and lavender to the south, marked the frontier[11] of eternal summer. He had been named to a post farther north, on the plateau itself. In the beginning, the

---

11. frontier: border.

The Arab took a piece of the cake, lifted it eagerly to his mouth, and stopped short.

"And you?" he asked.

"After you. I'll eat too."

The thick lips opened slightly. The Arab hesitated, then bit into the cake determinedly.

Detail of *A Seated Arab Boy* (1858), Frederick Goodall. Oil on canvas.
Copyright © Christie's Images, New York/SuperStock, Inc.

solitude and the silence had been hard for him on these wastelands peopled only by stones. Occasionally, furrows suggested cultivation, but they had been dug to uncover a certain kind of stone good for building. The only plowing here was to harvest rocks. Elsewhere a thin layer of soil accumulated in the hollows would be scraped out to enrich paltry village gardens. This is the way it was: bare rock covered three quarters of the region. Towns sprang up, flourished, then disappeared; men came by, loved one another or fought bitterly, then died. No one in this desert, neither he nor his guest, mattered. And yet, outside this desert neither of them, Daru knew,

could have really lived.

When he got up, no noise came from the classroom. He was amazed at the unmixed joy he derived from the mere thought that the Arab might have fled and that he would be alone with no decision to make. But the prisoner was there. He had merely stretched out between the stove and the desk. With eyes open, he was staring at the ceiling. In that position, his thick lips were particularly noticeable, giving him a pouting look. "Come," said Daru. The Arab got up and followed him. In the bedroom, the schoolmaster pointed to a chair near the table under the window. The Arab sat down without taking his eyes off Daru.

"Are you hungry?"

"Yes," the prisoner said.

Daru set the table for two. He took flour and oil, shaped a cake in a frying-pan, and lighted the little stove that functioned on bottled gas. While the cake was cooking, he went out to the shed to get cheese, eggs, dates, and condensed milk. When the cake was done he set it on the window sill to cool, heated some condensed milk diluted with water, and beat up the eggs into an omelette. In one of his motions he knocked against the revolver stuck in his right pocket. He set the bowl down, went into the classroom, and put the revolver in his desk drawer. When he came back to the room, night was falling. He put on the light and served the Arab. "Eat," he said. The Arab took a piece of the cake, lifted it eagerly to his mouth, and stopped short.

"And you?" he asked.

"After you. I'll eat too."

The thick lips opened slightly. The Arab hesitated, then bit into the cake determinedly.

The meal over, the Arab looked at the

schoolmaster. "Are you the judge?"

"No, I'm simply keeping you until tomorrow."

"Why do you eat with me?"

"I'm hungry."

The Arab fell silent. Daru got up and went out. He brought back a folding bed from the shed, set it up between the table and the stove, perpendicular to his own bed. From a large suitcase which, upright in a corner, served as a shelf for papers, he took two blankets and arranged them on the camp bed. Then he stopped, felt useless, and sat down on his bed. There was nothing more to do or to get ready. He had to look at this man. He looked at him, therefore, trying to imagine his face bursting with rage. He couldn't do so. He could see nothing but the dark yet shining eyes and the animal mouth.

"Why did you kill him?" he asked in a voice whose hostile tone surprised him.

The Arab looked away.

"He ran away. I ran after him."

He raised his eyes to Daru again and they were full of a sort of woeful interrogation.[12] "Now what will they do to me?"

"Are you afraid?"

He stiffened, turning his eyes away.

"Are you sorry?"

The Arab stared at him openmouthed. Obviously he did not understand. Daru's annoyance was growing. At the same time he felt awkward and self-conscious with his big body wedged between the two beds.

"Lie down there," he said impatiently. "That's your bed."

The Arab didn't move. He called to Daru: "Tell me!"

The schoolmaster looked at him.

"Is the gendarme coming back tomorrow?"

"I don't know."

"Are you coming with us?"

"I don't know. Why?"

The prisoner got up and stretched out on top of the blankets, his feet toward the window. The light from the electric bulb shone straight into his eyes and he closed them at once.

"Why?" Daru repeated, standing beside the bed.

The Arab opened his eyes under the blinding light and looked at him, trying not to blink.

"Come with us," he said.

In the middle of the night, Daru was still not asleep. He had gone to bed after undressing completely; he generally slept naked. But when he suddenly realized that he had nothing on, he hesitated. He felt vulnerable and the temptation came to him to put his clothes back on. Then he shrugged his shoulders; after all, he wasn't a child and, if need be, he could break his adversary in two. From his bed he could observe him, lying on his back, still motionless with his eyes closed under the harsh light. When Daru turned out the light, the darkness seemed to coagulate[13] all of a sudden. Little by little, the night came back to life in the window where the starless sky was stirring gently. The schoolmaster soon made out the body lying at his feet. The Arab still did not move, but his eyes seemed open. A faint wind was prowling around the schoolhouse. Perhaps it would drive away the clouds and the sun would reappear.

During the night the wind increased. The hens fluttered a little and then were silent. The Arab turned over on his side with his back to Daru, who thought he heard him moan. Then he listened for his guest's breathing, become heavier and more regular. He listened to that breath so close to him and mused without being able to go to sleep. In this room where he had been sleeping alone for a year, this presence bothered him. But it bothered him also by imposing on him a sort of brotherhood he knew well but refused to accept in the present circumstances. Men who share the same rooms, soldiers or prisoners,

---

12. **woeful interrogation:** sad questioning.

13. **coagulate:** thicken into a solid mass.

The Arab again stood framed in the doorway, closed the door carefully, and came back to bed without a sound.

When the prisoner made a second move, he stiffened, on the alert. The Arab was lifting himself slowly on his arms with almost the motion of a sleepwalker. Seated upright in bed, he waited motionless without turning his head toward Daru, as if he were listening attentively. Daru did not stir; it had just occurred to him that the revolver was still in the drawer of his desk. It was better to act at once. Yet he continued to observe the prisoner, who, with the same slithery motion, put his feet on the ground, waited again, then began to stand up slowly. Daru was about to call out to him when the Arab began to walk, in a quite natural but extraordinarily silent way. He was heading toward the door at the end of the room that opened into the shed. He lifted the latch with precaution and went out, pushing the door behind him but without shutting it. Daru had not stirred. "He is running away," he merely thought. "Good riddance!" Yet he listened attentively. The hens were not fluttering; the guest must be on the plateau. A faint sound of water reached him, and he didn't know what it was until the Arab again stood framed in the doorway, closed the door carefully, and came back to bed without a sound. Then Daru turned his back on him and fell asleep. Still later he seemed, from the depths of his sleep, to hear furtive steps around the schoolhouse. "I'm dreaming! I'm dreaming!" he repeated to himself. And he went on sleeping.

PAUSE & REFLECT How would you evaluate Daru's treatment of the Arab?

develop a strange alliance as if, having cast off their armor with their clothing, they fraternized[14] every evening, over and above their differences, in the ancient community of dream and fatigue. But Daru shook himself; he didn't like such musings, and it was essential to sleep.

A little later, however, when the Arab stirred slightly, the schoolmaster was still not asleep.

14. **fraternized:** associated in a friendly, brotherly way

When he awoke, the sky was clear; the loose window let in a cold, pure air. The Arab was asleep, hunched up under the blankets now, his mouth open, utterly relaxed. But when Daru shook him, he started dreadfully, staring at Daru with wild eyes as if he had never seen him and such a frightened expression that the schoolmaster stepped back. "Don't be afraid. It's me. You must eat." The Arab nodded his head and said yes. Calm had returned to his face, but his expression was vacant and listless.[15]

The coffee was ready. They drank it seated together on the folding bed as they munched their pieces of the cake. Then Daru led the Arab under the shed and showed him the faucet where he washed. He went back into the room, folded the blankets and the bed, made his own bed and put the room in order. Then he went through the classroom and out onto the terrace. The sun was already rising in the blue sky; a soft, bright light was bathing the deserted plateau. On the ridge the snow was melting in spots. The stones were about to reappear. Crouched on the edge of the plateau, the schoolmaster looked at the deserted expanse. He thought of Balducci. He had hurt him, for he had sent him off in a way as if he didn't want to be associated with him. He could still hear the gendarme's farewell and, without knowing why, he felt strangely empty and vulnerable. At that moment, from the other side of the schoolhouse, the prisoner coughed. Daru listened to him almost despite himself and then, furious, threw a pebble that whistled through the air before sinking into the snow. That man's stupid crime revolted him, but to hand him over was contrary to honor. Merely thinking of it made him smart with humiliation. And he cursed at one and the same

time his own people who had sent him this Arab and the Arab too who had dared to kill and not managed to get away. Daru got up, walked in a circle on the terrace, waited motionless, and then went back into the schoolhouse.

The Arab, leaning over the cement floor of the shed, was washing his teeth with two fingers. Daru looked at him and said: "Come." He went back into the room ahead of the prisoner. He slipped a hunting-jacket on over his sweater and put on walking-shoes. Standing, he waited until the Arab had put on his *chèche* and sandals. They went into the classroom and the schoolmaster pointed to the exit, saying: "Go ahead." The fellow didn't budge. "I'm coming," said Daru. The Arab went out. Daru went back into the room and made a package of pieces of rusk,[16] dates, and sugar. In the classroom, before going out, he hesitated a second in front of his desk, then crossed the threshold and locked the door. "That's the way," he said. He started toward the east, followed by the prisoner. But, a short distance from the schoolhouse, he thought he heard a slight sound behind them. He retraced his steps and examined the surroundings of the house; there was no one there. The Arab watched him without seeming to understand. "Come on," said Daru.

They walked for an hour and rested beside a sharp peak of limestone. The snow was melting faster and faster and the sun was drinking up the puddles at once, rapidly cleaning the plateau, which gradually dried and vibrated like the air itself. When they resumed walking, the ground rang under their feet. From time to time a bird rent the space in front of them with a joyful cry. Daru breathed in deeply the fresh morning light. He felt a sort of rapture[17] before the vast familiar

---

15. **listless:** lacking energy or enthusiasm.

16. **rusk:** a soft, sweet biscuit.

17. **rapture:** a strong feeling of delight or joy; ecstasy.

expanse, now almost entirely yellow under its dome of blue sky. They walked an hour more, descending toward the south. They reached a level height made up of crumbly rocks. From there on, the plateau sloped down, eastward, toward a low plain where there were a few spindly trees and, to the south, toward outcroppings of rock that gave the landscape a <u>chaotic</u> look.

Daru surveyed the two directions. There was nothing but the sky on the horizon. Not a man could be seen. He turned toward the Arab, who was looking at him blankly. Daru held out the package to him. "Take it," he said. "There are dates, bread, and sugar. You can hold out for two days. Here are a thousand francs too." The Arab took the package and the money but kept his full hands at chest level as if he didn't know what to do with what was being given him. "Now look," the schoolmaster said as he pointed in the direction of the east, "there's the way to Tinguit. You have a two-hour walk. At Tinguit you'll find the administration and the police. They are expecting you." The Arab looked toward the east, still holding the package and the money against his chest. Daru took his elbow and turned him rather roughly toward the south. At the foot of the height on which they stood could be seen a faint path. "That's the trail across the plateau. In a day's walk from here

WORDS TO KNOW
chaotic (kā-ŏt′ĭk) *adj.* showing great disorder or confusion

> **"In a day's walk from here you'll find pasturelands and the first nomads. They'll take you in and shelter you according to their law."**

you'll find pasturelands and the first nomads. They'll take you in and shelter you according to their law." The Arab had now turned toward Daru and a sort of panic was visible in his expression. "Listen," he said. Daru shook his head: "No, be quiet. Now I'm leaving you." He turned his back on him, took two long steps in the direction of the school, looked hesitantly at the motionless Arab, and started off again. For a few minutes he heard nothing but his own step resounding on the cold ground and did not turn his head. A moment later, however, he turned around. The Arab was still there on the edge of the hill, his arms hanging now, and he was looking at the schoolmaster. Daru felt something rise in his throat. But he swore with impatience, waved vaguely, and started off again. He had already gone some distance when he again stopped and looked. There was no longer anyone on the hill.

Daru hesitated. The sun was now rather high in the sky and was beginning to beat down on his head. The schoolmaster retraced his steps, at first somewhat uncertainly, then with decision. When he reached the little hill, he was bathed in sweat. He climbed it as fast as he could and stopped, out of breath, at the top. The rock-fields to the south stood out sharply against the blue sky, but on the plain to the east a steamy heat was already rising. And in that slight haze, Daru, with heavy heart, made out the Arab walking slowly on the road to prison.

A little later, standing before the window of the classroom, the schoolmaster was watching the clear light bathing the whole surface of the plateau, but he hardly saw it. Behind him on the blackboard, among the winding French rivers, sprawled the clumsily chalked-up words he had just read: "You handed over our brother. You will pay for this." Daru looked at the sky, the plateau, and, beyond, the invisible lands stretching all the way to the sea. In this vast landscape he had loved so much, he was alone. ❖

Connect to the Literature

1. **What Do You Think?**
   What do you **predict** will happen to Daru now that the Arab's kinsmen have threatened him?

   Comprehension Check
   • What crime has the Arab committed?
   • Why has Balducci brought the Arab to Daru?

Think Critically

2. Why do you think the Arab chooses to go to prison rather than go free? Explain your response.

3. **ACTIVE READING: MAKING INFERENCES** Review the inferences you recorded in your **READER'S NOTEBOOK**. How would you describe Daru's main conflict?

   > **THINK ABOUT**
   > • his duty to France
   > • his attitude toward the Arab's crime
   > • his reaction to the police orders
   > • his growing bond with the Arab

4. Contrast Daru and Balducci in their attitude toward the Arab.

5. **Irony** is a surprising contrast between expectation and reality. What is ironic about what happens to Daru at the end of the story?

6. How does the **setting**—both the historical context and the desert landscape—affect the plot of this story?

Extend Interpretations

7. **What If?** Imagine that Daru escorted the Arab to the nomads. How would your reaction to the story be different?

8. **Connect to Life** Daru is housing a murderer, yet he decides to go against the law and release his guest. How do you feel about a person's breaking the law in a situation like this?

LITERARY ANALYSIS: THEME

A **theme** is a central idea or message that a writer shares with the reader. To discover a story's theme, you might consider what happens to the main character. For example, at the end of this story, Daru has angered both Balducci—who represents the French authorities—and the local Arabs. These details suggest that the theme of this story has to do with the situation of an individual caught between larger, opposing forces.

Cooperative Learning Activity
Go back through the story and list events, sentences, or phrases that provide clues about Daru's situation as a French citizen living in Algeria. Consider how Balducci and the Arab represent opposite poles of Daru's conflict. Then write a sentence that states the story's theme in your own words. Share your thematic statement with a small group of classmates. Keep in mind that different readers may state the theme of a story in different ways.

Writing Options

1. Journal Entry Write a journal entry in which Daru expresses his thoughts after finding the threat scrawled on his classroom blackboard.

2. Story Epilogue Imagine that Daru and the Arab's kinsmen meet. Write an epilogue to the story telling what happens in this encounter.

Writing Handbook
See page R29: Narrative Writing.

3. Literary-Analysis Essay In a brief essay, discuss the use of foreshadowing in this story. First define foreshadowing as a literary technique. Refer to the **Glossary of Literary Terms,** beginning on page R91, if you need help. Next describe the outcome of the story, when Daru discovers that he is a marked man. Finally, provide details from the story that hint at this outcome.

Activities & Explorations

1. Role-Playing With a classmate, role-play a conversation between Daru and Balducci after the events described in the story. Before you begin, review their dialogue in the story and discuss their manner of speaking with each other. How might Balducci react to Daru's release of the Arab? What concerns might Daru have regarding his superiors and the local Arabs? ~ **SPEAKING AND LISTENING/PERFORMING**

2. Landscape Drawing Create a drawing of the setting for this story. Before you begin, list details from the story that help you visualize the desert plateau. ~ **ART**

Inquiry & Research

French Colonialism in Algeria
Prepare an oral report that explains some aspect of Algeria's colonial history. For example, you might focus on the efforts of Muslim residents to gain legal rights or on the development of the nationalist movement. Use maps and other visual aids in your presentation.

RESEARCH STARTER
CLASSZONE.COM

Vocabulary in Action

EXERCISE: CONTEXT CLUES Choose the correct word to complete each sentence.

1. The starving prisoner _____ ate the food given to him.

2. He was not the least bit _____ by Daru's watching him eat greedily.

3. The prisoner was _____, stubbornly refusing to change his course of action.

4. If the situation had been _____ rather than peaceful and orderly, he might have tried to escape.

5. He knew that then Daru might have turned from friend to _____, but the idea did not frighten him.

Building Vocabulary
For an in-depth lesson on using context clues, see page 674.

The Prison Experience

OVERVIEW

Freedom to Breathe 1261

The Prison Cell 1265

Standardized Test Practice:
Writing About Literature 1269

The 20th century was marked by two world wars and numerous other armed conflicts. Millions of people were injured, slain, or uprooted from their homes. Many others suffered the horrors of prisons and concentration camps—their freedom swept away in a tidal wave of repression.

This lesson includes two selections written by 20th-century authors who suffered as political prisoners. The first selection is a prose poem by the Russian writer Aleksandr Solzhenitsyn (sōl'zhə-nēt'sĭn); the second is a poem by the Palestinian writer Mahmud Darwish (mä-mōōd' där'wēsh). In the pages that follow, you will be asked to compare and contrast these two writers' views of the prison experience. Your comparisons will help you explore the writers' perspectives on this tragic ordeal.

Points of Comparison

Create a chart like the one shown, and fill it in after you read each selection. The topics listed will help you identify similarities and differences between the selections. Feel free to add other topics to your chart.

	"Freedom to Breathe"	"The Prison Cell"
Where is the speaker?		
How has imprisonment affected the speaker?		
What is the speaker's message about freedom?		
How strong is the speaker's spirit?		
Evidence of spiritual strength or weakness		

Standardized Test Practice: Comparison-and-Contrast Essay After you finish reading the two selections, you will be asked to write a comparison-and-contrast essay. Your chart will help you plan and develop the essay.

Freedom to Breathe

ALEKSANDR SOLZHENITSYN

**Aleksandr
Solzhenitsyn**
1918–

Prisoner and Literary Giant

Aleksandr Solzhenitsyn is one of the most famous writers to come from the Soviet Union. As a young man, he joined the Soviet army to fight in World War II (1939–1945), rising to the rank of captain. In the final year of the war, however, his life took an unexpected turn. After writing a letter critical of Stalin, he was stripped of his rank and was sentenced to a Soviet prison camp. He drew upon his ordeal in writing *One Day in the Life of Ivan Denisovich*. This novella tells of a prisoner in a forced labor camp during Stalin's regime. With this work, published in 1962, Solzhenitsyn burst onto the literary scene.

To get around government censorship, Solzhenitsyn had his writings smuggled out of the Soviet Union and published abroad. They earned him the Nobel Prize in Literature in 1970. Three years later, the first volume of *The Gulag Archipelago* was published in Paris. In this nonfiction work, Solzhenitsyn described the vast network of Soviet prison camps. The government, outraged at Solzhenitsyn, expelled him from the country. Only in 1994, after the collapse of the Soviet Union, did he again set foot in Russia.

Build Background

According to one critic, Solzhenitsyn's "deepest identity is that of a former political prisoner." In "Freedom to Breathe," he describes a simple pleasure that prison took away from him.

Connect to Your Life

What freedoms do you enjoy as a member of the society you live in? Are there some freedoms that you take for granted? Share your ideas with a small group of classmates.

Focus Your Reading

LITERARY ANALYSIS: DESCRIPTION
Writing that helps a reader picture scenes, events, or people is known as **description**. Description often involves the use of precise language and vivid, original phrases, as in this passage:

> *A shower fell in the night and now dark clouds drift across the sky, occasionally sprinkling a fine film of rain.*

Think about the effects created by the descriptive details as you read the prose poem.

ACTIVE READING: RECOGNIZING SENSORY DETAILS **Sensory details** are words and phrases that appeal to readers' senses of sight, smell, hearing, taste, or touch. For example, in the boldfaced passage above, the detail "a fine film of rain" appeals to the senses of sight and touch.

READER'S NOTEBOOK As you read, jot down sensory details and the sense or senses each appeals to.

Detail	Sense(s)
1.	1.
2	2.
3.	3.

Freedom to Breathe

Aleksandr Solzhenitsyn

Translated by Michael Glenny

Apple Tree (1904), Kasimir Malevich. Oil on canvas. Copyright © Russian State Museum, St. Petersburg, Russia/SuperStock, Inc.

A shower fell in the night and now dark clouds drift across the sky, occasionally sprinkling a fine film of rain.

I stand under an apple tree in blossom and I breathe. Not only the apple tree but the grass round it glistens with moisture; words cannot describe the sweet fragrance that pervades the air. I inhale as deeply as I can, and the aroma invades my whole being; I breathe with my eyes open, I breathe with my eyes closed—I cannot say which gives me the greater pleasure.

This, I believe, is the single most precious freedom that prison takes away from us: the freedom to breathe freely, as I now can. No food on earth, no wine, not even a woman's kiss is sweeter to me than this air steeped in the fragrance of flowers, of moisture and freshness.

No matter that this is only a tiny garden, hemmed in by five-story houses like cages in a zoo. I cease to hear the motorcycles backfiring, radios whining, the burble of loudspeakers. As long as there is fresh air to breathe under an apple tree after a shower, we may survive a little longer.

Connect to the Literature

1. **What Do You Think?** What are your impressions of the speaker?

Think Critically

2. **ACTIVE READING: RECOGNIZING SENSORY DETAILS**
   Review the details you recorded in your
    READER'S NOTEBOOK. Which sensory detail was most vivid for you? What sense or senses did it appeal to?

3. Why do you think the speaker believes that the most precious freedom is "the freedom to breathe freely"?

   THINK ABOUT
   - the sensations he experiences in the garden
   - what his experiences in prison might have been like

4. What does the last paragraph add to your understanding of this prose poem?

   THINK ABOUT
   - the setting that the speaker is in
   - whom the speaker might be referring to when he says "we" in the final sentence

Extend Interpretations

5. **Connect to Life** Think again about the freedoms you discussed for the Connect to Your Life activity on page 1261. Now that you've read the selection, have you changed your ideas about freedoms you take for granted?

LITERARY ANALYSIS: DESCRIPTION

Description is the process by which a writer creates in words a picture of a scene, an event, or a character. Good descriptive writing is rich in **sensory details,** or words and phrases that appeal to the reader's senses—sight, hearing, smell, taste, touch. Consider, for example, the phrase "glistens with moisture" in this sentence:

Not only the apple tree but the grass round it glistens with moisture.

The image appeals to the senses of sight and touch.

Paired Activity With a partner, look again at the sensory details you recorded in your
 READER'S NOTEBOOK. If you took out all the details that appeal to smell, hearing, taste, and touch, leaving only visual images, how would the prose poem be affected? What couldn't it communicate about freedom?

Choices & CHALLENGES

Writing Option

Sensory Description Think about a simple pleasure you enjoy—for example, taking a walk at sunset near a pond or lake. Then write a few paragraphs to describe this pleasure, using vivid sensory details.

Writing Handbook
See page R27: Description.

Activities & Explorations

1. Oral Interpretation Prepare an oral reading of this prose poem. Use the tone, pitch, and volume of your voice to convey the speaker's sense of delight in the garden. Choose appropriate background music to enhance the mood you wish to convey.
~ **PERFORMING**

2. Artistic Reflection Create a drawing, a painting, or some other artwork to express the ideas in "Freedom to Breathe." What is more challenging to convey in the artwork than in the prose poem? ~ **ART**

Inquiry & Research

Writers in Communist Russia Do research to find out more about conditions for writers in the Soviet Union under the totalitarian regimes of Joseph Stalin and his successors, especially Nikita Khrushchev. Share your findings in an oral report to the class.

Points of Comparison

Paired Activity With a partner, review "Freedom to Breathe," using the topics in your comparison-and-contrast chart to help you analyze the prose poem. Fill in the spaces pertaining to this selection.

	"Freedom to Breathe"	"The Prison Cell"
Where is the speaker?	in a tiny garden in a city	
How has imprisonment affected the speaker?		
What is the speaker's message about freedom?		
How strong is the speaker's spirit?		
Evidence of spiritual strength or weakness		

The speaker in Solzhenitsyn's prose poem—a former prisoner—is enjoying and reflecting on a freedom that was denied him in prison. In Mahmud Darwish's poem "The Prison Cell," the speaker is a prisoner struggling to cope with the conditions he is experiencing while behind bars.

Mahmud Darwish
1942–

Literary Reputation Mahmud Darwish is widely regarded as an important Arabic poet. The author of more than two dozen books, he has gained a reputation as a major voice of the Palestinian resistance to Israeli occupation in the Middle East. One reviewer has said: "Mahmud Darwish is a great poet. . . . Anyone unaware of that displays not only his ignorance of Arabic culture but also his ignorance of universal culture."

From Palestine to Exile Darwish knows firsthand the tragedy of life in a war zone. He was born in Barweh, a village in Palestine. It was raided by the Israelis when Darwish was six years old. He and his family narrowly escaped death and fled to Beirut, Lebanon. When they returned a year later, the village no longer existed. Darwish never forgot this experience. As a young man, he joined the Palestinian resistance movement, suffering arrest and imprisonment for his political activities. He left Palestine in 1971, coming home in 1996 after 25 years in exile.

His Poetry Darwish's poems are intense, dramatic, and realistic; many are controversial. Some of his poems are lyrical and have been set to music. Darwish's poetry is known throughout the Arab world and, in translation, by a larger audience.

Build Background

In the poem you are about to read, you will find details that reveal some of the conditions of the speaker's imprisonment. You will also find details that reveal how the speaker transforms these conditions through the force of his imagination. Part of the poem includes the speaker's dialogue with a prison guard. The lines of dialogue are preceded by a dash.

The Prison Cell

Mahmud Darwish

Translated by Ben Bennani

It is possible . . .
It is possible at least sometimes . . .
It is possible especially now
To ride a horse
5   Inside a prison cell
And run away . . .

It is possible for prison walls
To disappear,
For the cell to become a distant land
10   Without frontiers:

—What did you do with the walls?
—I gave them back to the rocks.
—And what did you do with the ceiling?
—I turned it into a saddle.
15   —And your chain?
—I turned it into a pencil.

The prison guard got angry.
He put an end to the dialogue.
He said he didn't care for poetry,
20   And bolted the door of my cell.

He came back to see me
In the morning;
He shouted at me:

Wall mural with a forest and man behind bars. Copyright © 1980 Cuchi White/Corbis.

—Where did all this water come from?
25 —I brought it from the Nile.
—And the trees?
—From the orchards of Damascus.
—And the music?
—From my heartbeat.

30 The prison guard got mad;
He put an end to my dialogue.
He said he didn't like my poetry,
And bolted the door of my cell.

But he returned in the evening:

35 —Where did this moon come from?
—From the nights of Baghdad.
—And the wine?
—From the vineyards of Algiers.
—And this freedom?
40 —From the chain you tied me with last night.

The prison guard grew so sad . . .
He begged me to give him back
His freedom.

27 Damascus: the capital of Syria (known for its apricot and nut orchards and its olive groves).

36 Baghdad (băg'dăd): the capital of Iraq (presented as a romantic setting in many literary works).

38 Algiers: the capital of Algeria (a major exporter of wine).

Connect to the Literature

1. What Do You Think? What were your thoughts or questions after reading this poem?

Comprehension Check
- Name two ways in which the speaker transforms the prison cell.
- What does the guard seek at the end of the poem?

Think Critically

2. How would you describe the relationship between the speaker and the guard?

 {
- how the guard talks to and behaves toward the speaker
- how you interpret what the guard begs of the speaker

3. In your opinion, how well does the speaker cope with prison conditions?

4. How would you describe the speaker's view of freedom?

Extend Interpretations

5. Connect to Life The speaker of this poem is endowed with a vivid imagination. The famous scientist Albert Einstein once stated, "Imagination is more important than knowledge." Do you agree or disagree with Einstein's statement? Support your opinion with examples from your experience.

Points of Comparison

Paired Activity Now that you have read and studied these two poems, work with a partner to fill in the spaces for "The Prison Cell" in your chart.

	"Freedom to Breathe"	"The Prison Cell"
Where is the speaker?	in a tiny garden in a city	inside a prison cell
How has imprisonment affected the speaker?		
What is the speaker's message about freedom?		
How strong is the speaker's spirit?		
Evidence of spiritual strength or weakness		

Standardized Test Practice

Writing About Literature

PART 1 Reading the Prompt

In writing assessments, you may be asked to compare and contrast works of literature that treat a similar subject. You are now going to practice writing an essay that requires this type of focus.

> **Writing Prompt**
> Being imprisoned is an ordeal that tests the strength of the human spirit. Unfortunately, this ordeal was all too common in the 20th century. Think about Solzhenitsyn's "Freedom to Breathe" and Darwish's "The Prison Cell." Compare and contrast the speakers and ❶ their messages about freedom. Which speaker do you think is stronger ❷ in spirit? Support your analysis with details from the two selections. ❸

STRATEGIES IN ACTION

❶ I have to **compare and contrast** the speakers and also their messages about freedom.

❷ I must **judge** which speaker is stronger in spirit.

❸ I need to include **details** from the selections to support my analysis.

PART 2 Planning a Comparison-and-Contrast Essay

- Review the comparison-and-contrast chart that you completed for the Points of Comparison features in this lesson.
- Using your chart, find examples to use as evidence for the points you develop in your essay. If necessary, review the selections again to identify more examples.
- Create an outline to organize your main points.

PART 3 Drafting Your Essay

Introduction Introduce the topic—the response to being imprisoned—and mention that it was an important theme for many writers in the 20th century. Then explain that you will be comparing two selections in terms of the speakers' response to imprisonment.

Body You might use the topics in your comparison-and-contrast chart as a guide to the key points of your comparison. In one paragraph, for example, you might compare and contrast the effect of imprisonment on each speaker. Within each paragraph you write, give specific details to back up your points.

Conclusion Wrap up your essay with a restatement of your thesis, or main idea, and a brief summary of your main points.

Revision Check your use of transitional words and phrases to connect your ideas within and between paragraphs. Words such as *likewise, both,* and *in the same way* signal similarities. *On the other hand, instead, nevertheless,* and *however* signal differences.

TEST PRACTICE

Chinua Achebe

OVERVIEW

Life and Times — 1270

Dead Men's Path
~ SHORT STORY — 1274

from An
Interview with
Chinua Achebe *by
Bill Moyers* — 1280

Keeper of the Vigil, *a
poem for Chinua Achebe
by Yusef Komunyakaa* — 1284

Civil Peace ~ SHORT STORY — 1286

The Author's Style — 1292

Author Study Project — 1293

"*Chinua Achebe creates
. . . a coherent picture
of coherence being
lost, of the tragic
consequences of the
African-European
collision.*"

—*Robert McDowell*

Africa's Premier Storyteller

1930–

*One of the 20th century's
most honored writers, Nigeria's
Chinua Achebe* (chĭn′oo-ä ä-chä′bä)
*helped pioneer native African
literature written in English. His
masterpiece* Things Fall Apart, *the first
major novel written in English by a native African, has
become a world classic. In his works, Achebe often depicts the
clash of cultures and its lingering effects in his native land.
His portrayal of Africa—haunting and lyrical—evokes a way
of life lost forever.*

STUDENT OF LITERATURE Chinua Achebe was born in
Ogidi, a village in Nigeria, which at the time was a colony of
Great Britain. His original name was Albert Chinualumogu
Achebe, the name "Albert" reflecting the cultural influence of
British rule. Achebe's earliest experience with literature came
from his mother, who told him folk tales from the African
oral tradition. His father, who had become a Christian as a
young man, taught at Ogidi's mission school, which Achebe

Countryside
in Nigeria

1930
Is born in Ogidi,
an Ibo village
in southeastern
Nigeria

1948
Starts attending
University
College in Ibadan,
Nigeria

HIS LIFE
HIS TIMES   **1930**   **1935**   **1940**   **1945**

1929
**U.S. stock market
crashes, marking the
start of a worldwide
economic depression.**

1939
**World War II
begins when
Germany
invades Poland.**

1945
**World War II
ends; United
Nations is
established.**

1948
**Mohandas
Gandhi is
killed by an
extremist
in India.**

attended as a young boy. Later, Achebe studied English literature at University College in Ibadan, Nigeria (where he dropped "Albert" and shortened his African name). At that time, stories about Africa were written mainly by Europeans, not by native Africans. Achebe realized the need for a new African literature. "Our story," he said, "could not be told for us by anyone else."

NIGERIA'S STRUGGLE FOR INDEPENDENCE

Nigeria, Africa's most populous nation, is home to many ethnic groups, each with its own language and customs. Achebe's background is Ibo (ē'bō), or Igbo. The Ibo come from southeastern Nigeria, and their language was Achebe's first tongue. By the time Achebe was eight, however, he had begun to study English, the language introduced with British colonial rule in the 19th century. Nigeria's relationship with Britain was stormy from the start, with many groups, including the Ibo, rebelling from time to time. After World War II, the pressure for self-rule grew even stronger. Finally, in 1960, Nigeria gained its independence. It became a republic three years later.

Chinua Achebe at home near Lagos in 1966

LITERARY *Contributions*

Fiction Achebe is best known for novels and short stories that explore the cultural conflicts of Africa, past and present. His novels and short story collections include

> *Things Fall Apart*
> *No Longer at Ease*
> *The Sacrificial Egg and Other Stories*
> *Arrow of God*
> *A Man of the People*
> *Girls at War and Other Stories*
> *Anthills of the Savannah*

Poetry & Nonfiction Achebe has also published poetry volumes, essay collections, and other nonfiction works, most of which focus on African life and culture. Among them are

> *Beware, Soul Brother and Other Poems*
> *Christmas in Biafra and Other Poems*
> *Morning Yet on Creation Day*
> *The Trouble with Nigeria*
> *Hopes and Impediments: Selected Essays, 1965–1987*
> *Another Africa*
> *Conversations with Chinua Achebe*
> *Home and Exile*

1954 Joins production staff of the Nigerian Broadcasting Corporation in Lagos

1958 Publishes *Things Fall Apart*, his first novel

1962 Becomes editor of the Heinemann African Writers Series

1964 Publishes *Arrow of God*, his third novel

1967 Travels in Africa, Europe, and the United States to win support for the Biafran cause

1972 Publishes *Girls at War and Other Stories*, which includes "Dead Men's Path" and "Civil Peace"

1950 — **1955** — **1960** — **1965** — **1970**

1957 Ghana becomes the first West African nation to achieve independence.

1960 Nigeria achieves independence from Great Britain.

1964 In the United States, a landmark civil rights law bans discrimination.

WE WANT BLACK POWER

1967 Civil War begins after a region in eastern Nigeria secedes as Biafra; the Nigerian poet Christopher Okigbo is killed.

1973 Rising oil prices around the world begin to bring newfound wealth to Nigeria.

Kwame Nkrumah, Ghana's first prime minister

NOVELIST FOR A NEW AFRICA Inspired by his love of language, Achebe sought to create a new African literature—one written in English by native Africans. He began writing stories and essays for his college newspaper. After graduating, he worked as a producer for the new Nigerian Broadcasting Corporation in Lagos, then Nigeria's capital. He wrote fiction in his spare time. In 1958, he published *Things Fall Apart,* a novel about a heroic Ibo leader who defies colonial rule. The novel gradually earned both critical and popular acclaim around the world.

CRUSADER FOR A LOST CAUSE Ever since Nigeria had won its independence, ethnic tensions had simmered in the new nation. In 1967, the mostly Ibo region in the east seceded from Nigeria and formed the independent republic of Biafra. A civil war erupted, involving widespread destruction and loss

of life. Achebe traveled the world, trying to raise funds for the Biafran cause. After three years of bloodshed and famine, the Ibo were defeated, and the Biafran region again became part of Nigeria.

LITERARY PURSUITS After the civil war, Achebe published poetry, stories, and essays; edited *Okike,* a magazine of African literature; and taught as a visiting professor at two New England universities. In 1976, he returned home to teach literature at the University of Nigeria. Five years later, he formed the Association of Nigerian Authors and served as its first president.

POLITICAL LIFE AND EXILE In the early 1980s, Achebe decided to take part in Nigerian politics. In 1983, he served as deputy national chairman of the People's Redemption Party (PRP). In 1985, however, a military ruler named Ibrahim Babangida (ē-brä′hēm bä-bän′gē-dä) came to power, banning many political parties, including the PRP.

In 1990, Achebe was seriously injured in a suspicious automobile accident in Nigeria, in which a military vehicle was said to have been involved. Concerned for his safety, Achebe

1975
Begins one-year visiting professorship at the University of Connecticut

1976
Begins serving as professor of literature at the University of Nigeria in Nsukka

1981
Founds the Association of Nigerian Authors and is elected its first president

1990
After recuperating from a serious car accident, begins teaching at Bard College in upstate New York

2000
Publishes his nonfiction work *Home and Exile*

CHINUA
ACHEBE
HOME AND EXILE

1975   1980   1985   1990   1995   2000

1989
The Berlin Wall, which has divided East Berlin from West Berlin, comes down.

1991
The city of Abuja becomes Nigeria's capital.

1994
In South Africa's first all-race elections, Nelson Mandela is elected to lead the nation.

decided to leave his native land. For six months he recuperated in Great Britain. He then came to the United States to teach at Bard College, in upstate New York.

Achebe has published more than 20 works—including novels, children's books, short story collections, and poetry volumes— in English, his second language. He calls language "mankind's greatest blessing," and the storyteller its "high priest." His mission as a storyteller, he says, is to enable his readers to see the world through a child's eyes. "The child . . . is new in the world, and everything is possible to him. The imagination hasn't been dulled by use and experience. Therefore, when you [write for] the adult, what you do is you give him back some of that energy and optimism of the child, that ability to be open and to expect anything."

Caricature of Achebe

 **AUTHOR LINK**
CLASSZONE.COM

 NetActivities: Author Exploration

A Literary Masterpiece: *Things Fall Apart*

Things Fall Apart has been called "the archetypal African novel." Achebe took the title from the opening lines of William Butler Yeats's poem "The Second Coming":

> Turning and turning in the widening gyre
> The falcon cannot hear the falconer;
> Things fall apart; the center cannot hold;
> Mere anarchy is loosed upon the world,

In this novel, Achebe describes what happens when traditional and colonial cultures collide. The novel begins with a depiction of traditional life among the Ibo people at the end of the 19th century and goes on to sketch the beginnings of European colonization and the conflicts it triggers. The main character is Okonkwo, a tribal leader. Brave, honest, and hard-working, he represents the cherished values of his culture. Clinging to his traditions, he refuses to adapt to European ways. For this hero, things do indeed fall apart, and his people's way of life is changed forever.

Ibo headdress made of carved and painted wood

DEAD MEN'S PATH

Chinua Achebe

Build Background

In the 19th century, when the British began to colonize Nigeria, most of the Ibo people followed a traditional religion. They worshiped a supreme creator (called Chukwu), an earth goddess, and several lesser divinities. According to Ibo tradition, dead ancestors had the power to guard the living. These traditional beliefs were scorned by the British colonizers. Most village schools were run by Christian missionaries who taught religion along with the three R's. Thus, many Ibo villagers came to accept Christianity as a means to a modern education and a successful life. The story you are about to read takes place in an Ibo village in 1949, when Nigeria was still a British colony. The main character is the principal of a village school. He does not respect the traditional beliefs of the villagers.

Connect to Your Life

In the name of progress, historic buildings may be torn down to make room for parking lots or shopping malls. Do you think your community should preserve its landmarks or replace them to keep pace with modern life? Discuss these questions with a small group of classmates.

Focus Your Reading

LITERARY ANALYSIS: CULTURAL CONFLICT

Cultural conflict is a struggle that arises between groups of people because of their opposing values, beliefs, or customs. In "Dead Men's Path," the headmaster of a village school believes in modern methods of education. This belief triggers a conflict with the villagers.

ACTIVE READING: UNDERSTANDING MOTIVATIONS

A character's **motivations** are the reasons why he or she acts, feels, or thinks in a certain way. Often a reader must make inferences—logical guesses or conclusions based on the evidence found in a story—to determine those reasons.

📖 **READER'S NOTEBOOK**   Make a chart like the one shown below for Michael Obi, the main character in the story. Then make a similar chart for the village priest. As you read, list several actions of each character, the motivations you infer, and the clues you use to make your inferences.

Michael Obi		
Actions	**Motivations**	**Clues**
accepts the position of headmaster with enthusiasm	wants to show older teachers that he can run a school better than they can	"outspoken in his condemnation of the narrow views of these older and often less-educated ones" (page 1275)

WORDS TO KNOW **Vocabulary Preview**

denigration   pivotal   zeal
eradicate   skeptical

Dead Men's Path

Chinua Achebe

Michael Obi's hopes were fulfilled much earlier than he had expected. He was appointed headmaster of Ndume[1] Central School in January 1949. It had always been an unprogressive school, so the Mission authorities decided to send a young and energetic man to run it. Obi accepted this responsibility with enthusiasm. He had many wonderful ideas and this was an opportunity to put them into practice. He had had sound secondary school education which designated him a "pivotal teacher" in the official records and set him apart from the other headmasters in the mission field. He was outspoken in his condemnation of the narrow views of these older and often less-educated ones.

"We shall make a good job of it, shan't we?" he asked his young wife when they first heard the joyful news of his promotion.

"We shall do our best," she replied. "We shall have such beautiful gardens and everything will be just *modern* and delightful . . ." In their two years of married life she had become completely infected by his passion for "modern methods" and his denigration of "these old and superannuated[2] people in the teaching field who would be better employed as traders in the Onitsha market."[3] She began to see herself already as the admired wife of the young headmaster, the queen of the school.

The wives of the other teachers would envy her position. She would set the fashion in everything . . . Then, suddenly, it occurred to her that there might not be other wives. Wavering between hope and fear, she asked her husband, looking anxiously at him.

"All our colleagues are young and unmarried," he said with enthusiasm which for once she did not share. "Which is a good thing," he continued.

"Why?"

"Why? They will give all their time and energy to the school."

Nancy was downcast. For a few minutes she became skeptical about the new school; but it was only for a few minutes. Her little personal misfortune could not blind her to her husband's happy prospects. She looked at him as he sat folded up in a chair. He was stoop-shouldered and looked frail. But he sometimes surprised people with sudden bursts of physical energy. In his present posture, however,

> He had many wonderful ideas and this was an opportunity to put them into practice.

---

1. **Ndume** (ən-doo'mä).

2. **superannuated:** ready for retirement.

3. **Onitsha market:** The city of Onitsha, in eastern Nigeria, is known for its huge market, where many kinds of items are sold or traded.

WORDS TO KNOW

pivotal (pĭv'ə-tl) *adj.* very important
denigration (dĕn'ĭ-grā'shən) *n.* the act of speaking ill of someone; defamation
skeptical (skĕp'tĭ-kəl) *adj.* doubtful

Silent Faces at the Crossroads (1967), Obiora Udechukwu. Oil on board, 121.5 cm × 73.5 cm. Collection and photo: the artist.

whole life into the work, and his wife hers too. He had two aims. A high standard of teaching was insisted upon, and the school compound was to be turned into a place of beauty. Nancy's dream-gardens came to life with the coming of the rains, and blossomed. Beautiful hibiscus and allamanda[4] hedges in brilliant red and yellow marked out the carefully tended school compound from the rank[5] neighborhood bushes.

One evening as Obi was admiring his work he was scandalized to see an old woman from the village hobble right across the compound, through a marigold flower-bed and the hedges. On going up there he found faint signs of an almost disused path from the village across the school compound to the bush on the other side.

"It amazes me," said Obi to one of his teachers who had been three years in the school, "that you people allowed the villagers to make use of this footpath. It is simply incredible." He shook his head.

"The path," said the teacher apologetically, "appears to be very important to them. Although it is hardly used, it connects the village shrine with their place of burial."

"And what has that got to do with the school?" asked the headmaster.

"Well, I don't know," replied the other with a shrug of the shoulders. "But I remember there was a big row[6] some time ago when we attempted to close it."

"That was some time ago. But it will not be used now," said Obi as he walked away. "What will the Government Education Officer think of

all his bodily strength seemed to have retired behind his deep-set eyes, giving them an extraordinary power of penetration. He was only twenty-six, but looked thirty or more. On the whole, he was not unhandsome.

"A penny for your thoughts, Mike," said Nancy after a while, imitating the woman's magazine she read.

"I was thinking what a grand opportunity we've got at last to show these people how a school should be run." Ndume School was backward in every sense of the word. Mr. Obi put his

---

4. **hibiscus and allamanda:** tropical shrubs with large, showy flowers.

5. **rank:** growing wildly or excessively.

6. **row** (rou): quarrel.

this when he comes to inspect the school next week? The villagers might, for all I know, decide to use the schoolroom for a pagan ritual during the inspection."

Heavy sticks were planted closely across the path at the two places where it entered and left the school premises. These were further strengthened with barbed wire.

Three days later the village priest of *Ani*[7] called on the headmaster. He was an old man and walked with a slight stoop. He carried a stout walking-stick which he usually tapped on the floor, by way of emphasis, each time he made a new point in his argument.

"I have heard," he said after the usual exchange of cordialities,[8] "that our ancestral footpath has recently been closed . . ."

"Yes," replied Mr. Obi. "We cannot allow people to make a highway of our school compound."

"Look here, my son," said the priest bringing down his walking-stick, "this path was here before you were born and before your father was born. The whole life of this village depends on it. Our dead relatives depart by it and our ancestors visit us by it. But most important, it is the path of children coming in to be born . . ."

Mr. Obi listened with a satisfied smile on his face.

"The whole purpose of our school," he said finally, "is to eradicate just such beliefs as that. Dead men do not require footpaths. The whole idea is just fantastic. Our duty is to teach your children to laugh at such ideas."

"What you say may be true," replied the priest, "but we follow the practices of our fathers. If you re-open the path we shall have nothing to quarrel about. What I always say is: let the hawk perch and let the eagle perch."

> "Our dead relatives depart by it and our ancestors visit us by it. But most important, it is the path of children coming in to be born . . ."

He rose to go.

"I am sorry," said the young headmaster. "But the school compound cannot be a thoroughfare. It is against our regulations. I would suggest your constructing another path, skirting our premises. We can even get our boys to help in building it. I don't suppose the ancestors will find the little detour too burdensome."

"I have no more words to say," said the old priest, already outside.

Two days later a young woman in the village died in childbed. A diviner[9] was immediately consulted and he prescribed heavy sacrifices to propitiate ancestors insulted by the fence.

Obi woke up next morning among the ruins of his work. The beautiful hedges were torn up not just near the path but right round the school, the flowers trampled to death and one of the school buildings pulled down . . . That day, the white Supervisor came to inspect the school and wrote a nasty report on the state of the premises but more seriously about the "tribal-war situation developing between the school and the village, arising in part from the misguided zeal of the new headmaster." ❖

---

7. *Ani* (ä′nē): the Ibo earth goddess.

8. **cordialities:** pleasantries.

9. **diviner:** a person who uses signs and omens to predict the future.

Connect to the Literature

1. What Do You Think? What do you **predict** will happen to Michael Obi after the supervisor files his report?

Comprehension Check
- What does the path through the school grounds connect?
- What happens to the school grounds after Michael Obi refuses to reopen the path?

Thinking Critically

2. Do you think the villagers were justified in their actions against Michael Obi? Why or why not?

3. How would you rate Michael Obi's performance as the headmaster of the village school?

THINK ABOUT
- his aims for the school
- his enthusiasm for his work
- whether he seems to care about the students
- his attitude toward the villagers' beliefs
- the ill will he creates between the village and the school

4. ACTIVE READING: UNDERSTANDING MOTIVATIONS Review the character charts that you made in your 📖 READER'S NOTEBOOK. In your opinion, how do Michael Obi's motivations differ from those of the village priest?

5. How would you describe the relationship between Michael Obi and his wife, Nancy?

Extend Interpretations

6. What If? What do you think would have happened to the school grounds if the young village woman had not died?

7. Connect to Life Explain the meaning of this proverb offered by the village priest: "Let the hawk perch and let the eagle perch." Then discuss how you might apply the proverb to situations in your school or community.

LITERARY ANALYSIS: CULTURAL CONFLICT

Cultural conflict occurs when customs, attitudes, or beliefs push groups of people in opposing directions. This conflict may arise from changes within a culture, from one culture's contact with other cultures, or from a combination of both. In "Dead Men's Path," contact with British culture has pushed some Nigerians—for example, Michael Obi's wife—in new directions:

> *In their two years of married life she had become completely infected by his passion for "modern methods" and his denigration of "these old and superannuated people in the teaching field. . . ."*

Paired Activity With a partner, look through the story for clues that help you understand the causes and effects of the cultural conflict between Michael Obi and the villagers. Then write a sentence or two to describe the conflict. Finally, discuss whether or not the conflict might be resolved and, if so, how.

Writing Option

Job Assessment Imagine that you are the supervisor who has just visited the village school. Write an assessment of Michael Obi's performance as headmaster. Use your response to question 3 on the preceding page as a starting point.

> ### Ndume Central School
>
> Performance Review
>
> Name: _Michael Obi_
>
> Job: _Headmaster of Ndume Central School_
>
> Starting Date: _January 1949_
>
> Rating : ☐ excellent ☐ good ☐ fair ☐ poor
>
> Assessment:_____
> _____
> _____
>
> Suggestions for Improvement:_____
> _____
> _____

Activities & Explorations

1. Artistic Interpretation Draw or paint sketches depicting the school grounds before and after the destruction. ~ **ART**

2. Role-Playing With another student, role-play the conversation that might have taken place between the visiting supervisor and Michael Obi. ~ **SPEAKING AND LISTENING/PERFORMING**

Inquiry & Research

Nigerian Culture Find out more about an aspect of Nigerian culture that interests you, such as its school system, its religions, or its literature. Share your findings in an oral report to your classmates. Use visual aids in your presentation.

RESEARCH STARTER
CLASSZONE.COM

Vocabulary in Action

EXERCISE: RELATED WORDS Write the letter of the word that is not related in meaning to the other words in the set.

1. (a) erase, (b) eradicate, (c) eliminate, (d) evoke

2. (a) essential, (b) unimportant, (c) pivotal, (d) crucial

3. (a) zeal, (b) enthusiasm, (c) complexity, (d) passion

4. (a) defamation, (b) denigration, (c) criticism, (d) destination

5. (a) skeptical, (b) overtired, (c) exhausted, (d) drowsy

Building Vocabulary

For a lesson on using a thesaurus to find synonyms, see page 558.

Chinua Achebe

PREPARING to *Read*

Build Background Bill Moyers has worked in the media for more than 25 years. Known especially for his documentaries on public television, he has interviewed prominent figures from all over the world. You are about to read part of a transcript of an interview with Chinua Achebe. It took place in the 1980s, when Achebe was still living in Nigeria.

MOYERS: How would you like for us to see Africa?

ACHEBE: To see Africa as a continent of people—just people, not some strange beings that demand a special kind of treatment. If you accept Africans as people, then you listen to them. They have their preferences. If you took Africa seriously as a continent of people, you would listen. You would not be able to sit back here and suggest that you know, for instance, what should be done in South Africa. When the majority of the people in South Africa are saying, "This is what we think will bring apartheid to an end," somebody sits here and says, "No, no, that will not do it. We know what will work." Margaret Thatcher[1] sits in Britain and says, "Although the whole of Africa may think that this works, I know that what will work is something else."

That's what I want to see changed. The traditional attitude of Europe or the West is that Africa is a continent of children. A man as powerful and enlightened as Albert

---

1. **Margaret Thatcher:** Great Britain's first woman prime minister, who served from 1979 to 1990.

FROM AN INTERVIEW WITH

CHINUA ACHEBE

by BILL MOYERS

Schweitzer[2] was still able to say, "The black people are my brothers—but my junior brothers." We're not anybody's junior brothers.

MOYERS: There is still a lot of Robinson Crusoe. Robinson Crusoe could never accept Friday[3] as anything but a child living in a primitive simplicity.

ACHEBE: That's right. But that's not really true, it's self-serving. What I'm suggesting is we must look at Africans as full-grown people. They may not be as wealthy or advanced in the same ways as you are here, but they're people who, in their history, also have had moments of great success—in social organization, for instance. If you grant that Africans are grown-up, a lot of other things will follow.

MOYERS: You once said that if you're an African, the world is turned upside down. Explain that.

ACHEBE: What I mean is, I look at the world, at the way it is organized, and it is inadequate. Whichever direction I look, I don't see a space I want to stay in. On our own continent, there are all kinds of mistreatment. The most recent, for instance, is the dumping of the toxic wastes from the industrialized world in Africa.

MOYERS: Many American companies and Western countries are dumping their toxic wastes in African countries, and they're often bribing governments to do it.

ACHEBE: Yes. The world is not well arranged, and therefore there's no way we can be happy with it, even as writers. Sometimes our writer colleagues in the West suggest that perhaps we

---

2. **Albert Schweitzer** (shwīt'sər): a French physician who lived from 1875 to 1965. He spent much of his life at a missionary hospital in present-day Gabon. He was awarded the 1952 Nobel Peace Prize.

3. **Robinson Crusoe . . . Friday:** Robinson Crusoe, the hero of Daniel Defoe's 1719 novel, is an English sailor shipwrecked on an island. He befriends a native and names him Friday.

Bill Moyers

1281

are too activist, we are too earnest. "Why don't you relax?" they say. "This is not really the business of poetry." About a month ago I was at an international conference of writers to celebrate the one thousandth year of Dublin. During the discussion everybody was saying that poetry has nothing to do with society or with history. Poetry is something personal, private, introspective. Now, obviously, poetry can be that.

MOYERS: But a poet is a member of society.

ACHEBE: Yes, yes. When you say poetry is only something personal, you are saying something outrageously wrong. So I took the opportunity to state the other case. I said that poetry can be as activist as it wants, if it has the willingness and the energy. And I gave them two examples.

Toward the end of the colonial period in Angola, there was a doctor practicing his medicine and writing very delicate, very sensitive poetry in his spare time. One day he saw one of the most brutal acts of the colonial regime, and he shut down his surgery, took to the bush, and wrote a poem which had the words "I wait no more. I am the awaited." It is said that the guerrillas who fought with him chanted lines

from his poetry. So I'm saying that these things are possible for poetry. Of course, a poet who becomes activist risks certain dangers, such as getting into trouble with those in power.

Here's another example: Some years ago, at a conference in Stockholm, a Swedish writer and journalist said to two or three African writers, "Say, you fellows are very lucky— your governments put you in jail. Here in Sweden nobody pays any attention to us, no matter what we write."

But, you see, the point is this: A poet who sees poetry in the light I'm suggesting is likely to fall out very seriously with the emperor. Whereas the poet in the West might say, "Oh no, we have no business with politics, we have no business with history, we have no business with anything—just what is in our own mind"—well, the emperor would be very, very happy.

MOYERS: So that's what you meant when you said once that storytelling is a threat to anyone in control.

ACHEBE: Yes, because a storyteller has a different agenda from the emperor.

MOYERS: And yet storytelling, poetry, literature didn't stop the brutalities that were visited on

your own Ibo people in the Biafran War and didn't stop Idi Amin[4] in Uganda, or Bokassa[5] in the Central African Republic.

ACHEBE: Yes, well, there's a limit to what story-telling can achieve. We're not saying that a poet can stop a battalion with a couple of lines of his poetry. But there are other forms of power. The storyteller appeals to the mind, and appeals ultimately to generations and generations and generations.

MOYERS: I love this line in *A Man of the People*—"The great thing, as the old people have told us, is reminiscence, and only those who survive can have it. Besides, if you survive, who knows? It may be your turn to eat tomorrow. Your son may bring home your share." The power of reminiscing is very important to you.

ACHEBE: If you look at the world in terms of storytelling, you have, first of all, the man who agitates, the man who drums up the people—I call him the drummer. Then you have the warrior, who goes forward and fights. But you also have the storyteller who recounts the event—and this is one who survives, who out-lives all the others. It is the storyteller, in fact, who makes us what we are, who creates history. The storyteller creates the memory that the survivors must have—otherwise their surviving would have no meaning. ❖

---

4. **Idi Amin:** the military ruler of Uganda from 1971 to 1979, who killed approximately 200,000 people during his regime.

5. **Bokassa:** the president of the Central African Republic from 1966 to 1979, known as erratic and violent.

Thinking Through the Literature

1. **Comprehension Check** According to Achebe, how should Western countries regard Africa?

2. **Comparing Texts** How do the ideas in this interview influence your interpretation of Michael Obi's conduct in "Dead Men's Path"?

3. On the basis of this interview, how do you think Achebe views his role as a writer?

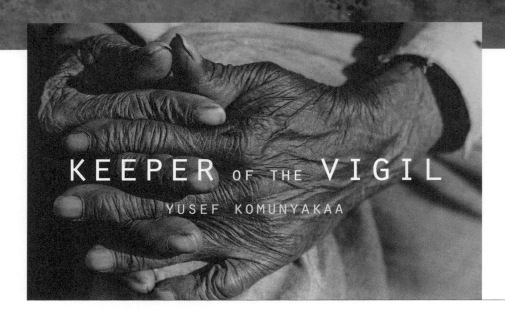

KEEPER OF THE VIGIL

YUSEF KOMUNYAKAA

PREPARING to *Read*

Build Background Chinua Achebe is revered by many writers around the world. Yusef Komunyakaa (kō'mən-yä'kə) wrote the following poem as a tribute to Achebe's literary vision.

When the last song
   was about to leave
dust in the mouth,

where termite-eaten
5   masks gazed down
in a broken repose, you

unearthed a language
   ignited by horror
& joy. A cassava

10   seed trembled in a pellet
of fossilized goat dung.
The lifelines on my palms

mapped buried footprints
   along forgotten paths
15   into Lagos. The past

& present balanced till
   the future formed a
wishbone: Achebe,

9 cassava (kə-sä'və): any of several plants having fleshy roots that yield a nutritious starch.

11 fossilized: changed into a fossil—a trace of an organism preserved in rock or sediment.

15 Lagos (lā'gŏs'): the largest city of Nigeria.

you helped me steal
20   back myself. Although
sometimes the right hand

wrestles the left, you
        showed me there's a time
for plaintive reed flutes

24 plaintive: sorrowful.

25   & another for machetes.
        I couldn't help but see
the church & guardtower

25 machetes (mə-shĕt′ēz): large
heavy knives with broad blades.

on the same picturesque
        hill. *Umuada* & *chi*
30   reclaimed my tongue

quick as palm wine
        & kola nut, praisesongs
made of scar tissue.

32 kola nut: a seed of a tropical
African evergreen plant.

—*for Chinua Achebe*

Civil Peace

CHINUA ACHEBE

Build Background

More than 250 ethnic groups call Nigeria home. The largest groups are the Hausa and Fulani in the north, the Yoruba in the southwest, and the Ibo in the southeast. When Nigeria gained its independence in 1960, these groups began to vie for power, often violently. In 1966, anti-Ibo riots erupted in the north, where Hausa and Fulani peoples resented Ibo influence on the government. Then, in 1967, the Ibo seceded from Nigeria to form the independent republic of Biafra. A civil war followed, causing massive hardship and devastation, especially in Biafra. It is estimated that more than 1.5 million Biafrans starved to death before Biafra surrendered in 1970 and was reintegrated into Nigeria. The story you are about to read takes place shortly after the end of the civil war.

WORDS TO KNOW **Vocabulary Preview**

amenable	imperious	monumental
dissent	inaudibly	

Connect to Your Life

Think about books, articles, films, or news accounts that describe the aftermath of a war. What do you think conditions are like for ordinary civilians after a war has been fought on their land?

Focus Your Reading

LITERARY ANALYSIS: DIALECT

A **dialect** is a form of a language that is spoken in a particular place or by a particular group of people. In "Civil Peace" some of the characters speak a dialect that differs markedly from standard English. Here are some words from that dialect:

am: it
commot: leave
katakata: trouble
na: is; it is

soja: soldiers
wetin: what are
wey de for inside: that went with it

Use the context to help you figure out the general meanings of sentences written in dialect. Reading these sentences aloud may help you understand them better.

ACTIVE READING: MAKING JUDGMENTS ABOUT CHARACTERS

When you read a story, you often judge the characters on the basis of what they say, do, think, or feel and how they react to events. In this story, Jonathan Iwegbu considers himself very lucky. As you read, think about whether or not you agree with him.

📖 **READER'S NOTEBOOK** On a chart like the one shown below, list Jonathan's blessings and misfortunes.

Jonathan's Luck	
Blessings	**Misfortunes**
He, his wife, and three of their children survive the war.	One of his children dies in the war.

Civil Peace
Chinua Achebe

Jonathan Iwegbu[1] counted himself extraordinarily lucky. "Happy survival!" meant so much more to him than just a current fashion of greeting old friends in the first hazy days of peace. It went deep to his heart. He had come out of the war with five inestimable[2] blessings—his head, his wife Maria's head and the heads of three out of their four children. As a bonus he also had his old bicycle—a miracle too but naturally not to be compared to the safety of five human heads.

The bicycle had a little history of its own. One day at the height of the war it was commandeered "for urgent military action." Hard as its loss would have been to him he would still have let it go without a thought had he not had some doubts about the genuineness of the officer. It wasn't his disreputable[3] rags, nor the toes peeping out of one blue and one brown canvas shoes, nor yet the two stars of his rank done obviously in a hurry in biro,[4] that troubled Jonathan; many good and heroic soldiers looked the same or worse. It was rather a certain lack of grip and firmness in his manner. So Jonathan, suspecting he might be amenable to influence, rummaged in his raffia bag and produced the two pounds with which he had been going to buy firewood which his wife, Maria, retailed to camp officials for extra stock-fish and corn meal, and got his bicycle back. That night he buried it in the little clearing in the bush where the dead of the camp,

including his own youngest son, were buried. When he dug it up again a year later after the surrender all it needed was a little palm-oil greasing. "Nothing puzzles God," he said in wonder.

He put it to immediate use as a taxi and accumulated a small pile of Biafran money[5] ferrying camp officials and their families across the four-mile stretch to the nearest tarred road. His standard charge per trip was six pounds and those who had the money were only glad to be

---

1. **Iwegbu** (ē-wĕg′bōo).
2. **inestimable:** priceless.
3. **disreputable:** in poor condition; not fit to be used.
4. **biro** (bîr′ō): ballpoint pen.
5. **Biafran money:** Biafra is a region in eastern Nigeria that fought unsuccessfully from 1967 to 1970 to establish itself as an independent republic.

WORDS TO KNOW
amenable (ə-mē′nə-bəl) *adj.* open to suggestion; responsive

rid of some of it in this way. At the end of a fortnight he had made a small fortune of one hundred and fifteen pounds.

Then he made the journey to Enugu[6] and found another miracle waiting for him. It was unbelievable. He rubbed his eyes and looked again and it was still standing there before him. But, needless to say, even that monumental blessing must be accounted also totally inferior to the five heads in the family. This newest miracle was his little house in Ogui[7] Overside. Indeed nothing puzzles God! Only two houses away a huge concrete edifice some wealthy contractor had put up just before the war was a mountain of rubble. And here was Jonathan's little zinc house of no regrets built with mud blocks quite intact! Of course the doors and windows were missing and five sheets off the roof. But what was that? And anyhow he had returned to Enugu early enough to pick up bits of old zinc and wood and soggy sheets of cardboard lying around the neighborhood before thousands more came out of their forest holes looking for the same things. He got a destitute carpenter with one old hammer, a blunt plane and a few bent and rusty nails in his tool bag to turn this assortment of wood, paper and metal into door and window shutters for five Nigerian shillings or fifty Biafran pounds. He paid the pounds, and moved in with his overjoyed family carrying five heads on their shoulders.

His children picked mangoes near the military cemetery and sold them to soldiers' wives for a few pennies—real pennies this time—and his wife started making breakfast akara balls[8] for neighbors in a hurry to start life again. With his family earnings he took his bicycle to the villages around and bought fresh palm-wine which he mixed generously in his rooms with the water which had recently started running again in the public tap down the road, and opened up a bar for soldiers and other lucky people with good money.

At first he went daily, then every other day and finally once a week, to the offices of the Coal Corporation where he used to be a miner, to find out what was what. The only thing he did find out in the end was that that little house of his was even a greater blessing than he had thought. Some of his fellow examiners who had nowhere to return at the end of the day's waiting just slept outside the doors of the offices and cooked what meal they could scrounge together in Bournvita tins.[9] As the weeks lengthened and still nobody could say what was what Jonathan discontinued his weekly visits altogether and faced his palm-wine bar.

But nothing puzzles God. Came the day of the windfall when after five days of endless scuffles in queues[10] and counter-queues in the sun outside the Treasury he had twenty pounds counted into his palms as ex-gratia[11] award for the rebel money he had turned in. It was like Christmas for him and for many others like him when the payments began. They called it (since few could manage its proper official name) *egg-rasher.*

As soon as the pound notes were placed in his palm Jonathan simply closed it tight over them and buried fist and money inside his trouser pocket. He had to be extra careful because he had seen a man a couple of days earlier collapse into near-madness in an instant before that oceanic crowd because no sooner had he got his twenty pounds than some heartless ruffian picked it off him. Though it was not

---

6. **Enugu** (ā-nōō'gōō): the capital city of Biafra.
7. **Ogui** (ō'gōō-ē).
8. **akara balls:** fried batter consisting mainly of mashed black-eyed peas.
9. **Bournvita tins:** cans that had contained a nutritional drink used to supplement children's diets.
10. **queues** (kyōōz): lines of waiting people.
11. **ex-gratia** (ĕks-grā'shə): given as a favor rather than as a legal right.

monumental (mŏn'yə-mĕn'tl) *adj.* very significant; astonishing

Indeed nothing puzzles God!

right that a man in such an extremity of agony should be blamed yet many in the queues that day were able to remark quietly on the victim's carelessness, especially after he pulled out the innards of his pocket and revealed a hole in it big enough to pass a thief's head. But of course he had insisted that the money had been in the other pocket, pulling it out too to show its comparative wholeness. So one had to be careful.

Jonathan soon transferred the money to his left hand and pocket so as to leave his right free for shaking hands should the need arise, though by fixing his gaze at such an elevation as to miss all approaching human faces he made sure that the need did not arise, until he got home.

He was normally a heavy sleeper but that night he heard all the neighborhood noises die down one after another. Even the night watchman who knocked the hour on some metal somewhere in the distance had fallen silent after knocking one o'clock. That must have been the last thought in Jonathan's mind before he was finally carried away himself. He couldn't have been gone for long, though, when he was violently awakened again.

"Who is knocking?" whispered his wife lying beside him on the floor.

"I don't know," he whispered back breathlessly.

The second time the knocking came it was so loud and imperious that the rickety old door could have fallen down.

"Who is knocking?" he asked then, his voice parched and trembling.

"Na tief-man and him people," came the cool reply. "Make you hopen de door." This was followed by the heaviest knocking of all.

Maria was the first to raise the alarm, then he followed and all their children.

"Police-o! Thieves-o! Neighbors-o! Police-o! We are lost! We are dead! Neighbors, are you asleep? Wake up! Police-o!"

This went on for a long time and then stopped suddenly. Perhaps they had scared the thief away. There was total silence. But only for a short while.

"You done finish?" asked the voice outside. "Make we help you small. Oya, everybody!"

"Police-o! Tief-man-o! Neighbors-o! we done loss-o! Police-o! . . ."

There were at least five other voices besides the leader's.

Jonathan and his family were now completely paralyzed by terror. Maria and the children

WORDS TO KNOW
imperious (ĭm-pîr′ē-əs) *adj.* urgent; pressing

sobbed <u>inaudibly</u> like lost souls. Jonathan groaned continuously.

The silence that followed the thieves' alarm vibrated horribly. Jonathan all but begged their leader to speak again and be done with it.

"My frien," said he at long last, "we don try our best for call dem but I tink say dem all done sleep-o. . . . So wetin we go do now? Sometaim you wan call soja? Or you wan make we call dem for you? Soja better pass police. No be so?"

"Na so!" replied his men. Jonathan thought he heard even more voices now than before and groaned heavily. His legs were sagging under him and his throat felt like sand-paper.

"My frien, why you no de talk again. I de ask you say you wan make we call soja?"

"No."

"Awrighto. Now make we talk business. We no be bad tief. We no like for make trouble. Trouble done finish. War done finish and all the katakata wey de for inside. No Civil War again. This time na Civil Peace. No be so?"

"Na so!" answered the horrible chorus.

"What do you want from me? I am a poor man. Everything I had went with this war. Why do you come to me? You know people who have money. We . . ."

"Awright! We know say you no get plenty money. But we sef no get even anini."[12] So derefore make you open dis window and give us one hundred pound and we go commot. Orderwise we de come for inside now to show you guitar-boy like dis . . ."

A volley of automatic fire rang through the sky. Maria and the children began to weep aloud again.

"Ah, missisi de cry again. No need for dat. We done talk say we na good tief. We just take our small money and go nwayorly. No molest. Abi we de molest?"

"At all!" sang the chorus.

"My friends," began Jonathan hoarsely. "I hear what you say and I thank you. If I had one hundred pounds . . ."

"Lookia my frien, no be play we come play for your house. If we make mistake and step for inside you no go like am-o. So derefore . . ."

"To God who made me; if you come inside and find one hundred pounds, take it and shoot me and shoot my wife and children. I swear to God. The only money I have in this life is this twenty-pounds egg-rasher they gave me today . . ."

"OK. Time de go. Make you open dis window and bring the twenty pound. We go manage am like dat."

There were now loud murmurs of <u>dissent</u> among the chorus: "Na lie de man de lie; e get plenty money. . . . Make we go inside and search properly well. . . . Wetin be twenty pound? . . ."

"Shurrup!" rang the leader's voice like a lone shot in the sky and silenced the murmuring at once. "Are you dere? Bring the money quick!"

"I am coming," said Jonathan fumbling in the darkness with the key of the small wooden box he kept by his side on the mat.

At the first sign of light as neighbors and others assembled to commiserate with him he was already strapping his five-gallon demijohn[13] to his bicycle carrier and his wife, sweating in the open fire, was turning over akara balls in a wide clay bowl of boiling oil. In the corner his eldest son was rinsing out dregs of yesterday's palm wine from old beer bottles.

"I count it as nothing," he told his sympathizers, his eyes on the rope he was tying. "What is *egg-rasher*? Did I depend on it last week? Or is it greater than other things that went with the war? I say, let *egg-rasher* perish in the flames! Let it go where everything else has gone. Nothing puzzles God." ❖

---

12. **anini:** any.
13. **demijohn:** a large glass or earthenware jar encased in wicker.

WORDS TO KNOW

1290
inaudibly (ĭn-ô′də-blē) *adv.* in a way that cannot be heard
dissent (dĭ-sĕnt′) *n.* disagreement

Connect to the Literature

1. What Do You Think?
After reading the story, what are your thoughts about Jonathan?

Comprehension Check
• How does Jonathan acquire the ex-gratia award money?
• What happens to this money?

Think Critically

2. ACTIVE READING: MAKING JUDGMENTS ABOUT CHARACTERS Review the chart you created in your **READER'S NOTEBOOK.** Do you agree with Jonathan's view of himself as lucky? Why or why not?

3. How would you describe Jonathan's attitude toward life?

> THINK ABOUT
> • the importance he places on his family's safety
> • how he supports his family during and after the war
> • his confrontation with the thieves
> • his reaction to the loss of his money

4. How would you explain the meaning of the **aphorism** "Nothing puzzles God"?

5. What does the story say to you about the aftermath of war for ordinary civilians?

Extend Interpretations

6. Critic's Corner In describing Achebe's fiction, the critic G. D. Killam has observed: "Sometimes his characters meet with success, more often with defeat and despair. Through it all the spirit of man and the belief in the possibility of triumph endure." Do you think this assessment applies to Jonathan? Cite details from the story to support your opinion.

7. Comparing Texts Imagine that Jonathan had been in Michael Obi's situation in "Dead Men's Path." How do you think Jonathan might have handled the conflict with the village priest?

8. Connect to Life Do you think Jonathan's attitude in the wake of the war's destruction and tragedy is common among the survivors of wars? Give reasons for your opinion.

LITERARY ANALYSIS: DIALECT

Dialect reflects the pronunciations, vocabulary, and grammatical rules that are typical of a region. In "Civil Peace," Achebe uses two dialects of English, the Nigerian dialect of the thieves and the near-standard dialect of Jonathan and his family. The leader of the thieves first uses the Nigerian dialect when Jonathan asks who is knocking on the door:

"Na tief-man and him people,"
came the cool reply.

or

"The thief and his people," came
the cool reply.

The thieves' dialect is markedly different from standard English:

"So wetin we go do now?
Sometaim you wan call soja?"

or

"So what are we going to do now?
Do you want to call for soldiers
awhile?"

Jonathan's own dialect is evident in this passage, in which he and his family raise the alarm about the thieves:

"Police-o! Thieves-o! Neighbors-o!
Police-o! We are lost. We are
dead! Neighbors, are you
asleep? Wake up! Police-o!"

Paired Activity Working with a partner, read aloud the dialogue between Jonathan and the thieves. Then discuss why you think Achebe chose to use contrasting dialects in his story.

Achebe's Cross-Cultural Style

Though English is his second, not his native, language, Chinua Achebe writes stories about Africa in English. His style, though, is all his own, suiting his African characters, settings, and themes. Many critics have praised him for creating an authentic Ibo prose style in English.

Key Aspects of Achebe's Style

- a focus on African people and traditional African values
- simple, straightforward diction, or word choice
- the use of ironic situations and mild satire to explore social issues
- the frequent use of African proverbs and folklore to help convey character and theme
- the use of different dialects to convey cultural differences among characters

Analysis of Style

Study the aspects of Achebe's style in the chart above and the passages from his works that appear at the right. Then complete the following activities:

- Find in the passages examples of each aspect of Achebe's style. For examples of irony or satire, explain what Achebe targets for mockery.
- Find additional examples of Achebe's style in "Dead Men's Path" and "Civil Peace."
- Decide which aspects of Achebe's style help convey the themes of his work.

Applications

1. **Imitating Style** Try writing the first few paragraphs of a sequel to either "Dead Men's Path" or "Civil Peace." Make sure to imitate the style of the author.

2. **Changing Style** Rewrite the dialogue between Jonathan and the thieves in "Civil Peace," but have the thieves use standard or near-standard English instead of Nigerian dialect. What qualities, if any, do you think are lost in the rewritten version?

3. **Comparing Styles** Compare and contrast Achebe's style with the style of the West African literature in Unit Four. What influences of these older forms do you detect in Achebe's writing?

---

from ***Things Fall Apart***

"I know what it is to ask a man to trust another with his yams, especially these days when young men are afraid of hard work. I am not afraid of work. The lizard that jumped from the high iroko tree to the ground said he would praise himself if no one else did."

---

from **"The Voter"**

The village already belonged *en masse* to the People's Alliance Party, and its most illustrious son, Chief the Honorable Marcus Ibe, was Minister of Culture in the outgoing government (which was pretty certain to be the incoming one as well). Nobody doubted that the Honorable Minister would be elected in his constituency. Opposition to him was like the proverbial fly trying to move a dunghill.

---

from **"Chike's School Days"**

Chike was very fond of "Ten Green Bottles." They had been taught the words but they only remembered the first and the last lines. The middle was hummed and hie-ed and mumbled:

Ten grin botr angin on dar war,
Ten grin botr angin on dar war,
Hm hm hm hm hm
Hm, hm hm hm hm hm,
An ten grin botr angin on dar war.

Writing Options

1. News Article Write a news account—one that might appear in the local paper—describing the theft of Jonathan's money. For an effective news article, be sure to include information telling who, what, where, when, why, and how.

Who?
What?
Where?
When?
Why?
How?

2. Essay About the Title In a brief essay, explain the different meanings of Achebe's title "Civil Peace." First, explain why the leader of the thieves calls the period "Civil Peace" and indicate what is ironic about the term. Then consider the other chief meaning of *civil,* and explain whether anything or anyone in the story is truly civil. Finally, explain how the title helps point to the story's central theme or themes.

Writing Handbook
See page R33: Analysis.

Vocabulary in Action

EXERCISE: CONTEXT CLUES Complete each sentence by choosing the appropriate Word to Know.

1. Jonathan was not particular; he was _____ to any plan that would help him rebuild his life.

2. He had seen _____ landowners lose their wealth in the war.

3. Though he too had suffered losses, most of his family had been saved through _____ luck.

4. In most situations, Jonathan preferred agreement rather than _____.

5. Though the thieves were murmuring _____, he became frightened and quickly gave in.

WORDS TO KNOW

amenable	imperious	monumental
dissent	inaudibly	

Building Vocabulary

For an in-depth lesson on context clues, see page 674.

Netscape: Welcome to Netscape

Back Forward Home Reload Images Open Print Find Stop

Go To:

Chinua Achebe

Author Study Project
A RADIO PROGRAM ON ACHEBE

Document: Done.

Working with a group of classmates, create a radio program about Chinua Achebe's life and achievements. Begin the program with a brief oral biography of Achebe. Then present an imaginary interview with the author, in which he discusses some of his literary works and key ideas. Review Bill Moyers's interview with Chinua Achebe for examples of probing questions that elicit in-depth responses. Conclude the radio program with oral readings from some of Achebe's works, including poems as well as passages from his fiction and essays. Rehearse the program thoroughly, and then present it to the rest of the class—your "live" studio audience. Have a classmate tape-record the presentation.

Primary Sources Review several books by Achebe to find suitable poems and excerpts for the final part of the radio program. Also, to help you with the interview, find actual interviews with Achebe in books or magazine articles or at sites on the World Wide Web. *Conversations with Chinua Achebe* would be a good printed source. Reliable Web sites would include those maintained by universities and cultural societies.

Secondary Sources Obtain information about Achebe and his writing from reference works, literary biographies, and reliable online sources. Again, reliable online sources would include Web sites maintained by universities and cultural societies.

RESEARCH STARTER
CLASSZONE.COM

from *Paula*

ISABEL ALLENDE

Isabel Allende
1942–

Creative Beginnings Born in Peru, Isabel Allende (ē-sä-běl′ ä-yěn′dě) moved with her mother to Santiago, Chile, at the age of three. Allende's mother recognized and nurtured her daughter's creativity from an early age, encouraging her to keep a journal and draw on a bedroom wall. The efforts paid off. Allende's love of language led her to become a journalist at the age of 17, working for Chilean television stations and magazines. However, she later claimed that her imagination was a "great handicap" in her work as a journalist because it prevented her from being objective.

Murder and Exile By the time she was 30, Allende felt settled and content with her work in Chile. In addition, her uncle and godfather, Salvador Allende, had been elected president of Chile in 1970. He died in 1973, however, during a military takeover led by General Augusto Pinochet (ou-gōos′tô pē-nô-chět′). Pinochet formed a dictatorship that remained in place until 1990. For a time, Isabel Allende stayed in Chile, secretly helping those who opposed the repressive new regime. When it became clear that her own life was in danger, she fled—first to Venezuela and later to the United States.

International Acclaim While in exile, Allende began writing a letter to her grandfather, who had remained in Chile. The letter, in which she recorded many of her family's stories and legends, became the basis of Allende's first novel, *The House of the Spirits*. Published in 1982, the novel became an international bestseller. Her other works include *Of Love and Shadows* (1984), *Eva Luna* (1987), *The Stories of Eva Luna* (1990), *Paula* (1994), and *Daughter of Fortune* (1999). Allende continues to write in Spanish, but her work has been translated into many languages, including English.

Connect to Your Life

Think of a powerful world event—involving war, death, disease, or politics—that captured your attention. Then get together with a partner and discuss why the event intrigued you.

Focus Your Reading

LITERARY ANALYSIS: AUTOBIOGRAPHY

An **autobiography** is a person's account of his or her own life. Autobiographies provide revealing insights into the characters of their writers, as well as the societies in which they lived. As you read the excerpt from *Paula,* look for details that help you learn about Isabel Allende and about conditions in Chile during Pinochet's military regime.

ACTIVE READING: RECOGNIZING AUTHOR'S PURPOSE

Recall that the term **author's purpose** refers to a writer's reason for writing something. An author's purpose may be to entertain, to inform, to express opinions, or to persuade. An author may accomplish more than one purpose in a piece of writing, but one purpose is usually the most important.

READER'S NOTEBOOK To help you recognize Allende's purpose, take notes about the following as you read the excerpt:

- the main subject of the writing
- the author's **tone,** or attitude toward the subject
- the details the author uses to develop her ideas
- what you know about why the author began writing this piece

WORDS TO KNOW **Vocabulary Preview**

implacable	osmosis	tedium
naive	subvert	

Build Background

Remembering the Dead In 1991 Allende's 27-year-old daughter Paula became seriously ill and fell into a coma. Allende stayed near her daughter's side throughout the year-long illness. During that time, she wrote the story of her own life, which she hoped that Paula herself would read one day. Tragically, the young woman never regained consciousness, dying at the age of 28. Allende later completed her autobiography, in which she interwove the story of Paula's death, and named the book after her daughter.

In this excerpt from *Paula,* Allende explains how she came to write her second novel, *Of Love and Shadows.* The novel, which takes place in an unnamed Latin American country, tells the story of a couple who find a mine filled with the dead bodies of citizens murdered by a military regime. The narrative is based on an incident that occurred after President Allende's government had been overthrown: the discovery of the bodies of 15 murdered men.

The deaths clearly had been arranged by the Chilean government. In 1973, when General Pinochet established his military dictatorship, he crushed any resistance to the government by having thousands of President Allende's supporters rounded up and secretly killed. These people became known as *desaparecidos* (dĕ-sä-pä-rĕ-sē'dôs), "the disappeared." The number of *desaparecidos* officially recognized by the Chilean government is 3,000, but many people believe the real number to be much higher.

from Paula

Isabel Allende

Translated by Margaret Sayers Peden

began *Of Love and Shadows* on January 8, 1983, because that day had brought me luck with *The House of the Spirits,* thus initiating a tradition I honor to this day and don't dare change; I always write the first line of my books on that date. When that time comes, I try to be alone and silent for several hours; I need a lot of time to rid my mind of the noise outside and to cleanse my memory of life's confusion. I light candles to summon the muses and guardian spirits, I place flowers on my desk to intimidate tedium and the complete works of Pablo Neruda[1] beneath the computer with the hope they will inspire me by osmosis—if computers can be infected with a virus, there's no reason they shouldn't be refreshed by a breath of poetry. In a secret ceremony, I prepare my mind and soul to receive the first sentence in a trance, so the door may open slightly and allow me to peer through and perceive the hazy outlines of the story waiting for me. In the following months, I will cross that threshold to explore those spaces and, little by little, if I am lucky, the characters will come alive, become more precise and more real, and reveal the narrative to me as we go along. I don't know how or why I write; my books are not born in my mind, they gestate[2] in my womb and are capricious creatures with their

own lives, always ready to subvert me. I do not determine the subject, the subject chooses me, my work consists simply of providing enough time, solitude, and discipline for the book to write itself. That is what happened with my second novel. In 1978, in the area of Lonquén,[3] some fifty kilometers from Santiago, they found the bodies of fifteen campesinos[4] murdered by the government and hidden in abandoned lime kilns. The Catholic Church reported the discovery and the scandal exploded before authorities could muffle it; it was the first time the bodies of *desaparecidos* had been found, and the wavering finger of Chilean justice had no choice but to point to the armed forces. Several *carabineros*[5] were accused, tried, and found guilty of murder in the first degree—and immediately set free by General Pinochet under a decree of amnesty.[6] The news was published around the world,

---

1. **Pablo Neruda** (pä′blō nĕ-rōō′dǝ): a Chilean poet who won the Nobel Prize for literature in 1971.
2. **gestate:** develop.
3. **Lonquén** (lôn-kĕn′).
4. **campesinos** (käm′pǐ-sē′nōz): peasants.
5. *carabineros* (kä-rä-bē-nĕ′rôs) *Chilean Spanish:* members of the national police force.
6. **amnesty:** a general pardon granted by a government, usually for political offenses.

WORDS TO KNOW

tedium (tē′dē-ǝm) *n.* boredom
osmosis (ŏz-mō′sĭs) *n.* an unconscious absorbing of facts or ideas
subvert (sǝb-vûrt′) *v.* to destroy or corrupt

Isabel Allende. Photograph by Acey Harper.

I light candles to summon the muses and guardian spirits, I place flowers on my desk to intimidate tedium.

which was how I learned of it in Caracas.[7] By then, thousands of people had disappeared in many parts of the continent, Chile was not an exception. In Argentina, the mothers of the *desaparecidos* marched in the Plaza de Mayo[8] carrying photographs of their missing children and grandchildren; in Uruguay, the names of prisoners far exceeded physical bodies that could be counted. What happened in Lonquén was like a knife in my belly, I felt the pain for years. Five men from the same family, the Maureiras,[9] had died, murdered by *carabineros*. Sometimes I would be driving down the highway and suddenly be assaulted by the disturbing vision of the Maureira women searching for their men, years of asking their futile questions in prisons and concentration camps and hospitals and barracks, like the thousands and thousands of other persons in other places trying to find their loved ones. In Lonquén, the women were more fortunate than most; at least they knew their men had been murdered, and they could cry and pray for them—although not bury them, because the military later scattered the remains and dynamited the lime kilns to prevent their becoming a site for pilgrimages and worship. One day those women

---

7. **Caracas** (kə-rä′kəs): the capital of Venezuela, where Allende was living in exile.
8. **Plaza de Mayo** (plä′sä dĕ mä′yô): a main square in Buenos Aires, the Argentine capital.
9. **Maureiras** (mou-rā′räz).

walked up and down a row of rough-hewn tables, sorting through a pitiful array—keys, a comb, a shred of blue sweater, a lock of hair, or a few teeth—and said, This is my husband, This is my brother, This is my son. Every time I thought of them, I was transported with implacable clarity to the times I lived in Chile under the heavy mantle of terror: censorship and self-censorship, denunciations, curfew, soldiers with faces camouflaged so they couldn't be recognized, political police cars with tinted glass windows, arrests in the street, homes, offices, my racing to help fugitives find asylum in some embassy, sleepless nights when we had someone hidden in our home, the clumsy schemes to slip information out of the country or bring money in to aid families of the imprisoned. For my second novel, I didn't have to think of a subject, the women of the Maureira family, the mothers of the Plaza de Mayo, and millions of other victims pursued me, obliging me to write. The story of the deaths at Lonquén had lain in my heart since 1978; I had kept every press clipping that came into my hands without knowing exactly why, since at that time I had no inkling that my steps were leading toward literature. So by 1983, I had at my disposal a thick folder of information, and knew where to find other facts; my job consisted of weaving those threads into a single cord. I was relying on my friend Francisco in Chile, whom I meant to use as model for the protagonist, a family of Spanish Republican refugees on whom to pattern the Leals,[10] and a couple of women I had worked with on the women's magazine in Santiago as inspiration for the character of Irene. I drew Gustavo Morante,[11] Irene's fiancé, from a Chilean army officer who followed me to San Cristobal Hill one noontime in the autumn of 1974. I was sitting under a tree with my mother's Swiss dog, which I used to take for walks, looking down on Santiago from the heights, when an automobile stopped a few

meters away and a man in uniform got out and walked toward me. I froze with panic; for a split second I considered running, but instantly knew the futility of trying to escape and simply waited, shivering and speechless. To my surprise, the officer did not bark an order to me but removed his cap, apologized for disturbing me, and asked if he could sit down. I still was unable to speak a word, but since arrests were always made by several men it calmed me to see that he was alone. He was about thirty, tall and handsome, with a rather naive, unlined face. I noticed his distress as soon as he spoke. He told me he knew who I was; he had read some of my articles, and hadn't liked them, but he enjoyed my programs on television. He had often watched me climb the hill and had followed me that day because he had something he wanted to tell me. He said that he came from a very religious family; he was a devout Catholic and as a young man had contemplated entering the seminary, but had gone to the military academy to please his father. He soon discovered he liked that profession, and with time the army had become his true home. "I am prepared to die for my country," he said, "but I didn't know how difficult it is to kill for it." And then, after a very long pause, he described the first detail he had commanded, how he was assigned to execute a political prisoner who had been so badly tortured he couldn't stand and had to be tied in a chair, how in a frosty courtyard at five in the morning he gave the order to fire, and how when the sound of the shots faded he realized the man was still alive and staring tranquilly into his eyes, because he was beyond fear.

"I had to approach the prisoner, put my pistol to his temple, and press the trigger. The blood splattered my uniform. It's something I can't tear

---

10. **Leals** (lĕ-älz′): a family in *Of Love and Shadows*.
11. **Gustavo Morante** (gōōs-tä′vô mô-rän′tĕ).

WORDS TO KNOW

implacable (ĭm-plăk′ə-bəl) *adj.* unable to be appeased; unyielding
naive (nī-ēv′) *adj.* innocent or childlike

"I am prepared to die for my country," he said, "but I didn't know how difficult it is to kill for it."

from my soul. I can't sleep, I am haunted by the memory."

"Why are you telling me this?" I asked.

"Because it isn't enough to have told my confessor, I want to share it with someone who may be able to make use of it. Not all the military are murderers, as is being said; many of us have a conscience." He stood, saluted me with a slight bow, put on his cap, and left.

Months later, another man, this one in civilian clothes, told me something similar. "Soldiers shoot at the legs to force the officers to fire the *coup de grace*[12] and stain themselves with blood, too," he said. I jotted down those memories and for nine years kept them at the bottom of a drawer, until I used them in *Of Love and Shadows*. Some critics considered the book sentimental, and too political; for me, it is filled with magic because it revealed to me the strange powers of fiction. In the slow and silent process of writing, I enter a different state of consciousness in which sometimes I can draw back a veil and see the invisible, the world of my grandmother's three-legged table.[13] It is not necessary to mention all the premonitions and coincidences recorded in those pages, one will suffice. Although I had abundant information, there

were large lacunae[14] in the story, because many of the military trials were conducted in secret and what was published was distorted by censorship. In addition, I was far from the scene and could not go to Chile to interrogate the involved parties as I would have done under other circumstances. My years as a journalist had taught me that it is in personal interviews that one obtains the keys, motives, and emotions of a story, no research in a library can replace the firsthand information derived from a face-to-face conversation. During those warm Caracas nights, I wrote the novel from the material in my file of clippings, a few books, some tapes from Amnesty International,[15] and the inexhaustible voices of the women of the *desaparecidos* speaking to me across distance and time. Even with all that, I had to call upon my imagination to fill in

12. *coup de grace* (ko͞o′ də gräs′) *French:* a death blow to a mortally wounded victim.

13. **my grandmother's three-legged table:** a table around which Allende's grandmother would sit with her friends and try to conjure up spirits of the dead.

14. **lacunae** (lə-kyo͞o′nē): gaps.

15. **Amnesty International:** a worldwide organization that works against human-rights violations and for the release of political prisoners.

Copyright © Luis Navarro Vega.

HUMANITIES CONNECTION This photograph shows Purisma Muñoz de Maureira mourning her husband and four sons at a mass for the victims of Lonquén.

"The dead told me,"

I replied,

but he did not believe me.

blanks. After she read the original, my mother objected to one part that to her seemed absolutely improbable: the protagonists, at night and during curfew, go by motorcycle to a mine sealed off by the military; they find a break in the fence and enter an area that is off-limits, dig into the mouth of the mine with picks and shovels, find the remains of the murdered, photograph them, return with the proof, and deliver it to the cardinal, who finally orders the tomb opened. "That's impossible," she said. "No one would dare run such risks at the height of the dictatorship." "I can't think of any other way to resolve the plot, just think of it as literary license,"[16] I replied. The book was published in 1984. Four years later, the list of exiles who could not return to Chile was abolished and for the first time I felt free to go back to my country to vote in a plebiscite[17] that finally unseated Pinochet. One night the doorbell rang in my mother's house in Santiago and a man insisted in talking with me in private. In a corner of the terrace, he told me he was a priest, that he had learned in the sanctity of the confessional about the bodies buried in Lonquén, had gone there on his motorcycle during curfew, had opened a sealed mine with pick and shovel, had photographed the remains and taken the proof to the cardinal, who ordered a group of priests, newspapermen, and diplomats to open the clandestine tomb.

"No one has any knowledge of this except the cardinal and myself. If my participation in that matter had been known, I'm sure I wouldn't be here talking with you, I would be among the disappeared. How did you learn?" he asked.

"The dead told me," I replied, but he did not believe me. ❖

---

16. **literary license:** a fiction writer's freedom to adjust or distort real-life situations.

17. **plebiscite** (plĕb′ĭ-sīt′): a direct vote of the people on an important issue.

Connect to the Literature

1. What Do You Think?
What is your reaction to Allende's conversation with the priest at the end of the excerpt?

Comprehension Check
- What had happened to the men whose bodies were discovered in Lonquén?
- What real events described in this selection did Allende use in *Of Love and Shadows?*

Think Critically

2. ACTIVE READING: RECOGNIZING AUTHOR'S PURPOSE
With a small group of classmates, compare the notes you recorded in your ▥ READER'S NOTEBOOK. As a group, decide on Allende's main **purpose** for writing the excerpt. What secondary purposes might she have had?

3. How would you describe Allende as a writer?

THINK ABOUT
- how she sets up her environment as she begins
- her decision to write about "the disappeared"
- her use of personal interviews rather than library research

4. Why do you suppose the Chilean army officer wanted Allende to write about his confession?

5. Irony is a surprising contrast between expectation and reality. What is ironic about the objection Allende's mother raises to the story of the sealed-off mine?

Extend Interpretations

6. Critic's Corner Many writers and critics believe that in order to create a good story, a writer must write about what he or she knows—that to write about events, characters, and settings not experienced at first hand almost always leads to failure. Do you agree? Could Allende have written *Of Love and Shadows* if she had never experienced Chile's political turmoil? Give reasons or examples to support your opinion.

7. Connect to Life Many people are working to obtain justice for "the disappeared" in Chile. What other atrocities around the world have you read or heard about? What are people doing to try to right these wrongs? If appropriate, you might want to write about the event you recalled in the Connect to Your Life on page 1295.

LITERARY ANALYSIS: AUTOBIOGRAPHY

An **autobiography** is a writer's first-person account of his or her own life. Typically, an autobiography focuses on the most significant events and people in the writer's life. The narrative reveals the writer's feelings about these events and people and provides some understanding of the society in which he or she lived. Think about what the following statement suggests about Allende and about Chile during the years of the military dictatorship:

Sometimes I would be driving down the highway and suddenly be assaulted by the disturbing vision of the Maureira women searching for their men, years of asking their futile questions in prisons and concentration camps and hospitals and barracks. . . .

Paired Activity Get together with a partner and review the excerpt from *Paula.* Identify other details that provide insights into Allende and life in Chile under Pinochet. Then think about the type of information a history text might convey about "the disappeared" in Chile. What details does Allende's autobiography contain that might not be included in a traditional history book? What additional information might you find in a history book?

Writing Options

1. Autobiographical Essay

Write an autobiographical essay in which you describe an important event, at your school or in your community, that you experienced personally. Be sure to express your feelings and opinions about the event.

Writing Handbook
See page R29: Narrative Writing.

2. Mother-and-Daughter Dialogue

Write a dialogue that might have taken place between Allende and her mother after the writer's conversation with the priest.

3. Letter to the Editor

Write a letter that Isabel Allende might have written to the editor of the newspaper that published the article about the deaths at Lonquén. Make sure that your letter is consistent with Allende's own feelings and opinions about the incident.

Activities & Explorations

Human-Rights Poster

Atrocities like those that Allende describes have happened—and continue to happen—around the world. Create a poster that a United Nations agency might use to promote respect for human rights. ~ **ART**

Inquiry & Research

Chile After Pinochet Do research to find out what happened in Chile after Pinochet's years in power. How was Pinochet removed from power? What happened to him? Who governs Chile now? Write a brief report in which you answer these questions.

RESEARCH STARTER
CLASSZONE.COM

Vocabulary in Action

EXERCISE: MEANING CLUES Use your knowledge of the Words to Know to answer the following questions.

1. If you are **implacable** during an argument, do you readily admit you are wrong, speak very loudly, or refuse to give in?

2. Is **tedium** likely to be a result of having nothing to do, going to an amusement park, or falling off a bicycle?

3. When you learn something by **osmosis,** have you most likely studied hard, copied someone else's work, or absorbed the information unconsciously?

4. Is a **naive** person one who is very innocent, very shrewd, or very stubborn?

5. If you **subvert** someone's plan, do you carry out the plan, spoil the plan, or praise the plan?

Building Vocabulary

For an in-depth lesson on context clues, see page 674.

THE DIAMETER OF THE BOMB

YEHUDA **AMICHAI**

Translated by
CHANA BLOCH and
STEPHEN MITCHELL

Yehuda Amichai
1924–2000

Israeli Homeland Yehuda Amichai (yə-hōō′də ä′mĭ-κhī′) is widely considered one of Israel's greatest poets. Born in Würzburg, Germany, Amichai was raised in the Orthodox Jewish tradition. To escape the persecution of Jews in Europe, his family emigrated to Jerusalem in 1936. There, Amichai became involved in Israel's struggle to win independence and define itself as a nation.

Soldier and Poet To a great extent, Amichai's poetry was influenced by his war experiences. He was a member of Britain's Jewish Brigade during World War II and fought in the Israeli army during the Arab-Israeli war of 1948. Many of his poems feature the images and terminology of warfare, and he treats such war themes as loss and destruction with ironic humor and understatement. His poetry rings true to soldiers themselves. According to one story, several Israeli students drafted to fight in the Arab-Israeli conflict of 1973 packed books of Amichai's poetry along with their rifles.

Amichai's first book of poetry was published in 1955. Over the course of his career, he wrote ten more volumes of poetry, as well as novels, short stories, and plays. Although Amichai's poetry is deeply rooted in his adopted homeland, his writing has become well-known outside Israel. His work has been translated into more than 30 languages.

In "The Diameter of the Bomb," Amichai describes the range of destruction caused by a terrorist's bomb. Like the other selections in this part of Unit Seven, the poem deals with the consequences of conflict. As you read it, ask yourself these questions:

1. What causes the bomb's circle of destruction to keep growing?

2. How does Amichai's attitude toward conflict and its devastation compare with the attitudes of other writers you've read in this part?

The diameter of the bomb was thirty centimeters
and the diameter of its effective range about seven
    meters,
with four dead and eleven wounded.
And around these, in a larger circle
5   of pain and time, two hospitals are scattered
and one graveyard. But the young woman
who was buried in the city she came from,
at a distance of more than a hundred kilometers,
enlarges the circle considerably,
10   and the solitary man mourning her death
at the distant shores of a country far across the sea
includes the entire world in the circle.
And I won't even mention the crying of orphans
that reaches up to the throne of God and
15   beyond, making
a circle with no end and no God.

Writing Workshop

Researching a topic in depth . . .

From Reading to Writing In this part, you have read works written in response to various 20th-century political conflicts. In coming to understand these works, a knowledge of the period's political and historical events is important. The 20th century offers a wide range of topics for a **research report,** an academic paper in which you explore a subject and present information you have gathered and synthesized. The skills you develop in writing a research report can help you outside school—gathering, evaluating, and making sense of information are critical in today's world.

For Your Portfolio

WRITING PROMPT Write a short research report about a historical or political topic or another topic that interests you.

Purpose: To share information and draw a conclusion about your topic

Audience: Your classmates, your teacher, or anyone who shares your interest in the topic

---

Basics in a Box

Research Report at a Glance

THESIS

INTRODUCTION	BODY	CONCLUSION	WORKS CITED
Presents the thesis statement	Presents evidence that **supports** the thesis statement	Restates the thesis	Lists the sources of information

RESEARCH

RUBRIC Standards for Writing

A successful research report should

- contain a strong introduction with a clear thesis statement
- contain evidence from primary and secondary sources that develops and supports the writer's ideas

- have a logical pattern of organization, with clear transitions between ideas
- contain a synthesis of ideas and end with a satisfying conclusion
- indicate the sources from which information was taken
- include a correctly formatted Works Cited list

Analyzing a Student Model

Richard Jones

Mr. Martin

English, period 2

25 May

Nigeria: Independence Was Not Enough

Nigeria as we know it has existed since 1914, when Great Britain combined its protectorates of Southern Nigeria and Northern Nigeria into a single colony. The British had been in the region for almost a hundred years at that point, first as traders and missionaries and eventually as rulers. In 1960, however, they handed the country back to the Nigerian people in a remarkably peaceful transfer of power ("Western Africa" 894, 903-904). However, the Nigerian struggle for successful self-government was far from over. In fact, the gaining of independence was the easiest step in Nigeria's painful struggle for democracy, a struggle that continues today.

When Nigeria became independent, its leaders faced an entirely new situation. Before the arrival of the British in the early 19th century, there was no country called Nigeria. The region had consisted of many independent states, ranging in size from small villages and chiefdoms to powerful empires. While the different states were connected by trade and geography, and sometimes by religion, they had never shared a common identity, and certainly not a central government (Falola 19-27).

Nationalism—the desire for an independent, unified Nigeria—arose in response to British colonial rule. Many Nigerians were unhappy with colonialism; they felt that the British were racist and patronizing and that the British influence in Nigeria was damaging to traditional values. The common desire for freedom from colonial rule united people and strengthened their sense of national identity (Falola 82).

RUBRIC IN ACTION

❶ This writer begins by giving a brief historical background.
Other Options:
• Begin with a provocative question.
• Start with an anecdote.

❷ Presents the thesis statement

❸ Uses parenthetical documentation to credit a source

LANGUAGE SKILLS

When the British had begun to govern Nigeria, they had taken control from the traditional leaders of the independent states. Under the British government a new Nigerian elite developed—black Nigerians with a European education and Western values. It was this elite that promoted the nationalist movement. The movement gained strength during the economic depression of the 1920s and 1930s and especially during World War II, when Nigerian troops fought for the British. At this point, Nigerians realized that they were helping the British fight for freedom and democracy on an international level but that they themselves enjoyed no such benefits (Falola 81-82, 88). The nationalist movement continued to grow, and after a series of peaceful constitutional changes, the British finally granted Nigeria its independence in 1960 (Falola 89).

This independence proved difficult. The new Nigerian state was troubled almost from the start. Different regions of the country struggled for power, and the country saw a series of six military coups over 20 years. In 1967, three eastern states tried to establish an independent state of Biafra, and a bloody civil war ensued, lasting for almost three years. The Biafran secession failed ("Western Africa" 904).

In addition to ferocious ethnic and regional rivalry, Nigeria has been plagued by great corruption in government. For years, the country's leaders have diverted billions of dollars of the nation's oil wealth to increase their personal fortunes (Maier 3). The majority of Nigerians, however, have remained among the poorest people in the world (Pulsipher 348). According to Karl Meier, an American journalist, the members of the Nigerian elite have served the Nigerian people little better than the British did: "Colonial Nigeria was designed in 1914 to serve the British Empire, and the independent state serves as a tool of plunder by the country's modern rulers" (xxiii).

What happened? "The trouble with Nigeria is simply and squarely a failure of leadership," wrote Chinua Achebe in his book The Trouble with Nigeria. "There is

④ Presents events in the rise of nationalism in chronological order

⑤ Uses a transitional phrase between paragraphs to connect ideas

⑥ Supports a key idea with a quotation
Other Options:
• Paraphrase a source.
• Summarize information.

nothing basically wrong with the Nigerian character. There is nothing wrong with the Nigerian land or climate or water or air or anything else. The Nigerian problem is the unwillingness or inability of its leaders to rise to the responsibility, to the challenge of personal example which are the hallmarks of true leadership" (1).

Works Cited

Achebe, Chinua. The Trouble with Nigeria. Enugu, Nigeria: Fourth Dimension, 1983.

Falola, Toyin. The History of Nigeria. Westport: Greenwood, 1999.

Maier, Karl. This House Has Fallen: Midnight in Nigeria. New York: PublicAffairs, 2000.

"Nigeria." Encyclopaedia Britannica Online. Vers. 99.1. 2000. Encyclopaedia Britannica. 16 May 2001 <http://www.eb.com:180/bol/topic?eu=120185&sctn=1&pm=1>.

Onishi, Norimitsu. "In the Oil-Rich Nigeria Delta, Deep Poverty and Grim Fires." New York Times 11 Aug. 2000, natl. ed.: A1+.

Pulsipher, Lydia Mihelič. World Regional Geography. New York: Freeman, 2000.

Soyinka, Wole. The Open Sore of a Continent: A Personal Narrative of the Nigerian Crisis. New York: Oxford UP, 1996.

"Western Africa." The New Encyclopaedia Britannica: Macropaedia. 15th ed. 1993.

Works Cited
- Identifies the information sources credited in the report
- Lists sources alphabetically, in most cases by authors' last names
- Contains complete publication information for each source
- Follows an established style for arranging and punctuating the information in entries

Need help with a Works Cited list?

See the **Writing Handbook**, p. R41

LANGUAGE SKILLS

Writing Your Research Report

❶ Prewriting and Exploring

Begin by exploring topics that interest you. Look through the selections in this unit—what interesting historical, political, or literary topics do they suggest? Think about the geographic and political backgrounds of the selections. Which ones deal with real-life events or people? (See the **Idea Bank** in the margin for more suggestions for finding a topic.) Choose one topic and follow the steps below to narrow it and define your research goal.

Planning Your Research Report

▷ **1. Focus your topic.** How broad is your topic? If it is too broad, you will find far more information on it than you can use. If it is too narrow, you might not find enough. For a too-broad topic, think about ways of dividing it into subtopics, as in this cluster diagram.

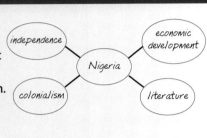

▷ **2. Set your goals.** What do you want to accomplish in your report? Do you want to entertain your readers, prove a point, share information, or provoke a response from your readers?

▷ **3. Identify your audience.** Who will read your report? What will interest them about your topic? What might they already know about it? What background information will you need to provide?

▷ **4. Write a working thesis statement.** A thesis statement is a sentence that explains what your report is about. It will guide your research and help you sort through and evaluate the information that you find. For now, you simply need a working thesis, which you can revise later.

❷ Researching

Begin your research by making a list of relevant, interesting, and researchable questions about your topic. Using these questions as a guide, gather and review a variety of reliable sources. You might start with general reference works (such as print or online encyclopedias) and move from there to books, periodicals, and reputable online sources for more-specific information.

Every source of information is either a primary or a secondary source. **Primary sources** provide direct, firsthand information about events. These sources include letters, journals, diaries, eyewitness accounts, and historical documents. **Secondary sources** present information derived or compiled from other sources; they offer interpretations, explanations, and comments about events. Newspapers, encyclopedias, and magazines, as well as many books, are secondary sources.

Evaluate Your Sources

Not all sources of information are equally valuable or reliable. The following questions can help you determine whether a source is a good one to use:

- **To what extent is the author's viewpoint biased**—that is, influenced by his or her position in society, political beliefs, gender, and ethnic background? Be sure to read materials from a variety of viewpoints.

- **How current is the source?** In quickly changing fields—such as technology, medicine, and present-day politics—it's particularly important to find up-to-date materials.

- **Is the source reliable?** This question is especially important when reviewing online publications.

Make Source Cards

When you have found sources of information relevant to your topic, make source cards. For each source, record the author, title, and complete publishing information on an index card. Follow the formats shown at the right, numbering the sources. You will use these cards later to credit sources in your report and to prepare your Works Cited list.

As technology begins to play a greater role in research and writing, many handbooks are beginning to recommend taking notes directly on the computer rather than using note cards; the fifth edition of the *MLA Handbook for Writers of Research Papers* has information about this approach. Ask your teacher before using this method of note taking.

Take Notes

As you read, keep your thesis statement and writing goals in mind. Take notes on any relevant information, using a separate index card for each piece of information. Write the number of the source on each note card, along with the page number on which you found the information. The example below shows two different note-taking strategies.

Paraphrase. Restate the material in your own words. This is a good strategy to use when taking detailed notes.

Source Number

Quotation. Copy the exact words and punctuation that appear in the source, enclosing them in quotation marks. Use a quotation when you need to emphasize a point or when the author's language is especially strong or clear.

Note Card

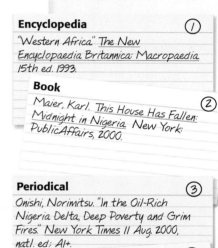

Encyclopedia (1)

"Western Africa." The New Encyclopaedia Britannica: Macropaedia. 15th ed. 1993.

Book (2)

Maier, Karl. This House Has Fallen: Midnight in Nigeria. New York: PublicAffairs, 2000.

Periodical (3)

Onishi, Norimitsu. "In the Oil-Rich Nigeria Delta, Deep Poverty and Grim Fires." New York Times 11 Aug. 2000, natl. ed.: A1+.

Internet (4)

"Nigeria." Encyclopaedia Britannica Online. Vers. 99.1. 2000. Encyclopaedia Britannica 16 May 2001 <http://www.ebcom:180/bol/topic?eu=120185&sctn=1&pm=1>.

Nigeria's Potential in Africa (2)

Nigeria has great potential: a wealth of natural resources, thousands of educated professionals, a resilient population. It could be a leader in Africa. "Nigeria was once the premier African voice, taking principled stands in the face of fierce Western opposition over important issues. . . . It lost that position through its own inept leadership to Nelson Mandela's South Africa." xxiv–xxv

Organize Your Material

Once you have gathered all of your information, it's time to organize your notes. A topic outline is one very good way of doing so. Begin by grouping your note cards into stacks of related ideas. Then think about how you want to arrange the ideas. You might choose chronological order for historical or biographical information, but there are other useful patterns of organization, such as cause and effect, comparison and contrast, and order of importance. Develop an outline based on the pattern you choose, and organize the notes in each stack accordingly.

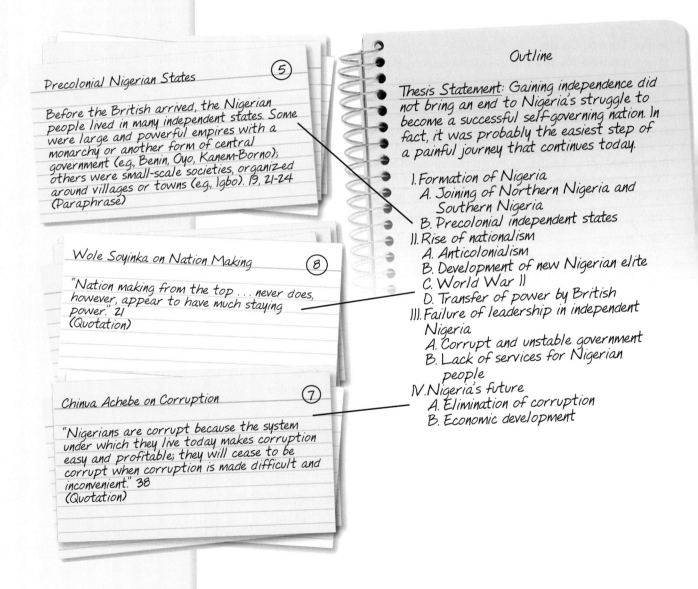

Precolonial Nigerian States ⑤

Before the British arrived, the Nigerian people lived in many independent states. Some were large and powerful empires with a central monarchy or another form of central government (e.g., Benin, Oyo, Kanem-Borno); others were small-scale societies, organized around villages or towns (e.g., Igbo). 19, 21-24 (Paraphrase)

Wole Soyinka on Nation Making ⑧

"Nation making from the top ... never does, however, appear to have much staying power." 21 (Quotation)

Chinua Achebe on Corruption ⑦

"Nigerians are corrupt because the system under which they live today makes corruption easy and profitable; they will cease to be corrupt when corruption is made difficult and inconvenient." 38 (Quotation)

Outline

Thesis Statement: Gaining independence did not bring an end to Nigeria's struggle to become a successful self-governing nation. In fact, it was probably the easiest step of a painful journey that continues today.

I. Formation of Nigeria
  A. Joining of Northern Nigeria and Southern Nigeria
  B. Precolonial independent states
II. Rise of nationalism
  A. Anticolonialism
  B. Development of new Nigerian elite
  C. World War II
  D. Transfer of power by British
III. Failure of leadership in independent Nigeria
  A. Corrupt and unstable government
  B. Lack of services for Nigerian people
IV. Nigeria's future
  A. Elimination of corruption
  B. Economic development

❸ Drafting

Begin drafting your report, using your outline as a guide. At the beginning of your report, you should state your main idea, or thesis; you will end with a restatement of this thesis and a summary of your main points. In the body of your report, which is the largest part, you should develop your ideas and support your thesis.

Settle on a Thesis Statement

After you've finished your research, revise your working thesis statement (if necessary) to reflect your findings.

Write Your Draft

As you draft your report, concentrate on getting your ideas on paper in clear, natural language. Follow your outline and refer to your notes as you write, keeping in mind that you may need to reorganize your material as you gather new information or discover a new way of thinking about it.

Develop your own analysis. Your report should be more than a collection of information. Analyze, synthesize, and draw conclusions from the information you've found, using facts, statistics, quotations, and examples as evidence to support your ideas.

Document your sources. After each quotation, paraphrase, or summary in your report, add (in parentheses) the name of the source's author—or its title if no author is credited—and the page number where you found the information. (If you mention the author's name in introducing the information, you need cite only the page number.) Use your note cards and source cards to identify the sources of the information you have used. If you do not credit the sources of the information in your report, you are guilty of plagiarism—the unlawful use of another's words or ideas. The Works Cited page at the end of your report will provide complete publishing information for each source.

Drafting Tip

Remember that your outline is only a tool. Feel free to reorganize your material at any time or collect new information as needed.

Need help documenting sources?

See the **Writing Handbook,** p. R40.

Reread What You've Written

Take a break from your writing. Then review your draft. Ask yourself the following questions:

- How can I make my thesis statement clearer?

- What additional information would support my thesis statement?

- What information, if any, is irrelevant?

- How can I improve the organization of the ideas in my report?

- What facts and documentation do I need to check?

Ask Your Peer Reader

- What did you find most interesting in my report?

- What did you learn about my topic?

- Which ideas need more explanation?

- Does the order in which I've presented my ideas make sense? Would another type of organization work better?

- What impression were you left with when you read my conclusion?

Need revising help?

Review the **Rubric**, p. 1306

Consider **peer reader** comments

Check **revision guidelines**, p. R19

❹ Revising

TARGET SKILL ▶ **PARAGRAPH BUILDING** Writing has unity when all the sentences in a paragraph support its central idea. As you revise your research report, delete any unrelated ideas.

> Nationalism—the desire for an independent, unified Nigeria—arose in response to British colonial rule. Many Nigerians were unhappy with colonialism; they felt that the British were racist and patronizing and that the British influence in Nigeria was damaging to traditional values. ~~The British had their own identity and traditional values.~~ The common desire for freedom from colonial rule united people and strengthened their sense of national identity (Falola 82).

❺ Editing and Proofreading

TARGET SKILL ▶ **USING COMMAS** Reports include a great deal of information. The correct use of commas can help your readers better understand relationships between ideas.

> For years, the country's leaders have diverted⁁billions of dollars⁁of the nation's oil wealth to increase their personal fortunes (maier 3). (CAP)
>
> The majority of Nigerians⁁ however, have remained among the poorest people in the World (Pulsipher 348). (lc)

Publishing IDEAS

• Share your report with the class in an oral presentation.

PUBLISHING OPTIONS
CLASSZONE.COM

❻ Making a Works Cited List

When you have finished revising and editing your report, make a Works Cited list and attach it to the end of your paper. See page R41 in the Writing Handbook for the correct format.

❼ Reflecting

FOR YOUR WORKING PORTFOLIO What did you learn about your working style and habits as you engaged in the process of writing a research report? Is there anything more you would like to know about your topic? Write some questions for further study, then attach them to your research report and save it in your **Working Portfolio.** 🗂

Read this opening from the first draft of a research report. The underlined sections may include the following kinds of errors:

- **comma errors**
- **capitalization errors**
- **misspelled words**
- **errors in parallelism**

For each underlined section, choose the revision that most improves the writing.

> When <u>European Colonizers</u> arrived in Africa, they saw an opportunity to
> ₍₁₎
> increase the <u>wealth, of their empires, by</u> exploiting the natural and human
> ₍₂₎
> resources of the African continent. <u>There</u> first influence in Africa came through
> ₍₃₎
> <u>trade and Christian missionary work, eventually</u> they came to rule over African
> ₍₄₎
> lands, <u>either directly or ruling them indirectly.</u> <u>In the 19th century, European</u>
> ₍₅₎ ₍₆₎
> <u>nations began</u> to fight among themselves for control of different African regions.
>
> They settled some of their disputes in the Berlin West Africa Conference of
>
> 1884–1885. There, European leaders decided who would have control over various
>
> parts of Africa. No African leaders were invited to participate in the conference.

1. **A.** European colonizers
   B. european colonizers
   C. european Colonizers
   D. Correct as is

2. **A.** wealth of their empires, by
   B. wealth, of their empires by
   C. wealth of their empires by
   D. Correct as is

3. **A.** They're
   B. Their
   C. There are
   D. Correct as is

4. **A.** trade and Christian missionary work, eventually,
   B. trade and Christian missionary work; eventually
   C. trade, and Christian missionary work; eventually
   D. Correct as is

5. **A.** either directly or indirectly
   B. either directly or to rule them indirectly
   C. either directly or without being direct
   D. Correct as is

6. **A.** In the 19th century, European nations, began
   B. In the 19th century—European nations began
   C. In the 19th century European nations, began
   D. Correct as is

Need extra help?

See the **Grammar Handbook:**

Quick Reference: Punctuation, p. R77

Quick Reference: Capitalization, p. R79

TEST PRACTICE

What's the Best Approach? In this book you have learned a number of word-attack strategies for determining the meaning of unfamiliar words. When you come across a new word in your reading, you can draw on any of these strategies. However, depending on the word and its context, you may find that some strategies are more useful than others. In reading the passage on the right, what strategy or strategies would you use to figure out the meaning of *superannuated?*

> In their two years of married life she had become completely infected by his passion for "modern methods" and his [criticism] of "these old and superannuated people in the teaching field who would be better employed as traders in the Onitsha market."
>
> —Chinua Achebe, "Dead Men's Path"

Strategies for Building Vocabulary

Follow the steps below to evaluate and choose the appropriate word-attack strategy or strategies for *superannuated.* In many cases you will find it most helpful to use a combination of strategies.

❶ **Evaluate the Word and Its Context** When considering word-attack strategies, you can ask yourself a few quick questions to determine which strategy would be the most useful:

- Does the context help me understand the word?
- Do I recognize any parts of the word?
- Does the word resemble other words that I know?

In general, you will probably find that context clues are the most useful guides. Even if context clues alone do not help you figure out a word's meaning, they should help you confirm or reject any guesses you make as you use other strategies.

❷ **Consider Each Strategy** Consider the usefulness of each of the following strategies for attacking the word *superannuated:*

- **Using context clues** "I can see from the context that *superannuated* is used to describe old teachers who are better suited to selling goods at the market than to teaching. That gives me some idea that the word must have to do with being old or unskilled, but I'm still not sure."
- **Recognizing word families or roots** "*Superannuated* might be related to *annual,* which means 'yearly.'"
- **Recognizing affixes** "I know the word *super,* which means 'excellent.' I also know it as a prefix meaning 'extra' or 'over and above,' as in *superfluous,* which means 'more than necessary.' If

I put the prefix together with the root, I can guess that *superannuated* means 'having extra years.' That fits with the context, which suggests old age."

- **Using reference tools** "When I check my guess in the dictionary, I find that *superannuated* means 'retired or ineffective because of advanced age.'"

❸ **Record and Use the Word** To make the word a part of your permanent vocabulary, write it down and make a point of using it in class discussions or other conversations during the next few days.

Use this table as a general guide.

Strategy	When to Use
Using context clues	• as a first strategy
Identifying roots	• when the word has many syllables (Polysyllabic words are more likely to have Greek or Latin roots.) • when you recognize the word's root
Identifying affixes	• when the word has a familiar beginning or ending
Recognizing word families	• when the word resembles familiar words
Using reference tools	• when you need to confirm your guess • when nothing else works

EXERCISE Choose five unfamiliar words from the selections in Unit Seven, and use the strategies listed above to try to determine their meanings. Write what you think each word means, and tell what strategy or strategies you used. Finally, if you haven't already done so, check the meanings in a dictionary.

Sentence Crafting | Varying Sentence Length

Grammar from Literature Skilled writers add interest and rhythm to their work by writing sentences of varying lengths. On page 559, you learned about using variety in sentence structure. Varying your sentence length is a similar skill. By varying the length of your sentences, you can improve the flow and rhythm of your writing. Read aloud the following passage from "The Guest" by Albert Camus, listening to the rhythm created by the different sentence lengths.

> Then he went through the classroom and out onto the terrace. The sun was already rising in the blue sky; a soft, bright light was bathing the deserted plateau. On the ridge the snow was melting in spots. The stones were about to reappear. Crouched on the edge of the plateau, the schoolmaster looked at the deserted expanse.

The long sentences create a smooth, rolling rhythm; the shorter sentences tend to produce a stronger beat. The following passage from Elie Wiesel's *The World Was Silent* contains two short sentences amid several much longer ones.

> Indescribable confusion reigned.
> Parents searched for their children, children for their parents, and lonely captives for their friends. The people were beset by loneliness. Everyone feared that the outcome of the journey would be tragic and would claim its toll of lives. And so one yearned to have the companionship of someone who would stand by with a word, with a loving glance.

The short sentences stand out against the longer ones, emphasizing the ideas of confusion and loneliness.

Pay special attention to sentence variety during revision. Look at each paragraph. Does the paragraph contain only long sentences? only short ones? Too many sentences of the same length can produce a rhythm that is droning or unnecessarily choppy.

Style Tip: Using Fragments for Stylistic Reasons
Although sentence fragments are generally considered incorrect, writers occasionally use them deliberately—to present dialogue or thoughts in a natural way, for example, or create emphasis. In the passage below, from *The World Was Silent,* the fragment at the end of the paragraph emphasizes a particularly striking image.

> So we all got up—even those who seemed to be dying—and wrapped our drenched blankets about our bodies. The scene was reminiscent of a congregation wrapped in prayer shawls, swaying to and fro in prayer. The snow, the car, even the sky (heaven?)—everything and everybody seemed to be swaying, worshiping, communing with God, uttering the prayer of life, the prayer of death. The sword of the Angel of Death was suspended above. A congregation of corpses at prayer.

WRITING EXERCISE The first of the following two paragraphs contains only short sentences; the second contains only long ones. Rewrite them so that they contain sentences of varying length. Feel free to change the wording in addition to combining or breaking up sentences. You might use one or two sentence fragments for effect.

Michael Obi was very proud of the new garden at Ndume Central School. His wife, Nancy, had planted it. She had used great care. She filled the school compound with beautiful flowers, hedges, and trees. Then the rains came. They turned the dusty grounds into a lush, green paradise. They looked rich and refined. The plants of the village were sloppy and untended. It was a sight to behold.

Imagine Obi's surprise, then, when he discovered that the villagers were using an old footpath across the school grounds, tracking through the marigolds as if the garden were not even there. He could not believe their ignorance, and he discussed it with one of the teachers, who told him that this was an old footpath connecting the village shrine with the burial ground. Obi found this unacceptable, and he planted heavy sticks and barbed wire across the path so that the villagers would not be able to use it ever again.

Responses to War and Conflict

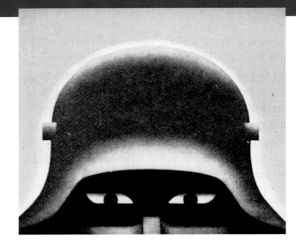

Reflect and Assess

Conflict has defined much of the 20th century, from international warfare to colonial struggles for independence to civil war. The selections in this part of Unit Seven were written in response to such times of turmoil. The following options will help you to review what you have learned.

Reflecting on the Literature

The Human Cost of Conflict What do human beings lose when countries go to war or when other great conflicts erupt? Working with a partner, review the selections in this part, and make a list of all that is lost by the major characters or people in each selection. Pay attention to both the physical effects and the psychological effects of conflict. After you have finished, compare your list with those of your classmates, and discuss what you have learned about the human consequences of conflict.

Reviewing Literary Concepts

Analyzing Tone *Tone* refers to a writer's attitude toward his or her subject. Working with a partner, choose four works in this part in which you can clearly identify the author's tone. How does the author feel about the war or conflict portrayed in his or her work? What evidence can you find in the selection that helps you to identify that tone? Share the results of your work with your classmates, and read aloud passages from each of the four selections to express the tone conveyed.

Building Your Portfolio

Writing Workshop and Writing Options Review the research paper that you wrote for the Writing Workshop on page 1306. In your judgment, how successful is the paper? Attach a cover note to your research paper in which you evaluate your work, noting its strengths and weaknesses. Then review the Writing Options that you completed in this part, and choose the one that best demonstrates your ability as a writer. Attach a note to your choice, explaining your judgment. Place the research paper and the Writing Option in your **Presentation Portfolio.**

Self **ASSESSMENT**

READER'S NOTEBOOK
Get together with a small group of classmates to review the following terms from this part of Unit Seven. In your group, discuss the meaning of each term, using the Glossary of Literary Terms (beginning on page 000) to check your understanding. For each term, find an example from a selection that illustrates its meaning, or discuss how an entire selection helps you to understand the term. Share your findings with other groups.

setting	speaker
Holocaust	dialogue
mood	author's purpose
colonialism	theme
cultural conflict	dialect

Setting **GOALS**

Reflect upon the progress that you have made this year as a writer and a reader. Write down two goals for yourself that you think can be reached by the end of the year.

Extend Your *Reading*

Things Fall Apart

CHINUA ACHEBE

This novel, set in colonial Nigeria between 1890 and 1915, explores the conflict between traditional tribal ways of life and European culture. Achebe presents two closely related tragedies, the personal tragedy of Okonkwo, a "great man" of his Ibo village, and the communal tragedy of his people.

Here are just a few of the related readings that accompany *Things Fall Apart:*

The Second Coming
WILLIAM BUTLER YEATS

Shooting an Elephant
GEORGE ORWELL

Genesis 22:1–19: The Sacrifice of Isaac
THE BIBLE

When Rain Clouds Gather

BESSIE HEAD

Set in Botswana in the mid-1960s, this novel focuses on a young South African man, Makhaya, who is trying to establish a new life for himself in a poverty-stricken village. Makhaya becomes involved in the villagers' struggles to adopt new agricultural techniques and to overcome rigid customs, a corrupt chief, and the unrelenting climate.

Here are just a few of the related readings that accompany *When Rain Clouds Gather:*

The Rain Came
GRACE OGOT

I Am Crying from Thirst
ALONZO LOPEZ

Some Monday for Sure
NADINE GORDIMER

And Even *More* . . .

Books

The Great War and Modern Memory PAUL FUSSELL
This landmark study of World War I focuses on the British army in the trenches, paying especially close attention to the experiences of writers.

The Stranger ALBERT CAMUS
In this short 1946 novel, a young man becomes involved in a senseless killing on a beach in Algeria. His trial reveals the absurdity of his predicament.

Other Media

The Greatest Generation
This is a compilation of Tom Brokaw's interviews with World War II veterans, as shown on *NBC Nightly News.* The interviews explore the experience of war and its effects on people's lives. (VIDEOCASSETTE)

Schindler's List
This 1993 Steven Spielberg film tells a true story about a German manufacturer who risks his life to save more than 1,000 Jews during World War II. (VIDEOCASSETTE)

One Day in the Life of Ivan Denisovich

ALEKSANDR SOLZHENITSYN

This novel provides a gripping account of the hardships of daily life in a Siberian labor camp. Based on the author's own experiences as a political prisoner in the Soviet Union, the novel caused an international stir when published in 1962.

PART 3 Critics and Dreamers:
Contemporary Nobel Prize Winners

Why It Matters

There is no literary award more prestigious than the Nobel Prize. The winners are considered the most important writers in the entire world, those who should be known outside of their own countries and languages. In Part 3, you will read poetry and fiction by Nobel Prize winners since 1970. Their works will introduce you to the provocative themes and styles associated with contemporary literature.

Alfred Nobel's Legacy

Dr. Alfred Bernhard Nobel (1833–1896) was a brilliant Swedish inventor and engineer who made a fortune from one of his most successful inventions—dynamite. After a newspaper mistakenly published Nobel's obituary and referred to him as a "merchant of death," Nobel decided to leave a different legacy. In his will, he established the **Nobel Prizes** to reward people "who, during the preceding year, shall have conferred the greatest benefit on mankind" in physics, chemistry, medicine, peace, and literature.

For Links to Nobel Prize Winners, click on:

HUMANITIES
CLASSZONE.COM

Benefiting Humanity

According to Nobel's will, the winner of the literature prize must have produced "the most outstanding work in an ideal direction." To select a **laureate,** a small Nobel committee judges nominations from professors, former laureates, and presidents of authors' groups. It then recommends candidates to the **Swedish Academy,** which makes the final vote. In Nadine Gordimer's Nobel diploma, the Academy acknowledged her writing's "very great benefit to humanity."

NADINE GORDIMER

SVERIGE

The Highest Literary Honor

One Nobel Prize is given to a poet, dramatist, or prose writer annually. In 1901, only 25 nominations were made in literature, yet today more than 200 writers are nominated each year. Not only is competition for the coveted prize fierce, but the award's value has grown since its creation. Worth about $40,000 in 1901, the prize is now worth about $1 million.

SVERIGE 5.50

DEREK WALCOTT

Recent Nobel Prize Winners

The names in blue are the writers whose work you will read in Part 3.

1971	Pablo Neruda	CHILE
1972	Heinrich Böll	WEST GERMANY
1976	Saul Bellow	CANADA/U.S.
1978	Isaac Bashevis Singer	POLAND/U.S.
1980	Czeslaw Milosz	POLAND/U.S.
1982	Gabriel García Márquez	COLOMBIA
1986	Wole Soyinka	NIGERIA
1987	Joseph Brodsky	U.S.S.R./U.S.
1988	Naguib Mahfouz	EGYPT
1990	Octavio Paz	MEXICO
1991	Nadine Gordimer	SOUTH AFRICA
1992	Derek Walcott	ST. LUCIA
1993	Toni Morrison	UNITED STATES
1994	Kenzaburo Oe	JAPAN
1995	Seamus Heaney	NORTHERN IRELAND
1996	Wislawa Szymborska	POLAND
1999	Günter Grass	GERMANY
2000	Gao Xingjian	CHINA

A Grand Ceremony

Writers receive the Nobel Prize in literature at a formal ceremony held in the Stockholm Concert Hall in Sweden on December 10, the anniversary of Alfred Nobel's death. The king of Sweden presents the winner with a gold medal, a diploma, and a certificate for the amount of the prize. The medal bears a portrait of Nobel on one side; on the other is a picture of a young man and a muse under a laurel tree.

The laureate's diploma is a work of art that captures the spirit of his or her writings. The photo at left shows the Polish poet Wislawa Szymborska receiving her prize in 1996.

The Nobel Prize and World Literature

The writing by the Nobel Prize winners in Part 3 reflects important trends and concerns in contemporary literature. Following are just some of the moral causes, political developments, and artistic movements that have shaped the pieces you will read.

Protesters demand the release of jailed antiapartheid leader Nelson Mandela.

Apartheid Literature

One important moral and political issue of the late 20th century was the struggle to end apartheid—the official system of racial segregation enforced in South Africa from 1948 to 1991.

Writers whose works carried an antiapartheid message include Nobel laureate **Nadine Gordimer,** playwrights Athol Fugard and Mbongeni Ngema, and novelist André Brink. By exposing the evils of racism, these writers helped bring change to their country.

Postcolonial Writing

The term **postcolonial writing** is often used to describe contemporary writing from India and other nations in Asia, Africa, and the Caribbean that were formerly European colonies. Usually written in colonial languages (such as English or French) instead of native languages, these works take on lingering issues within postcolonial societies—ethnic and religious conflicts, government instability, and questions of national and personal identity.

Nobel Prize winner **Wole Soyinka** and his fellow Nigerian **Chinua Achebe** are postcolonial writers who look critically at modern African society.

Eastern European Dissidents

From the end of World War II until the end of the 1980s, Eastern European nations such as Poland, Czechoslovakia, and Hungary were in the grip of the Soviet Union. In these countries, Communist leaders limited free speech. They controlled what writers could publish through censorship and the threat of imprisonment or exile. A number of writers protested against government repression and championed the causes of dignity and individuality.

Poet Czeslaw Milosz, a Nobel Prize winner in 1980, left Poland after becoming disillusioned with life under Communist rule. His countrywoman **Wislawa Szymborska** remained in Poland, publishing playful yet deeply thoughtful poems for 50 years before she, too, was awarded the Nobel Prize in 1996.

The Solidarity movement in Poland weakened Communist rule.

A work by Egyptian writer Naguib Mahfouz

The Latin American Boom

In the 1960s, Latin American novelists gained world attention with fresh, exciting work that drew on Western literary styles, such as surrealism, yet was distinctly Latin American. Some of these writers developed a new form, **magical realism,** which mixed fantasy and realism. It blended the traditions and perspectives of the Native American, European, and African cultures that mingle in the region.

Prominent writers associated with the Latin American boom in literature include Mexico's Carlos Fuentes, Argentina's Julio Cortázar, and Colombia's **Gabriel García Márquez,** a winner of the Nobel Prize.

Poetic Innovation

In the early 20th century, poets such as Ezra Pound and T. S. Eliot rebelled against traditional forms and themes in poetry. Poets today still seek new ways to express their unique visions of the world.

For a long time, Nobel judges tended to shy away from difficult, experimental literature. However, in recent years they have acknowledged innovative contemporary poets such as Chile's **Pablo Neruda,** who wrote both grand historical epics and odes to simple objects, and Mexico's **Octavio Paz,** whose complex work drew on European, Asian, and Native American philosophies.

Non-European Languages

As technology has turned the world into a "global village," readers have had more interest in foreign literature and more access to translations.

Long criticized for honoring only literature in European languages, the Nobel Prize now reflects a wider view of the world. Non-Western writers who have won in the past few years include Egyptian novelist **Naguib Mahfouz** (who writes in Arabic), Japanese novelist Kenzaburo Oe, and Chinese novelist Gao Xingjian.

Other Literary Awards

The **Booker Prize** is awarded to the best novel in English from Britain or from other present or former Commonwealth nations. **Margaret Atwood,** Canada's foremost writer, recently won the prize for her complex novel within a novel, *The Blind Assassin.*

The **Prix Goncourt** is given to French-language writers. Recent winners have included **Jean Echenoz,** author of the art-world mystery *I'm Gone;* and **Patrick Chamoiseau,** author of *Texaco,* an imaginative history of Martinique.

The **Pulitzer Prize** is a U.S. award for journalism, literature, and music. In 2000, **Jhumpa Lahiri** won the fiction prize for *Interpreter of Maladies,* a collection of short stories set in India and the United States.

Margaret Atwood

AMNESTY

Nadine Gordimer

Nadine Gordimer
1923–

Solitary Child Nadine Gordimer, one of South Africa's most notable authors, is known for her beautifully crafted novels and short stories dealing with themes of exile, alienation, the effects of racism, and life's missed opportunities. Born into a white middle-class family in the Transvaal province of South Africa, she spent much of her childhood in solitude because her mother worried excessively about the girl's health and often kept her at home.

To relieve her loneliness, Gordimer began to write when she was 9 years old. At 15, she published her first short story in a magazine. Almost from the beginning of her career, one critic notes, her precise ear for spoken language, her keen sense of social satire, and her strong moral purpose were evident.

Critic of Apartheid Much of Gordimer's writing is set in South Africa, and her work draws on the political situation there. Many of her characters have had to grapple with the injustices of apartheid (ə-pärt'hīt')—the official system of racial segregation that was in place from 1948 to 1991—and the process of healing since the government repealed apartheid laws. Because Gordimer openly criticized apartheid and exposed its tragic consequences in her fiction, three of her novels were banned by the South African government.

Although she used her talents and influence to oppose apartheid, she refused to let her writing become propaganda. Instead, she has said, she has always tried simply to portray the society in which she lives: "I thrust my hand as deep as it will go, deep into the life around me, and I write about what comes up."

Accolades and Achievements In 1974 Gordimer won the Booker Prize, England's most prestigious literary award, for her novel *The Conservationist.* In 1991 she received the Nobel Prize in literature. In addition, she has received honorary degrees from a number of universities in the United States and has been called "one of the most gifted practitioners of the short story anywhere in English."

Other Works
Six Feet of the Country
July's People
Jump and Other Stories

For a humanities activity, click on:

HUMANITIES
CLASSZONE.COM

Build Background

The Apartheid System "Amnesty" takes place in South Africa during the time of apartheid. Under apartheid, whites owned more than 80 percent of the land while making up less than 20 percent of the population. Black farm workers struggled to support themselves on small plots of poor farmland, some in designated tribal homelands and some on white-owned farms. Many members of rural families left home to seek industrial jobs in the towns and cities. Such jobs paid little.

Apartheid required blacks to carry passes, or identity papers, at all times and restricted where they could live and travel. In fact, this system regulated almost all aspects of the lives of blacks. It even specified the kinds of jobs blacks could hold and the schools they could attend.

Fighting Apartheid During this period many blacks, as well as some whites, actively opposed apartheid by staging boycotts, demonstrations, and strikes. To put down the resistance, the government arrested leaders of the antiapartheid movement and imprisoned them on Robben Island, off the coast of Cape Town. Among the prisoners there was Nelson Mandela, who later became the country's first black president. In 1991 the South African government finally ended apartheid and released the political prisoners held on Robben Island. The former prisoners were granted amnesty, or government pardon.

Robben Island

Connect to Your Life

In this story, a young woman waits for the man she loves to return home to her. Imagine waiting years to be with someone you love. What would you expect your relationship to be like once you were together again?

Focus Your Reading

LITERARY ANALYSIS: FIRST-PERSON POINT OF VIEW

"Amnesty" is told from the **first-person point of view**—that is, the narrator is a character in the story who describes the action in his or her own words. As you read the story, think about how the use of this point of view affects what you learn as a reader. Consider why Gordimer might have chosen this particular narrator and point of view.

ACTIVE READING: MAKING INFERENCES

When you read a story, you form ideas about a character, a relationship, or a way of life by making **inferences,** or logical guesses based on clues. Notice what this passage from "Amnesty" suggests about the culture the characters live in:

> *Also my parents were short of money. Two of my brothers who had gone away to work in town didn't send home; I suppose they lived with girlfriends and had to buy things for them.*

From the passage you can infer that in this culture, it is customary for sons who work in the towns to send some of the money they earn to their parents.

📖 **READER'S NOTEBOOK** As you read "Amnesty," pay attention to the details that give you insight into customs and conditions in South Africa and into the relationship between the two main characters. Stop after every third or fourth paragraph and jot down some inferences you've made.

Amnesty

Nadine Gordimer

When we heard he was released I ran all over the farm and through the fence to our people on the next farm to tell everybody. I only saw afterwards I'd torn my dress on the barbed wire, and there was a scratch, with blood, on my shoulder.

He went away from this place nine years ago, signed up to work in town with what they call a construction company—building glass walls up to the sky. For the first two years he came home for the weekend once a month and two weeks at Christmas; that was when he asked my father for me. And he began to pay. He and I thought that in three years he would have paid enough for us to get married. But then he started wearing that T-shirt, he told us he'd joined the union, he told us about the strike, how he was one of the men who went to talk to the bosses because some others had been laid off after the strike. He's always been good at talking, even in English—he was the best at the farm school, he used to read the newspapers the Indian wraps soap and sugar in when you buy at the store.

There was trouble at the hostel where he had a bed, and riots over paying rent in the townships[1] and he told me—just me, not the old ones—that wherever people were fighting against the way we are treated they were doing it for all of us, on the farms as well as the towns, and the unions were with them, he was with them, making speeches, marching. The third year, we heard he was in prison. Instead of getting married. We didn't know where to find him, until he went on trial. The case was heard in a town far away. I couldn't go often to the court because by that time I had passed my Standard 8[2] and I was working in the farm school. Also my parents were short of money. Two of my brothers who had gone away to work in town didn't send home; I suppose they lived with girl-friends and had to buy things for them. My father and other brother work here for the Boer[3] and the pay is very small, we have two goats, a few cows we're allowed to graze, and a patch of land where my mother can grow vegetables. No cash from that.

When I saw him in the court he looked beautiful in a blue suit with a striped shirt and brown tie. All the accused—his comrades, he said—were well-dressed. The union bought the clothes so that the judge and the prosecutor would know they weren't dealing with stupid *yes-baas*[4] black men who didn't know their rights. These things and everything else about the court and trial he explained to me when I was allowed to visit him in jail. Our little girl was born while the trial went on and when I brought the baby to court the first time to show him, his comrades hugged him and then hugged me across the barrier of the prisoners' dock and they had clubbed together to give me some money as a present for the baby.

---

1. **townships:** areas of South Africa set aside for blacks.
2. **Standard 8:** Standards are classes or grades in elementary schools. Standard 8 would have been the top level of elementary school.
3. **Boer:** a descendant of the Dutch colonists of South Africa.
4. *yes-baas:* "Yes, boss"—the words of someone who does not question authority.

We have two goats, a few cows we're allowed to graze, and a patch of land where my mother can grow vegetables.

the glass walls showed the pavement trees and the other buildings in the street and the colors of the cars and the clouds as the crane lifted him on a platform higher and higher through the sky to work at the top of a building.

He was allowed one letter a month. It was my letter because his parents didn't know how to write. I used to go to them where they worked on another farm to ask what message they wanted to send. The mother always cried and put her hands on her head and said nothing, and the old man, who preached to us in the veld[7] every Sunday, said tell my son we are praying, God will make everything all right for him. Once he wrote back, That's the trouble—our people on the farms, they're told God will decide what's good for them so that they won't find the force to do anything to change their lives.

After two years had passed, we—his parents and I—had saved up enough money to go to Cape

He chose the name for her, Inkululeko.[5]

Then the trial was over and he got six years. He was sent to the Island.[6] We all knew about the Island. Our leaders had been there so long. But I have never seen the sea except to color it in blue at school, and I couldn't imagine a piece of earth surrounded by it. I could only think of a cake of dung, dropped by the cattle, floating in a pool of rain-water they'd crossed, the water showing the sky like a looking-glass, blue. I was ashamed only to think that. He had told me how

5. **Inkululeko** (ĭn-kōō′lōō-lā′kō): a word meaning "freedom" in the Xhosa language of South Africa.

6. **the Island:** Robben Island, the site of a maximum-security prison from the mid-1960s to 1991. Most of its inmates were black political prisoners.

7. **veld:** an open grazing area in southern Africa.

Town[8] to visit him. We went by train and slept on the floor at the station and asked the way, next day, to the ferry. People were kind; they all knew that if you wanted the ferry it was because you had somebody of yours on the Island.

And there it was—there was the sea. It was green *and* blue, climbing and falling, bursting white, all the way to the sky. A terrible wind was slapping it this way and that; it hid the Island, but people like us, also waiting for the ferry, pointed where the Island must be, far out in the sea that I never thought would be like it really was.

There were other boats, and ships as big as

> We took the train back and we never went to the Island—never saw him in the three more years he was there. Not once.

buildings that go to other places, all over the world, but the ferry is only for the Island, it doesn't go anywhere else in the world, only to the Island. So everybody waiting there was waiting for the Island, there could be no mistake we were not in the right place. We had sweets and biscuits, trousers and a warm coat for him (a woman standing with us said we wouldn't be allowed to give him the clothes) and I wasn't wearing, any more, the old beret pulled down over my head that farm girls wear, I had bought relaxer cream[9] from the man who comes round the farms selling things out of a box on his bicycle, and my hair was combed up thick under a flowered scarf that didn't cover the gold-colored rings in my ears. His mother had her blanket tied round her waist over her dress, a farm woman, but I looked just as good as any of the other girls there. When the ferry was ready to take us, we stood all pressed together and quiet like the cattle waiting to be let through a gate. One man kept looking round with his chin moving up and down, he was counting, he must have been

afraid there were too many to get on and he didn't want to be left behind. We all moved up to the policeman in charge and everyone ahead of us went onto the boat. But when our turn came and he put out his hand for something, I didn't know what.

We didn't have a permit. We didn't know that before you come to Cape Town, before you come to the ferry for the Island, you have to have a police permit to visit a prisoner on the Island. I tried to ask him nicely. The wind blew the voice out of my mouth.

We were turned away. We saw the ferry rock, bumping the landing where we stood, moving, lifted and dropped by all that water, getting smaller and smaller until we didn't know if we were really seeing it or one of the birds that looked black, dipping up and down, out there.

The only good thing was one of the other people took the sweets and biscuits for him. He wrote and said he got them. But it wasn't a good letter. Of course not. He was cross with me; I should have found out, I should have known about the permit. He was right—I bought the train tickets, I asked where to go for the ferry, I should have known about the permit. I have passed Standard 8. There was an advice office to go to in town, the churches ran it, he wrote. But the farm is so far from town, we on the farms don't know about these things. It was as he said; our ignorance is the way we are kept down, this ignorance must go.

We took the train back and we never went to the Island—never saw him in the three more years he was there. Not once. We couldn't find the money for the train. His father died and I had to help his mother from my pay. For our people

---

8. **Cape Town:** the legislative capital of South Africa, in the extreme southeast portion of the country.

9. **relaxer cream:** cream to straighten the hair.

the worry is always money, I wrote. When will we ever have money? Then he sent such a good letter. That's what I'm on the Island for, far away from you, I'm here so that one day our people will have the things they need, land, food, the end of ignorance. There was something else—I could just read the word "power" the prison had blacked out. All his letters were not just for me; the prison officer read them before I could.

He was coming home after only five years!

That's what it seemed to me, when I heard—the five years were suddenly disappeared—nothing!—there was no whole year still to wait. I showed my—our—little girl his photo again. That's your daddy, he's coming, you're going to see him. She told the other children at school, I've got a daddy, just as she showed off about the kid goat she had at home.

We wanted him to come at once, and at the same time we wanted time to prepare. His mother lived with one of his uncles; now that his father was dead there was no house of his father for him to take me to as soon as we married. If there had been time, my father would have cut poles, my mother and I would have baked bricks, cut thatch,[10] and built a house for him and me and the child.

We were not sure what day he would arrive. We only heard on my radio his name and the names of some others who were released. Then at the Indian's store I noticed the newspaper, *The Nation*, written by black people, and on the front a picture of a lot of people dancing and waving—I saw at once it was at that ferry. Some men were being carried on other men's shoulders. I couldn't see which one was him. We were waiting. The ferry had brought him from the Island but we remembered Cape Town is a long way from us. Then he did come. On a Saturday, no school, so I was working with my mother,

hoeing and weeding round the pumpkins and mealies,[11] my hair, that I meant to keep nice, tied in an old *doek*.[12] A combi[13] came over the veld and his comrades had brought him. I wanted to run away and wash but he stood there stretching his legs, calling, hey! hey! with his comrades making a noise around him, and my mother started shrieking in the old style aie! aie! and my father was clapping and stamping towards him. He held his arms open to us, this big man in town clothes, polished shoes, and all the time while he hugged me I was holding my dirty hands, full of mud, away from him behind his back. His teeth hit me hard through his lips, he grabbed at my mother and she struggled to hold the child up to him. I thought we would all fall down! Then everyone was quiet. The child hid behind my mother. He picked her up but she turned her head away to her shoulder. He spoke to her gently but she wouldn't speak to him. She's nearly six years old! I told her not to be a baby. She said, That's not him.

The comrades all laughed, we laughed, she ran off and he said, She has to have time to get used to me.

He has put on weight, yes; a lot. You couldn't believe it. He used to be so thin his feet looked too big for him. I used to feel his bones but now—that night—when he lay on me he was so heavy, I didn't remember it was like that. Such a long time. It's strange to get stronger in prison; I thought he wouldn't have enough to eat and would come out weak. Everyone said, Look at him!—he's a man, now. He laughed and banged his fist on his chest, told them how the comrades exercised in their cells, he would run three miles a day, stepping up and down on one place on the

---

10. **thatch:** plant stalks or leaves used to make roofs.

11. **mealies:** corn.

12. *doek* (do͝ok): a headscarf worn like a turban.

13. **combi:** a multipurpose vehicle.

Sometimes in the daytime I do try to tell him what it was like for me, here at home on the farm, five years.

floor of that small cell where he was kept. After we were together at night we used to whisper a long time but now I can feel he's thinking of some things I don't know and I can't worry him with talk. Also I don't know what to say. To ask him what it was like, five years shut away there; or to tell him something about school or about the child. What else has happened, here? Nothing. Just waiting. Sometimes in the daytime I do try to tell him what it was like for me, here at home on the farm, five years. He listens, he's interested, just like he's interested when people from the other farms come to visit and talk to him about little things that happened to them while he was away all that time on the Island.

He smiles and nods, asks a couple of questions and then stands up and stretches. I see it's to show them it's enough, his mind is going back to something he was busy with before they came. And we farm people are very slow; we tell things slowly, he used to, too.

He hasn't signed on for another job. But he can't stay at home with us; we thought, after five years over there in the middle of that green and blue sea, so far, he would rest with us a little while. The combi or some car comes to fetch him and he says don't worry, I don't know what day I'll be back. At first I asked, what week, next week? He tried to explain to me: in the Movement it's not like it was in the union, where you do your work every day and after that you are busy with meetings; in the Movement you never know where you will have to go and what is going to come up next. And the same with money. In the Movement, it's not like a job, with regular pay—I know that, he doesn't have to tell me—it's like it was going to the Island, you do it for all our people who suffer because we haven't got money, we haven't got land—look, he said, speaking of my parents', my home, the home that has been waiting for him, with his child: look at this place where the white man owns the ground and lets you squat in mud and tin huts here only as long as you work for him—*Baba*[14] and your brother planting his crops and looking after his cattle, Mama cleaning his house and you in the school without even having the chance to train properly as a teacher. The farmer owns us, he says.

I've been thinking we haven't got a home because there wasn't time to build a house before he came from the Island; but we haven't got a home at all. Now I've understood that.

I'm not stupid. When the comrades come to this place in the combi to talk to him here I don't go away with my mother after we've brought them tea or (if she's made it for the weekend) beer. They like her beer, they talk about our culture and there's one of them who makes a point of putting his arm around my mother, calling her the mama of all of them, the mama of Africa. Sometimes they please her very much by telling her how they used to sing on the Island and getting her to sing an old song we all know from our grandmothers. Then they join in with their strong voices. My father doesn't like this noise traveling across the veld; he's afraid that if the Boer finds out my man is a political, from the Island, and he's holding meetings on the Boer's land, he'll tell my father to go, and take his family with him. But my brother says if the Boer asks anything just tell him it's a prayer meeting. Then the singing is over; my mother knows she must go away into the house.

I stay, and listen. He forgets I'm there when he's talking and arguing about something I can see is important, more important than anything we could ever have to say to each other when we're alone. But now and then, when one of the other comrades is speaking I see him look at me for a moment the way I will look up at one of my favorite children in school to encourage the child to understand. The men don't speak to me and I don't speak. One of the things they talk about is organizing the people on the farms—the workers, like my father and brother, and like his parents used to be. I learn what all these things are: minimum wage, limitation of working hours, the right to strike, annual leave, accident compensation,[15] pensions, sick and even maternity leave. I am pregnant, at last I have another child inside me, but that's women's business. When they talk about the Big Man, the Old Men,[16] I know who these are: our leaders are also back from prison. I told him about the child coming; he said, And this one belongs to a new country, he'll build the freedom we've fought for! I know he wants to get married but there's no time for that at present. There was hardly time for him to make the child. He comes to me just like he comes here to eat a meal or put on clean clothes. Then he picks up the little girl and swings her round and there!—it's done, he's getting into the combi, he's already turning to his comrade that face of his that knows only what's inside his head, those eyes that move quickly as if he's chasing something you can't see. The little girl hasn't had time to get used to this man. But I know she'll be proud of him, one day!

---

14. *Baba:* a title of respect for an aged man, here indicating the narrator's father.

15. **accident compensation:** money or medical benefits paid to someone who has been injured on a job.

16. **the Big Man, the Old Men:** Nelson Mandela and several of his elderly associates, who were freed from prison in the early 1990s.

How can you tell that to a child six years old? But I tell her about the Big Man and the Old Men, our leaders, so she'll know that her father was with them on the Island, this man is a great man, too.

On Saturday, no school and I plant and weed with my mother, she sings but I don't; I think. On Sunday there's no work, only prayer meetings out of the farmer's way under the trees, and

> **I'm watching the rat, it's losing itself, its shape, eating the sky, and I'm waiting. Waiting for him to come back.**

beer drinks at the mud and tin huts where the farmers allow us to squat on their land. I go off on my own as I used to do when I was a child, making up games and talking to myself where no one would hear me or look for me. I sit on a warm stone in the late afternoon, high up, and the whole valley is a path between the hills, leading away from my feet. It's the Boer's farm but that's not true, it belongs to nobody. The cattle don't know that anyone says he owns it, the sheep—they are grey stones, and then they

become a thick grey snake moving—don't know. Our huts and the old mulberry tree and the little brown mat of earth that my mother dug over yesterday, way down there, and way over there the clump of trees round the chimneys and the shiny thing that is the TV mast of the farmhouse—they are nothing, on the back of this earth. It could twitch them away like a dog does a fly.

I am up with the clouds. The sun behind me is changing the colors of the sky and the clouds are changing themselves, slowly, slowly. Some are pink, some are white, swelling like bubbles. Underneath is a bar of grey, not enough to make rain. It gets longer and darker, it grows a thin snout and long body and then the end of it is a tail. There's a huge grey rat moving across the sky, eating the sky.

The child remembered the photo; she said *That's not him.* I'm sitting here where I came often when he was on the Island. I came to get away from the others, to wait by myself.

I'm watching the rat, it's losing itself, its shape, eating the sky, and I'm waiting. Waiting for him to come back.

Waiting.

I'm waiting to come back home. ❖

Connect to the Literature

1. **What Do You Think?**
What is your impression of the narrator's life?

Comprehension Check
- Why has the narrator been separated from her fiancé for nine years?
- What does her fiancé do in the weeks after he returns home?

Think Critically

2. Describe the narrator's feelings about her fiancé.

3. How have the fiancé's political activities affected him? How have they affected the narrator and their child?

4. What is your opinion of the fiancé?

THINK ABOUT

- his commitment to the antiapartheid movement
- how he treats the narrator and their child
- how he treats the farm workers who come to talk with him

5. What do you think the narrator means at the end of the story when she says she is "waiting to come back home"?

6. **ACTIVE READING: MAKING INFERENCES** Review the list of inferences you made about customs and conditions in South Africa and about the relationship between the two main characters. What did you learn that was not directly stated in the story?

Extend Interpretations

7. **The Writer's Style** Sometimes Gordimer subtly uses description and figurative language to support themes of the story. For example, she belittles Robben Island by having the narrator compare it to a cake of cattle dung floating in a pool of rainwater. What ideas about South Africa are suggested to you by the description of the land and sky at the end of the story?

8. **Connect to Life** The narrator's fiancé tells her that he is in jail so that people's lives will be better in the future. In what way is your own life better because of someone else's effort and sacrifice for an important cause? Name the cause and, if possible, a specific person.

LITERARY ANALYSIS: FIRST-PERSON POINT OF VIEW

"Amnesty" is told from the **first-person point of view:** the narrator is a character in the story who tells everything in her own words. She is a simple country woman who at first has little political awareness. This simplicity is evident in the following description of her fiancé at a meeting of antiapartheid activists:

> *I stay, and listen. He forgets I'm there when he's talking and arguing about something I can see is important, more important than anything we could ever have to say to each other when we're alone.*

Using the first-person point of view usually ensures that readers will feel close to the narrator, but it also restricts readers to knowing only what the narrator understands and tells them, and no more. In this story, for example, readers don't know what the narrator's fiancé feels each time he leaves his family.

Cooperative Learning Activity
Gordimer could have chosen to write from the **third-person point of view**, referring to the young woman as *she*. She could have revealed only the young woman's thoughts **(third-person limited point of view)**. Or she could have revealed all the characters' thoughts **(third-person omniscient point of view)**. In small groups, discuss how the story would have been different if told from either of these third-person points of view. Judging by Gordimer's choice of narrator, what ideas do you think she wanted to present? How do you think she wanted to affect her readers?

Choices & CHALLENGES

Writing Options

1. Comparison-and-Contrast Essay Who has made the bigger sacrifices, the narrator or her fiancé? Write a brief essay comparing and contrasting the kinds of sacrifices made by the two characters.

Writing Handbook
See page R31: Compare and Contrast.

2. A Daughter's Diary Imagine that the couple's daughter is now a teenager and keeps a diary. Write an entry in which the daughter reflects on her relationship with her father and on the life he has led. Does she admire her father as her mother predicted she would?

3. Revealing Letter The narrator describes her fiancé as knowing "only what's inside his head." What does this mean? What does her fiancé fail to see and know about her? Write a letter to the fiancé telling him what he doesn't notice about the narrator.

Activities & Explorations

1. Waiting Portrait At the end of the story, the narrator describes what she sees as she sits "on a warm stone in the late afternoon" to think and to wait. Reread the passage and then draw or paint the scene you picture in your mind. In your drawing or painting, try to capture the mood of the passage. ~ ART

2. Debate on Self-Sacrifice Anyone devoted to working for a cause makes some personal sacrifices. In this story, is the fiancé sacrificing more than he should, or are all his sacrifices necessary? As a class, choose sides and debate this issue. ~ SPEECH

Inquiry & Research

1. Robben Island Prisoners Research the life of a well-known South African leader who was imprisoned on Robben Island, such as Nelson Mandela, Robert Sobukwe, or Walter Sisulu. Prepare an oral report telling about your subject's antiapartheid activities, years of imprisonment, and experiences after being freed.

2. Legacy of Apartheid Although apartheid ended in 1991, it continues to cast a long shadow over South Africa. Investigate current social problems in the country that are at least partly the legacy of apartheid and the racism it supported. Explain your findings in a cause-and-effect chart.

RESEARCH STARTER
CLASSZONE.COM

Farm Workers in the New South Africa

How has the end of apartheid changed life for landless black farm workers in South Africa? Many new laws have been passed to benefit them, but real change has been slow in coming.

Land Rights South Africa's new national constitution, adopted in 1996, states that "everyone has the right of access to land." The government has begun a land-reform program with three objectives:

1. the return of land to blacks who had it taken away from them by whites

2. the redistribution of white-owned land to blacks, either through government-assisted purchases by individuals or through voluntary donation by owners

3. the protection of blacks against eviction from white-owned land where they have lived and worked

So far, relatively little land has changed hands. Many rural people have been unaware of their new land rights; others have not known how to complete the forms needed to apply for land. The legal process has been slow, and judges, most of whom are white, tend to favor white landowners in disputes. Land remains too expensive for most black families to buy.

Mistreatment and Murders Conditions for workers on white-owned farms are not much improved, either. For example, from January to September 1999, the South African labor department received more than 4,000 complaints from farm workers against employers, citing such mistreatment as refusing to give workers time off, unfairly evicting them from their homes, preventing them from joining unions, replacing them with lower-paid immigrants, and verbally and physically abusing them. Mutual resentment has led to a wave of racial violence in rural areas that includes murders of black workers by white farmers and murders of white farmers by black workers. More than a thousand people have been killed on farms since 1996.

A Brighter Future? Amid the violence, though, there are a few signs of progress. The Centre for Rural Legal Studies, formed in 1991, runs projects designed to improve conditions for farm workers and set a minimum wage for them. It has trained paralegals and union leaders to help farm workers obtain their rights. Also, some visionary employers have experimented with new labor arrangements. The owner of the Nelson Creek winery, for example, donated land to black workers, which they used to produce their own successful brand of wine labeled New Beginnings.

Group Discussion What more do you think could be done to improve life for farm workers in South Africa? What ways can you think of to stop the racial violence on the farms?

AFTER THE DELUGE
WOLE SOYINKA

THE END AND THE BEGINNING
WISLAWA SZYMBORSKA

Wole Soyinka
1934–

Playwright and Prisoner In 1986 the Nigerian writer Wole Soyinka (wō'lĕ shô-yĭng'kə) became the first African to win the Nobel Prize in literature. His work blends traditional folklore and myths from his native Yoruba culture with Western literary forms. His first major play, *A Dance of the Forests,* was commissioned as a salute to Nigeria's independence. This humorous play warned that the end of colonial rule did not necessarily promise the end of Nigeria's problems.

In the mid-1960s, Soyinka became actively involved in the civil war between the Nigerian government and the Ibo ethnic group, who wanted to form their own country, Biafra. Accused of helping the Biafrans, Soyinka was arrested in 1967 and kept in solitary confinement for more than two years. He smuggled out fragments of writing that were later published as *Poems from Prison* and *The Man Died: Prison Notes of Wole Soyinka.* Since his imprisonment, he has had long periods of exile from Nigeria. His writing has become, in his words, "more and more preoccupied with the theme of the oppressive boot, the irrelevance of the color of the foot that wears it and the struggle for individuality."

**Wislawa
Szymborska**
1923–

Surprised to Win Wislawa Szymborska (vē-swä'vä shĭm-bôr'skə) was surprised when, one day in 1996, she learned that she had won the Nobel Prize in literature. That day the world "came crashing down" on her, she has said.

Szymborska has lived in the Polish city of Kraków since she was eight. She made her literary debut in 1945 with the publication of a poem in a newspaper. Since then, she has published 16 books of poetry, including 2 early collections she now disclaims because she was writing under pressure to praise communism. "I really wanted to save humanity," she has said, "but I chose the worst possible way. I did it out of love for mankind. Then I came to understand that you should not love mankind, but rather like people."

The poetry Szymborska has written since the loosening of Communist censorship in 1957 is praised for its sharp wit, keen observation, and simple language. Her work was largely unknown outside Poland until she won the Nobel Prize. The first English translation of her poems was *View with a Grain of Sand,* which appeared in 1995.

Build Background

The two poems you are about to read deal with the aftermath of catastrophic events—in "After the Deluge," a revolution, in "The End and the Beginning," a war. The authors of these poems have experienced such events firsthand. Soyinka has seen his native Nigeria torn by civil wars and ruled by military dictatorships for much of the time since the country achieved independence in 1960. Other African countries have undergone similar experiences, and Soyinka has not hesitated to criticize corrupt leaders.

Szymborska also has lived through war and dictatorship. She was a teenager when Germany invaded Poland during World War II. The war, with its brutality and hardships, was followed by a Communist dictatorship, which ruled Poland until 1989. After the end of Communist rule, people looked for new ways to organize their lives.

Warsaw, Poland, during World War II

Connect to Your Life

We in the United States are fortunate in never having been ruled by a dictatorship and not having had a war on our own soil since the Civil War. What changes would dictatorship and war at home have brought to us? Discuss this question with classmates.

Focus Your Reading

LITERARY ANALYSIS: TONE

The **tone** of a written work is an expression of the writer's attitude toward the work's subject. The tone of a literary work might be serious, humorous, admiring, or sarcastic, for example. Writers communicate tone largely through diction, or word choice. For example, "After every war / someone has to tidy up" has a tone different from that of the more serious "After every violent conflict / rebuilding must occur." Choice of details can also convey tone; for instance, if a poem mentioned only a leader's accomplishments and not his or her flaws, you might interpret the tone as admiring. As you read each of these poems, consider how you would describe the tone.

ACTIVE READING: EVALUATING

To evaluate is to make a judgment or form an opinion about something. As you read "After the Deluge," evaluate the former leader who is described in the poem. What kind of person is he? As you read "The End and the Beginning," evaluate the speaker's ideas about what must happen after a war. Do you agree with them?

📖 **READER'S NOTEBOOK** Be aware of your evaluations, or judgments, as you read. After every stanza record your reaction in your notebook.

"After the Deluge"	
Stanza 1	What a showoff!

After the Deluge

Wole Soyinka

Once, for a dare,
He filled his heart-shaped swimming pool
With bank notes, high denomination
And fed a pound of caviar to his dog.
5 The dog was sick; a chartered plane
Flew in replacement for the Persian rug.

He made a billion yen
Leap from Tokyo to Buenos Aires,
Turn somersaults through Brussels,
10 New York, Sofia and Johannesburg.
It cracked the bullion market open wide.
Governments fell, coalitions cracked
Insurrection raised its bloody flag
From north to south.

15 He knew his native land through iron gates,
His sight was radar bowls, his hearing
Electronic beams. For flesh and blood,
Kept company with a brace of Dobermans.
But—yes—the worthy causes never lacked
20 His widow's mite, discreetly publicized.

He escaped the lynch days. He survives.
I dreamt I saw him on a village
Water line, a parched land where
Water is a god
25 That doles its favors by the drop,
And waiting is a way of life.
Rebellion gleamed yet faintly in his eye

3 denomination: value.

7–10 He made . . . Johannesburg: He transferred money through major cities of the world— probably government funds that he stole and did not want traced.

11 bullion: gold.

13 insurrection: revolt; rebellion.

18 brace of Dobermans: pair of Doberman pinschers—medium-sized dogs often trained to attack intruders.

20 widow's mite: a small contribution by one who has little.

Falcon's Descent on the People (1992), Chike Aniakor. Pen, ink, and watercolor on paper. From the collection of the artist.

Traversing chrome-and-platinum retreats. There,
Hubs of commerce smoothly turn without
30 His bidding, and cities where he lately roosted
Have forgotten him, the preying bird
Of passage.

They let him live, but not from pity
Or human sufferance. He scratches life
35 From earth, no worse a mortal man than the rest.
Far, far away in dreamland splendor,
Creepers twine his gates of bronze relief.
The jade-lined pool is home
To snakes and lizards; they hunt and mate
40 On crusted algae.

29 hubs of commerce: centers of trade.

The End and the Beginning

Wislawa Szymborska

Translated by Stanislaw Baranczak and Clare Cavanagh

After every war
someone has to tidy up.
Things won't pick
themselves up, after all.

5   Someone has to shove
the rubble to the roadsides
so the carts loaded with corpses
can get by.

Someone has to trudge
10   through sludge and ashes,
through the sofa springs,
the shards of glass,
the bloody rags.

Someone has to lug the post
15   to prop the wall,
someone has to glaze the window,
set the door in its frame.

No sound bites, no photo opportunities,
and it takes years.
20   All the cameras have gone
to other wars.

The bridges need to be rebuilt,
the railroad stations, too.
Shirtsleeves will be rolled
25 to shreds.

Someone, broom in hand,
still remembers how it was.
Someone else listens, nodding
his unshattered head.
30 But others are bound to be bustling nearby
who'll find all that
a little boring.

From time to time someone still must
dig up a rusted argument
35 from underneath a bush
and haul it off to the dump.

Those who knew
what this was all about
must make way for those
40 who know little.
And less than that.
And at last nothing less than nothing.

Someone has to lie there
in the grass that covers up
45 the causes and effects
with a cornstalk in his teeth,
gawking at clouds.

Connect to the Literature

1. **What Do You Think?** What image from each poem stands out most in your mind?

Think Critically

2. **ACTIVE READING: EVALUATING** Give your own opinion of the former leader described in "After the Deluge." On what details is your opinion based? Look back at the reactions you recorded in your 📖 **READER'S NOTEBOOK**.

3. Reread the last stanza of "After the Deluge." What do the images in it suggest to you?

4. What must happen after the end of a war, according to the speaker in "The End and the Beginning"? Explain the speaker's argument in your own words.

> THINK ABOUT
> - what it might mean to "tidy up" (line 2)
> - what it might mean to "dig up a rusted argument / . . . and haul it off to the dump" (lines 34–36)
> - who replaces "Those who knew / what this was all about" (lines 37–38)
> - what is suggested by the image of someone lying "in the grass that covers up / the causes and effects" and "gawking at clouds" (lines 44–47)

5. **ACTIVE READING: EVALUATING** Do you agree with the speaker's ideas about what must happen after the end of a war?

Extend Interpretations

6. **Critic's Corner** One of Szymborska's translators, Stanislaw Baranczak, has interpreted the cleaning up in "The End and the Beginning" as a metaphor for forgetting. To him, the poem implies that people "never learn from history." Do you agree or disagree that this is true of people?

7. **Comparing Texts** How similar are the messages about political regimes in these two poems?

8. **Connect to Life** What issues or conflicts in the United States are most similar to the ones described in these poems?

LITERARY ANALYSIS: TONE

Tone is an expression of a writer's attitude toward his or her subject. Reading a literary work aloud, with expression, may help you identify its tone. The emotions you convey in your reading can often give you clues.

Writers convey particular tones by means of the words and details they use. For example, Nadine Gordimer's short story "Amnesty" has a serious, thoughtful, and sad tone. In a matter-of-fact way, the narrator shares details that give a picture of the limited scope of her life. One such detail is the fact that she has never seen the sea "except to color it in blue at school."

Paired Activity Work with a partner to identify the tone of each poem you have just read. To describe a tone, you may select an adjective from the following list of words or come up with one of your own. Review each poem for examples of word choices and details that contribute to the tone you have identified. Is the tone of each poem what you would expect, considering the poem's subject?

bitter	scornful
sad	angry
humorous	sarcastic
ironic	tongue-in-cheek
lighthearted	mocking

Choices & CHALLENGES

Writing Options

1. Poetic Portrait Write a poem that sharply characterizes a person, as Wole Soyinka does in "After the Deluge." Include telling details that reveal personality traits. If the person you chose is known to your classmates, leave out the name and see if they can guess who it is.

2. Editorial on Memory In an editorial, either agree or disagree with the assertion that people "never learn from history." Support your opinion with examples from world events.

Writing Handbook
See page R35: Persuasive Writing.

3. Comparison-and-Contrast Essay Write a brief essay comparing and contrasting "After the Deluge" and "The End and the Beginning." How are the poems similar or different in subject, tone, and theme?

Activities & Explorations

1. Dramatic Reading Prepare and present a dramatic reading of one of these two poems. You might work with a group to present "The End and the Beginning" as a choral reading, with separate voices speaking separate stanzas or particular lines. In your performance try to capture the tone you think the writer intended. ~ **PERFORMING**

2. Editorial Cartoon Draw an editorial cartoon mocking the leader described in "After the Deluge." You might create a caricature, a drawing in which distinctive features are deliberately exaggerated. Let images in the poem suggest ways of representing the leader. You might show him as a bird of prey, for example. ~ **ART**

3. Personal Interview If possible, interview someone who has personally witnessed a war or revolution, such as a veteran or an immigrant. Find out what the experience taught this person that he or she will never forget.
~ **SPEAKING AND LISTENING**

Communication Handbook
See page R52: Conducting an Interview.

Inquiry & Research

1. More by the Authors Find more poems by Wislawa Szymborska and choose two to share with the class. As an alternative, read a play by Wole Soyinka and present an oral review of it to the class.

2. Historical Time Line Investigate the history of either postcolonial Nigeria or postwar Poland and create a time line of major events. Do you see any connections between the events and the related poem?

3. Starting Over Investigate a country that has recently undergone a revolution or war. Report on what happened to its overthrown leaders or what rebuilding has been necessary.

RESEARCH STARTER
CLASSZONE.COM

Magical Realism

Mixing Reality and Fantasy

Magical realism is a category of fiction in which fantastic, unbelievable events take place in a realistic setting. Usually, magical realism is associated with Latin American fiction, but the term has been applied to writing from elsewhere.

In a magical realist work, characters accept supernatural or unlikely events without much question. To the reader, the amount of realistic detail makes the impossible seem possible. For example, in this passage from "A Very Old Man with Enormous Wings" by Gabriel García Márquez, a married couple accepts the sudden appearance of a winged man in their courtyard.

> *They both looked at the fallen body with mute stupor. He was dressed like a ragpicker. There were only a few faded hairs left on his bald skull and very few teeth in his mouth, and his pitiful condition of a drenched great-grandfather had taken away any sense of grandeur he might have had. His huge buzzard wings, dirty and half-plucked, were forever entangled in the mud. They looked at him so long and so closely that Pelayo and Elisenda very soon overcame their surprise and in the end found him familiar.*

A Latin American Form

In Latin American fiction, Argentina's Jorge Luis Borges and Cuba's Alejo Carpentier pioneered the use of magical realism, or *"lo real maravilloso,"* as Carpentier called it. In his opinion, magical realism best captured Latin America's unique and wondrous geography, history, and culture.

In the 1950s and 1960s, magical realism flowered in novels by such authors as Julio Cortázar and Carlos Fuentes. By far the best-known example of magical realism is the 1967 novel *One Hundred Years of Solitude* by Gabriel García Márquez (see Milestones in World Literature, page 1356).

Magical realism was originally an art term applied to dreamlike paintings such as *The Philosopher's Conquest* (1914) by Giorgio de Chirico.

Characteristics of Magical Realism

Although magical realist works can differ widely, they tend to share common characteristics.

Realistic Elements Works of magical realism, as you would expect, have realistic elements. Unlike fairy tales or some fantasies, they contain recognizable characters, believable dialogue, a true-to-life setting, and, often, accounts of actual historical events. The writer will often employ a matter-of-fact tone and rely heavily on sensory details to establish credibility.

Magical Elements Drawing on folklore and myths, magical realism also contains supernatural or mysterious elements. Ghosts may appear, dreams may come true, superstitions may prove warranted, people may even fly.

Humor and Exaggeration Magical realist fiction often includes humor and exaggeration. In "The Handsomest Drowned Man in the World," for instance, García Márquez uses exaggeration in describing the drowned man: "Not only was he the tallest, strongest, most virile, and best built man they had ever seen, but even though they were looking at him there was no room for him in their imagination."

Distortions of Time and Identity In works of magical realism, readers often encounter distortions of time and identity. In *One Hundred Years of Solitude*, the same sequence of events is periodically repeated. In addition, characters may change into other characters, and the usual distinctions between living and dead characters may be blurred.

Political and Social Commentary Finally, in many works of magical realism, writers directly or indirectly address important political and social issues, such as racism, tyranny, and conformity.

YOUR TURN Identify an example of magical realism that you have read in literature or seen in a film.

Magical Realism Worldwide

Magical realism is not a purely Latin American form. Works by many world writers, including some recent Nobel Prize winners, fall into the category. The U.S. writer Toni Morrison, who received the award in 1993, is noted for weaving the supernatural into her historical novels about African-American life. In her book *Song of Solomon* is an unforgettable woman named Pilate, who has no navel—a detail that suggests her disconnection from all other humans. The plot of Morrison's later novel *Beloved* revolves around a ghost—a child killed during slavery who returns to live with her family after emancipation. The German author Günter Grass, who won the Nobel Prize in 1999, is best known for his novel *The Tin Drum*. In this novel, Nazi Germany is presented through the eyes of a young boy who wills himself not to grow up.

Strategies for Reading: Magical Realism

1. Notice realistic elements, such as recognizable characters, believable dialogue, and true-to-life settings.

2. Watch for magical elements, including bizarre or impossible events and characters with supernatural abilities.

3. Look for humor and exaggeration, and notice the mood or atmosphere they create.

4. Do not be troubled by odd shifts in time and identity. Remember that events are not always presented in chronological order and that characters' identities may change.

5. **Monitor** your reading strategies and modify them when your understanding breaks down. Remember to use the strategies for active reading: **predict, visualize, connect, question, clarify,** and **evaluate.**

Handsomest
Drowned Man
in the
World

GABRIEL GARCÍA MÁRQUEZ

**Gabriel García
Márquez**
1928–

Tropical Roots Gabriel García Márquez (gär-sē′ə mär′kəs) was born in the small tropical town of Aracataca in Colombia, which he has fictionalized as the town of Macondo in his stories and novels. Raised by his grandparents until he was eight years old, García Márquez was influenced by his grandmother's unique storytelling style. She told fabulous legends and tales in a believable way, a technique García Márquez later borrowed in his writing. After his grandfather died, García Márquez returned to live with his parents and was sent away to school. Although he later enrolled in college, he abandoned his law studies to pursue a career as a journalist.

Accomplished Journalist In 1948, in the midst of political violence and riots in Colombia, García Márquez embarked on a career as a newspaper reporter. He eventually worked in France, England, and Venezuela as a freelance journalist and in 1959 helped establish a news agency for the Cuban government, working as its correspondent in Havana and New York City. Besides his novels and stories, García Márquez has published insightful works of nonfiction, such as *News of a Kidnapping* (1996). He frequently draws on his experience as a journalist in his fiction, bringing to life the political and social struggles of Latin America.

Lasting Legacy In 1982 García Márquez was awarded the Nobel Prize in literature. To date, his greatest literary achievement has been the monumental novel *One Hundred Years of Solitude,* which was published in 1967. An international success, this book traces several generations of a Colombian family and established García Márquez as a master of the style known as **magical realism.** (For more information on magical realism and *One Hundred Years of Solitude,* see Learning the Language of Literature on page 1344 and Milestones in World Literature on page 1356.)

Other Works
Chronicle of a Death Foretold
Love in the Time of Cholera

Build Background

The Colombian Coast "The Handsomest Drowned Man in the World" was first published in 1972 as part of a collection of short stories set along the Caribbean coast of northern Colombia. The stories take place in imaginary coastal towns and villages along the Guajira Peninsula, a hot, dry, sparsely populated region. To a visitor in the 1970s, the lives of the people there would have seemed as desolate as the landscape. The inhabitants lived in wooden huts and survived largely by raising goats or working at a few trades.

The Caribbean area of Colombia is rich in folklore that reflects the region's mixture of Hispanic, African, and Indian cultures. Roaming the coastal region as a young reporter, García Márquez absorbed this folklore. Its influence shows in both his novels and his short stories.

Salt miners on the Guajira Peninsula

Connect to Your Life

Have you ever met or heard of someone who made you want to live your own life differently? If so, tell a partner about this person and how he or she affected you. In the story you are about to read, the people of an isolated fishing village react to a stranger in a surprising way.

Focus Your Reading

LITERARY ANALYSIS: SYMBOL

A **symbol** is a person, a place, or an object that stands for something beyond itself, such as an idea or a feeling. For example, a dove is a symbol of peace, and a flag can be a symbol of a country. Such visual symbols have standard interpretations. In a literary work, however, you often have to figure out a symbol's meaning by noticing what else is linked to it. As you read this story, think about what the drowned man might represent.

ACTIVE READING: UNDERSTANDING CAUSE AND EFFECT

In a story, as in real life, a single cause may have more than one effect. In "The Handsomest Drowned Man in the World," for example, one event—the discovery of a drowned man—has many effects on the people of a small village.

📖 **READER'S NOTEBOOK** As you read the story, pay attention to the effects that the drowned man has on the people of the village. Jot down the effects in a chart like this one.

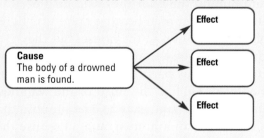

WORDS TO KNOW **Vocabulary Preview**

arid	improvise	virile
haggard	labyrinth	

The Handsomest Drowned Man in the World

Gabriel García Márquez

Translated by Gregory Rabassa

✳

The first children who saw the dark and slinky bulge approaching through the sea let themselves think it was an enemy ship. Then they saw it had no flags or masts and they thought it was a whale. But when it washed up on the beach, they removed the clumps of seaweed, the jellyfish tentacles, and the remains of fish and flotsam,[1] and only then did they see that it was a drowned man.

They had been playing with him all afternoon, burying him in the sand and digging him up again, when someone chanced to see them and spread the alarm in the village. The men who carried him to the nearest house noticed that he weighed more than any dead man they had ever known, almost as much as a horse, and they said to each other that maybe he'd been floating too long and the water had got into his bones. When they laid him on the floor they said he'd been taller than all other men because there was barely enough room for him in the house, but they thought that maybe the ability to keep on growing after death was part of the nature of certain drowned men. He had the smell of the sea about him and only his shape gave one to suppose that it was the corpse of a human being, because the skin was covered with a crust of mud and scales.

They did not even have to clean off his face to know that the dead man was a stranger. The village was made up of only twenty-odd wooden houses that had stone courtyards with no flowers and which were spread about on the end of a desertlike cape. There was so little land that mothers always went about with the fear that the wind would carry off their children and the few dead that the years had caused among them had to be thrown off the cliffs. But the sea was calm and bountiful and all the men fit into seven boats. So when they found the drowned man they simply had to look at one another to see that they were all there.

That night they did not go out to work at sea. While the men went to find out if anyone was missing in neighboring villages, the women stayed behind to care for the drowned man. They took the mud off with grass swabs, they removed the underwater stones entangled in his hair, and they scraped the crust off with tools used for scaling fish. As they were doing that they noticed that the vegetation on him came from faraway oceans and deep water and that his clothes were in tatters, as if he had sailed through labyrinths of coral. They noticed too that he bore his death with pride, for he did not have the lonely look of other drowned men who came out of the sea or that haggard, needy look

---

1. **flotsam:** wreckage or debris floating in the water.

1348

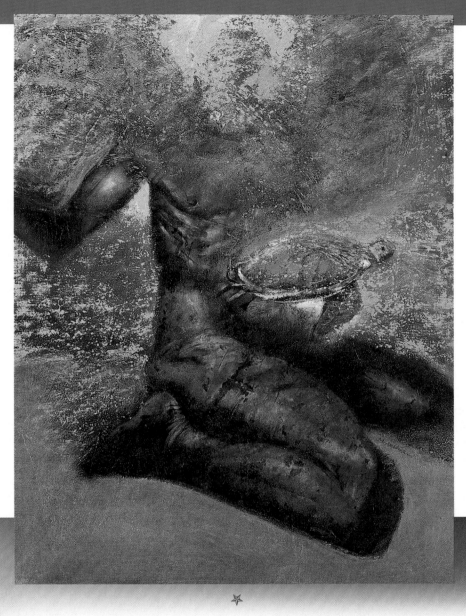

Man in Sand,
Marshall Arisman.

of men who drowned in rivers. But only when they finished cleaning him off did they become aware of the kind of man he was and it left them breathless. Not only was he the tallest, strongest, most <u>virile</u>, and best built man they had ever seen, but even though they were looking at him there was no room for him in their imagination.

They could not find a bed in the village large enough to lay him on nor was there a table solid enough to use for his wake. The tallest men's holiday pants would not fit him, nor the fattest ones' Sunday shirts, nor the shoes of the one with the biggest feet. Fascinated by his huge size and his beauty, the women then decided to make him some pants from a large piece of sail and a shirt from some bridal brabant linen[2] so that he could continue through his death with dignity. As they sewed, sitting in a circle and gazing at

2. **brabant linen:** cloth from a particular region of Belgium.

"He has the face
of someone called
Esteban."
It was true.
Most of them had only
to take another look
at him to see that
he could not have
any other name.

the corpse between stitches, it seemed to them that the wind had never been so steady nor the sea so restless as on that night and they supposed that the change had something to do with the dead man. They thought that if that magnificent man had lived in the village, his house would have had the widest doors, the highest ceiling, and the strongest floor, his bedstead would have been made from a midship frame held together by iron bolts, and his wife would have been the happiest woman. They thought that he would have had so much authority that he could have drawn fish out of the sea simply by calling their names and that he would have put so much work into his land that springs would have burst forth from among the rocks so that he would have been able to plant flowers on the cliffs. They secretly compared him to their own men, thinking that for all their lives theirs were incapable of doing what he could do in one night, and they ended up dismissing them deep in their hearts as the weakest, meanest, and most useless creatures on earth. They were wandering through that maze of fantasy when the oldest woman, who as the oldest had looked upon the drowned man with more compassion than passion, sighed:

Two Women and a Child (1926), Diego Rivera. Oil on canvas, 29 ³/₈" × 31 ⁵/₈" (74.6 cm × 80.3 cm). Gift of Albert M. Bender to the California Palace of the Legion of Honor. Copyright retained by the artist.

"He has the face of someone called Esteban."[3]

It was true. Most of them had only to take another look at him to see that he could not have any other name. The more stubborn among them, who were the youngest, still lived for a few hours with the illusion that when they put his clothes on and he lay among the flowers in patent leather shoes his name might be Lautaro.[4] But it was a vain illusion. There had not been enough canvas, the poorly cut and worse sewn pants were too tight, and the hidden strength of his heart popped the buttons on his shirt. After midnight the whistling of the wind died down and the sea fell into its Wednesday drowsiness. The silence put an end to any last doubts: he was Esteban. The women who had dressed him, who had combed his hair, had cut his nails and

---

3. **Esteban** (ĕ-stĕ′bän).
4. **Lautaro** (lou-tä′rô).

shaved him were unable to hold back a shudder of pity when they had to resign themselves to his being dragged along the ground. It was then that they understood how unhappy he must have been with that huge body since it bothered him even after death. They could see him in life, condemned to going through doors sideways, cracking his head on crossbeams, remaining on his feet during visits, not knowing what to do with his soft, pink, sea lion hands while the lady of the house looked for her most resistant chair and begged him, frightened to death, sit here, Esteban, please, and he, leaning against the wall, smiling, don't bother, ma'am, I'm fine where I am, his heels raw and his back roasted from having done the same thing so many times whenever he paid a visit, don't bother, ma'am, I'm fine where I am, just to avoid the embarrassment of breaking up the chair, and never knowing perhaps that the ones who said don't go, Esteban, at least wait till the coffee's ready, were the ones who later on would whisper the big boob finally left, how nice, the handsome fool has gone. That was what the women were thinking beside the body a little before dawn. Later, when they covered his face with a handkerchief so that the light would not bother him, he looked so forever dead, so defenseless, so much like their men that the first furrows of tears opened in their hearts. It was one of the younger ones who began the weeping. The others, coming to, went from sighs to wails, and the more they sobbed the more they felt like weeping, because the drowned man was becoming all the more Esteban for them, and so they wept so much, for he was the most destitute, most peaceful, and most obliging man on earth, poor Esteban. So when the men returned with the news that the drowned man was not from the neighboring villages either, the women felt an opening of jubilation in the midst of their tears.

> "Praise the Lord," they sighed, "he's ours!" The men thought the fuss was only womanish frivolity.

"Praise the Lord," they sighed, "he's ours!" The men thought the fuss was only womanish frivolity. Fatigued because of the difficult night-time inquiries, all they wanted was to get rid of the bother of the newcomer once and for all before the sun grew strong on that <u>arid</u>, windless day. They <u>improvised</u> a litter with the remains of foremasts and gaffs,[5] tying it together with rigging so that it would bear the weight of the body until they reached the cliffs. They wanted to tie the anchor from a cargo ship to him so that he would sink easily into the deepest waves, where fish are blind and divers die of nostalgia, and bad currents would not bring him back to shore, as had happened with other bodies. But the more they hurried, the more the women thought of ways to waste time. They walked about like startled hens, pecking with the sea charms on their breasts, some interfering on one side to put a scapular[6] of the good wind on the drowned man, some on the other side to put a wrist compass on him, and after a great deal of *get away from there, woman, stay out of the way, look, you almost made me fall on top of the dead man,* the men began to feel mistrust in their livers and started grumbling about why so many main-altar decorations for a stranger, because no

---

5. **gaffs:** hooks attached to poles, used for pulling fish out of the water.

6. **scapular:** a religious badge consisting of two pieces of cloth worn over the shoulders.

WORDS TO KNOW

arid (ăr′ĭd) *adj.* dry
improvise (ĭm′prə-vīz′) *v.* to make on the spur of the moment, using any resources available

matter how many nails and holy-water jars he had on him, the sharks would chew him all the same, but the women kept piling on their junk relics,[7] running back and forth, stumbling, while they released in sighs what they did not in tears, so that the men finally exploded with *since when has there ever been such a fuss over a drifting corpse, a drowned nobody, a piece of cold Wednesday meat.* One of the women, mortified by so much lack of care, then removed the handkerchief from the dead man's face and the men were left breathless too.

He was Esteban. It was not necessary to repeat it for them to recognize him. If they had been told Sir Walter Raleigh, even they might have been impressed with his gringo accent, the macaw on his shoulder, his cannibal-killing blunderbuss,[8] but there could be only one Esteban in the world and there he was, stretched out like a sperm whale, shoeless, wearing the pants of an undersized child, and with those stony nails that had to be cut with a knife. They only had to take the handkerchief off his face to see that he was ashamed, that it was not his fault that he was so big or so heavy or so handsome, and if he had known that this was going to happen, he would have looked for a more discreet place to drown in, seriously, I even would have tied the anchor off a galleon[9] around my neck and staggered off a cliff like someone who doesn't like things in order not to be upsetting people now with this Wednesday dead body, as you people say, in order not to be bothering anyone with this filthy piece of cold meat that doesn't have anything to do with me. There was so much truth in his manner that even the most mistrustful men, the ones who felt the bitterness of endless nights at sea fearing that their women would tire of dreaming about them and begin to dream of drowned men, even they and others who were harder still shuddered in the marrow of their bones at Esteban's sincerity.

That was how they came to hold the most splendid funeral they could conceive of for an abandoned drowned man. Some women who had gone to get flowers in the neighboring villages returned with other women who could not believe what they had been told, and those women went back for more flowers when they saw the dead man, and they brought more and more until there were so many flowers and so many people that it was hard to walk about. At the final moment it pained them to return him to the waters as an orphan and they chose a father and mother from among the best people, and aunts and uncles and cousins, so that through him all the inhabitants of the village became kinsmen. Some sailors who heard the weeping from a distance went off course and people heard of one who had himself tied to the mainmast, remembering ancient fables about sirens.[10] While they fought for the privilege of carrying him on their shoulders along the steep escarpment[11] by the cliffs, men and women became aware for the first time of the desolation of their streets, the dryness of their courtyards, the narrowness of their dreams as they faced the splendor and beauty of their drowned man. They let him go without an anchor so that he could come back if he wished and whenever he wished, and they all held their breath for the fraction of centuries the body took to fall into the abyss.

---

7. **relics:** objects that once belonged to a holy person.

8. **Sir Walter Raleigh . . . blunderbuss:** Sir Walter Raleigh (1552?–1618) was an English explorer. A macaw is a parrot, and a blunderbuss is a type of gun—short and not very accurate—that was used from the 1600s to the 1800s.

9. **galleon:** a type of large sailing ship in use from the 1400s through the 1600s, with three masts and two or more decks.

10. **ancient fables about sirens:** In the *Odyssey*, an ancient Greek epic, the hero Odysseus has himself tied to the mast of his ship to resist the Sirens, sweet-voiced nymphs who lure sailors to their destruction on the rocks.

11. **escarpment:** a steep slope or long cliff.

Burial of an Illustrious Man (1936), Mario Urteaga. Oil on canvas, 23″ × 32 1/2″ (58.4 cm × 82.5 cm). The Museum of Modern Art, New York. Inter-American Fund. Photograph copyright © 2001 The Museum of Modern Art, New York.

HUMANITIES CONNECTION Musicians and, likely, hired mourners are among this funeral procession of Quechua Indians in northern Peru.

They did not need to look at one another to realize that they were no longer all present, that they would never be. But they also knew that everything would be different from then on, that their houses would have wider doors, higher ceilings, and stronger floors so that Esteban's memory could go everywhere without bumping into beams and so that no one in the future would dare whisper the big boob finally died, too bad, the handsome fool has finally died, because they were going to paint their house fronts gay colors to make Esteban's memory eternal and they were going to break their backs digging for springs among the stones and planting flowers on the cliffs so that in future years at dawn the passengers on great liners would awaken, suffocated by the smell of gardens on the high seas, and the captain would have to come down from the bridge in his dress uniform, with his astrolabe, his pole star,[12] and his row of war medals and, pointing to the promontory of roses on the horizon, he would say in fourteen languages, look there, where the wind is so peaceful now that it's gone to sleep beneath the beds, over there, where the sun's so bright that the sunflowers don't know which way to turn, yes, over there, that's Esteban's village. ❖

---

12. **astrolabe** (ăs′trə-lāb′) . . . **pole star:** An astrolabe is an instrument formerly used to measure the altitude of stars, including the North Star, or pole star.

Connect to the Literature

1. **What Do You Think?**
Did this story turn out the way you expected? Explain.

Comprehension Check
- What do the villagers do with the body of the drowned man?
- By the end of the story, how do they want their village to be known?

Think Critically

2. **ACTIVE READING: UNDERSTANDING CAUSE AND EFFECT** Review the cause-and-effect chart you made in your ▐█▌ **READER'S NOTEBOOK**. What effects does the drowned man have on the villagers?

3. Why do you think the drowned man affects the villagers as he does?

THINK ABOUT

- the qualities the villagers attribute to him
- the nature of the villagers' lives and their environment

4. What are your own theories about who the drowned man is and where he came from? Support your response.

Extend Interpretations

5. **What If?** If the villagers had found out the identity of the drowned man, how might this knowledge have affected their reaction to him?

6. **The Writer's Style** What elements in this story make it an example of **magical realism?** Be specific.

7. **Connect to Life** The Connect to Your Life activity on page 1347 asked you to discuss a person who made you want to live your life differently. How do Esteban's effects on the villagers compare with this person's effects on you?

LITERARY ANALYSIS: SYMBOL

A person, a place, or an object that represents something beyond itself is known as a **symbol.** In a literary work, an element has symbolic meaning when it is used to stand for an abstract quality or idea. In the story "The Handsomest Drowned Man in the World," the drowned man comes to represent a number of qualities to the villagers. One of these qualities is beauty.

Cooperative Learning Activity
With a small group of classmates, brainstorm a list of qualities that the villagers associate with the drowned man. Then determine which two or three qualities or ideas the drowned man mainly symbolizes. Discuss the reasons for your choice.

Writing Options

1. Character Biography Write an imaginary biography of the drowned man, telling where he's from, what his life was like, how he drowned, and how he came to wash ashore in this Caribbean fishing village.

Writing Handbook
See page R29: Narrative Writing.

2. Interpretive Essay In a brief essay, explain what the drowned man symbolizes and what the overall theme of the story might be.

Activities & Explorations

1. Village Diorama Create a diorama of "Esteban's village," emphasizing the qualities of Esteban's that the villagers wanted to honor. ~ ART

2. Radio Recording Work with a group to record a dramatic reading of this story for a radio broadcast. Include sound effects and background music in your recording. ~ PERFORMING

Inquiry & Research

Magical Realist Anthology
Work with a group of classmates to find other magical realist stories from Latin America or elsewhere. For example, you might look for stories by Julio Cortázar, Isabel Allende, or Rosario Ferré. You could also use the Internet to guide you to lesser-known works. Gather your favorite stories in a class anthology. Write either a brief introduction for each story or a longer introduction for the whole collection.

RESEARCH STARTER
CLASSZONE.COM

Vocabulary in Action

EXERCISE: WORD MEANINGS For each sentence, write *Yes* if the italicized word seems to fit the meaning of the sentence. Write *No* if it does not seem to fit.

1. The children of the town found the body in a wide, open *labyrinth* on the beach.

2. Because of the water, the body's condition was very *arid*.

3. The man had been quite *virile*, judging from his great size and obvious strength.

4. Nothing fit him properly, so the villagers had to *improvise* in preparing him for burial.

5. The cliffs looked *haggard* after the townspeople planted them with flowers.

Building Vocabulary

For an in-depth lesson on recognizing word connotation and denotation, see page 1090.

Gabriel García Márquez

One Hundred Years of Solitude

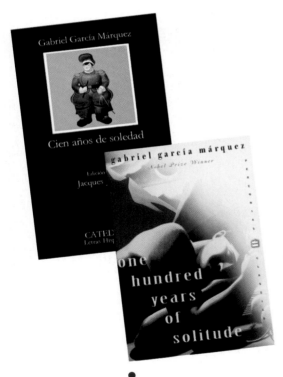

Above:
*English and Spanish editions
of the bestselling novel*

Pablo Neruda once called *One Hundred Years of Solitude* "the greatest revelation in the Spanish language since the *Don Quixote* of Cervantes." Written by the Colombian novelist Gabriel García Márquez and first published in 1967, *One Hundred Years of Solitude* has been translated into over 30 languages and has sold more copies than any other novel from Latin America.

The book traces six generations of the Buendía family. The family's patriarch, José Arcadio, and his wife, Úrsula, establish the town of Macondo, which García Márquez based on the Colombian coastal village of Aracataca, where he was born. In successive generations, the descendants of José Arcadio and Úrsula endure hardships—such as labor strikes, political strife, and murder—as well as the joys of family and community. The novel describes not only the rise and fall of the Buendía family but also the colorful history of Macondo.

While telling the story of one family in one town, *One Hundred Years of Solitude* also reflects the social, political, and economic history of Colombia and of Latin America in general. García Márquez weaves historical facts throughout his novel and alludes to real-life events from the late 16th century to the mid-20th century. Many occurrences in the story, including violent civil wars, oppressive dictatorships, and bloody massacres, parallel actual events in Colombia's past.

Left:
García Márquez wearing his masterwork

García Márquez drew on many of his own experiences in writing *One Hundred Years of Solitude.* He based some characters on family members and friends, adapted African and Caribbean myths and legends he heard as a youth, and borrowed his grandmother's technique of relating outrageous events in a deadpan tone. The novel's themes, structure, and vision were also shaped by such diverse works of literature as the Bible, Greek tragedies, Kafka's "Metamorphosis," the satires of François Rabelais, the family sagas of William Faulkner, and the experimental prose of Virginia Woolf.

A complex, sprawling work, *One Hundred Years of Solitude* consists of 20 unnumbered sections. It contains more than 50 characters (some of whom have the same names) and encompasses more than 400 years of history. García Márquez creates a world in which time is cyclical, with events repeating in different generations. He often uses flashbacks and foreshadowing in his narration. Furthermore, he employs a distinctive form called **magical realism** (see Learning the Language of Literature, page 1344) to capture his view of Latin America's marvelous reality. Throughout the novel, impossible things happen: characters rise to heaven, flowers rain from the sky, and the entire population of Macondo is plagued by insomnia and amnesia.

Below:
In Macondo, women have unearthly beauty and flowers rain from the sky.

Despite its complexity, this novel has achieved enormous popularity because of its accessible prose, lively pace, comical characters, and satirical tone. An international sensation, *One Hundred Years of Solitude* established a benchmark for magical realist fiction and gave new life to the novel form.

MILESTONE LINKS
CLASSZONE.COM

Left:
García Márquez in Sweden, receiving the 1982 Nobel Prize for his work

Odes BY *Pablo Neruda*

Pablo Neruda
1904–1973

Going His Own Way Pablo Neruda grew up as Neftalí Ricardo Reyes Basoalto in the rugged frontier town of Temuco, Chile. His father was a railroad worker, and his mother was a teacher who died shortly after his birth. Although Neftalí showed a talent for writing poetry by the time he was 10 years old, his friends and his father ridiculed his literary ambitions. He was encouraged instead by Gabriela Mistral (see page 1188), principal of the local girls' school, who would later become Chile's first Nobel laureate in literature. She gave him books and urged him to pursue his poetry. While still in his teens, he began to publish work under the pen name Pablo Neruda, which he took to avoid conflict with his family. Later, he made this his legal name.

Poet and Diplomat Neruda's first successful book was *Twenty Love Poems and a Song of Despair,* published when he was only 20. People still quote passionate verses from this book today. Celebrated as a poet but unable to support himself by writing, Neruda took a series of diplomatic posts in Asia and Europe. From 1927 through 1943, the Chilean government sent him as a consul to such countries as Burma, Java, Ceylon, Singapore, Cambodia, Argentina, Mexico, and Spain. In Spain, Neruda became involved in the Spanish civil war and experienced the assassination of his friend Federico García Lorca. The poems in *Residence on Earth* reflect Neruda's loneliness and sense of alienation during his time abroad.

Public Figure After returning to Chile, Neruda joined the Communist Party and was elected to the Chilean senate in 1945. After criticizing the president's policies, he was forced to leave Chile for several years to avoid arrest. He continued to write in exile and in 1950 completed his epic poem *Canto General,* about the history of Latin America. After he returned to Chile in 1952, his stature as a poet and public figure rose. He was even nominated for president in 1969. He withdrew his nomination in favor of the socialist candidate Salvador Allende but accepted an ambassadorship to France after Allende's victory.

While living in Paris, Neruda was awarded the 1971 Nobel Prize—"for a poetry that with the action of an elemental force brings alive a continent's destiny and dreams." In his acceptance speech he compared poetry to bread and a poet to a baker, an ordinary person who labors to share his product with all who need it. Two years later Neruda died of cancer, days after President Allende died during a coup. Thousands gathered in the streets for the poet's funeral, reciting his verses in defiance of surrounding government troops.

Other Works
One Hundred Love Sonnets
The House at Isla Negra

Build Background

Exalting Simple Subjects Neruda wrote in many forms, but his "elementary odes" are especially admired. An **ode** is a lyric poem that exalts, or praises, a person, an event, or an object. This literary form dates back to classical times, when the ancient Greek poet Pindar wrote odes in praise of Greek heroes and athletes. Traditionally, the language and tone of an ode are dignified and serious, and many odes follow a fixed pattern of stanzas and rhyme.

Pablo Neruda's odes break with this tradition. Because Neruda wanted to reach a mass audience of ordinary people, he wrote odes in simple language about the most common things in daily life, such as rain and salt. But although he wrote in free verse and used conversational language, he treated these subjects with a reverence usually reserved for loftier subjects.

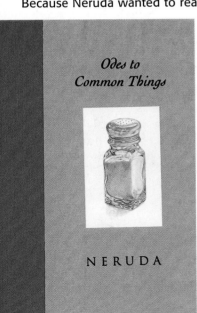

Odes to Common Things

NERUDA

Connect to Your Life

What sensations or memories do you associate with a lizard? a watermelon? In your notebook, freewrite for two minutes on each subject, jotting down whatever comes to your mind. Then read Neruda's poems to see what associations these subjects held for him.

Focus Your Reading

LITERARY ANALYSIS: STYLE

The term **style** refers to the distinctive way in which a work of literature is written. Such elements as word choice, sentence length, sentence structure, tone, and imagery are all expressions of a writer's style. Notice how Neruda creates a vibrant image through the choice and arrangement of words in these lines from "Ode to the Lizard":

> *By the*
> *water*
> *you are*
> *silent, slippery*
> *slime.*

As you read Neruda's odes, pay attention to his style of writing and think about what makes it distinctive.

ACTIVE READING: READING POETRY ALOUD

You'll notice that the lines in Neruda's odes are very short. By stretching the words out over many lines, Neruda forces the reader to focus on individual words and to savor each image. To appreciate the imagery, read the odes aloud softly and slowly to yourself, stopping every few lines to "see" what the poet is describing.

READER'S NOTEBOOK As you read each poem, copy down a passage that you especially like or one that you don't quite understand. Be prepared to examine it more closely with the class.

Ode to the Lizard

Pablo Neruda

Translated by Margaret Sayers Peden

On the sand
a
lizard
with a sandy tail.

5 Beneath
a leaf,
a leaflike
head.

From what planet,
10 from what
cold green ember
did you fall?
From the moon?
From frozen space?
15 Or from
the emerald
did your color
climb the vine?

On a rotting
20 tree trunk
you are
a living
shoot,[1]
arrow
25 of its foliage.
On a stone
you are a stone
with two small, ancient
eyes—

---

1. **shoot:** a new growth on a plant.

30   eyes of the stone.
     By the
     water
     you are
     silent, slippery
35   slime.
     To
     a fly
     you are the dart
     of an annihilating dragon.

40   And to me,
     my childhood,
     spring
     beside
     a lazy
45   river,
     that's
     you!
     lizard,
     cold, small
50   and green;
     you are a long-ago
     siesta
     beside cool waters,
     with books unopened.

55   The water flows and sings.

     The sky, overhead, is a
     warm corolla.[2]

---

2. **corolla** (kə-rôl′ə): the grouping of petals on a flower.

Ode to the Watermelon

Pablo Neruda

Translated by Robert Bly

The tree of intense
summer,
hard,
is all blue sky,
5 yellow sun,
fatigue in drops,
a sword
above the highways,
a scorched shoe
10 in the cities:
the brightness and the world
weigh us down,
hit us
in the eyes
15 with clouds of dust,
with sudden golden blows,
they torture
our feet
with tiny thorns,
20 with hot stones,
and the mouth
suffers
more than all the toes:
the throat
25 becomes thirsty,
the teeth,
the lips, the tongue:

we want to drink
waterfalls,
30 the dark blue night,
the South Pole,
and then
the coolest of all
the planets crosses
35 the sky,
the round, magnificent,
star-filled watermelon.

It's a fruit from the thirst-tree.
It's the green whale of the summer.

40 The dry universe
all at once
given dark stars
by this firmament of coolness
lets the swelling
45 fruit
come down:
its hemispheres open
showing a flag
green, white, red,
50 that dissolves into
wild rivers, sugar,
delight!

Las sandias [Watermelons] (1957), Diego Rivera.
Fundacion Dolores Olmedo, Mexico City.
Schalkwijk/Art Resource, New York.

Jewel box of water, phlegmatic[1]
queen
55 of the fruitshops,
warehouse
of profundity,[2] moon
on earth!
You are pure,
60 rubies fall apart
in your abundance,
and we
want
to bite into you,
65 to bury our
face
in you, and
our hair, and
the soul!
70 When we're thirsty
we glimpse you
like
a mine or a mountain

of fantastic food,
75 but
among our longings and our teeth
you change
simply
into cool light
80 that slips in turn into
spring water
that touched us once
singing.
And that is why
85 you don't weigh us down
in the siesta hour
that's like an oven,
you don't weigh us down,
you just
90 go by
and your heart, some cold ember,
turned itself into a single
drop of water.

---

1. **phlegmatic** (flĕg-măt′ĭk): calm; unemotional.
2. **profundity**: great depth, especially of feeling or meaning.

Thinking *through the* LITERATURE

Connect to the Literature

1. **What Do You Think?** What do you like or dislike about these poems? Support your opinion.

Think Critically

2. **ACTIVE READING: READING POETRY ALOUD**
Read aloud the passages you copied in your 📖 **READER'S NOTEBOOK.** Explain what impresses or confuses you about each passage.

3. What different things is a lizard compared to in the first ode? Discuss the qualities of a lizard that are brought out by these comparisons.

4. Images in the second ode associate a watermelon with a planet, stars, and what else? How do these images contrast with the images at the beginning of the poem?

5. What makes these poems **odes?**

   THINK ABOUT { • the definition of *ode* on page 1359
   • the **tone** of the poems

Extend Interpretations

6. **Critic's Corner** According to critic René de Costa, Neruda's odes contain "an element of humor, a delicate whimsicality" that distinguishes them from odes in the classical tradition. What passages can you find to support this observation?

7. **What If?** If "Ode to the Lizard" ended with line 39, how would the poem be affected? If "Ode to the Watermelon" began with line 38, how would the poem be affected?

8. **Connect to Life** How do your associations with lizards and watermelons compare with Neruda's?

LITERARY ANALYSIS: STYLE

An author's **style** is the particular way he or she writes. The term *style* refers not to what is said but rather to *how* it is said. Many elements contribute to the style of a poem, including word choice, arrangement of lines and stanzas, tone, figurative language, and imagery. For example, consider the word choice in Neruda's odes. With a few exceptions, Neruda uses simple, everyday, concrete words.

Paired Activity Work with a partner to create a "checklist" that characterizes Neruda's style in these odes. Describe as many distinctive features of his writing style as you can. If you're having trouble recognizing these features, you may find it helpful to compare Neruda's odes with other 20th-century poems you've read in Unit Seven, such as those by Rilke, García Lorca, and Mistral (pages 1151, 1152, and 1188).

> **You Know It's a Neruda Ode If . . .**
>
> **Word choice:** *it uses mostly simple, common, concrete words*
>
> **Length of lines:**
>
> **Tone:**
>
> **Kind of imagery:**

After you have completed your checklist, you might try to write our own ode in the style of a Neruda ode.

On Translating Neruda

Translating poems into another language is not easy. Margaret Sayers Peden, the translator of "Ode to the Lizard," wrote that in translating odes by Neruda, she tried to follow four commandments:

1. **Respect simplicity,** keeping the same level of language as in the originals, not using fancier words.
2. **Respect sound,** keeping the musical quality of the poems.
3. **Respect sense,** preserving the content, or what each poem "tells."
4. **Respect shape,** keeping the long, narrow form of the words on the page.

Look at Peden's translation beside the original Spanish poem, and see how she followed these commandments.

Margaret Sayers Peden

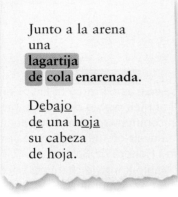

Junto a la arena
una
lagartija
de cola enarenada.

Debajo
de una hoja
su cabeza
de hoja.

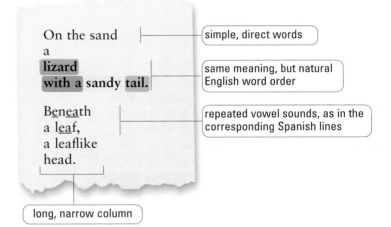

On the sand — simple, direct words
a
lizard
with a sandy tail. — same meaning, but natural English word order

Beneath — repeated vowel sounds, as in the corresponding Spanish lines
a leaf,
a leaflike
head.

long, narrow column

Peden said that "Respect sound" was the most difficult commandment to follow:

> *There is little a translator can do about lost sound values except to listen constantly and to try as nearly as possible to re-create those sounds or to substitute a similar series of resonances [sounds].*

Neruda himself worried about the sound of his poetry being lost in translation:

> *It seems to me that the English language, so different from Spanish and so much more direct, often expresses the meaning of my poetry but does not convey its atmosphere.*

Small Group Discussion Think about a poem you love. How much does the actual sound of the words contribute to the meaning or the beauty of the poem? Do you think that poem could be translated well into another language? Explain your opinion, using examples from the poem.

Half a Day

NAGUIB MAHFOUZ

Naguib Mahfouz
1911–

Promoting Arabic Fiction

When the Swedish Academy awarded Naguib Mahfouz (nä-gēb′ mä-fōōz′) the 1988 Nobel Prize in literature, it called him a writer who "has formed an Arabian narrative art that applies to all mankind." Mahfouz, from Egypt, was the first Arabic-language writer to receive the prize. He is credited with popularizing the novel and short story as literary forms in the Arab world, where poetry has traditionally been preferred. He was little known in the rest of the world before winning the Nobel honor. Although he had written more than 50 books, few had ever been translated.

Stories of Egypt

The youngest of seven children, Naguib Mahfouz was born in Cairo. After earning a degree in philosophy from the University of Cairo, he began a civil-service career and started to publish his fiction. His early works were historical novels set in ancient Egypt, but he turned his attention to modern Egypt beginning in 1945. He first gained acclaim with the 1957 publication of his "Cairo trilogy." These three books—*Palace Walk, Palace of Desire,* and *Sugar Street*—chronicle three generations of a middle-class Cairo family and serve as a history of Egypt since World War I. Full of memorable characters, precise detail, and social commentary, they have been compared to the novels of 19th-century realists such as Leo Tolstoy and Honoré de Balzac.

In the 1960s Mahfouz's style changed, becoming less realistic and more experimental, as you will see in the story "Half a Day." Still, his later works, like his earlier works, were concerned with the passage of time, the plight of the poor, and the clash of traditional and modern values—issues relevant to people worldwide.

Brutal Attack

Mahfouz has not been universally admired, however. At one point, certain Islamic leaders became angered by Mahfouz's support for peace with Israel and by his novel *Children of Gebalawi,* in which God and the prophets appeared as characters. These leaders called for Mahfouz's death, and in 1994, he was stabbed outside his home by an Islamic extremist. Mahfouz recovered, and his attacker was caught and executed. Afterward, Mahfouz continued to write, coming out with a new book on his 89th birthday.

Other Works

Miramar
Arabian Nights and Days

Background

A Century of Growth Nearly all of the stories that Naguib Mahfouz has written take place in Cairo, where the author has lived his entire life. In Mahfouz's lifetime, which spans most of the 1900s, Cairo has undergone vast changes, growing tremendously in both population and land area. In 1910, a year before Mahfouz was born, Cairo's population was 700,000. By the end of the century, more than 12 million people lived in the metropolitan area. Nearby cities had become absorbed as suburbs, and once-rural areas between the Nile River and the pyramids were as crowded as the city's center. In "Half a Day," Mahfouz hints, in an unusual way, at the degree of change he has seen in Cairo over his lifetime.

Because Cairo's history dates back more than 1,000 years, the city is a curious blend of the old and the new. The old quarters of the city have winding alleys with open-front shops, outdoor markets selling spices and rugs, and mosques built centuries ago. Modern sections feature Western-style high-rise apartment buildings, hotels, and shops.

Modern-day Cairo

Connect to Your Life

"Half a Day" begins with the narrator remembering his first day of school as a young boy. In what ways have you changed since your first day of school? In what ways has your community changed? Share your responses in a class discussion.

Focus Your Reading

LITERARY ANALYSIS: TITLE AND THEME
As you know, a **theme** is a central idea or message of a literary work. Often the **title** of a story or a poem gives you a clue to the work's theme. The title of Wislawa Szymborska's poem "The End and the Beginning," for example, suggests the new beginning that follows the end of a war. As you read "Half a Day," ask yourself, How does the title relate to the meaning of the story? What idea is the title referring to?

ACTIVE READING: CONNECTING WITH CHARACTERS
"Half a Day" is set in Cairo at an unspecified time in the past. Like some other stories you have read, it describes a culture that may be very different from your own. Still, you can make connections with the characters, because human beings share many of the same feelings and experiences despite cultural differences.

📖 **READER'S NOTEBOOK** As you read "Half a Day," try to identify with the feelings and experiences of the main character. Then, after you've finished the story, complete the following sentence in your notebook:

_____ in this

story reminds me of a time in my life when

_____.

WORDS TO KNOW **Vocabulary Preview**

cleave   intricate   majestically   misgiving   unmarred

Half a Day

Naguib Mahfouz

Translated by Denys Johnson-Davies

I proceeded alongside my father, clutching his right hand, running to keep up with the long strides he was taking. All my clothes were new: the black shoes, the green school uniform, and the red tarboosh.[1] My delight in my new clothes, however, was not altogether unmarred, for this was no feast day but the day on which I was to be cast into school for the first time.

My mother stood at the window watching our progress, and I would turn toward her from time to time, as though appealing for help. We walked along a street lined with gardens; on both sides were extensive fields planted with crops, prickly pears, henna trees,[2] and a few date palms.

"Why school?" I challenged my father openly. "I shall never do anything to annoy you."

"I'm not punishing you," he said, laughing. "School's not a punishment. It's the factory that makes useful men out of boys. Don't you want to be like your father and brothers?"

I was not convinced. I did not believe there was really any good to be had in tearing me away from the intimacy of my home and throwing me into this building that stood at the end of the road like some huge, high-walled fortress, exceedingly stern and grim.

When we arrived at the gate we could see the courtyard, vast and crammed full of boys and girls. "Go in by yourself," said my father, "and join them. Put a smile on your face and be a good example to others."

I hesitated and clung to his hand, but he gently pushed me from him. "Be a man," he said. "Today you truly begin life. You will find me waiting for you when it's time to leave."

I took a few steps, then stopped and looked but saw nothing. Then the faces of boys and girls came into view. I did not know a single one of them, and none of them knew me. I felt I was a stranger who had lost his way. But glances of curiosity were directed toward me, and one boy approached and asked, "Who brought you?"

"My father," I whispered.

"My father's dead," he said quite simply.

I did not know what to say. The gate was closed, letting out a pitiable screech. Some of the children burst into tears. The bell rang. A lady

---

1. **tarboosh** (tär-bōōsh'): a felt hat with a tassel on top.
2. **prickly pears, henna trees:** Prickly pears are cacti with pear-shaped, edible fruit. Henna trees are small, thorny trees with white flowers.

Retrato del pintor [Portrait of the painter] (1994), Diego Maqueria. Wax on paper.
Photograph copyright © Kactus Foto, Santiago, Chile/SuperStock, Inc.

We submitted to the facts, and this submission brought a sort of contentment. Living beings were drawn to other living beings, and from the first moments my heart made friends with such boys as were to be my friends and fell in love with such girls as I was to be in love with, so that it seemed my misgivings had had no basis. I had never imagined school would have this rich variety. We played all sorts of different games: swings, the vaulting horse, ball games. In the music room we chanted our first songs. We also had our first intro-duction to language. We saw a globe of the Earth, which revolved and showed the various continents and countries. We started learning the numbers. The story of the Creator of the universe was read to us, we were told of His present world and of His Hereafter, and we heard examples of what He said. We ate delicious food, took a little nap, and woke up to go on with friendship and love, play and learning.

As our path revealed itself to us, however, we did not find it as totally sweet and unclouded as we had presumed. Dust-laden winds and unex-pected accidents came about suddenly, so we had

came along, followed by a group of men. The men began sorting us into ranks. We were formed into an intricate pattern in the great courtyard surrounded on three sides by high buildings of several floors; from each floor we were over-looked by a long balcony roofed in wood.

"This is your new home," said the woman. "Here too there are mothers and fathers. Here there is everything that is enjoyable and beneficial to knowledge and religion. Dry your tears and face life joyfully."

to be watchful, at the ready, and very patient. It was not all a matter of playing and fooling around. Rivalries could bring about pain and hatred or give rise to fighting. And while the lady would sometimes smile, she would often scowl and scold. Even more frequently she would resort to physical punishment.

In addition, the time for changing one's mind was over and gone and there was no question of ever returning to the paradise of home. Nothing lay ahead of us but exertion, struggle, and perseverance. Those who were able took advantage of the opportunities for success and happiness that presented themselves amid the worries.

The bell rang announcing the

passing of the day and the end of work. The throngs of children rushed toward the gate, which was opened again. I bade farewell to friends and sweethearts and passed through the gate. I peered around but found no trace of my father, who had promised to be there. I stepped aside to wait. When I had waited for a long time without avail, I decided to return home on my own. After I had taken a few steps, a middle-aged man passed by, and I realized at once that I knew him. He came toward me, smiling, and shook me by the hand, saying, "It's a long time since we last met—how are you?"

With a nod of my head, I agreed with him and in turn asked, "And you, how are you?"

"As you can see, not all that good, the Almighty be praised!"

Again he shook me by the hand and went off. I proceeded a few steps, then came to a startled halt. Good Lord! Where was the street lined with gardens? Where had it disappeared to? When did all these vehicles invade it? And when did all these hordes of humanity come to rest upon its surface? How did these hills of refuse come to cover its sides? And where were the fields that bordered it?

High buildings had taken over, the street surged with children, and disturbing noises shook the air. At various points stood conjurers[3] showing off their tricks and making snakes appear from baskets. Then there was a band announcing the opening of a circus, with clowns and weight lifters walking in front. A line of trucks carrying central security troops crawled <u>majestically</u> by. The siren of a fire engine shrieked, and it was not clear how the vehicle would <u>cleave</u> its way to reach the blazing fire. A battle raged between a taxi driver and his passenger, while the passenger's wife called out for help and no one answered. Good God! I was in a daze. My head spun. I almost went crazy. How could all this have happened in half a day, between early morning and sunset? I would find the answer at home with my father. But where was my home? I could see only tall buildings and hordes of people. I hastened on to the crossroads between the gardens and Abu Khoda.[4] I had to cross Abu Khoda to reach my house, but the stream of cars would not let up. The fire engine's siren was shrieking at full pitch as it moved at a snail's pace, and I said to myself, "Let the fire take its pleasure in what it consumes." Extremely irritated, I wondered when I would be able to cross. I stood there a long time, until the young lad employed at the ironing shop on the corner came up to me. He stretched out his arm and said gallantly, "Grandpa, let me take you across." ❖

---

3. **conjurers** (kŏn′jər-ərz): trick players; magicians.

4. **Abu Khoda** (ə-bōō′ KHŏ′dä): a busy traffic area in Cairo.

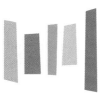

WORDS TO KNOW

majestically (mə-jĕs′tĭ-klē) *adv.* in a noble or stately way
cleave (klēv) *v.* to cut through; penetrate

COUNTING IN SEVENS

JUDITH WRIGHT

*Wright, a noted Australian poet, looks at the passage of time
from a woman's perspective.*

Seven ones are seven.
I can't remember that year
or what presents I was given.

Seven twos are fourteen.
5 That year I found my mind,
swore not to be what I had been.

Seven threes are twenty-one.
I was sailing my own sea,
first in love, the knots undone.

10 Seven fours are twenty-eight;
three false starts had come and gone;
my true love came, and not too late.

Seven fives are thirty-five.
In her cot my daughter lay,
15 real, miraculous, alive.

Seven sixes are forty-two.
I packed her sandwiches for school,
I loved my love and time came true.

Seven sevens are forty-nine.
20 Fruit loaded down my apple-tree,
near fifty years of life were mine.

Seven eights are fifty-six.
My lips still cold from a last kiss,
my fire was ash and charcoal-sticks.

25 Seven nines are sixty-three, seven tens are
        seventy,
Who would that old woman be?
She will remember being me,
but what she is I cannot see.

Yet with every added seven,
30 some strange present I was given.

Connect to the Literature

1. What Do You Think?
When did you first notice something unusual about the end of the story?

Comprehension Check
- How does the narrator feel about going to school for the first time?
- What is his experience at school like?
- What changes does the narrator notice after he leaves school?

Think Critically

2. How do you account for the changes the narrator witnesses after leaving school?

3. In your opinion, what does the school **symbolize** in this story?

THINK ABOUT
- the schoolteacher's advice to "dry your tears and face life joyfully"
- what happens to the narrator at the school
- what has changed when the narrator leaves the school

4. Do you see any other **symbols** in the story? Explain.

5. ACTIVE READING: CONNECTING WITH CHARACTERS
Share with a partner the sentence you completed in your 📖 **READER'S NOTEBOOK.** What universal human experiences does this story describe?

Extend Interpretations

6. Critic's Corner The critic Liz Brent has written that in "Half a Day" Mahfouz portrays the human experience of life as one "of being cast out of a paradise of early childhood into a harsh world of struggle and pain" to which we must submit. Do you agree that this is how Mahfouz portrays life?

7. Comparing Texts How is the narrator's experience of time in "Half a Day" similar to the speaker's in "Counting in Sevens"?

8. Connect to Life In your own life so far, have you experienced time as passing quickly or slowly? Explain.

LITERARY ANALYSIS: TITLE AND THEME

The **title** of a literary work often hints at the work's **theme,** or central message. One way to discover the theme of a literary work is to think about what happens to the main characters and to relate those experiences to the title. In "Half a Day," the narrator enters school as a young boy. After leaving the school at the end of the day, he discovers that the world has changed drastically. In this context, what does "half a day" represent? What does this story suggest about time and a person's life?

Cooperative Learning Activity
Get together with a small group of classmates and discuss the theme of "Half a Day." See if you can come up with another title that also hints at the theme. Share your group's title with the rest of the class.

Choices & CHALLENGES

Writing Options

1. School Memory In a personal narrative, describe a vivid memory you have of your early school days.

2. Interpretive Essay Some critics see "Half a Day" as an allegory—a story in which characters, events, and objects represent abstract ideas. Think again about the symbols you saw in the story. Write an interpretive essay explaining how "Half a Day" is an allegory. Tell what the narrator, the school, the teacher, the ringing bell, and other elements in the story might stand for.

Writing Handbook
See page R33: Analysis.

Activities & Explorations

1. Life on the Line Create an illustrated time line that reflects how a person's sense of the passage of time varies at different stages of life. ~ ART

2. Wordless Portrayal Present a pantomime in which you portray the narrator as a young boy going off to school and as an old man leaving the school. ~ PERFORMING

Inquiry & Research

1. Present-Day Cairo Find photographs, film footage, or travelers' descriptions of present-day Cairo. Bring them to class and discuss whether they match Mahfouz's description of Cairo at the end of "Half a Day."

2. More Mahfouz Read another short story by Mahfouz, either from *God's World* or from *The Time and the Place*. Report on it to your classmates, comparing and contrasting it with "Half a Day."

RESEARCH STARTER
CLASSZONE.COM

Vocabulary in Action

EXERCISE: CONTEXT CLUES Write the vocabulary word that best completes each sentence.

1. The classroom floor was freshly waxed and _____ before the first students entered.
2. The first-grade teacher strode _____ into the room, like a queen.
3. One child was full of _____, fearing that he would not learn to read.
4. Could that _____ pattern of lines on the paper actually be his last name?
5. At the end of the day, he would _____ a path through a crowd to reach his mother's waiting arms.

Building Vocabulary
For an in-depth lesson on using context clues, see page 674.

January First

OCTAVIO PAZ

Translated by *Elizabeth Bishop*

1
1 | 2 | 3 | 4 | 5 | 6 | 7 | 8 | 9 |10|11|12|13|14|15|16|17|18|19|20|21|22|23|24|25|26|27|28|29|30|31 | 1 | 2 | 3 | 4 | 5 | 6 | 7 | 8 | 9 |10|11|12|13|14|15|16|17|18

Octavio Paz
1914–1998

Early Promise Octavio Paz, who in 1990 would be the first Mexican to receive the Nobel Prize in literature, loved books from the time he was a young child. Paz was born on the outskirts of Mexico City during the Mexican Revolution. The war left his family in financial ruin, but Paz remembered his childhood as a kind of paradise: "I lived . . . in an old dilapidated house that had a junglelike garden and a great room full of books. . . . The garden soon became the center of my world; the library, an enchanted cave." He began writing as a teenager, publishing his first poem at 16 and his first book of poems, *Forest Moon,* at 19.

Mexican Voice Paz went on to become Mexico's most important modern writer in both poetry and prose. His travels to Europe, the United States, and Asia brought many influences to bear on his writing. Many of his works also reflect the influences of Spanish and Indian cultures on Mexican identity. His first prose work, *The Labyrinth of Solitude* (1950), was an exploration of Mexican culture and thought that brought him international recognition. Poetry was the most vital form of literature for Paz, however. In his poetry he sought to create unity out of the differences, divisions, and contradictions present in modern life. In his Nobel lecture, he observed, "All our ventures and exploits, all our acts and dreams, are bridges designed to overcome the separation and reunite us with the world and our fellow beings."

Other Works
Sun Stone
A Tree Within

In the poem you are about to read, the speaker faces the beginning of a new year. Paz uses familiar as well as unexpected images, words, and ideas to explore what it is like to enter a new day and year. As you read the poem, ask yourself the following questions:

1. *What does the speaker expect to do on January first?*
2. *What discoveries does the speaker make when he wakes up on the first day of the new year?*

*T*he year's doors open
like those of language,
toward the unknown.
Last night you told me:

5   tomorrow
we shall have to think up signs,
sketch a landscape, fabricate a plan
on the double page
of day and paper.

10   Tomorrow, we shall have to invent,
once more,
the reality of this world.

I opened my eyes late.
For a second of a second

15   I felt what the Aztec felt,
on the crest of the promontory,
lying in wait
for time's uncertain return
through cracks in the horizon.

20   But no, the year had returned.
It filled all the room
and my look almost touched it.
Time, with no help from us,

15 the Aztec: In the 15th and 16th centuries, the Aztec people inhabited the area that is now central and southern Mexico. They developed a complex calendar based on a cycle of 52 years. The beginning of every cycle was marked with ceremonies and celebrations.

16 promontory (prŏm′ən-tôr′ē): a high point of land jutting out into a body of water.

had placed
25   in exactly the same order as yesterday
houses in the empty street,
snow on the houses,
silence on the snow.

You were beside me,
30   still asleep.
The day had invented you
but you hadn't yet accepted
being invented by the day.
—Nor possibly my being invented, either.
35   You were in another day.

You were beside me
and I saw you, like the snow,
asleep among appearances.
Time, with no help from us,
40   invents houses, streets, trees
and sleeping women.

When you open your eyes
we'll walk, once more,
among the hours and their inventions,
45   and lingering among appearances,
we'll bear witness to time and its conjugations.
We'll open the doors of the day,
and enter the unknown.

46 conjugations (kŏn′jə-gā′shənz):
combinations.

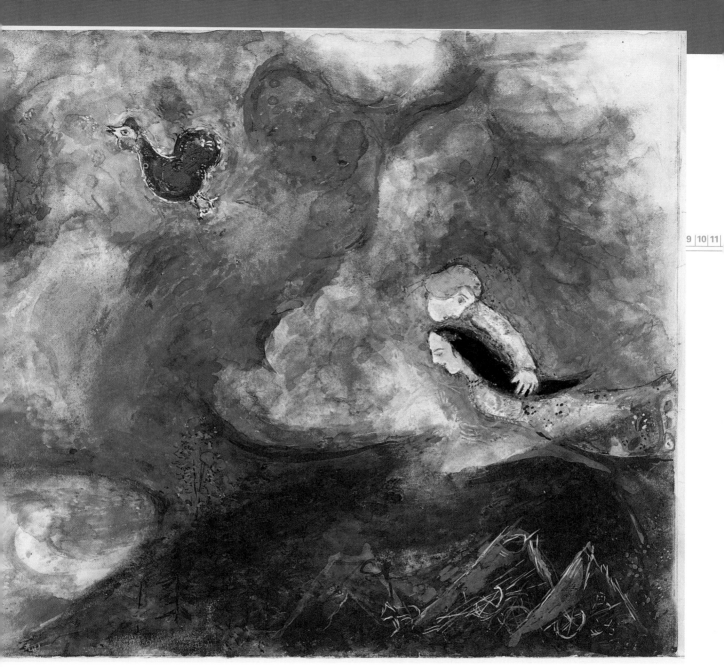

Aleko and Zemphira by Moonlight decor for *Aleko (Scene I)* (1942), Marc Chagall. Gouache, wash, brush, and pencil, 15 1/8″ × 22 1/2″ (38.4 cm × 57.1 cm). The Museum of Modern Art, New York. Acquired through the Lillie P. Bliss Bequest. Photography copyright © 2001 The Museum of Modern Art, New York.

Reflect and Assess

What did you learn about contemporary literature in Unit Seven, Part 3? Did you find the writing easier or more difficult to read than the writing of earlier eras? Use the following activities to clarify your thoughts.

Reflecting on the Literature

Critics and Dreamers This part was titled "Critics and Dreamers: Contemporary Nobel Prize Winners." Of the writers in this part, which would you classify as the critics? What are they criticizing? Which would you classify as the dreamers? What do they imagine? Create a chart that classifies the writers and explains why they belong in either category.

Reviewing Literary Concepts

Analyzing Styles Of the writers in this part, whose style appealed to you most? On a sheet of paper, name the writer and describe elements that contribute to his or her particular style, such as diction, tone, and figurative language. Then name the writer from Part 3 whose style is most different from this writer's, in your opinion. Note how their styles are different. Then compare your choices with your classmates'.

🗀 Building Your Portfolio

Writing Options Look back at the Writing Options you completed for this part, particularly any comparison-and-contrast or interpretive essays. Compare one of these with a similar assignment you did at the beginning of the year. Attach a cover sheet to the recent assignment, explaining how it shows your growth as a writer. Then place the work in your final **Presentation Portfolio.** 🗀

Self ASSESSMENT

📖 **READER'S NOTEBOOK**

In your own words, define each of the following terms or names. If you are unsure of any, go back through Part 3 or consult the **Glossary of Literary Terms** (page R91).

Alfred Nobel	symbol
apartheid	ode
Wole Soyinka	tone
magical realism	Pablo Neruda
first-person point of view	
postcolonial writing	

Setting GOALS

What reading and writing goals would you like to set for yourself for next year?

Extend Your *Reading*

LITERATURE CONNECTIONS
Kaffir Boy

MARK MATHABANE

In this memoir, Mathabane recalls growing up under apartheid in Johannesburg in the 1960s and 1970s. After his father is arrested and forced to labor on a white-owned farm, Mathabane's mother is determined that her son will get an education. Mathabane excels in school, but it is tennis—and the inspiration of players Arthur Ashe and Stan Smith—that ultimately help him escape apartheid.

These are some of the thematically related readings that are provided along with *Kaffir Boy*:

from **Makes Me Wanna Holler**
NATHAN MCCALL

A Message from Nelson Mandela to the Youth of America
NELSON MANDELA

LITERATURE CONNECTIONS
A Place Where the Sea Remembers

SANDRA BENÍTEZ

This best-selling magical realist novel is set in Santiago, Mexico. It consists of short, interrelated narratives, each focused on a single character. The work depicts the triumphs and tragedies of common people—a flower seller, a healer, a fisherman, a teacher, a midwife—whose lives are interwoven by fate and passion.

These are some of the thematically related readings provided along with *A Place Where the Sea Remembers*:

Talking to the Dead
JUDITH ORTIZ COFER

Death of a Young Son by Drowning
MARGARET ATWOOD

An Astrologer's Day
R. K. NARAYAN

And Even *More* . . .

Books
The Vintage Book of Contemporary World Poetry
EDITED BY J. D. MCCLATCHY
This is a collection of verse by 83 major poets, including the Nobel Prize winners in Unit 7 and others such as Czeslaw Milosz, Derek Walcott, and Seamus Heaney.

Short Stories by Latin American Women:
The Magic and the Real EDITED BY CELIA C. DE ZAPATA
Isabel Allende and Luisa Valenzuela are among the contributors to this anthology of magical realist fiction.

Other Media
The García Márquez Collection
Six made-for-TV films based on stories by Gabriel García Márquez, including "A Very Old Man with Enormous Wings." In Spanish with English subtitles.
Fox Lorber (VIDEOCASSETTES)

The Nobel Prize

BURTON FELDMAN

Feldman traces the history of the Nobel Prize and examines the controversies surrounding the award. In his chapter on the Nobel Prize in literature, he groups winners by the language in which they wrote and questions why many great writers were overlooked.

Student *Resource Bank*

Reading Handbook R2
Reading for Different Purposes R2
Reading for Information R4
Functional Reading R14
Enriching Your Vocabulary R16

Writing Handbook R18
The Writing Process R18
Building Blocks of Good Writing R22
Descriptive Writing R27
Narrative Writing R29
Explanatory Writing R31
Persuasive Writing R35
Research Report Writing R37
Business Writing R43

Communication Handbook R45
Inquiry and Research R45
Study Skills and Strategies R47
Critical Thinking R49
Speaking and Listening R50
Viewing and Representing R52

Grammar Handbook R55
Quick Reference: Parts of Speech R55
Nouns R56
Pronouns R57
Verbs R59
Modifiers R62
Prepositions, Conjunctions, and Interjections R64
Quick Reference: The Sentence and Its Parts R66

The Sentence and Its Parts R67
Phrases R69
Verbals and Verbal Phrases R69
Clauses R71
The Structure of Sentences R72
Writing Complete Sentences R73
Subject-Verb Agreement R74
Quick Reference: Punctuation R77
Quick Reference: Capitalization R79
Little Rules That Make a Big Difference R80
Commonly Confused Words R84
Grammar Glossary R85

Academic Reading Handbook R91
Analyzing Text Features R91
Understanding Visuals R95
Recognizing Text Structures R99
Reading in the Content Areas R109
Reading Beyond the Classroom R115

Glossary of Literary Terms R125

Glossary of Words to Know in English and Spanish R144

Pronunciation Key R155

Index of Fine Art R156

Index of Skills R163

Index of Titles and Authors R176

Reading for Different Purposes

You read for many different reasons. In a single day, you might read a short story for fun, a textbook for information to help you pass a test, and a weather map to find out if it will rain. For every type of reading, there are specific strategies that can help you understand and remember the material. This handbook will help you become a better reader in school, at home, and on the job.

Reading Literature

Before Reading

- Set a **purpose** for reading. What do you want to learn? Are you reading as part of an assignment or for fun? Establishing a purpose will help you focus.
- **Preview** the work by looking at the title and any images and captions. Try to **predict** what the work will be about.
- Ask yourself if you can **connect** the subject matter with what you already know.

During Reading

- **Check your understanding** of what you read. Can you restate the plot in your own words?
- Try to **connect** what you're reading to your own life. Have you experienced similar events or emotions?

- **Question** what's happening. You may wonder about events and characters' feelings.
- **Visualize,** or create a mental picture of, what the author describes.
- **Pause** from time to time to predict what will happen next.

After Reading

- **Review** your predictions. Were they correct?
- Try to **summarize** the work, expressing the **main idea** or the basic plot.
- **Reflect** on and evaluate what you have read. Did the reading fulfill your purpose?
- To **clarify** your understanding, write down opinions or thoughts about the work, or discuss it with someone.

Reading for Information

Set a Purpose for Reading

- Decide why you are reading the material—to study for a test, to do research, or to find out more about a topic that interests you.
- Use your **purpose** to determine how detailed your **notes** will be.

Look for Design Features

- Look at the **title** and at **subheads, boldfaced words** or phrases, **boxed text,** and any other text that is highlighted in some way.
- Use these **text organizers** to help you preview the text and identify the main ideas.
- Study photographs, maps, charts, and captions.

Notice Text Structures and Patterns

- Does the text make **comparisons?** Does it describe **causes and effects?** Is there a **sequence** of events?
- Look for **signal words** such as *same, different, because, first,* and *then* to help you see the organizational pattern.

Read Slowly and Carefully

- **Take notes** on the main ideas. State the information in your own words.
- Map the information by using a word web or another **graphic organizer.**
- Notice **unfamiliar words.** These are sometimes defined in the text.
- If there are **questions** accompanying the text, be sure that you can answer them.

Evaluate the Information

- Think about what you have read. Does the text make sense? Is it complete?
- **Summarize** the information—give the main points in just a few words.

Functional Reading

Identify the Audience, Source, and Purpose

- Look for clues that tell you whom the document is for. Is there an address or a title? Does the information in the document affect you?
- Look for clues that tell you who created the document. Is the source likely to be reliable?
- Think about the **purpose** of the document. Is it designed to show you how to do something? to warn you about something? to tell you about community events?

Read Carefully

- Notice **headings** or **rules** that separate one section from another.
- Look for numbers or letters that signal steps in a **sequence.** If you are reading directions, read them all the way through at least once before beginning the steps.
- Examine any charts, photographs, or other **graphics** and their captions.
- **Reread** complex instructions if necessary.

Evaluate the Information

- Think about whether you have found the information you need.
- Look for telephone numbers, street addresses, or e-mail addresses of places where you could find more information.

Reading for Information

Reading informational materials—such as textbooks, magazines, newspapers, and Web pages—requires special skills. As you read these materials, look for text organizers that can guide you to the main ideas, facts, terms, and names. Then think about how the information is organized. Using these strategies will help you read informational materials more quickly and with a clearer understanding.

Text Organizers

Look for headings, large or dark type, pictures, or drawings that signal the most important information on the page. These special features, called **text organizers,** help you understand and remember what you read.

Strategies for Reading

A First, look at the **title** and any **subheads.** These will tell you the main ideas.

B Many textbooks include a list of **objectives** or **key terms** at the start of each lesson. Keep these in mind as you read. They will help you focus on the most important facts and details.

C **Key terms** are often boldfaced or underlined where they first appear in the text. Be sure that you understand what they mean.

D Notice any **special features,** such as extended quotations or sidebar articles. These provide important details and can help you visualize the information.

E Look at the **visuals**—photographs, illustrations, charts, maps, time lines—and read their **captions.** Visuals often give information that is not in the main text.

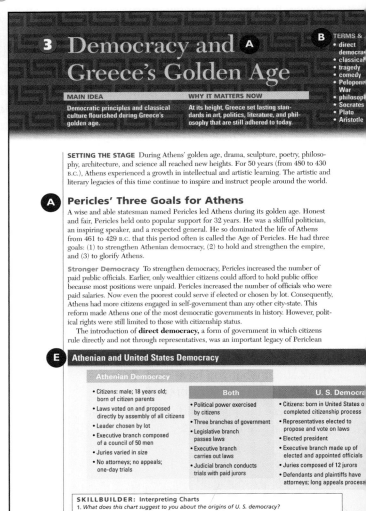

3 Democracy and Greece's Golden Age **A**

B TERMS &
• direct democracy
• classical
• tragedy
• comedy
• Peloponnesian War
• philosophy
• Socrates
• Plato
• Aristotle

MAIN IDEA
Democratic principles and classical culture flourished during Greece's golden age.

WHY IT MATTERS NOW
At its height, Greece set lasting standards in art, politics, literature, and philosophy that are still adhered to today.

SETTING THE STAGE During Athens' golden age, drama, sculpture, poetry, philosophy, architecture, and science all reached new heights. For 50 years (from 480 to 430 B.C.), Athens experienced a growth in intellectual and artistic learning. The artistic and literary legacies of this time continue to inspire and instruct people around the world.

A **Pericles' Three Goals for Athens**

A wise and able statesman named Pericles led Athens during its golden age. Honest and fair, Pericles held onto popular support for 32 years. He was a skillful politician, an inspiring speaker, and a respected general. He so dominated the life of Athens from 461 to 429 B.C. that this period often is called the Age of Pericles. He had three goals: (1) to strengthen Athenian democracy, (2) to hold and strengthen the empire, and (3) to glorify Athens.

Stronger Democracy To strengthen democracy, Pericles increased the number of paid public officials. Earlier, only wealthier citizens could afford to hold public office because most positions were unpaid. Pericles increased the number of officials who were paid salaries. Now even the poorest could serve if elected or chosen by lot. Consequently, Athens had more citizens engaged in self-government than any other city-state. This reform made Athens one of the most democratic governments in history. However, political rights were still limited to those with citizenship status.

The introduction of **direct democracy,** a form of government in which citizens rule directly and not through representatives, was an important legacy of Periclean

E **Athenian and United States Democracy**

Athenian Democracy	Both	U. S. Democracy
• Citizens: male; 18 years old; born of citizen parents	• Political power exercised by citizens	• Citizens: born in United States or completed citizenship process
• Laws voted on and proposed directly by assembly of all citizens	• Three branches of government	• Representatives elected to propose and vote on laws
• Leader chosen by lot	• Legislative branch passes laws	• Elected president
• Executive branch composed of a council of 50 men	• Executive branch carries out laws	• Executive branch made up of elected and appointed officials
• Juries varied in size	• Judicial branch conducts trials with paid jurors	• Juries composed of 12 jurors
• No attorneys; no appeals; one-day trials		• Defendants and plaintiffs have attorneys; long appeals process

SKILLBUILDER: Interpreting Charts
1. *What does this chart suggest to you about the origins of U. S. democracy?*
2. *What is the main difference between Athenian democracy and democracy in the United States?*

More Strategies for Reading Textbooks

- Before you begin the text, read any **questions** that appear at the end of the lesson or chapter. These will help you focus your reading.

- Read slowly and carefully. If you see an unfamiliar word and can't find a definition in the text or in a marginal note, check the **glossary** or a dictionary. Look for **pronunciation guides** as you read.

- Take **notes** as you read. These will help you understand new ideas and terms. Review your notes before a test to jog your memory.

- You may want to take notes in the form of a **graphic organizer,** such as a cause-and-effect chart or a sequence chart. The graphic organizer shown in the example is a comparison-and-contrast chart.

Athens. Few other city-states practiced this style of government. In Athens, male citizens who served in the assembly established all the important government policies that affected the polis. In a speech for the slain soldiers killed in the first year of the Peloponnesian War, Pericles expressed his great pride in Athenian democracy:

D **HISTORY MAKERS**

A VOICE FROM THE PAST

Our constitution is called a democracy because power is in the hands not of a minority but of the whole people. When it is a question of settling private disputes, everyone is equal before the law; when it is a question of putting one person before another in positions of public responsibility, what counts is not membership in a particular class, but the actual ability which the man possesses. No one, so long as he has it in him to be of service to the state, is kept in political obscurity because of poverty.

PERICLES, *Funeral Oration*

Athenian Empire Pericles tried to enlarge the wealth and power of Athens. He used the money from the Delian League's treasury to build Athens' 200-ship navy into the strongest in the Mediterranean. A strong navy was important because it helped Athens strengthen the safety of its empire. Athenian prosperity depended on gaining access to its surrounding waterways. It needed overseas trade to obtain supplies of grain and other raw materials.

Glorifying Athens Pericles also used money from the empire to beautify Athens. Without the Delian League's approval, he persuaded the Athenian assembly to vote huge sums of the league's money to buy gold, ivory, and marble. Still more money went to a small army of artisans who worked for 15 years (447–432 B.C.) to build one of architecture's noblest works—the Parthenon.

Greek Styles in Art

The Parthenon, a masterpiece of craftsmanship and design, was not novel in style. Rather, Greek artisans built the 23,000-square-foot building in the traditional style that had been used to create Greek temples for 200 years. In ancient times, this temple built to honor Athena contained examples of Greek art that set standards for future generations of artists around the world.

Greek Sculpture Within the Parthenon stood a giant statue of Athena, the goddess of wisdom and the protector of Athens. Pericles entrusted much of the work on the temple, including the statue of Athena, to the sculptor Phidias (FIDH-ee-uhs). The great statue of the goddess not only contained precious materials such as gold and ivory, it stood 38 feet tall!

Phidias and other sculptors during this golden age aimed to create figures that were graceful, strong, and perfectly formed. Their faces showed neither laughter nor anger, only serenity. Greek sculptors also tried to capture the grace of the idealized human body in motion. Their values of order, balance, and proportion became the standard of what is called **classical art.** **C**

Classical works such as the Parthenon and the statue of Athena showcased the pride that Athenians had for their city. (See History Through Art, page 122.)

Greek Drama

The Greeks invented drama and built the first theaters in the west. Theatrical productions in Athens were both an expression of civic pride and a tribute to the gods.

Pericles
4947–429 B.C.

Pericles came from a rich and high-ranking noble family. His aristocratic father had led the Athenian assembly and fought at the Battle of Salamis in the Persian Wars. His mother was the niece of Cleisthenes, an influential statesman.

Well known for his political achievements as a leader of Athens, some historians say Pericles the man was harder to know. One historian wrote,

[Pericles] no doubt, was a lonely man. Among the politicians, including his supporters, he had no friend. He avoided all social activity . . . [and] he only went out [of his home] for official business. . . .

H HISTORY
ishing
pinion
e do you
icles'
at
mocracy
ands of
eople"?

Strategies for Reading

A Read the **title** and any other **headings** to get an idea of what the article is about and how it is organized.

B As you read the main text, notice any **quotations.** Who is quoted? Is the person a reliable source on the subject?

C Notice text that is set off in some way, such as a passage in a **different typeface.** A quotation or statistic that sums up the article is sometimes presented in this way.

D Study **visuals,** such as graphs, charts, maps, and photographs. Read their captions and make sure you know how they relate to the main text.

A Summer Jobs Let Teens Cash In

by Kirsti MacPherson
Staff Writer

B "I am so excited to be working this summer," says 15-year-old Brianna Mason. "I already have plans for the money. Some of it I'll save for college, but I'm also going to get some new clothes and CDs."

Like many teenagers, Mason will increase the number of hours she works once summer vacation begins. According to this year's Summer Jobs Survey, conducted by Junior Achievement, Inc., the most popular summer jobs for teens are in retail sales (41 percent of respondents), restaurants and fast-food establishments (20 percent), offices (14 percent), baby-sitting (6 percent), arts and entertainment (4 percent), and manual trades (4 percent). The survey questioned 659 teenagers nationwide.

Teenagers struggle with the desire to spend and the need to save, just as other workers do. The Junior Achievement survey found that students working during the summer saved about a third of their earnings—about 17 times what the typical adult saved! Since parents pay for most food, clothing, and shelter needs, many teens can save for higher education, cars, and other big-ticket items.

A summer job can make a teenager feel independent and accomplished—and tired. "When you work so many hours in the summer, getting back to school is kind of a relief," Mason confesses.

C *Students working during the summer saved about a third of their earnings.*

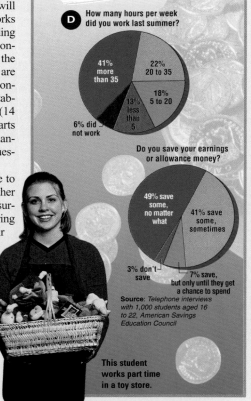

D How many hours per week did you work last summer?

- 41% more than 35
- 22% 20 to 35
- 18% 5 to 20
- 13% less than 5
- 6% did not work

Do you save your earnings or allowance money?

- 49% save some, no matter what
- 41% save some, sometimes
- 3% don't save
- 7% save, but only until they get a chance to spend

Source: Telephone interviews with 1,000 students aged 16 to 22, American Savings Education Council

This student works part time in a toy store.

Reading a Web Page

Strategies for Reading

(A) Look for the page's **Web address,** sometimes called a URL. If you think you will need to return to the page, write down the address or use the Web browser to "bookmark" the page or log it as a "favorite site."

(B) Read the **title** of the page to find out what topics the page covers. The blue page shown here is a search-engine page. It lists pages corresponding to responses to a student's search. The other page is one of the sites the search engine identified.

(C) Look for **menu bars** along the top, bottom, or side of the page. These tell you about other parts of the site. Instead of printing out every page of the site, read the text carefully and decide which pages contain information you need.

(D) Notice any **links** to related pages. Links are sometimes buttons or underlined words.

(E) Some sites have **interactive areas** where you can ask questions or tell the sites' creators what you think of their work.

Patterns of Organization

Reading any type of writing is easier if you understand how it is organized. A writer organizes ideas in a sequence, or structure, that helps the reader see how the ideas are related. Five important structures are the following:

- main idea and supporting details
- chronological order
- comparison and contrast
- cause and effect
- problem and solution

This page contains an overview of the five structures, which you will learn about in more detail on pages R9–R13. Each type has been represented graphically to help you see how ideas are organized in it.

Main Idea and Supporting Details

The main idea of a paragraph or a longer piece of writing is its most important point. Supporting details give more information about the main idea.

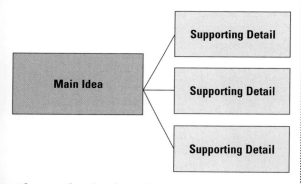

Chronological Order

Writing that is organized in chronological order presents events in the order in which they occur.

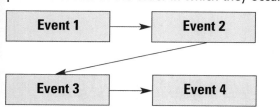

Comparison and Contrast

Comparison-and-contrast writing explains how two or more subjects are similar and how they are different.

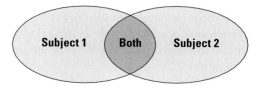

Cause and Effect

Cause-and-effect writing explains relationships between events. A cause is an event that gives rise to another event, called an effect. A cause may have more than one effect, and an effect may have more than one cause.

Single Cause with Multiple Effects

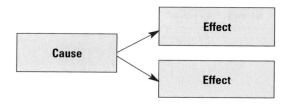

Multiple Causes with Single Effect

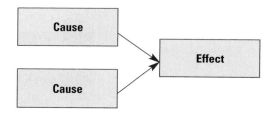

Problem and Solution

This type of writing describes a difficult issue and suggests at least one way of solving it. The writer provides reasons to support his or her solution.

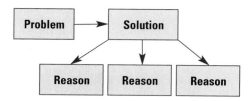

Main Idea and Supporting Details

The **main idea** of a paragraph is the basic point you should remember from your reading. The **supporting details** give you more information about the main idea. A main idea can be stated directly, or it can be implied. If it is stated, it can appear anywhere in the paragraph. Often it will be the first or the last sentence. An implied main idea is suggested by the details that are provided.

Strategies for Reading

- To find the **main idea,** ask, What is this paragraph about?
- To find **supporting details,** ask, What else do I learn about the main idea?

MODEL

Main Idea in the First Sentence

Main idea

Like his chosen last name, which means "man of steel" in Russian, Joseph Stalin was hard, cold, and dangerous. He began his climb to power in 1922, by installing his followers in key positions. By 1928, he had taken control of the Communist Party. The next year, he sent his main rival, Leon Trotsky, into exile. He then transformed the Soviet Union into a totalitarian state.

Supporting details

MODEL

Main Idea in the Last Sentence

Supporting details

A totalitarian government is a dictatorship in which one person has absolute control and one political party rules. The dictator uses propaganda (persuasive messages that often distort the truth) to convince people to support government policies. Citizens are expected to sacrifice their own goals for the good of the state and are severely punished if they show any opposition. A totalitarian government maintains its power by controlling every aspect of its citizens' lives.

Main idea

MODEL

Implied Main Idea

Implied main idea: Totalitarianism spread across the world during the 20th century.

In the 1920s and 1930s, Benito Mussolini in Italy and Adolf Hitler in Germany began creating their own totalitarian states. Hungary, Poland, Yugoslavia, Albania, Bulgaria, and Romania also fell into the hands of dictators. In 1949, Mao Zedong followed Stalin's example and established a totalitarian dictatorship in the People's Republic of China. Neighboring North Korea became a totalitarian state in 1948 and was ruled by the dictator Kim Il Sung until 1994.

PRACTICE AND APPLY

Less than 1 percent of the German population was made up of Jews. However, the Nazis blamed them for all of Germany's troubles. This led to a wave of anti-Jewish hatred across Germany. Beginning in 1933, the Nazis passed laws depriving Jews of most of their rights. Violence against Jews increased. On the night of November 9, 1938, Nazi mobs attacked Jews in their homes and destroyed thousands of Jewish-owned businesses. This rampage was called *Kristallnacht* ("night of broken glass"). The Nazis used a variety of methods in their quest to eliminate Jews from German life.

Read the paragraph above and then do the following activities:

1. Identify the main idea of the paragraph. Is it stated or implied?
2. List at least two details that support or expand on the main idea.

Chronological Order

Events discussed in **chronological order,** also called time order, are treated in the order they happen. Historical events are usually presented in chronological order. The steps of a process may also be presented this way.

Strategies for Reading

- Look for the **individual events or steps** in the sequence.
- Look for words or phrases that identify **time,** such as *in a year, three hours earlier, in 1957,* and *later.*
- Look for words that signal **order,** such as *first, afterward, then, before, finally,* and *next.*

MODEL

Time phrases

Event

Order words

    The development of language skills is one of the most important differences between humans and other living things. In an important study done in 1957, M. M. Lewis kept a record of his son's progress in understanding and speaking language—specifically, the word *flower.*

    The child's mother first named and pointed to different flowers in different situations. Over a period of time, the child watched, listened, pointed, and eventually named flowers himself.

    Lewis began the experiment when his son was 16 months and 12 days old. At that time, the mother brought the child close to a bowl of yellow jonquils and said, "Smell the pretty flowers." The child bent over and smelled the flowers, saying, "a . . . a . . . a." The next day, when the child was crawling around the room, his mother said, "Where are the flowers?" The child then crawled toward the jonquils and held out his hand.

    Three days later, in a room with pink tulips in a bowl, the mother said, "Baby, where's flowers?" Immediately after, the child pointed to the tulips. Five weeks later, however, the child did not respond to a picture of flowers in a book.

    When the child was 18 months and 14 days old, he saw a bowl of hyacinths through a window and responded, "fa, fa." When his mother wheeled him toward a bed of tulips the next day, asking "Where are the flowers?" he repeated "fa, fa" many times. Over the next week and a half, the child looked or reached toward a bowl of irises and a flowering cherry tree, naming both *fa fa.*

    After another month had passed, the child followed his mother's instructions to "pick a flower and give it to Daddy." Finally, three months later, aged 22 months and 26 days, the child was able to recognize images of flowers on a sugar cookie and on embroidered slippers and name them with his word for that object—*fa fa.* Although the child could not say *flower,* he recognized flowerlike things—in bowls, in gardens, on trees, and on cookies and shoes. With correction from his parents, the child eventually replaced *fa fa* with the word *flower.*

PRACTICE AND APPLY

Reread the model and then do the following activities:

1. List at least six words or phrases in the model that show order or time. Do not include those that have been identified for you.

2. Draw a time line beginning when the child was 16 months and 12 days old and ending when he was 22 months and 26 days old. Chart each event in his acquisition of language as described in the model.

Comparison and Contrast

Comparison-and-contrast writing explains how subjects are alike and different. This type of writing is usually organized by subject or by feature. In **subject organization,** the writer discusses one subject, then discusses the other. In **feature organization,** the writer compares a feature of one subject with the same feature of the other, then compares another feature of both, and so on.

Strategies for Reading

- Look for words and phrases that signal **comparisons,** such as *like, similarly, both, also,* and *in the same way.*
- Look for words and phrases that signal **contrasts,** such as *unlike, on the other hand, in contrast,* and *however.*

MODEL

> Whales are surprising creatures. Totally aquatic mammals, they belong to the order Cetacea, along with porpoises, dolphins, and narwhals. Cetaceans are divided into two main suborders, Mysticeti (baleen whales) and Odontoceti (toothed whales). Baleen whales include blue whales, humpback whales, right whales, and gray whales. Toothed whales include beaked whales, dolphins, porpoises, and narwhals.
>
> Baleen whales and toothed whales have many similar habits and behaviors. They live in oceans, seas, and rivers. Both types of whales often travel in groups, called schools or pods. They rise to the surface of the water to breathe through blowholes on the top of their head. Out of the water they are unable to move, and their lungs may be crushed by the weight of their bodies.
>
> Baleen whales and toothed whales have a number of physical differences, however. Adult baleen whales have baleen instead of teeth. Baleen is a thick curtain of hornlike plates that hang down from the roof

Subjects being compared

Comparison words and phrases

Contrast words and phrases

of the whales' mouth. Some baleen whales have teeth before birth, but these disappear as the young whale grows. The baleen acts as a filter that catches the small animals and plants that make up the whales' diet. Toothed whales, on the other hand, always have teeth. These teeth have sharp edges that are good for slicing and tearing the toothed whales' food—large fish, squid, and other whales.

Baleen whales have two blowholes. In contrast, toothed whales have only one blowhole. Baleen whale females tend to be larger than the males, while the opposite is true for toothed whales. Baleen whales have large tongues; toothed whales have small tongues. Unlike baleen whales, which usually have four digits in their flippers, toothed whales always have five digits.

Toothed whales figure out where they are by using reflected sound waves—a process called echolocation. However, baleen whales do not seem to navigate this way. Because whales spend much of their lives underwater, they are difficult to study, and they remain a fascinating mystery.

PRACTICE AND APPLY

Reread the model and then do the following activities:

1. Tell whether the model is organized by subject or by feature.

2. Draw a chart or a Venn diagram that shows at least three features that the writer compares or contrasts. (See the top of page R8 for an example of a Venn diagram.)

3. List at least six of the comparison and contrast words and phrases that the writer uses.

Cause and Effect

Cause-and-effect writing explains relationships between events. A **cause** is an event that brings about another event. An **effect** is something that happens as a result of the cause. A piece of cause-and-effect writing is usually organized in one of three ways:

1. starting with a cause or causes and explaining the effect(s)
2. starting with an effect or effects and explaining the cause(s)
3. describing a chain of causes and effects

Strategies for Reading

- To find the **effect** or **effects,** ask, What happened?
- To find the **cause** or **causes,** ask, Why did it happen?
- Look for words and phrases that signal **relationships between events,** such as *because, as a result, for that reason, so, consequently,* and *since.*

MODEL

Causes

Signal words

In the 1800s, new approaches to manufacturing caused dramatic changes around the world.

These sweeping changes, usually called the Industrial Revolution, began in the 1700s in Great Britain. First, inventors discovered ways to generate power by using the energy in flowing water and plentiful supplies of coal. They then created power-driven machinery. Because of these inventions, it was possible to create large quantities of manufactured goods.

Effects

As a result of improved nutrition, sanitation, and medical care, people lived longer, healthier lives. The resulting increase in population led to an increase in the number of workers available to work in the new factories. These businesses therefore grew, and their owners were able to build more factories, fund the

invention of more machines, and help industrialization spread.

One of the places where industrialization took hold was New England. This occurred because the United States had the necessary resources—rushing rivers, coal deposits, and many immigrants who were willing to work.

The first industry to be mechanized in the United States was the production of cloth. Samuel Slater, a British immigrant, established the first successful cloth mill in Rhode Island in 1793. Twenty years later, three Boston businessmen mechanized the entire process of manufacturing cloth. In 1822 they built a factory in Lowell, Massachusetts. Because of that factory, Lowell changed from a quiet village into a busy manufacturing center in only a few years.

Industrialization soon spread to other basic industries. Inventors discovered how to drill for oil and change it into fuel. A steel-making method called the Bessemer process was used to make steel from iron and coal cheaply and efficiently. These new uses for natural resources had lasting effects on the United States. A national network of railroads was established, new buildings and bridges sprang up, and new products—such as the tin-plated steel can, barbed wire, farm machinery, and the automobile— were invented.

PRACTICE AND APPLY

Reread the model and then do the following activities:

1. Identify the type of organization used in the model. (Choose from the three types listed at the beginning of this page.)
2. Create a list or chart that shows at least four causes mentioned in the model, along with their effects.
3. List at least four words and phrases the writer uses to signal causes and effects.

Problem and Solution

Problem-solution writing clearly presents the various aspects of a problem and offers a solution. Logical arguments are used to convince readers that the proposed solution will solve the problem.

Strategies for Reading

- To find the **problem,** ask, What is this writing about?
- To find the **solution,** ask, What suggestions does the writer offer to remedy the problem?
- Look for the **reasons** the writer gives to support the solution. Is the thinking behind them logical? Is the evidence presented strong and convincing?

MODEL

The sun rises over the Atlantic Ocean. Peach-colored rays shimmer on the crests of the waves as they tumble against the shore. Out for a brisk morning walk along the beach, you stop to enjoy the beauty—until you stumble over a discarded soft-drink can and step down hard on a sharp bottle cap. As you gaze along the sand, you wonder if it has been snowing, until you realize that those white patches are scraps of paper and plastic left by thoughtless picnickers. **Our parks and beaches are becoming garbage dumps.**

> **Problem**

It takes more than one person to create so much litter, and it will take more than one person to clean it up. **One solution is to organize a group of friends and neighbors into a "save-our-favorite-spot committee."** There are many advantages to this plan.

> **Solution**

First, almost anything is more fun if it's done with people you know and like. You might want to have everyone wear the same color T-shirt or a funny hat to draw the group members together. Second, although picking up trash is work, you can make a game

> **Reason**

of it by singing songs, telling jokes, or offering prizes to the people who find the most disgusting or the most creative pieces of trash.

Also, when a group of people take responsibility for their environment, other people notice. No one may pay attention to a solitary person picking up bottles and cans and papers, but one or two dozen happy, energetic people all working together and obviously having fun are going to send a strong message to anyone who sees them. "I don't want to be left out," many onlookers will think.

The first step in organizing such a cleanup group is identifying a park or beach or river that has become overrun with litter. Be sure to choose an area that can be cleared of debris in several hours. It's more important to do a thorough job of cleaning a local playground than to barely make a mark on a national forest.

Start out by recruiting people who you know well and who share your concern for the environment. If each of those people asks one or two others along, you'll soon have a large, willing work crew. You might even make some new friends.

Nothing succeeds like success, and your cleanup efforts will give rise to others. Go ahead and take the first step.

PRACTICE AND APPLY

Reread the model and then do the following activities:

1. List two reasons the writer gives to support the plan.
2. The fifth and sixth paragraphs give tips on how to organize a cleanup group. State two of the tips the writer suggests.

Functional Reading

Functional reading is reading to gain certain information, such as instructions for doing something. When you read a map, a memo, or a product manual, you are engaged in functional reading. These examples show how you can improve your functional-reading skills.

Transit Map

Strategies for Reading

A Read the **title** to learn what the map shows.

B Examine the **legend,** sometimes called a **key,** to find out what the symbols on the map mean.

C Study **geographic labels,** such as station and town names, so that you will know the specific stops on each route.

D Use the **compass rose** to determine direction. Some maps also include a **scale** to help you determine distance.

PRACTICE AND APPLY

Study the map and answer these questions:

1. What is the purpose of this map?

2. Explain what the symbols ⬤ and ♿ mean when used together.

3. Which stations on the Blue Line are accessible to commuters who use wheelchairs?

4. Does the Purple Line run north and south or east and west?

5. Is it possible to take the Orange Line from Henry Street to Anthony Street on a Sunday night? Why or why not?

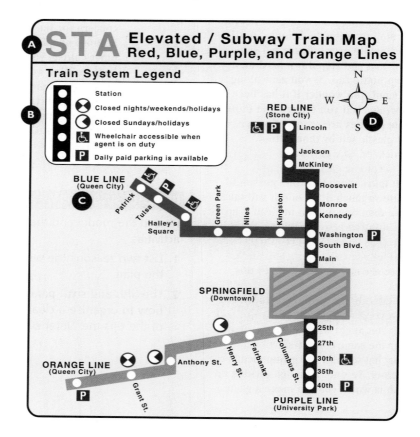

Workplace Document

Strategies for Reading

A Read the **title** to find out what the document is about. This document is a page from an employee manual.

B Notice any **introductory information** that tells who created the document or whom the document is for.

C Read any **charts** or other graphics carefully. A chart's **title** may be in the top row, in the column on the left, or in both places. The title may be in a different type size, color, or style.

D Look for **details** that explain what the document creator wants you to do.

E If you don't understand certain **terms** in the document, try to figure them out by analyzing their context (the words and sentences around the unknown terms), by breaking the words into parts, or by looking them up in a dictionary.

PRACTICE AND APPLY

Reread the document and answer these questions:

1. Who created this document?
2. Whom is the document for?
3. What is the purpose of the document?
4. What does *troubleshooting* mean?
5. According to the document, what should you do if the words you type do not appear on your computer screen?

A Computer Troubleshooting Guide

B All employees of the **Graziano Corporation** have access to the Computer Help Desk at extension 4315. If you have a problem with your computer or monitor, please follow these steps **BEFORE** calling the Help Desk.

Thank you,
The Help Desk Staff

C Problem	What to check
Nothing appears on computer monitor.	• Check that the power cord is properly connected. • Make sure the power switch is in the "On" position.
POWER and POWER SAVING lights are flashing.	• The monitor may have failed. Call the Help Desk immediately.
Picture is too dark.	• Adjust the dial marked "Brightness," located directly beneath the screen.
Picture is fuzzy.	• Adjust the dial marked "Contrast," located directly beneath the screen.
Picture bounces, or a wavy line moves through picture.	• Move electrical devices (heaters, fans, etc.) and magnets away from the computer. • If there is another computer in your workstation, move it away from this computer. • Move the computer away from the wall. Electrical wiring in the wall may be causing interference.
Typed words do not appear on screen.	• Make sure the keyboard and the computer are properly connected at both points.
E-mail program refuses to accept my password.	• Be sure you are entering the correct password. • Passwords are case sensitive. The computer does not consider a password in lowercase letters (jsmith430) the same as a password in capital letters (JSMITH430). Check the "Caps Lock" light in the upper right corner of your keyboard. If the light is on, press the "Caps Lock" button once and reenter your password.

Enriching Your Vocabulary

Even the best readers sometimes see unfamiliar words. These tips will help you figure out the meaning of a challenging word or phrase.

Use Context Clues

The **context** of a word consists of the punctuation marks, words, sentences, and paragraphs that surround the word. A word's context can give you important clues about its meaning.

> When I saw that my sister had spilled nail polish on my new jacket, I wasn't just angry—I was **apoplectic**. "Cindy! Get in here right now!" I yelled.

You can figure out from the context that *apoplectic* means "enraged" or "extremely angry."

See page 674 for more information on context clues, including definition, restatement, example, comparison, contrast, and inference clues.

Break Words into Parts

Breaking a word into its parts can help you understand it. When you see an unfamiliar word, try these strategies:

- Look for any prefixes or suffixes. Then remove them to try to isolate the **root**—the word part that contains the core meaning.
- Try to think of other words containing each prefix, suffix, or root. Think about what those words mean. Do they have anything in common?
- Consider the way the word is used in the sentence. Use the context and the word parts to make a logical guess about its meaning.
- Consult a dictionary to see whether your guess is correct.

Many words have roots that come from older languages, such as Greek, Latin, and Old English. Knowing the meaning of a root can help you determine the meaning of an unfamiliar word.

Root	Meaning	Examples
ast(e)r (Greek)	star	asterisk, astronomer
bibl (Greek)	book	bible, bibliography
dynam (Greek)	power, force	dynamic, dynamite
aud (Latin)	hear	audible, auditorium
fin (Latin)	limit, end	final, finished
flor (Latin)	flower	floral, florist
gress (Latin)	step	progress, regression
lin (Old English)	flax	linen, linseed
hus (Old English)	house	husband, husbandry
mer(e) (Old English)	sea, pool	mermaid, merman

A **prefix** is a word part that appears at the beginning of a word.

Prefix	Meaning	Examples
inter-	among, between	international, Internet
mis-	bad, badly, wrong	misfire, misguided
multi-	many, much	multicolored, multimillionaire
re-	again	renew, refreshing
trans-	across	transatlantic, transcontinental
un-	not	undo, unfinished

A **suffix** is a word part that appears at the end of a word.

Suffix	Meaning	Examples
-est	most	coldest, fastest
-hood	state or quality of	motherhood, neighborhood
-ish	relating to	childish, selfish
-ize	to make	computerize, standardize
-y	being, having	jumpy, sunny

Some words come from mythology (ancient legends and stories).

Your behavior is **narcissistic.** Please stop admiring yourself in the mirror!

Aunt Amanda has the **Midas touch.** She has started three businesses, all of which have made money.

Francine, our hockey goalie, looks like a **Valkyrie** when she puts on her helmet and padding. I wouldn't dare get in her way!

You can figure out these sentences quite easily if you are familiar with mythology. Narcissus was a character in Greek and Roman legend who fell in love with his own reflection. Midas was a mythical king who turned everything he touched into gold. Valkyries were women in Norse myths who rode onto battlefields and guarded the lives of warriors. When you see a word that you think may come from a myth or legend, use a dictionary to confirm your guess.

Understand Analogies

An **analogy** is a comparison between two things that are similar in some way. Analogies are sometimes used in nonfiction when unfamiliar subjects or ideas are explained in terms of familiar ones. Analogies often appear on tests as well, usually in a format like this:

BEGIN : END : : A) complete : total
B) start : continue
C) last : only
D) create : destroy
E) finish : final

Follow these steps to determine the correct answer.

- Read the part in capital letters as *"Begin is to end as . . ."*

- Read the answer choices as *"complete is to total," "start is to continue,"* and so on.

- Ask yourself how the words *begin* and *end* are related. (They are opposites, or antonyms.)

- Ask yourself which of the choices shows the same relationship. (*Complete* and *total* are synonyms, not antonyms. *Start* and *continue* aren't antonyms, either. *Last* and *only* don't

have opposite meanings, and neither do *finish* and *final.* Only *create* and *destroy* are opposites, so the answer is D.)

Here are some relationships that are often expressed in analogies.

Relationship	Example
Actor to action	WOLF : HOWL
Part to whole	MUSICIAN : ORCHESTRA
Word to synonym	FRIENDLY : PLEASANT
Word to antonym	BEGIN : END
Item to category	BRACELET : JEWELRY
Worker to tool	ARTIST : PAINTBRUSH
Action to object	READ : BOOK
Time sequence	DAWN : DUSK

Understand Denotations and Connotations

A word's **denotation** is its dictionary definition. Its **connotations** are the thoughts and feelings that the word evokes in people's minds. Good readers know that words can have precise shades of meaning. Make sure that you understand a word's connotations as well as denotations when you read it or use it in your writing.

Positive	Neutral	Negative
aroma	smell	stench
exotic	unusual	bizarre
bright, eye-catching	colorful	gaudy, garish, flashy

Learn Academic Vocabulary

Science, mathematics, and history have their own technical or specialized vocabularies. Use context clues and reference tools to figure out the meanings of specialized words.

This chemistry experiment will show you how to use a **catalyst,** a substance that speeds up a chemical reaction without being consumed itself.

If you cannot determine a word's meaning from its context, look for a definition or restatement of the word within the text. You can also consult a dictionary, a glossary, or an encyclopedia.

❶ The Writing Process

Different writers use different processes. Try out different strategies and figure out what works best for you. For some assignments, it is best to start by figuring out what you need to end up with, make a plan or outline, and stick to it. Other writing assignments may be more successful if you start by writing everything you know about the topic, allow things to get messy, and then reshape and revise the writing so it fits the assignment. Try both approaches and get to know yourself as a writer.

Also consider whether the assignment is high-stakes or low-stakes writing. When the success of the piece is very important, such as in a test, you might choose to focus on meeting the requirements or criteria of the assignment. When the purpose of the writing is to develop your ideas, there is more opportunity to experiment and take risks. Take into account the time factor as well. In a timed writing test, you may not have time to explore and revise.

Correct grammar and spelling are very important in your final product. You don't need to focus on these as you shape your ideas and draft your piece, but be sure you allow time for a careful edit before turning in your final piece.

❶.❶ Prewriting

In the prewriting stage, you explore your ideas and discover what you want to write about.

Finding Ideas for Writing
Try one or more of the following techniques to help you find a writing topic.

Personal Techniques

- Practice imaging, or trying to remember mainly sensory details about a subject—its look, sound, feel, taste, and smell.

- Complete a knowledge inventory to discover what you already know about a subject.

- Browse through magazines, newspapers, and on-line bulletin boards for ideas.

- Start a clip file of articles that you want to save for future reference. Be sure to label each clip with source information.

Sharing Techniques

- With a group, brainstorm a topic by trying to come up with as many ideas as you can without stopping to critique or examine them.

- Interview someone who knows a great deal about a subject.

Writing Techniques

- After freewriting on a subject, try looping, or choosing your best idea for more freewriting. Repeat the loop at least once.

- Make a list to help you organize ideas, examine them, or identify areas for further research.

Graphic Techniques

- Create a pro-and-con chart to compare the positive and negative aspects of an idea or a course of action.

- Use a cluster map or tree diagram to explore subordinate ideas that relate to a general subject or central idea.

Determining Your Purpose
Your purpose for writing may be to express yourself, to entertain, to describe, to explain, to analyze, or to persuade. To clarify it, ask yourself questions like these:

- Why did I choose to write about my topic?

- What aspects of the topic mean the most to me?

- What do I want others to think or feel after they read my writing?

LINK TO LITERATURE One purpose for writing is to express an opinion. For example, Thomas More wrote *Utopia* (page 794) to criticize the division between the wealthy and the poor in 16th-century Europe.

Identifying Your Audience

Knowing who will read your writing can help you focus your topic and choose relevant details. As you think about your readers, ask yourself questions like these:

- What does my audience already know about my topic?
- What will they be most interested in?
- What language is most appropriate for this audience?

1.2 Drafting

In the drafting stage, you put your ideas on paper and allow them to develop and change as you write.

Two broad approaches to this stage are discovery drafting and planned drafting.

Discovery drafting is a good approach when you are not quite sure what you think about your subject. You just plunge into your draft and let your feelings and ideas lead you where they will. After finishing a discovery draft, you may decide to start another draft, do more prewriting, or revise your first draft.

Planned drafting may work better for research reports, critical reviews, and other kinds of formal writing. Try making a writing plan or a scratch outline before you begin drafting. Then, as you write, you can fill in the details.

LINK TO LITERATURE Rarely does a successful writer achieve a final manuscript without several attempts and rewrites. Leo Tolstoy often relied on his wife, Sonya, for help with his manuscripts. As Sonya copied Leo's works in progress, she also offered opinions and suggestions on how to improve each draft. An excerpt from her diary appears on page 993.

1.3 Revising, Editing, and Proofreading

The changes you make in your writing during this stage usually fall into three categories: revising for content, revising for structure, and proofreading to correct mistakes in mechanics.

Use the questions that follow to assess problems and determine what changes would improve your work.

Revising for Content

- Does my writing have a main idea or central focus? Is my thesis clear?
- Have I incorporated adequate detail? Where might I include a telling detail, revealing statistic, or vivid example?
- Is any material unnecessary, irrelevant, or confusing?

WRITING TIP Be sure to consider the needs of your audience as you answer the questions under Revising for Content and Revising for Structure. For example, before you can determine whether any of your material is unnecessary or irrelevant, you need to identify what your audience already knows.

Revising for Structure

- Is my writing unified? Do all ideas and supporting details pertain to my main idea or advance my thesis?
- Is my writing clear and coherent? Is the flow of sentences and paragraphs smooth and logical?
- Do I need to add transitional words, phrases, or sentences to make the relationships among ideas clearer?
- Are my sentences well constructed? What sentences might I combine to improve the grace and rhythm of my writing?

Proofreading to Correct Mistakes in Grammar, Usage, and Mechanics

When you are satisfied with your revision, proofread your paper, looking for mistakes in grammar, usage, and mechanics. You may want to do this several times, looking for different types of mistakes each time. The following checklist may help.

Sentence Structure and Agreement
- Are there any run-on sentences or sentence fragments?
- Do all verbs agree with their subjects?
- Do all pronouns agree with their antecedents?
- Are verb tenses correct and consistent?

Forms of Words
- Do adverbs and adjectives modify the appropriate words?
- Are all forms of *be* and other irregular verbs used correctly?
- Are pronouns used correctly?
- Are comparative and superlative forms of adjectives correct?

Capitalization, Punctuation, and Spelling
- Is any punctuation mark missing or not needed?
- Are all words spelled correctly?
- Are all proper nouns and all proper adjectives capitalized?

WRITING TIP For help with identifying and correcting problems that are listed in the proofreading checklist, see the Grammar Handbook, pages R55–R90.

You might wish to mark changes on your paper by using the proofreading symbols shown in the chart below.

Proofreading Symbols

∧	Add letters or words.	╱	Make a capital letter lowercase.
⊙	Add a period.	¶	Begin a new paragraph.
≡	Capitalize a letter.	ϑ	Delete letters or words.
⊃	Close up space.	∩∪	Switch the positions of letters or words.
⋏	Add a comma.		

1.4 Publishing and Reflecting

Always consider sharing your finished writing with a wider audience. Reflecting on your writing is another good way to bring closure to a project.

Creative Publishing Ideas
Following are some ideas for publishing and sharing your writing:
- Post your writing on an electronic bulletin board or send it to others via e-mail.
- Create a multimedia presentation and share it with classmates.
- Publish your writing in a school newspaper or literary magazine.
- Present your work orally in a report, a speech, a reading, or a dramatic performance.
- Submit your writing to a local newspaper or a magazine that publishes student writing.
- Form a writing exchange group with other students.

WRITING TIP You might work with other students to publish an anthology of class writing. Then exchange anthologies with another class or another school. Reading the work of other student writers will help you get ideas for new writing projects and find ways to improve your work.

Reflecting on Your Writing
Think about your writing process and whether you would like to add what you have written to your portfolio. You might attach a note in which you answer questions like these:
- What did I learn about myself and my subject through this writing project?
- Which parts of the writing process did I most and least enjoy?
- As I wrote, what was my biggest problem? How did I solve it?
- What did I learn that I can use the next time I write?

1.5 Using Peer Response

Peer response consists of the suggestions and comments your peers or classmates make about your writing.

You can ask a peer reader for help at any point in the writing process. For example, your peers can help you develop a topic, narrow your focus, discover confusing passages, or organize your writing.

Questions for Your Peer Readers

You can help your peer readers provide you with the most useful kinds of feedback by following these guidelines:

- Tell readers where you are in the writing process. Are you still trying out ideas, or have you completed a draft?

- Ask questions that will help you get specific information about your writing. Open-ended questions that require more than yes-or-no answers are more likely to give you information you can use as you revise.

- Give your readers plenty of time to respond thoughtfully to your writing.

- Encourage your readers to be honest when they respond to your work. It's OK if you don't agree with them—you always get to decide which changes to make.

Tips for Being a Peer Reader

Follow these guidelines when you respond to someone else's work:

- Respect the writer's feelings.

- Make sure you understand what kind of feedback the writer is looking for, and then respond accordingly.

- Use "I" statements, such as "I like . . . ," "I think . . . ," or "It would help me if . . . ." Remember that your impressions and opinions may not be the same as someone else's.

WRITING TIP Writers are better able to absorb criticism of their work if they first receive positive feedback. When you act as a peer reader, try to start your review by telling something you like about the piece.

The chart below explains different peer-response techniques to use when you are ready to share your work.

Peer-Response Techniques

Sharing Use this when you are just exploring ideas or when you want to celebrate the completion of a piece of writing.

- *Will you please read or listen to my writing without criticizing or making suggestions afterward?*

Summarizing Use this when you want to know if your main idea or goals are clear.

- *What do you think I'm saying? What's my main idea or message?*

Replying Use this strategy when you want to make your writing richer by adding new ideas.

- *What are your ideas about my topic? What do you think about what I have said in my piece?*

Responding to Specific Features Use this when you want a quick overview of the strengths and weaknesses of your writing.

- *Are the ideas supported with enough examples? Did I persuade you? Is the organization clear enough for you to follow the ideas?*

Telling Use this to find out which parts of your writing are affecting readers the way you want and which parts are confusing.

- *What did you think or feel as you read my words? Would you show me which passage you were reading when you had that response?*

② Building Blocks of Good Writing

Whatever your purpose in writing, you need to capture your readers' interest, organize your ideas well, and present your thoughts clearly. Giving special attention to some particular parts of a story or an essay can make your writing more enjoyable and more effective.

2.1 Introductions

When you flip through a magazine trying to decide which articles to read, the opening paragraph is often critical. If it does not grab your attention, you are likely to turn the page.

Kinds of Introductions

Here are some introduction techniques that can capture a reader's interest:

- Make a surprising statement
- Provide a description
- Pose a question
- Relate an anecdote
- Address the reader directly
- Begin with a thesis statement

Make a Surprising Statement Beginning with a startling statement or an interesting fact can capture your reader's curiosity about the subject, as in the model below.

> MODEL
>
> September should be the seventh month, and October should be the eighth. Any Latin student knows that *septem* is "seven" and *octo* is "eight." Where did the calendar makers go wrong? The truth is that when the months acquired their names, during Roman times, the year started in March.

Provide a Description A vivid description sets a mood and brings a scene to life for your readers. Here, details about a lion observing possible prey set the tone for an essay on survival in the wild.

> MODEL
>
> Cool and cunning eyes followed the impala herd from a sturdy low-slung tree branch. The young female lion watched hungrily to see whether any of the impalas might be sickly or slower than the others. She kept every muscle quiet, though tense and ready to spring if an opportunity arose.

Pose a Question Beginning with a question can make your reader want to read on to find the answer. The following introduction asks questions about how the Holocaust could have happened.

> MODEL
>
> How could people and, indeed, entire nations stand by and allow the Holocaust to happen? As the Nazis rounded up and destroyed the Jewish populations of countless cities and towns throughout Europe, how could so many otherwise decent citizens merely watch in silence?

Relate an Anecdote Beginning with a brief anecdote, or story, can hook readers and help you make a point in a dramatic way. The anecdote below introduces an essay about the downside of self-closing shoe straps.

> MODEL
>
> My five-year old nephew, Ali, has never tied a shoelace. All his shoes have self-closing straps. Little boys already suffer because they are encouraged to develop large muscles by throwing and climbing, while little girls gain dexterity by dressing dolls and coloring in coloring books. Ali's younger sister, who has learned to tie bows on her doll clothes, may well have to stick around to tie the bows on Ali's gift packages and tie his bow tie for his tuxedo.

Address the Reader Directly Speaking directly to readers establishes a friendly, informal tone and involves them in your topic.

> MODEL
> If you've ever wondered how to avoid using pesticides in your garden, you can get answers from Natural Gardens, Inc. It's easy to protect the environment and have pest-free plants.

Begin with a Thesis Statement A thesis statement expressing a paper's main idea may be woven into both the beginning and the end of nonfiction writing. The following is a thesis statement that introduces an essay on the relationship between caring for pets and caring for children.

> MODEL
> Pet owners who are casual about their pets' health and safety are likely to be the same ones who are casual about the health and safety of their children.

WRITING TIP In order to write the best introduction for your paper, you may want to try more than one of the methods and then decide which is the most effective for your purpose and audience.

2.2 Paragraphs

A paragraph is made up of sentences that work together to develop an idea or accomplish a purpose. Whether or not it contains a topic sentence stating the main idea, a good paragraph must have unity and coherence.

Unity
A paragraph has unity when all the sentences support and develop one stated or implied idea. Use the following techniques to create unity in your paragraphs.

Write a Topic Sentence A topic sentence states the main ideas of a paragraph; all other sentences in the paragraph provide supporting details. A topic sentence is often the first sentence in a paragraph. However, it may also appear later in the paragraph or at the end, to summarize or reinforce the main idea, as shown in the model that follows.

> MODEL
> Plastic that does not rust, rot, or shatter is useful, of course, but does add to the ever-increasing problems of waste disposal. It is possible to add chemicals to plastic that make it dissolvable by other chemicals. There are plastics that slowly disintegrate in sunlight. Biodegradable plastic is available and should be preferred over nonbiodegradable plastic.

Relate All Sentences to an Implied Main Idea A paragraph can be unified without a topic sentence as long as every sentence supports the implied, or unstated, main idea. In the example below, all the sentences work together to create a unified impression of a swim meet.

> MODEL
> The swimmers were lined up along the edge of the pool. Toes curled over the edge, arms swung back in the ready position, and bodies leaned forward. The swimmers' eyes looked straight ahead. Their ears were alert for the starting signal.

Coherence
A paragraph is coherent when all its sentences are related to one another and flow logically from one to the next. The following techniques will help you achieve coherence in paragraphs:

- Present your ideas in the most logical order.
- Use pronouns, synonyms, and repeated words to connect ideas.
- Use transitional devices to show relationships between ideas.

In the model below, the writer used some of these techniques to create a unified paragraph.

> MODEL
> As we experience day and night repeatedly, it is hard to imagine the enormous significance of that change. We have day and night because our planet rotates on its axis. We have seasons because Earth revolves around our solar system's star, the sun. Our solar system, along with many others, rotates with the Milky Way galaxy. The universe is a gigantic structure of which our daily experiences of day and night, summer and winter, are tiny parts.

2.3 Transitions

Transitions are words and phrases that show the connections between details. Clear transitions help show how your ideas relate to one another.

Kinds of Transitions

Transitions can help readers understand several kinds of relationships:

- Time or sequence
- Spatial relationships
- Degree of importance
- Comparison and contrast
- Cause and effect

Time or Sequence Some transitions help to clarify the sequence of events over time. When you are telling a story or describing a process, you can connect ideas with such transitional words as *first, second, always, then, next, later, soon, before, finally, after, earlier, afterward,* and *tomorrow.*

> MODEL
> **Teaching a puppy to come when called takes patience from the owner and the puppy. First tie a lightweight rope to the dog's collar and go to a large play area. Play with the pup a while and then call to it. At the same time pull gently on the rope. Always praise the puppy for coming when called. Next allow the puppy to play again. Carry out this exercise several times a day.**

Spatial Relationships Transitional words and phrases such as *in front, behind, next to, along, nearest, lowest, above, below, underneath, on the left,* and *in the middle* can help readers visualize a scene.

> MODEL
> **On the porch, wicker chairs stand in casual disorder along the red wall of the house. Next to the red-and-white porch railing, orange day lilies nod in the breeze. Overhead, a flycatcher perches on a bare branch, alert for her next meal. Beyond the lawn, a small stream flows from beneath an arched stone bridge.**

Degree of Importance Transitional words such as *mainly, strongest, weakest, first, second, most important, least important, worst,* and *best* may be used to rank ideas or to show degrees of importance, complexity, or familiarity.

> MODEL
> **The Repertory Theater performed six plays last year. All the plays were exciting, but the most outstanding one was *Master Class.***

Comparison and Contrast Words and phrases such as *similarly, likewise, also, like, as, neither . . . nor,* and *either . . . or* show similarities between details. *However, by contrast, yet, but, unlike, instead, whereas,* and *while* show differences. Note the use of both types of transitions in the model below.

> MODEL
> **Like running and bicycling, swimming helps you maintain aerobic fitness; however, swimming has the added benefit of exercising muscles throughout your body.**

WRITING TIP Both *but* and *however* may be used to join two independent clauses. When *but* is used as a coordinating conjunction, it is preceded by a comma. When *however* is used as a conjunctive adverb, it is preceded by a semicolon and followed by a comma.

Cause and Effect When you are writing about a cause-and-effect relationship, use transitional words and phrases such as *since, because, thus, therefore, so, due to, for this reason,* and *as a result* to help clarify that relationship and to make your writing coherent.

> MODEL
> **Because the temperature dropped to 28 degrees after it rained for five hours, car door locks froze.**

Conclusions

A conclusion should leave readers with a strong final impression. Try any of these approaches.

Kinds of Conclusions
Here are some effective methods for bringing your writing to a conclusion:

- Restate your thesis
- Ask a question
- Make a recommendation
- Make a prediction
- Summarize your information

Restate Your Thesis A good way to conclude an essay is by restating your thesis, or main idea, in different words. The conclusion below restates the thesis introduced on page R23.

> MODEL
> Although each pet has a personality of its own just as each child does, there are many ways of encouraging the best behavior in each. Love, persistence, patience, and consistency make all the difference in training pets as well as in raising children.

Ask a Question Try asking a question that sums up what you have said and gives readers something new to think about. The question below concludes an appeal to halt funding for space exploration.

> MODEL
> Given all the evidence, can you imagine that continued investment in the space program will benefit future generations more than the same investment in the basic needs of those living now?

Make a Recommendation When you are persuading your audience to take a position on an issue, you can conclude by recommending a specific course of action.

> MODEL
> Today's youth are at risk of damaging their hearing by listening to very loud music. Consider turning down the bass and turning down the volume on your headphones.

Make a Prediction Readers are concerned about matters that may affect them and therefore are moved by a conclusion that predicts the future.

> MODEL
> If the government continues to spend money from Social Security taxes for current operations, we will create a disastrous burden of debt for future generations.

Summarize Your Information Summarizing reinforces the writer's main ideas, leaving a strong, lasting impression. The model below is a statement that summarizes a film review.

> MODEL
> The movie *The Postman* shows the tremendous influence of the Chilean poet Pablo Neruda on a young Italian man—not only in his love life but also in his acquired self-confidence and his dedication to a cause.

 Elaboration

Elaboration is the process of developing a writing idea by providing specific supporting details that are relevant and appropriate to the purpose and form of your writing.

- **Facts and Statistics** A fact is a statement that can be verified; a statistic is a fact expressed as a number. Make sure the facts and statistics you supply are from reliable, up-to-date sources. As in the model below, the facts and statistics you use should strongly support the statements you make.

> MODEL
> Our entire solar system speeds through the Milky Way galaxy at a speed of 180 miles a second. One could worry about the ability of any of us to stay in place with our feet on the ground. Or one could marvel at the magnificence of a universe that keeps everything whirling with such constancy.

- **Sensory Details** Details that show how something looks, sounds, tastes, smells, or feels can enliven a description, making readers feel they are actually experiencing what you are describing. Which senses does the writer appeal to in this paragraph?

MODEL

The campers lay as quiet as mice inside their tent as they considered the power of the massive beast they'd glimpsed through the tent flap. Snuffling and crackling brought news that the black bear had found something delectable inside the garbage can, probably leftover corncobs and pork-chop bones. The campfire smoke lingered, and the campers fervently hoped that the odors of grease and butter wouldn't bring the animal even closer to the tent.

- **Incidents** From our earliest years, we are interested in hearing "stories." One way to illustrate a point powerfully is to relate an incident or tell a story, as shown in the example below.

MODEL

Some of our most valuable sources of historical knowledge come from events that were disastrous for the people who were involved. The eruption of the volcano Vesuvius in A.D. 79 was a nightmare for the people of Pompeii. Many fled the city, but about 2,000 died, and their homes were buried under tons of volcanic ash. The long-buried remains have provided the modern world with detailed knowledge of everyday life in ancient Pompeii.

- **Examples** An example can help make an abstract or a complex idea concrete or can provide evidence to clarify a point for readers.

MODEL

The mere mention of the names of some writers causes distinct reactions, even from those who have not read the writers' works. For example, the mention of William Shakespeare causes many people to take in a sharp breath of admiration and others to think of something long and tedious. On the other hand, the name Edgar Allan Poe brings an involuntary shiver to almost everyone.

- **Quotations** Choose quotations that clearly support your points, and be sure that you copy each quotation word for word. Remember always to credit the source.

MODEL

In her book *How to Talk to Your Cat*, Patricia Moyes replies to certain authorities who claim that cats cannot smile: "I can only presume that these people have never owned a cat in the true sense of the word." She goes on to describe the cat's smile as a "relaxed upward tilting of the corners of the mouth" that occurs when the cat is feeling peaceful or pleased, perhaps while being stroked or while having happy dreams.

 2.6 Using Language Effectively

Effective use of language can help readers to recognize the significance of an issue, to visualize a scene, or to understand a character. The specific words and phrases that you use have everything to do with how effectively you communicate meaning. This is true of all kinds of writing, from novels to office memos. Keep these particular points in mind.

- **Specific Nouns** Nouns are specific when they refer to individual or particular things. If you refer to a *city*, you are being general. If you refer to *London*, you are being specific. Specific nouns help readers identify the who, what, and where of your message.

- **Specific Verbs** Verbs are the most powerful words in sentences. They convey the action, the movement, and sometimes the drama of thoughts and observations. Verbs such as *trudged, skipped,* and *sauntered* provide more-vivid pictures of actions than the verb *walked*.

- **Specific Modifiers** Use modifiers sparingly, but when you use them, make them count. Is the building *big* or *towering*? Are your poodle's paws *small* or *petite*? Once again, it is the more specific word that carries the greater impact.

❸ Descriptive Writing

Descriptive writing allows you to paint word pictures about anything and everything in the world, from events of global importance to the most personal feelings. It is an essential part of almost every piece of writing, including essays, poems, letters, field notes, newspaper reports, and videos.

RUBRIC — Standards for Writing

A successful description should
- have a clear focus and sense of purpose
- include sensory details and precise words that create vivid images, establish moods, or express emotions
- present details in a logical order

❸.❶ Key Techniques

Consider Your Goals What do you want to accomplish in writing your description? Do you want to show why something is important to you? Do you want to make a person or scene more memorable? Do you want to explain an event?

Identify Your Audience Who will read your description? How familiar are they with your subject? What background information will they need? Which details will they find most interesting?

Think Figuratively What figures of speech might help make your description vivid and interesting? What simile or metaphor comes to mind? What imaginative comparisons can you make? What living thing does an inanimate object remind you of?

MODEL
After the 10-mile hike, we pounced on the buffet table like starving lions. Some of us stuffed pieces of bread and morsels of roast beef into our mouths before we'd even finished filling our plates. By the time we flopped into chairs, we looked even more like scavenging carnivores, with our dripping hands and greasy mouths. But the predatory look in our eyes had abated somewhat.

Gather Sensory Details Which sights, smells, tastes, sounds, and textures make your subject come alive? Which details stick in your mind when you observe or recall your subject? Which senses does it most strongly affect?

MODEL
Light snowflakes brushed her cheek as she poised at the top of the mountain. After an admiring glance at the spots of bright color on the slope, she lifted both ski poles and crouched in preparation for the leap forward to start her fifth run through the powdery snow.

You might want to use a chart like the one shown here to collect sensory details about your subject.

Sights	Sounds	Textures	Smells	Tastes

Create a Mood What feelings do you want to evoke in your readers? Do you want to soothe them with comforting images? Do you want to build tension with ominous details? Do you want to evoke sadness or joy?

MODEL
It was always difficult to see the dangerous rocks just below the surface of the lake, but in the dark and without the light it was impossible. If only Guy had remembered the backup batteries. Although he had been on this lake only twice before, he had been confident he could run this fishing trip without incident. Now, as gray clouds gathered to cover even the faint light of the new moon, Guy worried not just about his summer job but also about the safety of his first paying customers.

3.2 Options for Organization

Spatial Order Choose one of these options to show the spatial order of a scene.

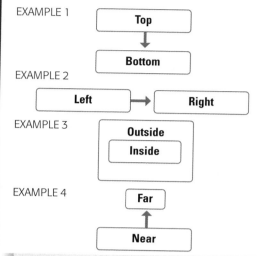

EXAMPLE 1

| Top |
| Bottom |

EXAMPLE 2

| Left | → | Right |

EXAMPLE 3

| Outside |
| Inside |

EXAMPLE 4

| Far |
| ↑ |
| Near |

MODEL
Thunder's nostrils quivered as he was led into the barn. How would this be as a place to spend nights from now on? In the stall to the left, the straw smelled fresh. Beyond that stall a saddle hung from rough boards. To the right of his stall was another, from which a mare looked at him curiously. So far, so good. From the far right, beyond two empty stalls, strode the barn cat.

WRITING TIP Use transitions that help the reader picture the relationship among the objects you describe. Some useful transitions for showing spatial relationships are *behind, below, here, in the distance, on the left, over,* and *on top.*

Order of Impression Order of impression is how you notice details.

| What first catches your attention |
| ↓ |
| What you notice next |
| ↓ |
| What you see after that |
| ↓ |
| What you focus on last |

MODEL
As her foot slipped on the pebbles, her first thought was of whether she would sprain an ankle sliding into the surf. Her heart began a dangerous thumping, but soon the soft sand provided a comfortable seat so that her body responded by calming down. She realized that the water was shallow and warm. Her hat would shade her eyes and prevent sunburn. By the time she remembered she had on dry-clean-only shorts, she'd decided that sitting in the surf while her friends gathered shells was a perfectly fine way to enjoy the beach.

WRITING TIP Use transitions that help readers understand the order of the impressions you are describing. Some useful transitions are *after, next, during, first, before, finally,* and *then.*

Order of Importance You might want to use order of importance as the organizing structure for your description.

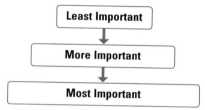

| Least Important |
| ↓ |
| More Important |
| ↓ |
| Most Important |

MODEL
Annaliese tried to imprint on her memory everything about the accident. She remembered unimportant details, like the song that was playing on her radio before the truck loomed up ahead. She remembered her panic as she steered into the guard rail. Gradually she recalled more important information—her conservative speed, the fact that the truck was on the wrong side of the road coming toward her, the driver's long beard. Finally, when she closed her eyes and really concentrated, she could remember the license plate number at eye level as the truck zoomed on by.

WRITING TIP Use transitions that help the reader understand the order of importance that you attach to the elements of your description. Some useful transitions are *first, second, mainly, more important, less important,* and *least important.*

④ Narrative Writing

Narrative writing tells a story. If you write a story from your imagination, it is a fictional narrative. A true story about actual events is a nonfictional narrative. Narrative writing can be found in short stories, novels, news articles, and biographies.

RUBRIC Standards for Writing

A successful narrative should

- include descriptive details and dialogue to develop the characters, setting, and plot.
- have a clear beginning, middle, and end.
- have a logical organization, with clues and transitions to help the reader understand the order of events.
- maintain a consistent tone and point of view.
- use language that is appropriate for the audience.
- demonstrate the significance of events or ideas.

4.1 Key Techniques

Identify the Main Events What are the most important events in your narrative? Is each event part of the chain of events needed to tell the story? In a fictional narrative, this series of events is the story's plot.

MODEL

Event 1	A railroad porter notices a woman boarding the train and pulling along a young child.
Event 2	Because the porter has the sense the child is frightened, he finds several excuses to appear at their compartment door.
Event 3	When he hears the child crying, he goes to the compartment and sees the glint of gunmetal inside a partially open market basket.
Event 4	The porter begins to plan how to identify the woman and child and to separate the child from the woman.

Describe the Setting When do the events occur? Where do they take place? How can you use setting to create mood and to set the stage for the characters and their actions?

MODEL

Bright spring sunshine highlighted the auburn hair of the child being pulled along by the matronly woman carrying a market basket. Joshua helped her up the steps onto the train. He stooped to lift the little girl at the same moment the woman jerked the small arm, so that the child stumbled up the stairs on her own.

Depict Characters Vividly What do your characters look like? What do they think and say? How do they act? What vivid details can show readers what the characters are like?

MODEL

Joshua hardly noticed the other passengers as his eyes followed the woman and child. His instincts warned him that something was wrong here.

WRITING TIP Dialogue is an effective way of developing characters in a narrative. As you write dialogue, choose words that express your characters' personalities and show how the characters feel about one another and about the events in the plot.

MODEL

"Hello, ma'am. I'm Joshua, and I'll be in soon to get your compartment ready for the night."

The woman's whisper sent chills down Joshua's spine. "Yeah, OK."

"Are you having a nice ride?" he asked the thin little girl.

"She likes the train," answered the woman.

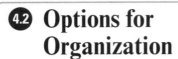 **Options for Organization**

Option 1: Chronological Order One way to organize a piece of narrative writing is to arrange the events in chronological order, as shown below.

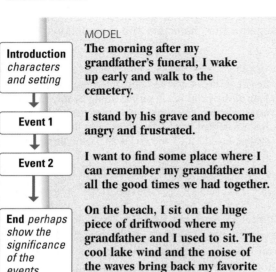

MODEL

Introduction *characters and setting*
The morning after my grandfather's funeral, I wake up early and walk to the cemetery.

Event 1
I stand by his grave and become angry and frustrated.

Event 2
I want to find some place where I can remember my grandfather and all the good times we had together.

End *perhaps show the significance of the events*
On the beach, I sit on the huge piece of driftwood where my grandfather and I used to sit. The cool lake wind and the noise of the waves bring back my favorite memories of him.

Option 2: Flashback It is also possible in narrative writing to arrange the order of events by starting with an event that happened before the beginning of the story.

Flashback
Begin with a key event that happened before the time in which the story takes place.

↓

Introduce characters and setting.

↓

Describe the events leading up to the conflict.

Option 3: Focus on Conflict When the telling of a fictional narrative focuses on a central conflict, the story's plot may follow the model shown below.

MODEL

Describe the main characters and setting.
The brothers arrive at the school gym long before the rest of the basketball team. Although the twins are physically identical, their personalities couldn't be more different. Mark is outgoing and impulsive, while Matt is thoughtful and shy.

Present the conflict.
Matt realizes his brother is missing shots on purpose and believes they will lose the championship.

Relate the events that make the conflict complex and cause the characters to change.
- Matt has a chance at a basketball scholarship if they win the championship.
- Mark needs money to buy a car.
- Matt and Mark have stood by each other no matter what.

Present the resolution or outcome of the conflict.
Matt retells a family story in which their grandfather chose honor and integrity over easy money. Mark plays to win.

Explanatory Writing

Explanatory writing informs and explains. For example, you can use it to evaluate the effects of a new law, to compare two movies, to analyze a piece of literature, or to examine the problem of greenhouse gases in the atmosphere.

5.1 Types of Explanatory Writing

There are many types of explanatory writing. Think about your topic and select the type that presents the information most clearly.

Compare and Contrast How are two or more subjects alike? How are they different?

> MODEL
> **Achilles and Hector are both fierce in battle, but while Hector can show his enemies mercy, Achilles is often cruel and blinded by rage.**

Cause and Effect How does one event cause something else to happen? Why do certain conditions exist? What are the results of an action or a condition?

> MODEL
> **Because the goddess Athena urges Achilles to suppress his anger, the great warrior does not kill Agamemnon.**

Analysis How does something work? How can it be defined? What are its parts?

> MODEL
> **Epics, such as Homer's *Iliad*, tell about events set in a distant and glorious past and present larger-than-life heroes who perform great deeds.**

Problem-Solution How can you identify and state a problem? How would you analyze the problem and its causes? How can it be solved?

> MODEL
> **Priam desperately wishes to have the body of his dead son, Hector, returned to him, but he must beg Achilles, his son's killer, to grant his wish.**

5.2 Compare and Contrast

Compare-and-contrast writing examines the similarities and differences between two or more subjects. You might, for example, compare and contrast two short stories, the main characters in a novel, or two movies.

Options for Organization

Compare-and-contrast writing can be organized in different ways. The examples that follow demonstrate feature-by-feature organization and subject-by-subject organization.

Option 1: Feature-by-Feature Organization

MODEL

Feature 1 — **I. Temperament**
    Subject A. Achilles: prone to angry outbursts and violent rages
    Subject B. Hector: tender with his wife and child

Feature 2 — **II. Fighting ability**
    Subject A. Achilles: ruthless and vengeful with his enemies
    Subject B. Hector: courageous but willing to show his enemies some mercy

Option 2: Subject-by-Subject Organization

MODEL

Subject A — **I. Achilles**
    Feature 1. Temperament: prone to angry outbursts and violent rages
    Feature 2. Fighting ability: ruthless and vengeful with his enemies

Subject B — **II. Hector**
    Feature 1. Temperament: tender with his wife and child
    Feature 2. Fighting ability: courageous but willing to show his enemies some mercy

WRITING TIP Remember your purpose for comparing and contrasting your subjects, and support your purpose with expressive language and specific details.

5.3 Cause and Effect

Cause-and-effect writing explains why something happened, why certain conditions exist, or what resulted from an action or a condition. You might use cause-and-effect writing to explain a character's actions, the progress of a disease, or the outcome of a war.

RUBRIC Standards for Writing

Successful cause-and-effect writing should
- clearly state the cause-and-effect relationship.
- show clear connections between causes and effects.
- present causes and effects in a logical order and use transitions effectively.
- use facts, examples, and other details to illustrate each cause and effect.
- use language and details appropriate to the audience.

Options for Organization

Your organization will depend on your topic and purpose for writing.

- If you want to explain the causes of an event such as the closing of a factory, you might first state the effect and then examine its causes.

Option 1: Effect to Cause Organization

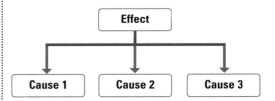

- If your focus is on explaining the effects of an event, such as the passage of a law, you might first state the cause and then explain the effects.

Option 2: Cause to Effect Organization

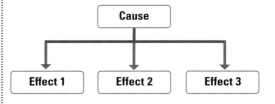

- Sometimes you'll want to describe a chain of cause-and-effect relationships to explore a topic such as the disappearance of tropical rain forests or the development of home computers.

Option 3: Cause-and-Effect Chain Organization

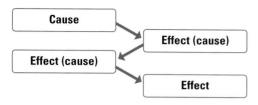

WRITING TIP Don't assume that a cause-and-effect relationship exists just because one event follows another. Look for evidence that the later event could not have happened if the first event had not caused it.

Problem-Solution

Problem-solution writing clearly states a problem, analyzes the problem, and proposes a solution to the problem. It can be used to identify and solve a conflict between characters, analyze a chemistry experiment, or explain why the home team keeps losing.

RUBRIC Standards for Writing

Successful problem-solution writing should
- identify the problem and help the reader understand the issues involved.
- analyze the causes and effects of the problem.
- integrate quotations, facts, and statistics into the text.
- explore possible solutions to the problem and recommend the best one(s).
- use language, tone, and details appropriate to the audience.

Options for Organization
Your organization will depend on the goal of your problem-solution piece, your intended audience, and the specific problem you choose to address. The organizational methods that follow are effective for different kinds of problem-solution writing.

Option 1: Simple Problem-Solution

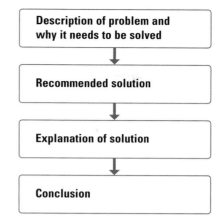

Option 2: Deciding Between Solutions

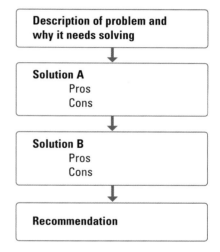

WRITING TIP Have a classmate read and respond to your problem-solution writing. Ask your peer reader: Is the problem clearly stated? Is the organization easy to follow? Do the proposed solutions seem logical?

Analysis

In writing an analysis, you explain how something works, how it is defined, or what its parts are. The details you include will depend upon the kind of analysis you write.

Process Analysis What are the major steps or stages in a process? What background information does the reader need to know—such as definitions of terms or a list of needed equipment—to understand the analysis? You might use process analysis to explain how to program a VCR or prepare for a test, or to explain the stages of an insect's life.

Definition Analysis What are the most important characteristics of a subject? You might use definition analysis to describe what an insect is, explain the characteristics of a sonnet, or outline the skills of an airplane pilot.

Parts Analysis What are the parts, groups, or types that make up a subject? Parts analysis could be used to explain the parts of an insect's body or the mechanics of an airplane.

RUBRIC **Standards for Writing**

A successful analysis should
- hook the readers' attention with a strong introduction.
- clearly state the subject and its parts.
- use a specific organizing structure to provide a logical flow of information.
- show connections among facts and ideas through subordinate clauses and transitional words and phrases.
- use language and details appropriate for the audience.

Options for Organization
Organize your details in a logical order appropriate for the kind of analysis you're writing.

Option 1: Process Analysis A process analysis is usually organized chronologically, with steps or stages in the order they occur.

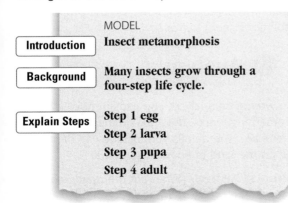

MODEL

Introduction	**Insect metamorphosis**
Background	**Many insects grow through a four-step life cycle.**
Explain Steps	**Step 1 egg** **Step 2 larva** **Step 3 pupa** **Step 4 adult**

Option 2: Definition Analysis You can organize the details in a definition or parts analysis in order of importance or impression.

MODEL

Introduce Term	**What is an insect?**
General Definition	**An insect is a small animal with an external skeleton, three body segments, and three pairs of legs.**
Explain Features	**Feature 1: external skeleton** **Feature 2: three body segments** **Feature 3: three pairs of legs**

Option 3: Parts Analysis The following parts analysis describes the major parts of an insect's body.

MODEL

| Introduce Subject | **An insect's body is divided into three main parts.** |
| Explain Parts | **Part 1: The head includes eyes, mouth, and antennae.**
Part 2: The thorax has the legs and wings attached to it.
Part 3: The abdomen contains organs for digesting food, eliminating waste, and reproducing. |

WRITING TIP Try to capture your readers' interest in your introduction. You might begin with a vivid description or an interesting fact, detail, or quotation. For example, an exciting excerpt from the narrative could open the process analysis.

An effective way to conclude an analysis is to return to your thesis and restate it in different words.

⑥ Persuasive Writing

Persuasive writing allows you to use the power of language to inform and influence others. It can take many forms, including speeches, newspaper editorials, billboards, advertisements, and critical reviews.

RUBRIC   Standards for Writing

Successful persuasion should
- state an issue and the writer's position
- contain opinions supported by facts or reasons
- have a reasonable and respectful tone
- answer opposing views
- contain sound logic and effective language
- conclude by summing up reasons or calling for action

6.1 Key Techniques

Clarify Your Position What do you believe about the issue? How can you express your opinion most clearly?

MODEL
Our city needs to find ways to decrease pollution, especially during the workweek.

Know Your Audience Who will read your writing? What do they already know and believe about the issue? What objections to your position might they have? What additional information might they need? What tone and approach would be most effective?

MODEL
Everyone wants to breathe clean air, at least cleaner than what we've had in our city lately. The smog is heavier during the workweek, when more people drive to work, more buses run, and businesses burn more fuel to heat or cool buildings.

Support Your Opinion Why do you feel the way you do about the issue? What facts, statistics, examples, quotations, anecdotes, or opinions of authorities support your view? What reasons will convince your readers? What evidence can answer their objections?

MODEL
Climate geographers from Arizona State University report that 45 statistical analyses have shown that along the eastern seaboard rainfall is highest on Saturdays, with an average of 658 millimeters per year, and lowest on Mondays, with an average of 538 millimeters per year. The researchers have found that pollution is also highest on Saturdays and lowest on Mondays.

Ways to Support Your Argument	
Statistics	Facts that are expressed in numbers
Examples	Specific instances that explain your point
Observations	Events or situations you yourself have seen
Anecdotes	Brief stories that illustrate your point
Quotations	Direct statements from authorities

Begin and End with a Bang How can you hook your readers and make a lasting impression? What memorable quotation, anecdote, or statistic will catch their attention at the beginning or stick in their minds at the end? What strong summary or call to action can you conclude with?

BEGINNING
A recent research report states that there is more rain on weekends than during the week. Scientists attribute this to the extra pollution that builds throughout the workweek.

CONCLUSION
We need to plan for more car-pooling, efficient heating and cooling, and consolidation of some bus schedules to improve our air quality—and provide better weekend weather.

6.2 Options for Organization

In a two-sided persuasive essay, you want to show the weaknesses of other opinions as you explain the strengths of your own.

The example below demonstrates one method of organizing your persuasive essay to convince your audience.

Option 1: Reasons for Your Opinion

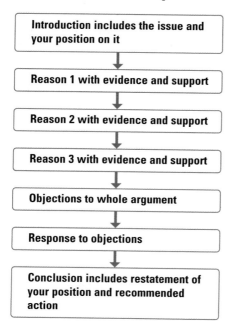

Introduction includes the issue and your position on it

↓

Reason 1 with evidence and support

↓

Reason 2 with evidence and support

↓

Reason 3 with evidence and support

↓

Objections to whole argument

↓

Response to objections

↓

Conclusion includes restatement of your position and recommended action

Option 2: Point-by-Point Basis

In the organization that follows, each reason and its objections are examined on a point-by-point basis.

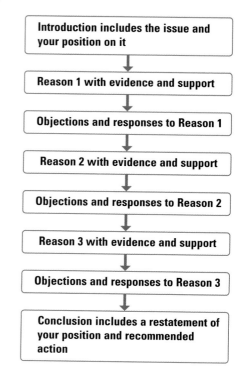

Introduction includes the issue and your position on it

↓

Reason 1 with evidence and support

↓

Objections and responses to Reason 1

↓

Reason 2 with evidence and support

↓

Objections and responses to Reason 2

↓

Reason 3 with evidence and support

↓

Objections and responses to Reason 3

↓

Conclusion includes a restatement of your position and recommended action

---

Beware of Illogical Arguments Be careful about using illogical arguments. Opponents can easily attack your argument if you present illogical material.

Circular reasoning—trying to prove a statement by just repeating it in different words

> Precipitation is heavier on weekends because of higher rainfall then.

Overgeneralization—making a statement that is too broad to prove

> Nobody is doing anything to reduce air pollution.

Either-or fallacy—stating that there are only two alternatives when there are many

> Either we cut weekday car travel by fifty percent or pollution will make our city unlivable.

Cause-and-effect fallacy—falsely assuming that because one event follows another, the first event caused the second

> The growing population of our region has caused the increase in air pollution.

❼ Research Report Writing

A research report explores a topic in depth, incorporating information from a variety of sources.

❼.❶ Key Techniques

Develop Relevant, Interesting, and Researchable Questions Asking thoughtful questions is an ongoing part of research. Begin with a list of basic questions that are relevant to your topic. Focus on getting basic facts that answer the questions *who, what, where, when,* and *why* about your topic. If you were researching the social context of Dickens's novels, you might develop a set of questions like these.

> MODEL
> **What were living conditions like in London during the 1800s?**
>
> **What happened to orphans?**

As you become more familiar with your topic, think of questions that might provide an interesting perspective to make readers think.

> MODEL
> **How did the legal system reflect society's values?**

Check that your questions are researchable. Ask questions that will uncover facts, statistics, case studies, and other documentable evidence.

Clarify Your Thesis A thesis statement is one or two sentences clearly stating the main idea that you will develop in your report. A thesis may also indicate the organizational pattern you will follow and reflect your tone and point of view.

> MODEL
> In *Oliver Twist*, instead of drawing clear lines between the dark underworld of London and the light of the more civilized world, Charles Dickens blurs the distinction, making good and evil in society difficult to define.

Document Your Sources You need to document, or credit, the sources where you find your evidence. In the example below, the writer uses and documents a quotation from the novel.

> MODEL
> In *Oliver Twist*, Dickens shows the intertwining of good and evil in the world. The narrator states, "Men who look on nature . . . and cry that all is dark and gloomy, are in the right; but the somber colours are reflections from their own jaundiced eyes and hearts. The real hues . . . need a clearer vision" (256–57).

Support Your Ideas You should support your ideas with relevant evidence—facts, anecdotes, and statistics—from reliable sources. In the example below the writer includes a fact about the conditions of workhouses.

> MODEL
> Oliver is condemned to a workhouse. The living conditions in workhouses were deliberately worse than those in prisons in order to discourage the poor from depending on the publicly funded institutions (Pool 245).

7.2 Gathering Information: Sources

You will use a range of sources to collect the information you need to develop your research paper. These will include both print and electronic resources.

General Reference Works To clarify your thesis and begin your research, consult reference works that give quick, general overviews of a subject. General reference works include encyclopedias, almanacs and yearbooks, atlases, and dictionaries.

Specialized Reference Works Once you have a good idea of your specific topic, you are ready to look for detailed information in specialized reference works. In the library's reference section, specialized dictionaries and encyclopedias can be found for almost any field. For example, in the field of literature, you will find specialized reference sources such as *Contemporary Authors* and *Twentieth-Century Literary Criticism.*

Periodicals Journals and periodicals are a good source for detailed, up-to-date information. Periodical indexes, found in print and online catalogs in the library, will help you find articles on a topic. The *Readers' Guide to Periodical Literature* indexes many popular magazines. More specialized indexes include the *Humanities Index* and the *Social Sciences Index.*

Electronic Resources Commercial information services offer access to reference works such as dictionaries and encyclopedias, databases, and periodicals.

The **Internet** is a vast network of computer networks. News services, libraries, universities, researchers, organizations, and government agencies use the Internet to communicate and to distribute information. The Internet gives you access to the World Wide Web, which provides information on particular topics and links you to related topics and resources.

A **CD-ROM** is a compact disc on which information is stored. Reference works on CD-ROMs may include text, sound, images, and video.

Databases are large collections of related information stored electronically. You can scan the information or search for specific facts.

RESEARCH TIP To find books on a specific topic, check the library's online catalog. Be sure to copy the correct call numbers of books that sound promising. Also look at books shelved nearby. They may relate to your topic.

7.3 Gathering Information: Validity of Sources

When you find source material, you must determine whether it is useful and accurate.

Credibility of Author Check whether an author has written several books or articles on the subject and has published in respected newspapers or journals.

Objectivity Decide whether the information is fact, opinion, or propaganda. Reputable works credit their sources of information.

Currency Check the publication date of the source to see whether the information is current.

Credibility of Publisher Seek information from a respected newspaper or journal, not from a tabloid newspaper or popular-interest magazine.

WEB TIP Be especially skeptical of information you locate on the Internet, since virtually anyone can post anything there. Read the URL, or Internet address. Sites sponsored by government agencies (*.gov*) or educational institutions (*.edu*) are generally more reliable.

7.4 Taking Notes

As you find useful information, record bibliographic information for each source on a separate index card. Then you are ready to take notes on your sources. You will probably use these three methods of note taking.

Paraphrase, or restate in your own words, the main ideas and supporting details in a passage.

Summarize, or rephrase in fewer words, the original material, trying to capture the key ideas.

Quote, or copy word for word, the original text if you think the author's own words best clarify a particular point. Use quotation marks to signal the beginning and the end of the quotation.

For more details on making source cards and taking notes, see the Writing Workshop on pages 1306–1315.

7.5 Options for Organization

Begin by reading over your note cards and sorting them into groups. The main-idea headings may help you find connections among the notes. Then arrange the groups of related note cards so that the ideas flow logically from one group to the next.

Like other forms of writing, research reports can be organized in different ways. For some topics, chronological order may work. For others, you may want to compare and contrast two things. Other possibilities are a cause-and-effect organization or a least-important-to-most-important one. If your material does not lend itself to any of these organizations, try a general-to-specific approach.

Whatever your organizational pattern, making an outline can help guide the drafting process. The subtopics that you located in sorting your note cards will be the major entries in your outline, preceded by Roman numerals. Make sure that items of the same importance are parallel in form. For example, in the topic outline below, entries I and II are both phrases. So are subentries A and B.

In a second kind of outline, shown below in Option 2, complete sentences are used instead of phrases for entries and subentries.

Option 1: Topic Outline

The Two Worlds of Oliver Twist
Introduction Dickens blurs the distinction between good and evil.
I. The underworld of London
   A. The criminal characters
     1. Sikes and Monks
     2. Fagin
   B. The good characters
II. The civilized world of London

Option 2: Sentence Outline

The Two Worlds of Oliver Twist
Introduction Dickens blurs the distinction between good and evil.
I. Dickens depicts the underworld of London by showing both evil criminal characters and those who commit crimes due to poverty or misfortune.
   A. The criminal characters are cruel and brutal.
     1. Sikes and Monks are characterized as men who will do anything to get what they want.
     2. Fagin's amorality is shown in his manipulating children into committing crimes.
   B. The good characters have believable human weaknesses and failings.
II. The civilized world of London is populated with people who are far from perfect.

7.6 Documenting Sources

When you quote, paraphrase, or summarize information from a source, you need to credit that source. Parenthetical documentation is the accepted method for crediting sources. You may choose to name the author in parentheses following the information, along with the page number on which the information is found.

> MODEL
> **Workhouses were purposely made "as grim and forbidding as possible" (Pool 245).**

In parenthetical documentation, you may also use the author's name in the sentence, along with the information. If you do, the parenthetical citation should consist only of the page number on which the information is found.

> MODEL
> **According to Pool, many poor children like Oliver Twist populated London in the 1800s (31).**

In either case, your reader can find out more about the source by turning to your Works Cited page, which lists complete bibliographical information for each source.

PUNCTUATION TIP When only the author and page number appear in parentheses, there is no punctuation between the two items. Also notice that the parenthetical citation comes after the closing quotation marks of a quotation, if there is one, and before the end punctuation of the sentence.

The examples above show citations for books with one author. The list that follows shows the correct way to write parenthetical citations for several kinds of sources.

Guidelines for Parenthetical Documentation

Work by One Author
Put the author's last name and the page reference in parentheses: **(Pool 191)**.

If you mention the author's name in the sentence, put only the page reference in parentheses: **(191)**.

Work by Two or Three Authors
Put the authors' last names and the page reference in parentheses: **(Mitchell and Deane 42)**.

Work by More Than Three Authors
Give the first author's last name followed by *et al.* and the page reference: **(Bentley et al. 122)**.

Work with No Author Given
Give the title or a shortened version and (if appropriate) the page reference: **("Hurried Trials" 742)**.

One of Two or More Works by Same Author
Give the author's last name, the title or a shortened version, and the page reference: **(Dunn, "But We Grow" 54)**.

Selection from a Book of Collected Essays
Give the name of the author of the essay and the page reference: **(Bayley 54)**.

Dictionary Definition
Give the entry title in quotation marks: **("Workhouse")**.

Unsigned Article in an Encyclopedia
Give the article title in quotation marks: **("English Literature")**.

WRITING TIP Presenting someone else's writing or ideas as your own is plagiarism. To avoid plagiarism, you need to credit sources. However, if a piece of information is common knowledge—information available in several sources—you do not need to credit a source.

7.7 Following MLA Manuscript Guidelines

The final copy of your report should follow the Modern Language Association (MLA) guidelines for manuscript preparation.

- The heading in the upper left-hand corner of the first page should include your name, your teacher's name, the course name, and the date, each on a separate line.
- Below the heading, center the title on the page.
- Number all the pages consecutively in the upper right-hand corner, one-half inch from the top. Include your last name before each page number.

- Double-space the entire paper.
- Except for the margins above the page numbers, leave one-inch margins on all sides of every page.

The Works Cited list at the end of your report is an alphabetized list of the sources you have used and documented. In each entry all lines after the first are indented an additional one-half inch.

WRITING TIP When your report includes a quotation that is longer than four lines, set it off from the rest of the text by indenting the entire quotation one inch from the left margin. In this case, you should not use quotation marks.

Works Cited
Models for Works Cited entries

Works Cited

Bayley, John. "Oliver Twist: 'Things As They Really Are.'" <u>Dickens and the Twentieth Century</u>. Ed. John Gross and Gabriel Pearson. London: Routledge, 1962. 49–64.

❶ Selection from a book of collected essays; note that publishers' names are shortened.

Bentley, Nicholas, et al. <u>The Dickens Index</u>. Oxford: Oxford UP, 1988.

❷ Book with more than three authors

Collins, Philip, ed. <u>Sikes and Nancy: A Facsimile</u>. London: Dickens, 1982.

❸ Book with editor but no single author

Dickens, Charles. <u>Oliver Twist</u>. New York: Bantam, 1981.

❹ Book with one author

Dunn, Richard J. "'But We Grow Affecting: Let Us Proceed.'" <u>Dickensian</u> 62 (1966): 53–55.

❺ Article in scholarly journal

---. <u>Oliver Twist: Whole Heart and Soul</u>. New York: Twayne, 1993.

❻ Second work by same author

Mitchell, B. R., and Phyllis Deane. <u>Abstract of British Historical Statistics</u>. Cambridge: Cambridge UP, 1962.

❼ Work with two authors

7.8 MLA Documentation: Electronic Sources

As with print sources, information from electronic sources, such as CD-ROMs or the Internet, must be documented in your Works Cited list. You may find a reference to a source on the Internet and then use the print version of the article. If so, document it as you do other printed works. However, if you read or print out an article on the Internet, document it as shown below for an electronic source. Although electronic sources are shown separately below, they should be included in the Works Cited list with print sources.

Internet Sources Works Cited entries for Internet sources include the same kind of information as those for print sources. They also include the dates you accessed the information and the electronic addresses of the sources. Some of the information about a source may be unavailable. Include as much as you can. For more information on how to write Works Cited entries for Internet sources, see the MLA guidelines posted on the Internet or access this document through the McDougal Littell Web site.

RESEARCH STARTER
CLASSZONE.COM

CD-ROMs Entries for CD-ROMs include the publication medium (CD-ROM), the distributor, and the date of publication. Some of the information shown may not always be available. Include as much as you can.

Works Cited

Models for Works Cited entries for electronic sources

Works Cited

"Charles Dickens." <u>Britannica Online</u>. Vers. 98.2. Apr. 1998.
    Encyclopaedia Britannica. 17 Sept. 1998
    <http://www.eb.com:180/bol/topic?eu114623&sctn=5>.

❶ Encyclopaedia entry from online version

Dickens, Charles. <u>Oliver Twist</u>. Ed. Andrew Lang. London,
    1897. <u>Electronic Text Center.</u> 1993. U of Virginia Library.
    14 June 1998 <http://etext.lib.virginia.edu/
    toc/modeng/public/DicOliv.html>.

❷ The complete text of the novel, available on the Internet; includes access date

<u>The Dickens Page</u>. Ed. Mitsuharu Matsuoka. 1995. Nagoya
    U. 14 June 1998 <http://lang.nagoya-u.ac.jp/
    ~matsuoka/Dickens. html>.

❸ Scholarly site; shows date you accessed it

Rosenberg, Brian. "Character and Contradiction in
    Dickens." <u>Nineteenth Century Literature—Electronic</u>
    <u>Edition</u> 47.2 (1992): 18 pp. 15 June 1998
    <http://www-ucpress.berkeley.edu:8080/scan/ncl-e/
    472/articles/rosenberg.art472.html>.

❹ Article in a scholarly journal available on the Internet; includes number of pages and access date

"Workhouse." <u>The Oxford English Dictionary</u>. 2nd ed. CD-
    ROM. Oxford: Oxford UP, 1992.

❺ Dictionary entry from CD-ROM version

8 Business Writing

The ability to write clearly and succinctly is an essential skill in the business world. As you prepare to enter the job market, you will need to know how to create letters, memos, and résumés.

RUBRIC

Standards for Writing

Successful business writing should

- have a tone and language geared to the appropriate audience.
- state the purpose clearly in the opening sentences or paragraph.
- use precise words and avoid jargon.
- present only essential information.
- present details in a logical order.
- conclude with a summary of important points.

8.1 Key Techniques

Think About Your Purpose Why are you doing this writing? Do you want to "sell" yourself to a college admissions committee or a job interviewer? Do you want to order or complain about a product? Do you want to set up a meeting or respond to someone's ideas?

Identify Your Audience Who will read your writing? What background information will they need? What questions might they have? What tone or language is appropriate?

Support Your Points What specific details clarify your ideas? What reasons do you have for your statements? What points most strongly support them?

Finish Strongly How can you best sum up your statements? What is your main point? What action do you want others to take?

8.2 Options

Model 1: Letter

Heading *Where the letter comes from and when*

#1 Andover Lane
Sunnydale, CA 93933
July 16, ____

Inside Address *To whom the letter is being sent*

Customer Service Representative
Bionic Bikes, Inc.
12558 Industrial Drive
Schaumburg, IL 60193

Salutation *Greeting*

Dear Customer Service Representative:

Body *Text of the message*

I was really pleased to get a Bionic Bike for my birthday in March. I've ridden it every day—to school, to the rec center, and everywhere.

The bike is great, but the handlebars are not comfortable. I think you should raise the angle of the hand grips about two inches so that riders can hold them comfortably while looking straight ahead.

Thank you for considering my suggestion.

Sincerely yours,
Marisa LaPorta

Closing

Model 2: Memo

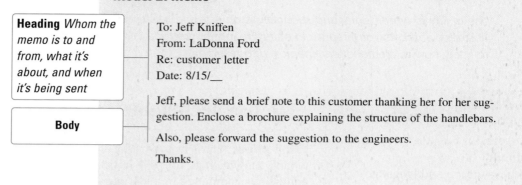

Heading *Whom the memo is to and from, what it's about, and when it's being sent*

To: Jeff Kniffen
From: LaDonna Ford
Re: customer letter
Date: 8/15/__

Body

Jeff, please send a brief note to this customer thanking her for her suggestion. Enclose a brochure explaining the structure of the handlebars.

Also, please forward the suggestion to the engineers.

Thanks.

Model 3: Résumé A well-written résumé is invaluable when you apply for a part-time or full-time job or to college. It should highlight your skills, accomplishments, and experience. Proofread your résumé carefully to make sure it is clear and accurate and free of errors in grammar and spelling. It is a good idea to save a copy of your résumé on your computer or on a disk so that you can easily update it.

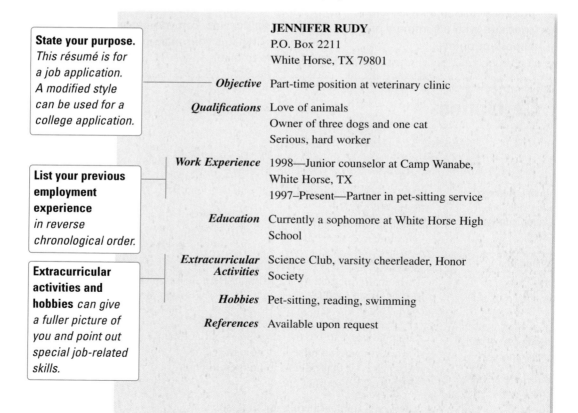

State your purpose. *This résumé is for a job application. A modified style can be used for a college application.*

List your previous employment experience *in reverse chronological order.*

Extracurricular activities and hobbies *can give a fuller picture of you and point out special job-related skills.*

JENNIFER RUDY
P.O. Box 2211
White Horse, TX 79801

Objective Part-time position at veterinary clinic

Qualifications Love of animals
Owner of three dogs and one cat
Serious, hard worker

Work Experience 1998—Junior counselor at Camp Wanabe, White Horse, TX
1997–Present—Partner in pet-sitting service

Education Currently a sophomore at White Horse High School

Extracurricular Activities Science Club, varsity cheerleader, Honor Society

Hobbies Pet-sitting, reading, swimming

References Available upon request

❶ Inquiry and Research

In this age of information, the ability to locate and evaluate resources efficiently can spell the difference between success and failure—in both the academic and the business worlds. Make use of print and nonprint information sources.

1.1 Finding Sources

Good research involves using the wealth of resources available to answer your questions and raise new questions. Knowing where to go and how to access information can lead you to interesting and valuable sources.

Reference Works

Reference works are print and nonprint sources of information that provide quick access to both general overviews and specific facts about a subject.

Dictionaries—word definitions, pronunciations, and origins

Thesauri—lists of synonyms and antonyms of words

Glossaries—collections of specialized terms, such as those pertaining to literature, with definitions

Encyclopedias—detailed information on nearly every subject, arranged alphabetically (*Encyclopaedia Britannica*). Specialized encyclopedias concentrate on specific subjects, such as music, economics, and science (*International Encyclopedia of Economics*).

Almanacs and Yearbooks—current facts and statistics (*The World Almanac and Book of Facts, Statistical Abstract of the United States*)

Atlases—maps and information about weather, agricultural and industrial production, and other geographical topics (*National Geographic Atlas of the World*)

Specialized Reference Works—biographical data (*Who's Who, Current Biography*), literary information (*Contemporary Authors, Book Review Digest, Cyclopedia of Literary Characters, The Oxford Companion to English Literature*), and quotations (*Bartlett's Familiar Quotations*)

Electronic Sources—Many of these reference works and databases are available on CD-ROMs, which may include text, sound, photographs, and video. CD-ROMs can be used on a home or library computer. You can subscribe to services that offer access to these sources online.

Periodicals and Indexes

One kind of specialized reference is a periodical.

- Some periodicals, such as the *Atlantic Monthly* and *Psychology Today,* are intended for a general audience. They are indexed in the *Readers' Guide to Periodical Literature.*

- Many other periodicals, or journals, are intended for specialized or academic audiences. These include titles as diverse as *American Psychologist* and *Studies in Short Fiction.* These are indexed in the *Humanities Index* and the *Social Sciences Index.* In addition, most fields have their own indexes. For example, articles on literature are indexed in the *MLA International Bibliography.*

Many indexes are available in print, CD-ROM, and online forms.

Internet

The Internet is a system of networks that connect computers. News services, libraries, universities, researchers, organizations, and government agencies use the Internet to distribute information and to communicate. The Internet can provide links to library catalogs, newspapers, government sources, and many of the reference sources described above. The Internet includes two key features:

World Wide Web—source of information on specific subjects and links to related topics

Electronic mail (e-mail)—communications link to other e-mail users worldwide

Other Resources

In addition to reference works found in the library and over the Internet, you can get information from the following sources: corporate publications, lectures, correspondence, and media such as films, television programs, and recordings. You can also observe directly, conduct your own interviews, and collect data from polls or questionnaires that you create yourself.

Evaluating Sources

Not all information is equal. You need to be a discriminating consumer of information and evaluate the credibility of a source, the reliability of the specific information included, and its value in answering your research needs.

Credibility of Sources

You must determine the credibility and appropriateness of each source in order to write an effective report or speech. Ask yourself the following questions:

Is the writer an authority? A writer who has written several books on a subject or whose name is included in numerous bibliographies may be considered an authoritative source.

Is the source reliable and unbiased? What is the author's motivation? For example, a defense of an industry in which the author has a financial interest may be biased. A profile of a writer or scientist written by a close relative or friend may also be biased.

WEB TIP Be especially skeptical of information you locate on the Internet, since virtually anyone can post anything there. Read the URL, or Internet address. Sites sponsored by government agencies (.gov) or educational institutions (.edu) are generally more reliable.

Is the source up-to-date? It is important to consult the most recent material, especially in fields, such as medicine and technology, in which there is constant research and development. Some authoritative sources have withstood the test of time, however, and should not be overlooked.

Is the source appropriate? For what audience is the material written? In general, look for information directed at the educated reader. Material geared to experts or to popular audiences may be too technical or too simplified and therefore not appropriate for most research projects.

Distinguishing Fact from Opinion

As you gather information, it is important to recognize facts and opinions. A **fact** can be proved to be true or false. You could verify the statement "Congress rejected the bill" by checking newspapers, magazines, or the *Congressional Record*. An **opinion** is a judgment based on facts. The statement "Congress should not have rejected the bill" is an opinion. To evaluate an opinion, check for evidence presented logically to support it.

Recognizing Bias

A writer may have a particular bias. This does not automatically make his or her point of view unreliable. However, recognizing an author's bias can help you evaluate a source. Recognizing that the author of an article about immigration is a Chinese immigrant will help you understand that author's bias. In addition, an author may have a hidden agenda that makes him or her less than objective about a topic. To avoid relying on information that may be biased, check an author's background and gather a variety of viewpoints.

Collecting Information

People use a variety of techniques to collect information during the research process. Try out several of those suggested below and decide which ones work best for you.

Paraphrasing and Summarizing

You can adapt material from other sources by quoting it directly or by paraphrasing or summarizing it. Paraphrasing involves restating the information in your own words. A paraphrase is often a simpler version but not necessarily a shorter version. Summarizing involves extracting the main ideas and supporting details and writing a shorter version of the information.

Remember to credit the source when you paraphrase or summarize. See "Research Report Writing" in the Writing Handbook, pp. R37–R42.

Strategies for Paraphrasing

1. Select the portion of the article you want to record.
2. Read it carefully and think about those ideas you find most interesting and useful to your research. Often these will be the main ideas.
3. Retell the information in your own words.

Strategies for Summarizing

1. Read the article carefully. Determine the main ideas.
2. In your own words, write a shortened version of these main ideas.

Avoiding Plagiarism

Plagiarism is copying someone else's ideas or words and using them as if they were your own. This can happen inadvertently if you are sloppy about collecting information and documenting your sources. Plagiarism is intellectual stealing and can have serious consequences.

How to Avoid Plagiarism

1. When you paraphrase or summarize, be sure to change entirely the wording of the original by using your own words.
2. Both in notes and on your final report, enclose in quotation marks any material copied directly from other sources.
3. Indicate in your final report the sources of any ideas that are not general knowledge—including those in the visuals—that you have paraphrased or summarized.
4. Include a list of works cited with your finished report. See "Research Report Writing" in the Writing Handbook, pp. R37–R42.

② Study Skills and Strategies

As you read an assignment for the first time, review material for a test, or search for information for a research report, you use different methods of reading and studying.

2.1 Skimming

When you run your eyes quickly over a text, paying attention to overviews, headings, topic sentences, highlighted words, and graphic features, you are skimming.

Skimming is a good technique for previewing material in a textbook or other source that you must read for an assignment. It is also useful when you are researching a self-selected topic. Skimming a source helps you determine whether it has pertinent information. For example, suppose you are writing a research report on Leo Tolstoy. Skimming an essay on the literature of Russia can help you quickly determine whether any part of it deals with your topic.

2.2 Scanning

To find a specific piece of information in a text, use scanning. To scan, place a card under the first line of a page and move it down slowly. Look for key words and phrases that signal the information you are looking for.

Scanning is useful in reviewing for a test or in finding a specific piece of information for a paper. Suppose you are looking for a discussion of Tolstoy's relationship with his family for your research report. You can scan a book chapter or an essay, looking for the key name *Sonya*.

2.3 In-Depth Reading

When you must thoroughly understand the material in a text, you use in-depth reading.

In-depth reading involves asking questions, taking notes, looking for main ideas, and drawing conclusions as you read slowly and carefully. For example, in researching your report on Tolstoy, you may find an essay on how Tolstoy's point of view changed in his later literature. Since this is closely related to your topic, you will read it in depth and take notes. You also should use in-depth reading for reading textbooks and literary works.

2.4 Outlining

Outlining is an efficient way of organizing ideas and is useful in taking notes.

Outlining helps you retain information as you read in depth. For example, you might outline a chapter in a history textbook, listing the main subtopics and the ideas or details that support them. An outline can also be useful for taking notes for a research report or in reading a piece of literature. The following is an example of a topic outline that summarizes, in short phrases, part of a chapter.

MAIN IDEA: **Leo Tolstoy was one of the world's greatest novelists.**

I. Early Years
  A. First publications
  B. Importance of wife and family
II. Major Novels
  A. *War and Peace*
  B. *Anna Karenina*
III. Later Years
  A. Change in religious beliefs and writing style
  B. Abandoned by wife and daughter
IV. Evaluations of Tolstoy
  A. Valued everyday reality
  B. Wrote about varied aspects of human existence
  C. On a constant search for the meaning of life

2.5 Identifying Main Ideas

To understand and remember any material you read, identify its main idea.

In informative material, the main idea is often stated. The thesis statement of an essay or article and the topic sentence of each paragraph often state the main idea. In other material, especially literary works, the main idea is implied. After reading the piece carefully, analyze the important parts, such as characters and plot. Then try to sum up in one sentence the general point that the story makes.

2.6 Taking Notes

As you listen or read in depth, take notes to help you understand the material. Look and listen for key words that point to main ideas.

One way to help you summarize the main idea and supporting details is to take notes in modified outline form. In using a modified outline form, you do not need to use numerals and letters. Unlike a formal outline, a modified outline does not require two or more points under each heading, and headings do not need to be parallel grammatically. Yet, like a formal outline, a modified outline organizes a text's main ideas and related details. The following modified outline describes methods of communication:

Preliterate Methods
- storytelling
- messengers
- smoke signals
- drums

Literate Methods
- writing
- printing press

Electronic Methods
- telegram
- telephone
- movies
- television
- Internet

Use abbreviations and symbols to make note taking more efficient. Following are some commonly used abbreviations for note taking.

w/	with	re	regarding
w/o	without	=	is, equals
#	number	*	important
&, +	and	def	definition
>	more than	Amer	America
<	less than	tho	although

③ Critical Thinking

Critical thinking includes the ability to analyze, evaluate, and synthesize ideas and information. Critical thinking goes beyond simply understanding something. It involves making informed judgments based on sound reasoning skills.

③.1 Avoiding Faulty Reasoning

When you write or speak for a persuasive purpose, you must make sure your logic is valid. Avoid these mistakes in reasoning, called **logical fallacies.**

Overgeneralization

Conclusions reached on the basis of too little evidence result in the fallacy called overgeneralization. A person who saw three cyclists riding bicycles without helmets might conclude, "Nobody wears bicycle helmets." That conclusion would be an overgeneralization.

Circular Reasoning

When you support an opinion by simply repeating it in different terms, you are using circular reasoning. For example, "Sport-utility vehicles are popular because more people buy them than any other category of new cars." This is an illogical statement because the second part of the sentence simply uses different words to restate the first part of the sentence.

Either-Or Fallacy

Assuming that a complex question has only two possible answers is called the either-or fallacy. "Either we raise the legal driving age or accidents caused by teenage drivers will continue to increase" is an example of the either-or fallacy. The statement ignores other ways of decreasing the automobile accident rate of teenagers.

Cause-and-Effect Fallacy

The cause-and-effect fallacy occurs when you say that event B was caused by event A just because event B occurred after event A.

A person might conclude that because a city's air quality worsened two months after a new factory began operation, the new factory caused the air pollution. However, this cause-and-effect relationship would have to be supported by more specific evidence.

③.2 Identifying Modes of Persuasion

Understanding persuasive techniques can help you evaluate information, make informed decisions, and avoid persuasive techniques intended to deceive you. Some modes of persuasion appeal to your various emotions.

Loaded Language

Loaded language is words or phrases chosen to appeal to the emotions. It is often used in place of facts to shape opinion or to evoke a positive or negative reaction. For example, you might feel positive about a politician who has a *plan.* You might, however, feel negative about a politician who has a *scheme.*

Bandwagon

Bandwagon taps into the human desire to belong. This technique suggests that "everybody" is doing it, or buying it, or believing it. Phrases such as "Don't be the only one" and "Everybody is" signal bandwagon appeal.

Testimonials

Testimonials present well-known people or satisfied customers who promote and endorse a product or idea. This technique taps into the appeal of celebrities or into people's need to identify with others just like themselves.

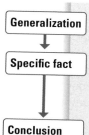

⓷ Logical Thinking

Persuasive writing and speaking require good reasoning skills. Two ways of creating logical arguments are deductive reasoning and inductive reasoning.

Deductive Arguments

A deductive argument begins with a generalization, or premise, and then advances with facts and evidence that lead to a conclusion. The conclusion is the logical outcome of the premise. A false premise leads to a false conclusion; a valid premise leads to a valid conclusion provided that the specific facts are correct and the reasoning is correct.

Generalization	We need to reduce our dependence on fossil fuels.
Specific fact	Cars that get very high mileage from using a mixture of gasoline and electric power are now available in some countries.
Conclusion	Congress should provide tax incentives for manufacturers and consumers to use cars that use gasoline/electric power.

You may use deductive reasoning when writing a persuasive paper or speech. Your conclusion is the thesis of your paper. Facts in your paper supporting your premise should lead logically to that conclusion.

Inductive Arguments

An inductive argument begins with specific evidence that leads to a general conclusion.

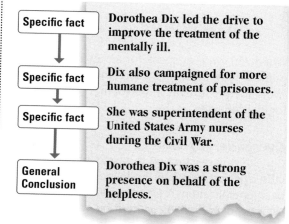

Specific fact	Dorothea Dix led the drive to improve the treatment of the mentally ill.
Specific fact	Dix also campaigned for more humane treatment of prisoners.
Specific fact	She was superintendent of the United States Army nurses during the Civil War.
General Conclusion	Dorothea Dix was a strong presence on behalf of the helpless.

The conclusion of an inductive argument often includes a qualifying term such as *some, often,* or *most*. This usage helps to avoid the fallacy of overgeneralization.

❹ Speaking and Listening

Good speakers and listeners do more than just talk and hear. They use specific techniques to present their ideas effectively, and they are attentive and critical listeners.

⓸ Giving a Speech

In school, in business, and in community life, giving a speech is one of the most effective ways of communicating. Whether you are trying to persuade, to inform, or to entertain, you may often speak before an audience.

Analyzing Audience and Purpose

In order to speak effectively, you need to know to whom you are speaking and why you are speaking. When preparing a speech, think about

how much knowledge and interest your audience has in your subject. A speech has one of two main purposes: to inform or to persuade. A third purpose, to entertain, is often considered closely related to these two purposes.

A speech **to inform** gives the audience new information, provides a better understanding of information, or enables people to use information in a new way. An informative speech is presented in an objective way.

In a speech **to persuade,** a speaker tries to change the actions or beliefs of an audience.

Preparing and Delivering a Speech

There are four main methods of preparing and delivering a speech.

Manuscript When you speak from **manuscript,** you prepare a complete script of your speech in advance and use it to deliver your speech.

Memory When you speak from **memory,** you prepare a written text in advance and then memorize it so you can deliver it word for word.

Impromptu When you give an **impromptu** speech, you speak on the spur of the moment without any special preparation.

Extemporaneous When you give an **extemporaneous** speech, you research and prepare your speech and then deliver it with the help of notes.

Points for Effective Speech Delivery

- Avoid speaking either too fast or too slow. Vary your **speaking rate** depending on your material. Slow down for difficult concepts. Speed up to convince your audience that you are knowledgeable about your subject.

- Speak loud enough to be heard clearly, but not so loud that your voice is overwhelming.

- Use a **conversational tone.**

- Use a change of **pitch,** or inflection, to help make your tone and meaning clear.

- Let your **facial expressions** reflect your message.

- Make **eye contact** with as many audience members as possible.

- Use **gestures** to emphasize your words. Don't make your gestures too small to be seen. On the other hand, don't gesture too frequently or wildly.

- Use **good posture**—not too relaxed and not too rigid. Avoid nervous mannerisms.

4.2 Analyzing, Evaluating and Critiquing a Speech

Evaluating speeches helps you make informed judgments about the ideas presented in a speech. It also helps you learn what makes an effective speech and delivery. Use these criteria to help you analyze, evaluate, and critique speeches.

CRITERIA — How to Evaluate a Persuasive Speech

- Did the speaker have a clear goal or argument?
- Did the speaker take the audience's biases into account?
- Did the speaker support the argument with convincing facts?
- Did the speaker use sound logic in developing the argument?
- Did the speaker use voice, facial expressions, gestures, and posture effectively?
- Did the speaker hold the audience's interest?

CRITERIA — How to Evaluate an Informative Speech

- Did the speaker have a specific, clearly focused topic?
- Did the speaker take the audience's previous knowledge into consideration?
- Did the speaker cite sources for the information?
- Did the speaker communicate the information objectively?
- Did the speaker present the information in an organized manner?
- Did the speaker use visual aids effectively?
- Did the speaker use voice, facial expressions, gestures, and posture effectively?

4.3 Using Active Listening Strategies

Listeners play an active part in the communication process. A listener has a responsibility just as a speaker does. Listening, unlike hearing, is a learned skill.

As you listen to a public speaker, use the following active listening strategies:

- Determine the **speaker's purpose.**
- Listen for the **main idea** of the message and not simply the individual details.
- **Anticipate the points** that will be made, taking into account the speaker's purpose and main idea.
- Listen with an open mind, but **identify faulty logic, unsupported facts,** and **emotional appeals.**

4.4 Conducting Interviews

Conducting a personal interview can be an effective way to get information.

Preparing for an Interview

- Read any articles by or about the person you will interview. This background information will help you get to the point during the interview.
- Prepare a list of questions. Think of more questions than you will need. Include some yes/no questions and some open-ended questions. Order your questions from most important to least important.

Participating in the Interview

- Listen interactively. Be prepared to follow up on a response you find interesting.
- Avoid arguments. Be tactful and polite.

Following Up on the Interview

- Summarize your notes while they are still fresh in your mind.
- Send a thank-you note to the interviewee.

5 Viewing and Representing

In our media-saturated world, we are immersed in visual messages that convey ideas, information, and attitudes. To understand and use visual representations effectively, you need to be aware of the techniques and the range of visuals that are commonly used.

5.1 Understanding Visual Messages

Information is communicated not only with words but with graphic devices. A **graphic device** is a visual representation of data and ideas and the relations among them.

Reading Charts and Graphs

In charts, information is organized in rows and columns. They are helpful in showing complex information clearly. When interpreting a chart, first read the title. Then analyze how the information is presented. Charts can take many different forms. The following chart compares

Dante's descriptions of sinners and their punishments in the *Inferno*.

Comparison and Contrast	
Sinners	**Punishment**
"souls unsure / whose lives earned neither honor nor bad fame"	"a blind life / So abject they envy any other fate"
those "who sinned in carnal things"	"All light is mute . . ." "hurricane of Hell"
those who betrayed their benefactors	"covered wholly by ice"

There are several different types of **graphs,** visual aids that are often used to display numerical information.

- A **circle graph** shows proportions in a whole.
- A **line graph** shows changes in data over a period of time. The following line graph shows changes in the area of the United States during the 19th century.

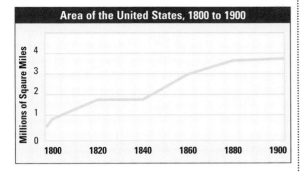

- A **bar graph** compares amounts. The following bar graph shows how many books Leo Tolstoy wrote in each period of his writing career.

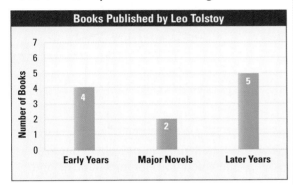

Interpreting Images

Speakers and writers often use visual aids to inform or persuade their audiences. These aids can be invaluable in helping you understand the information being communicated. However, you must interpret visual aids critically, as you do written material.

- **Examine photographs critically.** Does the camera angle or the background in the photo intentionally evoke a positive or negative response? Has the image been altered or manipulated?
- **Evaluate carefully the data presented in charts and graphs.** Some charts and graphs may exaggerate the facts. For example, a circle graph representing a sample of only ten people may be misleading if the speaker suggests that the data represent a trend.

5.2 Evaluating Visual Messages

When you view images, whether they are cartoons, advertising art, photographs, or paintings, there are certain elements to look for.

CRITERIA   How to Analyze Images

- Is color used realistically? Is it used to emphasize certain objects? to evoke a specific response?
- What tone is created by color and by light and dark in the picture?
- Do the background images intentionally evoke a positive or negative response?
- What is noticeable about the picture's composition—that is, the arrangement of lines, colors, and forms? Does the composition emphasize certain objects or elements in the picture?
- For graphs and charts, does the visual accurately represent the data?

5.3 Using Visual Representations

Tables, graphs, diagrams, pictures, and animations often communicate information more effectively than words alone do.

Use visuals with written reports to illustrate complex concepts and processes or to make a page look more interesting. Computer programs, CD-ROMs, and online services can help you generate

- **graphs** that present numerical information
- **charts** and **tables** that allow easy comparison of information
- **logos** and **graphic devices** that highlight important information
- **borders** and **tints** that signal different kinds of information
- useful **illustrations**
- **interactive animations** that illustrate difficult concepts

You might want to explore ways of displaying data in more than one visual format before deciding which will work best for you.

5.4 Making Multimedia Presentations

A multimedia presentation is an electronically prepared combination of text, sound, and visuals (such as photographs, videos, and animations). Your audience reads, hears, and sees your presentation at a computer, following different "paths" you have created to lead them through the information you have gathered.

Planning Presentations

To create a multimedia presentation, first choose your topic and decide what you want to include. Then plan how you want the audience to move through your presentation. For a multimedia presentation on the role of the hero in literature, you might include the following items:

- text defining *hero* and discussing elements of heroes

- a taped reading from *Sundiata,* describing the "Lion King," accompanied by photo of a painting of the African leader

- a taped reading from the *Iliad,* accompanied by a sequence of slides showing various images of Achilles

- a chart comparing two descriptions of a hero: one epic, one cultural

- a video interview with an author on the role of the hero in his or her work

- a video of Troy as seen from an explorer's viewpoint, with a voice-over discussing Homer's *Iliad*

- a series of short film clips showing various heroes from epic movies

You can choose one of the following ways to organize your presentation:

step by step, with only one path, or order, in which the user can see and hear the information

a branching path that allows users to make choices about what they will see and hear, and in what order

A flow chart can help you figure out the paths a user can take through your presentation. Each box in the flow chart that follows represents something about heroes for the user to read, see, or hear. The arrows on the flow chart show the possible paths the user can follow.

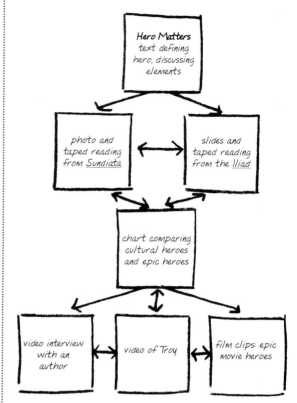

TECHNOLOGY TIP You can download photos, sound, and video from Internet sources onto your computer. This process lets you add elements that would usually require complex editing equipment.

Guiding Your User

Your user will need directions to follow the path you have planned for your multimedia presentation.

Most multimedia authoring programs allow you to create screens that include text or audio directions that guide the user from one part of your presentation to the next.

If you need help creating your multimedia presentation, ask your school's technology adviser. You may also be able to get help from your classmates or your software manual.

Grammar Handbook

1 Quick Reference: Parts of Speech

Part of Speech	Definition	Examples
Noun	Names a person, place, thing, idea, quality, or action	Margaret, Texas, knuckles, nature, beauty, beginning
Pronoun	Takes the place of a noun or another pronoun	
Personal	Refers to the ones speaking, spoken to, or spoken about	I, me, my, mine, we, us, our, ours, you, your, yours, she, he, it, her, him, hers, his, its, they, them, their, theirs
Reflexive	Follows a verb or preposition and refers to a preceding noun or pronoun	myself, yourself, herself, himself, itself, ourselves, yourselves, themselves
Intensive	Emphasizes a noun or another pronoun	(Same as reflexive pronouns)
Demonstrative	Points to one or more specific persons or things	this, that, these, those
Interrogative	Signals a question	who, whom, whose, which, what
Indefinite	Refers to one or more persons or things not specifically mentioned	both, all, most, many, anyone, everybody, several, none, some
Relative	Introduces a subordinate clause and relates it to a word in the main clause	who, whom, whose, which, that
Verb	Expresses action, condition, or state of being	
Action	Tells what the subject does or did, physically or mentally	run, reaches, listened, consider, decides, dreamed
Linking	Connects a subject to that which identifies or describes it	am, is, are, was, were, sound, taste, appear, feel, become, remain, seem
Auxiliary	Precedes and introduces a main verb	be, have, do, can, could, will, would, may, might
Adjective	Modifies a noun or pronoun	**strong** women, **two** epics, **enough** time
Adverb	Modifies a verb, an adjective, or another adverb	walked **out**, **really** funny, **far** away
Preposition	Relates one word to another (following) word	at, by, for, from, in, of, on, to, with
Conjunction	Joins words or word groups	
Coordinating	Joins words or word groups used the same way	and, but, or, for, so, yet, nor
Correlative	Work as a pair to join words or word groups used the same way	both . . . and, either . . . or, neither . . . nor
Subordinating	Joins word groups not used the same way	although, after, as, before, because, when, if, unless
Interjection	Expresses emotion	wow, ouch, hurrah

2 Nouns

A noun is a word used to name a person, place, thing, idea, quality, or action. Nouns can be classified in several ways. All nouns can be placed in at least two classifications. They are either common or proper. All are also either abstract or concrete. Some nouns can be classified as compound, collective, or possessive as well.

2.1 Common Nouns are general names, common to an entire group.

> EXAMPLES: *motor, tree, time, children*

2.2 Proper Nouns name specific, one-of-a-kind things. (See Quick Reference: Capitalization, page R79.)

> EXAMPLES: *Bradbury, Eastern Standard Time, Maine*

2.3 Concrete Nouns name things that can be perceived by the senses.

> EXAMPLES: *stadium, jacket, St. Louis, Wrigley Field*

2.4 Abstract Nouns name things that cannot be perceived by the senses.

> EXAMPLES: *intelligence, fear, joy, loneliness*

	Common	Proper
Abstract	beauty	Enlightenment
Concrete	planet	Mars

2.5 Compound Nouns are formed from two or more words but express single ideas. They are written as single words, as separate words, or with hyphens. Use a dictionary to check the correct spelling of a compound noun.

> EXAMPLES: *sunshine, call waiting, job-sharing*

2.6 Collective Nouns are singular nouns that refer to groups of people or things. (See Collective Nouns as Subjects, page R76.)

> EXAMPLES: *army, flock, class, species*

2.7 Possessive Nouns show who or what owns something. Consult the following chart for the proper use of the possessive apostrophe.

Category	Possessive Nouns Rule	Examples
All singular nouns	Add apostrophe plus *s*	Lily's, bass's, pitcher's, daughter-in-law's
Plural nouns not ending in *s*	Add apostrophe plus *s*	children's women's people's
Plural nouns ending in *s*	Add apostrophe only	witnesses' churches' males' Johnsons'

GRAMMAR PRACTICE

A. For each underlined noun, first tell whether it is common or proper. Then tell whether it is concrete or abstract.

1. The <u>legend</u> of Sundiata is loosely based on the true story of the man who established the Mali empire.

2. After he returned from years in exile, Sundiata united the <u>kingdoms</u> of the region.

3. The Mali territory, which eventually stretched from the <u>Atlantic Ocean</u> to what is now Nigeria, included <u>part</u> of the Niger River.

4. The tranquillity and peace established by <u>Sundiata</u> lasted for many years.

5. <u>Griots</u>, or trained storytellers, narrate the epic of Sundiata by reciting, chanting, and singing the story.

6. Valmiki, the author of the *<u>Ramayana</u>*, at first did not think himself worthy to tell the tale of Rama.

7. Rama, a strong and brave leader, prepares to do battle with the enemy who kidnapped Sita, Rama's <u>wife</u>.

8. Rama fights Ravana, a powerful <u>demon</u> with 10 heads and 20 arms.

9. In Indian <u>culture</u>, Rama represents values such as strength and leadership.

10. The *Ramayana*, while filled with <u>action</u> and intrigue, is a highly spiritual work as well.

B. 11–15. From the sentences above, write three compound nouns and two collective nouns.

C. Write the possessive forms of the following nouns.

16. Sundiata
17. kingdoms
18. Rama
19. tranquillity
20. values

21. Valmiki
22. arms
23. strength
24. Nigeria
25. storytellers

③ Pronouns

A pronoun is a word that is used in place of a noun or another pronoun. The word or word group to which the pronoun refers is called its antecedent.

3.1 *Personal Pronouns* are pronouns that change their form to express person, number, gender, and case. The forms of these pronouns are shown in the chart that follows.

	Nominative	Objective	Possessive
Singular			
First person	I	me	my, mine
Second person	you	you	your, yours
Third person	she, he, it	her, him, it	her, hers, his, its
Plural			
First person	we	us	our, ours
Second person	you	you	your, yours
Third person	they	them	their, theirs

3.2 *Pronoun Agreement* Pronouns should agree with their antecedents in number and person. Singular pronouns are used to replace singular nouns. Plural pronouns are used to replace plural nouns. Pronouns must also match the gender (masculine, feminine, or neuter) of the nouns they replace.

3.3 *Pronoun Case* Personal pronouns change form to show how they function in a sentence. Their forms are called *cases.* The three cases are **nominative, objective,** and **possessive.**

A nominative pronoun is used as a subject or a predicate nominative in a sentence.

An objective pronoun is used as a direct or indirect object or as an object of a preposition.

SUBJECT   OBJECT

He will lead them to us.

OBJECT OF PREPOSITION

A possessive pronoun shows ownership. The pronouns *mine, yours, hers, his, its, ours,* and *theirs* can be used in place of nouns.

> **EXAMPLE:** *This horse is mine.*

The pronouns *my, your, her, his, its, our,* and *their* are used before nouns.

> **EXAMPLE:** *This is my horse.*

USAGE TIP To decide which case to use in a comparison, such as *He tells better tales than (I or me),* fill in the missing words: *He tells better tales than I tell.*

WATCH OUT! Many spelling errors can be avoided if you watch out for *its* and *their.* Don't confuse the possessive pronoun *its* with the contraction *it's,* meaning "it is" or "it has." The homophones *they're* (contraction of *they are*) and *there* (place or expletive) are often mistakenly used for *their.*

3.4 *Reflexive and Intensive Pronouns* These pronouns are formed by adding *-self* or *-selves* to certain personal pronouns. Their forms are the same, and they differ only in how they are used.

Reflexive pronouns follow verbs or prepositions and reflect back on an earlier noun or pronoun.

> **EXAMPLES:** *He likes himself too much. She is now herself again.*

Intensive pronouns intensify or emphasize the nouns or pronouns to which they refer.

> **EXAMPLES:** *They themselves will educate their children. You did it yourselves.*

Singular	
First person	myself
Second person	yourself
Third person	herself, himself, itself

Plural	
First person	ourselves
Second person	yourselves
Third person	themselves

WATCH OUT! Avoid using *hisself* or *theirselves.* Standard English does not include these forms.

> **NONSTANDARD:** *The children sang theirselves to sleep.*
> **STANDARD:** *The children sang themselves to sleep.*

USAGE TIP Reflexive and intensive pronouns should never be used without antecedents.

> **INCORRECT:** *Read a tale to my brother and myself.*
> **CORRECT:** *Read a tale to my brother and me.*

3.5 Demonstrative Pronouns point out things and persons near and far.

	Singular	Plural
Near	this	these
Far	that	those

WATCH OUT! Avoid using the objective pronoun *them* in place of the demonstrative *those.*

> **INCORRECT:** *Let's dramatize one of them tales.*
> **CORRECT:** *Let's dramatize one of those tales.*

3.6 Indefinite Pronouns do not refer to specific persons or things and usually have no antecedents. The chart shows some commonly used indefinite pronouns.

Singular	Plural	Singular or Plural	
each	both	all	
either	few	any	
neither	many	more	none
another	several	most	some

Here is another set of indefinite pronouns, all of which are singular. Notice that, with one exception, each is spelled as one word:

anyone	everyone	no one	someone
anybody	everybody	nobody	somebody
anything	everything	nothing	something

USAGE TIP Since all these are singular, pronouns referring to them should be singular.

> **INCORRECT:** *Did everybody play their part well?*
> **CORRECT:** *Did everybody play her part well?*

If the indefinite pronoun can denote either a male or a female, *his or her* may be used to refer to it, or the sentence may be recast.

> **EXAMPLES:** *Did everybody play his or her part well?*
> *Did all the students play their parts well?*

GRAMMAR PRACTICE

Write the correct form of each incorrect pronoun in the sentences below.

1. In "Song of P'eng-ya," a family flees rebel troops who are chasing his.
2. The speaker of the poem carries the baby girl and lets the young boy walk by myself.
3. The family travels for days in unbearable conditions until she finally reaches the marsh.
4. Sun Tsai, an old friend of the speaker, and her wife help the family.
5. The vow between Sun Tsai and the speaker reinforces she loyalty.

3.7 Interrogative Pronouns tell a reader or listener that questions are coming. The interrogative pronouns are *who, whom, whose, which,* and *what.*

> **EXAMPLES:** *Who is going to rehearse with you? From whom did you receive the script?*

USAGE TIP *Who* is used as a subject, *whom* as an object. To find out which pronoun you need to use in a question, change the question to a statement:

> **QUESTION:** *(Who/Whom) did you meet there?*
> **STATEMENT:** *You met (?) there.*

Since the verb has a subject (*you*), the needed word must be the object form, *whom.*

> **CORRECT:** *Whom did you meet there?*

WATCH OUT! A special problem arises when you use an interrupter such as *do you think* within a sentence:

> **EXAMPLE:** *(Who/Whom) do you think will win?*

If you eliminate the interrupter, it is clear that the word you need is *who.*

3.8 *Relative Pronouns* relate, or connect, clauses to the words they modify in sentences. The noun or pronoun that a clause modifies is the antecedent of the relative pronoun. Here are the relative pronouns and their uses.

Replacing:	Subject	Object	Possessive
Persons	who	whom	whose
Things	which	which	whose
Things/persons*	that	that	whose

* *That* generally will not replace specific names, such as *Richard Wright.*

Often short sentences with related ideas can be combined by using a relative pronoun to create a more effective sentence.

> **SHORT SENTENCE:** *Amy won a swimming contest at the age of eight.*
> **RELATED SENTENCE:** *Amy did not plan to become a professional athlete.*
> **COMBINED SENTENCE:** *Amy, who won a swimming contest at the age of eight, did not plan to become a professional athlete.*

GRAMMAR PRACTICE

Choose the appropriate interrogative or relative pronoun from the words in parentheses.

1. Mrs. Linde, (who/whom) is an old friend of Nora's, stops by the Helmer house for an unexpected visit.
2. When Dr. Rank tells the ladies of a morally corrupt patient, Nora asks, "(Who/Whom) do you mean?"
3. Dr. Rank, (who/whom) is in love with Nora, asks her not to tell Torvald his secret.
4. Nora knows that Torvald, (who/whom) refuses to give Krogstad a position at the bank, would be devastated by the truth.
5. Fear, pride, and love are some of the factors (that/who) prevent Nora from telling Torvald about the loan from Krogstad.
6. Finally, Nora tells Torvald about her agreement with Krogstad, (who/whom) Torvald thinks is corrupt and loathsome.
7. Nora decides to leave her home after realizing that the man to (who/whom) she devoted her life did not understand her.

④ Verbs

A verb is a word that expresses an action, a condition, or a state of being. There are two main kinds of verbs: action and linking. Other verbs, called auxiliary verbs, are sometimes used with action verbs and linking verbs.

4.1 *Action Verbs* tell what action someone or something is performing, physically or mentally.

> **PHYSICAL ACTION:** *You hit the target.*
> **MENTAL ACTION:** *She dreamed of me.*

4.2 *Linking Verbs* do not express actions. Linking verbs link subjects to complements that identify or describe them. Linking verbs may be divided into two groups:

> **FORMS OF BE:** *She is our queen.*
> **VERBS THAT EXPRESS CONDITION:** *The writer looked thoughtful.*

4.3 *Auxiliary Verbs,* sometimes called helping verbs, precede action or linking verbs and modify their meanings in special ways. The most commonly used auxiliary verbs are forms of the verbs *be, have,* and *do.*

> **Be:** *am, is, are, was, were, be, being, been*
> **Have:** *have, has, had*
> **Do:** *do, does, did*

Other common auxiliary verbs are *can, could, will, would, shall, should, may, might,* and *must.*

> **EXAMPLES:** *I always have admired her.*
> *You must listen to me.*

4.4 *Transitive and Intransitive Verbs*
Action verbs can be either transitive or intransitive. A transitive verb directs the action towards someone or something. It has an object. An intransitive verb does not direct the action towards someone or something. It does not have an object. Since linking verbs convey no action, they are always intransitive.

> **Transitive:** *The storm sank the ship.*
> **Intransitive:** *The ship sank.*

4.5 **_Principal Parts_** Action and linking verbs typically have four principal parts, which are used to form verb tenses. The principal parts are the _present_, the _present participle_, the _past_, and the _past participle_.

If the verb is a regular verb, the past and past participle are formed by adding the ending -*d* or -*ed* to the present part. Here is a chart showing four regular verbs.

Present	Present Participle	Past	Past Participle
risk	(is) risking	risked	(has) risked
solve	(is) solving	solved	(has) solved
drop	(is) dropping	dropped	(has) dropped
carry	(is) carrying	carried	(has) carried

Note that the present participle and past participle forms are preceded by forms of _be_ and _have._ These principal parts cannot be used alone as main verbs and always need auxiliary verbs.

> **EXAMPLES**: _She once thought her mother was wasting her time._
> _Now she has stopped trying to be like everyone else._

The past and past participle of an irregular verb are not formed by adding -*d* or -*ed* to the present; they are formed in irregular ways.

Present	Present Participle	Past	Past Participle
begin	(is) beginning	began	(has) begun
break	(is) breaking	broke	(has) broken
bring	(is) bringing	brought	(has) brought
choose	(is) choosing	chose	(has) chosen
go	(is) going	went	(has) gone
lose	(is) losing	lost	(has) lost
see	(is) seeing	saw	(has) seen
swim	(is) swimming	swam	(has) swum
write	(is) writing	wrote	(has) written

4.6 **_Verb Tense_** The tense of a verb tells the time of the action or the state of being. An action or state of being can occur in the present, the past, or the future. There are six tenses, each expressing a different range of time.

Present tense expresses an action that is happening at the present time, occurs regularly, or is constant or generally true. Use the present part.

> **EXAMPLES**
> **NOW**: _This soup tastes delicious._
> **REGULAR**: _I make vegetable soup often._
> **GENERAL**: _Crops require sun, rain, and rich soil._

Past tense expresses an action that began and ended in the past. Use the past part.

> **EXAMPLE**: _The storyteller finished his tale._

Future tense expresses an action (or state of being) that will occur. Use _shall_ or _will_ with the present part.

> **EXAMPLE**: _They will attend the next festival._

Present perfect tense expresses action (1) that was completed at an indefinite time in the past or (2) that began in the past and continues into the present. Use _have_ or _has_ with the past participle.

> **EXAMPLE**: _Poetry has inspired readers throughout the ages._

Past perfect tense shows an action in the past that came before another action in the past. Use _had_ before the past participle.

> **EXAMPLE**: _Before we left, we had asked him to find a place to stay._

Future perfect tense shows an action in the future that will be completed before another action in the future. Use _shall have_ or _will have_ before the past participle.

> **EXAMPLE**: _They will have finished the novel before seeing the movie version of the tale._

4.7 **_Progressive Forms_** The progressive forms of the six tenses show ongoing action. Use a form of _be_ with the present participle of a verb.

> **PRESENT PROGRESSIVE**: _She is rehearsing her lines._
> **PAST PROGRESSIVE**: _She was rehearsing her lines._
> **FUTURE PROGRESSIVE**: _She will be rehearsing her lines._

PRESENT PERFECT PROGRESSIVE: *She has been rehearsing her lines.*
PAST PERFECT PROGRESSIVE: *She had been rehearsing her lines.*
FUTURE PERFECT PROGRESSIVE: *She will have been rehearsing her lines.*

WATCH OUT! Do not shift tenses needlessly. Watch out for these special cases.

- In most compound sentences and in sentences with compound predicates, use only one tense.

  INCORRECT: *I keyed in the password, but I get an error message.*
  CORRECT: *I keyed in the password, but I got an error message.*

- If one past action happens before another, do shift tenses—from the past to the past perfect:

  INCORRECT: *They wished they started earlier.*
  CORRECT: *They wished they had started earlier.*

GRAMMAR PRACTICE

Identify the tenses of the verbs in the following sentences. If you find an unnecessary tense shift, correct it.

1. The story "Iktomi and the Wild Ducks" is a Lakota trickster tale.
2. Iktomi decided he wants some ducks for breakfast.
3. After he tells the ducks to close their eyes for a dance, Iktomi will have been killing them.
4. However, one young duck had broken Iktomi's rule and opens his eyes.
5. He tells the other ducks to take off and they flew safely into the distance.

4.8 ***Active and Passive Voice*** The voice of a verb tells whether the subject of a sentence performs or receives the action expressed by the verb. When the subject performs the action, the verb is in the active voice. When the subject is the receiver of the action, the verb is in the passive voice.

Compare these two sentences:

ACTIVE: *Her sunglasses hid most of her face.*
PASSIVE: *Most of her face was hidden by her sunglasses.*

To form the passive voice, use a form of *be* with the past participle of the main verb.

WATCH OUT! Use the passive voice sparingly. It tends to make writing less forceful and less direct. It can also make the writing awkward.

AWKWARD: *She was given the handmade quilts by her mother.*
BETTER: *Her mother gave her the handmade quilts.*

There are occasions when you will choose to use the passive voice because

- you want to emphasize the receiver: *The king was shot.*
- the doer is unknown: *My books were stolen.*
- the doer is unimportant: *French is spoken here.*

4.9 ***Mood*** A verb's mood conveys the manner in which the verb expresses an idea. There are three moods.

The indicative mood states a fact or asks a question. You use this mood most often.

EXAMPLE: *His trust was shattered by the betrayal.*

The imperative mood is used to give a command or make a request.

EXAMPLE: *Be there by eight o'clock sharp.*

The subjunctive mood is used to express a wish or a condition that is contrary to fact.

EXAMPLE: *If I were you, I wouldn't get my hopes up.*

GRAMMAR PRACTICE

A. Identify the boldfaced verbs as active or passive.

1. The *Epic of Gilgamesh* **was written** more than 4,000 years ago.
2. It **is considered** one of the oldest quest stories.
3. Gilgamesh **explores** both his godlike side and his human side throughout the epic.
4. The death of his friend Enkidu **causes** Gilgamesh to break down and weep.
5. Utnapishtim and his family **had been saved** from the flood.

B. Identify the boldfaced verbs as indicative or subjunctive in mood.

6. Utnapishtim **gives** Gilgamesh advice before Gilgamesh meets with the gods.

7. If Utnapishtim **were** more trusting, he wouldn't have to test Gilgamesh's word.

8. After Utnapishtim **touched** Gilgamesh, Gilgamesh thought he had slept only moments.

9. The men **were leaving** when Utnapishtim's wife called out.

10. If Gilgamesh **were** a different kind of figure, he would not learn as much as he does during his quest.

⑤ Modifiers

Modifiers are words or groups of words that change or limit the meanings of other words. The two kinds of modifiers are adjectives and adverbs.

5.1 *Adjectives* An adjective is a word that modifies a noun or pronoun by telling which one, what kind, how many, or how much.

WHICH ONE: *this, that, these, those*
EXAMPLE: *These tomatoes have grown quickly.*

WHAT KIND: *tiny, impressive, bold, rotten*
EXAMPLE: *The bold officer stood in front of the crowd.*

HOW MANY: *some, few, thirty, none, both, each*
EXAMPLE: *Some of us had three helpings of sweet potatoes.*

HOW MUCH: *more, less, enough, scarce*
EXAMPLE: *There was enough chicken to serve everyone.*

The **articles** *a, an,* and *the* are usually classified as adjectives. These are the most common adjectives that you will use.

EXAMPLES: *The bridge was burned before the attack.*
A group of peasants led the procession in the town.

5.2 *Predicate Adjectives* Most adjectives come before the nouns they modify, as in the examples above. Predicate adjectives, however, follow linking verbs and describe their subjects.

EXAMPLE: *My friends are very intelligent.*

Be especially careful to use adjectives (not adverbs) after such linking verbs as *look, feel, grow, taste,* and *smell.*

EXAMPLE: *The weather grows cold.*

5.3 *Adverbs* modify verbs, adjectives, and other adverbs by telling where, when, how, or to what extent.

WHERE: *The children played outside.*
WHEN: *The author spoke yesterday.*
HOW: *We walked slowly behind the leader.*
TO WHAT EXTENT: *He worked very hard.*

Unlike adjectives, adverbs tend to be mobile words; they may occur in many places in sentences.

EXAMPLES: *Suddenly the wind shifted. The wind suddenly shifted. The wind shifted suddenly.*

Changing the position of adverbs within sentences can vary the rhythm in your writing.

5.4 *Adjective or Adverb* Many adverbs are formed by adding *-ly* to adjectives.

EXAMPLES: *sweet, sweetly; gentle, gently*

However, *-ly* added to a noun will usually yield an adjective.

EXAMPLES: *friend, friendly; woman, womanly*

5.5 *Comparison of Modifiers* The form of an adjective or adverb indicates the degree of comparison that the modifier expresses. Both adjectives and adverbs have three forms, or degrees: positive, comparative, and superlative.

The positive form is used to describe individual things, groups, or actions.

EXAMPLES: *The emperor's chariots are fast. Brenda's speech was effective.*

The comparative form is used to compare two things, groups, or actions.

EXAMPLES: *The emperor's chariots are faster than the senators' chariots. George's speech was more effective than Brenda's speech.*

The **superlative form** is used to compare more than two things, groups, or actions.

> **EXAMPLES:** *The emperor's chariots are the <u>fastest</u> in the empire.*
> *Antony's speech was the <u>most effective</u> of all.*

5.6 **Regular Comparisons** For one-syllable and some two-syllable adjectives and adverbs, the comparative and superlative forms are formed by adding -*er* and -*est*. All three-syllable and most two-syllable modifiers form their comparative and superlative forms by adding *more* and *most*.

Positive	Comparative	Superlative
small	smaller	smallest
thin	thinner	thinnest
sleepy	sleepier	sleepiest
useless	more useless	most useless
precisely	more precisely	most precisely

WATCH OUT! Note that spelling changes must sometimes be made to form the comparatives and superlatives of modifiers.

> **EXAMPLES:** *friendly, friendlier* (Change *y* to *i* and add the ending.)
> *sad, sadder* (Double the final consonant and add the ending.)

5.7 **Irregular Comparisons** Some commonly used modifiers have irregular comparative and superlative forms. You may wish to memorize them.

Positive	Comparative	Superlative
good	better	best
bad	worse	worst
far	farther *or* further	farthest *or* furthest
little	less *or* lesser	least
many	more	most
well	better	best
much	more	most

5.8 **Using Modifiers Correctly** Study the tips that follow to avoid common mistakes.

Farther* and *further *Farther* is used for distances; use *further* for everything else.

Avoiding double comparisons You make a comparison by using -*er*/-*est* or by using *more*/*most*. Using -*er* with *more* or using -*est* with *most* is incorrect.

> **INCORRECT:** *I like her <u>more better</u> than she likes me.*
> **CORRECT:** *I like her <u>better</u> than she likes me.*

Avoiding illogical comparisons An illogical or confusing comparison results if two unrelated things are compared or if something is compared with itself. The word *other* or the word *else* should be used in a comparison of an individual member with the rest of the group.

> **ILLOGICAL:** *Shakespeare's plays are more popular than those of any Elizabethan writer.* (Wasn't Shakespeare an Elizabethan writer?)
> **LOGICAL:** *Shakespeare's plays are more popular than those of any <u>other</u> Elizabethan writer.*

Bad* vs. *badly *Bad,* always an adjective, is used before a noun or after a linking verb to describe the subject. *Badly,* always an adverb, never modifies a noun. Be sure to use the right form after a linking verb.

> **INCORRECT:** *Ed felt badly after his team lost.*
> **CORRECT:** *Ed felt bad after his team lost.*

Good* vs. *well *Good* is always an adjective. It is used before a noun or after a linking verb to modify the subject. *Well* is often an adverb meaning "expertly" or "properly." *Well* can also be used as an adjective after a linking verb, when it means "in good health."

> **INCORRECT:** *Helen writes very good.*
> **CORRECT:** *Helen writes very well.*
> **CORRECT:** *Yesterday I felt bad; today I feel well.*

Double negatives If you add a negative word to a sentence that is already negative, the result will be an error known as a double negative. When using *not* or *-n't* with a verb, use *"any-"* words, such as *anybody* or *anything,* rather than *"no-"* words, such as *nobody* or *nothing,* later in the sentence.

> **INCORRECT:** *I don't have no money.*
> **CORRECT:** *I don't have any money.*
>
> **INCORRECT:** *We haven't seen nobody.*
> **CORRECT:** *We haven't seen anybody.*

Using *hardly, barely,* or *scarcely* after a negative word is also incorrect.

> **INCORRECT:** *They couldn't barely see two feet ahead.*
> **CORRECT:** *They could barely see two feet ahead.*

Misplaced modifiers A misplaced modifier is one placed so far away from the word it modifies that the intended meaning of the sentence is unclear. Place modifiers as close as possible to the words they modify.

> **MISPLACED:** *We found the child in the park who was missing.* (The child was missing, not the park.)
>
> **CLEARER:** *We found the child who was missing in the park.*

GRAMMAR PRACTICE

Choose the correct word from each pair in parentheses.

1. The *Iliad's* main character is Achilles, the (powerfulest/most powerful) soldier in the Trojan War.
2. The war begins after Paris takes Helen, the (most beautiful/beautifulest) woman in the world, away from Menelaus.
3. Paris (could/couldn't) hardly know that his rash action would cause a ten-year battle.
4. Nine years later, when the *Iliad* begins, Greek armies still hadn't defeated (no/any) Trojans.
5. Between Agamemnon and Achilles, Achilles is the (better/best) commander.
6. Achilles defects from Agamemnon, but Achilles' soldiers follow Achilles because they love him (well/good).
7. After his best friend, Patroclus, dies in battle, Achilles feels (bad/badly).

8. Achilles doesn't have (any/no) qualm about destroying Hector's body.
9. Achilles doesn't want (anyone/no one) but the Trojans to win the war.
10. Some Greeks think that Achilles is the (most good/best) leader they will ever have.

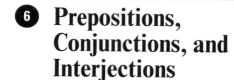

6 **Prepositions, Conjunctions, and Interjections**

6.1 ***Prepositions*** A preposition is a word used to show the relationship between a noun or a pronoun and another word in the sentence.

Commonly Used Prepositions			
above	down	near	through
at	for	of	to
before	from	on	up
below	in	out	with
by	into	over	without

The preposition is always followed by a word or group of words that serve as its object. The preposition, its object, and modifiers of the object are called a **prepositional phrase.** In each example below, the prepositional phrase is underlined and the object of the preposition is in boldface type.

> **EXAMPLES**
> *The future of the entire **kingdom** is uncertain.*
> *We searched through the deepest **woods.***

Prepositional phrases may be used as adjectives or as adverbs. The phrase in the first example is used as an adjective modifying the noun *future.* In the second example, the phrase is used as an adverb modifying the verb *searched.*

WATCH OUT! A prepositional phrase must be as close as possible to the word it modifies.

> **MISPLACED:** *We have clothes for leisure wear of many colors.*
> **CLEARER:** *We have clothes of many colors for leisure wear.*

6.2 *Conjunctions* A conjunction is a word used to connect words, phrases, or sentences. There are three kinds of conjunctions: **coordinating conjunctions, correlative conjunctions,** and **subordinating conjunctions.**

Coordinating conjunctions connect words or word groups that have the same function in a sentence. These include *and, but, or, for, so, yet,* and *nor.* Coordinating conjunctions can join nouns, pronouns, verbs, adjectives, adverbs, prepositional phrases, and clauses.

These examples show coordinating conjunctions joining words of the same function:

> **EXAMPLES**
>
> *I have many friends <u>but</u> few enemies.* (two direct objects)
>
> *We ran out the door <u>and</u> into the street.* (two prepositional phrases)
>
> *They are pleasant <u>yet</u> seem aloof.* (two predicates)
>
> *We have to go now, <u>or</u> we will be late.* (two clauses)

Correlative conjunctions are similar to coordinating conjunctions. However, correlative conjunctions are always used in pairs.

Correlative Conjunctions		
both . . . and	neither . . . nor	whether . . . or
either . . . or	not only . . . but also	

Subordinating conjunctions introduce subordinate clauses—clauses that cannot stand by themselves as complete sentences. The subordinating conjunction shows how the subordinate clause relates to the rest of the sentence. The relationships include time, manner, place, cause, comparison, condition, and purpose.

TIME	*after, as, as long as, as soon as, before, since, until, when, whenever, while*
MANNER	*as, as if*
PLACE	*where, wherever*
CAUSE	*because, since*
COMPARISON	*as, as much as, than*
CONDITION	*although, as long as, even if, even though, if, provided that, though, unless, while*
PURPOSE	*in order that, so that, that*

In the example below, the boldfaced word is the conjunction, and the underlined words are the subordinate clause:

> **EXAMPLE:** *We sing **because** <u>we are happy</u>.*

We sing is an independent clause because it can stand alone as a complete sentence. *Because we are happy* cannot stand alone as a complete sentence; it is a subordinate clause.

Conjunctive adverbs are used to connect clauses that can stand by themselves as sentences. Conjunctive adverbs include *also, besides, finally, however, moreover, nevertheless, otherwise,* and *then.*

> **EXAMPLE:** *She loved the fall; <u>however</u>, she also enjoyed winter.*

6.3 *Interjections* are words used to show strong emotion, such as *wow* and *cool*. Often followed by an exclamation point, they have no grammatical relationship to the rest of a sentence.

> **EXAMPLE:** *You've written a poem? <u>Great!</u>*

GRAMMAR PRACTICE

Label each of the boldfaced words as a preposition, a conjunction, or an interjection.

1. Chrétien de Troyes wrote poetry about King Arthur **and** the knights of the Round Table.

2. He is well-known **for** his Arthurian romances, **but** he also wrote a tale that mocks epic **and** romance customs.

3. **In** Chrétien's romance *Perceval: The Story of the Grail,* the main character is searching **for** his mother.

4. Perceval feels sad **because** she fainted **when** he left home.

5. Perceval meets a man **by** a river and asks him **for** directions.

6. He finds shelter **for** the night **in** an enormous castle. **Excellent!**

7. **While** he is inside the castle, Perceval observes a ritual full **of** mystery **and** magic.

8. He is afraid **of** interrupting the ceremony, **yet** he cannot turn away.

9. **After** he leaves, he meets a girl; she tells Perceval **of** future misfortunes **for** himself **and** others.

10. **In** the end, Perceval cannot believe he saw the Holy Grail **and** didn't know it. **Wow!**

❼ Quick Reference: The Sentence and Its Parts

The diagrams that follow will give you a brief review of the essentials of the sentence—subjects and predicates—and of some of its parts.

The writer's **pen** hit the floor.

The **complete subject** includes all the words that identify the person, place, thing, or idea that the sentence is about.

The complete predicate includes all the words that tell or ask something about the subject.

pen

hit

The **simple subject** tells exactly whom or what the sentence is about. It does not include any modifiers.

The simple predicate, or verb, tells what the subject does or is. It may be one word or several, but it does not include modifiers.

For his graduation, the family **had given** the young **Buddy** money.

A **prepositional phrase** consists of a preposition, its object, and any modifiers of the object. In this phrase, *for* is the preposition and *graduation* is its object.

subject

An indirect object is a word or a group of words that tells to whom or for whom or to what or for what about the verb. A sentence can have an indirect object only if it has a direct object. The indirect object always comes before the direct object in a sentence.

Verbs often have more than one part. They may be made up of a main verb, like *given*, and one or more auxiliary, or helping, verbs, like *had*.

A direct object is a word or group of words that tells who or what receives the action of the verb in the sentence.

⑧ The Sentence and Its Parts

A sentence is a group of words used to express a complete thought. A complete sentence has a subject and predicate.

8.1 *Kinds of Sentences* Sentences make statements, ask questions, give commands, and show feelings. There are four basic types of sentences.

Type	Definition	Example
Declarative	States a fact, wish, intent, or feeling	I read White's essay last night.
Interrogative	Asks a question	Did you like the essay?
Imperative	Gives a command or direction	Read this paragraph aloud.
Exclamatory	Expresses strong feeling or excitement	I wish I had thought of that!

WRITING TIP One way to vary your writing is to employ a variety of different types of sentences. In the first example below, each sentence is declarative. Notice how much more interesting the revised paragraph is.

SAMPLE PARAGRAPH: *You have to see Niagara Falls in person. You can truly appreciate their awesome power in no other way. You should visit them on your next vacation. They are a spectacular sight.*

REVISED PARAGRAPH: *Have you ever seen Niagara Falls in person? You can truly appreciate their awesome power in no other way. Visit them on your next vacation. What a spectacular sight they are!*

WATCH OUT! Conversation frequently includes parts of sentences, or **fragments.** In formal writing, however, you need to be sure that every sentence is a complete thought and includes a subject and a predicate. (See Correcting Fragments, page R73.)

8.2 *Complete Subjects and Predicates* A sentence has two parts: a subject and a predicate. The complete subject includes all the words that identify the person, place, thing, or idea that the sentence is about. The complete predicate includes all the words that tell what the subject did or what happened to the subject.

Complete Subject	Complete Predicate
The poets of the time	wrote about nature.
This new approach	was extraordinary.

8.3 *Simple Subjects and Predicates* The simple subject is the key word in the complete subject. The simple predicate is the key word in the complete predicate. In the examples that follow they are underlined.

Simple Subject	Simple Predicate
The <u>poets</u> of the time	<u>wrote</u> about nature.
This new <u>approach</u>	<u>was</u> extraordinary.

8.4 *Compound Subjects and Predicates* A compound subject consists of two or more subjects of the same verb. They are typically joined by the coordinating conjunction *and* or *or.*

> **EXAMPLE:** <u>*Tolstoy and Ibsen*</u> *write about families.*

A compound predicate consists of two or more predicates that have the same subject. They too are usually joined by the coordinating conjunction *and, but,* or *or.*

> **EXAMPLE:** *The homeowner <u>mowed the lawn</u> and watered the garden.*

8.5 *Subjects in Questions* In an interrogative sentence, the subject may appear after the verb or between parts of a verb phrase.

> **INTERROGATIVE:** *Did <u>Father</u> get up early?*
> **INTERROGATIVE:** *Why has that <u>book</u> sold so well?*

8.6 Subjects in Imperative Sentences

Imperative sentences give commands, requests, or directions. The subject of an imperative sentence is the person spoken to. While it is not stated, it is understood to be *you.*

> **EXAMPLE:** *(You) Please tell me what you're thinking.*

8.7 Subjects in Sentences That Begin with There and Here

When a sentence begins with *there* or *here*, the subject usually follows the verb. Remember that *there* and *here* are never the subjects of sentences. The simple subjects in the example sentences are underlined.

> **EXAMPLES**
>
> *Here is the <u>solution</u> to the mystery.*
>
> *There is no <u>time</u> to waste now.*
>
> *There were too many <u>passengers</u> on the boat.*

GRAMMAR PRACTICE

Copy each of the following sentences. Then draw one line under the complete subject and two lines under the complete predicate.

1. Sophocles wrote the play *Oedipus the King.*
2. The story begins with Oedipus ruling Thebes with his wife, Jocasta, at his side.
3. A plague causes Oedipus to search for a remedy to stop the outbreak.
4. The oracle tells the king that he must find the man who murdered Jocasta's first husband, Laius.
5. As Oedipus begins to investigate, his hidden past begins to point suspicion in a startling direction.
6. The truth is that Oedipus himself murdered Laius.
7. Laius and Jocasta are actually Oedipus' father and mother!
8. Jocasta hangs herself to spare herself the shame of being married to her own son.
9. In a guilt-stricken moment, the king blinds himself with pins.
10. Oedipus is a classic example of a tragic hero.

8.8 Complements

A complement is a word or group of words that completes the meaning of a predicate. A sentence may contain only a subject and a verb. Most sentences, however, require additional words placed after the verb to complete the meaning of the predicate. There are three kinds of complements: **direct objects, indirect objects,** and **subject complements.**

Direct objects are words or word groups that receive the action of action verbs. A direct object answers the question *what* or *whom.* In the examples that follow, the direct objects are underlined.

> **EXAMPLES**
>
> *The students asked many <u>questions</u>.*
> (asked what?)
>
> *The teacher quickly answered <u>them</u>.*
> (answered whom?)
>
> *The school accepted <u>girls and boys</u>.*
> (accepted whom?)

Indirect objects tell to or for whom or what the action of verbs is performed. Indirect objects come before direct objects. In the examples that follow, the indirect objects are underlined.

> **EXAMPLES**
>
> *My sister usually gave her <u>friends</u> good advice.* (gave to whom?)
>
> *Her brother sent the <u>post office</u> a heavy package.* (sent to what?)
>
> *His kind grandfather mailed <u>him</u> a new tie.* (mailed to whom?)

Subject complements come after linking verbs and identify or describe their subjects. Subject complements that name or identify the subjects of sentences are called **predicate nominatives.** These include **predicate nouns** and **predicate pronouns.** In the examples that follow, the subject complements are underlined.

> **EXAMPLES**
>
> *My friends are very hard <u>workers.</u>*
>
> *The best writer in the class is <u>she.</u>*

Other subject complements describe the subjects of sentences. These are called **predicate adjectives.**

EXAMPLE: *The pianist appeared very <u>energetic</u>.*

GRAMMAR PRACTICE

Write all of the complements in the following sentences and label each as a direct object, an indirect object, a predicate noun, a predicate pronoun, or a predicate adjective.

1. The statesman Thomas More was famous in 16th-century England.
2. He gave the world many important written works.
3. *Utopia* is a respected example of social criticism.
4. The main character in the story is Raphael Hythloday.
5. With More's encouragement, Hythloday speaks glowing words about Utopia.
6. Magistrates rule the country.
7. Gold has no value, and everything is free.
8. Experienced farmers teach everyone agriculture.
9. The happiest community is theirs.
10. *Utopia* seems better than 16th-century England.

❾ Phrases

A phrase is a group of related words that does not have a subject and predicate and functions in a sentence as a single part of speech.

9.1 *Prepositional Phrases* A prepositional phrase is a phrase that consists of a preposition, its object, and any modifiers of the object. Prepositional phrases that modify nouns or pronouns are called **adjective phrases.** Prepositional phrases that modify verbs, adjectives, or other adverbs are **adverb phrases.**

ADJECTIVE PHRASE: *The central character <u>of the story</u> is a wicked villain.*
ADVERB PHRASE: *He reveals his nature <u>in the first scene</u>.*

9.2 *Appositives and Appositive Phrases* An appositive is a noun or pronoun that usually comes directly after another noun or pronoun and identifies or provides further information about that word. An appositive phrase includes an appositive and all its modifiers. In the following examples, the appositive phrases are underlined.

EXAMPLES
This poem was written by Dante Alighieri, <u>a great poet.</u>

He wrote this poem, <u>one of the world's most famous,</u> as an exploration of sin and salvation.

Occasionally, an appositive phrase may precede the noun it tells about.

EXAMPLE: *<u>A great poet,</u> Dante Alighieri wrote one of the many poems we are studying.*

❿ Verbals and Verbal Phrases

A verbal is a verb form that is used as a noun, an adjective, or an adverb. A verbal phrase consists of a verbal, all its modifiers, and all its complements. There are three kinds of verbals: infinitives, participles, and gerunds.

10.1 *Infinitives and Infinitive Phrases* An infinitive is a verb form that usually begins with *to* and functions as a noun, adjective, or adverb. The infinitive and its modifiers constitute an infinitive phrase. The examples that follow show several uses of infinitive phrases. Each infinitive phrase is underlined.

NOUN: *<u>To know her</u> is my only desire.* (subject)
I'm planning <u>to walk with you.</u> (direct object)
Her goal was <u>to promote women's rights</u>. (predicate nominative)
ADJECTIVE: *We saw his need <u>to be loved.</u>* (adjective modifying *need*)
ADVERB: *She wrote <u>to voice her opinions.</u>* (adverb modifying *wrote*)

Like verbs themselves, infinitives can take objects (*her* in the first noun example), be made passive (*to be loved* in the adjective example), and take modifiers (*with you* in the second noun example).

Because *to*, the sign of the infinitive, precedes infinitives, it is usually easy to recognize them. However, sometimes *to* may be omitted.

> **EXAMPLE:** *Let no one dare [to] <u>enter</u> this shrine.*

10.2 *Participles and Participial Phrases*

A participle is a verb form that functions as an adjective. Like adjectives, participles modify nouns and pronouns. Present participles end in *-ing*, and most past participles end in *-ed* or *-en*. In the examples below, the participles are underlined.

> **MODIFYING A NOUN:** *The <u>dying</u> man had a smile on his face.*
> **MODIFYING A PRONOUN:** *<u>Frustrated</u>, everyone abandoned the cause.*

Participial phrases are participles with all their modifiers and complements.

> **MODIFYING A NOUN:** *The dogs <u>searching for survivors</u> are well trained.*
> **MODIFYING A PRONOUN:** *<u>Having approved your proposal</u>, we are ready to act.*

10.3 *Dangling and Misplaced Participles*

A participle or participial phrase should be placed as close as possible to the word that it modifies. Otherwise the meaning of the sentence may not be clear.

> **MISPLACED:** *The boys were looking for squirrels searching the trees.*
> **CLEARER:** *The boys searching the trees were looking for squirrels.*

A participle or participial phrase that does not clearly modify anything in a sentence is called a **dangling participle.** A dangling participle causes confusion because it appears to modify a word that it cannot sensibly modify.

Correct a dangling participle by providing a word for the participle to modify.

> **CONFUSING:** *Running like the wind, my hat fell off.* (The hat wasn't running.)
> **CLEARER:** *Running like the wind, I lost my hat.*

10.4 *Gerunds and Gerund Phrases*

A gerund is a verb form ending in *-ing* that functions as a noun. Gerunds can perform any of the function nouns perform.

> **SUBJECT:** *<u>Running</u> is my favorite pastime.*
> **DIRECT OBJECT:** *I truly love <u>running</u>.*
> **SUBJECT COMPLEMENT:** *My deepest passion is <u>running</u>.*
> **OBJECT OF PREPOSITION:** *Her love of <u>running</u> keeps her strong.*

Gerund phrases are gerunds with all their modifiers and complements. The gerund phrases are underlined in the following examples.

> **SUBJECT:** *<u>Wishing on a star</u> never got me far.*
> **OBJECT OF PREPOSITION:** *I will finish before <u>leaving the office</u>.*
> **APPOSITIVE:** *Her avocation, <u>flying airplanes</u>, finally led to full-time employment.*

GRAMMAR PRACTICE

Identify each underlined phrase as an appositive phrase, an infinitive phrase, a participial phrase, or a gerund phrase.

1. <u>Born into an aristocratic family</u>, Tolstoy was orphaned by the age of nine.

2. *War and Peace,* <u>Tolstoy's longest novel</u>, was published in 1869.

3. His attempt <u>to get rid of his property</u> brought about disagreements with his wife.

4. <u>Seeing the naked man sitting by the shrine</u> made Simon incredibly scared.

5. Michael gradually became a faster shoemaker than Simon, <u>his teacher</u>.

⓫ Clauses

A clause is a group of words that contains a subject and a verb. There are two kinds of clauses: independent clauses and subordinate clauses.

⓫.1 Independent and Subordinate Clauses

An independent clause can stand alone as a sentence, as the word *independent* suggests.

INDEPENDENT CLAUSE: *Johann Wolfgang von Goethe was one of the greatest German poets.*

A sentence may contain more than one independent clause.

EXAMPLE: *Johann Wolfgang von Goethe was one of the greatest German poets, but he also produced many scientific writings.*

In the example above, the coordinating conjunction *but* joins the two independent clauses.

A subordinate clause cannot stand alone as a sentence. It is subordinate to, or dependent on, an independent clause.

EXAMPLE: *Johann Wolfgang von Goethe is known as one of the greatest German poets, because his style has been widely imitated.*

Because his style has been widely imitated cannot stand by itself.

⓫.2 Adjective Clauses

An adjective clause is a subordinate clause used as an adjective. It usually follows the noun or pronoun it modifies.

EXAMPLE: *Sappho, who lived on Lesbos, wrote about intensely personal subjects.*

Adjective clauses are typically introduced by the relative pronouns *who, whom, whose, which,* and *that.* (See Relative Pronouns, page R59.) In the examples that follow, the adjective clauses are underlined.

EXAMPLES

One song that we like became our theme song.

Johann Wolfgang von Goethe, whose poems have touched many, was given a state funeral.

The candidate whom we selected promised to serve us well.

WATCH OUT! The relative pronouns *whom, which,* and *that* may sometimes be omitted when they are objects of their own clauses.

EXAMPLE: *Sappho is a poet [whom/that] many have read.*

⓫.3 Adverb Clauses

An adverb clause is a subordinate clause that is used as an adverb, to modify a verb, an adjective, or another adverb. It is introduced by a subordinating conjunction (see Subordinating Conjunctions, page R65).

Adverb clauses typically occur at the beginning or end of sentences. The clauses are underlined in these examples.

MODIFYING A VERB: *When we need you, we will call.*

MODIFYING AN ADVERB: *I'll stay here, where there is shelter from the rain.*

MODIFYING AN ADJECTIVE: *Roman felt better than he had felt in days.*

⓫.4 Noun Clauses

A noun clause is a subordinate clause that is used in a sentence as a noun. A noun clause may be used as a subject, a direct object, an indirect object, a predicate nominative, or an object of a preposition. Noun clauses are often introduced by pronouns such as *that, what, who, whoever, which,* and *whose* or by subordinating conjunctions such as *how, when, where, why,* and *whether.* (See Subordinating Conjunctions, page R65.)

USAGE TIP Because the same words may introduce adjective and noun clauses, you need to consider how the clause functions within its sentence.

To determine if a clause is a noun clause, try substituting *something* or *someone* for the clause. If you can do it, it is probably a noun clause.

EXAMPLES: *I know whose woods these are.* ("I know something." The clause is a noun clause, direct object of the verb *know.*)

Give a copy to whoever wants one. ("Give a copy to someone." The clause is a noun clause, object of the preposition *to.*)

GRAMMAR PRACTICE

Identify each underlined clause as an adjective clause, an adverb clause, or a noun clause.

1. The Hebrew God, <u>who created the world in six days</u>, told Adam and Eve not to eat from the tree of knowledge.

2. The serpent in the garden of Eden thought <u>it could convince Eve to take an apple</u>.

3. <u>When God found out Adam and Eve had disobeyed him</u>, he was very angry.

4. He seemed not to question <u>whether the two of them were truly sorry</u>.

5. God's decision, <u>which would last forever</u>, changed the entire fate of humankind.

⑫ The Structure of Sentences

When classified by their structure, there are four kinds of sentences: simple, compound, complex, and compound-complex.

12.1 ***Simple Sentences*** A simple sentence is a sentence that has one independent clause and no subordinate clauses. The fact that such sentences are called "simple" does not mean that they are uncomplicated. Various parts of simple sentences may be compound, and they may contain grammatical structures such as appositives and verbals.

EXAMPLES

Leo Tolstoy, a famous Russian novelist, wrote the classic War and Peace. (appositive)

Pablo Neruda, drawn to writing poetry at an early age, won celebrity at age 20. (participial and gerund phrases)

12.2 ***Compound Sentences*** A compound sentence contains two or more independent clauses. The clauses are joined together with a comma and a coordinating conjunction (*and, but, or, nor, yet, for, so*), a semicolon, or a conjunctive adverb with a semicolon. Like simple sentences, compound sentences do not contain any subordinate clauses.

EXAMPLES

The main character in the Inferno *goes to visit souls in Hell, but he eventually returns to where he began.*

Charles Baudelaire's poem "Invitation to the Voyage" has powerful images; however, the word voyage *does not appear anywhere in it.*

WATCH OUT! Do not confuse compound sentences with simple sentences that have compound parts.

EXAMPLE: *A subcommittee drafted a document and immediately presented it to the entire group.* (Here *and* signals a compound predicate, not a compound sentence.)

12.3 ***Complex Sentences*** A complex sentence contains one independent clause and one or more subordinate clauses. If a subordinate clause is used as a modifier, it usually modifies a word in the main clause, and the main clause can stand alone. However, a noun clause is a part of the independent clause; the two cannot be separated.

MODIFIER: *One should not complain <u>unless she or he has a better solution.</u>*

NOUN CLAUSE: *We sketched pictures of <u>whomever we wished.</u>* (Noun clause is the object of the preposition *of* and cannot be separated from the rest of the sentence.)

12.4 ***Compound-Complex Sentences*** A compound-complex sentence has two or more independent clauses and one or more subordinate clauses. Compound-complex sentences are, simply, both compound and complex. If you start with a compound sentence, all you need to do to form a compound-complex sentence is add a subordinate clause.

COMPOUND: *All the students knew the answer, yet they were too shy to volunteer.*

COMPOUND-COMPLEX: *All the students knew the answer that their teacher expected, yet they were too shy to volunteer.*

GRAMMAR PRACTICE

Tell whether each sentence is a simple sentence, a compound sentence, a complex sentence, or a compound-complex sentence.

1. Written by Heinrich Heine, "The Lorelei" is named for a cliff in Germany.
2. Legend claims a drowned maiden sings nearby, but in fact the sound is only an echo.
3. The woman's song is said to lure fishermen to their death.
4. Heine wanted to marry his cousin, but she rejected him and married another man.
5. After she refused him, Heine wrote this poem as a response.

⑬ Writing Complete Sentences

A sentence is a group of words that expresses a complete thought. In writing that you wish to share with a reader, try to avoid both sentence fragments and run-on sentences.

13.1 *Correcting Fragments* A sentence fragment is a group of words that is only part of a sentence. It does not express a complete thought and may be confusing to the reader or the listener. A sentence fragment may be lacking a subject, a predicate, or both.

> **FRAGMENT:** *Waited for the boat to arrive.* (no subject)
> **CORRECTED:** *We waited for the boat to arrive.*
> **FRAGMENT:** *People of various races, ages, and creeds.* (no predicate)
> **CORRECTED:** *People of various races, ages, and creeds gathered together.*
> **FRAGMENT:** *Near the old cottage.* (neither subject nor predicate)
> **CORRECTED:** *The burial ground is near the old cottage.*

In your writing, fragments are usually the result of haste or incorrect punctuation. Sometimes fixing a fragment will be a matter of attaching it to a preceding or following sentence.

> **FRAGMENT:** *We saw the two girls. Waiting for the bus to arrive.*
> **CORRECTED:** *We saw the two girls waiting for the bus to arrive.*
> **FRAGMENT:** *Newspapers appeal to a wide audience. Including people of various races, ages, and creeds.*
> **CORRECTED:** *Newspapers appeal to a wide audience, including people of various races, ages, and creeds.*

13.2 *Correcting Run-On Sentences*
A run-on sentence is made up of two or more sentences written as though they were one. Some run-ons have no punctuation within them. Others may use only a comma where a conjunction or stronger punctuation is necessary. Use your judgment in correcting run-on sentences, as you have choices. You can make two sentences if the thoughts are not closely connected. If the thoughts are closely related, you can keep the run-on as one sentence by adding a semicolon or a conjunction.

> **RUN-ON:** *We found a place by a small pond for the picnic it is three miles from the village.*
> **MAKE TWO SENTENCES:** *We found a place by a small pond for the picnic. It is three miles from the village.*
> **RUN-ON:** *We found a place by a small pond for the picnic it was perfect.*
> **USE A SEMICOLON:** *We found a place by a small pond for the picnic; it was perfect.*
> **ADD A CONJUNCTION:** *We found a place by a small pond for the picnic, and it was perfect.*

WATCH OUT! When you add a conjunction, make sure you use appropriate punctuation before it: a comma for a coordinating conjunction, a semicolon for a conjunctive adverb. (See Conjunctions, page R65.) A very common mistake is to use a comma instead of a conjunction or an end mark. This error is called a **comma splice**.

> **INCORRECT:** *He finished the apprenticeship, then he left the village.*
> **CORRECT:** *He finished the apprenticeship, and then he left the village.*

GRAMMAR PRACTICE

Rewrite the following paragraph, correcting all fragments and run-ons.

Omar Khayyám was born in Persia. To a well-off family. He was educated in the sciences and philosophy he later wrote a treatise on algebra. By using his knowledge of astronomy. Omar also helped the sultan reform the calendar. After a journey to Mecca, Omar returned to his hometown to teach. He wrote many works on many subjects but only. His prose writing survived. *The Rubáiyát of Omar Khayyám* by Edward FitzGerald made the world aware of Khayyám's poetry FitzGerald published his translation in 1859. *The Rubáiyát of Omar Khayyám* is. A collection of quatrains. One of the most famous poems contains the lines "A Jug of Wine, a Loaf of Bread—and Thou" Khayyám uses many metaphors in his poetry to convey certain themes.

14 Subject-Verb Agreement

The subject and verb of a sentence must agree in number. When the subject is singular, the verb must be singular; when the subject is plural, the verb must be plural.

14.1 Basic Agreement Fortunately, agreement between subject and verb in English is simple. Most verbs show the difference between singular and plural only in the third person of the present tense. In the present tense, the third-person singular form ends in *-s*.

Present-Tense Verb Forms	
Singular	**Plural**
I sleep	we sleep
you sleep	you sleep
she, he, it sleeps	they sleep

14.2 Agreement of Be The verb *be* presents special problems in agreement because this verb does not follow the usual verb patterns.

Forms of *Be*			
Present Tense		**Past Tense**	
Singular	**Plural**	**Singular**	**Plural**
I am	we are	I was	we were
you are	you are	you were	you were
she, he, it is	they are	she, he, it was	they were

14.3 Words Between Subject and Verb
A verb agrees only with its subject. When words come between a subject and its verb, ignore them when considering proper agreement. Identify the subject and make sure the verb agrees with it.

> **EXAMPLES**
> A <u>story</u> in the newspapers <u>tells</u> about the 1890s.
>
> <u>Dad</u> as well as Mom <u>reads</u> the paper daily.

14.4 Agreement with Compound Subjects Use a plural verb with most compound subjects containing the word *and*.

> **EXAMPLE:** <u>My father and his friends read</u> the paper daily.

You could substitute the plural pronoun *they* for *my father and his friends*. This shows that you need a plural verb.

If the compound subject refers to a unit, use a singular verb. Test this by substituting the singular pronoun *it*.

> **EXAMPLE:** <u>Peanut butter and jelly [it] is</u> my brother's favorite sandwich.

Use a singular verb with a compound subject that is preceded by *each*, *every*, or *many a*.

> **EXAMPLE:** <u>Each novel and short story seems</u> grounded in personal experience.

When subjects are joined by *or*, *nor*, or the correlative conjunctions *either . . . or* or *neither . . . nor*, make the verb agree with the noun or pronoun nearest the verb.

> **EXAMPLES**
> <u>Cookies or ice cream is</u> my favorite dessert.
>
> <u>Either Cheryl or her friends are</u> being invited.
>
> <u>Neither ice storms nor snow is predicted</u> today.

14.5 Personal Pronouns as Subjects
When using a personal pronoun as a subject, make sure to match it with the correct form of the verb *be*. (See the chart in section 14.2.) Note especially that the pronoun *you* takes the form *are* or *were*, regardless of whether it is singular or plural.

WATCH OUT! *You is* and *you was* are nonstandard forms and should be avoided in writing and speaking. *We was* and *they was* are also forms to be avoided.

> **INCORRECT:** *You was helping me. They was hoping for this.*
>
> **CORRECT:** *You were helping me. They were hoping for this.*

14.6 *Indefinite Pronouns as Subjects*

Some indefinite pronouns are always singular; some are always plural. Others may be either singular or plural.

Singular Indefinite Pronouns			
another	either	neither	one
anybody	everybody	nobody	somebody
anyone	everyone	no one	someone
anything	everything	nothing	something
each	much		

> **EXAMPLES**
>
> *Each of the writers was given an award.*
> *Somebody in the room upstairs is sleeping.*

The indefinite pronouns that are always plural are *both, few, many, others,* and *several*. These take plural verbs.

> **EXAMPLES**
>
> *Many of the books in our library are not in circulation.*
>
> *Few have been returned recently.*

Still other indefinite pronouns can be either singular or plural.

Singular or Plural Indefinite Pronouns			
all	enough	most	some
any	more	none	

The number of the indefinite pronoun *any* or *none* depends on the intended meaning.

> **EXAMPLES**
>
> *Any of these topics has potential for a good article.* (any one topic)
>
> *Any of these topics have potential for a good article.* (all of the many topics)

The indefinite pronouns *all, enough, some, more, most,* and *none* are singular when they refer to quantities or parts of something. They are plural when they refer to numbers of individual things. Context will usually give a clue.

> **EXAMPLES**
>
> *All of the flour is gone.* (referring to a quantity)
>
> *All of the flowers are gone.* (referring to individual items)

14.7 *Inverted Sentences* Problems in agreement often occur in inverted sentences beginning with *here* or *there*; in questions beginning with *why, where,* and *what*; and in inverted sentences beginning with a phrase. Identify the subject—wherever it is—before deciding on the verb.

> **EXAMPLES**
>
> *There clearly are far too many cooks in this kitchen.*
>
> *What is the correct ingredient for this stew?*
>
> *Far from the embroiled cooks stands the master chef.*

GRAMMAR PRACTICE

Locate the subject of each verb. Then choose the correct verb.

1. Many scholars (think/thinks) the *Aeneid* is the finest epic of ancient Rome.
2. (Is/Are) the Trojan prince Aeneas the ideal Roman?
3. There (is/are) 16 books in the *Aeneid*.
4. Book 2 begins after the Greeks (was/were) pushed back after Achilles' death.
5. A large wooden horse full of armed men (was/were) left in front of the gates of Troy.
6. After the Greeks sailed away, their deserted camps (was/were) raided by the Trojans.
7. The Trojan people (enjoy/enjoyed) their victory but did not know it was short-lived.
8. As soon as the Trojans (was/were) asleep, the Greek army returned, let the men out of the wooden horse, and attacked the city.
9. Troy (was/were) burned to the ground
10. Virgil wanted the *Aeneid* destroyed, but it (was/were) published at the emperor's request.

Grammar Handbook

14.8 Sentences with Predicate Nominatives

When a sentence contains a predicate nominative, use a verb that agrees with the subject, not the complement.

EXAMPLES

The <u>tales</u> of Aeneas <u>are</u> a great work of work literature. (*Tales* is the subject—not—and it takes the plural verb *are*.)

A great <u>work</u> of literature <u>is</u> the tales of Aeneas. (The subject is the singular noun *work*.)

14.9 Don't *and* Doesn't *as Auxiliary Verbs*

The auxiliary verb *doesn't* is used with singular subjects and with the personal pronouns *she, he*, and *it*. The auxiliary verb *don't* is used with plural subjects and with the personal pronouns *I, we, you*, and *they*.

SINGULAR

She <u>doesn't</u> want to be without her cane.
<u>Doesn't</u> the <u>school</u> provide help?

PLURAL

They <u>don't</u> know what it's like to be hungry.
Bees <u>don't</u> like these flowers by the door.

14.10 Collective Nouns as Subjects

Collective nouns are nouns that name a group of persons or things. *Team*, for example, is the collective name of a group of individuals. A collective noun takes a singular verb when the group acts as a single unit. It takes a plural verb when the members of the group act separately.

EXAMPLES

Our team usually wins. (The team as a whole wins.)

Our team vote differently on most issues. (The individual members vote.)

14.11 Relative Pronouns as Subjects

When a relative pronoun is used as a subject of its clause—*who, which,* and *that* can serve as subjects—the verb of the clause must agree in number with the antecedent of the pronoun.

SINGULAR: *Have you selected one of the poems <u>that</u> <u>is</u> meaningful to you?*

The antecedent of the relative pronoun *that* is the singular *one;* therefore, *that* is singular and must take the singular verb *is*.

PLURAL: *The younger redwoods, <u>which</u> <u>grow</u> in a circle around an older tree, are also very tall.*

The antecedent of the relative pronoun *which* is the plural *redwoods.* Therefore, *which* is plural, and it takes the plural verb *grow*.

GRAMMAR PRACTICE

Choose the correct verb for each of the following sentences.

1. "Metamorphosis" (involve/involves) a traveling salesman and his family.
2. Gregor (go/goes) to bed one night and wakes up the next morning changed into a bug.
3. It (was/were) a startling and unexpected transformation for both Gregor and his family.
4. They (was/were) terrified and confused by what Gregor had become.
5. Grete, Gregor's sister, (doesn't/don't) know what kind of food Gregor likes, so she brings him several choices.
6. Gregor merely (exists/exist) from day to day, gradually losing his appetite and his will to live.
7. The tension between Gregor and his family (rises/rise) with each passing day.
8. (Do/Does) everyone see Gregor as a man or as a monster?
9. The cleaning lady (finds/find) Gregor dead on the floor.
10. What do you think Franz Kafka (is/are) saying in this story?

⓯ Quick Reference: Punctuation

Punctuation	Function	Examples
End marks period, question mark, exclamation point	To end sentences	The games begin today. Who is your favorite contestant? What a play Jamie made!
	After initials and other abbreviations	Prof. Ted Bakerman, D. H. Lawrence, Houghton Mifflin Co., P.M., A.D., oz., ft., Blvd., St.

	After numerals and letters in outlines	I. Volcanoes
		  A. Central-vent
		    1. Shield

	Exception: P.O. abbreviations	NE (Nebraska), NV (Nevada)
Commas	Before conjunctions in compound sentences	I have never disliked poetry, but now I really love it.
	To separate items in a series	She is brave, loyal, and kind. The slow, easy route is best.
	To set off words of address	Oh wind, if winter comes . . . Come to the front, children.
	To set off parenthetical expressions	Well, just suppose that we can't? Hard workers, as you know, don't quit. I'm not a quitter, believe me.
	After introductory phrases and clauses	At the beginning of the day, I feel fresh. While she was out, I was here. Having finished my chores, I went out.
	To set off nonessential phrases and clauses	Ed Pawn, captain of the chess team, won. Ed Pawn, who is the captain, won.
	In dates and addresses	August 18, 2002. Send it by August 18, 2002, to Cherry Jubilee, Inc., 21 Vernona St., Oakland, Minnesota.
	In letter parts	Dear Jim, Sincerely yours,
	For clarity, or to avoid confusion	By noon, time had run out. What the minister does, does matter. While cooking, Jim burned his hand.
Semicolons	In compound sentences without coordinating conjunctions	The last shall be first; the first shall be last. I read the Bible; however, I have not memorized it.
	To separate items in series that contain commas	We invited my sister, Jan; her boyfriend, Don; my uncle Jack; and Mary Dodd.
	In compound sentences whose parts contain commas	After I ran out of money, I called my parents; but only my sister was home, unfortunately.

Punctuation	Function	Examples
Colons	To introduce lists	**Correct:** Those we wrote were the following: Dana, John, and Will. **Incorrect:** Those we wrote were: Dana, John, and Will.
	Before long quotations	Susan B. Anthony said: "Woman must not depend upon the protection of man. . . ."
	After salutations of business letters	To Whom It May Concern: Dear Ms. Costa:
	With certain numbers	1:28 P.M., Genesis 2:5
Dashes	To indicate abrupt breaks in thought	I was thinking of my mother—who is arriving tomorrow—just as you walked in.
Parentheses	To set off less important material	Throughout her life (though some might think otherwise), she worked hard. The temperature on this July day (would you believe it?) is 45 degrees!
Hyphens	In compound adjectives before nouns	She lives in a first-floor apartment.
	In compounds with *all-, ex-, self-, -elect*	The president-elect is a respected woman.
	In compound numbers (to ninety-nine)	Today, I turn twenty-one.
	In fractions	My cup is one-third full.
	Between prefixes and words beginning with capital letters	Is this a pre-Renaissance artifact?
	With words divided at the ends of lines	Finding the right title has been a challenge for the committee.
Apostrophes	In possessives of nouns and indefinite pronouns	my friend's book, my friends' books, anyone's guess, somebody else's problem
	For omitted letters in contractions or numbers in dates	don't (omitted *o*); he'd (omitted *woul*) the class of '99 (omitted *19*)
	In plurals of letters and numbers	I had two A's and no 2's on my report card.
Quotation marks	To set off a speaker's exact words	Sara said, "I'm finally ready." "I'm ready," Sara said, "finally." Did Sara say, "I'm ready"? Sara said, "I'm ready!"
	For titles of stories, short poems, essays, songs, book chapters	We read Mistral's "Time" and Joyce's "Eveline." My eyes watered when I heard "The Star-Spangled Banner."
Ellipses	For material omitted from a quotation	"Neither slavery nor involuntary servitude . . . shall exist within the United States. . . ."
Italics	For titles of books, plays, magazines, long poems, operas, films, TV series, recordings	*War and Peace, A Doll's House, Newsweek, Paradise Lost, La Bohème, ET, The Cosby Show, The Three Tenors in Concert*

⓰ Quick Reference: Capitalization

Category/Rule	Examples
People and Titles	
Names and initials of people	**A**lice **W**alker, **E. B. W**hite
Titles used with or in place of names	**P**rofessor Holmes, **S**enator Long, The **P**resident has arrived.
Deities and members of religious groups	**J**esus, **A**llah, **B**uddha, **Z**eus, **B**aptists, **R**oman **C**atholics
Names of ethnic and national groups	**H**ispanics, **J**ews, **A**frican **A**mericans
Geographical Names	
Cities, states, countries, continents	**C**harleston, **N**evada, **F**rance, **A**sia
Regions, bodies of water, mountains	**M**idwest, **L**ake **M**ichigan, **M**ount **M**cKinley
Geographic features, parks	**C**ontinental **D**ivide, **E**verglades, **Y**ellowstone **N**ational **P**ark
Streets and roads, planets	361 **S**outh **T**wenty-**T**hird **S**treet, **M**iller **A**venue, **J**upiter, **S**aturn
Organizations and Events	
Companies, organizations, teams	**M**onsanto, **E**lks, **C**hicago **B**ulls
Buildings, bridges, monuments	**A**lamo, **G**olden **G**ate **B**ridge, **L**incoln **M**emorial
Documents, awards	**C**onstitution, **W**orld **C**up
Special named events	**S**uper **B**owl, **W**orld **S**eries
Governmental bodies, historical periods and events	**S**upreme **C**ourt, **C**ongress, **M**iddle **A**ges, **B**oston **T**ea **P**arty
Days and months, holidays	**T**uesday, **O**ctober, **T**hanksgiving, **V**alentine's **D**ay
Specific cars, boats, trains, planes	**C**adillac, ***T**itanic, **O**rient **E**xpress*
Proper Adjectives	
Adjectives formed from proper nouns	**D**oppler effect, **M**exican music, **E**lizabethan age, **G**ulf coast
First Words and the Pronoun *I*	
The first word in a sentence or quotation	**T**his is it. **H**e said, "**L**et's go."
Complete sentence in parentheses	(**C**onsult the previous chapter.)
Salutation and closing of letters	**D**ear **M**adam, **V**ery truly yours,
First lines of most poetry The personal pronoun *I*	**T**hen am **I** **A** happy fly **I**f **I** live **O**r if **I** die.
First, last, and all important words in titles	***A** **T**ale of **T**wo **C**ities,* "**T**he **W**orld **I**s **T**oo **M**uch with **U**s"

⑰ Little Rules That Make a Big Difference

Sentences

Avoid sentence fragments. Make sure all your sentences express complete thoughts.

A sentence fragment is a group of words that does not express a grammatically complete thought. It may lack a subject, a predicate, or both. A fragment can be corrected by adding the missing element(s) or by changing the punctuation to make the fragment part of a sentence.

> **FRAGMENT:** *One of my heroes is Barbara Jordan. A Texas senator who had an impressive record and great dedication to justice.*

> **COMPLETE:** *One of my heroes is Barbara Jordan. She was a Texas senator who had an impressive record and great dedication to justice.* (adding a subject and a verb)

> **COMPLETE:** *One of my heroes is Barbara Jordan, a Texas senator who had an impressive record and great dedication to justice.* (changing the punctuation)

Avoid run-on sentences. Make sure all clauses in a sentence have the proper punctuation and/or conjunctions between them.

A run-on sentence consists of two or more sentences written as though they were one. Correct a run-on by making two separate sentences, using a semicolon, adding a conjunction, or rewriting the sentence.

> **RUN-ON:** *James Galway is a great musician, he plays the flute.*

> **CORRECT:** *James Galway is a great musician. He plays the flute.*

> **CORRECT:** *James Galway is a great musician; he plays the flute.*

> **CORRECT:** *James Galway, who plays the flute, is a great musician.*

Use end marks correctly. Use a period, not a question mark, at the end of an indirect question.

An indirect question is a question that does not reproduce the exact words of the original speaker. Note the difference between the following sentences, and observe that the second sentence ends with a period, not a question mark:

> **DIRECT:** *Lou asked, "What is that?"*

> **INDIRECT:** *Lou asked what it was.*

Do not use quotation marks around an indirect quotation within a sentence.

A direct quotation reproduces the speaker's exact words. An indirect quotation reports a speaker's statement in other words. Compare these sentences:

> **DIRECT:** *Jean said, "I'm going to be up all night writing my essay."* (quotation marks appropriate)

> **INDIRECT:** *Jean said that she was going to be up all night writing her essay.* (no quotation marks)

Phrases

Place participial and prepositional phrases as close as possible to the words they modify. Participial and prepositional phrases are modifiers—that is, they tell about some other word in a sentence. To avoid confusion, they should be placed as close as possible to the words that they modify.

> **INCORRECT:** *Tiny microphones are planted by agents called bugs.*

> **CORRECT:** *Tiny microphones called bugs are planted by agents.*

Avoid dangling participles. Make sure a participial phrase does modify a word in the sentence.

> **INCORRECT:** *Disappointed in love, a hermit's life seemed attractive.* (Who was disappointed?)

> **CORRECT:** *Disappointed in love, the man became a hermit.*

Clauses

Use commas to set off nonessential adjective clauses.

Do you need the clause in order to indicate precisely who or what is meant? If not, it is nonessential and should be set off with commas.

USE COMMAS: *Jim's dogs, who had barked from morning until night, were suddenly quiet.*

NO COMMAS: *The dogs who had barked from morning until night were suddenly quiet.*

Verbs

Don't use a past-tense form with an auxiliary verb or a past-participle form without an auxiliary verb. (See Auxiliary Verbs, page R59.)

INCORRECT: *I have saw her somewhere before.* (*Saw* is past tense and shouldn't be used with *have*.)

CORRECT: *I have seen her somewhere before.*

INCORRECT: *I seen her somewhere before.* (*Seen* is a past participle and shouldn't be used without an auxiliary.)

Shift tenses only when necessary.

Usually, when you are writing in the present tense, you should stay in the present tense; when you are writing in the past tense, you should stay in the past tense.

INCORRECT: *When Mr. Miller spoke at the fair, we all pay attention.*

CORRECT: *When Mr. Miller spoke at the fair, we all paid attention.*

Sometimes a shift in tense is necessary to show a logical sequence of actions or the relationship of one action to another.

CORRECT: *After he had told his story, everybody went to sleep.*

Subject-Verb Agreement

Make sure subjects and verbs agree in number.

INCORRECT: *Several operas by Wagner is based on the legend of Siegfried.*

CORRECT: *Several operas by Wagner are based on the legend of Seigfried.*

INCORRECT: *Wotan, as well as others in the operas, are looking for the Ring.*

CORRECT: *Wotan, as well as others in the operas, is looking for the Ring.*

INCORRECT: *Siegmund and Sieglinde was the parents of Siegfried.*

CORRECT: *Siegmund and Sieglinde were the parents of Siegfried.*

Use a singular verb with a noun that looks plural but has a singular meaning.

Some nouns that end in -s are singular, even though they look plural. Examples are *measles, news, Wales,* and words ending in -ics that refer to school subjects, sciences, or general practices.

EXAMPLES: *Has headquarters heard from you yet?*
Physics is available to everyone who qualifies to take it.

Use a singular verb with a title.

EXAMPLE: *The* Analects *is on my summer reading list.*
"Two Springs" was written by Li Chi'ng-chao.

Use a singular verb with a word of weight, time, or measure.

EXAMPLES: *Forty pounds is what my niece weighs now.*
One hundred dollars is the price of the new equipment.

Pronouns

Use personal pronouns correctly in compounds.

Don't be confused about case when *and* joins a noun and a personal pronoun; the case of the pronoun still depends upon its function.

INCORRECT: *Marlene and her will conduct the interview.*

CORRECT: *Marlene and she will conduct the interview.*

INCORRECT: *She asked Sunny and I to wait for her.*

CORRECT: *She asked Sunny and me to wait for her.*

INCORRECT: *Show Anne and they how to work the video recorder.*

CORRECT: *Show Anne and them how to work the video recorder.*

Usually, if you remove the noun and *and,* the correct pronoun will be obvious.

Use *we* and *us* correctly with nouns.

When a noun directly follows *we* or *us*, the case of the pronoun depends upon its function.

INCORRECT: *Us cheerleaders have many new cheers.*

CORRECT: *We cheerleaders have many new cheers.* (*We* is the subject.)

INCORRECT: *It makes a big difference to we players.*

CORRECT: *It makes a big difference to us players.* (*Us* is the object of *to.*)

Avoid unclear pronoun reference.

The reference of a pronoun is ambiguous when the reader cannot tell which of two preceding nouns is its antecedent. The reference is indefinite when the idea to which the pronoun refers is only weakly or vaguely expressed.

AMBIGUOUS: *Pablo Neruda, not Octavio Paz, wrote "Ode to a Lizard," and he [who?] also wrote "Ode to a Watermelon."*

CLEARER: *Pablo Neruda, not Octavio Paz, wrote "Ode to a Lizard," and Neruda also wrote "Ode to a Watermelon."*

INDEFINITE: *Neruda won a Nobel Prize in 1971, which is a prestigious award for writers.*

CLEARER: *In 1971, Neruda won a Nobel Prize, which is a prestigious award for writers.*

Avoid changes of person.

If you are writing in the third person—using pronouns such as *she, he, it, they, them, his, her, its*—do not shift to the second person—*you.*

INCORRECT: *The feudal laborer had to obey his lord, and you needed to obey the king as well.*

CORRECT: *The feudal laborer had to obey his lord, and he needed to obey the king as well.*

Use correct pronouns in elliptical comparisons.

An elliptical comparison is a comparison from which words have been omitted. In order to choose the proper pronoun, fill in the missing words. Note the difference below:

EXAMPLES: *I like Carlos better than* (I like) *her. I like Carlos better than she* (likes Carlos).

Don't confuse pronouns and contractions.

Possessive forms of personal pronouns do not contain apostrophes; neither does the relative pronoun *whose.* Whenever you are unsure whether to write *it's* or *its* or *who's* or *whose*, ask if you mean *it is/has* or *who is/has.* If you do, write the contraction. Do the same for *you're* and *your, they're* and *their*, except that the contraction in this case is for the verb *are.*

Modifiers

Avoid double comparisons.

A double comparison is a comparison made twice. In general, if you add *-er* or *-est* to a modifier, you should not also use *more* or *most* in front of it.

INCORRECT: *Juan cooks more better since he's taken the chef's course.*

CORRECT: *Juan cooks better since he's taken the chef's course.*

INCORRECT: *Now he's the most greatest cook in the class.*

CORRECT: *Now he's the greatest cook in the class.*

Avoid illogical comparisons.

Can you tell what is wrong with the following sentence?

Plays are more entertaining than any kind of performance art.

This sentence implies that plays are not a kind of performance art. To avoid such illogical comparisons, use *other* when comparing an individual member with the rest of its group.

Plays are more entertaining than any other kind of performance art.

To avoid another kind of illogical comparison, use *than* or *as* after the first member in a compound comparison.

ILLOGICAL: *Sophocles wrote as many great plays if not more than Aeschylus.* (As many great plays . . . than is incorrect.)

CLEARER: *Sophocles wrote as many great plays as Aeschylus, if not more.*

Avoid misplacing modifiers.

Modifiers of all kinds must be placed as close as possible to the words they modify. If you place them elsewhere, you risk being misunderstood.

MISPLACED: *Eveline thinks about the promise she made, before her death, to her mother.*

CLEARER: *Eveline thinks about the promise she made to her mother before her death.*

It isn't Eveline's death; it's her mother's.

Words Not to Capitalize

Do not capitalize *north, south, east,* and *west* when they are used to tell direction.

EXAMPLE: *London is east of New York City. Charleston is the capital of West Virginia.* (Here *West* is part of a proper name.)

Do not capitalize *sun* and *moon,* and capitalize *earth* only when it is used with the names of other planets.

EXAMPLES: *The sun and the moon are heavenly bodies in a solar system that includes Mars, Jupiter, and Earth.*

We now live on the earth, not in heaven.

Do not capitalize the names of seasons.

EXAMPLE: *The winter snows have nearly disappeared.*

Do not capitalize the names of most school subjects.

School subjects are capitalized only when they are names of specific courses, such as World History I. Otherwise, they are not capitalized.

EXAMPLE: *I'm taking physics, social studies, and a foreign language this year.*

Note: *English* and the names of other languages are always capitalized.

EXAMPLE: *Everybody takes English and either Spanish or French.*

GRAMMAR PRACTICE

Rewrite each sentence correctly.

1. Mrs. Kulpinsky asked Trish and I to help with the decorations.
2. Let's keep this information between we girls.
3. An award-winning collection of poems, Mary Oliver wrote *Dream Work.*
4. Babe Ruth who played for the New York Yankees hit 60 home runs in one season.
5. *The Producers,* starring Zero Mostel and Gene Wilder, are a funny movie.
6. We wanted to know what the speaker means.
7. Having written both plays and sonnets, millions of people admire William Shakespeare.
8. I like Anton Chekhov more better than Franz Kafka.
9. Preserving nature, a major concern of most citizens.
10. Stumbling forward at the finish line, the race was barely won by the shortest runner.

⓲ Commonly Confused Words

accept/except	The verb *accept* means "to receive or believe"; *except* is usually a preposition meaning "excluding."	The teams accept everyone except those who don't have at least a C average.
advice/advise	*Advise* is a verb; *advice* is a noun naming that which an adviser gives.	How did the manager advise the baseball player? Was the baseball player given good advice?
affect/effect	As a verb, *affect* means "to influence." *Effect* as a verb means "to cause." If you want a noun, you will almost always want *effect*.	How did the player's home run affect the crowd? Did it effect a change in their attitude? The effect was dramatic.
all ready/already	*All ready* is an adjective meaning "fully ready." *Already* is an adverb meaning "before or by this time."	Before the player's home run, the spectators were all ready to boo the home team. One had already talked of abandoning the team.
allusion/illusion	An allusion is an indirect reference to something. An illusion is a false picture or idea.	Modern literature has many allusions to the works of Shakespeare. The world's apparent flatness is an illusion.
among/between	*Between* is used when you are speaking of only two things. *Among* is used for three or more.	There is respect between Sally and Robert. "The Panther" is among my favorite Rilke poems.
bring/take	*Bring* is used to denote motion toward a speaker or place. *Take* is used to denote motion away from a person or place.	Bring the books over here, and I will take them to the library.
fewer/less	*Fewer* refers to a number of separate, countable units. *Less* refers to bulk quantity.	We have less literature and fewer selections in this year's curriculum.
leave/let	*Leave* means "to allow something to remain behind." *Let* means "to permit."	The librarian will leave some books on display but will not let us borrow any.
lie/lay	*Lie* means "to rest or recline." It does not take an object. *Lay* always takes an object.	Dogs love to lie in the sun. We always lay some bones next to him.
loose/lose	*Loose* (lo͞os) means "free, not restrained"; *lose* (lo͞oz) means "to misplace or fail to find."	Who turned the horses loose? I hope we won't lose any of them.
precede/proceed	*Precede* means "to go or come before." Use *proceed* for other meanings.	The drum major preceded the other band members. The band director proceeded to direct the national anthem.
than/then	Use *than* in making comparisons; use *then* on all other occasions.	I like Camus better than Kafka. We read one, then the other.
two/too/to	*Two* refers to a number. *Too* is an adverb meaning "also" or "very." Use *to* before a verb or as a preposition.	Meg had to go to town, too. We had too much reading to do. Two chapters is too much.

Grammar Glossary

This glossary contains various terms you need to understand when you use the Grammar Handbook. Used as a reference source, this glossary will help you explore grammar concepts and the ways they relate to one another.

A

Abbreviation An abbreviation is a shortened form of a word or word group; it is often made up of initials. (B.C., A.M., *Maj.*)

Active voice. *See* **Voice.**

Adjective An adjective modifies, or describes, a noun or pronoun. (*happy* camper, she is *small*)

A *predicate adjective* follows a linking verb and describes the subject. (The day seemed *long.*)

A *proper adjective* is formed from a proper noun. (*Jewish* temple, *Alaskan* husky)

The *comparative* form of an adjective compares two things. (*more alert, thicker*)

The *superlative* form of an adjective compares more than two things. (*most abundant, weakest*)

What Adjectives Tell	Examples
How many	*some* writers *all* players
What kind	*grand* plans *wider* streets
Which one(s)	*these* flowers *that* star

Adjective phrase. See **Phrase.**

Adverb An adverb modifies a verb, an adjective, or another adverb. (Clare sang *loudly.*)

The *comparative* form of an adverb compares two actions. (*more generously, faster*)

The *superlative* form of an adverb compares more than two actions. (*most sharply, closest*)

What Adverbs Tell	Examples
How	climb *carefully* chuckle *merrily*
When	arrived *late* left *early*
Where	climbed *up* moved *away*
To what extent	*extremely* upset *hardly* visible

Adverb, conjunctive. *See* **Conjunctive adverb.**

Adverb phrase. *See* **Phrase.**

Agreement Sentence parts that correspond with one another are said to be in agreement.

In *pronoun-antecedent agreement,* a pronoun and the word it refers to are the same in number, gender, and person. (*Bill* mailed *his* application. The *students* ate *their* lunches.)

In *subject-verb agreement,* the subject and verb in a sentence are the same in number. (A *child cries* for help. *They cry* aloud.)

Ambiguous reference An ambiguous reference occurs when a pronoun may refer to more than one word. (Bud asked his brother if *he* had any mail.)

Antecedent An antecedent is the noun or pronoun to which a pronoun refers. (If *Adam* forgets *his* raincoat, *he* will be late for school. *She* learned *her* lesson.)

Appositive An appositive is a noun or phrase that explains one or more words in a sentence. (Cary Grant, *an Englishman,* spent most of his adult life in America.)

An *essential appositive* is needed to make the sense of a sentence complete. (A comic strip inspired the musical *Annie.*)

A *nonessential appositive* is one that adds information to a sentence but is not necessary to its sense. (O. Henry, *a short story writer,* spent time in prison.)

Article Articles are the special adjectives *a, an,* and *the.* (*the* day, *a* fly)

The *definite article* (the word *the*) refers to a particular thing. (*the* cabin)

An *indefinite article* is used with a noun that is not unique but refers to one of many of its kind. (*a* dish, *an* otter)

Auxiliary verb. *See* **Verb.**

C

Clause A clause is a group of words that contains a verb and its subject. (*they slept*)

An *adjective clause* is a subordinate clause that modifies a noun or pronoun. (Hugh bought the sweater *that he had admired.*)

An *adverb clause* is a subordinate clause used to modify a verb, an adjective, or an adverb. (Ring the bell *when it is time for class to begin.*)

A **noun clause** is a subordinate clause that is used as a noun. (*Whatever you say* interests me.)

An **elliptical clause** is a clause from which a word or words have been omitted. (We are not as lucky as *they*.)

A **main (independent) clause** can stand by itself as a sentence. (*the flashlight flickered*)

A **subordinate (dependent) clause** does not express a complete thought and cannot stand by itself. (*while the nation watched*)

Clause	Example
Main (independent)	The hurricane struck
Subordinate (dependent)	while we were preparing to leave.

Collective noun. *See* **Noun.**

Comma splice A comma splice is an error caused when two sentences are separated with a comma instead of a correct end mark. (*The band played a medley of show tunes, everyone enjoyed the show.*)

Common noun. *See* **Noun.**

Comparative. *See* **Adjective; Adverb.**

Complement A complement is a word or group of words that completes the meaning of a verb. (The kitten finished the *milk*.) *See also* **Direct object; Indirect object.**

An **objective complement** is a word or a group of words that follows a direct object and renames or describes that object. (The parents of the rescued child declared Gus a *hero*.)

A **subject complement** follows a linking verb and renames or describes the subject. (The coach seemed *anxious*.) *See also* **Noun (predicate noun); Adjective (predicate adjective).**

Complete predicate The complete predicate of a sentence consists of the main verb plus any words that modify or complete the verb's meaning. (The student *produces work of high caliber*.)

Complete subject The complete subject of a sentence consists of the simple subject plus any words that modify or describe the simple subject. (*Students of history* believe that wars can be avoided.)

Sentence Part	Example
Complete subject	The man in the ten-gallon hat
Complete predicate	wore a pair of silver spurs.

Compound sentence part A sentence element that consists of two or more subjects, verbs, objects, or other parts is compound. (*Lou* and *Jay* helped. Laura *makes* and *models* scarves. Jill sings *opera* and *popular music*.)

Conjunction A conjunction is a word that links other words or groups of words.

A **coordinating conjunction** connects related words, groups of words, or sentences. (*and, but, or*)

A **correlative conjunction** is one of a pair of conjunctions that work together to connect sentence parts. (*either . . . or, neither . . . nor, not only . . . but also, whether . . . or, both . . . and*)

A **subordinating conjunction** introduces a subordinate clause. (*after, although, as, as if, as long as, as though, because, before, if, in order that, since, so that, than, though, till, unless, until, whatever, when, where, while*)

Conjunctive adverb A conjunctive adverb relates the clauses of a compound sentence. (*however, therefore, yet*)

Contraction A contraction is formed by joining two words and substituting an apostrophe for a letter or letters left out of one of the words. (*didn't, we've*)

Coordinating conjunction. *See* **Conjunction.**

Correlative conjunction. *See* **Conjunction.**

Dangling modifier A dangling modifier is one that does not clearly modify any word in the sentence. (*Dashing for the train, the barriers got in the way.*)

Demonstrative pronoun. *See* **Pronoun.**

Dependent clause. *See* **Clause.**

Direct object A direct object receives the action of a verb. Direct objects follow transitive verbs. (Jude planned the *party*.)

Direct quotation. *See* **Quotation.**

Divided quotation. *See* **Quotation.**

Double negative A double negative is the incorrect use of two negative words when only one is needed. (*Nobody didn't care.*)

End mark An end mark is any of several punctuation marks that can end a sentence. See the punctuation chart on page R77.

F

Fragment. *See* **Sentence fragment.**

Future tense. *See* **Verb tense.**

 G

Gender The gender of a personal pronoun indicates whether the person or thing referred to is male, female, or neuter. (My cousin plays the tuba; *he* often performs in school concerts.)

Gerund A gerund is a verbal that ends in *-ing* and functions as a noun. (*Making* pottery takes patience.)

 H

Helping verb. *See* **Verb (auxiliary verb).**

 I

Illogical comparison An illogical comparison is a comparison that does not make sense because words are missing or illogical. (My computer is *newer than Kay.*)

Indefinite pronoun. *See* **Pronoun.**

Indefinite reference Indefinite reference occurs when a pronoun is used without a clear antecedent. (My aunt hugged me in front of my friends, and *it* was embarrassing.)

Independent clause. *See* **Clause.**

Indirect object An indirect object tells to whom or for whom (sometimes to what or for what) something is done. (Arthur wrote *Kerry* a letter.)

Indirect question An indirect question tells what someone asked without using the person's exact words. (*My friend asked me if I could go with her to the dentist.*)

Indirect quotation. *See* **Quotation.**

Infinitive An infinitive is a verbal, usually preceded by *to,* that functions as a noun, an adjective, or an adverb. (He wanted *to go* to the play.)

Intensive pronoun. *See* **Pronoun.**

Interjection An interjection is a word or phrase used to express strong feeling. (*Wow! Good grief!*)

Interrogative pronoun. *See* **Pronoun.**

Intransitive verb. *See* **Verb.**

Inverted sentence An inverted sentence is one in which the subject comes after the verb. (*How was the movie? Here come the clowns.*)

Irregular verb. *See* **Verb.**

 L

Linking verb. *See* **Verb.**

 M

Main clause. *See* **Clause.**

Main verb. *See* **Verb.**

Modifier A modifier makes another word more precise. Modifiers most often are adjectives or adverbs; they may also be phrases, verbals, or clauses that function as adjectives or adverbs. (*small* box, smiled *broadly,* house *by the sea,* dog *barking loudly*)

An *essential modifier* is one that is necessary to the meaning of a sentence. (Everybody *who has a free pass* should enter now. None *of the passengers* got on the train.)

A *nonessential modifier* is one that merely adds more information to a sentence that is clear without the addition. (We will use the new dishes, *which are stored in the closet.*)

 N

Noun A noun names a person, a place, a thing, or an idea. (*auditor, shelf, book, goodness*)

An *abstract noun* names an idea, a quality, or a feeling. (*joy*)

A *collective noun* names a group of things. (*bevy*)

A *common noun* is a general name of a person, a place, a thing, or an idea. (*valet, hill, bread, amazement*)

A *compound noun* contains two or more words. (*hometown, pay-as-you-go, screen test*)

A *noun of direct address* is the name of a person being directly spoken to. (*Lee,* do you have the package? No, *Suki,* your letter did not arrive.)

A *possessive noun* shows who or what owns or is associated with something. (*Lil's* ring, a *day's* pay)

A *predicate noun* follows a linking verb and renames the subject. (Karen is a *writer.*)

A *proper noun* names a particular person, place, or thing. (*John Smith, Ohio, Sears Tower, Congress*)

Number A word is **singular** in number if it refers to just one person, place, thing, idea, or action, and **plural** in number if it refers to more than one person, place, thing, idea, or action. (The words *he, waiter,* and *is* are singular. The words *they, waiters,* and *are* are plural.)

 O

Object of a preposition The object of a preposition is the noun or pronoun that follows a preposition. (The athletes cycled along the *route.* Jane baked a cake for *her.*)

Object of a verb The object of a verb receives the action of the verb. (Sid told *stories.*)

Participle A participle is often used as part of a verb phrase. (had *written*) It can also be used as a verbal that functions as an adjective. (the *leaping* deer, the medicine *taken* for a fever)

The *present participle* is formed by adding -*ing* to the present form of a verb. (*Walking* rapidly, we reached the general store.)

The *past participle* of a regular verb is formed by adding -*d* or -*ed* to the present form. The past participles of irregular verbs do not follow this pattern. (*Startled,* they ran from the house. *Spun* glass is delicate. A *broken* cup lay there.)

Passive voice. *See* **Voice.**

Past tense. *See* **Verb tense.**

Perfect tenses. *See* **Verb tense.**

Person Person is a means of classifying pronouns.

A *first-person* pronoun refers to the person speaking. (*We* came.)

A *second-person* pronoun refers to the person spoken to. (*You* ask.)

A *third-person* pronoun refers to some other person(s) or thing(s) being spoken of. (*They* played.)

Personal pronoun. *See* **Pronoun.**

Phrase A phrase is a group of related words that does not contain a verb and its subject. (*noticing everything, under a chair*)

An *adjective phrase* modifies a noun or a pronoun. (The label *on the bottle* has faded.)

An *adverb phrase* modifies a verb, an adjective, or an adverb. (Come *to the fair.*)

An *appositive phrase* explains one or more words in a sentence. (Mary, *a champion gymnast,* won gold medals at the Olympics.)

A *gerund phrase* consists of a gerund and its modifiers and complements. (*Fixing the leak* will take only a few minutes.)

An *infinitive phrase* consists of an infinitive, its modifiers, and its complements. (*To prepare for a test,* study in a quiet place.)

A *participial phrase* consists of a participle and its modifiers and complements. (*Straggling to the finish line,* the last runners arrived.)

A *prepositional phrase* consists of a preposition, its object, and the object's modifiers. (The Saint Bernard does rescue work *in the Swiss Alps.*)

A *verb phrase* consists of a main verb and one or more helping verbs. (*might have ordered*)

Possessive A noun or pronoun that is possessive shows ownership or relationship. (*Dan's* story, *my* doctor)

Possessive noun. *See* **Noun.**

Possessive pronoun. *See* **Pronoun.**

Predicate The predicate of a sentence tells what the subject is or does. (The van *runs well even in winter.* The job *seems too complicated.*) *See also* **Complete predicate; Simple predicate.**

Predicate adjective. *See* **Adjective.**

Predicate nominative A predicate nominative is a noun or pronoun that follows a linking verb and renames or explains the subject. (Joan is a computer operator. The winner of the prize was *he.*)

Predicate pronoun. *See* **Pronoun.**

Preposition A preposition is a word that relates its object to another part of the sentence or to the sentence as a whole. (Alfredo leaped *onto* the stage.)

Prepositional phrase. *See* **Phrase.**

Present tense. *See* **Verb tense.**

Pronoun A pronoun replaces a noun or another pronoun. Some pronouns allow a writer or speaker to avoid repeating a proper noun. Other pronouns let a writer refer to an unknown or unidentified person or thing.

A *demonstrative pronoun* singles out one or more persons or things. (*This* is the letter.)

An *indefinite pronoun* refers to an unidentified person or thing. (*Everyone* stayed home. Will you hire *anybody*?)

An *intensive pronoun* emphasizes a noun or pronoun. (The teacher *himself* sold tickets.)

An *interrogative pronoun* asks a question. (*What* happened to you?)

A *personal pronoun* shows a distinction of person. (*I* came. *You* see. *He* knows.)

A *possessive pronoun* shows ownership. (*My* spaghetti is always good. Are *your* parents coming to the play?)

A *predicate pronoun* follows a linking verb and renames the subject. (The owners of the store were *they.*)

A *reflexive pronoun* reflects an action back on the subject of the sentence. (Joe helped *himself.*)

A *relative pronoun* relates a subordinate clause to the word it modifies. (The draperies, *which* had been made by hand, were ruined in the fire.)

Pronoun-antecedent agreement. *See* **Agreement.**

Pronoun forms

The *subject form* of a pronoun is used when the pronoun is the subject of a sentence or follows a linking verb as a predicate pronoun. (*She* fell. The star was *she.*)

The *object form* of a pronoun is used when the pronoun is the direct or indirect object of a verb or verbal or the object of a preposition. (We sent *him* the bill. We ordered food for *them.*)

Proper adjective. *See* **Adjective.**

Proper noun. *See* **Noun.**

Punctuation Punctuation clarifies the structure of sentences. See the punctuation chart below.

Quotation A quotation consists of words from another speaker or writer.

A *direct quotation* is the exact words of a speaker or writer. (Martin said, *"The homecoming game has been postponed."*)

A *divided quotation* is a quotation separated by words that identify the speaker. (*"The homecoming game,"* said Martin, *"has been postponed."*)

An *indirect quotation* reports what a person said without giving the exact words. (Martin said *that the homecoming game had been postponed.*)

Reflexive pronoun. *See* **Pronoun.**

Regular verb. *See* **Verb.**

Relative pronoun. *See* **Pronoun.**

Run-on sentence A run-on sentence consists of two or more sentences written incorrectly as one. (*The sunset was beautiful its brilliant colors lasted only a short time.*)

Sentence A sentence expresses a complete thought. The chart at the top of the next page shows the four kinds of sentences.

A *complex sentence* contains one main clause and one or more subordinate clauses. (*Open the windows before you go to bed. If she falls, I'll help her up.*)

A *compound sentence* is made up of two or more independent clauses joined by a conjunction, a colon, or a semicolon. (*The ship finally docked, and the passengers quickly left.*)

A *simple sentence* consists of only one main clause. (*My friend volunteers at a nursing home.*)

Punctuation	Uses	Examples
Apostrophe (')	Shows possession	Lou's garage Alva's script
	Indicates a contraction	I'll help you. The baby's tired.
Colon (:)	Introduces a list or quotation	three colors: red, green, and yellow
	Divides parts of some compound sentences	This was the problem: we had to find our own way home.
Comma (,)	Separates ideas	The glass broke, and the juice spilled all over.
	Separates modifiers	The lively, talented cheerleaders energized the team.
	Separates items in series	We visited London, Rome, and Paris.
Exclamation point (!)	Ends an exclamatory sentence	Have a wonderful time!
Hyphen (-)	Joins parts of some compound words	daughter-in-law, great-grandson
Period (.)	Ends a declarative sentence	Swallows return to Capistrano in spring.
	Follows many abbreviations	min. qt. Blvd. Gen. Jan.
Question mark (?)	Ends an interrogative sentence	Where are you going?
Semicolon (;)	Divides parts of some compound sentences	Marie is an expert dancer; she teaches a class in tap.
	Separates items in series that contain commas	Jerry visited Syracuse, New York; Athens, Georgia; and Tampa, Florida.

Kind of Sentence	Example
Declarative (statement)	Our team won.
Exclamatory (strong feeling)	I had a great time!
Imperative (request, command)	Take the next exit.
Interrogative (question)	Who owns the car?

Sentence fragment A sentence fragment is a group of words that is only part of a sentence. (*When he arrived. Merrily yodeling.*)

Simple predicate A simple predicate is the verb in the predicate. (John *collects* foreign stamps.)

Simple subject A simple subject is the key noun or pronoun in the subject. (The new *house* is empty.)

Split infinitive A split infinitive occurs when a modifier is placed between the word *to* and the verb in an infinitive. (*to quickly speak*)

Subject The subject is the part of a sentence that tells whom or what the sentence is about. (*Lou* swam.) *See* **Complete subject; Simple subject.**

Subject-verb agreement. *See* **Agreement.**

Subordinate clause. *See* **Clause.**

Subordinating conjunction. *See* **Conjunction.**

Superlative. *See* **Adjective; Adverb.**

Transitive verb. *See* **Verb.**

Unidentified reference An unidentified reference usually occurs when the word *it, they, this, which,* or *that* is used. (In California *they* have good weather most of the time.)

Verb A verb expresses an action, a condition, or a state of being.

An **action verb** tells what the subject does, has done, or will do. The action may be physical or mental. (Susan *trains* guide dogs.)

An **auxiliary verb** is added to a main verb to express tense, add emphasis, or otherwise affect the meaning of the verb. Together the auxiliary and main verb make up a verb phrase. (*will* intend, *could have* gone)

A **linking verb** expresses a state of being or connects the subject with a word or words that describe the subject. (The ice *feels* cold.) Linking verbs include *appear, be (am, are, is, was, were, been, being), become, feel, grow, look, remain, seem, smell, sound,* and *taste.*

A **main verb** expresses action or state of being; it appears with one or more auxiliary verbs. (will be *staying*)

The **progressive form** of a verb shows continuing action. (She *is knitting.*)

The past tense and past participle of a **regular verb** are formed by adding *-d* or *-ed.* (*open, opened*) An **irregular verb** does not follow this pattern. (*throw, threw, thrown; shrink, shrank, shrunk*)

The action of a **transitive verb** is directed toward someone or something, called the object of the verb. (Leo *washed* the windows.) An **intransitive verb** has no object. (The leaves *scattered.*)

Verbal A verbal is formed from a verb and acts as another part of speech, such as a noun, an adjective, or an adverb.

Verbal	Example
Gerund (used as a noun)	Lamont enjoys *swimming.*
Infinitive (used as an adjective, an adverb, or a noun)	Everyone wants *to help.*
Participle (used as an adjective)	The leaves *covering the drive* made it slippery.

Verb phrase. *See* **Phrase.**

Verb tense Verb tense shows the time of an action or the time of a state of being.

The **present tense** places an action or condition in the present. (Jan *takes* piano lessons.)

The **past tense** places an action or condition in the past. (We *came* to the party.)

The **future tense** places an action or condition in the future. (You *will understand.*)

The **present perfect tense** describes an action in an indefinite past time or an action that began in the past and continues in the present. (*has called, have known*)

The **past perfect tense** describes one action that happened before another action in the past. (*had scattered, had mentioned*)

The **future perfect tense** describes an event that will be finished before another future action begins. (*will have taught, shall have appeared*)

Voice The voice of a verb depends on whether the subject performs or receives the action of the verb.

In the **active voice** the subject of the sentence performs the verb's action. (We *knew* the answer.)

In the **passive voice** the subject of the sentence receives the action of the verb. (The team *has been eliminated.*)

Analyzing Text Features

Reading a Magazine Article

A **magazine article** is designed to catch and hold your interest. Learning how to recognize the items on a magazine page will help you read even the most complicated articles. Look at the sample magazine article as you read each strategy below.

Strategies for Reading

A Read the **title** and other **headings** to get an idea of what the article is about. Frequently, the title presents the article's main topic. Smaller headings may introduce subtopics related to the main topic.

B Note introductory text that is set off in some way, such as an **indented paragraph** or a passage in a **different typeface**. This text often summarizes the article.

C Pay attention to terms in **italics** or **boldface**. Look for definitions or explanations before or after these terms.

D Study **visuals**—photos, pictures, or maps. Visuals help bring the topic to life and enrich the text.

E Look for **special features**, such as charts, tables, or graphs, that provide more detailed information on the topic or on a subtopic.

PRACTICE AND APPLY

Use the sample magazine page at right and the tips above to help you answer the following questions.

1. What is the article's main topic?

2. What gives fireflies their "fire"?

3. What happens soon after a firefly mates?

4. How do the visuals help you understand the article?

5. What information appears in the box?

The Lure of Light

For humans, cosmic showers are awe-inspiring.
For fireflies, lights closer to home mean it's time to mate.

Also called "lightning bugs" and "glowworms," fireflies belong to the beetle family *Lampyridae*. Their **bioluminescent** "fire" comes from *luciferin* (a compound that reacts with oxygen) and *luciferase* (an enzyme that makes this reaction possible). Scientists are studying ways to use luciferase to "highlight" abnormal cells in people.

Most fireflies look for mates on warm summer evenings. Each species seems to have its own light signal. The male firefly flies around flashing his light signal. When the flightless female, perched on a plant, sees the appropriate signal, she responds by flashing her light. Then the male flies toward her, repeating his signal. . . .

Fireflies die within days after mating. Their young hatch as wormlike larvae. They hide (on land or underwater), eat, grow, **molt,** and grow some more. After several months, each larva buries itself in an underground chamber, where it transforms into an adult firefly. The adult then chews through its chamber wall, pushes up to the surface, and searches for a mate.

The lure of light begins again.

---

bioluminescent: emitting visible light (in a living organism)
molt: to shed a body covering

Reading a Textbook

The first page of a **textbook** lesson introduces you to a particular topic. The page also provides important information that will guide you through the rest of the lesson. Look at the sample textbook page as you read each strategy below.

Strategies for Reading

A Preview the **title** and other **headings** to find out the lesson's main topic and related subtopics.

B Look for a list of terms or **vocabulary words**. These words will be identified and defined throughout the lesson.

C Read the **main idea**, **objectives**, or **focus**. These items summarize the lesson and establish a purpose for your reading.

D Find words set in special type, such as **italics** or **boldface**. Also look for material in **parentheses**. Boldface is often used to identify the vocabulary terms in the lesson. Material in parentheses may refer you to another page or visual in the lesson.

E Notice text on the page that is set off in some way. For example, text placed in a tinted, or colored, box may be from a **primary source** or a **quotation** that gives firsthand knowledge or historical perspective on a topic.

F Examine **visuals**, such as photos and drawings, and their captions. Visuals can help the topic come alive.

PRACTICE AND APPLY

Use the sample textbook page and the tips above to help you answer the following questions.

1. What does this lesson focus on?

2. What vocabulary terms will be defined in the lesson?

3. Review the quotation. Who is being quoted?

4. Where did the Assyrians come from?

2 Assyria Dominates the Fertile Crescent

TERMS & NAMES
- Assyria
- Sennacherib
- Nineveh
- Ashurbanipal
- Medes
- Chaldeans
- Nebuchadnezzar

MAIN IDEA	WHY IT MATTERS NOW
Assyria developed a military machine, conquered an empire, and established imperial administration.	Some leaders still use military force to extend their rule, stamp out opposition, and gain wealth and power.

SETTING THE STAGE For more than two centuries, the Assyrian army advanced across Southwest Asia. It overwhelmed foes with its military strength. After the Assyrians seized control of Egypt, the Assyrian king Esarhaddon proclaimed, "I tore up the root of Kush, and not one therein escaped to submit to me." The last Kushite pharaoh retreated to Napata, Kush's capital city.

A Mighty Military Machine

Beginning around 850 B.C., **Assyria** (uh·SEER·ee·uh) acquired a large empire. It accomplished this by means of a sophisticated military organization and state-of-the-art weaponry. For a time, this campaign of conquest made Assyria the greatest power in Southwest Asia.

The Rise of a Warrior People The Assyrians came from the northern part of Mesopotamia. Their flat, exposed farmland made them easy to attack. Invaders swept down from the nearby mountains. The Assyrians may have developed their warlike behavior in response to these invasions. Lacking natural barriers such as mountains or deserts, they repelled invaders by developing a strong army. Through constant warfare, Assyrian kings built an empire that stretched from east and north of the Tigris River all the way to central Egypt.

One of these Assyrian kings, **Sennacherib** (sih·NAK·uhr·ihb), bragged that he had sacked 89 cities and 820 villages, burned Babylon, and ordered most of its inhabitants killed. Centuries later, in the 1800s, the English poet George Gordon, Lord Byron, romanticized the Assyrians' bloody exploits in a poem:

A VOICE ABOUT THE PAST
The Assyrian came down like a wolf on the fold,
And his cohorts were gleaming in purple and gold;
And the sheen of their spears was like stars on the sea,
When the blue wave rolls nightly on deep Galilee.
GEORGE GORDON, LORD BYRON, "The Destruction of Sennacherib"

This detail of a sandstone relief shows an Assyrian soldier with a shield and iron-tipped spear.

THINK THROUGH HISTORY
A. Analyzing Causes
What caused the Assyrians to develop a strong army and large empire.
Possible Answer:
No natural barriers to invasion, needed strong army to repel invaders, constant warfare produced large empire.

Military Organization and Conquest Assyria was a society which glorified military strength. Its soldiers were well equipped for conquering an empire. Making use of the iron-working technology of the time, the soldiers covered themselves in stiff leather and metal armor. They wore copper or iron helmets, padded loincloths, and leather skirts layered with metal scales. Their weapons were iron swords and iron-pointed spears. Infantry, archers, and spear throwers protected themselves with huge shields.

Advance planning and technical skill allowed the Assyrians to lay siege to enemy cities. When deep water blocked their passage, engineers would bridge the rivers with pontoons, or floating structures used to support a bridge. Tying inflated animal skins

Vocabulary
siege: a military blockade to force a city to surrender.

Understanding Visuals

Reading a Table

Tables hold a lot of information in an organized way. These tips can help you read a table quickly and accurately. Look at the example as you read each strategy in this list.

Strategies for Reading

A Read the **title** to find out the content of the table.

B Read the **introduction** to get a general overview of the information included in the table.

C Look at the **heading** of each row and column. To find specific information, find the place where a row and column intersect.

D Check the **credit** to see if the information is up-to-date and from a respected source.

B

A Planets of the Solar System

Each planet in our solar system is unique. As the table shows, these differing traits include mass, mean distance from the sun, revolution period, and surface gravity.

C	Mass (kg)	Mean Distance from the Sun (km)	Revolution Period (Earth time)	Surface Gravity (m/s²)
Mercury	3.3×10^{23}	57,909,175	87.97 days	3.69
Venus	4.87×10^{24}	108,208,930	224.7 days	8.86
Earth	5.9742×10^{24}	149,597,890	365.26 days	9.81
Mars	6.42×10^{23}	227,936,640	686.98 days	3.73
Jupiter	1.9×10^{27}	778,412,010	11.86 years	22.96
Saturn	5.69×10^{26}	1,426,725,400	29.46 years	11.38
Uranus	8.68×10^{25}	2,870,972,200	83.75 years	11.28
Neptune	1.02×10^{26}	4,498,252,900	163.72 years	11.67
Pluto	1.29×10^{22}	5,906,376,200	248 years	0.65

Source: National Aeronautics and Space Administration Jet Propulsion Laboratory Web site: http://www.jpl.nasa.gov/solar_system/planets/planets_index.html **D**

PRACTICE AND APPLY

Answer the following questions using the table of information and tips.

1. Which planet has the strongest surface gravity?

2. Which planet is about ten times farther from the Sun than Earth?

3. Which planet is more massive: Earth or Venus?

Reading a Map

To read a **map** correctly, you have to identify and understand its elements. Look at the example below as you read each strategy in this list.

Strategies for Reading

A Scan the **title** to understand the content of the map.

B Study the **key**, or **legend**, to find out what the symbols and colors on the map stand for.

C Study **geographic labels** to understand specific places on the map.

D Look at the **pointer**, or **compass rose**, to determine direction.

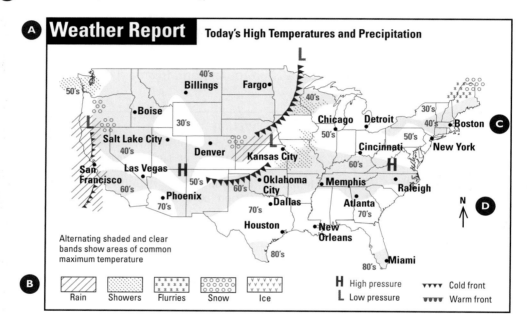

PRACTICE AND APPLY

Use the map to answer the following questions.

1. What is the purpose of this map?

2. What does the symbol ▼▼▼▼ mean?

3. In which cities is rain indicated?

4. What seems to be the relationship between rain and cold fronts?

5. List the names of the coldest cities in the country.

Reading a Diagram

Diagrams combine pictures with a few words to provide a lot of information. Look at the example on the opposite page as you read each of the following strategies.

Strategies for Reading

A Look at the **title** to get a quick idea of what the diagram is about.

B Study the **images** closely to understand each part of the diagram.

C Look at the **captions** and the **labels** for more information.

PRACTICE AND APPLY

Study the diagram, then answer the following questions using the strategies above.

1. What is this diagram about?

2. What is an updraft?

3. What are the two forces represented by the arrows in the Mature Stage?

4. Which force is growing stronger in this stage?

5. Why does the cloud begin to evaporate in the Dissipating Stage?

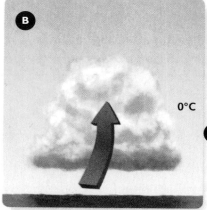

0°C

①

C **CUMULUS STAGE** Air rises and a cumulus cloud forms. The rising air is called an updraft. The updraft prevents precipitation from reaching the ground.

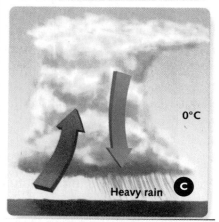

0°C

Heavy rain

②

MATURE STAGE The precipitation becomes heavy enough to fall through the updraft and reach the ground. The falling precipitation creates a downdraft.

0°C

Light rain

③

DISSIPATING STAGE
The downdraft weakens the updraft eventually cutting off the supply of moist air rising to the cloud. The cloud begins to evaporate.

Recognizing Text Structures

Main Idea and Supporting Details

The **main idea** in a paragraph is its most important point. **Details** in the paragraph support the main idea. Identifying the main idea will help you focus on the main message the writer wants to communicate. Use the following strategies to help you identify a paragraph's main idea and supporting details.

Strategies for Reading

- Look for the **main idea**, which is often the first sentence in a paragraph.
- Use the main idea to help you **summarize** the point of the paragraph.
- Identify specific **details**, including facts and examples, that **support** the main idea.

Creatures of the Night

 Main Idea — Bats are nocturnal animals—

Details — animals that are awake during the night and sleep during the day. Just before dusk, bats wake from their slumber. At dusk they begin their search for food; most eat insects, but some also eat fruit, pollen, or nectar. After feeding, bats rest, and then may eat again. Before dawn, they return to their roost for a good day's sleep.

PRACTICE AND APPLY

Read the following paragraph. List the main idea and three supporting details.

When a volcano erupts, it produces a molten rock called lava. Lava is extremely hot when it first escapes but hardens as it cools. There are two kinds of lava; one kind is fast and fluid, while the other is slow and sticky.

Problem and Solution

Does the proposed **solution** to a **problem** make sense? In order to decide, you need to look at each part of the text. Use the following strategies to read the text below.

Strategies for Reading

- Look at the beginning or middle of a paragraph to find the **statement of the problem**.
- Find **details** that explain the problem and tell why it is important.
- Look for the **proposed solution**.
- Identify the **supporting details** for the proposed solution.
- Think about whether the solution is a good one.

Safer Streets by Wanda Briggs

Statement of problem

The intersection at Fourth and D streets, two blocks from our school, is an accident waiting to happen. Cars speed down the street while students stand at the crosswalk. Every day there are a few drivers who barely slow down, creating a dangerous situation.

Explanation of solution

Currently there is no stop sign at this intersection. Although the intersection is two blocks away from the school, many students use it because D Street connects the school with the subway station. Every morning and afternoon, hundreds of students and teachers cross the intersection at Fourth and D Streets.

The city should put a stop sign at this intersection and station adult crossing guards there. The presence of a stop sign will be a signal to motorists, and the crossing guard will make sure that students know when it is safe to cross. These safety measures would make the streets safer for students and teachers as well as drivers.

PRACTICE AND APPLY

Read the text above. Then answer these questions.

1. What is the proposed solution in the third paragraph?
2. Identify at least one detail that supports the solution.
3. Do you think the solution is a good one? Explain why or why not.

Sequence

It's important to understand the **sequence**, or order of events, in what you read. It helps you know what happens and why. Read the tips below to make sure a sequence is clear to you. Then look at the example on the opposite page.

Strategies for Reading

- Read through the passage and think about what its **main steps**, or stages, are.
- Look for **words and phrases that signal time**, such as *today, Friday, that night, later,* or *at 3 o'clock.*
- Look for **words and phrases that signal order**, such as *first, second, now, after that,* or *finally.*

PRACTICE AND APPLY

Read the article on the next page, which describes how to make your own photographic print. Use the information from the article and the tips above to answer the questions.

1. List any words or phrases that signal time.

2. List any phrases in the article that signal order.

3. A flow chart can help you understand a sequence of events. Use the information from the article to copy and complete this flow chart.

---

1. Load and focus the image.

Put the *negative* in the enlarger.

Adjust the _____ knob.

2. Load and expose the paper.

Put the paper on the

_____.

Set the _____ and

push start.

3. Develop and fix the paper.

a. _____

b. _____

c. _____

How to Develop a Photograph

To make a black-and-white photographic print, you will need a photographic negative and a darkroom with an enlarger, photo paper, a printing easel to hold the paper, a clock or watch, and four trays with tongs. Each tray will contain one of four solutions: (1) developer; (2) a stop bath, or "stop"; (3) a fixing solution, or "fix"; and (4) water.

First, put the negative in the negative carrier of the enlarger. Switch the bulb on and adjust the size of the image on the easel. Then turn the focus knob until the image is sharp. Now, without moving the easel, turn off the bulb and place a sheet of photo paper on the easel. Set the timer on the enlarger to five seconds and expose the paper by pressing *start*.

After the paper has been exposed, remove it and place it in the developer tray for one minute. When the minute is up, remove the paper with tongs and place it in the stop bath for five seconds. Then move the paper to the fix tray and leave it there for three to five minutes. Once this time is up, the print has been "fixed" and you may view it in the light.

Look at the print to see whether it is too light or too dark. You may need to start again and adjust the time of exposure. Place the print in the water tray and start over with a new sheet of paper. If your first print was too dark, cut the time of exposure in half. If it was too light, double the time of exposure. Then repeat the remaining steps.

Cause and Effect

A **cause** is an event that brings about another event. An **effect** is something that happens as a result of the first event. Identifying causes and effects helps you understand how events are related. The tips below can help you find causes and effects in any reading.

Strategies for Reading

- Look for an action or event that answers the question "What happened?" This is the **effect**.
- Look for an action or event that answers the question "Why did it happen?" This is the **cause**.
- Identify words or phrases that **signal** causes and effects, such as *because, as a result, therefore, thus, consequently, since,* and *led to.*

PRACTICE AND APPLY

Read the cause-and-effect passage on the next page. Then answer the following questions. Notice that the first cause and effect in the passage are highlighted.

1. List any words in the passage that signal causes and effects. The first one is highlighted for you.
2. Sometimes a cause has more than one effect. List two problems that result when acid rain destroys the waxy coating on a plant's leaves.
3. Use three of the causes and effects in the **third** paragraph to copy and complete the following diagram.

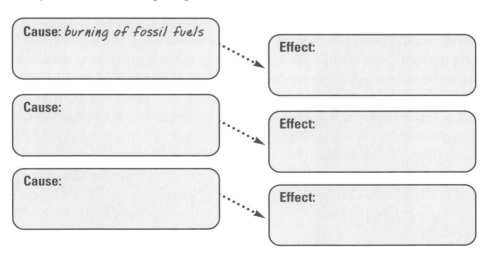

Cause: *burning of fossil fuels*

Effect:

Cause:

Effect:

Cause:

Effect:

Acid Rain

One of the more serious threats to our environment is acid rain. This term refers to polluted precipitation such as rain, sleet, snow, or fog. The acid in acid rain comes from sulfur dioxide and nitrogen oxides.

Effect The presence of sulfur **Signal word** dioxide and nitrogen oxides in the air is caused by the burning of fos- **Cause** sil fuels by automobiles, factories, and energy plants. Once released into the atmosphere, sulfur dioxide and nitrogen oxides react with the moisture in the air, producing nitric acid and sulfuric acid. In the last fifty years, taller smokestacks in urban areas have allowed acid pollutants to be blown great distances by the wind. For this reason acid rain has become a problem in rural as well as industrialized areas.

Acid rain can hinder a plant's growth and reproduction by damaging the roots, destroying nutrients in the soil, or inhibiting the plant's processing of nutrients. Acid rain also damages the protective waxy coating on a plant's leaves, thus making plants more vulnerable to disease and adverse weather conditions such as strong wind, heavy rain, or drought.

Another harmful effect of acid rain is that the water in rivers, lakes, and streams can become more acidic, threatening fish and other aquatic life. It also dissolves metals such as mercury and aluminum, which are found in the surrounding soil and rocks; these toxic elements are then carried into the water supply, where they can poison plants and wildlife. Acid rain can lead to serious health problems if people drink water contaminated with aluminum or eat fish tainted with mercury.

There are certain ways to counteract the effects of acid rain, such as adding lime to lakes and rivers, which temporarily reduces their acidity. However, this may have its own harmful side effects. It may be more effective to reduce the pollution at its source by removing sulfur and nitrogen compounds from fuel, or by burning less fossil fuel altogether.

Comparison and Contrast

Comparing two things means showing how they are the same. **Contrasting** two things means showing how they are different. Comparisons and contrasts are often used in science and history books to make a subject clearer. Use these tips to help you understand comparison and contrast in reading assignments, such as the article on the opposite page.

Strategies for Reading

- Look for **direct statements** of comparison and contrast: "These things are similar because . . . " or "One major difference is. . . ."
- Pay attention to **words and phrases that signal comparisons**, such as *also, both, is the same as,* and *in the same way.*
- Notice **words and phrases that signal contrasts**. Some of these are *however, still, but,* and *on the other hand.*

PRACTICE AND APPLY

Read the essay on the opposite page. Then use the information from the article and the tips above to answer the questions.

1. List any words and phrases that signal comparisons. A sample has been highlighted for you.
2. List any words and phrases that signal contrasts. A sample has been highlighted for you.
3. A Venn diagram shows how two subjects are similar and how they are different. Copy this diagram, which uses information from the essay to compare and contrast emotional and irritant tears. Add at least one similarity to the middle part of the diagram. Add at least one difference in each outer circle.

EMOTIONAL TEARS
caused by
strong feelings

BOTH
come from the
lacrimal glands

IRRITANT TEARS
caused by smoke,
onion vapors, foreign
substances

What Are Tears?

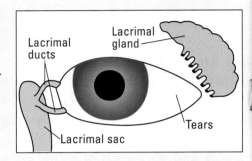

Humans shed two kinds of tears. Irritant tears occur in response to irritating physical stimuli, while emotional tears occur in response to sadness, anger, joy, or other intense emotions.

Comparison Both kinds of tears come from glands above the eyes called lacrimal glands. The fluid from the lacrimal glands moistens the eyes and keeps them clear of foreign particles. With each blink, a little bit of fluid is secreted from the glands. Tears form when the lacrimal glands produce more fluid than can drain through the available ducts.

Emotional tears occur when a strong feeling, such as grief, anger, or joy, causes the muscles around the lacrimal glands to tighten up **Contrast** and squeeze out excess fluid. These emotional tears differ from irritant tears, which occur in response to irritants such as smoke, onion vapors, or bits of dirt in the eye.

Irritant tears have a clear purpose —to wash the eye and keep it moist. What is the purpose of emotional tears? Scientist William Frey suspects that emotional tears might help relieve the body of chemicals that build up during stress.

He conducted a study in which he compared irritant tears with emotional tears. To produce irritant tears, he exposed people to grated onions and collected the resulting tears. Producing emotional tears was a little bit more complicated—what is the best way to make people cry without being mean to them? He finally decided to show them sad movies.

Frey found that emotional tears were in fact different from irritant tears. For one thing, people tended to shed many more emotional tears than irritant tears. And while both kinds of tears contained the element manganese, emotional tears had a much higher concentration of protein. However, the reason for this difference was not clear.

The mysterious causes and functions of tears are still being researched, but if you want to avoid shedding tears, stay away from onions and sad movies—at least that much is clear.

Argument

An **argument** is an opinion backed up with reasons and facts. Examining an opinion and the reasons and facts that back it up will help you decide if the opinion makes sense. Look at the argument on the right as you read each of these tips.

Strategies for Reading

- Look for words that **signal an opinion**: *I believe; I think; in my view; they claim, argue,* or *disagree.*
- Look for reasons, facts, or expert opinions that **support** the argument.
- Ask yourself if the argument and reasons **make sense**.
- Look for overgeneralizations or other **errors in reasoning** that may affect the argument.
- Think about the **accuracy** of the information.

PRACTICE AND APPLY

Read the argument on the next page, and then answer the questions below.

1. List any words that signal an opinion.
2. List any words or phrases that give the writer's opinion.
3. The writer presents both sides of the argument. Copy and complete the chart below to show the two sides. One example has been provided for you.

Reasons for	Reasons Against
1. Bicycles produce less air pollution than cars.	

More Rights for Bikes

By Maxine Fujita

I believe bicyclists should have as much claim to city streets as automobiles. In my view, it is time to encourage bicycle riding by increasing the number of bike lanes and by changing motorists' attitudes toward bicycle riders.

The advantages of riding a bicycle rather than driving a car are clear. For one thing, automobile exhaust adds to already grave air pollution problems in our cities. By choosing to ride a bike instead of drive, we help keep our air clean. We also keep our streets quiet. Although we often forget about noise pollution, few people would miss the constant revving of car engines and honking of horns if our streets were filled with bicycles. Cycling also provides great exercise. If more people rode bikes, our population would have healthier hearts, lungs, and legs.

There are those who oppose bicycle traffic. They say the streets were made for cars, so cars have

more right to be on the streets. They claim that cyclists are a nuisance and a danger because they interfere with auto traffic and are hard to see. They themselves don't want to cycle because it's too strenuous, too cold, too wet, too far, or too dangerous.

I'm not saying that bicycling is for everyone, but I am saying it's a safer, healthier, environmentally friendly alternative to driving. So join me in supporting more bike lanes and increased respect for the people who use them.

Reading in the Content Areas

Social Studies

Social studies class becomes easier when you understand how your textbook's words, pictures, and maps work together to give you information. Following these tips can make you a better reader of social studies lessons. As you read the tips, look at the sample lesson on the right-hand page.

Strategies for Reading

A First, look at any **headlines** or **subheads** on the page. These give you an idea of what each section covers.

B Make sure you know the meaning of any boldfaced or underlined **vocabulary terms**. These terms often appear on tests.

C Carefully read the text and think about **ways the information is organized**. Social studies books are full of sequence, comparison and contrast, and organization by geographic location.

D Look closely at **maps** and **map titles**. Think about how the map and the text are related.

E Read any **study tips** in the margins or at the bottom of the page. These let you check your understanding as you read.

PRACTICE AND APPLY

Carefully read the textbook page at right. Use the information from the page and from the tips above to answer these questions.

1. What are the two main subjects covered on this page? What secondary subject is covered?
2. List and define the three vocabulary terms.
3. Give three examples of uplands.
4. On the map, which river empties into the North Sea?
5. Read the "Geographic Thinking" question in the left margin. Which paragraph in the text contains the answer to this question?

off the Balkan Peninsula from the rest of Europe. Historically, they also have isolated the peninsula's various ethnic groups from each other.

(A) UPLANDS Mountains and uplands differ from each other in their elevation. **(B) Uplands** are hills or very low mountains that may also contain mesas and high plateaus. Some uplands of Europe are eroded remains of ancient mountain ranges. Examples of uplands include the Kjølen (CHUR·luhn) Mountains of Scandinavia, the Scottish highlands, the low mountain areas of Brittany in France, and the central plateau of Spain called the **Meseta** (meh·SEH·tah). Other uplands border mountainous areas, such as the Central Uplands of Germany, which are at the base of the Alps. About one-sixth of French lands are located in the uplands called the **Massif Central** (ma·SEEF sahn·TRAHL).

BACKGROUND
Brittany is a region located on a peninsula in northwest France.

(A) Rivers: Europe's Links

Traversing Europe is a network of rivers that bring people and goods together. These rivers are used to transport goods between coastal harbors and the inland region, aiding economic growth. Historically, the rivers also have aided the movement of ideas.

(C) Two major castle-lined rivers— the Danube and the Rhine—have served as watery highways for centuries. The Rhine flows 820 miles from the interior of Europe north to the North Sea. The Danube cuts through the heart of Europe from west to east. Touching 9 countries over its 1,771-mile length, the Danube River links Europeans to the Black Sea.

Many other European rivers flow from the interior to the sea and are large enough for ships to traverse. Through history, these rivers helped connect Europeans to the rest of the world, encouraging both trade and travel. Europeans have explored and migrated to many other world regions.

Rivers of Europe

ATLANTIC OCEAN
North Sea
Thames R. London Rotterdam
Nantes Paris Cologne R. Warsaw
Seine R. Bonn Wroclaw
Bay of Biscay Loire R. Rhine R. Bratislava
Lyon Vienna Budapest
Lisbon Belgrade Danube R.
Tagus R. Rome Black Sea
Mediterranean Sea

0 250 500 miles
0 250 500 kilometers
Azimuthal Equidistant Projection

SKILLBUILDER: Interpreting Maps
❶ MOVEMENT Which rivers empty into the North Sea? Into the Mediterranean Sea?
❷ PLACE What port is at the mouth of the Rhine?

(E) 🌐 **Geographic Thinking**

Seeing Patterns
▶ How does the direction in which European rivers flow aid in linking Europeans to the world?

Answer: Because they flow toward seas, the rivers help Europeans to travel to other regions.

Science

Reading a **science** textbook becomes easier when you understand how the explanations, drawings, and special terms work together. Use the strategies below to help you better understand your science textbook. Look at the examples on the opposite page as you read each strategy in this list.

Strategies for Reading

A Preview the **title** and **headings** on the page to see what scientific concepts will be covered.

B Read the **key idea, objectives,** or **focus**. These items summarize the lesson and establish a purpose for your reading.

C Look for **boldfaced** and **italicized** words that appear in the text. Look for **definitions** of those words.

D Carefully examine any **pictures** or **diagrams**. Read the **captions** and evaluate how the graphics help to illustrate and explain the text.

E Many science textbooks discuss **scientific concepts** in terms of **everyday events** or **experiences**. Look for these places and consider how they improve your understanding.

PRACTICE AND APPLY

Use the sample science page and the tips above to help you answer the following questions.

1. What scientific concepts will be covered in this lesson? Where on the page did you find this information?
2. Define the key term *fault.*
3. Why do you think the earthquake model described in the third paragraph is called the *elastic-rebound theory?*
4. What are two things the diagram tells you about earthquakes?

10.1

 KEY IDEA

Most earthquakes result from the strain that builds up at plate boundaries.

KEY VOCABULARY

- earthquake
- fault
- focus
- epicenter
- body waves
- P waves
- S waves
- surface waves

How and Where Earthquakes Occur

More than 3 million earthquakes occur each year, or about one earthquake every ten seconds. Most of these are too small to be noticeable. Each year, however, a number of powerful earthquakes occur. Because such earthquakes are among the most destructive of natural disasters, it is important to understand how and where earthquakes occur in order to prevent the loss of lives and property.

Causes of Earthquakes

An **earthquake** is a shaking of Earth's crust caused by a release of energy. Earthquakes can occur for many reasons. The ground may shake as a result of the eruption of a volcano, the collapse of a cavern, or even the impact of a meteor. The cause of most major earthquakes is the strain that builds up along faults at or near boundaries between lithospheric plates. A **fault** is a break in the lithosphere along which movement has occurred.

Most of the time, friction prevents the plates from moving, so strain builds up, causing the plates to deform, or change shape. Eventually, the strain becomes great enough to overcome the friction, and the plates move suddenly, causing an earthquake. The plates then snap back to the shapes they had before they were deformed, but at new locations relative to each other. This model of an earthquake is called the elastic-rebound theory.

The point at which the first movement occurs during an earthquake is called the **focus** of the earthquake. The focus is the point at which rock begins to move or break. It is where the earthquake originates and is usually many kilometers beneath the surface. The point on Earth's surface directly above the focus is the **epicenter** of the earthquake. News reports about earthquakes usually give the location of the epicenters.

 EARTHQUAKE These rows of lettuce were displaced by an earthquake in California in 1979.

Focus and Epicenter of an Earthquake

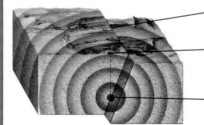

FAULT Most earthquakes originate at faults along plate boundaries.

EPICENTER The epicenter is the point on Earth's surface directly above the focus.

FOCUS Energy is released at the focus and travels away from it in all directions.

The depth at which an earthquake originates depends upon the type of plate boundary involved. At divergent boundaries, such as the Mid-Atlantic Ridge, earthquakes tend to occur within 30 kilometers of the surface. Earthquakes also tend to occur at shallow depths along transform boundaries. At subduction boundaries, however, where plates plunge beneath other plates, the focus of an earthquake can be located as far as

Mathematics

Reading in **mathematics** is different from reading in history, literature, or science. Use the strategies below to help you better understand your mathematics textbook. Look at the examples on the opposite page as you read each strategy in the list.

Strategies for Reading

A Preview the **title** and **headings** on the page to see what mathematics concepts will be covered.

B Find and read the **goals** or **objectives** for the lesson. These will tell you the most important points to know.

C Read **explanations** carefully. Sometimes a concept is explained in more than one way to make sure you understand it.

D Look for **special features**, such as study or vocabulary tips. They provide more help or information.

E Study any **worked-out solutions** to sample problems. These are the key to understanding how to do the homework assignment.

PRACTICE AND APPLY

Use the sample mathematics page and the strategies above to help you answer the following questions.

1. What is the title of the lesson?

2. What learning goals should you have as you work through this lesson?

3. List and define the vocabulary words that appear in the explanation at the top of the page.

4. Why is the relation in Example 1a *not* a function?

5. Where is the origin in a coordinate plane?

6. What is the name that is given to the first number in an ordered pair?

2.1

Functions and Their Graphs

GOAL 1 REPRESENTING RELATIONS AND FUNCTIONS

What you should learn

GOAL 1 Represent relations and functions.

GOAL 2 Graph and evaluate linear functions, as applied in **Exs. 55 and 56**.

Why you should learn it

▼ To model **real-life** quantities, such as the distance a hot air balloon travels in **Example 6**.

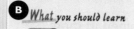

A **relation** is a *mapping*, or pairing, of input values with output values. The set of input values is the **domain**, and the set of output values is the **range**. A relation is a **function** provided there is exactly one output for each input. It is not a function if at least one input has more than one output.

Relations (and functions) between two quantities can be represented in many ways, including mapping diagrams, tables, graphs, equations, and verbal descriptions.

EXAMPLE 1 Identifying Functions

Identify the domain and range. Then tell whether the relation is a function.

a. Input Output
-3 → 3
1 → -2
1 → 1
4 → 4

b. Input Output
-3 → 3
1 → 1
3 → 1
4 → -2

SOLUTION

a. The domain consists of −3, 1, and 4, and the range consists of −2, 1, 3, and 4. The relation is not a function because the input 1 is mapped onto both −2 and 1.

b. The domain consists of −3, 1, 3, and 4, and the range consists of −2, 1, and 3. The relation is a function because each input in the domain is mapped onto exactly one output in the range.

• • • • • • • • • •

A relation can be represented by a set of **ordered pairs** of the form (x, y). In an ordered pair the first number is the **x-coordinate** and the second number is the **y-coordinate**. To graph a relation, plot each of its ordered pairs in a **coordinate plane**, such as the one shown. A coordinate plane is divided into four **quadrants** by the **x-axis** and the **y-axis**. The axes intersect at a point called the **origin**.

STUDENT HELP

▶ **Study Tip**
Although the origin O is not usually labeled, it is understood to be the point $(0, 0)$.

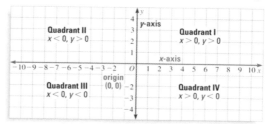

Quadrant II
$x < 0, y > 0$

Quadrant I
$x > 0, y > 0$

y-axis

x-axis

origin
$(0, 0)$

Quadrant III
$x < 0, y < 0$

Quadrant IV
$x > 0, y < 0$

Reading Beyond the Classroom

Reading an Application

Reading and understanding an **application** will help you fill it out correctly and avoid mistakes. Use the following strategies to help you understand any application. Look at the example on the next page as you read each strategy.

Strategies for Reading

A **Begin at the top**. Scan the application to understand the different sections.

B Look for special **instructions for filling out** the application.

C Note any **request for materials** that must be attached to the application.

D Watch for **sections you don't have to fill in** or **questions you don't have to answer**.

E Look for difficult or confusing words or abbreviations. Look them up in a dictionary or ask someone what they mean.

PRACTICE AND APPLY

Imagine that you are applying for a Social Security card. Read the application on the next page. Then answer the following questions.

1. Where should you send the completed form?
2. Which questions can you skip if you have never before applied for or received a Social Security card?
3. In which section of the application should your phone number be entered?
4. What is the penalty for deliberately giving false information?
5. What should be written in section 8B of the application?

SOCIAL SECURITY ADMINISTRATION
Application for a Social Security Card

Form Approved
OMB No. 0960-0066

STEP 1 Complete and sign the application using BLUE or BLACK ink. Do not use pencil or other colors of ink. Please print legibly.

STEP 2 Submit the completed and signed application with all required original documents to any Social Security office. To find out what documents are needed, please visit www.ssa.gov/online.

1	NAME — TO BE SHOWN ON CARD	First	Full Middle Name	Last
	FULL NAME AT BIRTH IF OTHER THAN ABOVE	First	Full Middle Name	Last
	OTHER NAMES USED			

2 MAILING ADDRESS Do Not Abbreviate

Street Address, Apt. No., PO Box, Rural Route No.

City	State	Zip Code

3 CITIZENSHIP (Check One)

☐ U.S. Citizen ☐ Legal Alien Allowed To Work ☐ Legal Alien **Not** Allowed To Work (See Instructions On Page 1) ☐ Other (See Instructions On Page 1)

4 SEX

☐ Male ☐ Female

5 RACE/ETHNIC DESCRIPTION (Check One Only - Voluntary)

☐ Asian, Asian-American or Pacific Islander ☐ Hispanic ☐ Black (Not Hispanic) ☐ North American Indian or Alaskan Native ☐ White (Not Hispanic)

6 DATE OF BIRTH _____ Month, Day, Year

7 PLACE OF BIRTH (Do Not Abbreviate) _____ City _____ State or Foreign Country _____ FCI

☐ Office Use Only

8
A. MOTHER'S MAIDEN NAME —	First	Full Middle Name	Last Name At Her Birth
B. MOTHER'S SOCIAL SECURITY NUMBER —	☐☐☐–☐☐–☐☐☐☐		

9
A. FATHER'S NAME —	First	Full Middle Name	Last
B. FATHER'S SOCIAL SECURITY NUMBER —	☐☐☐–☐☐–☐☐☐☐		

10 Has the applicant or anyone acting on his/her behalf ever filed for or received a Social Security number card before?

☐ Yes (If "yes", answer questions 11-13.) ☐ No (If "no", go on to question 14.) ☐ Don't Know (If "don't know", go on to question 14.)

11 Enter the Social Security number previously assigned to the person listed in item 1. — ☐☐☐–☐☐–☐☐☐☐

12 Enter the name shown on the most recent Social Security card issued for the person listed in item 1. —
First	Middle Name	Last

13 Enter any different date of birth if used on an earlier application for a card. — _____ Month, Day, Year

14 TODAY'S DATE _____ Month, Day, Year

15 DAYTIME PHONE NUMBER (___) _____ Area Code   Number

DELIBERATELY FURNISHING (OR CAUSING TO BE FURNISHED) FALSE INFORMATION ON THIS APPLICATION IS A CRIME PUNISHABLE BY FINE OR IMPRISONMENT, OR BOTH.

16 YOUR SIGNATURE ▶

17 YOUR RELATIONSHIP TO THE PERSON IN ITEM 1 IS:

☐ Self ☐ Natural Or Adoptive Parent ☐ Legal Guardian ☐ Other (Specify)

DO NOT WRITE BELOW THIS LINE (FOR SSA USE ONLY)

EVIDENCE SUBMITTED	SIGNATURE AND TITLE OF EMPLOYEE(S) REVIEWING EVIDENCE AND/OR CONDUCTING INTERVIEW
	DCL DATE

Reading a Public Notice

Public notices can tell you about events in your community and give you valuable information about safety. When you read a public notice, follow these tips. Each tip relates to a specific part of the notice on the opposite page.

Strategies for Reading

A Read the notice's **title**, if it has one. The title often gives the main idea or purpose of the notice.

B See if there is a logo, credit, or other way of telling **who created the notice**.

C Ask yourself, **"Who should read this notice?"** If the information in it might be important to you or someone you know, then you should pay attention to it.

D Look for **instructions**—things the notice is asking or telling you to do.

E See if there are details that tell you how you can **find out more** about the topic.

PRACTICE AND APPLY

The notice on the opposite page is from a state government agency. Read it carefully and answer the questions below.

1. Who is the notice from?
2. Who is the notice for?
3. What does the notice ask readers to do?
4. Where should proposals be sent?
5. What two things will be done with the proposals?
6. According to the notice, what kind of projects is the state looking to enact?

ⓑSTATE WATER CONTROL BOARD

The energy challenge facing our state is real. Every citizen needs to take immediate action to reduce energy consumption. For a list of simple ways you can reduce demand and cut your energy costs, see our website at www.stategovxyz.gov.

ⓐ PUBLIC NOTICE REQUESTING PROJECT PROPOSALS
FOR THE BEACH CLEANUP ACT (BCA)

ⓒ **ATTENTION:** COASTAL BIOLOGISTS, VOLUNTEER BEACH MONITORS, AND CONCERNED CITIZENS

The State's coastal beach monitoring programs indicate that beach pollution is widespread and too often exceeds acceptable levels, resulting in beach postings and closures. The major goal of the BCA is to reduce health risks and increase the public's access to clean beaches.

The State wants your proposals. The State Water Control Board (SWCB) is in the process of identifying traditional and innovative projects that will result in a reduction of coastal beach ⓓ contamination. These projects will be located in the areas of the state where beach postings and closures have been most prevalent. Project proposals that are submitted to the SWCB will be placed on a list and will be eligible for loans and grants, as they become available. During the fiscal year 2001–2002, loan moneys will be available through the State Fund for:

- development and implementation of programs to control pollution from nonpoint sources and stormwater drainage;
- publicly-owned capital improvement projects that benefit water quality;
- implementation of estuary enhancement programs.

Additionally, it is possible that a grant program may become available for local diversions, catch basins, filtration systems, and other projects that will reduce untreated runoff from reaching coastal waters. However, the SWCB will continue to seek funding for projects that will result in significant and steady decreases in beach postings and closures.

In preparing this list, we are seeking information on viable projects that will help us attain our goal of providing clean and healthy coastal beaches for all that reside in and visit our state. ⓓ Enclosed is a list of items and considerations that will be necessary for a timely review of all projects submitted. Priority will be given to projects that can be in place and in operation by July 2004. With your assistance, we plan to have an initial list of projects compiled by mid-April, 2003. Projects will be reviewed as they are received by staff for concurrence with the BCA's intent and completeness of information. We will post more information on our website at www.swcb.xyz.gov as it becomes available.

Project Proposals should be sent to:

> State Water Control Board
> Loans & Grants Branch
> P.O. Box 1234
> San Pedro, CA 90202

ⓔ If you have any questions, please contact Dr. John Smith, Clean Beaches Coordinator for the SWCB at (555) 555-1111 or jsmith@exec.swcb.xyz.gov.

Reading a Web Page

If you need information for a report, project, or hobby, the World Wide Web can probably help you. The tips below will help you understand the **Web pages** you read. As you look at the tips, notice where they match up to the sample Web page on the right.

Strategies for Reading

A Notice the page's **Web address**, or URL. You may want to write it down in case you need to access the same page at another time.

B Look for **menu bars** along the top, bottom, or side of the page. These guide you to other parts of the site that may be useful.

C Look for **links** to other parts of the site or to related pages. Links are often shown as underlined words.

D Use a **search** feature to quickly find out whether a certain kind of information is contained anywhere on the site.

E Many sites have a link that allows you to **contact** the creators with questions or feedback.

PRACTICE AND APPLY

Read the Web page on the next page. Then use the information from the page and the tips above to answer the questions.

1. What is the Web address?
2. If you wanted to know whether the ClassZone site contained any information about adjective clauses, how would you go about finding out?
3. Read the paragraph under "Topic." Then look at the thought bubbles below it. What would you expect to find if you clicked on "Write About It"?
4. What people, besides students, might find this site helpful?
5. In your own words, summarize the content under "Topic".

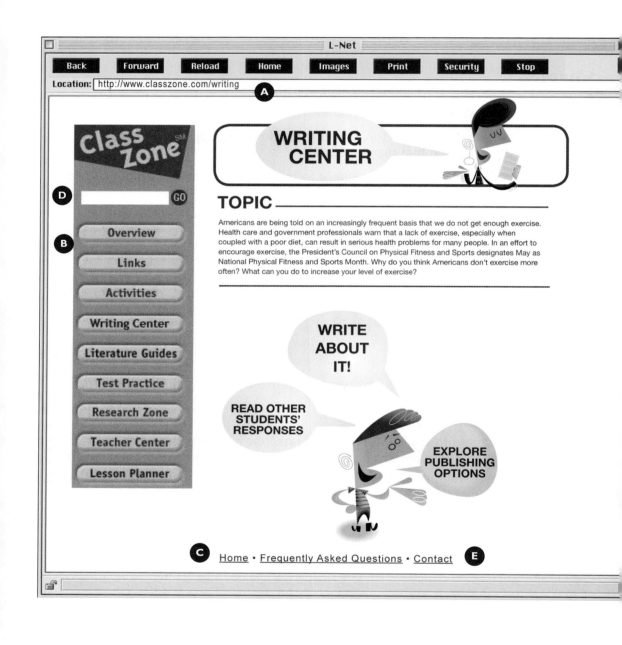

L-Net

Back　Forward　Reload　Home　Images　Print　Security　Stop

Location: http://www.classzone.com/writing

Class Zone℠

GO

- Overview
- Links
- Activities
- Writing Center
- Literature Guides
- Test Practice
- Research Zone
- Teacher Center
- Lesson Planner

WRITING CENTER

TOPIC

Americans are being told on an increasingly frequent basis that we do not get enough exercise. Health care and government professionals warn that a lack of exercise, especially when coupled with a poor diet, can result in serious health problems for many people. In an effort to encourage exercise, the President's Council on Physical Fitness and Sports designates May as National Physical Fitness and Sports Month. Why do you think Americans don't exercise more often? What can you do to increase your level of exercise?

WRITE ABOUT IT!

READ OTHER STUDENTS' RESPONSES

EXPLORE PUBLISHING OPTIONS

Home • Frequently Asked Questions • Contact

Reading Technical Directions

Reading **technical directions** will help you understand how to use the products you buy. Use the following tips to help you read a variety of technical directions.

Strategies for Reading

A Look carefully at any **diagrams** or **other images** of the product.

B **Read all the directions** carefully at least once before using the product.

C Notice **headings** or **rules** that separate one section from another.

D Look for **numbers** or **letters** that give the steps in sequence.

E Watch for **warnings** or **notes** with more information.

PRACTICE AND APPLY

Use the above tips and the technical directions on the next page to help you answer the following questions.

1. How will you know that the digital camera has taken a picture?
2. Into what part of the digital camera do you insert the plug labeled CAM?
3. What is the first thing you must do to download a picture?
4. What is the name of the software application that allows you to "view" and "get" images on your computer?
5. For what do you need the CD-ROM?

Digital Camera Instructions

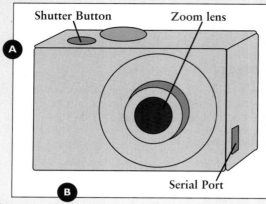 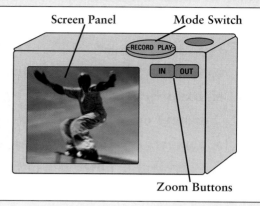

A. Taking Pictures
1. Turn the Mode Switch to RECORD.
2. Compose the image on the Screen Panel using the Zoom Buttons.
3. Press the Shutter Button halfway. This will freeze the image on the Screen Panel.
   NOTE: You will feel the button settle into a notch when it is halfway depressed.
4. If satisfied with the frozen image, press the Shutter Button fully to take the picture.
   NOTE: The camera will emit a beep to show that the picture has been taken.

B. Connecting to Your Computer
1. Locate the provided connecting cable.
2. Insert the plug labeled CAM into the camera's Serial Port.
3. Insert the plug labeled CPU into the serial port labeled CAM1 at the rear of your computer.

C. Installing Software
1. Locate the provided CD-ROM.
2. Insert the CD-ROM into your computer's CD-ROM drive and double-click on the INSTALL icon when it appears on your desktop.
3. The CD-ROM will install the necessary digital camera software over a period of up to five minutes.

D. Downloading Pictures
1. Turn the Mode Switch to PLAY.
2. Start the CamPics software by double-clicking the CamPics application icon.
3. Once the CamPics application has launched, select View Image from the Camera menu.
4. Select an image by either double-clicking on the individual image or clicking on the Get Images icon.
5. When an image has finished downloading, you may print, edit, organize, or transfer it to another host. The images are in JPEG format making them accessible to many applications.

Product Information: Safety Guidelines

Safety guidelines are facts and recommendations provided by government agencies or product manufacturers offering instructions and warnings about safe use of these products. Learning to read and follow such guidelines is important for your own safety. Look at the sample guidelines as you read each strategy below.

Strategies for Reading

A The **title** identifies what product the safety guidelines focus on.

B This section lists **recommendations** that product owners and users should follow in order to ensure safe usage of the product.

C This section lists the **hazards** associated with the product.

D This section includes the phone number and e-mail address where dangerous products or product-related injuries can be reported.

Ⓐ Spa Safety Information

The U.S. Consumer Product Safety Commission (CPSC) recommends these safety precautions for spa owners and users.

Ⓑ
1. Always use a locked safety cover when the spa is not in use and keep young children away from spas unless there is constant adult supervision.
2. Maintain the dual drains and covers required by current safety standards.
3. Regularly have a professional check your spa and make sure it is in safe working condition.
4. Locate the cut-off switch for your pump so you can turn it off in an emergency.
5. Be aware that consuming alcohol while using a spa could lead to drowning.
6. Keep the temperature of the water in the spa at 104° Fahrenheit or below.

Ⓒ CPSC warns about these **hazards** related to spas, hot tubs, and whirlpools:
Drownings—Since 1980, the CPSC has reports of 700 deaths in spas and hot tubs. About one-third of those were drownings by children under age five.
Hair Entanglement—Since 1978, CPSC has reports of 49 incidents (including 13 deaths) in which people's hair was sucked into the suction fitting (drain) of a spa, hot tub, or whirlpool, causing the victim's head to be held under water.
Hot Tub Temperatures—CPSC knows of several deaths from extremely hot water (approximately 110 degrees Fahrenheit) in a spa. High temperatures can lead to unconsciousness.

Ⓓ To report a dangerous product or a product-related injury, please contact info@cpsc.gov, or call the CPSC's hotline at (800) 638-2772.

PRACTICE AND APPLY

Read the safety guidelines to help you answer these questions.

1. What is the major cause of spa deaths?
2. What should you always do when a spa is not in use?
3. Why does the CPSC recommend that water temperature in a spa should be kept at 104 degrees Fahrenheit or below?
4. What e-mail address should you write to about a dangerous spa or a spa-related injury?
5. What temperature should the water in a spa be kept at?

Reading a Television Schedule

Knowing how to read a **television schedule** accurately will help you figure out the times of your favorite programs. Look at the example as you read each strategy on this list.

Strategies for Reading

A Scan the **title** to know what the schedule covers.

B Look for **labels** that show **dates** or **days of the week** to help you understand how the weekly or daily schedule works.

C Look for **expressions of time** to know what hours or minutes are listed on the schedule.

D Study the **labels** identifying the different channels listed on the schedule.

E Look at **program titles** to see what shows are playing at a given time on a given channel.

A Afternoon Programming Schedule   **B** July 19, 2002

	1:00 P.M.	1:30 P.M.	2:00 P.M.	2:30 P.M.	3:00 P.M.	3:30 P.M.	4:00 P.M.
2 NMXX	Antique Timezone **E**		Trixie Bear	Ken Marx	Who's That Head?		News
6 NPRR	Judge Gus	Judge Edna	The Stanleys		Town Noise		News
7 NABQ	Women's Soccer (cont.)		U.S. Shot Put Finals		Infomercial	Space Time	Starmix
8 NHH	Movie: Condor's Revenge				Movie: The Road to Ruin		
11 EPS	Too Many Tomatoes		Cook Karl	Fast Times	Travel Log	Travel Log	Mexican Cuisine
13 MP&Z	My Dad	Jessica's World	Tears	Infomercial	News	News	Carrie C
18 WOW	Kids Kraft		Movie: KeeKee and Sammy				Kids News
19 PBJ	Jam City	Keevo	Behind the...	Behind the...	Storyback	Storyback	Dance Party

Pay Channels listed in **BOLD**

PRACTICE AND APPLY

Answer the following questions using the television schedule and the strategies on this page.

1. What time span is covered by this schedule?

2. List the pay channels.

3. How many movies are listed on this schedule?

4. If you watched channel 6 from 1:30 to 2:00 and then watched channel 11 from 2:00 to 2:30, what two programs did you view?

Glossary of Literary Terms

Act An act is a major unit of action in a play. Acts are sometimes divided into scenes; each scene is limited to a single time and place.

Examples: Shakespeare's plays all have five acts. Many plays from the 19th century, such as Henrik Ibsen's *A Doll's House,* have three acts. Contemporary plays usually have two or three acts, although some have only one.

Allegory An allegory is a work with two levels of meaning—a literal one and a symbolic one. In an allegory, most of the characters, objects, and events stand for abstract qualities. Like a fable or parable, an allegory is often used to express generalizations about human existence and teach religious or moral lessons.

Example: Dante's *Inferno* has many allegorical elements. At the beginning of Canto I, Dante is struggling to emerge from a dark wood and reach a sun-drenched mountain. The wood represents Dante's spiritual confusion; the mountain symbolizes heaven, or paradise.

See page 759.

Alliteration Alliteration is the repetition of consonant sounds at the beginning of words. Alliteration occurs in everyday speech and in all forms of literature. Poets, in particular, use alliteration to emphasize certain words, to heighten mood, to underscore meaning, and to enhance rhythm. Notice the repeated *s* and *f* sounds in the following lines:

> How craven <u>s</u>o to <u>s</u>trike me <u>s</u>tricken <u>s</u>o
> Yet <u>f</u>rom you <u>f</u>ully armed conceal his bow!
> —Francesco Petrarch, "Sonnet 3"

See pages 927, 1154.
See also **Assonance; Consonance.**

Anecdote An anecdote is a brief story that focuses on a single revealing event, sometimes taken from the life of a real person. The event is meant to illustrate a particular truth or teaching.

Example: In tale 30 of Sadi's *Gulistan,* an innocent man appeals to the angry king who has condemned him to death. The man points out that if he is executed, the king will suffer from guilt forever. The anecdote teaches that people may come to regret acts committed in anger.

See page 433.

Antagonist The antagonist in a work of literature is the character or force against which the main character, or **protagonist,** is pitted. The antagonist may be another character, something in society or nature, or even an internal force within the protagonist.

Examples: In the Indian epic *Ramayana,* the antagonist is Ravana, the demon ruler of Lanka, who battles against Rama. In James Joyce's "Eveline," the main character struggles within herself to make an important decision about her future.

See also **Conflict; Protagonist.**

Aphorism *See* **Maxim.**

Assonance Assonance is the repetition of a vowel sound within nonrhyming words. *Sweet dreams* and *high and mighty* are examples of assonance. Writers of both poetry and prose use assonance to give their work a musical quality and unify stanzas and passages. Notice the examples of assonance in the following lines:

> The sinking m<u>oo</u>n floods the rafters of my
>   r<u>oo</u>m
> and still I s<u>ee</u>m to s<u>ee</u> it lighting your face.
>   —Tu Fu, "Dreaming of Li Po"

See page 1154.
See also **Alliteration; Consonance.**

Audience The audience of a piece of writing is the person or persons intended to read or listen to it. Every writer has an audience in mind when he or she is writing. The intended audience of a work influences a writer's choice of form, style, and tone and the details included.

Example: Virginia Woolf originally wrote

"Professions for Women" as a speech to be delivered to an organization of professional women. Woolf chose words that were suited to her audience.

See page 1164.

Author's Purpose Authors write for one or more of the following purposes: to inform, to express an opinion, to entertain, or to persuade. For instance, the purpose of a newspaper article is to inform; the purpose of a comic strip is to entertain.

Example: Elie Wiesel wrote *The World Was Silent* to inform readers about the horrors of the Holocaust and to persuade them to resist evil that made these horrors possible.

See pages 243, 802, 1242.

Autobiography An autobiography is a writer's account of his or her own life and is, in almost every case, told from the first-person point of view. Generally, an autobiography focuses on the most significant events and people in the writer's life over a period of time and on the ways in which those events and people affected the writer. Isabel Allende's *Paula* is an autobiography. Shorter autobiographical narratives include such private writings as **journals, diaries, memoirs,** and **letters.** Sei Shōnagon's *The Pillow Book* is a diary that provides important information about Japan during the Heian period. Elie Wiesel's *The World Was Silent* is a memoir about his experiences of the Holocaust.

See page 1302.
See also **Diary.**

Ballad A ballad is a narrative poem that was originally meant to be sung. Traditional folk ballads were composed by unknown authors and passed down orally. The ballads usually begin abruptly, focus on single tragic incidents, contain dialogue and repetition, and imply more than they actually tell. Typically, a ballad consists of four-line stanzas, with regular rhythm and rhyme. The rhythm often alternates between four-stress and three-stress lines, and the rhyme scheme usually is *abcb* or *aabb.*

A **literary ballad** is written by a single author

in conscious imitation of the folk-ballad style. Heinrich Heine's "The Lorelei" is a literary ballad from the Romantic period.

See page 913.
See also **Narrative Poem; Rhyme; Rhythm.**

Biography A biography is an account of a person's life written by another person. The writer of the biography, or biographer, often researches his or her subject in order to present accurate information. A biographer may also draw upon personal knowledge of his or her subject. Although a biographer—by necessity and by inclination—presents a subject from a certain point of view, a skilled biographer strives for a balanced treatment, highlighting weaknesses as well as strengths, failures as well as achievements.

Blank Verse Blank verse is unrhymed poetry written in iambic pentameter. Each line has five metrical feet, and each foot has an unstressed syllable followed by a stressed syllable. Because iambic pentameter resembles the natural rhythm of spoken English, it has been considered the most suitable meter for dramatic verse in English. Shakespeare's plays are written largely in blank verse. The following line is an example of blank verse:

> The world is too much with us; late and soon
> —William Wordsworth,
> "The World Is Too Much with Us"

See also **Meter; Sonnet.**

Character Characters are the people who participate in the action of a work. The most important characters are the **main characters.** Less prominent characters are known as **minor characters.** In Sophocles' *Oedipus the King,* Oedipus and Jocasta are main characters; Antigone and Ismene are minor characters.

Whereas some characters are two-dimensional, with only one or two dominant traits, a fully developed character possesses many traits, mirroring the psychological complexity of a real person. In longer works of fiction, main characters often undergo change as the plot unfolds. Such characters are called **dynamic characters,** as opposed to **static**

characters, who remain the same. In Henrik Ibsen's *A Doll's House,* Nora is a dynamic character because she transforms from a clinging wife to an independent woman. Torvald is a static character who primarily responds to Nora's words and actions.

See pages 532, 1043.
See also **Characterization.**

Characterization *Characterization* refers to the techniques that writers use to develop characters. There are four basic methods of characterization:

1. A writer may describe the physical appearance of a character. In "The Jay," Yasunari Kawabata describes Yoshiko: "The job of putting on her makeup went fairly pleasantly. Her eyebrows and lips all became unbearably winsome. Her kimono, too, went on easily."

2. A character's nature may be revealed through his or her own speech, thoughts, feelings, or actions. In Kawabata's story, the narrator reveals Yoshiko's distress over her brother's change of attitude toward their stepmother: "Hearing this suddenly, Yoshiko could not say a word. Her face paled, and she began to tremble."

3. The speech, thoughts, feelings, and actions of other characters can be used to develop a character. The father's comments help readers understand Yoshiko better: "I've caused you a great deal of trouble. I told the young man's mother that you're a girl with these circumstances and that, rather than treating you like a bride, she should try to bring back the happy days of your childhood."

4. The narrator can make direct comments about the character's nature. The narrator of Kawabata's story comments, "She had dreaded marriage on her father's account, but, when it came down to the actual talks, it was not that dreadful after all."

See pages 126, 648, 844, 952.
See also **Character.**

Climax *See* **Plot.**

Comedy A comedy is a dramatic work that is light and often humorous in tone, usually ending happily with a peaceful resolution of the main conflict. Shakespeare's *A Midsummer Night's Dream* is a comedy.

See also **Drama.**

Conflict Conflict is a struggle between opposing forces and is the basis of plot in dramatic and narrative literature. The conflict provides the interest or suspense in a short story, drama, novel, narrative poem, or nonfiction narrative. **External conflict** occurs when a character is pitted against an outside force, such as another character, a physical obstacle, or an aspect of nature or society. **Internal conflict** occurs when the struggle takes place within a character.

Examples: In Nadine Gordimer's "Amnesty," the narrator's fiancé is in conflict with the repressive white society of South Africa. In Johann Wolfgang von Goethe's *Faust,* the main character wages an external conflict with the devil and an internal conflict with his own confused desires.

See pages 143, 640, 1172, 1278.
See also **Antagonist; Plot.**

Connotation *Connotation* refers to the particular associations, images, or feelings evoked by a word, in contrast to **denotation,** which is the literal or dictionary meaning of the word. *Kitten,* for example, is defined as "a young cat." However, the word also suggests, or connotes, images of softness, warmth, and playfulness.

Example: In Léopold Sédar Senghor's "And We Shall Be Steeped," the speaker describes some African art as "pure primordial masks distant and yet present." The word *primordial* connotes the vast culture and history of Africa.

See page 1186.

Consonance Consonance is the repetition of consonant sounds within and at the ends of words, as in "last but not least" and "a stroke of luck." Consonance is often used together with assonance, alliteration, and rhyme to create a musical quality, to emphasize certain words, or to unify a poem. The repetition of the *t* sound in the following lines helps create a slower, more thoughtful pace:

> When to the sessions of sweet silent thought
> I summon up remembrance of things past,
> I sigh the lack of many a thing I sought,
> —William Shakespeare, "Sonnet 30"

See page 1154.
See also **Alliteration; Assonance.**

Contrast Contrast is a stylistic device in which one element is put into opposition with another. The opposing elements might be contrasting structures, such as sentences of varying lengths or stanzas of different configurations. They could also be contrasting ideas or images juxtaposed within phrases, sentences, paragraphs, stanzas, or sections of a longer work of literature. Writers use contrast to clarify or emphasize ideas and to elicit emotional responses from the reader.

Example: Much of the power of Tu Fu's poem "Jade Flower Palace" lies in the contrast between images of a flourishing palace, with its "dancing girls" and "gold chariots," and images of a ruined palace, with its "broken tiles" and "shattered pavements."

See pages 123, 393.

Creation Story *See* **Myth.**

Cultural Hero *See* **Hero.**

Denotation *See* **Connotation.**

Denouement *See* **Plot.**

Description Description is writing that helps the reader picture scenes, events, and characters. It helps the reader understand exactly what someone or something is like. To create description, writers often use sensory images—words and phrases that enable the reader to see, hear, smell, taste, or feel the subject described—and figurative language. Effective description also relies on precise nouns, verbs, adjectives, and adverbs, as well as carefully selected details. The following passage contains clear details and images:

> The snow! The hurt men struggled from the ranks,
> hid in the bellies of dead horse, in stacks
> of shattered caissons. By the bivouacs,
> one saw the picket dying at his post,
> still standing in his saddle, white with frost,
> the stone lips frozen to the bugle's mouth!
> —Victor Hugo, "Russia 1812"

See pages 97, 1263.
See also **Figurative Language; Imagery.**

Dialect A dialect is the form of a language spoken in a particular place by a distinct group of people. Dialects vary in pronunciation, vocabulary, colloquial expressions, and grammatical constructions. Writers use dialect to establish setting, to provide local color, and to develop characters.

Example: The thieves in Chinua Achebe's story "Civil Peace" speak in a Nigerian dialect of English, which highlights the contrast between the thieves and Jonathan Iwegbu.

See page 1291.

Dialogue Written conversation between two or more people, in either fiction or nonfiction, is called dialogue. Writers use dialogue to bring characters to life and to give readers insights into the characters' qualities, personality traits, and reactions to other people. Realistic, well-paced dialogue also advances the plot of a narrative.

Dialogue in **drama** is critical to an understanding of the playwright's story or message. How the dialogue is read or performed will determine to a great extent the reactions of the reader or audience to the play. Dramatists use **stage directions** to indicate how they intend the dialogue to be interpreted by the actors. In Henrik Ibsen's *A Doll's House,* the words *clapping her hands* and *unperturbed* are stage directions used to indicate how Nora is supposed to react to her husband at the beginning and at the end of the play.

See pages 896, 1230.
See also **Characterization; Drama.**

Diary A diary is a writer's personal day-to-day account of his or her experiences and impressions. Most diaries are private and not intended to be shared. Some, however, have been published because they are well written and provide useful perspectives on historical events or on the everyday life of particular eras. Sei Shōnagon's *Pillow Book,* a sort of diary she kept while serving as lady in waiting to Empress Sadako, is a collection of character sketches, lists, anecdotes, and poems. It provides a vivid glimpse into the lives of the Japanese nobility during the Heian period.

See page 506.
See also **Autobiography.**

Diction Diction is a writer's choice of words, a significant component of style. Diction encompasses both the words used and the way the writer arranges them. Diction can be described in terms such as *formal* or i*nformal, technical* or *common, abstract* or *concrete, literal* or *figurative.*

Examples: The diction in Plato's *Apology* is formal, which is appropriate for a serious speech. The lofty, elevated diction in Goethe's *Faust* suits the drama's subject and themes. By contrast, the simple and concrete diction in Voltaire's *Candide* helps establish the humorous tone of the narrative.

See pages 539, 1164.
See also **Connotation; Style.**

Didactic Literature Didactic literature is literature that instructs its readers. Writers use didactic literature to teach lessons about how to live a moral life. Writers communicate their views about what is right and wrong by focusing on qualities such as honesty, courage, wisdom, and kindness. Sometimes they state their ideas directly; at other times, they present their teachings by means of examples. These teachings are expressed in various forms, including maxims, anecdotes, and parables.

See page 432.
See also **Anecdote; Maxim; Parable.**

Drama Drama is literature that develops plot and character through dialogue and action; in other words, drama is literature in play form. Dramas are meant to be performed by actors who appear on a stage, before radio microphones, or in front of television or movie cameras.

Unlike other forms of literature, such as fiction and poetry, a drama requires the collaboration of many people in order to come to life. In an important sense, a drama in printed form is an incomplete work of art. It is a skeleton that must be fleshed out by a director, actors, set designers, and others who interpret the work and stage a performance. When the members of an audience become caught up in a drama and forget to a degree the artificiality of the play, the process is called "suspension of disbelief."

Most plays are divided into acts, with each act having an emotional peak, or climax, of its own. The acts sometimes are divided into scenes; each scene is limited to a single time and place. Shakespeare's plays have five acts. Contemporary plays usually have two or three acts, although some have only one act.

Realistic drama of the 19th century is drama in which life is presented objectively and honestly. The characters usually belong to the middle or lower class, and they tend to be ordinary people dealing with everyday problems. *A Doll's House* is one of the first examples of realistic drama.

See pages 260, 1019.
See also **Act; Dialogue; Stage Directions.**

Dramatic Irony See **Irony.**

Epic An epic is a long narrative poem on a serious subject, presented in an elevated or formal style. It traces the adventures of a great hero. Most epics share some or all of the following characteristics:

1. The **epic hero** is a figure of high social status and often of great historical or legendary importance.
2. The actions of the hero often determine the fate of a nation or group of people.
3. The hero performs exceedingly courageous, sometimes even superhuman, deeds that reflect the ideas and values of the era.
4. Supernatural beings and events complicate the plot.
5. The setting is large in scale, involving more

than one nation and often a long and dangerous journey through foreign lands.

6. The main character often gives long, formal speeches.

7. The poem treats universal ideas, such as good and evil, life and death.

The Epic of Gilgamesh, the *Mahabharata,* the *Ramayana,* the *Iliad,* the *Aeneid, Sundiata,* and *The Song of Roland* are all epics.

See pages 120, 176, 181.

Epic Hero *See* **Epic.**

Epic Simile *See* **Simile.**

Epithet An epithet is a brief phrase that points out traits associated with a particular person or thing. Homer's *Iliad* contains many examples of epithets, such as the references to Achilles as "the swift runner" and to Hector as "the gallant captain."

See pages 126, 223.

Essay An essay is a brief work of nonfiction that offers an opinion on a subject. The purpose of an essay may be to express ideas and feelings, to analyze, to inform, to entertain, or to persuade.

Some essays are formal and impersonal, and the major argument is developed systematically. Other essays are informal, personal, and less rigidly organized. The informal essay often includes anecdotes and humor.

Exposition *See* **Plot.**

Extended Metaphor Like any metaphor, an extended metaphor is a comparison between two essentially unlike things that nevertheless have something in common. It does not contain the word *like* or *as.* In an extended metaphor, two things are compared at length and in various ways—perhaps through a stanza, a paragraph, or even an entire work. The likening of God to a shepherd in Psalm 23 is an example of an extended metaphor.

See page 810.
See also **Figurative Language; Metaphor; Simile.**

External Conflict *See* **Conflict.**

Fable A fable is a brief tale, in either prose or verse, told to illustrate a moral or teach a lesson. Often, the moral of a fable appears in a distinct and memorable statement near the tale's beginning or end.

Falling Action *See* **Plot.**

Fantasy *Fantasy* is a term applied to works of fiction that display a disregard for the restraints of reality. The aim of a fantasy may be purely to delight or may be to make a serious comment. Some fantasies include extreme or grotesque characters. Others portray realistic characters in a realistic world who only marginally overstep the bounds of reality.

Examples: In *The Thousand and One Nights,* Sindbad voyages to islands inhabited by fantastic creatures. Gabriel García Márquez uses elements of fantasy in "The Handsomest Drowned Man in the World" to present the story's theme of the importance of heroes and great dreams.

Fiction A work of fiction is a narrative that springs from the imagination of a writer, though it may be based on actual events and real people. The writer shapes his or her narrative to capture the reader's interest and to achieve desired effects. The two major types of fiction are novels and short stories. The basic elements of fiction are characters, setting, plot, and theme.

See also **Novel; Short Story.**

Figurative Language Figurative language is language that communicates ideas beyond the literal meanings of the words. A figurative expression is not literally true, but rather creates an impression in the mind of the reader. Writers use figurative language to create effects, to emphasize ideas, and to evoke emotions. Figurative language appears in poetry and prose as well as in spoken language. Special types of figurative language, called figures of speech, include simile, metaphor, personification, and hyperbole.

Example: In Rabindranath Tagore's story "The Artist," the narrator uses a simile and personification to describe a scene in a painting: "The waves of the river looked like a flock of hungry seals just on the point of swallowing the boat. The clouds seemed to cheer them on and float their shawls overhead. . . ."

See page 903.

See also **Hyperbole; Metaphor; Personification; Simile; Understatement.**

First-Person Point of View *See* **Point of View.**

Flashback A flashback is an account of a conversation, an episode, or an event that happened before the beginning of a story. By revealing significant thoughts, experiences, or events in a character's life, a flashback can help readers understand a character's present situation. Flashbacks may take the form of reminiscences, dream sequences, or descriptions by third-person narrators; they usually interrupt the chronological flow of a story. Flashbacks may contain foreshadowing or other clues to the outcome of a story.

Folk Ballad *See* **Ballad.**

Folk Tale A folk tale is a story that is handed down, usually by word of mouth, from generation to generation. Folk tales reflect the unique characteristics of the regions they come from, showing how the inhabitants live and what their values are. Many involve supernatural events, and most suggest morals. Often, things happen in threes in folk tales. Leo Tolstoy's "What Men Live By" is a version of a Russian folk tale.

Foreshadowing Foreshadowing is a writer's use of hints or clues to indicate events that will occur later in a narrative. This technique often creates suspense and prepares readers for what is to come.

Example: In *Sundiata,* the epic hero's inability to walk foreshadows his later transformation.

See page 995.

Form When applied to poetry, the term *form* refers to all the principles of arrangement in a poem—the ways in which the words and images are organized and patterned to produce a pleasing whole, including the length and placement of lines and the grouping of lines into stanzas. Elements of form—such as the sound devices of rhythm, rhyme, alliteration, consonance, and assonance—work together with elements such as figurative language and imagery to shape a poem, convey meaning, and create a total experience for the reader. The term *form* can also refer to a type of poetry, such as the sonnet or the haiku. William Wordsworth's "The World Is Too Much with Us" and "My Heart Leaps Up" provide good examples of the poet's artful use of form.

See also **Structure.**

Frame Story A frame story exists when a story is told within a narrative setting or frame—hence, creating a story within a story.

Examples: The collection of tales in *The Thousand and One Nights* are set within a frame story. "Federigo's Falcon" and the other tales in Boccaccio's *Decameron* are presented within a similar framework.

Free Verse Free verse is poetry that does not contain regular patterns of rhyme and meter. The lines in free verse often flow more naturally than do rhymed, metrical lines and thus achieve a rhythm more like everyday speech. Much of the poetry written in the 20th century is free verse. Notice the natural flow of these free-verse lines:

> On the sand
> a
> lizard
> with a sandy tail.
> —Pablo Neruda, "Ode to the Lizard"

Haiku Haiku is a form of Japanese poetry that embodies three qualities greatly valued in Japanese art: precision, economy, and delicacy. Nature is a particularly important source of inspiration for Japanese haiku poets, and details from nature are often the subject of their poems. The rules of haiku are strict—in only 17 syllables, arranged in three lines of 5, 7, and 5 syllables, the poet must create a clear picture that will evoke a strong emotional response in the reader. The poems of Matsuo Bashō, Yosa Buson, and

Kobayashi Issa are examples of haiku.

See page 540.
See also **Tanka.**

Hero A hero, or **protagonist,** is a central character in a work of fiction, drama, or epic poetry. A traditional hero possesses good qualities that enable him or her to triumph over an antagonist who is bad or evil in some way.

The term *tragic hero,* first used by the Greek philosopher Aristotle, refers to a central character in a drama who is dignified or noble. According to Aristotle, a tragic hero possesses a defect, or **tragic flaw,** that brings about or contributes to his or her downfall. This flaw may be poor judgment, pride, weakness, or an excess of an admirable quality. The tragic hero, Aristotle noted, recognizes his or her flaw and its consequences, but only after it is too late to change the course of events. Oedipus in Sophocles' *Oedipus the King* is a tragic hero.

In a quest story, a **quest hero** goes on a journey and tries to achieve a goal, such as bringing back a valuable object or acquiring knowledge. This type of hero usually has special powers or special friends that help (or hinder) him or her on the journey. Gilgamesh is a quest hero.

A **culture hero** is a larger-than-life figure who represents the values of his or her culture. Such a hero ranks somewhere between ordinary human beings and the gods. The role of a culture hero is to provide a noble image that will inspire and guide the actions of mortals. Aeneas in the *Aeneid* is a culture hero.

See pages 33, 330, 380.
See also **Epic; Protagonist; Tragedy.**

Humor In literature there are three basic types of humor, all of which may involve exaggeration or irony. **Humor of situation** is derived from the plot of a work. It usually involves exaggerated events or situational irony, which occurs when something happens that is different from what was expected. **Humor of character** is often based on exaggerated personalities or on characters who fail to recognize their own flaws, a form of dramatic irony. **Humor of language** may include sarcasm, exaggeration, puns, or verbal irony, which occurs when what is said is not what is meant. In *Candide,* Voltaire uses all three kinds of humor, including absurd situations, ridiculous characters, and ironic descriptions.

See page 856.

Hyperbole Hyperbole is a figure of speech in which the truth is exaggerated for emphasis or for humorous effect. The expression "I'm so hungry I could eat a horse" is an example of hyperbole. The following example of hyperbole has a humorous effect:

> In short, our gentleman became so immersed in his reading that he spent whole nights from sundown to sunup and his days from dawn to dusk in poring over his books, until, finally, from so little sleeping and so much reading, his brain dried up and he went completely out of his mind.
> —Miguel de Cervantes, *Don Quixote*

Iambic Pentameter *See* **Blank Verse; Meter; Sonnet.**

Imagery Imagery consists of words and phrases that re-create vivid sensory experiences for the reader. The majority of images are visual, but imagery may also appeal to the senses of smell, hearing, taste, and touch. Effective writers of both prose and poetry frequently use imagery that appeals to more than one sense simultaneously.

Examples: The expression "I hugged her to my chest, muffling her mouth" from Tu Fu's "Song of P'eng-ya" appeals to the senses of sight, touch, and sound. In Charles Baudelaire's "Invitation to the Voyage," the lines "Flowers of rarest bloom / Proffering their perfume" appeal to the senses of sight and smell.

See pages 380, 459, 470, 546, 605, 913.

Internal Conflict *See* **Conflict.**

Irony Irony is a contrast between what is expected and what actually exists or happens. This incongruity often has the effect of surprising the reader or viewer. There are three main types of irony.

Situational irony occurs when a character or the reader expects one thing to happen but something else actually happens. In Boccaccio's "Federigo's Falcon," Federigo's expectations and dreams are repeatedly overturned. In Leo Tolstoy's "How Much Land Does a Man Need?" it is ironic that Pakhom dies just as he is about to get his land.

Verbal irony occurs when a writer or character says one thing but means another. In Goethe's *Faust,* Mephisto speaks about man, claiming, "I have no wish to cause him further woe," while he intends to destroy Faust.

Dramatic irony involves a contrast between what a character knows and what the reader or audience knows. In Sophocles' *Oedipus the King,* Oedipus claims that he never saw King Laius, not realizing—as the reader does—that he is the king's son and that he killed Laius long ago.

See pages 330, 792, 1006.

Italian (Petrarchan) Sonnet *See* **Sonnet**.

Legend
A legend is a story handed down from the past, especially one that is popularly believed to be based on historical fact. "The First Bard Among the Soninke" is a legend that explains about Soninke society. Though legends often incorporate supernatural elements and magical deeds, they claim to be stories of real human beings and are often set in particular times and places. These characteristics separate legends from myths.

See page 631.
See also **Myth**.

Literary Ballad *See* **Ballad**.

Lyric Poem
In ancient Greece, a lyre was a musical instrument, and *lyric* became the name for a song accompanied by music. In ordinary speech, the words of a song are still called lyrics. In literature, a lyric poem is any short poem in which a single speaker expresses his or her personal thoughts and feelings. In a love lyric, such as Sappho's "He Is More Than a Hero," the speaker expresses romantic love. In other lyrics, a speaker may meditate on nature or explore personal issues, such as those addressed by Li Ch'ing-chao's "Two Springs" and "On Plum Blossoms."

See page 231.

Magical Realism
Magical realism refers to a style of writing that often includes exaggeration, unusual humor, magical and bizarre events, dreams that come true, and superstitions that prove warranted. Magical realism differs from pure fantasy in combining fantastic elements with realistic elements, such as recognizable characters, believable dialogue, a true-to-life setting, a matter-of-fact tone, and a plot that sometimes contains historic events. Magical realism is usually associated with Latin American fiction, but the term has also been applied to writing from other parts of the world. The best-known example of magical realism is the 1967 novel *One Hundred Years of Solitude* by Gabriel García Márquez.

See page 1344.

Maxim
A maxim is a short, concise statement that expresses a general truth or rule of conduct. Maxims condense important ideas into memorable language that gets the reader's attention. Some maxims are phrased in a particularly pointed and witty way. Because of their clever yet simple structure, such maxims—sometimes called **aphorisms**—are easy to recall and memorize. An example is Confucius' statement "To study without thinking is futile. To think without studying is dangerous."

See pages 432, 439.

Memoir *See* **Autobiography**.

Metaphor
A metaphor is a figure of speech that makes a comparison between two things that are basically unlike but have something in common. Unlike a simile, a metaphor does not contain the word *like* or *as.* In the following lines, the phrase "preying bird of passage" is a metaphor for the poem's subject, a former leader:

> Hubs of commerce smoothly turn without
> His bidding, and cities where he lately roosted
> Have forgotten him, the preying bird
> Of passage.
> —Wole Soyinka, "After the Deluge"

See page 598.
See also **Extended Metaphor; Figurative Language; Simile**.

Meter Meter is the repetition of a regular rhythmic unit in poetry. The meter of a poem emphasizes the musical quality of the language. Each unit of meter is known as a foot, consisting of one stressed syllable and one or two unstressed syllables. In representations of meter, a stressed syllable is often indicated by the symbol ´, an unstressed syllable by the symbol ˘. Four basic types of metrical feet are the **iamb,** an unstressed syllable followed by a stressed syllable (˘ ´); the **trochee,** a stressed syllable followed by an unstressed syllable (´ ˘); the **anapest,** two unstressed syllables followed by a stressed syllable (˘ ˘ ´); and the **dactyl,** a stressed syllable followed by two unstressed syllables (´ ˘ ˘).

Two words are used to identify the meter of a line of poetry. The first word describes the predominant type of metrical foot in the line. The second word describes the number of feet in the line: dimeter (two feet), trimeter (three feet), tetrameter (four feet), pentameter (five feet), hexameter (six feet), and so forth. These lines illustrate iambic pentameter, perhaps the most common meter in English poetry:

> Whĕn ín dĭsgráce wĭth Fórtŭne ańd mĕn's eýes
>
> Ĭ áll ălóne bĕweép my oútcăst státe
>
> —William Shakespeare, "Sonnet 29"

See page 817.
See also **Free Verse; Rhythm.**

Modernism Modernism is a literary and artistic movement that developed in the early decades of the 20th century. The modernists felt disconnected from the social, religious, and artistic traditions of the past because the modern world, with its violence, skepticism, and loss of ideals, seemed different from that of previous generations. To reflect this unsettling new world, modernist writers experimented with original literary styles and forms.

See page 1106.

Mood Mood is the feeling, or atmosphere, that a writer creates for the reader. The writer's use of connotation, imagery, and figurative language, as well as sound and rhythm, help to develop mood. Notice how the author makes use of all these techniques to create a bleak and lonely mood in the following lines:

> Thin mists drift over One-Fold Mountain—
> Folds of faintly dyed cloth;
> In a cloudless sky a doleful wind.
> Lonely mountain vista,
> Remote and friendless landscape.
> —Zeami Motokiyo, *The Deserted Crone*

See pages 470, 1180, 1230.
See also **Tone.**

Myth A myth is a traditional story, usually concerning some superhuman being or unlikely event, that was once widely believed to be true. Myths were passed down from one generation to the next; the original authors are unknown. Frequently, myths attempt to explain features of the natural world, to support social customs, or to guide people through life. For some peoples, myths were both a kind of science and a religion. In addition, myths served as literature and entertainment, just as they do to modern audiences.

Some of the most famous myths in the Western tradition originated among the ancient Greeks and Romans. Norse mythology, consisting of myths from Scandinavia, is also important in literature. Native Americans have produced fascinating myths of various kinds, as have the peoples of Africa and Asia.

Many Greek stories were based on myths that would have been familiar to the audience. In Ovid's *Metamorphoses,* the poet retells many of the important Greek and Roman legends and myths.

A **creation story** is a particular kind of myth that tells how the earth and human beings were created. The Fulani tale "How the World Was Created from a Drop of Milk" is an example of a creation story, as are the important Mayan work *Popol Vuh* and the opening chapters of Genesis in the Hebrew Bible.

See pages 404, 627.
See also **Legend.**

Narration See **Narrative; Narrator; Point of View.**

Narrative A narrative is any type of writing that is primarily concerned with relating an event or a series of events. A narrative can be imaginary, like a short story or a novel, or it can be factual, like a newspaper account or a work of history. Isabel Allende's autobiography *Paula* is an example of narrative nonfiction.

Narrative Poem A narrative poem tells a story. Like a short story or a novel, a narrative poem has the elements of characters, setting, plot, and point of view, all of which combine to develop a theme.

Examples: Epics, such as Homer's *Iliad* and Virgil's *Aeneid,* are narrative poems, as are ballads. Victor Hugo's "Russia 1812" is an example of a 19th-century narrative poem.

See pages 399, 920.

Narrator The narrator of a literary work is the person or voice that tells the story. The narrator can be a character in the story or a voice outside the action.

Examples: In Naguib Mahfouz's "Half a Day," the narrator takes part in the incidents he recounts. The narrator of Franz Kafka's "The Metamorphosis" is, on the other hand, observant but detached.

See also **Point of View; Speaker.**

Naturalism An extreme form of realism, naturalism in fiction involves the depiction of life objectively and precisely, without idealizing. Naturalism originated in France in the late 1800s. Like the realist, the naturalist accurately portrayed the world. However, heavily influenced by new scientific theories, the naturalist created characters who were victims of environmental forces and internal drives beyond their control. Émile Zola was the foremost writer of the naturalistic movement.

See page 943.
See also **Realism.**

Neoclassicism Neoclassicism refers to a movement in Europe during the late 17th and 18th centuries, marked by a revival of classical tastes and forms. Neoclassicists respected order, reason, and rules and viewed humans as limited and imperfect. They valued the intellect over emotions and society over the individual. The neoclassicists wrote tightly controlled poetry in the classical mold and witty satiric essays.

See page 878.
See also **Romanticism.**

Noh Drama Noh drama began in 14th-century Japan as religious drama and was perfected in the late 14th and early 15th centuries by Kanami Kiyotsugu and his son Zeami Motokiyo. Influenced by the simplicity and discipline of Zen Buddhism, Noh actors wear masks and use formal language, mime, and stylized gestures to express meaning. *The Deserted Crone* is an example of a Noh drama.

See page 519.

Nonfiction Nonfiction is prose writing that is about real people, places, and events. Unlike fiction, nonfiction is largely concerned with factual information, although the writer shapes the information according to his or her purposes and viewpoint. Although the subject matter of nonfiction is not imaginative, the writer's style may be individualistic and innovative. Types of nonfiction include autobiographies, biographies, letters, essays, diaries, journals, memoirs, and speeches. Examples include Sei Shōnagon's diary *The Pillow Book* and Virginia Woolf's speech "Professions for Women."

See also **Autobiography; Biography; Diary; Essay.**

Novel A novel is an extended work of fiction. Like a short story, a novel is essentially the product of a writer's imagination. The most obvious difference between a novel and a short story is length. Because the novel is considerably longer, a novelist can develop a wider range of characters and a more complex plot.

Omniscient Point of View *See* **Point of View.**

Onomatopoeia The word *onomatopoeia* literally means "name making." It is the process of creating or using words that imitate sounds. *Buzz* (of a bee), *honk* (of a car horn), and *peep* (of a chick) are onomatopoetic, or echoic, words. Onomatopoeia as a literary technique goes beyond the use of simple echoic words. Writers, particularly poets, choose words whose sounds suggest their denotative and connotative meanings: for example, *whisper, kick, gargle, gnash,* and *clatter.*

Parable A parable is a brief story that is meant to teach a lesson or illustrate a moral truth. A parable is more than a simple story, however. Each detail of the parable corresponds to some aspect of the problem or moral dilemma it deals with. The story of the Prodigal Son in the New Testament is a classic parable.

See pages 433, 516.
See also **Wisdom Literature.**

Paradox A paradox is a statement that seems to contradict itself but, in fact, reveals some element of truth. Religious and spiritual writings often contain paradoxes. Such paradoxes shake readers out of their normal ways of thinking and point them toward a higher level of understanding.

Examples: The sentence "There was neither death nor immortality then" in the *Rig Veda* is a paradox. The *Tao Te Ching* contains many paradoxes, including "The Tao never does anything, yet through it all things are done."

See pages 119, 445.

Parallelism Parallelism is the use of similar grammatical constructions to express ideas that are related or equal in importance. The parallel elements may be words, phrases, sentences, or paragraphs. Parallelism occurs in the following lines:

> Did He not find you in error and guide you?
> Did He not find you poor and enrich you?
> —**Koran**

See page 581.
See also **Repetition.**

Parody A parody imitates or mocks another work or type of literature. Like caricature in art, parody in literature mimics a subject or a style. The purpose of a parody may be to ridicule through broad humor. On the other hand, a parody may broaden understanding of or add insight to the original work. Some parodies are even written in tribute to a work of literature.

Example: *Don Quixote* by Miguel de Cervantes parodies the romance genre. The novel mocks romances by having Don Quixote attempt to fulfill chivalric ideals in a realistic setting.

Personification Personification is a figure of speech in which human qualities are attributed to an object, animal, or idea. Writers use personification to make feelings and images concrete for the reader. In the following lines, the winds are personified:

> How could I leave the sound of singing winds,
> The strong clean scent that breathes from off
>   the sea,
> Or shut my eyes forever to the spring?
> —Sara Teasdale, "Helen of Troy"

See also **Figurative Language; Metaphor; Simile.**

Petrarchan (Italian) Sonnet *See* **Sonnet.**

Plot Plot is the sequence of actions and events in a narrative. Usually, the events of a plot progress because of a conflict, or struggle between opposing forces. Although there are many types of plots, most include the following stages:

1. The **exposition** lays the groundwork for the plot and provides the reader with essential background information. Characters are introduced, the setting is described, and the major conflict is identified. Although the exposition generally appears at the opening of a work, it may also occur later in the narrative.
2. In the **rising action,** complications usually arise, causing difficulties for the main characters and making the conflict more difficult to resolve. As the characters struggle to find solutions to the conflict, suspense builds.
3. The **climax** is the turning point of the action, the moment when interest and intensity reach their peak. The climax of a work usually involves an important event, decision, or discovery that affects the final outcome.
4. The **falling action** consists of the events that

occur after the climax. Often, the conflict is resolved, and the intensity of the action subsides. Sometimes this phase of the plot is called the **resolution** or the **denouement** (dā′nōō-män′). *Denouement* is from a French word that means "untying"—in this stage the tangles of the plot are untied and mysteries are solved.

See page 589.
See also **Conflict**.

Poetry Poetry is language arranged in lines. Like other forms of literature, poetry attempts to re-create emotions and experiences. Poetry, however, is usually more compressed and suggestive than prose. Because poetry frequently does not include the kinds of explanation found in prose, it tends to leave more to the reader's imagination. Poetry also may require more work on the reader's part to unlock meaning.

Many poems are divided into stanzas, or groups of lines. The stanzas usually contain the same number of lines. Some poems have definite patterns of meter and rhyme. Others rely more on the sounds of words and less on fixed rhythms and rhyme schemes. The use of imagery and figurative language is also common in poetry.

See also **Figurative Language; Form; Free Verse; Imagery; Meter; Repetition; Rhyme; Rhythm; Stanza**.

Point of View *Point of view* refers to the narrative method used in a short story, novel, or work of nonfiction. The three most common points of view are first person, third person omniscient, and third person limited.

In **first-person point of view,** the narrator is a character in the work, narrating the action as he or she perceives and understands it. A first-person narrator tends to involve the reader in the story and to communicate a sense of immediacy and personal concern. Two short stories using first-person narration are "Amnesty" by Nadine Gordimer and "Half a Day" by Naguib Mahfouz.

In **third-person point of view,** events and characters are described by a narrator outside the action. In **third-person omniscient point of view,** the narrator is omniscient, or all-knowing, and can see into the mind of more than one character. The use of a third-person omniscient narrator gives the writer great flexibility and provides the reader with access to all the characters and to events that may be occurring simultaneously. In Boccaccio's "Federigo's Falcon," the use of a third-person omniscient narrator allows the reader insight into the private thoughts and motivations of both Federigo and Monna Giovanna.

When a writer uses a **third-person limited point of view,** the narrator tells the story from the perspective of only one of the characters. The reader learns only what that character thinks, feels, observes, and experiences. "The Guest" by Albert Camus is told from a third-person limited point of view. The writer's use of this point of view accentuates Daru's isolation and conflict.

See pages 1148, 1172, 1333.
See also **Narrator**.

Prose Generally, *prose* refers to all forms of written or spoken expression that are organized and that lack regular rhythmic patterns. Prose is characterized by logical order, continuity of thought, and individual style. Prose style varies from one writer to another, depending on such elements as word choice, sentence length and structure, use of figurative language, and tone.

Examples: Examples of prose include the Mayan *Popol Vuh,* the historical writings of Thucydides, and the fiction of Leo Tolstoy.

See also **Poetry**.

Protagonist The central character in a story, novel, or play is called the protagonist. The protagonist is always involved in the central conflict of the plot and often changes during the course of the work. The force or person who opposes the protagonist is the antagonist.

Examples: In the *Song of Roland,* the protagonist is Roland, a warrior who battles many enemies. The protagonist in Ibsen's *A Doll House* is Nora, who faces several antagonists, including her husband and the expectations and conventions of 19th-century society.

See also **Antagonist; Hero**.

Proverb A proverb is a short, well-known saying that expresses a widely held belief. Proverbs, which are used in every culture, serve to warn, encourage, and console people. "Look before you leap" is an example of a familiar proverb.

Quest Hero *See* **Hero.**

Quest Story In a quest story, a hero goes on a journey, achieves a goal, or undergoes a personal transformation. A quest hero usually has special powers or special friends that help (or hinder) him or her on the journey. The quest story is common to many cultures. *The Epic of Gilgamesh* may be the oldest quest story in existence.

See page 47.

Realism In literature, *realism* has both a general meaning and a special meaning. As a general term, *realism* refers to any effort to offer an accurate and detailed portrayal of actual life. More specifically, realism refers to a literary movement of the 19th century. The realists based their writing on careful observations of ordinary life, often focusing on the middle or lower classes. They attempted to present life objectively and honestly, without the sentimentality or idealism that had characterized earlier literature, particularly fiction. Typically, realists developed their settings in great detail in an effort to re-create specific times and places for the reader. Guy de Maupassant and Leo Tolstoy are both considered realists.

See pages 942, 952, 1019.
See also **Naturalism.**

Realistic Drama *See* **Drama.**

Repetition Repetition is a technique in which a sound, word, phrase, or line is repeated for emphasis. The use of repetition often helps to reinforce meaning and to create an appealing rhythm. Repetition can also unify a poem by creating a clear structure. Note the use of repetition in the following lines:

> We pick ferns, we pick ferns,
> for the ferns are sprouting now:
> oh to go home, to go home
> before the year is over!
> —"We Pick Ferns, We Pick Ferns"

See pages 451, 927.
See also **Parallelism.**

Resolution *See* **Plot.**

Rhyme Words rhyme when the sounds of their accented vowels and all succeeding sounds are identical, as in *tether* and *together.* For true rhyme, the consonants that precede the vowels must be different. Rhyme that occurs at the end of lines of poetry is called **end rhyme,** as in Dante's rhyming of *ease* and *seas* in the *Inferno.* End rhymes that are not exact but approximate are called **off rhyme,** as in the words *on* and *sun* in Heinrich Heine's "The Lorelei." Rhyme that occurs within a single line is called **internal rhyme,** as in the phrase *stunned and numb* in Rainer Maria Rilke's "The Panther."

Rhyme Scheme A rhyme scheme is the pattern of end rhyme in a poem. The pattern is charted by assigning a letter of the alphabet, beginning with the letter *a,* to each line. Lines that rhyme are given the same letter. The following example has an *abba* rhyme scheme:

> What good it is to me if long ago   *a*
> you eloquently praised my golden hair,   *b*
> compared my eyes and beauty to the flare   *b*
> of two suns where, you say, love bent the bow *a*
> —Louise Labé, "Sonnet 23"

See page 927.

Rhythm *Rhythm* refers to the pattern or beat of stressed and unstressed syllables in a line of poetry. Poets use rhythm to bring out the musical quality of language, to emphasize ideas, to create mood, to unify a work, and to reinforce subject matter.

See also **Meter.**

Rising Action *See* **Plot.**

Romance The romance has been a popular narrative form since the Middle Ages. Generally, the term *romance* refers to any imaginative story concerned with noble heroes, gallant love, a chivalric code of honor, daring deeds, and supernatural events. Romances usually have faraway settings, depict events unlike those of ordinary life, and idealize their heroes as well as the eras in which the heroes lived. Medieval romances are sometimes lighthearted in tone, usually consist of a number of episodes, and often involve one or more characters in a quest.

Example: Chrétien de Troyes's "Perceval: The Story of the Grail" is an example of a medieval romance. Its story of a knight who visits an unusual castle includes adventure, mysterious rituals, and a shocking supernatural secret.

See page 722.

Romanticism *Romanticism* refers to a literary movement that flourished in Europe in the first half of the 19th century. Romantic writers looked to nature for their inspiration, idealized the distant past, and celebrated the individual. In reaction against neoclassicism, their treatment of subjects was emotional rather than rational, imaginative rather than analytical.

See page 878.
See also **Neoclassicism.**

Sacred Literature *See* **Scripture.**

Satire Satire is a literary technique in which ideas, customs, behaviors, or institutions are ridiculed for the purpose of improving society. Satire may be gently witty, mildly abrasive, or bitterly critical, and exaggeration may be used in it to force readers to see something in a more critical light. Often, a satirist will distance himself or herself from a subject by creating a fictional speaker—usually a calm, and often a naive, observer—who can address the topic without revealing the true emotions of the writer. The title character of Voltaire's *Candide* is an example of such an observer.

See page 856.

Scripture Texts that convey the traditions, beliefs, and rituals of particular religions are often referred to as scriptures, or sacred literature. Scripture often has a special status in the culture from which it springs. It may be seen as divinely inspired and may be used in worship and viewed with reverence. It may also be a work of great beauty and artistry. More than many other kinds of literature, scripture is likely to have teaching as one of its main purposes. What it teaches generally has to do with a culture's most important concerns: the basic principles of morality, the meaning of human existence, and the relationship between the human and the divine. The Hebrew Bible, the *Rig Veda,* and the Koran are examples of scripture.

See page 74.

Setting Setting is the time and place of the action of a short story, novel, play, narrative poem, or nonfiction narrative. In addition to time and place, however, setting may include the larger historical and cultural contexts that form the background for a narrative. Setting is one of the main elements in fiction and often plays an important role in what happens and why.

Examples: Torvald's "tastefully but not expensively furnished" home in Ibsen's *A Doll's House* reflects the social and cultural environment of 19th-century Europe. The setting in Victor Hugo's "Russia 1812" is essential to the historical context of the narrative poem; the setting functions almost as a character.

See pages 532, 920, 1062, 1212.
See also **Fiction.**

Shakespearean (English) Sonnet *See* **Sonnet.**

Short Story A short story is a work of fiction that can be read in one sitting. Generally, a short story develops one major conflict. The basic elements of a short story are setting, character, plot, and theme.

A short story must be unified; all the elements must work together to produce a total effect. This unity of effect is reinforced through an appropriate title and through the use of symbolism, irony, and other literary devices.

Simile A simile is a figure of speech that compares two things that are basically unlike yet have something in common. Unlike a metaphor, which implies or suggests a comparison, a simile states it by means of the word *like* or *as.* Both poets and prose writers use similes to intensify emotional response, stimulate vibrant images, provide imaginative delight, and concentrate the expression of ideas. In his short story "Civil Peace," Chinua Achebe uses a simile to describe the sound of the head thief's voice:

> "Shurrup!" rang the leader's voice like a lone shot in the sky and silenced the murmuring at once.
>
> —Chinua Achebe, "Civil Peace"

An **epic simile** is a long comparison that often continues for a number of lines. Here is an example of an epic simile:

> Like powerful stallions sweeping round the
>   post for trophies,
> galloping full stretch with some fine prize at
>   stake,
> a tripod, say, or woman offered up at funeral
>   games
> for some brave hero fallen—so the two of
>   them
> whirled three times around the city of
>   Priam. . . .
>
> —Homer, *Iliad*

See also **Figurative Language; Metaphor.**

Situational Irony *See* **Irony.**

Soliloquy In a dramatic work, a soliloquy is a speech in which a character speaks his or her thoughts aloud. The character is usually on the stage alone, not speaking to other characters and perhaps not even consciously addressing the audience. (If there are other characters on stage, they are ignored temporarily.) The purpose of a soliloquy is to reveal a character's inner thoughts, feelings, and plans to the audience. In this soliloquy from Goethe's *Faust,* Mephisto reveals his ironic attitude toward the Lord:

> I like to see the Old Man now and then
> And try to be not too uncivil.
> It's charming in a noble squire when
> He speaks humanely with the very Devil.
>   —Johann Wolfgang von Goethe, *Faust*

See page 896.

Sonnet A sonnet is a lyric poem of 14 lines, commonly written in **iambic pentameter.** For centuries the sonnet has been a popular form because it is long enough to permit development of a complex idea yet short and structured enough to challenge any poet's skills. Sonnets written in English usually follow one of two forms.

The **Petrarchan,** or **Italian, sonnet,** introduced into English by Sir Thomas Wyatt, is named after Francesco Petrarch, the 14th-century Italian poet. This type of sonnet consists of two parts, called the **octave** (the first eight lines) and the **sestet** (the last six lines). The usual rhyme scheme for the octave is *abbaabba.* The rhyme scheme for the sestet may be *cdecde, cdccdc,* or a similar variation. The octave generally presents a problem or raises a question, and the sestet resolves or comments on the problem.

The **Shakespearean,** or **English, sonnet** is sometimes called the Elizabethan sonnet. It consists of three **quatrains,** or four-line units, and a final couplet. The typical rhyme scheme is *abab cdcd efef gg.* In the English sonnet, the rhymed couplet at the end of the sonnet provides a final commentary on the subject developed in the three quatrains. Shakespeare's sonnets are the finest examples of this type of sonnet.

Some poets have written series of related sonnets on a single subject. These are called **sonnet sequences,** or **sonnet cycles.** Toward the end of the 16th century, writing sonnet sequences became fashionable, with a common subject being love for a beautiful but unattainable woman. Petrarch wrote sonnet sequences to the mysterious Laura.

See page 804.
See also **Meter; Poetry.**

Sound Devices *See* **Alliteration; Assonance; Consonance; Onomatopoeia; Repetition; Rhyme; Rhyme Scheme; Rhythm.**

Speaker The speaker in a poem is the voice that "talks" to the reader. The speaker is not necessarily the writer; he or she may be a creation of the writer, much like a character in a play.

Examples: In "To Helen" by Edgar Allan Poe, the speaker may be addressing Helen of Troy or another woman who reminds the speaker of the legendary beauty. In Anna Akhmatova's poem "I Am Not One of Those Who Left the Land," the speaker may be closely identified with the poet herself, who refused to leave Russia after the Communists took control.

See pages 59, 387, 1218.

Speech A speech is a talk or public address. The purpose of a speech may be to entertain, to explain, to persuade, or to inspire, or it may be any combination of these aims. Plato's *Apology* and Virginia Woolf's "Professions for Women" are both speeches.

See page 254.

Stage Directions The stage directions in a dramatic script serve as a kind of instructional manual for the director, actors, and stage crew as well as for the general reader. Often the stage directions are printed in italic type, and they may be enclosed in parentheses or brackets.

Stage directions serve a number of important functions. They may describe the scenery or setting as well as lighting, costumes, props, music, and sound effects. Most important, the stage directions usually provide hints to the performers on how the characters look, move, and speak.

See also **Drama.**

Stanza A stanza is a group of lines that form a unit in a poem. In traditional poems, the stanzas usually have the same number of lines and often have the same rhyme scheme and meter. In the 20th century, poets have experimented more freely with stanza form, sometimes writing poems that have no stanza breaks at all.

Stream of Consciousness *Stream of consciousness* refers to a style of fiction that takes as its subject the flow of thoughts, responses, and sensations of one or more characters. A stream-of-consciousness narrative is not structured as a coherent, logical presentation of ideas. Rather, the connections between ideas are associative, with one idea suggesting another.

A character's stream of consciousness is often expressed as an interior monologue, a record of the total workings of the character's mind and emotions. An interior monologue may reveal the inner experience of the character on many levels of consciousness, often represented through a sequence of images and impressions. Virginia Woolf and James Joyce make extensive use of stream of consciousness in their fiction.

See also **Characterization; Point of View; Style.**

Structure Structure is the way in which the parts of a work of literature are put together. In poetry, structure involves the arrangement of words and lines to produce a desired effect. A common structural unit in poetry is the stanza, of which there are numerous types. In prose, structure is the arrangement of larger units or parts of a selection. Paragraphs, for example, are a basic unit in prose, as are chapters in novels and acts in plays. The structure of a poem, short story, novel, play, or nonfiction work usually emphasizes certain important aspects of content.

See also **Form.**

Style Style is the particular way in which a piece of literature is written. Style is not what is said but how it is said. It is the writer's uniquely individual way of communicating ideas. Many elements contribute to style, including word choice, sentence length, tone, figurative language, use of dialogue, and point of view. A literary style may be described in a variety of ways, such as formal, conversational, journalistic, wordy, ornate, poetic, or dynamic.

Examples: In Sei Shōnagon's *Pillow Book,* the writer uses a humorous, conversational style. In the excerpt from Elie Wiesel's *The World Was Silent*, the author uses simple words, short sentences, imagery, and dialogue to convey his horrifying experiences.

See page 1364.

Supernatural Elements Supernatural elements are beings, powers, or events that are unexplainable by known forces or laws of nature. In the *Ramayana,* Rama and Ravana battle each other with the aid of supernatural powers. In Chrétien de Troyes's narrative poem *Perceval: The Story of the Grail,* supernatural events occur in the magical castle.

Surprise Ending A surprise ending is an unexpected twist in the plot at the end of a story. The surprise may be a sudden turn in the action or a revelation that gives a different perspective to the entire story.

Example: The final paragraph of Luigi Pirandello's story "War," which provides a sudden, shattering perspective on war and loss, is an example of a surprise ending.

Suspense Suspense is the tension or excitement readers feel as they are drawn into a story and become increasingly eager to learn the outcome of the plot. Suspense is created when a writer purposely leaves readers uncertain or apprehensive about what will happen.

Example: In *The Spy,* Bertolt Brecht uses suspense-building techniques to help create doubt about the son's loyalty.

Symbol A symbol is a person, place, object, or activity that represents something beyond itself. Certain symbols are commonly used in literature, such as a journey to represent life or night to represent death. Other symbols, however, acquire their meanings within the contexts of the works in which they occur.

Examples: Torvald's house in Ibsen's *A Doll's House* may symbolize the societal restrictions from which Nora must free herself. In Federico García Lorca's poem "The Guitar," the guitar may symbolize human grief or longing.

See pages 927, 1180, 1354.

Tanka Tanka are Japanese lyric poems that express single thoughts or tell brief stories. *Tanka* means "short song," and a traditional tanka poem consists of just 31 syllables divided among five lines. The first and third lines contain 5 syllables each; the remaining lines contain 7 syllables each. Love, nature, and time are frequent themes in these poems. Tanka was the dominant form of Japanese verse from the 700s until the 1500s. Eventually, tanka inspired the more concise verse form known as haiku.

See also **Haiku.**

Theme A theme is a central idea or message in a work of literature. A theme should not be confused with a work's subject, or what the work is about. Rather, a theme is a perception about life or human nature shared with the reader. Sometimes the theme is directly stated within a work; at other times it is implied, and the reader must infer the theme. There may be more than one theme in a work. In *Oedipus the King,* for example, the themes include the immutability of fate, the blinding nature of power, and the conflict between father and son.

One way to discover the theme of a literary work is to think about what happens to the central characters. The importance of those events, stated in terms that apply to all human beings, is often the theme. In poetry, imagery and figurative language also help convey theme. In Omar Khayyám's *Rubáiyát,* for example, metaphors are used to convey such themes as time's passing quickly.

See pages 397, 598, 903, 972, 1081, 1258, 1372.

Third-Person Point of View

See **Point of View.**

Title The title of a literary work introduces readers to the piece and usually reveals something about its subject or theme. Although works are occasionally untitled or, in the case of some poems, merely identified by their first line, most literary works have been deliberately and carefully named. Some titles are straightforward, stating exactly what the reader can expect to discover in the work. Others suggest possibilities, perhaps hinting at the subject and forcing the reader to search for interpretations.

Examples: The title of Tolstoy's story "How Much Land Does a Man Need?" poses—as the reader discovers—an ironic question. "The Handsomest Drowned Man in the World," the title of a story by Gabriel García Márquez, intrigues the reader and hints at the story's magical realism.

See page 1372.

Tone Tone is an expression of a writer's attitude toward a subject. Unlike mood, which is intended to shape the reader's emotional response, tone reflects the feelings of the writer. The language and details a writer chooses help establish the tone, which might be playful, serious, bitter, angry, or detached, among other possibilities. To identify the tone of a work, you might find it helpful to read the work aloud. The emotions you convey in reading should give you clues to the tone of the work.

Examples: Rumi uses a joyful tone to describe a bird's song in "Birdsong from Inside the Egg." In the poem "Prayer to Masks," Léopold Sédar Senghor uses a solemn, intense tone to celebrate his African heritage.

See pages 605, 823, 1218, 1342.
See also **Mood.**

Tragedy A tragedy is a dramatic work that presents the downfall of a dignified character who is involved in historically or socially significant events. The main character, or **tragic hero,** has a **tragic flaw,** a quality that leads to his or her destruction. The events in a tragic plot are set in motion by a decision that is often an error in judgment caused by the tragic flaw. Succeeding events are linked in a cause-and-effect relationship and lead inevitably to a disastrous conclusion, usually death. A tragic hero evokes both pity and fear in readers or viewers: pity because readers or viewers feel sorry for the character, and fear because they realize that the problems and struggles faced by the character are perhaps a necessary part of human life. At the end of a tragedy, a reader or viewer generally feels a sense of waste, because humans who were in some way superior have been destroyed. Shakespeare's plays *Romeo and Juliet, Hamlet,* and *Macbeth* are tragedies, as are *Oedipus the King* and *Antigone* by the Greek dramatist Sophocles.

See page 330.
See also **Hero.**

Tragic Flaw *See* **Hero; Tragedy.**

Tragic Hero *See* **Hero; Tragedy.**

Trickster Tale A trickster tale is a humorous folk tale about an animal or person who creates mischief by trying to outwit others. Neither all good nor all bad, a trickster may be a culture hero, a clever deceiver, or a fool. Trickster tales often explain how some feature of the world or society came to be. The tales are found in West Africa and all over the world. The stories of Anansi and Iktomi are examples of trickster tales.

See page 651.

Understatement Understatement is a technique of creating emphasis by saying less than is actually or literally true. Understatement is the opposite of hyperbole, or exaggeration. One of the primary devices of irony, understatement can be used to develop a humorous effect, to create biting satire, or to achieve a restrained tone.

Verbal Irony *See* **Irony.**

Voice The term *voice* refers to a writer's unique use of language that allows a reader to "hear" a human personality in his or her writing. The elements of style that determine a writer's voice include sentence structure, diction, and tone. For example, some writers are noted for their reliance on short, simple sentences, while others make use of long, complicated ones. Certain writers use concrete words, such as *lake* or *cold,* which name things that you can see, hear, feel, taste, or smell. Others prefer abstract terms like *memory,* which name things that cannot be perceived with the senses. A writer's tone also leaves its imprint on his or her personal voice.

Wisdom Literature Wisdom literature is writing that teaches rules for living and conveys scholarly learning. Wisdom literature often takes the form of parables, brief stories that are meant to teach lessons or illustrate moral truths. Some parables contain paradoxes, or contradictions, designed to make the reader question conventional logic. Zen parables are examples of wisdom literature.

See page 516.
See also **Parable; Paradox.**

Glossary of Words to Know
In English and Spanish

A

abate (ə-bāt′) *v.* to lessen in intensity
  abatir *v.* disminuir la intensidad

abiding (ə-bī′dĭng) *adj.* enduring
  abide *v.*
  duradero *adj.* perdurable; resistente **durar** *v.*

abject (ăb′jĕkt′) *adj.* very low or miserable in condition
  abyecto *adj.* de condición muy baja o miserable

ablution (ə-blōō′shən) *n.* a washing or cleansing of the body
  ablución *s.* lavado o limpieza del cuerpo

acute (ə-kyōōt′) *adj.* intense
  agudo *adj.* intenso

adversary (ăd′vər-sĕr′ē) *n.* an opponent; enemy
  adversario *s.* opositor; enemigo

affable (ăf′ə-bəl) *adj.* pleasant; agreeable
  afable *adj.* amable; agradable

affront (ə-frŭnt′) *n.* an open insult
  afrenta *s.* insulto frontal

allot (ə-lŏt′) *v.* to give as a share or portion
  repartir *v.* dar una parte o porción

amenable (ə-mē′nə-bəl) *adj.* open to suggestion; responsive
  receptivo *adj.* abierto a sugerencias; dispuesto a aceptar razones

amiably (ā′mē-ə-blē) *adv.* in a friendly manner; pleasantly
  amigablemente *adv.* de manera amistosa; amablemente

anguish (ăng′gwĭsh) *n.* agony
  angustia *s.* agonía

annihilation (ə-nī′ə-lā′shən) *n.* a ceasing to exist; total destruction
  aniquilación *s.* destrucción total

appall (ə-pôl′) *v.* to horrify
  asombrar *v.* asustar; horrorizar

arid (ăr′ĭd) *adj.* dry
  árido *adj.* seco

assent (ə-sĕnt′) *n.* agreement
  asentimiento *s.* consentimiento

assert (ə-sûrt′) *v.* to express forcefully and positively
  afirmar *v.* expresar fuerte y positivamente

assiduously (ə-sĭj′ōō-əs-lē) *adv.* diligently
  asiduamente *adv.* diligentemente

avail (ə-vāl′) *v.* to be of use to; help
  beneficiar *v.* ser de utilidad; ayudar

avidly (ăv′ĭd-lē) *adv.* eagerly
  ávidamente *adv.* ansiosamente

B

banish (băn′ĭsh) *v.* to force to leave a place or country
  desterrar *v.* expulsar de su tierra o del lugar donde vive

basking (băs′kĭng) *n.* warming oneself pleasantly **bask** *v.*
  calentamiento *s.* asoleo **calentarse** *v.*

benediction (bĕn′ĭ-dĭk′shən) *n.* a blessing
  bendición *s.* gracia

benevolent (bə-nĕv′ə-lənt) *adj.* intended to promote the happiness of others; kindly
benévolo *adj.* con la intención de promover la felicidad de otros; bondadoso

bitterness (bĭt′ər-nĭs) *n.* a feeling of disgust or resentment
rencor *s.* sentimiento de repugnancia o resentimiento

blandly (blănd′lē) *adj.* in an easygoing, unconcerned way
suavemente *adj.* de modo fácil; despreocupadamente

boundless (bound′lĭs) *adj.* without limits; infinite
ilimitado *adj.* sin límites; infinito

C

calculating (kăl′kyə-lā′tĭng) *adj.* crafty; scheming
calculador *adj.* tramposo; intrigante

candid (kăn′dĭd) *adj.* frank; blunt; straightforward
cándido *adj.* franco; honesto; directo

candor (kan′dər) *n.* frankness; openness
candor *s.* franqueza; apertura

capricious (kə-prĭsh′əs) *adj.* acting on whim; unpredictable
caprichoso *adj.* que actúa por impulso; imprevisible

chagrin (shə-grĭn′) *n.* a feeling of disappointment or humiliation
mortificación *s.* sentimiento de desilusión o humillación

chaotic (kā-ŏt′ĭk) *adj.* showing great disorder or confusion
caótico *adj.* que muestra gran desorden o confusión

chronic (krŏn′ĭk) *adj.* lasting for a long time; continual
crónico *adj.* que dura mucho tiempo; continuo

clandestine (klăn-dĕs′tĭn) *adj.* secret
clandestino *adj.* secreto

cleave (klēv′) *v.* to cut through; penetrate
cortar *v.* partir; penetrar

commend (kə-mĕnd′) to express approval of; praise
alabar *v.* expresar aprobación; halagar

compel (kəm-pĕl′) *v.* to force or pressure
compeler *v.* forzar o presionar

comply (kəm-plī′) *v.* to agree to a request or carry out an order; obey
cumplir *v.* aceptar una petición o llevar a cabo una orden; obedecer

compulsion (kəm-pŭl′shən) *n.* an irresistible impulse to act
compulsión *s.* impulso irresistible a actuar

compulsory (kəm-pŭl′sə-rē) *adj.* required
obligatorio *adj.* requerido

condiment (kŏn′də-mənt) *n.* a spice or other substance used as a seasoning
condimento *s.* especia u otra substancia usada para sazonar

confiscate (kŏn′fĭ-skāt′) *v.* to seize by authority
confiscar *v.* tomar por la fuerza

confounded (kən-foun′dĭd) *adj.* confused; befuddled
atolondrado *adj.* confundido; aturdido

conjecture (kən-jĕk′chər) *n.* a conclusion based on guesswork
conjetura *s.* conclusión basada en suposiciones

connive (kə-nīv′) *v.* to fail to take action; secretly cooperate
disimular *v.* hacerse de la vista gorda; cooperar secretamente

convention (kən-vĕn′shən) *n.* a social custom
convención *s.* costumbre social

credence (krē´dns) *n.* belief; trust
crédito *s.* confianza

culmination (kŭl´mə-nā´shən) *n.* a high point or climax
culminación *s.* punto alto o clímax

culpable (kŭl´pə-bəl) *adj.* deserving of blame
culpable *adj.* que tiene la culpa

D

defile (dĭ-fīl´) *v.* to treat in a shameful way; destroy the beauty or honor of
mancillar *v.* tratar de manera humillante; destruir la belleza o el honor

dejectedly (dĭ-jĕk´tĭd-lē) *adv.* sadly; in a depressed way
abatidamente *adv.* tristemente; de manera deprimida

delusion (dĭ-lōō´zhən) *n.* a false idea or belief
ilusión *s.* idea o creencia falsa

demoralizing (dĭ-môr´ə-lī´zĭng) *adj.* weakening to one's spirit or discipline; disheartening **demoralize** *v.*
desmoralizador *adj.* que debilita el espíritu o la disciplina; descorazonador **desmoralizar** *v.*

denigration (dĕn´ĭ-grā´shən) *n.* the act of speaking ill of someone; defamation
denigración *s.* acto de hablar mal de alguien; difamación

denounce (dĭ-nouns´) *v.* to condemn publicly
denunciar *v* condenar públicamente

derisively (dĭ-rī´sĭv-lē) *adv.* in a mocking or jeering manner
burlonamente *adv.* de manera burlona, irónica

desolate (dĕs´ə-lĭt) *adj.* barren; empty; dismal
desolado *adj.* desierto; vacío; empobrecido

despair (dĭ-spâr´) *n.* complete loss of hope
desesperación *s.* pérdida completa de esperanza

despondent (dĭ-spŏn´dənt) *adj.* sad; depressed
desalentado *adj.* triste; deprimido

diminish (dĭ-mĭn´ĭsh) *v.* to lessen
disminuir *v.* reducir

din (dĭn) *n.* a loud, confused noise
estrépito *s.* ruido fuerte, confuso

discern (dĭ-sûrn´) *v.* to perceive with the eyes or intellect
discernir *v.* percibir con los ojos o el intelecto

disconcerted (dĭs´kən-sûr´tĭd) *adj.* embarrassed or confused **disconcert** *v.*
desconcertado *adj.* avergonzado o confundido **desconcertar** *v.*

discourse (dĭs´kôrs´) *n.* talk; conversation
discurso *s.* charla; conversación

discretion (dĭ-skrĕsh´ən) *n.* a sense of carefulness and restraint in one's actions or words
discreción *s.* cuidado de las palabras o actos

disdain (dĭs-dān´) *v.* to look down on or treat with contempt
desdeñar *v.* menospreciar o tratar con desprecio

disparage (dĭ-spăr´ĭj) *v.* to speak in a slighting way of; belittle
menoscabar *v.* hablar con desprecio; desacreditar

dissent (dĭ-sĕnt´) *n.* disagreement
disensión *s.* desacuerdo

dissipated (dĭs´ə-pā´tĭd) *adj.* participating excessively in sensual or foolish pleasures
disipado *adj.* dedicado excesivamente a placeres sensuales o necios

dissuade (dĭ-swād') *v.* to persuade not to; discourage
disuadir *v.* convencer de no hacer algo; desalentar

docile (dŏs'əl) *adj.* obedient; easily led or managed
dócil *adj.* obediente; fácil de dirigir o manejar

donor (dō'nər) *n.* a person who gives or contributes something
donador *s.* persona que da o contribuye

E

edifying (ĕd'ə-fī'ĭng) *adj.* intended to improve morally; instructing **edify** *v.*
edificante *adj.* con la intención de mejorar moralmente; instructivo **edificar** *v.*

emaciated (ĭ-mā'shē-ā'tĭd) *adj.* unnaturally thin **emaciate** *v.*
enflaquecido *adj.* anormalmente flaco **enflaquecer** *v.*

equilibrium (ē'kwə-lĭb'rē-əm) *n.* a stable or balanced condition
equilibrio *s.* estabilidad

eradicate (ĭ-răd'ĭ-kāt') *v.* to get rid of; eliminate
erradicar *v.* eliminar

esoteric (ĕs'ə-tĕr'ĭk) *adj.* understood by only a certain group
esotérico *adj.* entendido sólo por cierto grupo

explicit (ĭk-splĭs'ĭt) *adj.* clear; definite
explícito *adj.* claro; definido

F

fleeting (flē'tĭng) *adj.* happening or passing swiftly
efímero *adj.* que sucede o pasa rápidamente

foreboding (fôr-bō'dĭng) *n.* a sense of evil or danger to come
presentimiento *s.* sensación de que se acerca un mal o peligro

formidable (fôr'mĭ-də-bəl) *adj.* hard to overcome
formidable *adj.* difícil de superar

fortitude (fôr'tĭ-tōōd') *n.* courage
fortaleza *s.* valentía

futile (fyōōt'l) *adj.* useless
futil *adj.* inútil

G

gaping (gā'pĭng) *adj.* staring open-mouthed **gape** *v.*
boquiabierto *adj.* pasmado **mirar con la boca abierta** *v.*

gaunt (gônt) *adj.* thin and drawn
demacrado *adj.* flaco y sin energía

genial (jēn'yəl) *adj.* pleasant; agreeable
genial *adj.* agradable; jovial

grave (grāv) *adj.* serious
grave *adj.* serio

H

haggard (hăg'ərd) *adj.* looking worn and exhausted
macilento *adj.* que se ve agotado

hapless (hăp'lĭs) *adj.* unfortunate
desgraciado *adj.* infortunado

harrowing (hăr'ō-ĭng) *adj.* extremely distressing
aflictivo *adj.* extremadamente inquietante

haughty (hô'tē) *adj.* overly proud; tending to look down on others
arrogante *adj.* demasiado orgulloso; tendiente a despreciar a los demás

heedless (hēd'lĭs) *adj.* thoughtless; unmindful
desatento *adj.* descuidado; despreocupado

hinder (hĭn'dər) *v.* to keep from doing something
obstaculizar *v.* impedir que algo se haga

honed (hōnd) *adj.* finely sharpened
hone *v.*
afilado *adj.* bien pulido **afilar** *v.*

humanely (hyōō-mān'lē) *adv.* in a compassionate or sympathetic way
humanamente *adv.* de manera compasiva o apiadada

I

ignoramus (ĭg'nə-rā'məs) *n.* a foolish or ignorant person
ignorante *s.* tonto o sin conocimientos

illustrious (ĭ-lŭs'trē-əs) *adj.* well known and respected
ilustre *adj.* conocido y respetado

imbued (ĭm-byōōd') *adj.* filled or inspired
imbue *v.*
imbuido *adj.* lleno o inspirado **imbuir** *v.*

imminent (ĭm'ə-nənt) *adj.* about to happen
inminente *adj.* a punto de suceder

impassive (ĭm-păs'ĭv) *adj.* revealing no emotion; expressionless
impasible *adj.* que no revela ninguna emoción; inexpresivo

imperceptibly (ĭm'pər-sĕp'tə-blē) *adv.* in a barely noticeable way
imperceptiblemente *adv.* de manera que apenas se nota

imperious (ĭm-pîr'ē-əs) *adj.* urgent; pressing
imperioso *adj.* urgente; que presiona

impervious (ĭm-pûr'vē-əs) *adj.* unable to be affected
impenetrable *adj.* que no puede ser afectado

implacable (ĭm-plăk'ə-bəl) *adj.* unable to be appeased; unyielding
implacable *adj.* incapaz de ser apaciguado; que no cede

improvise (ĭm'prə-vīz') *v.* to make on the spur of the moment, using any resources available
improvisar *v.* hacer en el momento, usando los recursos a la mano

inane (ĭn-ān') *adj.* pointless; silly
anodino *adj.* sin sentido; tonto

inaudibly (ĭn-ô'də-blē) *adv.* in a way that cannot be heard
inaudiblemente *adv.* de manera que no se puede oír

incantation (ĭn'kăn-tā'shən) *n.* a set of words chanted or sung as part of a religious ritual
conjuro *s.* serie de palabras dichas o cantadas como parte de un ritual religioso

incarnation (ĭn'kär-nā'shən) *n.* a bodily form taken on by a spirit
encarnación *s.* forma corporal que toma un espíritu

incessantly (ĭn-sĕs'ənt-lē) *adv.* continually; without stopping
incesantemente *adv.* continuamente; sin parar

incompatibility (ĭn'kəm-păt'ə-bĭl'ĭ-tē) *n.* a lack of harmony; conflict
incompatibilidad *s.* falta de armonía; conflicto

incongruous (ĭn-kông'grōō-əs) *adj.* not appropriate; out of place
incongruente *adj.* inapropiado; fuera de lugar

incredulous (ĭn-krĕj'ə-ləs) *adj.* unwilling to believe; skeptical
incrédulo *adj.* que no desea creer; escéptico

indifferent (ĭn-dĭf'ər-ənt) *adj.* having no particular interest or concern
indiferente *adj.* que no tiene interés particular

indigent (ĭn′dĭ-jənt) *adj.* without money; very poor
indigente *adj.* sin dinero; muy pobre

indignation (ĭn′dĭg-nā′shən) *n.* anger caused by something mean or unjust
indignación *s.* ira ante maldad o injusticia

indolent (ĭn′ də-lənt) *adj.* lazy
indolente *adj.* flojo

indulgence (ĭn-dŭl′jəns) *n.* a giving in to someone's wishes or desires
indulgencia *s.* ceder a los deseos de alguien

ineffectually (ĭn′ĭ-fĕk′chōō-ə-lē) *adv.* in a useless manner
ineficazmente *adv.* de manera inútil

inevitably (ĭn-ĕv′ĭ-tə-blē) *adv.* unavoidably
inevitablemente *adv.* de manera que no es posible evitar

inextricably (ĭn-ĕk′strĭ-kə-blē) *adv.* in a way that one cannot get out of
inextricablemente *adv.* sin posibilidad de zafarse

infatuation (ĭn-făch′ōō-ā′shən) *n.* a foolish, unreasonable attraction
encaprichamiento *s.* atracción tonta e irracional

ingenuity (ĭn′jə-nōō′ĭ-tē) *n.* cleverness
ingenio *s.* agudeza

inhospitable (ĭn-hŏs′pĭ-tə-bəl) *adj.* unfriendly or unwelcoming to a guest
inhospitalario *adj.* persona o lugar que no acoge

innuendo (ĭn′yōō-ĕn′dō) *n.* an indirect hint or reference, usually negative
alusión *s.* insinuación o referencia indirecta, generalmente negativa

insatiable (ĭn-sā′shə-bəl) *adj.* impossible to satisfy
insaciable *adj.* imposible de satisfacer

interminable (ĭn-tûr′mə-nə-bəl) *adj.* unending
interminable *adj.* sin fin

intermittently (ĭn′tər-mĭt′nt-lē) *adv.* with stops and starts; on and off
intermitentemente *adv.* con detenciones y arranques; prendido y apagado

intervene (ĭn′tər-vēn′) *v.* to come between; get involved in order to help
intervenir *v.* interponerse; involucrarse para ayudar

intransigence (ĭn-trăn′sĭ-jəns) *n.* a condition of being stubborn and uncompromising
intransigencia *s.* terquedad; rigidez

intricate (ĭn′trĭ-kĭt) *adj.* complex
intrincado *adj.* complejo

intrigue (ĭn′trēg′) *n.* a secret scheme; plot
intriga *s.* plan secreto; complot

invincible (ĭn-vĭn′sə-bəl) *adj.* unable to be conquered
invencible *adj.* que no es posible conquistar

J

jauntily (jôn′tĭ-lē) *adv.* in a lively, carefree manner
garbosamente *adv.* de manera vivaz y desenvuelta

jocular (jŏk′yə-lər) *adj.* funny; comic
jocoso *adj.* chistoso; cómico

jubilant (jōō′bə-lənt) *adj.* extremely joyful
jubiloso *adj.* sumamente alegre

L

labyrinth (lăb′ə-rĭnth′) *n.* a confusing network of passages; maze
laberinto *s.* red confusa de pasajes

lament (lə-měnt′) *v.* to express grief
or sorrow
lamentar *v.* expresar dolor o pena

lavishly (lăv′ĭsh-lē) *adv.* very freely and
abundantly
copiosamente *adv.* de manera muy libre
y abundante

lethargy (lěth′ər-jē) *n.* inactivity; sleepy
dullness
letargo *s.* inactividad; modorra con sueño

lithe (līth) *adj.* limber and graceful
ágil *adj.* flexible y gracioso

loathed (lōthd) *adj.* intensely hated **loathe** *v.*
aborrecido *adj.* odiado intensamente
aborrecer *v.*

lucid (lōō′sĭd) *adj.* clear; easily
understood
lúcido *adj.* claro; entendido fácilmente

M

majestically (mə-jěs′tĭ-klē) *adv.* in
a noble or stately way
majestuosamente *adv.* en forma noble
o señorial

malicious (mə-lĭsh′əs) *adj.* evil; wicked
malicioso *adj.* malo; malvado

meagerly (mē′gər-lē) *adv.* poorly; scantily
magramente *adv.* pobremente;
escasamente

menace (měn′ĭs) *n.* a threat
amenaza *s.* peligro

misgiving (mĭs-gĭv′ĭng) *n.* a feeling
of doubt; concern
recelo *s.* sentimiento de duda;
desconfianza

monumental (mŏn′yə-měn′tl) *adj.* very
significant; astonishing
monumental *adj.* muy significativo; asombroso

mortify (môr′tə-fī′) *v.* to embarrass
or humiliate
mortificar *v.* avergonzar o humillar

musing (myōō′zĭng) *adj.* thoughtfully
questioning or meditating **muse** *v.*
meditabundo *adj.* pensativo
o meditativo **meditar** *v.*

N

naive (nī-ēv′) *adj.* lacking worldliness and
sophistication
ingenuo *adj.* carente de mundo y
sofisticación

nominally (nŏm′ə-nə-lē) *adv.* apparently (but
usually not in reality); seemingly
nominalmente *adv.* aparentemente;
por cumplir las apariencias

novice (nŏv′ĭs) *n.* a beginner in a job
or activity
novato *s.* nuevo en un empleo

O

oblivion (ə-blĭv′ē-ən) *n.* a state of being
forgotten
olvido *s.* falta de recuerdo

oblivious (ə-blĭv′ē-əs) *adj.* not aware;
unmindful
olvidadizo *adj.* abstraído; que no recuerda

obstinate (ŏb′stə-nĭt′) *adj.* stubborn
obstinado *adj.* terco

ominous (ŏm′ə-nəs) *adj.* threatening;
signaling evil to come
ominoso *adj.* amenazador; que señala mal por
venir

omission (ō-mĭsh′ən) *n.* an act of leaving out,
passing over, or neglecting
omisión *s.* acto de dejar fuera, de olvidar o
relegar

ordain (ôr-dān′) *v.* to establish by decree or law
  ordenar *v.* establecer por decreto o ley

osmosis (ŏz-mō′sĭs) *n.* an unconscious absorbing of facts or ideas
  ósmosis *s.* forma inconsciente de absorber hechos o ideas

P

paltry (pôl′trē) *adj.* insignificant; almost worthless
  miserable *adj.* insignificante; casi sin valor

parrying (păr′ē-ĭng) *n.* a warding off or turning aside **parry** *v.*
  esquivador *s.* el que evita un golpe o se hace a un lado **esquivar** *v.*

peer (pîr) *n.* an equal
  par *s.* igual

pensive (pĕn′sĭv) *adj.* thoughtful; moody
  pensativo *adj.* abstraído; melancólico

perpetual (pər-pĕch′ōō-əl) *adj.* lasting for an indefinitely long time
  perpetuo *adj.* que dura por un tiempo indefinidamente largo

petty (pĕt′ē) *adj.* of no importance; trivial
  insignificante *adj.* sin importancia; trivial

pittance (pĭt′ns) *n.* a small reward; tiny amount
  miseria *s.* pequeña recompensa; pequeña cantidad

pivotal (pĭv′ə-tl) *adj.* very important
  axial *adj.* muy importante

plight (plīt) *n.* a bad or unfortunate situation; predicament
  apuro *s.* situación mala o desafortunada

presumption (prĭ-zŭmp′shən) *n.* bold or outrageous behavior
  presunción *s.* conducta atrevida o engreída

prevail (prĭ-vāl′) *v.* to hold out against; triumph over
  prevalecer *v.* predominar; triunfar

prevalent (prĕv′ə-lənt) *adj.* widely or commonly occurring
  frecuente *adj.* que ocurre en forma generalizada o común

primordial (prī-môr′dē-əl) *adj.* first-existing; original
  primordial *adj.* que existió primero; original

pristine (prĭs′tēn′) *adj.* pure; uncorrupted
  prístino *adj.* puro; incorrupto

prodigious (prə-dĭj′əs) *adj.* impressively great; stupendous
  prodigioso *adj.* grandioso; estupendo

protrude (prō-trōōd′) *v.* to jut out; project
  proyectar *v.* resaltar

R

rash (răsh) *adj.* hasty and careless
  imprudente *adj.* temerario y descuidado

recoil (rĭ-koil′) *v.* to pull back in fear or surprise
  retroceder *v.* retirarse por temor o sorpresa

reconcile (rĕk′ən-sīl′) *v.* to bring into agreement or harmony; cause to accept
  reconciliar *v.* llegar a un acuerdo o armonía; llevar a aceptar

recourse (rē′kôrs′) *n.* something turned to for help or protection
  recurso *s.* algo que se busca para obtener ayuda o protección

refuge (rĕf′yōōj) *n.* protection; comfort
  refugio *s.* protección; amparo

reiterated (rē-ĭt′ə-rā′tĭd) *adj.* repeated **reiterate** *v*
  reiterado *adj.* repetido **reiterar** *v.*

relinquish (rĭ-lĭng′kwĭsh) *v.* to give up; hand over
renunciar *v.* ceder; entregar

repose (rĭ-pōz′) *v.* to rest
reposar *v.* descansar

reprehensible (rĕp′rĭ-hĕn′sə-bəl) *adj.* deserving of blame
reprensible *adj.* que merece reproche

reproach (rĭ-prōch′) *n.* blame; criticism
reproche *s.* culpa; crítica

reprove (rĭ-proōv′) *v.* to scold
reprobar *v.* regañar

reputable (rĕp′yə-tə-bəl) *adj.* of good reputation; honorable
intachable *adj.* de buena reputación; honorable

resolute (rĕz′ə-loōt′) *adj.* resolved; determined
resuelto *adj.* decidido; determinado

respite (rĕs′pĭt) *n.* a rest
respiro *s.* descanso

retort (rĭ-tôrt′) *v.* to reply quickly or sharply
replicar *v.* responder rápida o tajantemente

retract (rĭ-trăkt′) *v.* to take back; withdraw
retractar *v.* revocar; retirar

revelation (rĕv′ə-lā′shən) *n.* a making known; exposure
revelación *s.* divulgación; exposición

reverberate (rĭ-vûr′bə-rāt′) *v.* to reflect a noise; resound
reverberar *v.* reflejar un ruido; resonar

revile (rĭ-vīl′) *v.* to abuse verbally; criticize harshly
vilipendiar *v.* insultar; criticar duramente

ruse (roōs) *n.* a trick
artificio *s.* truco

S

scrutinizing (skroōt′n-ī′zĭng) *n.* observing or inspecting with great care **scrutinize** *v.*
escrutinio *s.* observación o inspección muy cuidadosa **inspeccionar** *v.*

sinister (sĭn′ĭ-stər) *adj.* having an evil disposition or intent
siniestro *adj.* con disposición o intención mala

skeptical (skĕp′tĭ-kəl) *adj.* doubtful
escéptico *adj.* dudoso

sloth (slôth) *n.* laziness
pereza *s.* flojera

solace (sŏl′ĭs) *n.* comfort in sorrow or distress
solaz *s.* consuelo en la pena o el dolor

spurn (spûrn) *v.* to reject in a scornful way
desdeñar *v.* rechazar con desdén

stature (stăch′ər) *n.* status or importance gained by growth or achievement
estatura *s.* importancia ganada por desarrollo y logros

stifle (stī′fəl) *v.* to hold back; repress
sofocar *v.* ahogar; reprimir

stoically (stō′ĭ-klē) *adv.* in a manner showing no emotion
estoicamente *adv.* sin mostrar emoción

stupor (stoō′pər) *n.* a dazed condition, almost without sense or feeling
estupor *s.* embotamiento

subvert (səb-vûrt′) *v.* to destroy or corrupt
subvertir *v.* destruir o corromper

suffused (sə-fyoōzd′) *adj.* overspread; filled **suffuse** *v.*
inundado *adj.* lleno **inundar** *v.*

sumptuous (sŭmp′choō-əs) *adj.* costly; magnificent
suntuoso *adj.* costoso; magnífico

superfluous (sŏŏ-pûr′flŏŏ-əs) *adj.* more than is needed; unnecessary
superfluo *adj.* más de lo necesario; innecesario

surmise (sər-mīz′) *n.* a conclusion based on little evidence; guess
suposición *s.* conclusión basada en poca evidencia; conjetura

swarthy (swôr′thē) *adj.* having a dark complexion
moreno *adj.* de piel oscura

T

taciturn (tăs′ĭ-tûrn′) *adj.* not talkative
taciturno *adj.* retraído; que no habla

tactless (tăkt′lĭs) *adj.* not sensitive to what is appropriate in dealing with people and situations
imprudente *adj.* falto de tacto en el trato con personas y situaciones

tangible (tăn′jə-bəl) *adj.* capable of being felt or perceived; concrete
tangible *adj.* capaz de ser sentido o percibido; concreto

tedium (tē′dē-əm) *n.* boredom
tedio *s.* aburrimiento

teem (tēm) *v.* to be filled to overflowing
rebosar *v.* llenar más allá del tope

tenuous (tĕn′yŏŏ-əs) *adj.* thin or flimsy
tenue *adj.* delgado o delicado

tranquilly (trăng′kwə-lē) *adv.* calmly; peacefully
tranquilamente *adv.* serenamente; pacíficamente

transit (trăn′sĭt) *n.* passage
tránsito *s.* pasaje

tumult (tŏŏ′mŭlt′) *n.* a disorderly noisiness or disturbance
tumulto *s.* ruido o disturbio desordenado

U

undeterred (ŭn′dĭ-tûrd′) *adj.* not discouraged
imparable *adj.* resuelto a seguir adelante a pesar de obstáculos

undulating (ŭn′jə-lā′tĭng) *adj.* moving with a wavelike motion **undulate** *v.*
ondulante *adj.* con movimiento como ola **ondular** *v.*

unimpeded (ŭn′ĭm-pē′dĭd) *adj.* not held back or obstructed
sin impedimento *adj.* sin detención; sin obstrucción

unintelligible (ŭn′ĭn-tĕl′ĭ-jə-bəl) *adj.* unable to be understood
ininteligible *adj.* incapaz de ser entendido

unmarred (ŭn-märd′) *adj.* not damaged or injured
intacto *adj.* sin daño; ileso

unscrupulous (ŭn-skrŏŏ′pyə-ləs) *adj.* lacking a sense of right and wrong
inescrupuloso *adj.* sin noción del bien y el mal

unvanquished (ŭn′văng′kwĭsht) *adj.* undefeated
inconquistable *adj.* indomable

V

versatility (vûr′sə-tĭl′ĭ-tē) *n.* an ability to do many things well
versatilidad *s.* capacidad para hacer muchas cosas bien

vindictive (vĭn-dĭk′tĭv) *adj.* having a strong tendency toward revenge
vengativo *adj.* con fuerte tendencia a la venganza

virile (vîr′əl) *adj.* masculine; full of manly strength
viril *adj.* masculino; lleno de fuerza masculina

vitality (vī-tăl′ĭ-tē) *n.* strength of mind or body; energy
  vitalidad *s.* fuerza de mente y cuerpo; energía

vivacity (vĭ-văs′ĭ-tē) *n.* liveliness
  vivacidad *s.* viveza; intensidad

W

waive (wāv) *v.* to voluntarily give up; abandon
  ceder *v.* rendirse voluntariamente; abandonar

warily (wâr′ĭ-lē) *adv.* watchfully; cautiously
  desconfiadamente *adv.* cuidadosamente; cautamente

waver (wā′vər) *v.* to have difficulty in making a decision
  titubear *v.* tener dificultad para tomar una decisión

wittingly (wĭt′ĭng-lē) *adv.* knowingly; intentionally
  intencionadamente *adv.* a sabiendas; a propósito

writhe (rīth) *v.* to twist about; squirm
  retorcer *v.* torcer; enchuecar

Z

zeal (zēl) *n.* enthusiasm; fervor
  fervor *s.* entusiasmo; dedicación

Pronunciation Key

Symbol	Examples	Symbol	Examples	Symbol	Examples
ă	at, gas	m	man, seem	v	van, save
ā	ape, day	n	night, mitten	w	web, twice
ä	father, barn	ng	sing, anger	y	yard, lawyer
âr	fair, dare	ŏ	odd, not	z	zoo, reason
b	bell, table	ō	open, road, grow	zh	treasure, garage
ch	chin, lunch	ô	awful, bought, horse	ə	awake, even, pencil,
d	dig, bored	oi	coin, boy		pilot, focus
ĕ	egg, ten	ŏŏ	look, full	ər	perform, letter
ē	evil, see, meal	ōō	root, glue, through		
f	fall, laugh, phrase	ou	out, cow		**Sounds in Foreign Words**
g	gold, big	p	pig, cap	KH	*German* ich, auch;
h	hit, inhale	r	rose, star		*Scottish* loch
hw	white, everywhere	s	sit, face	N	*French* entre, bon,
ĭ	inch, fit	sh	she, mash		fin
ī	idle, my, tried	t	tap, hopped	œ	*French* feu, cœur;
îr	dear, here	th	thing, with		*German* schön
j	jar, gem, badge	*th*	then, other	ü	*French* utile, rue;
k	keep, cat, luck	ŭ	up, nut		*German* grün
l	load, rattle	ûr	fur, earn, bird, worm		

Stress Marks

′ This mark indicates that the preceding syllable receives the primary stress. For example, in the word *language*, the first syllable is stressed: lăng′gwĭj.

′ This mark is used only in words in which more than one syllable is stressed. It indicates that the preceding syllable is stressed, but somewhat more weakly than the syllable receiving the primary stress. In the word *literature*, for example, the first syllable receives the primary stress, and the last syllable receives a weaker stress: lĭt′ər-ə-chŏŏr′.

Adapted from *The American Heritage Dictionary of the English Language,* fourth edition. Copyright © 2000 by Houghton Mifflin Company. Used with the permission of Houghton Mifflin Company.

Index of Fine Art

x, 14–15	Nakht hunting with his family (18th dynasty).
xiv, 418–419	*Moonlight on the River Seba,* Andō Hiroshige.
xviii *top,* 684–685	*Primavera* [Spring] (c. 1481), Sandro Botticelli.
xviii *bottom,* 732	Detail of *Dante Alighieri* (1500–1503), Luca Signorelli.
xx, 868–869	*Dance at the Moulin de la Galette, Montmartre* (1876), Pierre Auguste Renoir.
xxi, 954 *top*	*Portrait of Leo Tolstoy,* Ilya Yefimovich Repin.
8	*Katada Bay Moon* (19th century), Yoshitoshi Taiso.
11	*Seven Spring Herbs* (c. 1918), Kaburaki Kiyokata.
12	*Toba (Su Tung-p'o)* (1820–1832), Katsushika Hokusai.
18	Mask of King Sargon of Akkad.
19 *top*	*Hanging Gardens of Babylon* (c. 1960), Mario Larrinaga.
20	Pharaoh Khafre (fourth dynasty).
21 *left*	Detail of Queen Ankhesenamen and King Tutankhamen (18th dynasty).
21 *right*	Bust of Nefertiti.
22	King Solomon, Anagni Cathedral, Italy.
26 *right*	Detail of the stele of the Law Code of Hammurabi (c. 1792–1750 B.C.).
27	Gold mask of Tutankhamen.
30	Detail of *Moses Receiving the Ten Commandments* (16th century), Raphael.
32, 44	Statue of a hero, possibly Gilgamesh, taming a lion (722–705 B.C.).
35	Gilgamesh and Enkidu slaying Humbaba.
38	Sumerian bull-headed lyre.
52–53	Nakht scroll (18th dynasty).
55	Relief of Akhenaten offering a sacrifice to Aten, the sun god (c. 1350 B.C.).
56	Painted limestone statue of Kat-Tep and his wife, Hetepheres (fourth dynasty).
58	Relief from the tomb of Vizier Ramose (18th dynasty), Thebes.
61	Gray granite statue of Pady-mahes (745–656 B.C.).
64	Jonah in the fish's mouth. Illumination from the Kennicott Bible.
65	*The Creation of Adam,* Michelangelo Buonarroti.
69	*The Judgement of Adam and Eve: "So Judged He Man"* (1807), William Blake.
72	The building of the Ark (Gen. 6:13–17), the Flood (Gen. 8:6–11), leaving the Ark (Gen. 8:18–19), the sacrifice of Noah (Gen. 8:20–9:15) (c. 1250 A.D.).
76 *bottom,* 83	*The Creation of Man,* Diego Rivera.
77	Mayan cylindrical vessel decorated with mythological scene (seventh to eighth century A.D.).
80	Detail of the Bonampak fresco cycle.
88, 89	David, the young shepherd, plays his pipe and a bell (I Samuel 16:5–11). French manuscript illustration.
91	Detail of *St. John the Baptist in the Wilderness,* Geertgen tot Sint Jans.
94	*Summer, or Ruth and Boaz* (1660), Nicolas Poussin.
98	*The Return of the Prodigal Son* (1773), Pompeo Baton.
102 *top*	Statue in the Horse Court of the Temple of Vishnu at Srirangam.
102–103 *bottom*	Statue of Shiva, Madurai.
104 *top*	The Aryan god of war, Indra, seated on an elephant (c. 1825).
105	Buff sandstone head of the Buddha (fifth century).
106 *top*	Detail from Ranganatha Temple fresco.

106 *bottom* — Battle between armies of Arjuna and Tamradhvaia Brahma and deities in sky (1598), Nakib Khan Mughal.

107 *right* — Detail of illustration of Krishna playing flute to a woman beneath a willow tree (1710).

109 — Sculpture of dancing Shiva.

110 *left* — Statue of a priest–king of Mohenjo–Daro.

111 — Sculptured head of Alexander the Great.

116 — Woodcarving of Indra, King of Three Worlds, from the Temple Car.

118 — Statue of Agni, fire god.

120 — Rama.

125 — *Drona at the Well*, Bhaktisiddhanta.

128 *top* — Detail of the head of Krishna, attributed to Sahib Ram.

130 — Detail of Valmiki teaching the *Ramayana* in Dandak Forest.

133, 158 — Rama fights Ravana.

137 — Rama cuts off Ravana's heads.

140 — Rama and Sita enthroned.

141 — Rama and the archer in a carriage attack Ravana.

142 — *Saint George and the Dragon* (17th century).

148 — Kanduri cloth from Ultar Pradesh (c. 1900).

163 *bottom* — Statue of Athena (c. 340–330 B.C.).

164 — *Achilles and the Body of Patroclus (The Spoils of War)* (1986), David Ligare.

165 *top* — Detail of Alexander Sarcophagus (late fourth century B.C.).

166 *left* — Detail of marble grave stele of a youth and a little girl (c. 530 B.C.).

166 *bottom center* — Vase painting of Greek family (mid-fifth century B.C.), attributed to the Harrow Painter.

167 *top* — Vase painting of potter at work.

168–169 — Bronze statue of Zeus or Poseidon (460 B.C.).

169 — *School of Athens* (1508), Raphael.

170 — Marble statue of Demosthenes (c. 280 B.C.).

171 *center* — Parthenon façade reconstruction (1879–1881).

171 *bottom* — Vase painting of woman playing a lyre.

172 *top* — Greek terracotta black-figured vase (about 540 B.C.), attributed to the Amasis Painter.

173 — Roman bust of Aristotle.

176 — *Achilles Kills Hector* (1630), Peter Paul Rubens.

179 — *The Judgment of Paris* (16th century), Giulio Romano.

193, 342 — Fresco of Athena restraining Achilles from killing Agamemnon (1757), Giambattista Tiepolo.

196 — Vase painting of soldier leaving his family for battle.

199 — Greek bust of Zeus.

205 — Pallas de Velletri, attributed to Kresilas.

214 — Roman sarcophagus sculpture, showing Achilles dragging Hector's corpse.

219 — Roman sarcophagus sculpture, showing Priam begging Achilles for Hector's body.

228 — Greek sculpture of a maenad (late fifth century B.C.).

234–235 — Marble sculpture of fallen warrior.

237 — Marble bust of Pericles (c. 425 B.C.).

241 — Vase painting of Athenians voting.

249 — Roman mosaic of the school of Plato.

252 — Fresco of Socrates (first century B.C.).

329	Sphinx of Taharqa.
345 *center left*	*Baptism of Christ in Jordan River* (1240), unknown artist.
345 *bottom right*	Roman marble relief of an officer of the Praetorian Guard (early second century A.D.).
346 *top*	Portrait bust of Emperor Augustus.
348 *left*	Portrait bust of Cicero.
348 *bottom*	Detail of Roman bas-relief from Avignon.
349 *top right*	Encaustic portrait of Roman woman.
349 *bottom*	Detail of mosaic from Cicero's villa (first century A.D.), Dioscurides of Samos.
351 *top*	Marble statue of Emperor Augustus (21 B.C.–14 A.D.).
351 *bottom*, 356	*Virgil and the Muses* (third century A.D.), Roman mosaic from Sousse.
352	Statue of Romulus and Remus being suckled by a she-wolf.
364	Sculpture of Laocoön (first century B.C.).
371	*The Death of Priam* (1787–1792), Antonio Canova.
385	*Helen of Troy* (1863), Dante Gabriel Rossetti.
388	Detail of *Helen of Troy* (late 19th–early 20th century), Evelyn de Morgan.
394, 410	Wall painting of Pasquius Proculus and his wife.
395	Pompeiian household shrine fresco.
399	*Sky and Water I* (1938), M. C. Escher.
401	*The Fall of Icarus* (17th century), Jacob Peter Gowy.
403	*Landscape with the Fall of Icarus* (c. 1558), Pieter Brueghel the Elder.
405 *left*	Man in an ornithopter, Leonardo da Vinci.
407	Portrait bust of laurel-crowned ruler.
420 *bottom*	Camel (eighth century A.D.) from tomb of Cungpu.
421 *bottom*	Terra-cotta sculptures of soldiers from the tomb of Shih Huang Ti.
422 *bottom*	Shang bronze ritual vessel.
423 *top*	Terra-cotta sculpture of kneeling soldier from the tomb of Shih Huang Ti.
424 *left*	Detail of *The Thirteen Emperors* (seventh century A.D.).
424 *right*	Painting of rice farmers.
425 *top*	Painting of paper shop.
425 *center*	Gilt bronze statue of female servant carrying a lantern.
425 *bottom*	Tomb figure of equestrienne on horse (eighth century A.D.).
427 *top*	Detail of *Nine Dragons* (c. 1244), Chen Rong.
427 *center*	Jade sculpture of dragon (Chou dynasty).
429 *right*	Detail of Bayeux Tapestry (c. 11th century A.D.).
436	Painting of Confucius.
438	*A Literary Gathering*, Han Huang.
442	Detail of *Lady with Fan* (mid-19th century), Ju Qing.
443	Lao-tzu riding an ox (early/middle 16th century), Zhang Lu.
444	Ming dish, porcelain with overglaze enamel decoration (16th century).
447	Figure of sitting woman.
448	Bronze horseman (second century A.D.).
450	Ink drawing of mountain scene.
455	Woman writing a letter (1640), Min Qiji.
456	*Li Po* (Southern Sung dynasty), Liang Kai.
458	*Early Spring*, Kuo Hsi.
465	Ceramic jar with dragon (c. 1426–1435).
466	Bronze running horse (Han dynasty).
467	Stone head, tomb of Antiochus I of Commagene.
469	Circular box with garden scene, Yung Lo.

473, 484	*Spring Morning in the Han Palace,* Qui Ying.
475	Detail of *The Old Plum* (1647), attributed to Kano Sansetsu.
486 *bottom left*	*Fishermen Netting Sole* (1853), Andō or Utagawa Hiroshige.
488 *left*	Portrait of Emperor Saga.
489 *top*	Detail of statue of Tokugawa Ieyasu at Toshogu Shrine, Nikko.
490 *left*	*The Emperor Go-Yōzei* (early 17th century), Kano Takanobu.
491 *top*	Detail of screen painting, showing armorers at work (16th century).
492 *top right*	*Moonlit Landscape* (15th century), Saiyo.
493 *top*	Statue of the Great Buddha in Kamakura.
494 *top right*	Detail of Japanese screen.
498 *top,* 505, 560	Detail of *Five Beautiful Women* (early 19th century), Katsushika Hokusai.
498 *left center*	Detail of *The Poetess Sei Shōnagon with the Eizan* (19th century), Kikugawa.
500	*Woman and a Cat,* Utagawa Kunimasa.
502	*Three Women Reading a Letter,* Katsukawa Terushige.
509 *top*	Fan painting (court lady) (c. 1650–1700).
509 *right center*	*Prince Genji with His Lover in a Boat Admiring the Snow in the Garden,* Utagawa Hiroshige.
515	Carving of Zen priest Hoto Kokushi.
518, 520 *left,* 522, 523, 529	*Fukai* mask (18th century).
520 *center,* 525, 527 *left,* 531	*Uba* mask (Edo period).
520 *right,* 527 *right*	*Uba* mask (19th century).
524	"Kasugayama" writing box (Muromachi period).
528	*Kariginu,* Noh costume.
530	*Chukei* fan.
534	*The Poetess Ono no Komachi, Cherry Tree, Full Moon* (c. 1820s), Hokkei.
537	Detail of *Pastimes and Observances of Four Seasons,* Maruyama Okyo.
538	*Poet Saigyō Viewing the Moon* (c. 1637), Iwasa Katsumochi.
549	*The Rhythm of a Corner* (1957), W. Eugene Smith.
566 *right*	Relief from Persepolis of Darius I giving audience (c. 490 B.C.).
566–567	Manuscript illustration of cavalry fighting on camels.
568 *center*	Persian manuscript illustration of mounted ruler.
568 *right*	Manuscript illustration of woman making bread.
569 *top*	Scholars in the House of Wisdom.
569 *bottom*	Persian princess writing a letter, detail of a 17th-century fresco.
587	Sindbad carried by the roc, Edmund Dulac.
592 *bottom*	Illustration from *Shahnameh* manuscript (early 14th century).
593	Illustration from Iranian manuscript of the *Shahnameh.*
596, 610	Detail of *Fête champêtre* [Picnic on the grass] (c. 1610), Riza.
601	*Prayer in the Mosque* (19th century), Jean-Léon Gérôme.
603	Manuscript illustration of a cow bowing to Rumi.
606, 609	Illustration from manuscript of the *Kulliyat* (collected works) of Sadi (c. 1600–1605), attributed to Aqa Riza.
613 *bottom*	Bronze leopard from Benin.
615	French aquatint of African slave embarkation (1794).
616 *bottom*	Detail of sculpture of Dahomean king (before 1889).
617 *right*	Bronze head of queen mother from Benin.
620 *right*	Bronze head of Yoruba king or god.
621	Detail of *Cardinal Chigi Caring for Plague Victims* (18th century).

629, 676	Five terra-cotta horseback riders.
635	Seated terra-cotta figure (early 13th century).
639	Terra-cotta horse and rider.
646	Wood sculpture of Shango priest and fellow worshipers, Lamidi Fakeye.
655	*Akunitam* cloth (mid/late 20th century).
686 *top*	Detail of *August: Mowing Wheat, Binding Sheaves* (c. 1515), Simon Bening.
686 *bottom*	Venice, from a manuscript of Marco Polo's *Travels*.
688 *bottom*	Relic of Charlemagne.
688–689	*Prise de Jérusalem par les Croisés* (19th century), Emile Signol.
689 *bottom*	The Wife of Bath, from a manuscript of Chaucer's *Canterbury Tales*.
690 *left*	Detail of *January* from *Très Riches Heures du Duc de Berry* (early 15th century), Limbourg brothers.
690 *right*	*June* from *Très Riches Heures du Duc de Berry* (early 15th century), Limbourg brothers.
693 *left*	Detail of *Arthur Draws the Sword from the Stone*, Walter Crane.
698	Illustration of Charlemagne's army departing for Spain (14th century).
701	Knights being driven off by a town's defenders (c. 1250).
704, 770	Knights attacking a town gate (c. 1250).
708	Perceval at the castle of the wounded Fisher King.
710	*Perceval in Quest of the Holy Grail*, Ferdinand Leeke.
711	Galahad, Boort, Perceval, and his sister arriving at an island (15th century).
713	Manuscript illustration of a banquet scene (13th century).
715	Detail of *Mystery of the Holy Grail*, W. Hauschild.
719	*The Forest Crossed by Perceval to Liberate Amfortas at the Castle of the Grail*, Christian Jank.
721	*Lancelot and Guinevere: The Dawn of Love* (1867), after Gustave Doré.
727	*The Werewolf of Eschenbach, Germany* (1685).
730	Werewolf attacking its victim (15th century).
734	Detail of *The Meeting of Dante with Beatrice* (1883), Henry Holiday.
735	*Dante with his Poem* (1465), Domenico di Michelino.
738	Virgil rescuing Dante from the three beasts (15th century).
743	*Inscription over the Gate* (1824–1827), William Blake.
746	The circle of the simoniacs, after Gustave Doré.
751	*Dante's Dream* (1871), Dante Gabriel Rossetti.
754	*Dante and Virgil in the Ninth Circle of the Inferno*, Gustave Doré.
757	*Beata Beatrix* (1864–1870), Dante Gabriel Rossetti.
760	*Dante Alighieri* (14th century), unknown artist.
772 *top*	*Queen Elizabeth I* (16th century), unknown artist.
772 *bottom*	Sailing ships at Antibes, France (c. 1750).
773 *top*	"Vitruvian man" (c. 1487), Leonardo da Vinci.
773 *bottom*	Detail of *David* (1501–1504), Michelangelo.
774	St. Peter's Basilica, Rome (17th century).
775	*Louis XIV, King of France* (c. 1701), Hyacinthe Rigaud.
776 *top*	*Lorenzo de Medici* (16th century), Girolamo Macchietti.
776 *bottom*	*Martin Luther* (1533), Lucas Cranach the Elder.
777 *bottom*	Detail of marketplace in Antwerp (17th century).
778	*Sir Isaac Newton* (1710), Sir James Thornhill.
779 *top*	*The Art of Painting* (c. 1666), Jan Vermeer.
780 *top*	The Manciple, from a manuscript of Chaucer's *Canterbury Tales*.
780 *bottom*	Detail of *The Last Supper* (c. 1495), Leonardo da Vinci.
781	*Peter the Great of Russia* (1838), Paul Delaroche.

784 *bottom* *Giovanni Boccaccio* (14th century), unknown artist.

787 *La Pia de Tolommei* (1868–1880), Dante Gabriel Rossetti.

789 Painting of peregrine falcon.

797 *How Utopians Breed Chickens by Incubation,* François van Bleyswyck.

799 *How the Island of Utopia Is Shaped like a Crescent,* François van Bleyswyck.

804 Detail of *St. Madeleine Reading* (16th century).

807 *Petrarch's First Sight of Laura* (1884), William Cave Thomas.

808 *Old Woman Reading* (1665), Rembrandt Harmensz van Rijn.

814 *Love Among the Ruins* (1894), Sir Edward Burne-Jones.

815 *Sir Henry Percy,* Nicolas Hilliard.

821 *top,* 822, 866 *Mary Magdalen* (c. 1540), Jan van Scorel.

824 *Sister Juana Inés de la Cruz* (1750), Miguel Cabrera.

828 *top,* 831 *Don Quixote on Horseback,* Honoré Daumier.

833 Don Quixote in his library, Gustave Doré.

839 Detail of *Don Quixote and the Dead Mule* (1867), Honoré Daumier.

841 *Don Quixote and the Windmill,* after Gustave Doré.

850 Uniforms of imperial cavalry (18th century).

852 *The Stolen Kiss* (late 1780s), Jean-Honoré Fragonard.

855 Assassination of Albrecht Wallenstein, duke of Friedland (18th century).

870 *top* *Portrait of Jean Jacques Rousseau* (18th century), Maurice Quentin de la Tour.

870 *bottom* *Hadleigh Castle* (1829), John Constable.

871 *bottom* Detail of *Bonaparte Crossing the Great Saint-Bernard Pass* (1800–1801), Jacques Louis David.

872–873 *top* *Napoleon's Retreat from Moscow* (19th century), Adolf Northen.

874 *bottom* *Moroccan Caid* (1837), Eugène Delacroix.

875 *top* *Llanthony Abbey, Monmouthshire* (1834), Joseph Mallord William Turner.

875 *bottom* *Ludwig van Beethoven* (19th century), Josef Karl Stieler.

878 *The Wanderer Above the Sea of Clouds* (1818), Caspar David Friedrich.

895 *Johann Wolfgang von Goethe* (1828), J. K. Stieler.

899 *William Wordsworth* (1818), Benjamin Robert Haydon.

900 *View of a Harbour* (c. 1830), Peter De Wint.

901 *The Passing Shower* (1868), George Inness.

905 *top,* 907 *Foggy River* (1990), Florence Brown Eden.

911 *Loreley* (1864), Eduard Jakob von Steinle.

917 *On the March from Moscow* (19th century), John Laslett Pott.

918 *Napoleon Bonaparte During Campaign in France* (1864), Ernest Meissonier.

922 *right* *The Absinthe Drinker* (c. 1875–1876), Edgar Degas.

924, 932 *On Board a Sailing Ship* (1818–1819), Caspar David Friedrich.

926 *La grande famille* [The great family] (1963), René Magritte.

928 *top right,* 931 *Two Heads Among Flowers* (c. 1905), Odilon Redon.

928 *center left* Detail of *Un coin de table* [Table corner] (1872), Henri Fantin-Latour.

935 *top* *Das Eisenwalzwerk: Moderne Cykopen* [The rolling mill: A modern behemoth] (1872–1875), Adolph von Menzel.

936 *bottom* Detail of *Queen Victoria* (1900), Bertha Muller.

937 *right* *Louis Pasteur, French Chemist and Biologist, in His Laboratory* (1885), Albert Gustaf Aristides Edelfelt.

938 *The Thinker* (1880–1882), Auguste Rodin.

942 *top* *Paying the Harvesters* (1882), Léon Lhermitte.

944 *left* *Portrait of Guy de Maupassant* (19th century), François Nicolas Feyen-Perrin.

949, 1092 *The Peasants of Flagey Returning from the Fair, Ornans* (1850–1855), Gustave Courbet.

954 *bottom*	Detail of *Queen Victoria* (1838), Sir George Hayter.
957 *top*	*Leo Tolstoy Writing* (1891), Ilya Yefimovich Repin.
960	*Tolstoy in the Field of Labour* (1889), after Ilya Yefimovich Repin.
965	*The Harvest,* Paul Serusier.
969	*Motherland* (1886), Apollinarii Mikhailovich Vasnetsov.
978	*The House in Gray* (1917), Marc Chagall.
983	*Still-Life with Lamp* (1910), Marc Chagall.
987	*Grain Harvest* (1908), Natalya Sergeyevna Goncharova.
991	*The Dream* (1939), Marc Chagall.
1001	*Doppelbildnis Benesch* [Double portrait of Otto and Heinrich Benesch] (1913), Egon Schiele.
1011	*The Summer Elephant* (mid-18th century), unknown artist.
1016 *bottom*	Detail of *View of the Nevsky Prospect near the Anichkov Bridge* (1886), Alexander Karlovitch Beggrow.
1098 *top*	*The Jazz Singer* (1997), Gil Mayers.
1101 *top right,* 1216 *bottom*	*Portrait of Anna Andreevna Akhmatova* (1914), Natan Isaevich Altmann.
1102 *bottom right*	*Family Group* (1947), Henry Moore.
1105 *right*	*Man Leaning on a Table* (1916), Pablo Picasso.
1106	*Nude Descending a Staircase (No. 2)* (1912), Marcel Duchamp.
1111	*Hidden Resemblance* (1991), Elizabeth Barakah Hodges.
1118	*Der Irrenwarter von Saint-Remy* [The asylum attendant from Saint-Remy] (1889), Vincent van Gogh.
1128	*Portrait of Mlle Ravoux* (late 19th century), Vincent van Gogh.
1133	*Nächtlicher Lärm* [Nightly noise] (1919), Georg Scholz.
1136	*Le lessive* [The wash] (early 20th century), Maria Blanchard.
1140	*Die Skatspieler* [Skat players] (1920), Otto Dix.
1161	*La reve II* [The dream], Balthus.
1169, 1198	*Fishergirl, Newlyn,* Alexander Stanhope Forbes.
1170	*St. Patrick's Close, Dublin,* Walter Osborne.
1184	Zaire-Angola wood mask (20th century).
1209	*Self-Portrait,* Käthe Kollwitz.
1217	*Mujer de la tierra* [Woman from the earth] Maria Eugenia Terrazas.
1223	*Femme à la robe noir* [Woman in a black dress] Tamara de Lempicka.
1226	*Portrait of Prince Eristoff* (1925), Tamara de Lempicka.
1246	Detail of *Portrait of a Man* (1942), Mario Mafai.
1252	Detail of *A Seated Arab Boy* (1858), Frederick Goodall.
1262	*Apple Tree* (1904), Kasimir Malevich.
1276	*Silent Faces at the Crossroads* (1967), Obiora Udechukwu.
1339	*Falcon's Descent on the People* (1992), Chike Aniakor.
1344	*The Philosopher's Conquest* (1914), Giorgio de Chirico.
1349	*Man in Sand,* Marshall Arisman.
1350	*Two Women and a Child* (1926), Diego Rivera.
1353	*Burial of an Illustrious Man* (1936), Mario Urteaga.
1363	*Las sandias* [Watermelons] (1957), Diego Rivera.
1369, 1378	*Retrato del pintor* [Portrait of the painter] (1994), Diego Maqueria.
1377	*Aleko and Zemphira by Moonlight,* decor for *Aleko* (Scene I) (1942), Marc Chagall.

Index of Skills

Literary Concepts

Act, R91

Allegory, 736, 759, R91

Alliteration, 923, 927, 1150, 1154, R91

Allusion, 648

Anapest, R100

Anecdote, 433, R91

Antagonist, R91

Aphorism. *See* Maxim.

Archetype, 31

Assonance, 1150, 1154, R91

Audience, 1157, 1164, R91

Author's purpose, 233, 243, 795, 802, 1233, 1242, 1295, R92

Autobiography, 1295, 1302, R92

Ballad, 910, 913, R92

Bible as literature, 63

Biography, R92

Blank verse, R92

Character, 88, 158, 194, 200, 212, 223, 519, 532, 999, 1043, 1367, 1372, R92. *See also* Motivation.

  minor, 261, 1043, R92

Characterization, 123, 126, 643, 648, 829, 844, 945, 952, R93

Chivalry, 709, 844. *See also* Honor.

Chorus, 261

Clever deceiver, 650

Climax, 589, R102

Comedy, R93

Conflict, 131, 143, 194, 583, 633, R93

  external, 633, 640

  internal, 633, 640, 1167, 1172

Connotation, 1183, 1186, R93

Consonance, 1150, 1154, R93

Contrast, R94

Couplet, 805, 810

Courtly love, 785

Creation literature, 62, R100

Culture hero, 359, 381, 650, R98

Dactyl, R100

Denotation, 1183, 1186, R93

Denouement, R103

Description, 88, 97, 1261, 1263, R94

Detail, 88

Deus ex machina, 261

Dialect, 1286, 1291, R94

Dialogue, 881, 896, 1221, 1230, R94

  Socratic, 247

Diary, 499, 506, R94

Diction, 535, 539, 1157, 1164, R95

Didactic literature, 432–433, R95. *See also* Values in literature.

Drama, 256–260, 330, 943, 1019, 1062, 1081, R95. *See also* Act; Dialogue; Stage directions; Theater, ancient.

Dramatic irony, 330, R99

Ending

  surprise, R108

  unhappy, 145

Epic, 30, 32–33, 120–121, 122, 143, 176–177, 356–357, 696–697, 881, R95. *See also* Heroic literature.

Epic hero, 33, 100, 120, 123, 145, 177, 181, 200, 223, 357, 640, 697, 707

Epic simile, 223, 380, R106

Epithet, 120, 123, 126, 223, R96

Essay, R96

Event, 88, 97

Exposition, 589, 829, R102

Extended metaphor, 806, 810, R96

Fable, R96

Falling action, 589, R102

Fantasy, R96

Fate, 610

Fiction, R96. *See also* Novel; Short story.

Figurative language, 899, 903, 932, R96. *See also* Metaphor; Simile.

Flashback, 153, R30, R97

Foil, 380, 844

Folk tale, 650, 976, R97

Fool, 650

Foot, metrical, 817, R100

Foreshadowing, 194, 633, 976, 995, 1081, R97

Form, poetic, R97

Fragment, literary, 227

Frame story, 785, R97

Free verse, R97

Genre, 881

Haiku, 541, 547, R97

Hero, R98
    culture, 359, 380, 650, R98
    epic, 33, 100, 120, 123, 145, 177, 181, 200, 223,
        357, 640, 697, 707
    Quixotic, 829
    romantic, 879
    tragic, 261, 330, 342, R98
Heroic literature, 30. *See also* Epic; Hero.
Honor, 770, 844
Humanism, 100
Humor, 849, 856, R98
Hymn, 30
Hyperbole, R98
Iamb, R100
Iambic pentameter, 813, 817
Imagery, 330, 380, 410, 453, 459, 463, 470, 535, 541,
    546, 560, 601, 903, 913, R98
Irony, 330, 999, 1006, 1092, R98
    dramatic, 330, R99
    situational, 785, 792, 1006, R98
Lai, 724
Legend, 30, 628, 631, R99
Lyric poetry, 227, 231, R99.
        See also Ode; Sonnet; Tanka.
Magical realism, 1344–1345, R99
Maxim, 432, 435, 439, R99
Metaphor, 594, 598, 810, 899, 903, R99
    extended, 806, 810, R96
Meter, 813, 817, 881, R100
Modernism, 1104–1107
Mood, 463, 470, 535, 539, 560, 1180, 1220, 1230, R100
Moral tale, 996. *See also* Values in literature.
Motivation, 261, 1167, 1274
Myth, 30, 399, 404, 627, R100
Narrative, R101
Narrative poetry, 399, 915, R101
Narrator, 856, 915, R101
National epic, 356, 696
Naturalism, 943, R101
Neoclassicism, 878, R101
Noh drama, 519, R101
Nonfiction, R101. *See also* Autobiography; Biography; Diary;
    Essay.
Novel, 829, R101
Ode, 393, 446, 1359
Omniscient narrator, 1148
Onomatopoeia, R101

Optimism, 849
Oral literature, 30, 446, 618, 676, 696
Oration, 233
Parable, 30, 433, 516, R102
Paradox, 114, 119, 441, 445, R102
Parallelism, 577, 581, R102. *See also* Parallelism *under*
    Grammar, Usage, and Mechanics.
Parody, 829, R102
Personification, 899, 903, R102
Petrarchan sonnet, 804, R106
Philosophical romance, 795
Plot, 62, 261, 583, 589, 792, R102. *See also* Conflict;
    Ending; Exposition.
Poetry, 463, 470, 601, 605, 910, 1150, 1154, 1216, R103.
    See also Ballad; Epic; Haiku; Lyric poetry; Meter;
    Narrative poetry; Ode; Refrain; Sonnet; Stanza; Tanka.
Point of view, 499, 943, 1109, 1148, 1172, 1198, 1325,
    1333, R103
Postcolonial writing, 1322
Praise song, 642–643, 648
Prayer, 30
Prose, R103
Protagonist, R103
Proverb, 30, 664, R104
Psalm, 30
Quatrain, 805, R106
Quest, 31, 33, 47, 709, R104
Quixotic hero, 829
Realism, 942–943, 945, 996, 998, 1092, R104
    in drama, 1019, 1062, 1081
Refrain, 927
Repetition, 446, 451, 923, 927, R104
Resolution, R103
Rhyme, R104
Rhyme scheme, 804, 881, 923, 927, R104
Rhythm, R104. *See also* Meter.
Rising action, 589, R102
Romance, 708, 709, 722, 770, 829, R105
    philosophical, 795
Romantic hero, 879
Romanticism, 878–879, 898, 932, R105
Sacred literature, 30, 64, 74, R105
Satire, 849, 856, R105
Scene, dramatic, 88, 97
Scripture. *See* Sacred literature.
Setting, 88, 97, 231, 519, 532, 915, 1062, 1207, 1212, R105
Shakespearean sonnet, 804, 813, R106

Short story, 944, R105

Simile, 899, 903, R105

    epic, 223, 380, R106

Situational irony, 785, 792, 1006, R98

Socratic dialogue, 247

Soliloquy, 896, R106

Sonnet, 804–805, 811, 820, 866, R106

    meter in, 813, 817, R106

    Petrarchan, 804, R106

    Shakespearean, 804, 813, R106

Sound device, 923, 927, 1150, 1154. *See also* Repetition;
    Rhyme scheme.

Speaker, 51, 59, 231, 383, 387, 1216, 1218, R106

Speech, 247, 254, R107

Stage directions, 334, 335, 336, 1019, 1081, R94, R107

Stanza, R107

Stream of consciousness, R107

Structure, R107

Style, 176, 380, 760, 996, 1198, 1359, 1364, 1378, R107

Supernatural element, R107

Surprise ending, R108

Suspense, R108

Symbol, 759, 910, 913, 927, 1062, 1175, 1180,
    1347, 1354, R108

Symbolist, 923

Tanka, 534–535, R108

Theater, ancient, 260–261

Theme, 223, 393, 397, 594, 598, 610, 903, 958, 972,
    1081, 1245, 1258, 1367, 1372, R108

Title, 1367, 1372, R108

Tone, 59, 594, 601, 823, 1216, 1218, 1318, 1337, R109

Tragedy, 259, 330, R109

Tragic flaw, 261, 330, R98

Tragic hero, 261, 330, 342, R98

Transformation, 399

Translation, 61, 225, 461, 599, 811, 1063, 1155

Trickster tale, 650, 651

Trochee, R100

Trouvère, 696

Understatement, R109

Unhappy ending, 145

Values in literature, 410, 432, 628, 676, 999, 1006, 1008

Voice, R109

Wisdom literature, 30, 511, 516, R109

Reading and Critical Thinking Skills

Active reading, 33, 64. *See also* Clarifying; Connecting;
    Evaluating; Predicting; Questioning; Strategies for
    reading; Visualizing.

Adaptation for film, television, or another medium. *See*
    Comparing literature to adaptations in other media.

Allegory, analyzing, 736, 759

Argument, logic of, R50

Audience, analyzing, 1157, 1164

Author's purpose, analyzing, 233, 243, 795, 802, 1233,
    1242, 1295, 1302

Autobiography, analyzing, 1295, 1302

Bandwagon appeal, R49

Bias, recognizing, R46

Brainstorming. *See* Brainstorming *under* Writing Skills,
    Modes, and Formats.

Cause and effect, analyzing, 33, 47, 624, 1347, 1354

Cause-and-effect fallacy, R49

Character, responding to, 123, 126, 519, 532, 643, 648, 829,
    945, 952, 999, 1006, 1081, 1207, 1212, 1291, 1367,
    1372. *See also* Motivation.

Chronological relationship, 624

Circular reasoning, R49

Clarifying, 227, 231, 261, 736, 759, 813, 817, 881,
    896, 1175, 1180

Classifying and categorizing
    characters, 131, 143, 849, 995, 1043, 1167, 1207,
        1245, 1274, 1286
    with chart, 382, 387, 390, 535, 539, 540, 546, 550, 605,
        640, 650, 657, 662, 759, 795, 820, 823, 826, 829,
        896, 898, 904, 952, 998, 1007, 1014, 1164, 1260,
        1264, 1268, R52
    with diagram, 920
    with flow chart, 709, R54
    with word web, 1230

Comparing literature to adaptations in other media, 591,
    723, 921

Comparing texts, 59, 74, 97, 119, 126, 143, 243, 254, 330,
    382, 387, 390, 397, 404, 445, 451, 470, 516, 532,
    539, 540, 547–549, 598, 599, 605, 627, 631,
    650–662, 722, 792, 810, 811, 817, 820, 823, 826,
    844, 856, 898, 904, 913, 920, 927, 998, 1007, 1155,
    1172, 1198, 1242, 1264, 1291, 1342. *See also*
    Classifying and categorizing.

Conclusions, drawing, 598, 795, 802, 899, 903, 958, 972,
    1216, 1218, R50

Conflict, analyzing, 583, 633, 640, 1167, 1172, 1274, 1278
Connecting. *See also* Character, responding to.
   to authors' experiences, 1233, 1242
   to history, 18, 104, 164, 346, 422, 488, 566, 688, 774, 873, 937, 1203
   to humanities, 44, 53, 55, 56, 65, 72, 80, 116, 118, 133, 137, 193, 196, 214, 219, 249, 252, 364, 371, 385, 407, 438, 443, 447, 448, 458, 466, 467, 469, 473, 512, 515, 527, 528, 538, 580, 587, 596, 603, 629, 635, 646, 655, 701, 704, 713, 715, 730, 738, 746, 754, 807, 855, 883, 891, 900, 917, 919, 949, 960, 991, 1011, 1111, 1128, 1228
   to modern world, 28–29, 47, 49, 59, 97, 112–113, 145, 174–175, 223, 231, 243, 245, 254, 330, 354–355, 380, 397, 404, 405, 430–431, 439, 445, 459, 468, 470, 471, 496–497, 506, 516, 517, 532, 539, 574–575, 581, 589, 591, 598, 605, 622–623, 627, 631, 648, 649, 694–695, 707, 722, 723, 759, 782–783, 792, 802, 803, 806, 844, 856, 896, 920, 921, 927, 939, 952, 995, 1006, 1043, 1062, 1083, 1148, 1154, 1164, 1172, 1175, 1180, 1186, 1187, 1212, 1218, 1219, 1230, 1242, 1243, 1258, 1268, 1333, 1335, 1342, 1354, 1364, 1372
   to personal experience, 33, 51, 88, 114, 119, 123, 126, 131, 143, 181, 227, 233, 247, 261, 359, 383, 399, 435, 441, 446, 453, 463, 499, 511, 519, 533, 541, 577, 583, 594, 601, 624, 628, 633, 640, 642, 651, 709, 736, 785, 795, 813, 817, 829, 849, 881, 899, 910, 915, 923, 945, 958, 976, 999, 1019, 1109, 1150, 1157, 1167, 1207, 1216, 1221, 1233, 1261, 1263, 1274, 1286, 1291, 1295, 1325, 1337, 1347, 1359, 1367
   to science and technology, 574–575, 782–783, 937, 1096
Connotation, 1183, 1186
Constituent relationship, 624
Contrast, 123, 126, 393, 397
Cooperative learning activities, 74, 75, 86, 97, 119, 143, 231, 243, 255, 330, 380, 387, 390, 404, 439, 445, 459, 470, 507, 516, 517, 532, 539, 546, 550, 581, 589, 598, 605, 627, 631, 640, 648, 657, 662, 707, 722, 759, 792, 802, 803, 810, 811, 817, 823, 844, 856, 896, 903, 913, 920, 927, 952, 972, 995, 1006, 1014, 1043, 1062, 1081, 1154, 1155, 1164, 1172, 1180, 1186, 1212, 1218, 1230, 1242, 1258, 1263, 1264, 1278, 1291, 1302, 1333, 1342, 1354, 1364, 1372
Credibility of information sources, 181. *See also* Bias, recognizing.

Critical response, 47, 59, 74, 86, 119, 126, 143, 223, 330, 380, 387, 390, 397, 439, 445, 451, 459, 470, 506, 516, 532, 581, 627, 631, 640, 648, 657, 662, 707, 722, 759, 802, 810, 817, 823, 826, 844, 856, 896, 903, 1014, 1043, 1062, 1164, 1172, 1180, 1186, 1212, 1218, 1230, 1242, 1258, 1263, 1268, 1302, 1333, 1342, 1354, 1364, 1372
Cross-cultural comparison. *See* Comparing texts; Connecting; Cultural values and characteristics, identifying and comparing.
Cultural conflict, analyzing, 1274, 1278
Cultural values and characteristics, identifying and comparing, 51, 59, 62, 628, 631, 676, 820, 898, 1187, 1278, 1292. *See also* Comparing texts; Connecting.
Deductive argument, R50
Denotation, 1183, 1186
Description, analyzing, 88, 97, 1261, 1263
Details, interpreting, 541, 546, 945, 952
Diagramming. *See* Classifying and categorizing.
Dialect, analyzing, 1286, 1291
Dialogue, analyzing, 245, 255, 881, 896, 1221, 1230
Diary, analyzing, 499, 506
Diction, analyzing, 823, 1157, 1164
Drama, analyzing, 261, 330, 1019, 1043, 1062, 1081
Dramatic irony, analyzing, 261, 330
Either-or fallacy, R49
Evaluating, 181, 223, 435, 439, 1337, 1342
Exposition, analyzing, 829
Extending interpretation. *See* Interpretations, extending.
Fact and opinion, R46
Faulty reasoning, R49
Figurative language, analyzing, 899
Foreshadowing, analyzing, 976, 995, 1081
Generalization, R50. *See also* Overgeneralization.
Goals, setting, 100, 158, 342, 410, 484, 560, 610, 676, 770, 866, 932, 1092, 1198, 1318, 1378
Hierarchical relationship, 624
Historical context, 1221, 1230
Humor, analyzing, 849, 856
Imagery, analyzing, 453, 459, 463, 470, 535, 541, 601, 605, 707, 908
Inductive argument, R50
Inferences, making, 114, 383, 387, 397, 1245, 1325. *See also* Conclusions, drawing; Generalization; Predicting.
Internal conflict, analyzing, 1167, 1172
Interpretations, extending, 47, 59, 74, 143, 231, 330, 380, 390, 397, 539, 589, 598, 605, 627, 648, 651, 707,

722, 759, 792, 802, 817, 826, 844, 856, 896, 913, 927, 952, 972, 995, 1006, 1043, 1062, 1081, 1148, 1154, 1164, 1172, 1180, 1186, 1212, 1218, 1230, 1242, 1258, 1263, 1268, 1278, 1291, 1302, 1333, 1342, 1354, 1364, 1372

Irony, analyzing, 785, 792, 972, 999, 1006, 1092

Judgments, making, 849, 856, 1286, 1291

Legend, analyzing, 628, 631

Loaded language, R49

Main ideas, recognizing, 233, 243, 413, 511, 516, 1157, 1164, R48

Maxim, evaluating, 435, 439

Mood, analyzing, 463, 470, 535, 539, 908, 913, 1180, 1221, 1230

Motivation, analyzing, 1167, 1172, 1274, 1278

Myth, analyzing, 399, 404, 614, 624, 627

Narrator, responding to, 856. *See also* Speaker, analyzing.

Oral reading. *See* Oral reading *under* Speaking and Listening.

Overgeneralization, R49

Parable, analyzing, 511, 516

Paradox, analyzing, 114, 119, 441, 445

Parallelism, analyzing, 577, 581

Paraphrasing, 247, 254, 760, 813, 881, 1183, R46

Persuasion, modes of, R49

Plot, analyzing, 583, 589, 633, 640, 829

Poetry, analyzing, 463, 470, 601, 605, 910, 1150, 1154, 1216. *See also* Strategies for reading.
    lyric, 227, 231
    meter in, 813, 817
    narrative, 915, 920
    reading aloud and, 446, 451, 1359, 1364
    repetition in, 446, 451
    sound devices in, 923, 1150, 1154

Point of view, analyzing, 499, 506, 1198
    first-person, 1109, 1148, 1325, 1333
    omniscient, 1148, 1333
    third-person, 1109, 1148, 1333

Predicting, 359, 380, 633, 640, 785, 792, 976, 995

Problems and solutions, 583, 589

Questioning, 261, 414, 519, 532, 577, 581, 697, 707

Reading aloud, 446, 451, 1359, 1364

Reasoning, faulty, R49

Sacred literature, analyzing, 64, 74, 576–577

Satire, analyzing, 849, 856

Scanning, R47

Sensory language, 707, 908, 923, 927, 1261, 1263. *See also* Imagery, analyzing.

Setting, analyzing, 519, 532, 1062, 1207, 1212

Skimming, 414, R47

Speaker, analyzing, 51, 383, 387, 598, 806, 823, 1216, 1218

Speech, analyzing, 245, 255

Strategies for reading
    didactic literature, 433
    early literature, 31
    epic, 121, 177
    Greek drama, 261, 330
    magical realism, 1345
    modernist literature, 1107
    narrative poetry, 399
    realistic drama, 1019, 1043, 1062, 1081
    realistic literature, 943
    romance, 709, 722
    sacred literature, 64
    sonnet, 805
    standardized tests, 412–414

Style, analyzing, 380, 390, 404, 581, 707, 760, 810, 913, 920, 996, 1081, 1148, 1198, 1212, 1292, 1354, 1359, 1364, 1378

Summarizing, 511, 516, 881

Symbols, analyzing, 1175, 1180, 1347, 1354

Symbols, interpreting, 910, 913, 1347

Synthesizing, 643, 648

Testimonial, R49

Theme, analyzing, 393, 397, 594, 598, 651, 657, 958, 1081, 1245, 1258, 1367, 1372

Title, 1367, 1372

Tone, analyzing, 601, 605, 823, 1216, 1218, 1318, 1337, 1342

Translation, art of, 61, 225, 461, 599, 811, 1063, 1155, 1365

Values, conflicting, 1008

Visualizing, 88, 97, 261, 453, 459, 915, 920, 1019, 1109, 1148

Vocabulary. *See entries under* Vocabulary Skills.

Wisdom literature, analyzing, 511, 516

Word order, 881

Vocabulary Skills

Affix, 340, 864, 1316

Analogies, 507, 761, 768

Antonyms, 127, 331, 803

Appositive, 674

Base word, 864

Building vocabulary, strategies for, 156, 340, 482, 558, 674, 768, 864, 1090, 1196, 1316

Comparison clue, 674

Connotation, 558, 1090

Context clues, 144, 156, 224, 590, 674, 793, 845, 897, 1007, 1149, 1165, 1181, 1213, 1259, 1293, 1316, 1355, 1373

Contrast clue, 674

Definition clue, 674

Denotation, 1090

Dictionary, use of, 156, 340, 558, 1316

Etymology, 340, 558, 1196

Example clue, 674

Homographs, 482

Homonyms, 482, 1088

Homophones, 482

Inference clue, 674

Meaning clues, 244, 255, 381, 533, 1231, 1303

Multiple-meaning word, 156

Prefix, 864

Related words, 641, 953, 1279

Root, 340, 864, 1196

Suffix, 864

Synonyms, 48, 127, 331, 558, 857

Thesaurus, 558

Word family, 1196, 1316

Word part, 340, 1196

Word relationships, 768

Grammar, Usage, and Mechanics

Abbreviation, R85

Accept and *except*, R84

Active voice, 766, 1194, R61, R90

Adjective, R62–R64, R85

Adjective clause, 1197, R71, R81, R85

Adjective phrase, 1197, R88

Adverb, 675, R62–R64, R85
   conjunctive, R65, R86

Adverb clause, 1091, R71, R85

Adverb phrase, 675, R88

Advice and *advise*, R84

Affect and *effect*, R84

Agreement
   pronoun-antecedent, R57, R85
   subject-verb, 672, R74–R76, R81, R85

All ready and *already*, R84

Allusion and *illusion*, R84

Ambiguous pronoun reference, R82, R85

Among and *between*, R84

Antecedent, R58, R85, R88

Apostrophe, R78

Appositive, 674, R69, R85, R88

Article, R85

Bad and *badly*, R63

Between and *among*, R84

Bring and *take*, R84

But and *however*, R24

Capitalization, 557, R79, R83
   of directions, R83
   of first words, R79
   of geographic names, R79
   of organizations and events, R79
   of people and titles, R79
   of planets and heavenly bodies, R83
   of proper adjectives, R79
   of school subjects, R83
   of seasons, R83

Case, R57

Clause
   adjective, 1197, R71, R81, R85
   adverb, 1091, R71, R85
   independent, 1091, R71, R72, R86
   noun, 865, R71, R86
   subordinate, 1091, R71, R72, R86

Colon, R78

Comma, 481, 1314, R77, R81

Comma splice, R73, R86

Comparison

    of adjectives and adverbs, R62–R63

    double, R63, R82

    elliptical, R82

    illogical, R63, R83, R87

Complement, R86. *See also* Direct object; Indirect object;
    Predicate nominative.

Conjunction, R65, R86

Conjunctive adverb, R65, R86

Contraction, R86

Coordinating conjunction, R65, R86

Correlative conjunction, R65, R86

Dangling participle, 157, R70, R80

Dash, R78

Definite article, R85

Direct object, R66, R68, R86, R89

Double comparison, R63, R82

Double negative, 557, R64, R86

Effect and *affect,* R84

Ellipses, R78

End marks, 481, R77, R80, R86

Except and *accept,* R84

Exclamation point, R77

Fewer and *less,* R84

Fragment, 559, R67, R73, R80, R89

Future tense, R60, R90

Gender, R87

Gerund, R70, R87

Good and *well,* R63

Homophones, misspelled, 1088, 1089

However and *but,* R24

Hyphen, R78

Illusion and *allusion,* R84

Imperative mood, R61

Indefinite article, R85

Indefinite pronoun reference, R82, R87

Independent clause, 1091, R71, R72, R86

Indicative mood, R61

Indirect object, R66, R68, R87, R89

Indirect question, R87

Infinitive, R69, R87

    split, R90

Interjection, R65, R87

Italics, R78

Leave and *let,* R84

Less and *fewer,* R84

Lie and *lay,* R84

Loose and *lose,* R84

Modifier, R62–R64, R82–R83, R87

    misplaced, R64, R70, R80, R83, R86

Mood, R61

Noun, R56, R87

    abstract, R56, R87

    collective, R56, R76, R87

    common, R56, R87

    compound, R56, R87

    concrete, R56

    of direct address, R87

    possessive, R56, R87, R88

    predicate, R68, R87

    proper, R56, R87

Noun clause, 865, R71, R86

Number, R87

Object

    direct, R66, R68, R86, R89

    indirect, R66, R68, R87, R89

    of preposition, R87

Parallelism, 157, 483, 577, 581

Parentheses, R78

Participle, 341, R60, R70, R88

    dangling, 157, R70, R80

Parts of speech, R55. *See also names of individual parts*
    of speech.

Passive voice, R61, R90

Past tense, R60, R81, R90

Perfect tenses, R60, R90

Period, R77

Person, R82, R88

Phrase

    adjective, 1197, R88

    adverb, 675, R88

    appositive, R69, R85, R88

    gerund, R70, R88

    infinitive, R69, R88

    participial, R70, R80, R88

    prepositional, R64, R66, R80, R88

Possessive

    noun, R56, R87, R88

    pronoun, R57, R88

Precede and *proceed,* R84

Predicate, R66, R67, R86, R88, R90

Predicate nominative, R68, R76, R88

Preposition, R64, R88
    object of, R87
Prepositional phrase, R64, R66, R80, R88
Present tense, R60, R90
Proceed and *precede,* R84
Progressive verb forms, R60
Pronoun, R57–R59, R81–R82, R88
    agreement with antecedent, R57, R85
    contraction confused with, R82
    demonstrative, R58, R88
    indefinite, R58, R75, R88
    intensive, R57, R88
    interrogative, R58, R88
    personal, R57, R74, R81, R88
    possessive, R57, R88
    predicate, R68, R88
    reference of, R82, R85, R87, R90
    reflexive, R57, R88
    relative, R59, R76, R89
Punctuation, R77, R89. *See also names of individual*
        punctuation marks.
Question mark, R77
Quotation, R89
Quotation mark, R78, R80
Run-on sentence, R73, R80, R89
Semicolon, 481, R77
Sentence, 483, 559, 769, 1317, R66–R76, R89–R90
    complex, 559, R72, R89
    compound, 559, R72, R86, R89
    declarative, R67
    exclamatory, R67
    fragment, 559, R67, R73, R80, R89
    imperative, R67, R68
    independent clause in, 1091, R71, R72, R86
    interrogative, R67
    inverted, R75, R87
    run-on, R73, R80, R89
    simple, R72, R89
    subordinate clause in, 1091, R71, R72, R86
Series, 157
Split infinitive, R90
Subject, R66, R67, R86, R89, R90
    compound, R67, R74
Subject-verb agreement, 672, R74–R76, R81, R85
Subjunctive mood, R61
Subordinate clause, 1091, R71, R72, R86

Subordinating conjunction, R65, R86
Take and *bring,* R84
Tense, R60, R90
    shifts in, R81
Than and *then,* R84
Two, too, and *to,* R84
Unidentified pronoun reference, R90
Us and *we,* R82
Verb, 556, 557, R59–R62, R90.
        See also Gerund; Infinitive; Participle.
    action, R59, R90
    agreement with subject, 672, R74–R76, R81, R85
    auxiliary, R59, R66, R76, R81, R90
    intransitive, R59
    linking, R59, R90
    main, R66, R90
    transitive, R59
Verbal, R69–R70, R90
Verb phrase, R88
Voice, 556, 766, 1194, R61, R90
We and *us,* R82
Well and *good,* R63

Writing Skills, Modes, and Formats

Abbreviations, use of, R48
Active voice, use of, 766, 1194
Analysis, 331, R31, R33. *See also* Definition analysis;
        Parts analysis; Process analysis.
Anecdote, 669, 859, R22
Argument. *See* Persuasive writing.
Audience, identifying, 153, 336, 555, 765, 861, 1087,
        R19, R27, R35, R43
Autobiography, 60, 150–154, 1303
Biography, 641, 1355
Brainstorming, 153, 555, 861, 1087
Business writing, R43–R44
Capitalization, R20
Cause and effect, 1084, 1312, R24, R31, R32
    fallacy of, R36
Characterization, 153, R29
Character sketch, 533, 641
Chronological order, 153, 671, 1308, 1312, R30
Circular reasoning, R36
Clarifying, R35, R37
Coherence, R23

Comparison and contrast, 62, 144, 381, 391, 551, 650, 663, 793, 827, 898, 909, 1015, 1269, 1312, 1334, 1343, R24, R31

Conclusion, 153, 391, 551, 663, 827, 909, 1015, 1086, 1192, 1269, R25

Conflict, 333, 336, R30

Definition analysis, R34

Degree of importance, R24

Descriptive writing, 668–672, R27–R28
autobiographical essay, 1303
biographical article, 641
diary, 331, 857, 1082, 1149, 1334
job assessment, 1279
journal, 1259
letter, 845, 993, 1082, 1334
news story, 973
personality profile, 668–672
personal response, 1165, 1213
reminiscence, 127

Detail, use of, 672, 827, 1269

Dialogue, 153, 335, 337, 669, 897, 1303, R29

Direct address, R23

Documenting sources, 1307, 1309, 1311, 1313, 1314, R37, R40, R41, R42

Drafting, 336, 391, 479, 551, 555, 663, 765, 827, 861, 909, 1015, 1087, 1193, 1269, 1313, R19

Dramatic writing, 332–338
dialogue, 335, 337, 897, 1303
fairy tale theater, 336
monologue, 127
scene, 255, 332–338, 793
stage directions, 334, 335, 336

Editing. See Revising and editing.

Either-or fallacy, R36

Elaboration, R25

Essay questions, answering. See Writing for assessment.

Example, R26

Explanatory writing, 997, R31–R34. See also Research report.
ancient values essay, 224
cause-and-effect essay, 904, 953, 1082–1088
character analysis, 1181, 1213
compare-and-contrast essay, 62, 144, 381, 391, 551, 650, 663, 793, 827, 898, 909, 1015, 1269, 1334, 1343
definition essay, 144, 244, 1165
essay questions, 416–417
guide-for-living comparison, 75

literary analysis, 1149, 1173, 1190–1194, 1259, 1355
research plan, 1231
subject analysis, 762–766
title essay, 1293

Facts and statistics, using, 555, 556, 861, R25, R35, R37

Feature-by-feature organization, R32

Feedback. See Peer response.

Figurative language, R27

Flashback, 153, R30

Focus, maintaining, 154. See also Main idea.

Goal, R27

Hook, 861, R35

Incident, R26

Interview, 381

Introduction, 151, 333, 391, 551, 663, 763, 765, 827, 909, 1015, 1191, 1269, R22–R23, R34

Letter, business, R43

List, 507

Main event, R29

Main idea, R23

Mapping ideas, 1087

Memo, R44

Modern Language Association guidelines, R41, R42

Mood, 336, R27

Narrative writing, R29
adventure, 590
autobiography, 60, 150–154
biography, 641, 1355
children's story, 973
different ending, 1213
epic adventure, 48
epilogue, 1259
folk tale, 997
legend, 533
news article, 1293
pillow book, 507
satire, 857
story of ambition, 897

Note taking, 1311, R38–R39, R48

Order of importance, 671, 1312, R28

Order of impression, R28

Organization, 153, 336, 391, 551, 663, 671, 765, 827, 909, 1015, 1190, 1269, 1306, 1312, 1313, R28, R30, R31, R32, R33, R36, R39, R48

Outline, 765, 1312, 1313, R39, R48

Overgeneralization, R36

Parable, 517

Paragraphs, constructing, 1314, R23

Paraphrasing, 760, 1311, R39, R46

Parts analysis, R34

Peer reader, 153, 338, 556, 671, 765, 862, 1088, 1193, 1313, R21, R33

Persuasive writing, R35
   advice column, 1173
   editorial, 255, 1343
   essay, 590
   Homeric argument, 224
   letter to the editor, 1303
   maxim, 997
   memo, 1231
   problem-solution essay, 552–556, 1181, R31, R33
   speech, 845, 858–862, 953

Plagiarism, 1313, R40, R47

Plot, 153, 460

Poetry
   epic, 144
   lyric, 476–480
   mood poem, 460
   nature poem, 904
   portrait, 1334
   praise poem, 60
   rhythm in, 480

Point-by-point organization, R36

Portfolio, building, 100, 153, 154, 158, 336, 342, 410, 479, 480, 484, 517, 555, 560, 610, 668, 671, 672, 676, 762, 765, 766, 770, 858, 861, 866, 932, 1084, 1088, 1092, 1190, 1193, 1198, 1310, 1314, 1378

Prediction, R25

Prewriting, 153, 336, 479, 555, 671, 765, 1087, 1193, 1310, R18

Problem-solution writing, 552–556, 1181, R31, R33

Process analysis, R33, R34

Prompts, writing, 150, 391, 476, 551, 663, 668, 762, 827, 858, 909, 1015, 1190, 1269, 1306

Proofreading, 154, 417, 480, 556, 672, 766, 1088, 1194, 1314, R19–R20

Publishing, 154, 338, 480, 672, 766, 862, 1068, 1088, 1094, 1314, R20

Punctuation, 480, 481, 1314, R20, R40. *See also* Punctuation *under* Grammar, Usage, and Mechanics.

Purpose, R43

Questions, use of, 1308, 1311, R22, R25, R37

Quotation, 481, 827, R26, R39, R41

Recommendation, R25

Redundancy, avoiding, 766

Research report, 1306–1314, R37–R42

Restatement, R25

Résumé, R44

Revising and editing, 154, 155, 337, 339, 417, 480, 481, 556, 557, 663, 672, 673, 766, 767, 827, 909, 1088, 1089, 1194, 1195, 1314, 1315, R19

Rhythm, 480

Rubrics. *See* Standards for evaluating writing.

Run-on sentences, avoiding, 154

Sensory details, 151, 153, 478, R26, R27

Sentence structure, 865, 1091, 1197, R20
   variety in, 769, 1317

Setting, 153, R29

Signal words, 391, 551, 663

Sound devices, 480

Sources, 1310. *See also* Sources *under* Inquiry and Research.
   CD-ROMs, R38, R42
   databases, R38
   documenting, 1307, 1309, 1311, 1313, 1314, R37, R40, R41, R42
   electronic, R38
   gathering, 1087, R38
   Internet, 1311, R38, R42
   online catalogs, R38
   periodicals, R38
   reference works, R38
   validity of, 1311, R38, R46

Spatial relationships, R24, R28

Specific language, R26

Speech, 845, 858–862, 953

Stage directions, 334, 335, 336

Standards for evaluating writing
   autobiography, 150
   business writing, R43
   cause-and-effect essay, 1084, R32
   description, R27
   dramatic scene, 332
   explanatory writing, R31
   literary interpretation, 1190
   lyric poetry, 476
   narration, R29
   personality profile, 668
   problem-solution essay, 552
   research report, 1306, R37
   speech, 858
   subject analysis, 762

Statistics. *See* Facts and statistics, using.
Subject-by-subject organization, R32
Summarizing, R25, R39, R46
Surprise, R22
Thesis statement, 765, 1191, 1307, 1313, R23, R37
Time or sequence, R24
Topic sentence, R23
Transitions, 1088, 1269, 1308, R24, R28
Translating, 461
Visual aids, 859, 862, R53
Word order, 769
World Wide Web, R38
Writing for assessment, 87, 391, 412–417, 551, 663, 678–683, 827, 909, 1015, 1269
Writing prompts. *See* Prompts, writing.

Inquiry and Research

Almanac, R45
Atlas, R45
Bias, R46
Biographical sources, 761, R45
Catalog, online, R38
CD-ROMs, R38, R42
Databases, R38
Dictionary, R45
Electronic mail, R45
Encyclopedia, R45
Glossary, R45
Historical sources, 761
Humanities Index, R45
Indexes, R45
Internet, 997, R38, R45, R46
MLA International Biography, R45
Note taking, 1311
Periodical index, R45
Periodicals, R45
Plagiarism, avoiding, R47
Primary sources, 997, 1293, 1310
Readers' Guide to Periodical Literature, R45
Reference works, R45
Report and research topics
    apartheid, 1334
    Aristophanes, 255
    Bible, 75
    bibliography, 1149
    Brecht, Bertolt, 1231
    Cairo, 1373
    canine communication, 507
    Ch'ang-an, 460
    character profile, 761
    Chile, 1303
    chivalry, 845
    colonialism, 1259
    communes, 973
    Communist Russia, 1264
    courtly love, 793
    cultural diversity, 1187
    epics in performance, 144
    Faust, 897
    grieving process, 1213
    griot tradition, 641
    Holocaust, 1243
    human flight, 405
    interactive map, 761
    Islamic empires, 590
    Japanese family, 1181
    Joyce, James, 1173
    Lisbon earthquake, 857
    magical realism, 1355
    Mahabharata, 127
    Mahfouz, Naguib, 1373
    Mali, 641
    mental health, 845
    Nigeria, 1279, 1343
    Oedipus complex, 331
    papyrus, 60
    peasant life, 953
    Pericles, 244
    refugees, 471
    revolution, 1343
    Roman culture, 381
    Shakespearean Noh plays, 533
    Sumerians, 48
    Tolstoy, Leo, 973, 997
    Tolstoy, Sonya, 997
    Troy, 224
    Voltaire's world, 857
    women's history, 1082, 1165, 1173
    Wordsworth and Coleridge, 904
    World War I, 1213
    Wu, Empress, 460
    Yoruba religion, 649
    youth movements, 1231

Research report. *See* Research report *under* Writing Skills, Modes, and Formats.

Research starters, 48, 60, 75, 127, 144, 224, 244, 255, 331, 381, 405, 460, 471, 507, 533, 590, 641, 649, 761, 793, 803, 845, 857, 897, 904, 973, 997, 1082, 1083, 1149, 1165, 1173, 1181, 1213, 1231, 1243, 1259, 1264, 1279, 1293, 1303, 1311, 1334, 1355

Secondary sources, 997, 1293, 1310

Social Science Index, R45

Sources, 1293, R45–R47

    bias in, R46

    biographical, 761, R45

    documenting, 1309, 1313

    electronic, 997, R38, R45, R46

    evaluating, 413, R46

    fact and opinion in, R46

    historical, 761

    primary, 997, 1293, 1310

    secondary, 997, 1293, 1310

World Wide Web. *See* Internet.

Yearbook, R45

Speaking and Listening

Active listening, strategies for, R52

Audience, identifying, R50

Debate, 75, 244

Dialogue, 255, 1173, 1181, 1334

Dramatic presentation, 144, 284, 328, 332–338, 973, 997, 1063, 1149. *See also* Performance planning.

Dramatic reading, 127, 460, 761, 1343, 1355

Extemporaneous speech, R51

Eye contact, R51

Facial expression, R51

Film score, 460

Gesture, R51

Group discussion, 49, 145, 517, 591, 921, 1083, 1219, 1243, 1335, 1365

Impromptu speech, R51

Improvisation, 845, 1082, 1231

Interpretation, 338

Interview, 507, 953, 1343, R52

Multimedia presentation, R54

Newscast, 857

Noh performance, 533

Oral reading, 381, 760, 1264

Oration, 233

Panel discussion, 590

Pantomime, 1373

Performance planning, 337–338

Pitch, R51

Poetry, reading aloud, 446, 451

Readers Theater, 1213

Rehearsal. *See* Performance planning.

Role-playing, 331, 1259, 1279

Song, 857

Speaking rate, R51

Speech

    delivery of, 861–862, 1165, R50–R51

    evaluation of, R51

Storytelling, 641, 793

Tone, R51

Trial, mock, 973

Viewing and Representing

Bar graph. *See* Graphs.

Chart, R52, R53

Comparing visual images. *See* Visuals, comparing.

Creative response

    artistic interpretation, 1264, 1279

    Bible storyboard, 75

    caricature, 255

    city plan, 48

    comic book, 144

    diorama, 1355

    editorial cartoon, 1343

    family tree, 1181

    hieroglyphics, 61

    illustration, 48, 224, 507, 590, 793, 904, 1149, 1173, 1213, 1373

    landscape painting, 460, 1259

    movie review, 641

    multimedia display, 1181

    news display, 997

    photo biography, 997

    photo essay, 1165

    portrait, 897, 1334

    poster, 1231, 1303

    pyramid cutaway, 60

    set design, 1082

    storyboard, 381

    theater model, 331

    time line, 1343, 1373

    town banner, 953

Graphic devices. *See* Visuals.

Graphs, R52–R53

Line graph. *See* Graphs.

Multimedia presentation, R54

Photographs, interpreting, R53

Visuals, R52

    comparing, 284, 328, 1042, 1080

    evaluating and interpreting, R53

    on Internet, 997, R54

    using, R53

Assessment

Comparison-and-contrast essay, 87, 391, 551, 663, 827, 909, 1015, 1269

Essay questions, answering, 416–417, 682–683

Grammar and usage, 155, 339, 481, 557, 673, 767, 863, 1089, 1195, 1315

Multiple-choice questions, answering, 415, 681

Portfolio, 100, 158, 342, 410, 484, 560, 610, 676, 770, 866, 932, 1092, 1198, 1318, 1378

Revising and editing, 155, 339, 417, 481, 557, 673, 683, 767, 863, 1195

Self-assessment, 100, 158, 342, 410, 484, 560, 610, 676, 770, 866, 932, 1092, 1198, 1318, 1378

Short-answer questions, answering, 416, 682

Standardized test practice, 87, 155, 339, 382, 391, 412–417, 481, 551, 557, 673, 767, 863, 909, 1015, 1089, 1195, 1315

Test questions, strategies for reading, 412–414, 678–683

Vocabulary, 48, 144, 224, 244, 255, 331, 381, 507, 533, 641, 761, 793, 803, 845, 897, 953, 1006, 1082, 1149, 1165, 1181, 1213, 1231, 1259, 1279, 1293, 1303, 1355, 1373

Writing about literature, 87, 155, 339, 382, 391, 412–417, 481, 551, 557, 673, 767, 863, 909, 1015, 1089, 1195, 1315

Index of Titles and Authors

Page numbers that appear in italics refer to biographical information.

A

Achebe, Chinua, *1270, 1274, 1280, 1286*
Adoration of the Disk, 50
Aeneid, from the, 356
After the Deluge, 1336
Akhenaten, King, 50
Akhmatova, Anna, *1216*
Albatross, The, 922
Alighieri, Dante, *732, 736, 757*
Allende, Isabel, *1294*
All Quiet on the Western Front, about, 1214
All Stories Are Anansi's, 651
Amichai, Yehuda, *1304*
Amnesty, 1324
Analects, from the, 434
Anansi Plays Dead, 651
Andreas Capellanus, 791
And we shall be steeped . . . , 1182
Annals, from the, 406
Apology, from the, 246
Arrow of the Blue-Skinned God, from, 141
Artist, The, 1008
Art of Courtly Love, The, from, 791
As I look at the moon, 534
Autumn Song, 928

B

Bashō. *See* Matsuo Bashō.
Baudelaire, Charles, 922
Better to live, Licinius, . . . , 392
Bhagavad-Gita, about, 128
Birdsong from Inside the Egg, 600
Blank, Jonah, 141
Boccaccio, Giovanni, *784*
Book of Odes, from the, 446
Book of the Dead, from the, 50
Borges, Jorge Luis, 843
Brahman's Dream, The, 146
Brecht, Bertolt, *1220*
Buson. *See* Yosa Buson.

C

Camus, Albert, *1244*
Candide, from, 848
Cervantes, Miguel de, *828*
Chekhov, Anton, *999*
Ch'ing-chao. *See* Li Ch'ing-chao.
Chrétien de Troyes, *708*
Chuang Tzu, 444
Civil Peace, 1286
Confucius, *434*
Counting in Sevens, 1371
Cruz, Juana Inés de la, *824*

D

Dante. *See* Alighieri, Dante.
Darwish, Mahmud, *1265*
Dead Men's Path, 1274
Decameron, from the, 784
Deserted Crone, The, 518
Diameter of the Bomb, The, 1304
Doll's House, A, 1018
Don Quixote, from, 828
Dostoyevsky, Fyodor, *1016*
Dreaming of Li Po, 462

E

End and the Beginning, The, 1336
Epic of Gilgamesh, The, from, 32
Eveline, 1166
Expiation, The, from, 914

F

Faust, from, 880
Federigo's Falcon, 784
Ferdowsi, *592*
First Bard Among the Soninke, The, 628
Fish Rejoice, The, 444
Freedom to Breathe, 1261
Fu. *See* Tu Fu.

G

García Lorca, Federico, *1152*
García Márquez, Gabriel, *1346, 1356*
Gazing at the Lu Mountain Waterfall, 452
Genesis, from, 63
Gilgamesh. See *Epic of Gilgamesh, The*.
Goethe, Johann Wolfgang von, *880, 895*
Gordimer, Nadine, *1324*
Grasmere Journals, from the, 902
Grasses, The, 600
Greek Drama, about, 256
Green Willow, 8
Guest, The, 1244
Guitar, The, 1152
Gulistan, from the, 606

H

Haiku (Japanese), 541
Haiku (Tablada), 547
Haiku (Wright), 547
Half a Day, 1366
Handsomest Drowned Man in the World, The, 1346
Hebrew Bible, from the, 63, 88
Heine, Heinrich, *910*
He Is More Than a Hero, 226
Helen of Troy, 383
History of the Peloponnesian War, from, 232
Homer, *178*
Horace, *392*
How Much Land Does a Man Need?, 958
How the World Was Created from a Drop of Milk, 624
Hugo, Victor, *914*

I

I Am Not One of Those Who Left the Land, 1216
Ibsen, Henrik, *1018*
Iktomi and the Wild Ducks, 658
Iktomi Takes Back a Gift, 658
Iliad, from the, 178
I'm going downstream on Kingswater Canal, 50
Inferno, from the, 736
Interview with Chinua Achebe, from, 1280
In this world, 534
Invitation to the Voyage, 922
Ise, Lady, *534*
Issa. See Kobayashi Issa.
I've gone to him, 534

J

Jade Flower Palace, 462
January First, 1374
Jay, The, 1174
Joyce, James, *1166*

K

Kafka, Franz, *1108*
Kawabata, Yasunari, *1174*
Keeper of the Vigil, 1284
Khayyám. See Omar Khayyám.
Ki Tsurayuki, *534*
Kobayashi Issa, *541, 545*
Komachi. See Ono Komachi.
Komunyakaa, Yusef, 1284
Koran, from the, 576

L

Labé, Louise, *821*
Landscape with the Fall of Icarus, 403
Lao-tzu, *440*
Lay of the Were-Wolf, The, 724
Letter from Leo Tolstoy to N. A. Nekrasov, 974
Letter to His Friends (Goethe), from, 895
Li Ch'ing-chao, *472*
Li Po, *452*
Lorca. See García Lorca, Federico.
Lorelei, The, 910

M

Mahabharata, from the, 122
Mahfouz, Naguib, *1366*
Marie de France, *724*
Márquez. See García Márquez, Gabriel.
Martí, José, *905*
Matsuo Bashō, *541*
Maupassant, Guy de, *944*
Metamorphoses, from, 398
Metamorphosis, 1108
Mistral, Gabriela, *1188*
Molière, *846*
More, Sir Thomas, *794*
Motokiyo. See Zeami Motokiyo.
Moyers, Bill, 1280
Mulberry on the Lowland, 446
Murasaki Shikibu, Lady, *508*
Musō Soseki, *510*
My Heart Leaps Up, 899
Myth, 329

N

Nefertiti, Princess, 50
Neruda, Pablo, *1358*
New Testament, from the, 98
Novels of Fyodor Dostoyevsky, about, 1016

O

Ode to the Lizard, 1358
Ode to the Watermelon, 1358
Oedipus the King, 258
Old Testament, from the, 63, 88
Omar Khayyám, *594*
One Hundred Years of Solitude, about, 1356
Ono Komachi, *534*
On Plum Blossoms, 472
Ovid, *398*
Ozymandias, 467

P

Panchatantra, from the, 146
Panther, The, 1150
Parable of the Prodigal Son, 98
Paula, from, 1294
Paz, Octavio, *1374*
Perceval: The Story of the Grail, from, 708
Pericles' Funeral Oration, 232
Petrarch, Francesco, *806*
Piece of String, A, 944
Pillow Book, The, from, 498
Pirandello, Luigi, *1206*
Plato, *246*
Plays of Molière, about, 846
Plays of Shakespeare, about, 818
Po. *See* Li Po.
Poe, Edgar Allan, *388*
Popol Vuh, from, 76
Praise Songs for Orishas, 642
Prayer to Masks, 1182
Prison Cell, The, 1265
Problem, A, 999
Professions for Women, 1156
Psalm 23, 88
Psalm 104, 88

R

Ramayana, from the, 130
Remarque, Erich Maria, *1214*
Rig Veda, from the, 114
Rilke, Rainer Maria, *1150*
Rimbaud, Arthur, *928*
River-Merchant's Wife: A Letter, The, 452
Ronsard, Pierre de, *808*
Rubáiyát, from the, 594
Rukeyser, Muriel, 329
Rumi, *600*
Russia 1812, 914
Ruth, Book of, 88

S

Sachs, Nelly, 1241
Sadi, *606*
Saigyō, *534*
Sappho, *226*
Second Voyage of Sindbad the Sailor, The, 582
Sei Shōnagon, *498*
Seize the Day, 392
Senghor, Léopold Sédar, *1182*
Shahnameh, about, 592
Shakespeare, William, *812*, 818
Shaman Song, 905
Shelley, Percy Bysshe, 467
Simple Verses, from, 905
Sleeper in the Valley, The, 928
Slow, the Weaver, 146
Soldier of Urbina, A, 843
Solzhenitsyn, Aleksandr, *1261*
Some say thronging cavalry . . ., 226
Song of P'eng-ya, 462
Song of Roland, The, from, 696
Sonnet 3 (Petrarch), 806
Sonnet 23 (Labé), 821
Sonnet 29 (Shakespeare), 812
Sonnet 30 (Shakespeare), 812
Sonnet 64 (Shakespeare), 812
Sonnet 165 (Cruz), 824
Sonya Tolstoy's Diary, from, 993
Sophocles, *258*
Soyinka, Wole, *1336*
Spring of My Life, The, from, 545
Spring rains weaving, 534
Spy, The, 1220
Still Night Thoughts, 452
Sundiata: An Epic of Old Mali, from, 632
Szymborska, Wislawa, *1336*

T

Tablada, José Juan, *547*
Tacitus, 406
Tagore, Rabindranath, *1008*
Tale of Genji, The, about, 508
Tao Te Ching, from the, 440
Teasdale, Sara, *383*
Thousand and One Nights, The, from, 582
Thucydides, *232*
Time, 1188
To Aphrodite of the Flowers, at Knossos, 226
To Helen, 388
To Hélène, 808
Tolstoy, Leo, *954, 958, 974, 976*
Tolstoy, Sonya, 993
Tsurayuki. *See* Ki Tsurayuki.
Tu Fu, *462*
Two Springs, 472

U

Utopia, from, 794
Uvavnuk, *905*

V

Verlaine, Paul, *928*
Virgil, *356*
Vita Nuova, La, from, 757
Voltaire, *848*

W

War, 1206
We Pick Ferns, We Pick Ferns, 446
West African Proverbs, 664
What Men Live By, 976
Whenever I leave you, I go out of breath, 50
When in early summer . . . , 1241
Wiesel, Elie, *1232*
Williams, William Carlos, 403
Woolf, Virginia, *1156*
Wordsworth, Dorothy, 902
Wordsworth, William, *899*
World Is Too Much with Us, The, 899
World Was Silent, The, from, 1232
Wright, Judith, 1371
Wright, Richard, *547*

Y

Yosa Buson, *541*

Z

Zeami Motokiyo, *518*
Zen Teachings and Parables, 512

Acknowledgments *(continued)*

Simon & Schuster: Excerpts from *Popol Vuh: The Mayan Book of the Dawn of Life,* translated by Dennis Tedlock. Copyright © 1985, 1996 by Dennis Tedlock. Reprinted with the permission of Simon & Schuster.

Excerpt from the Gospel According to Luke, from *The Bible, Designed to Be Read as Living Literature,* edited by Ernest Sutherland Bates. Copyright © 1936 by Simon & Schuster. Copyright renewed © 1965 by Simon & Schuster. Reprinted with the permission of Simon & Schuster.

Jewish Publication Society: The Book of Ruth, from *Tanakh, the Holy Scriptures: The New JPS Translation According to the Traditional Hebrew Text.* Copyright © 1985 by the Jewish Publication Society. Reprinted by permission of the Jewish Publication Society.

University of Chicago Press: Excerpt from "Arjuna, the Mighty Archer," from *The Mahabharata,* translated by J. A. B. van Buitenen. Copyright © 1973 by the University of Chicago. Reprinted by permission of the University of Chicago Press.

"Slow, the Weaver" and "The Brahman's Dream," from *The Panchatantra,* translated by Arthur W. Ryder. Copyright © 1925 by the University of Chicago, renewed © 1953 by Mary E. Ryder and Winifred Ryder. Reprinted by permission of the University of Chicago Press.

Bantam Books: Excerpts from *The Bhagavad-Gita,* translated by Barbara Stoler Miller. Copyright © 1986 by Barbara Stoler Miller. Reprinted by permission of Bantam Books, a division of Random House, Inc.

Viking Penguin: "Rama and Ravana in Battle," from *The Ramayana* by R. K. Narayan. Copyright © 1972 by R. K. Narayan. Used by permission of Viking Penguin, a division of Penguin Putnam Inc.

Houghton Mifflin: Excerpts from *Arrow of the Blue-Skinned God: Retracing the Ramayana Through India* by Jonah Blank. Copyright © 1992 by Jonah Blank. Reprinted by permission of Houghton Mifflin Company. All rights reserved.

Emily Craighead: "I'm Gonna Wash That Dye Right Outta My Hair" by Emily Craighead, from *Best Illinois Student Poetry and Prose, 1996 (Illinois English Bulletin* 84.1 [Fall 1997]). Copyright © 1996 by Emily Craighead. Reprinted by permission of the author.

Unit Two

Houghton Mifflin: Excerpt from entry s.v. "hero" in *The American Heritage Dictionary of the English Language,* fourth edition. Copyright © 2000 by Houghton Mifflin Company. Reprinted by permission of Houghton Mifflin Company.

Viking Penguin: Excerpts from the *Iliad* by Homer, translated by Robert Fagles. Copyright © 1990 by Robert Fagles. Used by permission of Viking Penguin, a division of Penguin Putnam Inc.

Oedipus the King, from *The Three Theban Plays* by Sophocles, translated by Robert Fagles. Copyright © 1982 by Robert Fagles. Used by permission of Viking Penguin, a division of Penguin Putnam Inc.

Farrar, Straus and Giroux: "Some say thronging cavalry . . ." by Sappho, from *Sappho, a Garland: The Poems and Fragments of Sappho,* translated by Jim Powell. Copyright © 1993 by Jim Powell. Reprinted by permission of Farrar, Straus and Giroux, LLC.

University of California Press: "He Is More Than a Hero" by Sappho, from *Sappho: A New Translation* by Mary Barnard. Copyright © 1958 by The Regents of the University of California, renewed © 1986 by Mary Barnard. Reprinted by permission of the Regents of the University of California and the University of California Press.

Schocken Books: "To Aphrodite of the Flowers, at Knossos" by Sappho, from *Sappho and the Greek Lyric Poets,* translated by Willis Barnstone. Copyright © 1962, 1967, 1988 by Willis Barnstone. Used by permission of Schocken Books, a division of Random House, Inc.

Penguin Books: "Pericles' Funeral Oration," from *History of the Peloponnesian War* by Thucydides, translated by Rex Warner (Penguin Classics, 1954). Copyright © 1954 by Rex Warner. Reproduced by permission of Penguin Books Ltd.

Excerpt from *The Annals of Imperial Rome* by Tacitus, translated by Michael Grant (Penguin Classics, 1956; sixth revised edition, 1989). Copyright © 1956, 1959, 1971, 1973, 1977, 1989, 1996 by Michael Grant Publications, Ltd. Reproduced by permission of Penguin Books Ltd.

Princeton University Press: Excerpt from the *Apology* by Plato, translated by Hugh Tredennick, from *The Collected Dialogues of Plato*, edited by Edith Hamilton and Huntington Cairns. Copyright © 1961 by Princeton University Press. Reprinted by permission of Princeton University Press.

ICM: "Myth" by Muriel Rukeyser, from *The Collected Poems of Muriel Rukeyser*. Copyright © 1978 by Muriel Rukeyser. Reprinted by permission of International Creative Management, Inc.

Random House: Excerpts from the *Aeneid* by Virgil, translated by Robert Fitzgerald. Copyright © 1981, 1982, 1983 by Robert Fitzgerald. Reprinted by permission of Random House, Inc.

Scribner: "Helen of Troy" by Sara Teasdale, from *The Collected Poems of Sara Teasdale*. Copyright © 1937 by The Macmillan Company. Reprinted with the permission of Scribner, a division of Simon & Schuster.

University of Michigan Press: "Seize the Day" by Horace, from *Horace's Odes and Epodes*, translated by David Mulroy (Ann Arbor: University of Michigan Press, 1994). Copyright © 1994 by the University of Michigan Press. Reprinted by permission of the University of Michigan Press.

University of Chicago Press: "Better to live, Licinius, . . ." by Horace, from *The Odes and Epodes of Horace*, translated by Joseph P. Clancy. Copyright © 1960 by the University of Chicago Press. Reprinted by permission of the University of Chicago Press.

Indiana University Press: Excerpt from *Metamorphoses* by Ovid, translated by Rolfe Humphries. Copyright © 1955 by Indiana University Press. Reprinted by permission of Indiana University Press.

New Directions: "Landscape with the Fall of Icarus," from *Collected Poems 1939–1962*, Volume II, by William Carlos Williams. Copyright © 1953 by William Carlos Williams. Reprinted by permission of New Directions Publishing Corp.

Sarah Delaney: "Ancient Greece Revived in Rome; Colosseum Reopens as Theater with Staging of *Oedipus Rex*" by Sarah Delaney, from the *Washington Post*, July 20, 2000. Copyright © 2000 by Sarah Delaney. Reprinted by permission of the author.

Unit Three

W. W. Norton & Company: Excerpts from *The Analects of Confucius*, translated by Simon Leys. Copyright © 1997 by Pierre Ryckmans. Reprinted by permission of W. W. Norton & Company, Inc.

HarperCollins Publishers: Chapters 37, 44, and 68 from *Tao Te Ching: A New English Version with Foreword and Notes* by Stephen Mitchell. Translation copyright © 1988 by Stephen Mitchell. Reprinted by permission of HarperCollins Publishers, Inc.

Four haiku by Yosa Buson and four haiku by Kobayashi Issa, from *The Essential Haiku: Versions of Bashō, Buson, and Issa*, edited and with an introduction by Robert Hass. Copyright © 1994 by Robert Hass. Translations copyright © 1994 by Robert Hass. Reprinted by permission of HarperCollins Publishers, Inc.

Pantheon Books: "The Fish Rejoice" by Chuang Tzu, from *Chinese Fairy Tales and Fantasies*, translated and edited by Moss Roberts. Copyright © 1979 by Moss Roberts. Used by permission of Pantheon Books, a division of Random House, Inc.

Grove/Atlantic: "Mulberry on the Lowland," from *The Book of Songs*, translated by Arthur Waley. Copyright © 1937 by Arthur Waley. Used by permission of Grove/Atlantic, Inc.

Columbia University Press: "We Pick Ferns, We Pick Ferns," from the *Book of Odes*, and "Dreaming of Li Po" and "Song of P'eng-ya" by Tu Fu, from *The Columbia Book of Chinese Poetry*, translated and edited by Burton Watson. Copyright © 1984 by Columbia University Press. Reprinted by permission of the publisher.

"Still Night Thoughts" by Li Po, translated by Burton Watson, from *The Columbia Anthology of Traditional Chinese Literature,* edited by Victor H. Mair. Copyright © 1994 by Columbia University Press. Reprinted by permission of the publisher.

Excerpts from *The Pillow Book of Sei Shōnagon,* translated and edited by Ivan Morris. Copyright © 1967 by Ivan Morris. Reprinted by permission of Columbia University Press.

"The Deserted Crone" by Zeami Motokiyo, translated by Stanleigh H. Jones, Jr., from *Twenty Plays of the Nō Theatre,* edited by Donald Keene. Copyright © 1970 by Columbia University Press. Reprinted by permission of the publisher.

New Directions Publishing Corp.: "The River-Merchant's Wife: A Letter" by Li Po, translated by Ezra Pound, from *Personae: The Collected Shorter Poems of Ezra Pound.* Copyright © 1926 by Ezra Pound. Reprinted by permission of New Directions Publishing Corp.

"Gazing at the Lu Mountain Waterfall" by Li Po, from *The Selected Poems of Li Po,* translated by David Hinton. Copyright © 1996 by David Hinton. Reprinted by permission of New Directions Publishing Corp.

"Jade Flower Palace" by Tu Fu, from *One Hundred Poems from the Chinese,* translated by Kenneth Rexroth. Copyright © 1971 by Kenneth Rexroth. Reprinted by permission of New Directions Publishing Corp.

"Two Springs" and "On Plum Blossoms" by Li Ch'ing Chao, from *Li Ch'ing-Chao: Complete Poems,* translated by Kenneth Rexroth. Copyright © 1979 by Kenneth Rexroth and Ling Chung. Reprinted by permission of New Directions Publishing Corp.

Hanging Loose Press: "Harlemite Easter" by Shakira Hightower, from *Bullseye: Stories and Poems by Outstanding High School Writers.* Copyright © 1995 by Hanging Loose Press. Reprinted by permission of Hanging Loose Press.

"Revolution" by Susan Gray, from *Bullseye: Stories and Poems by Outstanding High School Writers.* Copyright © 1995 by Hanging Loose Press. Reprinted by permission of Hanging Loose Press.

Michael Brinker: "Yellow" by Michael Brinker, from *Virginia Writing* 9.2 (June 1995). Copyright © 1995 by Michael Brinker. Reprinted by permission of the author.

Shambhala Publications: "Aim in Life," "Contamination of Virtue," and "Hypocritical Scholars," from *Dream Conversations on Buddhism and Zen* by Musō Kokushi (Musō Soseki), translated by Thomas Cleary. Copyright © 1994 by Thomas Cleary. Reprinted by arrangement with Shambhala Publications, Inc., Boston (www.shambhala.com).

Four haiku by Matsuo Bashō, from *The Essential Bashō,* translated by Sam Hamill. Copyright © 1998 by Sam Hamill. Reprinted by arrangement with Shambhala Publications, Inc., Boston (www.shambhala.com).

Charles E. Tuttle: "Publishing the Sutras" and "Right & Wrong," translated by Nyogen Senzaki and Paul Reps, from *Zen Flesh, Zen Bones: A Collection of Zen and Pre-Zen Writings,* compiled by Paul Reps. Copyright in Japan © 1957 by Charles E. Tuttle Co., Inc. Reprinted by permission of Charles E. Tuttle Co., Inc., of Boston, Massachusetts, and Tokyo, Japan.

Doubleday: Tanka by Ono Komachi, Lady Ise, Ki Tsurayuki, and Saigyō, translated by Burton Watson, and excerpt from *The Spring of My Life* by Kobayashi Issa, translated by Hiroaki Sato, from *From the Country of Eight Islands: An Anthology of Japanese Poetry,* edited and translated by Hiroaki Sato and Burton Watson. Copyright © 1981 by Hiroaki Sato and Burton Watson. Used by permission of Doubleday, a division of Random House, Inc.

Dutton: "Dry Leaves" and "Flying Fish" by José Juan Tablada, translated by W. S. Merwin, from *New Poetry of Mexico* by Octavio Paz and Mark Strand. Copyright © 1970 by E. P. Dutton & Co., Inc. Copyright © 1966 by Siglo XXI Editores, S.A. Used by permission of Dutton, a division of Penguin Putnam Inc.

Arcade Publishing: Three haiku from *Haiku: This Other World* by Richard Wright. Copyright © 1998 by Ellen Wright. Reprinted by permission of Arcade Publishing, New York, New York.

Unit Four

Penguin Books: Excerpts from *The Koran*, translated by N. J. Dawood (Penguin Classics, 1956; fifth revised edition, 1990). Copyright © 1956, 1959, 1966, 1968, 1974, 1990, 1995 by N. J. Dawood. Reprinted by permission of Penguin Books Ltd.

"The Second Voyage of Sindbad the Sailor," from *Tales from the Thousand and One Nights,* translated by N. J. Dawood (Penguin Classics, 1954; revised edition, 1973). Copyright © 1954, 1973 by N. J. Dawood. Reprinted by permission of Penguin Books Ltd.

Coleman Barks: "Birdsong from Inside the Egg" and "The Grasses" by Rumi, from *The Essential Rumi,* translated by Coleman Barks. Copyright © 1995 by Coleman Barks. Reprinted by permission of Coleman Barks.

Reed Educational & Professional Publishing: "How the World Was Created from a Drop of Milk," from *The Origin of Life and Death: African Creation Myths,* edited by Ulli Beier. Copyright © 1966 by Heinemann Educational Books Ltd. and Ulli Beier. Reprinted by permission of Reed Educational & Professional Publishing Ltd.

The Emma Courlander Trust: "The First Bard Among the Soninke," retold by Ousmane Sako and Harold Courlander, from *The Crest and the Hide and Other African Stories of Heroes, Chiefs, Bards, Hunters, Sorcerers and Common People* by Harold Courlander. Copyright © 1982 by Harold Courlander. Reprinted by permission of The Emma Courlander Trust.

"All Stories Are Anansi's" and "Anansi Plays Dead," from *The Hat-Shaking Dance and Other Tales from the Gold Coast* by Harold Courlander. Copyright © 1957 by Harold Courlander. Reprinted by permission of The Emma Courlander Trust.

Pearson Education: Excerpt from *Sundiata: An Epic of Old Mali* by D. T. Niane, translated by G. D. Pickett. Copyright © 1965 by Longman Group Limited. Reprinted by permission of Pearson Education Limited.

Viking Penguin: "Iktomi and the Wild Ducks" and "Iktomi Takes Back a Gift," from *American Indian Trickster Tales* by Richard Erdoes and Alfonso Ortiz. Copyright © 1998 by Richard Erdoes & the Estate of Alfonso Ortiz. Used by permission of Viking Penguin, a division of Penguin Putnam, Inc.

Hippocrene Books: Excerpts from *African Proverbs* by Gerd de Ley. Copyright © 1999 by Hippocrene Books, Inc. Reprinted by permission of Hippocrene Books.

The Free Press: Excerpts from "Edison's Curse," from *Sleep Thieves: An Eye-Opening Exploration into the Science and Mysteries of Sleep* by Stanley Coren. Copyright © 1996 by Stanley Coren. Reprinted and edited with the permission of The Free Press, a division of Simon & Schuster, Inc.

Unit Five

W. W. Norton & Company: Excerpts from *The Song of Roland,* translated by Frederick Goldin. Copyright © 1978 by W. W. Norton & Company, Inc. Reprinted by permission of W. W. Norton & Company, Inc.

Excerpt from the *Decameron* by Giovanni Boccaccio, translated by Mark Musa and Peter Bondanella. Copyright © 1982 by Mark Musa and Peter Bondanella. Used by permission of W. W. Norton & Company, Inc.

Boydell & Brewer: Excerpt from *Perceval: The Story of the Grail* by Chrétien de Troyes, translated by Nigel Bryant. Translation copyright © 1982 by Nigel Bryant. Reprinted by permission of Boydell & Brewer Ltd.

Farrar, Straus and Giroux: Excerpts from *The Inferno of Dante: A New Verse Translation* by Robert Pinsky. Translation copyright © 1994 by Robert Pinsky. Reprinted by permission of Farrar, Straus and Giroux, LLC.

Indiana University Press: Excerpts from *Dante's Vita Nuova,* translated by Mark Musa. Copyright © 1973 by Indiana University Press. Reprinted by permission by of Indiana University Press.

Columbia University Press: Excerpt from *The Art of Courtly Love* by Andreas Capellanus, translated by John Jay Parry. Copyright © 1941 by Columbia University Press. Reprinted by permission of the publisher.

Yale University Press: Excerpts from *Utopia* by St. Thomas More, edited by Edward Surtz, S.J. Copyright © 1964 by Yale University. Reprinted by permission of Yale University Press.

Oxford University Press: Excerpt from "Sonnet 3" by Francesco Petrarch, from *Selections from the Canzoniere and Other Works,* translated by Mark Musa (Oxford World's Classics, 1999). Translation copyright © 1985 by Mark Musa. Reprinted by permission of Oxford University Press.

Schocken Books: "Sonnet 23" by Louise Labé, translated by Willis Barnstone, from *A Book of Women Poets from Antiquity to Now,* edited by Aliki Barnstone and Willis Barnstone. Copyright © 1980 by Schocken Books. Used by permission of Schocken Books, a division of Random House, Inc.

Fondo de Cultura Económica: "Sonnet 165" by Sor Juana Inés de la Cruz, from *Obras Completas de Sor Juana Inés de la Cruz,* edited by Alfonso Méndez Plancarte. Copyright © by Fondo de Cultura Económica. Reprinted by permission of Fondo de Cultura Económica.

Viking Penguin: Excerpts from *Don Quixote* by Miguel de Cervantes Saavedra, translated by Samuel Putnam. Copyright © 1949 by The Viking Press, Inc. Used by permission of Viking Penguin, a division of Penguin Putnam Inc.

Alastair Reid: "A Soldier of Urbina," translated by Alastair Reed, from *Selected Poems* by Jorge Luis Borges. Translation copyright © 1999 by Alastair Reid. Reprinted by permission of Alastair Reid.

Random House: Excerpt from *Candide* by Voltaire, translated by Richard Aldington. Copyright © 1928 by Random House, Inc. Used by permission of Random House, Inc.

Unit Six

Doubleday: Excerpts from *Goethe's Faust,* translated by Walter Kaufmann. Copyright © 1961 by Walter Kaufmann. Used by permission of Doubleday, a division of Random House, Inc.

New Directions Publishing Corp.: Excerpt from letter of March 1, 1788, by Johann Wolfgang von Goethe, translated by Berthold Biermann, from *Goethe's World as Seen in Letters and Memoirs,* edited by Berthold Biermann. Copyright © 1949 by New Directions. Reprinted by permission of New Directions Publishing Corp.

Penguin Books: Excerpt from *The Grasmere Journal* by Dorothy Wordsworth (Michael Joseph, 1987). Text copyright © 1987 by the Wordsworth Trust. Reprinted by permission of Penguin Books Ltd.

Arte Público Press: "I know of Egypt and Niger," from *Versos Sencillos/Simple Verses* by José Martí, translated by Manuel A. Tellechea (Houston: Arte Público Press—University of Houston, 1997). Copyright © 1997 by Arte Público Press. Translation copyright © 1997 by Manuel A. Tellechea. Reprinted with permission from the publisher.

HarperCollins Publishers: "Shaman Song" by Uvuvnuk, translated by Jane Hirshfield, from *Women in Praise of the Sacred,* edited by Jane Hirshfield. Copyright © 1994 by Jane Hirshfield. Reprinted by permission of HarperCollins Publishers, Inc.

Kensington Publishing: "The Lorelei" by Heinrich Heine, from *The Poetry and Prose of Heinrich Heine,* translated by Aaron Kramer. Copyright © 1948 by the Citadel Press. Reprinted by permission of Citadel Press/Kensington Publishing Corp. (www.kensingtonbooks.com). All rights reserved.

Farrar, Straus and Giroux: "Russia 1812" by Victor Hugo, translated by Robert Lowell, from *Imitations.* Copyright © 1959 by Robert Lowell. Copyright renewed © 1987 by Harriet, Sheridan, and Caroline Lowell. Reprinted by permission of Farrar, Straus and Giroux, LLC.

Harcourt: "L'Invitation au Voyage" ("Invitation to the Voyage") by Charles Baudelaire, translated by Richard Wilbur, from *Things of This World.* Copyright © 1956 and renewed 1984 by Richard Wilbur. Reprinted by permission of Harcourt, Inc.

Oxford University Press: "The Albatross," from *The Flowers of Evil* by Charles Baudelaire, translated and annotated by James McGowan, with an introduction by Jonathan Culler (Oxford World's Classics, 1998). Translation copyright © 1993 by James McGowan. Reprinted by permission of Oxford University Press.

Louis Simpson: "Autumn Song" by Paul Verlaine, translated by Louis Simpson. Copyright © 1988 by Louis Simpson. Reprinted by permission of the author.

Dutton Signet: *A Doll's House* by Henrik Ibsen, from *Henrik Ibsen: The Complete Major Prose Plays,* translated by Rolf Fjelde. Copyright © 1965, 1970, 1978 by Rolf Fjelde. Used by permission of Dutton Signet, a division of Penguin Putnam Inc.

Unit Seven

Schocken Books: "Metamorphosis" by Franz Kafka, translated by Willa and Edwin Muir, from *Franz Kafka: The Complete Stories,* edited by Nahum N. Glatzer. Copyright © 1946, 1947, 1948, 1949, 1954, 1958, 1971 by Schocken Books. Used by permission of Schocken Books, a division of Random House, Inc.

Random House: "The Panther" by Rainer Maria Rilke, from *The Selected Poetry of Rainer Maria Rilke,* translated by Stephen Mitchell. Copyright © 1982 by Stephen Mitchell. Used by permission of Random House, Inc.

"After the Deluge," from *Mandela's Earth and Other Poems* by Wole Soyinka. Copyright © 1988 by Wole Soyinka. Used by permission of Random House, Inc.

Robert Bly: "The Guitar" by Federico García Lorca, from *Lorca and Jiménez: Selected Poems,* translated by Robert Bly (Boston: Beacon Press, 1973, 1997). Copyright © 1997 by Robert Bly. Reprinted by permission of Robert Bly.

"Ode to the Watermelon" by Pablo Neruda, translated by Robert Bly, from *Neruda and Vallejo: Selected Poems,* edited by Robert Bly. Copyright © 1971 by Robert Bly. Reprinted by permission of Robert Bly.

HarperCollins Publishers: Excerpt from "The Panther" by Rainer Maria Rilke, from *Selected Poems of Rainer Maria Rilke,* translated by Robert Bly. Copyright © 1981 by Robert Bly. Reprinted by permission of HarperCollins Publishers, Inc.

Excerpt from *Paula* by Isabel Allende, translated by Margaret Sayers Peden. Copyright © 1994 by Isabel Allende. Translation copyright © 1995 by HarperCollins Publishers, Inc. Reprinted by permission of HarperCollins Publishers, Inc.

"The Handsomest Drowned Man in the World," from *Leaf Storm and Other Stories* by Gabriel García Márquez, translated by Gregory Rabassa. Copyright © 1971 by Gabriel García Márquez. Reprinted by permission of HarperCollins Publishers, Inc.

Harcourt: "Professions for Women," from *The Death of the Moth and Other Essays* by Virginia Woolf. Copyright © 1942 by Harcourt, Inc., and renewed 1970 by Marjorie T. Parsons, Executrix. Reprinted by permission of the publisher.

"The End and the Beginning," from *View with a Grain of Sand* by Wislawa Szymborska, translated by Stanislaw Baranczak and Clare Cavanagh. Copyright © 1993 by Wislawa Szymborska. English translation copyright © 1995 by Harcourt, Inc. Reprinted by permission of the publisher.

Viking Penguin: "Eveline," from *Dubliners* by James Joyce. Copyright © 1916 by B. W. Huebsch. Definitive text copyright © 1967 by the Estate of James Joyce. Used by permission of Viking Penguin, a division of Penguin Putnam Inc.

North Point Press: "The Jay," translated by Lane Dunlop, from *Palm-of-the-Hand Stories* by Yasunari Kawabata, translated by Lane Dunlop and J. Martin Holman. Translations copyright © 1988 by Lane Dunlop and J. Martin Holman. Reprinted by permission of North Point Press, a division of Farrar, Straus and Giroux, LLC.

Penguin Books: "Prayer to Masks" by Léopold Sédar Senghor, from *The Penguin Book of Modern African Poetry,* edited by Gerald Moore and Ulli Beier (Penguin Books, 1963; third edition, 1984). Copyright © 1963, 1968, 1984 by Gerald Moore and Ulli Beier. Reprinted by permission of Penguin Books Ltd.

Joan Daves Agency/Writers House: "Time" by Gabriela Mistral, from *Selected Poems of Gabriela Mistral,* translated by Doris Dana (Baltimore: Johns Hopkins University Press, 1971). Copyright © 1961, 1964, 1970, 1971 by Doris Dana. Reprinted with the permission of Joan Daves Agency/Writer's House, Inc., New York, on behalf of the proprietors.

The Pirandello Estate and Toby Cole: "War," translated by Samuel Putnam, from *The Medals and Other Stories* by Luigi Pirandello. Copyright © 1939 by E. P. Dutton & Company. Reprinted by permission of the Pirandello Estate and Toby Cole, Agent.

Arcade Publishing: "The Spy," translated by John Willett, excerpt from the original work *Furcht und Elend des Dritten Reiches (Fear and Misery of the Third Reich)* by Bertolt Brecht. Copyright © 1957 by Suhrkamp Verlag, Frankfurt am Main. Translation copyright © 1983 by Stefan S. Brecht. Reprinted with permission of Arcade Publishing, New York, N.Y.

Farrar, Straus and Giroux: "When in early summer . . . ," translated by Ruth and Matthew Mead, from *The Seeker and Other Poems* by Nelly Sachs, translated by Ruth and Matthew Mead and Michael Hamburger. Translation copyright © 1970 by Farrar, Straus & Giroux, Inc. Reprinted by permission of Farrar, Straus and Giroux, LLC.

"Freedom to Breathe," from *Stories and Prose Poems* by Alexander Solzhenitsyn, translated by Michael Glenny. Translation copyright © 1971 by Michael Glenny. Reprinted by permission of Farrar, Straus and Giroux, LLC.

"January First" by Octavio Paz, from *The Complete Poems: 1927-1979* by Elizabeth Bishop. Copyright © 1979, 1983 by Alice Helen Methfessel. Reprinted by permission of Farrar, Straus and Giroux, LLC.

Alfred A. Knopf: "The Guest," from *Exile and the Kingdom* by Albert Camus, translated by Justin O'Brien. Copyright © 1957, 1958 by Alfred A. Knopf, a division of Random House, Inc. Used by permission of Alfred A. Knopf, a division of Random House, Inc.

Ben Bennani: "The Prison Cell" by Mahmud Darwish, translated by Ben Bennani. Copyright © 1992 by Ben Bennani. Reprinted by permission of Ben Bennani.

Doubleday: Excerpt from interview with Chinua Achebe, from *Bill Moyers: A World of Ideas* by Bill Moyers. Copyright © 1989 by Public Affairs Television, Inc. Used by permission of Doubleday, a division of Random House, Inc.

"Half a Day," from *The Time and the Place and Other Stories* by Naguib Mahfouz, translated by Denys Johnson-Davies. Copyright © 1991 by the American University in Cairo Press. Used by permission of Doubleday, a division of Random House, Inc.

Wesleyan University Press: "Keeper of the Vigil," from *Pleasure Dome* by Yusef Komunyakaa. Copyright © 2001 by Yusef Komunyakaa. Reprinted by permission of Wesleyan University Press.

University of California Press: "The Diameter of the Bomb" by Yehuda Amichai, from *The Selected Poetry of Yehuda Amichai*, translated by Chana Bloch and Stephen Mitchell. Copyright © 1996 by The Regents of the University of California. Reprinted by permission of the Regents of the University of California and the University of California Press and Hana Amichai.

"Ode to the Lizard" by Pablo Neruda, from *Selected Odes of Pablo Neruda*, translated by Margaret Sayers Peden. Copyright © 1990 by The Regents of the University of California, © Fundación Pablo Neruda. Reprinted by permission of the Regents of the University of California and the University of California Press.

Farrar, Straus and Giroux and Penguin Books Canada: "Amnesty," from *Jump and Other Stories* by Nadine Gordimer. Copyright © 1991 by Felix Licensing, B.V. Reprinted by permission of Farrar, Straus and Giroux, LLC, and Penguin Books Canada Limited.

Tom Thompson: "Counting in Sevens," from *A Human Pattern: Selected Poems* by Judith Wright (Sydney: ETT Imprint, 1996). Copyright © 1996 by Tom Thompson. Reprinted by permission of Tom Thompson.

The editors have made every effort to trace the ownership of all copyrighted material found in this book and to make full acknowledgment for its use. Omissions brought to our attention will be corrected in a subsequent edition.

Art Credits

Mary Evans Picture Library; *right* Israel Antiquities Authority; **26** *left* Copyright © PhotoDisc/Getty Images; *right* Detail of the stele of the Law Code of Hammurabi (c. 1792–1750 B.C.). Diorite. Musée du Louvre, Paris. Photograph by Hervé Lewandowski. Réunion des Musées Nationaux/Art Resource, New York; **27** Robert Harding Picture Library; **28** *top right* Copyright © Nathan Benn/Corbis; *bottom left* Copyright © Spencer Grant/Stock Boston/PictureQuest; **28–29** Copyright © Herbert Hartmann/The Image Bank; **29** *top right* Copyright © Michael St. Maur Sheil/Corbis; *bottom right* Copyright © Michael Newman/PhotoEdit; **30** Detail of *Moses Receiving the Ten Commandments* (16th century), Raphael. Vatican City, Vatican State. Photograph copyright © David Lees/Corbis; **31** Copyright © Photofest; **32** Detail of statue of a hero, possibly Gilgamesh, taming a lion (722–705 B.C.). Musée du Louvre, Paris. Photograph copyright © Erich Lessing/Art Resource, New York; **33** Copyright © G. Tortoli/Ancient Art & Architecture Collection; **44** Statue of a hero, possibly Gilgamesh, taming a lion (722–705 B.C.). Musée du Louvre, Paris. Photograph copyright © Erich Lessing/Art Resource, New York; **76** *top* Copyright © Craig Aurness/Corbis; *bottom* Detail of *The Creation of Man*, Diego Rivera. Page from *Popol Vuh*, watercolor on paper. Copyright © 2001 Banco de México Diego Rivera & Frida Kahlo Museums Trust. Av. Cinco de Mayo No. 2, Col. Centro, Del. Cuauhtémoc 06059, México, D.F./The Bridgeman Art Library; **78** Copyright © Craig Aurness/Corbis; **80** Detail of the Bonampak fresco cycle. Photograph copyright © Doug Stern/NGS Image Collection; **81** Copyright © Craig Aurness/Corbis; **88** The Granger Collection, New York; **100** Detail of the building of the Ark (Gen. 6:13–17), the Flood (Gen. 8:6–11), leaving the Ark (Gen. 8:18–19), the sacrifice of Noah (Gen. 8:20–9:15) (c. 1250 A.D.). The Pierpont Morgan Library/Art Resource, New York. **101** *left* From *Conversations with Mummies* by Rosalie David and Rick Archbold. Cover copyright © 2000 The Madison Press Limited, a division of HarperCollins, Inc.; *right* From *The Illustrated Hebrew Bible* by Ellen Frankel. Copyright © 1999 Stewart Tabori & Chang, a division of U.S. Media Holdings, Inc.; **102** *top* Sculpture from the Horse Court of the Temple of Vishnu at Srirangam. Photograph by Wim Swaan. Library, Getty Research Institute, Los Angeles. Wim Swaan Photograph Collection (96.P.21); *bottom, left to right* Copyright © Dinodia Picture Agency; Copyright © John and Lisa Merrill/Stone; Copyright © Will Curtis/Stone Images; **102–103** *bottom* Copyright © Robert Frerck/Odyssey/Chicago; **103** *top* Copyright © Alison Wright/Corbis; **104** *top* The Aryan god of war, Indra, seated on an elephant (c. 1825). Victoria & Albert Museum, London/Art Resource, New York; *bottom* Mohenjo-Daro seal. Karachi Museum, Pakistan. Robert Harding Picture Library; **105** *bottom* Head of the Buddha (fifth century). Buff sandstone. National Museum of India, New Delhi/The Bridgeman Art Library; **106** *top* Detail from Ranganatha Temple fresco. Photograph copyright © Gian Berto Vanni/Corbis; *bottom* Battle between armies of Arjuna and Tamradhvaia Brahma and deities in sky (1598), Nakib Khan Mughal. By permission of The British Library/The Art Archive; **107** *left* Copyright © Corbis; **110** *left*, Priest-king of Mohenjo-Daro. Karachi Museum, Pakistan. Scala/Art Resource, New York; *right* From *The Upanishads,* translated by Eknath Easwaran, founder of the Blue Mountain Center of Meditation. Copyright © 1987. Reprinted by permission of Nilgiri Press, Tomales, California; **111** Copyright © Araldo de Luca/Corbis; **112** *top* Copyright © Rick Smolan/Stock Boston/PictureQuest; *center* Copyright © Jim Pickerell/Stock Connection/PictureQuest; *bottom* Copyright © Sisse Brimberg/NGS Image Collection; **113** *top* Copyright © 1963 Bob Adelman/Magnum Photos; *bottom* NASA; **121** Wolverine and Spider-Man: Trademark and copyright © 2001 Marvel Characters, Inc. Used with permission; **122** Copyright © Barnaby Hall/Photonica; **125** *Drona at the Well*, Bhaktisiddhanta. From *Art Treasures of the Mahabharata,* written and illustrated by Bhaktisiddhanta. Copyright © 2000. Used with permission from Torchlight Publishing; **128** *top* Copyright © Dwarkadas Thanvi/Dinodia Picture Agency; *bottom* Copyright © Images of India/Dinodia Picture Agency; **129** *top, Henry David Thoreau* (1817–1862), Benjamin D. Maxium. Daguerreotype. National Portrait Gallery, Smithsonian Institution, Washington, D.C., Gift of an anonymous donor; *bottom* From *Bhagavad Gita: A New Translation* by Stephen Mitchell. Harmony Books, a division of Random House, Inc.; **130** Copyright © The British Museum, London; **145** *bottom* Copyright © Michael Newman/PhotoEdit/PictureQuest; **159** *left* From *Folktales from India,* edited by A. K. Ramanujan. Pantheon Books, a division of Random House, Inc.; *right* From *The Eternal Cycle: Indian Myth.* Duncan Baird Publishers, London.

Unit Two
162 *top* Copyright © George Hunter/H. Armstrong Roberts; *bottom* The Granger Collection, New York; **163** *top* Photograph copyright © Erich Lessing/Art Resource, New York; *bottom* Statue of Athena (c. 340–330 B.C.). National Archaeological Museum, Athens/The Bridgeman Art Library; **164** *Achilles and the Body of Patroclus (The Spoils of War)* (1986), David Ligare. Oil on canvas, 60″ × 78″. Private collection, Los Angeles; **165** *top* Alexander Sarcophagus (late fourth century B.C.). Archaeological Museum, Istanbul, Turkey. Photograph copyright © Erich Lessing/Art Resource, New York; **166** *top right* The Granger Collection, New York; *left center* Detail of grave stele of a youth and a little girl (c. 530 B.C.). Marble, 3′ 10 ¹¹/₁₆″ (432.4 cm). The Metropolitan Museum of Art, New York. Frederick C. Hewitt Fund, 1911, Rogers Fund, 1921, Munsey Funds, 1936, 1938, and Anonymous Gift, 1951. Photograph copyright © 1997 The Metropolitan Museum of Art; *bottom center* Vase painting of Greek family (mid-fifth century B.C.), attributed to the Harrow Painter. Photograph by Bastòn Design; **167** *top center* Copyright © Ashmolean Museum, Oxford, England; *bottom left* Photograph copyright © Erich Lessing/Art Resource, New York; *bottom right* Copyright © The British Museum, London; **168–169** Poseidon (460 B.C.). Bronze, 195 cm. National Archaeological Museum, Athens, Greece. Photograph copyright © Erich Lessing/Art Resource, New York; **169** *School of Athens* (1508), Raphael. Stanza della Segnatura, Vatican City, Vatican State. Photograph copyright © Erich Lessing/Art Resource, New York; **170** Demosthenes (c. 280 B.C.). Marble, 79 ½″ (202 cm). Ny Carlsberg Glyptothek, Copenhagen, Denmark. Copyright © Ole Haupt; **171** *top* Copyright © SuperStock, Inc.; *center* Parthenon façade reconstruction (1879–1881). École Nationale Superieure des Beaux-Arts, Paris; *bottom* Staatliche Antikensammlungen und Glyptothek, Munich, Germany; **172** *top* Greek black-figured vase (about 540 B.C.), attributed to the Amasis Painter. Terracotta, 6 ¾″ (17.1 cm). The Metropolitan Museum of Art, New York. Fletcher Fund, 1931 (31.11.10). Photograph copyright © 1999 The Metropolitan Museum of Art; *bottom* Copyright © Manfred Morgenstern; **173** Musei Capitolini, Rome. Scala/Art Resource, New York; **174** *Olympic runner* Copyright © PhotoDisc/Getty Images; **174–175** *bottom* NASA; **175** *top* Copyright © PhotoDisc/Getty Images; *bottom* Copyright © Camerique Stock Photography/H. Armstrong Roberts; **176** Photograph copyright © 1998 Wood River Gallery/PictureQuest; **178** *left* Art Resource, New York; *right* The Art Archive; **179** *Judgement of Paris,* Giulio Romano. Palazzo Ducale, Mantua, Italy/SuperStock; **183** *background* Copyright © Hugh Sitton/Stone; *foreground* Photograph copyright © Erich Lessing/Art Resource, New York; **189** Copyright © Kathleen Campbell/Stone; **199** *background* Copyright © Steve Satushek/The Image Bank; **205** *background* Copyright © Michael Busselle/Stone; **214** *background* Copyright © Kim Heacox/Stone; *foreground* Copyright © Chris Hellier/Corbis; **219** *background* Copyright © George Grigoriou/Stone; *foreground* Copyright ©

Chris Hellier/Corbis; **225** *top* Photograph by Mary Gross; *bottom* From the *Iliad* by Homer, translated by Robert Fagles. Copyright © 1991 Penguin Classics, a division of Penguin Putnam, Inc.; **226** The Granger Collection, New York; **232** Museo Nazionale, Naples, Italy/Art Resource, New York; **238** Copyright © Michael Townsend/Stone; **245** *top* AP/Wide World Photos; *bottom* Adil Bradlow/AP/Wide World Photos; **246** The Granger Collection, New York; **256** *top* Copyright © R. Sheridan, Ancient Art and Architecture; *bottom* Scala/Art Resource, New York; **257** *top* Copyright © Donald Cooper/Photostage; *bottom* Andromeda Oxford Ltd.; **258** *left* The Granger Collection, New York; **260–261** Classical Greek theatre. Illustration by Gerda Becker from *The Living Stage*. Copyright © 1990 by Kenneth Macgowan and William Melnitz. Reprinted/adapted by permission of Allyn & Bacon; **263, 266** Copyright © Photofest; **270** Photograph copyright © 1996 Colin Willoughby/Arena. StageImage, San Francisco; **277** Copyright © Merlyn Severn/Hulton Archive by Getty Images; **284** *top* Copyright © Photofest; *bottom* Copyright © Robbie Jack/Corbis; **290, 292** Pier Paolo Cito/AP/Wide World Photos; **295** Copyright © Merlyn Severn/Hulton Archive by Getty Images; **310** Photograph Copyright © 1996 Colin Willoughby/Arena. StageImage, San Francisco; **312** Copyright © Merlyn Severn/Hulton Archive by Getty Images; **318** Old Vic Archive, University of Bristol Theatre Collection, England; **325** Copyright © Photofest; **328** *clockwise from top left* Courtesy of Hartford Stage. Photograph by T. Charles Erickson; Courtesy of Hartford Stage. Photograph by T. Charles Erickson; Copyright © Photofest; Copyright © The Kobal Collection/Universal; **332** Copyright © PhotoDisc/Getty Images; **343** *left* TV Books, New York; *right* From *The Ancient City* by Peter Connolly and Hazel Dodge; **344** *bottom left* Copyright © Grazia Neri/Camera Press Digital/Retna Ltd. USA; **345** *top right* Copyright © Dennis Degnan/Corbis; *center left* Baptism of Christ in Jordan River (1240), unknown artist. Ancient Art & Architecture Collection; *bottom right* Officer of the Praetorian Guard (early second century A.D.). Roman marble relief. Musée du Louvre, Paris. Photograph by Hervé Lewandowski. Réunion des Musées Nationaux/Art Resource, New York; **346** *top right* Musei Capitolini, Rome. SEF/Art Resource, New York; *bottom* Copyright © Archivo Iconografico, S.A./Corbis; **347** Copyright © Elio Ciol/Corbis; **348** *top* Copyright © Araldo De Luca; *bottom* Museo della Civiltà Romana, Rome. Scala/Art Resource, New York; **349** *top left* Copyright © Michael Holford; *top right* Copyright © The British Museum, London; *bottom* Detail of mosaic from Cicero's villa (first century A.D.), Dioscurides of Samos. Museo Archeologico Nazionale, Naples, Italy. Scala/Art Resource, New York; **350** Marcello Bertinetti/White Star Archive; **351** *top* Emperor Augustus (21 B.C.–14 A.D.). Marble, 204 cm. Vatican City, Vatican State. Photograph copyright © Erich Lessing/Art Resource, New York; *bottom* Virgil and the muses (third century A.D.). Roman mosaic from Sousse. Musée National du Bardo, Le Bardo, Tunisia/The Bridgeman Art Library; **352** Copyright © Araldo de Luca/Corbis; **353** *top* From *Meditations* by Marcus Aurelius, translated by Maxwell Staniforth. Copyright © 1987 Viking Press/Penguin Classics, a division of Penguin Putnam Inc.; *bottom* Copyright © Ding Jun/New China Pictures/Sovfoto/Eastfoto/PictureQuest; **354** *clockwise from top* AP/Wide World Photos; Copyright © Joseph Sohm/ChromoSohm Inc./Corbis; Copyright © Photofest; **354–355** Copyright © Tom Carroll/Phototake/PictureQuest; **355** *left* Copyright © Tony Freeman/PhotoEdit/PictureQuest; *right* Copyright © Kevin Fleming/Corbis; **356** Detail of Virgil (third century A.D.). Roman mosaic from Sousse. Musée National du Bardo, Le Bardo, Tunisia/The Bridgeman Art Library; **361** Copyright © Photofest; **364** Nimatallah/Art Resource, New York; **367** Copyright © Bettman/Corbis; **371** Copyright © Mimmo Jodice/Corbis; **379** Copyright © The Kobal Collection; **383** Copyright © Underwood and Underwood/Corbis; **388** *left* The Edgar Allan Poe Museum of the

Poe Foundation, Richmond, Virginia; **392** Museo Nazionale Romano delle Terme, Rome/Art Resource, New York; **394** Photograph copyright © Erich Lessing/Art Resource, New York; **398** The Granger Collection, New York; **399** Copyright © 2001 Cordon Art, Baarn, Holland; **405** *left* Man in an ornithopter, Leonardo da Vinci. Bibliothèque de l'Institut de France, Paris/Art Resource, New York; *top right* Photograph copyright © Judy MacReady; *bottom right* Photograph copyright © Steve Finberg; **406** Culver Pictures; **407** *background* Illustration by Eileen Wagner; *foreground* Art Resource, New York; **408** Illustration by Eileen Wagner; **410** Photograph copyright © Erich Lessing/Art Resource, New York; **411** *right* From *The Roman Way* by Edith Hamilton. Used by permission of W. W. Norton & Co., Inc.

Unit Three

420 *top* Tortoise shell with inscription. Academia Sinica, Taipei, Taiwan, Republic of China; *bottom* Camel (eighth century A.D.) from tomb of Cungpu, Shaanxi province, China. Pottery with three-color glaze, 47.5 cm. Genius of China Exhibition/The Art Archive; **421** *top* Copyright © Dallas and John Heaton/Stock Boston; *bottom* Copyright © O. Louis Mazzatenta/NGS Image Collection; **422** *top* China Pictorial Photo Service; *bottom* Shang bronze ritual vessel, 13″. Copyright © The Image Bank; **424** *left* Detail of *The Thirteen Emperors* (seventh century A.D.). Handscroll, ink and color on silk, 20 3/16″ × 209 1/16″ (51.3 cm × 531 cm). Denman Waldo Ross Collection. Courtesy of Museum of Fine Arts, Boston; *right* Courtesy of the Freer Gallery of Art, Smithsonian Institution, Washington, D.C., F1954.21, section 10; **425** *top*, Paper store. Bibliothèque Nationale de France, Paris; *center* Wen Wu Publishing; *bottom* Equestrienne on horse (eighth century). Buff earthenware with traces of polychromy, 56.2 cm × 48.2 cm. The Art Institute of Chicago. Gift of Mrs. Pauline Palmer Wood, 1970.1073. Photograph copyright © 2001 The Art Institute of Chicago. All rights reserved; **426** Copyright © Archivo Iconographico, S.A./Corbis; **427** *bottom* "The Cold Food Observance" (11th century A.D.), Su Shih. Collection of the National Palace Museum, Taipei, Taiwan, Republic of China; **428** Cast bronze sword of the late Eastern Shou period. Copyright © The British Museum, London; **429** Detail of Bayeux Tapestry (c. 11th century A.D.). Wool embroidery on linen. Musée de la Tapisserie, Bayeux, France/The Bridgeman Art Library; **430** *clockwise from top right* Copyright © PhotoDisc/Getty Images; Photograph by Sharon Hoogstraten; Copyright © Bruce Burkhardt/Corbis; Copyright © FoodPix; **431** *clockwise from top left* Copyright © 1996 Louis Jacobs, Jr./Mira; Copyright © 2000 Jeff Hunter/The Image Bank; Copyright © PhotoDisc/Getty Images; **434** *bottom* Copyright © Wang Lu/China Stock; **440** The Granger Collection, New York; **441** Copyright © Wolfgang Kaehler/Corbis; **452** *top* Copyright © Clive Druett/Papilio/Corbis; *bottom* Copyright © Stock Montage/SuperStock, Inc.; **454, 457, 458** *top* Copyright © Clive Druett/Papilio/Corbis; **462** *left center* Copyright © Liu Liqun/China Stock; **465** *left* Ceramic jar with dragon (c. 1426–1435 A.D.). Porcelain and blue underglaze, 19″ (48.3 cm). The Metropolitan Museum of Art, New York. Gift of Robert E. Tod, 1937 (37.191.1). Photograph copyright © 1987 The Metropolitan Museum of Art; **467** Copyright © Gordon Gahan/NGS Image Collection; **471** *right, top to bottom* Copyright © Howard Davies/Corbis; Copyright © Howard Davies/Corbis; Copyright © Peter Turnley/Corbis; *bottom left* Copyright© Chris Hondros/Getty News Services; **472** *top* Copyright © Corbis; *bottom* Copyright © Liu Liqun/China Stock; **475** Detail of *The Old Plum* (1647), attributed to Kano Sansetsu. Colors and gold leaf on paper, 68 3/4″ × 191 1/8″ (174.5 cm × 485.3 cm). The Metropolitan Museum of Art, New York. The Harry G. C. Packard Collection of Asian Art, Gift of Harry G. C. Packard and Purchase, Fletcher, Rogers, Harris Brisbane Dick and Louis V. Bell Funds, Joseph Pulitzer Bequest and the Annenberg Fund, Inc., Gift, 1975 (1975.268.48). Photograph copyright © 1983 The Metropolitan Museum of Art; **484** Detail of *Spring Morning in the Han Palace*. Qui Ying. Collection of the National Palace Museum, Taiwan, Republic of China; **485** *left* From *A Floating Life: The Adventures of Li Po* by Simon Elegant. The Ecco Press, New Jersey; *right* From *What Life Was Like in the Land of the Dragon: Imperial China (960–1368 A.D.)*. Copyright © Time-Life Books; **486** *clockwise from top right* Copyright © Sylvain Grandadam/Stone; Japanese National Tourist Organization/The Bridgeman Art Library; *Fishermen Netting Sole* (1853), Andō or Utagawa Hiroshige. Color woodblock print. Blackburn Museum and Art Gallery, Lancashire, United Kingdom/The Bridgeman Art Library; **487** *top* Copyright © 1961 Burt Glinn/Magnum Photos; *bottom* Sotheby's Picture Library, London; **488** *top* Gyobutsu-Imperial Collections; **488–489** *bottom* Collection of the Tokyo National Museum; **489** *top* Copyright © Ric Ergenbright/Corbis; **490** *left, The Emperor Go-Yozei* (early 17th century), Kano Takanobu. Hanging scroll, ink and color on silk, 42 1/8″ × 23 5/8″ (107 cm × 60.1 cm). Sennyuji Temple, Kyoto, Japan; *right* Kyoto National Museum, Japan; **491** *top* Werner Forman Archive/Art Resource, New York; *bottom* Koyasan Society for the Preservation of Cultural Properties, Museum Reihokan, Koyasan, Japan; **492** *bottom* Copyright © Image Eye/Pacific Press; **493** *top* Copyright © Sakamoto Photo Research Laboratory/Corbis; *bottom* Copyright © Bruce Burkhardt/Corbis; **494** *center, The Tale of Genji*, Lady Murasaki Shikibu. Ancient Art & Architecture Collection; **495** Copyright © PhotoDisc/Getty Images; **496** *top, center* Copyright © FoodPix; *bottom* Copyright © PhotoDisc/Getty Images; **496–497** Copyright © 1991 Roberto Soncin Gerometta/Photo 20-20/Picture Quest; **497** *top* Copyright © Robert Holmes/Corbis; *bottom* Copyright © 1989 Peter Gould/Images Pictures; **498** *top* Detail of *Five Beautiful Women* (early 19th century), Katsushika Hokusai. Gouache and ink on silk. Seattle (Washington) Art Museum, Margaret E. Fuller Purchase Fund. Photograph by Susan Dirk; *left center* Detail of *The Poetess Sei Shōnagon with the Eizan* (19th century), Kikugawa. Copyright © Angers Museum/Giraudon, Paris/SuperStock, Inc.; **508** *bottom* Copyright © 2002 Kozo Furui/Orion Press; **512** *right* Copyright © 1996 Rene Burri/Magnum Photos; **517** *left* From *Zen and the Art of Motorcycle Maintenance* by Robert M. Pirsig. Copyright © 2000 Perennial Classics, a division of HarperCollins Publishers; *center* Copyright © Eric Pearle/FPG International; *right* Copyright © David and Peter Turnley/Corbis; **518, 520** *left, Fukai* mask (18th century). Noh mask of painted Japanese cypress, 20.9 cm × 13.6 cm. The Tokugawa Art Museum, Nagoya, Japan; **520** *center, Uba* mask (Edo period). Polychromed wood, 21.2 cm × 14.1 cm. Collection of the Tokyo National Museum; *right, Uba* mask (19th century). Polychromed wood, 20.3 cm × 13.6 cm. Collection of the Tokyo National Museum; **521** Copyright © Morton Beebe, S.F./Corbis; **522, 523** *Fukai* mask (18th century). Noh mask of painted Japanese cypress, 20.9 cm × 13.6 cm. The Tokugawa Art Museum, Nagoya, Japan; **524** "Kasugayama" writing box (Muromachi period). Wood with *maki-e* lacquer, 22.7 cm × 20.6 cm. Nezu Art Museum, Tokyo; **525, 527** *left, Uba* mask (Edo period). Polychromed wood, 21.2 cm × 14.1 cm. Collection of the Tokyo National Museum; **527** *right, Uba* mask (19th century). Polychromed wood, 20.3 cm × 13.6 cm. Collection of the Tokyo National Museum; **529** *Fukai* mask (18th century). Noh mask of painted Japanese cypress, 20.9 cm × 13.6 cm. The Tokugawa Art Museum, Nagoya, Japan; **531** *Uba* mask (Edo period). Polychromed wood, 21.2 cm × 14.1 cm. Collection of the Tokyo National Museum; **534** *The Poetess Ono no Komachi, Cherry Tree, Full Moon* (c. 1820s), Hokkei. Woodcut, Surimono print. William Bridges Thayer Memorial, Spencer Museum of Art, University of Kansas, Lawrence, Kansas; **536** Photograph by Sharon

Hoogstraten; **541** Copyright © Shinya Yoshimori/Photonica; **542** Copyright © Alan Sirulnikoff/Photonica; **543** *left* Copyright © Jane Booth Vollers/Photonica; *right* Copyright © Corbis; **544** Copyright © Kevin Schafer/Corbis; **545** Copyright © Corbis; **547** *top* Copyright © Masao Ota/Photonica; *bottom right* Archive Photos; **548** Copyright © Masao Ota/Photonica; **561** *left* From *As I Crossed a Bridge of Dreams* by Lady Sarashina, translated by Ivan Morris. Copyright © 1989 Penguin Classics, a division of Penguin Putnam, Inc.; *right* From *Legends of the Samurai* by Hiroaki Sato. Illustration copyright © 1995 by Murakami Tamotsu. Jacket design by Michael Hornburg is reprinted by permission of The Overlook Press.

Unit Four

562–563 Copyright © 1999–2001 Gerard Del Vecchio/Stone; **564** *top* Copyright © Archivo Iconografico, S.A./Corbis; *bottom* Copyright © Chris Bradley/Axiom; **565** *top* Copyright © Nabeel Turner/Stone; *bottom* Copyright © Owen Franken/Stock Boston/PictureQuest; **566** *left* SEF/Art Resource, New York; **566–567** *bottom* By permission of The British Library (1008782.011); **567** *top* SEF/Art Resource, New York; **568** *top right* By permission of The British Library (1007628.011); *center* Musée Reza Abbasi, Teheran, Iran; *bottom left* Copyright © Alistair Duncan/Dorling Kindersley; **569** *top* Bibliothèque Nationale de France, Paris; *bottom left* Dagli Orti/Palace of Chihil Soutoun, Isfahan/The Art Archive; *bottom right* Copyright © Adam Woolfitt/Robert Harding Picture Library; **570** *top* The Granger Collection, New York; *bottom left* Copyright © Marvin E. Newman; *bottom right* Copyright © I. Perlman/Stock Boston; **571** *top* Copyright © PictureQuest; *bottom* Copyright © Bojan Brecelj/Corbis; **573** *top* Dagli Orti/Galleria degli Uffizi, Florence, Italy/The Art Archive; *bottom* Copyright © 2000 British Library Board; **574** *clockwise from top* Copyright © Bettman/Corbis; Copyright © Lawrence Wigdale/Stone; Copyright © James L. Amos/Corbis; **575** *left* NASA; *right* John Clarke (University of Michigan) and NASA; **577** Copyright © A. Ramey/PhotoEdit; **580** Copyright © Burstein Collection/Corbis; **587** Illustration by Edmund Dulac. Copyright © 1998 by Ragnarok Press; **591** *top* Copyright © Photofest/Jagarts; *bottom right* Copyright © Photofest; **592** *top* Roloff Beny/National Archives of Canada/PA211051; *bottom* Leaf from a *Shahnameh* manuscript (early 14th century). Colors and gold on paper, 6″ × 4 ⁷/₈″. The Metropolitan Museum of Art, New York. Purchase, Joseph Pulitzer Bequest, 1934 (34.24.1). Photograph Copyright © The Metropolitan Museum of Art; **593** Garrett Islamic manuscript, Third Series 310. Property of Princeton University Library; **594** Culver Pictures; **599, 600** *left* The Granger Collection, New York; **601** *Prayer in the Mosque* (19th century), Jean-Léon Gérôme. Oil on canvas, 35″ × 29 ¹/₂″ (88.9 cm × 74.9 cm). The Metropolitan Museum of Art, New York. Catharine Lorillard Wolfe Collection, Bequest of Catharine Lorillard Wolfe, 1887 (87.15.130). Photograph copyright © 1980 The Metropolitan Museum of Art; **611** *left* From *Night & Horses & the Desert,* edited by Robert Irwin. The Overlook Press; *right* From *The Essential Rumi,* translations by Coleman Barks with John Moyne; **612** *top* Copyright © Aldona Sabalis/Photo Researchers, Inc.; *bottom* Copyright © NGS Image Collection; **613** *top, left to right* Copyright © Explorer/Robert Harding Picture Library; Photograph by Eliot Elisofon, 1959. Image no. C 2 YRB 10.4 (2060). Eliot Elisofon Photographic Archives/National Museum of African Art, Smithsonian Institution, Washington, D.C.; Copyright © Nik Wheeler; *bottom* The Metropolitan Museum of Art, New York. The Michael C. Rockefeller Memorial Collection, Gift of Nelson A. Rockefeller, 1972 (1978.412.321). Photograph copyright © 1983 The Metropolitan Museum of Art; **614** The Art Archive; **615** The Granger Collection, New York; **616** *top* Copyright © Daniel Laine-Cosmos/Matix; *bottom* Statue of the king Glélé (c. 1889), Huntondji.

Brass, 105 cm. Photograph copyright © Hughes Dubois/Archives Musée Dapper, Paris; **617** *left* Copyright © Michael Holford/The British Museum, London; *right* The British Museum, London/Art Resource, New York; **618** From *Jali Kunda: Griots of West Africa & Beyond*, edited by Matthew Kopka and Iris Brooks. Photograph by Daniel Laine-Cosmos/Matrix. Cover copyright © 1996 Ellipsis Arts; **619** *top* Copyright © M&E Bernheim/Woodfin Camp; *right* Copyright © Lorna Stanton/Anthony Bannister Photo Library; **620** *left* Courtesy of Royal Pavilion Museum and Art Gallery, Brighton, England. Photograph copyright © Geoff Dann/Doring Kindersley; *right* Yoruba bronze head. Museum of Mankind, London/The Bridgeman Art Library; **621** Copyright © Gianni Dagli Orti/Corbis; **622** *left* Copyright © Mitchell Gerber/Corbis; *top right* Copyright © Steve Vidler/eStock Photography/PictureQuest; **622–623** *bottom* Copyright © Barbara Alper/Stock Boston/PictureQuest; **623** *top* Copyright © Stephen McBrady/PhotoEdit/PictureQuest; *right* From *Anansi the Spider* by Gerald McDermott. Copyright © 1972 by Landmark Production, Inc. Reprinted by permission of Henry Holt and Company, L.L.C.; **633** Copyright © Papilio/Corbis; **635** Seated figure (early 13th century). Terracotta, 10″ (25.3 cm). The Metropolitan Museum of Art, New York. Purchase, Buckeye Trust and Mr. and Mrs. Milton F. Rosenthal Gifts, Joseph Pulitzer Bequest, and Harris Brisbane Dick and Rogers Funds, 1981 (1981.218). Photograph copyright © 1984 The Metropolitan Museum of Art; **642** *top* Copyright © PhotoDisc/Getty Images; *center* Copyright © Storm Pirate Productions/Artville/Picture Quest; *bottom* Copyright © Peter Johnson/Corbis; **643** Henning Christoph/Das Fotoarchiv; **644** Copyright © PhotoDisc/Getty Images; **645** Copyright © Storm Pirate Productions/Artville/Picture Quest; **647** Copyright © Peter Johnson/Corbis; **649** *top* Copyright © 1996 BMG Entertainment; *center* Copyright © Sony Music Entertainment; *bottom* Copyright © Musica del Sol; **659, 660** Illustrations copyright © 1998 by Richard Erdoes; **677** *left* From *The Hero with an African Face* by Clyde W. Ford. Used by permission of Bantam Books, a division of Random House, Inc.; *right* From *Jali Kunda: Griots of West Africa & Beyond*, edited by Matthew Kopka and Iris Brooks. Cover copyright © 1996 Ellipsis Arts.

Unit Five

686 *top* Detail of *August: Mowing Wheat, Binding Sheaves* (c. 1515), Simon Bening. The Pierpont Morgan Library/Art Resource, New York; *bottom* The Bodleian Library, University of Oxford, England. MS Bodl. 264, fol. 218r; **687** *top* Copyright © Cathedral Treasury, Aachen, Germany/ET Archive, London/SuperStock, Inc.; **687** *bottom* Copyright © The Board of Trustees of the Armouries/Royal Armouries, Leeds, England; **688** *bottom* Copyright © Cathedral Treasury, Aachen, Germany/ET Archive, London/SuperStock, Inc.; **688–689** *Prise de Jérusalem par les Croisés* (19th century), Emile Signol. Musée de Versailles, France. Copyright © Collection Viollet, Paris; **689** *bottom* Copyright © The Huntington Library, Art Collections, and Botanical Gardens, San Marino, California/SuperStock, Inc.; **690** *left* Detail of *January* from *Très Riches Heures du Duc de Berry* (early 15th century), Limbourg brothers. Victoria & Albert Museum, London/The Bridgeman Art Library; *left, June* from *Très Riches Heures du Duc de Berry* (early 15th century), Limbourg brothers. Victoria & Albert Museum, London/The Bridgeman Art Library; **691** *top* From the Saint-Chapelle, Paris. Photograph by Graydon Wood, 1993. Philadelphia Museum of Art. Gift of Mrs. Clement Biddle Wood in memory of her husband; *center left* Bildarchiv der Österreichische Nationalbibliothek, Vienna, Austria; *bottom right* Copyright © Angelo Hornak/Corbis; **692** Copyright © Corbis; **693** *left* Detail of *Arthur Draws the Sword from the Stone* by Walter Crane. From *King Arthur's Knights: The Tales Re-Told for Boys and Girls*. London: T. C. and E. C. Jack, 1911. Courtesy of the Newberry Library, Chicago; *right, Joan of Arc* (15th century), unknown artist. Archives Nationales, Paris/Giraudon/Art Resource, New York; **694** *top* Copyright © Gregor M. Schmid/Corbis; *bottom right* Copyright © PhotoDisc/Getty Images; **694–695** *top* Copyright © Photofest; **695** *bottom left* Ian Jones/AP/Wide World Photos; *bottom right* Used with permission of HRH The Prince of Wales; **701, 704** The Granger Collection, New York; **711** Galahad, Boort, Perceval, and his sister arriving at an island (15th century). Manuscript illumination from *The Romance of Saint Graal*. Photograph copyright © Gianni Dagli Orti/Corbis; **713** Bibliothèque Nationale de France, Paris; **723** *top* Cover art by Braldt Bralds. From *The Mists of Avalon* by Marion Zimmer Bradley. Copyright © 1982, 2001 Marion Zimmer Bradley and The Ballantine Publishing Group, a division of Random House Inc; *center* Hallmark Entertainment/Shooting Star; *bottom* Warcraft® II image courtesy of Blizzard Entertainment; **724** *bottom*, **730** The Granger Collection, New York; **732** Detail of *Dante Alighieri* (1500–1503), Luca Signorelli. Fresco. Duomo, Orvieto, Italy/Scala/Art Resource, New York; **733** *top* Scala/Art Resource, New York; *bottom left, bottom right* The Granger Collection, New York; **734** Detail of *The Meeting of Dante with Beatrice* (1883), Henry Holiday. Walker Art Gallery, Liverpool, England/The Bridgeman Art Library; **760** *Dante Alighieri* (14th century), unknown artist. Portraitgalerie, Schloss Ambras, Innsbruck, Austria. Photograph copyright © Erich Lessing/Art Resource, New York; **771** *right* From *A Distant Mirror: The Calamitous 14th Century* by Barbara W. Tuchman; **772** *top* Copyright © Dagli Orti/Miramare Palace, Trieste/The Art Archive; *bottom* Copyright © Explorer, Paris/SuperStock, Inc.; **773** *top* Copyright © Bettman/Corbis; *bottom* Copyright © Galleria dell'Accademia, Florence, Italy/SuperStock, Inc.; **774** Scala/Art Resource, New York; **775** Copyright © Arte & Immagini srl/Corbis; **776** *top* Copyright © Archivo Iconografico, S.A./Corbis; *bottom* Copyright © SuperStock, Inc.; **777** *top* Copyright © Corbis; *bottom* Copyright © Speltdoorn; **778** *Sir Isaac Newton* (1710), Sir James Thornhill. Trinity College, Cambridge, England; **779** *top* Copyright © Kunsthistorisches Museum, Vienna, Austria/SuperStock, Inc.; *bottom* Copyright © Christel Gerstenberg/Corbis; **780** *top* Copyright © The Huntington Library, Art Collections, and Botanical Gardens, San Marino, California/SuperStock, Inc.; *bottom* Copyright ©

EdimÈdia/Corbis; **781** Copyright © SuperStock, Inc.; **782** *top* Copyright © Lester Lefkowitz/FPG International; *bottom foreground* Copyright © Reuters NewMedia Inc./Corbis; **783** *left* Copyright © Mehau Kulyk/Science Photo Library/Photo Researchers, Inc.; *right* Copyright © 1998 Mark Burnett/Stock Boston/PictureQuest; **784** *top* Copyright © Junko Yamada/Photonica; *bottom, Giovanni Boccaccio* (14th century), unknown artist. Portraitgalerie, Schloss Ambras, Innsbruck, Austria. Photograph copyright © Erich Lessing/Art Resource, New York; **787** *right,* **788, 790** Copyright © Junko Yamada/Photonica; **794** *top background* Copyright © Roy Morsch/Corbis Stock Market; *center* Scala/Art Resource, New York; **797** *background,* **799** *background* Copyright © Roy Morsch/Corbis Stock Market; **803** From *Is It Utopia Yet?* by Kat Kincade. Copyright © 1994 by Twin Oaks Publishing; **804** Copyright © SuperStock, Inc.; **805** Copyright © PhotoDisc/Getty Images; **806** The Granger Collection, New York; **807** *Petrarch's First Sight of Laura* (1884), William Cave Thomas. Fine Art Photographic Library Ltd., London; **808** *left* Giraudon/Art Resource, New York; **812** The Granger Collection, New York; **818** *top* Copyright © National Portrait Gallery, London/SuperStock, Inc.; *center* Copyright © Photofest; **819** From *The Globe Restored: A Study of the Elizabethan Theatre* by C. Walter Hodges. Illustration by the author. Copyright © Native American Books; **821** *top* Detail of *Mary Magdalene* (c. 1540), Jan van Scorel. Oil on panel, 67 cm × 76.5 cm. Rijksmuseum, Amsterdam, Netherlands; *bottom, Portrait of Louise Labé* (1555), Dubouchet. Engraving. Private Collection/Roger-Viollet, Paris/The Bridgeman Art Library; **828** *top* Detail of *Don Quixote on Horseback,* Honoré Daumier. Neue Pinakothek, Munich, Germany. Giraudon/Art Resource, New York; *bottom* The Granger Collection, New York; **833** *Don Quixote in His Study,* Gustave Doré. Illustration in *History of Don Quixote* by Miguel de Cervantes, edited by J. W. Clark; **842** Copyright © Albert Normandin/Masterfile; **846, 847** *top* Copyright © Archivo Iconografico, S.A./Corbis; **847** *bottom* Copyright © Gianni Dagli Orti/Corbis; **848** *top* Uniforms of imperial calvary (18th century). Watercolor. Heeresgeschichtliches Museum, Vienna, Austria. Photograph Copyright © Erich Lessing/Art Resource, New York; *bottom* The Granger Collection, New York.

Unit Six

870 *top*, *Portrait of Jean Jacques Rousseau* (18th century), Maurice Quentin de la Tour. Pastel. Musée Antoine Lecuyer, Saint-Quentin, France/Giraudon/The Bridgeman Art Library; *bottom*, *Hadleigh Castle* (1829), John Constable. Oil on canvas, 122 cm × 164.5 cm. Yale Center for British Art, Paul Mellon Collection/The Bridgeman Art Library; 871 *top* Copyright © Hulton-Deutsch Collection/Corbis; *bottom* Detail of *Bonaparte Crossing the Great Saint-Bernard Pass* (1800–1801), Jacques-Louis David. Oil on canvas. Copyright © Musée National du Château de Malmaison, Rueil Malmaison, France/Lauros-Giraudon, Paris/SuperStock, Inc.; 872 *bottom* Copyright © Gianni Dagli Orti/Corbis; 872–873 *top*, *Napoleon's Retreat from Moscow* (19th century), Adolf Northen. Courtesy of Sotheby's Picture Library, London; 874 *top* The Granger Collection, New York; *bottom*, *Moroccan Caid* (1837), Eugene Delacroix. Oil on canvas. Musée des Beaux-Arts, Nantes, France/The Bridgeman Art Library; 875 *top*, *Llanthony Abbey, Monmouthshire* (1834), Joseph Mallord William Turner. Watercolor over pencil on white paper, 11 $\frac{13}{16}$″ × 16 $\frac{3}{4}$″. Indianapolis (Indiana) Museum of Art, Bequest of Kurt F. Pantzer, Sr.; *bottom* Copyright © Dagli Orti/Beethoven House, Bonn, Germany/The Art Archive;

876 From *Frankenstein* by Mary Shelley. Used by permission of Puffin Books, an imprint of Penguin Putnam Books for Young Readers, a division of Penguin Putnam, Inc.; 877 *left* Historical and Ethnological Museum of Greece; *bottom* Courtesy of the Seneca Falls (New York) Historical Society; 880 *top* Copyright © 1989 Ron Scherl/StageImage; *bottom* Giraudon/Art Resource, New York; 899 *William Wordsworth* (1818), Benjamin Robert Haydon. Courtesy of the National Portrait Gallery, London; 902 Silhouette of Dorothy Wordsworth, unknown artist. The Wordsworth Trust; 905 *top*, *Foggy River* (1990), Florence Brown Eden. Copyright © Gallery Contemporanea, Jacksonville, Florida/SuperStock, Inc.; *bottom left* The Granger Collection, New York; *bottom right* Werner Forman Archive/Anchorage (Alaska) Museum of History and Art/Art Resource, New York; 910 The Granger Collection, New York; 911 *top*, 912 Copyright © 1987 by Curtis Music Press. International copyright secured. All rights reserved; 914 *top background* Copyright © Phil Schermeister/Corbis; *center* The Granger Collection, New York; *bottom* Copyright © Hulton-Deutsch Collection/Corbis; 915 Fotomas Index, Kent, England; 918 *Campaign in France, 1814* (1864), Ernest Messonier. Oil on wood, 20 $\frac{1}{8}$″ × 29 $\frac{7}{8}$″. Bequest of Alfred Chauchard, 1909. Photograph by Dagli Orti/Musée d'Orsay Paris/The Art Archive; 919 *background* Copyright © Phil Schermeister/Corbis; 921 *top*, *Les Misérables*, Palace Theatre, London. Copyright © 1999 Michael Le Poer Trench/Arena Images/StageImage; *bottom left* Hulton Archive by Getty Images; *bottom right* Sherrill Milnes as Rigoletto. Copyright © 1973 Ron Scherl/StageImage; 922 *top* The Granger Collection, New York; 928 *top left* Copyright © 1999 Visual Language; *top right* Detail of *Two Heads Among Flowers* (c. 1905), Odilon Redon. Oil on canvas, 24″ × 19 $\frac{3}{4}$″. Private collection, Cambridge, Massachusetts; *bottom* Detail of *Un coin de table* [Table corner] (1872), Henri Fantin-Latour. Oil on canvas, 160 cm × 225 cm. Musée d'Orsay, Paris. Photograph copyright © Erich Lessing/Art Resource, New York; 929 Copyright © 1999 Visual Language; 933 *left* From *Les Misérables* by Victor Hugo, translated by Lee Fahnestock and Norman MacAfee. Copyright © 1987 by Lee Fahnestock and Norman MacAfee. Used by permission of Dutton Signet, a division of Penguin Putnam Inc; *right* From *The Sorrows of Young Werther* by Johann Wolfgang von Goethe. Copyright © Penguin Classics, a division of Penguin Putnam, Inc.; 934 *top* Copyright © Barbara Galasso. Courtesy George Eastman House; *bottom* Copyright © PictureQuest; 935 *top*, *Das Eisenwalzwerk: Moderne Cyklopen* [The rolling mill: A modern behemoth] (1872–1875), Adolph von Menzel. Oil on canvas, 158 cm × 254 cm. Staatliche Museen zu Berlin/Preussischer Kulturbesitz, Nationalgalerie. Photograph by Klaus Göken; *bottom* Copyright ©

PhotoDisc/Getty Images; **936** *bottom center* The Granger Collection, New York; **936–937** *top* Copyright © Hulton-Deutsch Collection/Corbis; **937** *right* Copyright © PictureQuest; **938** *The Thinker* (1880–1882), Auguste Rodin. Copyright © Christie's Images/SuperStock, Inc.; **939** *left* Copyright © PictureQuest; *right* Copyright © Carolyn Iverson/Science Source/Photo Researchers; **940, 941** *top and bottom* The Granger Collection, New York; **942** *top, Paying the Harvesters* (1882), Léon Lhermitte. Oil on canvas, 251 cm × 272 cm. Musée d'Orsay, Paris. Photograph copyright © Erich Lessing/Art Resource; *bottom, left to right* The Granger Collection; The Granger Collection; Copyright © Bettmann/Corbis; Copyright © Bettman/Corbis; Copyright © Erich Lessing/Art Resource, New York; Private collection/Ken Walsh/The Bridgeman Art Library; Sovfoto/Eastfoto; **944** *Portrait of Guy de Maupassant* (19th century), François-Nicolas Feyen-Perrin. Châteaux de Versailles et de Trianon, Versailles, France. Réunion des Musées Nationaux/Art Resource, New York; **954** *top* Scala/Art Resource, New York; *center left (signature)* The Granger Collection, New York; *bottom center* Copyright © Nick Wiseman/Eye Ubiquitous/Corbis; *bottom right Queen Victoria* (1838), Sir George Hayter. Picture Library, National Portrait Gallery, London; **955** *left* Copyright © Bettman/Corbis; *right* Sovfoto/Eastfoto; **956** *left* The Granger Collection, New York; *right* Copyright © Novosti Photo Library, London; **957** *top* Copyright © The State Russian Museum/Corbis; *bottom* From *War and Peace* by Leo Tolstoy, translated by Ann Dunnigan. Copyright © 1968 by Ann Dunnigan. Introduction copyright © 1968 by New American Library. Used by permission of Dutton Signet, a division of Penguin Putnam Inc; **958, 959, 961, 963, 964, 966, 967, 968, 970, 974** Copyright © PhotoDisc/Getty Images; **975** Photograph by Sharon Hoogstraten; **976** Copyright © Mark Douet/Stone; **993, 994** *background* Photograph by Sharon Hoogstraten; **996** Scala/Art Resource, New York; **999** *bottom* Sovfoto/Eastfoto; **1008** *left* Wirephoto/*The New York Times*, 8/7/1941; *right* Copyright © 1999 Visual Language; **1016** *top* The Granger Collection, New York; *bottom, View of the Nevsky Prospect near the Anichkov Bridge* (1886), Alexander Karlovitch Beggrow. 605 mm × 895 mm. The State Museum of the History of St. Petersburg, Russia; **1017** *top* Copyright © NBC/Hallmark Entertainment/Upton, Oliver/The Kobal Collection; *bottom* From *The Brothers Karamazov* by Fyodor Dostoyevsky. Foreword by Manuel Komroff, edited by Manuel Komroff, translated by Constance Garnett. Copyright © 1957 by Manuel Komroff, editing and foreword. Used by permission of Dutton Signet, a division of Penguin Putnam; **1018** *top* The Dolls House Emporium; *bottom* Reproduced by permission of Elizabeth Banks/Castle Museum and Art Gallery, Nottingham, England/The Bridgeman Art Library; **1020–1022** *top* The Dolls House Emporium; **1023** *bottom* Copyright © Photofest; **1023–1028** *top* The Dolls House Emporium; **1028** *bottom* Copyright © The Kobal Collection; **1029–1036** *top* The Dolls House Emporium; **1036** *bottom* Copyright © Photofest; **1037–1041** *top* The Dolls House Emporium; **1042** *left, top to bottom* Copyright © Photofest; Philip Rinaldi Publicity/Public Relations, New York; Copyright © Photofest; *right* Copyright © Photofest; **1044–1045** *top* The Dolls House Emporium; **1045** *bottom* Copyright © The Kobal Collection; **1046–1051** *top* The Dolls House Emporium; **1051** *bottom* Copyright © Photofest; **1052–1058** *top* The Dolls House Emporium; **1058** *bottom* Copyright © Photofest; **1059–1061** *top* The Dolls House Emporium; **1061** *bottom* Copyright © Photofest; **1063** Copyright © PhotoDisc/Getty Images; **1064–1072** *top* The Dolls House Emporium; **1072** *bottom* Copyright © Photofest; **1073–1078** *top* The Dolls House Emporium; **1078** *bottom* Copyright © Photofest; **1079** The Dolls House Emporium; **1080** Copyright © Photofest; **1083** Copyright © PhotoDisc/Getty Images; **1093** *right* Detail of *A Family Gathering in an Orchard* (1890), Théo Van Rysselberghe. Kröller-Müller Museum, Otterlo, Netherlands. Used with permission of The Kröller-Müller Foundation. From the cover of *Anton Chekhov: Five Plays,* translated by Ronald Hingley.

Unit Seven

1096 *top right* NASA; *center left* Copyright © Hulton Archive by Getty Images/ PictureQuest; *bottom right* Copyright © Corbis; **1097** Copyright © 2000 Jeffrey Aaronson/Network Aspen; **1098** *top* Copyright © Gil Mayers/SuperStock, Inc.; *bottom* Copyright © Bettmann/Corbis; **1099** *top* Copyright © Joseph Sohm/ ChromoSohm Inc./Corbis; **1099** *bottom* Greg English/AP/Wide World Photos; **1100** *left* Copyright © Steve Northup/TimePix; *right* AP/Wide World Photos; **1101** *clockwise from top left* Culver Pictures; *Portrait of the Russian Poet Anna Andreevna Akhmatova* (1914), Natan Isaevich Altmann. Oil on canvas. State Russian Museum, St. Petersburg, Russia/The Bridgeman Art Library; Copyright © Y. Karsh/Woodfin Camp; Coward of Camberra; AP/Wide World Photos; **1102** *bottom left, La chaise longue* [The long chair] (1928), Le Corbusier. Chrome-plated tubular steel, painted steel, fabric, and leather, 24″ × 62 ⁵/₁₆″ × 19 ⁹/₁₆″. The Museum of Modern Art, New York. Gift of Thonet Industries, Inc. Photograph copyright © 2001 The Museum of Modern Art, New York; *bottom right, Family Group* (1947), Henry Moore. Copyright © Christie's Images/Corbis; **1102–1103** *top* Copyright © Chaplin/United Artists/The Kobal Collection; **1103** *top right* Copyright © Angelo Hornak/Corbis; *bottom* Copyright © Barbara Morgan. Courtesy George Eastman House; **1104** *top* Copyright © Bettmann/Corbis; *bottom* Copyright © Hulton-Deutsch Collection/Corbis; **1105** *left* Kluver/Martin Montparnasse Archive; *right, Man Leaning on a Table* (1916), Pablo Picasso. Oil on canvas, 78 ³/₄″ × 52″ (200 cm × 132 cm). Private collection, Switzerland. Photograph copyright © 2002 Estate of Pablo Picasso/Artists Rights Society (ARS), New York; **1106** *Nude Descending a Staircase (No. 2)* (1912), Marcel Duchamp. Oil on canvas, 57 ⁷/₈″ × 35 ¹/₈″. Philadelphia Museum of Art, The Louise and Walter Arensberg Collection, 1950. Photograph copyright © Burstein Collection/Corbis; **1108** *bottom* Culver Pictures; **1123** Detail of poster for *Das Kabinett des Dr. Caligari* (1920), Ernst Ludwig Stahl and Otto Arpke. Color lithograph. Deutsches Historisches Museum, Berlin. Copyright © A. Psille/S. Ahlers; **1140** *Die Skatspieler* [Skat players] (1920), Otto Dix. Oil on canvas and collage, 110 cm × 87 cm. Nationalgalerie Staatliche Museen zu Berlin. Purchased with funds of the Verein der Freunde der Nationalgalerie und des Bundes; **1150** The Granger Collection, New York; **1151** Photograph copyright © 2000 Stone Images; **1152** *left* Photograph by Rogelio Robles Romero Saavedra. Fundacion Federico García Lorca; *right* Copyright © Daniel E. Arsenault Photography/The Image Bank/Picture Quest; **1156** *top* Photograph by Sharon Hoogstraten; *center* Copyright © Gisele Freund/Photo Researchers; **1158, 1160, 1162** Photograph by Sharon Hoogstraten; **1166** The Granger Collection, New York; **1174** Copyright © Y. Karsh/Woodfin Camp; **1176, 1177** *Two Japanese Women, ca. 1890.* Copyright © Michael Maslan Historic Photographs/Corbis; **1182** *top background* Copyright © Martin B. Withers/Frank Lane Picture Agency/Corbis; *center* Copyright © P. Jordan/Getty News Services; **1184** *top* Mask (20th century), Zaire-Angola. Wood, 9″ (22.8 cm). From Zaire River coastal region. Kimbell Art Museum, Fort Worth, Texas. Photograph by Michael Bodycomb; **1184** *bottom*, **1185** *top* Copyright © Martin B. Withers/Frank Lane Picture Agency/Corbis; **1187** *right* Copyright © Michael Newman/PhotoEdit; **1188** *top background* Copyright © 1999 Stockbyte/PictureQuest; *center* Culver Pictures; **1198** Detail of *Fishergirl, Newlyn* (date unknown), Alexander Stanhope Forbes. Copyright © Christie's Images; **1199** *right* From *Siddhartha* (jacket cover) by Hermann Hesse, copyright. Used by permission of Bantam Books, a division of Random House, Inc.; **1200** *top* AKG Photo; **1201** *top* McDougal Littell File Photo; *bottom* Copyright © Peter Turnley/Corbis; **1202** Copyright © Bettmann/Corbis; **1203** *top* Copyright © UPI/Bettmann/Corbis; *bottom* Copyright © Hulton-Deutsch Collection/Corbis; **1204** *top left* Sovfoto/Eastfoto; *top right* Copyright © Hulton Archive by Getty Images;

Art Institute of Chicago/The Art Archive; **1345** From *The Tin Drum* by Günter Grass. Copyright © Vintage International, a division of Random House, Inc.; **1346** *top background* Copyright © Stock Image/ImageState; *bottom* Copyright © Piero Pomponi/Getty News Services; **1347** Copyright © Jeremy Horner/Corbis; **1356** *top to bottom* Copyright © Piero Pomponi/Getty News Services; From *Cien años de solidad* by Gabriel García Márquez. Edición de Jacques Joset. Copyright © Catedra Letras Hispánicas; From *One Hundred Years of Solitude* by Gabriel García Márquez. Copyright © 1998 Perennial Classics, a division of HarperCollins Publishers, Inc.; **1357** *top to bottom* Copyright © Colita/Corbis; Illustration by Thomas Woodruff; Bjorn Elgstrand/AP/Wide World Photos; **1358** *top* Copyright © Steve Satushek/The Image Bank; *bottom* AP/Wide World Photos; **1359** From *Odes to Common Things* by Pablo Neruda. Copyright © Bulfinch Press, a division of Little, Brown and Company, a division of Time Warner; **1360** Copyright © Steve Satushek/The Image Bank; **1365** Copyright © Aritz Parra/Adelante!; **1366** AP/Wide World Photos; **1367** Copyright © Robert Holmes/Corbis; **1374** AP/Wide World Photos; **1378** Detail of *Retrato del pintor* [Portrait of the painter] (1994), Diego Maqueria. Wax on paper. Copyright © Kactus Foto, Santiago, Chile/SuperStock, Inc.

Reading Handbook

R2 *bottom right: background, top, center* Copyright © PhotoDisc/Getty Images; *bottom* Copyright © Corbis; **R3** NASA; **R6** *background, top, center* Copyright © PhotoDisc/Getty Images; *bottom* Copyright © Corbis; **R7** NASA. **R94** © Michael Holford/British Museum, London; **R96** Mapquest.com; **R102, R104, R108** © PhotoDisc; **R110** Mapquest.com; **R112** © Courtesy NOAA/NGDC; **R114** © Matin de Lausanne/Corbis-Sygma.

The editors have made every effort to trace the ownership of all copyrighted material found in this book and to make full acknowledgment for its use. Omissions brought to our attention will be corrected in a subsequent edition.

Multicultural Advisory Board *(continued)*

Janna Rigby Clovis High School, Clovis, California

Noreen M. Rodriguez Trainer for Hillsborough County School District's Staff Development Division, Independent Consultant, Gaither High School, Tampa, Florida

Olga Y. Sanmaniego English Department Chairperson, Burges High School, El Paso, Texas

Liz Sawyer-Cunningham Los Angeles Senior High School, Los Angeles, California

Michelle Dixon Thompson Seabreeze High School, Daytona Beach, Florida

Teacher Review Panels *(continued)*

CALIFORNIA *(continued)*

Gail Kidd Center Middle School, Azusa School District

Corey Lay ESL Department Chairperson, Chester Nimitz Middle School, Los Angeles Unified School District

Myra LeBendig Forshay Learning Center, Los Angeles Unified School District

Dan Manske Elmhurst Middle School, Oakland Unified School District

Joe Olague Language Arts Department Chairperson, Alder Middle School, Fontana School District

Pat Salo Sixth Grade Village Leader, Hidden Valley Middle School, Escondido Elementary School District

FLORIDA

Judith H. Briant English Department Chairperson, Armwood High School, Hillsborough County School District

Beth Johnson Polk County English Supervisor, Polk County School District

Sharon Johnston Learning Resource Specialist, Evans High School, Orange County School District

Eileen Jones English Department Chairperson, Spanish River High School, Palm Beach County School District

Jan McClure Winter Park High School, Orange County School District

Wanza Murray English Department Chairperson (retired), Vero Beach Senior High School, Indian River City School District

Shirley Nichols Language Arts Curriculum Specialist Supervisor, Marion County School District

Debbie Nostro Ocoee Middle School, Orange County School District

Barbara Quinaz Assistant Principal, Horace Mann Middle School, Dade County School District

OHIO

Glyndon Butler English Department Chairperson, Glenville High School, Cleveland City School District

Ellen Geisler English/Language Arts Department Chairperson, Mentor Senior High School, Mentor School District

Dr. Paulette Goll English Department Chairperson, Lincoln West High School, Cleveland City School District

Loraine Hammack Executive Teacher of the English Department, Beachwood High School, Beachwood City School District

Marguerite Joyce English Department Chairperson, Woodridge High School, Woodridge Local School District

Sue Nelson Shaw High School, East Cleveland School District

Dee Phillips Hudson High School, Hudson Local School District

Carol Steiner, English Department Chairperson, Buchtel High School, Akron City School District

Nancy Strauch English Department Chairperson, Nordonia High School, Nordonia Hills City School Dictrict

Ruth Vukovich Hubbard High School, Hubbard Exempted Village School District

TEXAS

Dana Davis English Department Chairperson, Irving High School, Irving Independent School District

Susan Fratcher Cypress Creek High School, Cypress Fairbanks School District

Yolanda Garcia Abilene High School, Abilene Independent School District

Patricia Helm Lee Freshman High School, Midland Independent School District

Joanna Huckabee Moody High School, Corpus Christi Independent School District

Josie Kinard English Department Chairperson, Del Valle High School, Ysleta Independent School District

Mary McFarland Amarillo High School, Amarillo Independent School District

Gwen Rutledge English Department Chairperson, Scarborough High School, Houston Independent School District

Bunny Schmaltz Assistant Principal, Ozen High School, Beaumont Independent School District

Michael Urick A. N. McCallum High School, Austin Independent School District

Manuscript Reviewers *(continued)*

Beverly Ann Barge Wasilla High School, Wasilla, Alaska

Louann Bohman Wilbur Cross High School, New Haven, Connecticut

Rose Mary Bolden J. F. Kimball High School, Dallas, Texas

Lydia C. Bowden Boca Ciega High School, St. Petersburg, Florida

Angela Boyd Andrews High School, Andrews, Texas

Judith H. Briant Armwood High School, Seffner, Florida

Hugh Delle Broadway McCullough High School, The Woodlands, Texas

Stephan P. Clarke Spencerport High School, Spencerport, New York

Kathleen D. Crapo South Fremont High School, St. Anthony, Idaho

Dr. Shawn Eric DeNight Miami Edison Senior High School, Miami, Florida

JoAnna R. Exacoustas La Serna High School, Whittier, California

Linda Ferguson English Department Head, Tyee High School, Seattle, Washington

Ellen Geisler Mentor Senior High School, Mentor, Ohio

Ricardo Godoy English Department Chairman, Moody High School, Corpus Christi, Texas

Meredith Gunn Secondary Language Arts Instructional Specialist, Katy, Texas

Judy Hammack English Department Chairperson, Milton High School, Alpharetta, Georgia

Robert Henderson West Muskingum High School, Zanesville, Ohio

Martha Watt Hosenfeld English Department Chairperson, Churchville-Chili High School, Churchville, New York

Janice M. Johnson Assistant Principal, Union High School, Grand Rapids, Michigan

Eileen S. Jones English Department Chair, Spanish River Community High School, Boca Raton, Florida

Paula S. L'Homme West Orange High School, Winter Garden, Florida

Bonnie J. Mansell Downey Adult School, Downey, California

Linda Maxwell MacArthur High School, Houston, Texas

Ruth McClain Paint Valley High School, Bainbridge, Ohio

Rebecca Miller Taft High School, San Antonio, Texas

Deborah Lynn Moeller Western High School, Fort Lauderdale, Florida

Bobbi Darrell Montgomery Batavia High School, Batavia, Ohio

Bettie Moody Leesburg High School, Leesburg, Florida

Margaret L. Mortenson English Department Chairperson, Timpanogos High School, Orem, Utah

Marjorie M. Nolan Language Arts Department Head, William M. Raines High School, Jacksonville, Florida

Julia Pferdehirt Freelance Writer, Former Special Education Teacher, Middleton, Wisconsin

Cindy Rogers MacArthur High School, Houston, Texas

Pauline Sahakian English Department Chairperson, San Marcos High School, San Marcos, Texas

Jacqueline Y. Schmidt Department Chairperson and Coordinator of English, San Marcos High School, San Marcos, Texas

David D. Schultz East Aurora High School, East Aurora, New York

Milinda Schwab Judson High School, Converse, Texas

John Sferro Butler High School, Vandalia, Ohio

Brad R. Smedley English Department Chairperson, Hudtloff Middle School, Lakewood, Washington

Faye S. Spangler Versailles High School, Versailles, Ohio

Rita Stecich Evergreen Park Community High School, Evergreen Park, Illinois

GayleAnn Turnage Abilene High School, Abilene, Texas

Ruth Vukovich Hubbard High School, Hubbard, Ohio

Kevin J. Walsh Dondero High School, Royal Oak, Michigan

Charlotte Washington Westwood Middle School, Grand Rapids, Michigan

Tom Watson Westbridge Academy, Grand Rapids, Michigan

Linda Weatherby Deerfield High School, Deerfield, Illinois